The Military Cross to Flying Personnel of Great Britain and the Empire 1914-1919

The Military Cross
to
Flying Personnel
of
Great Britain and the Empire
1914-1919

with service and biographical details of recipients

Hal Giblin
and
Norman Franks

SAVANNAH
2008

First published 2008

Published by Savannah Publications
90 Dartmouth Road, Forest Hill, London SE23 3HZ, UK
British Library Cataloguing in Publication Data

A CIP catalogue record is available from the British Library
ISBN 1 902366 43 3
EAN 9781902366432

Printed in the UK by Print Solutions Partnership
Cover design by Reggie Freeman

Dedication

For Hal Giblin

a much missed husband, father, grandfather, friend and colleague

Preface

Although I had known Hal Giblin for around 40 years, we only actually met on about eight occasions, although it seems we spent months talking on the telephone. With him living near Liverpool, and myself in north Surrey and then East Sussex, it was always going to be difficult to meet. However, our friendship and mutual admiration for each other grew apace.

We had been involved in three books together before he suggested, some eight years ago, that we work on a book recording Royal Flying Corps and Royal Air Force recipients of the Military Cross. I readily agreed, not knowing then that it would take those eight years, and certainly not even thinking that when the work was done, Hal would no longer be with us.

His very great knowledge of the Great War was exceptional. Once, when we were in Northern France, he would point constantly to locations and tell me that it had been there that such-and-such an action had taken place, or that this was where someone had won a Victoria Cross, or been killed, of whatever. I just could not keep up with his scale of knowledge.

Over those eight years we gathered as much information on the men who had been awarded the Military Cross while serving with the flying services during the First World War. Hal's circle of friends included many historians who were keen medal collectors, and help from them and from the almost unique collection of school registers and history books within his library, we combined our knowledge, with the main RFC/RAF information coming from many visits to the National Archives in Kew, Surrey. The more we found, the happier we became, and the reader and researcher will discover much fascinating material within the biographies in this book.

When Hal died on 20 May 2005, he had just about finished putting all the biographies on disk. He had spent the last three years of his life assembling all this together before cancer took him from us. He was a wonderful chap, a good friend, and a fabulous husband and father. Anyone who says the good die young, ought to remember that at least Hal had lived for 70 years.

Unfortunately most of the names of the people who helped him with his research for this book were in his head, so it is with great regret that I cannot list all those helpers. I hope they know who they are and are pleased to have assisted. Those I do know I can list, but the list should be much longer. They are:

Frank 'Bill' Bailey, Paul Baillie, Mike Blackburn, Marcus J. Boret, Marjorie Jill Caster, the late Frank Cheesman, Andrew Cormack, Joe Devereux, Air Vice Marshal Peter Dye, Nick Forder, Geoff Houghton, Kevin Kelly, Jim Kenny, Stuart Leslie, Bob Lynes, Tony Mellor-Ellis, Charles Noon, Rob O'Brien, Mike O'Connor, Michael Partridge, Henry Pickthorn, Walter Pieters, Simon Pile, Marc Privett, Bob Rogers, Wing Commander Jim Routledge, Graham Saunders, Mike Schoemann, Stewart M. Simpson, Lieutenant Colonel Neil Smith, Sir Freddie Sowrey, Jeff Taylor, Stuart Tucker, Brian Turner, Mary Tyler, John Umney, Ann Wheeler *et al.*

We also acknowledge the help of staff at the National Archives, especially William Spencer, and at the RAF Museum, Hendon. Hal was also in touch with many schools and libraries up and down the country as well as others in Australia, Canada, and New Zealand. Because there are many I cannot name, thank you to everyone who gave their time to search old records in their care.

Norman Franks
July 2008

Abbreviations

1 AM	Air Mechanic 1st Class
2 AM	Air Mechanic 2nd Class
2 Lt	Second Lieutenant
A/	Acting
(A)	Air
AA	Anti-Aircraft
AAF	Australian Air Force
AAF	Auxiliary Air Force
AAG	Assistant Adjutant-General
AAP	Aircraft Acceptance Park
AASF	Advanced Air Striking Force
ACAS	Assistant Chief of Air Staff
AD	Air Depot
ADC	Aide de Camp
ADGB	Air Defence of Great Britain
AF	Air Force
AFC	Air Force Cross
AFC	Australian Flying Corps
AHQ	Air Headquarters
AIF	Australian Imperial Forces
AIMechE	Associate of the Institute of Mechanical Engineers
AMICE	Associate Member of the Institution of Civil Engineers
ANZAC	Australian & New Zealand Army Corps
AOA	Air Officer Administration
AOC	Air Officer Commanding
AOC	Army Ordnance Corps
AOC-in-C	Air Officer Commanding in Chief
APC	Armament Practice Camp
ARIBA	Associate of the Royal Institute of British Architects
ASD	Aircraft Supply Depot
ASO	Air Staff Officer
ATC	Air Training Corps
BA	Bachelor of Arts
BASc	Bachelor of Arts and Science
BBC	British Broadcasting Corporation
BC	Balloon Company
BC	British Columbia
BCh	Bachelor of Surgery
Bde	Brigade
BEA	British European Airways
BEF	British Expeditionary Force
BM	Bachelor of Medicine
BOAC	British Overseas Airways Corporation
BP	British Petroleum
BSc	Bachelor of Science
BSc (Eng)	Bachelor of Science (Engineering)
bt	Baronet
CAB	Civilian Air Board
CAF	Canadian Air Force
CAF	Citizens Air Force
CAG	Combat Air Group
CAMC	Canadian Army Medical Corps
Capt	Captain
CASC	Canadian Army Service Corps
CB	Companion of the Order of the Bath
CBE	Commander of the Order of the British Empire
CC	County Councillor
CCS	Casualty Clearing Station
CDF	Chief of the Defence Force
CEF	Canadian Expeditionary Force
CFA	Canadian Field Artillery
CFI	Chief Flying Instructor
CFS	Central Flying School
ChM	Master of Surgery
C-in-C	Commander-in-Chief
Col	Colonel
CIE	Companion of the Order of the Indian Empire
CM	Master of Surgery
CMG	Companion of the Order of St Michael and St George
COTC	Canadian Officer Training Corps
CTO	Chief Technical Officer
CVO	Commander of the Royal Victorian Order
D/	Deputy
DAAG	Deputy Assistant Adjutant General
DAC	Divisional Ammunition Column
DC	District of Columbia
DCL	Doctor of Civil Law
DCM	Distinguished Conduct Medal
DFC	Distinguished Flying Cross
DL	Deputy Lieutenant
DLI	Durham Light Infantry
DM	Doctor of Medicine
DPM	Diploma in Psychological Medicine
DSc	Doctor of Science
DSO	Distinguished Service Order
EA	Enemy Aircraft
EGM	Empire Gallantry Medal
ENSA	Entertainers National Service Association
FBI	Federation of British Industry
FMS	Federated Malay States
FO	Foreign Office
FRAeS	Fellow of the Royal Aeronautical Society
FRCP	Fellow of the Royal College of Physicians
FRCPE	Fellow of the Royal College of Physicians Edinburgh
FRCS	Fellow of the Royal College of Surgeons
FRGS	Fellow of the Royal Geographical Society
FRIBA	Fellow of the Royal Institute of British Architects

FRS	Fellow of the Royal Society
FSA	Fellow of the Society of Antiquaries
FTS	Flying Training School
GB	Great Britain
GBE	Knight Grand Cross of the Order of the British Empire
GC	George Cross
GCB	Knight Grand Cross of the Order of the Bath
GCSI	Knight Grand Commander of the Star of India
GHQ	General Headquarters
GOC	General Officer Commanding
GPO	General Post Office
GSO	General Staff Officer
GTS	Glider Training Squadron
HA	Hostile Aircraft
HAC	Honourable Artillery Company
HD	Home Defence
HLI	Highland Light Infantry
HM	His Majesty
HMS	His Majesty's Ship
HMAS	His Majesty's Australian Ship
HQ	Headquarters
IAF	Independent Air Force
idc	Imperial Defence College
IF	Independent Force
ITS	Initial Training Squadron
JP	Justice of the Peace
KB	Kite Balloon
KBE	Knight Commander of the Order of the British Empire
KBS	Kite Balloon Section/Squadron
KC	King' Counsel
KCB	Knight Commander of the Order of the Bath
KCMG	Knight Commander of the Order of St Michael and St George
KCVO	Knight Commander of the Royal Victoria Order
KG	Knight of the Order of the Garter
KLR	King's (Liverpool Regiment)
KOYLI	King's Own Yorkshire Light Infantry
KSLI	King's Shropshire Light Infantry
KRRC	Kings Royal Rifle Corps
LDS	Licenciate of Dental Surgery
lbs	pounds (weight)
LLB	Bachelor of Laws
LLD	Doctor of Laws
LRB	London Rifle Brigade
LRCP	Licentiate of the Royal College of Physicians
Lt	Lieutenant
Ltnt	Lieutenant
MA	Master of Arts
Maj	Major
MB	Bachelor of Medicine
MBE	Member of the Order of the British Empire
MC	Military Cross
MCC	Marylebone Cricket Club
MD	Doctor of Medicine
MEF	Middle East Forces
MFJ	Marine-feld Jagdstaffel
MG	Machine Gun
MGC	Machine Gun Corps
MID	Mention in Despatches
MIMechE	Member of the Institute of Mechanical Engineers
MLA	Member Legislative Assembly
MM	Military Medal
MP	Member of Parliament
MRAeS	Member of the Royal Aeronautical Society
MRCS	Member of the Royal College of Surgeons
MVO	Member of the Royal Victorian Order
NATO	North Atlantic Treaty Organisation
NCO	Non Commissioned Officer
NSW	New South Wales
NTC	National Telephone Company
NZ	New Zealand
OBE	Officer of the Order of the British Empire
OC	Officer Commanding
OGPU	(trans) All-Union State Political Administration (Soviet Secret Police)
OM	Order of Merit
OMRS	Orders & Medals Research Society
OOC	Out of Control
OSS	Office of Strategic Service
OTC	Officer Training Corps
psa	Graduate of the RAF Staff College
QFI	Qualified Flying Instructor
QM	Quarter Master
Qr Mr	Quarter Master
qv	quod vide (literally, which see)
RA	Royal Artillery
RAAF	Royal Australian Air Force
RAC	Royal Automobile Club
RAE	Royal Aircraft Establishment
RAeC	Royal Aero Club
RAF	Royal Air Force
RAFO	Reserve of Air Force Officers
RAFVR	Royal Air Force Volunteer Reserve
RAMC	Royal Army Medical Corps
RAS	Reserve Aerodrome Squadron
RC	Reserve Company
RCA	Royal College of Art
RCAF	Royal Canadian Air Force
RCAFA	Royal Canadian Air Force Association
RCM	Royal College of Music
RDI	Royal Designer for Industry
RE	Royal Engineers
RFA	Royal Field Artillery
RFC	Royal Flying Corps
RGA	Royal Garrison Artillery
Rgt	Regiment
RHA	Royal Horse Artillery
R Ir Fus	Royal Irish Fusiliers
RMA	Royal Military Academy

RMA	Royal Marine Artillery
RMC	Royal Military College
RN	Royal Navy
RNAF	Royal Naval Air Force
RNAS	Royal Naval Air Service
RNLI	Royal National Lifeboat Institution
RNZAF	Royal New Zealand Air Force
RNVR	Royal Navy Volunteer Reserve
RS	Reserve Squadron
RWF	Royal Welsh Fusiliers
SA	South Africa
SAAC	South African Air Corps
SAAF	South African Air Force
SAFO	Senior Air Force Officer
SAI	South African Infantry
SASO	Senior Air Staff Officer
SBO	Senior British Officer
Scot Rif	Scottish Rifles
SIS	Special Intelligence Service
SO	Staff Officer
Sqd	Squadron
SR	Special Reserve
SS	Steam Ship
SWB	South Wales Borderers
T/	Temporary
(T)	Training Branch
TA	Territorial Army
TD	Territorial Decoration
TDS	Training Depot Squadron
TF	Territorial Force
TS	Training Squadron
UCL	University College London
UK	United Kingdom
UN	United Nations
USA	United States of America
USAAC	United States Army Air Corps
USAS	United States Air Service
USS	United States Ship
VC	Victoria Cross
VD	Volunteer Decoration

A

ACKLAND, William Henry Dyke

The eldest son of Admiral Sir William Alison Dyke Ackland (2nd Baronet) CVO, JP, DL, FRGS and Lady Emily Anna (née Smith) of 'Wilmead', Middle Warberry Road, Torquay, he was born on 16 May 1888. Educated at Eton (1902-06), and at Christ Church, Oxford, from where he graduated BA in 1909. A pre-war volunteer, he was gazetted Second Lieutenant to 1 Royal Devon Yeomanry on 11 March 1914. Gained his Royal Aero Club Certificate (Number 773) flying a Vickers machine at the Vickers School, Brooklands, on 22 April 1914. Mobilised with the rest of the TF as soon as war came on 4 August 1914, he soon afterwards successfully sought secondment to the RFC. His pilot training duly completed, he was confirmed and gazetted Flying Officer on 27 March 1915. Posted overseas shortly afterwards, he joined 5 Squadron in France. On 20 June 1915, Ackland and his Observer of the day, Second Lieutenant R V de Halpert, in Vickers FB5, '1642', were attacked by a large German biplane. De Halpert fired 50 rounds into the enemy machine that was seen to 'dive down, erratically, to the ground'. During their return flight to their airfield after this incident, the FB5 was hit by a shell burst which set the fuel tank alight. Although both occupants were severely burnt and despite most of the framework having been destroyed by fire, Ackland somehow contrived to land the Vickers safely. The Order of St George, 4th Class, was conferred on Ackland by the Czar of Russia, *London Gazette* of 25 August 1915. His MC was announced in the *London Gazette* of 14 January 1916 (no citation). Although no formal citation was published in the *Gazette*, research has unearthed the original recommendation for the award: 'On many occasions he attacked German aeroplanes with determination and skill and succeeded in wrecking three. Lieutenant Ackland was badly burnt owing to his machine catching fire during a fight with a German aeroplane. He made a most skilful landing in our lines'.

He was also Mentioned in Despatches in the same *Gazette*. Ackland married, on 26 April 1916, Margaret Emily Barclay, with whom he had three daughters. Although his operational career was curtailed by the severity of his wounds, he stayed with the flying service in an instructing capacity, attaining the rank of Major by the end of the war. The award of an Air Force Cross came in the *London Gazette* of 8 February 1919. In the post-war years he commanded, with the rank of Major, 381 (Thorverton) Battery, Royal Devon Yeomanry, from 1923-30 and, as Lieutenant Colonel, commanded 96 (Royal Devon Yeomanry) Field Brigade, Royal Artillery (TA), from 1931 (awarded the Territorial Decoration). In civilian life, he became a director of W H Smith and Son, Booksellers and Newsagents, with homes at both Barnes Wood, Welwyn, Herts, and at Seaview House, Isle of Wight. On the death of his father, he became Sir William, 3rd Baronet).

ADAMS, Haddon Clifford

The son of Ironmongers Clerk, Henry C Adams and Alice L Adams, of 29 Gladstone Villas, Salisbury Road, St Clement, Ipswich, he was born on 9 November 1898. Educated at Ipswich Municipal Secondary School. He enlisted as a Private soldier into Suffolk Regiment in 1916. Picked out for a commission, he was gazetted Second Lieutenant to the RFC on 13 September 1917. His pilot training duly completed, he was confirmed and gazetted Flying Officer on 20 December following. Sent out to 12 Squadron (RE8s) on 23 February 1918. On 21 March 1918, the first day of the German spring offensive, Adams and his Observer of the day, Lieutenant Edward Campbell Batchelor (qv), in RE8, 'B2273', were both wounded when their machine was shot up by an enemy

Scout during a photo-reconnaissance patrol. His MC was announced in the *London Gazette* of 22 June 1918, the citation for which graphically reflects his gallantry on this and other patrols: 'For conspicuous gallantry and devotion to duty. Whilst on contact patrol, he was attacked by seven hostile scouts, and by skilful manoeuvring he enabled his Observer to shoot one of them down in flames. During the same fight he was attacked by 10 hostile machines which made repeated dives at him. He handled his machine with great coolness and skill, and finally he and his Observer drove down one of the enemy machines in flames. Later, while engaged in photographic work, he was attacked by a formation of 20 hostile scouts. He beat off their attacks with great skill and enabled his Observer to shoot down one of the enemy machines, which burst into flames and broke into pieces. He has shown magnificent courage and resource on many occasions'.

For his part in these actions, his Observer, Edward Batchelor, also received the MC. Adams left the RAF, via the Unemployed List, on 19 February 1919. He was known to be living in Springfield, Illinois, USA, during the 1920s.

ADAMS, Ralph Newton

The first son of Stockbroker, Harry Newton Adams and Mrs Adams, of 8 Stanley Crescent, Kensington, London, he was born on 21 October 1895. Educated at St Andrew's, Eastbourne, and at Charterhouse, where he was a member of the OTC. Gazetted Second Lieutenant to 7 (Extra Reserve) Battalion, Royal Fusiliers, on 18 April 1914, he was called to the colours in the early days of the war and proceeded to the front with 4 Battalion of his regiment in the December following. Having contracted dysentery in the trenches during January 1915, he was invalided home in the following month. Once recovered, he sought secondment to the RFC, which came in September 1915. Gained his Royal Aero Club Certificate (Number 1967) on 15 October 1915. Passing successfully through his formal training at the CFS, he accompanied as a 'founder member' the FE2b-equipped 23 Squadron to France on 16 March 1916. Rapid advancement to Captain and Flight Commander came on 8 July 1916. His MC was announced in the *London Gazette* of 27 July 1916: 'For conspicuous gallantry and skill. With Second Lieutenant Vernon [qv] as Observer, he attacked a flight of six enemy machines within the enemy's lines and caused one to fall in flames. He was then joined by another of our machines, and together they drove off the remainder, one falling out of control. Previously, with Second Lieutenant Cloete [qv] as his Observer, he brought down an enemy machine, which turned upside down'.

On 10 October 1916, Adams and his Observer of the day, Second Lieutenant G J Ogg, in FE2b, '4918', were engaged in an aerial combat over Achiet le Grand. Adams was hit and mortally wounded early in the fight, slumping, unconscious, over the controls. Despite this severe encumbrance, his Observer, in mortal danger of his life, somehow contrived at least a partially controlled crash-landing, into a shell-hole near to Meaulte. Ralph Adams was buried at Guillemont with full military honours. However, his grave was subsequently lost in the heavy fighting in the area, and hence he is commemorated on the Flying Services Memorial, Arras, France.

ADDENBROOKE-PROUT, Reginald

A Staff, not a flying, award

From Croydon, Surrey, he was born on 23 December 1893. His brother, Harold, would also serve with the RAF and be awarded the Air Force Cross. Reginald was educated at Whitgift Grammar School, where he was a Sergeant in the OTC. Training as an Analytical Explosives Chemist when the war came in August 1914, he volunteered immediately and was enlisted as a Private soldier (Number 9757) into the Royal Army Medical Corps. Proceeding to France in September 1914, he served as a Operating Theatre Assistant and Dresser. Picked out for a commission, he was gazetted Second Lieutenant to the RGA on 2 October 1914. Sent first to 9 Divisional Heavy Battery in France, he later served, from 8 February 1915, with 115 (Howitzer) Battery, RGA. His uncle, Major W H S Addenbrooke, Royal Engineers, was also serving in France at this time at the Head Quarters of 24 Division. Reginald was seconded to the RFC early in August 1915, but, after receiving some training as an Observer with 1 Squadron, was struck down with enteritis on the 22nd of the same month. Once recovered, he was, on 11 September, again attached to the RFC in France but then, two days later, returned to the UK for pilot training. This intention was short-lived, however, as it was found, in January 1916, that he had 'eye problems' and was unfit for flying duties. He transferred instead, to Staff duties with the RFC and was, eventually, formally gazetted as Adjutant, on 13 November 1916. His MC was announced in the New Year *London Gazette* of 1 January 1918 (no citation). Although no formal citation was published in the *Gazette*, research has unearthed the original recommendation for the award: 'For conspicuous good work as Staff Officer, RFC, at Headquarters, GHQ Wing. The influence of his keenness and spirit has been felt throughout the Wing. His energy is unlimited and it is with difficulty he can be restrained from working all night as well as all day. His main endeavour is to help others and he works unceasingly with the object in view entirely regardless of himself. His work has been invaluable'.

This recommendation, dated 20 October 1917, was made by General Trenchard himself, and to the main text he added a pencilled note: '....he carried out last year the work of an observer for six months with the greatest keenness and dash and was taken from this work to become a Staff Officer'. It has to be assumed from this, that he worked as an Observer sometime between January 1916, when he was pronounced, 'unfit for flying duties' and November 1916, when he was graded an Adjutant. Addenbrooke-Prout was, by the end of the war, promoted to Major, made an OBE, and created Chevalier, Légion d'Honneur by the French.

AITKEN, Robert Stanley

The son of Mr and Mrs R Aitken, of 32 King's Avenue, Muswell Hill, London, he was born on 4 April 1896. Educated at Highgate School (1909-12). He enlisted as a Private soldier into 15 Battalion, London Regiment (Civil Service Rifles) (TF) in 1914. Picked out for a commission, he was gazetted Second Lieutenant to the East Anglian Battery (Essex), RGA (TF), on 14 December 1915. After service with the Gunners, he successfully sought secondment to the RFC. His pilot training duly completed, he was confirmed and gazetted Flying Officer on 29 August 1916. Sent out to France and 42 Squadron, soon after qualifying for his 'Wings'.

His MC was announced in the *London Gazette* of 26 July 1917: 'For conspicuous gallantry and devotion to duty. On several occasions he made most valuable reconnaissances of the enemy's line, and on two successive days he engaged and severely damaged hostile batteries, working under most adverse weather conditions'.

Aitken served subsequently with 52 and 7 Squadrons in France before being posted as a Flying Instructor in the UK in 1918. Staying on in the RAF after the war, he commanded 41 and 25 Fighter Squadrons between 1928 and 1930. Awarded the OBE in 1937. He was appointed Air Attaché in Shanghai, China, between 1938 and 1940, before, as a specialist in Signals, becoming the Director of Signals in the Air Ministry. Next he was appointed Chief Signal Officer, Air Defence of Great Britain and Fighter Command, from 1940 to 1942, reaching the rank of A/Air Vice-Marshal (Technical). A CBE came in 1942, after which he served as AOC, 60 Group 1942-43; Chief Signal Officer, Mediterranean Allied Air Force 1942-43 and Air Staff Officer in Charge, Mediterranean Allied Air Force, Central Mediterranean Force, 1944-45. At the end of the war, he was made CB and, in 1946, the Americans made him an Officer of the Legion of Merit. He was also Mentioned in Despatches on two occasions. Retiring finally from the RAF in 1946, his technical skills were put to use as a Director of the Radio & Television Trust Ltd and of Airmec Laboratories Ltd; he was also appointed President of the Radar Association. Air Vice-Marshall Aitken lived, in the early 1950s, at 111 Old Brompton Road, London SW7.

AIZLEWOOD, Leslie Peech

The son of Solicitor, Albert Percy Aizlewood and his wife, Florence Shaw Aizlewood, of Blenheim House, Doncaster Road, Rotherham, Yorkshire, he was born in April 1895. Educated privately, and at Uppingham School, Rutland (1909-1912). After Uppingham, Leslie studied mechanical and electrical engineering at Sheffield University and at Parkgate Iron and Steel Works. Before the war, he became involved with his local (Rotherham) TF unit, being commissioned into 5 Battalion, York and Lancaster Regiment (TF). Mobilised in August 1914, he helped to get his battalion up to standard before accompanying it to France on 13 April 1915. Following a period at home recovering from wounds he had received in the trenches in July 1915, he took flying lessons and was rewarded with the Aviators Certificate (Number 2742) of the Royal Aero Club on 18 March 1916. His formal pilot training duly completed, he was confirmed and gazetted Flying Officer on 17 May following. Sent out to 32 Squadron (DH2s) in France in July 1916. In the September following, he single-handedly attacked five enemy machines for which action he was awarded the MC, announced in the *London Gazette* of 20 October 1916: 'For conspicuous gallantry and skill. Seeing five hostile machines, he manoeuvred to get between them and their lines; then, diving on one of them, he reserved his fire till he was only twenty yards off. The hostile machine fell out of control, but he was so close to it that he collided with it, breaking his propellor and damaging his machine. Though it was barely controllable, he managed to get it back to our lines'.

Shortly after this incident, Aizlewood was promoted to A/Captain and Flight Commander. He was wounded in a fight with the German Ace, Werner Voss, on 10 February 1917, (Voss claimed Aizlewood as the sixth of his victories), and he was obliged to return to England to recuperate. His wounds healed, he was next appointed to help with the establishment of new aerodromes in Scotland and England and, indeed, received a Mention in Despatches for this work, *London Gazette* of 13 March 1918. On 29 September 1918, by then a Major, Aizlewood was killed in a flying accident over the sea off Saltburn in Yorkshire. His body was recovered and buried with full military honours near to his home aerodrome at Marske-in-Cleveland (St Germain), Yorkshire. The award of an Air Force Cross was announced posthumously in the New Year *London Gazette* of 1 January 1919.

ALDRED, John William

The son of Coal Merchant, John Aldred and Louisa Aldred (née Clarke), of Stafford Road, Eccles, Lancashire, he was born on 26 April 1884. Gazetted Second Lieutenant to 11 Battalion, King's Own Royal Lancaster Regiment, on 29 November 1915. He served in the trenches in France and Flanders with the King's Own, before securing secondment to the RFC. Having trained as an Observer, he was posted to BE2c-equipped 5 Squadron with which unit he flew operationally from 30 August 1916 to 3 April 1917, claiming two victories and earning the first of his MCs, announced in the *London Gazette* of 26 March 1917: 'For conspicuous gallantry during an aerial combat with two hostile scouts, he drove one of the hostile machines down and succeeded in driving the other hostile machine back over the enemy's lines. He displayed great courage and determination throughout'.

Returning to the UK, he trained as a Pilot and after qualifying for his full 'Wings', returned again to the front on 21 October 1917, this time joining the Sopwith Camel-equipped 70 Squadron. Three more victories followed before he was promoted to Captain and Flight Commander and sent as such to 3 Squadron (Camels) on 3 April 1918. During the next month he claimed a further three victories and his efforts were rewarded with a Bar to his MC which came in the *London Gazette* of 16 September 1918: 'For conspicuous gallantry and devotion to duty whilst taking part in offensive patrols. During recent operations he has destroyed four enemy aircraft and drove down three others out of control. He also did much successful low bombing and firing at low targets. He did splendid service'.

Aldred finally left the service and returned to civilian life on 5 April 1919.

ALLEN, Laurence Wilfred

The son of Cycle Mechanic, Joseph Allen and Lillie Allen, of 83 Moor Street, Coventry, he was born on 14 September 1892. A pre-war volunteer, he had enlisted as a Private soldier (Number 1377) into 7 Battalion, Royal Warwickshire Regiment (TF). Allen accompanied his battalion to France and served in the trenches as a Sergeant from 22 March 1915. Picked out for a commission, he was gazetted Second Lieutenant to 6 Battalion, Royal Warwickshire Regiment (TF) on 20 November 1915. After further service as a subaltern in the trenches, he successfully sought secondment to the RFC late in 1916. He accompanied the BF2a-equipped 48 Squadron to France as a 'founder member' as soon as his observer training was completed in March 1917. On 24 May 1917, flying with Captain J H T Letts (qv) in Bristol Fighter, 'A3350', he was involved in a particularly fierce combat with an enemy machine. Although his Pilot escaped injury in this action, Allen himself was slightly wounded. In a hectic period during the months of April, May and June 1917, Allen claimed no less than ten victories. His MC was announced in the *London Gazette* of 26 May 1917: 'For conspicuous gallantry and devotion to duty when acting as an Observer. On many occasions he has helped to shoot down and destroy hostile machines. He has shown the greatest courage and skill on all occasions, frequently clearing difficult jams in the middle of a fight'.

He subsequently became a Pilot and, in the post-war years, became a Class 'A' Reservist in the RAF. His grading was dropped to Class 'C' in 1926 when, on 17 February of that year, whilst flying a Wolf (G-EDHJ), he was slightly injured in a crash at Whitby aerodrome. Allen subsequently relinquished his commission in the Reserve in September 1926.

ALLISON, John Oliver

The son of Mr and Mrs Joseph Allison, of Maxwell, Ontario, he was born on 8 October 1891. Educated at Maxwell Public and High Schools and at Toronto University (1914-16), where he studied medicine and was also a member of the OTC. In May 1916, he was gazetted Lieutenant and appointed to the 162 Battalion (Western Ontario Regiment) as Signalling Officer. Seconded to the RFC in England in January 1917, he completed his pilot training at the CFS in the following March. Sent out to Egypt in April 1917, he was next posted to Mesopotamia and 30 Squadron, on 17 August following. He was attacked and shot down in flames by three enemy aircraft while machine-gunning Turkish troops on the ground at Altun Kipri, on the Lesser Zab River, on 15 May 1918. His passenger in this flight, was an officer of the Mapping Section, RFC HQ, Lieutenant Francis Wright Atherton, MC, RFA attached RAF, whom he had volunteered to take over the Turkish dispositions to obtain some first-hand information. Atherton had won his MC as an Flying Officer Observer, RFA, in the summer of 1916. The belated announcement of Allison's MC came in the *London Gazette* of 11 January 1919: 'For conspicuous gallantry and devotion to duty. Often he descended to within a few hundred feet of the ground and regardless of danger, bombed and machine-gunned the enemy. On one occasion he carried out four bombing raids in one day at low altitudes'.

John Allison's remains were never recovered and hence he is commemorated on the Basra Memorial, Iraq.

ALLPORT, Jack Manning

The son of Mr and Mrs R Allport, of 6 Middlehead Road, Mosman, New South Wales, Australia, he was born in North Sydney on 13 July 1895. A Motor Mechanic and Despatch Clerk, he enlisted as a Gunner (Number 18626) into the AIF on 4 January 1916. His basic training completed, he embarked at Sydney aboard the SS *Argyllshire* (Transport A8) on 11 May 1916, bound for the Middle East as part of 26 Battery, 7 Field Artillery Brigade. After service in Egypt and Palestine, he was sent to the UK as a candidate for the flying service. Gazetted Second Lieutenant to RFC, via the Special List, on 17 March 1917. Having trained first as an Observer, he served briefly at the front in May 1917, with 5 Squadron (RE8s) before training as a Pilot. Confirmed and gazetted Flying Officer on 4 September 1917, he was next sent out to 2 Squadron with which unit he flew mainly photographic reconnaissance patrols. During one such sortie on 18 February 1918, Allport, by then promoted to Captain and Flight Commander, and his Observer of the day, Lieutenant A W Hammond (qv), were attacked by six enemy scouts. In the ensuing melée, Hammond shot down in flames one of the six, whilst another disintegrated in the air under his fire. Allport's MC citation reflects the circumstances of this and other actions he was involved in, *London Gazette* of 22 April 1918: 'For conspicuous gallantry and devotion to duty. On one occasion during night flying he made four trips during a period of four hours, dropping 60 bombs on his two objectives with excellent results. On a later occasion whilst on photographing work, he was attacked by six enemy machines, but by skilful manoeuvring he enabled his Observer to shoot down in flames one enemy machine, another falling to pieces in the air. On several occasions he has carried out his tasks of photographing hostile battery positions and calibrating our long-range batteries on their targets under the most unfavourable conditions and with excellent results, showing a magnificent example to the whole squadron'.

His tour with '2' duly completed, he returned to the UK in the late spring of 1918, where he saw out the remainder of the war as an Instructor. Allport returned to Australia and civilian life on 1 January 1919. During the Second World War, he served initially as a Sub Lieutenant in the Royal Australian Navy Volunteer Reserve at HMAS *Rushcutter*, Sydney, from 8 July 1942. He was later posted as Liaison Officer, Naval Auxiliary Patrol, HMAS *Penguin*, and promoted to Lieutenant. His appointment in the RANVR was finally terminated on 18 June 1946, and Allport took up residence with his wife at 11 Clifton Street, Clifton, New South Wales.

ANDERSON, William Kennedy

The son of William and Mary Ann Anderson, of Lindsay, Ontario, Canada, he was born in 1892. Educated at McMaster University (1911-14). Gazetted Lieutenant to 109 Battalion, Canadian Infantry, on 23 July 1916, he subsequently served with the CEF in France with, successively, 42 and 156 Battalions. Seconded to the RFC on 15 March 1917, he trained as an Observer and was sent out as a Probationary to 15 Squadron (RE8s) on 23 April following. His 'apprenticeship' satisfactorily completed, he was confirmed and gazetted Flying Officer (Observer) on 2 June 1917. Injury curtailed his tour with '15,' and he returned to the Home Establishment on 20 September 1917. His MC was announced in the New Year *London Gazette* of 1 January 1918 (no citation).

Anderson was killed in a flying accident at 20 TS, Harlaxon, near Nottingham, on 7 January 1918. His parents succeeded in getting his body returned home to Canada, and hence William Anderson is buried in Lindsay (Riverside) Cemetery, Ontario.

ANDREWS, John Oliver

The son of Brewer, John Andrews and Mrs Andrews, of Waterloo, Liverpool, he was born on 20 July 1896. Educated at Owens School (1908-11), at Manchester High School (1911-12), and at Manchester University. Gazetted Second Lieutenant to 15 Battalion, Royal Scots, on 9 October 1914. Seconded to the RFC, he trained as an Observer and was sent out as such to 5 Squadron (Avro 504s) in France in June 1915. Taking lessons at the Le Crotoy School in France, he gained his Royal Aero Club Certificate (Number 1924) on 19 October 1915. His formal pilot training duly completed, he was confirmed and gazetted Flying Officer on 30 April 1916. Sent out to 24 Squadron (DH2s) soon after qualifying for his full 'Wings', he achieved seven victories between 21 July and 22 November 1916, being promoted to A/Captain and Flight Commander in the process. The first of his MCs was announced in the *London Gazette* of 20 October 1916: 'For conspicuous gallantry and skill. He is a fine leader of offensive patrols, and has himself shot down four enemy machines. On one occasion he got within 25 yards of an enemy machine and under heavy fire brought it down a wreck'.

Andrews led the three-machine 24 Squadron patrol to which Major Lanoe Hawker, VC, famously attached himself on 23 November 1916. The RFC patrol had just engaged two enemy two-seaters when they were themselves attacked by a formation of enemy Scouts which included, amongst their number, Manfred von Richthofen. In the ensuing fight, Hawker, on this, his last active combat patrol before taking a Staff job, fell to the Red Baron. John Andrews, too, came close to being downed, his fuel tank was shot through and his engine hit, but he was saved by the intervention of Second Lieutenant R H M S Saundby (qv) who successfully beat off his attacker.

The Bar to his MC came in the *London Gazette* of 11 December 1916: 'For conspicuous gallantry in action. He showed great courage and determination in leading successful patrols and attacks on hostile aircraft, and has now accounted for his ninth machine. On one occasion he followed a machine down to 800 feet and on another, he went down to 500 feet'.

The King of Montenegro conferred that country's Silver Medal for Bravery upon Andrews, *London Gazette* of 31 October 1916. The French, too, weighed in with a Croix de Guerre. Andrews was also Mentioned in Despatches on three occasions during the Great War. Following a short rest at home, he was sent out to the Sopwith Pup-equipped 66 Squadron as a Flight Commander. Five more victories were achieved between 30 April and 11 July 1918 and he was awarded a gallantry Distinguished Service Order in the *London Gazette* of 26 July 1917. Promoted to Major, Andrews went on to commanded 209 Squadron in 1918. In the following year, after receiving a permanent commission in the RAF, he led 221 Squadron in the Mediterranean and in South Russia. Service in India followed in 1920. In 1923, he married Bertha Hambrook, with whom he would have two sons. Andrews instructed at the Imperial Defence College, and held a variety of important Staff positions, before going on to serve throughout the Second World War. His Second World War appointments included AOC, 12 (Fighter) Group, and AOA, HQ, Flying Training Command. He was created CB in 1942. Andrews finally retired in 1945, with the rank of Air Vice-Marshal. He died in 1989.

ARCHER, Robert Alexander

The son of Captain R H Archer RN and Mrs Archer, of Horndean, Hampshire, he was born on 14 September 1892. A pre-war officer of the Regular Army, he was gazetted Second Lieutenant to the Royal Artillery on 20 December 1912. Developing an interest in flying, he gained his Royal Aero Club Certificate (Number 434) in a Bristol machine at the Bristol School, Brooklands, on 4 March 1913. Secondment to the RFC eventually came in the second year of the war and, after a brief period of service at the front as an Observer with 6 Squadron, he trained as a Pilot and was formally confirmed and gazetted Flying Officer on 9 June 1915. His MC, presumably for his work as an Observer, was announced in the *London Gazette* of 23 June 1915 (no citation). Archer continued to serve with 6 Squadron, but now as a Pilot. On 10 September 1915, he and his Observer, Lieutenant G A Parker (qv), in BE2c '2031', although shot up and damaged, still managed to drive off an attacking Albatros after firing one drum at about 150 yards. His tour with '6' completed, he returned to the UK for a rest and instructing duties. In July 1916, Archer was sent to join 42 Squadron, then at Filton, before accompanying that unit to France as a 'founder member' on 8 August following. His first tour with '42' completed in 1917, he spent a period instructing at the CFS before eventually rejoining '42', now re-equipped with RE8s, at the front in March 1918. Apparently deciding he had had enough of the flying service, Archer reverted to the Royal Field Artillery in August 1918.

ARCHIBALD, Max Stansfield Eaton

The son of Mr & Mrs P McGregor Archibald, of Truro, Nova Scotia, Canada he was born on 23 July 1887. Educated locally at Truro, and also at McGill University, from where he graduated BSc with Honours in Mining Engineering in 1910. His first job was in the Transvaal, where he spent four years working for a living, whilst still continuing to study for his Diploma in Mine Management. When war came in 1914, he made his way to England as soon as he could, and was gazetted Second Lieutenant to the Royal Engineers late in 1915. On 23 April 1916, he was a Mine-Tunnelling Officer, and following a foray into enemy territory to blow up one of their mines, he was seriously wounded in the foot by shrapnel when returning to his own lines. For his gallantry in this affair, he was Mentioned in Sir Douglas Haig's Despatches of 22 June 1916. After convalescing in the UK, he was granted three months leave of absence to visit his home in Canada. Returning to England, he next successfully sought secondment to the RFC. Having trained as an Observer, he was sent out to join 18 Squadron (DH4s) in February 1918. On 12 May 1918, his DH4 received a direct hit from ground fire. The exploding shell knocked out one of the struts in between the planes and, at the same time, badly shattered Archibald's arm. The Pilot landed on the first available airfield and the seriously wounded Archibald was rushed to a Field Hospital at Aeq, where he died two hours after his arrival. His MC was announced posthumously in the *London Gazette* 16 September 1918: 'For conspicuous gallantry and devotion to duty. He has taken part in fourteen successful bombing raids, twenty-five successful low bombing reconnaissance flights, and eleven successful photographic flights. On one occasion he was attacked by ten enemy scouts, and drove down one completely out of control. He has engaged enemy troops from low altitudes, and his excellent work, good spirits, and total disregard of danger have been a fine example to all'.

Max Archibald is buried in Aubigny Communal Cemetery Extension, France.

ARKELL, Anthony John

The son of the Reverend John Norris Arkell and Elenor Jessy Arkell (née Bunting), he was born at Hinxhill, Kent, on 29 July 1898. Educated at Bradfield College (1912-16), and at Queen's College, Cambridge (1919-20 and again in 1938). Gazetted Second Lieutenant to the RFC, via the Special Lists, on 12 August 1916. His formal training duly completed, he was confirmed and gazetted Flying Officer on 4 January 1917. Posted to 'B' Flight, 50 HD Squadron at Throwley, Tony Arkell found himself combating, mostly at night and in darkness, Zeppelin raids on the east coast of England. Night flying in those early days was risky; simply taking off or landing in the dark, fraught with danger. He later transferred briefly to 112 Squadron, who also operated from Throwley. As the Zeppelin menace receded due to the effective work of the HD squadrons, a new problem arose, with the onset of the Gotha bomber raids. On the night of 19/20 May 1918, Arkell who had survived to become one of the most experienced night-flying HD Pilots was, by this time, operating out of North Weald with 39 Squadron. Taking off in a Bristol Fighter, 'C4636' (dubbed 'Devil in the Dusk' by its Pilot) with 1 AM Albert Thomas Charles Stagg (Number 10652) as his Gunner/Observer, Arkell had been patrolling for just over an hour when, at 00.05 am, and north of Hainault, he glimpsed the glowing exhausts of a Gotha bomber a thousand feet below him. The citation for his MC, announced in the *London Gazette* of 31 May 1918, is eloquent testament to what happened next: 'For conspicuous gallantry when, during a hostile aeroplane raid, he and his Observer, Private Stagg, while on patrol, sighted a Gotha machine at a height of 10,000 feet. He opened fire at a range of 200 yards and so manoeuvred his machine as to give his Observer, despite a vigorous fire being continually poured onto his machine from the enemy aeroplane, the target which offered best possible advantage for attack. Private Stagg then opened a heavy fire upon the enemy aeroplane at close range, as a result of which the enemy machine burst into flames and crashed to the ground. Lieutenant Arkell showed the utmost coolness and courage during the engagement, the result of which was to cause the enemy machine to be brought down'.

When their bullet-riddled Brisfit landed – the Gotha had put up a spirited resistence – Arkell was unstinting in his praise for his experienced and gallant Gunner. Albert Stagg later received the Military Medal, *London Gazette* of 31 May 1918, from the hands of Major General F C Heath-Caldwell. On what was a successful night for the RAF, three Gothas were brought down and a fourth crashed of its own volition. Tony Arkell went on to live an interesting life after leaving the service in 1919. First of all, he returned to Oxford to finish his degree. In 1920 he joined the Sudan Political Service, an ideal location to cultivate his great passion for archaeology. His many and varied appointments over the next few decades can be summarised as follows: Assistant District Commissioner, Darfur Province, 1921-24; Acting Resident, Dar Masalit, 1925-26; District Commissioner, Kosti (White Nile Province), 1926-29; DC, Sennar (Blue Nile Province), 1929-32; Acting Deputy Governor, Darfur Province, 1932-37; Commissioner, Archaeology and Anthropology, Sudan Government, 1938-48; Chief Transport Officer, Sudan Government, 1940-44; Editor, *Sudan Notes and Records*, 1945-48; Archaeological Adviser to the Sudan Government, 1948-53; Lecturer in Egyptology, University College, London, 1948-53; accompanied the British Ennedi Expedition in 1957; First President of Philosophical Society of Sudan, 1947 (Honorary Life Member, 1949); Honorary Member, German Archaeological Institute, 1953; Member of Council, Society of Antiquities, 1956-57; Member of Committee, Egypt Exploration Society. Arkell received the MBE for his outstanding services to archaeology in 1928. In 1931, he was also awarded the Order of the Nile (4th Class) by the Egyptian Government. He married, firstly, in 1928, Dorothy Davidson (died 1945) with whom he had one son and one daughter, and, secondly, Joan Margaret Burnell (née Andrews). Returning to Oxford in 1938, he graduated B.Litt, and also secured a Diploma in Anthropology in the same year.

After the Second World War, a Doctorate in Literature (Oxon) was achieved in 1955. He next took the decision to become a man of the cloth and entered Cuddesdon College, becoming deacon in 1960 and priest in 1961. His many other accomplishments, in no particular order, included: Fellow of the Society of Arts; Vicar of Cuddington with Dinton in the Diocese of Oxford, 1963-71; Reader in Egyptian Archaeology, University of London, 1953-63; Curator of the Flinders Petrie Collection of Egyptian Antiquities at University College, London, 1948-63; Honorary Assistant Curate, Great Missenden, 1960-63. Arkell also published a number of books and wrote many articles. He lived, latterly, at Cuddington, Colam, Little Badow, Essex. The Reverend Tony Arkell died on 26 February 1980.

ARNISON, Charles Henry

The stepson of Brewers Manager, William Eley, and the son of Elizabeth Eley, of 21 Lansdown Parade, Cheltenham, Gloucester, he was born on 13 January 1893. Educated locally, he was apprenticed as an engineer in May 1913. Volunteering as soon as war came in August 1914, he enlisted as a Private soldier (Number 2454) into the Gloucestershire Hussars Yeomanry. On 14 September 1915, he was sent out to Gallipoli as part of a reinforcing draft. Following the evacuation from the Peninsula, he served with his regiment in Egypt. His engineering experience no doubt helped his application for a transfer to the flying service and, early in 1917, he was accepted as an Officer Cadet. Gazetted Second Lieutenant to the RFC, via the General List, on 26 May 1917. His pilot training duly completed, he was confirmed and gazetted Flying Officer on 28 June 1917. Joining 62 Squadron in England on 12 October 1917, Arnison eventually accompanied the Bristol Fighter-equipped unit to France as a 'founder member', on 23 January 1918. On 3 May 1918, he had an extremely close call when, during an aerial combat, his Observer, Lieutenant Samuel Parry, Royal Engineers attached RFC, was killed. Less than two weeks later on 16 May 1918, Arnison was forced down during a combat over Corbie with Leutnant Hans Kirschstein of Jasta 6, becoming the twelfth of the German Ace's 27 victories. Once again, Arnison's Observer, Charles Douglas Wells, from Norfolk, who had won an MC in the trenches with 7 Battalion, King's Own, was killed. Arnison, wounded in the back, crawled out of the wreckage of the crashed Brisfit just before it was shelled to matchwood. His MC was announced in the *London Gazette* of 16 September 1918: 'For conspicuous gallantry and devotion to duty. He has destroyed four enemy aircraft and driven down four others completely out of control. He has always shown the greatest skill, keenness and gallantry, and has largely been instrumental in the fine achievements of his Squadron'.

Staying on in the RAF after the war, he suffered the indignity of a Court Martial on 15 September 1919 and, although he was found guilty, he was allowed to continue in the service. Whilst serving with 12 Squadron on the Rhine as part of the Occupation Force, his right eye was injured in an accident on 6 June 1920, and this may have led to his leaving the RAF in October 1920.

ARNOT, Arthur Alison McDonald

The son of Gordon Alison Arnot and Janey Wood Arnot, of 6 Dryburgh Gardens, Kelvinside, Glasgow, he was born in 1899. Educated at Hill Head High School, Glasgow, where he excelled at games and literature, becoming Editor and Business Manager of the school magazine. Leaving school at Easter 1917, he was immediately accepted into the RFC as a Cadet. After receiving his commission, he gained his 'Wings' in near record time and was in France flying with the Camel-equipped 3 Squadron by November 1917. In February 1918, he was allowed to return home to enjoy a short leave. On 12 April 1918, he was promoted to A/Captain and Flight Commander and, in the afternoon of that same day, he was last seen patrolling in Sopwith Camel, 'B5580', over Aveluy Wood at 1740 hours. Writing to his parents, his Squadron Commander inferred that he had been shot-up in the air, saying: 'He could have landed on the German side in safety at any time, but preferred to try and get home to being taken prisoner'. His MC was announced posthumously in the *London Gazette* of 22 June 1918: 'For conspicuous gallantry and devotion to duty. When engaging hostile troops with bombs and machine-gun fire, he was attacked by a large number of enemy aircraft. He engaged the hostile machines in a most gallant manner, one of which he destroyed. On a previous occasion he shot down another enemy plane, which fell in flames. During the last four months, he has carried out offensive patrols at very low altitudes under adverse weather conditions with conspicuous skill and success'.

Arthur Arnot is buried in Knightsbridge Cemetery, Mesnil-Martinsart, Somme, France.

ASHCROFT, Reginald Bruce

From Derby, he was born on 25 February 1893. He was in college studying English in 1914, 1915 and for most of 1916, before he was eventually gazetted Second Lieutenant to 4 (Extra Reserve) Battalion, Sherwood Foresters, on 5 August 1916, followed by an immediate attachment to the 17 Battalion of his regiment, the 'Welbreck Rangers'. Successfully seeking secondment to the RFC, he was, after training and initial probationary service as an Observer, confirmed and gazetted Flying Officer (Observer) on 10 March 1917. Sent out to 9 Squadron in France, he became one of the unit's most effective Observers, particularly adept at the low-level strafing of ground targets. The first of his MCs was announced in the *London Gazette* of 26 September 1917, details in the *Gazette* of 9 January 1918: 'For conspicuous gallantry and devotion to duty. He rendered invaluable assistance to our infantry in the attack, flying several times through heavy barrage and using his machine-gun at a very low altitude. He has consistently done splendid work in contact patrols and in attacking enemy infantry from low altitudes'.

The Bar to his MC came in the *London Gazette* of 27 October 1917, details in the *Gazette* of 18 March 1918: 'For conspicuous gallantry and devotion to duty in attacking enemy troops from an extremely low altitude; on one occasion he attacked from the rear at a height of about 150 feet, the enemy who were holding up our infantry'.

His tour with '9' completed, Ashcroft returned to the Home Establishment on 28 October 1917, and was appointed an Assistant Instructor. Later, in March 1918, he was graded as an Equipment Officer, 3rd Class, at No 5 School of Military Aeronautics, Denham, where he saw out the remainder of the war.

ATKEY, Alfred Clayburn

From Minebow, Saskatchewan, Canada, he was born in Toronto, Ontario, on 16 August 1894. He was working as a journalist with the *Toronto Evening Telegram* when war broke out in August 1914. With 38 victories, Atkey would become the most successful two-seater Ace on the British side. Volunteering directly into the flying service whilst still in Canada, he was, upon arrival in England, duly gazetted Second Lieutenant to the RFC on 19 October 1916. Once qualified he was sent out to 18 Squadron (DH4s) in France on 8 September 1917. The first of his eventual 38 victories on 4 February 1918, was perhaps a little slow in coming but once he got started, there was no stopping him! Eight more victories came with '18', before he was posted as a Flight Commander and A/Captain to the BF2b-equipped 22 Squadron late in April 1918. The first of his MCs was announced in the *London Gazette* of 22 June 1918: 'For conspicuous gallantry and devotion to duty. When engaged on reconnaissance and bombing work, he attacked four scouts, one of which he shot down in flames. Shortly afterwards he attacked four two-seater planes, one of which he brought down out of control. On two previous occasions his formation was attacked by superior numbers of the enemy, three of whom in all were shot down out of control. He has shown exceptional ability and initiative on all occasions'.

His Observer in at least one of the actions described in this citation was J M Brisbane (qv). After arriving at '22', Atkey teamed up with Londoner Lieutenant Charles Gass (qv) of the Poplar and Stepney Rifles (17 Battalion, London Regiment (TF)) to deadly effect. In the course of just one month the pair would account for no less than 29 hostiles. They were involved, with Squadron colleagues John Gurdon and John Thornton, in one of the most famous aerial battles of all time. The action, known for obvious reasons as, 'Two against Twenty', occurred on 7 May 1918, when the two 22 Squadron Brisfits took on no less than 20 enemy Scouts. Atkey and his partner claimed five of the Germans, whilst Gurdon and Thornton accounted for three others. The pair would do well again just two days later with five more victories on a single day. On another occasion, when a section of a top plane was shot away, Gass climbed out onto a lower wing to balance the Bristol Fighter as Atkey nursed it back to base. His remarkable tour with '22' completed, Atkey returned to the Home Establishment in June 1918. Described as, 'expert in gunnery, bombing, photography, reconnaissance', he was sent as an Instructor to No 1 Flight School, on 21 August 1918. The Bar to his MC came in the *London Gazette* of 16 September 1918: 'For conspicuous gallantry and devotion to duty. During recent operations he destroyed seven enemy machines. When engaged with enemy aircraft, often far superior in numbers, he proved himself a brilliant fighting pilot and displayed dash and gallantry of the highest order'.

Returning to Canada, he finally left the service in 1919. Atkey served again in the Second World War, this time as a Link Instructor with the RCAF. Alfred Atkey died on 29 January 1971.

ATKINSON, Rupert Norman Gould

The son of China trader J B Atkinson and his wife, Amelia Sophie, of 17 Waldeck Avenue, Bedford, he was born on 17 July 1896 in Shanghai, China. Educated at Marlborough (1910-14), he was about to go up to Cambridge when war intervened. He initially enlisted as a Private soldier into the Middlesex Regiment, before being picked out for a commission and gazetted Second Lieutenant to 15 Battalion of that same regiment on 2 December 1914. In the following year, he was seconded to the West African Regiment in the Cameroons, spending nine months there before being invalided home in April 1916. Transferring to the RFC, he gained his Royal Aero Club Certificate (Number 3646) on 28 September 1916. His formal training duly completed, he was confirmed and gazetted Flying Officer on 1 November following. His first operational posting was to 10 Squadron, with which unit he would spend the next year. His MC was announced in the *London Gazette* of 18 October 1917, details in the *Gazette* of 7 March 1918: 'For conspicuous gallantry and devotion to duty. This officer has done a large amount of successful artillery work, has taken part in many night bombing raids, and has continually distinguished himself by his fearlessness and determination in descending to low altitudes in order to attack hostile infantry and machine guns. On one occasion, also he successfully attacked and drove down a hostile balloon'.

Following a short rest, Atkinson was sent to the DH9-equipped 98 Squadron in January 1918 and accompanied that unit to France as a 'founder member' in the following April. Atkinson achieved two victories with '98' in May 1918, before being posted as a Senior Flight Commander to 206 Squadron (also DH9s) in June. Three further victories came to Atkinson between 30 August and 14 October 1918. The first of his two DFCs was gazetted on 2 November 1918, the Bar following in the *London Gazette* of 4 June 1919, both awarded for his leadership and gallantry. He was also Mentioned in Despatches around this time. The Belgians awarded him a Croix de Guerre which was announced in the *London Gazette* of 15 July 1919, but, by this time, Atkinson was already dead. He had arrived in England in February 1919, for a short leave but was struck down by Spanish influenza, a contemporary pandemic which would claim many more millions of lives than did the Great War itself. Robert Atkinson died at his widowed mother's home at High Kelton, Berkhampsted, on 7 March 1919, the very day he was due to return to his unit in Germany. It was tragically ironic that, after surviving more than one thousand combat hours, he should be wiped out by 'flu. He is buried in Great Berkhamstead (St Peter) Church Cemetery, Hertfordshire.

AUSTIN, Ronald Albert

The son of Mr and Mrs Albert S Austin of 'Eilyer', Lake Bolac, Victoria, Australia, he was born on 21 June 1893. Educated at Melbourne Grammar School, and at Cambridge University. A sheep station manager, he enlisted as a Private soldier (Number 2930) into 8 Australian Light Horse Regiment, on 20 March 1916. His basic training completed, he embarked at Melbourne aboard the SS *Hymettus* on 12 September 1916, as part of 21 Reinforcement Group for 8 LH Regiment in the Middle East. After arriving in Egypt, Austin served with 3 LH Training Regiment, before being accepted as a volunteer into the flying service, and sent on to Aeronautics School in the UK, on 1 February 1917. Gazetted Second Lieutenant to the RFC on 5 May 1917. Austin duly received his 'Wings' and was gazetted Pilot, AFC, on 31 May 1917. After brief service with 27 RS and 23 Reserve Wing in the UK, he was sent out to fly operationally with 1 Squadron, AFC, in Egypt and Palestine. On 26 June 1917, following a bombing raid on the Turkish Fourth Army HQ, the engine of a BE flown by Lieutenant C le Brun Brown (qv), seized up, forcing him to land in the desert. Austin, also in a BE, and Captain A T Cole (qv), in a Martinsyde, landed alongside their stranded comrade and while Cole burnt the abandoned BE, Austin took off with le Brun Brown aboard. Cole joined his comrades in the air and the two machines set off again for their base. However, some time later, south east of Beersheba, Austin's engine also seized, forcing him to land. Again, Cole came down and at first tried to take off again with both le Brun Brown and Austin as his passengers. When this failed, he attempted to take just one of them up, but was again unable to do so when his undercarriage broke under the strain. The three stranded airmen buried a camera and their machine guns, and set off across the desert towards the British lines, where, fortunately, they were rescued by a patrol of Australian Light Horse. The Official History relates how, on 29 November 1917, Austin and his Observer, Lieutenant G Findlay, flying an RE8, with an accompanying RFC Bristol Fighter, shot down out of control, two enemy aircraft during an engagement in the area of Tul Keram. The same source also credits Austin and Lieutenant L W Sutherland (qv), in a 1 Squadron, AFC Bristol Fighter, with shooting down an Albatros on 3 January 1918 – the first enemy machine to be confirmed as destroyed in air combat by the squadron. Austin was promoted to A/Captain and Flight Commander on 1 February 1918. His MC was announced in the *London Gazette* of 26 March 1918 (no citation).

The recommendation for his MC states that it was for actions in November 1917, when he undertook photographic missions near Jerusalem despite heavy anti-aircraft fire, and also for leading many bombing raids. Austin was captured by Arabs on 19 March 1918, when he and his Observer, Lieutenant O M Lee, in a Bristol Fighter, landed to pick up Major A J Evans, whose 142 Squadron Martinsyde had been forced down near Kerak, with engine trouble. Austin broke a wheel whilst landing, and the three stranded officers could only set fire to their machines and surrender to some unfriendly Arabs, who subsequently handed them over to the Turks. Austin was repatriated on 21 November 1918, arriving in England on the Christmas Day following. He finally left the service to return to Australia on 4 March 1919. Austin was rejected on health grounds by the RAAF in the Second World War, but was able to enlist in the Australian Military Forces at Mortlake on 18 April 1942, before being promoted to Captain with 7 Garrison Battalion, Volunteer Defence Corps. His appointment was eventually terminated after the war on 31 October 1945.

AYRE, Ronald Henderson

From St Johns, Newfoundland, he was born on 9 April 1898. The Ayre family were to suffer grievously on 1 July 1916, the first day of the Battle of the Somme, when three of their number, all officers with the Newfoundland Regiment, were killed in action. Ronald, like the other Ayre boys, was educated at Leys School, Cambridge (1911-16). Going into the service almost straight from school, he was gazetted Second Lieutenant to the RFC, via the Special Lists, on 5 August 1916. Still only 18 years old, he was kept back in England until the summer of 1917, when he was sent out to 27 Squadron. 'The Flying Elephants' were in process of changing over from their Martinsydes to DH4s as the winter came. Ayre, who flew both types, made an immediate impression and had been promoted A/Captain and Flight Commander by 8 October 1917, his MC announced shortly afterwards in the *London Gazette* of 27 October 1917, details in the *Gazette* of 18 March 1918: 'For conspicuous gallantry and devotion to duty. During a period of five months he took part in many successful bombing raids. On one occasion he bombed an enemy airship shed and on another occasion bombed a railway station from a height of 500 feet. He derailed part of a train, and then engaged the occupants with machine-gun fire. He displayed the greatest gallantry and determination'.

Ayre was allowed to return to Canada to take up instructing duties on 27 February 1918, the sole member of the family to survive the Great War. Subsequently qualified BA. Ronald Ayre died on 26 December 1967.

B

BABINGTON, Philip

The fourth son of Charles H Babington and Grace Damaris Babington (née Tremayne), of Croan, Wadebridge, Cornwall, he was born in February 1894. Two of his brothers fell in the Great War - Lieutenant Hugh Babington, DSC, RN, HMS *Fox*, died on 27 November 1919, age 27, and 2 Lieutenant Ralph Vivian Babington, 3 Coldstream Guards, killed in action on 9 October 1917, age 19. An elder brother, John, flew with the RNAS in the Great War, and eventually became Air Marshal Sir John Babington, KCB, CBE, DSO, etc, although he changed his surname to 'Tremayne' in 1945. Philip's remaining brother, Gervase Babington, North Somerset Yeomanry attached Fife and Forfar Yeomanry, also won an MC, before going on to serve with the RAF. Philip was educated at Eton (1907-13). Volunteering immediately war came, he was gazetted Second Lieutenant to 9 (Cyclist) Battalion, Hampshire Regiment (TF), on 31 August 1914. Keen for secondment to the RFC, he gained his Royal Aero Club Certificate (Number 1036) on 7 January 1915. His formal pilot training duly completed, he was confirmed and gazetted Flying Officer on 1 April following. Babington first served operationally with BE2c-equipped 2 Squadron, mainly co-operating with the artillery and undertaking photographic reconnaissance sorties. Awarded the MC in the Birthday Honours *London Gazette* of 3 June 1916 (no citation). Promoted to A/Major, he commanded 46 Squadron (Sopwith Pups) on the Western Front in 1916 and 1917. Returning to the UK, he commanded 141 Squadron at Rochford and Biggin Hill from 1 January 1918. A brief appointment to the command of an RAF Wing came later in 1918. He was Mentioned in Despatches on three occasions during the Great War. He was also awarded the Air Force Cross, *London Gazette* of 1 January 1919. He married in 1918, Joan Daniell (OBE 1946), with whom he had one son (Flying Officer Henry Christopher Babington, 157 Sqd, RAFVR, who was killed on active service on 19 May 1942, age 20) and three daughters. Staying on in the RAF after the war, he commanded 39 Squadron at Biggin Hill, from 1 July 1919. His many other subsequent appointments, promotions and honours included: Staff Officer, HQ, Egyptian Group, 1921; OC, 5 FTS, 1925; Wing Commander, 1925; Group Captain, 1931; Assistant Commandant, RAF College, Cranwell, 1931-35: Air Commodore, 1936; Director of Postings, Air Ministry, 1936-40; Air Vice-Marshal, 1939; Air Member for Personnel, 1940-42; CB, 1941; AOC, Flying Training Command, 1942-45; Air Marshal, 1942; KCB, 1943. Sir Phillip finally retired with the rank of Air Marshal in December 1945, he and Lady Babington settling into the family home at Glebe House, Chiddingstone, Kent, until his death on 25 February 1965.

BAILLIE, William

The son of Daniel and Marion Baillie, of Knapdale, Motherwell, he was born on 16 April 1891. Educated at Glasgow High School, he left in 1908 to enter the offices of Messrs Wright & Co., Solicitors of Motherwell, before, later, transferring to Messrs Robb & Crosbie of George Street, Glasgow. Volunteering as soon as the war came, he enlisted as a Private soldier into 10 Battalion, Black Watch (Royal Highland Regiment) on 12 September 1914. Picked out for a commission, he was gazetted Second Lieutenant to the same battalion on 17 November 1914. Seconded to the RFC late in 1915, he served in Egypt as a Probationary with 14 Squadron before being formally confirmed and gazetted Flying Officer (Observer) on 1 April 1916, earning, in the process, a Mention in Despatches which was announced in the *London Gazette* of 26 September 1916. Returning from Egypt, he formally qualified as a Pilot on 1 June 1916 and was sent to FE2b-equipped 11 Squadron in France in October 1916. In an aerial engagement on 5 April 1917, he was severely wounded, but was awarded the MC for his share in the fight, *London Gazette* of 11 May 1917: 'For conspicuous gallantry and devotion to duty. Although very severely wounded during a combat with hostile aircraft, he succeeded in bringing his own machine back and effected a safe landing'.

After eight months in hospital, he resumed flying, mainly as an Instructor. He was with 78 Squadron, 49 Wing RAF, when, on 1 April 1919, he met with a motor accident in London and died in Queen Alexander's Hospital five days later. William Baillie is commemorated in Dalziel (Airbles) Cemetery, Lanarkshire (Special Memorial), and is buried in Dalziel (Old Manse Road) Burial Ground.

BAILLIEU, Reginald Francis

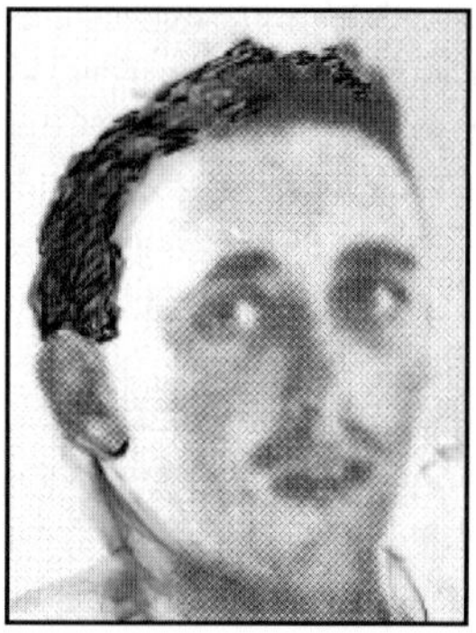

The son of Mr and Mrs George Baillieu, of 'Talana', 109 Westbury Street, East St Kilda, Victoria, Australia, he was born in Queenscliff, Victoria, on 17 March 1896. He enlisted as a Private soldier (Number 154) into the AIF on 1 February 1916. Quickly promoted to Sergeant, he embarked at Melbourne aboard the SS *Orsova* (Transport A67) on 16 March 1916, bound for the Middle East as part of 'B' Flight, 1 Squadron, AFC. Arriving in Egypt on 16 April 1916, he trained as a Pilot and was subsequently gazetted Pilot and Second Lieutenant, AFC, on 24 June following. Baillieu served with 1 Squadron, AFC in Egypt and Palestine. On 19 March 1917, Baillieu and his Observer, Ross Smith (qv), landed and rescued a 14 Squadron Pilot who had come down within sight of the enemy, both receiving the MC for their selfless bravery, *London Gazette* of 11 May 1917: 'For conspicuous gallantry and devotion to duty. Accompanied by his Observer, he descended to the rescue of a pilot who had been forced to land and who had set his machine on fire. He landed safely on difficult ground, and, despite the close proximity of the enemy, succeeded in rescuing the pilot and carrying off his two passengers under close and heavy rifle fire'. Baillieu was eventually be presented with the insignia of his MC by the King at an investiture held at Buckingham Palace on 15 January 1918.

On 13 July 1917, Baillieu and his Observer Lieutenant A E Barbe, Highland Light Infantry attached RFC, narrowly escaped disaster when their BE was shot about by an enemy Scout attacking out of the fierce desert sun. He was promoted to A/Captain and Flight Commander on 15 August 1917. His tour with 1 AFC completed on 27 September 1917, he shortly afterwards embarked for England. His appointment terminated, he was allowed to return home to Australia on 24 June 1918. Baillieu served subsequently as a Second Lieutenant in the Militia in the 1920s. Reginald Baillieu died on 18 January 1965.

BAKER, Brian Edmund

The son of Mr and Mrs E Baker, of Queen's Hill House, Hertford, he was born on 31 August 1896. Educated at Haileybury School (1910-14). Gazetted Second Lieutenant to 15 Battalion, Rifle Brigade, on 9 January 1915 with a secondment to the RFC coming in the following September. Gained his Royal Aero Club Certificate (Number 1938) on 25 October 1915. His formal pilot training duly completed, he was confirmed and gazetted Flying Officer on 7 December 1915. He was sent to BE2-equipped 13 Squadron in France with a mere 12 hours flying time in his logbook. His tour with '13' completed, he returned to the Home Establishment, before accompanying 48 Squadron to France as a 'founder member' and Flight Commander on 8 March 1917. On 22 July 1917, his Bristol Fighter intercepted and sent down one of a formation of Gothas returning from a bombing raid over England. Just five days later, with his Observer, Lieutenant G R Spencer, in BF2b, 'A7170', he gained another of his 12 victories by shooting down Vizefeldwebel Brandt of MFJa1. His MC was announced in the *London Gazette* of 25 August 1917: 'For conspicuous gallantry and devotion to duty. He led his patrol with great skill against a hostile formation, which he attacked, accounting for five enemy machines out of six. Later he drove down a hostile machine in flames and attacked and destroyed another by diving 7,000 feet on to it and firing at such close range as to nearly collide with it. His gallantry has been at all times of great value to his squadron'.

His continuing successes were marked by the award of a gallantry Distinguished Service Order, *London Gazette* of 4 March 1918. His tour with '48' completed, he returned to instructing duties in the UK. Baker's outstanding work as an Instructor in the later months of the war was rewarded with the Air Force Cross, *London Gazette* of 1 January 1919. He was also Mentioned in Despatches, *London Gazette* of 20 May 1918. The French, too, showed their appreciation with a Croix de Guerre, *London Gazette* of 18 April 1918. Baker was granted a permanent commission in the RAF in 1919. He married, in 1926, Jaimsie Derby Robinson, with whom he had two daughters. He played Soccer for the RAF XI, from 1926 to 1930, captaining the team in the '28, '29 and '30 seasons. As he progressed through his RAF career, his many appointments, promotions and honours included: CFI, RAF Training Base, Leuchars, 1932-34: CFI, HMS *Eagle*, 1934: CFI HMS *Courageous*, 1936; Commanding RAF Gosport, 1937-38 and RAF Leuchars 1938; AOC, 51 Group, 1940-41; AOC, RAF Iceland, 1941; AOC, 16 Group, 1941-42 and 19 Group, 1943-44; CB, 1943; KBE, 1944; Order of the White Lion and Military Medal (Czechoslovakia), 1944; Polonia Restituta (Poland), 1944; AOC, East Africa, 1945; SASO, HQ, Middle East, 1945; Commander of the Legion of Merit (USA), 1946; AOC Transport Command, 1947-50. He retired from the RAF with the rank of Air Marshal in 1950. Taking a great interest in the work of the Royal National Lifeboat Institution, he was made Life Governor of that institution. Air Marshal Sir Brian Baker lived at 3 Howard Place, St Andrews, Fife, Scotland, until his death on 8 October 1979.

BAKER, George Brindley Aufrere

The son of Colonel Walter Way Baker, Royal Engineers, and Mrs Baker, he was born in Canada on 25 July 1894. Educated at Cheltenham College (1908-10). Gazetted Second Lieutenant to 7 Battalion, Royal Berkshire Regiment, on 23 December 1914. Anxious to transfer to the RFC, Baker gained his Royal Aero Club Certificate (Number 2729) on 6 April 1916. His formal training duly completed, he was confirmed and gazetted Flying Officer on 31 May following. He first served operationally with the BE12-equipped 19 Squadron from July 1916. His MC was announced in the *London Gazette* of 4 June 1917 (no citation). Although no formal citation was published in the *Gazette*, research has unearthed the original recommendation for the award: 'March 1917, Has led a great many offensive patrols and successful bomb raids and has set a fine example by his dash and initiative'.

Promoted to A/Captain, he joined 23 Squadron as a Flight Commander in October 1917. Further tours with 85 Squadron and with 52 Squadron followed before the end of the war. The French awarded him the Croix de Guerre at this time. Staying on in the RAF, he was given a permanent commission and appointed Flight Lieutenant in 1919, and further promoted to Squadron Leader in 1923. He married, in 1924, Charlotte Marian Anderson, with whom he had one daughter. Baker served in Egypt from 1927 to 1932, being promoted to Wing Commander in 1931. An Air Vice-Marshal by 1941, he was created CB in 1942 and CBE in 1943. His appointments during the Second World War included Chief of Staff, Mediterranean Allied Air Force, 1944-45 and Director of Training (Plans) in 1945. Retiring with the rank of Air Vice-Marshal in 1946, he lived with his family at Queen Anne Cottage, Friday Street, Henley-on-Thames, Oxfordshire, until his death on 23 October 1968.

BAKER, John Wakeling

The elder son of the Reverend F V Baker, DD,BA, and Mrs Baker, he was born in Winnipeg, Canada, on 23 October 1897. Educated at Eastbourne College (1911-15), and at the Royal Military Academy, Woolwich. Gazetted Second Lieutenant into the RGA on 19 February 1916, he was a Gunner Liaison Officer attached to 34 Squadron, before being seconded to the RFC in the following year. Having trained as an Observer, he was sent to serve as such with 4 Squadron (RE8s) in France. His MC was announced in the *London Gazette* of 26 July 1918: 'For conspicuous gallantry and devotion to duty in carrying out low-flying reconnaissances and contact patrols under heavy machine-gun, rifle and anti-aircraft fire, when he remained in the air for long hours, often under abnormally bad weather conditions and often in darkness or thick mist. On one occasion he fired into enemy troops and transport, causing great confusion, and he remained over their lines taking notes until quite dark, when he returned with his machine riddled with bullets. On every flight he obtained most important information, which was dropped at headquarters, and throughout the period his work has been magnificent'.

Staying on in the RAF after the war, he served in Germany and in the UK between 1919 and 1922. Next he served with 60 Squadron on the North West Frontier, 1923-28. Baker was awarded a Distinguished Flying Cross, *London Gazette* of 20 November 1925, for his services in Waziristan in 1925. He married in 1927, Hilary Bonham-Carter, with whom he had three sons and one daughter. As his career advanced, his many appointments, promotions and honours included: Staff Officer, HQ, Air Defence of Great Britain, 1928; RAF Staff College, 1931; CO, 33 Squadron, Middle East, 1935-36; Imperial Defence College, 1938; Director of

Bombing Operations at the Air Ministry, 1941-43; CB, 1942; SASO, Air Command, SE Asia, 1943-44; AOC, Air (Fighter) Group, 1945-46; Director General of Personnel, Air Ministry, 1946-48; AOC-in-C, Coastal Command, 1948-49; KCB, 1949; C-in-C Controller of Aircraft, Ministry of Supply, 1953-56; Air ADC to the Queen, 1952-56; GBE, 1956. He was also Mentioned in Despatches on a number of occasions. He retired with the rank of Air Chief Marshal in 1956, living in retirement at 10 The Glebe, Chislehurst, Kent. Air Marshal Sir John Wakeling Baker died on 10 March 1978.

BAKER, Valentine Henry

The youngest son of Mr and Mrs J M Baker, of Llanfairfechan, North Wales, he was born on 24 August 1888. Educated at St Deiniols School, Bangor. When the war came, he joined the RNAS (Armoured Cars Section) as a despatch rider. As a qualified mechanic, he was given swift advancement to Chief Petty Officer with the RNAS Armoured Car Brigade, a unit he served with during the disastrous Gallipoli campaign. He was wounded in action on 8 May 1915, at Sedd-el-Bar in the Dardanelles, receiving a rifle bullet in the neck. The bullet was left in situ as it caused him no inconvenience, and removing it may have created complications. He was discharged as unfit from the RNAS, but once recovered, he again sought active service and was subsequently gazetted Second Lieutenant to 12 Battalion, Royal Welsh Fusiliers on 5 November 1915, with a secondment to the RFC coming in the following June. His formal pilot training duly completed, he was confirmed and gazetted Flying Officer on 25 September 1916. He served briefly with 23 Squadron before going on to the FE8-equipped 41 Squadron, newly arrived in France in October 1916. His MC was announced in the *London Gazette* of 26 July 1917: 'For conspicuous gallantry and devotion to duty. In a large number of aerial combats he showed the greatest daring and determination. On one occasion alone, he flew at a low altitude over the enemy's lines, attacking and dispersing enemy artillery, infantry and transport, and returned with a valuable reconnaissance report concerning the retiring enemy'.

He married, in 1916, an old school friend, Dilys Eames, with whom he had one daughter. His tour with '41' completed, he returned to the Home Establishment and was next appointed Flight Commander to 46 TS, in August 1917. Baker saw out the remainder of the war as an Instructor, his outstanding work in this field being recognised by the award of an Air Force Cross in the *London Gazette* of 3 June 1918. During 1920 and 1921, he served in the Secret Codes Department at the Air Ministry. After leaving the RAF in 1921, his first civilian aviation job was representing Vickers-Armstrong in the Dutch East Indies. Based in Java, he acted as a Flying Instructor and consultant to the Dutch Naval and Military Air Forces. After three years in the Far East, he returned to England briefly, before going out to Chile, where he again demonstrated the latest A-W models and also gave flying instruction. Returning to England, he became an Instructor at the Lancashire Flying Club, and later Chief Instructor at the London Aeroplane Club at Stag Lane Aerodrome, Edgware. In 1929 he opened his own school, becoming Chief Pilot and Instructor for the Airwork School of Flying at Heston Aerodrome. In 1934, Baker joined with an old friend and colleague, James Martin, to form a new venture, the Martin-Baker Aircraft Company Limited. As well as testing the Company's prototypes, Baker continued to give lessons to select clients, including the then Prince of Wales, the Duke of Kent and the Air Minister, Lord Londonderry. Two of his better known lady pupils were Lady Drummond Hay and Amy Johnson. The Martin-Baker Company are now, of course, in the forefront of ejection seat and other escape systems, development and manufacture. 'Bake' Baker was killed in September 1942, whilst testing the prototype of a new fighter plane, the Martin Baker Mark III, when the engine failed soon after he had taken off.

BALCOMBE-BROWN, Rainsford

The son of Edward Balcombe-Brown and Eliza M Balcombe-Brown, he was born on 27 February 1895 in Barnwood Village, Gloucestershire. After his birth, the family moved to New Zealand, taking up residence at Upper Hutt, Wellington. Educated at Wanganui School, NZ, and, returning to England, at Oriel College, Oxford, where he was a member of the OTC (Sergeant). Volunteering as soon as war came, he was gazetted Second Lieutenant to the Royal Field Artillery, via the Special Reserve, on 15 August 1914. Seconded to the RFC in the spring of 1915, he trained as a Pilot and was confirmed and gazetted Flying Officer on 13 July following. Sent out to join 1 Squadron in France, he was soon intensely involved in operational flying. On 7 September 1915, he and his Observer, Lieutenant T McK Hughes, were involved in a remarkable incident. Their Morane L, '1894', was attacked from the rear by two Albatroses between Ypres and Courtrai. As the Morane was armed only with a forward-firing machine gun, their peril was extreme. Hughes, deciding on a nothing-to-lose ruse, fully extended a telescope they were carrying and pointed it at the pursuing enemy machines, whilst Balcombe-Brown blazed away pointlessly, but noisily, on the impotent forward-firing machine gun. Both enemy machines immediately sheered away from the perceived threat, leaving the intrepid pair to make good their escape. Balcombe-Brown was promoted to A/Captain and Flight Commander on 12 December 1915. He became something of a balloon busting specialist as his MC, announced in the *London Gazette* of 27 July 1916, reflects: 'For conspicuous gallantry and skill. He attacked an enemy kite balloon and brought it down in flames. He was flying a type of machine unfamiliar to him owing to the absence through wounds of the regular pilot. At dawn he commenced to learn the machine, and the same evening brought down the kite'.

His tour with '1' completed, he returned to the UK for a rest and, subsequently, an appointment as an Instructor. Next, he was promoted to A/Major and given command of the crack 56 Squadron (SE5As). At 1130 on 2 May 1918, Major Balcombe-Brown, in SE5A, 'C1796', was seen to be in aerial combat with hostile aircraft over Martinpuich. From the available evidence, it would appear that he was shot down by Leutnant Erich Löwenhardt of Jasta 10, the eighteenth of the German Ace's remarkable 54 victories. Rainsford Balcombe-Browne is buried in Carnoy Military Cemetery, France.

BALFOUR, Harold Harrington

The son of Colonel and Mrs N H Balfour of Belton, Camberley, Surrey, he was born on 1 November 1897. Educated at Chilverton Elms, Dover and at the Royal Naval College, Osborne. Despite his original aspirations to join the Royal Navy, Balfour was gazetted to a Regular Army battalion of the King's Royal Rifle Corps on 1 November 1914. Transferred to 10 Battalion of his regiment, he became frustrated with the tedium of the training routine and applied for secondment to the RFC. Borrowing £75 from his father, he learnt to fly at the Ruffy-Baumann School, Hendon, where he gained the Royal Aero Club Certificate (Number 1399) on 5 July 1915. Accepted into the RFC, he completed his formal training at Shoreham and then at Gosport, where he was confirmed and gazetted Flying Officer on 15 May 1916. He served with 60 Squadron in France in 1916, then equipped with single-seater Morane monoplanes. His tour with '60' terminated for the most bizarre of reasons. Balfour trapped and injured both his hands when a deck chair he was sunning himself on, collapsed! Once recovered, he test-flew machines at Martlesham, and instructed at Upavon. He returned again to the front as a Flight Commander with 43 Squadron but, soon afterwards in April 1917, was injured when the Strutter he was flying over Vimy Ridge was shot down by ground fire. The first of his MCs was announced in the *London Gazette* of 26 May 1917: 'For conspicuous gallantry and devotion to duty on many occasions. He has carried out many valuable reconnaissances under very adverse conditions. He has shot down two hostile machines'.

Recovered from his injuries, he served briefly with 40 Squadron before going again to '43', now re-equipped with Sopwith Camels. He gained two victories with '43', before returning again to England in the spring of 1918. A Bar to his MC was announced in the *London Gazette* of 22 April 1918 :'For conspicuous gallantry and devotion to duty. On three occasions during one month he had destroyed one hostile machine and driven down two others completely out of control. On one occasion, flying at a very low altitude, under extremely adverse weather conditions, he carried out a reconnaissance, in which he bombed two guns and silenced them, bombed large bodies of troops in a market square, and fired into the hangars and huts in a hostile aerodrome, several casualties being observed. He has at all times shown himself to be a leader of exceptional dash and ability, and offensive patrols led by him have constantly attacked enemy formations with marked gallantry and determination'.

The French also showed their appreciation by conferring a Croix de Guerre upon him. After a spell as Chief Fighting Instructor at No 3 Fighting School at Driffield, he went on, in the same capacity, to Bircham Newton, Norfolk, where he saw out the war with the rank of Major. After the war, he briefly commanded a training school in Norfolk, before being appointed to a post at the RAF College, Cranwell. He also saw service in the Middle East before finally leaving the RAF in 1923. After a period in the USA and in Canada, he returned to the UK determined to enter the world of politics. He progressed well and in the year before the Second World War broke out, was Parliamentary Under-Secretary of State for Air; also a Privy Counsellor. He continued to fly whenever he was able, adding time to his logbook with flights in Hurricanes, Spitfires, Whirlwinds and Typhoons. In 1944, he was appointed Resident Minister to West Africa before returning to the UK in the following year to enter the House of Lords. Ennobled, he took the title Lord Balfour of Inchrye. His publications included 'An Airman Marches' and 'Wings Over Westminster' as well as numerous articles. Lord Balfour was President of the Cross and Cockade Society from 1975 to 1984. He died in September 1988

BALL, Albert VC

The son of Alderman Albert Ball, JP, and Mrs Harriet Mary Ball, of Sedgley House, The Park, Nottingham, he was born on 14 August 1896. Educated at Nottingham High School and at Trent College. Volunteering immediately war broke out, he first enlisted as a Private soldier in 2/7 Battalion, Sherwood Foresters (TF) - 'The Robin Hoods'. Two months later, on 28 October 1914, Ball was gazetted Second Lieutenant into his own battalion. Keen to fly, Ball would frequently make the round trip by motorcycle from his camp in Luton to Hendon aerodrome until, eventually, he was awarded the Aviators Certificate of the Royal Aero Club (Number1898) on 15 October 1915. Transfer to the RFC and an intensive course of further training followed his successful acquisition of a 'ticket', until he was confirmed and gazetted Flying Officer on 29 January 1916. Ball was first sent to the front on 18 February 1916, joining 13 Squadron to fly reconnaissance machines. His subsequent prowess is well documented elsewhere, the chronicle of his brilliance perhaps best illustrated by the honours showered upon his young and slight shoulders. His MC was announced in the *London Gazette* of 27 June 1916: 'For conspicuous skill and gallantry on many occasions, notably when, after failing to destroy an enemy kite balloon with bombs, he returned for a fresh supply, went back and brought it down in flames. He has done great execution among the enemy aeroplanes. On one occasion he attacked six in one fight, forced down two and drove the others off. This occurred several miles over the enemy lines'.

The first of his Distinguished Service Orders came with the announcement in the *London Gazette* of 22 September 1916, that he had been created a Companion of the Order: Shortly afterwards, he was promoted to Captain and a second Bar to his Distinguished Service Order was announced in the *London Gazette* of 25 November 1916. Still only 20 years of age, Ball was presented with the honorary freedom of his native city, Nottingham. In August 1916, the Tsar of Russia had conferred upon him the Order of St George. After his death, the President of France added the Cross of the Chevalier of the Légion d'Honneur to his many awards. Ball became the first British officer to receive the Medal and Diploma of the Aero Club of America. He had also been Mentioned in Despatches on a number of occasions but the ultimate accolade was presented posthumously, the award of the Victoria Cross being announced in the *London Gazette* of 3 June 1917: 'For most conspicuous and consistent bravery, from 25 April to 6 May 1917, during which period Captain Ball took part in twenty-six combats in the air and destroyed eleven hostile aeroplanes, drove down two out of control and forced several others to land. Flying alone, on one occasion he fought six hostile machines, twice he fought five and once four. When leading two other British planes he attacked an enemy formation of eight – on each of these occasions he brought down at least one enemy plane, and several times his plane was badly damaged. On returning with a damaged plane he had always to be restrained from immediately going out in another'.

The quintessential British ace, Albert Ball, gained no less than 44 victories in his brief combat career. He was with the crack SE5-equipped 56 Squadron by the time of his death in action. On the evening of 7 May 1917, members of his patrol had had a sequence of inconclusive skirmishes with a number of enemy aircraft and, as a consequence, had been split up, completely losing contact with each other. The sky was busy that evening, Sopwith Triplanes from 8 Squadron, RNAS, and Spads from 19 Squadron, also being engaged at one time or another by the Jasta 11 Pilots. Lothar von Richthofen sparred with at least one of the Triplanes, before engaging two of the SE5s, one of which may well have been Ball's. Certainly Ball was last seen chasing a red Albatros Scout into a large bank of cloud. What happened after that last sighting remains a matter of speculation. It is possible, even probable, that Ball became disorientated in the cloud, and came out of it too low to correct his dive before his machine ploughed into the ground. He lived for a few minutes after the crash, dying in the arms of a young French woman, Madame Sieppe Coulon, who had hurried to the scene. The death of so significant a figure led, inevitably, to speculation regarding the circumstances surrounding his demise and, as is often the case, some of the speculators invented circumstances to fit their own scenarios, whilst others were loathe to let the truth get in the way of a good story! There was, understandably, a reluctance on the British side to believe that Ball could have been bested in combat or even that he could have been guilty of a simple error of judgement. Lothar von Richthofen had originally claimed a Triplane on this day and at this time, the claim clearly recorded as such in the Nachrichtenblatt. The fact is, of course, that no Triplanes were lost on this particular evening. The news of Ball's death quickly reached Berlin and as the location of his wrecked SE5 was similar to that of Lothar's 'phantom' Triplane, it hardly took a quantum leap of imagination to link the two. The propaganda value to the German High Command was immense. Manfred von Richthofen had, in November 1916, bested the great British ace Major Lanoe Hawker in combat, and now the Red Baron's brother, Lothar, had destroyed the current leading British ace, Albert Ball. Whatever the truth of the matter, Lothar was formally credited with the victory over Albert Ball by the German Air Service. Certainly Lothar von Richthofen knew he had been in a fight that day, his Albatros had been hit and with his engine giving him trouble, he had been forced to land, although he was himself unhurt. Albert Ball was buried by the German Air Service with full Military Honours, in Annoeullin Communal Cemetery, German Extension, France (Fr. 1279).

BANKS, Charles Chaplin

The elder son of C P and Helen Agnes Banks, of Arnold House, Llandulas, Denbighshire, although the family originally came from Kendall, Westmorland. Educated at Shrewsbury (1908-13), and at Trinity College, Oxford (MA). He was working as a schoolmaster when the war came in August 1914. Gazetted Second Lieutenant to 5 (Flintshire) Battalion, Royal Welsh Fusiliers (TF) on 10 December 1914. He served through the miseries of the Gallipoli campaign, from the landings at Suvla on 9 August 1915, through to the final evacuation. His younger brother, Arthur, newly arrived from Sandhurst, was killed on 22 June 1916 during a German raid on the 2 Royal Welsh Fusiliers trenches in France. Seconded to the RFC in 1917, Charles first served with the Camels of 44 Squadron on Home Defence duties. He shared, with Captain G H Hackwill (qv), in the destruction of a Gotha bomber on 28 January 1918, for which feat he was awarded the MC, *London Gazette* of 8 February 1918: 'For conspicuous gallantry when he engaged and shot down a Gotha raiding London. During the engagement which lasted a considerable time, they were continually under fire from the enemy machine'.

Banks next joined 43 Squadron (Sopwith Camels) at the front on 8 February 1918 and soon afterwards became a Flight Commander. He served out the war with '43', the unit converting to Sopwith Snipes in September 1918. Banks added three more victories in the new machine to the nine he had already achieved in Camels. His sixth victory on 31 May 1918, when he shot down a Friedrickshafen two-seater, was remarkable in that it occurred at night, still a rare occurrence at that time. Banks was awarded the Distinguished Flying Cross for his further exploits in the *London Gazette* of 8 February 1919. He was also Mentioned in Despatches on two occasions, *London Gazettes* of 20 December 1917 and 15 July 1919. Banks returned to teaching after the war, retiring in 1958. 'Sandy' Banks' son was also a Fighter Pilot in the Second World War. Shot down over Italy, he fought alongside local partisans until captured by the Germans and executed.

BARKER, William George VC

The son of Mr and Mrs G W J Barker, of Winnipeg, Manitoba, Canada, he was born on 3 November 1894. Educated at Dauphin College, Manitoba. Volunteering almost immediately after leaving school, he enlisted into the Canadian Mounted Rifles. An accomplished horseman and a very good shot, he was soon promoted Corporal and attached to the machine gun section of his regiment. In the spring of 1915, he accompanied his regiment to England and immediately sought a transfer to the RFC. First inducted as a mechanic, he later trained as an Observer/Gunner and, in December 1915, was posted to the BE2c-equipped 9 Squadron. Credited with sending down a Fokker monoplane early in the New Year, he was next gazetted Second Lieutenant, via the Special Lists, on 2 April 1916. Sent out first to 4 Squadron on 7 April 1916, he transferred to 15 Squadron on 18 July following. His second victory, a Roland destroyed, came on 15 August 1916. His 'apprenticeship' satisfactorily completed, he was confirmed and gazetted Flying Officer (Observer) on 22 September 1916. His first MC for contact patrol work over Bapaume in November 1916, was announced in the *London Gazette* of 10 January 1917: 'For conspicuous gallantry in action. He flew at a height of 500 feet over the enemy's lines, and brought back most valuable information. On another occasion, after driving off two hostile machines, he carried out an excellent reconnaissance'.

He returned to the UK for pilot training on 16 November 1916 and, after qualifying for his full 'Wings', returned to 15 Squadron on 24 February 1917. A Bar to his MC, in recognition of his new role in artillery collaboration, came in the *London Gazette* of 18 July 1917: 'For conspicuous gallantry and devotion to duty. He has done continuous good work in co-operation with the artillery, and has carried out successful reconnaissances under most difficult and dangerous conditions'.

Wounded slightly by 'Archie' in August 1917, he returned to the Home Establishment and, once recovered, instructed pupils for six months, whilst continually agitating for a posting to an active Scout squadron. His agitations extended even to 'beating-up' Whitehall at very low level, deliberately singling out the Air Ministry for special attention. The Air Ministry's reaction to this challenge could have gone either way, but, in the event, they granted him his wish and sent him to join 28 Squadron, then newly equipped with Camels and about to leave for France on 8 October 1917. Later in the same month, '28' moved to Droglandt in Flanders – intended for use in the aerial support of the Third Battle of Ypres (Passchendaele), which had commenced earlier on 31 July 1917. Barker had claimed three victories before 26 October, when, unexpectedly, '28' was ordered to the Italian front, arriving at Ghedi on 14 November 1917, its role defined as bomber escorts. Victories and distinctions continued to come Barker's way. He was awarded a Distinguished Service Order, announced in the *London Gazette* of 5 January 1918. Another Bar to his MC followed in the *London Gazette* of 24 April 1918, details in the *Gazette* of 16 September 1918: 'For conspicuous gallantry and devotion to duty. When leading patrols he on one occasion attacked eight hostile machines, himself shooting down two, and on another occasion seven, one of which he shot down. In two months he himself destroyed four enemy machines and drove down one, and burned two balloons'.

A Bar to his Distinguished Service Order followed in the *London Gazette* of 20 July 1918, this for his continued prowess in destroying enemy aircraft. The Allies, too, recognised his worth, the French with a Croix de Guerre, *London Gazette* of 26 May 1918, and the Italians with the Silver Medaglia al Valore Militare. He was also Mentioned in Despatches on three occasions during the Great War. Barker, having left '28', flew with 66, 139 and 201 Squadrons before the end of the war. Perhaps surprisingly, bearing in mind the length and intensity of his combat career, Barker survived the war having amassed no less than 52 victories. Almost inevitably, the ultimate accolade of the Victoria Cross was bestowed upon him, the largely self-explanatory citation appearing in the *London Gazette* of 30 November 1918: 'On the morning of 27 October 1918, this officer observed an enemy two-seater over the Fôret de Mormal. He attacked this machine, and after a short burst it broke up in the air. At the same time a Fokker biplane attacked him, and he was wounded in the right thigh, but managed, despite this, to shoot down the enemy aeroplane in flames. He then found himself in the middle of a large formation of Fokkers, who attacked him from all directions, and was again severely wounded in the left thigh, but succeeded in driving down two of the enemy in a spin. He lost consciousness after this, and his machine fell out of control. On recovery he found himself again being attacked heavily by a large formation, and singling out one machine, he deliberately charged and drove it down in flames. During this fight his left elbow was shattered and he again fainted, and on regaining consciousness he found himself still being attacked, but, not withstanding that he was severely wounded in both legs and his left arm shattered, he dived on the nearest machine and shot it down in flames. Being greatly exhausted, he dived out of the fight to regain our lines, but was met by another formation which attacked and endeavoured to cut him off, but after a hard fight he succeeded in breaking up this formation and reached our lines, where he crashed on landing. This combat, in which Major Barker destroyed four enemy machines (three of them in flames), brought his total successes up to fifty machines destroyed, and is a notable example of the exceptional bravery and disregard of danger which this very gallant officer has always displayed throughout his distinguished career'.

Having left the RAF in April 1919, Barker returned to Canada and attempted to launch an aviation business with fellow Canadian aviator and VC holder, Billy Bishop (qv). This venture failed and Barker entered the new Canadian Air Force in 1920. Leaving the RCAF in 1924, he started a wholesale tobacco business. This enterprise, too, was less than successful and certainly not helped by a spell of ill health. In January 1930, he was pleased to rejoin the aviation industry, being appointed to the newly formed Fairchild Aviation Company of Canada. On 12 March 1930, he set off from Rockcliffe Airfield, Ottawa, on a routine test of one of the company's machines, when, suddenly and unaccountably, it stalled and crashed into a river. William George Barker,VC, one of the truly great Pilots of the First World War, was buried with appropriate honours in Mount Pleasant Cemetery, Ottawa.

BARLOW, Leonard Monteagle

The son of Leonard and Katharine Barlow, of 'Ben Varne', 132 Onslow Gardens, Wallington, Surrey, he was born at Highbury, London, on 5 June 1898. Educated at Wallington Modern School (1906-12), and privately (1913). He entered the City and Guilds Technical College, Finsbury, with a Scholarship in October 1913, and took a two-year course in electrical engineering. Barlow was awarded the prestigious Salomans Scholarship in 1915, and subsequently became engaged on research work. He was also awarded the College Certificate in Electrical Engineering at this time. Having attained his 18th birthday, he immediately volunteered and was subsequently gazetted Second Lieutenant to the RFC, via the Special Reserve, on 8 July 1916. His pilot training duly completed, he was confirmed and gazetted Flying Officer on 14 October following. Joining 56 Squadron, then stationed at London Colney on 8 February 1917, he subsequently accompanied the newly SE5-equipped unit to France as a 'founder member' on 8 April following. During five months in combat, Barlow would amass 20 victories between 24 April and 1 October 1917, including one 'trio' and three 'doubles' on single days. He made full use of his engineering expertise and soon acquired the nickname of 'The Gadget King'. One of his more successful 'gadgets' was the coupling up of both his Vickers and his Lewis guns to fire simultaneously from the same trigger. A brilliant air fighter, once, over Houthoulst Forest, he single-handedly engaged four enemy Scouts. Within three minutes, he had shot three of the four hostiles down – one Albatros DV and two Pfalz DIIIs – the fourth surviving Albatros having beaten a hasty retreat. The feat elicited a congratulatory telegram from Hugh Trenchard: 'I congratulate you on doing the 'hat trick' yesterday; it was splendid work'. The first of his three MCs was announced in the *London Gazette* of 25 August 1917: 'For conspicuous gallantry and devotion to duty when engaged on aerial combat. He has set a fine example of courage and dash in attacking and destroying hostile machines. He also attacked and stopped a goods train, silenced a machine gun on an enemy aerodrome, and dispersed troops on the roads from a very low altitude'.

The first Bar to his MC came in the *London Gazette* of 18 October 1917, details in the *Gazette* of 7 March 1918: 'For conspicuous gallantry and devotion to duty in aerial combats over a considerable period, during the course of which he destroyed six enemy machines and drove down three out of control. He has taken part in over 60 offensive patrols of which he has led 10. His gallantry and skill have been most marked and consistent'.

His second Bar was announced in the *London Gazette* of 27 October 1917, details in the *Gazette* of 22 March 1918: 'For conspicuous gallantry and devotion to duty in aerial combats. In the course of a fortnight he destroyed seven enemy machines; on one occasion he attacked four enemy scouts and shot one down in flames, and two others, which were seen to crash. He showed the greatest gallantry, dash and skill'.

His tour with '56' completed, the 19 year old Barlow was sent back to the UK for a rest on 21 October 1917. Following a short leave, he was posted as a Chief Instructor to the School of Aerial Fighting on 6 November 1917. He was next appointed a Test Pilot at the Aeroplane Experimental Station at Martlesham Heath, Suffolk. As part of his routine testing duties, he took off in a Sopwith Dolphin on 5 February 1918. Shortly after take-off, defects developed which caused the machine to suddenly burst into flames. On 28 September 1918, some months after his death, his MC and two Bars were presented to his father and mother at a special ceremonial parade before the Guards Battalions at Wellington Barracks, London. Leonard Monteagle Barlow is buried in Bandon Hill Cemetery, Surrey.

NB: The RAF Museum Hendon has his medals in its collection: MC and Two Bars, British War Medal 1914-20, and Victory Medal 1914-19.

BARNES, Henry Farquharson

Born in London on 9 February 1898, he was a sugar planter in Zululand, Natal, South Africa, when war came. Returning to England, he volunteered as soon as he was old enough, and was subsequently gazetted Second Lieutenant to the RGA, via the Special Reserve, on 27 September 1915. The first of his MCs was earned with the Gunners on the Western Front and announced in the *London Gazette* of 1 January 1917 (no citation). He would subsequently receive the insignia of his award from the hands of the King during an investiture held at Buckingham Palace on 9 January 1918. He had, in the meantime, secured secondment to the RFC, and the Balloon Service. He first served operationally with 23 KBS, from 7 April 1917, before joining 25 KBS on 15 June following. His last operational posting was to 16 KB Company, which came on 7 July 1918, and it was during his stint with this unit that he earned a Bar to his MC, announced in the *London Gazette* of 8 February 1919: '16 Balloon Company, France. During the operations from 21 August to 1 October this officer's balloon was very heavily shelled (one balloon being totally destroyed), and was subjected to attacks by hostile aircraft. Lieutenant Barnes, however, kept it well forward and rendered very valuable assistance to our artillery, showing conspicuous skill and determination throughout'.

Henry Barnes was finally demobilised on 9 July 1919, returning to his civilian work in South Africa soon afterwards.

BARNETT, John Canning Lethbridge

The only son of the Reverend Canon H B Barnett and Mrs Barnett, of The Vicarage, Bracknell, Berkshire, he was born on 27 May 1894. Educated at Eton (1907-12), he had gone up to Christchurch College, Oxford (1912-14) by the time the war came. Interrupting his studies, he volunteered immediately, and was gazetted Second Lieutenant to 4 Battalion, Oxfordshire and Buckinghamshire Light Infantry (TF), on 14 September 1914. Sent to France to serve in various Staff positions, he was subsequently formally gazetted an 'Aide-de-Camp' in the *London Gazette* of 21 September 1915. Seeking secondment to the RFC, he gained his Royal Aero Club Certificate (Number 4338) on 25 February 1917. After formally qualifying for his 'Wings' two months later, he was eventually sent out to the BF2b-equipped 11 Squadron in June 1917. On 20 November 1917, Barnett and his Observer/Gunner, Corporal J Mason, narrowly escaped disaster when their Bristol Fighter, 'A7153', was badly shot up. Barnett continued to fly operationally with '11' until January 1918, when his health broke down and forced his return to the UK. His MC was announced in the *London Gazette* of 4 February 1918, details in the *Gazette* of 5 July 1918: 'For conspicuous gallantry and devotion to duty. When information was urgently needed, he volunteered to go out on patrol in a gale of wind and most difficult conditions. The patrol was successful, and valuable information was obtained. On another occasion he made a reconnaissance in a thick fog, flying at a height of 40 feet, and was heavily fired on from the ground. He showed the greatest courage and determination'.

Barnett had the distinction of being presented with his Cross by HM the King at an investiture held at Buckingham Palace on 9 March 1918. Unfortunately, his ill-health persisted and he was forced to relinquish his commission on 3 September 1919.

BARNETT, Percy John

The son of Operative Miller, John V Barnett and Florence J Barnett, of 'The Laurels', Stapleton, Bristol, he was born on 2 September 1895. Educated at Bristol Grammar School (1910-13), where he was a member of the OTC. After completing his education, he moved to London, living at Northwood and working as a clerk. When the war came, he enlisted as a Private soldier into 24 (2 Sportsmans) Battalion, Royal Fusiliers. Picked out for a commission, he was gazetted Second Lieutenant into 23 (1 Sportsmans) Battalion of the same regiment on 25 September 1915. Barnett served in the trenches from April 1916, before returning to England as a possible candidate for the RFC. In order to advance his ambitions, he took flying lessons at his own expense, and was rewarded with the Royal Aero Club Aviators Certificate (Number 3611) on 15 September 1916. His formal training duly completed, he was confirmed and gazetted Flying Officer on 13 November following. A posting to 55 Squadron, then stationed at Castle Bromwich, came early in 1917, and he accompanied the DH4-equipped unit to France as a 'founder member' on 6 March following. Barnett survived a particularly 'hairy' crash on 10 June 1917, when his DH4, 'A7469', came down near to Alveringhem. Barnett was unscathed, although his Observer, 2Lt R M Dixon, was wounded in the incident. His MC was announced in the *London Gazette* of 17 September 1917: 'For conspicuous gallantry and devotion to duty on many occasions. His reconnaissance work has been particularly daring and successful owing to the pluck and determination with which he has faced bad weather and attacks from hostile aircraft in order to obtain his information. He has taken part in ten successful bomb raids, and his keenness on all occasions has set a splendid example to others'.

His tour with '55' completed early in 1918, he returned to the Home Establishment and to instructing duties.

BARR, Eric Noel Douglas

The son of Henry B Barr and Louisa B Barr, of 'The Oaks', Weyhill Road, Andover, Southampton, he was born in Colyford, Devon, in December 1892. Educated at Bradfield College (1907-10). Gazetted Second Lieutenant to the Royal Field Artillery on 19 May 1915. He served with 60 Howitzer Battery, RFA, before successfully seeking secondment to the RFC. Barr trained as an Observer and was sent out as a Probationary to 30 Squadron in Mesopotamia on 17 May 1916. His 'apprenticeship' satisfactorily completed, he was confirmed and gazetted Flying Officer (Observer) on 15 August following. On 30 August 1916, Barr and his Pilot, Lieutenant T E Lander (qv), spotted another BE2c, flown by Lieutenant the Honourable J H B Rodowney, under heavy attack from a Fokker Scout over Shumran aerodrome. Although technically disadvantaged, they engaged the Fokker and damaged it sufficiently to oblige the enemy Pilot to withdraw. His MC was announced in the *London Gazette* of 14 November 1916: 'For conspicuous gallantry and skill in an encounter with an enemy machine. By skilful manoeuvring Second Lieutenant Barr and Lieutenant Lander drove the enemy machine behind the enemy's lines in a damaged condition'.

His tour with '30' completed on 3 December 1916, he returned to the UK. Taking flying tuition, he gained his Royal Aero Club Certificate (Number 4481) on 16 April 1917. Formal qualification for his official

'Wings' followed, and he served briefly as a Pilot with 38 and 76 HD Squadrons, before ill health overtook him in December 1917. So badly was his health affected, that he was obliged to relinquish his commission and leave the service on 12 June 1918.

BARRACLOUGH, Noel Edgar

The younger son of Mr and Mrs Norman Charles Barraclough, of Russell Road, Kensington, London, he was born on 29 December 1894. Educated at Westminster School (1908-13) and at King's College, Cambridge. Interrupting his university studies, he enlisted as a Private soldier into 16 (Public Schools) Battalion, Middlesex Regiment, and accompanied that unit to France in November 1915. Singled out for a commission, his wish to join the flying service was realised when he was gazetted Second Lieutenant to the RFC, via the Special Lists, on 5 August 1916. He qualified for his 'Wings' at the year's end and was sent out to the RE8-equipped 6 Squadron early in the New Year of 1917. On 31 July 1917, the first day of the third Battle of Ypres, Barraclough and his Observer of the day, Lieutenant H J Snowden, in RE8, 'A111', were shot up and damaged. Snowden was wounded in the incident but, fortunately, Barraclough emerged unscathed. This action is referred to in the citation for his MC, which was announced in the *London Gazette* of 26 September 1917, details in the *Gazette* of 9 January 1918: 'For conspicuous gallantry and devotion to duty. For several months he has done work of a consistently high order as a pilot, continually harassing the enemy's infantry with machine-gun fire and remaining on one occasion for two hours in extremely bad weather at a very low altitude on patrol before an offensive. On this occasion his Observer was wounded by the intense fire to which his machine was subjected. His photographic reconnaissances and artillery observation have on all occasions been accurate and valuable'.

After leaving the service in 1919, Barraclough resumed his education and was eventually admitted a Solicitor in practice in London, in October 1921. In the same month he married Marjorie Delicia Hill, of North Gate, Regent's Park, London.

BARRATT, Arthur Sheridan

The eldest son of Charles Henry and Harriet T Barratt of 60 St John's Road, Clifton, Bristol, he was born in India on 25 February 1891. Educated at Clifton College (1905-09), at the Royal Military Academy, Woolwich and at the Staff College, Camberley. Barratt's younger brother, Corporal Charles Herbert Barratt, 31 (Indian) Signal Company, Royal Engineers, a 22 year old despatch rider, was killed in action in France on 26 September 1915. A professional soldier, Arthur was gazetted Second Lieutenant to the Royal Artillery in December 1910. Developing an interest in aviation, and sensing the importance of the flying service to future artillery operations, he gained the Royal Aero Club Certificate (Number 756) in a Bristol machine of the Bristol School at Salisbury Plain on 26 March 1914. His formal training duly completed, he was confirmed and gazetted Flying Officer on 30 June following. Barratt attracted the unfortunate sobriquet, 'Ugly', at this time, a nickname that stayed with him for the remainder of his life. Although something of an intellectual – he passed the Staff College examinations at an unusually early age and, hence, served mainly in Staff positions – he did, however, gain operational experience with 3 Squadron in 1915. He was promoted to A/Captain and Flight Commander on 11 June 1915. On 22 July 1915, during a gale, he successfully ranged 19 Siege Battery, RGA, onto a long-range gun that the Germans had concealed within the walls of a factory with a sliding roof. His MC was announced in the *London Gazette* of 1 January 1916 (no citation). Promoted to A/Major, he subsequently commanded 6 Squadron from September

1916, and 49 Squadron from April 1917. Promoted to A/Lieutenant Colonel in June 1917, he was given command of 3 (Corps) Wing, RFC.

After the Great War, Barratt's career progressed rapidly, his many subsequent appointments, promotions and honours included: CMG, 1919; Chief Instructor at the RAF Staff College, Andover; Group Captain, 1928; Command of 1 (Indian) Group, Peshawar, 1930-31; Air Commodore, 1932; SASO, HQ, RAF India, 1932-34; Director of Staff Duties, Air Ministry, 1935; Commandant RAF Staff College, Andover, 1936-39; Air Vice-Marshal, 1936; CB, 1937; Air Marshal, 1939; AOC-in-Chief, British Air Forces in France, 1940; KCB, 1940; AOC-in-C, Army Co-operation Command, 1940-43; AOC-in-C, Technical Training Command, 1943-45; Inspector-General of the RAF, 1945-47; and he was also Mentioned in Despatches on four occasions. His foreign awards included: Officer de l'Ordre de la Couronne (Belgium); Restituta Militari 2nd Class (Poland); and the Grand Cross Légion d'Honneur and the Croix de Guerre (France). He was appointed Air Chief Marshal in 1946, before finally retiring in 1947. Civilian honours bestowed upon him included: Gentleman Usher to the Sword of State, 1946, and Deputy Lieutenant of the County of Hampshire. He married, firstly, in 1916, Norah Lillian Crewe (dissolved in 1948), with whom he had one daughter. And, secondly, in 1949, Judith Rhoda Cartmell, widow of Terence Horsley. He lived after his retirement at The Old Vicarage, Hambledon, Hampshire. Air Chief Marshal Sir Arthur Barratt died on 4 November 1966.

NB: The RAF Museum Hendon has his medals in its collection: MC, 1914 Star with Bar (Lieut RA attd RFC)*, British War Medal 1914-20, Victory Medal 1914-19* (Lt Col RAF)*, 1939-45 Star, Defence Medal 1939-45, War Medal 1939-45 with MID, Silver Jubilee Medal 1935, Coronation Medal 1937, Order of the Crown of Belgium (Officier, Badge), Order of the Légion d'Honneur (Officier, Badge, France), Croix de Guerre avec Palme 1914-18 (Belgium), Croix de Guerre avec Palme, 1939 (France).*

BARRINGTON, Croker Edmund

The only son of Mr and Mrs Croker Barrington, of Barrington's Bridge, co Limerick, Ireland, he was born in Dublin on 2 September 1897. Educated at Rugby (1911-15), and at the Royal Military Academy, Woolwich, from whence he was gazetted Second Lieutenant to the Royal Field Artillery on 19 February 1916. He successfully sought secondment to the RFC and, following training, served as an Observer with the BE2e-equipped 34 Squadron from September 1916. Returning to the UK, he trained as a Pilot and gained his Royal Aero Club Certificate (Number 4378) on 14 March 1917, the same day that he was confirmed as Flying Officer. He served in France as a Pilot with 3 Squadron, from April 1917. On 3 May 1917, he was fortunate to survive when his Morane P, 'A6698', received multiple hits from rifle and shell fire. Although managing to get the machine back over the lines with some difficulty, the Morane was wrecked in landing, the fuselage breaking into two. Promoted to A/Captain and Flight Commander in December 1917, just days before his tour with '3' was completed, he returned to the Home Establishment. After a spell in the UK in the early months of 1918, he served briefly with 70 Squadron before transferring as Commander of 'N' Flight, 15 Squadron, in June 1918. His MC was announced in the *London Gazette* of 5 July 1918: 'For conspicuous gallantry and devotion to duty. He attacked enemy transport with bombs from a height of 50 feet,, two of his bombs exploding in the rear of the column. He led his formation successfully on many occasions in very bad weather conditions and obtained valuable information'.

Research has unearthed the original recommendation for this award, which was sent to the OC, 13 Wing, RFC, on 29 November 1917: 'This officer was an observer for 9 months in 34 Squadron, before going home to learn to fly. He joined this Squadron 20 April 1917, and has previously been recommended for his excellent work in adverse weather and conducting shoots from low altitudes. (No award). He carried out several very valuable contact patrols in May 1917, and has always worked unceasingly and in a fearless manner, regardless of weather. During recent operations he has shown great initiative in gaining information while leading his formation in attacks with bombs and machine-gun fire on ground targets'.

Apparently, his CO must have been 'tipped the wink' that this wording was inadequate and likely to fail, and there is a further, amended, recommendation in existence, that not only, 'beefed things up' somewhat, but also omits mention of a previously failed recommendation. This amendment is signed by R Raymond-Barker, CO, 'In the Field', on 3 December 1917: 'During the recent operations this Officer has worked unceasingly, absolutely regardless of weather, in effecting successful reconnaissances, and attacks at enemy ground targets at under 100 feet, and bringing back valuable information. On one occasion, in very misty weather, he attacked a convoy of six limbers with four bombs at a height of 50 feet, two exploding at the rear of the column. On this occasion, owing to the low height he was carrying out his work he returned with 50 yards of telegraph cable round his propeller, together with some small branches of trees in his undercarriage. On two separate occasions this Officer has safely led his formation back in misty weather when the weather had got so bad that other machines could not leave the aerodrome'.

Barrington returned to service with the Royal Artillery after the war.

BATCHELOR, Edward Campbell

From Dundee, Scotland, he was born in 1895. He served in France as a Gunner with the Royal Field Artillery from 19 April 1915. Picked out for a commission, he was gazetted Second Lieutenant to 'C' Battery (City of Dundee), Royal Field Artillery (TF) on 30 September 1915. After further service in France with the Gunners, he successfully sought secondment to the RFC. He trained as an Observer and was sent out as such to the RE8-equipped 12 Squadron on 3 March 1918. Some eighteen days later, on 21 March 1918, the first day of the German spring offensive, he and his Pilot, Second Lieutenant H C Adams (qv), in RE8, 'B2273', came under heavy attack from an enemy formation. The citation for his MC reflects his and Adams' gallantry on that day: *London Gazette* of 22 June 1918: 'For conspicuous gallantry and devotion to duty. When attacked three times by a hostile formation and though wounded in the arm, he continued to work his gun and succeeded in shooting down two enemy machines which vanished in the clouds spinning. An observer reported that at this time and place he saw two enemy machines burst into flames and crash to earth. By his coolness and skill on this occasion he saved his machine and pilot. On a later occasion, on seeing two hostile scouts above him, he attacked and shot down one of them, which eventually crashed to earth. His gallantry and valuable services have been most marked'.

After recovering from the effects of his wounds, he was not able to fly operationally again, but, instead, worked in an administrative capacity, until finally leaving the service in 1919.

BATE, Basil Dixon

The son of J C Bate, Coroner of Wallasey and West Cheshire, and Mrs Bate, of Dee Banks, Chester, he was born in May 1898. Educated at Arnold House School, and at Hoylake College. After leaving school, he became an engineering pupil at the Hydraulic Engineering Works, Chester. In May 1916, as soon as he reached the age of 18, he enlisted as a Driver in the RFC. Picked out for a commission, he was gazetted Second Lieutenant to the RFC, on 14 March 1917. Put to work in an engineering workshop, he decided to try for the flying branch, and began taking lessons at his own expense, thus gaining his Royal Aero Club Certificate (Number 4750) on 31 May 1917. Armed with this, he was allowed to transfer and to undertake formal pilot training which culminated with him being confirmed and gazetted Flying Officer on 16 August 1917. He flew operationally with 18 Squadron (DH4s) from August 1917, before returning in January 1918, for rest and recuperation. Back home in Chester for a well earned leave, he gave the local press a resumé of his flying experiences to date: 'He has shot down 2 Hun machines totally out of control and driven down 7 Hun machines. Not long ago he went out on photography and met a formation of 3 enemy aircraft about 35 miles over the enemy lines. A fierce fight ensued and he shot down the leader of the formation. Lieutenant Bate continued taking photographs and met another formation of 4 enemy aircraft which he succeeded in driving away. He still persisted in taking photographs and encountered a third formation of 9 aircraft. A short fight followed and our hero returned to our lines whither the enemy did not follow. He secured excellent photographic results. The machine had no fewer than 40 bullet holes through it and as one control was shot away, he was not able to reach his own aerodrome but managed to land on our side of the lines. He had another adventure while out taking photographs recently. Meeting a loose Hun balloon at 15,000 feet, he shot it down and followed it. It came down on our side and stuck on top of a tree. It was got down. There was no one in it but was carrying propaganda to cause disaffection to the French civilians. Lieut Bate and his comrade took all the papers and the gas bag and brought it home in their machine'.

Bate's MC was announced in the *London Gazette* of 4 February 1918, details in the *Gazette* of 5 July 1918: 'For conspicuous gallantry and devotion to duty. He carried out a photographic reconnaissance of several distant hostile aerodromes, in the course of which he encountered in all fifteen hostile aeroplanes, and took part in many combats, destroying at least one of the enemy machines. He completed the whole of his reconnaissance, and returned with his machine much damaged by the enemy's fire'.

Bate's elder brother, motor driver Roger Bate, served with the British Red Cross in Italy, and was awarded a medal for his services. Basil Bate left the RAF on 19 February 1919.

BATES, Frederic Alan

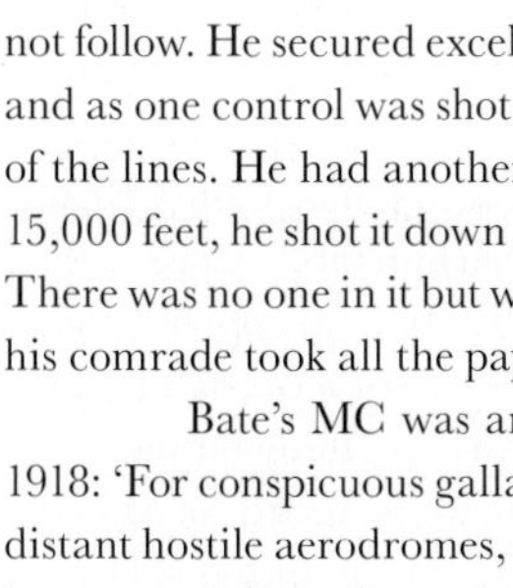

The fourth son of Sir Edward Percy Bates, Bart, and Lady Constance Bates, of Gyrn Castle, Llanasa, Flintshire, he was born on 16 August 1884. Educated at Winchester (1898-1903), and at Trinity College, Cambridge. The Bates family owned large holdings in the Cunard Steam-Ship Company, in T & J Brocklebank Ltd, and in Cunard White Star and so, after completing his education, Frederic took up a position in the Head Offices of the various companies at Cunard Buildings, Liverpool, whilst living at 'Beechenhurst', Allerton, Liverpool. When the war came, he immediately volunteered and was gazetted Second Lieutenant to his local Yeomanry regiment, the Denbighshire Hussars (TF), on 8 September 1914. After service with the Yeomanry, he successfully sought secondment to the RFC at the end of 1916. His formal pilot training duly completed, he was confirmed and gazetted

Flying Officer on 13 February 1917. Sent out to the MEF and 14 Squadron on 27 June 1917. Bates kept a diary during his service with '14' and this gives some fascinating insights into the day-to-day experiences of airmen on this front. Bates was obviously deeply impressed by the chivalry and skill of their opponents. He records how, on 11 July 1917, a Hun recco machine escorted by a Scout single-seater dropped a message near to the aerodrome to say they had buried Captain Charles Alfred Brookes of the Australian Squadron with due military honours, and that Second Lieutenant Claude Henry Vautin was a prisoner. They said how much they enjoyed the company of the latter and that they, 'were showing him the country!'. They also said that Vautin wanted his kit, and asked that it be dropped from a 2c at Huj. They guaranteed they would not attack the machine if it flew a straight course and dropped a smoke bomb to identify itself. Vautin's kit was duly dropped the following day, without molestation. Bates, by then the 'C' Flight CO, relates how, on 7 November 1917, the squadron dropped one and a quarter tons of bombs during the advance on Gaza. He goes on to say that just three days later, he and two friends drove into Gaza in a Ford car, taking their lunch along, 'just like Cook's tourists'. They inspected with professional interest, the strafed and wrecked Turkish trenches and Hun positions their handiwork had helped reduce to ruin. On 28 November 1917, Bates was acting as Observer to Lieutenant W J Mitchell, when their BE2c was hit by rifle fire. Bates was unhurt in the incident, although unfortunately, Mitchell was wounded. On 9 December 1917, the civilian authorities surrendered Jerusalem to Allenby's forces, and Bates landed the first British aeroplane within the boundaries of the Holy City. Despite appalling weather, the 14 Squadron personnel enjoyed a passable Christmas dinner in a memorable location. Unfortunately, Bates was quite badly injured in an aero accident on 30 December 1917. His MC was announced in the *London Gazette* of 18 July 1918: 'For conspicuous gallantry and devotion to duty. He flew over an enemy battery which was firing on our positions, dived on to it and silenced it with his machine guns. He showed splendid courage and resource'.

His second operational tour was as CO, 47 Squadron, on the Salonika front, joining that unit with the rank of Major on 1 August 1918. His tour with '47' completed, he returned to the UK on 5 January 1919. He was Mentioned in Despatches on four occasions during the Great War. The Greeks awarded him the 3rd Class version of their Military Cross for his services in Salonika, *London Gazette* of 10 October 1919. In final appreciation of his services during the last months of the war, Bates was awarded the Air Force Cross, *London Gazette* of 3 June 1919 (Salonika). Leaving the service early in 1919, Bates joined the boards of the various family businesses as a director. Extending his interests over the years, he was subsequently also invited onto the boards of Martin's Bank, Port Line Ltd, Cunard House Ltd and Edward Bates & Sons Ltd. His civil appointments included Deputy Lieutenant of Flintshire and High Sheriff of the same county in 1935. He married, in 1932, Barbara Fair of Preston. His one book, 'Dingle Stalk', was published posthumously in 1960. Frederic Bates died at the Mayfair Hotel, Westminster, London, on 24 June 1957.

BAYLY, Leonard Joseph St George

From Bircham, Newton, Norfolk. A pre-war Regular Army soldier, he was a Gunner (Number 58339) in the Royal Field Artillery when war came, and accompanied his Battery to the front on 22 September 1914, thus earning the 1914 Star. Marked out for swift advancement, he was gazetted Second Lieutenant to the RGA on 23 January 1915. Transferring to the RFC, he was, after training, confirmed and gazetted Flying Officer (Observer) on 10 November 1915. Following a brief period of operational service at the front, he returned to the UK, gaining his Royal Aero Club Certificate (Number 3280) on 31 May 1916, before formally qualifying for his full 'Wings' shortly afterwards. Sent out to 17 Squadron in Salonika on 22 August 1916, he served with that unit until 10 January 1917, during which time the French conferred a Croix de Guerre upon him. His next tour, from 3 February 1917 to 7

October 1917, was with 30 Squadron in Mesopotamia. His MC was announced in the *London Gazette* of 1 January 1918, 'for distinguished service rendered, Military Operations in Mesopotamia', but carried no published citation. Bayly was also Mentioned in Despatches. He was next appointed CO, School of Aeronautics, in Egypt in 1918. Bayly stayed on in the RAF after the war, but died on 23 October 1927, at the Watford Peace Memorial Hospital, Watford, Hertfordshire. He had, by then, attained the rank of Squadron Leader.

BEANLANDS, Bernard Paul Gascoigne

The son of Canon and Mrs Beanlands, of Wickhurst Manor, Weald, Kent, he was born in Victoria, British Columbia, Canada, on 9 September 1897. Educated at Oundle (1909-14), and at the Royal Military College, Sandhust. From Sandhurst he was gazetted Second Lieutenant to 1 Battalion, Hampshire Regiment, on 23 December 1914. He went to the front for the first time in January 1915, and fought with his battalion throughout the Second Battle of Ypres, and beyond. Returning to the UK, he successfully sought secondment to the RFC, gaining his Royal Aero Club Certificate (Number 2473) on 20 February 1916. His formal pilot training duly completed, he was confirmed and gazetted Flying Officer on 31 May following. He first flew operationally with the Sopwith 1½ Strutter-equipped 70 Squadron before, having gained one victory, he was sent as a Flight Commander to the single-seaters of 24 Squadron (DH5s). Eight further victories followed, his MC being announced in the *London Gazette* of 10 January 1918 (no citation). Although no formal citation for his MC appeared in the *Gazette*, research has unearthed the original recommendation for the award, put forward on 18 November 1917, by CO, 14 Wing, RFC, Joubert de la Ferte: 'On 25 August near Belle Eglise, while leading a patrol of four De Hav 5s, he dived on a formation of 2-seater EAs over the enemy lines. He attacked one but after firing about 30 rounds his gun jammed and he drew off to clear it. He rejoined the fight and observed one of the other pilots in difficulties with one of the EA on his tail, immediately attacked it and drove it down to 2,000ft, when it fell out of control. Confirmation was received that this machine burst into flames and crashed. On 15 November near Nieuport, while leading a patrol of 8 De Hav 5s he engaged a formation of 7 DIII scouts. During the fight he drove one down out of control. He then attacked another DIII scout which was over our lines above the clouds and drove it down out of control. This machine crashed in our lines and the pilot was made prisoner. On several occasions Captain Beanlands has brought EA down out of control over the enemy lines, but unfortunately these have never been confirmed owing to poor visibility'.

24 Squadron had re-equipped with SE5As by 21 March 1918, the first day of the German spring offensive. On that day, Beanlands was forced to land his SE5A, 'C1798', after the machine was shot up. Worse was to come on the following day when another SE5A, 'D272', was shot from under him. Seriously wounded, Beanlands returned to the UK for treatment. Although his medical condition was somewhat complicated by the onset of septicaemia, he was eventually able to return to duty as an Examining Wing Officer to 18 Wing, RAF. He was killed in an accident while flying at Northolt on 8 May 1919. Bernard Beanlands is buried in Sevenoaks (St Nicholas) Churchyard, Kent.

NB: His group of medals are known to be in a private collection: MC, 1914-15 Star, British War Medal 1914-20, and Victory Medal 1914-19.

BEAUFORT, Victor Alexandre

The son of Major Francis Beaufort, RA, and Mrs Beaufort, of Bovey Tracey, South Devon, he was born on 23 June 1890. Educated at St David's, Reigate, and at Wellington College (1904-05). Joined, initially, 3 (Special Reserve) Battalion, Devon Regiment, in 1908, before passing into the Regular Army via 1 Devons in 1911. Before leaving for the front, he married Enid Margaret Robin of Jersey. Beaufort accompanied 'C' Company of his battalion to France aboard the SS *Reindeer* on 21 August 1914, thus earning the 1914 Star. He was seriously wounded on 26 September 1914, during a ten-day defence of primitive trenches near to Fort Conde. Due to the effects of his wounds, he was unable to return to his regiment and so was employed in an administrative capacity at the War Office until September 1915. He began agitating for a more active role and, on 15 January 1916, was accepted for service in France with 1 KBS. Still not enjoying good health, he was again hospitalised on 28 March 1916. Sufficiently recovered, he was sent for light duties with the KB Depot in July 1916. Next, in May 1917, he was sent out to Palestine as CO, 21 BC. Injured in a balloon accident on 24 March 1918, he was taken for treatment to No 77 Casualty Clearing Station in Jaffa. His MC was announced in the *London Gazette* of 11 April 1918, (no citation) other than: '....military operations culminating in the capture of Jerusalem'. Back in service, he continued his command of 21 BC until 13 February 1919. Returning to the UK in 1919, with the rank of Acting Major, he helped to organise the London, Paris aerial route for the post-war Peace Conference in the French capital. For these services he was rewarded with the OBE (Military), *London Gazette* of 3 June 1919, and twice Mentioned in Despatches. His last military appointment was as Adjutant of 4 Battalion, Devon Regiment (TF) from 1920 to 1923. In 1927, he married, secondly, Miss W C Thompson, and the pair settled in the USA from 1931. Beaufort died on 15 March 1957.

BEAVER, Wilfred

The son of Shoemaker, John Beaver and Flora Beaver (née Robins), of Lansdown Road, Mangotsfield, Gloucestershire, he was born in Bitton, Gloucestershire, on 10 May 1897. When the war came in August 1914, he was a 17 year old dental student living with an uncle in Montreal, Canada. Although under-age, he was amongst the first to volunteer and, by adding two years to his age, was allowed to enlist into the CEF in September 1914. Beaver served with 1 Canadian Heavy Battery on the Western Front from 1915 until February 1917. Commissioned into the RFC, he trained as a Pilot and was sent out to the Bristol Fighter-equipped 20 Squadron in France, arriving in October 1917. Beaver quickly established himself as an exceptional and aggressive two-seater Pilot, being appointed to Flight Commander during the heavy fighting of the German spring offensive which began on 21 March 1918. He was ably supported in his endeavours by a number of Observer/Gunners including Sergeant E A Deighton DCM, and Corporal M B Mather DCM. In all Beaver claimed no less than 19 victories. His MC was announced in the *London Gazette* of 11 April 1918: 'For conspicuous gallantry and devotion to duty. During the last five months he has destroyed five hostile machines and has brought down completely out of control, six others. During the recent operations he had performed exceptionally good work in bombing and firing upon hostile troops from very low altitudes. He has displayed marked gallantry and resource and has proven himself a patrol leader of great dash and ability'.

Married in April 1919, he left the RAF shortly afterwards before sailing for the USA with his new wife. Intending to settle in that country, he applied for permanent residence status. Once established, Beaver purchased an Avro aircraft and, in June 1919, flew from New York to Kentucky in a record 13½ hours. In the following September, he started his own commercial aviation company in Mississippi, an enterprise which endured until 1922, when he was unfortunate enough to write-off his one and only machine. Turning to a less exciting and more prosaic way of earning a living, he joined the Delta and Pine Land Company (Lumber), a job which entailed him in crossing to England from time to time. Divorced in 1922, he married for a second time in 1924, changing his employment to another lumber company in the same year. His second marriage produced a son and a daughter. Beaver became a naturalised US citizen in 1926 whilst living in Michigan. He moved, in 1927, to New Mexico and to another employer in the lumber business, before going on to Memphis in 1929, when he became District Sales manager with the Bruce Lumber Company, a post which lasted for 12 years. Settled, at last, he took up flying again, eventually founding the Civil Air Guard at Jamestown, New York, and, in June 1942, joined the USAAC. Given the rank of Major, he served in England with 447 Bomb Group, 8 Air Force, (B17s), and flew at least 25 missions before ending the war with a Bronze Star and the rank of full Colonel. He served as a Reserve Officer through some of the 'Cold War' years from 1949 to 1955. Having returned to his job in the Lumber Company, he finally retired in April 1961. Wilfred Beaver died of heart failure on 21 August 1986, at West Point, Mississippi, Hospital. He was buried with full military honours in Columbus, Mississippi.

BEDWELL, James Robert

The son of GPO Inspector, Charles William Bedwell and Fanny Bedwell (née St Clair Adamson), of 7 Arlington Square, Islington, London, he was born on 11 January 1888. When war came, he was employed as a clerk in the London Stock Exchange. Enlisting initially as a Gunner (Number 864) into the RGA, he was eventually picked out for a commission and gazetted Second Lieutenant to 2 London Battery (Heavy), RGA (TF) on 20 June 1915. Going to the front with the Artillery for the first time on 18 January 1917, he soon afterwards decided to try for the Balloon Service. After training, he was sent as an Observer to 20 KBS in France in June 1917. His MC was announced in the New Year *London Gazette* of 1 January 1918 (no citation). Subsequently, he served, with the rank of Major, as Commanding Officer of, successively, 4 and 2 Balloon Companies. Bedwell left the service, via the Unemployed List, on 7 April 1919, returning to work in the London Stock Exchange. He died at his home, 25 Shirehall Lane, London, on 17 March 1949.

BEGG, Malcolm Glassford

The son of Mr and Mrs Robert Begg, of Buenos Aires, Argentina, he was born on 27 January 1896. Educated at Northdown Hill School, at Marlborough (1910-14), and at Gonville and Caius College, Cambridge, where he studied medicine. Interrupting his studies, he obtained a commission in the Rifle Brigade, being gazetted Second Lieutenant to 6 (Reserve) Battalion of that regiment on 3 February 1915. After service at the front with the Rifle Brigade, he successfully sought secondment to the RFC and was, after training, confirmed and gazetted Flying Officer (Observer) on 24 February 1916. He was sent to France in the same month to the BE2e-equipped 9 Squadron. He had at least one narrow escape when, on 3 September 1916, his BE2e, '5817', had a longeron shot through. Begg and his Pilot, Second Lieutenant S W Mann, both escaped unscathed in the incident. His first MC was announced in the *London Gazette* of 22 September 1916: 'For conspicuous gallantry and skill in contact work. A close reconnaissance was required of a certain locality and he came down to 700 feet and obtained valuable information under a heavy fire from the ground'.

The 'close reconnaissance' referred to was during the intense fighting on 8 August 1916, when 55 West Lancashire Division (TF) in particular, was attempting to take the village of Guillemont on the Somme. Begg went out on two successive patrols with different Pilots, to obtain the information demanded. On the first patrol, he was able to locate a particular battalion by means of the mirrors and tin plates fixed to the Tommies' backs.

The Bar to his MC came in the *London Gazette* of 14 November 1916: 'For conspicuous gallantry in action. He has on many occasions carried out successful contact patrol work at low altitudes, rendering most valuable reports and displaying great courage and determination'.

Returning to the UK, Begg underwent pilot training, and after receiving his full 'Wings', was sent out to the RE8-equipped 63 Squadron in Mesopotamia. On 25 September 1917, Begg and his Observer, Lieutenant L N Baillon, in RE8, 'A4334', set off on their very first patrol, a reconnaissance from Samarrah up the Tigris River, and were shot down by an Halbestadt scout over Tekrit. Both crewmen were uninjured, but were taken prisoner by the Turks. Repatriated on 16 December 1918, Malcolm Begg left the RAF early in 1919. He completed a degree course at Cambridge, and went on to become a stockbroker in the London Stock Exchange, with offices at 6 Princes Street, Bank, in the City of London. He lived at 15b Albion Mews, Albion Street, London W2.

BELGRAVE, James Dacres

The second son of Mr and Mrs Dalrymple J Belgrave, of County End, Chinnor Hill, Oxfordshire, he was born on 27 September 1896, at Pitt Street, Kensington, London. Educated at Bedford Grammar School, where he was an outstanding member of the OTC, he passed into Sandhurst on 18 August 1914, with a prize Cadetship. Gazetted to a Regular Army battalion of the Oxfordshire and Buckinghamshire Light Infantry on 16 December 1914, he was subsequently ordered to northern France on 31 May 1915, to join 'D' Company, 2 Battalion of his regiment. Wounded and gassed (almost certainly, by our gas) on the first day of the Battle of Loos, on 25 September 1915, he remained in hospital in France until he recovered his health. His request for a transfer to the RFC was granted in the summer of 1916. His pilot training completed, he was confirmed and gazetted Flying Officer on 27 October 1916. Posted first to the 1½ Strutters of 45 Squadron, he had gained six victories by the end of May 1917. His first MC was announced in the *London Gazette* of 18 July 1917: 'For conspicuous gallantry and devotion to duty. On at least five occasions he successfully engaged and shot down hostile aeroplanes, and has consistently shown great courage and determination to get to closest range - an invaluable example to a fighting squadron'.

His tour with '45' completed, he returned to the UK, and was posted to Home Defence duties with 61 Squadron. He had two unproductive brushes with Gotha bombers over the following months. In April 1918, he returned to the front as a Flight Commander with 60 Squadron. Picking up where he left off, he gained a further 12 victories between 15 May and 13 June 1918, including three 'doubles' on single days. On 13 June 1918, Belgrave, in SE5A, 'D5988', was last seen on the tail of an enemy two-seater during a dawn patrol east of Albert. Initially posted as 'Missing', he was subsequently pronounced killed in action. A Bar to his MC was announced posthumously in the *London Gazette* of 16 September 1918: 'For conspicuous gallantry and devotion to duty whilst leading offensive patrols. In four days he destroyed two enemy machines and drove down four others. The odds were heavy against him, and he did magnificent work'.

James Dacres Belgrave is buried in the Grove Town Cemetery, Meaulte, Somme, France.

BELL, David Cockburn

From East Finchley, London, he was born on 16 January 1884. He worked as a clerk in the London Stock Exchange from 1901 to September 1914, when he enlisted as a Private soldier (Number 2510) into 28 Battalion, London Regiment (Artists Rifles) (TF). The Artists Rifles was, in effect, an Officers Training Unit and, subsequently, Bell became one of the many commissioned from its ranks, being gazetted Second Lieutenant to 3/9 Battalion,

Middlesex Regiment (TF), on 21 May 1915. Seconded to the RFC in October 1916, he trained as a Balloon Observer. Sent out to Italy in 1917, his MC was announced in the *London Gazette* of 4 March 1918, details in the *Gazette* of 16 August 1918: 'For conspicuous gallantry and devotion to duty. When on observation duty, together with another officer, in a balloon, which was set on fire by an enemy machine, he remained in the burning balloon endeavouring at very great risk to himself to get his companion, who had been rendered insensible by a bullet wound in the head, overboard in his parachute. Being unable to do this, he was compelled to abandon his companion, whose death was subsequently found to have been due to the bullet wound, and to jump from the burning balloon'.

He was also awarded the Bronze Medaglia al Valore Militare by the Italians. Bell next served with 33 Section, 9 BC, from 6 April 1918. Returning to the Home Establishment on 31 January 1919, he finally left the service, via the Unemployed List, with the rank of Captain on 15 March 1919.

BELL, Douglas John

The son of Herbert and Christine Bell, of Johannesburg, and of the Rest Mine, Pilgrim's Rest, Transvaal, South Africa, he was born on 16 September 1893. He enlisted as a Trooper into the Transvaal Light Horse, when war came in August 1914, and subsequently served in the German South West Africa campaign. Crossing to the UK at his own expense, he was gazetted Second Lieutenant (on probation) to the RFC, via the Special Reserve, on 17 June 1916. Following pilot training, he was confirmed and gazetted Flying Officer on 22 September 1916. In the following October, Bell was sent to France to fly Martinsydes G100s with 27 Squadron. He shared, with John Gilmour, the distinction of becoming the highest scoring Ace to fly the Martinsyde G100s. Bell claimed three victories before March 1917, when he was promoted to Flight Commander. His first MC was announced in the *London Gazette* of 18 June 1917: 'For conspicuous gallantry and devotion to duty when in command of a long-distance bomb raid. Owing to his good leadership and skill a large ammunition dump was destroyed. Later, he single-handedly carried out a difficult mission and succeeded in reaching his objective under extremely adverse weather conditions'.

His tour with '27' completed, he returned to the UK and Home Defence duties with 78 Squadron. On the night of the 28/29 August 1917, he shot up a marauding Gotha, which may have gone down into the North Sea. In the absence of independent confirmation, however, the claim was not allowed. Although that particular Gotha was never confirmed, Bell successfully claimed another – the first for a HD Squadron – on the evening of 25 September 1917. Bell and his Observer, Lieutenant G G Williams, attacked the Gotha south of Brentwood and continued to pursue it until it crashed into the North Sea. He eventually returned to France in the last year of the war, this time as a Flight Commander with 3 Squadron (Sopwith Camels). The Bar to his MC came in the *London Gazette* of 13 May 1918: 'For conspicuous gallantry and devotion to duty. He has led his formation with great skill and has destroyed three enemy aeroplanes and has driven down two others, one of which was seen to be completely out of control. The high state of efficiency which his Flight has attained is due to his splendid example and fearless leadership'.

Bell achieved a further 17 victories between 13 March and 27 May 1918, before, soon after registering the 20th of his total success on 27 May 1918, he was shot down and killed. Bell, in Sopwith Camel, 'C6730', had been attacking a German two-seater over Thiepval, when the end came. His remains were never recovered and hence he is commemorated on the Flying Services Memorial, Arras, France.

BELL, Hilliard Brooke

The son of Sarah Bell, he was born in Chatham, Toronto, Canada, on 9 March 1897. Educated at St Andrew's College, and at the University of Toronto, where he was a member of the COTC. He enlisted as a Gunner into 67 (University of Toronto) Battery, Canada Field Artillery, before being gazetted Lieutenant into the Canadian Field Artillery in November 1916. He next trained as a Pilot at Camp Borden during the spring of 1917. Agreeing to relinquish his commission in the Canadian Army, he was gazetted Second Lieutenant to the RFC on 23 July 1917. Bell's formal pilot training duly completed, he was confirmed and gazetted Flying Officer on 15 September following. His first active service posting, on 13 October 1917, was to 66 Squadron (Sopwith Camel F1s), then operating over the Ypres, Roulers and Menin sector. soon after his arrival, '66' was transferred to the Italian front, arriving there in December 1917. Bell achieved ten victories between 16 December 1917 and 4 July 1918, during which time he was promoted to A/Captain and Flight Commander. His MC was announced in the *London Gazette* of 16 September 1918: 'For conspicuous gallantry and devotion to duty. He destroyed five enemy machines and drove one down out of control. He is a very fine patrol leader and an excellent officer. His work is thoroughly good, all round'.

Bell was also Mentioned in Despatches, and awarded the Bronze Medaglia al Valore Militare (Italy), *London Gazette* of 2 November 1918. He left the RFC to return to Canada in 1919. He subsequently qualified as a lawyer, embarking upon a distinguished career which would eventually see him appointed a KC (King's Counsel). Hilliard Bell, KC, died in Toronto on 16 September 1966.

BELL, Walter Dalrymple Maitland

Born in 1880. Gazetted Second Lieutenant to the RFC, via the Special Reserve, on 15 August 1915, the same day that he gained his Royal Aero Club Certificate (Number 1594). His formal training completed, he was confirmed and gazetted Flying Officer on 11 November 1915. He served first with 26 'South African' Squadron from 23 December 1915, accompanying that unit to Mombasa on 31 January 1916. East Africa was a 'home from home' for Bell who was described by his CO, Major Kenneth Reid van der Spuy (qv), as 'the world's greatest elephant hunter'. 'Kamaroja' Bell later wrote the definitive book on big game hunting, 'The Wanderings of an Elephant Hunter'. His intimate knowledge and experience of the country proved invaluable, and the fact that he also proved to be one of the squadron's best Pilots, came as a bonus. The first of his MCs was announced in the *London Gazette* of 26 June 1916, (no citation). His tour with '26' completed on 23 August 1916, he was eventually posted to 47 Squadron in Salonika. Bell it was who, on 23 December 1916, following a combat with an enemy two-seater over the Macedonian front, gained the first victory for '47'. A Bar to his MC came in the *London Gazette* of 3 March 1917: 'For conspicuous gallantry in action. He has on several occasions displayed great courage and determination in aerial combats with enemy machines'.

Walter Bell survived the Great War to return to Africa and big game hunting. He died on 30 June 1956.

BELL-IRVING, Angus

From Deuman Island, British Columbia, Canada, he was born on 24 May 1890, a cousin to Alan (qv) and Duncan (qv) Bell-Irving. Volunteering for service with the CEF, he first served with 48 Canadian Infantry Battalion. Accepted for the flying service, he was gazetted Second Lieutenant to the RFC, via the Special Lists, on 5 August 1916. His formal pilot training duly completed, he was confirmed and gazetted Flying Officer on 7 December following. Posted to the Sopwith Pup-equipped 66 Squadron in the UK in January 1917, he accompanied the unit to France as a 'founder-member' and a Flight Commander, in the following March. His MC was announced in the *London Gazette* of 9 January 1918: 'For conspicuous gallantry and devotion to duty. During the last five months he has taken part in many offensive patrols, the majority of which have entailed very heavy fighting. He has on numerous occasions attacked enemy formations double the strength of his own and dispersed them. On one occasion by his gallantry and self-sacrifice he saved another machine from certain destruction during continuous and severe fighting with ten enemy machines, returning to his lines with his own machine so shot about that it was unfit for further use. His gallantry and devotion to duty have on all occasions deserved the highest praise'.

His tour with '66' completed, he returned to the Home Establishment on 7 September 1917. Bell-Irving spent the remainder of the war in various training posts, enjoying a particularly lengthy spell with 7 TDS, which earned him a Mention in Despatches, *London Gazette* of 22 January 1919. He finally left the RAF, via the Unemployed List, on 12 July 1919.

BELL-IRVING, Alan Duncan

From Vancouver, British Columbia, Canada, he was born on 28 August 1894 and known to his family as Duncan. Educated in Canada and at Loretto (1911-14), where he was a member of the OTC (Company Sergeant Major). Duncan's brothers also served the Empire well – Henry, a Lieutenant in the RNVR, DSC; Richard, a Captain in the Canadian Land Forces, later a Wing Commander in the RAF and Commandant of No 1 School of Aerial Gunnery; Roderick, a Major and Second in command of the Manitoba Regiment who served on the Western Front and was killed in action, DSO, MC; Malcolm (qv); and Aeneas, Lieutenant RGA, served on the Western Front, Mentioned in Despatches and in the Second World War, Lieutenant Colonel Royal Canadian Artillery, OBE, ED. Duncan was gazetted Second Lieutenant to 1 Battalion, Gordon Highlanders, on 22 January 1915. Seconded to the RFC later in the year, he trained as an Observer and was sent out as such to 7 Squadron. On 15 September 1915, Duncan and his Pilot, Second Lieutenant N J Bengough, in a BE2c, were shot down, but, fortunately, both escaped injury. Three months later on 14 December, Bell-Irving and his Pilot, Captain O M Guest, were shot down by a Fokker on the Allied side of the lines, an unusual occurrence in that most aerial combats took place over German territory. Both crewmen were wounded in the air, Bell-Irving receiving further injuries in the subsequent crash. Once recovered, he took flying lessons, gaining his Royal Aero Club Certificate (Number 2664) on 31 March 1916. His formal pilot training duly completed, he was confirmed and gazetted Flying Officer on 15 May following. In the same month, he was sent out to 60 Squadron in France. Bell-Irving claimed seven victories, including one balloon, before being shot down yet again on 21 October 1916. Luckily, he escaped physical injury on this occasion. However, he was downed again less than three weeks later on November 9, almost certainly by Leutnant Otto Walter Hohne of Jasta 2, and on this occasion he was wounded. The first of his MCs had come in the *London Gazette* of 20 October 1916: 'For gallantry and skill in attacking a hostile balloon at 1,000 feet under heavy fire and bringing it down in flames. On a previous occasion he brought down a hostile machine'.

The Bar to his MC came in the *London Gazette* of 10 January 1917: 'For conspicuous gallantry in action. He displayed great courage and skill escorting a bombing raid. He engaged seven enemy machines and drove them off. Afterwards, though his own machine was damaged, he continued to fight against superior numbers of the enemy.

Bell-Irving was also awarded a Croix de Guerre avec Palme, by the French, *London Gazette* of 1 May 1917. Following a spell in hospital, he served as an Instructor before going on to command the School of Special Flying at Gosport. Leaving the RAF in 1919, he returned to Canada and to the family's insurance business, eventually becoming President of Bell-Irving Insurance Agencies Ltd, Vancouver. He joined the RCAF Auxiliary as a Squadron Leader on 1 October 1932. He was promoted to Wing Commander in 1937, and to Group Captain in 1940. During the Second World War, Bell-Irving actively served with the RCAF, reaching the rank of Air Commodore. He was awarded a civil OBE, *London Gazette* of 6 July 1946. Duncan Bell-Irving died on 24 April 1965 at his home, 380 Keith Road, West Vancouver, BC, Canadaage 71.

NB: The Royal Canadian Air Force Memorial Museum, Toronto, Canada, has his medals and logbook in its collection.

BELL-IRVING, Malcolm McBean

From Vancouver, British Columbia, Canada, he was born in 1892. Educated at University School, Victoria, British Columbia, and at Loretto, Edinburgh (1904-07). When the war came, he immediately left his job at a cannery in Alaska, and departed for England at his own expense. As a preamble to getting his wish to join the RFC, he gained his Royal Aero Club Certificate (Number 928) on 9 October 1914. Thought to be the first Canadian volunteer to be given a commission, he was gazetted Second Lieutenant to the RFC, via Special Reserve, on 21 October 1914. His formal training completed, he was given his 'Wings' and sent out to 1 Squadron in France in the spring of 1915. He was involved in the very early days of air 'fighting', even before the advent of machine guns. After many, largely inconclusive, aerial combats during 1915, he was, on 19 December, wounded in the hand by shell splinters when his Morane L, '5069', was hit by anti-aircraft fire soon after he had sent an enemy machine down, 'smoking', over Quesnoy. The events of this day, when he successfully engaged three enemy machines before he was himself wounded in a combat with a fourth, earned him a gallantry Distinguished Service Order, announced in the *London Gazette* of 22 January 1916. He was also Mentioned in Despatches. Returning to England for treatment to his wounds, he found himself in the same London hospital (Lady Ridley's) as his brother, Duncan. Eventually returning to active service, he and his Observer of the day, Second Lieutenant A W Smith, in Morane BB, '5164', were both wounded when their machine was shot down on 17 June 1916. The most serious of Bell-Irving's wounds – a bullet to the head – proved inoperable at the time and by remaining in situ, would cause him many problems. His MC was announced in the *London Gazette* of 27 July 1916: 'For conspicuous gallantry when on a photographic reconnaissance. When very severely wounded in the head by fire from an anti-aircraft gun, and half blinded by blood, he steered for the nearest aerodrome and, feeling he could not last out, landed safely in a small field well within our lines. After giving orders for the safe delivery of his photographs he collapsed. His pluck and skill saved his Observer'.

He was returned to Canada after a prolonged convalescence and, in April 1917, was sent to Camp Borden and 98 TS. Shortly after this, he underwent an operation to remove the bullet in the head which was causing him so much distress. Despite being grounded as a consequence of his medical condition, he was again sent to Camp Borden, this time to command 78 TS. Returning to England, he was soon allowed to fly once more, but the wisdom of this decision came into question when he was seriously injured in a crash at Gosport early in 1918. Once again he suffered serious head injuries and, furthermore, his left leg had to be amputated above the knee. 'Mick' Bell-Irving relinquished his commission due to ill-health on 26 October 1918, the severity of his wounds rendering him incapable of future employment, military or civil. He married in 1921, and lived in Victoria, BC, until his death in 1950.

BELLAMY, Franklyn

Originally from London, he was educated at Plymouth College, where he was a member of the OTC. Gazetted Second Lieutenant to the New Armies on 21 December 1914, with an immediate attachment to 10 Battalion, Durham Light Infantry. A transfer to 16 Battalion of the same regiment followed on 12 March 1915. He next successfully sought secondment to the RFC, going first for training to Harrow on 12 May 1915. Gained his Royal Aero Club Certificate (Number 1364) on 30 June 1915. His formal training continued at Fort George where, on 4 August 1915, he was involved in an accident. This setback was hardly significant, however, as he was confirmed and gazetted Flying Officer just two days later. Bellamy accompanied 17 Squadron to Egypt on 22 November 1915, and served with that unit in the Middle East, until going south to the Sudan with 'C' Flight in the late spring of 1916. On 12 May he flew a BE2c on the first reconnaissance flight at the opening of the Darfur campaign. The flight took him to El Fasher, the main base for the Sultan of Darfur's operations against the Sudan. His service in this campaign entitled him to the Khedive's Sudan Medal 1910-20, with two clasps, Darfur 1916 and Fasher. His MC was announced in the *London Gazette* of 25 September 1916 and is slightly unusual in that it mentions his squadron in the preamble: 'Attached 17 Sqd RFC: For conspicuous gallantry and skill. When unable to reconnoitre owing to clouds, he descended to 200 feet under heavy fire. Though his instruments were broken and his petrol tank pierced, he eventually returned safely. On another occasion, when forced to descend, he repaired his engine under sniping fire, carried out his bombing and again returned safely'.

He was also Mentioned in Despatches on two occasions, *London Gazettes* of 25 September and 25 October 1916. His health apparently broke down as he was subsequently pronounced, 'Unsuitable for RFC' and ceased to be employed on 9 September 1916, eventually being granted Retired Pay as Honorary Lieutenant (Army) on 1 September 1917. Bellamy received the Silver War Badge (Number 240530) following his discharge. He lived, after he left the services in 1917, at 'Brewlands', Glenisla, Blyth.

BENBOW, Edwin Louis

The second son of Joseph Benbow, the Director of the Botanical Gardens in La Mortola, Ventimiglia, Italy, and Mrs Jan Caroline Benbow, he was born in Abbotsbury, Dorset, on 10 December 1895. Educated at Menton College, France, and at Castle House School, Weymouth. Gazetted Second Lieutenant to 4 Reserve Brigade, Royal Field Artillery, along with his brother, E W Benbow, on 7 October 1914. 'Lobo' Benbow served with his Battery on the Western Front from 2 February 1915, before successfully achieving a secondment to the RFC in the following December. His formal pilot training completed, he was confirmed and gazetted Flying Officer on 10 March 1916. Oddly, Benbow gained his Royal Aero Club Certificate (Number 3109) at Ruislip on 21 June following, thus reversing the usual progression. His first operational posting was to 4 Squadron as an Observer but once a Pilot he went to 40 Squadron, notable in that he was the only Pilot to fly the dreadful FE8 in combat with a measure of success, amassing an impressive total of eight victories between 20 October 1916 and 6 March 1917. His MC was announced in the *London Gazette* of 13 February 1917: 'For conspicuous gallantry in action. He has on several occasions displayed great courage and skill, and has destroyed four enemy machines under difficult conditions'.

Wounded in the air by anti-aircraft fire on 21 March 1917, he still succeeded, despite his injuries, in reaching the Canadian lines at Vimy Ridge. Once recovered, he had a spell as an Instructor in the UK, before being posted as a Flight Commander to Billy Bishop's newly formed 85 Squadron (SE5As). He had been in France for only a month when, on 30 May 1918, on patrol in SE5A, 'C1862', he was shot down and killed by Oberflugmeister Kurt Schonfelder of Jasta 7, the seventh of the German Ace's eventual 13 victories, and the first loss for '85'. Edwin Benbow is buried in Dulhallow Advance Dressing Station Cemetery, Ypres, Belgium.

BENJAMIN, Maurice Arthur

The son of Michael and Rose Amelia Benjamin (née Keyzor), who came, originally, from Maida Vale, London, Maurice was born in Port Elizabeth, South Africa, on 10 July 1883. His parents had moved to South Africa soon after they were married in 1882, and their two sons, Maurice and Harold, were born in that country. The family, however, decided to return to England while the boys were still young. At the turn of the new century, the Benjamins were living at 21 Essendine Road, Paddington, London, and Maurice was working as a Publisher's Clerk in the city. The family still had connections in South Africa, and Maurice decided to return to his place of birth and try his luck there. By the time war came in August 1914, Maurice had secured a managerial position with South African Theatres Ltd. Returning to England, he was gazetted Second Lieutenant (on probation) to the RFC on 8 July 1916. He trained as an Observer and despite his relatively advanced age – he was approaching 34 – accompanied the BF2a-equipped 48 Squadron to France as a 'founder member' on 8 March 1917. He enjoyed almost immediate success and his MC was announced in the *London Gazette* of 18 July 1917, mainly as a reward for two particularly successful actions on the previous 25 and 27 April: 'For conspicuous gallantry and devotion to duty. He helped to attack two large hostile machines, one of which was seen to crash to the ground. Previously he helped to engage three hostile scouts, one of which he destroyed and the remainder dispersed. He has helped to destroy four hostile machines in all'.

Benjamin went on to achieve a further four victories by 15 June 1917, before eventually returning to the UK at the end of his tour. Deciding to train as a Pilot, he gained his Royal Aero Club Certificate (Number 5883) on 3 February 1918, and was confirmed and gazetted Flying Officer on the same day. Promoted to T/Captain in August 1918, he saw out the war as an Instructor in England. Maurice's closest friend during the war years, was his first cousin, Leonard Keysor, who, as a Private soldier (later Lieutenant) with 1 Battalion (NSW), Australian Imperial Force, had won the Victoria Cross at Lone Pine, Gallipoli, on 7 August 1915, *London Gazette* of 15 October 1915. He finally left the RAF, via the Unemployed List, on 12 October 1919. He later married Stella, with whom he had one daughter, Maureen. Following the death of his mother in 1920, Benjamin decided to return to South Africa, taking up his old job with South African Theatres Ltd. In the fullness of time, he became known as a pioneer and innovator in the theatrical and cinema industry in South Africa. He was credited with bringing the 'talkies' to Durban, as well as being largely responsible for the building of the Playhouse Cinema in that city. Benjamin brought many leading stars of the stage and the concert platform to perform in South Africa, including Dame Sybil Thorndyke, Sir Thomas Beecham, Sir Harry Lauder and the prima ballerina, Pavlova. He eventually retired as Assistant General Manager of African Consolidated Theatres. Maurice Benjamin died in Natal in 1966.

BENNETT, John

The son of Steam Ship Company Manager, John Bennett and Elizabeth Bennett, of 19 Heber Terrace, Goole, Yorkshire, he was born on 20 October 1895. He worked as a Marine Engineer for 18 months with Earles Shipbuilders of Hull, before joining the services. Gained the Royal Aero Club Certificate (Number 7036) on 26 August 1916. Sent to Russia to help train its Pilots but when the Revolution began in July 1917, he helped evacuate his unit, driving across Russia, Finland and Sweden to Bergen. For this he received the MC, *London Gazette* of 1 January 1918 (no citation). Back in the UK, he served at No 2 School of Air Gunnery in May 1918, then to 59 TS. Went to France on 2 October 1918 as a Bristol Fighter Pilot, but hospitalised on 21 October 1918, he was subsequently invalided back to the UK. Left the RAF via the Unemployed List, on 3 February 1919.

NB: The RAF Museum Hendon has his MC (single) listed, inexplicably, as 'in Russia' in its collection.

BENNETT, Leonard James

The son of Farmer, William S Bennett and Harriet Bennett, of 'Leigh', Milverton, Somerset, he was born on 30 March 1892, the family living later in Finsbury Park, London, and in Maidstone, Kent. James was one of four brothers, one having died from TB in the pre-war years. His brother, Second Lieutenant Robert Davis Bennett, RFC, was killed whilst testing a machine at 1 ASD, France, on 7 December 1917. The remaining brother, Edward Hamilton Bennett, after enlisting as a Private soldier into the Royal Welsh Fusiliers, and being wounded as a Sergeant in the trenches in 1916, was gazetted Second Lieutenant into a Regular Army battalion of his own regiment in March 1917. James was an accomplished athlete, winning the City of London's Albion Club's Gold Medal for running in 1911, 1912 and 1913. A volunteer Seaman in the Royal Naval Volunteer Reserve, he served with the Royal Naval Division in the retreat from Antwerp in 1914, thus earning the 1914 Star. Picked out for a commission, he was gazetted Sub-Lieutenant to the RNVR, on 16 September 1916, before later successfully seeking transfer to the RNAS. Sent to the Dunkirk Seaplane Station on 20 March 1917, he qualified as an Observer a month later on 21 April. On 25 May 1918, Bennett and his Pilot, Flight Lieutenant C Laurence, were obliged, due to engine failure, to set down their Short 184 (9060) onto the North Sea, to the north of Dunkirk, and twenty miles from the nearest land. Unfortunately, despite the remoteness of their situation, they found that they had alighted within half a mile of a surfaced U-boat! The U-boat, obviously suspecting some sort of trap, immediately crash-dived. Presumably after scanning the situation with his periscope, and satisfying himself that the stranded flyers posed no threat, the submarine's captain brought his vessel to the surface and took Laurence and Bennett into captivity. Most of this little drama had been observed by the crew of an airborne RNAS machine who, because they were not carrying bombs to use against the U-boat, were helpless to intervene. Bennett was confined in Karlsruhe on 8 June 1917, before being consigned to the dreaded Holzminden on 11 December of the same year. Bennett was one of the eleven men who, famously, made good their escapes, initially via the celebrated tunnel, in the summer of 1918. A feat which brought him an MC, announced in the 'Escapers Gazette', *London Gazette* of 16 December 1919: '....in recognition of gallantry in escaping from captivity whilst Prisoners of War'. After the war, Bennett worked for Selfridge's in London for a while, before setting up his own Import/Export business in the capital. In the Second World War, Bennett joined MI6 in a civilian capacity, lecturing at RAF bases about various methods of escape and evasion techniques, after having been shot down. James Bennett died on 10 June 1983.

BENTLEY, Richard Reed

From Clapham, South London, he was born on 20 November 1897. Educated at St Catherine's College, Richmond, and at St Dunstan's, Catford, where he was a member of the OTC. He was farming in Canada when the war came. He enlisted as a Private Soldier into 34 Battalion, Canadian Infantry, at Sarnia, Ontario, on 9 August 1915. Crossing to the UK, he was promoted to Corporal, and was serving at the Canadian MG Depot, Risborough, Kent, in 1916. Picked out for a commission, he was gazetted Second Lieutenant to the RFC on 5 April 1917 and, following training, was confirmed and gazetted Flying Officer on 23 July following. Sent out to 59 Squadron (RE8s) in France soon after qualifying for his 'Wings'. Promoted to Flight Commander and A/Captain on 10 March 1918. His MC was announced in the *London Gazette* of 18 January 1918, details in the *Gazette* of 25 April 1918: 'For conspicuous gallantry and devotion to duty. When information was urgently required during an attack and several attempts to obtain it had been unsuccessful owing to exceptionally bad weather conditions, he went out and succeeded in gaining the necessary information, flying at a height of about 50 feet under heavy rifle and machine-gun fire. He had already made a flight under similar conditions on the same day. His pluck and determination are a fine example to his Squadron'.

Research has unearthed the original recommendation for this award, which is a little more detailed than is the official citation: 'HQ, 3 Brigade, RFC. For skill and gallantry. On November 20th [1917] information was urgently required as to the position of our troops and the condition of certain bridges. Several attempts had been made to get this information but had been unsuccessful owing to the exceptionally bad weather conditions. Finally 2nd Lieutenant Bentley went out at 2.30pm and in spite of the fact that the clouds and mist were only at 50 feet he succeeded in obtaining the information required, in the course of a flight lasting one hour, and in the face of very heavy machine-gun and rifle fire. This was the second occasion on which this officer had completed successful reconnaissance that day, the first being carried out in the morning under very similar weather conditions. This officer again carried out a successful contact patrol on 21st instant, also under very bad weather conditions. His pluck and determination have been a fine example to his squadron'.

Bentley left the RAF, via the Unemployed List, in September 1919. He eventually went to South Africa and was accepted into the SAAF, serving as an Instructor from 1923 to 1928. Bentley was awarded an Air Force Cross, *London Gazette* of 11 November 1927, for a record breaking flight from England to Cape Town. Subsequently flew three other trans-Africa flights during 1928 and 1929. Bentley became the first Flying Instructor to the Liverpool and District Aero Club in 1928. He was known to be living in London in 1935. Died May 1994.

BINNIE, Alan

The son of Mr and Mrs Binnie of Quikindi, New South Wales, Australia, he was born in Seton Mains, Haddingtonshire, Scotland, on 22 August 1898. Travelling to the UK when the Great War came, he was gazetted Second Lieutenant to 9 (Reserve) Battalion, Royal Scots Fusiliers, on 11 March 1915. Binnie fought with 29 Division in the Gallipoli campaign, before returning to the UK, where he successfully sought secondment to the RFC. His pilot training duly completed, he was confirmed and gazetted Flying Officer on 18 November 1916, before, unusually, gaining his Royal Aero Club Certificate (Number 6235) nine days later on 27 November 1916. An extremely brave and resourceful Pilot, he quickly made a name for himself with the elite Nieuport Scout-equipped 60 Squadron. On 14 April 1917, Binnie led an offensive patrol over Douai, where, during an attack on a German two-seater, his Nieuport,

'A6772', came under the guns of Lothar von Richthofen, the Red Baron's younger brother. Von Richthofen's machine-gun fire shattered the Australian's left arm, as Binnie reached up to his wing-mounted Lewis gun. Blood splattered the instrument panel and, to make matters worse, the Nieuport caught fire. Binnie afterwards vaguely recalled attempting to extinguish the flames as he glided down. When, eventually, he regained consciousness, he found himself surrounded, not only by the wreckage of his Nieuport, but also by a large number of German soldiers, equally surprised as he, that he was still alive. He was driven straight to a military hospital where, subsequently, his left arm was amputated at the shoulder following the onset of gangrene. His MC was announced in the *London Gazette* of 26 May 1917 during the period he was receiving medical treatment in a German military hospital: 'For conspicuous gallantry and devotion to duty. He came down to 50 feet and attacked a hostile kite balloon on the ground. He has on previous occasions shot down and destroyed three enemy machines'.

Binnie remained in captivity until early in 1918, when he was exchanged for an equally badly injured German soldier. Upon arrival in England, he was sent to Lady Caernavon's Hospital at 48 Bayswater Road, London, for further medical treatment. The insignia of his MC was presented to him by the King at an investiture held at Buckingham Palace on 15 January 1918. Before long, however, the seemingly indestructible Alan Binnie was agitating for a return to duty. After a refresher course at the CFS in November 1918, and despite the loss of his left arm, he was soon flying again. Binnie served again in the Second World War, first in the Western Desert as adjutant of 3 (RAAF) Squadron, before then going on to New Guinea, where, as a Lieutenant Colonel (Number NX12184) attached to AIF, HQ, 2 Al Group, Australian HQ, he met his death in the crash of a 60 Squadron (RAAF) aircraft on 25 March 1945. He is buried in Lae War Cemetery, Papua New Guinea.

BINNING, Keith Riddell

The son of Mr and Mrs J T Binning, of Ely House, Queen's Park, Chester, he was born in Liverpool on 2 February 1894. Keith's father had business interests in both Burma and in Liverpool. Educated at Haileybury (1908-11). After leaving school in 1911, he worked as a motor trader in one of the family's businesses in West Derby, Liverpool, until April 1914, when he took up a position with the Imperial Bank of Persia. He was gazetted Second Lieutenant to 20 Battalion, Manchester Regiment (5 City 'Pals') on 19 December 1914. Seconded to the RFC in September 1915, he trained as a Pilot and was duly confirmed and gazetted Flying Officer on 18 November following. Binning accompanied 15 Squadron to France as a 'founder member' on 23 December 1915. He was promoted to A/Captain and Flight Commander in the following summer. His MC was announced in the *London Gazette* of 20 October 1916: 'For conspicuous gallantry and skill, notably when he made two contact patrol flights over the enemy's trenches at a height of under 1,000 feet. His machine was repeatedly hit by machine-gun and rifle fire, but he rendered exact reports of the positions of our own and the enemy's troops. On another occasion he did similar fine work'.

His tour with '15' completed, he returned to the UK for a period before being sent out to Salonika on 20 February 1917, where he remained until the end of the war. His services on that front were ultimately recognised by the Greeks with an award of Officer de L'Ordre de Georges, *London Gazette* of 5 April 1919, by which time he held the rank of Major. Binning finally left the RAF, via the Unemployed List, on 15 July 1919. He worked at his father's firm in Rangoon, from 1920 to 1934. Binning married, in 1925, Beryl Augusta Geraldine May Talbot. In later life he was appointed as the Director of the Technical Research Works at 38 Grosvenor Gardens, London SW1, whilst living at 16 Wetherby Gadens, London, SW15. He served in the Home Guard during the Second World War. Keith Binning became the licensee of the Queen Head Inn, Clackmore, Buckinghamshire, from 1954 until his death in Buckingham Hospital on 19 December 1958.

BIRCH, William Claud Kennedy

The only son of Colonel William James Alexander Birch and Mrs Dora Birch, of Compton Lodge, Walton-on-Thames, he was born in Landour, Mussoorie, India, on 24 August 1891. Educated at Berkhampstead School, at the Hermitage, Rochester, and at the Royal Military College, Sandhurst. Gazetted Second Lieutenant to a Regular Army battalion of the Yorkshire Regiment (Green Howards), on 4 March 1911. Developing an interest in aviation, he gained his Royal Aero Club Certificate (Number 375) in a Graham White machine at Hendon on 17 December 1912. Seconded to the RFC in September 1913, Birch subsequently accompanied 3 Squadron to France as part of the original RFC contingent in August 1914, thus earning the 1914 Star. He was reported 'Missing' in January 1915, having been forced to land inside enemy territory, but managed to evade capture and get back to the British lines. Birch took part in what was one of the first ever 'planned' bombing raids, when, at 06.00 on 10 March 1915, a Flight of three 3 Squadron machines attacked buildings which were reputed to house a German divisional headquarters in Fournes. His MC was announced in the *London Gazette* of 1 January 1916 (no citation). Birch returned to duty with the Green Howards in April 1915 and, in the absence of a published citation for his MC, the authors were not entirely certain that it was, in fact, a reward for his flying services. Happily, however, research has unearthed the original recommendation for the award, which removes all doubt: 'Has performed the arduous duty of ranging for artillery day after day under very active anti-aircraft gun fire, and was never satisfied until his task was completed although his machine was repeatedly hit'.

Birch was subsequently appointed Adjutant to his battalion in June 1917. At the beginning of the New Year of 1918, he was a Major and in temporary command of his battalion. He was killed in unusual circumstances when a fire broke out in Hedge Tunnel, near Loos, on 5 January 1918. Having first escaped from the smoke-filled tunnel safely himself, he almost immediately plunged back into its depths when he realised that some of his men were missing. His body was eventually recovered, and he is buried in Railway Dugouts Burial Ground, Zillebeke, Ypres, West-Vlaaderen, Belgium.

BIRKS, Gerald Alfred

The second of the seven children of William Massey Birks and Miriam Childs Birks (née Gifford), of Montreal, Canada, he was born on 30 October 1894. Educated at Montreal High School, at Lower Canada College and in the Department of Architecture, McGill University. An athlete of some ability, he represented McGill in several of the skiing disciplines. Considered too young to accompany his choice of regiment, 73 Royal Highlanders of Canada (Black Watch), to the front in 1915, he instead managed, by 'pulling strings', to get to England as a driver with the YMCA. He worked mainly in the Folkestone area, before being called to his regiment, then on the Ypres Salient, in August 1916. Lieutenant Birks later accompanied the Canadian Black Watch to the Somme, where he was wounded in the leg by a sniper in November 1916. Following a spell in a London hospital, he was allowed to return to Montreal to convalesce. RFC recruiters were active in Canada at this time, and Birks presented himself as a candidate. The fact that he was obliged to relinquish his commission and start again as a Cadet, with the rank of Second Class Mechanic, did not deter him for a moment, and, after passing a medical in which his colour blindness went undetected, he was sent to Camp Mohawk, Deseronto, for flying training. After no more than sixteen hours in the air, he was transferred to Camp Borden, where he began instructing noviciates! Commissioned into the RFC, he was next sent to Hooton Park, near Chester, at the end of 1917, and from there to Castle Bromwich, where he continued to expand his experience and flying time, until, in March 1918, he was he was sent out to Italy and 66 Squadron, as a Camel Pilot. Despite the comparative brevity of his operational career, he accumulated 12 victories between 18 March and 21 June 1918, a feat which earned him the MC and Bar. Amongst his victims was the Commander of Flik 55j, the noted Hungarian Ace, Josef Kiss (19 victories), who he shot down on 24 May 1918. Birks also sent down a second Austro-Hungarian Ace, Lieutenant Patzelt (five victories). Both his MCs were announced in the *London Gazette* of 16 September 1918, MC: 'For conspicuous gallantry and devotion to duty in destroying six enemy aeroplanes, two of which fell on our side of the lines'.

Bar to his MC: 'For conspicuous gallantry and devotion to duty in destroying four enemy aeroplanes, two of which were destroyed in one fight'.

After leaving the RAF and returning to Canada, he joined the family business, managing Henry Birks & Sons, a jewellery and silver store, in Winnipeg until 1929, when he entered into an investment banking partnership in Montreal. He married twice, and had three children and seven grandchildren.

In 1981, Gerald Birks, by then in his mid-eighties, was hale and hearty enough to attend a Great War Aces re-union in Paris, where he met a few old friends and adversaries. Gerald Birks died in Toronto on 26 May 1991.

BISHOP, Edwin Leslie

The younger son of Councillor T Bishop and Mrs Bishop, of The Lodge, Greenhill Road, Moseley, Birmingham, he was born on 27 July 1890. After completing his education, he served an engineering apprenticeship in Droitwich, leaving only to enlist as a Private soldier (Number 14/363) into 14 Battalion, Royal Warwickshire Regiment (1 Birmingham 'Pals') in first weeks of the war. Picked out as 'officer material' he was gazetted Second Lieutenant to 6 (Reserve) Battalion, Worcestershire Regiment, on 13 February 1915. Subsequently transferring to 3 Battalion, he served in the trenches of the Ypres Salient, before being wounded at Hooge on 26 September 1915. Once recovered, he decided to try for the RFC, and to help his cause, duly qualified for the Royal Aero Club Certificate (Number 3779) on 14 October 1916. His formal training duly completed, he was confirmed and gazetted Flying Officer on 7 January 1917. Sent to the front, he joined 16 Squadron on 30 January following. On 21 April, he had a narrow escape when on an Artillery Observation patrol over Vimy, his BE2g, 'A2888', received a direct hit from anti-aircraft fire, causing him to crashland. Although his machine was wrecked and his Observer, Second Lieutenant C N Milligan, wounded, Bishop himself was unscathed. Again, just nine days later on 30 April, his machine, BE2e, 'A2768', was shot up and damaged during a photo-reconnaissance. Fortunately both Bishop and his Observer, Second Lieutenant P A B Lytton, were unharmed. Sadly however, Percy Lytton was killed in the following February whilst serving with 58 Squadron. Bishop's luck changed on 12 June 1917, when he was hospitalised with a poisoned hand before being sent home for rest and recuperation. His MC was announced in the *London Gazette* of 18 July 1917: 'For conspicuous gallantry and devotion to duty. When engaged with another pilot taking important photographs, they were attacked by a superior number of hostile machines. The other pilot was forced to land, and he himself was driven down close to the ground, but, despite the presence of the hostile machines, he climbed once more and succeeded in taking a large number of most valuable photographs'.

Bishop remained in the UK, and saw out the war as an Instructor with a number of training squadrons, reaching the rank of A/Captain. He finally left the RAF, via the Unemployed List, on 14 September 1919.

BISHOP, William Avery VC

The third son of William A Bishop and Margaret Louise Bishop (née Greene), of Grey County, Ontario, he was born in Owen Sound, on 8 February 1894. Educated at the Owen Sound Collegiate and at the Royal Military College, Kingston. A pre-war member of a militia unit, the Mississauga Horse of Toronto, he was, soon after the war came, gazetted Lieutenant into 7 Canadian Mounted Rifles, a cavalry unit of 2 Canadian Division. Despite the temporary setback of a bout of pneumonia, he nevertheless left Canada for the UK on 9 June 1915. Soon after arriving in England, he caught the aviation 'bug' and agitated for a secondment to the flying service. Having trained as an Observer at Netheravon, he was sent to France, and the RE7-equipped 21 Squadron on 1 January 1916. A relatively uneventful tour of duty lasted until May, when he was hospitalised with a knee injury sustained in a crash-landing at his home aerodrome. After recovering his fitness and following a convalescent leave back home in Canada, his wish to train as a Pilot was granted and he reported to the CFS, Upavon, for instruction. Never an apt pupil, it was, apparently, largely due to the patience of one of his Instructors, the Norwegian, Tryggve Gran (qv), that he finally secured his 'Wings', being confirmed and gazetted Flying Officer on 8 December 1916. Sent, initially, to 37 Squadron for Home Defence duties, he very soon asked for a transfer to the Western Front as he particularly disliked night-flying – an essential element of Home Defence. On 9 March 1917, he was posted to the Nieuport Scout-equipped 60 Squadron. The first of his many victories was achieved on 25 March 1917, when he shot down an Albatros but, in so doing, accidentally over-choked his engine with oil. A mishap that caused him to make an emergency landing in the front lines, although fortunately, on the right side. After his first victory, others accumulated at an incredible rate – two in March were followed by twelve in April, followed by eight in May, followed by....and so on.

His MC was announced in the *London Gazette* of 27 May 1917: 'For conspicuous gallantry and devotion to duty. He attacked a hostile balloon on the ground, dispersed two of the crew, and destroyed the balloon, and also drove down a hostile machine, which attacked him. He has on several other occasions brought down hostile machines'.

On 2 June 1917, Bishop undertook a lone dawn attack on an enemy airfield, later recounting how he swept the target with machine-gun fire, shooting an Albatros into the ground as it attempted to take off to confront him. Yet another Albatros, again trying to get aloft, swerved away from his fire only to crash into a tree on the perimeter. By this time two other Germans had succeeded in getting airborne, and now attacked him from different directions. Having managed to dispose of one of these, he fired at the other and, without waiting to judge the effect, promptly 'legged it' for home. When he finally arrived at his home field, his mechanics reported that his Nieuport was, 'shot to ribbons'. Shortly after this escapade, the first of his gallantry Distinguished Service Orders was announced in the *London Gazette* of 18 June 1917. Some weeks, and many more victories later, Bishop was informed that he was to receive the Victoria Cross for his lone sortie on 2 June1917. The citation for his VC was published in the *London Gazette* of 11 August 1917: 'For most conspicuous bravery, determination and skill. Captain Bishop, who had been sent out to work independently, flew, first of all, to an enemy aerodrome; finding no machine about, he flew on to another aerodrome about three miles south-east, which was at least twelve miles the other side of the line. Seven machines, some with their engines running, were on the ground. He attacked these from about fifty feet, and a mechanic, who was starting one of the engines, was seen to fall. One of the machines got off the ground, but at a height of 60 feet Capt Bishop fired fifteen rounds into it at very close range, and it crashed to the ground. A second machine got off the ground, into which he fired thirty rounds at 150 yards range, and it fell into a tree. Two more machines then rose from the aerodrome. One of these he engaged at the height of 1,000 feet, emptying the rest of his drum of ammunition. This machine crashed 300 yards from the aerodrome, after which Capt Bishop emptied a whole drum into the fourth hostile machine and then flew back to his station. Four hostile scouts were about 1,000 feet above him for about a mile of his return journey, but they would not attack. His machine was very badly shot about by machine-gun fire from the ground'.

His victory tally standing at an amazing 47, Bishop returned to the UK in September to receive from the hands of the King at Buckingham Palace, not only the Victoria Cross, but also the insignia of the MC and the Distinguished Service Order. Almost immediately after the investiture, he was promoted to Major, and a Bar to his Distinguished Service Order was announced in the *London Gazette* of 26 September 1917. During a trip home to Canada, he married his fiancée, Margaret Burden, in Toronto, on 17 October 1917. A Mention in Despatches, *London Gazette* of 7 November 1917, was added to his collection of honours. An instructing stint at the Aerial Gunnery School, was followed, in March 1918, by an appointment as CO, 85 Squadron, then at Hounslow. Taking '85' to France on 22 May, he proceeded to claim yet further victories, bringing his total to 72 by 19 June 1918. Returning to England for the last time in the war, he would soon receive yet further accolades in the shape of a Distinguished Flying Cross, *London Gazette* of 2 July 1918, a Croix de Guerre avec Palmes, and a Chevalier, Légion d'Honneur from the French, both *London Gazette* of 2 November 1918. Next, he was promoted to Lieutenant Colonel, and appointed to supervise the formation of the Canadian Corps Wing (later to become the RCAF). The urgency for all of this fizzled out somewhat with the welcome intervention of the Armistice on 11 November 1918. The international aviation community showered him with honours, including the Special War Medal of the Aero Club of America, the Special Medallion of the Imperial Air Committee of Great Britain and the Gold Medal of the Aero Club of France. Anxious to get back home to his wife, Bishop was demobilised in Canada early in 1919. He joined the lecture tour circuit around the US for a while, before linking up with another VC flyer, W G (George) Barker (qv), in an air charter venture. This enterprise sadly failed, and after living in England for a spell, Bishop returned to Canada having secured employment on the board of an oil company. Still having retained connections with the RCAF, he was made an Air Vice-Marshal in 1936, going on to become head, with the rank of Air Marshal, of the Air Advisory Committee in 1938, and, after the coming of the Second World War, Director of Recruiting from January 1940. Stress and general poor health obliged him to leave the RCAF in 1945, his services marked by the award of the CB in the previous year. He returned to the oil industry, before finally retiring in 1952. His publications were 'Winged Warfare 1918'; 'The Flying Squad'; 'Hunting the Huns in the Air' and 'Winged Peace'. Air Marshal Billy Bishop VC died on 11 September 1956, at his home in Palm Springs, Florida.

Footnote: It has to be said that the award of Bishop's VC, and his remarkable combat career generally, have, over the years, been the subject of often quite bitter controversy. The main, but not only, reason, seems to stem from the departure, on this occasion, from the strictly observed and stringently applied conventions that usually surround the final approval of the award of a Victoria Cross. The high levels of independent corroboration, invariably demanded, were completely overlooked in Bishop's case. In the event, Bishop's version of events was accepted without question and without witness.

BLACKBURN, Harold

The son of School Master, Edwin W Blackburn and Sarah J Blackburn, of Carcroft Board School, Carcroft Road, Owston, Yorkshire, he was born in Dymock, Gloucestershire, on 19 January 1879. He was a Bicycle Maker and Repairer in the early years of the twentieth century but had, in the pre-war years, served as an officer with the Argyll and Sutherland Highlanders, and is noted in the early *Army Lists* of the Great War period as 'Major, 12 (Service) Battalion, 12 October 1914, retired pay'. In the same lists he is shown as being confirmed and gazetted a Flying Officer on 29 August 1914, with the rank of a Second Lieutenant of the Special Reserve. He had obviously accepted a drastic reduction in rank in his desire to serve with the RFC.

In fact, he was amongst the pioneers of flight, having gained his Royal Aero Club Certificate (Number 79) in a Bristol machine at Brooklands, on 9 May 1911. Although not related to the Robert Blackburn, the famous designer and manufacturer of aeroplanes, he did, nonetheless, work for the industrialist, particularly after the Blackburn School moved south from Filey in Yorkshire to Hendon, in 1912. Blackburn was employed at the school as an Instructor, and was also deeply involved in the aeroplane racing side of the business. Having joined the RFC when the war came, he served in France from 25 September 1914, thus earning the 1914 Star, but appears to have been mainly employed on administration duties. A more active role was found for him when he was sent out to Palestine with 14 Squadron in November 1915, not only a 'founder member', but also as a Captain and Flight Commander ('C' Flight). His MC was announced in the *London Gazette* of 14 January 1916 (no citation). Although no formal citation was published in the *Gazette*, research has unearthed the original recommendation for the award: 'Has carried out many dangerous bombing expeditions under heavy anti-aircraft gun fire. To ensure hitting the objective he frequently returned over the same course several times thereby greatly increasing the accuracy of the enemy's fire. This officer shows great determination in ranging artillery fire and is not satisfied until his task is completed'.

His tour with '14' completed on 8 July 1916, he was next promoted to Major and appointed CO, 22 RS, at Ismailia in the Nile Delta. Blackburn returned to the Home Establishment on 16 February 1917, taking up a number of Instructing and Staff jobs in both the UK and in France before the end of the war. For his services in this regard, he was awarded the Air Force Cross, *London Gazette* of 3 June 1919, his rank by then, a Wing Commander and T/Lieutenant Colonel. Blackburn was also Mentioned in Despatches on four occasions during the Great War years. Staying on in the RAF after the war, he commanded the Inland Area Depot at Henlow in 1923, before going on to command the Aircraft and Armament Establishment at Martlesham Heath between 1924 and 1928. Harold Blackburn finally retired from the RAF, with the rank of Wing Commander, on 28 September 1929.

BLACKIE, William Matthew

From Toronto, Canada, he was born on 1 May 1893. Following service with the CEF, he was accepted as a candidate for the flying service. Gazetted Second Lieutenant to the RFC on 24 May 1917. His pilot training duly completed, he was confirmed and gazetted Flying Officer on 6 July following. His first operational tour was with 35 Squadron (AWFK8s), a unit he joined in France on 1 August 1917, becoming a Flight Commander and A/Captain on 25 February 1918. After a brief rest in the UK, he was sent out next to 10 Squadron (also AWFK8s) on 4 March 1918. His MC was announced in the *London Gazette* of 22 April 1918: 'For conspicuous gallantry and devotion to duty. When on a special reconnaissance of two small hostile works, he dived to within 300 feet of the ground, dropped his bombs near the works and then engaged with machine-gun fire a number of men who were running for cover. On a previous occasion he carried out a very successful night bombing raid under the most adverse conditions. He has always shown great determination, and has set a splendid example to his squadron'. His second operational tour ended on 4 June 1918, when he returned to the Home Establishment.

In September 1918, Blackie was given a home posting to Canada, as an Instructor on AWFK8s. Returning to the UK after the war, he went again to France in January 1919, before finally leaving the RAF, via the Unemployed List, on 12 July 1919. Blackie served thereafter in the RCAF.

BLAYNEY, Charles Edward

From Auckland, New Zealand, he was born on 14 May 1891. He was employed in the motor business in Auckland from January 1912 until September 1915, when he left for England intent on joining the RFC. Gazetted Second Lieutenant, on probation, to the Military Wing, RFC, Special Reserve on 3 January 1916. Gained the Royal Aero Club Certificate (Number 2757) on 19 April 1916. His formal pilot training duly completed, he was confirmed and gazetted Flying Officer on 28 July following, the very same day that he was first sent out to the front. Whatever occurred next is unclear, but whatever it was, it resulted in him being sent back to the UK on 23 August 1916 for 'further instruction'. Presumably following that further instruction, he was sent next to 38 HD Squadron in October 1916. Blayney next joined 100 Squadron on 14 February 1917, and accompanied that unit, the first designated night-bombing squadron, to France in the following month. He obviously had, by now, honed his skills, as he was promoted to A/Captain and Flight Commander on 23 July 1917 just five days after his MC had been announced in the *London Gazette*: 'For conspicuous gallantry and skill on many occasions in successfully bombing stations and trains at very low altitudes. He has at all times displayed the greatest bravery and skill'.

Blayney completed his tour with '100', and returned to the Home Establishment on 12 September 1917. The insignia of his MC was presented to him by the King at an investiture held at Buckingham Palace on 9 March 1918. On 27 March, he returned to the front, this time as a Flight Commander with another night-bombing unit, 83 Squadron. His final tour completed, he returned to the Home Establishment for the last time on 23 August 1918. Charles Blayney left the RAF, via the Unemployed List, on 3 June 1919.

BLENKIRON, Alfred Victor

From London, he was born on 4 July 1896. Gazetted Second Lieutenant into a Regular Army battalion of the Somerset Light Infantry on 19 October 1915. Successfully seeking secondment to the RFC early in 1916, he trained as an Observer and flew with 22 Squadron in France from March 1916 to August 1916. A brief posting to 23 Squadron in October 1916, was followed by a transfer to 25 Squadron in December 1916. On 29 January 1917, Blenkiron and his Pilot, Second Lieutenant A W Shirtcliffe, in FE2b, 'A782', were attacked during a photo-reconnaissance patrol by a formation of Halberstadts, over Harnes, at 10,000 feet. Despite being wounded in the thigh, and the engine of the BE shot-up, Blenkiron despatched one of the enemy machines down out of control, as, indeed, the citation for his MC relates, *London Gazette* of 3 March 1917: 'For conspicuous gallantry in action. Although wounded, he fired his machine-gun with great skill and brought down an enemy machine, thereby enabling his pilot to bring his machine safely home. On another occasion he displayed great courage when observing on patrol, and brought down a hostile machine'.

Once recovered, he trained as a Pilot, first gaining his Royal Aero Club Certificate (Number 4842) on 3 June 1917, the same day that he formally qualified for his full 'Wings'. Returning to the front, he joined the SE5s of the crack 56 Squadron on 3 December 1917. Blenkiron achieved two further victories with '56', before returning to the UK and joining the newly-formed Camel-equipped 151 (Night Fighter) Squadron. Returning yet again to France late in the war, he claimed the last of his five victories on the night of 14/15 August 1918. Spotting an enemy bomber silhouetted and trapped in the night sky by searchlights, he closed in to give the nocturnal intruder several short bursts which caused it to fall in flames near to Bapaume.

BLENNERHASSET, Giles Noble

From Leoville, Sligo, Ireland, he was born on 16 April 1895. Educated at Sligo Grammar School. Already a married man when he entered the Inns of Court OTC on 9 September 1915 (Number 6/4/6115), he was gazetted Second Lieutenant into the Royal Irish Fusiliers on 1 June 1916, before successfully seeking secondment to the RFC later in the same year. His training as an Observer completed, he was sent out as a Probationary to 18 Squadron in France, on 31 December 1916. Flying in FEs and DH4s with '18', he claimed eight victories between 4 February and 23 May 1917, his MC announced in the *London Gazette* of 26 July 1917: 'For conspicuous gallantry and devotion to duty. He has shown great skill and courage when acting as escort in attacking hostile formations. On one occasion he attacked two hostile machines, driving down both out of control. Later, he forced three other machines down'.

His tour with '18' completed, he returned to the Home Establishment on 19 July 1917. Blennerhasset next trained and qualified as a Pilot, subsequently serving with 78 HD Squadron. After '78', he served successively with 112, 153 and 39 HD Squadrons. A posting to India with 48 Squadron, came at the end of 1919. After returning home in October 1920, he resigned his commission, before leaving the RAF on 22 January 1921.

BLOFELD, Hamilton

From 43 Sydenham Road, south east London, he was born on 29 August 1896. Educated at Felsted (1911-13). An engineering apprentice prior to volunteering his services, he was gazetted Second Lieutenant to RFC, via the Special Reserve, on 1 August 1916. Gained his Royal Aero Club Certificate (Number 3421) on 17 August 1916. His formal training duly completed, he was confirmed and gazetted Flying Officer on 29 November following. Sent out to join the artillery observation unit, 42 Squadron, on 23 April 1917. On 27 May 1917, his RE8, 'A3200', whilst directing a shoot near to Comines, came under heavy attack from hostile aircraft. Although the 'Harry Tate' was badly shot up, and Blofeld and his Observer, Second Lieutenant W A Hamilton, wounded – severely so, in Blofeld's case – they nevertheless still contrived to land behind British lines. Blofeld's right arm was shattered, the nerves severed and three pieces of bone had to be extracted. He had a bullet through his body and liver, not to mention 20 other relatively minor wounds. The citation for his MC, *London Gazette* of 26 July 1917, reflects the circumstances of this incident: 'For conspicuous gallantry and skill. Whilst registering a long-range gun, he was attacked by five Albatros Scouts, and was severely wounded in several places, the Observer being shot through the wrist. The petrol tank being pierced, he flew back to his own aerodrome, and was unconscious when taken out. His courage and skill saved both their lives'.

Blofeld was so badly wounded that he did not fly operationally again, although he did serve briefly with No 5 School of Aeronautics in 1918, before finally leaving the RAF on 12 February 1919. An Engineer by profession, he became, in later life, a director of Kartret Engineering Company of 7 Carteret Street, London SW1, whilst living at 61 Jermyn Street, London SW1.

BLOUNT, Charles Hubert Boulby

The son of Major C H Blount, RA, and Mrs Blount, he was born in Kampti, Central Provinces, India, on 26 October 1893. Educated at Harrow (1907-12), and at the Royal Military College, Sandhurst. Gazetted Second Lieutenant to 2 Battalion, Queen's Regiment, Royal West Surreys, in 1913, joining that battalion in Bermuda in the same year. On 4 October 1914, Blount crossed to France as a Platoon Commander with 'B' Company, 2 Queen's, thus earning the 1914 Star. After service in the trenches, he successfully sought secondment to the RFC early in 1916. Gained the Royal Aero Certificate (Number 2599) on 20 March 1916. His formal training duly completed, he was confirmed and gazetted Flying Officer on 17 June 1916. He accompanied the BE2e-equipped 34 Squadron to France in the same month that he qualified as a Pilot. On 22 July 1916, Blount and his Observer of the day, Second Lieutenant Sydney Thomas Pearson (qv), despite poor weather, completed an extremely valuable patrol on a line from Bazentin-le-Petit to High Wood, spotting and plotting a new, and previously unknown, elaborate enemy trench system. Their discovery caused alterations to the planning for the upcoming second phase of the Somme Offensive in the British sector. Appointed a Flight Commander on 7 November 1916, his MC was announced in the *London Gazette* of 14 November 1916: 'For conspicuous gallantry and skill. He has organised the contact patrol work of the new Squadron, and has carried out valuable work in the air himself. On one occasion he flew for a long time at about 500 feet under heavy fire to locate a battalion which was lost'.

Blount was, on 27 May 1917, appointed as acting CO, 34 Squadron, and, just two months later on 26 June, was promoted to Major and confirmed in that appointment. In the November of the same year, Blount took 34 Squadron to Italy as Commanding Officer. Returning to the Home Establishment on 29 April 1918, he went on to command the Artillery and Infantry Co-operation School and, later, 2 Wing, RAF, in France, and on the Rhine, as part of the Occupation Force in 1919. Further awards came from the Allies – the French awarded a Croix de Guerre, July 1918; the Belgians made him an Officer of the Order of the Crown, July 1918; and the Italians gave him a Silver Medaglia al Valore Militare, November 1918. He married, in 1918, Beatrice Joan Melbourne, with whom he had two sons. Staying on in the RAF after the war, his many appointments, promotions and honours thereafter included: OC, 4 Squadron, 1920; OBE, 1924; RAF Staff College, 1925; Wing Commander, 1925; OC, 7 Squadron, 1926; Staff, Directorate of Operations and Intelligence, 1927; OC, 70 Squadron in Iraq, 1930; Group Captain, 1932; Commandant, Army School of Co-operation, 1933; SASO, 2 (Bomber) Group, 1936; Air Commodore, 1937; AOC, 4 and 22 Groups, 1938 and 1939; Air Vice-Marshal, 1939. After the evacuation from France in 1940, he was appointed AOC, 22 Group in the UK, and made a CB. He was killed in a flying accident, when a DH Hertfordshire he was travelling in as a passenger, crashed in North London shortly after taking off from Hendon, on 23 October 1940. Air Vice-Marshal Charles Blount is buried in Essendon (St Mary) Churchyard, Hertfordshire.

BOLITHO, Thomas Gerald Glyn

From Penzance, Cornwall, he was born on 21 May 1890. An Engineer, he worked in Canada from 1911 to 1915, before returning to the UK to be gazetted Second Lieutenant to the RFC, via the Special Reserve, on 1 November 1915. Appointed an Assistant Equipment Officer on 6 December 1915, he soon sought transfer to the Balloon Service. Transferring to the Balloon Wing, he first saw active service with 2 Section, between March and December 1916. Next, he was posted to 9 Section, a unit with which he remained until August 1917. A short history of 9 Section contains the following entry: 'The first day the Drachen-type balloon ascended it was attacked by three hostile planes and burnt. Lieutenant Bolitho parachuted successfully. A new balloon was soon inflated and two days later was unsuccessfully attacked by hostile planes. The following day, whilst the balloon was in the air, it was again attacked by hostile planes....and Lieut Bolitho made a safe descent by parachute. He afterwards received the MC'. His MC was announced in the *London Gazette* of 17 April 1917: 'For conspicuous gallantry and devotion to duty when his balloon was attacked by a hostile aeroplane. He saw his Observer safely out, and then descended by parachute himself. He has at all times set a fine example, and has done much to preserve a high standard of efficiency in his section'.

Bolitho was compelled to take to his parachute on four separate occasions, a total which was equalled by only one other Balloon Officer. By the summer of 1917, he had completed 325 hours operational duty, in itself a major feat, given the dangers and stresses of the job. He commanded 11 BC in 1918, for which he received a Distinguished Flying Cross, *London Gazette* of 1 January 1919 (no citation).

NB: His medals were offered for sale by Buckland Dix & Wood on 7 April 1994: MC, Distinguished Flying Cross, British War Medal 1914-20, and Victory Medal 1914-19.

BOND, William Arthur

The son of Mr and Mrs Arthur Bond, of 'Sherwood', Carisbrooke Road, Stoneygate, Leicester, he was born on 27 June 1889. When the war came, he was a sub-editor with the Paris *Daily Mail.* Amongst the first to volunteer his services, he was accepted as a Trooper (Number 4845) into 20 Hussars in September 1914. Picked out for a commission, he was gazetted Second Lieutenant to 11 Battalion, King's Own Yorkshire Light Infantry, on 11 March 1915. He served in Gallipoli as a replacement officer attached to another regiment, before being invalided home because of sickness. After regaining his health in March 1916, he was sent out to France to join 7 Battalion of his own regiment. The first of his MCs was won in the trenches with 7 King's Own Yorkshire Light Infantry, and announced in the *London Gazette* of 24 June 1916. In this incident, he suffered wounds when bringing in another, even more severely wounded officer, over 200 yards of a no-man's land swept by machine-gun fire. Once recovered, he next successfully sought secondment to the RFC, and was sent for training in August 1916. Gained the Royal Aero Club Certificate (Number 3913) on 23 November 1916, and was confirmed and gazetted Flying Officer on the same day. Sent out again to France early in 1917, this time to join the Nieuport XVII-equipped 40 Squadron. Bond achieved five victories between 10 May and 9 June 1917. On 22 July 1917, however, his Nieuport, 'B1688', was shot down by anti-aircraft fire over Sallaumines, a wing being completely blown off and the rest of the machine breaking up in the air. A Bar to his MC was announced posthumously in the *London Gazette* of 16 August 1917: 'For conspicuous gallantry and devotion to duty. While on patrol he attacked at close range a hostile machine, which was sent down out of control. Shortly afterwards he attacked another, which stalled and fell sideways. On another date he flew over the lines at about 50 feet and attacked a hostile balloon, bringing it down in flames'.

In 1918, Bond's wife, Aimee (née McHardy), of 33 Cavendish Square, Oxford Street, London, published his letters in a well received book, 'An Airman's Wife' (republished by Grub Street in 2005). William Bond's remains were never recovered and hence he is commemorated on the Flying Services Memorial, Arras, France.

BORET, John Auguste

The son of Mr and Mrs Boret, of 25 Barrow Gate Road, Chiswick, London W4, he was born on 28 March 1898. Educated at Westcliffe College (1907-13), and at Hitchen Grammar School (1914). He enlisted early in the war as a Private soldier (Number 3586) into 28 Battalion, London Regiment (Artists Rifles). Picked out for a commission, he was gazetted Second Lieutenant to 4 Battalion, Queen's Regiment, Royal West Surreys (TF), on 10 October 1915, whilst still only 17 years old. Transferring to the RFC on 14 August 1916, he was, after training, confirmed and gazetted Flying Officer on 1 February 1917. Having served with 7 and 11 Squadrons during training, he was sent, on 5 February 1917, as a fully fledged Pilot for Home Defence duties with 51 Squadron. A transfer to 100 Squadron, then at Hingham, came on 16 March following. Boret accompanied the night-bombing 100 Squadron to France as a 'founder member' on 24 March 1917. He served a full and rigorous tour with '100', before finally returning to the Home Establishment on 18 November 1917. His MC was announced in the *London Gazette* of 7 March 1918: 'For conspicuous gallantry and devotion to duty on many occasions. He has taken part in forty-one bombing raids, many of which were carried out at a very low altitude and in bad weather. He has successfully inflicted considerable damage upon his objectives'.

In actual fact, Boret had flown 47 bombing raids between April and October 1917, so perhaps his MC recommendation had been in the pipe-line for some time before he had completed his tour. After a rest, he was, on Boxing Day 1917, sent again to 51 Squadron for Home Defence duties. A month later, he joined 33 Squadron for just six days, before being posted on to 36 Squadron as an A/Captain and Flight Commander. He was awarded the Air Force Cross, *London Gazette* of 21 September 1918, for a sea patrol on the NE coast of England After the war, he held various training posts before being sent for a course of instruction to the School of Technical Training on 5 April 1919. Granted a permanent commission in the RAF on 1 August 1919, he then held various administration posts before going to RAF HQ, India, on 16 March 1920. He served next with 28 Squadron, before eventually returning to the UK in December 1922. Administration duties again intervened before he joined 32 Squadron in January 1924. In March 1929, he underwent a Coastal Reconnaissance Course at Calshot. An exchange with a Pilot from the RCAF for Special Duties was just one of the many and varied posts he held until he was sent to command 41 Squadron, on 1 May 1933. This command lasted just five months, before he was again sent off on a specialist course – this time, one concerning Anti-Gas tactics. Boret returned to command 41 Squadron in Aden on 4 October 1935, the tour ending on 11 August 1936, with a return to the Home Establishment. Promoted Wing Commander on 1 October 1937. A series of Staff posts followed, and when the Second World War came in September 1939, he was on Air Staff Operations duties at HQ, Fighter Command. Sent next to command 61 Fighter Wing on 18 October 1939. Six weeks later, on 29 November, he was appointed to the command of 60 Wing in France, comprising as it did: 1, 73, 85 and 87 Squadrons. The stress and strain of those times told on him, and he suffered a breakdown on 18 May 1940. Two days later, he and his Staff were evacuated in a Sabena SM73P airliner (271 Squadron) from Norrent-Fontes to RAF Kenley. Once recovered, he undertook further Staff duties before being sent to command Tangmere on 22 July 1940. An OBE (Military) was conferred in the *London Gazette* of 1 January 1941. Having commanded Tangmere throughout the Battle of Britain, he was next sent to command Portreath on 22 April 1941. Various commands followed, including AOC, HQ, 13 Group and AOC, 88 Group. He was created CBE in the *London Gazette* of 2 June 1943. Boret served in the newly liberated Norway from 7 May 1945, until 25 November 1945, receiving in recognition, the Order of

St Olav, 2nd Class with Star, *London Gazette* of 1 January 1946, conferred upon him in person by His Majesty the King of Norway. He was also honoured, subsequently, by the President of the United States, with the Legion of Merit, Degree of Commander, *London Gazette* of 15 March 1946. He had also twice been Mentioned in Despatches during the war years, *London Gazettes* of 11 June 1942 and 14 June 1945. Air Vice-Marshal Boret's last post was that of Director of Air Force Welfare in the Air Ministry in 1946. 'Jack' Boret died on 26 April 1964.

BOTT, Alan John

From Stoke-on-Trent, he was born on 14 January 1893. He was working in the capital and living at 2a Artillery Mansions, Victoria Street, London, when he joined the Inns of Court OTC on 12 April 1915 (Number Sq/3220). Gazetted Second Lieutenant to the RGA on 22 July 1915. Seconded to the RFC, he trained as an Observer and accompanied the Sopwith Strutter-equipped 70 Squadron to France as a Probationary and 'founder member' in July 1916. His 'apprenticeship' satisfactorily completed, he was confirmed and gazetted Flying Officer on 26 September following. The first of his MCs was announced in the *London Gazette* of 20 October 1916: 'For conspicuous gallantry and skill. As observer he has been in many fights, and furnished many good reports. On one occasion, when his pilot was gliding back to our lines after his engine had been hit and stopped, he drove off an attacking aeroplane and put out with his hands a fire started by anti-aircraft guns. On another occasion, after driving down one hostile aeroplane, he fired at another, which dived and collided with a third. The last one fell vertically'.

The first of the two incidents mentioned in the MC citation, referred to an occasion when, on 24 August 1916, Bott and his Pilot of the day, Second Lieutenant A M Vaucour (qv), in Strutter, 'A890', were hit by anti-aircraft fire which caused a fire in a section of the fuselage. Bott tore away the ignited material in an attempt to extinguish the flames. Partially successful, they headed for home, but were then attacked by two enemy aircraft. Their engine hit and stopped, Bott kept the attackers away with his machine gun, as they glided back to a forced-landing in the British lines. Surprisingly, both crewmen were unharmed in this action. Bott next trained as a Pilot and, once qualified, was sent out to the newly formed 111 Squadron (Nieuport XVIIs) in Palestine in the late summer of 1917. His Nieuport XVII was shot down on 22 April 1918, and Bott was wounded and taken prisoner by the Turks. Remarkably, he subsequently escaped from captivity and made his way to the British lines on the Salonika front. For this feat he was awarded a Bar to his MC in the 'Escapers Gazette', *London Gazette* of 16 December 1919: '....in recognition of gallantry in escaping from captivity whilst Prisoners of War'. Bott was also Mentioned in Despatches. Perhaps surprisingly, he waited until 28 June 1928, before securing his Royal Aero Club Certificate. Bott became an author, journalist and publisher of some note. Between 1920 and 1926, he was the Special Correspondent and Drama Critic for a number of journals. In 1926, he was appointed Editor of *The Graphic*, and remained so until 1932. He later became Chairman of the Book Society Ltd, and Founder and Chairman of The Reprint Society Ltd, Avalon Press Ltd, and, most notably, in 1944, Pan Books Ltd. His publications included: 'An Airman's Outings', 1917; 'Eastern Flights', 1920; 'Our Fathers', 1931; 'Our Mothers' (with Irene Clephane), 1932; 'The Londoner's England', 1947. He lived at 26 Hans Court, London SW1. Alan Bott died on 17 September 1952.

BOULTBEE, Beauchamp St John

The son of the Reverend and Mrs F C Boultbee, of Huntingdon, he was born on 8 March 1895. He was an undergraduate at Christ College, Cambridge, when the war came. Interrupting his studies for the duration, he volunteered for service and was gazetted Second Lieutenant to the New Armies on 23 November 1914. Boultbee served in the trenches with 1 Battalion, Northamptonshire Regiment, before successfully seeking secondment to the RFC, which came in December 1915. His pilot training duly completed, he was confirmed and gazetted Flying Officer on 30 June 1916. He was sent out to France and to 8 Squadron, just five days after he qualified for his 'Wings'. His tour with '8' completed, he was next sent to 12 Squadron as an A/Captain and Flight Commander on 13 March 1917. His MC was announced in the *London Gazette* of 18 June 1917: 'For conspicuous gallantry and devotion to duty while on contact patrols. He descended to a height of 400 feet and attacked a large party of the enemy. He subsequently effected a safe landing, in spite of very adverse weather conditions. He has on many previous occasions done fine work'.

His second tour completed, he returned to the Home Establishment for a rest on 23 May 1917. His next posting was to 39 HD Squadron, in August 1917, where he was employed in countering the Gotha incursions against England. Injured in a crash at Gosport on 25 March 1918, he did not return to operational flying. Given a permanent commission in the RAF after the war, he served in the UK and later, successively, with 48 and 5 Squadrons in India. Hospitalised in January 1921, he finally decided to relinquish his RAF commission and return to the Army on 10 March 1921.

BOURDILLON, Robert Benedict

The son of Mr and Mrs Francis William Bourdillon, of Buddington, Midhurst, Sussex, he was born on 8 September 1889. Educated privately, at Balliol College, Oxford, and at St Mary's Hospital, London. Graduated BA (Natural Science) in 1912, the first of many degrees, and was teaching at Balliol when war came. Fluent in French, he was gazetted Second Lieutenant to the Special Lists as an Interpreter, on 6 August 1914. He served in various Staff positions, but then decided to try for the flying service. Gained his Royal Aero Club Certificate (Number 1976) on 29 October 1915 at the CFS, Upavon, but, despite this, was kept on the Staff, rated as an Equipment Officer, 1st Class. Described as possessing, 'exceptional foresight and inventive genius', Bourdillon had largely been responsible for the invention of the standard CFS bomb-sight, and had also helped to design a most effective 40lb phosphorus bomb. Early in 1917, he trained as a Pilot and, after formally qualifying for his 'Wings', was sent out to 27 Squadron, the 'Flying Elephants', on 11 April 1917. Not only did he prove to be a highly effective Bomber Pilot, but he also did much to develop a system of flying above the clouds purely on instruments. The system he devised greatly assisted his colleagues in 27 Squadron, who were frequently called upon to make long-distance bombing raids in poor weather. He also employed what would later be called 'Pathfinder' tactics, going in ahead of his formation at very low level to mark the target with his bombs. His first brief, but highly eventful, tour with '27' was curtailed on 2 May 1917, when he was hospitalised. His MC was announced in the *London Gazette* of 26 September 1917, details in the *Gazette* of 9 January 1918: 'For conspicuous gallantry and devotion to duty on long distance bomb raids. He has in all taken part in 17 successful raids, many of which were on distant objectives and in unfavourable weather, and has been exceptionally successful in attacking railways, frequently descending to very low altitudes with the greatest determination in order to make sure of his aim. He has set a fine example by his courage and offensive spirit'.

Recovering his health, he returned again to '27' on 3 July 1917, before, his tour completed, finally leaving for the Home Establishment on 28 August following. Back in the UK, he continued to work as an Experimental Officer, work which garnered him an Air Force Cross, *London Gazette* of 3 June 1918, and promotion to the rank of Lieutenant Colonel. Returning to Oxford after the war, he went on to enjoy an extremely distinguished medical career. His many academic distinctions included MA, 1919; BM and BCh, 1925; DM, 1935. His appointments included Fellow and Praelector in Chemistry, University College, Oxford, 1919-21; Dean, University College,

Oxford, 1920-21; House Physician and later Assistant, Medical Unit, St Mary's Hospital, 1925-26; National Institute for Medical Research, Hampstead, 1925-46; Director, Electro-Medical Research Unit Stoke Mandeville, 1946-54. He was created a CBE in 1946. He married in 1922, Harriet Ada Barnes, with whom he had two sons. After retirement he lived at Ganges, British Columbia, Canada. Robert Bourdillon died on 3 March 1971.

BOWMAN, Geoffrey Hilton

The son of Dr G Bowman, MD, and Mrs Bowman, of 'Monifieth', Old Trafford, Manchester, he was born on 2 May 1891. Educated at Haileybury (1905-09), at Manchester University and at Trinity College, Cambridge. Interrupting his studies when the war came, he was gazetted Second Lieutenant to the Royal Warwickshire Regiment on 15 August 1914. He served two tours in the trenches with 1 Battalion of his regiment, and was wounded on one occasion. Bowman was seconded to the RFC on 20 March 1916. His formal pilot training duly completed, he was confirmed and gazetted Flying Officer on 29 June following. Six days after qualifying for his 'Wings', he was sent out to 29 Squadron in France. Bowman gained two victories, of a sort, in the DH2s of '29'. During the action involving his first victory, he actually collided head-on with his opponent. Unlike that of his adversary, Bowman's machine actually survived the encounter and he was, therefore, judged to have 'won on points.' After shooting down a kite balloon on 29 September 1916, he attempted, for some unaccountable reason, to land alongside the wreckage. What was never a good idea, turned out to be even less so, when he crashed his machine in the process. Unsurprisingly, after this, he was sent home for a rest. Returning to France as an A/Captain and Flight Commander with the crack 56 Squadron on 11 May 1917, he flew his new SE 5 with devastating effect, achieving five victories in June and a further eight in July. He continued to accumulate successes throughout 1917. The first of his MCs was announced in the *London Gazette* of 17 September 1917: 'For conspicuous gallantry and devotion to duty. He has taken part in many offensive patrols, which he led on 20 occasions, in the course of which four enemy aircraft were destroyed and 12 others driven down out of control. Although outnumbered by five to one on one occasion, he handled his patrol of four machines with such skill and gallantry that after a very severe fight he was able to withdraw them without loss, having destroyed at least two enemy machines and driven down one out of control. His fearlessness and fine offensive spirit have been a splendid example to others'.

The Bar to his MC came in the *London Gazette* of 27 October 1917: 'For conspicuous gallantry and devotion to duty in leading 25 offensive patrols in two months, shooting down five enemy aircraft and showing marked skill as a leader'.

'Beery' Bowman – an unusually florid countenance was the main reason for the unfortunate sobriquet – was promoted to Major, and sent to command 41 Squadron on 9 February 1918. Despite a High Command order effectively grounding Bowman (he was too experienced and valuable to risk), he still managed to accumulate at least nine further victories, taking him to an impressive total of 32. Inevitably, he was awarded the Distinguished Service Order, *London Gazette* of 26 March 1918. The Belgians also weighed in with the award of the Croix de Guerre, *London Gazette* of 15 July 1919. In 1919, Bowman was involved in the Allied Intervention in Russia, and awarded a Distinguished Flying Cross, *London Gazette* of 3 June 1919. Having secured a permanent commission in the RAF, he rose to the rank of Wing Commander in 1929. Retiring in 1934, he joined the RAE in the following year. Recalled in 1939, he served for a further two years in the Second World War before finally retiring in 1941. He died on 25 March 1970.

BOYD, Owen Tudor

The son of Alfred Black Pringle Boyd and Mary Tudor Boyd, of Egginton Hall, Egginton, Derbyshire, he was born in Marylebone, London, on 30 August 1889. Educated at the Forest School and at Eton. Gazetted Second Lieutenant to the Indian Army on 20 January 1909. He was attached to 5 Cavalry (formerly 5 Bengal Cavalry) when the war came in August 1914. Boyd successfully sought secondment to the RFC early in 1916. His pilot training duly completed, he was confirmed and gazetted Flying Officer on 25 April 1916. He was sent out to the Martinsyde G100-equipped 27 Squadron, 'The Flying Elephants', soon after qualifying for his 'Wings'. Because of his seniority and maturity he was quickly confirmed as a Flight Commander, *London Gazette* of 9 June 1916. A determined and aggressive Pilot, his 'sterling work' with '27', particularly in bombing enemy aerodromes and other targets, was rewarded with the MC, announced in the *London Gazette* of 20 August 1916: 'For conspicuous gallantry when on a bombing raid in unfavourable weather. He descended to less than 1,000 feet and bombed a train, which he afterwards attacked with his machine gun, though heavily attacked by rifle and machine-gun fire'.

Promoted to A/Major, he was posted to the command of 66 Squadron (Sopwith Pups) on 19 January 1917. Leaving '66' in June 1917, he was appointed to a number of Staff posts before being sent to command 72 Squadron in Mesopotamia, from 7 July 1918. On 6 January 1919, he was appointed to the command of 31 Wing, RAF. He was Mentioned in Despatches, *London Gazette* of 5 June 1919, and also awarded the OBE (Military) and the Air Force Cross, in the same year, both announced in the *London Gazette* of 10 October 1919. Boyd finally left Mesopotamia to return to the UK on 22 May 1920. He married in 1921, Ira Marjorie, with whom he had one son. Boyd's many appointments, promotions and honours thereafter, included: Staff Officer, Directorate of Operations and Intelligence, 1921-23; Wing Commander, 1923; Commandant, School of Army Co-operation, 1923; Attended Army Staff College, Camberley, 1926; Directing Staff, Army Staff College, 1928; Group Captain, 1930; Deputy Director of Staff Duties, 1930; OC, RAF, Aden, 1931; SASO, HQ, Fighting Area, 1934; Air Commodore, 1934; AOC, Central Area, RAF, 1935-36; Air Vice-Marshal, 1937; Director of Personnel Services, Air Ministry, 1936-38; AOC, Balloon Command, 1938; CB, 1939; Deputy AOC in C, HQ, RAF Middle East (designate) and A/Air Marshal, 1940. On 20 November 1940, Boyd was in a Wellington bomber, 'T2873', of 214 Squadron, en route to Cairo to take up a post as Deputy AOC-in-C, when, due to a navigational error which resulted in a shortage of petrol, it was forced to land in Sicily and all aboard were taken into captivity. After nearly three years as a prisoner of war, Boyd was one of six high-ranking officers who tunnelled out of the Castle Vincigliata, near Florence, in September 1943. Two of the six made good their escape to Switzerland, but the other four, including Boyd, were re-captured. Nothing daunted, however, Boyd, in company with General Sir Richard Connor and Lieutenant General Sir Philip Neame, made yet another, and this time successful, attempt in the following year. Back in Britain by February 1944, Boyd was appointed to command 93 Group, Bomber Command. His private life was somewhat complicated and, soon after his wife divorced him in July 1944, he died of a massive heart attack at Hendon on 5 August following. Air Marshal O T Boyd is buried in the City of Westminster (Paddington) Mill Hill Cemetery, London.

BOYLE, Allan

From Patrickhill, Glasgow, he was born on 21 July 1892. An Apprentice Engineer with the Clyde Shipbuilding Company from 1909 to 1913. After serving his Articles, he secured employment as an Engineer with the Robertson Engineering Company from 1913 until 1914. Gazetted Second Lieutenant to the Royal Field Artillery on 30 November 1914, he went to France for the first time on 1 July 1915. Seconded to the RFC, he trained as an Observer and was sent out as such to the BE2g-equipped 16 Squadron in the early spring of 1917. On 30 April 1917, Boyle and his Pilot, Second Lieutenant V F Stewart, in BE2g, 'A2851', during a photo-reconnaissance sortie over Arras, were brought down by an enemy machine. Although their machine was wrecked, both crewmen were, remarkably, unscathed. Sadly, Vernon Stewart, a Geordie from Newcastle, would be killed in action on 13 May following. Boyle's MC was announced in the *London Gazette* of 26 September 1917, details in the *Gazette* of 9 January 1918: 'For conspicuous gallantry and devotion to duty when engaged upon artillery observation work. By his determination and fearlessness he has been most successful in this important service, in addition to which he has carried out several successful contact patrols at low altitudes, although subjected to attack from hostile machines and heavy machine-gun fire from the ground, which considerably damaged his machine'.

His tour with '16' completed, Boyle returned to the Home Establishment and was sent to instruct at No 1 School of Air Gunnery, on 6 September 1917. Next, he undertook pilot training with 25 and 50 TS, qualifying for his full 'Wings' on 18 December 1917. In 1918, he was posted as an Instructor at the Wireless School, his outstanding work in this field being acknowledged with an Air Force Cross, *London Gazette* of 1 January 1919. Boyle finally left the RAF, via the Unemployed List, with the rank of Captain on 26 September 1919.

BRADFORD, Jocelyn Ernle Sydney Patton

The son of Captain Sydney Sheridan Bradford and Beryl Angelica Selby Bradford, of 11 Bryanston Street, Park Lane, London W1, he was born on 4 December 1897. Educated at St Bees (1912-14). Bradford's widowed mother, the Lady Controller of Women Staff, at the Air Ministry, was awarded an MBE for her outstanding war work during the Great War. Jocelyn was gazetted Second Lieutenant to a Regular Army battalion of the Duke of Wellington's (West Riding) Regiment, on 16 June 1915. Transferring to the Balloon Service, he was gazetted a Balloon Officer on 22 June 1916. Sent to France and to 15 KBS, on 5 July 1916, he served with that unit briefly before transferring and training as an Aeroplane Observer. He was sent next to 15 Squadron later in the same summer of 1916. His MC was announced in the *London Gazette* of 26 July 1917: 'For conspicuous gallantry and devotion to duty. On three separate occasions his accurate information enabled our artillery to engage and destroy enemy guns and emplacements. He afterwards attacked and inflicted serious damage upon a hostile battery, using his machine-gun from a very low altitude'. Bradford was also Mentioned in Despatches on no less than four occasions during the Great War.

His tour with '15' completed, he returned to the Home Establishment on 14 June 1917. His next appointment of note was as an Instructor at No 1 School of Aeronautics in November 1917. Posted finally to the Air Ministry as an Administration Officer, in October 1918, he did not fly operationally again. Bradford finally left the RAF, via the Unemployed List, on 19 April 1919. He would be awarded the MBE in later life.

BRAND, Christopher Joseph Quintin

The son of Mr and Mrs E C J Brand, he was born in Beaconsfield, near Kimberley, South Africa, on 25 May 1893. Brand's father was a Detective Inspector with the Johannesburg CID. Christopher was educated at the Marist Brothers School, Johannesburg. Travelling to England, he was gazetted Second Lieutenant to the RFC, via the Special Reserve, on 15 March 1916. Gained his Royal Aero Club Certificate (Number 2685) on 30 March 1916. His formal training duly completed, he was confirmed and gazetted Flying Officer on 14 May following. Sent out to 1 Squadron (Nieuport XVIIs) in France, he achieved seven victories between 4 March and 1 May 1917. His MC was announced in the *London Gazette* of 26 April 1917: 'For conspicuous gallantry and devotion to duty whilst on patrol with one other machine. He attacked a formation of five hostile machines and shot one of them down in flames. On another occasion he brought down two hostile machines. He has at all times shown great courage and initiative'.

On the day of his seventh victory, he was himself wounded in the hand when his Nieuport Scout, 'A6668', was shot up and damaged. Returning to the UK, he was appointed a Flight Commander with 112 HD Squadron on 30 July 1917. He was Mentioned in Despatches, *London Gazette* of 20 December 1917, for his work on Home Defence duties. In May 1918, his eighth victory was achieved by shooting down a Gotha during one of the last German bomber-plane raids on England in the Great War. He received the Distinguished Service Order for this feat, *London Gazette* of 31 May 1918. Brand was promoted to A/Major and appointed Squadron Commander of 151 Squadron (Sopwith Camels), and took this unit out to France, on 9 July 1918 – the first ever dedicated night-fighter squadron. Four more victories, taking his total to 12, were achieved with '151' before the war. He received the Distinguished Flying Cross for his further outstanding work in the last weeks of the war, *London Gazette* of 3 December 1918. Staying on in the RAF, Brand, known as 'Flossie', and his fellow South African and Co-Pilot, Pierre van Ryneveld (qv), received knighthoods (KBEs) for completing, in 1920, the first ever flight from London to Capetown. In fact, the pair needed three aeroplanes to achieve this pioneering feat. First they crashed their original Vimy machine, Silver Queen, alongside the Nile in Egypt. They were then forced to return to Cairo to pick up another Vimy, Silver Queen II, which, in its turn, they proceeded to crash near to Bulawayo. The flight was finally completed in a borrowed DH9, the only machine available. Brand married, in 1920, Marie Vaughan, with whom he had two sons and one daughter. His many other appointments, promotions and honours thereafter included: A degree course at Cambridge, 1920-23; Staff, 5 Wing, Inland Area, 1923; OC, 56 Squadron, 1923; Senior Technical Officer, RAE, 1925; Principal Technical Officer, RAE, 1927; Engineering Officer, Aircraft Depot, Iraq, 1929; Wing Commander, 1929; seconded to Egyptian Government as Director-General of Aviation, 1932; Group Captain, 1935; Director of Repair and Maintenance, 1936; Air Commodore, 1938; Air Vice-Marshal, 1940; and AOC, 10 (Fighter) Group, during the Battle of Britain. He retired from the RAF in 1943, going to live at 'Quo Vadis', Umtail, Rhodesia. Air Vice-Marshal Sir Quintin Brand died in Rhodesia on 7 March 1968.

BRANDON, Alfred deBathe

The son of Mr and Mrs Alfred deB Brandon, of New Zealand, he was born on 21 July 1883. Educated at Wellington College, New Zealand, and at Trinity College, Cambridge. Gazetted Second Lieutenant to the RFC, via the Special Reserve, on 8 December 1915. His pilot training duly completed, he was confirmed and gazetted Flying Officer on 24 February 1916. Oddly, he gained his Royal Aero Club Certificate (Number 1905) on 17 October 1916, some months after formally receiving his 'Wings', a reverse of the usual scenario. Posted for Home Defence duties to BE2c-equipped 19 Reserve Aerodrome Squadron, at Hainault, in March 1916. Brandon had been with 19 RA Squadron for little over a week when, on the night of 31 March/1 April, he located and attacked a German airship, the *L15*. The enemy airship had just been hit by ground fire when Brandon chanced upon the scene. He climbed and attacked with Ranken darts, but with little effect. He then decided to have a go with an incendiary bomb, not an easy thing to do, but in manoeuvring to come around again, he lost his quarry in the darkness. Brandon and another Pilot, Claude A Ridley (qv), who had also unsuccessfully attacked and then lost the *L15*, both received MCs for their efforts. Brandon's MC was announced in the *London Gazette* of 16 May 1916: 'For conspicuous gallantry and skill in dropping bombs on a Zeppelin at night'.

The elusive *L15*, badly damaged by ground fire, eventually came down into the North Sea. On the night of 23/24 September 1916, Brandon had another opportunity to finish off a Zeppelin. *L33* had just completed its attack on east London, when a ground-fired shell hit a gas cell behind the control gondola. The explosion caused a massive escape of hydrogen gas which, in turn, caused a loss of both buoyancy and trim. Brandon took off and intercepted the damaged airship, only to be beset by a number of mechanical problems of his own. He did manage one attack, lacing the underside of the Zeppelin with a drum of Brock bullets, but to no apparent effect. His second pass had to be aborted when, after firing no more than nine rounds, his machine gun jammed. By the time he had sorted matters out, he had lost the airship in the stygian blackness. For this attempt, as well as for other outstanding work, he was awarded the Distinguished Service Order, *London Gazette* of 4 October 1916. In the event, *L33* came to ground at Little Wigborough, north of the Blackwater estuary, her crew setting her ablaze before being taken prisoner by a local policeman. Brandon, by now a leading Home Defence specialist, commanded 50 Squadron in 1917 and 1918.

BREARLEY, Norman

From Geelong, Victoria, Australia, he was born on 22 December 1890. His family later moved to Perth, and he received much of his advanced education at the Technical School in that city. After the war came, he volunteered for 35 West Australia Engineers, on 2 November 1914, receiving promotion to Sergeant a month later. Brearley sailed for England in the New Year and was gazetted Second Lieutenant to 3 (Reserve) Battalion, King's Liverpool Regiment on 12 October 1915. Anxious to seek acceptance into the RFC, he gained his Royal Aero Club Certificate (Number 2231) at the Military School, Thetford, on 20 December 1915. Seconded to the RFC, he completed his formal training and was confirmed and gazetted Flying Officer on 21 April 1916. A natural flyer, he had passed easily through pilot training and was soon instructing others in the art. His first posting to an operational unit came in June 1916, when he joined the DH2-equipped 29 Squadron. His MC was announced in the *London Gazette* of 22 September 1916: 'For conspicuous gallantry and devotion to duty. He went out to attack an enemy kite balloon, and managed to get immediately above his objective. He then pretended that he had been hit by anti-aircraft fire and side-slipped down to 1,500 feet, when he suddenly dived at the balloon, which was being hauled down, and fired into it until he almost touched it. When at 300 feet from the ground the balloon burst into flames and was entirely destroyed. He then returned'.

On 9 November 1916, Brearley in DH2, '7928', was shot through both lungs with a armour-piercing bullet – probably by Leutnant Hans von Keudall of Jasta 1 – and crashlanded in no-man's land. After laying doggo overnight, he somehow contrived to gain the safety of the Allied lines, despite his severe injuries. A further appreciation of the work he had done in France came with the award of a Distinguished Service Order, announced in the *London Gazette* of 10 January 1917. He was also Mentioned in Despatches, *London Gazette* of 12 May 1917. After receiving treatment in England, he was, eventually, allowed to return to Australia for rest and recuperation, having been deemed, 'unfit for further service for six months'. Whilst at home, he took the opportunity to marry his fiancée, Violet Stubbs, who would return to England with him later in 1917. Somehow wangling his way back into flying, albeit at low level due to breathing difficulties, he first became an Instructor at Gosport and then took command there in 1918. His efforts at Gosport were marked by the award of an Air Force Cross, *London Gazette* of 1 January 1919. After leaving the RAF, he purchased two Avro 504 aircraft and a spare engine, all of which he shipped home to Australia to become the basis of his burgeoning company, West Australia Airways. He eventually sold his business interests in 1936, and settled into retirement. However, as soon as the Second World War came in 1939, he joined the RAAF and was appointed CO, No 4 Services FTS, at Geraldton. Resuming his well-earned retirement in 1945, he immersed himself in local community matters, whilst always maintaining his life-long association with aviation. He was knighted in 1970 for his services to flying – commercial and military. In the following year, he published his autobiography, 'Australian Aviator' (Rigby Publishing). Sir Norman Brearley died on 9 June 1989.

BRETT, Reginald de Renzie

Born in Dublin on 20 May 1897. Educated at the Engineering High School, Dublin, (1910-12), and at Paynbroke Technical School (1912-14), in the Irish capital. He was working in Canada as an engineer when war came. Gazetted Lieutenant to Lord Strathcona's Horse on 5 October 1916. Transferring to the RFC, he trained as an Observer before being sent out as such to the DH9-equipped 55 Squadron on 1 May 1917. His first tour ended on 13 September 1917, when he returned to the Home Establishment. His MC was subsequently announced in the *London Gazette* of 1 January 1918 (no citation). Although no citation was published in the *Gazette*, research has unearthed the original recommendation for the award: '22 September 1917 – For consistent good work as an observer in a fighting squadron. He has personally accounted for the destruction of three enemy aircraft. He has shown great skill in photographic reconnaissance and his work and example generally have been of a high order'.

He next trained as a Pilot in the UK, and having gained his 'Wings', returned to 55 Squadron in that capacity on 26 January 1918. Brett received the insignia of the MC from the hands of the King at an investiture held in Buckingham Palace on 9 March 1918. Reginald Brett finally left the RAF, via the Unemployed List, in 1919, returning to live and work in Toronto, Canada.

BREWER, Charles Herbert

The son of Alfred Herbert Brewer, Doctor of Music, and Mrs Brewer of 7 Palace Yard, Gloucester, he was born on 21 May 1895. Educated as a day boy at Cheltenham College (1909-13). Brewer entered Guy's Hospital to study medicine in 1913. When war came, he immediately enlisted as a Private soldier (Number 1260) into 28 Battalion, London Regiment (Artists Rifles). Picked out for a commission, he was gazetted Second Lieutenant to 2 Battalion, Bedfordshire Regiment, on 15 December 1914. Brewer served in the trenches with 2 Beds until 17 June 1915, when he was wounded and returned to the UK to recover. Seconded to the RFC, he trained as an Observer and was sent out as a Probationary to the MEF and 14 Squadron, on 20 July 1916. His 'apprenticeship' satisfactorily completed, he was confirmed and gazetted Flying Officer (Observer) on 1 September following. His tour with '14' completed, he returned to the UK to train as a Pilot and, once qualified, subsequently accompanied the FE2b-equipped night-bombing 58 Squadron to France as a 'founder member' on 11 January 1918. On 10 March 1918, 58 Squadron was engaged in the relatively new art of night reconnaissance, tasked in this instance of assessing the degree of activity on the Lille-Valenciennes railway line. In the murk and fog, Brewer and his colleagues were forced to descend to less than 300 feet to carry out their work. Inevitably, they were met by heavy anti-aircraft fire and the radiator of Brewer's FE2b, 'B484', was hit, forcing a crash-landing in no-man's land. Brewer, his jaw broken, crawled out of the upside down wreckage of the FE. His Observer, Second Lieutenant D S Broadhurst, was trapped and unconscious, and it was only with the greatest difficulty that Brewer was able to extricate him, though under fire from the enemy trenches the whole time. Whilst dragging Broadhurst to the shelter of a deep shell-hole, Brewer was shot in the thigh. Two hours later, with Broadhurst now fully conscious, the two airmen crawled to the safety of the British trenches. His MC was announced in the *London Gazette* of 13 May 1918: 'For conspicuous gallantry and devotion to duty. He set out to make a special railway reconnaissance, and though the weather conditions became very bad he continued his task with the greatest determination. His engine began to fail when he was a long distance over the enemy's lines. By skilful piloting, he succeeded in crossing the enemy's trenches, but the machine crashed in 'No Man's Land' and turned completely over. Heavy machine-gun fire was opened by the enemy, and though his jaw was broken he extricated the observer, who was pinned under the machine and was unconscious, and dragged him to a shell-hole in the face of the enemy's fire. He showed splendid courage and resource'.

His injuries precluded him from returning to operational flying and he left the RAF early in 1919. In later life Charles Brewer was employed by BBC, Cardiff, as an Assistant Director and lived at Millers Green, Gloucester.

BREWSTER-JOSKE, Clive Alexander

Born in Fiji of Australian parentage in October 1896, he was educated in Melbourne, Victoria. As soon as war broke out, he immediately made arrangements to travel to the UK, leaving Australia in September 1914. Gazetted Second Lieutenant to the Motor Machine Gun Service, Royal Artillery (the fore-runner of the Tank Corps) on 15 June 1915, he served with his unit at the front as part of 37 Division, from the July following. Seconded to the RFC on 13 November 1915, he trained as an Observer, and was sent out as a Probationary to 1 Squadron in France. His 'apprenticeship' satisfactorily completed, he was confirmed and gazetted Flying Officer (Observer) on 27 February 1916. Brewster-Joske claimed one victory with '1' before, his tour completed, returning to the UK for pilot training. Qualifying for his full 'Wings' in August 1916, he next flew operationally in 1917 with the Sopwith Pups of 46 Squadron, gaining seven further victories and winning that unit's first gallantry award. His MC was announced in the *London Gazette* of 18 March 1918: 'For conspicuous gallantry and devotion to duty in taking part in twenty-nine air fights, in which he has destroyed seven hostile machines'.

Brewster-Joske served out 1918 and the reminder of the war in a Home Establishment posting, before returning home to Fiji in 1919, where he subsequently became a figure of some prominence. At the outbreak of the Second World War, Brewster-Joske commanded the Fiji Military Forces with the rank of Lieutenant Colonel. A transfer to the RAAF followed in 1940, and he was immediately given a post in 'Training and Administration', with the rank of Group Captain. Clive Brewster-Joske died in 1947.

BRIDGEMAN, Orlando Clive

The third son of Colonel the Hon F C Bridgeman and Mrs Bridgeman, of Neachley, Shifnal, Shropshire, he was born in 1898. His father would, later, become a Brigadier General and, later still, the Earl of Bradford. Orlando, known always as 'Bridget', was, like his father before him, educated at Harrow (1912-16). Gazetted Second Lieutenant to the RFC, via the General List, on 17 March 1917. Having qualified for his 'Wings', he was sent out to the Camels of 70 Squadron in the late summer of 1917. On 25 August 1917, Bridgeman had the dubious distinction of being shot down by Hermann Goring, and becoming the Germans Ace's twelfth victory. Once recovered from the wounds received in that encounter, he was promoted to A/Captain and Flight Commander and sent out to 80 Squadron (Sopwith Camel F1s) in France. Bridgeman attained Ace status by gaining five victories between 16 March and 27 June 1918. On 10 May 1918, despite his own valiant efforts, his squadron was badly mauled by elements of the Richthofen Circus, although, of course, the Red Baron himself was dead by then. Bridgeman's MC, apparently the first and only one awarded to 80 Squadron, was announced in the *London Gazette* of 16 September 1918: 'For conspicuous gallantry and devotion to duty. The patrol he was leading was attacked by twenty or thirty enemy aeroplanes of which he destroyed two himself, and by skilful manoeuvring enabled two others to be 'crashed' by officers of his patrol. His tactics and gallantry undoubtedly prevented what might have been a severe reverse to his patrol. On many occasions his work in attacking troops and other ground targets from low altitudes has been excellent, and his example and skilful leadership have been of great value to his Squadron'.

His tour with '80' completed, he returned to the UK in August 1918, going on to join 204 TDS as an Instructor. Leaving the RAF in 1919, Bridgman lived at 6 Pelham Close, South Kensington, London. 'Bridget' Bridgeman died tragically early on 21 December 1931, from blood poisoning.

BRISBANE, John Miller

The eldest son of Major T F Brisbane and Mrs Brisbane, of Edinburgh, he was born in 1897. Educated at George Watson's Boy College (1904-14), where he was a member of the OTC. He had started a career in Banking when the war came in 1914. Brisbane initially enlisted as a Trooper into the Lovat's Scouts Yeomanry (TF). Picked out for a commission, he was gazetted Second Lieutenant to 4 Battalion, Royal Scots (Edinburgh Rifles) (TF) on 15 October 1915. He served in the trenches with his regiment, before successfully seeking secondment to the RFC, in July 1917. After training as an Observer, he was sent out as such to the DH4-equipped 18 Squadron in the following September. Brisbane flew with several notable and extremely effective and successful Pilots such as A C Atkey (qv) and H R Gould (qv). His MC was announced in the *London Gazette* of 22 June 1918: 'For conspicuous gallantry and devotion to duty. When on a low flying bombing patrol, he engaged four hostile scouts, one of which he destroyed. Later, when four two-seater enemy machines attacked his patrol he shot one down completely out of control. On the following day, when returning from a low bombing reconnaissance, his machine was attacked by twelve hostile scouts. He fired several hundred rounds into one of these, and it was seen to crash to earth. He is a patrol leader of great dash'.

Returning to the Home Establishment on 4 May 1918, he was seriously injured in an aeroplane accident on 6 September 1918, the resultant injuries effectively ending his operational career. John Brisbane left the RAF, via the Unemployed List, on 9 May 1919.

BRISCO-OWEN, Clarence Morland

The son of Physician, Robert Brisco-Owen and Sarah Hannah Brisco-Owen, of Haulfre, Llangoed, Anglesey, Wales, he was born on 7 July 1878. Educated at the University of Wales, Cardiff. Having trained as a Civil Engineer, he gained a position as Assistant Engineer in the Military Works Service, India. Later transferring to the Public Works Department, Government of India, he was appointed an Executive Engineer to the Imperial Branch of that department. As his career progressed, he occupied other important posts, including Manager of the Gondal Porbander State Railways, India, and Assistant Agent for Northwestern Railway, India. He also managed various railway construction projects in the sub-continent. His distinguished public services were marked in 1911, the year of the Delhi Durbar, by an award of the Kaisar-I-Hind Medal in Silver. Returning to the UK in the second year of the war, he was immediately gazetted Captain to the Royal Engineers on 23 October 1915, and sent out to France in command of a Field Company. He won the first of his MCs for, 'supervising repairs to a railway for twelve hours under heavy fire....', *London Gazette* of 10 January 1917. Seconded to the RFC, he trained as an Observer and was sent out to France in an advisory Staff capacity, his great experience in engineering to be put to use in aerial observation. A Bar to his MC came in the *London Gazette* of 17 September 1917: 'For conspicuous gallantry and devotion to duty in making numerous daring reconnaissances of enemy wire and trenches at very low altitudes, during which he and his pilot constantly emptied their drums into the enemy trenches, undeterred by violent machine-gun fire. He secured information of the utmost value, which could not have been obtained by any other means'.

His stint finished, he returned to the Home Establishment at the end of 1917. Brisco-Owen was presented with the insignia of his MC and Bar by the King in an investiture held at Buckingham Palace on 16 March 1918. He was next, on 5 April 1918, appointed in an advisory capacity to the British War Mission in the USA, where he saw out the remainder of the war. He finally left the service, via the Unemployed List, on 14 January 1919, returning to India with his wife, Ada Henrietta. Clarence Brisco-Owen contracted, and died of, cholera in Rawalpindi on 12 September 1919, and is buried at Rawalpindi (West Ridge) Cemetery.

BRITTON, Arthur Frederick

The son of Mr and Mrs Britton, of 46 Norfolk House Road, Streatham, London, he was born on 2 October 1888. A Clerk with the Seaman's Insurance Company, he was a pre-war volunteer with 5 London Regiment (London Rifle Brigade) (TF), from April 1908, until the term of his engagement expired in April 1913. When the war came, he immediately enlisted as a Trooper (Number 1796) into 1/1 Surrey Yeomanry. Picked out for a commission, he was gazetted Second Lieutenant to the New Armies, via the General List, on 27 November 1915. A brief attachment to 9 (Reserve) Battalion, Somerset Light Infantry, was followed by a formal secondment to the newly forming MGC on 13 March 1916. Britton served in France with the MGC from 18 July 1916. He next transferred to the RFC on 28 April 1917 and, following training, was sent out as a Probationary Observer to the DH4-equipped 57 Squadron in the following June. An Observer Ace, Britton achieved six victories between 3 July and 27 July 1917. On 27 July 1917, Britton and his Pilot, Captain L Minot (qv), in DH4, 'B3963', fought and sent down an Albatros out of control. Britton received a calf wound in this combat. On 18 August, Britton and his Pilot, Lieutenant D S Hall, in DH4, 'A7535', were fortunate to escape injury when their machine was hit by anti-aircraft fire and forced to crashland. Britton was, however, severely wounded just two days later during a photo-reconnaissance over Pilchem Ridge. His left leg had to be amputated above the knee as a consequence of this second wounding. His MC was announced in the *London Gazette* of 1 January 1918 (no citation), and the further award of a French Croix de Guerre came on 18 June 1918. His widowed mother wrote a moving letter to Lord Derby, the Minister of War, asking for Arthur to be released from further service. She explained that all four of her sons had volunteered as soon as war had broken out. Lieutenant Edward W Britton, 20 Durham Light Infantry, had been killed at Klein Zillebeke on 31 July 1917; another had been wounded at Delville Wood, and the fourth was serving in Salonika. In the event, Arthur was given six months leave at home to comfort and sustain his mother. Because of his disability, Britton was grounded and posted as an Administration Officer before prematurely leaving the service, with the rank of Honorary Lieutenant, on 28 September 1918. Unfortunately, as a consequence of his severe injuries, his health deteriorated to such an extent that he died on 19 February 1919.

BROADBERRY, Edric William

The son of Civil Engineer, Arthur Edward Broadberry and Amy Lucy Broadberry (née Dubois), of 'Elmlea', Willoughby Lane, Tottenham, Middlesex, he was born on 14 December 1894. A pre-war volunteer, he had been commissioned into 7 Battalion, Essex Regiment (TF). With the rest of the TF, Broadberry was mobilised immediately upon the outbreak of war on 4 August 1914. He accompanied his battalion when it landed at Suvla Bay on the Gallipoli Peninsula, on 12 August 1915, serving in that unhappy place until the evacuation in the following December. After a period of garrison duty on the Suez Canal, he could no longer stand the stupefying boredom and successfully applied for a transfer to the RFC. His pilot training completed at RFC HQ, Aboukir, he was confirmed and gazetted Flying Officer on 8 November 1916. A transfer to the UK was followed by a posting to the prestigious 56 Squadron in France, on 20 April 1917. Broadberry achieved eight victories between 12 May and 11 July 1917. On 12 July 1917, he was shot down and wounded in the leg. In the early morning of that day, Broadberry and his SE5A, 'A8918', were bested in a combat over Menin, his opponent was almost certainly Leutnant Kurt Küppers of Jasta 6. Broadberry's MC was announced in the *London Gazette* of 1 January 1918 (no citation). Although no formal citation was published in the *Gazette*, research has unearthed the original recommendation for the award: 'For great energy and determination during the period 20 April 1917 to 12 July 1917, on which date he was wounded and admitted to hospital. During this period he took part in many offensive patrols. He destroyed one enemy aeroplane and drove down five others completely out of control. His work invariably showed coolness, determination and courage'.

Although he did not return to combat flying, he did stay on in the RAF after the war and, by 1936, was a Squadron Leader at the Air Observers School at North Coates. Broadberry eventually attained the rank of Group Captain during the Second World War, before finally retiring in 1947. Group Captain Edric Broadberry died at his home, Walnut Tree Farm House, Wattisfield, Diss, Norfolk, on Boxing Day 1967.

BROADWAY, John Hartgill

From West Knoyle, Wiltshire, he was born on Christmas Day, 1893. Educated at Stourpaine House School, Blandford. After leaving school, he followed his father into farming. Gazetted Second Lieutenant into 3 (Reserve) Battalion, Dorset Regiment on 18 November 1915. Seconded to the RFC, he gained his Royal Aero Club Certificate (Number 3369) on 19 August 1916. His formal pilot training completed, he was confirmed and gazetted Flying Officer on 13 September 1916. He was sent out to 17 Squadron in Salonika, just one week after qualifying. Broadway was first Mentioned in Despatches for his work over this front in the *London Gazette* of 21 July 1917, with his MC following in the *London Gazette* of 27 October 1917, details in the *Gazette* of 18 March 1918: 'For conspicuous gallantry and devotion to duty. He attacked a party of six enemy machines, driving one down over the enemy's lines. He has always set a splendid example of courage and devotion to duty'.

He was, for a period, attached to, and flew with, a French squadron, Escadrille N506, and claimed a victory with that unit on 21 August 1917. For this success, he was mentioned in the Ordre Generale No 46, before receiving the Croix de Guerre, *London Gazette* of 17 December 1917. His tour with '17' completed, he returned to the Home Establishment early in 1918. 'Jack' Broadway next served with 3 and 34 Training Depot Squadron in the UK, before being hospitalised in October 1918. This bout of ill-health precluded any possibility of a return to operational flying before the end of the war. He finally left the RAF, via the Unemployed List, on 12 April 1919, and returned to farming. Broadway died at his home, 'St Bernard's', Shawford, Winchester, on 18 February 1965.

BROOKS, Douglas Charles Morris

The son of Alfred B Brooks, JP, and Mrs Alexander Amelia Florence Brooks (née Smith), of 'Goldsmiths', Langdon Hills, Essex, he was born at Grays, Essex, on 2 January 1897. Educated at Bootham College (1903-13), and at King's College, Cambridge (1914-15), where he studied structural engineering. Interrupting his studies in 1915, he, as a member of a Quaker family, joined the Friends Ambulance Unit in France. Apparently later deciding upon more militant service, he was gazetted Second Lieutenant into the RFC in April 1917. After qualifying for his 'Wings', he served briefly in the UK before being sent out to France and the Bristol Fighter-equipped 11 Squadron on 24 November 1917. On 9 March 1918, Brooks and his Observer of the day, Lieutenant H R Kinkaid (qv), carried out a valuable long-range reconnaissance in poor weather conditions, shooting down an enemy machine in the process. His MC was announced in the *London Gazette* of 22 June 1918: 'For conspicuous gallantry and devotion to duty. During the recent operations he succeeded, despite the most adverse climatic conditions, in completing a long-distance reconnaissance over the enemy's lines, returning with the most valuable and important information. Previous to this he has brought down completely out of control one hostile machine. He has displayed great gallantry and determination and has rendered services of great value'.

Brooks' success on 9 March 1918 was the first of at least three victories with this Observer. His tour with '11' completed, he returned to the Home Establishment in January 1918. Posted to Biggin Hill on 14 March 1918, he served at that station until 24 June 1918, when he was sent out again to 11 Squadron in France. His second tour came to an end three months later, whereupon he was posted as an Instructor to No 3 Flying School, on 29 September 1918. He married, in 1918, Beryl Anderson. For his outstanding services as an Instructor, he was awarded the Air Force Cross, *London Gazette* of 3 June 1919. Resuming his studies at Cambridge in 1919, Brooks graduated and was subsequently admitted AMIStructE. In 1920, he was given a contract to erect a refrigeration plant in Port Said. From that small beginning, he set up as an Engineer and Constructor in Egypt, living at 32 Soliman Pasha, in that city. Some of his major projects over the subsequent years, included the building of the British Government Barracks in Cairo, as well as a large camp at Ismailia. Brooks was also responsible for building the British Consulate at Alexandria and the first skyscraper in Cairo for Shell Oil. Other contracts he completed, included a huge electric installation for the improved drainage of the Nile Delta; the overland cable from Port Said to Suez for the Eastern Telegraph Company; the harbour works at Haifa; the rebuilding of the Qasr-el-Nil Bridge in Cairo; the erection of several steel bridges in the Sudan; a large brickworks near Baghdad; and, in association with Balfour Beatty, the Kut Barrage in Mesopotamia (now Iraq).

BROWN, Alfred John

Originally from Deal, Kent, he enlisted as a Private soldier (Number 4766) into 28 Battalion, London Regiment (Artists Rifles) (TF). Picked out for a commission, he was gazetted Second Lieutenant to 3/6 (Cyclists) Battalion, Royal Sussex Regiment (TF), on 11 July 1916. Seconded to the RFC in October 1916, he qualified for his 'Wings' and was immediately sent to France and the DH2-equipped 24 Squadron, on 14 March 1917. After a relatively slow start, he improved with experience, achieving eight victories between 21 September 1917 and 13 March 1918 – the first two in DH5s and the remaining six in the cockpit of an SE5A. He was also promoted to A/Captain and Flight Commander during this period. His MC was announced in the *London Gazette* of 22 June 1918: 'For conspicuous gallantry and devotion to duty. While on patrol he and his patrol attacked two enemy two-seater machines, one of which was driven down out of control, the other being seriously damaged. On the following day he attacked a hostile reconnaissance machine, which he forced to land in our lines. On a later occasion he volunteered to attack a hostile aerodrome in foggy weather. He dropped four bombs from a height of 200 feet, which blew in the sides of one of the hangars, and then attacked horse and motor transport on the road, finally engaging enemy troops in the main street of a village with machine-gun fire. He has shown great skill and daring as a leader of offensive patrols'.

His tour with '24' completed, he returned home for a rest and instructing duties on 15 March 1918. Refreshed, he went out again to France on 4 August 1918, this time as a Flight Commander to the Sopwith Dolphin-equipped 23 Squadron. Four days later, on the opening day of the Battle of Amiens, the 'Black Day of the German Army', Brown's Dolphin, 'C8074', was shot up by machine-gun fire from the ground and he was forced to land. On 31 August 1918, Brown and two of his colleagues were shot up by elements of Jasta 11. Brown and Lieutenant W N L Cope, although forced to land, managed to do so without injury. Their colleague, Second Lieutenant C H A Bridge, however, died of wounds after his Dolphin was brought down in flames. Brown transferred to the Administration Branch in February 1919, before shortly afterwards, on 11 March 1919, relinquishing his commission due to ill-health. He was issued with a Silver War Badge as a consequence of his infirmity, his eligibility published in the *London Gazette* of 25 July 1919. Brown lived, in the immediate post-war years, at 'St Neots', London Road, Deal, Kent.

BROWN, Clifford le Brun

The son of Mr and Mrs William le Brun Brown, of Tarrongyle, New South Wales, Australia, he was born in Patterson, NSW, on 14 September 1892. Brown was working as a Station Overseer in Inverell, NSW, when he enlisted as a Private soldier (Number 996) into the AIF in Brisbane on 30 June 1915. His basic training completed, he embarked at Brisbane aboard the SS *Hymattus* on 17 September 1915, bound for the Middle East as part of 4 Reinforcement Group for 11 Light Horse Regiment. Promoted to Corporal on 13 December 1915, he was subsequently wounded in action in Egypt whilst serving with Composite Light Horse Regiment on 18 March 1916. Once recovered, le Brun Brown secured a secondment to the flying service and was attached to 68 (Australian) Squadron on 5 January 1917. Picked out for a commission, he was gazetted Second Lieutenant to the RFC on 30 April 1917. His pilot training duly completed, he was confirmed and gazetted Flying Officer on 8 June following. On 26 June 1917, Brown was involved in an extraordinary series of misadventures following an eight-machine 1 AFC Squadron bombing raid on the Turkish Fourth Army Headquarters. During the return flight, the engine on Brown's BE seized-up and stopped, forcing him to land. Captain A T Cole (qv) in an accompanying Martinsyde and Lieutenant R A Austin (qv) in another BE, seeing his plight, both landed their machines alongside Brown. After setting fire to his BE, Brown climbed in with Austin, who immediately took-off, as did Cole in his Martinsyde.

Resuming their homeward journey, all seemed perfectly well until suddenly, in the vicinity of Beersheba, the engine on Austin's engine seized and stopped, forcing yet another landing. The accompanying Cole also came down, taxiing up alongside Austin's stationary BE. The ground they had alighted on was bad, uneven and rock-strewn. Cole loaded both Brown and Austin aboard his Martinsyde, but, what with the additional weight and the bad ground, could not get airborne. He next tried with just one passenger, but this, too, failed. After lifting off to no more than ten feet, the machine dropped back to the ground, breaking the under-carriage. The now disconsolate trio stripped out their machine guns and a camera, then, having buried them, set off on foot for the lines. Whilst all this drama was being enacted below them, the remaining – still airborne – members of the original formation had hovered above, reluctant to leave their comrades to their fate. Now, suddenly, two of these machines, flown by Lieutenants J H Butler and L M Potts, found themselves out of petrol and oil. This pair, too, were forced to land near Khalasa. After leaving their machines unburnt and intact in hope of future salving, Butler and Potts, in their turn, were lifted off by two others of the patrol and eventually got home safely. Their abandoned machines, however, were stripped bare by Arabs and only the engines could be recovered. Happily, the perambulating trio of Brown, Cole and Austin, were picked up by a patrol of the Light Horse and guided to safety. Five of the original eight machines had been lost in the course of this patrol, and not one as the result of enemy action. Brown's MC was announced in the *London Gazette* of 11 April 1918 (no citation): '.... military operations culminating in the capture of Jerusalem'.

The recommendation for the award cites his, 'outstanding gallantry and devotion to duty when on numerous occasions his work as a Pilot during bombing and photographic reconnaissances has been invaluable'.

His tour with 1 AFC completed, he left Suez for the UK on 28 April 1918. Leaving the service on 30 November 1918, he eventually returned to Australia on 24 July 1920, and became a Mining Engineer. In 1939, he was working and living in Misima Island, Papua New Guinea. He served again in the Second World War, this time as a Flight Lieutenant with 1 Radio Installation and Maintenance Unit, at Croydon, NSW, until he was finally discharged on 6 October 1944. Clifford le Brun Brown died on 15 November 1972.

BROWN, Frederic Elliot

From Quebec, Canada, he was born in 1895. He came to the UK early in 1915 and was gazetted, initially, to 3 (Reserve) Battalion, Royal Dublin Fusiliers in April. Posted next to 8 Battalion of his regiment, he accompanied that unit to France in December 1915. After service in the trenches, he was seconded to the RFC in the summer of 1916. Having trained as an Observer he joined BE2c-equipped 12 Squadron as such in August 1916. The French were the first to recognise his services with an award of a Croix de Guerre, *London Gazette* of 14 July 1917. His tour with '12' completed in April 1917, he returned to the UK for pilot training. Having qualified for his full 'Wings', he was sent out to the SE5A-equipped 84 Squadron on 1 November following. Brown achieved ten victories between 8 November 1917 and 22 March 1918, including a 'treble' and a 'double' on single days. On 16 February 1918, he attacked a formation of four enemy Scouts, shooting down one immediately. Turning his attention to another, his tracers were seen to strike and it spun away completely out of control. His engine began to give him trouble and he turned for home. As he crossed the lines, he stumbled across a solitary two-seater LVG, into which he fired 150 rounds from as close as thirty yards range. The stricken LVG fell away and was seen to crash. Brown was promoted to A/Captain and Flight Commander in February 1918. His tour with '84' was curtailed when he was injured in a landing crash on 31 March following. The first of his MCs was announced in the *London Gazette* of 22 April 1918: ' For conspicuous gallantry and devotion to duty. Whilst leading a patrol of five machines, on observing four hostile scouts diving on one of our formations, he at once engaged them, driving one of them down completely out of control, while his formation dispersed the others. Later, on sighting another hostile scout, he engaged it and forced it down spinning and out of control. While returning to his aerodrome, he observed an enemy two seater, and although his engine was running badly and might have failed him at any moment, he attacked it and drove it down in a vertical nose dive. Previous to this, he had driven down one other machine, which was seen to crash, and a third completely out of control. He is a most daring and skilful pilot'.

The Bar to this came in the *London Gazette* of 22 June 1918:' For conspicuous gallantry and devotion to duty in attacking enemy aircraft. During an engagement between fourteen of our scouts and about forty enemy scouts, he shot down two enemy machines completely out of control. On another occasion, he attacked a formation of seven enemy scouts and destroyed one of them. He has destroyed two other enemy machines and driven down one other out of control. His courage and initiative have been a source of inspiration to all'.

The injuries he received in the crash at the end of March 1918, spelt the end of his combat flying and he saw out the remainder of the war instructing in the UK. Returning to Canada in 1919, he subsequently became a respected and successful businessman, living and working in Montreal. Frederic Brown died in Toronto on 15 September 1971.

BROWN, John

The son of Hugh Brown and Maggie Brown (née Gibb), of Govan, Glasgow, he was born on 29 March 1890. Educated at the Universities of Glasgow and Göttingen, Germany, his particular field of study being in magnetic electrical research, MA, BSc 1911. His first employment was as University Assistant to the Physics Professor, at University Court, Glasgow. Next, from 1913 to 1915, he was appointed Assistant Master (Science and Maths) at Bellahouston Academy. He was gazetted Second Lieutenant to the RFC, via the Special Reserve, on 30 November 1915, and further gazetted Assistant Equipment Officer (Wireless) on 21 December 1915. A wireless expert, he first served on the Western Front from 20 April to 15 September 1916, with 13 Squadron. His expertise needed elsewhere, he was sent out to RFC Headquarters in Egypt. and from there he was detached to HQ, Palestine Brigade. His MC was announced in the *London Gazette* of 1 January 1918 (no citation).

Brown was also promoted to A/Captain on 1 January 1918. He was Mentioned in Despatches on four occasions during the Great War, *London Gazette*s of 1 December 1916 (Egypt), 28 June 1917, 12 January 1918 (Sir A Murray) and 5 June 1919 (Allenby). He was also appointed MBE (Military) in the Birthday Honours *London Gazette* of 3 June 1919. Brown's last service appointment was to the Air Ministry in London from January 1919, until he finally left the RAF in the October of the same year. Brown briefly returned to his teaching post at Bellahouston Academy before, late in 1919, securing a position as Assistant to the Professor of Natural Philosophy at Glasgow University. Within weeks, he was appointed a District Inspector, London County Council, serving in that post for six years before being promoted to a succession of increasingly senior positions in the education field: Assistant Education Officer, 1925-36; Chief Inspector, 1936-47; Deputy Education Officer, 1947-51; and Education Officer, 1951-56. His publications included, 'Teaching Science in Schools', 1926. He lived at 74 Ryecroft Road, London SW16. John Brown died on 24 August 1977.

BROWN, Ralph Seath Stark

From Dowanhill, Glasgow, he was born on 26 October 1888. Educated at Glasgow Academy and at Glasgow University. Admitted a Solicitor in January 1910, he practised in Glasgow until war came in August 1914. Brown enlisted as a Private soldier into 9 (Glasgow Highland) Battalion, Highland Light Infantry (TF) in August 1914. Picked out for a commission, he was gazetted Second Lieutenant to 15 Battalion, Highland Light Infantry, on 1 September 1914. Brown accompanied his battalion to France on 23 November 1915, serving in the trenches until his request for secondment to the RFC was granted in January 1916. Having trained as an Observer, he was sent out as a Probationary to 3 Squadron in March 1916. On 21 July 1916, Brown, with Lieutenant Green, in a Morane Parasol, shared a success over a Fokker with two DHs of 24 Squadron. His 'apprenticeship' satisfactorily completed, he was confirmed and gazetted Flying Officer (Observer) on 29 September 1916. His tour with '24' ending on 9 December 1916, Brown returned to the UK to train, after a rest, as a Pilot. Having qualified for his full 'Wings', he returned to the front in October 1917, this time to the Camel F1-equipped 3 Squadron. Promoted Captain and Flight Commander in December 1917, his operational career came to an end on 3 January 1918 when he was wounded in action. His MC was announced in the *London Gazette* of 4 February 1918, details in the *Gazette* of 5 July 1918: 'For conspicuous gallantry and devotion to duty. He bombed and wrecked a hangar on an enemy aerodrome, damaged five enemy machines which were on the ground, and scattered a party of mechanics with machine-gun fire from a height of 100 feet. He then attacked three large transport wagons, and damaged them all. On another occasion he bombed a convoy of twelve limbers, destroyed some of them, and completely disorganised the personnel with machine-gun fire from a height of 20 feet. He also carried out reconnaissances at a very low altitude in most difficult weather. He showed magnificent skill and determination'.

Research has unearthed the original recommendation for this award, made by his CO and addressed to the OC, 13 Wing, RFC, which contains additional items of interest: 'This officer was previously an observer in this Squadron and did nine months steady Artillery work. He returned to 3 Squadron as a Pilot, on 12 October 1917, and has always shown himself exceedingly willing and fearless. On 20 November 1917 he bombed and wrecked a hangar in CAUDRY aerodrome, raked 5 EA on the ground, damaging the machines and dispersing a party of mechanics from a height of 100 feet, with machine-gun fire. He then attacked three large Transport Waggons, the first of which bolted, three horses were killed in the second, and the third ran into a ditch and was overturned. Two days later Lieut. Brown dropped three bombs on a convoy of about twelve limbers from 100 feet, scoring at least one direct hit, and completely disorganising the personnel with heavy MG fire from 20 feet. On later occasions he has shown great skill in carrying out reconnaissances at below 100 feet, and returning home with the required information'.

Brown finally relinquished his commission due to ill-health, on 29 March 1919.

BROWN, William Henry

From Victoria, British Columbia, Canada, he was born on 12 March 1894. Brown volunteered for service with 1 Canadian Signal Corps, in the early weeks of the war. After two years active service with the CEF in France, he transferred to the RFC. After training, he qualified as a Pilot before accompanying, on 23 September 1917, the SE5A-equipped 84 Squadron to France as a 'founder member'. After a disastrous start, the squadron personnel slowly found their feet. Brown, in particular, enjoyed considerable success, achieving nine victories between 26 November 1917 and 3 April 1918, including two 'doubles' on single days. He was also promoted to A/Captain and Flight Commander. His MC was announced in the *London Gazette* of 22 June 1918: 'For conspicuous gallantry and devotion to duty. Whilst bombing an enemy aerodrome, his squadron was attacked by a formation of forty enemy scouts. He engaged one of these with the result that it dived straight to the ground. He was then attacked by another machine, and by skilful piloting, he succeeded in firing at close range behind its tail, with the result that it fell on its back and went down out of control. Later, whilst leading a low flying attack on enemy troops, he dropped four bombs from a very low altitude, scattering the enemy in all directions and then at a height of 300 feet, engaged them with machine-gun fire. Shortly afterwards he attacked two enemy two-seater planes, crashing them both to earth. In addition to these, he has shot down out of control four other hostile machines, and has displayed throughout the recent operations marked gallantry and skill'.

His tour with '84' completed, Brown returned to the Home Establishment on 8 April 1918, never again to return to combat flying.

BROWNELL, Raymond James

The son of Mr and Mrs William Percival Brownell, of 'Carolside', Newtown, Tasmania, Australia, he was born on 17 May 1894. Educated at Scotch College, Melbourne, just across the Bass Straight from his island home. He was working as a Clerk when he enlisted as a Gunner (Number 2058) into 9 Battery, 3 Field Artillery Brigade, AIF, at Pontville on 12 September 1914. Brownell embarked at Brisbane aboard the SS *Rangitara* (Transport A22), on 25 September 1914, bound for the Middle East. He subsequently served in Egypt and in Gallipoli. Promoted to Sergeant on 24 February 1916, he next accompanied his unit to France and Flanders in mid-April 1916. For his meritorious services in establishing and maintaining communications with Brigade HQ on 21/22 July 1916, near Pozières, on the Somme, Brownell was awarded the Military Medal, *London Gazette* of 16 November 1916. Accepted as a volunteer for the flying service, he was sent as a Cadet to Denham in England, on 16 November 1916. Gazetted Second Lieutenant to the RFC on 17 March 1917. His pilot training duly completed, he was confirmed and gazetted Flying Officer on 19 June following. Sent out to 45 Squadron (Sopwith Camels) in France on 25 August 1917, he achieved five victories between 10 September and 27 October 1917, before accompanying the same unit to Italy in the following November. Promoted to A/Captain and Flight Commander on the intervening 11 February 1918, he went on to gain a further seven victories on the Italian front between 31 December 1917 and 18 April 1918. His MC was announced in the *London Gazette* of 4 March 1918 (no citation).

Brownell's tour with '45' completed, he returned to the Home Establishment on 21 April 1918. Following a period of instructing duties, he embarked for Hobart and home aboard the SS *Friederichstruhe* on 9 July 1919. Accepted into the Royal Australian Air Force on 13 September 1921, his subsequent appointments, promotions and honours in what would prove to be a distinguished career, included: Squadron Leader, 1927; Wing Commander, 1936; OC, RAAF, Western Australia, 1939; Commander, RAAF, Far East, at Sembawang, Malaya, 1940-41; Commanding 1 Training Group, 1941-42; Air Commodore, 1942; Commanding RAAF, Western Area, 1943-45; Commanding 495 Group, South West Pacific Area, 1945; CBE, 1945. He finally retired in 1947, going on to live later at 3 Alexandra Avenue, Claremont, Western Australia. His autobiography, 'From Khaki to Blue', was published shortly after his death, on 12 April 1974.

BROWNING, Lancelot Harold

The son of schoolmaster, B P Browning and Mrs Browning, he was born in Bournemouth on 25 September 1897. Educated at Rosehill School, Banstead, and at Wellington College (1911-14). Gazetted Second Lieutenant to the Royal Field Artillery, on 28 July 1915. Seconded to the RFC on 17 May 1916, he was, following observer training, posted out to 30 Squadron in Mesopotamia on 6 June 1916. His 'apprenticeship' satisfactorily completed, he was confirmed and gazetted Flying Officer (Observer) on 15 August following. His tour with '30' completed on 10 January 1917, he was next sent to RFC HQ, Egypt, for pilot training. After qualifying for his full 'Wings', he eventually returned to 30 Squadron, still based in Mesopotamia, on 7 December 1917. His MC was announced in the *London Gazette* of 15 October 1918, an unusually late 'gazetting' and one of the last to the RFC/RAF, other than, of course, those in the 'Escapers Gazette' of 16 December 1919: 'For conspicuous gallantry and daring whilst carrying out independent bombing behind the enemy's lines. He was attacked by a fast enemy scout machine, which by skilful piloting and accurate shooting he drove down to its aerodrome. No sooner had the enemy aeroplane landed than Lt Browning dropped a bomb, completely obliterating the pilot who had begun to run away, and damaged his machine. He then continued bombing and while doing so was attacked by two more enemy scouts, both of which he drove off. He showed fine skill and courage throughout'.

Promoted to Captain, he returned again to Egypt on 3 July 1918, before being posted on to 111 Squadron, on 3 September 1918. His brief tour with '111' completed on 23 November following, he returned to the UK. Staying on in the RAF after the war, he again returned to Mesopotamia in May 1919, this time as a member of 63 Squadron. He was awarded the Distinguished Flying Cross, *London Gazette* of 10 July 1920, for his services during the Kurdistan campaign. Lance Browning's career ended on 2 August 1928, when he was killed in a flying accident involving a 3 Squadron Woodcock aircraft at Holbeach Ranges.

BRUCE, Talbot Baines

Born in Adelaide, on 20 August 1897, he later lived in Hyde Park, South Australia. Educated at Saint Peter's College, Adelaide. Having served with the Australian Imperial Forces, he transferred and was gazetted Second Lieutenant to the RFC, via the Special Lists, on 8 July 1916. His pilot training duly completed, he was confirmed and gazetted Flying Officer on 10 October following. Bruce was sent out to 3 Squadron in France in the spring of 1917. On 6 November 1917, Bruce was a member of a Flight of four Camels which were caught in atrocious conditions – strong westerly winds and poor visibility. Following a frantic exchange of hand signals in the air, all four agreed to land near to Namur, basically with the express purpose of finding out just exactly where they where! Once down, Bruce was alone in being unable to take off again, as his engine could not be coaxed to restart. The remaining three Camels did manage to get airborne, only to be driven down again a hundred miles further on, near to Rheims. So disorientated were they, that they had been flying south and not, as they thought, west. All three Pilots were taken captive. In the meantime, Bruce had burnt his Camel, 'B6392', and, with the help of a young Belgian, exchanged his uniform for civilian clothes. Still undetected by the German Army, he decided to take his chance in avoiding capture. His adventures over the next 13 weeks – he crossed the German/Dutch border on 1 February 1918 – are recounted in a book he wrote in 1930, aptly enough entitled 'Missing'. He chose the title after being shown a telegram his mother, then living at Dalewood Cottage, Mickleham, near Dorking, had received from the War Office on 10 November 1917: 'Regret to inform you 2nd Lt T B Bruce, General List and RFC 3 Squadron, is reported missing November 6th. This does not necessarily mean either killed or wounded. Further report sent immediately received'. Once back in England, Bruce was invited to Buckingham Palace to relate the circumstances of his escape to the King. His MC was announced in the so-called 'Escapers Gazette', *London Gazette* of 16 December 1919: '....in recognition of gallantry in escaping from captivity whilst Prisoners of War'. Bruce remained in the RAF after the war, and had attained the rank of Squadron Leader by 1936.

BRYSON, Oliver Campbell GC

The younger son of George Alexander Bryson, JP, and Mrs Bryson, of 'Gorse Meadow', Brent Green, Worcestershire, he was born on 18 August 1897. Educated at Lickey Hills School, Birmingham, at Uppingham (1910-15), and at Trinity College, Cambridge. He was gazetted Second Lieutenant to the Dorset Yeomanry on 19 April 1915. Bryson joined his regiment in Egypt on 17 November 1915, one of a welcome draft of ten replacement officers for the losses the Dorset Yeomanry had suffered in the disastrous Gallipoli campaign. Bryson served in the desert campaign, before being wounded in the famous and successful cavalry charge made by the Dorset Yeomanry at Agagia, on 26 February 1916. After recovering from his wounds in a military hospital in Egypt, he transferred to the RFC, learning to fly with the training squadrons of the MEF. Gained his Royal Aero Club Certificate (Number 4284) on 26 December 1916, and was confirmed and gazetted Flying Officer on the same day. Having shortly afterwards returned to the UK, he was involved in an act of great gallantry that earned him the award of the Albert Medal (he would, in 1972, exchange his AM for the highly prestigious, George Cross - the highest award for civilian gallantry). The citation for the Albert Medal, *London Gazette* 11 January 1918, reads: 'On 15 March 1917, Lieutenant Bryson, with another officer as passenger, was piloting an aeroplane at Wye Aerodrome when, owing to a sideslip, the machine crashed to the ground and burst into flames. On disentangling himself from the burning wreckage Lieutenant Bryson at once went back into the flames, dragged the other man from the machine, and, not-withstanding his own injuries, which were undoubtedly aggravated by his gallant efforts to rescue his brother officer from the fire, tried to extinguish the fire on the other man's clothing'.

Bryson was next posted to 19 Squadron (Spads) in France in July 1917, gaining a total of 12 victories between 25 August 1917 and 8 March 1918, and being promoted to A/Captain and Flight Commander in the process. His MC was announced in the *London Gazette* of 4 February 1918: 'For conspicuous gallantry and devotion to duty. He made several difficult flights in most unfavourable weather, and destroyed several hostile machines. He has proved himself a determined and undaunted leader, and set a splendid example of courage on all occasions'.

On 9 January 1918, Bryson was presented with the insignia of both his Albert Medal and his MC by the King at an investiture held at Buckingham Palace. Staying on in the RAF after the war, Bryson commanded a squadron of heavy bombers of the North Russian Expeditionary Force during the Allied Intervention in Russia in 1919, for which he received the Distinguished Flying Cross, *London Gazette* of 18 November 1919, for, amongst other things: '....[flying] a Snipe machine with exceptional skill and daring'. He also saw active service in India during 1928-31, gaining a Bar to his Distinguished Flying Cross, *London Gazette* of 26 June 1931 for: '....gallant and distinguished service rendered in connection with the operations on the North West Frontier of India between 23 April and 12 September 1930'. He finally retired from the RAF in August 1943, with the rank of Group Captain, his extraordinary bravery reflected by the range of his gallantry awards – GC, MC, DFC and Bar. Oliver Bryson died on 27 March 1977.

NB: The RAF Museum Hendon has his medals in its collection: George Cross, MC, Distinguished Flying Cross & Bar, Albert Medal, Bronze (engraved: Presented by His Majesty to Lieutenant Oliver Campbell Bryson, 1st Dorset Yeomanry and Royal Flying Corps for gallantry in endeavouring to save life on 15th March 1917*), 1914-15 Star* (2 Lt Dorset Yeo)*; British War Medal 1914-20, Victory Medal 1914-19 with MID* (Capt RAF)*, India General Service Medal 1908-35 (2nd issue), with clasp, North West Frontier 1930-31* (S/L RAF)*, Defence Medal 1939-45, War Medal 1939-45, and Coronation Medal 1937.*

BRYSON, Robert Edwards

From Glasgow, he was born on 25 April 1886. Educated at Hillhead High School, Glasgow. When war came in August 1914, Bryson was living and working in London. He soon enlisted as a Private soldier (Number 3458) into 28 Battalion, London Regiment (Artists Rifles) (TF). Picked out for a commission, he was gazetted Second Lieutenant to 12 Battalion, Cameronians (Scottish Rifles) on 5 April 1915. Bryson served in the trenches with the Scottish Rifles and was, apparently, recommended for, although did not receive, an MC for gallantry during a raid on the enemy's trenches. Seconded to the RFC in January 1917, he trained as a Pilot and, qualifying for his 'Wings', was sent out to the RE8-equipped 52 Squadron on 18 April 1917. He was heavily involved in reconnaissance and photographic patrol work throughout the remainder of 1917, and was promoted to A/Captain and Flight Commander at the year's end. On 21 March 1918, the first day of the German spring offensive, Bryson, in RE8, 'A4259', was severely wounded when his machine was hit by machine-gun fire from the ground at St Quentin. Despite the 'Harry Tate' being alight and badly damaged, Bryson, with the help of his Observer of the day, Lieutenant B T Head, nursed the stricken machine back over the lines to safety. His MC was announced in the *London Gazette* of 22 June 1918: 'For conspicuous gallantry and devotion to duty. When on contact patrol work he was subjected to the most severe machine-gun and rifle fire from the ground, and received a serious wound. Despite this, and the most adverse weather conditions, he succeeded in locating the enemy positions, landing his machine safely behind our lines and bringing back most valuable information. By his disregard of personal danger and unfailing devotion to duty he has set a splendid example to all ranks'.

Because of the severity of his wounds, Bryson was unable to return to operational flying and finally left the service, via the Unemployed List, in April 1919.

BUCK, Geoffrey Sebastian

The son of Dr Percy Carter Buck and Lucy Elizabeth Buck, of 'Steep Hill', Waldron Road, Harrow-on-the-Hill, he was born on 17 May 1897. Educated at Dragon School, Oxford (1905-10), and at Winchester (1910-14). An all-round sportsman, he was an excellent swimmer, a good footballer, boxer and cricketer. As well as editing *The Wykehamist*; he won his Lords cap in 1914, and played in the Commoner Rugby XV and the Second Cricket XI (Association). Buck scored 150 runs in the two innings of the 1914 Winchester vs Eton match. He actually left school with still a year to run, so anxious was he to get into the war. Gazetted Second Lieutenant to 1 City of London Battalion, London Regiment (Royal Fusiliers) (TF) on 10 November 1914. His first posting was to Malta, but, in March 1915, he was sent to the trenches in France. After 16 months in the trenches, he was seconded to the RFC. Gained the Royal Aero Club Certificate (Number 3368) on 19 August 1916. His formal training duly completed, he was confirmed and gazetted Flying Officer on 21 September 1916, the same day that he was sent out to the BE12-equipped 19 Squadron in France. He was Mentioned in Despatches in the *London Gazette* of 12 May 1917. His tour with '19' ended on 14 July 1917, the day after he had sent an Albatros D down out of control, over Brebières, whilst flying Spad VII, 'A6649'. His MC was announced in the *London Gazette* of 25 August 1917: 'For conspicuous gallantry and devotion to duty. He has taken part in many offensive patrols and has led seventeen, frequently attacking hostile troops on the ground. He has also successfully attacked and destroyed hostile aircraft, on several occasions, setting a fine example of dash and determination'.

Buck's next posting was to 39 HD Squadron, before going on to be employed as a Ferry Pilot with 215 Squadron. Buck was sent out again to France on 4 July 1918, this time as a Flight Commander with the Handley Page bomber-equipped 215 Squadron, part of the Independent Air Force. On 3 September 1918, when returning from a night-bombing raid, he crashed into a petrol tank tower at Rambervillers, near Nancy, and was instantaneously killed. The award of a Distinguished Flying Cross, for bringing his machine home from a raid on enemy territory through a heavy thunderstorm, was posthumously announced in the *London Gazette* of 2 November 1918. Captain Geoffrey Buck is buried in Charmes Military Cemetery, Essegney, Vosges, France.

BUCKINGHAM, Reginald Eric

Born in Stanmore, New South Wales on 23 September 1895. A Farmer and an Orchardist, pre-war he had begun to study medicine at Sydney University when the war came. Interrupting his studies, he journeyed to England to offer his services to the flying service. Gazetted Second Lieutenant to the RFC, via the Special Lists, on 13 May 1916. After training with 26 RS, amongst others, he was confirmed and gazetted Flying Officer on 28 June 1916. Following a brief attachment to 53 Squadron in July 1916, he accompanied 47 Squadron to Salonika as a 'founder member' in August 1916. His MC was announced in the *London Gazette* of 3 June 1917 (no citation).

The French, too, acknowledged his services with a Croix de Guerre, *London Gazette* of 1 June 1917. Promoted to Captain and Flight Commander on 21 November 1917, he was taken ill and invalided to Egypt suffering with malaria, just one week later. Attached to 193 TS, on 12 December 1917, he was allowed to 'take it easy' for a while. His next posting, on 28 July 1918, was to 32 Training Wing, before being allowed a recuperative leave of absence in Australia from 6 October. After returning to the UK, and reporting for duties as an Instructor to No 5 Flying School, on 25 February 1919, he was finally allowed to leave for home on 28 May 1919. Taking up his studies once again at Sydney University, he duly qualified MB and ChM in 1926, before becoming FRCS, Edinburgh, in 1929. During the Second World War, he served as a part-time Medical Officer with the rank of Flight Lieutenant, RAAF, at 6 Stores Depot, before finally being discharged from those duties on 1 May 1947. In 1948, he was appointed the Ear, Nose and Throat Surgeon at Dubbo Base Hospital, New South Wales. In 1966, Reginald Buckingham retired, with his wife, Susan, to their home at 'Finisterre', Avalon Beach, New South Wales. He was brother to William Buckingham (qv).

BUCKINGHAM, William

Born in Sydney, New South Wales, on 7 April 1893. Living in Petersham, NSW, he worked in the office of a commodity importer from 1911 to December 1915, when he left for the UK intent on joining the flying service. He was accepted as a Cadet at Oxford, before being gazetted Second Lieutenant to the RFC on 13 May 1916. His pilot training duly completed, he was confirmed and gazetted Flying Officer on 31 July 1916, and sent out to 15 Squadron for his first tour in August 1916. On 15 April 1917, he, with another Pilot, Second Lieutenant W R Cox (qv) acting as his Observer, volunteered to go out in atrocious weather to gather badly needed information for the Staff. Both men received the MC for their gallantry; Buckingham's was announced in the *London Gazette* of 26 May 1917: 'For conspicuous gallantry and devotion to duty. He displayed great courage and initiative in carrying out a patrol in heavy rain, with clouds at 500 feet, during an enemy attack. He obtained valuable information and undoubtedly contributed largely to the successful repulse of the enemy'.

His tour with '15' completed, he returned to the UK in June 1917, by now an Acting Captain and Flight Commander. He undertook various instructing duties before going out again in 1918, this time to the Bristol Fighter-equipped 48 Squadron. On 1 October 1918, Buckingham and his Observer, Lieutenant Tom Beck, MC, Highland Light Infantry, in BF2b, 'E2265', were shot down during an aerial combat over Thielt. Sadly, Beck, who had won his MC with the 2 Highland Light Infantry, died of the wounds he had received in the combat shortly after they came down. Buckingham, unscathed, was taken as a prisoner of war. Fortunately, Buckingham's imprisonment was relatively short-lived, as he was repatriated some ten weeks later on 13 December 1918. Returning to Australia in 1919, he married, and lived with his wife at Lucinda Avenue, Pymble, New South Wales. In the Second World War, he served with the rank of Squadron Leader with 23 Squadron, ATC, at Chatswood, Sydney. He was brother to Reginald E Buckingham (qv).

BUCKLEY, Sidney Earl

The son of Major Thomas William Buckley, MD, and Mrs Buckley, of Madeley Manor, Newcastle under Lyme, he was born on 6 December 1893. Educated at Rugby (1908-11), and at Queen's College, Oxford. After graduating from Oxford, Buckley secured a position as a Farm Manager, living at Nuptown, Warfield, Bracknell, Berkshire. He offered his services as soon as war came, and was gazetted Second Lieutenant to 5 Battalion, Northamptonshire Regiment (Pioneers) on 26 August 1914. He served briefly at the front with 5 Northants from May 1915, but was seconded to the RFC in the following July. He trained as an Observer, and was sent out to join 16 Squadron as a Probationary later in the same year. Buckley flew with, amongst others, Lieutenant D W Grinnell-Milne (qv), the two inconclusively confronting a double-fuselage machine over Loos on 16 November 1915. On 30 November following, Buckley was flying with Second Lieutenant H S Ward in a BE2c, '1717', on a photo-reconnaissance, when they were attacked by a hostile machine and sent down into the German lines. Both men were taken prisoner, but, amazingly, both would eventually escape. Ward, wounded in the incident, would get away in April 1916, whilst Buckley, who was unhurt, would escape in company with Lieutenant A J Evans (qv), and make his way all the way home to England, arriving there on 16 June 1917. Buckley is said to have helped others escape while he was in captivity. Gazetted Staff Lieutenant 3rd Class on 10 September 1917, he served out the remainder of the war in the Intelligence Corps, no doubt his experiences as a prisoner-of-war and his subsequent escape were put to good use; he was Mentioned in Despatches for this work. His MC was announced in the 'Escapers Gazette', *London Gazette* of 16 December 1919: '....in recognition of gallantry in escaping from captivity whilst Prisoners of War'.

BULMAN, Paul Ward Spencer

The son of the Reverend Thomas Bulman, Canon Emeritus of St Albans, and Mrs Bulman, he was born in Luton on 8 April 1896. Educated at Bedford School. He enlisted as a Private soldier into the Honourable Artillery Company (TF) on 15 March 1916, serving with a Reserve Battalion in the UK, until he was gazetted Second Lieutenant to the RFC on 2 May 1917. Gained his Royal Aero Club Certificate (Number 4727) on 25 May 1917. After completing his formal training he was given his 'Wings' and sent out for his first tour to the Sopwith Camel-equipped 46 Squadron. Wounded in action on 29 January 1918, he returned to the UK to recover. As soon as he was fit enough, he next joined the Camels of 3 Squadron at the front. He appears to have become a highly successful ground-strafing specialist, an art he had ample opportunity to practise throughout the fraught days of the German spring offensive which commenced on 21 March 1918. His MC was announced in the *London Gazette* of 4 February 1918: 'For conspicuous gallantry and devotion to duty. On five occasions, in most difficult weather conditions, he dropped bombs and fired on enemy infantry from a low altitude, inflicting heavy casualties. During these flights he frequently obtained valuable information, and twice drove off enemy machines, which attempted to interfere. He showed the greatest initiative and resource'.

The Bar to his MC was announced in the *London Gazette* of 22 June 1918: 'For conspicuous gallantry and devotion to duty. On four successive days, when on low bombing patrol, out of a total of sixteen bombs dropped on enemy troops and transport, he obtained eight direct hits and seven others within ten yards of his objective, inflicting the most severe casualties on the enemy. Within the last fortnight, he has shot down out of control two enemy planes and has forced two others to land. He has displayed the utmost skill and gallantry, and his courage and efficiency have afforded a splendid example to his squadron'.

After completing his tour with '3', he was employed in a succession of instructing and testing posts for which he received the first of his Air Force Crosses, *London Gazette* of 2 November 1918. Bulman was employed as an Experimental Test Pilot at the RAE, Farnborough, from 1919 to 1925. He married, in 1920, Constance Dorothy Wiseman, to whom he had one son. The award of a Bar to his Air Force Cross came in the *London Gazette* of 12 July 1921 and the value of his work was so exceptional, that he was given a second Bar in the following year, *London Gazette* of 3 June 1922. Bulman held a series of increasingly important positions in the aviation world, including Chief Test Pilot at Hawker Aircraft Ltd. In the Second World War, he was given the rank of Group Captain and appointed as Head of Air Test Branch, British Air Commission, in Washington, from 1941 to 1942. Created CBE in 1943, he was also elected a Fellow of the Royal Aeronautical Society. He lived at 'Lyedale', Woodham Road, Woking, Surrey. Group Captain Paul Bulman died on 6 May 1963.

BULMER, George William

Born on 1 September 1898 in Dixon, Illinois, USA, of British parents. By 1910, his family had settled in Toronto, Canada, and, after completing his education, he practised as an accountant in that city. He joined the RFC in Ottawa in April 1917, although he actually finished off his pilot training in the UK. His pilot training completed, he was confirmed and gazetted Flying Officer 24 December 1917. Sent out the Bristol Fighter-equipped 22 Squadron in France just five days later. Bulmer achieved ten victories between 6 March and 10 July 1918. Promoted Captain and Flight Commander in the intervening May, he, on occasions, actually led the squadron. His MC was announced in the *London Gazette* of 16 September 1918: 'For conspicuous gallantry and devotion to duty as a fighting pilot. In recent operations he has destroyed seven enemy machines and an observation balloon. By his tenacity and zeal he set a magnificent example to his squadron'.

His tour with '22' completed, he returned to the UK on 20 August 1918, before finally leaving the service. Bulmer left for Toronto and his accountancy job, on 13 April 1919. In 1925, Bulmer returned to live in his birthplace, Dixon, Illinois, and remained resident there, and later in Chicago, for more than 40 years. His only publication, 'Clouds of Glory', deals with his flying career. In the spring of 1970, he moved to Phoenix, Arizona. Bulmer's son became one of the officers on the USS *Nautilus*, the first US nuclear submarine. George Bulmer died in San Diego, California, on 5 April 1987.

BUNTINE, Walter Horace Carlyle

Born of British parents at East St Kilda, Australia, on 10 October 1895. Educated at Caulfield Grammar School, East St Kilda, and at Melbourne University, where he was in the second year of a medical degree course when he enlisted as a Private soldier into the Australian Army Medical Corps, on 15 May 1915. An athlete of some note, he was first in pole vaulting at the Victoria Championships in March 1915. His basic training duly completed, he embarked aboard No 1 Hospital Ship, on 17 July 1915, bound for the UK. He had, by then, been promoted to Corporal. Arriving in England, he was picked out for a commission and gazetted Second Lieutenant to 4 Battalion, Nottinghamshire and Derbyshire Regiment on 20 September 1915. Seconded to the RFC, he first gained his Royal Aero Club Certificate (Number 2892) on 16 May 1916, his final examination flight taken in a Maurice Farman biplane at Thetford, Norfolk. His formal training duly completed, he was confirmed and gazetted Flying Officer on 2 July following. Sent out, shortly afterwards, to the FE2b-equipped 11 Squadron in France. On 9 September 1916, Buntine was severely wounded when his FE2b, '6988', was shot up whilst acting as an escort to a bombing raid on an ammunition dump, near Irles. Fortunately, his Observer on this occasion, Sergeant G J Morton (Number 2173), was unhurt. Morton would receive the Military Medal, *London Gazette* of 21 October 1916, for his part in this action, whilst Buntine would receive the MC, announced in the *London Gazette* of 20 October 1916: 'For conspicuous gallantry and skill. As escort to a bombing raid he attacked seven hostile machines, one of which fell to the ground. Later he was attacked by three enemy machines, his own machine being damaged and himself severely wounded. With great skill he managed to land in our lines, though most of his propeller was shot away and his machine otherwise much damaged'.

Buntine was also Mentioned in Despatches at this time. The gun shot wound he received in the right arm, resulted in a compound fracture of the humerus. After recovering at least some of his fitness, he was allowed to return to Australia on furlough, arriving there on 5 December 1916. Shortly before he was due to return to the UK, the Australian Forces requested that he be allowed to remain there in order to continue with his medical studies at Melbourne University, but the request appears to have been turned down. He sailed again for the UK in April 1917, and upon arrival was posted to the instructional staff at the Turnberry North British Flying School in Scotland. Once back in the UK, he was obliged to attend several medical boards as he was still having difficulty with his wounded arm. On 19 June 1917, he was a passenger in an FE2b, 'A817', at No 1 Auxiliary School of Air Gunnery at Turnberry. The machine crashed from 450 feet, and both occupants were killed. Walter Buntine is buried in Girvan (Doune) Cemetery, Ayrshire, UK.

BURBURY, Arthur Vivian

Born on 20 May 1896, he was the son of Company Secretary, Arthur Burbury and Mrs Burbury, of 32 Campden Hill Gardens, West Kensington, London. Educated at Colet Court Prep School, at St Paul's School (1908-14), and at the Royal Military College, Sandhurst. He enlisted as a Private soldier (Number 2345) into 28 Battalion, London Regiment (Artists Rifles) from which unit he was first sent to Sandhurst and then gazetted Second Lieutenant to 2 Battalion, Yorkshire Regiment (Green Howard) on 14 July 1915. Gained his Royal Aero Club Certificate (Number 1555) on 10 August 1915. Seconded to the RFC, he was appointed a Staff Lieutenant and then, despite his RAeC 'ticket', was gazetted a Balloon Officer on 1 October 1915, obviously earmarked for Intelligence work. He served with a KBS in France from December 1915 to October 1916, his MC being won in an incident that occurred at Caftet Wood on 15 September 1916 and announced in the *London Gazette* of 14 November 1916: 'For conspicuous gallantry and devotion to duty. When observing from a balloon at a height of 3,000 feet the cable was cut by a shell. He destroyed his papers, ripped the balloon, a most difficult operation in the air, and then got down in his parachute'.

The full circumstances of this incident were as follows: On 15 September 1916, when observing the advance of an offensive by 6 Division against the Quadrangle Redoubt, the Royal Artillery officer in charge of the Battery above which Burbury was positioned, warned him that his balloon cable was beginning to lean towards the path of the trajectories of some 6-inch Howitzers. As Burbury considered that he was ideally sited to observe the attack, and given that nearby trees and telephone wires would have restricted his re-positioning, he informed the Gunners that he would run the risk of remaining where he was. Minutes later, a Howitzer shell cut through his cable and he was immediately drifting on the wind towards the enemy's lines. Conscious that his balloon was of a type unknown to the enemy, he decided to use the emergency 'rip panel' to deflate the balloon, before he baled out – a risky business, indeed. In the event, his efforts were rewarded when the partially deflated balloon fell into the British frontline trenches. Meanwhile, he had taken the precaution of destroying his maps and papers, before landing by parachute inside his own lines. For this he received an immediate MC and, from the French, a Croix de Guerre. Next, he decided it was time to make use of his flying expertise and, having received his formal training, was confirmed and gazetted Flying Officer on 16 March 1917 and sent out to 1 Squadron in France almost immediately afterwards. On 26 April 1917, piloting Nieuport XVII, 'A6671', he had just destroyed an enemy balloon, and was in the process of attacking a second, when he was himself shot down by anti-aircraft fire. He was taken prisoner of war and remained so until his repatriation on 14 December 1918. His language skills invaluable, Burbury served in Archangel, North Russia, (Staff Officer 4th Class) as part of the Allied Intervention Force from June to September 1919. He also served briefly in Ireland, before leaving the RAF and going on to King's College, Cambridge, to complete his interrupted education. From Cambridge, he graduated BA (Honours) and MA in Modern Languages, in 1921. He married, first, in 1920, Maisie Martin; secondly in 1924, Joan Storm, and thirdly in 1938, Edith Payne (one son, two daughters). On 16 February 1923, he passed a competitive examination and was granted a Civil Service Certificate as 3rd Secretary in the Foreign and Diplomatic Service, His first overseas posting in the Diplomatic Service was to Copenhagen in 1922, before a transfer to Moscow came in 1924. In 1924, his language skills were rewarded with a special allowance for a knowledge of Russian. He was sent next to Riga in 1927 and then to Brussels later in the same year. An appointment to the Foreign Office, London, and a promotion to 2nd Secretary came at the end of 1927. His next posting was to Helsingfors, as acting Chargé d'Affaires from 1929 to 1931. He was granted yet another allowance for knowing Finnish in 1931. Burbury's last foreign posting was to Athens in 1932, before he finally retired in 1936. Turning his hand to teaching languages and translating, he also acted in stage and radio plays and wrote the novel, 'The Higher The Fewer'. When the Second World War came in 1939, he was appointed a Foreign Press Censor at the Ministry of Information. After the fall of Germany in 1945, Burbury worked as a translator for the American Forces in that occupied country. The multi-talented Arthur Burbury died in Germany on 8 November 1949.

NB: His medals were offered for sale by Buckland Dix & Wood on 7 April 1994: MC, 1914-15 Star (2Lt Yorks Regt), *British War Medal 1914-20, Victory Medal 1914-19 with MID* (Lieut, RAF), *1939-45 Star, Defence Medal 1939-45, War Medal 1939-45, and Croix de Guerre avec Palme (France).*

BURCHETT, James Godfrey

Born in England in 1892, he had been ranching in the Argentine for five years when the war came in 1914. He returned to the UK in 1916 with his wife, Edith, setting up home in Mortlake Road, Kew Gardens, London, before enlisting as a Private soldier into the Royal Fusiliers. Picked out for a commission, he was gazetted Second Lieutenant to the RFC on 26 April 1917. His pilot training duly completed, he was confirmed and gazetted Flying Officer on 14 June 1917. After several months service in the UK, he was sent out to France and the RE8-equipped 15 Squadron in December 1917. His MC was announced in the *London Gazette* of 16 April 1918, details in the *Gazette* of 22 June 1918: 'For conspicuous gallantry and devotion to duty. During ten days' operations he showed splendid courage and skill in carrying out reconnaissances and contact patrols at low altitude and under heavy rifle and machine-gun fire. He obtained valuable information as to the enemy's movements, and attacked enemy troops and transport with machine-gun fire. He also bombed enemy batteries with excellent results'.

His tour with '15' completed, he returned to the Home Establishment before, following a rest, he went out to the front again, this time to 52 Squadron. Hospitalised on 13 July 1918, he did not again return to operational flying. Once recovered, he was posted for instructional duties to 15 TDS, in October 1918. James Burchett left the service, via the Unemployed List, with the rank of Captain on 10 May 1919.

BURD, John Marsh

The son of Surgeon, George Vanhouse Burd, and Isabella Burd (née Harris), of East Street, Okehampton, Devon, he was born in 1896. Gazetted Second Lieutenant to the Royal Field Artillery on 10 February 1915. He landed at Suvla Bay in Gallipoli, with the Gunners on 8 August 1915. After the evacuation, Burt returned to the UK and was seconded to the RFC in the spring of 1916, gaining his Royal Aero Club Certificate (Number 3868) on 1 October following. His pilot training duly completed, he was confirmed and gazetted Flying Officer on 25 October 1916. Served with 55 Squadron, becoming a Flight Commander, from April to December 1917. His MC was announced in the *London Gazette* of 17 December 1917, details in the *Gazette* of 23 April 1918: 'For conspicuous gallantry and devotion to duty as a leader of long-distance bomb raids. When returning from a raid he attacked ten enemy aeroplanes which were engaged with another of our formations. He shot down two and his Observer another, and he then brought his formation back without loss. In six raids he only lost one machine. He has been leader in seventeen operations and deputy leader in eleven'. John Burd survived the Great War.

BURDICK, Frederick William

The son of William Edward and Agnes Louisa Mary Burdick of 10 Breakspeare Rd, Brockley, London, and later of 158 Engleheart Road, Catford, Kent, he was born in 1896. Educated at Colfe's Grammar School (1908-11). He enlisted as a Private soldier in 20 Battalion, County of London Regiment (Blackheath and Woolwich) (TF) in August 1914. Picked out for a commission, he was gazetted Second Lieutenant to 2 London Division, Cyclist Companies (TF), on 10 December 1915. Burdick led 6 Platoon, 60 (London) Divisional Cyclist Company to France on 25 June 1916, serving in the area of St Eloi and later on the Somme. Seconded to the RFC, he trained as a Pilot and was subsequently confirmed and gazetted Flying Officer on 20 October 1916. Sent out to France and 5 Squadron, soon after he qualified for his 'Wings', he completed his first, and largely uneventful, tour on 21 May 1917, before returning then to the Home Establishment. Burdick was next sent out to the AWFK8-equipped 10 Squadron on 13 October 1917. On 8 December 1917, Burdick and his Observer of the day, Second Lieutenant L M Fenelon, in AWFK8, 'B5784', were forced to land after their machine was shot-up during an aerial combat – fortunately, both men were unscathed in the ensuing crash-landing. He was fortunate again on the following 29 April 1918, when, this time with Probationary Air Gunner C Liston acting as his Observer in AWFK8, 'B3327', he was again forced to crashland, the 'Big Ack' being damaged by shell fire. The same pair were in trouble again on 3 May following, when their AWFK8, 'C3641', was hit by machine-gun fire from the ground. This time, however, Burdick was able to bring the damaged machine back to his home field without further mishap. Promoted to A/Captain and Flight Commander on 3 June 1918, he was sent as such to the RE8-equipped 4 Squadron. He appeared to have left his luck behind at 10 Squadron, for, on 16 June following, Burdick and his Observer, Lieutenant Stanley C Shillingford, 2 Royal Fusiliers attached RFC, in RE8, 'B6656', were shot down by anti-aircraft fire during a photo-reconnaissance patrol. Both men were killed in the air, their bodies being discovered many miles apart. Burdick's MC was announced posthumously in the *London Gazette* of 16 September 1918: 'For conspicuous gallantry and devotion to duty. This officer has carried out several contact patrols and brought in accurate information, and has bombed and machine-gunned enemy troops from a low altitude, under bad weather conditions. He has also carried out many successful flights, and on one occasion landed his machine after a direct hit from a shell'.

Frederick Burdick is buried in Aval Wood Military Cemetery, Vieux-Berquin, Nord, France.

BURGE, Philip Scott

The son of William A and Grace Burge, of 82 Holbein House, Sloane Square, London, he was born on 24 July 1894, in Potters Bar, Middlesex. Educated at Marlborough (1909-1913). He enlisted as a Private soldier (Number Stk 1182) into 10 Battalion, Royal Fusiliers, a battalion recruited mainly from the staff of businesses located in the City of London, and hence known as, 'The Stockbrokers Battalion'. He served in France from July 1915, winning a Military Medal in the trenches, announced in the *London Gazette* of 1 September 1916. Picked out for a commission, he was gazetted Second Lieutenant to the RFC, via the General List, in October 1916. His pilot training duly completed, he was confirmed and gazetted Flying Officer on 24 May 1917. Burge accompanied the DH5-equipped 64 Squadron to France as a 'founder member' on 15 October 1917. '64' re-equipped with SE5As in January 1918, and Burge flew this excellent machine with deadly effect, achieving 11 victories between 23 March and 22 July 1918. On 17 March 1918, Burge in SE5A, 'B673.A', was shot up during an aerial combat. Despite some damage to his machine, he was able to land at his own aerodrome without further mishap. In this fight, Leutnant Fritz Rumey of Jasta 5 claimed Burge, albeit a shade optimistically, as the tenth of his eventual 45 victories. However, on 24 July 1918, Burge, by then promoted to A/Captain and Flight Commander, was shot down in flames and killed by Unteroffizer Marat Schumm of Jasta 52, during a dogfight over Senlis. His MC was announced posthumously in the *London Gazette* of 16 September 1918: 'For conspicuous gallantry and devotion to duty. This officer is a brilliant fighting pilot, and has destroyed six enemy machines. His dash and determination when engaged in combat with the enemy, often numerically superior, has set a fine example to the remainder of his formation'.

Philip Burge is buried in Dud Corner Cemetery, Loos, France.

BURGESS, David Luther

From Forfar, Ontario, he was born in Kleinberg, Ontario, on 28 January 1891. Burgess worked as a Financial Estate Broker prior to being gazetted Lieutenant to 188 Canadian Infantry Battalion, on 12 October 1916. He served in the trenches with the CEF, firstly with 15 Battalion, and later with 52 Battalion. Seconded to the RFC in April 1917, he trained as an Observer and was sent out to 25 Squadron in France, on 30 May following. On 7 July 1917, Burgess and his Pilot, Captain James F Morris (qv), in a recently acquired DH4, 'A7505', claimed the squadron's first victory in this type of aircraft, sending down an Albatros DV out of control. Burgess would go to achieve a further six victories, all in the company of Captain Morris, before his tour with '25' was completed on 20 October 1917. His MC was announced in the *London Gazette* of 26 September 1917, details in the *Gazette* of 9 January 1918: 'For conspicuous gallantry and devotion to duty in aerial fighting and on photography. As Observer he has taken a large number of very successful photographs in spite of bad weather and continual opposition from the enemy. On four occasions at least he has assisted his pilot to drive down and destroy hostile aircraft'.

Posted next to the Middle East, he learnt to fly and was awarded his full 'Wings' at Amria, Egypt. Returning again to the UK in 1918, he was sent as an Instructor to 34 TDS, then at Scampton in Lincolnshire. He was presented with the insignia of his MC by the King at an investiture held at Buckingham Palace on 13 February 1919. Burgess finally relinquished his commission on 3 March 1919 and returned home to Canada, where he entered the Civil Service. An active member of the Canadian Legion for the rest of his life, he became President of that organisation in 1959-60. David Burgess died in Ottawa on 30 November 1960, then in his seventieth year.

BURKETT, George Thomas William

The son of Mr and Mrs George Burkett, of 113 Clarke Street, South Melbourne, Victoria, Australia, he was born in Warragui, Victoria, on 16 June 1896. Burkett trained and worked as an electrical engineer pre-war. He enlisted in the AIF in Melbourne, on 20 February 1915. His basic training completed on 17 April 1915, he embarked at Melbourne aboard the SS *Hororatia* (Transport 'A20') bound for the Middle East, as a Gunner with 5 Reinforcement Group for 1 Divisional Ammunition Column. Once arrived in Alexandria, the Group was sent to camp near to Heliopolis, Egypt. Promoted to Sergeant, Burkett transferred to 2 Field Artillery Brigade, on 6 September 1915, accompanying that unit to Gallipoli shortly afterwards. Following the evacuation from the dreaded Peninsula, he was next posted to 4 Division Artillery in Egypt, on 27 February 1916. From Egypt, he was sent with 2 Field Artillery Brigade, to France and Flanders on 7 March 1916. Gazetted Second Lieutenant to the RFC on 16 March 1917, he secured his Royal Aero Club Certificate (Number 4459) on 31 March following. His formal training duly completed, he was confirmed and gazetted Flying Officer on 29 May 1917. Burkett was sent out to the FE2d-equipped 20 Squadron in France, just three days later on 2 June 1917. On 27 July 1917, Burkett, with his Observer, Second Lieutenant T A M S Lewis (qv), in FE2d, 'A6512', became heavily embroiled in a fierce dogfight over Menin. Both men were wounded in the combat, but, despite this, continued to fight on. Lewis, whose wounds would afterwards cause him to lose his leg, fired his gun from a supine position to good effect as Burkett's MC citation avows, *London Gazette* of 26 September 1917, details in the *Gazette* of 9 January 1918: 'For conspicuous gallantry and devotion to duty. With his patrol he engaged a superior force of enemy machines, and although wounded early in the engagement, continued to fight. He brought down two hostile machines, and drove off two more whilst returning to our lines with his own machine badly damaged. In spite of this, however, he succeeded in making a good landing. He displayed splendid dash and coolness under very trying circumstances'.

After recovering from the effects of his wounds, Burkett served with various training depot squadrons until finally leaving the service, via the Unemployed List, on 11 November 1919. He married, in June 1924, Adelaide Henrietta. Burkett became a Bus Superintendent in Melbourne, living later in Minnewarre, near Young, New South Wales. During the Second World War, he was appointed a Captain in the Australian Military Forces. From May 1942, he served briefly with Australian Army Ordnance Corps at Caulfield, Melbourne, before going on to a post at 1 Tank Workshops, on 25 July 1942. Captain George Burkett joined the Retired List on 1 September 1942.

BURNAND, Robert Moverly

The son of Mr and Mrs R J Burnand, of 'Sandhurst', Alnmouth, Northumberland, he was born in September 1896. Educated at Uppingham (1911-15). Burnand's brother, Richard, also served in the Great War, as a Major in the MGC – OBE, MID – subsequently becoming the Supreme Court Judge, Sir Richard Burnand, KB, CBE. Robert was gazetted Second Lieutenant to the RFC, via the General List on 5 August 1916. His pilot training duly completed, he was confirmed and gazetted Flying Officer on 9 February 1917. Sent out to the RE8-equipped 16 Squadron in France, soon after qualifying for his 'Wings'. On 15 August 1917, Burnand and his Observer of the day, Second Lieutenant N V Harle, in RE8, 'A3648', were fortunate to be able to return to their aerodrome unscathed, after their machine had been hit by ground-based machine-gun fire whilst on an Artillery Observation patrol. His MC was announced in the *London Gazette* of 26 September 1917, details in the *Gazette* of 8 January 1918: 'For conspicuous gallantry and devotion to duty as pilot in an artillery squadron. He has a very large number of successful artillery shoots to his credit, and has specially distinguished himself in carrying out exceptionally long flights during which he has attacked hostile infantry from a low altitude and furnished most valuable information to our artillery regarding the dispositions of the enemy. He has always set a fine example of fearlessness and determination'.

His tour with '16' completed early in 1918, he returned to the Home Establishment and was next posted to 8 TDS as an Instructor. Burnand finally left the RAF, via the Unemployed List, on 5 May 1919. He worked in the Insurance business in London, living at 33 Gerrard Road, Harrow, Middlesex. During the Second World War, he served as a Lieutenant in the Royal Army Pay Corps. Robert Burnand retired from business in 1960, living, in retirement, at Rookery Cottage, Gatton Park, Reigate.

BURNS, James Rattray

The second son of Solicitor and Town Clerk, James Burns and Jessie Kerr Burns (née Rattray) of Stanley House, Motherwell, Scotland, he was born 25 April 1888. Educated in Motherwell and at Edinburgh University (1907-08), where he studied Law. After graduating LLB, he was admitted and practised as a Solicitor. Gazetted Second Lieutenant to 6 Battalion, Cameronians (Scottish Rifles) (TF) on 30 September 1914. Burns was promoted to Lieutenant in April 1915, the same month that he secured a secondment to the RFC. His pilot training completed, he was confirmed and gazetted Flying Officer on 7 March 1916. He served very briefly in France, before going out to 30 Squadron in Mesopotamia, on 2 July 1916. On 1 February 1917, Burns and his Observer, Lieutenant L Beevor-Potts, in a BE2c, were attacked by a Fokker over the Hai Salient, whilst registering for the artillery. The British pair made short work of the enemy machine, bringing it down with no more than five shots. The brief encounter was witnessed by British troops in the act of assaulting the Turkish third line in the Hai Salient. It was a timely boost for the Tommies, who greeted the victory with wild cheering. His MC was announced in the *London Gazette*

of 17 March 1917, details in the *Gazette* of 26 April 1917: 'For conspicuous gallantry and devotion to duty when co-operating with the Artillery. He attacked a hostile machine, and by skilful manoeuvring forced it down out of control'.

His tour with '30' completed, he went next to RFC HQ, Egypt and was killed there in an accident at 193 TS, Amria, on 10 June 1917. James Rattray Burns is buried in Alexandria (Hadra) War Memorial Cemetery, Egypt.

BUSK, Clifford Westly

The son of Mr and Mrs R W Busk, of Longdown House, Hindhead, he was born on 19 March 1898. Educated at Marlborough (1912-14), and at Sandhurst. From Sandhurst, he was gazetted Second Lieutenant to a Regular Army battalion of the Suffolk Regiment on 7 April 1916. Seconded to the RFC, he trained as an Observer and accompanied the Sopwith Strutter-equipped 70 Squadron to France as a Probationary and 'founder member', in July 1916. Busk achieved a victory on 6 September 1917, when, with Captain W D S Sanday (qv) as his Pilot in Strutter, 'A3431', he sent down a Roland CII in flames over Elincourt. On the following day he was confirmed and gazetted Flying Officer (Observer). His MC was announced in the *London Gazette* of 20 October 1916: 'For conspicuous gallantry and skill. He has taken part in many reconnaissances and fights, and on one occasion shot down an enemy aeroplane. On another occasion, when his pilot's control wires were cut and the machine went into a spin, he helped to restore stability by leaning far out on the upper side, and remained in this position until the machine got home'.

His tour with '70' completed in the spring of 1917, he returned to the Home Establishment and qualified as a Pilot. Busk was employed at the CFS as an Instructor of exceptional merit until the end of the war. Staying on in the RAF, he instructed at Sealand from 1919 to 1923. Posted to 60 Squadron in India in 1923, he remained on that station until 1927. His next appointment was as Armament Officer, 25 Group, from 1928 to 1933. He was awarded the Air Force Cross, *London Gazette* of 1 March 1929. Busk served on the Staff of Air HQ, Iraq, as a Squadron Leader from 1933 to 1935, before acting in a similar post as a Wing Commander at HQ, Flying Training Command until 1938. Promoted to Group Captain in 1940, he was next appointed the Deputy Director Training (Armament) at the Air Ministry from 1940 to 1943. Busk became the first Commandant of the Empire Air Armament School in 1944, before, in 1946, being appointed AOA, Reserve Command. Created CB, 1947. His last post was as Air Force Adviser Officer, UK Service Liaison Staff, in Ottawa, Canada. Clifford Busk retired in that post with the rank of Air Commodore in 1950. He lived, in retirement, at Farvane Cottage, Little Sandhurst, Camberley, Surrey. Air Commodore Clifford Busk died on 23 October 1970.

C

CAHUSAC, Edmund Barry

Born on 10 March 1895 in Yokohama, Japan, where his father was in business. Educated at Chefoo School, China. The Cahusac family had, for several generations, served in the Indian Army; Edmund's uncle (DSO) and grandfather both attained senior rank. Edmund joined the Inns of Court OTC (Number 6/4/5158), on 29 July 1915, from whose ranks he was gazetted Second Lieutenant to 3 Battalion, South Staffordshire Regiment, on 20 December 1915. Seconded to the RFC, he completed his pilot training and was confirmed and gazetted Flying Officer on 24 September 1916. Proceeded to the front and 2 Squadron on 16 October 1916. His MC was announced in the *London Gazette* of 11 May 1917: 'For conspicuous gallantry and devotion to duty. He carried out a successful artillery observation on a hostile battery in very adverse weather. He worked for two and a half hours at a height of 1,500 feet to 3,000 feet under very heavy fire. On another occasion, while engaged with photography he drove off three hostile scouts and completed his work'.

His tour with '2' completed, he returned to the Home Establishment for, initially, rest and recuperation before taking up instructing duties there. Promoted to A/Captain and Flight Commander, Cahusac returned to the front on 21 February 1918, as a 'founder member' with the Sopwith Dolphin-equipped 79 Squadron. On 27 March following, Cahusac in Sopwith Dolphin, 'C3967', were posted as 'Missing', one of five members of the squadron who may have fallen to elements of the Richthofen 'Wing' or 'Flying Circus'. Fortunately, however, he was later reported to have been taken as a prisoner of war and was physically unharmed. Repatriated on 24 December 1918, he was taken quite seriously ill early in the New Year. Edmund Cahusac eventually left the service, via the Unemployed List, in March 1920, taking up residence at 171 Castellian Mansions, Maida Vale, London W9.

CAIRNS, James

From Dundee, Scotland, he was born on 19 May 1896. He studied Engineering at the Herriot Watt College, Edinburgh. Cairns enlisted as a Sapper in the City of Dundee Fortress Engineers, Royal Engineers (TF) in 1914, and accompanied his unit to France on 24 June 1915. Picked out for a commission, he was gazetted Second Lieutenant to his own unit on 16 October 1915. After successfully seeking secondment to the RFC, which came in September 1916, he trained as a Pilot and was eventually sent out as such to 42 Squadron in France on 14 March 1917. His MC was announced in the *London Gazette* of 26 September 1917, details in the *Gazette* of 8 January 1918: 'For conspicuous gallantry and devotion to duty. He has been continuously successful and skilful for five months, doing his own piloting and observing. He has frequently ranged two or more batteries simultaneously and brought back numerous valuable reconnaissance reports. He has also displayed the utmost fearlessness and a fine offensive spirit in attacking and destroying enemy strong points and ammunition dumps, acting in conjunction with our artillery. His work has, on all occasions, been marked by accuracy and the highest degree of initiative and energy'.

He was promoted to A/Captain and Flight Commander in October 1917 and accompanied his unit to the Italian front on 17 November following. His tour with '42' completed, he returned to the Home Establishment on 1 February 1918 and, after a rest, was appointed to various instructing posts in the UK. Cairns finally left the RAF, via the Unemployment List, on 13 January 1919.

CALDWELL, Keith Logan

The son of Merchant, David Robert Caldwell and Mary Dunlop Caldwell (née McKerrow), of Wellington, New Zealand, he was born on 16 October 1895. The Caldwells moved to Auckland when Keith was still quite young. Educated at King's College, Auckland, at Rose Hill in England and at Wanganui Collegiate School. He was working as a bank clerk in Auckland when the war came in August 1914. Caldwell unsuccessfully volunteered for service with the Infantry as soon as war broke out. Still living in New Zealand in September 1915, he learnt to fly at his own expense, first in a flying boat and then in a Caudron converted as a seaplane. He left for England in December 1915 and, not long after arriving, secured a commission, being gazetted Second Lieutenant to the RFC, via the Special Reserve, on 15 April 1916. Following his formal training, he was appointed Flying Officer and awarded his 'Wings' on 17 July 1916. Just two days later, he left for France and the BE2-equipped 8 Squadron. He flew many operational missions with '8', claiming one victory over a Roland CII on 18 September 1916, before, in the November following, he was ordered to 60 Squadron. Eight further victories, seven in Nieuports and one in a SE5A, and the award of an MC were achieved before, in September 1917, he was sent to the Special School of Flying at Gosport. His MC was announced in the *London Gazette* of 17 September 1917: 'For conspicuous gallantry and devotion to duty when leading offensive patrols. On one occasion he led a patrol of five machines against twelve hostile aircraft, all of which he drove down out of control. He has personally destroyed five hostile machines, and has had over fifty contests in the air, in all of which he has displayed splendid skill and fearlessness, and has set a excellent example to his squadron'.

Training roles at the Aerial Gunnery School at Ayr and at the CFS occupied the next few months, before he was promoted to Major, and given command of 74 Squadron, taking that unit to France in April 1918. His handling of '74', 'Tiger Squadron', was outstandingly successful, the unit claiming over 200 enemy aircraft during the eight months of his command. 'Grid' Caldwell himself achieved a total of 25 victories by the end of the war, adding a Distinguished Flying Cross and Bar, *London Gazette*s of 3 December 1918 and 1 January 1919, and a Belgian Croix de Guerre to the MC, he had won earlier. Undoubtedly an exceptional Pilot, his marksmanship, by his own admission, left something to be desired. Had his aim been as good as his flying ability, he would, undoubtedly, have been amongst the very greatest Aces of the Great War. After the war, he returned to farming in New Zealand, marrying, in 1925, Dorothy Helen Gordon, the sister of one of his former 74 Squadron colleagues, with whom he had two sons and two daughters. Keen to keep his aviation interests alive, he was an active member of a local flying club throughout the 1920s and 1930s. When the Second World War came in 1939, Caldwell served in the RNZAF, attaining the rank of Air Commodore, and was created a CBE. Air Commodore Keith Caldwell died in New Zealand on 28 November 1980.

CALLAGHAN, Joseph Creuss

The eldest of the three sons of Mr and Mrs J P Callaghan, of 'Ferndene', Stradbrook, Blackrock, County Dublin, Ireland, he was born on 4March 1893. All three Callaghan boys would enter the RFC and all would be killed. His youngest brother, Eugene, a Pilot with 19 Squadron, was killed in action on 26 August 1916. The other brother, Stanilaus, who had been held captive for a week by Sein Feiners during the 1916 Easter Rebellion in Dublin, was killed in a flying accident at Camp Borden, Canada, on 27 June 1917. Joseph, like his brothers, was educated at Belvedere College, Dublin, and at Stonyhurst. 'Casey', as Joseph was known, was working in Texas when the war came in August 1914. Making his way home as soon as he could, he was gazetted Second Lieutenant to 7 Battalion, Royal Munster Fusiliers, on 3 January 1915. Seconded to the RFC in September 1915, he trained as a Pilot and was confirmed and gazetted Flying Officer on 25 January 1916. Sent out to France in February 1916, his first operational posting was to 18 Squadron. On 26 April 1916, Callaghan and his Observer, fellow Irishman James Mitchell, in FE2b, '5232', were returning from a photo-reconnaissance patrol when they were suddenly caught between four enemy aircraft. Second Lieutenant Mitchell managed to send down one of the attacking machines, a Fokker E, before he was killed. The FE2b's engine was knocked out, and some controls shot away in the onslaught. Despite his dire situation, Callaghan glided his stricken machine to a safe landing near to the Château de la Haie. Usually in the company of Observer/Gunner Sergeant B Ankers (Number 3464), Callaghan became an effective and specialist Night-Bombing Pilot, a comparatively rare art at the time. On 9/10 October 1916, Callaghan and Ankers, attacked two searchlights with machine-gun fire, extinguishing one of them. Exactly one month later, the same pair dropped bombs onto an enemy aerodrome with great effect. On the following night, they bombed a railway station and again caused two searchlights to be extinguished with their machine-gun fire. Ankers, who was awarded the Distinguished Conduct Medal, *London Gazette* of 11 December 1916, would go on to be commissioned into the RFC, attaining the rank of Captain and Flight Commander with 23 Squadron. Callaghan's MC was announced in the *London Gazette* of 13 February 1917: 'For conspicuous gallantry in action. He displayed marked courage and skill on several occasions in carrying out bombing operations. On one occasion he extinguished a hostile searchlight'.

His tour with '18' completed, he returned to the UK in January 1917, whereupon he was sent as an Instructor to No 2 School of Aerial Gunnery, at Turnbury in Scotland. Whilst in Scotland, he flew over to Dublin on three occasions to visit his mother. Promoted to Major, he took out the Sopwith Dolphin-equipped 87 Squadron to the front in April 1918. Callaghan gained four further victories, before he was himself shot down and killed by Leutnant Franz Büchner, the Commanding Officer of Jasta 13, becoming the seventh of the German Ace's eventual 40 victories. A squadron colleague writing to Callaghan's parents, described his last fight: 'He was last seen with a patrol of 60 Squadron, and then a tremendous fight started, and he went into the thick of it, as he always would. Captain Maxwell, 56 Squadron, saw one machine fighting about twenty-five Germans, but the machine was hit before he could arrive close enough'. Joseph Creuss Callaghan is buried in Contay British Cemetery, Contay, France.

CAMBRAY, William Charles

The son of Produce Broker's Clerk, William C Cambray and Carrie Cambray, of 2 Derwent Grove, Camberwell, London, he was born in Herne Hill, south-east London, on 12 November 1894. He worked in Insurance in the City of London between 1912-14. Cambray enlisted, pre-war, as a Private soldier (Number 672) into 5 Battalion, London Regiment (London Rifle Brigade) (TF), and was mobilised along with the rest of the TF on 4 August 1914, the day war began. He accompanied his battalion to France, with the rank of a Lance Corporal, on 23 September 1915. Picked out for a commission, he was gazetted Second Lieutenant to 2 Battalion, London Regiment (TF) on 7 November 1915. He joined the 2 Londons on the Somme in August 1916, one of seven much needed replacement officers following the losses suffered by the battalion in the Battle of Gommecourt. On 9 September, 56 Division attacked Ginchy, and Cambray distinguished himself during a German counter-attack when, as the only officer still alive and unwounded, he took command of 'B' Company and succeeded in leading it forward to one of its objectives. Seconded to the RFC in the spring of 1917, he trained as an Observer and, qualifying on 28 March 1917, was sent out as such to FE2d-equipped 20 Squadron in April. Cambray became an Observer Ace, gaining six victories between 31 May and 21 September 1917. His MC was announced in the *London Gazette* of 17 September 1917: 'For conspicuous gallantry and devotion to duty whilst acting as an Observer to offensive patrols. On four occasions, at least, he has shot down enemy scouts and also had numerous indecisive combats, in all of which he has displayed the greatest gallantry'.

His tour with '20' completed, he returned to the Home Establishment on 9 October 1917, where he was posted to instructing duties. Cambray received the insignia of his MC from the hands of the King at an investiture held at Buckingham Palace in January 1918. After leaving the service on 22 April 1919, Bill Cambray did not fly again until 1967 and he was, by then, living in Queensland!

CAMPBELL, Patrick Colin

The son of Major and Mrs E P Campbell of 'Ardachuidh', Colintraire, Argyllshire, Scotland, he was born on 6 November 1889. Educated at Bradfield College (1904-07). He worked as a Mechanical Engineer in Glasgow for two years, followed by a further year in Alexandria, Scotland, before being gazetted Second Lieutenant to 4 (Extra Reserve) Battalion, Argyll and Sutherland Highlanders, on 3 October 1914, with an immediate transfer to a Regular Army battalion of the Black Watch. Campbell served in the trenches in 1915, before being seconded to the RFC in the November of the same year. Gained the Royal Aero Club Certificate (Number 2017) on 8 November 1915. His formal training duly completed, he was confirmed and gazetted Flying Officer on 24 February 1916. Sent out to France and 18 Squadron in April 1918. On 16 September 1916, Campbell and his Observer of the day, Second Lieutenant W A Mackay, damaged and drove down an LVG near to Combles on the Somme. His MC was announced in the *London Gazette* of 14 November 1916: 'For conspicuous skill and gallantry on many occasions. On one occasion, seeing a cavalry patrol held up, he came down to 600 feet, dropped bombs on the enemy and enabled his Observer to enfilade the hostile trench with machine-gun fire. Finally, his engine was put out of action by rifle fire from the ground'.

On 10 November 1916, Campbell and his Observer/Gunner, 1 AM O F Watts, dropped bombs to good effect upon an enemy aerodrome, before, during their return flight to base, attacking four trains in Quent station, with machine-gun fire. On the following night, the same pair again attacked a succession of moving trains. Two drums of tracers (Buckingham ammunition) were expended, and one of the trains set alight. 1 AM Oliver Frederick Watts (Number 2073) was awarded a posthumous Military Medal for his part in these raids, announced in the *London Gazette* of 22 January 1917, as the 23 year old, from Aston, Birmingham, was killed in action on 27 November 1916. Campbell's tour with '18' completed in December 1917, he returned to the Home Establishment and duties there with, successively, 64 and 28 Squadrons. Promoted to A/Captain and Flight Commander, he next accompanied the Camel-equipped 28 Squadron to France on 8 October 1917. Campbell was hospitalised for some reason on 25 October, and this heralded the end of his operational career. He subsequently held various instructional posts in the UK, for which he received a Mention in Despatches. Patrick Campbell finally left the RAF, via the Unemployed List, with the rank of Captain on 18 April 1919.

NB: His medals were offered for sale by Christie's (lot 545) on 27 November 1990: MC (inscribed: Lieut P C Campbell/ Somme/18.11.16*), 1914-15 Star* (2LT/A & S H'ldrs), *British War Medal 1914-20, and Victory Medal 1914-19 with MID* (Capt RFC). *It is a mystery as to why his MC is inscribed, '18/11/1916', when his* Gazette *date was earlier on '14/11/16'.*

CAMPBELL, William Charles

Born in Bordeaux on 27 April 1889, the son of a Scottish father and a French mother. Gazetted Second Lieutenant to the RFC, via the Special Reserve, on 10 August 1916. He gained his Royal Aero Club Certificate (Number 3806) on 1 November 1916, being confirmed and gazetted Flying Officer on the same day. A 33 year old Wine Importer, Campbell was considerably older than most of his fellow Pilots when he was sent out to join 1 Squadron (Nieuport XVIIs) on 1 May 1917. Despite his relatively advanced years, he was to prove himself a truly exceptional Fighter Pilot. Campbell had arrived in France to join '1' in the company of his best friend, Lieutenant T H Lines. Lines was shot down and taken prisoner on 18 May 1917, an event which greatly affected Campbell. Fellow Pilot Stuart Keith-Jopp recorded in his diary, 'At dinner Campbell cursed and damned, walking all round the table until we turned him out and had more drinks. He continued outside, and the next morning went out and shot down a balloon in revenge against orders'. This was to be the first of five balloons claimed by Campbell, thus making him the first acknowledged 'balloon buster' Ace in the RFC. In addition to his balloons, Campbell would also shoot down 18 hostiles between mid-May and the end of 31 July 1917, when he was wounded. On 31 July 1917, Campbell, in Nieuport Scout, 'A4724', was shot up and wounded in the thigh by Oberleutnant Eduard Ritter von Dostler of Jasta 6, the 21st of the German Ace's eventual 26 victories. Campbell's MC and Bar were both announced in the *London Gazette* of 16 August 1917 – MC: 'For conspicuous gallantry and devotion to duty. He attacked an enemy balloon, bringing it down in flames and returned to our lines at about 20 feet from the ground under heavy fire. On another occasion he attacked and dispersed a column of infantry from a very low altitude. He has shown great courage and initiative throughout'.

Bar to MC: 'For conspicuous gallantry and devotion to duty. He has repeatedly shown great fearlessness and skill in attacking and destroying enemy aircraft, on one occasion destroying three within one hour. He has also attacked and dispersed enemy troops from a low altitude, at all times showing the utmost disregard for personal safety'.

His gallantry and brilliance as a fighter Ace also earned him the Distinguished Service Order, *London Gazette* of 17 September 1917. Following this outstanding tour, and once recovered from his wound, Campbell was ordered home to take up a post as an Instructor, yet another appointment in which he would excel, eventually becoming Chief Instructor, School of Military Aeronautics. After leaving the RAF in 1919, Campbell embarked on a successful business career. Living in Hove, Sussex, he occupied a seat on a number of boards of nationally known companies. He became, in time, Deputy Chairman of Crosse and Blackwell (Holdings) Ltd; Chairman of British Vinegars Ltd; Chairman of Champion & Slee Ltd; Chairman of Sarsons Ltd; and Chairman of Plaistow Ltd. He was also Chairman of his local football team, Brighton and Hove Albion Football Club. William Campbell died in Hove on 26 February 1958.

CAMPBELL-MARTIN, Peter Clifford

The son of Henry Torrence Campbell-Martin and Adeline Campbell-Martin, he was born on 6 November 1896, in Calcutta, India. Gazetted Second Lieutenant to a Regular Army battalion of the Sherwood Foresters, on 19 July 1916. Seconded to the RFC in July 1917, he trained as an Observer, before joining the DH4-equipped 25 Squadron in France, as a Probationary, on 22 August following. His 'apprenticeship' satisfactorily completed, he was confirmed and gazetted Flying Officer (Observer) on 15 October 1917. On 3 February 1918, Campbell-Martin and his Pilot, Lieutenant E G Green (qv), in DH4, 'A7873', were ordered to bomb Melle Station. On the return leg back to their base, their machine was attacked and shot down over Mariakerke,

Ghent, by Leutnant Otto Löffler of Jasta 2, the second of the German Ace's eventual 15 victories. Green was badly wounded in the stomach, whilst Campbell-Martin suffered only slight wounds to the neck and leg. Green landed the smouldering DH4 near to Grand St Bigard. After he and Green exited the machine, Campbell-Martin was able to completely finish it off by setting it alight with his Very pistol. Campbell-Martin would afterwards claim that in this fight, he had shot down an Albatros in flames, and also forced a Dr1 to crashland in a near-by field. Green and Campbell-Martin were taken prisoner and spirited away to detention camps. On 10 April 1918, Campbell-Martin contrived an escape whilst being transferred from the infamous Holzminden camp to another camp in Landshut. It took him nearly four months of evasion, before he finally reached the UK on 16 August 1918. He was received in audience by the King at Buckingham Palace, on 18 September following. His MC was announced in the so-called 'Escapers Gazette', *London Gazette* of 16 December 1919: '....in recognition of gallantry in escaping from captivity whilst Prisoners of War'.

Campbell-Martin served in Northern Ireland, before joining the F2b-equipped 105 Squadron at St Omer in April 1919. He married, firstly, Monica Mary O'Hea' on 6 August 1919, at the Church of the Holy Ghost, Nightingale Square, Wandsworth, the couple setting up home in South Kensington, London. At a Court Martial convened at Baldonnel, Ireland, Campbell-Martin was found guilty of four charges concerning a pay list he should have ascertained as being accurate and being privy to the making of a false statement. He was dismissed the Service in November 1920, his medals forfeited. Campbell-Martin then appears to have returned to live and work in India, joining a Volunteer unit there and eventually qualifying for an Efficiency Medal (1930), with clasp, India. He married, secondly, Emily Barbara, from Kensington, London. When the Second World War came in 1939, Campbell-Martin was commissioned Flying Officer into the RAFVR, and trained as an Air Gunner. On 17 October 1941, the 44 year old Campbell-Martin was the rear-gunner in a 40 Squadron Wellington bomber, 'Z8862 BL-B', detailed to attack Duisberg, Germany, after taking off at 01.06 hours from Alconbury. Five members of the crew were killed in the crash when the Wellington was brought down over Germany – Sergeant J A Lamb, Sergeant J A Jacques, RCAF, Sergeant A H Harman, Flight Sergeant P L Henningan, DFM, and Flying Officer P C Campbell-Martin. All are buried in Reichswald Forest War Cemetery, Germany. The Pilot and sole survivor, Squadron T G Kirby-Green, was shot by the Gestapo on 29 March 1944, one of the 50 officers executed following the mass escape from Stalag Luft III – the famous Great Escape – and is buried in Poznan Old Garrison Cemetery, Poland.

NB: The RAF Museum Hendon has a group of medals in its collection, presented by the Campbell-Martin family: MC, 1914-15 Star (original naming removed), British War Medal 1914-20, Victory Medal 1914-19 (both unnamed), Efficiency Medal 1930, with bar, India (un-named), and Croix de Guerre 1914-18 (France). The Museum catalogue adds the following note: 'From the absence of naming on these medals this is presumed to be a re-constructed group following the loss of the originals'.

CARBERY, Douglas Hugh Moffatt

Born in Ambala, India, on 26 March 1894, he returned to England in 1913 to live in Suffolk under the guardianship of Sir William and Lady Austin, following the death of his father. Educated at the King's School, Bruton, Somerset, he had almost completed his further studies at the Royal Military Academy, Woolwich, when war came on 4 August 1914. Eight days later on 12 August, he passed out near the top of his intake, and was, by his own choice, gazetted Second Lieutenant to the Royal Horse Artillery. He went to France with 96 Battery, RHA, but transferred, in January 1915, to 'E' Battery RHA. Carbery served through the Battles of St Eloi and Neuve Chapelle, before returning to 96 Battery during the Second Battle of Ypres, and was wounded with that unit on 14 May 1915. Recovering quickly, he returned to the front, only to be wounded yet again in the following July, when the top of one of his fingers was shot off whilst he was peering through a pair of field glasses – an unfortunate wound for an aspiring pianist!. Transferring to the RFC on 20 April 1916, he began pilot training with 19 TS. Gained his Royal Aero Club Certificate (Number 3383) on 31 July 1916. His formal training duly completed, he was confirmed and gazetted Flying Officer on 4 August following. Sent to France, he served first with the BE2e-equipped 52 Squadron. He achieved two victories, including the first ever for the squadron on 25 January 1917, before briefly transferring to 9 Squadron as a Flight Commander. His MC was announced in the *London Gazette* of 26 March 1917: 'For conspicuous gallantry and devotion to duty while engaged in artillery observation. He was attacked by four hostile machines which he succeeded in driving off and continued to carry out his observations. Later, he was again attacked by several hostile machines and succeeded in bringing one of them down. He has previously done good work'.

He was also Mentioned in Despatches in May 1917. Carbery would later be presented with the insignia of his MC by the King, at an investiture held at Buckingham Palace on 15 January 1918. Following a stint in the UK as an Instructor with 15 TS, he joined 59 Squadron (RE8s) at the front in August 1918, claiming a further four victories before the cessation of hostilities. On 28 August 1918, Carbery flew his most celebrated operational flight with Lieutenant J B V Clements. During the morning of that day, they sent down an enemy two-seater. An hour or so later at 07.15, they sighted a German 77mm gun team galloping in retreat to Bapaume, and immediately signalled the RA to open fire. Getting no immediate response, they took it upon themselves to attack the gun team with two 25 lb bombs. Two limbers were destroyed, before Carbery turned and swooped to strafe the gun team from 300 feet, inflicting severe casualties on men and horses. Half an hour later, the intrepid pair finished off this sortie with a low level strafe of Bapaume town square, wreaking havoc amongst 200 enemy troops paraded there. In the meantime the gun that Carbery and Clements had shot-up and all but wrecked, had been captured by advancing British troops and would, eventually, find its way to stand outside the RAF College, Cranwell, as a presentation piece. (Sadly, 'Carbery's Gun', as it became known, was removed to be melted down for scrap at the commencement of the Second World War. The Tommies who captured the gun in August 1918, also presented a broken wheel from one of the limbers to Carbery and Clements, an item which became something of a mascot for 59 Squadron. In 1939, Carbery's and Clement's exploit was immortalised when, with the authority of the King, the broken wheel emblem became the 59 Squadron badge). The first of Carbery's Distinguished Flying Crosses for, amongst other things, 'displaying remarkable courage and skill in attacking hostile batteries', was announced in the *London Gazette* of 3 December 1918. After the war, he stayed on in the RAF, serving with 31 Squadron in India and Afghanistan and adding a Bar for Afghanistan to his Distinguished Flying Cross, *London Gazette* of 12 July 1920. Following unrest in Amritsar and Gujanwala, punitive measures were considered necessary. Aircraft of 52 Wing, including Carbery's, dropped bombs into the thick of a mob, and sprayed it with machine-gun fire. In May 1919, 31 Squadron was sent to the Frontier to join the Waziristan operation. On 9 May, the squadron bombed Dakka inflicting 600 casualties. Three machines of '31' were hit by ground fire and forced to land fortunately, for the crews involved, in friendly territory. Carbery wrote off the squadron's one and only, highly prized, Armstrong Whitworth FK 8. Later in the same month, Carbery made a night bombing raid on the Amir's palace in Jalalabad. Because of the weight of his bomb load, he could not fly over the mountains and was forced to negotiate the Khyber Pass by night. Successfully reaching the target, he gained four direct hits. The Amir was shaken by this demonstration, and soon the Afghan envoy, Abdul Rahman Khan, was attempting to come to terms with General Barrett at Dakka. Carbery assumed command of '31' on 10 August and, on 11 September following, bombed the village of Chora to destruction. The Bar to his Distinguished Flying Cross followed, but, back in England, questions were being posed about the punitive severity of the suppression of the insurrection and, as a consequence of these misgivings, both General Dyer, who had ordered the mass shooting of the rebels in the streets of Amritsar, and Carbery, himself, were sent home under a cloud. Carbery decided to revert to his Army roots and his former regiment, the Royal Artillery, was delighted to have him back. He did return to India to serve with the Mountain Artillery and was, at one point, under the direct command of a certain Bernard Law Montgomery, who, even then, insisted that all his officers did early morning exercises! Carbery, a high goal polo player and a natural sportsman, who had represented 'The Shop' at cricket, hockey and rugby, did not feel the need to prove his physical fitness and failed to turn up for the compulsory exercises. Monty responded by challenging Carbery to a game of squash. Three sets to nil later, Carbery confessed to the bemused and defeated 'Monty', that he, Carbery, was the current Champion of the All India Amateur Squash Club! After much service in India between the wars, he also served in West Africa and in Burma during the Second World War, before retiring in 1946, with the rank of Brigadier, going on to live at 'Redgate', Lanner House, Lanner, Cornwall. Brigadier Douglas Carbery died on 27 April 1959, at the Redruth Miners and General Hospital, Cornwall.

NB: Carbery's medals were offered for sale by Sotheby's (lot 609) on 15 September 1990: MC, Distinguished Flying Cross & Bar, British War Medal 1914-20, Victory Medal 1914-19 with MID (Capt RAF), *Indian General Service 1908-35, with clasps, Afghanistan N.W.F. 1919, Waziristan 1919-21, North West Frontier 1930-31* (Flt Lt RAF), *1939-45 Star, Burma Star 1941-45, Defence Medal 1939-45, and War Medal 1939-45.*

CARDEN, Percy Theodore

The son of Major General George Carden and Mary Gertrude Carden (née Baline), he was born at Earl's Court, London, on 14 December 1892. Educated at Wellington College (1899-1903), and at Corpus Christi College, Oxford, from where he graduated with Honours in Law. A practising Barrister, he was called to the Bar – Lincoln's Inn and Inner Temple – in 1908. When the war came, he enlisted as a Private soldier into 18 (Public Schools) Battalion, Royal Fusiliers, in 1914. This battalion went to France on 27 November 1915, but when the great need for replacement officers was realised, it was brought home in April 1916, with the great majority of its members being subsequently commissioned. Carden, in fact, had already returned to the UK and had been gazetted Second Lieutenant to the RFC on 4 February 1916. He undertook training as an Observer and was duly sent out as a Probationary to BE2c-equipped 12 Squadron in the April following. On 20 May 1916, Carden and his Pilot of the day, Lieutenant Farrow, in BE2c, '2731', 'saw off' a two-seater that had been forced down to their level by two FEs of 23 Squadron. The unfortunate German airmen fell out of their machine, before it crashed to earth, near to Beaumetz. His 'apprenticeship' satisfactorily completed, Carden was confirmed and gazetted Flying Officer (Observer) on 7 July 1916. One month later on 7 August, Carden and his Pilot, Lieutenant McArthur, silenced a hostile anti-aircraft battery with their bombs. On 1 November 1916, Carden and his Pilot, Captain J R Philpott (qv), caused great confusion and casualties amongst a large party of enemy infantry. Carden's tour with '12', was interrupted when he was appointed Brigade Intelligence Officer, 12 Corps, Wing HQ, from December 1916 to February 1917. He returned briefly to his squadron, before being posted next to the Home Establishment, where he commenced pilot training in December 1917, qualifying early in the following New Year. His MC was announced, rather belatedly, in the *London Gazette* of 25 April 1918: 'For conspicuous gallantry and devotion to duty. When acting as Observer he made a successful wire reconnaissance along a corps front at a height of 300 to 800 feet under heavy machine-gun and rifle fire. On another occasion, while observing during a reconnaissance patrol, he and his pilot had four encounters with enemy aeroplanes, in one of which they were attacked at 800 feet by five enemy scouts. He kept up a continuous fire, and drove off the enemy, and completed a valuable reconnaissance. He showed the greatest keenness and determination at his work'.

Carden served out the rest of the war as a Pilot with several units, including 120 Squadron, mainly flying mail-carrying machines. He finally left the RAF, via the Unemployed List, in January 1919, returning to London to practise law. In 1930, he married Marjorie Ruth Scott of Maida Vale, the couple living at 78

Leith Mansions, in the London district. When the Second World War came in 1939, he was recalled as a Flight Lieutenant, RAFVR. Percy Carden died whilst on active service, on 12 February 1942, at the RAF Hospital, Kirkham, near Preston, Lancashire, and is buried nearby in Kirkham (St Michael) Churchyard Extension.

NB: His medals were offered for sale by Dix Noonan Webb (lot 1306) on 15 December 2000: MC, 1914-15 Star (Pte, Royal Fusiliers), *British War Medal 1914 20, Victory Medal 1914 19* (Lieut RFC), *Defence Medal 1939-45, and War Medal 1939-45.*

CAREY-THOMAS, William Warren

The son of Mr and Mrs Charles Carey-Thomas, he was born in Cardiff, South Wales, on 14 November 1885. Educated at Rossall School, Fleetwood, Lancashire. He went to South Africa in 1907, working with Rand Mines Ltd, until the outbreak of war in 1914. Volunteering first for the South African Forces, he was eventually sent, with other candidates, to the UK for flying training. Gazetted Second Lieutenant to the RFC, via the Special Lists, on 31 July 1915, he gained, at his own expense, his Royal Aero Club Certificate (Number 1918) on 15 October 1915. Going on to formal pilot training, he was confirmed and gazetted Flying Officer on 6 January 1916. Appropriately enough, he was sent out to 26 (South Africa) Squadron in East Africa, on 9 June 1916. In the African campaign, Carey-Thomas served with Kenneth Reid Van der Spuy (qv), even acting as the great man's Observer on occasions. The aerial war in this part of the world was markedly different from that in France and Flanders. On one occasion, Carey-Thomas, on a reconnaissance with another officer in a BE2c, ran short of petrol. Landing on a small, remote, emergency landing field, they decided to take a stroll down to a near-by river to collect some water. Pushing their way through the high reeds and elephant grass edging the river bank, they suddenly came face to face with two lions. Beating a hasty retreat, they climbed back into the BE, and spent an uncomfortable wide-awake night clutching their revolvers. Carey-Thomas' MC was announced in the *London Gazette* of 3 June 1917 (no citation).

His tour with '26' completed, he returned to the Home Establishment on 30 January 1918. When the war ended, Carey-Thomas, who had also been twice Mentioned in Despatches, joined the newly formed South African Aviation Force, going on to command a squadron with the rank of Major. In 1922, South Africa was torn apart by the Rand Industrial Revolt, when gold miners staged an all-out and concerted strike which quickly escalated into violence and soon bordered upon civil war. Because of Carey-Thomas' familiarity with the area around Witwatersrand – he had been a senior mine official there before the war – van der Spuy detailed him for special observer duties on 10 March 1922. An hour after take-off, he was shot through the heart by rifle fire from the ground, the first ever SAAF casualty.

CARPENTER, Peter

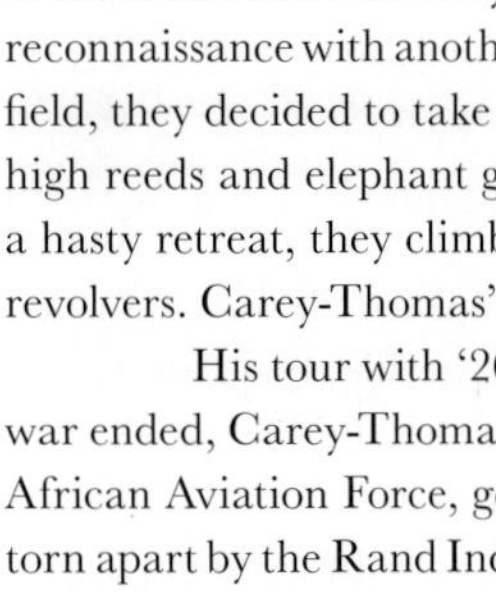

The son and one of the nine children of Boat Pilot, Peter Carpenter and Jane Carpenter, of 35 Clive Street, Canton, Cardiff, he was born 6 December 1892. A milling and engineering student in Cardiff, he first served as a Lance Corporal (Number 8188) with a battalion of the Royal Fusiliers. He entered the RFC as a Cadet in January 1917, and was subsequently gazetted Second Lieutenant on 17 March following. His pilot training duly completed, he was confirmed and gazetted Flying Officer on 16 June 1917. Sent out to 45 Squadron (Sopwith Camels) in France in the summer of 1917, he gained eight victories between 20 September 1917 and 26 January 1918. Promoted to A/Captain and Flight Commander, he was next posted out to 66 Squadron in Italy, on 27 February 1918. Carpenter went on to achieve a further 16 victories on this front between 27 February and 25 October 1918. On 30 March 1918, Carpenter involved in a fight with a number of Austro-Hungarian Scout planes, for which Alan Jerrard was awarded the Victoria Cross. Carpenter's first MC was announced in the *London Gazette* of 4 March 1918, details in the *Gazette* of 16 August 1918: 'For conspicuous gallantry and devotion to duty. Within a period of the last three months he has brought down six enemy machines, four of which were observed to crash to the ground, the remaining two being shot down completely out of control. The offensive tactics pursued by this daring and skilful officer have produced most excellent results'.

The Bar to his MC came in the *London Gazette* of 16 September 1918: 'For conspicuous gallantry and devotion to duty. He led an offensive patrol against seven of the enemy; three were destroyed. Again he led a patrol of three machines against six of the enemy; two of whom were destroyed and one driven down out of control. Later, with two other pilots, he engaged twelve hostile machines, of which three were destroyed and one driven down out of control. He shot down seven machines himself'.

For his leadership and outstanding success as a Scout Pilot, he was also awarded the Distinguished Service Order in the same *London Gazette* of 16 September 1918. The Italians, too, showed their appreciation with the award of a Italian Bronze Medaglia al Valore Militare, *London Gazette* of 2 November 1918. Hospitalised on 4 December 1918, Carpenter was sent home for further treatment on 6 January 1919. In hospital yet again in Swanage on 21 March 1919, he finally left the RAF, via the Unemployment List, on 3 May 1919.

CASTER, William Samuel

The son of William George Caster and Alice Elizabeth Caster (née Dell), he was born in Peterborough, on 8 November 1896. Educated at King's School, Peterborough, and at Wellingborough School. In 1912, he commenced training as a 'Premium Apprentice' in Engineering, at the Great Eastern Railway Works, in Stratford. Volunteering his services, he was gazetted Second Lieutenant to the Huntingdon Cyclist Battalion (TF) on 7 March 1915. Seconded to the RFC, he trained as an Observer and, in January 1916, was sent out as a Probationary to 17 Squadron in the Middle East. His 'apprenticeship' satisfactorily completed, he was confirmed and gazetted Flying Officer (Observer) on 1 April 1916. Caster served with '17' and, briefly, with 14 Squadron until 15 July 1916, whereupon he returned to the UK to undertake pilot training. Once qualified for his full 'Wings', he was sent out in September 1916, to the Martinsyde Elephant-equipped 27 Squadron in France. Caster was promoted Captain and Flight Commander in March 1917, shortly before his MC was announced in the *London Gazette* of 26 April 1917: 'For conspicuous gallantry and devotion to duty. He led a successful long-distance raid, and brought six machines safely back in very bad weather. On another occasion, while leading a long-distance bomb raid, he engaged five hostile machines'.

His tour with '27' completed, he returned to the UK for a rest and later to take up a post as an Instructor at the CFS, Upavon. Sent out next to Egypt in January 1918, he instructed at the Aerial Fighting School, at Heliopolis. Returning to the UK at the end of the war, he obtained a permanent commission in the RAF. His many subsequent appointments, honours and promotions included: OC, Workshops and Transport at the CFS, Upavon, 1919; Instructor at No 4 FTS, Manston, 1921; Instructor and Communications Pilot with 24 Squadron at Kenley, also responsible for flight testing of Pilots for civil licence, 1922; Flight Commander with 30 and 70 Squadrons in Iraq, 1924; with 70 Squadron and responsible for carrying mail between Iraq and Egypt, 1924-25; Squadron Leader 1926; Chief Test Pilot, Aircraft Depot, Aboukir, Egypt, 1927; OC, Experimental Flying Section at the RAE, Farnborough, 1928 (the first Pilot to be catapulted in a heavy bomber and also flew many experimental prototypes); Senior Staff Officer, Policy and Administration, Coastal Command, 1933; Wing Commander, 1934; OC, Aircraft Repair Depot, Iraq, 1938; Air HQ, Iraq, 1941; President of the Air Crew Selection Board, later going to the command of RAF, Detling, Kent and later again to Northern Ireland to open up a Flying Boat Operational Training Unit, 1942; Mentioned in Despatches, 1942; and Command of RAF

Mountbatten, a unit equipped with Sunderland Flying Boats for patrol and rescue, 1944. Caster finally retired from the RAF with the rank of Group Captain on 13 March 1946. Following his retirement, Caster joined the Ministry of Civil Aviation, and was appointed Airport Manager at Northolt. Over the next 15 years, he served, successively, as Airport Commandant at Turnhouse, at Heathrow and at Speke, Liverpool. He worked later as Operations Officer at HQ, Heston, and was heavily involved in the development of Gatwick Airport. Retiring from the Ministry in 1962, he became the Honorary Secretary General of the Parachute Association. Group Captain William Caster died on 16 November 1979.

CATCHPOLE, Basil Everard

The third son of Company Secretary, Arthur Everard Catchpole, and Marie Catchpole (née Harmer), of 18 Riggindale, Streatham, London, he was born on 30 January 1896. Like so many others in the first decade of the twentieth century, the family emigrated, the Catchpoles choosing Canada. They settled in British Columbia, where Basil completed his education before joining, in August 1912, the Mission Junction, BC, branch of the Canadian Bank of Commerce. Two years later, soon after the war came, the young clerk volunteered for service on 18 December 1914, as a Gunner (Number 83865) with 15 Battery, Canadian Field Artillery. After service with the CEF, he was eventually picked out for a commission and gazetted Second Lieutenant to the RFC on 21 June 1917. His pilot training duly completed, he was confirmed and gazetted Flying Officer on 14 August following. Sent out to 8 Squadron (AWFK8s) in the same month that he qualified, he completed his first, largely routine, tour early in 1918. In April 1918, he was promoted to A/Captain and Flight Commander and posted to the command of 'L' Flight, 21 Squadron (RE8s). His MC was one of the last announced to the flying service, the unusually detailed citation appearing in the *London Gazette* of 16 September 1918: 'For conspicuous gallantry and devotion to duty. This officer has been observing for artillery during the last eight months, often flying at low altitudes over enemy lines under heavy anti-aircraft and machine-gun fire. The following is three consecutive day's work: (1) While on patrol, flying at 400 ft, he fired 900 rounds under intense anti-aircraft and machine-gun fire; (2) carried out two very successful shoots, observing on hostile batteries, dropped four bombs, and saw several large explosions, also fired 800 rounds into farms, orchards and trenches; (3) left the ground in the dark on artillery patrol and located accurately 20 hostile batteries. In the afternoon he did four good shoots in two flights, causing explosions in every case. He flew for eight hours this day. He has always set a splendid example in his squadron'.

The award of a Distinguished Flying Cross, for setting, 'a magnificent example of courage and determination', came in the *London Gazette* of 2 November 1918, as, indeed, did the announcement that the French had awarded him a Croix de Guerre avec Palme. Catchpole returned to the Home Establishment on 18 December 1918 and, after actively considering the possibility of making the RAF his career, decided against it, and resigned his commission in November 1919.

CAVE, Francis Oswin

From Petersfield, Hampshire, he was born on 27 August 1897. Educated at the Oratory School, and at the Royal Military College, Sandhurst, from where he was gazetted Second Lieutenant to a Regular Army battalion of the Rifle Brigade on 15 October 1915. Cave served with 6 (Reserve) Battalion of his regiment in Sheerness for the remainder of 1915, and into 1916. Seconded to the RFC in March 1916, he gained his Royal Aero Club Certificate (Number 2881) on 13 May 1916. After completing his formal training, he was confirmed and gazetted Flying Officer on 22 June following. Sent out to 4 Squadron in France almost immediately after qualifying, he proved an efficient Artillery Co-operation Pilot. On 10 October 1916, Cave and his Observer, Lieutenant Duke, in co-operation with the 8 inch Howitzer-equipped 33 Siege Battery, RGA, obtained eight direct hits on an enemy battery, destroying three gunpits and blowing up large quantities of ammunition. On 1 November 1916, the same pair arrived too late to save a 7 Squadron BE2d, under attack from an enemy machine but still extracted some revenge by sending the offending German down. His tour with '4' completed in February 1917, he returned to the Home Establishment. His MC was announced in the Birthday Honours *London Gazette* of 3 June 1917 (no citation). Although no formal citation appeared in the *Gazette*, research has unearthed the original recommendation for the award: '12 March 1917: 5th Brigade, RFC: 'For exceptionally good work as a Flying Officer from July 1916 to February 1917 during which time he has carried out an enormous amount of contact patrol work and Artillery observation, often in excessively bad weather. This Officer had always shown the greatest determination in carrying out his work under the most difficult conditions and has set a very fine example'. Cave served in various administration posts until finally returning to the front on 31 October 1918, this time with the SE5A-equipped 94 Squadron. Relinquishing his RAF commission in October 1919, he reverted to his Rifle Brigade roots, serving with 2 Battalion of his regiment in Ireland through the 'Troubles' of 1919 to 1922. Next he served 1 Battalion, Rifle Brigade, in India from 1922 to 1930, followed by two years in the Regimental Depot in the UK. Detached to the Sudan Defence Force in 1933, he served with that unit with the rank of Major, until 1943. Cave was awarded the OBE in 1942 and the Egyptian Government conferred the Order of the Nile upon him. His next posting was to the Special Force (Chindits) in India and Burma, with which unit he served from 1943 to early 1944. Promoted to Lieutenant Colonel on 30 March 1944, he finally retired from the Army with the rank of Honorary Colonel, on 6 January 1945. He had been Mentioned in Despatches on three occasions during his distinguished career. Entering Holy Orders after his retirement from the Army, Francis Cave became a Roman Catholic priest, teaching at the Sacred Heart College, Sunningdale, Berkshire, and was eventually elevated to Monsignor, and appointed a Personal Prelate to the Pope. He lived at 19 Melton Court, London SW7.

CAVE, Thomas Walford

The eldest son of the Reverend T S Cave, MA, Vicar of St James's Church, Handsworth, Birmingham, and Mrs Cave. A pre-war TF volunteer, he was gazetted Second Lieutenant to 3 North Midland Brigade, RFA, on 1 July 1914. Mobilised with the rest of the TF on 4 August 1914, he served in France with his unit before eventually achieving secondment to the RFC in 1917. He trained as an Observer and was sent out as such to 35 Squadron (AWFK8s) in France, on 25 October 1917. On 6 March 1918, Cave and his Pilot of the day, Second Lieutenant Evan Pybus (qv), shot down an enemy machine out of control. His tour with '35' ended on 13 April 1918, and his MC was announced a month later in the *London Gazette* of 13 May 1918: 'For conspicuous gallantry and devotion to duty. While engaged in taking photographs of an enemy area he was slightly wounded by anti-aircraft fire. In spite of this and the enemy's fire, 17 photographs were taken. Later, while he was again taking photographs over the enemy's lines, his machine was attacked by 12 enemy machines. He shot down one of them completely out of control, after which several photographs were taken. On three occasions, in the course of flights lasting four hours or more, he ranged a siege battery most effectively on hostile batteries, with the result that several gun pits were destroyed and three explosions were caused. He showed splendid determination and initiative'.

The wound referred to in the citation was slight, but to the eye, and he was obliged to return home for treatment. Cave did not return again to operational flying during the Great War, but did remain in the RAF after the war. With the rank of Flight Lieutenant, he served with the RAF School of Photography, at Farnborough, in 1920 and 1921.

CHADWICK, Reginald

The son of Carpet Weaver, James T Chadwick, and Emma Chadwick, of 7 Holts Yard, Rochdale, he was born on 26 September 1897. His family later owned a Paper Mill in Salford, where he had worked since leaving school in 1911. When war came in August 1914, he volunteered immediately, joining the Royal Engineers as a Sapper (Number 29650). Promoted to Corporal, he was sent out to France as a motor cycle despatch rider on 8 November 1914, thus qualifying for the 1914 Star. Attached to the Lahore Signal Company, Indian Corps, he earned a Distinguished Conduct Medal, *London Gazette* of 3 June 1916, for carrying messages under heavy fire on three separate occasions. At the same time, the Emperor of Japan bestowed upon him the Order of the Rising Sun, 4th Class. Picked out for a commission, he was gazetted Second Lieutenant to the RFC, via the Special Lists, on 17 August 1915. He gained his Royal Aero Club Certificate (Number 2540) on 2 March 1916. His formal pilot training duly completed, he was confirmed and gazetted Flying Officer on 30 April following. Sent out to 11 Squadron in France in the following month, he proved an aggressive and resolute FE2b Pilot. On 17 June 1916, Chadwick and his Observer, Second Lieutenant W A Wedgwood, attacked a formation of no less than eight hostiles, successfully picking off two of the trailing enemy machines. Promoted to A/Captain and Flight Commander in September 1916, Chadwick was sent to 25 Squadron, leading many patrols and successfully laying claims to further enemy machines sent down. On 25 September 1916, came the event which was to win him his MC. During an attack upon enemy airfields and troop and ammunition trains, Chadwick and his Observer of the day, Sergeant C Brown (Number 1863), descended to a low height and deposited six 20-lbs bombs onto a train. The engine was hit and leapt off the rails, causing the leading coaches to telescope one into another. German troops leapt from the wrecked carriages and fled in all directions, whilst Chadwick and Brown strafed them. Chadwick said later that there were so many troops that it would have been difficult to miss, and large numbers were killed or wounded. Chadwick's MC was announced in the *London Gazette* of 14 November 1916: 'For conspicuous gallantry in action. He dived down to a low altitude, attacking a train, displaying great courage and determination'.

For his gallantry in this and other actions, Sergeant Brown received the Military Medal, *London Gazette* of 27 October 1916. His tour with '25' completed in December 1916, Chadwick returned to the Home Establishment, where he was, subsequently, seconded to Staff duties. Promoted to Major, and later Lieutenant Colonel, he never returned to operational flying. Chadwick finally left the RAF, via the Unemployed List, on 14 April 1919.

CHALMERS, James Lauder

From Midlothian in Scotland, he was born on 12 March 1890. He worked as a 'Paper Maker' in Leith from 1907 until 1914. Anxious to join the flying service, he gained his Royal Aero Club Certificate (Number 1411) on 8 July 1915, and was subsequently gazetted Second Lieutenant to the RFC, via the Special Lists, on 16 August following. His formal pilot training duly completed, he was confirmed and gazetted Flying Officer on 3 November 1915. He was sent out to 9 Squadron in France on 19 December 1915. On 21 July 1916, Chalmers and his Observer of the day, Lieutenant H B Cox, spotted 50 German soldiers walking behind a hedge between Leuze Wood and Guillemont. Diving down, they opened fire, scattering the unfortunate infantrymen. Chalmers was promoted to A/Captain and Flight Commander in August 1916. His MC was announced in the *London Gazette* of 20 October 1916: 'For conspicuous gallantry and skill. He has done much fine counter-battery work, often flying very low under heavy fire from the ground. On one occasion one of our shells broke the main spar of his machine. On another, in one flight, he dealt effectively with four enemy batteries'.

His tour with '9' completed, he returned to the UK to take up instructing duties in the late autumn of 1916. Appointed a Squadron Commander in August 1917, he served with various training depot squadrons until leaving the RAF, via the Unemployed List, with the rank of Major, on 10 July 1919. He was Mentioned in Despatches in August 1919. James Chalmers was known to be living in Edinburgh during the 1920s.

CHAMPION deCRESPIGNY, Hugh Vivian

The son of Mr and Mrs Philip Champion deCrespigny of Victoria, Australia, he was born on 8 April 1897, in Elsternwick, Melbourne. Educated at Brighton, Victoria, and at University College, Melbourne. He enlisted as a Private soldier into the Australian Army in August 1914, having previously been a Second Lieutenant in 46 Battalion, Australian Senior Cadets. Allowed to make his way to the UK, he was gazetted Second Lieutenant to the RFC, via the Special Reserve, on 26 February 1915, the same day that he gained his Royal Aero Club Certificate (Number 1099) at the Military Aviation School, Brooklands. After completing his formal pilot training, he was confirmed and gazetted Flying Officer on 16 July 1915. He accompanied the Vickers FB5-equipped 11 Squadron, the first dedicated 2-seater 'fighter' squadron, to France as a 'founder member' on 25 July 1915. Champion deCrespigny progressed rapidly and was an Acting Captain by March 1916. His MC was announced in the *London Gazette* of 16 May 1916: 'For conspicuous gallantry and skill, notably when he attacked five enemy machines over the enemy's lines. He drove away one and brought down another to the ground badly hit. His own machine was then crippled by the fire of the remaining three, but after emptying one more drum at them he brought his machine down safely in our lines'.

Still not yet 19 years old, he was next promoted to A/Major and appointed to the command of 29 Squadron from 22 March 1917 until 21 July 1917, and again later in that year between 4 October to 20 November. His next command was of the Camel-equipped 65 Squadron, which he assumed on 3 June 1918. The award of a Distinguished Flying Cross came in the *London Gazette* of 3 December 1918, in which he was described, without exaggeration, as 'a brilliant and gallant officer'. The French, too, showed their appreciation with the Croix de Guerre and Bronze Star, *London Gazette* of 5 April 1919. He was, in fact, singled out to received both his MC and his Distinguished Flying Cross from the hands of the King at an investiture held at Buckingham Palace on 4 December 1919. Staying on in the RAF, he embarked upon what was to be a distinguished career. His many appointments, promotions and honours included: service in India with 97 (later re-numbered 60) Squadron and then later commanded 60 Squadron in Waziristan; Officer Commanding 39 Squadron from 1925 to 1930; service on the North West Frontier in 1930 (Mentioned in Despatches); Commanded 2 (Indian) Wing Station as a Wing Commander, at Risalpur, from 1930 to 1933; Air Staff HQ, Inland Area from 1934 to 1936; Group Captain, 1936; joined the Air Staff HQ, Bentley Priory, 1936; appointed Air Vice-Marshal commanding the 25 Armament Group, in September 1939; AOC, Iraq and Persia, 1942-43; CB, 1943; and AOC, 21 Group, 1943-44. He married in 1926, Sylvia Ethel (née Usher), dissolved in 1951, five sons including one adopted. In the first General Election after the war in 1945, he stood as the Labour Party Candidate for Newark-on-Trent Parliamentary Division. He was appointed as Regional Commissioner for Schleswig-Holstein Control Commission in Occupied Germany from 1946 to 1947. Air Vice-Marshal Hugh Champion deCrespigny died on 20 June 1969.

NB: His medals were offered for sale by Dix Noonan Webb (lot 1095) on 4 December 2001: CB, MC, Distinguished Flying Cross, 1915 Star (2Lt RFC*), British War Medal 1914-20, Victory Medal 1914-19 with MID* (Major RAF), *India General Service Medal 1908-35, with clasps, Mahsud 1919-20, Waziristan 1921-24, Waziristan 1925, North West Frontier 1930-31* (Flt Lt RAF)*, Africa Star 1940-43, Defence Medal 1939-45, War Medal 1939-45, Coronation Medal 1937, and Croix de Guerre (France).*

CHAPMAN, Charles Meredith Bouverie

The elder son of William Charles Newton Chapman and Alice Maud Chapman, of Heppington, Canterbury, Kent, he was born in 1892. Educated at Harrow and at Sandhurst, before being gazetted to a Regular Army battalion of the Buffs (East Kent Regiment) in 1913. He accompanied 1 Battalion of his regiment to France in September 1914, serving through the early battles of the war, before being sent home with trench fever in the summer of 1915. To enhance his chances of a secondment to the RFC, he learnt to fly whilst still on sick leave, qualifying for his Royal Aero Club Certificate (Number 1491) on 31 July 1915. The RFC accepted him and, after completing his formal training, he was confirmed and gazetted Flying Officer on 1 April 1916. Sent out to 24 Squadron (DH2s) in France on the same day that he qualified for his 'Wings'. On 20 July 1916, Chapman with three other DH Scouts of his squadron, led by Captain Chamberlain, encountered an enemy formation comprising five LVGs, three Rolands and three Fokkers, over Flers. During the ensuing melée, Chapman rescued his colleague, Lieutenant McKay, who, having had his engine hit, was unable to deal with a persistently attacking Fokker. Chapman dived to the rescue over High Wood, sending the German machine down in flames. Chapman achieved two further victories with '24' before his MC was announced in the *London Gazette* of 22 September 1916: 'For conspicuous gallantry and skill in action against enemy aeroplanes. On one occasion he attacked three LVG's and one Fokker, shooting the latter down. Later, during an air battle with eleven enemy machines, he brought another Fokker down'.

Following a brief rest period in the UK, he was promoted to A/Captain and Flight Commander, and sent out to 29 Squadron (Nieuport Scouts) in the spring of 1917. Three further victories accrued to him in May and June, before he was promoted to Major, and given command of his squadron in the following month. The fifth of his victories on 4 June 1917, was particularly notable in that he forced down into the Allied lines, an Albatros DIII, flown by Leutnant George Simon of Jasta 11, the German Pilot being taken into captivity. The Belgians decorated him at this time, appointing him Chevalier de l'Ordre of Leopold, *London Gazette* of 24 September 1917, and awarding him a Croix de Guerre. Chapman's seventh and last victory, came on 17 September 1917. Two weeks later on 1 October, 29 Squadron's airfield at Poperinghe, in Belgium, was attacked and bombed by German raiders. Whilst directing anti-aircraft fire, Major Charles Chapman was struck by bomb splinters and died shortly afterwards. He is buried in nearby Mendinghem Military Cemetery, Poperinghe, Belgium.

CHAPPELL, Roy Williamson

Born on the last day of 1896, he was educated at Brighton College (1911-13). He was living and working in South Africa when the war came in August 1914, and responded by immediately enlisting as a Trooper (Number D8745) into the ranks of a locally raised cavalry regiment, and volunteering to serve in the German South Africa campaign. He next travelled to England at his own expense at the end of 1915, before entering the Inns of Court OTC (Number 6/9030) on 20 January 1916. Following training, he was gazetted Second Lieutenant to the RFC on 17 June 1916. An apt pupil, he gained the Royal Aero Club Certificate (Number 3329) on 17 July 1916. His formal pilot training duly completed, he was confirmed and gazetted Flying Officer on 24 August following. In September 1916, he was posted to the Martinsyde G100-equipped 27 Squadron in France, a unit with which he flew many bombing sorties, as well as claiming two victories. His tour with '27' completed, he returned to England in May 1917, taking up a post as an Instructor at the CFS. In the following October he was again sent to the front, this time as a Flight Commander with 41 Squadron (SE5As). A highly successful tour gained him a further nine victories between 2 February and 16 May 1918, including two 'doubles' on single days. His MC was announced in the *London Gazette* of 22 June 1918: 'For conspicuous gallantry and devotion to duty. He showed the greatest skill and courage in leading patrols, with the result that during four days' operations the formations which he led destroyed nineteen enemy aeroplanes and drove down seven others, the fate of which was not observed, owing to the intensity of the fighting. He has destroyed altogether five enemy machines, and has driven down seven others out of control'.

His tour with '41' completed, he returned to the Home Establishment to be based at Turnberry, where he saw out the remainder of the war. Staying on in the RAF, he served with 24 Squadron, before going out to Iraq and 84 Squadron in 1922. He next became a Test Pilot at Henlow in 1924, before going out to the British Embassy in Tokyo for a three-year stint as a 'Language Officer'. In 1930, he returned again to Japan, giving instruction in air fighting to the Japanese Navy. After next serving briefly in Palestine, by now a Squadron Leader, he once again returned to Japan in 1934, this time as Air Attaché with the rank of Wing Commander. A further promotion to Group Captain followed in 1938. When the Second World War came in September 1939, he was appointed Deputy Director of Intelligence. In 1941, he was promoted to Group Captain, becoming Air Attaché in Bangkok. Returning to the UK, he again served with Intelligence units until finally retiring in 1946, with the rank of Air Commodore. Air Commodore Roy Chappell lived, in retirement, in Sussex and died on 7 February 1982.

CHARLEY, Reginald Morse

The son of Journalist/Author, James Smith Charley, and Eva Charley (née Morse), of Brook House, Awre, Gloucestershire, he was born in Blakeney, Gloucester, in 1892. Charley qualified as an Electrical Engineer in 1911. Three years later in February 1914, he went to Pittsburgh to take up a job representing the English Electric Company in the USA. During 1915, he crossed into Canada, intent on joining the RFC. He qualified for the North American version of the Royal Aero Club Certificate (Number Am 486) on 2 May 1916, at the Curtiss School in Toronto, after taking lessons at Newport News, Virginia, USA. Crossing the Atlantic, he was gazetted Second Lieutenant to the RFC, via the Special Reserve, on 14 June 1916. His formal pilot training duly completed, he was confirmed and gazetted Flying Officer on 30 September following. His first posting was to 59 Squadron in Narborough, from whence he was sent on to the Sopwith Pup-equipped 54 Squadron at Castle Bromwich, before accompanying that unit to France as a 'founder member' on Christmas Eve 1916. Charley achieved five victories between 26 April and 12 November 1917, and was promoted to A/Captain and Flight Commander in the process. His MC was announced in the *London Gazette* of 25 April 1918: 'For conspicuous gallantry and devotion to duty. He attacked a hostile balloon which was eventually brought down in flames. With four other pilots he attacked eight enemy scouts and drove two down. He has driven down four other enemy aircraft, usually fighting with his patrol against greatly superior numbers'.

He was also awarded the Croix de Guerre by the French. Charley received the insignia of his MC from the hands of the King at an investiture held at Buckingham Palace on 16 March 1918. Having returned to the Home Establishment in November 1917, he was eventually posted to the Armament Experimental Station, at Orfordness, where he saw out the war. Leaving the RAF in 1919, he returned to the USA to continue his career as Transformer Sales Manager for the English Electric Company. Reginald Charley retired in 1960, going to live in North Wales before moving later to Yorkshire, where he eventually died in 1986.

CHERRY, Robert Graeme

The son of Colonel Henry Aitken Cherry, Northumberland Fusiliers, and Mrs Cherry, of 'The Heath', Upton by Severn, Worcestershire, he was born on 22 March 1886. Educated at Charterhouse (1899-1904), and at the Royal Military Academy, Woolwich. Gazetted Second Lieutenant to the Royal Artillery on 7 October 1907. By the time war came in August 1914, Cherry had attained the rank of Captain and was, shortly afterwards on 7 October 1914, formally gazetted an ADC. He had married by this time and had set up home with his wife in Folkestone. As an Artillery officer with Staff duties, he had a professional interest in aviation matters and, deciding to extend his involvement, gained his Royal Aero Club Certificate (Number 1253) on 30 April 1915. He was formally seconded to the RFC in May 1915 and, following further training in the UK with 9 Squadron and a stint at the CFS, Upavon, he was given his 'Wings' and sent to 25 Squadron in September 1915, before accompanying that FE2b-equipped unit to France as a 'founder member' on 20 February 1916. Not surprisingly in view of his maturity and military experience, he advanced rapidly through to Flight Commander, gazetted 16 March 1916, to Major and Squadron Commander. He continued to command '25' throughout the Somme battles and on to the Arras offensive, before finally returning to the Home Establishment on 4 June 1917. His MC was announced in the New Year *London Gazette* of 1 January 1917 (no citation). Although no formal citation was published in the *Gazette*, research has unearthed the original recommendation for the award: 'T/Maj R G Cherry. For exceptional good service and continued devotion to duty during the last six months. As officer commanding a fighting squadron he has, by the personal interest he always takes in all details of his command and the example he has shown his pilots in the air, helped to gain that moral ascendancy over hostile aircraft that his Squadron undoubtedly possesses'.

Cherry was also recommended to receive the Russian Order of St Stanislaus, 3rd Class, with Swords, on 18 August 1916, which was formally sanctioned and announced in the *London Gazette* of 15 February 1917. Posted to Eastern Wing HD, on 28 August 1917, he was promoted to Lieutenant Colonel on 9 October following. Cherry was injured in an aero accident on 29 November 1917. Once recovered, his next posting was to 50 Wing, RFC, on 25 February 1918, before moving, just after the war on 16 November 1918, to 13 Group, RAF. Lieutenant Colonel Cherry finally relinquished his commission on 12 September 1919.

CHICK, John Stanley

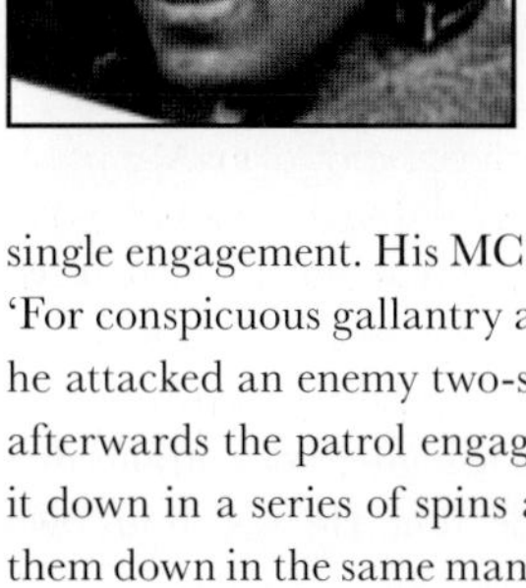

From Pontardawe in Wales, he was born on 22 September 1897. When war came in August 1914, he immediately enlisted as a motor-cycle despatch rider (Number 72484), Royal Engineers, going to France for the first time, with the rank of Corporal, on 29 October 1914, thus earning the 1914 Star. Picked out for a commission, he was gazetted Second Lieutenant to the RFC on 3 May 1917. Gained his Royal Aero Club Certificate (Number 4735) shortly afterwards on 27 May. His formal pilot training duly completed, he was confirmed and gazetted Flying Officer on 25 June following. He was sent out to the BF2b-equipped 11 Squadron in France, shortly after qualifying for his 'Wings'. Chick achieved 16 victories between 1 January and 15 May 1918, including, on 12 March, in company with Second Lieutenant Percy Douglas no less than five enemy machines sent down out of control in a single engagement. His MC, with its outstanding citation, was announced in the *London Gazette* of 13 May 1918: 'For conspicuous gallantry and devotion to duty. While leading a patrol of four machines over the enemy lines, he attacked an enemy two-seater machine, which his Observer drove down completely out of control. Shortly afterwards the patrol engaged nineteen enemy machines; he dived on to the upper-most machine, and drove it down in a series of spins and side-slips completely out of control. He then attacked two others and brought them down in the same manner, while his Observer drove down another out of control. On another occasion his formation, consisting of five machines, attacked twenty-five enemy aeroplanes. He destroyed one of the enemy, and drove down another out of control. He set a magnificent example of courage and skill'.

His tour with '11', and, indeed, his operational career, was curtailed when he was injured in a crash on 20 June 1918. Staying on in the RAF after the war, he flew with the RAF Acrobatic Team in 1923, 1929 and 1930. His expertise as a Pilot was acknowledged with the award of an Air Force Cross in 1926. He had attained the rank of Wing Commander by 1939, when the Second World War came. John Chick was Officer Commanding, RAF Luqa, during the siege of Malta in 1942. Wing Commander Johnny Chick died at Essex County Hospital, Colchester, on 21 January 1960.

CHIDLAW-ROBERTS, Robert Leslie

Born in May 1896. He graduated from the Royal Military College, Sandhurst, to be gazetted Second Lieutenant to a Regular Army battalion of the Hampshire Regiment on 16 June 1915. Seconded almost immediately to the RFC, he trained as an Observer and served as such with 2 Squadron in France. Training next as a Pilot, he gained his Royal Aero Club Certificate (Number 2527) on 23 January 1916. His formal training duly completed, he was confirmed and gazetted Flying Officer on 21 April following. He was sent out to 18 Squadron and served with that unit, mainly flying by night, for eight months before being posted to the SE5As of 60 Squadron in August 1917. Chidlaw-Roberts achieved nine victories with '60' between 14 September 1917 and 9 January 1918. The second of these victories, on 16 September 1917, was over Leutnant Alfred Bauer of Jasta 17, and only a week later, he was heavily involved in the famous aerial battle that culminated with the German Ace, Werner Voss, going down to his death. Voss left his mark on Chidlaw-Roberts SE5A by shooting holes in its rudder. Chidlaw-Robert's MC was announced in the *London Gazette* of 4 February 1918, details in the *Gazette* of 9 July 1918: 'For conspicuous gallantry and devotion to duty. He constantly attacked superior numbers of enemy aeroplanes. On one occasion he repeatedly attacked five enemy machines, diving among them and attacking each in turn at short ranges. On three other occasions he brought down enemy machines. He showed great skill and courage'.

On 9 January 1918, Chidlaw-Roberts also shared in the final battle and demise of the great Max Muller, CO, Jasta 'Boelcke', and an Ace with 36 victories. Sent home for a rest shortly after the fight with Muller, he instructed at 28 TS, before returning to France in the last summer of the war, this time to command 'A' Flight, 40 Squadron. The last of his ten victories was registered against a kite balloon, sent down under his guns on 29 September 1918. He would, however, continue operational flying during the Allied Intervention in Russia in 1919. Chidlaw-Roberts served again in the RAF in the Second World War. He died at his home near Winchester on 1 June 1989.

CHILD, Arthur James

A Staff, not a flying, award

The son of Mr and Mrs J T Child of Highgate, London, he was born on 19 April 1888. Educated at Marlborough (1901-05), and at University College, London, from where he graduated BSc. A pre-war volunteer, he enlisted as a Private soldier into 28 Battalion, London Regiment (Artists Rifles) and had, by 4 August 1914, when he was mobilised, attained the rank of Sergeant. A prime candidate for a commission, he was gazetted Second Lieutenant to the Artists Rifles on 17 October 1914. He remained in England, helping to train the high-grade entrants into his regiment – the Artists Rifles being, to all intents and purposes, an Officer Cadet unit. He was, at his own request, seconded to the RFC in the late summer of 1915. Having trained as an Observer, he was sent out as such to 8 Squadron. In the course of research, a previously unpublished recommendation for a Mention in Despatches he received around this time has been unearthed: '11 March 1916 - 8 Squadron. For continuous good work as an Observer from 15 September 1915 to 26 January 1916. On 29 December 1915 when on reconnaissance duty escorted by another machine, they were attacked by six Fokkers. The escort machine was immediately shot down and was followed by two of the hostile machines. One of the remainder was driven off, the other three kept up the attack for 13 minutes. Both machine-guns being temporarily out of order the pilot dived to within 20 feet of the ground and the reconnaissance was continued from that height. Lieut Child managed to get one of the machine-guns into working order again and the fight was kept up with the hostile machines till they finally gave it up about a mile from the line'.

Child's Pilot in this incident was William Sholto Douglas (qv). Their BE2c, '4087', and another, '2039', crewed by Second Lieutenant D A Glen and Sergeant E Jones, were attacked by a formation of Fokkers led by Oswald Boelcke, and including Immelmann and Leffers. '2039' was sent down, with David Glen killed and Jones taken as prisoners-of-war. Considering the quality of their opposition, it was nothing short of a miracle that Sholto Douglas and Arthur Child not only escaped with their lives, but were also able to give such a good account of themselves. What is difficult to understand, is why Sholto Douglas should receive the MC for this action, whilst Child was rewarded with only a Mention in Despatches. Progressing into Staff and technical work, Child was eventually awarded an MC in the New Year *London Gazette* of 1 January 1918 (no citation). Although no citation was published in the *Gazette*, research has unearthed the original recommendation for the award: 'Has served in the RFC since September 1916. During the past eight months he has been Brigade Major to this Brigade. His first hand knowledge of aviation no less than his zeal and tact, has enabled him to carry out his many and varied duties in a highly efficient manner. His responsibilities are great and cover a very wide-range of subjects. He has been a very real help during the period of great activities'.

Arthur Child had attained the rank of Lieutenant Colonel, when he was made an OBE in the *London Gazette* of 3 June 1919. The Italians admitted him a Cavaliere, Order of St Maurice and St Lazarus, in the same year. He lived, in the 1930s and beyond, at 'Heathbourne', Bushey Heath.

CHILD, James Martin

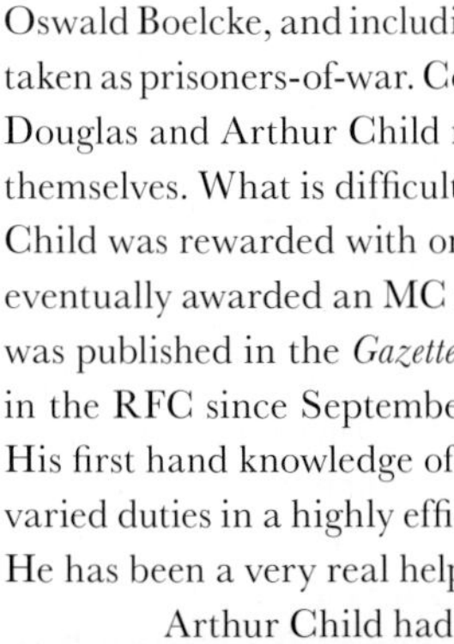

The son of Accountant, Tylney Harris Child and Mrs Child, of 83 Kings Road, Leytonstone, Essex, he was born on 20 October 1893. Educated at Leyton County High School, Essex. After leaving school, he emigrated to Canada, entering the service of the Canadian Bank of Commerce on 27 November 1912. When the war came he was employed at the Oak Bay Avenue, Victoria, British Columbia, branch of the bank, and it was from there that he enlisted as a Private soldier on 20 November 1914, for service with 2 Canadian Overseas Contingent. Once in England, he was picked out for a commission and gazetted Second Lieutenant to 13 Battalion, Durham Light Infantry, on 3 March 1915. Child would subsequently, however, be given a permanent commission into a Regular Army battalion of the Manchester Regiment. Seconded to the RFC, gained his Royal Aero Club Certificate (Number 2377) on 31 January 1916. His formal pilot training duly completed, he was confirmed and gazetted Flying Officer on 2 March following. He served briefly with 4 Squadron, before joining 19 Squadron in July 1916, initially flying BE12s and later Spads. He achieved three victories with '19', and was promoted to A/Captain and Mentioned in Despatches for his efforts. After a rest, he next joined the newly formed SE5A-equipped 84 Squadron as a Flight Commander, gaining a further five victories between 21 October and 30 November 1917. His MC was announced in the *London Gazette* of 9 July 1918: 'For conspicuous gallantry and devotion to duty. While leading a patrol he encountered four enemy scouts, one of which he destroyed. On another occasion he attacked one of two enemy two-seater machines which he encountered over the enemy's lines. He disabled the machine and skilfully turned it towards our own lines, where the enemy pilot was forced to land and he and his Observer were taken prisoner. On another occasion he attacked five enemy scouts, one of which he destroyed. He showed the greatest judgment and determination'.

To impress a number of Italian Generals and dignitaries visiting the Western Front, the RFC was asked by the French authorities to provide an exhibition flight. Captain Child was chosen to perform and subsequently warmly congratulated for his efficiency and skill. He also received, for his considerable efforts, the Order of Leopold (Chevalier) and the Croix de Guerre from the Belgians. His tour with '84' completed in February 1918, he returned to England to instruct and to take a well-earned rest. Tragically, James Child was killed in a training accident at Turnberry, on 23 August 1918. His brother, Jack, was also killed in a flying accident on 3 November 1918, age 29. James and Jack are both buried in Chingford Mount Cemetery, Essex.

CHIPPINDALE, Hugh Arthur

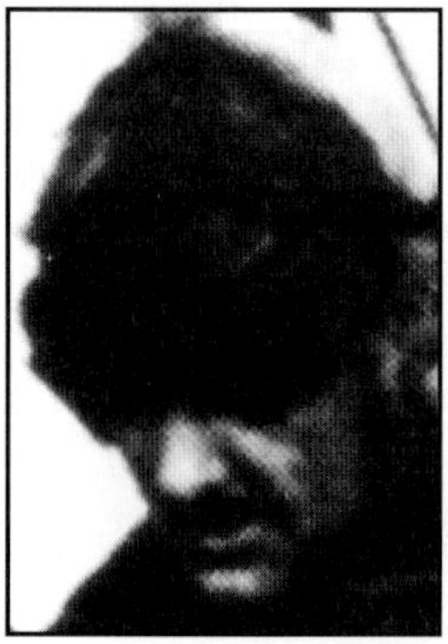

Originally from Leeds, he was gazetted Second Lieutenant to the Sheffield-based 3 West Riding Ammunition Column, Royal Field Artillery (TF), on 7 September 1915. Following service with the RFA in France, he was seconded to the RFC. Having trained as an Observer, he joined the RE8-equipped 15 Squadron on 30 December 1917. He fought with '15' through the fraught days of the German spring offensive which commenced on 21 March 1918. On 25 March 1918, Chippindale and his Pilot, Second Lieutenant Hobbs (qv), were attacked by a formation of enemy scouts, their number variously estimated at seven and eleven. Fighting furiously, they succeeded in sending one of the enemy down in flames, before making good their escape. Both men received the MC for their resource and gallantry on this day, *London Gazette* of 22 June 1918: 'For conspicuous gallantry and devotion to duty. While carrying out a reconnaissance, he and his pilot were attacked by eleven hostile scouts. They succeeded in destroying one of these, drove off the remainder, and then completed the reconnaissance. Later, when information was urgently needed during an engagement, he and his pilot carried out a most successful reconnaissance, flying at a very low altitude under continuous rifle and machine-gun fire from the ground. They located hostile batteries, and enabled very effective counter-battery work to be carried out, and also engaged ground targets with bombs and machine-gun fire. He showed splendid courage and skill'.

His tour with '15' completed on 12 June 1918, Chippindale returned to the Home Establishment. His operational flying over for the remainder of the war, he was finally demobilised from the RAF on 29 January 1919. Hugh Chippindale died in Bridlington, Yorkshire, on 11 April 1977.

CHRISTIE, Malcolm Grahame

The third son of Banker, J A Christie and Mrs Christie, of 'The Chantry', Stanmore, he was born in Edgbaston, Warwickshire, in 1881. Educated at Leamington Preparatory School, at Malvern College (1894-97), and at Aachen University, from where he graduated, with first class honours, DSc (Doktor-Ingenieur). When the war came he was an Associate Professor at the Imperial College of Science, Kensington, London. Determined to join the flying service, he gained his Royal Aero Club Certificate (Number 954) on 27 October 1914. Next he was gazetted a probationary Second Lieutenant to the RFC on 20 November 1914, before being confirmed in that rank on 4 February 1915. His formal pilot training completed, he was confirmed and gazetted

Flying Officer on 24 April following. He accompanied 12 Squadron to France as a 'founder member' on 6 September 1915, subsequently flying mainly RE7s on reconnaissance and artillery observation. His MC was announced in the Birthday Honours *London Gazette* of 3 June 1916 (no citation). Although no formal citation was published in the *Gazette*, research has unearthed the original recommendation for the award: 'This officer has shown consistent good work and zeal as a Flight Commander with the squadron at Headquarters. He has set an excellent example of untiring energy and drive during the past Winter. He has also done much useful work over the lines'.

After returning to the UK, Christie served on Home Defence duties, energetically commanding 50 Squadron with the rank of Major, from the latter part of 1916. Christie it was who introduced the first specialised colour scheme for night fighters. He was awarded the Distinguished Service Order in the *London Gazette* of 24 January 1917. Christie formed 100 Squadron on 23 February 1917, and commanded the unit until 10 December 1917. Promoted to Lieutenant Colonel, he next commanded 49 Wing in the UK in 1918, and later was Commandant of No 2 School of Bombing and Aerial Navigation, at Andover. Created CMG in 1919. Staying on in the RAF, his many subsequent appointments, honours and promotions included: Air Attaché in Washington, 1922 to 1926 and, similarly, in Berlin, 1927 to 1930. Christie retired from the RAF with the rank of Group Captain, in 1930. Enthusiastically entering the business world, he became the General Manager and a Director of the Otto Coke-Oven Company of Leeds, and President of the Otto Coking Corporation of New York. He was also an Honorary Lecturer at Leeds University. His publications included, 'The Nitrogen Compounds in Coal'. He lived at 58 Cranmer Court, Sloane Avenue, London, SW3. Group Captain Malcolm Christie died on 3 November 1971.

CLARKE, Arthur Ramsey Stanley – see Arthur Ramsey **STANLEY-CLARKE**

CLARKE, Edward Denman

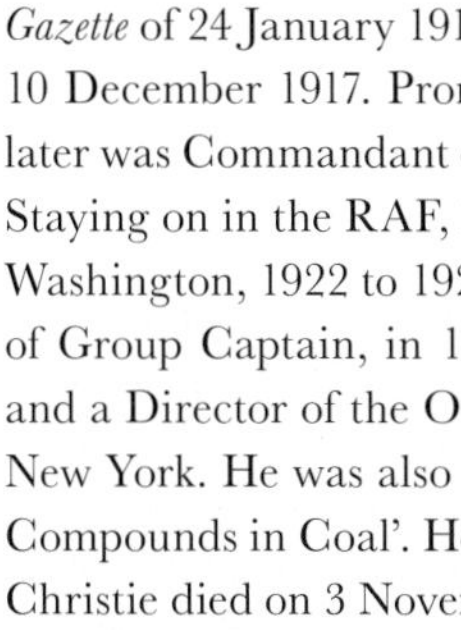

The son of Mr and Mrs Alexander F Clarke, of Midgham House, near Reading, Berkshire, he was born on 21 May 1898. Educated at Wixenford School, and at Eton. Gazetted Second Lieutenant to the RFC, via the Special Reserve, on 17 June 1916. His pilot training duly completed, he was confirmed and gazetted Flying Officer on 22 August following. Still only 18 years old, he was held back in the UK until 12 August 1917 when he joined 45 Squadron at the front, first flying Sopwith Strutters, before changing to Camels. Clarke achieved six victories between 23 August and 20 October 1917, before receiving a flesh wound to his left upper arm from ground fire on 26 October 1917. His MC was announced in the *London Gazette* of 17 December 1917, details in the *Gazette* of 23 April 1918: 'For conspicuous gallantry and devotion to duty. He has shot down five enemy machines. In an attack he repeatedly dived to within fifty feet of the enemy infantry, firing between 500 and 600 rounds. Though struck by a piece of shell, which wounded him in both arms and shattered both petrol tanks, he succeeded in gliding back behind our lines'.

Research has unearthed the original recommendation for this award, which was made by Brigadier General T I Webb-Bowen, on 30 October 1917, and is considerably more informative than is the published citation: 'This officer was posted to his squadron on 12 August 1917 and is only 19 years of age. He has shown considerable skill and daring. On 3 September 1917 he shot down an Albatros Scout in flames between Comines and Becelaere. On 20 September 1917 he destroyed another Albatros Scout at Passchendaele. On 29 September 1917 he destroyed an Albatros two-seater east of Zillebeke. On 23 August 1917, 14 September 1917 and 20 October 1917 he shot down enemy machines out of control. On the morning of 26 October 1917 he repeatedly dived down behind the German lines and within 50 feet of the enemy infantry east of Passchendaele firing between 500 and 600 rounds. When all his ammunition was spent on this occasion he was struck by a piece of shell which wounded him in the left arm and shattered both his petrol tanks. He was at this time at 500 feet being about to return. He just managed to glide back behind our front line and landed his machine intact in a shell hole'.

In March 1918, after recovering his fitness, he was posted to 3 TDS as an Instructor, never again to return to operational flying. Although he left the RAF in 1919, he still remained in the aviation industry. He worked in Canada from 1920 until 1935, living at 3738 Angus Drive, Vancouver, BC, before returning to the UK to join Saunders Roe Limited in 1936, living at 'Crossways', Rinstead, Isle of Wight. In the following year, he was appointed Managing Director of Saunders Roe, a position he held until his retirement in 1960. He was appointed CBE in 1956. He married, in 1946, Maureen Cowle Leitch, with whom he had two sons and one daughter. Edward Denman Clarke died on 5 September 1966, at the Royal Isle of Wight County Hospital.

CLARKE, Sidney Herbert

The son of Stockbroker, Charles Herbert Clarke and Edith Mary Clarke, of 'Langsmead', Pyrford, Woking, Surrey (later, 'Highcroft', 1 Parkside Avenue, Wimbledon Common, London), he was born in Islington, London, on 15 December 1895. Educated at Marlborough College (1910-14), where he was a member of the OTC, and at Caius College, Cambridge. When war came, he interrupted his studies at Cambridge to volunteer, and was almost immediately gazetted Second Lieutenant to 3 Battalion, Wiltshire Regiment, on 15 August 1914. Still only 18 years old, he was kept back in England. Seconded to the RFC early in 1916, he trained as an Observer and, in March, was sent as a Probationary to the FE2b-equipped 22 Squadron, then stationed at Gosport. Clarke subsequently accompanied '22' to France as a 'founder member' on 1 April 1916. On 25 August 1916, Clarke and his Pilot, Captain J H S Tyssen (qv), in FE2b, '4289', were forced to land after their fuel tank was holed during an aerial combat over Combles with two Fokkers. Their tracers were seen to strike one of the enemy aircraft. Clarke's first MC was announced in the *London Gazette* of 14 November 1916: 'For conspicuous skill and gallantry. He has done fine photographic work, often working far over the lines and being attacked by superior numbers of enemy machines. On one occasion, with another officer, he brought down one of five enemy machines which had attacked him'.

His tour with '22' completed, he returned to the UK and commenced pilot training. Having gained his full 'Wings', he served briefly with 16 RS, before going out to France again, this time to join 16 Squadron (RE8s) on 28 April 1917. Advancement to Flight Commander and A/Captain came on 10 July 1917. On 2 September 1917, Clarke was at 1 Aircraft Depot, when that establishment was subjected to a heavy bombing raid by enemy aircraft. He was mortally wounded by an exploding bomb, and taken to 10 Stationery Hospital, where he died within hours. The Bar to his MC was posthumously announced in the *London Gazette* of 26 September 1917, details in the *Gazette* of 9 January 1918 : 'For conspicuous gallantry and devotion to duty in carrying out contact patrols, reconnaissances, and artillery observation. He has frequently engaged bodies of hostile infantry at low altitudes, causing them heavy casualties, and although continually subjected to attacks from hostile machines and heavy machine-gun fire from the ground, which considerably damaged his machine, he completed his work in every case. On one occasion he took some exceptionally successful and valuable photographs of the enemy's wire from a height of 1,200 feet, and has also carried out a number of successful shoots in co-operation with artillery'.

Sidney Clarke is buried in Longuenesse (St Omer) Souvenir Cemetery, France.

CLAYSON, Percy Jack

The son of John Henry Clayson and Georgiana Clayson (née Darby), of 77 Kitto Road, Deptford, London, he was born in Peckham on 7 June 1896. Clayson volunteered for service with the RNAS when war came. Going to France in December 1914, he served there as an mechanic for 30 months. Picked out for a commission, he was gazetted Second Lieutenant to the RFC on 30 September 1917, the same day that he gained his Royal Aero Club Certificate (Number 5617), and was confirmed and gazetted Flying Officer. Clayson joined 1 Squadron (Nieuport Scouts) at the front on 31 October 1917. His squadron re-equipped with SE5As in January 1918, and after a slow start, Clayson's successes mounted at an incredible rate. He achieved 29 victories between 16 February and 14 July 1918, including a 'treble' and three 'doubles' on single days. Unsurprisingly, he was promoted to Captain and Flight Commander in April 1918. On 9 June 1918, Clayson and his patrol forced Gefreiter Preiss of Jasta 14 to land, where he was taken into captivity. His MC was announced in the *London Gazette* of 22 June 1918: 'For conspicuous gallantry and devotion to duty. When on low flying offensive patrol, he engaged an enemy scout and shot it down, with the result that it crashed to earth. He has brought down several enemy machines, one of which he forced to land in our lines, and has engaged massed enemy troops and transport from very low altitudes with machine-gun fire, inflicting heavy casualties. He has displayed the most marked determination, courage and skill'.

The award of the newly introduced Distinguished Flying Cross followed in the *London Gazette* of 2 July 1918, this for leading his patrols with great skill and gallantry. He was sent home to rest on 3 August, seeing out the remainder of the war as an Instructor. Clayson stayed on in the RAF after the war, flying with 6 and 70 Squadrons in the 1920s. He served again in the Second World War. 'Pip' Clayson died in Glasgow on 9 December 1970.

NB: His medals were offered for sale by Christie's (lot 215) on 30 April 1991: MC, Distinguished Flying Cross, 1914-15 Star (AM1 RNAS), *British War Medal 1914-20, Victory Medal 1914-19* (Capt RAF), *Defence Medal 1939-45, and War Medal 1939-45.*

CLEAR, Edwin Arnold

The son of Railway Car Attendant, Ernest William Clear, and Amy Alice Clear (née Madell), of 76 Jackson Road, East Barnet, Hertfordshire, he was born on 28 May 1896. Enlisting into the RFC, he served in the Middle East for 20 months as a Mechanic, before he was selected as potential officer material and given flying training in Egypt. Gazetted Second Lieutenant to the RFC on 28 April 1917. His formal pilot training duly completed, he was confirmed and gazetted Flying Officer on 27 June following. Returning to the UK in September 1917, he was posted to the SE5A-equipped 84 Squadron on 19 October following, '84' having arrived in France only the month before. Clear achieved 12 victories between 29 January and 28 May 1918, including three 'doubles' on single days. All 12 of his 'kills' were confirmed as destroyed. His MC was announced in the *London Gazette* of 22 June 1918: 'For conspicuous gallantry and devotion to duty. During an encounter between one of our patrols and nine enemy machines, he observed an enemy tri-plane which was about to attack his patrol leader from the rear. He at once dived to the attack, firing on the enemy machine, which turned to avoid him and collided with an enemy scout. The two enemy machines crashed to earth locked together. On the following day, during an engagement between twelve of our machines and about thirty enemy scouts, he attacked an enemy tri-plane which he observed beneath him. He dived after it, and following it down, eventually destroyed it. He has destroyed seven enemy machines, and has proved himself a most enterprising and courageous pilot'.

His tour with '84' completed, he returned to the Home Establishment and instructing duties on 15 June 1918. He was given a permanent commission in 1919, and stayed on in the RAF until ill-health forced his retirement, with the rank of Flying Officer, in January 1935.

CLEAVER, Charles Thornton

The son of Mr and Mrs R S Cleaver, of 10 Hayman's Green, West Derby, Liverpool, he was born on 12 November 1893. Educated at Repton School (1908-11). He was working in the cotton trade in Liverpool when war came, and he immediately enlisted as a Private soldier (Number 3218) into 10 (Scottish) Battalion, King's Liverpool Regiment (Liverpool Scottish) (TF), in August 1914. After training in Edinburgh and Tunbridge Wells, he accompanied the original Liverpool Scottish contingent to France on 1 November 1914, thus earning the 1914 Star. He served in the trenches for some months and was slightly wounded, before being selected as an officer candidate. This selection probably saved his life, for it meant that he was elsewhere when the Liverpool Scottish fought its first major action at Hooge on 16 June 1915, sustaining many casualties. Having trained as an Observer, he was gazetted Second Lieutenant to the RFC, via the Special Lists, on 21 June 1915, joining 3 Squadron as a Probationary in the same month. His 'apprenticeship' satisfactorily completed, he was confirmed and gazetted Flying Officer (Observer) on 22 November following. Cleaver earned a reputation as an exceptional Observer Officer, surviving – just – the Fokker menace in late 1915, and continuing on throughout the remaining years of the war. On 5 August 1915, Cleaver and his Pilot, Lieutenant C A Ridley (qv), narrowly escaped with their lives when their FE2a, '4227', suffered up to 50 hits from the machine gun of an enemy aircraft. On 11 October 1915, Cleaver and his Pilot of the day, Captain M Barratt, celebrated a shared victory over an enemy Albatros by recklessly landing alongside the downed machine. He was wounded in the air by a rifle bullet in the foot on 9 October 1916, and was laid up in hospital when his first MC was announced in the *London Gazette* of 20 October 1916: 'For conspicuous gallantry and skill. He has shown great dash in contact patrol work at very low altitudes. On one occasion he obtained good information of a trench flying at 500 ft under heavy fire from rifles and machine guns'.

Once recovered, he returned to 3 Squadron, and was wounded in the air again, and again by rifle fire from the ground, on 3 May 1917. A Bar to his MC, as a consequence of his gallantry on the occasion of his second wounding, came in the *London Gazette* of 18 June 1917: 'For conspicuous gallantry and devotion to duty. When flying at low altitude on reconnaissance patrol, he was wounded in the arm. He continued flying for some time, gaining most valuable information. On landing he insisted on being taken to Headquarters to impart the results of his reconnaissance'.

The wound in his arm healed, he returned yet again to France in July 1917 and served there until December 1918, winning, on 11 October, a Distinguished Flying Cross, *London Gazette* of 8 February 1919. Cleaver and his Pilot, Captain A F Peacey, were jointly awarded the Distinguished Flying Cross for 'a most daring and successful contact patrol flying at an average height of fifty feet in the face of extremely heavy machine-gun fire....'. The gallant Charles Cleaver left the RAF, via the Unemployed List, on 15 January 1919, returning to Liverpool and the cotton shipping business.

CLEMENT, Carleton Main

The son of the Hon. Justice W H P Clement and Mrs Elsie L Clement, of Toronto, Ontario and of Vancouver, British Columbia, Canada, he was born in Toronto, on 15 May 1896. Educated at Vancouver Public and High Schools, at Victoria College (1912-13) and at Toronto University He resigned his Militia commission to enlist as a Private soldier into 47 (BC) Battalion, CEF, going overseas in June 1915. After serving in the trenches, he was picked out for a commission and gazetted Second Lieutenant to the RFC, on 29 April 1916. He gained his Royal Aero Club Certificate (Number 2563) on 16 June 1915, and was confirmed and gazetted Flying Officer on the same day. He was sent out to 22 Squadron soon after qualifying for his 'Wings', and despite having to fly the near obsolete FE2b, still managed to accrue eight victories. He was promoted to A/Captain and Flight Commander on 26 December 1916. Research has unearthed a recommendation for the MC which, in the event, was not awarded: 'Brigadier General J H W Becke, DSO, commanding 4 Brigade, RFC : 'Festing 5 April 1917: For skill and determination. This officer has taken all the photographs of the Hindenburg Line opposite this front, a total of 200 negatives. This was completed in five flights. On each occasion his machine was attacked by hostile aircraft'. A handwritten note scribbled across this document, indicated that the GOC (General Trenchard), thought the deeds related were not up to the standard required for an 'Immediate Award', and hence it was disallowed. Clement was, however, Mentioned in Despatches at this time, and a Croix de Guerre avec Palme, was afterwards forthcoming from the French, *London Gazette* of 14 July 1917. After his squadron was re-equipped with Bristol Fighters in July 1917, Clement continued to accrue victories, adding a further six between 29 July and 12 August 1917, including four on a single day in company with Lieutenant R B Carter. On 19 August 1917, Clement and his Observer, fellow Canadian, Ralph Barr Carter, were killed in action during an offensive patrol over Langemarck, when their Bristol F2b, 'A7172', was hit by ground fire from Leutnant Böhner's Flakzug 99. Clement's MC was posthumously announced in the New Year *London Gazette* of 1 January 1918 (no citation). Although no formal citation appeared in the *Gazette*, research has unearthed the original recommendation for the award, and this one was approved by Trenchard: 'For consistent gallantry and skill as a leader of offensive patrols. Since the beginning of this year Captain Clement has continuously led his flight with great success, only losing two machines. On 12 August he shot down and destroyed a hostile machine. On 9 May he destroyed another hostile machine. He has in addition shot down five EA out of control. He has taken an active part in the destruction of four other EA. He has led many successful reconnaissances. The dash and spirit shown by this officer has been of the highest order and he has set a very fine example. Captain Clement was reported missing on 19 August 1917'.

Carleton Clement's remains were never found and hence he is commemorated on the Flying Services Memorial, Arras, France.

CLISDAL, John

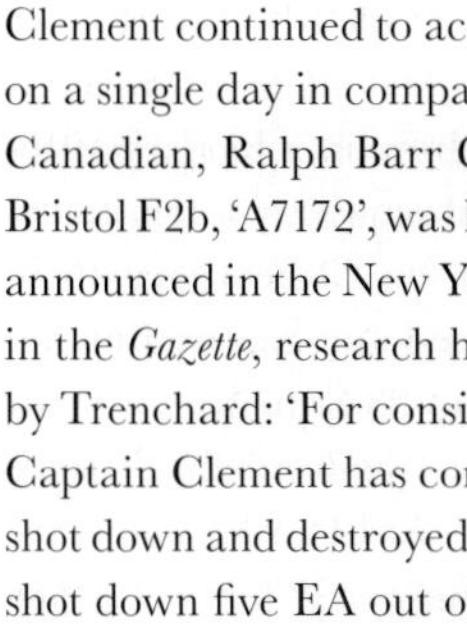

From Bangor, County Down, Ireland, he was born on 1 March 1883. He served first as a volunteer with the Imperial Yeomanry during the last year of the Boer War in 1902. Staying on in South Africa, he joined the Cape Mounted Rifles in 1904, initially as a Trooper. Clisdal was involved in resisting the Chief Bambata-led Zulu Rebellion in Natal in 1906 (Natal Medal 1906, with clasp, 1906). He was also present at Umtala in 1912, and was promoted to Sergeant in the following year. Arriving in the UK in the summer of 1915, he was promoted Lieutenant, South African Mounted Rifles on 31 July 1915 and was, on the same date, given a Lieutenancy, via the Special List, after requesting service with the RFC. As a preamble to that end, he secured his Royal

Aero Club Certificate (Number 1786) at Castle Bromwich on 24 September 1915. His formal pilot training duly completed, he was confirmed and gazetted Flying Officer on 6 December following. Sent to 26 (South African) Squadron in the same month, he accompanied that unit to Mombasa, East Africa, on 31 January 1916. Clisdal, promoted to A/Captain and Flight Commander on 22 November 1916, served in East Africa with '26' until 28 July 1917, when he was ordered back to the UK. His MC was announced in the 'Birthday Honours' *London Gazette* of 3 June 1917 (no citation).

Clisdal served out the war and beyond as an Instructor, eventually leaving the RAF with the rank of Captain, via the Unemployed List, on 9 August 1919. After returning to South Africa, he served, from 1922, with the South African Field Artillery, and the SAPGA, with the rank of Captain. In 1925, Clisdal was the Commander of the Royal Guard during a troop inspection in Cape Town by the Prince of Wales. John Clisdal died in Johannesburg, on 9 June 1939.

CLOETE, Dirk

The son of Mr and Mrs Louis Cloete, of 'Glen Kirk', Wynberg, near Cape Town, South Africa, he was born on 17 July 1888. Educated at the Diocesan College, Rondesbosch (1899-1901). Played cricket for Western Provinces in the match against the British Touring XI in 1910. After completing his education, he became a viniculturist, an active member of the burgeoning South African wine industry. After fighting with the South African forces in German South West Africa in the early months of the war, he arrived in the UK in the winter of 1915. Gazetted to the RFC, via the Special Reserve, on 13 December 1915. Having first trained as an Observer, he was sent to the FE2b-equipped 23 Squadron on 5 January 1916. After service on the Western Front as an Observer, he subsequently learnt to fly, gaining his Royal Aero Club Certificate (Number 2509) on 28 February 1916. His formal pilot training duly completed, he was confirmed and gazetted Flying Officer on 16 May following and immediately returned to 23 Squadron. On 20 May 1916, Cloete and his Observer, Corporal P Havens, in FE2b, '6351', shared in the squadron's first victory when an Aviatik that had been attacking his colleagues, Captain R N Adams (qv) and 1 AM D A R Chapman, was sent down to crash in Adinfer Wood. Cloete's MC was announced in the *London Gazette* of 27 July 1916: 'For conspicuous gallantry and skill. When one of our machines, piloted by Captain Adams, was engaged with six other machines, he dived into one of the enemy, drove it down out of control, and then assisted in driving away the remainder. Previously, when acting as Observer to Captain Adams, he brought down an enemy machine, which turned upside down'.

Eleven days later on 31 May, Cloete and his Observer of the day, Second Lieutenant C E Pither, in FE2b, '6354', were one of seven 23 Squadron machines that fought out a frantic and damaging battle against three Fokkers. Although greatly outnumbering the German machines, the FE2b aircraft were frankly outclassed. Sent back to the UK in September 1916, he suffered a prolonged period of ill-health, and following a series of hospitalisations, was eventually posted, on 8 August 1917, to the School of Special Flying at Gosport as an Instructor. He next commanded training at Shoreham, although his doctors continued to limit his flying to heights below a ceiling of 3,000 feet. His services as an Instructor were duly recognised by the award of an Air Force Cross, *London Gazette* of 3 June 1919. Cloete was also Mentioned in Despatches on two occasions during the Great War. Staying on in the RAF after the war, he served with 114 Squadron in India with the rank of Major. Seconded to the South African Air Force on 21 July 1921, he served mainly as an Instructor with that force until 1923, although he did assist in the operations against the insurgent miners in the Rand Revolt. Promoted Squadron Leader, RAF, on 1 January 1926, he commanded 9 Squadron until 18 June 1926. Retiring from the RAF in 1927, he settled in Southern Rhodesia, farming tobacco. An appointment as Air Advisor to the Southern Rhodesian Government in 1928, was followed by others as Staff Officer, Air Service, and Director of Civil Aviation, Southern Rhodesia, and Registrar of Aircraft, Northern Rhodesia. Cloete served again with the RAF in the Second World War. Based in South Africa from 1940 to 1942, he was next sent to the UK, where he saw out the remainder of the war. Returning to South Africa in 1946, he was appointed a Member of the Civil Aviation Council, and remained so until his retirement in 1950. He died in Cape Town on 15 May 1970. Remarkably, and for some unknown reason, his name remained in the *RAF Lists* until 1980.

COATES, William Alexander

A Staff, not a flying, award

From Melborne, Australia, he was born on 3 March 1887. He was living with his wife, Florence, in Swan Street, Burnley, Victoria, and working as a Machinist, when he enlisted into 1 Squadron, AFC, at Laverton on 25 June 1915. Quickly promoted to Sergeant, Air Mechanic, he eventually embarked at Melbourne aboard the SS *Orsova*, on 16 March 1916, bound for the Middle East. Once in Egypt, he was picked out for a commission and gazetted Second Lieutenant to the RFC on 11 June 1916. Sent next to Aboukir for flying instruction, his progress was delayed somewhat by illness. Once recovered, he was confirmed and gazetted Flying Officer on 21 December 1916. Sent to 67 (Australian) Squadron, on 31 December 1916, he subsequently became attached to 57 RS, RFC, from 4 January 1917, but fell sick once more in the following February. Recovered again, he joined 'C' Flight, 1 AFC Squadron, in April 1917. Presumably because of his indifferent health, he came off flying and was appointed an Equipment Officer on 8 August 1917. His tour in the Middle East completed, he left Alexandria for England aboard the SS *Indarra* on 20 February 1918. His MC was announced in the *London Gazette* of 11 April 1918 (no citation), although the *Gazette* makes clear that it was for: '....military operations culminating in the capture of Jerusalem'. The recommendation for the award reads: 'For untiring devotion to duty and ability in organisation. The work of this officer has been largely responsible for the high standard of efficiency and valuable achievements of his Squadron'.

Coates was promoted to A/Captain on 1 June 1918. He was next appointed Commanding Officer of the Aeroplane Repair Section at Upavon from 1 June 1918, before a posting to the Headquarters of the AIF in London came on 23 September 1919. Coates was promoted to A/Major and appointed a Liaison Officer with the Air Ministry on 1 February 1920 and was awarded the Air Force Cross in the same year. He returned to Australia in 1921, and was eventually accepted into the RAAF as a Flight Lieutenant at 1 Aircraft Depot, Laverton, in 1922. He finally left the RAAF on 17 March 1923. Coates served again in the Second World War, this time as a Captain with 17 Garrison Battalion, Australian Military Forces, from June 1941 until 26 August 1943.

COCHRANE, James Aikman

From Glasgow, he was born on 24 June 1888. He worked as a Civil Engineer from 1913 to 1914, before enlisting as a Private soldier (Number S/14823) into 7 Battalion, Cameron Highlanders, when the war came. Accompanying his battalion to France on 9 July 1915, he fought in the trenches and was wounded on Hill 70, during the first day of the Battle of Loos, 25 September 1915. Picked out for a commission, he was gazetted Second Lieutenant to 4 Battalion, Royal Scots Fusiliers (TF). Next, he successfully sought secondment to the Kite Balloon Service, RFC, which came in the autumn of 1916. Cochrane was gazetted BC Commander, on 16 June 1917, his MC being announced in the New Year *London Gazette* of 1 January 1918 (no citation). Although no formal citation was published in the *Gazette*, research has uncovered the original recommendation for the award: '6 October 1917 For the last year he has shown himself a most capable Officer, both on the ground and in the balloon. He has himself carried out much valuable work in observing for the artillery, and the sections under his command have been raised to a very high standard of efficiency. He had always set a splendid example'.

Cochrane was also awarded the Order of Leopold by the Belgians, and the Croix de Guerre avec Palme by the French. Coates subsequently commanded, with the rank of Major, 8 Kite BC in 1918.

COCHRAN-PATRICK, William John Charles Kennedy

The son of Sir Neil James and Lady Eleanora Kennedy Cochran-Patrick, he was born in Edinburgh on 25 May 1896. Educated at Wellington College (1909-13), where he was Head of House, at Trinity College, Cambridge, and at the Royal Military College, Sandhurst. Gazetted Second Lieutenant to a Regular Army battalion of the Rifle Brigade on 15 February 1915. Gained his Royal Aero Club Certificate (Number 1199) on 27 April 1915, which helped him to secure a secondment to the flying service. His formal training duly completed, he was confirmed and gazetted Flying Officer on 11 June following. A naturally gifted Pilot, he was appointed an Instructor at the CFS before going out to 1 Aircraft Depot, St Omer France, as a Test Pilot on Christmas Eve 1915. It was from St Omer, that he won the first of his MCs. On 26 April 1916, flying a Nieuport powered by a 110hp Le Rhone engine with a Lewis gun with a bowden wire trigger fixed to the top plane, he spotted the anti-aircraft defences at St Omer shooting at something above him. Circling up and round, he got behind and below the offending LVG and opened fire at 200 yards. Having expended one drum without effect, he had to change to another and circled away to give himself the time to do so. Attacking again, this time at closer range, another drum went the way of the first. Nothing daunted, he dropped away to re-arm yet again and then came back for a third attempt. This time it took just 20 rounds to send the enemy machine down in a spiralling nosedive, its engine full on. The LVG fell near to Flêtre, its Pilot and Observer both having been killed in the air prior to the crash. C-P landed alongside his victim to confirm this, the first of his eventual 21 victories. His MC was announced in the *London Gazette* of 16 May 1916: 'For conspicuous skill and determination. He climbed and attacked an enemy machine at 14,000 feet, and although he failed in his first and second attacks, he went for it again a third time, shot both pilot and observer and brought it down. He followed it down and landed alongside'.

From St Omer, he was sent to 70 Squadron (Sopwith Strutters) then commanded by Major A W Tedder, of later eminence. C-P's next two victories were particularly desperate affairs, involving the death of his Observer on both occasions. On 14 September 1916, C-P and his Observer, Irishman Second Lieutenant Edward William Burke, in Sopwith Strutter, 'A897', were involved in an aerial combat with elements of Jasta 2, including Oswald Boelcke himself. C-P managed to get the damaged 'Strutter' down safely, but the 18 year old Burke had been killed in the air. Despite this trauma, C-P was back up on the following day, 15 September 1916. A significant day in that it heralded the third phase of the Battle of the Somme, when tanks were used for the first time in the history of warfare. It was not a good day for 70 Squadron. They were again confronted by the peerless Oswald Boelcke and Jasta 2. Although giving a good account of themselves in driving down three of the enemy machines, '70' lost some good men on that day. C-P and his Observer, Captain Ferdinand Goncalves Gelday, Northumberland Fusiliers attached RFC, in Sopwith Strutter, 'A1913', were badly shot about and forced to land at the first opportunity. Gelday, from Bury, Lancashire, was mortally wounded in the air and died in hospital later the same day. In the spring of 1917, C-P was promoted to Captain and Flight Commander, and sent to the Spad VII-equipped 23 Squadron. A highly effective Scout-Pilot, he gained a further 18 victories between 22 April and 16 July 1917, becoming one of the first RFC Aces to exceed 20 victories. The Bar to his MC came in the *London Gazette* of 16 August 1917: 'For conspicuous gallantry in attacking hostile aircraft. Within two months he brought down two hostile machines in flames, and four others completely out of control. In addition he has driven several others down in a damaged condition'.

In the following month, he was awarded the Distinguished Service Order, *London Gazette* of 17 September 1917. He was also Mentioned in Despatches on two occasions during this period. In August 1917, he was promoted to Major and sent to command 60 Squadron. Next, on 29 December 1917, C-P was appointed to a Staff position with the Training Division of the Air Board at the Air Ministry, London. He married, firstly in 1918, Ella Cross, and, secondly in 1924, Naterlie Tanner, with whom he had one son. His final appointment, shortly before his retirement from the RAF in 1919, was to 1 Aircraft Depot, St Omer, where it had all started. In his civilian life, he made a career in Aerial Survey, still a comparatively new discipline. He was directly and personally involved in the aerial surveys of British Guiana and Venezuela in 1921, of Burma in 1924-25, of the Upper Zambesi River in 1927, of Iraq in 1928, of Rhodesia in 1930 and of South Africa in 1932. Elected to Fellowships of the Royal Aeronautical Society and of the Royal Geographical Society. William John Charles Kennedy Cochran-Patrick was killed piloting a De Havilland Dragon at Baragwanath Airport, near Johannesburg, South Africa, on 26 September 1933. Bound for Livingstone, Rhodesia, with Sir Michael Oppenheimer Bt, a famous financier and adventurer as his passenger, the Dragon he was piloting had barely reached 250 feet when it stalled and hurtled straight into the ground, erupting into a huge fireball. He was 37.

COCK, Geoffrey Hornblower

The second son of Tanner, James Cock, and Adeline Anna Cock (née Oldroyd), of Kingsland, St Julian, Salop, he was born in Shrewsbury, Salop, on 7 January 1896. Cock was a Day Boy at Shrewsbury School from 1909 to 1912. He enlisted as a Private soldier (Number 6099) into 28 Battalion, London Regiment (Artists Rifles), late in 1915, before being gazetted Second Lieutenant to the RFC, via the General List, on 2 June 1916. His pilot training duly completed, he was confirmed and gazetted Flying Officer on 7 September 1916. Cock accompanied the Sopwith Strutter-equipped 45 Squadron to France as a 'founder member' on 12 October 1916. By May 1917, he was an experienced operational Pilot, commanding 'B' Flight of his squadron. The award of an MC was announced in the *London Gazette* of 26 July 1917 with, seemingly, a low-level strafing incident that occurred on the Gapaard-Oostaverne Road on 6 June 1917, particularly impressing his superiors: 'For conspicuous gallantry and devotion to duty. On many occasions he showed great courage and determination in attacking and destroying hostile aircraft, and in dispersing hostile troops from a low altitude. His skill as a formation leader has set a fine example to other pilots of his squadron'.

The most successful of the Strutter Pilots, he had flown 97 sorties and gained 13 victories by 22 July 1917, when he and his Observer, Lieutenant M Moore, in Strutter, 'B2576', were shot down into the German lines by Hauptmann Willi Reinhard of Jasta 11, the first of the German Ace's eventual 20 victories. Despite a gallant but failed attempt at escape for which he was Mentioned in Despatches, Cock remained a prisoner until finally repatriated in December 1918. Staying on in the RAF after the war, he commanded 9 Squadron at Boscombe Down in 1935. After service in Egypt and Iraq, he eventually retired with the rank of Group Captain on 1 July 1943. Died 16 February 1980.

COLE, Adrian Trevor

The son of Robert Hodgson Cole, MD, LLB, and Mrs Cole of Melbourne, Australia, he was born on 19 June 1895. Educated at the Church of England Grammar Schools at Geelong and at Melbourne, Victoria. Known, inevitably, as King Cole, he was sent to Egypt with the AFC in 1917, joining the then 67 Squadron, RFC, later to become 1 AFC Squadron. After an inauspicious start, when he was shot down by ground fire on 21 April 1917, over Tel el Sheriba, and subsequently dramatically rescued from the desert floor by Captain R Williams, who landed nearby to pick him up, he believed his luck must change. However, two months later on 26 June, he found himself attempting to return the favour by rescuing not one, but two, of his colleagues, each of whom had been forced to land their machines through mechanical faults. After taking off, the combined weight of the three men proved too much for his Martinsyde, its engine spluttered to a halt, and the machine crash-landed. After a long walk in the direction of the British lines, the three airmen were picked up intact by a patrol of Australian Light Horse. His fortunes did change, however, and he soon proved himself a brave and resourceful Pilot, his MC being announced in the *London Gazette* of 16 August 1917: 'For conspicuous gallantry and devotion to duty. With another officer he attacked and disorganised six enemy machines that were about to attack our cavalry with bombs. The engagement was continued until all six machines were forced to return to their lines. His skill and courage on all occasions have been worthy of the highest praise'.

His next posting, this time to the Western Front, came in the summer of 1918, when he joined 2 AFC (SE5As) as a Flight Commander. Cole achieved ten victories between 2 June and 28 October 1918, and was awarded the Distinguished Flying Cross, *London Gazette* of 8 February 1919. Returning to Melbourne, he married his cousin, Katherine Shaw, with whom he had two sons and one daughter. Cole first tried his hand at business in 1919, but then, in 1920, joined the RAAF as a Flight Lieutenant. Over what would prove a distinguished career, his various appointments, promotions and honours included: Director of Training for three years; Commandant, 1 Aircraft Depot for three years; Air Member for Supply on the Air Board for three years; OC, RAAF Richmond, for two years; passed RAF Staff College, 1924; Organiser and Deputy Chairman of the McRobertson-Miller Annual Air Race – England to Australia – from 1932 to 1934; CBE, 1937; Imperial Defence College, 1938; AOC, Central Area, Sydney, from 1939 to 1940. Cole was detached for special duty to the RAF in 1940. He served in the Middle East and on the Home Front in Britain. He was actively involved as Fighter Controller during the disastrous commando raid on Dieppe on 19 August 1942, wounded and awarded the Distinguished Service Order. Cole retired with the rank of Air Vice-Marshal, going to live at 47 Caroline Street, South Yarra, Victoria, Australia. Air Vice-Marshal Adrian Cole died on 14 February 1966.

COLE, Edwin Stuart Travis

The son of Timber Labourer, Edwin Cole, and Sussanah Cole, of 10 Hanover Street, Bristol, he was born on 26 December 1894. Educated at Merchant Venturers School, Bristol. Anxious to join the flying service, he gained his Royal Aero Club Certificate (Number 2160) on 14 December 1915. Gazetted Second Lieutenant to the RFC on 29 April 1916, he was, after completing his formal training, confirmed and gazetted Flying Officer on 21 July following. Sent out to 60 Squadron on 5 August 1916, he apparently soon fell foul of that unit's CO, Jack Scott (qv), who lost little time in passing him on to 1 Squadron, despite him having gained one victory over a Roland CII on 15 September. Cole did well with 1 Squadron – by then newly equipped with Nieuport XVII Scouts – achieving a further seven victories between 4 March and

1 May 1917. In particular, on 1 May 1917, he was responsible for sending down the German Ace, Alexander Kutscher, newly appointed CO, Jasta 28. Elated, Cole landed alongside the wrecked Albatros, cautiously taking a photograph from behind a tree, before warily approaching the enemy machine, only to find Kutscher shot through the heart. His tour with '1' completed, he was ordered to return to the Home Establishment for rest and recuperation on 5 June 1917, however, he almost did not make it. On hearing of his leave, he decided to give a display of aerial acrobatics by way of a celebratory last farewell. In diving between a high chimney and a building, he failed to see a power cable stretched from one to the other. His propellor was smashed and his undercarriage 're-arranged', but still he managed to land, personally still intact. His MC was announced in the *London Gazette* of 18 June 1917: 'For conspicuous gallantry and devotion to duty. On one occasion he, in a scout, attacked and brought down an enemy two-seater bi-plane. He has brought down two hostile balloons. He has at all times set a splendid example of courage and initiative'.

Cole spent the remainder of the war as an Instructor. After leaving the RAF, he ran a garage in Malmesbury for many years, the rudder off Kutscher's Albatros proudly and prominently displayed on a wall. He served again in the Second World War, mainly on flying duties. In 1940, he was one of the relatively few survivors of a hare-brained attempt to fly a formation of Blenheims and Hurricanes bound for the Middle East, clear across occupied France. Those who were not brought down soon aborted the attempt and returned home, Cole among them.

COLIN, Jean Pierre (also known as John Peter Colin)

The second son of Mr and Mrs Anthony Colin, he was born in London in 1894. Educated at Tonbridge School (1909-11). Colin disliked his French forenames and adopted the Anglicised versions, John Peter. Gazetted Second Lieutenant to 14 Battalion, Middlesex Regiment, on 17 June 1915, before transferring to the RFC, via the General List, on 1 August following. Having trained as an Observer, he was confirmed and gazetted Flying Officer (Observer) on 10 August 1916. Sent out to France, he served first with 42 Squadron, until hospitalised on 1 January 1917. Once recovered, he trained as a Pilot and his next operational experience was in that capacity with the RE8-equipped 5 Squadron, flying at the front with that unit from June 1917. On 29 July 1917, Colin was fortunate to escape injury or worse, when he and his Observer of the day, Private W Milton, in RE8, 'A3683', were hit by anti-aircraft fire during an Artillery Observation patrol above Vimy Ridge. In fact, Milton was wounded in the air but Colin, unscathed, brought them back safely. He was promoted to A/Captain and Flight Commander in December 1917. His tour with '5' completed, he returned to the Home Establishment in April 1918. His MC was announced in the *London Gazette* of 22 June 1918: 'For conspicuous gallantry and devotion to duty. When on a special reconnaissance of enemy troops at a very low altitude, he took numerous valuable photographs, dropped bombs on a battery of artillery proceeding along a road, the majority of the horses and personnel of which were killed, and engaged with machine-gun fire massed formations of enemy infantry, causing a general stampede across the open fields. His repeated gallant efforts and consistent devotion to duty under adverse conditions have afforded a very fine example to his Flight'.

Colin did not return to operational flying, and finally left the RAF, via the Unemployed List, in April 1919.

COLLETT, Clive Franklyn

The son of Horace and Alice Collett, of Tauranta, New Zealand, he was born on 28 August 1886. He enlisted in the RFC in 1914, gaining his Royal Aero Club Certificate (Number 1057), on 29 January 1915, whilst still in the ranks. Picked out for a commission, he was gazetted Second Lieutenant to the RFC, via the Special Reserve, on 25 March 1915. His formal pilot training duly completed, he was confirmed and gazetted Flying Officer two months later on 25 May. He served briefly with 18 Squadron in France early in 1916, but suffered an accident when ferrying a machine from France to England. Once recovered, he became a Test Pilot in England. Collett was involved in the development of the parachute at this time, surviving an experimental leap from the cockpit of BE2c in January 1917. Sent out again to France in July 1917, he joined 70 Squadron, just newly re-equipped with Sopwith Camels. Collett achieved 11 victories between 27 July and 9 September 1917, including three on the last of these dates. However, immediately after gaining the third of these victories, Collett, in Camel, 'B2341', was himself shot up and wounded in the hand, probably by Leutnant Ludwig Hanstein of Jasta 35. Amongst the three Germans Collett sent down during his last combat day was Leutnant Karl Hammes of Jasta 35, who would, in later life, enjoy some fame as a star of the Vienna Opera. Hammes' operatic fame, however, was destined to be cut short when he was killed in action whilst serving with the Luftwaffe over Poland, during the opening days of the Second World War. Collett's MC was announced in the *London Gazette* of 26 September 1917, details in the *Gazette* of 9 January 1918: 'For conspicuous gallantry and devotion to duty as a leader of offensive patrols during a period of three weeks. He has on numerous occasions attacked large formations of enemy aircraft single-handed, destroyed some, and driven others down out of control. He has led his formation with great skill, and has on several occasions extricated them from most difficult positions, and in every engagement his gallantry and dash have been most marked'.

A Bar to his MC came in the *London Gazette* of 18 October 1917, details in the *Gazette* of 7 March 1918: 'For conspicuous gallantry and devotion to duty in leading offensive patrols against enemy aircraft. Within a period of three weeks he successfully engaged and destroyed five enemy machines (three of them in one day), attacking them from low altitudes with the greatest dash and determination. His brilliant example was a continual source of inspiration to the squadron in which he served'.

After having recovered from his wounds in England, Collett again took to testing aircraft for the RFC. Tragically, he was killed whilst flying a captured Albatros Scout over the Firth of Forth in Scotland, on 23 December 1917. Clive Collett is buried in Edinburgh (Comely Bank) Cemetery, Edinburgh.

COLLIER, Henry Waldo

The son of Mr and Mrs Henry C Collier of St John's Hill, Wanganui, New Zealand, he was born on 31 October 1893. Anxious to serve in the flying service, he travelled half-way around the world and learnt to fly at his own expense, being awarded the Royal Aero Club Certificate (Number 3863) on 20 November 1916. His initiative was rewarded when he was gazetted Second Lieutenant to the RFC on 19 January 1917. Following formal training, he was confirmed and gazetted Flying Officer on 18 August following. Sent out to 42 Squadron (RE8s) in Belgium on 2 September 1917, he accompanied the unit to Italy on 17 November following. His squadron returned to the Western Front in March 1918. On 7 April 1918, Collier and his Observer of the day, Lieutenant E C Musson, in RE8, 'B876' survived a combat with the German Ace, Herman Göring. Although Collier managed to get the machine back safely, Eric Musson was wounded in the air. On 13 April 1918, less than a week after his brush with Göring, Collier was again involved in an aerial battle, sustaining wounds which resulted in him being sent back to the London Hospital for treatment on 20 April following. His work during the dire days of the spring offensive was acknowledged by the award of the MC, announced in the *London Gazette* of 26 July 1918: 'For conspicuous gallantry and devotion to duty. During recent operations this officer carried out a contact patrol in a thick mist at a height of only 150 feet under heavy machine-gun and rifle fire, and flew daily during the misty weather at low altitudes bringing back much useful information of the enemy and harassing them with machine-gun fire and bombs. It was greatly due to his magnificent work that Headquarters were kept informed of the enemy's movements during a difficult phase of the battle. By his gallant and cheerful spirit at a time when the Squadron was suffering heavy casualties, he set a splendid example to the others'.

Once recovered, Collier was promoted to A/Captain and sent to the School of Artillery Co-operation on 7 November 1918. Henry Collier finally left the RAF, via the Unemployed List, on 29 July 1919, and returned home to New Zealand.

COLLIER, Samuel

The son of Auctioneer and Valuer, Edwin Collier, and Selina Collier, of 41 Sheffield Road, Glossop, Derbyshire, he was born on 14 October 1895. Educated at Glossop Grammar School (1909-1914) and at Manchester University, where he was a member of the OTC. Interrupting his studies, he was gazetted Second Lieutenant to 6 Battalion, Manchester Regiment (TF), on 31 October 1914. Following service in Gallipoli and Egypt with 6 Manchesters in 1915, Collier was seconded to the RFC in July 1916. After qualifying as a Pilot, he served first on Home Defence duties, joining the Sopwith Strutter-equipped 43 Squadron at Northolt in December 1916, before its departure to the front in the following month. He was promoted to A/Captain and Flight Commander in February 1917. '43' converted to F1 Camels in September 1917, just four months before Collier departed for Staff duties with HQ, 21 Wing, RFC, in January 1918. His MC was announced in the New Year *London Gazette* of 1 January 1918 (no citation). Although no formal citation was published in the *Gazette*, research has unearthed the original recommendation for the award: 'For six months this Officer did consistently good work. By his courage and skill he has on several occasions been responsible for successful photographic and fighting patrols. He carried out many low flying missions during the above period. He has always set a fine example by his fearless leadership and skilful handling of his Flight'.

Collier's final operational posting came on 7 September 1918, when he was sent out, again as a Flight Commander, to the Bristol Fighter-equipped 22 Squadron. He, with his Observer, J V Scottorn, was responsible for bringing down at least one enemy machine before he was hospitalised on 5 November 1918. Captain Collier finally left the RAF, via the Unemployed List, on 26 April 1919.

COLLINS, Lewis Isaac

From Dundee, he was born on 7 November 1894. Gazetted Second Lieutenant to 11 (Reserve) Battalion, Yorkshire Regiment (Green Howards), on 27 September 1915. Collins served with his regiment until being seconded to the RFC on 27 March 1917. After training as an Observer, he was eventually sent out as such to the DH4-equipped 18 Squadron in France. An Observer Ace, he achieved five victories between 25 March and 17 June 1918, all in company with his usual Pilot, Captain D A Stewart MC (qv). His MC was announced in the *London Gazette* of 16 September 1918: 'For conspicuous gallantry and devotion to duty. He has carried out twelve successful bombing raids, and fifteen low bombing and reconnaissance flights, and ten successful photographic flights. He has carried out many low-flying, harassing and bombing patrols of great value. In addition he has destroyed two enemy machines, on one occasion being attacked by three of the enemy'.

His tour with '18' completed on 13 July 1918, he returned to the Home Establishment, where he saw out the remainder of the war. Lewis Collins finally left the Service, via the Unemployed List, on 25 February 1919.

CONINGHAM, Arthur

Although born in Brisbane, Australia, on 19 January 1895, Arthur Coningham spent most of his formative years in Wellington, New Zealand. Educated at Wellington College, New Zealand. Volunteering his services as soon as war came in August 1914, he served first with the Canterbury Mounted Rifles in Samoaand then, later in 1915, in Egypt and in Gallipoli. So badly infected with Typhoid was he, that he was invalided out of the service and sent home to New Zealand in 1916. After regaining his health, he paid his own fare to the UK and once there, volunteered for the flying service, being gazetted Second Lieutenant to the RFC, via the Special Reserve, on 8 August 1916. Following the usual pilot training, he was confirmed and gazetted Flying Officer on 28 November following. His combat career commenced with 32 Squadron, with which unit he achieved ten victories – nine of those in the less-than-nimble DH 5. On 30 July 1917, Coningham in DH5, 'A9179', was slightly wounded in the head during an aerial combat. His MC was announced in the *London Gazette* of 17 September 1917 : 'For conspicuous gallantry and devotion to duty in attacking enemy aircraft. On numerous occasions he had displayed great dash and a fine offensive spirit in engaging the enemy at close range, and driving them down completely out of control'.

The award of a gallantry Distinguished Service Order followed almost immediately in the *London Gazette* of 26 September 1917. He was also Mentioned in Despatches at around this time, *London Gazette* of 7 November 1917. After a spell in the UK, he was promoted to A/Major, and placed in command of 92 Squadron (SE5As), taking that unit to France in June 1918. Although, along with all Squadron COs, he was discouraged from risking himself in combat, still he managed to notch up yet another four victories, picking up another wound in the process. He was awarded a Distinguished Flying Cross, announced in the Birthday Honours *London Gazette* of 3 June 1919. Coningham stayed on in the RAF after the war, his nickname, 'Maori', had slowly corrupted to 'Mary', a sobriquet he remained saddled with for the rest of his life! He served in Kurdistan during 1923, for which he was Mentioned in Despatches. Coningham participated in a pioneering flight from Cairo to Kano, in 1925, for which he received the Air Force Cross. He married, in 1932, Lady Nancy Frank, the widow of Sir H G Frank, with whom he had one daughter. In the Second World War he held, among other appointments, that of AOC, Western Desert Air Force, from 1941 to 1943, responsible for providing air support to the Eighth Army, including during the Battle of Alemein. He was knighted (KCB), 1942. Coningham commanded the Allied Tactical Air Forces during the Allied captures of Tunisia, Pantelleria, Sicily and southern Italy, 1943-44, going on to command 2 Tactical Air Force in England and in Normandy, during the crucial years of 1944-45. He was credited with being the originator and architect of 'tactical air forces', for he it was who devised an air-power doctrine which was adopted by General Eisenhower and embraced by the USAF. Created KBE in 1946. He was appointed to command RAF, Flying Training Command, from 1945 to 1947, retiring from the RAF in the same year. Air Marshal Sir Arthur Coningham died when a Avro Tudor of British South America Airways disappeared without trace during a flight to Bermuda on 30 January 1948.

CONRAN, Eric Lewis

From Brisbane, Queensland, Australia, he was born on 22 August 1887. He was living and working in London, when he became a pre-war member of the TF, being gazetted Lieutenant into 2 County of London Yeomanry on 12 August 1912. One of the early flyers, he gained his Royal Aero Club Certificate (Number 342), flying a Caudron of the Ewen School at Hendon, on 22 October 1912. His formal pilot training duly completed, he was confirmed and gazetted Flying Officer on 17 April 1913. Conran flew a 3 Squadron Bleriot Parasol to France as part of the original RFC contingent on 13 August 1914, thus earning the 1914 Star. His machine was looked after by Air Mechanic J T B McCudden, who would later achieve immortality as a supreme fighter Ace and holder of the Victoria Cross. McCudden's notes of the period mention that one morning, Lieutenant Conran 'left the aerodrome in the Bleriot Parasol to bomb Laon railway station, with the following load of bombs: 16 hand grenades, two shrapnel bombs, each one in a rack outside the fuselage, out of which the Pilot had to throw them by hand, and a Melinite bomb tied onto an upper fuselage with string, so that when he wanted to unload this bomb he had to cut the string first with a knife and push the bomb overboard'. Captain Charlton (later Brigadier General L E O Charlton, DSO) and Lieutenant Conran were, on 24 August 1914, responsible for bringing in information which led to the order for the great retreat from Mons. They were on reconnaissance when they spotted the German enveloping movements at Peruwelz and Charleroi. Had these enemy movements gone undetected, the British Army may well have been decimated. It was largely due to this intelligence that the RFC was elevated from being a force 'on probation', to taking its place, henceforth, as 'the eyes of the Army'. During the following month, Conran was given a permanent commission in the Regular Army, being gazetted Second Lieutenant to 21 Lancers and, shortly afterwards, promoted Lieutenant. He was next promoted to A/Captain and Flight Commander, on 28 November 1914. Conran's MC was amongst the very first to be announced, appearing in the *London Gazette* of 1 January 1915 (no citation). He was also twice Mentioned in Despatches at this time, *London Gazettes* of 19 October 1914 and 5 January 1915. On 26 March 1915, whilst flying a Morane L, '1872', of 3 Squadron, he was seriously wounded by shrapnel in the back and arm, and sent home to England for treatment. Once recovered, he was promoted to A/Major and given command of the Experimental Flight at the CFS. In April 1916, he became the first CO, the newly raised Nieuport two-seater-equipped 46 Squadron, at Wyton. In the following month, he was sent out again to France, this time to command 29 Squadron. Conran later went on to serve in Egypt, Palestine and Iraq, before finally returning home to HQ, 7 Group, RAF, at Andover on 13 April 1922. The Order of the Nile, Commander grade, was conferred upon him by the Egyptian Government, *London Gazette* of 18 November 1919. He fell sick on 4 November 1923 and died at 16 Langham Street, Marylebone, London, on 6 January 1924.

NB: His medals were offered for sale by Buckland Dix & Wood (lot 355) on 27 July 1995: MC, 1914 Star (Lt 2/Co of London Yeo)*, British War Medal 1914-20, Victory Medal 1914-19* (Major RAF)*, General Service Medal 1918-62, with clasp, Iraq* (Sqd Ldr RAF)*, Order of the Nile (Commander's neck badge in silver-gilt and enamel, Egypt). The group had been sold earlier by Sotheby's (lot 548) on 4 March 1982.*

COOK, William Wallace

Born in Palmerston, New Zealand, on 19 February 1890. Educated at Palmerston North District High School (1904-13). Making his way to the UK, he learnt to fly at his own expense, gaining his Royal Aero Club Certificate (Number 3864) on 20 November 1916. This qualification gave him the appropriate entrée, and he was subsequently gazetted Second Lieutenant to the RFC, via the Special Reserve, on 19 January 1917. Following the usual training, he was confirmed and gazetted Flying Officer on 14 June following. Cook first served with

HD Squadrons in 1917, and again in early 1918. On the night of 24/25 September 1917, Cook was on patrol in a 76HD Squadron BE2e, (A8663), when he encountered no less than three Zeppelins in succession. First he met *L55*, then *L41*, both of which outpaced him with relative ease. His third encounter was with *L42*, and this time he got close enough to launch an attack. Although Cook was certain that he scored hits on the airship's hull, still it climbed away from him to safety. On this patrol, he was airborne for more than five hours, no small feat in itself. His pluck and determination in this sortie, which failed mainly because of ill luck, earned him his MC. In fact, Cook rated a *London Gazette* announcement all to himself on 11 October 1917: 'His Majesty the King has been graciously pleased to approve the award of the MC to Lieutenant William Wallace Cook, New Zealand Forces and RFC : For conspicuous gallantry and skill in an attack on a Zeppelin. He ascended from his station during strong wind, thick mist and low clouds and showed great determination, eventually giving up the attack sixty miles out to sea. His return journey was hazardous, but with great skill he eventually effected a landing in a field within a quarter of a mile of the coast, having been in the air for five and a half hours'.

Transferring to the FE2b-equipped night-bombing 148 Squadron, on 1 March 1918, he accompanied that unit to France as a 'founder member' on 25 April following. Wounded in action on 15 May 1918, he was taken to No 1 Casualty Clearing Station for treatment. Cook returned to the Home Establishment on 15 September 1918. Repatriated to New Zealand on 2 October 1919, he finally left the RAF, via the Unemployed List, on 14 November following.

COOKE, Douglas Graham

From London, he was born on 26 July 1895. Gazetted Second Lieutenant to the RFC on 24 May 1917. Gained his Royal Aero Club Certificate (Number 4825) on 16 June 1917. Following the successful completion of his formal training, he was confirmed and gazetted Flying Officer on 10 September following. Sent out to the Bristol Fighter-equipped 20 Squadron in the same month, he struck up a productive and effective partnership with H G Crowe (qv) and other Observers, gaining 13 victories between 22 January and 19 May 1918, including four doubles on single days. Cooke was promoted to A/Captain and Flight Commander in the intervening April. His MC was announced in the *London Gazette* of 26 July 1918: 'For conspicuous gallantry and devotion to duty when engaged in many low bombing patrols and low reconnaissances. On one occasion, when important information was required, he flew along the front for ten miles at 100 feet, being subjected the whole way to heavy fire from the ground, and on the same day on another front twelve miles at 300 feet, each time returning with the information and his machine much shot about. He has destroyed several hostile machines in air combats, and has invariably displayed the highest courage and splendid fighting spirit'. Cooke survived the Great War.

COOPER, Horace Arthur

The son of Mr and Mrs A P Cooper, of Chapeltown, Leeds. Gazetted Second Lieutenant to the RFC in April 1917. Having trained as an Observer, he joined the F2b-equipped 48 Squadron at the front in September 1917. On 8 March 1918, Cooper with Captain N C Millman (qv), in Bristol F2b, 'B1190', were heavily engaged in combats with Albatros DVs. They claimed one down out-of-control in the morning and claimed another that same day – again down out-of-control – over Bohain. Cooper's MC was announced in the same *Gazette* as was Millman's, the *London Gazette* of 22 June 1918: 'For conspicuous gallantry and devotion to duty while as an Observer on an offensive patrol. He shot down completely out of control one of the twelve machines which had attacked his patrol, on another day, during a day-light bombing raid on a hostile aerodrome, he engaged with machine-gun fire from a low altitude hostile machines and personnel on the aerodrome. Previous to this he and his pilot voluntarily proceeded on a low flying reconnaissance, from which they returned with the most valuable and important information. He has brought down in all three enemy machines, and has at all times displayed the utmost keenness and efficiency in his work'.

In fact, Horace Cooper shared five of Millman's victories, and so qualified as an Observer Ace in his own right. Cooper returned to the Home Establishment on 22 March 1918 and saw out the remainder of the war in a series of instructing posts, before finally leaving the RAF, via the Unemployed List, in February 1919.

COOPER, James Percy Carré

From West Byfleet, Surrey, he was born on 18 January 1883. A married man, he was Works Manager at A Darracq & Company of Fulham, from 1913 to 1915. Gazetted Second Lieutenant to the RFC on 30 April 1915, the same day that he gained his Royal Aero Club Certificate (Number 1208). Following formal training he was confirmed and gazetted Flying Officer on 23 August following. Posted to 5 Squadron in November 1915, his first tour ended in March 1916, when he returned to the Home Establishment. His MC was announced in the *London Gazette* of 3 June 1916 (no citation). Although no citation was published in the *Gazette*, research has uncovered the original recommendation for the award: 'J P C Cooper. Although Captain Cooper has never been called upon by circumstances for any particularly noticeable achievement, he has, during four months, carried out a "lion's share" of the most disagreeable and most dangerous part of the routine work. This he has done most efficiently and his example has been, and is, extremely valuable to the squadron in which he is serving'.

Promoted to A/Captain, he was appointed an Instructor at the CFS in July 1916. Further advancement to T/Major came in December 1916. Sent out again to France on 6 March 1917, he joined 9 Squadron briefly before being transferred to a Staff position with 14 Wing HQ, RFC, just six days later. He commanded the Armament Experimental Station at Orfordness later in 1917, before going out to France again in March 1918, as CO of the Aerial Ranges there. Mentioned in Despatches, *London Gazette* of 8 November 1918. Invested as OBE (Military Division) announced in the *London Gazette* of 1 January 1919. He was also appointed Officer of the Order of the Star by the Roumanians. Cooper finally left the RAF, via the Unemployed List, on 1 May 1919. He next entered the Department of the Controller General of Civil Aviation in February 1920. In the mid-1930s he was the Inspector of Accidents, in charge of the Accidents Branch, RAF. James Cooper died in Falmouth Hospital, Cornwall, on 8 December 1961.

COOPER, John Henry

From Oban in Scotland, he was born on 28 May 1894. He studied engineering at the Technical College, Glasgow, from 1912 to 1914, obtaining a Diploma in Naval Architecture. Gazetted Second Lieutenant to 5 Battalion (Renfrewshire), Argyll and Sutherland Highlanders (TF), on 8 August 1915. Helped no doubt by his engineering knowledge, he became an Instructor on machine guns, before securing a secondment to the RFC late in 1916. After the appropriate training, he was confirmed and gazetted Flying Officer on 15 March 1917. His first operational posting was to 12 Squadron, arriving in France within days of having put up his 'Wings'. Recovering from wounds received whilst on a contact patrol on 10 April 1917, he was next transferred to the Camel-equipped 46 Squadron in June 1917. On 20 November 1917, he returned from a low-level bombing raid on a factory with a souvenir of that establishment's metal chimney dangling from his damaged lower wing! In fact, Cooper's Camel was so badly knocked about on this occasion, that he was forced to land the moment he crossed the British lines, ending up, rather ignominiously, nose first in a trench. Cooper's MC, one of five awarded to 46 Squadron on the same day, was announced in the *London Gazette* of 4 February 1918: 'For conspicuous gallantry and devotion to duty. He assisted to bomb an enemy aerodrome, and destroyed some billets close to it. On another occasion he flew over the enemy's lines in a very thick mist and bombed some enemy transport, completely destroying one wagon and scattering the remainder with machine-gun fire. He then bombed and blew up a factory. His machine was badly hit, and returned to our lines with the greatest difficulty in very bad weather conditions. Later, in the course of three fights, he dropped bombs and fired 1700 rounds on enemy infantry from a low altitude. He showed the greatest courage and determination'.

Cooper, or 'Hootsmon' as he was fondly known, crashed another Camel visiting the Naval 8 Squadron aerodrome at St Eloi on 15 December 1917. Badly concussed, he was sent home to recover. He was presented with his MC by the King at an investiture held at Buckingham Palace on 14 June 1919. The admiring citizens of his home town of Oban, also marked his distinction by presenting him with an inscribed gold fountain pen. Staying on in the RAF after the war, he married in December 1919. Cooper served with 28 Squadron in Ambala in 1921, before resigning his commission in the same year.

NB: His medals were offered for sale by Dix Noonan Webb (lot 483) on 29 November 1996: MC, British War Medal 1914-20, Victory Medal 1914-19 (Lieut RFC), *Defence Medal 1939-45, and War Medal 1939-45. The group was offered for sale again (lot 1473) on 20 September 2002.*

COWAN, Sidney Edward

The youngest son of P C Cowan, DSc, and Mrs Cowan, of 33 Ailesbury Road, Dublin, Ireland, he was born in Downpatrick on 23 August 1897. His father was the Chief Engineering Inspector of the Local Government Board for Ireland. Sidney was educated at Castle Park, Dalkey, at Marlborough College (1911-14), and at Trinity College, Dublin. Interrupting his studies at Trinity, he volunteered and was gazetted to the RFC, via the Special Lists, on 23 August 1915, the same day that he gained his Royal Aero Club Certificate (Number 1639). After the usual formal training, he was confirmed and gazetted Flying Officer on 14 October following. A 'founder member' of 24 Squadron (DH2s), he went out to the front with that unit on 7 February 1916. Cowan was one of the first Fighter Pilots – still a new concept in the autumn and winter of 1915. On 9 August 1916, Cowan in DH2, '5964', was wounded in the forehead and temporally blinded by cockpit splinters, when his machine was shot up during a combat over Flers. By the time he collided with another British machine and fell to his death on 17 November 1916, he had achieved seven victories, been promoted to Captain and awarded no less than three MCs and still was only 19 years old. The first of his MCs was announced in the *London Gazette* of 31 May 1916. 'For conspicuous gallantry and skill. He dived on to an enemy machine in the enemy's lines and drove it to the ground, where it was smashed, and then circled around firing at the pilot and Observer as they ran for shelter. Although forced to land through his engine stopping he contrived to restart it and got back under heavy fire'.

The first Bar to his MC came in the *London Gazette* of 20 October 1916: 'For conspicuous gallantry and skill. He has done fine work in aerial combat, and has shot down four enemy machines'. The second Bar was announced in the *London Gazette* of 14 November 1916: 'For conspicuous gallantry in action. He fought a long contest with seven enemy machines, finally bringing one down in flames. He has displayed great skill and gallantry throughout'.

A fellow Old Marlburian wrote from France to Cowan's parents to report that he had discovered Sidney's original grave at Ablairzevelle, 12 miles south east of Arras: 'It is railed in, and a cross at the head bears an inscription which, when translated from the German, reads: In memory of a gallant English officer, Captain S E Cowan, killed in an air combat'. Sidney's brother, Captain Philip Cowan, was also a Scout Pilot and he, too, was killed in action just a year later on 8 November 1917. After the Great War, Sidney Cowan's body was re-interred by the Imperial War Graves Commission and is now buried in Cagnicourt British Cemetery, France.

COWPER, Andrew King

The fifth son of Surveyor, Percival Cowper and Mrs Cowper, of Bingara, New South Wales, Australia, he was born on 16 November 1898. He was a fourth generation descendant of William Cowper, the eighteenth century poet. His family were in England, and living at 23 Jevington Gardens, Eastbourne, in January 1913, when Andrew entered Eastbourne College. Cowper played in the College Rugby XV and Cricket XI, in 1915 and 1916, and also had become a prefect by the time he left in December 1916. He first enlisted as a Private soldier into the Royal Sussex Regiment, almost as soon as he left school. Picked out for a commission, he was gazetted Second Lieutenant to the RFC on 10 May 1917. His pilot training duly completed, he was confirmed and gazetted Flying Officer on 12 August following. Posted out to 24 Squadron in France just two weeks later on 26 August 1917. Cowper gained his first two victories flying a DH5 fighter, but his successes increased dramatically once the squadron was re-equipped with SE5As, early in the last year of the war. Between 21 March 1918 (the opening day of the German spring offensive) and 1 April following, he had taken part in more than 20 highly successful ground attack sorties against the advancing enemy infantry and transport. His machines, it was reported, often had their planes and centre sections riddled with bullet holes. By the time he left for the Home Establishment on 11 April 1918, he had achieved a total of 19 victories and no less than three quite outstanding MC citations would be announced in the following weeks. The first of his MCs was announced in the *London Gazette* of 22 April 1918: 'For conspicuous gallantry and devotion to duty. Whilst leading a patrol of six machines he observed four hostile tri-planes, one of which he attacked, succeeding in causing it to break up in the air. The remaining three enemy machines were destroyed by the rest of the patrol. On the return journey he encountered an enemy scout, and shepherding it by the most skilful piloting west of the lines, forced it to land undamaged on one of our aerodromes. On a later occasion, during three separate combats, he and his patrol brought down one machine completely out of control and two others with their observers wounded, and later in the same day three other machines completely out of control. Previously to this he had assisted in destroying six other enemy scouts, displaying at all times the greatest courage and determination'.

The first of two Bars came in the *London Gazette* of 22 June 1918: 'Within a short period he has himself destroyed three enemy planes and has driven down four others completely out of control. During the recent operations he has further destroyed two hostile machines, and has attacked in the most daring manner and with the greatest effect enemy troops and transport. On all occasions his gallantry and skill have been of the highest order'.

His second Bar was announced in the same *London Gazette* of 22 June 1918: 'He bombed enemy troops who were entrenching, and caused great havoc and confusion. He made repeated and determined attacks, in spite of heavy hostile fire, and eventually forced the enemy to retire from their trench. He returned to his aerodrome for more bombs and ammunition, and, going out a second time, attacked enemy troops and transport and threw them into confusion. He went out on two other occasions on the same day with equal success. Later, while co-operating with an infantry attack he obtained four direct hits with bombs on an encampment and forced several parties of the enemy to retire from the front line. He showed magnificent dash and determination'.

Cowper's exuberance went unchecked after his return to the UK. He was court-martialled at Harleston on 16 September 1918, accused of creating a disturbance at the Gaiety Theatre, London, on the night of 14/15 August 1918, during a performance of a review called 'Going Up', which starred Joseph Coyne, Evelyn Laye and Ruby Miller. In the event, our hero was acquitted. Cowper did not fly in combat again, having been hospitalised from November 1918, with a form of tuberculosis said to be brought on by flying at altitude without oxygen. Once recovered in January 1919, he was sent to serve with 79 Squadron in Germany, as part of the Army of Occupation. In June 1919, he sailed for India with 48 Squadron. Cowper was arraigned before yet another Court Martial in Quetta, India, but this time the nature of the charges have been lost in the mists of time. However, on this occasion he was severely reprimanded and warned as to his future conduct. Cowper finally left the RAF to return to Australia on 19 February 1920. Taking over his parents' sheep station, Wiliga, at Coonamble, NSW, he married in 1924 and had two sons, Leon and Henry, both of whom, like their mother, would eventually predecease Andrew. The Cowpers were forced to leave their sheep property by prolonged droughts and they moved to Sydney to become Horticulturists. He served again in the Administration and Special Duties Branch of the RAAF during the Second World War, being demobilised with the rank of Squadron Leader on 2 March 1945. Andrew Cowper died on 25 June 1980.

COX, George Montague

Born in Calcutta, India, on 31 October 1892. Gazetted Second Lieutenant to 9 (Reserve) Battalion, Royal Berkshire Regiment, on 18 December 1914. Cox proceeded to France for the first time when he was sent out to re-enforce the badly depleted 8 Battalion of his regiment on 18 October 1915. After a stint in the trenches, he was seconded to the RFC in the summer of 1916 and, having successfully completed his pilot training, was confirmed and gazetted Flying Officer on 13 December following. He served as an Instructor in the UK before accompanying the Camel-equipped 65 Squadron to France, as a 'founder member', on 27 October1917. By the early summer of 1918 he had gained five victories and the status of Ace, as well as receiving the MC, mainly for his effectiveness during the difficult days that followed the German spring offensive, *London Gazette* of 26 July 1918: 'For conspicuous gallantry and devotion to duty. On numerous occasions during the recent operations he has descended to very low altitudes, and has attacked with bombs and machine-gun fire enemy troops forming up for attack. Thanks to his dash and intrepidity hostile bodies of troops have suffered very severe casualties and have been scattered in all directions. He has in all destroyed four hostile machines, and has at all times displayed the great gallantry'.

Posted next to the command of 2 Test Flight in France 2 ASD, he remained with that unit until the end of the war. Cox stayed on in the RAF to become a highly respected Flying Instructor with many hours flying time in his logbook, his appointments including instructing at the de Havilland School for the RAF Reserve, during the 1930s.

COX, Wilfred Reseigh

The son of Walter R Cox, JP, and Mrs Cox, of Falmouth, Devon, he was born on 15 July 1895. Gazetted Second Lieutenant to 8 Battalion, Duke of Cornwall's Light Infantry, on 8 October 1914. Seconded to the RFC in June 1916, he trained as a Pilot and was confirmed and gazetted Flying Officer on 23 December following. Sent out to 15 Squadron, he appears to have volunteered to act as Observer to Second Lieutenant W Buckingham (qv), on 15 April 1917, when the weather was particularly atrocious, but information on the enemy's movements was badly needed by the Staff. He and Buckingham both received the MC for their gallantry, *London Gazette* of 26 May 1917: 'For conspicuous gallantry and devotion to duty. He displayed great courage and initiative in carrying out a patrol in heavy rain, with clouds at 500 feet during a recent attack. He obtained valuable information, and undoubtedly contributed to the successful repulse of the enemy'.

Cox would eventually become an Instructor of some distinction, his expertise being recognised by the award of the Air Force Cross, *London Gazette* of 3 June 1919.

CREEK, Frederick Norman Smith

The son of Mr and Mrs Arthur Frederick Creek, of 16 Greenbank Crescent, Darlington, he was born on 12 January 1898. Educated at Darlington Grammar School and, after resuming his studies following the end of the war, at Trinity College, Cambridge (1919-21), from where he graduated BA. Having enlisted as a Private soldier (Number 25712) into the Durham Light Infantry in 1916, he served in the trenches before being picked out for a commission and gazetted Second Lieutenant to 5 Battalion, Durham Light Infantry (TF), on 1 March 1917. Seconded to the RFC in August 1917, he trained as an Observer and was subsequently confirmed and gazetted Flying Officer (Observer) on 4 November following. Sent out to the DH4-equipped 25 Squadron in December 1917, he served with that unit until June 1918, when he returned to the Home Establishment. His MC was announced in the *London Gazette* of 13 May 1918: 'For conspicuous gallantry and devotion to duty. He carried out several successful reconnaissances of enemy aerodromes and railways, and obtained valuable information often under the most difficult weather conditions. On one occasion he took several photographs of an enemy aerodrome though he was attacked by an enemy machine and subjected to anti-aircraft fire. He displayed the greatest skill and determination'.

No mean cricketer, he represented the RAF in the Army game in September 1919. Taking leave of the RAF in 1919, he again took up a place at Trinity College, Cambridge, where he gained Football Blues, in 1919 and 1921, and played for England in the Wales game of 1921. Creek formally and finally relinquished his RAF commission on 1 September 1921. He lived, in the 1930s, at 'Skelwyth', West Lavington, Wiltshire. In the Second World War, he was re-commissioned as an acting Pilot Officer, RAFVR (T) (personal number 61810), on 13 March 1941, going on to serve through to 1945. Frederick Creek lived, post-Second War, at 'Elmsdale', Richings Park, Iver, Buckinghamshire.

CROLE, Gerard Bruce

The son of G L Crole, KC, and Mrs Crole, of 1 Royal Circus, Edinburgh, he was born on 7 June 1894. Educated at Edinburgh Academy (1899 -1912), at Edinburgh University, and at University College, Oxford, from where he graduated BA. A sportsman of some note, he gained Blues by representing Oxford at both Rugby Union and at golf. Gazetted Second Lieutenant to the Royal Field Artillery on 4 January 1915, he served in France with the Gunners in 1915. Seconded to the RFC, he served as an Observer with 'A' Flight, 1 Squadron, from 25 February 1916 to 15 September 1916; first as a Probationary before being confirmed and gazetted Flying Officer (Observer) on the intervening 1 July. He next trained as a Pilot and was subsequently posted to the Nieuport XVII-equipped 40 Squadron at the front on 3 June 1917. Crole achieved five victories in the two months between 25 June and 23 August 1917. His MC was announced in the *London Gazette* of 26 September 1917, details in the *Gazette* of 9 January 1918: 'For conspicuous gallantry and devotion to duty in aerial fighting on many occasions. By his determination and fine offensive spirit in attacking hostile aircraft he has continually proved his superiority over the enemy, destroying several enemy machines and driving many others down out of control'.

Promoted to A/Captain and Flight Commander, he was next sent out to 43 Squadron on 13 September 1917. On the morning of 22 November 1917, Crole, in Sopwith Camel, 'B6267', was shot down by Leutnant Fritz Rumey of Jasta 5, over Marcoing, the third of the German Ace's eventual 45 victories. Wounded and taken prisoner, he would remain in captivity until his repatriation on 18 December 1918. Despite the privations of captivity, Crole was fit enough to play Rugby for the RAF in the British Army Football Tournament, before finally leaving the service on 6 May 1919. He subsequently represented Scotland in full Internationals against France, England and Ireland, in the 1920 season. A cricketer of no small skill, he also represented the Gentlemen of Scotland as a middle order batsman against the Gentlemen of Ireland in 1920. Crole qualified and practised as a Solicitor in the post-war years. He married Katharine Margaret House in 1921. Gerald Crole lived mainly at Auchlunkart House, Mulben, Banffshire, but died in Aberdeen on 3 March 1965.

CROOK, Joseph Alan Howard

The oldest son of John Higgs Howard Crook and Florence Cecilia Crook (neé Keep), of Carlton, Bedfordshire, he was born on 12 July 1897, in Liphook, Hampshire. Educated at Winchester (1911-15), where, as an accomplished horseman, he rode in the annual Steeplechase. Learning to fly at his own expense, he gained his Royal Aero Club Certificate (Number 1202) on 30 April 1915. Next, he was gazetted Second Lieutenant to the RFC, via the Special Reserve, on 26 July 1915, and ordered to report, in the first instance, to Brooklands. Following training at the CFS and elsewhere, he was confirmed and gazetted Flying Officer on 11 September following. Crook joined 21 Squadron at Netheravon, just ten days after qualifying, before accompanying that RE7-equipped unit to France as a 'founder member' on 23 January 1916. He next transferred as a Flight Commander to the Nieuports of 11 Squadron. On 18 June 1916, Crook, in company with Second Lieutenant W A C Morgan (qv), in a DH of 24 Squadron, engaged a hostile formation, variously reported as consisting of six or nine machines. Their combined efforts forced one of the enemy machines down into the British lines, near to Terre Mesnil, east of Doullens, the enemy Pilot and Observer being taken prisoner. Crook and Morgan both received the MC for this feat – Crook's announced in the *London Gazette* of 27 July 1916: 'For conspicuous gallantry. He attacked and drove down to 6,000 feet a hostile machine, and finally, assisted by another aeroplane, he brought it to the ground. He has previously done excellent work, often under heavy anti-aircraft fire'.

His tour with '11' completed, he returned to the Home Establishment in August 1916, taking up a post at the School of Air Gunnery. Crook would subsequently serve with both 8 and 12 Squadrons before joining, briefly and with the rank of Major, the newly formed 99 Squadron in the UK in August 1917. Next, he was appointed to the command of No 3A School of Air Gunnery in September 1917. He subsequently served on the Staff of 14 Wing, RAF, before assuming command of 45 Squadron on 28 July 1918, for which services he was Mentioned in Despatches. He returned again to the Home Establishment in the following October, where he saw out the remainder of the war. Crook left the RAF, via the Unemployed List, on 4 April 1919. Emigrating to America in 1921, he took up fruit farming in California. He married, on 12 October 1927, Margaret Jeannie Russell. Returning to the UK in time for the outbreak of the Second World War, he lived briefly in London and in Weston-super-Mare. Crook successfully applied for the RAFVR on 9 July 1940, subsequently serving at the Air Ministry from 1941 to 1945, his home during these years being at Clifton Park, Bristol.

CROWDEN, Roy Charles

From London, he was born on 5 April 1899. Having theatrical aspirations from an early age, he attended a stage school with other emerging talents such as Noel Coward and Gertrude Lawrence, soon becoming a child actor of some repute. He appeared on the London stage and on the 'silver screen' under the name of Roy Royston, before enlisting into the RFC in May 1917. Picked out for a commission, he was gazetted Second Lieutenant in August 1917 and, following training, was given his 'Wings' in the following December. Sent out to the Sopwith Camel-equipped 54 Squadron in the first month of the New Year. A diary he kept through this period records his experiences and emotions in graphic, if somewhat extravagant, language. After his first air fight on 19 January 1918, he wrote : 'Huns and Camels all over the place. Poor old Fritz, died of fright and so did I on quite the first scrap... Returned home OK, except for a piece of Archie in my plane, frightful excitement'.

On the following day there was even more, 'frightful excitement' as he, effectively, shot himself down: 'Took up new machine that is to be mine. Gear turned wrong [and] shot the propeller to pieces'.

In March 1918, Crowden observed that the famed Manfred von Richthofen, the Red Baron himself, was operating from an aerodrome just ten miles, as the crow, or a Dr.I, flies, from his own field. He soon built up his flying time, and during his 13th sortie was to participate in a massed bombing and strafing raid against Busigny airfield: 'Went down to 400 feet, dropped bombs. Think I got something like 6 direct hits....then the fun commenced....we played hell all the way back. To see the old Hun run like hell was damn funny. We swept so low we were on the Hun before he knew where he was. Charged over the trenches at about 6 feet, scared the Hun stiff!'

Due to the success of this raid, others were planned. On 17 March, Crowden again raided Busigny, but this time the Germans were waiting. A subsequent less than jolly entry in his diary opens with: '5 of our Squadron missing.....' and concludes, 'Fuck the war'.

The great German spring offensive, the 'Kaiser's Battle', commenced on 21 March 1918, and Crowden was obliged to concentrate on low-level ground attacks in an attempt to relieve the immense pressure on the Tommies. However, on the second day of the Offensive, he claimed his first victory: 'I dived next firing like blazes and he started to go down into the ground. Was seen later by McLean on the ground'.

Flying up to five sorties a day, he was soon nearly exhausted but still he managed a second victory claim on 31 March, this time his victim was a Pfalz scout. The RFC ceased to exist on this day, the RAF coming into being on 1 April 1918. Grateful to be sent on leave, he made the best of his time at home before rejoining '54' at Clairmaris on 11 April. A noted 74 Squadron Pilot, 'Taffy' Jones, would observe at the time: 'Major R S

Maxwell, commanding 54, looks the same type as Mick (Mannock); and besides his friends Lieutenants Howe, Legger and 'Digger' Moore, 'Roy Royston, the famous actor', is in the Squadron. Royston, I am told, is full of guts. He loves strafing, for which he was recently awarded the MC. They appear to be a full-out crowd, and it is easy to see why, when they have such a fizzing CO'.

After his very first flight from his new airfield, Crowden crashed on landing, not, it appears, an unusual occurrence on this oddly 'L'-shaped aerodrome. After their intensive exertions, '54' was at last taken out of the front line and temporarily retired to a field near to Calais on the coast. Crowden's diary records that he met, 'two topping girls in Calais', the only fly in his ointment at this time being the appearance of a new Flight Commander, who he describes as being, 'the finest shit I have ever met'.

His MC was announced in the *London Gazette* of 22 June 1918: 'For conspicuous gallantry and devotion to duty during operations. Observing a column of enemy troops marching along the road, he descended to a very low altitude, bombed them, and threw the column into complete confusion. Later on the same day, he attacked and caused heavy casualties to enemy infantry who are advancing across country. On another occasion he attacked one of six enemy scouts and destroyed it. He showed great determination and a splendid offensive spirit'.

Back again into the fray on 2 June 1918, he narrowly escaped disaster after chasing two German two-seaters over the lines, only to run into a formation of eight Albatros scouts. On 5 June, he claimed a third victory, whilst defending kite balloons from the attentions of 14 enemy aircraft. Twelve days later, he claimed another hostile down out of control. His last claim came on 5 July and, although his friend and colleague, Lieutenant Spence, saw the enemy machine going down out of control, he could not confirm that it had crashed. By the middle of July, Crowden's diary suggests that he was near the end of his tether. On 16 July, on patrol over Courtheizy, he witnessed his friend Spence's Camel struck by ground fire. Seconds before the Camel exploded, Spence waved an arm at Crowden, whether in despair or by way of a farewell, he could not decide. The entry in his diary reflects his state of mind: 'I don't think I can go on much longer. Spence incident has rather put the wind up me'.

He snatched a short leave in Paris at the end of the month, 'a most charming place, but too full of French whores who are rather crude'.

Crowden finally left for the Home Establishment on 1 September 1918, where he saw out the remainder of the war, before finally leaving the RAF in March 1919. Returning to the stage, he trod the boards again as 'Roy Royston', enjoying moderate success. In the Second World War, he served briefly with the RAFVR, before joining the Entertainers National Service Association (ENSA), to entertain the troops, although it has to be said that the lads themselves interpreted the acronym a little less flatteringly as, 'Every Night Something Atrocious'. Crowden finally retired from the theatre in 1950, trying his hand at running a chain of launderettes in Australia. Returning to the UK, he could, in the years before his death in 1976, be found dispensing pints from behind the bar at the Plough Inn in Tolworth.

NB: His medals were offered for sale by Sotheby's (lot 608) on 15 September 1990: MC, British War Medal 1914-20, and Victory Medal 1914-19.

CROWE, Cyril Marconi

The son of Edward and Mrs Crowe, of 'Greenholme', Eaglescliffe, Co Durham, and 'Denni', Redcar, Yorkshire, he was born on 6 January 1894. Educated at Mill Hill School, London (1907-11), where he was a member of the OTC. Soon after the war started, he gained his Royal Aero Club Certificate (Number 898) on 8 September 1914. Gazetted Second Lieutenant to the RFC, via the Special Reserve, on 1 October following. Having served initially as an Observer with 4 Squadron, he afterwards completed his formal pilot training and was confirmed and gazetted Flying Officer on 24 April 1915. Known as 'Billy', he next served briefly with 8 Squadron, arriving at the front on 4 December 1915 and leaving on 4 February 1916. Next he spent a year with 16 Squadron, joining that unit in March 1916. He was, by April 1917, when he joined 56 Squadron as a Flight Commander, a very experienced airman. Flying SE5s, Crowe finally came into his own, doing much to develop the 'dive and climb' tactic that made the SE5 such a formidable adversary. By the following June, he had gained nine victories. His MC was announced in the *London Gazette* of 18 July 1917: 'For conspicuous gallantry and skill as a leader of offensive patrols, many times attacking hostile formations single-handed, and descending to low altitudes under heavy anti-aircraft fire. He was remarkable for the destruction of several enemy machines'.

The insignia of his MC would eventually be presented to him by the King in an investiture held at Buckingham Palace. On the day that Albert Ball was killed, 7 May 1917, Crowe came very close to death himself, having his goggles shot off his face! Returning to the UK in August 1917, he spent the next seven months instructing at the CFS and was promoted to the rank of A/Major in the process. A further brief spell with 56 Squadron produced another five victories between March and July 1918. Following the death of the redoubtable Jimmy McCudden, Crowe was sent out to command 60 Squadron on 9 July 1918. Just three weeks later, on the night of 29 July 1918, he was involved in a serious motor accident when his two passengers were killed (one of whom was another MC recipient, O J F Scholte (qv)). Following an inquiry, Crowe was deemed to have borne some responsibility for the crash, and a subsequent court-martial reduced him to the rank of Captain for one month. His final posting of the war was to the command of 85 Squadron, with which unit he claimed his 15th and final victory on 16 September 1918. Crowe was awarded the Distinguished Flying Cross for, amongst other things, his brilliant leadership, gallantry and skill, *London Gazette* of 21 September 1918. Leaving the RAF in 1919, he lived, post-war, at 'The Hollis', Saltburn by the Sea, West Yorkshire. He served again during the Second World War, achieving the rank of Wing Commander. 'Billy' Crowe died in 1974.

CROWE, Henry George

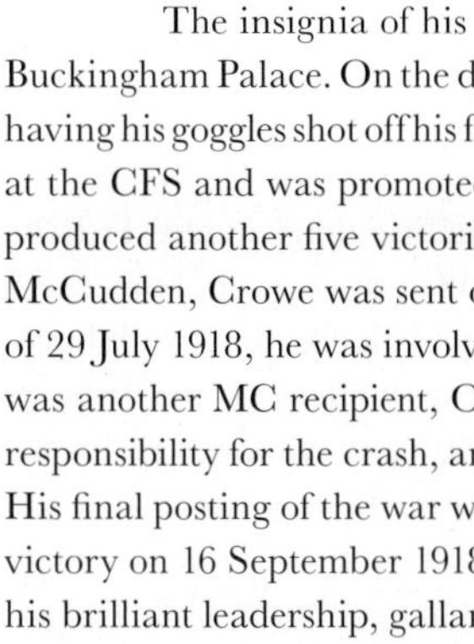

Born in Donnybrook, Dublin on 11 June 1897, he was educated at schools in Colwyn Bay in Wales, and Cheltenham in England, before going up to Trinity College, Dublin, for a degree course in Engineering. He attended the Royal Military College, Sandhurst, from where he was gazetted Second Lieutenant to the Royal Irish Regiment on 19 July 1916, afterwards being posted to 6 Battalion of his regiment in France in September 1916. He served in the trenches for almost a year, before securing a transfer to the RFC. Because of the shortage of Observers, his application for pilot training was refused and, as soon as he qualified for his 'Wing', he was sent out to the Bristol Fighters of 20 Squadron in November 1917 His service with 20 Squadron was 'charmed' to say the least. Aside from being responsible for eight victories over adversaries with various 'drivers', he was himself shot down on no fewer than six occasions. His MC was announced in the *London Gazette* of 26 July 1918: 'For conspicuous gallantry and devotion to duty when taking part in many low-flying bomb raids and reconnaissances as an Observer. On every occasion he brought back very accurate and valuable information. On three occasions his machine was shot down by enemy fire, but he continued his work, and his great fearlessness and fine spirit have been an invaluable example to others. He has taken part in several air combats and has been responsible for the destruction of many hostile machines'.

He finally realised his ambition, and after qualifying for his full 'Wings' was posted as a Pilot to 106 Squadron in Ireland, serving there through the troubled years of 1919 and 1920. Crowe qualified rather belatedly for his Royal Aero Club Certificate (Number 7911) on 25 November 1920. Staying on in the RAF, he went on to serve in Iraq with 39 Squadron during 1925-27 and in Amman, during 1927-28. Following a course at the RAF Staff College in 1929, he commanded 23 Squadron at Biggin Hill in the mid-1930s. During the Abyssinian crisis in 1935, he took over 74 Squadron, then handily placed in Malta. A Group Captain by the second year of the Second World War, he was sent out to command 223 Group in India in 1942. He was created CBE in the *London Gazette* of 8 June 1944. Crowe retired as an Air Commodore in 1945. A stalwart of the RAF Association, and of the RAF Benevolent Fund, he lived out his life in Thornton-le-Dale, North Yorkshire. 'Hal' Crowe died on 26 April 1983.

CRUIKSHANK, Guy Lindsey

The son of James and Marie Cruikshank, of 44 Cyril Mansions, Battersea, London, and 4 Devonshire House, Devonshire Place, Eastbourne, he was born in 1890. Educated at the King's School, Rochester (1904-07), at Emmanuel College, Cambridge and at Sandhurst. Gazetted Second Lieutenant to the Gordon Highlanders on 1 December 1908. Developing an interest in aviation, he gained a French 'ticket' qualification (Number Fr 1520) on 9 August 1913. Seconded to the RFC in 1913, he accompanied the original RFC contingent to France as a member of 3 Squadron in August 1914, thus earning the 1914 Star. Guy's brother, Eric Onslow Cruikshank, Wiltshire Regiment, had also won a 1914 Star, before he was killed in action during the Battle of the Aisne on 19 September 1914. Guy's MC was announced in the *London Gazette* of 23 June 1915 and, although no formal citation was published in the *Gazette*, research has unearthed the original recommendation for the award: 'On the 26th April this Officer was ordered to bomb the Station at Roubaix, which was done, and he came down to under 500 feet in order to do so. His machine was hit in many places, but he managed to successfully bring it back to the English lines'.

In this same raid and in similar circumstances, Second Lieutenant W B Rhodes Moorhouse, 2 Squadron, won, posthumously, the first Victoria Cross awarded to the flying service. Cruikshank was responsible for making the first successful attempt at landing a secret service agent behind the enemy's lines, on 29 September 1915. He was awarded the Distinguished Service Order for this feat announced in the *London Gazette* of 4 November 1915, the intriguing citation reading: 'For conspicuous gallantry in France on 29 September 1915, when he successfully carried out a special mission, involving great risk'.

Following a lengthy period of active service at the front, Cruikshank was at last given a prolonged rest before joining the CFS as an Instructor in 1916. He was sent out again to France in the summer of 1916, this time accompanying the newly raised Sopwith Strutter-equipped 70 Squadron as a Flight Commander and 'founder member'. '70' was commanded by a certain Major A W Tedder. On 8 July following, Cruikshank came close to disaster when his Strutter, '5719', was shot up over St Omer. His Observer, 18 year old Londoner, Second Lieutenant Andrew J T Cruickshank, was mortally wounded in the air, and died later in hospital at St Omer. On the same day, another 70 Squadron Strutter, 'A384', manned by Captain D M V Veitch and Lieutenant J L Whitty, was shot down in flames, these casualties being the first of the war for 70 Squadron. On 6 September, Cruikshank accounted for two EAs on the same patrol. Dawn on 15 September 1916, heralded the third phase of the Battle of the Somme, when an infantry assault in the area of the hamlets of Flers and Courcelette, would be supported, for the first time ever in the history of warfare, by tanks. In the air, 70 Squadron was charged with a dawn offensive patrol, and destined to experience what the Official History called 'some of the bloodiest fighting of the day'. Cruikshank, who led the patrol, was well aware of the reputation of the great German ace, Oswald Boelcke, and had openly expressed a wish to meet him in combat. It is extremely doubtful that he knew the identity of the Pilot of the enemy machine he swooped upon over Havrincourt Wood, but, in the event, it was, indeed, the redoubtable Boelcke. After a fierce and 'brilliant duel', Boelcke shot the Strutter to pieces in the air, its debris, as well as its occupants, Cruikshank and his Observer, Lieutenant R A Preston, being scattered over Havrincourt Wood. The MC Rudolph Preston had won in the trenches with the Lincolnshire Regiment would be announced in the *London Gazette* one week after his death. A formal recommendation for one of the two Mentions in Despatches Cruikshank received during the Great War has been unearthed by research, dated 16 October 1916, it reads: 'From 6 September 1916 he set a splendid example of gallantry and devotion to duty. His skill and untiring energy were of the greatest value throughout the whole period. (This officer was reported missing on 15 September 1916)'. Guy Cruikshank is buried in Hesbecourt Communal Cemetery, Somme, France.

CUBBON, Francis Richard

Born on 29 November 1892, he was brought up by his grandmother and guardian, Mrs Hull, of 45 Wolfington Road, West Norwood, London. Educated at Dulwich College (1906-10) and at the Royal Military College, Sandhurst, from where he passed out 23rd in 1911. He was gazetted Second Lieutenant to the Indian Army on 6 September 1911, before being posted to the Unattached List. Cubbon served for a year attached to the York and Lancaster Regiment in Karachi, before being posted to 72 Punjabis, for service on the North West Frontier. After the rigours of the Frontier, he was, in November 1915, invalided home to the UK. Once recovered, he was first attached to the Royal Warwickshire Regiment before successfully seeking secondment to the RFC in October 1916. After training as an Observer, he was sent to the FE2d-equipped 20 Squadron in France in April 1917, almost immediately teaming up with Captain F J H Thayre (qv) – a pairing which proved to be a formidable fighting unit. Cubbon was credited with an incredible 21 victories achieved between 24 April and 7 June 1917. On 9 June 1917, Thayre and Cubbon in FE2d, 'A6430', were engaged in bombing over Comines when they were shot down, whether by ground fire or in aerial combat is not clear. Although subsequently, their deaths were confirmed by the German Air Service in a note dropped on a British airfield, their graves were never discovered. Cubbon's MC and Bar were both announced posthumously in the same *London Gazette* of 18 July 1917, both citations extolling his remarkable marksmanship: MC: 'For conspicuous gallantry and devotion to duty. He has shown great pluck and determination when acting as observer, on several occasions displaying fine marksmanship and coolness against superior numbers of the enemy'.

Bar to his MC: 'For conspicuous gallantry and devotion to duty. When acting as an observer on an offensive patrol, he displayed great skill and courage against superior numbers of the enemy. Throughout the action he backed up his pilot with a remarkable display of marksmanship'.

Because his remains were never recovered, Francis Richard Cubbon is commemorated on the Flying Services Memorial, Arras, France.

CUDEMORE, Charles William

Born on 19 November 1897, his family lived at 'The Châlet', Loughton, Essex. Joined the Inns of Court OTC on 12 November 1914 (Number2/2072), attaining the rank of Corporal before being gazetted Second Lieutenant to the King's Shropshire Light Infantry on 21 June 1915. Kept back in the UK because of his age, he eventually succeeded in securing a transfer to the RFC in December 1916. After putting up his 'Wings' in the spring of 1917, he was sent out to join the Nieuport XVII-equipped 40 Squadron at the front on 23 April 1917. Cudemore achieved two victories with 40 Squadron, before joining 29 Squadron on 20 July following. Three more victories came with '29', before a posting to the Home Establishment followed on 8 October 1917. His MC was announced in the *London Gazette* of 18 October 1917, details in the *Gazette* of 7 March 1918: 'For conspicuous gallantry and devotion to duty in attacking enemy aircraft and kite balloons. He has brought down at least three enemy machines and three kite balloons, and has taken part in numerous other engagements. He has consistently set a fine example of pluck and determination in all his attacks'.

After a relatively long period out of the firing line, Cudemore returned to the front and 64 Squadron, as a Flight Commander with the rank of Captain, in August 1918. No less than ten further victories followed before the end of the war on 11 November. He was awarded a Distinguished Flying Cross in the *London Gazette* of 3 June 1919. Charles' younger brother, John Richardson Cudemore, also served in the RAF, after going through the route of the Inns of Court OTC and being commissioned into 5 Battalion, London Regiment. After the war, Charles emigrated to British Columbia, Canada, and there joined the RCAF. He flew and instructed at Brough CFS, between 1926 and 1929. In August 1940, his address was Portman Square, London, having previously lived at Westcliffe-on-Sea, Essex, in Battersea, London SW11 and in Chipstead, Surrey, since leaving Canada.

CURLEWIS, Ivan

Born on 27 December 1895, in Arcadia, Pretoria, South Africa. Gazetted Second Lieutenant to the RFC, via the Special Reserve, on 17 January 1916. Gained his Royal Aero Club Certificate (Number 2472) on 19 February 1916. Having completed his formal training, he was confirmed and gazetted Flying Officer on 11 May following, the same day that he was posted to 5 Squadron at the front. After the briefest acquaintance with '5', he was transferred to the DH2-equipped 29 Squadron in June. On 1 October, using the specialised 'Buckingham' bullets, he brought down a hostile balloon in flames, despite the intense ground fire put up by its defenders. His MC was announced in the *London Gazette* of 14 November 1916: 'For conspicuous gallantry in action. He attacked an enemy machine which he drove off. Later, he destroyed an enemy machine, and brought down a balloon under very heavy fire, displaying great courage and determination throughout'.

On 9 November 1916, Curlewis was on patrol with others of his squadron, when they encountered a formation of the new German Albatros DII fighters with disastrous effect. Four DH2s, including Curlewis' 'A2543', were shot down in short order. Curlewis, badly wounded and taken prisoner, was claimed as a victory by Leutnant Hans von Keudell of Jasta 1. Curlewis lost a leg in this action and, through the intervention of the International Red Cross, was repatriated on 9 January 1918, to be fitted with an artificial limb. He was further repatriated to his home in South Africa in the following March. Ivan Curlewis was finally forced to relinquish his commission, due to ill-health occasioned by wounds, on 22 July 1919.

CURPHEY, William George Sellar

The son of Civil Servant, William Salvador Curphey and Mrs Curphey, of 87 Canfield Gardens, Hampstead, Middlesex, he was born in 1895. Educated at Glasgow Academy, at University College School, Hampstead and at London University, where he was a member of the OTC. He enlisted as a Private soldier into the Royal Berkshire Regiment in the early weeks of the war, before being picked out for a commission and gazetted Second Lieutenant to his own regiment on 16 November 1914. Curphey was seconded to the RFC in November 1915 and, after gaining his 'Wings', accompanied the DH2-equipped 32 Squadron to France as a 'founder member' on 28 May 1916. His MC was announced in the *London Gazette* of 14 November 1916: 'For conspicuous skill and gallantry. He brought down an enemy machine and two days later attacked and brought down another. He has recently attacked formations of hostile aircraft and driven them down'.

Promoted to A/Captain and Flight Commander on 9 January 1917, a Bar to his MC came in the *London Gazette* of 12 March 1917: 'For conspicuous gallantry in action. He, with a patrol of four machines, attacked a hostile formation of ten machines. After a prolonged fight he drove one enemy machine down. Later, although wounded, he again led another attack on a hostile machine and succeeded in bringing it down. He has on many previous occasions done fine work'.

On 4 February 1917, Curphey in DH2, 'A2536', fell foul of the German ace, Erwin Böhme. Curphey had already accounted for an Albatros down out of control, when Böhme attacked him. Slightly wounded in the head, Curphey was forced to peel away and dive for the British lines. Having recovered from the slight wounds he had received, he was soon in the air again, claiming his sixth victory on 7 February. On 14 May 1917, Curphey and two of his colleagues successfully attacked three enemy balloons some six miles behind the lines. After turning for home, they were pounced upon by an equal number of hostile machines. An Albatros on Curphey's tail was shot up – and down – by Lieutenant St Cyprian Churchill Tayler, the second of his eventual ten victories before he, too, was killed in action, a victim of Leutnant Heinrich Kroll of Jasta 24, on 17 March 1918. Tayler's intervention was in vain, however, as Curphey was immediately afterwards hit by fire from Hauptmann Franz Walz, leader of Jasta Boelcke. Curphey was desperately unlucky, his DH2, 'A2622', bursting into flames a mere 20 feet from the ground. He died the following day in a German field hospital at Bouchain. Had he lived, he was due to be appointed to his Majority within weeks, a promotion which would, effectively, have brought his combat flying to an end. William Curphey is buried in the Caberet-Rouge Cemetery, France (Fr924).

CURRIE, John Clive

From Melbourne, Victoria, he was born on 24 May 1893. Employed as a Grazier on a sheep station pre-war, he attempted to enlist into the ranks of the AIF late in 1914, but was refused on medical grounds. Not content with this, he travelled to the UK at his own expense and, upon arrival, enlisted as a Private soldier (Number 4681) into 14 Battalion, London Regiment (London Scottish) on 20 April 1915. Sent out to the front as part of a re-enforcing draft on 5 July 1915, he was wounded in action during the Battle of Loos in September 1915. Following hospitalisation in France and in England, he was posted to the Regimental Depot on 25 November 1915. Picked out for a commission, he was gazetted Second Lieutenant to the Royal Field Artillery on 26 November 1915. Returning to the front, he again served in France and Flanders, this time with the Gunners, before being gassed in December 1916. Once partially recovered, Currie was seconded to the RFC, first charged with administration duties, but then, as his health improved, training as an Observer at the Wireless and Observer School at Brooklands from 30 March 1917. His training completed, he was sent out to the RE8-equipped 5 Squadron as a Probationary on 8 May following. Currie's probationary period satisfactorily completed, he was formally confirmed and gazetted Flying Officer (Observer) on 1 July 1917. His MC was announced in the *London Gazette* of 17 September 1917: 'For conspicuous gallantry and devotion to duty when acting as Observer to another officer. They faced a violent thunderstorm, accompanied by a gale of wind and blinding rain, which had compelled all other machines to return to their aerodromes or to make forced landings, in order to locate the position of our infantry in the front lines. This they successfully did, having spent one and a half hours in the air under fearful conditions, and returned with an accurate and valuable report to Headquarters'.

Brought down by a hostile on 24 September 1917, he received injuries which required field hospital treatment. Currie returned to the Home Establishment for rest and recuperation on 1 October 1917. Posted to the Artillery and Infantry Co-operation School on 7 November 1917, he did not again return to active service. He married, in England, in 1918, Joanna Fraser. Currie finally left the RAF on 21 January 1919, before returning to Australia with his wife and child on 21 May following. They lived at Gala Cottage, Lismore, Victoria, and he continued to serve in the local part-time militia. When the Second World War came, he enlisted into the AIF on 20 February 1940, and was subsequently appointed Quarter Master at the Infantry General Base Depot, Melbourne. He embarked, with the rank of Captain, from Melbourne on 14 April 1940, bound for the Middle East on troopship *Y1*, arriving at Kantara on 18 May. His next appointment, on 17 July 1940, was to HQ, 1 Corps, Suneid, as Camp Commandant. He was next posted to Suez as Draft Conducting Officer, on 28 August 1940. On 31 October 1940, he was sent to 22 Militia Battalion, and from that post to Liaison Officer duties, which commenced on 26 January 1942. John Currie finally left the service to revert to the Retired List, on 23 May 1943.

CUTHBERT, Cuthbert Ross

Enlisting as a Trooper (Number 1984) in the Royal Canadian Dragoons, he arrived in France as part of the CEF on 7 February 1915. Successfully responding to a call for officer candidates, he was gazetted Second Lieutenant to the Royal Field Artillery, via the Special Reserve, on 26 July 1915. Following further service at the front with the Gunners, he was seconded to the RFC in the autumn of 1917. After completing his observer training, he was sent out as a Probationary to the RE8-equipped 12 Squadron on 11 November 1917. His MC citation erroneously refers to Cuthbert as being a Pilot. In fact, both his Pilot, J L S Hanman (qv), and Cuthbert himself, were, confusingly, given identical citations. The main incident for which they were rewarded, occurred on the first day of the great German spring offensive on 21 March 1918. The MCs were both announced in the *London Gazette* of 22 June 1918: 'For conspicuous gallantry and devotion to duty. While on contact patrol he and his Observer [sic], noticing the enemy massing for an attack, sent down a call to open fire, which was answered, with the result that the enemy was driven back to their trenches. This was done on two later occasions, until finally the enemy were repulsed with heavy casualties. A hostile two-seater plane was then attacked, with the result that the latter dived very steeply, smoke issuing from it. His consistent gallantry and good work have proved invaluable'.

Research has unearthed the original recommendation for this award, which provides some further detail: '3rd Brigade HQ, RAF, 1 April 1918 [the first day of the new Service]. For consistent gallantry and good work during the recent operations, March 21st to March 31st, 1918. Lieutenant Cuthbert, with 2nd Lieutenant Hanman as Pilot, has shown the greatest gallantry and skill during the recent battle. They have together completed many successful contact patrols at a very low altitude under heavy fire from rifles and machine guns. On March 24th, while on contact patrol over St Leger and flying at 500 feet, they observed the enemy massed for an attack. An SOS call was sent, which was answered, and the enemy were driven back to their trenches. Ten minutes later another concentration was seen, and another SOS call sent with the same result; fifteen minutes later the enemy massed again and another SOS call was sent, and the enemy heavily engaged by our artillery. They were dispersed with heavy casualties. Both Pilot and Observer attacked these troops with machine-gun fire from 500 feet, entirely breaking up the enemy attack, which never reached our trenches. Lieutenant Cuthbert and 2nd Lieutenant Hanman then attacked an enemy two-seater which appeared, apparently to do a contact patrol with the enemy. After a good burst from Lieutenant Cuthbert's gun the enemy aeroplane dived very steeply, with smoke issuing from the fuselage. He was followed down to 50 feet, and was then lost sight of in the mist, and is believed have crashed near Croisilles'. Cuthbert's tour with '12' ended in May 1918, whereupon he returned to the Home Establishment. Cuthbert finally relinquished his commission, and left the RAF to return to Canada in February 1919.

CUTHBERTSON, George Chapman

The son of George William and Ethel Margaret Cuthbertson, of Manor House, Heighington, County Durham, he was born in 1896. Gazetted Second Lieutenant to 12 (Tee-side Pioneers) Battalion, Yorkshire Regiment (The Green Howards), a 'Pals' Battalion, on 10 February 1915. By then promoted to Lieutenant, Cuthbertson landed in France with his unit on 2 June 1916, as Second-in-Command of 'W' Company. He served in the trenches until securing a secondment to the RFC in the autumn of 1916. Following pilot training, he was confirmed and gazetted Flying Officer on 25 January 1917. Cuthbertson served in the UK as an Instructor before being sent out to the Sopwith Pup-equipped 54 Squadron on 23 October 1917. '54' evolved to Camels in December 1917, and Cuthbertson enjoyed some moderate success with the new vehicle. On 2 February 1918, he tackled a Jasta 11 Fokker Tri-plane which, in its turn, was attacking a Camel – the Fokker was seen to break up in the air. On 1 March, he sent a hostile down out of control. On 1 April, however, his Camel, 'D6529', was badly shot up in the air, and Cuthbertson received a serious throat wound. After the inevitable crash-landing, the Camel was found to be unsalvable. Eight days later, George Cuthbertson died in hospital as a consequence of his wounds. His MC was posthumously announced in the *London Gazette* of 22 April 1918: 'For conspicuous gallantry and devotion to duty. During a period of two months he has destroyed two enemy machines, one of which was a tri-plane, and sent down one other completely out of control. He has also carried out at very low altitude several valuable reconnaissances at a long distance behind the enemy lines, and has set an example of the greatest pluck and determination to all ranks'.

George Cuthbertson is buried at St Sever Cemetery, Rouen, France.

D

DANBY, Charles David

The son of Charles Percy Clemson Danby and Frances Danby, of Manchester, he was born on 10 July 1887. A qualified Consulting Engineer, he worked for the Egyptian Civil Service from 1912 to 1914. Returning to the UK, he was gazetted Second Lieutenant to the Electrical Engineering Section, Tyneside, Royal Engineers (TF), on 26 January 1915. Gained his Royal Aero Certificate (Number 1324) on 31 May 1915, and was confirmed and gazetted Flying Officer on the same day. Sent out to the BE2c-equipped 6 Squadron on 30 September 1915. These were busy times and Danby had a number of close calls flying in co-operation with the Artillery. On 4 November 1915, for example, Danby and his Observer, Second Lieutenant Howey, fought a prolonged battle with two Albatroses but, after 20 minutes of shooting at each other, the fight ended with all ammunition expended, but no damage whatsoever inflicted on any of the three machines. On 20 January following, however, Danby, this time with Lieutenant Price acting as Observer, was convinced that he had brought down an Aviatik over Polygon Wood. His MC was announced in the *London Gazette* of 30 March 1916: 'For excellent work, under bad weather conditions, when taking photographs both before and during operations'. (After his death in 1918, the *Illustrated London* News credited Danby with being, 'one of the first to take photographs over the enemy's lines'.)

Following his first tour with 6 Squadron, Danby rested in the UK, before going out as a Flight Commander with 1 Squadron on 5 January 1917. This proved to be a short-lived posting as he was admitted to hospital in France on 25 January following, before being sent home for further treatment. Once recovered, he served in the North East of England on Home Defence duties with 252 Squadron, in the summer of 1918, but was killed in a flying accident at Seaton Carew, Durham, on 18 July. Charles Danby is buried in Hartlepool (Stanton) Cemetery, Durham.

NB: His medals were offered for sale on eBay in July 2003: MC, 1914-15 Star, British War Medal 1914-20, and Victory Medal 1914-19 with MID.

DANBY, Cyril Stone

From West Bridgford, Nottingham, he was born on 26 May 1891. When the war came he was a self-employed Manufacturer in his home city. Gazetted Second Lieutenant to the RFC in March 1915, he qualified for his 'Wings' and was sent to 15 Squadron, then stationed at Dover, in the following May. He accompanied '15' to France as a 'founder member' on 23 December 1915, his first operational tour extending to July 1916. Gazetted Flight Commander and promoted to Acting Captain on 13 July 1916, his MC was announced in the New Year *London Gazette* of 1 January 1917 (no citation). Although no formal citation was published in the *Gazette*, research has unearthed the original recommendation for the award made by Brigadier General C A H Longcroft, commanding 5th Brigade, RFC: 'For exceptional brilliant work as a pilot in co-operation with the Artillery from January to July 1916. Lieut Danby has always shown the greatest dash and determination, frequently carrying out his work under the most difficult conditions'.

His tour with '15' completed, Danby worked as an Instructor in the UK, before going out to serve in the Adriatic theatre of war during 1917 and 1918. He next joined 113 Squadron in Palestine with the rank of Major, in February 1919. Danby spent the last months of his service in various administrative posts, before finally leaving the RAF in December 1919. A married man, he returned to live in his native Nottingham in the post-war years.

NB: His British War Medal 1914-20 was offered for sale by Lockdales of Ipswich in January 2005.

DANIEL, Hector Cyril

Born in South Africa on 19 October 1898. 'Daisey' Daniel was yet another South African who returned to the home country at his own expense, as soon as war came. He was, apparently, 'well-connected' as he was, soon after arriving, gazetted Second Lieutenant to 17 (Duke of Cambridge's Own) Lancers, on 23 December 1914. Although at first kept back in the UK because of his extreme youth, he eventually served in France with his regiment before being seconded to the RFC in the autumn of 1917. After learning to fly and putting up his 'Wings', he was sent out to join the Camel-equipped 43 Squadron at the front on 22 November 1917. He achieved nine victories between 17 February and 30 May 1918, including a 'double' and a 'trio' on single days. His tour with '43' completed, he was next posted to a training unit in the UK as an Instructor, in the last summer of the war. His MC was announced in the *London Gazette* of 26 July 1918: 'For conspicuous gallantry and devotion to duty in numerous aerial encounters. On one occasion he completely destroyed three enemy aeroplanes on the same day. He has in addition crashed three others and sent down two out of control. He has always displayed the greatest skill, keenness and courage in aerial fighting and his services have been of inestimable value to his patrol leader'.

Daniel was also subsequently awarded an Air Force Cross, *London Gazette* of 3 June 1919, in recognition of the outstanding work he had performed during his time at Major H H Balfour's No 3 Air Fighting School, in Norfolk. Daniel finally left the RAF, via the Unemployed List, on 10 August 1919. Returning to South Africa in 1921, he joined the newly formed South African Air Force and, by 1939, was the Director of Air and Technical Services with the rank of Lieutenant Colonel, then SASO, East Africa, advancing to Brigadier (and CBE) by the end of the Second World War in 1945, at which time he became OC, Natal Command. Not long afterwards, he terminated his own life, whilst a patient in a Pretoria hospital.

DANIELL, Thomas Edward St Clare

A Staff, not a flying, award

From London, he was born on 7 August 1886. Educated at Felsted (1897-1905) and at Exeter College, Oxford, from where he graduated BA in 1908. Admitted a Solicitor in February 1912, he was employed as Managing Clerk with Messrs Mackrell & Ward of 33 Wallbrook, London EC. A married man, he lived, pre-war, with his wife in Weybridge, Surrey. On 30 August 1914, he enlisted as a Private soldier (Number 1868) into 28 Battalion, London Regiment (Artist Rifles) (TF). He had served in France with his regiment and had attained the rank of Sergeant by the time he was gazetted Second Lieutenant to the RFC on 8 September 1915. An administrator of outstanding ability, he advanced through the ranks rapidly: Captain, January 1916; A/Major, June 1916; Deputy Assistant Director of Aircraft Equipment with the rank of Major, February 1917; Assistant Director and Lieutenant Colonel, March 1917; and Deputy Director and A/Colonel, April 1918. He served in the UK and in France throughout this period. His MC was announced in the New Year *London Gazette* of 1 January

1917 (no citation). Although no formal citation was published in the *Gazette*, research has unearthed the original recommendation for the award: 'From Feb 1916 until the present time he has displayed remarkable organising ability in the development of the Stores Section, 2 Aircraft Depot. He is extremely hard working, possessing patience and coolness. The fighting on the Somme has caused exceptional demands on the Stores Section of the Depot. These demands, which have invariably been met with promptness, are received at all hours of the day and night. He is cheerful under all conditions'.

Daniell was also Mentioned in Despatches on three occasions during the Great War. A recommendation for the earliest of these 'Mentions' has also been unearthed: '15 March 1916. This officer has carried the duties of Stores Officer, first in 1 Air Depot and latterly in charge of the Spares Section, 2 Air Depot, with much zeal and capacity. In the position of Stores Officer, he has shown considerable power of command and organisation'.

The award of an OBE to Daniell was gazetted on 7 June 1918, which was later transferred to the Military division on 15 April 1919. Daniell finally left the RAF in 1919, subsequently taking up residence with his wife at 42 Coleherne Court, South Kensington, London SW5.

NB: His medals were offered for sale by Glendining's (lot 382) on 19 September 1989: OBE (first type, Britannia in obverse centre), MC, 1914-15 Star (1868 Pte T E StC Daniell, 28/Lon R)*, British War Medal 1914-20, and Victory Medal 1914-19* (Major RFC).

DAVEY, Horace Balfour

The son of Lieutenant Colonel the Hon R S Davey and Mrs Davey, of Staffordshire, he was born in Umballa on 14 February 1894. A pre-war volunteer officer with 6 Battalion, North Staffordshire Regiment (TF), he was mobilised with the rest of the TF on the day war was declared, being promoted to Lieutenant just three weeks later on 26 August 1914. After serving in France with 1/6 South Staffs, Davey transferred to the RFC in the summer of 1915. Having trained as an Observer, he was sent out to BE2c-equipped 2 Squadron and fought through the worst days of the so-called 'Fokker Scourge'. He next trained as a Pilot, qualifying for his Royal Aero Club Certificate (Number 2752) on 6 March 1916. His formal pilot training duly completed, he was confirmed and gazetted Flying Officer on 6 May following. His first operational posting as a Pilot, just five days after qualifying, was to the FE2b-equipped 25 Squadron. Davey gained five victories and the status of Ace with '25', before being sent to 11 Squadron as A/Captain and Flight Commander on 10 August 1916. His MC was announced in the *London Gazette* of 25 November 1916: 'For conspicuous gallantry in action. He led a reconnaissance of six machines with great courage and skill. Later, although attacked by ten hostile machines, he continued to carry out this reconnaissance. He has previously done fine work'.

A further victory with '11' preceded a home posting, which was followed by a promotion to A/Major and command of 59 TDS, where he remained until May 1918. In that same month he was again sent out to 11 Squadron, this time as CO of that unit. His command of '11' extended to July 1919, whereupon he was appointed to the Staff, going on to serve with the RAF until September 1921, when he relinquished his commission. Davey lived, post-war, in Hampstead, North London.

DAVIDSON, Charles Robert

The son of Lieutenant Colonel C F H Davidson, 93 Highlanders, and Mrs Davidson, of Folkestone, he was born in Poona, India, on 2 November 1896. Educated at Dover College (OTC), at Oundle (OTC) and at the University of London. He enlisted as a Private soldier into 10 Battalion, Royal Fusiliers (Stockbrokers Battalion), in the early days of the war. Davidson subsequently contrived a transfer to his father's old regiment and accompanied 11 Battalion, Argyll and Sutherland Highlanders to France on 9 July 1915. He fought in the Battle of Loos, distinguishing himself on the first day, 25 September 1915, for which he received a Mention in Despatches, *London Gazette* of 1 January 1916. Transferring to the RFC, he was sent to Aboukir in Egypt, where he trained as an Observer. The inevitable commission came when he was gazetted Second Lieutenant to the Highland Light Infantry on 31 May 1916, with an immediate secondment to the RFC. His probationary period over, he was formally confirmed and gazetted Flying Officer (Observer) on 4 September 1916. A chance to train as a Pilot had presented itself around this time and, following qualification, he put up his full 'Wings' shortly before being sent to 14 Squadron early in 1917. When, later in the same year, 111 Squadron was raised as a specialised fighter unit for the MEF, Davidson was one of those selected for the new unit. Before leaving '111' through wounds received in action on 9 January 1918, he had gained two victories flying Vickers FB19 Scouts, and a further four victories in a Bristol Fighter, 'A7192'. On 9 January 1918, he and his Observer of the day, Captain J J Lloyd-Williams, were involved in an aerial combat and although Davidson was shot, agonisingly, through the ankle, he still managed to land his Brisfit without further mishap. His MC was announced in the *London Gazette* of 14 January 1918 - the graphic details appearing in the *Gazette* of 22 April 1918: 'For conspicuous gallantry and devotion to duty. He forced a hostile aeroplane to land, and, descending to a low altitude despite heavy rifle fire, shot down one of the occupants as he was escaping from the machine. On two later occasions he forced an enemy machine to land, and drove down another, which was last seen diving into country where it was impossible to land. Finally, though his ankle was fractured by a bullet during an air combat, he landed without injury either to his Observer or his machine'.

Davidson was invalided to the UK in March 1918, where he saw out the remainder of the war.

DAVIDSON, Donald Alistair Leslie

The elder son of Colonel W Leslie Davidson, CB, Royal Artillery, who died on active service in France in 1915, and Lady Theodora Davidson, sister of the Earl of Albemarle, who occupied a 'Grace and Favour' residence inside Hampton Court Palace, he was born in 1891. The young Davidson acted as Page of Honour to HM King Edward VII, from 1902 to 1908. Educated at Wellington College (1905-08) and at McGill University, Montreal, Canada. Learning to fly at his own expense, Davidson qualified for the Royal Aero Club Certificate (Number 1201) on 30 April 1915, the same day that he was gazetted Second Lieutenant to the RFC, via the Special Reserve. Three months later on 22 July 1915, his formal pilot instruction completed, he was confirmed and gazetted Flying Officer and able to put up his 'Wings'. Sent out to 30 Squadron in the Middle East, he served from 27 December 1915 to 6 May 1916 in that theatre of war. His duties included assisting the relief force in the failed attempts to raise the siege on the British garrison of Kut-al-Amara, which finally fell to the Turks in April 1916. Indeed, Donald was wounded in an aerial combat while dropping food to the beleaguered garrison. His MC was announced in the *London Gazette* of 24 June 1916, details in the *Gazette* of 27 July 1916: 'For conspicuous gallantry and determination. When attacked by an enemy fighting scout, his machine was heavily damaged, the control being shot away, and he himself being wounded in three places. He succeeded, however, with great skill in reaching his aerodrome and landing safely, after which he had to be lifted out and carried to hospital'.

He was also Mentioned in Despatches at this time. Davidson was invalided home because of the severity of his wounds. Once recovered, he was eventually able to return to active service and was subsequently posted to the Spad VII-equipped 19 Squadron in France early in 1917. On 30 April 1917, his Spad VII, 'B1592', was reportedly, 'blown up in the air'. The King and Queen expressed their deep sympathy to his widowed mother, 'for the dear boy who had already rendered such gallant service', whilst Queen Alexandra sorrowed for 'her dear Page of Honour'. Donald Davidson's remains were never recovered and hence he is commemorated on the Flying Services Memorial, Arras, France.

DAVIES, Frederick Harry

From South London, he was born on 30 October 1897. He was employed as a Timber Agent's Clerk in the City of London, during 1914 and 1915. Davies enlisted as a Private soldier (Number 760760) into 28 Battalion, London Regiment (Artists Rifles) (TF), in 1916. Transferring as an Officer Cadet to the flying service in October 1916, he was subsequently gazetted Second Lieutenant to the RFC on 28 February 1917. Having qualified as a Pilot, he was sent out to France and the RE8-equipped 13 Squadron, on 22 August 1917. On 11 March 1918, Davies and his Observer, Second Lieutenant E M Cleland, when engaged on an artillery patrol, were attacked by no fewer than five Albatros Scouts. Not only did Davies extricate them from an almost certain death situation, but Cleland also managed to shoot one of their feared adversaries down to crash near Sailly. His MC was announced in the *London Gazette* of 13 May 1918: 'For conspicuous gallantry and devotion to duty. Whilst on artillery observation duty he engaged a hostile scout, which he succeeded in sending down out of control. He then continued to observe for the shoot, and successfully accomplished his task. Later, whilst again on artillery patrol, though attacked by five hostile aeroplanes, he, by successful manoeuvring, enabled his observer to fire several bursts into the leader of the formation, whose machine was seen to go down in a vertical nose-dive and crash to earth. Continuing the fight against the remaining four hostile machines, he eventually forced them away, and succeeded in ranging on and neutralizing three hostile batteries. He set a magnificent example of skill and determination'.

Promoted to A/Captain and Flight Commander on 12 May 1918, he completed his tour with '13', and returned to the Home Establishment in the following July. Davies served, post-war, in Cologne with the Army of Occupation, before finally leaving the RAF, via the Unemployed List, in October 1919.

DAVIS, Harold Eborall

The son of Bedstead Manufacturer, William Harry and Florence Catherine Davis (née Harfield), of 'Woodville', Park Hill, Moseley, Worcestershire, he was born on 26 July 1890. Educated at Marlborough (1905-08). A Mechanical Engineer by profession, he was employed by Birmingham Corporation in the city's Electrical Tramways Engineering Shops, before going to work for three years prior to the outbreak of war in the Anchor Works, Birmingham. Volunteering immediately, he was gazetted Second Lieutenant to the New Armies, General List, on 22 September 1914, with an attachment to 9 Battalion, South Staffordshire Regiment. Proceeded to France in June 1915, he was attached to 23 Divisional Tunnelling Company. Davis was wounded in the trenches in the Arras area in September 1915. After recovering his health and fitness, Davis succeeding in securing a secondment to the RFC and, following training, was confirmed and gazetted Flying Officer on 13 December 1916. Sent out to the FE2b-equipped 25 Squadron soon after qualifying for his 'Wings'. On 14 April 1917 – 'Bloody April' – he and his Observer, Lieutenant Norman Walter Morrison, were engaged in a fierce combat with Leutnant Karl Emil Schäfer, then of Jasta 11. Schäfer sent the RFC machine down in flames, claiming it as the 18th of his eventual 30 victories. Miraculously, Davis managed to get the burning FE2b down to a controlled landing. It does appear, however, that his Observer, the 19 year old Norman Morrison, from Reigate, Surrey, fell or leapt from the burning machine, as his body was never recovered. Davis escaped with burns to his face and hands, and a shrapnel bullet wound to his left leg. His MC, the citation for which reflects the circumstances of this encounter, was announced in the *London Gazette* of 18 June 1917: 'For conspicuous gallantry and devotion to duty. He carried out a valuable reconnaissance over the enemy lines, flying for half an hour at a height of 500 feet. Although attacked by five hostile machines he succeeded in completing his task, effecting a safe landing. He was himself badly burned, but rendered a valuable report'.

When, eventually, Davis recovered, he was posted as an Instructor to Rochford aerodrome. On 19 June 1918, Davis was killed in an aerial accident, whilst instructing a pupil. The pupil survived, but was severely injured. Harold Davis is buried in Rochford (St Andrew) Churchyard, Essex.

DAVIS, John Ogilvie

The son of Dr and Mrs L Davis, of London, SW he was born on 24 June 1891. Educated at Wellington College (1904-07) and at Magdalen College, Cambridge. A note in Davis' records states that, as a civilian, he was, during the course of the Turko-Italian war in 1912, entrusted with the delivery of confidential despatches from Rome to London. He was gazetted probationary Flight Sub-Lieutenant to the RNAS on 17 April 1915, with an immediate posting to the Kite Balloon Service. An appointed to Overseeing Duties at 5 KBS at Roehampton followed next. He was promoted to Flight Lieutenant on 31 August 1915, the day after he accompanied No 8 KBS, to France, as its Commanding Officer. On 14 April 1916, Brigadier General E B Ashmore, Commanding 4 Brigade, RFC, reported on Davis' progress in the service: 'This officer is attached to No 8 KBS and is an able and successful Observer. On one occasion he made a parachute descent from a balloon. Has done well in Command of the Section'.

On 25 May 1916, Davis wrote to Major P K Wise, OC, 3 KBS, requesting his release from the RNAS and asking for a transfer to the RFC, with the rank of Captain and Flight Commander – the same seniority of rank he held in the RNAS. The letter was forwarded and endorsed by recommendation to 1 Wing RFC. Davis' wish was granted and his RNAS commission terminated on 26 May 1916, upon his formal transfer to the Army. He was then appointed to a temporary commission on the General List with the rank of Captain, to take effect from 26 May 1916, but with seniority back-dated to 17 April 1915. His appointments as a Balloon Officer with effect from 26 May 1916 and as a Flight Commander from 27 May 1916 were also promulgated and confirmed. His MC was announced in the New Year *London Gazette* of 1 January 1917 (no citation). Although no formal citation was published in the *Gazette*, research has unearthed the original recommendation for the award: 'For exceptional good service and devotion to duty in command of a KBS in France since 31-8-15. He has done much to increase the efficient co-operation of kite balloons with artillery'.

Davis next served at the Balloon Training Wing, before proceeding to BC HQ, Salonika on 12 January 1917, having been promoted to Major in the previous month.

His Salonika tour completed, he returned to the Home Establishment on 22 June 1918. Davis was Mentioned in Despatches for his services in Salonika, *London Gazette* of 11 June 1918, and also received a Croix de Guerre from the French, *London Gazette* of 21 September 1918. On 29 July 1918, he was appointed to command 3 Balloon Squadron, 7 Balloon Wing, South East Area. Next, he was sent to 2 Balloon Training Wing, on 16 September, where he saw out the remainder of the war. His final posting was to Crystal Palace on 17 February 1919, from where he departed the service, via the Unemployed List, just two days later. Davis lived, post-Great War, at 1 Elyston Mansions, Pelham Crescent, London SW, before going to live and work in Chile. His last-known address, in 1962, was Correo el Golf, Las Condes, Santiago, Chile.

DAVIS, Walter Ernest

From Gloucester, he was born on 1 October 1896. Gazetted Second Lieutenant to a Regular Army battalion of the Gloucestershire Regiment on 26 March 1917. Transferring to the RFC, he first trained as an Observer, going out in that capacity to 51 Squadron in July 1917, before eventually joining the FE2b-equipped night-bombing 102 Squadron in November following. His MC was announced in the *London Gazette* of 4 February 1918, the details appearing in the *Gazette* of 5 July 1918: 'For conspicuous gallantry and devotion to duty during three months service as an observer in a night-flying squadron. He has taken part in many long-distance night bomb raids, and has on all occasions shown great courage and determination, which have been a splendid example to the rest of the squadron'.

Research has unearthed the original recommendation for this award which is rather more informative than is the published citation: 'W E Davis. 102 Sqn 19/12/17: For conspicuous gallantry and devotion to duty. 2/Lt Davis has had three months service as an observer in a night flying squadron. On 30/9/17 bombs were dropped from 1,000 feet on Dechy Dump from the machine in which he was flying. On 9/10/17 Menin Station was bombed by his machine from 800 feet. On 20/10/17 when bombing a lighted German aerodrome an EA was seen about to leave the ground at Bissenghem. It was destroyed by a bomb from his machine and a second bomb set fire to a patrol store. On 21/10/17 two bombs were dropped on troops at Moorslede, who were engaging his machine with rifle fire and machine-gun fire. On 7/11/17 he assisted to bomb Gontrude aerodrome from 750 feet after which his machine followed a German aeroplane to its aerodrome. He made observations, subsequently attacking. These observations were, in the circumstances, a very fine piece of work and contained valuable information. 2/Lt Davis has taken part in many long distance night raids and he has shown on all occasions great courage and determination, which have been a fine example to the rest of his squadron'.

Davis next trained as a Pilot, and after gaining his 'Wings', returned to fly with 51 Squadron in whose service he remained until 1919, when he reverted again to his Army career with the Gloucestershire Regiment.

DAVISON, Hiram Frank

From Leeds County, Ontario, he was born on 12 January 1894. He worked as a travelling salesman in Saskatchewan, prior to joining the Canadian Horse Artillery. Davison served with the CEF in France before responding to a call for volunteers for the flying service. Gazetted Second Lieutenant to the RFC in July 1917, he was, after training, confirmed and gazetted Flying Officer on 31 October following. Sent out to the Bristol Fighter-equipped 22 Squadron in March 1918. A highly successful Brisfit Pilot, he achieved no less than 11 victories, all with Lieutenant J L Morgan (qv), between 6 March and 29 March 1918, six occurring during the frantic days immediately following the onset of the German spring offensive on the 21st of that month. He was himself wounded on 13 April 1918, when he was hit by machine-gun fire; a wound which, ironically, may have prolonged his life, for he did not recover sufficiently to return to combat flying before the war ended on 11 November following. His MC was announced in the *London Gazette* of 22 June 1918: 'For conspicuous gallantry and devotion to duty. During four days' operations he destroyed two enemy aeroplanes, and drove down two out of control, while his Observer destroyed one and drove down another out of control. He also assisted other members of his Squadron in destroying enemy machines. He showed splendid courage and leadership, and set an excellent example to his comrades'.

Research has unearthed the original recommendation for this award, which provides further detail: '3rd Brigade HQ, RAF, 6 April 1918. For skill and gallantry. During recent operations between March 25th and March 29th 1918, this officer destroyed two enemy aircraft, one crashing at Hangard, the other falling in flames at Montauban. He also drove two enemy aeroplanes down out of control, one at Havrincourt and the other at Albert. During the same period he manoeuvred his machine so that his Observer crashed one enemy aircraft at Albert and drove another down out of control at Hangard. In addition to inflicting losses on the enemy, this officer has been the means of enabling other members of his formation to destroy enemy aircraft. On many occasions he has turned back to help other members of his squadron when they have been in trouble, and in this way has helped to save pilots and machines which might have been lost. 2nd Lieutenant Davison has proved himself keen and reliable, and has always set an excellent example to the other officers of his squadron. Up to date he has destroyed five enemy aircraft and driven five others down out of control'.

Hiram Davison died in London, Ontario, in January 1974.

DAVISON, James Frederick

Originally from London, he was born on 14 June 1882. Formerly an officer of the Black Watch (Royal Highlanders) with Staff qualifications, he had retired from the Army and was working abroad when the war came in August 1914. Returning to the UK to offer his services, he was immediately given a Captaincy, via the Special Lists, on 12 September 1914, being employed, initially, in the Infantry Records Office, York. Anxious for a more active role, he somehow contrived, despite his age, to secure a secondment to the RFC, in the autumn of 1916. After training as an Observer, he was sent out to 16 Squadron as a Probationary in October 1916. His 'apprenticeship' duly completed, he was confirmed and gazetted Flying Officer (Observer) on 15 November following. Davison was Mentioned in Despatches, *London Gazette* of 15 May 1917. He served as the specialist Squadron Artillery Officer during this period. His MC was announced in the New Year *London Gazette* of 1 January 1918 (no citation). Although no formal citation was published in the *Gazette*, research has unearthed the original recommendation for the award: 'J F Davison, 16 Sqn. For gallantry, perseverance and conspicuous devotion to duty. As an Observer and Squadron Artillery Intelligence Officer, he has performed his duties most conscientiously. (Previously MiD)'.

His tour with '16' completed, Davison next served in various Staff positions during 1918. After the war with the Central Powers was over, he joined the South Russia Mission on 12 April 1919, as part of the Allied Intervention Force, serving in Constantinople and Egypt in the following year. Returning to the Home Establishment on 20 August 1920, he finally left the RAF, via the Unemployed List, on 5 October following.

DAY, James

From Marden, Kent, where his father was a landowner, he was born on 1 September 1897. Educated at Clifton College, Margate. He worked as a Superintendent in his father's business, before applying for the RFC in October 1916. Called up in February 1917, he reported first to Denham, before being sent as a Cadet to Oxford on 4 April 1917. Gazetted Second Lieutenant to the RFC on 10 May following. After training, he was confirmed and gazetted Flying Officer on 30 June 1917. Day accompanied the night-flying FE2b-equipped 102 Squadron to France as a 'founder member' on 18 September 1917. He completed an intensive, if largely routine, tour and returned to the Home Establishment on 7 April 1918. His MC was announced in the *London Gazette* of 22 June 1918: 'For conspicuous gallantry and devotion to duty. In one night he made five consecutive raids over the enemy's lines, during which period he dropped over half a ton of bombs on his two objectives. He also, during these raids, engaged with machine-gun fire from low altitude enemy billets in the same neighbourhood. He has rendered exceptionally valuable service, and has taken part in numerous bombing raids by night, almost all of which have been most successful'.

The French, too, showed their appreciation of his exceptional ability in this relatively new form of warfare, with the award of a Croix de Guerre, *London Gazette* of 17 August 1918. James Day finally left the RAF, via the Unemployed List, in February 1919.

DEACON, George Raymond Albert

From Swindon, he was born on 18 May 1888. Educated at Dean Close School (1901-04). Employed as a Bank Clerk, he was heavily involved in motor racing in the pre-war years. He enlisted as a Private soldier (Number 2384) into 1/8 Battalion, Worcestershire Regiment (TF), on 5 September 1914. Deacon landed in France with his battalion on 1 April 1915 and served in the trenches until 2 October following. Picked out for a commission, he was gazetted Second Lieutenant to the New Armies (General List) with an immediate attachment to 9 Battalion, Royal Sussex Regiment, on 3 October 1915. He was hospitalised for a hernia operation in April 1916. Once recovered, he took flying lessons at the London and Provincial School, Hendon, in the hope that the qualification would get him into the RFC. Gained the Royal Aero Club Certificate (Number 3120) on 22 June 1916. Following completion of his formal training at the CFS, he was confirmed and gazetted Flying Officer on 15 September following. He went to 15 Squadron on 30 March 1917 and for a period was with C Flight, working with Colonel T E Lawrence. On 8 August he moved to 111 Squadron where he stayed till December 1918. Deacon subsequently served in Egypt and Palestine, his MC, for his services during the capture of Jerusalem, was announced in the *London Gazette* of 11 April 1918 (no citation). He was also Mentioned in Despatches during this period. Immediately post-war he was on Special Duties in Khartoum before returning to 111 Squadron till June 1919, at which time he went to 113 Squadron. Staying on in the RAF after the war, he had attained the rank of Squadron Leader by 1927, and was employed as the Chief Signals Officer in Iraq, and later Wing Commander OBE. He died in the late 1950s.

DEANE, William

The son of Chair Maker, George Deane and Mrs Deane, of Myrtle House, Stokenchurch, Buckinghamshire, he was born in High Wycombe on 27 July 1896. Educated at the Royal Grammar School, High Wycombe (1907-14) and at the Royal College of Science (University of London OTC) until June 1915, when he left to receive a commission in 4 Battalion, Norfolk Regiment (TF) on 13 July 1915. Deane served with his battalion in Egypt from January 1917, before securing a secondment to the RFC in that theatre of war in the spring. He learnt to fly at RFC HQ, Egypt, and was subsequently confirmed and gazetted Flying Officer on 10 June 1917. Deane was next sent to the RE8-equipped 52 Squadron in France in July 1917. On 26 February 1918, Deane, by then a Captain and a Flight Commander, and his Observer of the day, Second Lieutenant T A W Foy, were engaged on an Artillery Observation patrol when their RE8, 'B3434', was hit by anti-aircraft fire. Although their machine came down to crash heavily, both crewmen survived unscathed. This was not the case, however, when, almost a month later on 23 March, Deane, alone in an RE8 (the weight saved by the absent Observer enabling him to carry more bombs) was attacked by four hostiles. On this occasion, Deane was severely wounded, but still managed to bring the 'Harry Tate' back to his own field. His MC was announced in the *London Gazette* of 22 June 1918: 'For conspicuous gallantry and devotion to duty. He attacked massed enemy troops, dropping bombs on them and inflicting very severe casualties. He was then attacked by four enemy machines, and severely wounded; but by displaying great endurance he succeeded in landing his machine safely at his aerodrome. His work in conjunction with the artillery, and his handling of his flight, have been brilliant, and by his exceptional courage and devotion to duty he set an extremely fine example to his Squadron'.

Deane's wounds precluded his return to operational flying before the war. He stayed on in the RAF after the war, receiving a permanent commission on 1 August 1919. He served with 20 Squadron in India in 1919, and again in the following year, until 20 March 1920, when he was killed on active service. William Deane's remains were never recovered and hence he is commemorated on the Delhi Memorial (India Gate), India.

DEAR, Frank Henry

From Ladywell, South East London. He was gazetted Second Lieutenant to 4 Battalion, Royal Sussex Regiment (TF) on 19 June 1915. Dear secured a secondment to the RFC in the autumn of 1916 and, following training, was confirmed and gazetted Flying Officer on 12 January 1917. Sent out to East Africa and 26 (South African) Squadron on 27 February 1917. His MC was announced in the *London Gazette* of 4 February 1918, details in the *Gazette* of 5 July 1918: 'For conspicuous gallantry and devotion to duty. His machine caught fire while he was engaged on a reconnaissance, while he was endeavouring to put the fire out his machine got into a spinning nose-dive. With great difficulty he got the fire under control and righted his machine when only a few hundred feet from the ground. He then carried out his reconnaissance. He showed great coolness and skill'.

His tour with '26' completed on 23 February 1918, he returned to the Home Establishment. Dear did not return to operational flying before the end of the war, and eventually left the RAF, via the Unemployed List, on 5 September 1919. Frank Henry Dear died at his home at 11 Tower Road, Orpington, Kent, on 29 February 1972.

deCOURCY, John Arthur Gerald

The son of the Hon Robert C S deCourcy and Mrs Katherine deCourcy (née Harris), of Waipukurua, New Zealand, he was born in Ivybridge, Devon, on 2 February 1894. Educated at Glenalmond (1908-11), at Trinity College, Dublin and at the Royal Military Academy, Woolwich. Gazetted Second Lieutenant to the Royal Artillery in 1911. Seconded to the RFC in 1915, he first served as a Probationary Observer with 3 Squadron from 26 October 1915. With his Artillery background, he was obviously well qualified to conduct co-operation and co-ordination from the air. Research has uncovered the original recommendation for a Mention in Despatches he received during this period: '11 March 1916: For conspicuously good work as an observer since 26 October 1915. The Corps to which the Squadron is attached has frequently remarked on his excellent reports. He has done good work in connection with Artillery'. Keen to become a Pilot, he gained his Royal Aero Club Certificate (Number 2646) on 5 May 1916. His formal training duly completed, he was confirmed and gazetted Flying Officer on 10 June following. His MC was announced in the *London Gazette* of 10 January 1917: 'For conspicuous gallantry in action. He has located numerous hostile batteries, and by directing the fire of our howitzers has been instrumental in destroying them. On one occasion he drove off three hostile machines'.

The French, too, showed their appreciation with the award of the Croix de Guerre, *London Gazette* of 1 May 1917. DeCourcy would go on to serve with, and command, both 3 and 12 Squadrons before the end of the war. Staying on in the RAF after the war, he held the rank of Squadron Leader in 1919 and, among other appointments, commanded 70 Squadron in Iraq. DeCourcy also commanded the Officers Engineering Course at Henlow. Promoted to Wing Commander in 1928, he retired from the RAF in 1938. DeCourcy subsequently lectured in Engineering Processes and in the Superintending of Engineering Workshops at Cambridge University. He lived, at this time, with his wife, Anna Felicia, at The White House, Barton, Cambridgeshire. When the Second World War came in September 1939, he was taken back into the RAF with the rank of Group Captain, going on to command the HQ Unit, 43 Group, Maintenance Command. Group Captain John deCourcy died on active service on 30 December 1940 and is buried in Barton (St Peter) Churchyard, Cambridgeshire.

deCRESPIGNY, Hugh Vivian Champion – **see** Hugh Vivian **CHAMPION deCRESPIGNY**

de CRUCE GRUBB, Richard Raymond

A Staff, not a flying, award

The son of Mr and Mrs S R Grubb, of Clogheen, County Tipperary, Ireland. Educated at Wellington College (1900-04) and at Sandhurst. Gazetted Second Lieutenant to 3 (King's Own) Hussars in 1905. Passed Staff College. Married Ruth Leney, with whom he had two sons, living at Castle Green, Clogheen, County Tipperary, Ireland. He served during the Great War on secondment to the Head Quarters of the Intelligence Corps, and on the Staff of the RFC. His MC was announced in the New Year *London Gazette* of 1 January 1917 (no citation). Although no formal citation was published in the *Gazette*, research has unearthed the original recommendation for the award, this made by Brigadier General D leG Pitcher, Commanding Officer, 1 Brigade, RFC: 'For exceptional good service and continued devotion to duty as Brigade Major since 30 January 1916. This officer has never spared himself in his endeavours to increase the efficiency of his own Staff work and that of those under him. The services that he has rendered have been invaluable'.

De Cruce Grubb also received two Mentions in Despatches for his Staff work and, again, a recommendation for one of these has been unearthed: '10 March 1916: For continually good work from 26 October 1915 to March 1916 on the Staff of the 1 Brigade, RFC. He has done particularly well in working out the details of organisation of the new RFC Brigade system'.

After the end of the Great War, he returned again to 3 Hussars and actually commanded the regiment from 1932 to 1936. De Cruce Grubb retired from the Army in 1938, becoming Chairman of Tipperary Products Ltd. He was soon in uniform again, however, his qualities as a GSO I ensuring him an immediate posting to the Staff of 18 Division, the moment the Second World War came in 1939.

DELL-CLARKE, George Courtney

The son of George Dell Clarke and Emma Priscilla Clarke, of 47 Richmond Park Avenue, Bournemouth, he was born in Kobe, Japan, on 12 January 1896. The Dell Clarke family had lived for many years at 38 Nakayamate, Kobe, Japan, and after completing his education, George took up a post as a Merchant Shipping Manager in that city. When the war came, he made his way back to the UK, and was gazetted Second Lieutenant to 3 (Reserve) Battalion, Loyal North Lancashire Regiment, on 26 August 1915. Anxious to join the RFC, he learnt to fly at his own expense and gained his Royal Aero Club Certificate (Number 2727) on 3 April 1916. Completing his formal training, he was confirmed and gazetted Flying Officer on 6 August following. Sent out to 14 Squadron in the Middle East on 19 February 1917. Dell-Clarke suffered two traumatic experiences in quite rapid succession in the first few weeks of his combat flying. The first of these is referred to in the citation for his MC which was announced later in the *London Gazette* of 26 April 1917: 'For conspicuous gallantry and devotion to duty when his machine was set on fire. Although himself severely burned, he landed and extinguished the flames in his machine. Later, although his machine was in a dangerous condition, he flew it back to his aerodrome and handed in his reconnaissance report'.

He was wounded in action again on 28 March 1917, when, during an aerial combat, the Martinsyde he was flying was shot down into the sea at Garza Khan, Yunis. Apart from his physical wounds, he also fell victim to a nervous breakdown which lasted for most of 1917, and on through to February 1918. Recovered at last, he was posted with the rank of Captain to 60 Squadron in France on 7 July 1918. During his third practice flight on 16 July 1918, Dell-Clarke was involved in what would prove to be a fatal crash. He took off in SE5A, 'D5992', at

15.20 and five minutes later half-rolled into the ground from low level for reasons unknown. Badly injured with multiple fractures to the skull, he died in the near-by No 21 Casualty Clearing Station, within hours. George Dell-Clarke was buried at Wavans British Cemetery, France, with full military honours, the service conducted by the Reverend J B Simpson, the padre attached to the Casualty Clearing Station.

DEMPSEY, James Arthur Dermot

Originally from Hindhead, Surrey. A Regular Army officer, he was gazetted, pre-war, to the Royal Irish Fusiliers. Seconded to the RFC in the summer of 1916, he was, after training, confirmed and gazetted Flying Officer on 25 October following. He served with 14 Squadron in the Middle East from 28 October 1916 until 29 June 1917, being slightly wounded in Egypt on the intervening 26 March. He was Mentioned in Despatches and awarded the MC, the announcement for which appeared in the New Year *London Gazette* of 1 January 1918, (no citation). James Dempsey left the RAF and reverted to the Royal Irish Fusiliers after the war. *The Times* of 24 June 1920, carried the following announcement: 'MC Award Cancelled. The King has directed that the award of the MC to Temporary Captain James Arthur Dermot Dempsey, Royal Irish Fusiliers (formerly RFC) which was gazetted on 1 January 1918, shall be cancelled and his name erased from the Register in consequence of his having been removed from the Army'.

DENING, Douglas Montgomery

From London, he was born on 8 June 1877. A married man in 1914, he and his wife lived in North London. He worked as a Shipping Agent in the Strand, from 1906 to 1913. Volunteering as soon as war came, he was enlisted as a Trooper into King Edward's Horse. Picked out for a commission, he was subsequently gazetted Second Lieutenant to the Royal Field Artillery on 11 December 1914. Dening served in France with the RFA from February 1915. Seconded to the RFC in 1917, he became a Kite Balloon Officer. Promoted to Balloon Commander in 1918, his MC was announced in the *London Gazette* of 26 July 1918: 'For conspicuous gallantry and devotion to duty. With a party of men, five of whom had already been wounded, he repeatedly returned to a balloon position, which was being heavily shelled, to save stores and supervise the removal of the balloons. Owing to the roads being under heavy fire he was unable to effect his purpose until the following day, when he went up again, although subjected to heavy fire, and succeeded in getting the balloon and other stores safely away'.

Having left the RAF in 1919, he lived and worked in Brazil in the immediate post-war years. In June 1922, he was prosecuted in Rio de Janeiro, for 'irregular wearing of RAF uniform'. Tragically, Douglas Dening was drowned under unknown circumstances on 7 November 1922.

DENISON, Amos Allan

From Scarborough, Yorkshire, he was born on 5 September 1895. He appears to have disliked his first forename, as 'Amos' hardly ever appears in any documentation relating to him. Gazetted Second Lieutenant to the New Armies (General List) on 3 November 1915. Seconded to the RFC, he trained as a Pilot and was subsequently confirmed and gazetted Flying Officer on 16 September 1916, the same day that he gained his Royal Aero Club Certificate (Number 4392). He accompanied the FE8-equipped 41 Squadron to France as a 'founder member' on 15 October 1916. On 24 January 1917, Denison, on patrol in FE8, '6453', was attacked by two hostiles. Despite being severely wounded in the arm, he continued the fight, driving down one of the enemy machines. He continued to fight the remaining enemy machine until the engine of his FE8 was hit and immobilised. Breaking off the combat, he glided across the lines to bring his machine down reasonably intact. This action marked the end of Denison's operational flying, his efforts rewarded by an MC, announced in the *London Gazette* of 3 March

1917: 'For conspicuous gallantry in action. Although wounded, he continued single-handed to fight two enemy machines, and succeeded in bringing one of them down. Later, although his machine was badly damaged, he effected a successful landing. He has at all times displayed marked courage and initiative'.

After recovering from his wounds, Denison continued to serve in administration posts to such good effect that he was appointed MBE in the *London Gazette* of 1 January 1919. Allan Denison finally left the RAF, due to ill-health in August 1919. He lived, between the World Wars, in York.

DENNING, Charles Ffolliott

From London, he was born in 1897. After completing his education in 1913, he joined the Great Eastern Railway Company, becoming a clerk in the Continental Department in Liverpool Street Station, London. As soon as he was old enough, he volunteered his services, and was gazetted Second Lieutenant to 3 (Reserve) Battalion, Royal West Surrey Regiment, on 7 June 1915. Seconded to the RFC, he gained his Royal Aero Club Certificate (Number 3357) on 10 April 1916. Going on to complete his formal training, he was confirmed and gazetted Flying Officer on 11 May following. Sent out to Salonika in December 1916, he joined 47 Squadron as an operational Pilot. He was not only the first '47' Pilot to bring down an enemy machine, he was also the first squadron member to win an MC. On 19 January 1917, Denning, in a BE12, was acting as escort to a reconnaissance machine when he came across a two-seater Albatros. Although in the slower machine, Denning, by clever manoeuvring, got behind and above his speedier opponent. His first burst of fire damaged the enemy's controls and it began to descend. Denning followed, firing the occasional burst to discourage any thoughts of escape. The Albatros landed inside the Allied lines, about a mile and a half from Kilindir. The exuberant Denning immediately set down his BE12 alongside his conquest, only to find that the German crew had, upon landing, set their Albatros alight. Leaping from his cockpit, Denning rushed over to the burning machine and managed to extinguish the flames before too much damage was done. The enemy aeroplane was eventually dismantled and taken away for detailed examination. His MC was announced in the *London Gazette* of 17 April 1917: 'For conspicuous gallantry and devotion to duty when acting as escort to a reconnaissance machine. He attacked a hostile machine and succeeded in forcing it to land. Later, he landed beside the hostile machine, which was on fire, and extinguished the fire'.

Denning was subsequently credited with two other hostiles, 'driven down' before completing his tour with '47'. Returning to the UK in 1918, he served as a Captain with 30 TDS. Charles Denning finally left the RAF, via the Unemployed List, in April 1919.

DIAMOND, Julius

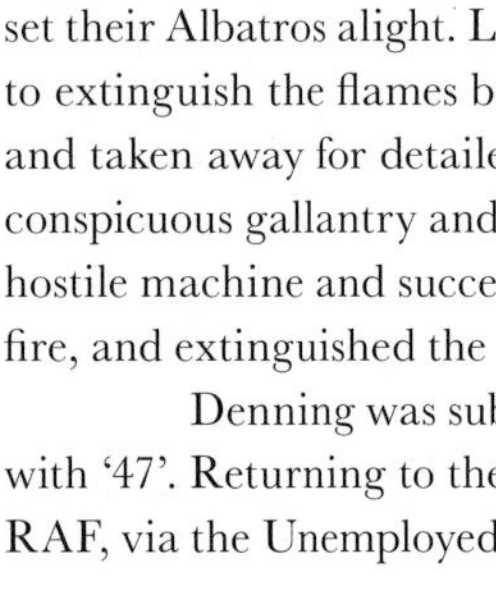

One of nine children, he was born on 5 September 1896 in Leeds, the family moving, in 1912, to live at 43 Abbotsford Road, Glasgow. Educated at Glasgow University, where he was a member of the OTC. Gazetted Second Lieutenant to 3 (Reserve) Battalion, King's Own Scottish Borderers, on 11 June 1915. Subsequently promoted to Lieutenant on 21 May 1916, and attached to 19 (Labour) Battalion, Royal Scots. Seconded to the RFC in the summer of 1917, he trained as an Observer before being sent out to the RE8-equipped 7 Squadron. On 8 October 1917, Diamond and his Pilot, 19 year old Second Lieutenant Cyril Beaven Wattson, from Stoke Newington, in RE8, 'A4315', were on an artillery observation patrol when they were attacked by a hostile and sent down to their deaths south west of Terhand Their last wireless transmission was timed at 08.50 am. Almost certainly, their nemesis was Vizefeldwebel Reichenbach, Jasta B who claimed an RE at this time. Diamond's outstanding work as an Observer was marked by the award of an MC, announced posthumously in the *London Gazette* of 18 October 1917, details in the *Gazette* of 7 March 1918: 'For conspicuous gallantry and devotion to duty in co-operating with our artillery often under most adverse conditions. On two occasions he ranged our siege batteries on hostile battery positions causing numerous fires and explosions'.

Julius Diamond's remains were never recovered and hence he is commemorated on the Flying Services Memorial, Arras, France.

DIX, Ralph St John

From Ebury Street, London, he was educated at Bedford Grammar School, where he was a member of the OTC. Gazetted Second Lieutenant to 1/25 (County of London) Cyclists Battalion, London Regiment, on 15 August 1914. Reorganised from a Cyclists Battalion to an infantry unit, the 1/25 Londons, including Ralph Dix, sailed for India aboard the White Star liner *Ceramic* on 3 February 1916. After a spell of the stupefying heat and boredom suffered by Garrison troops in India, he successfully sought secondment to the RFC. Going to Egypt in the spring of 1917, he trained there as a Pilot and was subsequently confirmed and gazetted Flying Officer on 27 June following. Returning to the UK from the Middle East Brigade in July 1917, he eventually accompanied the AWFK8-equipped 82 Squadron to France as a 'founder member' on 20 November 1917. On 21 March 1918, the first day of the German spring offensive, Dix and his Observer of the day, Lieutenant R M Montgomery, dived onto an enemy two-seater which was performing contact-patrol work and sent it down to crash just north of La Folie. On 26 March 1918, the same pairing, in AW FK8, 'C8448', were themselves shot down to a crash landing. Dix was unscathed in the action, but Montgomery was wounded. Having completed his tour with '82', Dix returned to the UK for a brief rest. His work during the dark days of the German Offensive was rewarded with the first of his MCs, announced in the *London Gazette* of 22 June 1918: 'For conspicuous gallantry and devotion to duty. While on a reconnaissance which lasted four hours he attacked enemy infantry with machine-gun fire and bombs. Though he was attacked by eight enemy scouts, one of which he shot down out of control, he obtained very valuable information. He did excellent work throughout the operations, flying at very low altitudes, and never spared himself in his determination to obtain accurate information and to inflict losses on the enemy'.

Next, in April 1918, he was sent out as an A/Captain and Flight Commander to 35 Squadron, continuing to work on the familiar AWFK8s until he was wounded in the arm by ground-based machine-gun fire on 19 May following. Having got his machine back to base, he insisted upon making his full report before being taken away for treatment, as the citation for the Bar to his MC, announced in the *London Gazette* of 16 September 1918, testifies: 'For conspicuous gallantry and devotion to duty in co-operation with artillery and reconnaissances at low altitudes. While on contact patrol, he observed two hostile trench mortars in action, and getting no reply from the artillery, he dived at them, silencing both after firing about 200 rounds. Later, he drove off two hostile two-seaters. After this he was wounded in the arm, attacking a trench mortar battery, but got safely back to his aerodrome, making an excellent report before being taken to the Casualty Clearing Station. His energy and courage inspired his Flight to a firm sense of duty'.

It is interesting to note that the gallantry he displayed in achieving this Bar to his MC occurred after the formation of the RAF on 1 April 1918 and at a time when the Distinguished Flying Cross was an option available to the authorities. The wounds he received on 19 May 1918 precluded his return to operational flying before the end of the war in the following November. Ralph Dix finally left the RAF, via the Unemployed List, in July 1919.

DIXON, Charles Herbert

From Hampstead in London, he was born on 9 July 1894. After completing his education he worked as a Commercial Traveller for a Sheffield company from December 1912 to August 1914, when the war came. Volunteering immediately, he was gazetted Second Lieutenant to 3 (Reserve) Battalion, the King's Own Yorkshire Light Infantry, on 15 August 1914. In the knowledge that learning to fly would help him to realise his RFC ambitions, he took lessons at his own expense at the Ruffy-Baumann School at Hendon, duly qualifying for his Royal Aero Club Certificate (Number 1480), on 29 July 1915. Seconded to the RFC in the following month, he completed his formal training and was confirmed and gazetted Flying Officer on 18 October following. He accompanied the FE2b-equipped 25 Squadron to France as a 'founder member' in February 1916. Dixon progressed rapidly to Flight Commander and Captain with '25', and was confirmed as such in the *Gazette* of 17 May 1916. On 1 August 1916, Dixon and his Observer of the day, Second Lieutenant J B Hinchcliffe, were fortunate to escape with their lives when their FE2b, '6990', was hit by anti-aircraft fire during a bombing raid in the area of La Bassée. Hinchclifee was wounded in the action, but Dixon emerged unscathed. Dixon's MC was announced in the *London Gazette* of 10 January 1917: 'For conspicuous gallantry in action. He deliberately made himself a bait for a hostile machine, thereby enabling two of our machines to approach unseen and shoot down the enemy machine. He has carried out many bombing raids with great courage and success'.

Promoted to T/Major in May 1917, Dixon was appointed to command 29 Squadron in the following November. Injured in an accident on 15 September 1918, he was able to return to his SE5A-equipped command just two weeks later to see out the remainder of the war, and beyond. Posted to the Home Establishment in January 1919, his services were further rewarded with the Distinguished Flying Cross, *London Gazette* of 1 January 1919, and, from the French, he received the Croix de Guerre, *London Gazette* of 15 July 1919. Charles Dixon resigned his commission, with the rank of Major, on 24 December 1919.

DIXON-SPAIN, Gerald

From Hythe, Kent, he was born on 11 May 1889. Dixon-Spain qualified and worked as a Draughtsman with a firm of architects in London from 1909 to 1911. He next trained as a school teacher, married his wife and went to live and work in Walton-on-the-Hill, Surrey. Unusually, and no doubt because of his age and experience, he was given an immediate Captaincy in 23 (1 Sportsmans) Battalion., Royal Fusiliers, on 10 June 1915. He commanded a Company in the trenches in France from November 1915, before securing a secondment to the RFC in the summer of 1916. After training as an Observer, he was sent out to 20 Squadron in France as a Probationary in July 1916. He there struck up a productive partnership with Second Lieutenant G P S Reid (qv), claiming at least three victories. His 'apprenticeship' satisfactorily completed, he was formally confirmed and gazetted Flying Officer (Observer) on 30 August following. His MC, issued in conjunction with Reid's, was announced in the *London Gazette* of 26 September 1916: 'For conspicuous gallantry on many occasions. Captain Dixon-Spain with Second Lieutenant Reid [qv] as his Pilot attacked and drove back a hostile machine. A few minutes later four hostile machines were seen, three of which were attacked, one after another, and driven back, the fourth being accounted for by another patrol. Another time they attacked two hostile machines, shot one down and drove the other back. Two days later they attacked two more machines, of which one is believed to have been destroyed, the other being pursued back to its aerodrome'.

After completing his tour with '20', Dixon-Spain was appointed to an Instructing post in the UK in July 1917. Rapid promotion to Chief Instructor at both the RFC Armaments School and No 1 School of Aerial Gunnery, came in the following month. His next posting in 1918, with the rank of Major, was to the Air Ministry in London. Dixon-Spain was awarded an OBE (Military) in the *London Gazette* of 3 June 1919. He finally left the RAF, via the Unemployed List, on 15 May 1919. During the Second World War, Gerald Dixon-Spain served again, this time commissioned as a Lieutenant into the Royal Army Service Corps.

DODDS, Robert

From Hamilton, Ontario, Canada, he was born on 11 March 1892. An engineering student prior to the war, he enlisted into the Canadian Army in 1915. Picked out for a commission, he was gazetted Lieutenant to the Canadian Local Forces on 23 August 1915. Following service in the trenches with 129 Battalion, CEF, he transferred to the RFC in October 1916. His formal training duly completed, he was confirmed and gazetted Flying Officer on 27 March 1917. Sent out to France and the F2b-equipped 48 Squadron on 12 July following. Dodds served with '48' throughout the remainder of 1917, and was promoted to Captain and Flight Commander early in the New Year of 1918. An accomplished Brisfit Pilot, Bob Dodds accumulated more than 11 victories before his MC was announced in the *London Gazette* of 13 May 1918: 'For conspicuous gallantry and devotion to duty. He has destroyed or driven down eleven enemy machines. On one occasion while on a one-machine patrol he attacked three enemy scouts, but owing to his gun jamming he was forced to withdraw from the attack. Though under heavy fire from the pursuing enemy he succeeded in remedying the defect, and then turned and attacked the enemy again. He destroyed one of them and drove down another out of control. Later, he led a bombing raid on an enemy aerodrome, and under intense machine-gun fire from the ground dived to within 100 feet of the hangars before releasing his bombs. Though his machine was damaged he remained at a height of 200 feet until the rest of his formation had dropped their bombs. His magnificent example of pluck and determination was of the greatest value to his squadron'.

His tour with '48' completed, he was, in May 1918, sent home to Canada to instruct at Camp Mohawk. Returning to the UK in September 1918, he was appointed Examining Officer at the School of Aerial Fighting. Dodds finally left the RAF, via the Unemployed List, on 4 April 1919, returning home to Canada immediately afterwards. He later became a leading figure in the world of Canadian Transport. Robert Dodds died in Hamilton, Ontario, on 8 December 1980.

DODSON, Leonard

Born in 1894, he and his parents lived at 50 West Heath Drive, Hampstead, London. Educated at London University, from where he graduated BSc. Gazetted Second Lieutenant to 9 Battalion, South Staffordshire Regiment, on 19 September 1914. Dodson accompanied his battalion of Pioneers to France on 24 August 1915, and served there in the trenches until June 1916, when he secured a secondment to the RFC. Having trained as a Pilot, he was confirmed and gazetted Flying Officer on 18 September following. He was sent out to the FE2d-equipped 25 Squadron in France, exactly one week after qualifying, and was soon heavily involved in the intense work of an active front-line squadron. His first victory appears to have been over a Halberstadt Scout he sent down to a forced landing near to Sallaumines on 4 December 1916. His MC, announced in the *London Gazette* of 26 April 1917, credits him with other victories: 'For conspicuous gallantry and devotion to duty. He has continuously shown great courage and determination in graphing the enemy's positions under the most trying conditions, and has brought down three enemy machines'.

In fact, by the time his MC was published in the *Gazette*, Dodson had been shot down, wounded and taken prisoner. On 3 April 1917, Dodson and his Observer of the day, Second Lieutenant H S Richards, in FE2d, 'A6371', were claimed over Lens by Leutnant Karl Emil Schäfer, then of Jasta 11, the ninth of the German Ace's eventual 30 victories. Dodson's Observer, Harry Richards, 15 Sherwood Foresters attached RFC, from Wolviston, County Durham, would die shortly after the FE crashed to earth. Dodson, however, although wounded, would survive to be taken into captivity and remain so until his repatriation on 22 December 1918. Leonard Dodson relinquished his commission and left the RAF in July 1919.

DOUGLAS, William Loudon

From Barnes Common, London SW13, he was born on 11 April 1895. Although he worked as an Import Merchant with the family firm, William Douglas & Son of Putney, from 1912, he always aspired to be an Engineer. Gazetted Second Lieutenant to 17 Battalion, London Regiment (Poplar and Stepney Rifles) (TF) on 31 July 1915. After service with his battalion at the front, he was seconded to the RFC in the spring of 1917. He gained his Royal Aero Club Certificate (Number 4721) on 22 May 1917, the same day that he was confirmed and gazetted Flying Officer. Just four days later, he was sent out to the RE8-equipped 16 Squadron. His MC was announced in the *London Gazette* of 26 September 1917, details in the *Gazette* of 9 January 1918 :'For conspicuous gallantry and devotion to duty in carrying out a large number of very successful photographic reconnaissances. He has repeatedly displayed the greatest fearlessness and determination, attacking enemy troops from a low altitude, and disregarding the attacks of hostile machines in superior numbers and adverse weather conditions, in order to obtain satisfactory photographs'.

Douglas was presented with his MC by the King at an investiture held at Buckingham Palace on 9 January 1918. Having completed his tour with '16', Douglas was next sent as Flight Commander and A/Captain to 4 Squadron, another RE8 unit, on 11 January 1918. His brief tour with '4' curtailed, he returned to the Home Establishment for a rest in February 1918, before joining No 1 Observer School of Gunnery as an Instructor. William Douglas left the RAF, via the Unemployed List, on 20 April 1919.

DOUGLAS, William Sholto

The son of Captain Robert Langton Douglas and Mrs Douglas, of Tonbridge, Kent, he was born on 23 December 1893. Educated at Tonbridge School (1908-13) and at Lincoln College, Oxford. Gazetted Second Lieutenant to the Royal Field Artillery, via the Special Reserve, on 15 August 1914. He went to the front for the first time with 'Z' Battery, 5 Brigade, RFA, 8 Division, on 5 November 1914, and was slightly wounded during the First Battle of Ypres in the same month. Leaving the RFA on Christmas Day 1914, he became formally attached to 2 Squadron, RFC, on Boxing Day. Douglas served with '2' as an Observer until 25 May 1915 and was involved in the Battles of Neuve Chapelle in March and Festubert in May. Douglas then gained his Royal Aero Club Certificate (Number 1301) on 2 June 1915. His formal pilot training duly completed, he was confirmed and gazetted Flying Officer on 23 July 1915. Posted out to the BE2c-equipped 8 Squadron just weeks ahead of its next major engagement, the Battle of Loos, which commenced on 25 September 1915. He was promoted to Flight Commander and T/Captain on 27 December 1915, before returning to the UK on 2 January 1916. He was

Mentioned in Despatches in the *London Gazette* of 1 January 1916. His MC was announced in the *London Gazette* of 14 January 1916 (no citation). Although no formal citation was published in the *Gazette*, research has unearthed the original recommendation for the award: 'Gallantry in action. On 29 December 1915, Lieut Douglas and Lieut (J) Child, Observer, when on reconnaissance over Cambrai escorted by another machine, were attacked by six Fokker aeroplanes. Their escort was almost immediately shot down and followed to the ground by two Fokkers. Lieuts Douglas and Child succeeded in defeating the first aeroplane which attacked them; this machine was last seen out of control and nose diving. After fighting the remaining three Fokkers for 15 minutes, both machine guns were put temporarily out of action so Lieut Douglas dived to within 20 feet of the ground. The enemy followed to within 1,000 feet of the ground from which height they made dives at our machine, these attacks were driven off by one gun which had by that time been repaired. Half way to the British lines two Fokkers gave up the fight. Lieuts Douglas and Child immediately started climbing to attack the remaining Fokker; on seeing this the other two at once returned so Lieuts Douglas and Child resumed their original height. The three German machines returned when within a mile of the lines. Lieuts Douglas and Child endeavoured to climb to cross the lines but were unable to get higher than 800 owing to their engine having been hit. They crossed the lines at this height under heavy rifle fire, machine-gun and Field Artillery fire and landed their machine safely in the French lines south west of Arras'.

In this incident, Douglas and Child's BE2c, '4087', and another BE2c, '2039', crewed by Second Lieutenant D A Glen and Sergeant E Jones, had been attacked by a formation of Fokkers led by Oswald Boelcke and including Immelmann and Leffers. '2039' was sent down with David Glen killed and Jones taken prisoner. Considering the quality of their opposition, it was nothing short of a miracle that Sholto Douglas and Arthur Child not only escaped with their lives, but were also able to give such a good account of themselves. What is difficult to understand is why Sholto Douglas should receive the MC for this action, whilst Child was rewarded with only a Mention in Despatches. Douglas next served as an Instructor at Montrose until April. Appointed as CO, 43 Squadron, with Home Defence duties, from April 1916 until 21 January 1917, when he led the Sopwith Strutter-equipped unit out to France. Douglas fought through and survived 'Bloody April', and the Battle of Arras, but was wounded in the air above Vimy Ridge on 5 May 1917. He returned to Home Service and medical attention until September 1917, when he was appointed CO, 84 Squadron, then at Libourne. '84' crossed to France in September, leading this unit till the Armistice. His last appointment in the Great War was as CO, 39 Wing, at Cranwell from 9 November 1918, until he left the RAF, via the Unemployed List, on 21 April 1919. He added the Distinguished Flying Cross, *London Gazette* of 2 February 1919 and the French Croix de Guerre, *London Gazette* of 15 July 1918, to his honours and had been Mentioned in Despatches on three occasions, *London Gazettes* of 1 January 1916, 20 May 1918 and 8 November 1918. Douglas next tried his hand as Chief Pilot of Handley Page Transport Ltd in 1919, but, in the event, decided to return to the RAF. He married, first in 1919, May Howard (dissolved in 1932); secondly in 1933, Joan Leslie (dissolved 1954); and thirdly in 1955, Hazel Walker, with whom he had one daughter. Returning to the RAF, he was given a short-service commission as a Squadron Leader, on 25 March 1920, swiftly followed by a permanent commission on 25 November 1920, thus crossing the threshold into what would prove to be an illustrious career. Promotions came as follows: Wing Commander, 1925; Group Captain, 1932; Air Commodore, 1936; Air Vice-Marshal, 1938; Air Marshal, 1940; Air Chief Marshal, 1942; and Marshal of the RAF, 1946. His many appointments included Directorate of Air Training in the Air Ministry, 1926-27; OC, RAF in the Sudan, 1929-32; Instructor at the Imperial Defence College, 1932-36; Director of Staff Duties, Air Ministry, 1936-37; Assistant Chief of Air Staff, 1938; Deputy Chief of the Air Staff, 1940; AOC-in-Chief, Fighter Command, 1940; AO C-in-C, Middle East, 1942; AO C-in-C, Coastal Command, 1944; Air C-in-C, British Air Forces in Germany, 1945; C-in-C, British Forces in Germany and Military Governor of the British Zone and British Member of the Allied Control Council, 1946-47. Honours flowed: CB, 1940; KCB, 1941; GCB, 1946; Chief Commander of the Legion of Merit (USA), 1944; Distinguished Service Medal (Naval) USA, 1945; Second Class Order of the White Lion of Czechoslovakia, 1942; Knight Commander (2nd Class) Polonia Restituta of Poland, 1942; Order of the White Eagle (with Swords) (1st Class) of Yugoslavia, 1944; Grand Cross of the Order of St Olaf (Norway), 1945; Grand Cross of the Order of Orange Nassau (Holland) 1945; Grand Cross of the Order of the Phoenix (Greece), 1945; Grand Cross of the Order of the Crown (Belgium), 1946; Created 1st Baron of Dornock, 1948. His civil appointments and academic honours included: Honorary Fellow of Lincoln College, Oxford, 1941; Deputy Lord Lieutenant of London; Chairman of Horizon Travel Associates Ltd 1964; Companion, Royal Aeronautical Society, 1950; Honorary. Liveryman, Dyers' Company; Liveryman, Guild of Air Pilots and Air Navigators; Vice President, Amateur Athletics Association. He lived, in retirement, at 'Shepherds Holt', Denham, Buckinghamshire. Published 'Years of Combat', 1963; 'Years of Command', 1966. Marshal of the RAF Lord Douglas of Kirtleside died on 29 October 1969.

Lord DOUNE, Francis Douglas Stuart-Gray

The eldest son of Morton, the 17th Earl of Moray, and Edith Douglas (née Palmer), of 31 St James Place, London, SW1, and Donibristle Park, Aberdour, Fife, and Castle Stuart, Inverness-shire, and Darnaway Castle, Forres, Morayshire, and Doune Lodge, Doune, Perthshire, he was born on 10 July 1892. Educated at Eton (1906-10), and at Trinity College, Cambridge. Gazetted Second Lieutenant to the Scottish Horse Yeomanry (TF) on 25 May 1914. Seconded to the RFC, he gained his Royal Aero Club Certificate (Number 1774) on 21 September 1915, shortly before formally qualifying for his 'Wings'. Sent to 25 Squadron, then at Montrose, in the November following. Accompanied '25' to France as a 'founder member' in February 1916. On 29 April 1916, Doune and his Observer, Second Lieutenant R V Walker (qv), in FE2b, '5209', on patrol between Hulluch and La Bassée, fought an intense, prolonged, but eventually successful, duel with a Fokker. The two men received their respective MCs for this feat, *London Gazette* of 31 May 1916: 'For conspicuous gallantry and skill. When on patrol duty with Second Lieutenant Walker he sighted a Fokker machine 1,000 feet below them. Second Lieutenant Lord Doune at once dived, and, when within 60 yards, Second Lieutenant Walker opened fire. Lord Doune then headed straight for the Fokker, which had to rise steeply to avoid a collision. Second Lieutenants Walker and Lord Doune then both opened fire and shot away one wing of the Fokker, which fell behind our lines'.

Any victory over a Fokker was seen not just as a material gain, but also a psychological boost, the Fokker menace was badly damaging morale at that time. The menace, however, was in decline, and it would be another 25 Squadron FE2b, crewed by Lieutenant G R McCubbin and Corporal J H Waller, which would send the great Ace, Max Immelmann, down to his death on 18 June 1916. On 7 June 1916, Lord Doune and Walker, were hit by anti-aircraft fire and forced down at Essars. Walker suffered wounds to his face, but Lord Doune escaped unscathed. However, he was injured just nine days later on 16 June 1916, the very day he was promoted to Captain and Flight Commander. Once recovered, he served for a period with the HD Wing, before going out again to France on 14 March 1917. He appears not to have flown operationally before returning briefly to the UK again on 5 June 1917. Doune next took up duties as a Liaison Officer at the Cavalry Corps HQ, France on 25 July following. Returning to the Home Establishment on 5 December 1917, he served for six months in the UK, before going out to a Staff job in France on 21 May 1918. He served as an ADC in the Army of Occupation HQ on the Rhine, from 29 December 1918, until returning to the UK on 22 July 1919. He was Mentioned in Despatches at this time. Lord Doune finally relinquished his commission and returned to civilian life on 10 March 1920. He married, in 1924, Barbara Archibald-Murray of New York, with whom he had three daughters. He succeeded his father, the 17th Earl, upon that gentleman's death in 1930, assuming the further titles of Lord Abernathy and Strathearn, Lord Doune, Baron of St Colme and Baron Stuart. Became Lord Lieutenant of the County of Moray in 1935. He was appointed to the Forestry Commission in 1942 and served as Chairman of the Police Committee for Moray and Nairn County Council from 1934. Francis Douglas Stuart-Gray, 18th Earl of Moray, died on 9 July 1943, the day before his 51st birthday.

DOWNING, Herbert George

The son of Richard and Lucy Downing, of 'Broadfield', Gomshall, Guildford, Surrey, he was born in 1893. Educated at Framlingham College (1905-06). Gazetted Second Lieutenant to the RFC on 5 September 1916. He trained as an Observer and was sent as a Probationary to 57 Squadron, then stationed at Copmanthorpe in the October following. His 'apprenticeship' satisfactorily completed, he was confirmed and gazetted Flying Officer (Observer) on 2 December 1916, before accompanying the FE2d-equipped 57 Squadron to France as a 'founder member', just ten days later. His MC was announced in the *London Gazette* of 18 June 1917: 'For conspicuous skill and gallantry as an Observer. On one occasion when on patrol, by holding his fire until very short range and by skilful co-operation with his pilot, he succeeded in shooting down two hostile machines'.

His tour with '57' completed, he returned to the Home Establishment and trained as a Pilot. Having qualified for his full 'Wings', he was sent out to France again, this time to the Nieuport XXVII-equipped 29 Squadron. On 6 November 1917, Downing in Nieuport XXVII, 'B6779', was involved in an aerial combat, probably with Vizefeldwebel Stumpf of Jasta 6, and sent down in the area of Zonnebeke. Herbert Downing's remains were never recovered and hence he is commemorated on the Flying Services Memorial, Arras, France.

DREWITT, Herbert Frank Stacey

From Christchurch, New Zealand, he was born on 25 March 1895. Educated at Waitaki Boys High School. Gained his Royal Aero Club Certificate (Number 3917) on 1 December 1916, in the soon-to-be realised hope of gaining acceptance into the flying service. Gazetted Second Lieutenant to the RFC, via the Special Reserve, on 19 January 1917. His formal pilot training duly completed, he was confirmed and gazetted a Flying Officer on 1 June 1917. Sent out to France and the Spad-equipped 23 Squadron, shortly after qualifying for his 'Wings'. Drewitt enjoyed considerablesuccess with '23', gaining no less than seven victories between 17 October 1917 and 16 March 1918, having been promoted to Flight Commander and Captain on the intervening 28 December. On 17 March 1918, Drewitt was fortunate indeed to get down safely after his Spad VII, 'B6738', had its propellor shot off by anti-aircraft fire. A week later on 24 March, Drewitt's Spad XIII, 'B6862', was shot up in the air and burning away around him, when he managed to effect a relatively safe landing. His MC was announced in the *London Gazette* of 22 June 1918: 'For conspicuous gallantry and devotion to duty. He, with another pilot, persistently attacked a large body of hostile cavalry, with the result that great confusion was caused, many casualties inflicted, and the horses stampeded in all directions. On a later occasion he engaged with machine-gun fire from a low altitude two hostile field batteries which were shelling our infantry. He has destroyed in all six enemy machines and has brought down out of control six others. He has displayed exceptional skill and gallantry'.

His tour with '23' completed, he returned to the Home Establishment for a well-earned rest. Drewitt next joined 79 Squadron in France, flying that unit's newly acquired Sopwith Dolphins, but without the success he had enjoyed in Spads. Following a period as an Instructor in the UK, he was awarded the Air Force Cross in the Birthday Honours *London Gazette* of 3 June 1919. He married, post-war, Edith Rosalyne from Liverpool. He returned to New Zealand, and took up farming, but then, in 1925, came back to England, living with his wife at 14 Rutherford Road, Wavertree, Liverpool. Herbert Drewitt died at the early age of 31 on 4 January 1927 from an illness said to have been contracted during his war service.

DRUMMOND, Roy Maxwell

The eldest son of Mr and Mrs John Maxwell Drummond, of Hawthornden, Western Australia, he was born on 2 June 1894, in Perth, Western Australia. Educated at Scotch College, Perth. He enlisted as a Private soldier into the Australian Medical Corps, serving with the AIF in Egypt and Gallipoli in 1914 and 1915. Gazetted Second Lieutenant to the RFC on 15 April 1916 and, following training in Egypt, was confirmed and gazetted Flying Officer on 4 July following. Drummond performed outstandingly in Palestine with 1 Squadron, AFC. His MC was announced in the *London Gazette* of 16 August 1917: 'For conspicuous gallantry and devotion to duty. With another officer he attacked and disorganised six enemy machines that were about to attack our cavalry with bombs. The engagement was continued until all six machines were forced to return to their lines. His skill and courage on all occasions have been worthy of the greatest praise'.

Drummond served next as a Flight Commander with 111 Squadron, with which unit he claimed eight victories between 12 December 1917 and 27 March 1918, the first five in Bristol Fighters, the remaining three in Nieuports. Later, he would be appointed to command 145 Squadron. Two gallantry Distinguished Service Orders were bestowed, the first published in the *London Gazette* of 26 March 1918, details in the *Gazette* of 24 August 1918, the Bar in the *Gazette* of 26 July 1918. Drummond was also twice Mentioned in Despatches during this period. Staying on in the RAF after the war, he served in the Sudan during 1919 and 1920, receiving the Khedive's Sudan Medal 1910-22, with one clasp. Awarded the OBE in 1921. He attended the RAF Staff College in 1923, and qualified psa. He married, in 1929, Isabel Rachael Mary Drake-Brockman, with whom he had one son and two daughters. Drummond held various Staff posts with the RAAF and RAF between the wars. He also attended the Imperial Defence College in 1930, before shortly afterwards being promoted to Wing Commander. He commanded RAF Northolt in 1936. Created CB in 1941 and promoted to Air Vice-Marshal. Drummond was next appointed Deputy Air Officer Commander-in-Chief, RAF, Middle East, serving there from 1941 to 1943. Knighted (KCB), 1943, he was formally appointed Deputy to Lord Tedder, and promoted to Air Marshal. Became Air Member for training on the Air Council from 1943. On 27 March 1945, Drummond in a Liberator 'Commando' (which had once been Winston Churchill's personal aircraft), of 45 Group Communications Squadron, was killed in an air accident, when en route for Canada. Air Marshal Sir Roy Drummond's remains were never recovered and hence he is commemorated on the Runnymede Memorial, Surrey; he was always known as 'Peter'.

DUFF, Ian Archibald James

The son of the Reverend Charles Edmund Duff, Vicar of Hardwicke, Hereford, and of Mrs Duff, he was born on 20 January 1895. Educated at Aldenham (1908-14), where he was Head of School (1913), a member of the OTC and editor of the school magazine, *The Aldenhamian*. Entered Trinity Hall, Cambridge, as an Exhibitioner in 1913. Volunteering immediately the war came, he was gazetted Second Lieutenant to 3 (Reserve) Battalion, Dorsetshire Regiment, on 29 August 1914, with a subsequent transfer to 4 Dorsets (TF). Successfully applying for a transfer to the RFC, he was accepted for observer training in December 1915. He first flew operationally in France with 5 Squadron and was wounded there in action on 9 April 1916, when his BE2c was hit by an anti-aircraft shell. Training next as a Pilot, he was confirmed and gazetted Flying Officer on 18 September 1916 and sent out to France as a 'founder member' of FE8-equipped 41 Squadron on 16 October following, before, soon afterwards, falling victim to a severe bout of influenza. His next posting, on 1 May 1917, was to 51 HD Squadron in the UK. Service in France with 102 Squadron commenced on 18 September 1917 and, despite being wounded on 27 October 1917, when '102', in company with 101 Squadron, bombed German aerodromes and rail junctions, Duff stayed on to complete the tour in April 1918. His MC was announced in the *London Gazette* of 4 February 1918, details in the *Gazette* of 9 July 1918: 'For conspicuous gallantry and devotion to duty. He frequently bombed dumps, aerodromes, and railway stations, and on one occasion obtaining a direct hit on an engine. He took part in many long-distance night bombing raids, always dropping his bombs from a low altitude. He showed great courage and determination'.

In addition to the award of his MC, he was also Mentioned in Despatches, *London Gazette* of 22 January 1919. After the war, he returned to Cambridge, subsequently graduating BA before going on to qualify as a Civil Engineer (AMICE). Duff secured a position in the Research Department of Shell-Mex and BP, in Shell-Mex House, London. He married his wife, Onich from Inverness-shire, the couple going on to live at Woodside Cottage, Oakley Green, Windsor.

DUFFUS, Chester Stairs

The son of Mr and Mrs W Stairs Duffus, of Halifax, Nova Scotia, he was born in Blackheath, South London, on 1 March 1891. Educated at Oundle (1905-09) Although his parents had chosen to live in Canada, Duffus was invited onto the board of the London Spinning Company in Deptford in April 1912 and remained as a director with that firm until August 1915, when he decided to volunteer his services. Gazetted Second Lieutenant to the RFC, via the Special Reserve, on 17 November 1915, having already gained his Royal Aero Club Certificate (Number 2003) just ten days earlier. Going on to complete his formal training, he was confirmed and gazetted Flying Officer on 24 February 1916. Sent to the FE2b-equipped 22 Squadron, then stationed at Gosport, immediately after qualifying for his 'Wings', he subsequently accompanied that unit to France as a 'founder member' on 1 April 1916. A successful and aggressive Pilot, he gained five victories between 17 August and 11 December 1916. A detailed account of an aerial fight involving Duffus and his Observer of the day, Corporal Arthur Winterbottom (Number 3192), which occurred on 22 August 1916, still exists: 'While on defensive patrol we saw an FE2b doing photography north of Le Sars. We followed this machine, going east of it, when he saw 5HA, type E, coming from Bapaume, evidently with the intent to attack the photographic machine. We dived at the HA, opening fire at 500 yards. The HA immediately split up their formation, diving and making off in all directions. We closed with one machine, firing two drums into it and actually set it on fire, but after a few seconds the flames went out. The hostile machine dived rapidly for the ground. We then engaged another machine, firing one drum at it, but could not get close to it. All five hostile machines made for the ground'. (Arthur Winterbottom would be killed in action on 22 September following, the award of a French Croix de Guerre posthumously announced in the *London Gazette* of 9 December 1916). On 30 September 1916, Duffus and his Observer of the day, Corporal F Johnson, Number 6391, were fortunate to survive after a drum of their Lewis gun ammunition fell into the propellor of their FE2b, '6931', forcing them to land hurriedly! (Johnson, a Pilot in his own right although an Observer on this occasion, would go on to win a Distinguished Conduct Medal and Bar as a Sergeant Pilot). Duffus' MC was announced in the *London Gazette* of 14 November 1916: 'For conspicuous skill and gallantry in fights with hostile aircraft. On one occasion, after hard fighting, he brought down a hostile machine in flames on our side of the lines'.

His tour with '22' completed, he returned to the Home Establishment on 22 December 1916, subsequently serving with 46 RS at the CFS, before being appointed to command, with the rank of A/Major, 46 TS, from June 1917. He next commanded 25 Squadron at the front in 1918. Duffus was awarded the OBE (Military Division) in the *London Gazette* of 1 January 1919. He finally left the RAF, via the Unemployed List, on 10 April 1919. Chester Duffus married Evelyn Ursula Coles, of Brora, Sutherland, and returned to take up his directorship with the London Spinning Company, the couple living at Corner House, Brentwood, Essex.

DUIGAN, John Robertson

From Terang, Victoria, Australia, he was born on 31 May 1882. An electrical engineer by profession, he was keenly interested in aviation and, in 1910, along with his brother, Reginald, became not only the first to build an aeroplane in Australia, but also, on 16 July of that year, the first Australian to fly. Duigan journeyed to England in 1912, gaining his Royal Aero Club Certificate (Number 211) on 30 April, flying an Avro at the Avro School at Brooklands. He was gazetted Lieutenant to the Australian Imperial Force on 14 March 1916, with an immediate posting to flying training at Point Cook. He embarked from Melbourne on the Transport *Ulysses*, with 'C' Flight, 2 Squadron, AFC, on 25 October 1916, arriving in England on 24 December following. Duigan undertook instructing duties with 30 TS from 5 August 1917, with a promotion to Captain and Flight Commander coming on 15 August following. His first operational duty came when he was sent out to France in command of 'C' Flight, 3 Squadron, AFC, on 10 December 1917. Duigan it was, who, on 22 April 1918, when piloting an RE8 with Lieutenant A S Paterson, MM, acting as his Observer, spotted for the first time the huge German railway gun which was shelling Amiens from Harbonnières. The great gun was eventually captured in the massive Allied offensive of 8 August 1918, the Black Day of the German Army, and subsequently taken to Australia for public display. During a photographic patrol over Villers Bretonneux on 9 May 1918, Duigen and Paterson, were attacked by four German tri-planes. Both men escaped with wounds as their RE8 was sent down over Cachy, to be claimed later by Leutnant Franz Hemer of Jasta 6, the eighth of the German Ace's eventual 18 victories. Duigan's MC, the citation for which makes graphic reference to this action, was announced in the *London Gazette* of 16 September 1918: 'For conspicuous gallantry and devotion to duty. While on reconnaissance he was attacked by four enemy scouts. Although wounded, he manoeuvred his machine with great skill, his Observer using the rear machine-gun with the result that one scout was shot down out of control. Three others continued the attack, eventually setting fire to his tail plane: after which he landed behind the front line, helped to remove the Observer, who had been wounded five times, and salved the photographic plates in spite of being wounded three times himself. '

Evacuated to England for hospital treatment on 16 May 1918, he would not again return to operational flying. Duigan returned to Australia on 19 April 1919, leaving the service on 15 July following, although still remaining on the Reserve of Officers in Victoria. He lived, in the 1930s, at Dandenong Road, Murrumbeena, Victoria, and later, in Yarrawonga, Victoria. Australian aviation pioneer, John Robertson Duigan, died on 11 July 1951.

DUNCAN, Harold Forrester

The son of Major and Mrs J F Duncan, of 'Polkemmet', Helensburgh, Dumbartonshire, Scotland, he was born on 9 October 1894. Educated at Sedbergh (1910-11). Gazetted Second Lieutenant to 3/5 (City of Glasgow) Battalion, Highland Light Infantry (TF), with an immediate attachment to 9 Battalion, on 5 February 1915. Harold's younger brother, Alan Mellish Duncan, also educated at Sedbergh, served with the Highland Light Infantry in the trenches and was badly wounded, but, fortunately, survived the war. Seconded to the RFC early in 1917, Harold trained as an Observer and was sent out as such to the Sopwith Strutter-equipped 70 Squadron. On 24 March 1917, a patrol of 70 Squadron Strutters, including Duncan and his Pilot, Captain A G Saxby, in 'A956', were attacked by 12 enemy scouts. Five of the Strutters were badly shot up and damaged. Duncan, who was wounded in two places, put up an outstandingly courageous fight, so much so that, although he would die of his wounds five days later, his Pilot and his CO, Major A W Tedder, no less, ensured his bravery was rewarded with the MC, announced posthumously in the *London Gazette* of 26 April 1917: 'For conspicuous gallantry and devotion to duty during an aerial combat. Although twice wounded, he continued firing until his gun was hit and put out of action. He then kept in communication with his pilot during the remainder of the action, and continually informed him as to the whereabouts of hostile aircraft'.

Harold Duncan is buried in Gezaincourt Communal Cemetery Extension, Somme, France.

DUNCAN, Richard

Born on 3 September 1888. He was living in Prince Albert, Saskatchewan, when the war came in 1914, having been employed on Survey and Construction work for the Canadian Government for the previous two years. Gazetted Lieutenant to 32 (Reserve) Battalion, Canadian Infantry, on 24 September 1914. He served in France with the CEF until 16 August 1916, when he presented himself to the RFC for appraisal. Gained his Royal Aero Club Certificate (Number 3702) on 17 October 1916, in the confidant hope that this would secure him a permanent secondment to the RFC. His formal pilot training duly completed, he was confirmed and gazetted Flying Officer on 11 December following. Sixteen days after qualifying for his 'Wings', he was sent out to 5 Squadron in France. His tour with '5' lasted until 23 November 1917, an unusually long spell of duty with one unit. In the course of it, he was promoted to Flight Commander and Captain and received the MC, announced in the *London Gazette* of 17 September 1917: 'For conspicuous gallantry and devotion to duty in carrying out the duties of artillery pilot. When a hostile attack was imminent he carried out a reconnaissance at a very low altitude which enabled him to observe and report upon the position of the enemy infantry well behind their front line. He also accurately located their artillery, although his machine was much damaged by fire from the ground. He displayed splendid fearlessness and determination'.

After a period instructing in the UK, he was posted to the RE8-equipped 106 Squadron, based in Ireland at the time of the 'troubles'. He was Mentioned in Despatches in the *London Gazette* of 28 August 1919, presumably for his services during this period in Ireland. Duncan finally relinquished his commission on 8 July 1919.

DUNCAN, William James Arthur

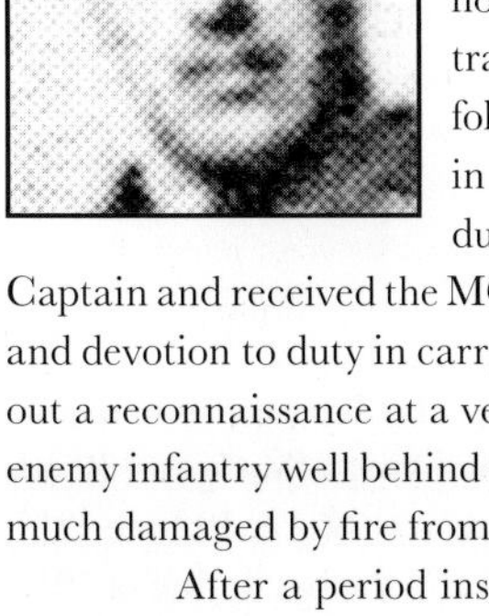

From Sault Ste Marie, Ontario, Canada, he was born on 4 July 1891. Duncan broke into professional ice hockey in Vancouver, prior to the outbreak of the Great War. He happened to be in the east of Canada when he first 'joined up', enlisting into 228 (Sportsmans) Battalion, Canadian Infantry, of Toronto. While his unit remained in Canada, Duncan played hockey with the battalion team in the National Hockey Association series, and was considered to be one of the best defence men in the game. Late in 1916, he proceeded overseas with his unit and, having once arrived in England, transferred quickly to the RFC. He trained as a Pilot in the summer of 1917 and, once qualified for his 'Wings', was sent out to the crack SE5A-equipped 60 Squadron, in the following September. Duncan, despite his considerable bulk and consequent difficulty in 'shoe-horning himself into a cockpit', would become a significant and valued member of '60', one of the few entrusted with a 'roving commission' to seek out and fight the enemy. In all, he was credited with 11 victories between 6 November 1917 and 5 June 1918. The seventh of his victories, which came on 1 April 1918, was probably his most notable in that he brought down Vizefeldwebel Weimer of Jasta 56, inside the Allied lines. Weimer, mortally wounded in the fight, was taken prisoner, only to die shortly afterwards. Very few German aircraft actually came down on the Allied side of the lines throughout the Great War. Duncan landed alongside his victim on this occasion, staying long enough to see him loaded into an ambulance, before taking off again and returning to his own aerodrome. Appointed a Flight Commander in May 1918, he returned to the Home Establishment for a well earned rest at the end of the following month. His MC was announced in the *London Gazette* of 26 July 1918: 'For conspicuous gallantry and devotion to duty. On one occasion he attacked and shot down an enemy plane which had been engaged at firing at our infantry. He then led his patrol over the enemy's lines, dived down to an altitude of 100 feet, and attacked large numbers of hostile infantry with machine-gun fire, causing the utmost panic amongst them and inflicting heavy casualties. His continuous gallantry and initiative have been most conspicuous'.

A Bar to his MC followed in the *London Gazette* of 16 September 1918: 'For conspicuous gallantry and devotion to duty. This officer sighted fifteen enemy scouts attacking eight of ours and immediately joined in, destroying one enemy aeroplane, which fell with a wing off. He then attacked and drove down three other machines, maintaining the fight until the eight had got back to their lines. He has also, with another office, destroyed an Albatros scout, which he followed down to a height of 200 feet, in spite of heavy machine-gun fire from the ground'.

Following his return to Canada in 1919, he would become one of the leading professional ice hockey players of the post-war era, the star defence man of the Vancouver Hockey Team. 'Art' Duncan died in Aurora, Ontario on 15 April 1975.

DURNO, Robert Stewart

The son of a Scottish father, he was born in Toronto, Canada, on 9 May 1892. Educated at Farquharson School, Toronto (1911-12), and at Toronto University. Durno listed his pre-service occupations as Stock and Bonds Salesman and Chauffer. He enlisted into the Canadian Army Service Corps (Number 3189), on 19 June 1915, rising to the rank of Staff Sergeant. He suffered some ill-health at the close of 1915 and the beginning of 1916, first with appendicitis and then with a 'social' disease. Having served in France with the CEF, he answered a call for volunteers for the flying service in December 1916 and was subsequently gazetted Second Lieutenant to the RFC, via the General List, on 13 April 1917. After completing his pilot training, he was confirmed and gazetted Flying Officer on 29 July following. Sent out to the RE8-equipped 5 Squadron in the month after he qualified. Soon in the thick of it, he and his Observer of the day, Second Lieutenant G Cooke, claimed an Albatros Scout, down out of control, on 25 September 1917. A re-occurrence of ill-health put him in hospital on 14 October 1917 and he was unable to return to his squadron until the Christmas Eve of 1917. Durno and Lieutenant R D Stewart in RE8, 'C4552', had an extremely close call on 25 March 1918, when their machine was set alight in a combat over Ayette. Three days later on 28 March, Durno and Second Lieutenant R H Boyd successfully claimed an EA down and crashed. On 21 April, this time with Captain L Oerbling acting as his Observer, he was lucky to survive the resultant crash-landing when the engine on their RE8, 'C5069', failed completely. His MC was announced in the *London Gazette* of 22 June 1918: 'For conspicuous gallantry and devotion to duty. When on photographic work he succeeded, despite the most constant and severe fire from the ground, in taking sixteen photographs from a height of 1,300 feet. On the following day he took part in a low-flying attack on hostile formations of troops, as a result of which, though his machine was riddled with bullets, he was forced to land, but succeeded in doing this behind our front line. He has set a splendid example to his Flight'.

On 27 June 1918, Durno and his Observer of the day, Second Lieutenant F W P Clark, were both injured during a take-off. He was promoted to Captain and Flight Commander in August 1918 and, perhaps surprisingly in view of his past experiences, saw out the war without further mishap. Robert Durno finally left the RAF, via the Unemployed List, on 29 September 1919.

DURRAND, William

Born on 25 May 1883 in Wick, Scotland, his family moved to Edmonton, Alberta, Canada, when he was still an infant. He enlisted first into 8 Battalion, Canadian Infantry, but later transferred and fought with 66 Battalion, then in France with the CEF. Responding to a call for volunteers for the flying service, he was subsequently gazetted Second Lieutenant to the RFC, via the Special List, on 28 August 1916. After completing his pilot training, he was confirmed and gazetted Flying Officer on 1 March 1917. Posted to 20 Squadron in the spring of 1917, he claimed four victories during the summer months, flying the FE2d. On 8 June 1917, he and his Observer of the day, Sergeant Edward Harper Sayers (Number 12315), had the controls of their FE2d, 'A1965', partially shot away by anti-aircraft fire and were fortunate to regain their home field without further mishap. (Sayers, an Ace Gunner with six victories, would receive a French Médaille Militaire in the *London Gazette* of 14 July 1917). On 6 July 1917, six FE2d aircraft of 20 Squadron were attacked by Jasta 11, led by Manfred von Richthofen himself. Before long, other German aircraft joined in, and at one time up to 40 enemy machines were attacking the hapless RFC formation. '20' however, gave an excellent account of itself, before it was reinforced and rescued by four Triplanes from 10 (Naval) Squadron. Three of the FEs were damaged, including 'A6419', crewed by Durrand and his Observer of the day, Lieutenant Stuart Fowden Trotter, Fort Gary Horse, attached RFC. Although Durrand emerged unscathed from the dogfight, Trotter, a Londoner, died from his wounds soon after they crashlanded. In this same fight, the Red Baron also came close to death, receiving a head wound which rendered him unconscious for a time. Coming to, just 500 feet from the ground, he contrived a safe landing near to Wervicq. It has been said that Manfred von Richthofen was never quite the same man after this, although he went on to claim many more victories. Following his squadron's conversion to Bristol Fighters, Durrand's successes continued, particularly after he formed a partnership with Lieutenant Albert Edward Woodbridge. Durrand survived the war with a total of eight victories and the MC, which was announced in the *London Gazette* of 17 December 1917: 'For conspicuous gallantry and devotion to duty. As a patrol leader he is dashing and determined. He has shot down seven enemy machines'.

Returning to Canada, Durr and formed and ran his own construction company in the post-war years. He died of a stroke in Kenmore, New York, USA, on 12 October 1939, whilst helping to erect the US Government buildings in that area.

E

ECCLES, Henry Ernest Karslake

The son of Dr G T Eccles and Mrs Eccles, of Hove, Sussex, he was born on 3 December 1894. Educated at Epsom College (1910-12), at the University of London (member of the OTC) and at St Bartholomew's Hospital, London. He was a medical student at the University of London and at St Bart's, when he volunteered his services, being gazetted Second Lieutenant to the RFC, via the Special Lists, on 3 June 1916. Gained his Royal Aero Club Certificate (Number 3313) on 7 August 1916. His formal pilot training duly completed, he was confirmed and gazetted Flying Officer on 29 January 1917. Eccles was sent out with the FE2b-equipped night-bombing 100 Squadron, as a 'founder member' on 21 March 1917. On the night of 6/7 May 1917, Eccles and his Observer, Second Lieutenant R J Housden from London, in FE2b, '4989', were part of an eight machine raid on Dorignies Aerodrome. Forty-two bombs were dropped from an average height of 400 feet, setting hangars alight. A further three bombs were dropped on a large factory near to the aerodrome, causing a fire. The squadron lost one machine in the raid and Eccles was wounded during the return flight. The nature of his injuries are not known, but appear to have been severe, as he is described in several sources as being 'invalided' after this, his last operational flight. His MC was announced in the *London Gazette* of 18 June 1917: 'For conspicuous gallantry and devotion to duty. He has shown great skill and gallantry in carrying out night raids on the enemy lines. He has also caused material damage to enemy railways while flying at a low altitude'

Eccles was eventually presented with his MC by the King at an investiture held at Buckingham Palace on 15 January 1918. Having regained some fitness in 1918, he was then posted to Administration duties and remained in that capacity until finally leaving the RAF, via the Unemployed List, in October 1919. Returning to his medical studies, he duly qualified and practised in the profession for the remainder of his life, whilst living at 10 Dyke Close, Hove.

EGLINGTON, Dudley Charles

From Enfield, Middlesex, he was born on 11 July 1895. Eglington was a Medical Student living and studying in Wallington, Surrey, during 1913 and 1914. His mother had re-married by this time and was now Mrs E A Hilditch. A pre-war volunteer, he had enlisted on 15 April 1913, age 17, as a Private soldier (Number 1187) into 28 Battalion, London Regiment (Artists Rifles). Mobilised with the rest of the TF in August 1914, he accompanied his battalion to France on 28 October following, thus earning the 1914 Star. The Artists Rifles detachment in France was effectively designated as an Officers Training Unit. The OTU, first based in Bailleul, moved later, in April 1915, to St Omer. Eglington himself was gazetted Second Lieutenant to 2 Battalion, Black Watch (Royal Highlanders), on 20 March 1915. He fought with his battalion at the Battle of Auber's Ridge in May 1915 and at the Battle of Loos, which commenced on 25 September following, being wounded by shrapnel to the left foot on 8 October 1915. He was wounded again during the Battle of the Somme in August 1916. Once recovered, he was seconded to the RFC, at his own request, at the beginning of 1917. Having trained as an Observer, he was sent out as a Probationary to the Sopwith Strutter-equipped 45 Squadron in February 1917. His 'apprenticeship' duly completed, he was confirmed and gazetted Flying Officer (Observer) on 4 March following. On 20 May 1917, Eglington and his Pilot of the day, Captain Christopher Hutchinson Jenkins, Royal Sussex Regiment, in Strutter, 'A8246', were engaged in combat by a formation of Albatros Scouts. Although Eglington managed to send one of the enemy down, Jenkins was wounded in the air. The graphically worded citation to his MC, published in the *London Gazette* of 16 August 1917, tells the remainder of the story: 'For conspicuous gallantry and devotion when acting as an observer. In the course of a fight with several Albatros Scouts, in which he shot down one, the pilot was wounded and fell over the control lever insensible, causing the machine to dive with the engine full on. He climbed out, standing outside the fuselage on the lower plane, dragged the pilot back, and switching off the engine, pulled the machine out of its dive. Not being a trained pilot, his act exhibited great fearlessness and skill'.

Remarkably, Eglington was physically unscathed in the incident, but his Pilot, Christopher Jenkins from West Ealing, died of his wounds two days later on 22 May. On 16 June1917, Eglington, this time flying with Second Lieutenant W A Wright, was again fortunate to escape injury when their Strutter, 'A1021', was shot up and badly damaged, possibly by Leutnant Schubert of Jasta 6. Eglington later transferred to the Balloon Service, serving operationally with 7 BC, in January 1918. His next posting, from 25 February 1918, was as an Instructor at the School of Aeronautics. Eglington finally left the RAF, via the Unemployed List, on 4 April 1919. Taking up his medical studies again, he eventually qualified and was, by 1923, a Surgeon Lieutenant in the Royal Navy.

ELLIS, Alfred William Leslie

From Malvern, Melbourne, Australia, he was born in Steiglitz, Victoria, on 4 October 1894. Educated at Scotch College, Melbourne. An Engineer by training. He gained his Royal Aero Club Certificate (Number 2193) on 20 October 1915 and was commissioned Second Lieutenant into the AIF on the same day. He left Melbourne for the Middle East on 23 November 1915, but, soon after arriving there, was sent on to the UK on 11 January 1916. His formal pilot training completed, he was confirmed and gazetted Flying Officer on 21 May 1916 and almost immediately posted back out to 1 Squadron, AFC, in Egypt. Ellis flew in support of the ground actions in the Egyptian theatre from 11 June 1916, often co-operating with machines of 14 Squadron, RFC. Promoted to A/Captain and Flight Commander on 23 December 1916, he was sent next to 68 Squadron, RFC. On 19 January 1917, Ellis flew as an escort to the first ever reconnaissance over the rear echelons of the Turkish Army, stretching back to famous towns such as Bethlehem, Jerusalem and Jericho. A further posting to 67 (Australian) Squadron followed on 26 February 1917. Next, on 16 September 1917, he joined details of the AFC who were then based at Moascar, Egypt. Returning again to the UK on 27 September 1917, he was, soon afterwards, sent to 30 TS, arriving on 31 October following. His MC was announced in the New Year *London Gazette* of 1 January 1918 (no citation).

He instructed at Gosford from 29 December 1917 to 14 January 1918, receiving a Mention in Despatches for his services there, *London Gazette* of 14 January 1918. He was promoted to A/Major followed on 28 January 1918. Sent out to 10 Wing, RFC, and operations in France on 10 March 1918, he transferred, in swift succession, to 2 Squadron on 12 March 1918 and then to 4 Squadron, just six days later. Returning again to the UK, he was appointed to the command 8 TS on 27 March 1918. Ellis was confirmed in the rank of Major and Squadron Commander on 27 April following. Two weeks after the war he was sent out briefly to 4 Squadron in France. Back to England again on 12 March 1919, he was next selected to command 4 Command Depot, RAF, Hurdcott. Appointed to the selection committee for the new Australian Air Force, he left the RAF to return to Australia on 8 August 1919. Ellis served again in the Second World War, this time with the rank of Wing Commander (Number 260048). He was appointed Administration Officer at 3 RAAF Hospital, before finally leaving the service on 15 December 1945.

EMMETT, Edwin Cheere

The younger son of William Cheere Ayliff Emmett and Johanna Elisabetta Emmett (née Botha), he was born in South Africa on 5 October 1890 and was a nephew of General Botha. Emmett was one of a small band of officers selected to form the nucleus of the South African Aviation Corps, when the decision was taken by the Union to set up a flying unit before the outbreak of the Great War. The pioneers of SA military aviation were ten young men who learnt to fly in a primitive pusher type biplane at an airfield near Kimberley, in 1913, seven years before the SAAF finally came into being on 1 February 1920. Hundreds of applications were received following the Government's call for candidates in a notice published in a *SA Government Gazette* of 10 May 1913. From the hundreds who replied, ten pupils, including Emmett, were selected to undergo initial flying training at Compton Paterson's Aviation School at Alexanderfontein, six miles east of Kimberley. The ten received instruction on a Paterson biplane and, on 22 April 1914, the *Government Gazette* announced that six of them had been appointed as probationary Lieutenants in the South African Aviation Corps. Emmett was amongst the six, all of whom were then sent to England to complete their flying training. Emmett took the test for his pilot licence, flying a Maurice Farman aircraft at Upavon, on 9 July 1914 and successfully gained his Royal Aero Club Certificate (Number 832). When the expected war came at last, he was attached to 3 Squadron, RFC. He accompanied the original RFC contingent to France on 8 August 1914, and, upon arrival, had the misfortune of crashing and writing-off his machine. This small disaster he shared in common, on the same day, with fellow-Springbok, Kenneth van der Spuy (qv). Soon after their arrival in France, Emmett and his colleague, Lieutenant Basil Turner, were re-directed back to Walvis Bay in South Africa to recruit ground personnel for the SA unit. Aircraft and other equipment finally began to arrive at Walvis Bay in March 1915 and the SAAC first went into action during the campaign in German South West Africa. The introduction of their Henry Farman aircraft had a dramatic effect on the progress of the campaign. General Botha, who had previously depended on mounted men for reconnaissance work and who had, until now, never been quite sure where, in the huge expanses of South West Africa, the enemy was deployed, declared, 'Now I can see for hundreds of miles'. When the campaign in German South West came to a close, the SAAC was demobilised in Cape Town on 31 July 1915. However, the Corps was remobilised during August and transferred, en bloc, to the UK, where it emerged as 26 (South African) Squadron, RFC. Emmett, himself, had re-joined his old comrades in England on 7 October 1915. Though the new squadron embarked again for Africa in December 1915, Emmett was not amongst them, having already departed to join the Staff of General Sir H Smith-Dorrien. It was not long, however, before he did re-join '26', arriving to take part in the squadron's bombing operations in East Africa during February 1916. Emmett flew for nine months in East Africa, before returning to England from Dar-es-Salaam, via South Africa, in December 1916. He was then given three months leave on medical grounds, which makes it all the more certain that his MC, announced in the *London Gazette* of 1 February 1917 (no citation), can only have been in recognition of his services in East Africa.

In November 1917, Emmett was serving in Egypt as a Flight Commander with the School of Aerial Gunnery at Heliopolis. Early in 1918, he transferred to an operational squadron, although still serving in Egypt. Emmett was gazetted Captain, RAF (Overseas Contingent serving with the RAF) on 1 April 1918, with a further promotion to A/Major coming on 13 November following. He was awarded the Distinguished Flying Cross in the *London Gazette* of 8 February 1919, this, for amongst other things: '....taking a series of oblique photographs of the enemy's lines, compelled to fly at a very low altitude in the face of heavy machine-gun fire'. Emmett was also Mentioned in Despatches on two occasions during the Great War, *London Gazettes* of 30 June 1916 (East Africa) and 11 January 1919 (Egypt). He was subsequently given a permanent commission in the post-war RAF. By 1928, he was a Squadron Leader, commanding 19 Squadron at RAF Duxford. Further advancement to Wing Commander came in 1935 and to Group Captain in 1938. He served as a Lecturer at Cranwell during the Second World War. Edwin Emmett retired from the RAF in October 1943, but was then recalled for duty until 28 March 1945.

NB: His medals were offered for sale by Dix, Noonan and Webb (lot 408) on 18 June 1997: MC, Distinguished Flying Cross, 1915 Star (SA Aviatn C), *British War Medal 1914-20, and Victory Medal 1914-19 with MID* (Capt RAF), *and Coronation Medal, 1937.*

EVANS, Alfred John

The elder son of Alfred Henry Evans, a master at Winchester, and of Isobel Aimée Evans (née Du Boulay), he was born in Newbury, Berkshire, on 1 May 1889. Educated at Winchester (1902-08) and at Oriel College, Oxford, where he took a 'second' in History in 1912. In 1913, he joined Edward Lloyd Ltd, paper manufacturers. Commissioned as a Staff Officer, he served with the Intelligence Corps in France in 1914. On 22 January 1915, he appears to have been the passenger in a Morane L, '1845', which was being delivered to 3 Squadron's base in France, when it was forced to come down behind enemy lines. Evans made his way to the neutral Dutch border, seeking internment in Holland in preference to capture by the Germans. Aspects of this affair remain mysterious and unexplained to this day. First, just who was the Morane's Pilot, and how did he fare in all of this? Secondly, how did Evans get so rapidly away from internment in Holland? International law would have required him to be held there until hostilities were over. Whatever the facts of the matter, Evans was soon back in England, being confirmed and gazetted Flying Officer (Observer) on 15 April 1915. He was sent out next to 1 Squadron in France in the following month. The first of his two MCs was announced in the *London Gazette* of 14 January 1916 (no citation). Although no citation was published in the *Gazette*, research has unearthed the original recommendation for the award: 'Lt Evans did exceptionally good work as an observer from 20th May to October 10th. On September 25th when observing for artillery over Pont á Vendin under heavy fire, he was attacked by a German with a machine gun. He kept the German off with a revolver while he completed his observation'.

Alfred Evans' Pilot on 25 September 1915, the first day of the Battle of Loos, was Lieutenant R A Saunders (qv), who also received the MC for his gallantry on this day.

Evans next trained as a Pilot and, soon after receiving his 'Wings', was sent out to 3 Squadron in that capacity in February 1916. On 14 July 1916, Evans and his Observer of the day, Lieutenant H O Long, in Morane LA, 'A120', were fortunate to escape with their lives when they were attacked and shot up by an enemy machine using explosive bullets. Evans was unscathed in the incident but Long was slightly wounded in the face. Just two days later, the same crew in Morane LA, 'A197', were forced to land near to La Transloy, behind the German lines, and were taken as prisoners-of-war. Evans was sent to Gutersloh, before transferring to Clausthal in the Harz Mountains, and it was from here that he made his first escape attempt. In company with a Belgian officer, he cut through the wire of the compound at night, making a successful getaway. The pair boarded a train separately, but the Belgian was subsequently re-captured. Evans managed to make his way to Dusseldorf, from where he boarded a tram to Crefeld. He then started the long walk to Holland. Evans had almost made the Dutch border, when he was caught. The Germans sent him next to Fort 9, at Ingolstadt, on the Danube. Fort 9 was a so-called 'strafe camp' where would-be escapers were kept under high-level security. Despite their German captors' best efforts, many escape attempts were made by the incorrigible inmates. Evans once tried a daylight charge across the frozen moat which failed as, indeed, did a similar attempt at night. A tunnel, started in the winter, collapsed when the spring thaw caused a subsidence. However, his persistence was rewarded when, during a transfer to Zorndoff, Evans and Lieutenant S E Buckley MC (qv), with the connivance of other prisoners-of-war, jumped in darkness from a moving train in the vicinity of Nuremburg. After 18 days of travelling at night and holing up during the daylight hours, Evans and Buckley made their way to the Swiss frontier, which they crossed successfully at Barzheim. After returning to England and enjoying a long leave, Evans was eventually sent out to Palestine. It was considered too dangerous for him to serve again on the Western Front, in the event of re-capture by the Germans. Promoted to A/Major, he was given command of 142 Squadron. On 19 March 1918, he was returning from a bombing raid on the Kutrani station on the Hedjaz railway in Martinsyde G102, 'A3960', when his engine failed, and he was forced to land. Having set his aircraft alight in the prescribed manner, he was captured by Arabs with Ottoman sympathies and delivered into the hands of the Turks. After one failed attempt at escape, he was sent to Constantinople where he remained in captivity for seven months. Just before the armistice, Evans successfully bribed a doctor to send him, with other genuinely invalided officers, to Smyrna for exchange with Turkish officer prisoners. The Bar to his MC came in the 'Escapers Gazette', *London Gazette* of 16 December 1919: '....in recognition of gallantry in escaping from captivity whilst Prisoners of war'. He was also Mentioned in Despatches during the Great War. Evans left the service in 1919; marrying, on 2 October of the same year, Marie Rose Galbraith. Their son, John Michael Evans, born in 1920 and also educated at Winchester, became a professional actor. In 1921, Alfred Evans published the first of his books, 'The Escaping Club', which described his escaping exploits in Germany and his experiences as a captive of the Turks. In the same year, he played cricket for Kent and for the MCC. He was also selected to play for England in the Lord's Test against Australia in 1921. Evans tried his hand as a Stockbroker in 1928, and became General Manager of Filastic Ltd in 1933, living in the heart of London at Flat 10, 20 Bryanston Street, W1. Volunteering to serve again in the Second World War, he was gazetted Pilot Officer to the RAFVR in 1940 and had become a Squadron Leader by 1944. He served in Occupied Germany in 1946 and worked for the Foreign Office in 1947. In 1946 he added 'Escape and Liberation 1940-45' to his other published works which included, 'Why Not Prosperity?' Alfred John Evans died in London on 18 September 1960.

EVERIDGE, James

Born in Surrey on 25 August 1881. A pre-war volunteer, he was gazetted to the Surrey Yeomanry (TF) in 1909 and had attained the rank of Captain by the time the war came in August 1914. Despite having already served for five years in the Surrey Yeomanry, he was pronounced unfit for further service due to deafness. Still anxious to serve, he learnt to fly at his own expense, gaining his Royal Aero Club Certificate (Number 1485) on 29 July 1915. Although holding a pilot's licence, the RFC accepted him for observer training and he was subsequently, in October 1915, sent to 9 Squadron in France as a Probationary. His 'apprenticeship' satisfactorily completed, he was duly confirmed and gazetted Flying Officer (Observer) on 1 May 1916. His tour with '9' completed, he returned to the UK for pilot training on 6 June 1916. Having qualified for his full 'Wings' in the following August, he was then employed as a Test and Ferry Pilot. Following a further spell as an Instructor with 83 Squadron, he was sent out to 63 Squadron in Mesopotamia, on 7 May 1917. After completing an 11 month tour with '63', during which he was promoted to A/Captain and Flight Commander, he was sent to RAF HQ, Egypt. Promoted to A/Major, he next commanded 30 Squadron in Mesopotamia from 25 April 1918 until 2 May 1919. His MC was announced in the *London Gazette* of 11 January 1919 (Mesopotamia): 'For conspicuous gallantry and devotion to duty. He performed bold and daring work on reconnaissance, artillery co-operation, and contact patrol, and also carried out many successful bombing raids by day and night. He rendered excellent service'.

Staying on in the RAF after the war, he eventually attained the rank of Wing Commander, before retiring on 5 August 1929. He served throughout the Second World War from 1 September 1939 to 10 September 1945 in the RAFVR. Wing Commander James Everidge died on 3 April 1979.

EYCOTT-MARTIN, Harold Ross

From Hayward's Heath, Sussex, he was born on 2 January 1897, but was living in Norwood, south east London when war came. Educated at Tonbridge School (1911-15). Gazetted Second Lieutenant to the Royal Engineers on 26 October 1915. A secondment to the RFC came in August 1916. Following pilot training, he was confirmed and gazetted Flying Officer on 28 February 1917. Eycott-Martin's first operational posting to 41 Squadron in May 1917, came to an abrupt end when he crashed his FE8 during a take-off just one week after arriving. Once recovered, he was sent to Italy and the Sopwith Camels of 66 Squadron on 7 February 1918. On 30 March 1918, he was involved in the action for which Alan Jerrard would be awarded the Victoria Cross. Eycott-Martin's not inconsiderable contribution to the proceedings was two Albatros DIIIs sent down and destroyed. He survived the war as an Ace, achieving eight victories over German and Austrian machines between 21 February and 22 June 1918. His MC was announced in the *London Gazette* of 16 September 1918: 'For conspicuous gallantry and devotion to duty. In a patrol with two other machines he attacked nineteen of the enemy. Of the six enemy aircraft destroyed on this occasion he destroyed two. On two other occasions he has destroyed an enemy machine'.

Harold Eycott-Martin finally left the RAF, via the Unemployed List, in October 1919 and went to live in America with his wife the following year.

F

FAIRCLOUGH, Arthur Bradfield

From Toronto, Ontario, Canada, he was born on 25 July 1896. A clerk with Wood Gundy & Company, financiers, he was a volunteer member of the Queen's Own Rifles Militia in Canada when the war came. His former Militia unit mobilised as 166 Overseas Battalion, CEF, and sailed for England in October 1916. Fairclough, in the meantime, had been gazetted Lieutenant to the Canadian General List (Machine Gun Dept) on 26 September 1916. Once in the UK, Fairclough sought secondment to the RFC, gaining his Royal Aero Club Certificate (Number 4597) on 24 April 1917. His formal pilot training duly completed, he was confirmed and gazetted Flying Officer on 23 May following. Posted to the Spad-equipped 19 Squadron in France on 15 November 1917, he was almost immediately successful, achieving his first nine victories before the end of the year. Following something of a lull in January and February 1918, 19 Squadron was re-equipped with Sopwith Dolphins and Fairclough went on to gain a further five victories by 2 May. His MC was announced in the *London Gazette* of 13 May 1918: 'For conspicuous gallantry and devotion to duty. During four months he has destroyed four enemy machines, and had driven down two others completely out of control. When engaged with hostile aircraft he has at all times displayed the utmost dash and courage'.

A transfer to 23 Squadron as Captain and Flight Commander came in May 1918 and, still flying Dolphins, Fairclough achieved a further five victories to make his grand total for the Great War, a remarkable 19. His tour with '23' completed, he returned to the Home Establishment in July 1918 and was posted back home to Canada later in the same month. Following a short leave of absence, he was posted as an Instructor to the School of Special Flying (43 Wing, RAF Canada). He finally left the RAF, struck off strength, RAF Canada, on 15 April 1919. Arthur Fairclough died on 9 December 1968.

FAIRWEATHER, Reginald Michael Duff

From Balckhull, Midlothian, he was born on 21 May 1895. Educated at Loretto (1909-12), where he was a member of the OTC, and at the University of Edinburgh (1912-14), where he studied the Arts. Volunteering as soon as the war came, he enlisted as a Private soldier into 9 Battalion, Royal Scots, the 'Dandy Ninth' (so-called because they were the only kilted battalion of the Royal Scots) in September 1914. Picked out for a commission, he was gazetted Second Lieutenant to 4 (Reserve) Battalion, Highland Light Infantry, on 12 July 1915. He was sent to France and 17 Battalion (Glasgow Chamber of Commerce) of his regiment, surviving the Battle of the Somme before successfully seeking secondment to the RFC late in 1916. He trained as an Observer and was duly confirmed and gazetted Flying Officer (Observer) on 2 January 1917. He was sent out to the RE8-equipped 7 Squadron in France on 1 May 1917. His MC was announced in the *London Gazette* of 9 January 1918: 'For conspicuous gallantry and devotion to duty when co-operating with artillery. He has carried out an exceptional number of successful shoots during the last eight months on one occasion ranging a howitzer on a hostile battery, destroying the ammunition and wrecking the battery position. He has consistently shown great skill in carrying out his duties as Observer'.

His tour with '7' completed, he returned to the Home Establishment on 14 September 1917. He spent the rest of the war in various training and administrative posts. Reginald Fairweather finally left the RAF, via the Unemployed List, on 15 April 1919.

FARRINGTON, Frank Cecil

A pre-war Regular Army soldier, he served in India with 'Q' Battery, Royal Horse Artillery, in 1910 and 1911, before transferring to 'X' Battery, RHA, whilst continuing to serve in India until 1914. Following extensive service with the Royal Artillery on the Western Front, he was picked out for a commission and gazetted Second Lieutenant to the Royal Field Artillery on 2 March 1917. After serving as an officer with A/291 Battery, RA, he successfully sought secondment to the RFC in the autumn of 1917. Having trained as an Observer, he was sent out to the RE8-equipped 13 Squadron late in 1917. On 6 January 1918, he and his Pilot, Lieutenant F R McCall (qv), whilst on artillery work, were attacked by an Albatros Scout. Farrington's close-range and accurate response sent the enemy machine crashing down into the barbed-wire defences in front of the German trenches near Noyelles. On 6 March following, the same pair successfully claimed another enemy machine, this time down out-of-control. His MC was announced in the *London Gazette* of 26 July 1918: ' For conspicuous gallantry and devotion to duty. On several occasions during heavy hostile attacks, he has sent down calls to the artillery to engage hostile infantry forming up to attack. Thanks to his skill in discovering enemy formations, and to his speed in communicating the requisite information to the artillery, the most severe casualties were inflicted on the enemy, the failure of their attacks largely due to his splendid work. On numerous other occasions his work has proved of exceptional value, and he has at all times set a magnificent example to all ranks of his squadron'.

Staying on in the RAF after the war, he served with 12 Squadron, then part of the Army of Occupation on the Rhine, from 1919 until 1922, when he qualified as a Pilot. He then served with 4 Squadron from 1922 to 1925. Next, he was sent to 6 Squadron and served in Iraq until 1928. From 1928 to 1931, he instructed at the School of Army Co-operation An appointment to 2 Army Co-operation Squadron, lasted from 1931 until he retired, with the rank of Flight Lieutenant, on 20 August 1933. Recalled for duty in 1939, he served throughout the war as a Squadron Leader in the Air Ministry Ward Room. Frank Farrington finally left the RAF in 1946 with the honorary rank of Wing Commander.

NB: His medal were offered for sale by Christie's (lot 74) on 17 November 1987: MC, 1914-15 Star (Bmbr RHA), *British War Medal 1914-20, Victory Medal 1914-19* (Lt RAF), *Defence Medal 1939-45, and War Medal 1939-45.*

FELLOWES, Cuthbert Dorset

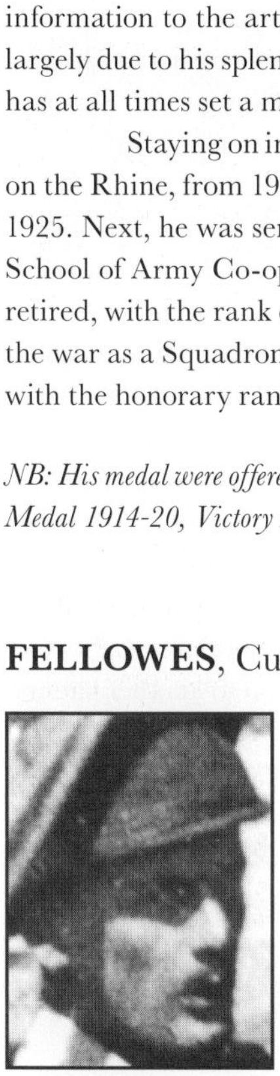

The son of Rear Admiral Sir T H B Fellowes, KCB, JP, and Lady Fellowes, of Woodfield, Stevenage, Hertfordshire, he was born on 26 March 1893. Educated at Haileybury (1907-09). He worked as a cattle rancher in Southern Rhodesia from January 1909 to September 1914. Making his way home to England, he was gazetted Second Lieutenant to the Staffordshire Yeomanry (TF) on 8 December 1914. Successfully seeking secondment to the RFC, he was, after pilot training, confirmed and gazetted Flying Officer on 23 October 1916. Sent out first to 14 Squadron in the Middle East, he earned his MC, with its possibly unique citation, with that unit. He was also promoted to A/Captain and Flight Commander, 'A' Flight. His MC was announced in the *London Gazette* of 26 September

1917, details in the *Gazette* of 9 January 1918: 'For conspicuous gallantry and devotion to duty. In order to save an aeroplane which had fallen between our lines and those of the enemy he twice crawled over 300 yards of open ground in full view of the enemy, started up the engine and lying flat on the ground, allowed the machine to pass over him. He then ran after it and gained the pilot's seat. The machine left the ground, and as all the controls had been shot away, he shut off the engine, and drove it out of range of the enemy guns. He has displayed consistent gallantry in numerous air combats'.

General Allenby asked for two further squadrons to reinforce the RFC and AFC squadrons in the area. Fellowes took his 'A' Flight as the nucleus of the newly forming 111 Squadron in Palestine on 1 August 1917. Due to a bout of ill health, he was returned to the Home Establishment just two months later in October 1917. Fellowes was presented with his MC by the King in an investiture held at Buckingham Palace on 9 January 1918, the same day that the details of the unusual circumstances of his award were published in the *Gazette*. After recovering his health, he was posted to the CFS at Upavon in March 1918. Promoted to the rank of Major in 1918, he continued with instructing duties and his outstanding services were rewarded with an Air Force Cross, *London Gazette* of 2 November 1918. He finally left the RAF, via the Unemployed List, on 1 July 1919. Fellowes rejoined the Yeomanry with the rank of Major on 7 January 1921. Having qualified as a Chartered Land Agent, he was subsequently appointed Agent to the estates of Lord Rothschild and Lord Jowitt. He married, in 1930, Elspeth, the daughter of Colonel A K Slessor, and sister of the future Marshal of the RAF, Sir John Slessor. Cuthbert and Elspeth Fellowes lived at Little Welnetham Hall, Bury St Edmunds, Suffolk.

FENTON, Cecil Gordon

Born in Sligo, Ireland, on 26 March 1887 or 1889 or 1894, all three dates appear in his records. The Fenton family appears to have emigrated to New Zealand in the first instance; his father, Samuel, living at Huntley Avenue in Auckland. His mother, however, lived for some time at 153 Rubert Street, Collingwood, Victoria, Australia. A Carpenter by trade, Fenton alternated between New Zealand, Australia and Fiji; his wife, in the meantime, lived mainly in Melbourne, but sometimes in New Zealand. Cecil Fenton enlisted into the AIF in Melbourne on 17 August 1914 and was sent to Broadmeadows for basic training. He embarked at Melbourne aboard the SS *Hororatia* on 19 October 1914, bound for the Middle East as a Band Sergeant with HQ, 7 Battalion, 2 Brigade, 1 Division. Arriving in Alexandria, he and his unit were sent to a camp at Mena, Egypt. He served in Gallipoli from the first day of the ANZAC landings on 25 April 1915. Fenton was appointed Orderly Room Sergeant on 13 May following. After the evacuation, he was sent next to 59 Battalion, AIF, on 24 February 1916. Accepted for service with the RFC in November 1916, he flew, after training, as an Observer/Gunner, with the artillery observation 42 Squadron on the Western Front from 16 January 1917. Subsequently gazetted Second Lieutenant to the RFC, via the Special Reserve, on 4 April 1917, he was confirmed as a Flying Officer (Observer) on 16 May following. His MC was announced in the *London Gazette* of 18 January 1918, details in the *Gazette* of 25 April 1918: 'For conspicuous gallantry and devotion to duty. In spite of frequent thunderstorms, and the use of smoke screens by the enemy, he ranged a battery on a hostile battery position, obtaining eight good hits, destroying two gun-pits, and causing a large explosion. He afterwards ranged them on to another battery, destroying a gun-pit, obtained three direct hits on a farm full of troops, and then silenced four batteries. On at least two other occasions he ranged the battery with remarkable success'.

He served again in Egypt from 18 October 1917, alternating between operational duties and training responsibilities. Fenton next trained and qualified as a Pilot at 58 TS, on 26 February 1918. Returning to the Home Establishment on 13 June 1918, he was, shortly afterwards, posted to 46 TD as an Assistant Flying Instructor. He finally left the RAF, via the Unemployed List, on 8 May 1919. Fenton eventually returned to Australia on 1 July 1921. He served again in the Second World War, performing part-time duties with the Royal Australian Air Force.

FERGUSON, Gerald William

From Devon, he was born on 27 December 1891. Educated at Newton College, Devon. Gazetted Second Lieutenant to the RFC on 13 February 1917. Having trained as a Pilot, he was confirmed and gazetted Flying Officer on 8 May 1917, joining the RE8-equipped 16 Squadron at the front shortly afterwards. His MC was announced in the *London Gazette* of 27 October 1917, details in the *Gazette* of 18 March 1918: 'For conspicuous gallantry and devotion to duty. As pilot in an artillery squadron, whilst on artillery observation, he was attacked by several hostile machines, two of which he drove off, the remainder breaking off the combat. Again, whilst on artillery patrol he attacked and drove down an enemy machine out of control. On a third occasion while engaged on artillery work, observing a party of enemy infantry, he dived on them, firing, and sent a wireless call to the artillery, which opened fire. This officer has shown exceptional capabilities as an artillery pilot, frequently carrying out his work at a low altitude, observation being otherwise impossible owing to low cloud'.

On 6 January 1918, Ferguson and his Observer, Lieutenant F W Howitt, in RE8, 'A4300', were hit successively by ground fire and then in aerial combat. Their engine cut out and they crashed inside the British lines, wrecking the RE8. Although Howitt was unscathed, Ferguson was wounded. After recovering his health and fitness, he was appointed to an instructing post. Ferguson's expertise in this discipline was recognised by the award of an Air Force Cross, *London Gazette* of 3 June 1919. Gerald Ferguson remained in aviation after the Great War and was, in the 1930s, the Navigation Instructor to the Airwork School of Flying.

FERGUSON, William Bruce

The son of Charles and Martha M Ferguson, of Ameliasberg, Ontario, Canada, he was born on 12 August 1896. He worked as a farmer prior to joining the Canadian forces. Although originally gazetted Lieutenant to 1 Canadian Pioneer Battalion on 23 August 1916, he actually served in France with 9 Canadian Railway Troops, before being seconded to the RFC in March 1917. Having trained as an Observer, he was confirmed and gazetted Flying Officer (Observer) on 11 April 1917, before being posted to the RE8-equipped 6 Squadron on 20 May following. On 16 August 1917, Ferguson and his Pilot, Second Lieutenant G Nicholas, whilst on counter-battery patrol, were attacked by five enemy machines. Ferguson's fire destroyed one of the attackers and, with the help of a Spad that happened upon the scene, dispersed the remaining four. His MC was announced in the *London Gazette* of 19 November 1917, details in the *Gazette* of 22 March 1918: 'For conspicuous gallantry and devotion to duty. He has continuously done valuable work in locating targets and ranging and observing artillery fire, and was responsible on several occasions for the destruction of hostile batteries by our artillery. He successfully took part in several aerial combats while engaged in this work, and showed great initiative and determination throughout'

His tour with '6' completed on 8 December 1917, he returned to the UK for a rest and subsequent transfer to 198 (N) TS, a night-flying training unit. He was drowned in an aeroplane accident on 7 July 1918, when the aeroplane he was travelling in fell into the River Thames. William Ferguson is buried in Hornchurch (St Andrew's) Churchyard, Essex.

FERNIHOUGH, Frank

The son of Mr and Mrs C B Fernihough, of Park Avenue, Southport and of Wigan, he was born in 1896. Educated at Moncton Combe School (1910-13). Volunteering immediately war came, he was gazetted Second Lieutenant to 'A' Battery, 1 Welsh (Howitzer) Brigade, Royal Field Artillery (TF), on 20 August 1914. Seeking secondment to the RFC in 1915, he gained his Royal Aero Club Certificate (Number 1946) on 6 September of that year. His formal pilot training duly completed, he was confirmed and gazetted Flying Officer on 28 October following. Fernihough served first at the front with the BE2c-equipped 7 Squadron, at the height of the so-called, 'Fokker Scourge'. On 14 December 1915, Fernihough and his Observer of the day, Lieutenant Moffatt, in BE2c, '4100', were attacked by two Fokkers, but lived to 'tell the tale', after fighting them both off. His tour with '7' completed, he returned to the UK and was posted to instructing duties. Promoted to A/Captain and Flight Commander, he was sent out to 2 Squadron in the late spring of 1917. His MC was announced in the *London Gazette* of 17 September 1917: 'For conspicuous gallantry and devotion to duty in artillery observation and patrol work. He has continually distinguished himself by his fearlessness and determination to gain information, undeterred by hostile fire or adverse weather conditions, remaining unshaken through some very trying experiences, during one of which his machine was very badly hit and his Observer's leg was shot away. He has furnished information of the greatest value on numerous occasions'.

Remaining in the RAF after the Great War, he rose to the rank of Wing Commander in 1935 and Group Captain in 1938. He continued to serve in the RAF throughout the Second World War. Frank Fernihough died in 1954.

FERRIE, Robert Leighton Moore

The son of Mr and Mrs Robert B Ferrie of Hamilton, Ontario, Canada, he was born in 1898. Accepted into the flying service whilst still in Canada, he was, upon arrival in England, gazetted Second Lieutenant to the RFC, via the Special Reserve, on 19 December 1916. Having trained as a Pilot, he was given his 'Wings' and sent out to the Sopwith Camel-equipped 46 Squadron on 13 June 1917. '46' was heavily committed throughout the autumn and early winter battles of 1917, Third Ypres and Cambrai. Ferrie claimed at least two victories and was promoted to A/Captain and Flight Commander. On 3 January 1918, Ferrie in Sopwith Camel, 'B2516', was bested in a combat over Metz-en-Coutre and sent down to his death. His MC was announced posthumously in the *London Gazette* of 5 July 1918: 'For conspicuous gallantry and devotion to duty. He led his flight with great skill and determination in very bad weather, and dropped bombs on an enemy aerodrome from a height of 400 feet, destroying one shed and badly damaging another. On two later occasions he bombed villages and attacked enemy infantry with his machine-gun from a low altitude. He has brought down two enemy machines and assisted in destroying others. He has shown great courage and resource at all times'.

Bob Ferrie is buried in Izel-les-Hameau Communal Cemetery, France.

FIELDING-JOHNSON, William Spurett

The son of Mr and Mrs Fielding-Johnson, of Tadcote Hall, Leicester, he was born on 26 September 1892. A pre-war volunteer, he was gazetted Second Lieutenant to the Leicestershire Yeomanry (Prince Albert's Own) (TF) on 16 March 1913. Fielding-Johnson was mobilised with the rest of the TF when war came in August 1914. He accompanied his regiment to France on 3 November 1914, thus earning the 1914 Star, one of the relatively few yeomen to do so. Fielding-Johnson won his first MC whilst serving with 7 Cavalry Brigade in France, *London Gazette* of 3 July 1915. Seconded to the RFC, he trained as an Observer and was sent out to 3 Squadron as a Probationary on 16 October 1915. On 26 October 1915, Fielding-Johnson and his Pilot of the day, Second Lieutenant R J Lilywhite, in Morane N, '5077', on escort duty to a photo-reconnaissance patrol, fought a series of successive mini aerial battles with five separate Aviatiks over Lille, without apparent damage to either side. His 'apprenticeship' satisfactorily completed, he was duly confirmed and gazetted Flying Officer (Observer) 19 December following. His Pilot crashed their Morane Parasol on 19 January 1916, and Fielding-Johnson was quite badly injured. Once recovered, he trained as a Pilot, serving briefly with 72 Squadron, before, in October 1917, joining the crack SE5-equipped 56 Squadron. By the time he returned to England in April 1918, he had gained six victories, been promoted to A/Captain and Flight Commander, and had gained a Bar to his MC, *London Gazette* of 13 May 1918: 'For conspicuous gallantry and devotion to duty. Whilst escorting machines of another squadron which were engaged in bombing work, with one other officer he attacked ten enemy scouts. He destroyed two of them and forced another to land. On another occasion, when leading a patrol of six machines, he attacked ten enemy scouts. He destroyed one and his patrol accounted for three others. A few minutes later, in conjunction with another officer, he destroyed an enemy two-seater machine of a new type. As a Flight Commander he showed great skill and by his daring and good leadership set a splendid example to the officers of his Flight'.

He was also twice Mentioned in Despatches, *London Gazettes* of 3 July 1915 and 1 January 1916. Fielding-Johnson finally left the RAF, via the Unemployed List, on 25 April 1919. He lived, post-war, at Barrow on Sea, near Loughborough, Leicestershire. During the Second World War, the indefatigable Fielding-Johnson managed to see service as an Air Gunner and Acting Squadron Leader (Number 73613) with the RAFVR, receiving a Distinguished Flying Cross for his efforts, *London Gazette* 22 September 1942. William Spurett Fielding-Johnson MC and Bar, DFC, then living at Manor Farm, Compton Basset, near Calne, Wiltshire, died on 11 February 1953, in the offices of the family business, Messrs Fielding and Johnson, Westbond Street, Leicester.

FILLEY, Oliver Dwight

The son of Iron Manufacturer, Oliver Brown Filley and Mrs Filley, of St Louis, Missouri, USA, he was born on 15 January 1883. Educated at Rugby School, England (1897-1901) and at the Harvard University School of Mines (1906-09). Having once graduated from Harvard as a Mining Engineer, he worked first in Mexico before securing a position in Rhodesia. He was living and working in Rhodesia when war came in August 1914. Like all his family, a confirmed Anglophile, Filley made his way to England in 1915, determined to join the flying service. He learnt to fly at his own expense, gaining the Royal Aero Club Certificate (Number 1101) on 2 March 1915, the same day that he was accepted and gazetted Second Lieutenant to the Military Wing, RFC. His formal training duly completed, he was confirmed and gazetted Flying Officer on 22 May following. He was sent out to the Avro 504-equipped 1 Squadron in France soon after he qualified. On 6 July 1915, he and his Observer, Lieutenant Lambert Playfair, 1 Royal Scots, in Avro

504, '4223', were involved in an aerial combat with two Aviatiks over St Julien. The Avro's engine was hit and Playfair was mortally wounded. Filley, however, somehow got the machine down, escaping unscathed. His MC, specifically for this incident, was announced in the *London Gazette* of 26 July 1915: 'For conspicuous gallantry and devotion to duty. On 6 July 1915, when he and his observer were co-operating with artillery, although they were not in a fighting machine, they attacked German aeroplanes, and, after driving them away, resumed their artillery work. Finally, two hostile aeroplanes came up simultaneously, and, although they had only five rounds of ammunition left, they at once proceeded to attack. The Observer, Lieutenant Lambert Playfair, 1 Royal Scots and RFC, was killed in the act of firing and the engine damaged, but Second Lieutenant Filley landed safely in our lines'.

Wounded in November 1915, he returned to England for hospital treatment. After recovering his health and fitness, he served successively with 32, 34 and 48 Squadrons, all stationed in the UK, between January and September 1916, having been promoted to A/Captain in the intervening February. Next, he returned to France to join the Martynsyde G100-equipped 27 Squadron in September 1916. On 27 October 1916, Filley was wounded in the air during a brief skirmish with an enemy machine. Once recovered in January 1917, he was ordered to Canada. Promoted to A/Major, he reported for duty at the RFC Depot at Camp Borden in April 1917. As the United States had entered the war on 6 April 1917, Filley decided to resign his RFC commission in September (granted honorary rank of Captain), and return to his own country. He had been Mentioned in Despatches on two occasions during his service with the RFC. His experience invaluable to the USAS, he was immediately commissioned Lieutenant Colonel into the Aviation Section, Signal Corps, in October 1917, and posted to Washington DC. His next posting, in December 1917, was to the School for Aerial Observers at Fort Sill, Oklahoma, as Commanding Officer. He relinquished this post in March 1918, before, in the following month, sailing for France where he was assigned to HQ, Services of Supply, Air Service. In June, he was transferred to the Night Bombardment Section, Air Service HQ, 3 Base Section, in England. One month later he was designated Officer in Command, Mobilization and Training, Night Bombardment Section. In the same month he was appointed Officer Commanding, Chichester Area, in which post he saw out the remainder of the war. In December 1918, he returned briefly to Air Service HQ, 3 Base Section, until proceeding home to the US in the following January. Deciding upon a change of profession, he became, in 1921, a Stockbroker with Messrs Post and Flagg, a New York Stock Exchange brokerage house. Filley retired in 1942, going to live at Bernarsville, New Jersey. Active in the local community, he was, amongst other things, President of the Library Board and a Vestryman at St Bernard's Protestant Episcopal Church. His clubs included the exclusive Knickerbocker of New York. Oliver Dwight Filley died at his home in New Jersey on 18 January 1961.

FINDLAY, Thomas Irving

From Toronto, Canada, he enlisted as a Gunner into 26 Battery, Canadian Field Artillery, in March 1915. Transferring to 25 Battery, Canadian Field Artillery, he accompanied this unit to France in February 1916. Once in France and Flanders with the CEF, he was posted to serve with 'Z' Battery, Trench Mortar Group, 2 Canadian Division, from April 1916. Picked out for a commission, he was gazetted Lieutenant to the Canadian Artillery on 7 July 1916. Wounded in action at Ypres on 26 July 1916, he was sent to England for medical treatment. Once recovered, he was sent out to re-join 25 Battery, Canadian Field Artillery, in January 1917. Successfully seeking secondment to the RFC in August 1917, he trained as an Observer. Findlay accompanied the AWFK8-equipped 82 Squadron to France as a 'founder member' on 20 November following. He flew operationally over Kemmel, St Eloi, Ypres, Vimy and Hill 70 during the fraught days of the German spring offensive. Findlay and his Pilot, Captain G I Paterson, had narrowly avoided disaster on 21 March 1918, when their 'Big Ack' was shot up by machine-gun fire from the ground. On 2 April, however, the same pair were not so fortunate. Flying in AWFK8, 'C8524', during a reconnaissance patrol, they were attacked and shot down by Leutnant Franz Piechulek of Jasta 56, the sixth of the German Ace's eventual 14 victories. George Irving Paterson, a fellow Canadian from Saskatchewan, Alberta, was killed outright, whilst Findlay was seriously wounded. Findlay's MC was announced in the *London Gazette* of 26 July 1918: 'For conspicuous gallantry and devotion to duty. On one occasion, under adverse climatic conditions, he carried out, during a flight of three hours at an altitude of 300 feet, a most valuable reconnaissance. During recent operations his working in attacking enemy troops from low altitude has been of the greatest value and he set a splendid example of energy and determination to all ranks of his squadron'.

Invalided out of the service as a consequence of his wounds in October 1918, he returned to University College, Toronto, to continue his war-interrupted education.

FIRTH, John Charles Bradley

The son of Mr and Mrs J B Firth, of Nottinghamshire, he was born on 8 August 1894. Educated at Wellington College (1908-12). Gazetted Second Lieutenant to the King's Shropshire Light Infantry on 29 August 1914, he was Transport Officer with the advance party of 5 Battalion when it departed for France on 19 May 1915. Firth was one of the many casualties 5 King's Shropshire Light Infantry suffered on 25 September 1915, the first day of the Battle of Loos, receiving wounds from which he would not recover until the following May. A further spell in the trenches preceded a secondment to the RFC in December 1916. Having trained as a Pilot, he was confirmed and gazetted Flying Officer on 17 April 1917. He joined the Sopwith Strutter-equipped 45 Squadron in France within days of qualifying as a Pilot. Firth gained two victories in Strutters before, on 22 July 1917, he and his Observer, Second Lieutenant J H Hartley, Royal Munster Fusiliers, were attacked by elements of Jasta 11 and badly shot up. James Hartley, a Lancastrian, was killed in the air but, Firth, unscathed, managed to get the damaged machine down safely. '45' swopped their Strutters for Camels on 25 July 1917 and Firth prospered in the new machine, achieving a further seven victories between 25 September and 15 November 1917, being promoted to A/Captain and Flight Commander on the intervening 8 October. His squadron was sent to the Italian front on 17 November 1917, where Firth would gain two further victories by 27 March 1918. His MC was announced in the *London Gazette* of 18 February 1918, details in the *Gazette* of 18 July 1918: 'For conspicuous gallantry and devotion to duty. He has on various occasions, during a period of two months, completely destroyed two enemy planes and shot down out of control seven others. The latter, by reason of the manner in which they were observed to go to earth, were probably all rendered useless for further service. He has set a fine example as a patrol leader, and has displayed much skill and courage'.

His tour with '45' completed, he returned to the UK for a rest on 10 April 1918. The Italians showed their appreciation of his services by awarding him their Bronze Medaglia al Valore Militare. Firth was next posted to the CFS as an Instructor in July 1918, a position in which he saw out the remainder of the war. His efforts in this field were rewarded with a Mention in Despatches, *London Gazette* of 4 February 1919. After leaving the RAF in 1919, he entered the steel business, becoming a director of Firth and Lotus Howard Ltd. Firth, his wife and two children, lived at Spital House, Blyth, Worksop, Notts. John Firth died under tragic circumstances on 23 August 1931.

FISH, William Raymond

The son of Henry and Mary Edith Fish, of 'Sunnydene', Woodford Green, Essex, he was born in 1894. Gazetted Second Lieutenant to 7 Battalion, Suffolk Regiment, on 23 January 1916. He served in France with his battalion and survived the first day of the Battle of the Somme on 1 July 1916. Securing a secondment to the RFC in November 1916, he was, after training, confirmed and gazetted Flying Officer on 3 March 1917. He was sent out to the DH5-equipped 32 Squadron in France in the summer of 1917. Fish survived a close call on 10 August 1917, when his DH5, 'A9396', was hit in the air over Kemmel, by a shell. Despite damage to his machine, Fish landed it safely on the right side of the lines. On 16 October following, he again diced with death when, after an aerial combat in DH5, 'A9209', he was forced down to crash into some shell holes. Although his machine was comprehensively wrecked, Fish again emerged unscathed. He was promoted to A/Captain and Flight Commander on 18 September 1917. His luck ran out to some extent on 19 November, when he was wounded in action. Once recovered, he was sent as a Flight Commander to the Sopwith Camel-equipped 54 Squadron in time to be heavily involved in the German spring offensive. On 27 March 1918, his Camel, 'C1574', was hit by machine-gun fire from the ground in the vicinity of Albert. Although initially reported 'missing in action', he appears to have been found by the Germans and treated in hospital until his death on 2 June 1918. Both of his MCs were announced posthumously in the *London Gazette* of 22 June 1918 – MC: 'For conspicuous gallantry and devotion to duty. While on reconnaissance, observing a number of enemy troops and transport on a road, he engaged these, diving on them from a height of 500 feet. He was throughout subjected to the most violent machine-gun and rifle fire from the ground, but he succeeded in scattering the enemy in all directions and inflicted heavy casualties on them. He has also destroyed several enemy machines, and his personal example and determination have been of the greatest value to his Squadron'.

Bar to MC: 'For conspicuous gallantry and devotion to duty. While leading a patrol in very bad weather he saw the enemy's infantry advancing in an attack on our trenches, which he knew were not strongly held. There were nine enemy scouts patrolling above their lines, but he led his patrol down immediately beneath them and under heavy machine-gun fire from the ground, concentrated his fire on the enemy infantry. Largely owing to his determined and courageous action the enemy's attack was repulsed'.

William Fish is buried in Ebbinghem Military Cemetery, France.

FITZ MORRIS, James – see J **MORRIS**

FLEMING, Austin Loyd

From Toronto, Canada, he was born on 7 August 1894. Educated locally, he traded as a Stockbroker from September 1913, until December 1915, when he decided to enlist into 1 Battalion, Canadian Railway Troops. Having crossed to the UK, he responded to a call for volunteers for the flying service and was subsequently gazetted Second Lieutenant to the RFC, via the Special Reserve, on 17 November 1916. His pilot training duly completed, he was confirmed and gazetted Flying Officer on 13 May 1917. Following service with 6 Training Wing at Maidstone, Kent, he was posted to France and the Sopwith Pup-equipped 46 Squadron on 8 June 1917. On 3 July 1917, Fleming was involved in a tragic 'friendly fire' incident when, mistaking a 1 Squadron Nieuport, piloted by Second Lieutenant Tom Littler, for an enemy Albatros Scout, he shot down and killed the 19 year old from Brixham, Devon. Fleming was sent back to the Home Establishment, 'under a cloud', on the following day. After a largely inconclusive high level enquiry, Fleming was posted to the Palestine front. Attached to 111 Squadron, he went on to enjoy considerable success, achieving a total of eight victories between 17 January and 12 April 1918, the first two in a BF2b, the remainder in a SE5A. His MC was awarded after his fifth victory when he attacked, on 29 January 1918, a German two-seater which was being escorted by two Scout planes. He killed the Pilot of the two-seater in the air, but the Observer managed to land the machine behind the British lines, where he was taken prisoner of war. Fleming's MC was announced in the *London Gazette* of 13 May 1918: 'For conspicuous gallantry and devotion to duty. He attacked a formation of three enemy machines and forced the leading machine, which was a two seater, to land, although the other two were attacking him from behind. He then attacked and destroyed another of the enemy machines and engaged the third, which succeeded in escaping He destroyed four enemy machines during one month and showed splendid courage and skill on many occasions'.

(Forty-one years later, Fleming presented the Spandau machine-gun he had taken from the downed two-seater in this incident, to his old Squadron). Fleming was injured on 11 September 1918, returning to the UK for treatment. Given three months leave in Canada, the war ended before he could return to operational flying. He finally left the RAF, via the Unemployed List, on 1 June 1919. After the Great War, Fleming lived in Palm Beach, Florida, for a number of years before returning to England in 1924 to sell vacuum cleaners. He served again as an Administration Officer with the RAF during the Second World War. Austin Fleming died in Malaga, Spain, on 26 January 1969.

FLETCHER, Albert

A Staff, not a flying, award

Born in Plumstead, Kent, in January 1881. He enlisted as a Sapper in the Royal Engineers in 1899, eventually training as a Driver. Fletcher subsequently served with the Air Battalion, Royal Engineers, from 1911 to 1912, whereupon he became one of the first – Service Number 4 – to transfer to the newly formed RFC on 13 May, of that latter year. His rank, by this time, was Company Quarter-Master Sergeant. On 16 June 1913, his rank having advanced to Sergeant Major, he gained his Royal Aero Club Certificate (Number 519) at Montrose in a Maurice Farman. Fletcher accompanied the original RFC contingent to France, arriving there on 16 August 1914, thus earning the 1914 Star. Picked out for a commission, he was, very shortly after arriving in France, gazetted Lieutenant Quartermaster to the RFC on 23 August 1914. After long service in Administration in France and Flanders, his MC was announced in the New Year *London Gazette* of 1 January 1917, (no citation). Although no formal citation was published in the *Gazette*, research has uncovered the original recommendation for the award: 'For excellent work in connection with the organisation and working of 4 Army Aircraft Park. Major Fletcher has produced a very high efficiency in this new unit'.

By the time of the formation of the RAF on 1 April 1918, Fletcher, the former Sapper, had attained the rank of A/Brigadier General. In 1919, he was awarded both the CMG and the CBE in recognition of his outstanding services. Two years later in 1921, Fletcher was given command of the RAF's Aircraft Park in Iraq, with the rank of Wing Commander. A Group Captain in 1922, he went on to become Deputy Director of Organisation, Air Ministry, between 1918 and 1930, before retiring in the latter year with the honorary rank of Air Commodore. He married first, Ethel Mary Futcher, who died in 1934, and, secondly, Doris Maud Norman, with whom he had one son. When the Second World War came in 1939, Fletcher was appointed Deputy Director of Personnel at the Air Ministry from 1939 to 1943 and then AOC, Administration, Transport Command, from 1943 to 1944. His final job in the service, before retiring for the second time in 1945, was as Liaison Officer between Transport Command, RAF, and the civilian airline, BOAC, He lived, in retirement, at 22 Goldsmith Avenue, London W3. Air Commodore Arthur Fletcher died at Neasdon Hospital, Willesden, Middlesex, on 29 January 1956.

FLOYER, Ernest Ayscoghe

The son of Chartered Surveyor, Ernest A Floyer and Mrs Floyer, of 3 Gainsborough Road, Ipswich, he was born on 30 June 1888. Educated at Haileybury (1901-05). He was, like his father, a Chartered Surveyor, and he worked in India prior to the Great War, where he was also a part-time volunteer with the Assam Valley Light Horse. He was mobilised to serve on attachment to 1/8 Gurkha Rifles, during the Abor Expedition of 1911-12, for which he received the India General Service Medal 1908-35, with clasp, Abor 1911-12. When the Great War came, he tidied up his affairs and responsibilities before offering his services. Gazetted Second Lieutenant to the Indian Army Reserve of Officers on 20 November 1914. Posted to Egypt in 1915, he served on attachment to 17 Cavalry Regiment, Indian Army, before successfully seeking secondment to the RFC, which came late in 1915. After the appropriate training, he was confirmed and gazetted Flying Officer (Observer) on 1 February 1916. Next, he gained his Royal Aero Club Certificate (Number 3038) on 2 June 1916, formally qualifying for his full 'Wings' shortly afterwards. Attached to the Middle East Brigade, RFC, he was sent to 14 Squadron on 12 August 1916. Floyer was a member of the BE2c-equipped 'C' Flight, 14 Squadron, who made up part of the 'Arabian Detachment' of the Hejaz Expedition, sent to support Captain T E Lawrence, Lawrence of Arabia, in his special operations against the Turks. After a false start, the detachment landed at Rabegh on 17 November 1916. Because of the soggy state of the aerodrome as a consequence of heavy winter rain, it was not until 6 January 1917, that the first bombing mission could be mounted. On that day, Floyer, in company with Major A J Ross and Captain T Henderson (qv), dropped twenty-four Hales bombs on the enemy encampment at El Hajah. However, an unacceptable number of the bombs failed to explode, rendering the raid virtually useless. Still, it was a start and as the weather improved so did the raiding and patrolling increase. On 5 March 1917, Floyer and his Observer, Second Lieutenant C B Palmer, were forced to land their DH1A in the wilderness, by the German Ace, Oberleutnant G Felmy, flying an Albatros DIII. The pair managed to burn their aircraft before being taken prisoner. Felmy, renowned for his chivalry, dropped a letter on 14 Squadron's aerodrome, advising of their capture, and inviting a drop of some clothing and shaving kits, whilst guaranteeing that a British machine arriving at a nominated time on the following day would not be molested. Floyer's MC was announced in the *London Gazette* of 8 August 1917 (no citation).

He was also Mentioned in Despatches around this time, *London Gazette* of 17 September 1917. Floyer was repatriated from Turkey before the end of the war on 6 October 1918. He subsequently relinquished his commission in the RAF, reverting to the Indian Army Reserve of Officers on 17 March 1919. He married, in 1926, Dorothy Castle, from Fruitvale, British Columbia, Canada. Ernest Floyer lived, post the Second World War, at Marinyn Estate, Kericho, Kenya.

FOOT, Ernest Leslie

The son of Dr Ernest and Mrs Foot, of Pulborough, Sussex, he was born on 19 May 1895. Educated at Epsom College (1906-12). He had lived and worked in London from January 1913, and was studying railway administration and control at London Bridge, when the war came in August 1914. Volunteering immediately, he was gazetted Second Lieutenant to 9 (Reserve) Battalion, Oxfordshire and Buckinghamshire Light Infantry. His brother, Douglas, would be killed in action with 8 Royal Berkshire Regiment on 13 October 1915. Ernest successfully sought secondment to the RFC early in 1915. Having trained as an Observer, he flew as a Probationary with the BE2c-equipped 4 Squadron in the summer of 1915. On 21 July 1915, Foot and his Pilot, Lieutenant O G W G Lywood, in BE2c, '1800', were attacked and shot up. Although their machine crashed, both occupants emerged from the wreckage unscathed. Next he returned to the UK to train as a Pilot, gaining his Royal Aero Club Certificate (Number 2257) on 20 December 1915. His formal pilot training duly completed, he was confirmed and gazetted Flying Officer on 10 February 1916. He served initially in this new capacity with 8 Squadron in France from March 1916, before being posted to 11 Squadron as a Flight Commander, three months later. 'Feet' Foot was Albert Ball's best friend and, although not as prolific as the great young Ace, he gained three victories in the FE2b of 11 Squadron before being sent to 60 Squadron on 16 September 1916, again as a Flight Commander. Two more victories followed, including, on 28 September, the first ever victory achieved by the RFC Pilot in a new French-built fighter, the Spad VII. On 26 October 1916, Foot was himself shot down in flames over Serre by Leutnant Hans Imelman of Jasta 2. Amazingly, despite flames licking around him, Foot managed to crash-land the Nieuport Scout, 'A 162', and step out of the cockpit unscathed. His MC was announced in the *London Gazette* of 14 November 1916: 'For conspicuous skill and gallantry. When flying a single-seater scout, he dived on to five hostile machines, which were flying at about 2,500 feet, and drove one of them down to the ground as a wreck. On many other occasions he has shown determination when fighting enemy machines'.

Foot was also twice Mentioned in Despatches during the Great War. Sent home for a rest in November, his next posting, on 10 March 1917, was to the newly-forming 56 Squadron at London Colney, where he became one of the original Flight Commanders of that famous squadron. Unfortunately (or perhaps fortunately?) he was injured in a car accident the evening before '56' was due to start for France, and would never fly in combat again. Foot spent most of the rest of the war instructing at the School of Special Flying, Gosport. Leaving the RAF, he went into Civil Aviation and was killed in an aerial accident on 23 June 1923, the wing of a Bristol Monoplane M1D (G-EAUP) tearing away, causing it to crash near to Chertsey.

NB: The RAF Museum Hendon has his single MC in its collection.

FORBES, Ellert Webster

Born on 31 March 1895, he was the third son of John Webster Forbes and Mrs Forbes, of 'The Hawthornes', Birchfield, Birmingham, and the youngest brother of Leslie Frederick Forbes (qv), another 'flying MC' winner. His other brother, Captain Stanley W Forbes, served in the trenches with the Royal Warwickshire Regiment. Ellert was educated at Lickey Hills School, Birmingham, and at Shrewsbury (1909-13). He was managing a leather works in Walsall, Staffordshire, when the war came in August 1914. A pre-war volunteer, he was gazetted Second Lieutenant to 6 Battalion, Royal Warwickshire Regiment (TF) on 29 June 1914, and hence was mobilised with the rest of the TF when war came on 4 August 1914. Ellert Forbes accompanied his battalion to France on 22 March 1915, and was subsequently wounded in the trenches during the following May. After recovering from the effects of his wounds, he successfully sought secondment to the RFC on 15 December 1915. Having trained as an Observer, he served briefly as a Probationary with 20 Squadron and with 25 Squadron in England, before almost immediately reverting to '20' in time to accompany that FE2b-equipped unit to France as a 'founder member' on 23 January 1916. His 'apprenticeship' satisfactorily completed, he was confirmed and gazetted Flying Officer (Observer) on 9 April 1916. On 16 May 1916, Forbes and his Pilot, Lieutenant Trafford Jones, in FE2b, '6359', were attacked by three Fokkers. Trafford Jones, from Toronto, Canada, was killed in the air, whilst Forbes received wounds to the chest. The citation of Ellert Forbes' MC, the first to be won by 20 Squadron, graphically, if succinctly, describes the circumstances, *London Gazette* of 24 June 1916: 'For conspicuous gallantry and skill. He was acting as observer when attacked by two enemy aeroplanes and was wounded in the chest. On recovering from the shock he saw that his pilot was killed. Climbing into the pilot's seat he succeeded in bringing his machine back from behind the enemy's lines and landing safely'.

Taken to hospital after he landed, he wrote to his parents on the following day:

> 17 May 1916:
> Isn't it extraordinary it is exactly a year ago since I was in this hospital, exactly to the day. I came here last night. [He had been wounded in the trenches with the 6th Warwicks exactly a year before].
>
> Well! my wound is slight, just where the heart is, it hasn't penetrated a lung and hasn't touched my heart, lucky isn't it? Presumably the bullet is still here. I am to be X-Rayed today and if I know the result by the time I post this I will let you know.
>
> Well, as to how I got it I am not going to give you great details.
>
> My pilot and I were fighting three Fokkers when I was wounded. I fell into the bottom of the nacelle and finding I wasn't dead, I got up to use my machine gun again only to find the machine was out of control and diving. I looked round to see my pilot leaning over the controls, a mass of blood, stone dead. I grabbed hold of the joy stick and managed to right the machine but found that it was partly uncontrollable owing to several wires shot through. How I managed to get back over the German lines I don't know, but several times the machine got out of control altogether. The engine stopped owing to seizure, the radiator having been punctured. God knows how I did it, but I got down and was about to land, I had meantime got into the pilot's seat and was sitting on top of the pilot. I was about 300 feet from the ground when the machine got out of control again and went hell for leather at a cottage. I managed to miss the cottage but hit a clump of trees at about 80 miles an hour. I remember whizzing through the air and skimming along a ploughed field head over heels, several people came to my rescue and bandaged up my chest and chin which is gashed. I have cracked three molar teeth on the left side and am stiff and bruised all over, but am capable to walk if they would let me.
>
> This all occurred about 7am yesterday.
>
> Now there is no need to worry at all and I hope to be in England very soon.

Once recovered from the effects of his wounds, Ellert was posted to Staff duties in the UK, eventually serving with the Air Ministry in London, before finally leaving the RAF, via the Unemployed List, with the rank of Major, in January 1920. After returning to civilian life, he again joined the TF, returning to his old battalion, 6 Warwicks, and reverting to the rank of Captain. He was promoted Major on 16 February 1928 and awarded the Territorial Decoration on 16 February 1929. When the Second World War came in 1939, he was employed 'extra-regimentally' with the Royal Artillery. He lived in retirement with his wife in Chilham, Kent. Ellert Forbes died on 25 July 1967.

NB: His medals were offered for sale by Glendinings (lot 351) on 28 March 1990: MC, 1914-15 Star (Lt R War R), *British War Medal 1914-20, Victory Medal 1914-19* (Capt RFC), *Defence Medal 1939-45, and Territorial Decoration (George V).*

FORBES, Leslie Frederick

The son of John Webster Forbes and Mrs Forbes, of 'The Hawthorns', Birchfield, Birmingham, he was born on 13 June 1892. His brother, Ellert Webster Forbes (qv), also won a 'flying MC'. Another brother, Captain Stanley W Forbes, served in the trenches with the Royal Warwickshire Regiment. Leslie was educated at Lickey Hills School, Birmingham, and at Shrewsbury (1906-09). After leaving school, he trained as a manufacturing engineer. When war came, he enlisted as a Private soldier (Number 13059) into 5 Battalion, King's Shropshire Light Infantry, on 18 August 1914. Forbes served in the trenches through the severe fighting in the Ypres Salient from 21 May 1915 to 11 November 1915, when he returned to the UK to be commissioned. Gazetted Second Lieutenant to the RFC on 18 November 1915. He next gained his Royal Aero Club Certificate (Number 2619) on 24 March 1916. His formal pilot training duly completed, he was confirmed and gazetted Flying Officer on 6 May following. Forbes was sent to France to join the Martinsyde G100-equipped 27 Squadron soon after qualifying for his 'Wings'. On 23 September 1916, six Martinsyde Elephants were attacked over Cambrai by elements of Jagdstaffel 2, led by Oswald Boelcke, and numbering amongst its number, a certain Manfred von Richthofen. Three of the Elephants were sent down within minutes. Leslie Forbes, having exhausted all of his ammunition, in desperation and frustration, flew his machine directly at the Albatros flown by Leutnant Hans Reimann. Reimann fell to his death but, amazingly, Forbes' Elephant, despite extensive damage, remained airborne. Forbes subsequently crash-landed at the first friendly airfield he encountered, Bertangles, the home of 24 Squadron. After deliberately steering the machine into a small tree to arrest its careering slide, Forbes sustained a dislocated shoulder, a fracture of the head of the humerus, as well as a number of fractured ribs. His MC was announced in the *London Gazette* of 20 October 1916: 'For conspicuous gallantry and ability in attacking hostile machines and bombing railway lines, especially on one occasion, when he descended to 350 feet in order to accomplish his object'.

Once recovered in April 1916, Forbes returned to duty as a Captain with 16 RS, going on to see out the remainder of the war in instructing and administration posts. Staying on in the RAF after the war, his many appointments and promotions during a distinguished career included: served on the Staff in Mesopotamia from 1920 to1922; served with 2 Squadron in England from 1922 to 1924; service with 99 (Bomber) Squadron in 1925 and with 7 Squadron (Bomber) from 1926 to 1927; command of 1 Section, 2 Armoured Car Company, in Amman in Transjordan, 1927-30; command of No 4 FTS at Abu Suier, 1930; promotion to Wing Commander in 1933 and advancment to Group Captain on 1 January 1936. Group Captain Forbes served with the RAF General Duties Branch throughout the Second World War, before finally retiring in 1945.

FORSYTH, Eric Mortimer

The son of Dr Alec Forsyth, MB, and Mrs Forsyth, of Chacewater, Cornwall, he was born on 12 April 1899. Educated at Lancing College (1914-17), where he was a Sergeant in the OTC. His brother, Ian, served as an officer in the Gurkhas in the Great War. As soon as he was old enough, Eric volunteered his services and was gazetted Second Lieutenant to the RFC on 19 July 1917. Having trained as a Pilot, he was confirmed and gazetted Flying Officer on 20 October following. He served as a Scout Pilot with 1 Squadron (SE5As) in France, from 5 December 1917, and had been credited with at least one victory when he returned to the Home Establishment for a well earned rest on 14 August 1918. His MC was announced in the *London Gazette* of 26 July 1918: 'For conspicuous gallantry and devotion to duty. He has on many occasions displayed the utmost courage and fearlessness in bombing enemy troops, and engaging them with machine-gun fire from low altitude, and in bombing huts and lorries. On one occasion he was sent out to do a special reconnaissance, and flying at a particularly low altitude, and in very bad weather, he successfully obtained the most valuable information'.

Leaving the RAF in 1919, still only 20-years old, he entered Pembroke College, Cambridge, to complete his interrupted education.

FOWLER, Harold

Born in Liverpool, England in 1887, his family moved to New York, whilst he was still a schoolboy. After graduating from Columbia University in 1908, he became a partner in the New York Stock Exchange firm of White, Weld and Company. In 1913, he was invited by the then US Ambassador to Great Britain, Walter Hines Page, to become his secretary. When the war came in August 1914, Fowler made strenuous attempts to be accepted into the British Army. Eventually, thanks mainly to a recommendation from the General Officer commanding the London District, he was accepted and gazetted Second Lieutenant to the Royal Field Artillery on 3 February 1915 and served with the Gunners on the Western Front in the same year, thus earning a 1914-15 Star. Promotion to Lieutenant came on 1 January 1916. Seconded to the RFC, he trained as an Observer, eventually being confirmed and gazetted Flying Officer (Observer) on 19 April 1916. In 1916 he was with 26 Squadron during July, October and November 1916. He next trained as a Pilot, qualifying for his full 'Wings' on 28 July following. Posted out to 2 Squadron in France on 24 January 1917, he was quickly promoted to T/Captain on 22 February following. Transferring as a Flight Commander to BE2c-equipped 12 Squadron soon after this, Fowler and his Observer, Lieutenant F E Brown, Royal Dublin Fusiliers attached RFC, were credited with sending a Halberstadt Scout down in flames on 25 February 1917. On 2 April 1917, the same pair in BE2c, '2521', were engaged in combat during an artillery observation patrol over Cité Calonne, by an Albatros. Following a series of prolonged exchanges, the fight petered out when the German machine broke off and turned for home. Having survived through 'Bloody April' and beyond, Fowler was able to return to the Home Establishment on 11 June 1917. His MC was announced in the *London Gazette* of 18 July 1917: 'For conspicuous gallantry and devotion to duty. He has done invaluable service in co-operating with the artillery. On one occasion he descended to 300 feet, and turned our guns on to parties of hostile troops. During the advance he was able to furnish much valuable information'.

As the USA had entered the conflict on 6 April 1917, Fowler was allowed to resign his commission, with the rank of Honorary Lieutenant, on 16 June following. His combat experience invaluable to the USAS, he was gladly accepted into the American Army. During his service with the USAS, he was wounded, and decorated with the Distinguished Service Medal. For his subsequent work as a Liaison Officer between the USAS and the RAF, he was awarded the Distinguished Service Order and created CMG by the British. (His 1914-15 Star, British War Medal 1914-20 and Victory Medal 1914-19 were, according to a note at the Public Records Office, delivered to him in 1929). He was also decorated by the French and the Belgians. Following the Armistice, he became the Commanding Colonel of the US Third Army Air Service. After the war, Fowler returned to his Stock Exchange interests in New York city. A horseman of some repute, he entered as a Gentleman rider and rode his own horse, Pop Ahead, in the Grand National steeplechase at Aintree, in the city of his birth, in 1927. At 40 to 1, he was not given much chance of success by the pundits, who, in the event, proved correct as his horse fell and failed to complete the most exacting course in world steeplechasing. He tried again in the following year, this time with Scotch Eagle, one of 42 starters, but rated as a rank outsider at 100 to 1. The 1928 Grand National, run over heavy ground and in a mist, was one of the most eventful in the race's long and distinguished history. Many horses, including Scotch Eagle, fell at the treacherous Canal Turn, and the race was eventually won by another 100 to 1 shot, Tipperary Tim. As well as steeplechase riding, Fowler enjoyed big game hunting in Africa and in Alaska. Fowler was a close friend of Fiorello H La Guardia, a famous Mayor of New York city. In fact, Fowler led the political Fusion movement which was largely instrumental in securing the election of La Guardia in 1933 and again in 1937. Fowler himself was the First Deputy Police Commissioner in NYC from 1934 until 1937. In that post he had responsibilities for the city traffic and during his tenure crusaded successfully for a reduction in traffic accidents, injuries and deaths. He also headed the Honor Board, which was responsible for decorating heroic New York policemen. An active member of the American Legion, he was Commander of Air Service Post 501 in 1939 and 1940. In 1941, Fowler crossed the Atlantic to serve as a volunteer Personnel Officer for American citizens in the Royal Canadian Air Force in Great Britain. In 1942, he was given the honorary rank of Group Captain, RCAF, and served on the Staff of the Commander of the RCAF in the UK. Later that same year, he became a US Army Air Force Colonel and was appointed to serve on the operational staff of Major General James E Chaney in London. In the following year he was appointed Air Attaché at the US Embassy in London. Returning to his business interests in New York after the war, he lived, in the 1950s, with his wife, Thyrza Benson Flagg Fowler, in his Southampton, Long Island, home during the summer and at his Palm Beach, Florida, home in the winter months. Colonel Harold Fowler died in a hospital in Palm Beach, Florida, on 17 January 1957.

FOX, John Bertram

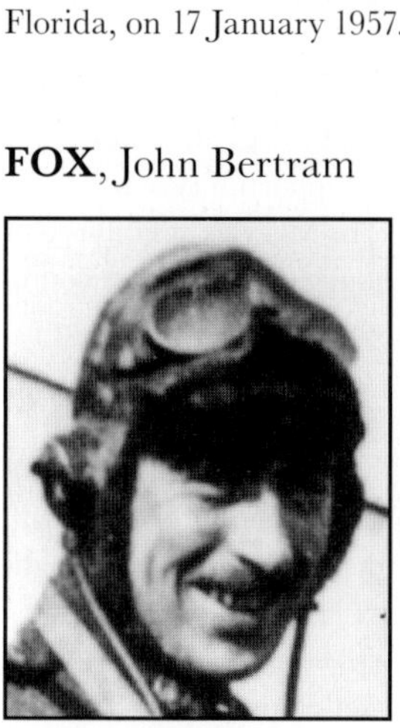

The son of the Assistant Postmaster General of Ceylon (Indian Civil Service), he was born on 24 July 1893. Educated at St Edward's School, Newara, Elyia, Ceylon, and at the Dollar Institution School, Dollar, Scotland (1906-11). Fox was working in Canada when the war came in August 1914. He immediately volunteered, enlisting as a Private soldier into the Machine Gun Section of 3 Canadian Infantry Battalion. Serving in France with the CEF in 1915, he transferred, on 8 July, to 1 Canadian Division Signals Company, as a motor-cycle despatch rider. Responding to a call for volunteers for the flying service, he was subsequently gazetted Second Lieutenant to the RFC on 5 April 1917. After training as a Pilot, he was confirmed and gazetted Flying Officer on 24 May following. He was sent out to the DH4-equipped 55 Squadron in France, soon after qualifying for his 'Wings'. On 5 September 1917, Fox and his Observer, 2 AM S L Leyland (Number 94425) were credited with sending an enemy Scout down out of control. His MC was announced in the *London Gazette* of 13 May 1918: 'For conspicuous gallantry and devotion to duty. During a period of two months he led his formation on six long distance bombing raids into enemy territory. On the last occasion, although engaged by three separate hostile formations, he dropped his bombs with excellent effect over his objective and brought the whole of his formation back to the aerodrome intact. His formation accounted for three enemy aeroplanes destroyed and four driven down out of control. He has carried out upwards of forty successful operations, his skill and leadership being of the highest order'.

Leyland, from Wallasey, was subsequently awarded a Military Medal in the *London Gazette* of 12 December 1917. John Fox survived the war with the rank of Captain.

FOX-RUSSELL, Henry Thornbury

The son of Physician and Surgeon, Dr William Fox-Russell and Ethel Maria Fox-Russell, of 5 Victoria Terrace, Holyhead, Anglesey, he was born in 1897. Educated at St Bee's, Cumberland (1909-10). Volunteering as soon as war came, he was gazetted Second Lieutenant to 1/6 (Carnarvon & Anglesey) Battalion, Royal Welsh Fusiliers (TF), on 20 August 1914. Initially considered too young for active service overseas, he was held back and transferred to 2/6 RWF, before 1/6 sailed for Gallipoli. Second thoughts prevailed, however, and he was allowed to join his battalion on the dreaded Peninsula soon after they arrived there in August 1915. Following the evacuation from the Dardanelles, he was stationed in Egypt. He eventually sought secondment to the RFC in Egypt and was subsequently sent back to the UK. Having qualified as a Pilot, he was made Assistant Instructor at Thetford, before being posted to the newly forming 64 Squadron at Sedgeford. Fox-Russell subsequently accompanied the DH5-equipped '64' to France as a Flight Commander and 'founder member' on 15 October 1917. On 23 November following, Fox-Russell in DH5, 'A9490', was a member of a 64 Squadron patrol which was attacked and badly shot up by the so-called 'Flying Circus'. Fox-Russell's machine had its tail shot off over Boulon Wood and he was extremely fortunate to survive the subsequent crash with nothing more than a severe shaking. Twenty minutes later, another DH5 of his squadron, 'A9299', came down to crash within his sight. He immediately went to the Pilot's aid, despite very heavy machine-gun fire from the enemy trenches. The Pilot, Lieutenant J A V Boddy, had broken both of his legs in the crash and it was only with great difficulty that Fox-Russell extricated him from the wreckage and carried him to safety. Boddy, it transpired, had been shot down by none other than Manfred von Richthofen himself, the Red Baron's 62nd victory. The unfortunate Boddy subsequently had one of his legs amputated, but still survived the war. Sent home for a rest after his shooting down, Fox-Russell took the opportunity of belatedly qualifying for his Royal Aero Club Certificate (Number 4649) on 27 December 1917. His MC was announced in the *London Gazette* of 4 February 1918, details in the *Gazette* of 5 July 1918: 'For conspicuous gallantry and devotion to duty. He formed one of a patrol which silenced an enemy battery. He dropped bombs on to two of the guns, silenced others with his machine gun and then engaged transport on a road. The operation was carried out under heavy fire and very difficult weather conditions. On another occasion he dropped bombs and fired 300 rounds on enemy trenches from a height of 100 feet. His machine was then hit by a shell and crashed in front of our advanced position. He reached the front line and while there saw another of our machines brought down. He went to the assistance of the pilot, who was badly wounded, extricated him under heavy fire and brought him to safety. He showed splendid courage and initiative'.

Henry's brother, Captain John Fox-Russell, MC, Royal Army Medical Corps attached 1/6 Battalion, Royal Welsh Fusiliers, was awarded a posthumous Victoria Cross after his death in action in Palestine, during the Third Battle of Gaza on 6 November 1917, just a couple of weeks before Henry won his MC. When, in 1918, Henry's tour with '64' was completed, he was appointed as an Instructor at Hooton in Cheshire, not too far from his Welsh home, where he saw out the remainder of the war. Tragically, he was killed in a flying accident at Hooton on 18 November 1918, just one week after the war ended. Henry Fox-Russell is buried in Holyhead (St Seirol) Churchyard, Anglesey.

FRANKLYN, Adrian Winfrid

From Hounslow in Middlesex, he was born on 1 April 1899. Gazetted Second Lieutenant to the RFC on 12 August 1917. Having trained as a Pilot, he was confirmed and gazetted Flying Officer on 12 November following. Sent out to the Camel-equipped 3 Squadron on 19 January 1918, he achieved seven victories between 22 March and 5 September. His MC was announced in the *London Gazette* of 22 June 1918: 'For conspicuous gallantry and devotion to duty. On one occasion he silenced an enemy battery which had been most active, and on the following day shot down a hostile plane, which finally crashed to earth. He has on numerous occasions successfully attacked enemy aircraft on the ground, and by accurate bombing and machine-gun fire has inflicted heavy casualties on personnel and a very considerable amount of damage to material. His skill and gallantry have been of the highest order'.

An Ace and the holder of an MC, he was still only 19 years old when the war ended. Research has unearthed a 3 Squadron recommendation, dated 9 October 1918, for the award of the Belgian Chevalier de l'Ordre de Leopold: 'This officer has been with the Squadron since 20 January 1918, and has always rendered most excellent service. During the German Offensive of March/April 1918 he was continuously involved in low bombing, and during the present offensive has led his Flight with great courage and dash, and has achieved very effective results, displaying fine leadership. – EA accounted for: 2 crashed; 2 Out of control. Awarded MC on 4 April 1918'.

Unfortunately, the recommendation does not appear to have been acted upon. Franklyn stayed on in the RAF after the war, serving with 3 Squadron in India in 1921. He was promoted to Flight Lieutenant in 1931 and Squadron Leader in 1936, at which time he was serving aboard HMS *Furious* on armament duties. Franklyn finally retired from the RAF, with the rank of Group Captain, in 1948. Group Captain Adrian Franklyn died on 9 June 1986.

FRASER, Harold Livingstone

From Rockhampton, Queensland, Australia, he was born in 1891. An Overseer on a sheep station pre-war, he enlisted into the AIF in Blackwell on 15 January 1915. After training, he embarked aboard the SS *Malkuta* (Transport A57) at Newcastle, NSW, on 17 May 1915, bound for the Middle East as part of 5 Reinforcement Group for 5 Light Horse Regiment, 2 Light Horse Brigade. Arriving in Alexandria, the Group was sent to camp Heliopolis in Egypt. Promoted to Corporal on 16 October 1915 and to Sergeant on 11 July 1916. Accepted as a Cadet into the flying service on 27 January 1917, he was subsequently gazetted Second Lieutenant to the RFC on 27 April following. After qualifying for his 'Wings', he was posted for operational service to 1 Squadron, AFC, on 15 June 1917. Fraser survived an eventful tour with 1 AFC, including, in January 1918, having his machine hit (once seriously) during three successive flights over the so-called 'hottest corner of all' at Tul Keram and Kalkilieh. His MC was announced in the *London Gazette* of 11 April 1918 (no citation): '....military operations culminating in the capture of Jerusalem'.

Fraser was able to return to Australia on 30 July 1918, his appointment terminated.

FREEMAN, Russell Herbert

The son of William Robert Freeman and Anne F C Freeman, of 103 Westbourne Terrace, Paddington, London, he was born in Christchurch, Oxford, on 27 January 1894. Educated at Winchester (1907-12), in Germany and at Christ Church College, Oxford (1912-14). His brother, Wilfred (qv), was also a 'flying MC' winner. Volunteering as soon as war came, he was gazetted Second Lieutenant to 3 Battalion, Worcestershire Regiment, in August 1914. He proceeded to France on 1 January 1915, and served in the trenches until the spring, when he was invalided home suffering with paratyphoid. Once recovered, he applied for secondment to the RFC, taking his Royal Aero Club Certificate (Number 2452) on 9 February 1916. After completing his formal training, he was confirmed and gazetted Flying Officer on 16 May following. Sent out to Egypt and 14 Squadron, he arrived on 19 June 1916. Freeman was involved in a famous incident on 2 November 1916, when he landed his Martinsyde 'Elephant' in the desert alongside a crashed colleague's machine and, taking off again, carried the downed Pilot, Captain F F R Minchin (qv), sitting astride the engine cowl, to safety. His MC was announced in the *London Gazette* of 26 January 1917: 'For conspicuous gallantry in action. He attacked and drove off an enemy aeroplane which had forced one of our machines to land. Later, he landed and rescued the pilot under very difficult conditions. He set a fine example of courage and initiative'.

The French, too, showed their appreciation of his services with an award of a Croix de Guerre, *London Gazette* of 21 May 1917. On 24 June 1917, Freeman and Lieutenant S K Muir (qv), each in a Martinsyde Elephant, took part in an extremely, for those days, long-distance bombing raid with the intention of cutting the Damascus-to-Medina railway by bombing a bridge four miles south of Qal'at el Hasa. At one point during the flight the airmen had, 'in simultaneous view, the Dead Sea, the River Jordan, the Mediterranean and the Red Sea'. In the event, they failed to bring down the bridge, but succeeded in displacing some of the track. In part, the raid was undertaken to demonstrate the wide range of British power to those tribesmen who had not yet committed themselves to either the Turkish or the Allied cause. The flight covered a distance of 350 miles and took more than five hours, but was successfully executed without loss. Freeman was Mentioned in Despatches for this feat, *London Gazette* of 6 July 1917. His tour with '14' completed, he returned to the UK and, after enjoying a short leave, was appointed an Instructor at the CFS, with the rank of A/Major and Squadron Commander. Sent out next to France to command the Sopwith Camel-equipped 73 Squadron, he was killed in action just three weeks later on 21 July 1918. His Camel, 'D1918', fell victim to Leutnant Harry von Bülow-Bothkamp of Jasta 36, the sixth and last of the German Ace's victories. Russell Freeman is buried in Raperie British Cemetery, Villemontoire, Aisne, France.

FREEMAN, Wilfred Rhodes

The third son of William Robert Freeman and Anne F C Freeman, of 29 Cambridge Square, London W, he was born on 18 July 1888. Educated at Rugby (1902-06) and at the Royal Military College, Sandhurst. Gazetted Second Lieutenant to 2 Battalion, Manchester Regiment, on 2 February 1908. Developing an interest in aviation, he gained his Royal Aero Club Certificate (French version, Number Fr 1404) on 21 July 1913. Wilfred's brother, Russell H Freeman (qv), also won a 'flying' MC. Seconded to the RFC in 1913, Wilfred accompanied 2 Squadron to France with the original RFC contingent in August 1914, thus earning the 1914 Star. On 12 September 1914, Freeman was acting as Observer to Lieutenant Leonard Dawes, Middlesex Regiment, in BE2, '384', when their engine was hit by machine-gun fire from the ground. Their wings, undercarriage and propeller badly damaged, they were forced to land in a small wood. They soon realised that they were surrounded by columns of enemy infantry and cavalry, and decided to lie low until nightfall. Once darkness fell, they made their way to the River Aisne, some eight miles distant. Arriving at the riverbank, at 03.00, they lay down to sleep. They were wakened by gunfire some three hours later and soon realised they were almost directly in front of a German position which was being heavily shelled by the Royal Artillery. Slipping into the Aisne, they swam to the other bank where they found a deserted farm house where they could dry their clothes. Making their way towards the sound of the British guns, they eventually connected with elements of the Third Cavalry Brigade, who fed and watered them. Two days after taking off, they were stood in front of their CO, Major C J Burke, Royal Irish Regiment, who gave them a severe dressing down for taking a machine up, manned by two Pilots, something strictly against Standing Orders. Freeman won his MC over the trenches on the first day of the Battle of Neuve Chapelle on 10 March 1915, announced in the *London Gazette* of 27 March 1915: 'For gallantry, ability, and very valuable work performed. Located the position of German batteries on 10th instant, and conveyed the information by wireless messages from his aeroplane to our artillery, and, although his propeller and planes were pierced by the enemy's bullets, he remained aloft for more than five hours during this day'.

Indeed, this might very well qualify as being the first 'flying' MC to carry a published citation. His tour with '2' completed, Freeman was subsequently employed in various Staff posts, rising inexorably through the senior ranks. The award of a Distinguished Service Order was announced in the *London Gazette* of 23 November 1916. He was also appointed Chevalier, Légion d'Honneur by the French, and Mentioned in Despatches on three occasions during the Great War. He married first, in 1915, Gladys Mews, with whom he had one son and one daughter, and secondly, in 1935, Elizabeth Richmond, with whom he had two daughters. Staying on in the RAF after the war, his many appointments, honours and promotions during a distinguished career included: Lecturer at the RAF Staff College at Andover, 1923; Deputy Director of Operations and Intelligence at the Air Ministry from 1927 to 1928; Chief Staff Officer Inland Area, 1930; AOC, Palestine and Transjordan from 1930 to 1933; CB, 1932; Command of the RAF Staff College from 1933 to 1936; Member of the Air Council for Research Development and Production from 1936 to 1940; KCB, 1937; Air Chief Marshal, 1940; Chief Executive, Ministry of Aircraft Production from 1942 to 1945; GCB, 1942; 1st Baronet, created 1945; Fellow of the Royal Aeronautical Society. Freeman inherited and lived in his late parents' home at 103 Westbourne Terrace, London W. Air Chief Marshal Sir Wilfred Freeman died on 15 May 1953.

FREW, Mathew Brown

The son of Harry Lorimer Frew and Annie Brown Frew, of Rutherglen, Glasgow, Scotland, he was born on 7 April 1895. Educated at Hutcheson's Grammar School, Glasgow. He enlisted as a Private soldier into the Highland Light Infantry in 1914, serving in the trenches in France from January 1915 until March 1916. After a spell in the UK, he was accepted for transfer to the flying service in August 1916 and was subsequently gazetted Second Lieutenant to the RFC on 26 September following. His pilot training duly completed, he was confirmed and gazetted Flying Officer on 6 April 1917. 'Bunty' Frew was sent out to the Sopwith Strutter-equipped 45 Squadron in France on 28 April 1917. Frew, first serving in France and Flanders, and then later on the Italian front, achieved no less than 23 victories, mainly flying a Camel between 5 June 1917 and 4 February 1918, collecting, in the process, a plethora of gallantry awards. He almost did not make it beyond the 28 July 1917, when he, and his Observer of the day, Lieutenant George A Brooke, in Sopwith Strutter, 'A8228', were counted amongst the victories, specifically the 19, attained by the great German Ace, Oberleutnant Max Müller. However, despite severe damage to their machine, both Frew and Brooke escaped unscathed. Frew had gained 16 victories by the time his squadron moved to the Italian front on 17 November 1917. The first of his MCs, awarded for his prowess on the Western Front, was announced in the *London Gazette* of 7 March 1918: 'For conspicuous gallantry and devotion to duty on patrol, showing a fine offensive spirit in many combats. He has shot down four enemy aeroplanes, and on one occasion leading his formation to attack twenty-two Albatros Scouts, and himself shooting one down '.

He was soon in his stride on the Italian front, achieving seven more victories between 11 January and 4 February 1918, including a 'trio' on a single day. The Bar to his MC came in the *London Gazette* of 23 April 1918: 'For conspicuous gallantry and devotion to duty in shooting down three enemy machines in two days. He has destroyed eight enemy machines and driven down many others out of control'.

A gallantry Distinguished Service Order followed in the *London Gazette* of 4 March 1918, details in the *Gazette* of 16 August 1918, this for, amongst other things, accounting for three enemy machines in the same fight. He was also Mentioned in Despatches for his services in Italy, *London Gazette* of 23 April 1918. In addition to the British awards, Frew was honoured by the Italians with the Silver Medaglia al Valore Militare. On 15 January 1918, his Camel was hit in the air by AA fire, and he injured his neck in the subsequent forced landing. This injury persisted and he was obliged to return home to the UK a month later. After a short period of recovery, he was transferred to a training role at the CFS and it was for his outstanding work in this field that he later received the Air Force Cross, *London Gazette* of 3 June 1919. Frew, not surprisingly in view of his record, remained in the RAF after the war. His many subsequent appointments, honours and promotions during a distinguished career included: Air Staff HQ, 7 Group RAF, 1920; Staff Instructor, Ground Wing, RAF, 1920; QFI, Flying Wing, RAF Cadet College; Flight Commander, 6 Squadron, 1921; QFI, 4 FTS, RAF, 1923; Staff, Armament and Gunnery School, 1925; Squadron Leader, 1927; CFI, 1 FTS, RAF; Air Staff, Operations HQ, Iraq, 1931, adding a Bar to his Distinguished Service Order whilst serving in North Kurdistan during 1931-32, *London Gazette* of 6 October 1933; OC, 111 Squadron, 1933; OC, 10 Squadron, 1934; Wing Commander, 1934; OC, RAF Hornchurch, 1937; SASO, HQ, 23 (Training) Group, 1938. A Group Captain at the commencement of the Second World War in 1939, he served in various capacities being appointed a CB in 1943, and promoted to Air Vice-Marshal by the end of the war. He was also honoured by the Greeks with the Commander of the Royal Order of George I of Greece with Swords, 1943, and by the Belgians with the Military Cross, 1st Class, 1945. Created KBE in 1948, he retired shortly afterwards to spend the rest of his days in Pretoria, South Africa. Air Vice-Marshal Sir Matthew Frew died in South Africa on 28 May 1974.

FROST, Oliver Harry

A Technical, not a flying, award

Gazetted Second Lieutenant to 10 Battalion, Middlesex Regiment (TF) on 2 May 1915. Seconded to the RFC, he was gazetted an Equipment Officer, 2nd Class, on 1 November 1916. His MC was announced in the New Year *London Gazette* of 1 January 1918 (no citation). Although no formal citation was published in the *Gazette*, research has unearthed the original recommendation for the award: 'O H Frost, Duke of Cambridge's Own. HQ 1 Bde, RFC. For devotion to duty and perseverance. This Officer, whilst in command of the photographic work of the 1st Brigade, RFC, for the past year, has, by his zeal and energy raised this work to a high standard'.

Frost had, previously, been Mentioned in Despatches for his photographic work in France. Furthermore, Frost's name was also submitted, in January 1919, for a Roumanian decoration for his work as Brigade Photographic Officer from September 1916 to December 1918.

FRY, William Mays

Born in Brentford, Middlesex, on 14 November 1896, he spent most of his early life in Taunton, Somerset. Educated at Brighton College (arrived and left in 1913). When war came in August 1914, he was living and working in London. He immediately enlisted as a Private soldier (Number 9960) into 1/5 (City of London) Battalion (TF), the London Rifle Brigade. He subsequently accompanied his battalion's original contingent to France on 5 November 1914, thus earning the 1914 Star. Fry personally witnessed and, indeed, took part in the famous 'Christmas truce' of 1914. However, he was not long at the front. When it was discovered that he was under the age of 19, the minimum age for service in a theatre of war, he, and other under-age boys, were sent home. Picked out as officer material, he was, after the appropriate training, gazetted Second Lieutenant to the Shropshire Light Infantry on 10 June 1915. Seconded to the RFC in December 1915, he gained his Royal Aero Club Certificate (Number 3003) on 24 May 1916. His formal pilot training duly completed, he was confirmed and gazetted Flying Officer on 16 June following. Ten days later, he was sent out to France and the BE2c-equipped 12 Squadron. After a short period with '12', he was asked if he would like to try his hand as a Scout Pilot with 11 Squadron. 'C' Flight of 11 Squadron was, following the Battle of the Somme, transferred en bloc to 60 Squadron, with Fry, and a certain Albert Ball, being two of the Pilots involved. Fry flew with '60' as deputy to the legendary 'Billy' Bishop, through the summer of 1917, achieving five victories between 2 May to 16 June. His MC was announced in the *London Gazette* of 16 August 1917: 'For conspicuous gallantry and devotion to duty. Diving to a very low altitude, and under heavy fire, he emptied all his ammunition into the retreating enemy. During the past month he has brought down four hostile machines. He has done consistent good work as a pilot'.

Sent home for a rest, he was soon making a nuisance of himself by agitating for a quick return to the front. Following a spell with the still forming 87 Squadron in the UK, he was given command of a Flight in the Spad-equipped 23 Squadron in France. Fry enjoyed considerable success with '23', gaining five further victories between 20 November 1917 and 23 January 1918. On 6 January 1918, Fry shared in the downing of the German Ace, Walter von Bulow-Bothkamp (28 victories). In this incident, Fry scored hits on von Bulow's Albatros DV, '2080/17', but the actual coup de grace was performed by Canadian Lieutenant Francis G Quigley, DSO, MC and Bar (qv), of 70 Squadron, with the German Ace crashing to his death into the front lines of the Ypres Salient, east of Passchendaele. Fry finished the war with an extremely creditable 11 victories, the last of which came whilst he was serving with the Dolphins of 79 Squadron. Fry stayed on in the RAF after the war, rising to the rank of Wing Commander before retiring in the 1930s. He returned, of course, for service throughout the Second World War. He published his biography, 'Air of Battle' (1974). Wing Commander William Fry died in South East London on 4 August 1992.

Footnote: Fry, in his later life, became involved in the controversy regarding the 'validity' of William Avery Bishop's Victoria Cross. As a former comrade of Bishop, Fry openly added to the doubts that had always existed about the award and, for expressing those doubts, he was widely attacked and accused of cowardice, not least from the floor of the Canadian Parliament. Fry decided to say no more at the time but, instead, entrusted a statement of the events, as he remembered them, into the hands of the eminent aviation historian, Alex Revell, for publication after his death. Revell, albeit reluctantly, kept his promise and the statement, in its entirety, was duly published in the Journal of the Cross and Cockade Society, *Volume 32, Number 1, 2001.*

FULLARD, Philip Fletcher

The son of Mr and Mrs Thomas Fletcher Fullard, he was born in Hatfield, London, on 27 June 1897. Educated privately and at Norwich Grammar School. Excelling in sports, he was signed up by Norwich City FC, and was playing centre-half in that Club's reserve team when war came in August 1914. Still only 18 years old, he joined the Inns of Court OTC on 30 August 1915 (Number 6/5/5884) and was eventually gazetted to the RFC, via the Special List, on 4 August 1916. His pilot training duly completed, he was confirmed and gazetted Flying Officer on Boxing Day 1916. Such was his flying ability that as soon as he had formally qualified, he was immediately appointed an Instructor at Upavon. As a consequence of his training role in England, he did not arrive in France and with the Nieuport Scout-equipped 1 Squadron until May 1917. As well as his natural flying ability, his careful attention to detail made him a formidable fighting Scout Pilot. Maintaining and servicing his own machine guns, he had the unusual distinction of never once suffering a jam. One of the truly great Aces of the Great War, he never has, then or now, received the acclaim his record merits. Remarkably, he accumulated no less than 40 victories between 26 May 1917 and 15 November 1917, including seven 'doubles' and two 'trios' on single days. His MC and Bar were both announced in the same *London Gazette* of 26 September 1917, details in the *Gazette* of 9 January 1918, MC: 'For conspicuous gallantry and devotion to duty when engaged in aerial combat. He has on four occasions attacked and destroyed enemy aircraft, and has in addition engaged in 25 indecisive combats, in which he has shown fine leadership, great dash and determination to close with the enemy'.

Bar to the MC: 'For conspicuous gallantry and devotion to duty. He has on many occasions displayed the utmost dash and fearlessness in attacking enemy aircraft at close range and in destroying at least eight hostile machines during a period of about ten days. His determination and fine offensive spirit have in almost every instance resulted in a disaster to the enemy'.

A gallantry Distinguished Service Order came in the *London Gazette* of 26 November 1917, but a recommendation for a Bar to this, made on 19 November 1917, was never acted upon. Fullard was also Mentioned in Despatches at this time, *London Gazette* of 7 November 1917. Two days after gaining his 40th victory on 15 November 1917, he broke a leg playing football. The Imperial German Air Service could not get him, but, apparently, an overly robust opposing centre-forward could! The bone was slow in knitting and the war was almost over before he regained his fitness. The Americans honoured him with their Medal of the Aero Club of America in November 1918. His outstanding work as an Instructor was recognised by the award of an Air Force Cross, *London Gazette* of 3 June 1919. The Belgians, too, showed their appreciation with a Croix de Guerre. Staying on in the RAF after the war, he was given a plum posting to the USA in 1919, going there to promote the sale of Victory Loan Bonds along with other distinguished Pilots like A W Beauchamp-Proctor, H W Woollett and G J C Maxwell, all MC winners, of course. Returning to the UK, he crossed the Channel again, this time to join the Army of Occupation in the Rhineland. Employed on the Staff, Fullard spent three years in Iraq, followed by a period at the Staff College at Quetta, in India. A Squadron Leader by 1929, he was given command of 2 Squadron four years later in 1933. Fullard attained the rank of Air Commodore during the Second World War, commanding 246 Group, RAF, for a period. He added a CBE to his distinctions, before finally retiring in 1947. Air Commodore Philip Fullard helped to run a successful engineering business until his death on 24 April 1984.

FULLJAMES, Reginald Edgar Gilbert

From Southsea, Hampshire, he was born on 13 November 1896. He was a student studying in London, when he joined the Inns of Court OTC (Number 6/3/6433) on 24 September 1915. Having successfully completed his officer training, he was gazetted Second Lieutenant to the RFC on 7 July 1916. His formal pilot training duly completed, he was confirmed and gazetted Flying Officer on 4 November following. He was sent out to France and 6 Squadron in the same month that he qualified for his 'Wings'. Fulljames served with this artillery co-operation unit until December 1917, being promoted to Captain and Flight Commander in the intervening November. However, so badly affected by stress was he, that, in January 1918, he was taken off flying duties altogether. His MC was announced in the *London Gazette* of 18 October 1917, details in the *Gazette* of 8 March 1918: 'For conspicuous gallantry and devotion to duty during six months' continuous work with the artillery. During a battle he carried out four most valuable reconnaissances, bringing back information of our front line and directing artillery on to enemy infantry and farm buildings where they were concentrating. During 19 days he had only one failure in 12 flights'.

Happily, he had sufficiently recovered to receive the insignia of his MC from the hands of the King at an investiture held at Buckingham Palace on 16 March 1918. Fulljames lived, post-war, at 'St Briavel', Queen's Grove, Southsea, Hampshire.

G

GALLEY, Edward David George

From Bath, Somerset, he was born on 14 June 1896. Gazetted Second Lieutenant to the Army Service Corps on 12 May 1915, he served in France with his unit from 24 November following. Seconded to the RFC in September 1916, he trained as an Observer and was sent out to the FE2b-equipped 22 Squadron as a Probationary in the November following. On 6 February 1917, Galley and his Pilot, Lieutenant W N McDonald, in FE2b, '4971', had an extremely close call when, over Flers, their machine was shot down and wrecked by Paul Bona of Jasta 1, the fourth of the German Ace's eventual six victories. On 24 March following, he was again on the wrong end of an aerial combat. Captain W E Salter and Galley in FE2b, '4986', were shot up over Hendecourt by Vizefeldwebel Patermann. Salter managed to get them back without further mishap, but Galley was wounded in the air. After recovering from the effects of his wounds, he trained as a Pilot and was sent out to 41 Squadron in that capacity on 24 November 1917. From '41', he was promoted to A/Captain and sent to SE5A-equipped 56 Squadron as a Flight Commander early in the New Year of 1918. He was fortunate again on 23 March 1918, when his SE5A, B59 '3', was shot up and damaged in the air. Yet again on the following day, he was in the thick of things and his SE5A, 'B666', was shot about, although Galley himself was unscathed. Returning to the Home Establishment in May, he was destined never to return to combat flying. His MC was announced in the *London Gazette* of 22 June 1918: 'For conspicuous gallantry and devotion to duty. Attacking on one occasion, 14 enemy scouts, he shot down one of these, which was confirmed to have crashed. On a later occasion, he engaged from a low altitude a large convoy on the road, and after diving down from 800 feet fired all his ammunition into its midst. He then returned to his aerodrome for a further supply of ammunition, and again attacked transport on the same road with the most effective results. He has not only led his flight with signal success, but has on occasion led the whole squadron patrols in the most daring and efficient manner'.

Over the remaining months of 1918, he was appointed to a series of instructing posts, his outstanding services in this field eventually being recognised by the award of an Air Force Cross, *London Gazette* of 1 January 1919.

GARDNER, George Dudley

The son of Mr and Mrs G J E Gardner of Alverton House, Northallerton, Yorkshire, he was born on 29 July 1896. Educated at Giggleswick School, Yorkshire (1911-13). Gazetted Second Lieutenant to 4 Battalion, Yorkshire Regiment (Green Howards) (TF), on 12 September 1914. Seconded to the RFC, he gained his Royal Aero Club Certificate (Number 1630) on 7 August 1915. His formal pilot training duly completed, he was confirmed and gazetted Flying Officer on 2 September following. Sent to Egypt on 12 December 1915, he would, subsequently, serve mainly on the Salonika front. His MC was announced in the New Year *London Gazette* of 1 January 1918, (no citation). On 13 March 1918, Gardner took over command of 47 Squadron. Having suffered bouts of malaria in 1917 and 1918, Gardner was finally invalided home in the summer of 1918. He was Mentioned in Despatches on three occasions during the Great War and received the Silver Medaglia al Valore Militare from the Italians, *London Gazette* of 26 May 1919. Gardner finally left the RAF, via the Unemployed List, on 8 April 1919.

GASS, Charles George

From Chelsea, London, he was born on 18 April 1898. Having enlisted as a Private soldier into 24 (County of London) Regiment (The Queen's) (TF), he served, from June 1916, with the Second Line Battalion of that unit, in France, in Salonika and in Egypt, rising to the rank of Sergeant. Picked out for a commission, he was gazetted Second Lieutenant to 17 (County of London) Battalion (Poplar and Stepney Rifles) (TF), in October 1917. Seconded to the RFC, he trained as an Observer and was sent out as a Probationary to the Bristol Fighter-equipped 22 Squadron on 26 March 1918. Gass formed a formidable partnership with Captain Alfred Atkey (qv), who, with other Pilots, helped him to gain no less than 39 victories between 22 April and 13 August 1918, which made him the leading Gunner/Observer Ace of the Great War. On one occasion, after sustaining damage to their Brisfit and, whilst Atkey struggled to control the machine, Gass was obliged to climb out onto one of the wings to enable his Pilot to achieve balance and some stability. His MC, surprisingly his only award, was announced in the *London Gazette* of 16 September 1918: 'For conspicuous gallantry and devotion to duty. During many engagements, generally against heavy odds, he destroyed five enemy aircraft. He showed great ability and an entire disregard for personal danger'.

Charles Gass survived the war and, in later years, lived again in London.

GAVIN, Alexander Gordon Douglas

From Partick, Scotland, he was born on 23 December 1892, his family moving later to Barrhead, Glasgow. Educated at Merchiston Castle School (1907-09) and at Peterhouse College, Cambridge, where he was a member of the OTC. He was studying medicine at St Thomas Hospital, London, in 1915, when he volunteered his services for the war effort. Gazetted Second Lieutenant to 3 (Reserve) Battalion, Black Watch (Royal Highlanders), on 12 July 1915. Seconded to the RFC, he trained as a Balloon Officer and was confirmed as such in the *London Gazette* of 17 December 1915. Sent out to France in January 1916, he served with 9 KBS until 4 November 1916. His MC was announced in the *London Gazette* of 27 July 1916: 'For conspicuous presence of mind and unselfish courage. When his balloon broke loose and drifted fast towards the enemy's lines, he instructed his passenger in the use of the parachute and helped him out of the basket. He then destroyed all his papers, and descended by his own parachute, landing under machine-gun fire close to the trenches. His passenger also landed safely'.

Having returned to the Home Establishment in November 1916, Gavin availed himself of a provision which allowed medical students to resign their commissions and resume their studies. Doctors were needed more than ever.

GAVIN, Stanford

Originally from Romsey, Hampshire, his family later moved to Earl's Court, London, SW. Gazetted Second Lieutenant to 5 (Prince of Wales) Battalion, Devonshire Regiment (TF), on 29 May 1915. He served with 3 Line Battalion of his unit in the UK, before seeking secondment to the RFC on 24 January 1916. Gavin trained as a Balloon Officer and was gazetted as such on 24 February 1916. Sent first to 4 KBS on 3 March 1916, he later transferred, on 31 July following, to 12 KBS. He was wounded in the foot during an action on 28 May 1917, the limb subsequently having to be amputated. The citation for his MC reflects his gallantry on this and other occasions, *London Gazette* of 26 July 1917: 'For conspicuous gallantry and devotion to duty. As Observing Officer in the artillery he showed great ability and conspicuous courage under shell fire. On two occasions he was compelled to parachute down from burning balloons, but this in no way lessened his enthusiasm. The loss of a foot necessitated his being sent home, and his valuable services have been greatly missed'.

Despite his infirmity, he continued to serve in the UK until finally leaving the RAF, via the Unemployed List, on 3 June 1919. After the Great War, he became a farmer, living at Upper House Farm, near Henley-on-Thames. When the Second World War came, he again, despite his infirmity, he applied for an RAFVR commission on 26 July 1940. He lived, at that time, at Church Farm House, Shippon, Abingdon, Buckinghamshire.

GAWLER, Douglas Reginald

From Perth, Western Australia, he was in the UK when war came in August 1914. Volunteering immediately, he was gazetted Second Lieutenant to 11 Battalion, Royal Scots, on 22 September 1914. He served in France with his regiment from 23 June 1915, before eventually gaining secondment to the RFC in the spring of 1916. His pilot training duly completed, he was confirmed and gazetted Flying Officer on 12 August following. He was next sent out to 16 Squadron for artillery co-operation duties in France, soon after qualifying for his 'Wings'. On 20 September 1916, Gawler and his Observer, Lieutenant Gorges, with well directed machine-gun fire from a height of 3,000 feet, managed to silence two out of three anti-aircraft guns that had been firing on them. Promoted to Captain in August 1916, he was appointed a Flight Commander on 6 April 1917. His MC was announced in the *London Gazette* of 11 May 1917: 'For consistent good work while carrying out artillery observation and for gallantry on many occasions. On one occasion he continued his observation work in spite of being attacked by several hostile machines and in spite of being under very heavy fire'.

Having returned to the Home Establishment, Gawler was promoted to T/Major on 1 December 1917, and sent as a Senior Instructor to the Wireless and Observer School, where he saw out the remainder of the war. Douglas Gawler finally left the service in January 1919.

GEDDES, Alaister Cosmo Burton

The elder son of Professor Patrick Geddes and Anna Morton Geddes, of 14 Ramsey Gardens, Edinburgh, he was born on 18 June 1891. Educated at Edinburgh Academy, at University College, Dundee, and at Edinburgh University (1908-14) from where he graduated BSc. As part of his degree course, he sailed with the Fisheries Board Boat, *Goldseeker*, in 1908, and accompanied the Scottish Arctic Expedition to Spitzbergen in 1909. A staff member with Cities and Town Planning Exhibitions in Ghent, Belgium, and India, in 1914 and 1915. Gazetted Flight Sub-Lieutenant to the RNAS in 1915, he was sent to France in the August of that year. Transferring to the Kite Balloon Service of the RFC in 1916, he served first with 6 KBS before going on, successively to 10 KBS and 13 KBS. Quickly achieving promotion, he was, by 5 December 1916, an Acting Major and BC Commander (a rank rated equivalent to Squadron Commander in the flying service). On one occasion when Artillery HQ was receiving more than its fair share of attention from the German heavy guns, Geddes was asked by the Staff to identify the source. When he reported the offending battery was ten miles behind the lines and that it was taking a full 45 seconds for the shells to arrive, he was scoffed at and told that he had seen the sun striking glasswork or an ammunition explosion in the distance. Unruffled, and still up in his balloon, Geddes accurately predicted the arrival of the next round, which promptly demolished the HQ's front door. As they raced to their dug-outs, the Staff radioed their thanks and apologies! His MC was announced in the New Year *London Gazette* of 1 January 1917 (no citation). Although no citation was published in the *London Gazette*, research has unearthed the original recommendation for the award: 'For exceptional good work in command of a KBS. This officer has consistently carried out the duties of a Kite Balloon Observer with marked skill and ability during the last 12 months'.

The French, too, honoured Geddes with a Croix de Chevalier de la Légion d'Honneur, the announcement appearing in the *London Gazette* of 1 June 1917. He was commanding 17 Kite BC on 19 April 1917, when he was killed in action. Alaister Geddes is buried in Vaux Australian Field Ambulance Cemetery, Vaulx-Vraucourt, France.

GEORGE, Robert Allingham

The son of William and Mary George, he was born at 7 Denny Street, Cromarty, on 25 July 1896, the family later moving to Invergordon. Educated at Invergordon Academy and at Roskeen School. During the Great War years, Robert's father was the Recruiting Officer at Invergordon Town Hall. Perhaps unsurprisingly, therefore, Robert enlisted as a Private soldier (Number 1311) into 4 Battalion, Seaforth Highlanders (Ross-shire Territorials) (TF), and landed in France with that unit on 7 November 1914, thus earning the 1914 Star. He served in the trenches in 1914 and 1915, before being gazetted Second Lieutenant to 11 (Reserve) Battalion, Gordon Highlanders on 4 January 1916. Seconded to the RFC later in the same year, he trained as a Pilot and was subsequently confirmed and gazetted Flying Officer on 10 February 1917. Sent out to AWFK8-equipped 35 Squadron in France on 5 April 1917, he served with that unit, latterly as a Flight Commander, until 17 March 1918, when he returned to the Home Establishment. His MC was announced in the *London Gazette* of 26 March 1918, details in the *Gazette* of 24 August 1918: 'For conspicuous gallantry and devotion to duty. He has done valuable work in ranging batteries, bombing at night, and in attacking enemy troops with machine-gun fire, often under the most adverse weather conditions. On one occasion he ranged a siege battery on a hostile battery, destroying four of its gun pits and causing fires and explosions. His splendid example has been an inspiration to his Squadron'.

Staying on in the RAF with a permanent commission after the war, he went on to enjoy a highly successful career. He served on the North West Frontier of India from 1919 to 1924, before going on to the RAF Staff Cadet College at Cranwell, where he instructed until 1930. He married, in 1927, Sybil Elizabeth Baldwin, with whom he had three sons and one daughter. George graduated from the RAF Staff College in 1931 (psa). In the early 1930s, he commanded 33(B) Squadron, one of the first to be equipped with Hawker Hart day bombers, and it was under his direction that the squadron did much to develop the technique of dive bombing. From the command of '33', he went on to occupy a series of senior appointments, including: SASO, Singapore, 1934-37; Air Attaché, Turkey, Greece and RAF Middle East, 1939-44; AOC, Iraq and Persia, 1944-45; and Air Attaché in Paris, 1945-52. Knighted, 1952, his many honours included: CBE, 1944; CB, 1948; KBE, 1952; Knight of St John, 1953; KCVO, 1954; and KCMG, 1958. The Greeks conferred the Order of King George I upon him in 1942, and the French made him a Commandeur of the Légion d'Honneur in 1952. George finally retired from the RAF with the rank of Air Vice-Marshal on 26 May 1952. Other honorary positions he held included: Honorary Colonel of the South African Scottish Regiment, and President of St John's Ambulance Brigade No 1 (Prince of Wales's) District. The King appointed him Governor of South Australia, 1953-60 and he was a Director of the Bank of Adelaide. His homes in the UK were at 6 Campden House Close, London W8, and at Holm Farm House, Rowlands Castle, Hampshire. Air Vice-Marshal Sir Robert George died in a London hospital on 13 September 1967, a few hours after being involved in a road accident.

GIBBONS, George Everard

From Stourbridge, he was born on 15 February 1895. Educated at Bromsgrove School. After leaving school he worked for his family's firm, Gibbons Brothers, Gas Engineers, Debtail Works, Dudley. Gazetted to 10 Battalion, North Staffordshire Regiment, on 23 February 1915. He transferred to the RFC in 1916, and having trained as an Observer was sent out as a Probationary to the BE2e-equipped 8 Squadron. His 'apprenticeship' satisfactorily completed, he was confirmed and gazetted Flying Officer (Observer) on 15 November 1916. On 11 April 1917, Gibbons and his Pilot, Second Lieutenant E J E Stafford, narrowly escaped death when their BE2e, 'A2813', was attacked and sent down to crash by enemy Scouts. Although Stafford was wounded in the air, Gibbons escaped unscathed. Later in 1917, Gibbons undertook pilot training and after qualifying on 8 August 1917, eventually joined 62 Squadron then stationed at Filton in the UK. Gibbons accompanied the Bristol F2b-equipped 62 Squadron to France as a 'founder member' on 23 January 1918. Flying mainly with either Lieutenant S A W Knight or Lieutenant T Elliot, he gained no less than seventeen victories between 12 March and 4 September 1918, including four 'doubles' and one 'trio' on single days. His MC was announced in the *London Gazette* of 16 September 1918: 'For conspicuous gallantry and devotion to duty. He has lately destroyed three enemy machines and driven down others out of control. He has always shown great gallantry and keenness, and has commanded his flight with distinction, performing invaluable services in training young officers in the squadron'.

Gibbons was later awarded a Distinguished Flying Cross- announced in the *London Gazette* of 3 December 1918, this for an incident on 4 September 1918 (wrongly stated as 4 August in the citation) when elements from 32 and 62 Squadrons, escorting bombers from 107 Squadron in the course of a raid on Valenciennes station, were attacked by more than twenty enemy scouts. Gibbons and his Observer, Second Lieutenant T Elliott, in attempting to rescue of two of their hard-pressed colleagues, W K Swayze and W E Hall in Brisfit in 'D7945', shot down a Fokker DVII, before returning to the main scrap and accounting for another. Gibbons was slightly injured in an aeroplane accident on 28 February 1919. He finally left the service, via the Unemployed List, on 15 April 1919.

GIBBS, Frederick John

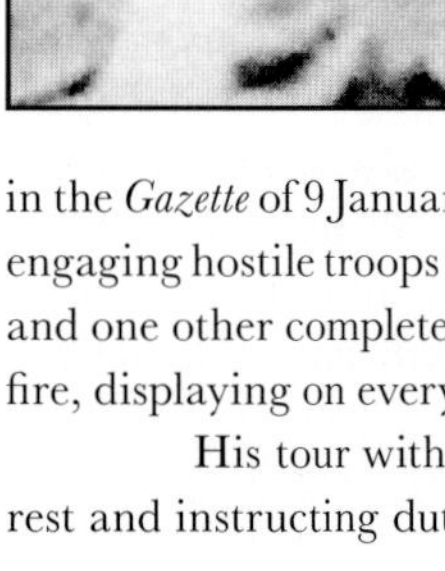

From Walsall, Staffordshire, he was born on 8 September 1894. He trained as a teacher at the Saltney College, Birmingham, from September 1913 to July 1914. When the war came in August 1914, he was a married man living and teaching in Barnsley, Yorkshire. Gazetted Second Lieutenant to a Regular Army Battalion of the South Staffordshire Regiment on 4 June 1915, he was immediately attached to 6 Battalion, Royal Welsh Fusiliers. Successfully seeking secondment to the RFC in the summer of 1916, he was, after the appropriate training, confirmed and gazetted Flying Officer on 29 November 1916. Posted to the Spad VII-equipped 23 Squadron in France on 4 April 1917, he achieved ten victories between 2 June and 2 October 1917, including two 'doubles' on single days. His MC was announced in the *London Gazette* of 26 September 1917, details in the *Gazette* of 9 January 1918: 'For conspicuous gallantry and devotion to duty in attacking enemy aircraft and engaging hostile troops from the ground. He has in all driven down five enemy machines, which were destroyed, and one other completely out of control. He has also attacked and silenced a hostile battery with machine-gun fire, displaying on every occasion the same dash and determined offensive spirit'.

His tour with '23' completed at the end of 1917, he returned to the Home Establishment for a short rest and instructing duties. Following a prolonged stint as an Instructor with 91 and 93 Squadrons, and with various training depot squadrons, all based in the UK, he returned to the front once more. This time he joined the SE5A-equipped 64 Squadron, during the penultimate month of the war. One last victory against an LVG C over Estreaux, on 29 October 1918, raised his final total to 11. Returning to the Home Establishment on 24 February 1919, Gibbs finally left the RAF, via the Unemployed List, on 28 March following.

GIBBS, Gerald Ernest

The son of Ernest William Cecil Gibbs and Fanny Wilhelmina Gibbs, he was born in Kent on 3 SBareptember 1896. Educated at Kingston Grammar School. Volunteering as soon as war came, he enlisted as a Private soldier (Number 6795) into 5 Battalion, East Surrey Regiment (TF), leaving England on 30 October 1914, bound for service on the North West Frontier of India. Picked out for a commission, he returned to the UK and was gazetted Second Lieutenant to Kitchener's New Armies on 18 November 1915, with an immediate posting to 7 Battalion, Wiltshire Regiment, in Salonika. He then secured a secondment to the RFC in the following summer. Having trained as a Pilot in Aboukir, Egypt, he was confirmed and gazetted Flying Officer on 11 October 1916. Kept back initially as an Instructor, it was early 1917, before he was sent to an operational unit, joining the BE2c-equipped 17 Squadron, then in Macedonia. Evolving gradually to the infinitely superior SE5As, he eventually began accumulating victories, the first coming on 28 January 1918. A further eight victories were achieved before 4 May, when the unit's Scout planes were incorporated into the newly formed 150 Squadron, basically an amalgam of Flights from 17 and 47 Squadrons. His three MCs, each with a graphic citation, were all announced in the spring and summer of 1918 – MC, *London Gazette* of 26 March 1918, details in the *Gazette* of 24 August 1918: 'For conspicuous gallantry and devotion to duty. On one occasion he pursued an enemy aeroplane to a very low altitude over the enemy lines and succeeded in driving his opponent to the ground. On a later occasion he and another pilot fought a hostile machine to within two hundred feet of the ground over hostile territory, where it fell, completely wrecked. He has displayed consistent gallantry and determination in action'.

Bar to MC, *London Gazette* of 22 June 1918: 'For conspicuous gallantry and devotion to duty. On one occasion he bombed an enemy aerodrome from a height of 100 feet, and, descending to 20 feet fired 200 rounds into the hangars. Later, on the same day, he engaged two enemy scouts and one two-seater machine, all three of which he drove down, the latter going down out of control from a height of 2,000 feet. On another occasion he pursued seven hostile scouts single-handed, one of which he succeeded in shooting down. He is a pilot of exceptional dash and resource'.

Second Bar to MC, *London Gazette* of 16 September 1918: 'For conspicuous gallantry and devotion to duty. While on patrol he engaged and pursued a hostile two-seater. After repeatedly diving on the enemy machine, the hostile Observer waved a white flag and was allowed to land. He landed beside it and took both occupants prisoner and the machine intact. Later, he encountered two enemy scouts and a two-seater. The scouts fled, and after a prolonged fight, shot down and crashed the two-seater, both occupants being killed. He has given repeated examples of skill, determination and pluck, and has accounted for ten enemy machines'.

The French, too, honoured him with the Chevalier Légion d'Honneur, *London Gazette* of 21 September 1918, and the Croix de Guerre. Striken with malaria, Gibbs was sent home to the UK in June 1918 and it would be beyond the Armistice before he eventually recovered his health sufficiently to join 29 Squadron in France as a Flight Commander. Securing a permanent commission in the RAF, he embarked upon what would prove to be a highly successful career, his many appointments, promotions and honours including: Aide-de-Camp to Marshal of the RAF Sir Hugh Trenchard (later 1st Viscount Trenchard), 1927-28; member, Air Staff Plans, Air Ministry, under Group Captain C F A Portal (later 1st Viscount Portal of Hungerford) (qv), and then later Group Captain

A T Harris (later Marshal of the RAF Sir Arthur Harris Bt), 1930 to 1934; Squadron Leader, 1930; service in Iraq, Palestine, Sudan and Kenya; Wing Commander, 1936; CO, 47 Squadron, Sudan and Kenya; SASO, 11 Group, Fighter Command, from 1940 to 1941, including during the Battle of Britain; Air Commodore, 1941; Director of Overseas Operations in the Air Ministry from 1942 to 1943; Group Captain, 1942; SASO, HQ, 3 Tactical Air Force, South-East Asia, 1943 to 1944; Chief ASO to Admiral Mountbatten (later Earl Mountbatten of Burma), at Supreme HQ, South East Asia Command, 1945 to 1946; CBE, 1945; Air Vice-Marshal, 1946; SASO, HQ, RAF Transport Command, 1946 to 1948; CIE, 1946; Head of Service Advisors to UK Delegation, and Chairman UK Members of Military Staff Committee, United Nations, 1948 to 1951; Chief of Air Staff and Commander in Chief, Indian Air Force, 1951 to 1954; Air Marshal, 1951; knighted (KBE), 1954. He married, in 1938, Margaret Jean Bradshaw, with whom he had one son and one daughter. Gibbs finally retired with the rank of Air Marshal in 1954 and lived thereafter at 'Lone Oak', 170 Coombe Lane West, Kingston-upon-Thames, Surrey. He published, 'Survivor's Story' in 1956 (Hutchinson, London). Air Marshal Sir Gerald Gibbs died on 13 October 1992 in Kingston, Surrey.

GILCHRIST, Euan James Leslie Warren

Originally from London, he was born on 8 September 1893. He studied at Cape University, South Africa, from 1910 to 1914, graduating BA in the unlikely combination of Science and Literature. Volunteering immediately the war came, he was commissioned into the Cape Garrison Artillery and actively served in the German East Africa campaign. In the autumn of 1915, he made his way to the UK at his own expense and was gazetted Second Lieutenant to 9 Lancers, via the Special Reserve, on 22 November 1915. Securing secondment to the RFC almost immediately, he gained his Royal Aero Club Certificate (Number 2609) on 9 March 1916. His formal training completed, he was confirmed and gazetted Flying Officer on 19 May following. He joined 46 Squadron in the UK on 25 June 1916, but was, in the following month, sent out to 60 Squadron in France, in time for the Battle of the Somme. He opened his account with the sending down of a hostile balloon under hazardous circumstances on15 September 1916, for which feat he received the MC. His award was announced in the *London Gazette* of 20 October 1916: 'For conspicuous gallantry and skill when he attacked a hostile balloon and brought it down in flames, although under heavy fire and attacked by six hostile machines'.

Promoted to A/Captain in December 1916, he broke his leg in a crash-landing on the 11th day of the same month. Once recovered, he was sent as an Instructor to the School of Special Flying at Gosport, where he served out the remainder of 1917, and the early months of the following year, being promoted A/Major in the intervening January 1918. Gilchrist commanded the renowned 56 Squadron from 5 May to 17 December 1918 and was awarded the Distinguished Flying Cross for outstanding leadership in general and for consistent bravery, in particular on 1 August 1918, when he bombed and machine-gunned an enemy airfield from a height of just ten feet, *London Gazette* of 3 December 1918. Euan Gilchrist finally left the RAF, via the Unemployed List, on 14 September 1919.

GILL, Napier John

A Staff, not a flying, award

The youngest son of Barrister, Robert Thomas Gill and Mrs Gill, of 60, The Drive, Hove, Sussex and of Airleywight House, Bankfoot, Perthshire, he was born in Kensington, London, on 5 April 1890. Educated at Summer Fields (1900-04), at Rugby (1904-06), and at the Royal Military Academy, Woolwich. Gazetted Second Lieutenant to the RGA in 1910. He married, on 14 March 1912, Daisy Cotton, the pair taking up residence at 1 Chester Place, Hyde Park West, London W. Gill learnt to fly at Brooklands in a Deperdussin monoplane, gaining his Royal Aero Club Certificate (Number 174) on 16 January 1912. Seconded to the RFC in 1913, he attended the Third Course at the CFS, Upavon. He was appointed Flight Commander in December 1914 and, in September 1915, Brigade Major to Brigadier General J F A Higgins, then in command of III Brigade, RFC, in France. His MC was announced in the New Year *London Gazette* of 1 January 1917 (no citation). Although there was no published citation, research has unearthed the original recommendation for the award: 'Captain N J Gill. (3 Brigade): Has done exceptionally good work from April to October 1916, as Brigade Major. His energy and great ability have been most valuable. Has previously done very good work as Wing Adjutant during the campaign'.

He was promoted, very shortly after the announcement of his MC, to T/Lieutenant Colonel. Remaining on the Staff to the end of the war and beyond, he was made CBE in the New Year *London Gazette* of 1 January 1919. Gill would, amongst other appointments, command the Aeroplane and Armament Experimental Establishment at Martlesham Heath from 1922 until 1924, when he was posted to a course at London University. In September 1925, he was appointed to HQ, Iraq Command for Technical Staff duty. In December 1927, he was made Deputy Director of Technical Development at the Air Ministry. He also assisted around this time with the preparation of RAF entrants to the Schneider Trophy. Promoted to Group Captain in January 1928. In January 1932, he was appointed SASO at Coastal Area and promoted to Air Commodore. In July 1936, he was appointed Air Officer in charge of Administration, Fighter Command. He was created a CB in the New Year Honours of 1936. Gill was placed on the Retired List on 1 January 1937. After leaving the RAF, he worked with Boulton Paul Aircraft from 1937 to 1942, living at 33 Palace Mansions, London W14. Air Commodore Napier Gill died on 20 October 1948, age58.

NB: His medals were offered for sale through C J & A J Dixon's catalogue in the spring of 2002: CB, CBE, MC, 1914-15 Star (Capt RGA), *British War Medal 1914-20, Victory Medal 1914-19* (Major RFC), *Jubilee Medal 1935.*

GILMOUR, John Ingles

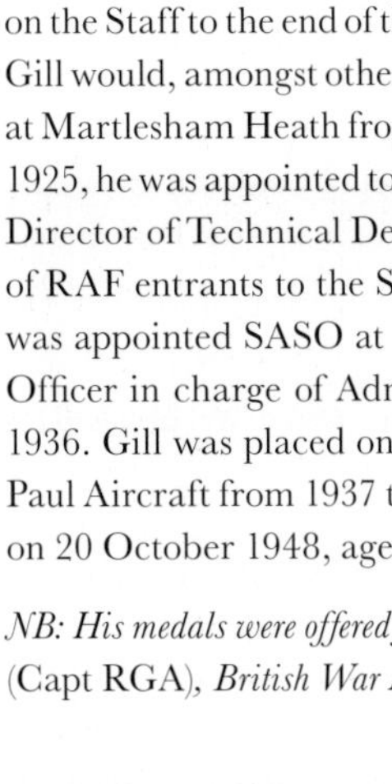

From Helensburgh, Dumbartonshire, he was born on 28 June 1896. Educated at Loretto (1910-14), where he was a Sergeant in the OTC, and represented the school in the Rugby XV. Gazetted Second Lieutenant to a Regular Army battalion of the Argyll and Sutherland Highlanders on 22 December 1915, with an almost immediate secondment to the RFC. Gained his Royal Aero Club Certificate (Number 2888) on 17 March 1916. After completing his formal pilot training, he was confirmed and gazetted Flying Officer on 12 June following. Sent out to the Martinsyde G100 Elephant-equipped 27 Squadron shortly after qualifying for his 'Wings', he was soon acknowledged as one of the leading exponents, if not the leading exponent, of using this fairly cumbersome machine as a fighter aircraft. He gained three victories with '27' between 15 and 26 September 1916, the first of the amazing 39 victories he would go on to achieve before the end of the war. The first of his MCs, announced in the *London Gazette* of 26 May 1917, was, in fact, in recognition of his bombing and reconnaissance exploits: 'For conspicuous gallantry and devotion to duty in carrying out long-distance bombing machines. On one occasion although his engine began to fail, he continued to lead his formation, and succeeded in bringing back most valuable information'.

In the winter of 1917, he was posted as a Flight Commander to the Sopwith Camel-equipped 65 Squadron, where he found his true niche and became one of the truly great Aces of the Great War. His successes included a 'pair' on 18 December 1917, a 'trio' on 4 January 1918, and an astounding 'quintet' on 1 July 1918. All five victories on this summer day were over Scout planes, two Fokker DVIIs, two Albatros DVs and a Pfalz DIII. A Bar to his MC came in the *London Gazette* of 26 July 1918: 'For conspicuous gallantry and devotion to duty when engaging hostile aircraft. Within a week he crashed to the ground four enemy machines, and at all times, when on patrol, he never hesitated to attack any enemy in sight. His consistent dash and great fearlessness have been of the highest praise. In all he has ten hostile machines to his credit'.

A gallantry Distinguished Service Order came to him in the *London Gazette* of 3 August 1918, this for, 'successfully accounting for 5 enemy machines in one day'.

(As a minor point of historical interest, Gilmour is the first MC recipient to be described in the *London Gazette* as belonging to the RAF, rather than the RFC.)

The third of his MCs was announced in the *London Gazette* of 16 September 1918: 'For conspicuous gallantry and devotion to duty in his leadership of offensive patrols. This officer has lately successfully engaged seven enemy machines, destroying five and shooting down two out of control. He has done splendid service'.

Following a rest from combat flying, he was promoted to A/Major, and sent out to command 28 Squadron in Italy, in October 1918. Fortunately, the Great War would end within weeks and John Gilmour could count himself among the survivors of that terrible conflict. He was Mentioned in Despatches for his services in Italy, *London Gazette* of 31 December 1918. The French showed their appreciation by appointing him Chevalier de Légion d'Honneur. Given a permanent commission and substantive rank of Captain in the RAF in August 1919, his post-war appointments included Air Attaché in the British Embassy in Rome and the command of 216 Squadron in the Middle East. John Gilmour died in 1928.

NB: His medals were offered for sale by Sotheby's (lot 543) on 28 June 1984: Distinguished Service Order; MC & two Bars, British War Medal 1914-20, and Victory Medal 1914-19 with MID (Capt RAF).

GIRVAN, Cuthbert Colin Gemmill

From Stockport, Cheshire, he was born on 13 July 1898. Gazetted Second Lieutenant to 2 Battalion, Lancashire Fusiliers on 24 December 1915. Girvan secured a secondment to the RFC at the end of 1916 and, after training as an Observer, was sent to a HD unit on 1 February 1917. His first overseas posting was to the RE8-equipped 6 Squadron in France on 20 April following. Girvan was severely wounded in the thigh during the course of a combat patrol on 7 June 1917, the opening day of the Battle of Messines, and it was for his gallant conduct on that day that he received his MC, *London Gazette* of 16 August 1917: 'For conspicuous gallantry and devotion to duty. When on patrol he flew for two and a half hours at a height of 500 feet, gaining and dropping valuable information at headquarters. Although severely wounded and fainting from loss of blood, he handed in his report before finally collapsing'.

After more than a month in a hospital in France, he was finally considered well enough to be sent home to the UK for further treatment on 23 September 1917. He never returned to operational flying, and finally left the service, via the Unemployed List, on 30 April 1919.

GLEN, John McGowan

The son of Mr and Mrs Glen, of Glengowan House, Caldercruix, he was born in New Monkland, Lanarkshire, on 7 January 1896. Educated at Loretto (1906-08). He was gazetted Second Lieutenant to a Regular Army battalion of the Royal Scots on 11 November 1915, but was, almost immediately, posted to serve with 1/4 Battalion (TF) of his regiment. He appears to have gravitated towards a Staff/Intelligence career, holding the rank of Staff Captain by the end of the war. He was, however, attached as an Observer to 1 Squadron, Australian Flying Corps, in the Middle East from 4 October 1916 to 10 June 1917. On 25 February 1917, Glen and his Pilot, Captain Adrian Trevor Cole (qv), in a BE, directed by wireless the fire of a French battleship during a ship-to-shore bombardment of the Turkish-held port of Jaffa. His MC was announced in the New Year *London Gazette* of 1 January 1918 (no citation). Staying on in the RAF after the war, Glen married Grace Couteroy, setting up home in Bettws-y-Coed, Carnarvonshire. John McGowan Glen, by then a Flight Lieutenant, RAF, died at his home in North Wales on 17 July 1924.

GLENN, Walter William

Born on 16 December 1897, in Stamford, London, his family moving later to Purley, Surrey. Educated at Bedford Modern School. He was gazetted Second Lieutenant to the Royal Field Artillery on 26 August 1916, before, soon afterwards, securing a secondment to the RFC. After training as an Observer, he served initially in the UK and was confirmed as a Flying Officer (Observer) on 2 December 1916. Sent out to the FE2d-equipped 57 Squadron in France on 20 March 1917. On 8 April 1917, he and his Pilot were shot up in the air, but despite being badly wounded, Glenn used his machine gun to great effect as, indeed, the citation for his MC, *London Gazette* of 26 May 1917, testifies: 'For conspicuous gallantry and devotion to duty. He saved one of our machines from being destroyed, and drove down a hostile machine out of control. Later, although severely wounded, he succeeded in bringing down a second hostile machine'.

Glenn subsequently had his left leg amputated at the knee as a consequence of the wounds he suffered on 8 April 1917 (he would, ultimately, receive a compensation payment amounting to £250 for the loss of that limb). Glenn was not able to resume his operational duties. After leaving the RAF, he was employed as a Transport Officer with the Department of Civil Aviation. Walter Glenn who, at the time, resided at 78 Clarkenhouse Road, Sheffield, died at the Kenwood Hotel in that city, on 6 June 1932.

GLENNY, Arthur Willoughby Falls

Gazetted Second Lieutenant to the Army Service Corps on 13 January 1915, he served in France with his unit in 1915. Seconded to the RFC, he trained as an Observer and was sent out as a Probationary to the BE2c-equipped 6 Squadron late in 1915. On 19 December 1915, Glenny and his Pilot of the day, Second Lieutenant Cooper, in BE2c, '4501', were attacked over Elverdinghe by a Fokker and two or three Aviatiks. After a running fight, the BE2c's petrol tank was holed and they were forced to land, albeit without injury to either occupant. Glenny's 'apprenticeship' satisfactorily completed, he was confirmed and gazetted Flying Officer (Observer) on 2 February 1916. He next trained as a Pilot, gaining his Royal Aero Club Certificate (Number 3205) on 1 July following. His formal pilot training duly completed, he qualified for his full 'Wings' on 4 August 1916. Glenny was next posted to Home Defence duties, serving with BE2c-equipped 50 Squadron stationed at Dover. Promoted to A/Captain and Flight Commander, Glenny was sent out to France and the RE8-equipped 7 Squadron on 25 May 1917. The first of his MCs was announced in the *London Gazette* of 17 September 1917: 'For conspicuous gallantry and devotion to duty when in co-operation with our artillery. By dint of great perseverance, skill and very gallant flying he has accomplished splendid work under very difficult circumstances. On one occasion, during a gale of wind, he successfully ranged three of our heavy batteries upon an enemy battery, which was completely obliterated. He has consistently set a very fine example to his squadron'.

Glenny was presented with the insignia of his MC by the King at an investiture held at Buckingham Palace in the spring of 1918. On 11 April 1918, Glenny and his Observer of the day, Second Lieutenant J P Bosman, in RE8, 'B6489', were hit from the ground by machine-gun fire over Nieppe. Forced to land, they abandoned the 'Harry Tate' to its fate and made their way to the British lines to pass on the valuable information they had gleaned during the patrol. To save it falling into the hands of the enemy, the RE8 was later burnt by the Tommies. The Bar to his MC came in the *London Gazette* of 26 July 1918: 'For conspicuous gallantry and devotion to duty, both in reconnaissance and as an Artillery Observer. On one occasion, although shot down, he brought in valuable information. On several occasions, he conducted several knock-out shoots with various batteries, obtained excellent photographs, and did much work of a very high standard'.

Glenny would also be awarded the Distinguished Flying Cross, *London Gazette* of 3 December 1918, this for, amongst other things, handling his machine with such skill that he managed to avoid the attentions of 12 enemy Scouts on 16 May 1918. After the enemy machines had been driven off by others, he returned to his patrol and succeeded in taking 15 graphs over the Corps' counter-battery area. The Belgians also showed their appreciation of his services with an award of their Croix de Guerre, *London Gazette* of 15 July 1919. Staying on in the RAF after the war, he was awarded a permanent commission in the rank of Captain, on 1 August 1919. Glenny's distinguished career in the RAF included the following appointments, promotions and honours: Flight Commander, 20 Squadron, 1919; Staff Officer, HQ, RAF, India, 1921; OC, 28 Squadron, 1922; Squadron Leader, 1922; Squadron Commander, School of Army Co-operation, 1924; attended RAF Staff College, 1926; Staff Officer, HQ, Wessex Bombing Area, 1927; Senior RAF Officer, HMS *Hermes*, 1930; Wing Commander, 1931; Attended Senior Officers War Course, 1933; attended Imperial Defence College, 1934; Staff Officer, HQ, 22 Group; Staff Officer, Deputy Directorate of Equipment (Supply and Movement), 1935; Deputy Director of Staff Duties, 1936; A/Group Captain, 1936; Aircraft Depot, India, 1938; OC, 1 (Indian) Group, RAF. Glenny attained the rank of Acting Air Commodore during the Second World War. He was Mentioned in Despatches in the *London Gazette* of 25 October 1940. Glenny retired from the RAF, retaining the rank of Air Commodore. Air Commodore Arthur Glenny died of tuberculosis in Davos, Switzerland, in 1947.

GODFREY, Albert Earl

He was born in Killarney, Manitoba, Canada, on 27 July 1890, his family moving to Vancouver whilst he was still young. A pre-war volunteer, he joined 6 Regiment, Duke of Connaught's Own Rifles, as a drummer boy in 1902. A Mechanical Engineer by profession, he worked in Vancouver and in Seattle, Washington, USA, from 1908 to 1914. Having a personal interest in aviation, he was actually building his own aeroplane when war was declared. Attempting to join the RFC, he was informed that unless he could pay for his own flying lessons and then present himself as a qualified Pilot, he would not be considered. Not having the necessary funds, he joined, instead, 11 Canadian Mounted Rifles. A transfer to 1 Canadian Pioneers preceded embarkation for the UK in November 1915. He served in the trenches with the CEF for more than six months, before a request to join the RFC as an Observer was granted in the summer of 1916. Picked out for a commission, he was gazetted Second Lieutenant to the RFC, via the Special List, on 28 August 1916. He was sent out to 25 Squadron as a Probationary, gaining the first of his victories against a Roland D west of Douai on 16 October 1916. His 'apprenticeship' satisfactorily completed, he was confirmed and gazetted Flying Officer (Observer) on 28 October 1916. He trained next as a Pilot and, after qualifying for his full 'Wings', was sent to the Nieuport XVII-equipped 40 Squadron. Godfrey personally fitted two Lewis guns to his Nieuport, thus doubling its rate of fire. This improvised device enabled him to achieve, at one stage, three victories in three days. In all, 13 further victories fell to his credit between 28 May and 22 August 1917. His MC was announced in the *London Gazette* of 26 July 1917: 'For conspicuous gallantry and devotion to duty in constantly attacking hostile machines at close range, regardless of personal risk or of their being in superior numbers'.

His tour with '40' completed, he returned to the Home Establishment in September 1917. Service with 44 and 78 HD Squadrons preceded a transfer back to Canada in April 1918. His outstanding service on Home Defence was eventually acknowledged with the award of an Air Force Cross, *London Gazette* of 1 January 1919. Just before he left for Canada, the insignia of his MC was presented to him by the King at an investiture held at Buckingham Palace. Godfrey joined the newly forming RCAF in 1919. In 1926, Godfrey accompanied, as Co-Pilot and Navigator, the American sportsman and millionaire, J Dalzell McKee, in the first ever float plane flight across Canada. In gratitude for the help he had received in this pioneering flight, McKee presented and endowed the Trans-Canada Trophy to the RCAF. By the beginning of the Second World War, 'Steve' Godfrey held the rank of Group Captain. He finally retired from the RCAF in 1944. Air Vice-Marshal A E Godfrey died on 1 January 1982.

GONNE, Michael Edward

The younger son of Henry and Grace Gonne of 'Homestead', Ringwood, Hampshire, he was born on 23 October 1898. Educated at Westminster School and at Sandhurst. He was gazetted Second Lieutenant to the Royal Fusiliers on 27 October 1916, with an immediate secondment to the RFC. After pilot training courses at Oxford and at Hendon, he was confirmed and gazetted Flying Officer on 23 May 1917 and briefly posted to RFC HQ, Egypt, shortly afterwards. A transfer to 54 Squadron (Sopwith Pups) in France came in July 1917. Flying Sopwith Pups and later Camels, he achieved five victories between 25 September 1917 and 25 January 1918, thus earning the status of Ace. He was promoted to A/Captain and Flight Commander in the intervening December. His MC was announced in the *London Gazette* of 4 March 1918, details in the *Gazette* of 16 August 1918: 'For conspicuous gallantry and devotion to duty. He is a daring and skilful leader of patrols and has led his flight throughout a large amount of fighting – often against superior numbers far over the enemy's lines, he has destroyed five enemy machines'.

After injuring himself testing a machine on 28 January 1918, he was sent home to the UK to recover. He spent some months instructing before requesting a return to the front and 54 Squadron. Michael Gonne in Camel, 'D6575', was last seen over the Somme crossing at Brie, then some15 miles behind the lines. He was reported missing on 8 August 1918, the so-called 'Black Day' of the German Army, and it was later established that he had died on that same day in a German Field Hospital at Villers Carbonnel. Michael Gonne is buried in Heath Cemetery, Harbonnières, France.

GOODFELLOW, Cecil Stuart

Born in Stoke-on-Trent on 27 December 1881, he was living in nearby Newcastle-under-Lyne, Staffordshire, when the war came in August 1914. Enlisting as a Sapper (Number 54433) into the Royal Engineers early in the war, he later served as a motor-cycle despatch rider with the rank of Corporal. Sent out to the 16 Signal Company, RE, in France, a unit attached to the Guards Divisional Signals, he served on the Western Front from 22 August

1915 to 28 October 1916. Seconded to the flying service, he had already undergone observer training when he was gazetted Second Lieutenant to the RFC, via the Special Lists, on 29 October 1916, being confirmed and gazetted Flying Officer (Observer) on the same day. Sent out to the artillery-co-operating 15 Squadron (BEs) in France, Goodfellow flew on more than one occasion with his Flight Commander, Captain W G Barker (qv), who would, in 1918, be awarded the Victoria Cross. Indeed, the citation for Goodfellow's MC, announced in the *London Gazette* of 18 July 1917, is similar to Barker's citation for the first Bar to his MC, announced in the same *Gazette*: 'For conspicuous gallantry and devotion to duty. He has done valuable and consistent good work in co-operating with the artillery. He has carried out numerous patrol flights under most adverse weather conditions, and has set a splendid example to his squadron throughout'.

Goodfellow next trained as a Pilot, qualifying for his full 'Wings' in September 1917. He continued to fly in this new capacity with 15 Squadron, although he was, by now, piloting RE8s. Cecil Goodfellow survived the Great War and, indeed, served again in the RAF in the Second World War. In 1982, after Cecil's death, his widow, Irene, enquired of the Air Ministry if she was entitled to an enhanced pension in recognition of her late husband's entitlement to a MC. She also pointed out that although he had not been disabled as a consequence of his combat career, he had, in fact, survived no less than 12 crashes!

GOODRICH, Frank Edward

The son of Albert F and Elizabeth Goodrich, of 16 Central Street, Hallowell, Maine, USA, he was born in 1889. Learning to fly at his own expense, he gained his Royal Aero Club Certificate (Number 1623) on 20 August 1915. Armed with this qualification, he applied for a commission in the flying service and was subsequently gazetted Second Lieutenant to the RFC, via the Special Lists, on 10 September following. His formal training duly completed, he was confirmed and gazetted Flying Officer on 7 December 1915. Sent to France on 19 December 1915, he joined the Morane LA-equipped 3 Squadron. On 21 February 1916, Goodrich and his Observer, Second Lieutenant C W Short, in Morane LA, '5120', had a narrow escape when their rudder and elevator controls were shot away by anti-aircraft fire over La Bassée. Goodrich managed to get the machine down without further mishap. His tour with '3' completed in March 1916, he returned to the UK for a well-earned rest. His MC was announced in the Birthday Honours *London Gazette* of 3 June 1916 (no citation). Although no formal citation was published in the *Gazette*, research has unearthed the original recommendation for the award: 'For conspicuous gallantry and skill. He has shown exceptional keenness as a pilot from December 19th 1915 to March 1916. He did very well on February 21st when he succeeded in bringing his machine down safely, after both rudder and elevator controls had been shot away'.

Goodrich next accompanied 60 Squadron to the front on 28 May 1916. He was killed in a flying accident on 12 September 1916 and is buried in Aubigny Communal Cemetery Extension, Pas de Calais.

GOODWIN, Laurence Frank

The elder son of Commercial Traveller, John Goodwin and Mrs Goodwin, of 8 Chestnut Road, Moseley, Birmingham, he was born on 12 June 1896. Educated at the Grammar School, Derby, and at King Edward's School, Camphill, Birmingham (1911-12). A clerk in the Civil Service from 1912, he was living at 89 Osborne Road, Forest Gate, London E7, and working in central London when the war came in August 1914. Enlisting immediately, he joined 2/15 London Regiment (Prince of Wales Civil Service Rifles) as a Private soldier (Signaller) on 28 August 1914. Goodwin was taken onto the staff of the Inns of Court OTC as an Instructor in Signalling, later in 1914. He eventually became a candidate for a commission himself, entering the OTC as a Cadet with the rank of Sergeant (Number 6/6846) on 16 October 1915. Because of his expertise in signalling, he logically enough applied for a commission in the Royal Engineers. In the event, however, he was eventually gazetted Second Lieutenant to 7 Battalion, Northamptonshire Regiment, on 25 October 1916. His own battalion was in Salonika at this time, but replacements were urgently needed by other battalions of the 'Steelbacks' in France and in Flanders and so he was sent out to the Western Front. After serving through some months of hard fighting in France, he secured, late in 1917, a secondment to the RFC. After training as an Observer, he joined the RE8-equipped 52 Squadron in France on 4 February 1918. He served through the early days of the great German spring offensive, indeed, on the first day of the massive onslaught, 21 March 1918, he and his Pilot, Second Lieutenant J H Reeves, in RE8, 'B6519', were fortunate to escape serious injury or worse, when their machine was forced to crashland after being hit by fire from the ground. He lasted less than six weeks at the front, before being returned traumatised to the Home Establishment on 13 April following. He had, however, earned an MC in his brief career of operational flying, *London Gazette* of 22 June 1918: 'For conspicuous gallantry and devotion to duty. On one occasion he flew for over two hours from a height varying from 50 to 200 feet, bombing and engaging with machine-gun fire enemy troops and transport, the while inflicting the most severe casualties on them. His keenness and dash are exceptional, and he has rendered since the commencement of the present operations the most meritorious service'.

Following a prolonged period of treatment, he was, after being reviewed by a Medical Board, invalided out of the service on 28 October 1918.

GORDON, John Rutherford

From Gilberton, South Australia, he was born on 18 June 1895. He served, initially as a Sergeant, with 10 Battalion, Australian Expeditionary Force, in Gallipoli, before being picked out for a commission and gazetted Second Lieutenant on 4 August 1915. Struck down by typhoid fever, he was evacuated from the Peninsula and sent home to Australia. His fitness having been reviewed by a Medical Board, he was subsequently invalided out as being unfit for further service with the infantry. Despite this pronouncement, Gordon himself pushed for inclusion in the AFC and, in the summer of 1917, duly qualified as an Observer, after failing to become a Pilot. On Christmas Day 1917, he was sent to the BF2b-equipped 62 Squadron, RFC, then in the UK, and preparing to go to the front. He subsequently accompanied '62' to France as a 'founder member' on 23 January 1918. During the ensuing year, flying mainly with the Ace Bristol Fighter Pilot, William Staton (qv), he was credited with no less than 15 victories between 21 March and 8 June 1915. His tour with'62' completed, he returned to the Home Establishment, where he subsequently qualified, at last, as a Pilot. His MC was announced in the *London Gazette* of 22 June 1918: 'For conspicuous gallantry and devotion to duty when, as Observer on an offensive patrol, he shot down and destroyed three hostile machines. Previous to this he had shot down two enemy tri-planes, one of which crashed to the ground in flames. He has also effectively and repeatedly scattered massed bodies of enemy troops by accurate shooting from a height of 100 feet. His skill and daring have been of the highest order'.

Gordon eventually returned to Australia and went on to join the RAAF after the war. He served as a Wing Commander during the Second World War. John Rutherford Gordon died on 11 December 1978.

GORDON-DAVIS, Cecil

Born on 9 February 1897, his family had connections in both London and in Devon, before they emigrated to South Africa in the early years of the new century. Educated at Rondesbosch High School, Cape Town. Returning to the UK at his own expense, he was gazetted Second Lieutenant to a Regular Army battalion of the North Staffordshire Regiment on 7 April 1916, with an immediate secondment to the RFC. Gained his Royal Aero Club Certificate (Number 3054) on 6 May 1916. His formal training duly completed, he was confirmed and gazetted Flying Officer on 24 June following. Sent out to the FE2d-equipped 20 Squadron in France on 28 June 1916. On 6 September 1916, Gordon-Davis and his Observer of the day, Corporal Birch, engaged an enemy machine over Passchendaele and drove it down. On 3 February 1917, Gordon-Davis and his Observer, Captain R M Knowles, Norfolk Regiment attached RFC, engaged, single-handedly, no less than seven enemy aircraft over Wervicq, driving one down out of control. His MC was announced in the *London Gazette* of 12 March 1917: 'For conspicuous gallantry and devotion to duty. He brought down a hostile machine. Later, during the same flight, he attacked four enemy machines, split up their formation, and brought one of them down. He set a splendid example of courage and determination in the face of superior forces'.

His tour with '20' completed, he returned to the Home Establishment on 14 May 1917. Gordon-Davis served thereafter as an Instructor with various training squadrons, until finally leaving the services, via the Unemployed List, on 18 April 1919.

GORDON-SCAIFE, Thomas Earle – see Thomas Earle Gordon **SCAIFE**

GORRINGE, Frank Clifton

Born on 30 September 1890, in Eastbourne, Sussex, he was working in Canada when war came in 1914. Volunteering his services early in the war, he served in France with 5 Battalion, Canadian Infantry, CEF. Transferring to the RFC, he flew operationally as a Gunner with the Sopwith Strutters of 43 Squadron. On 16 January 1917, he was gazetted Second Lieutenant to the RFC, and confirmed and gazetted Flying Officer (Observer) on the same day. Having aspirations to be a Pilot, he gained his Royal Aero Club Certificate (Number 5035) on 29 July 1917, and soon afterwards commenced his formal training. After qualifying for his full 'Wings', he was sent out to the Camel-equipped 70 Squadron in November 1917. A highly accomplished Scout Pilot, he achieved 14 victories between 7 November 1917 and 18 February 1918, including two 'doubles' on single days. His MC was announced in the *London Gazette* 4 March 1918, details in the *Gazette* of 16 August 1918: 'For conspicuous gallantry and devotion to duty. He has destroyed several enemy machines, and has shot down others out of control. On several occasions also has forced enemy aeroplanes to land, and has shown fine qualities of leadership and a keen offensive spirit'.

Following a period of rest in the UK, Gorringe instructed aspiring Scout Pilots before going out again to the front on 25 October 1918, this time as a Flight Commander with 210 Squadron (Camel 2.F1s). He showed great gallantry on 9 November 1918, when he made a dangerous landing behind the advancing British troops to give them a detailed and first hand account of the dispositions of the enemy troops in front of them. For this act of gallantry he was awarded a Distinguished Flying Cross, *London Gazette* of 8 February 1919.

GOSSAGE, Ernest Leslie

The eldest son of Lieutenant Colonel E F Gossage, VD, and Mrs Gossage, of 'Beachside', Allerton, Liverpool and 'Winwood', Budley Salterton, Devon, he was born on 3 February 1891. Educated at Rugby (1905-09) and at Trinity College, Cambridge. Gazetted Second Lieutenant to the Royal Field Artillery in 1912. When the war came, he proceeded to France with XXVth Brigade, RFA. Desirous of a transfer to the flying service, he gained his Royal Aero Club Certificate (Number 1120) on 10 March 1915. His formal pilot training duly completed, he was confirmed and gazetted Flying Officer on 12 May following. He next served in France with FE-equipped 6 Squadron on artillery observation duties, and was promoted to A/Captain and Flight Commander on 5 September 1915. His MC was announced in the *London Gazette* of 30 March 1916: 'For consistent good and zealous work under bad weather conditions, both on patrol and when co-operating with the artillery in operations resulting in the capture of the enemy's positions'.

His tour with '6' completed, he returned to the Home Establishment. Next, he was promoted to A/Major on 1 June 1916 and appointed to the command of 56 Squadron, then a HD unit based at London Colney. On 24 August 1916, he was sent out to command 8 Squadron on the Western Front. Further advancement to the command of 1 (Corps) Wing, RFC, with the rank of Lieutenant Colonel, came on 5 December 1917. He married in 1917, Eileen Gladys O'Brien, with whom he had two sons (one of whom would be killed on active service in the Second World War). Gossage was awarded the Distinguished Service Order in the Birthday Honours *London Gazette* of 3 June 1919 and was Mentioned in Despatches on four occasions during the Great War. Staying on in the RAF after the war, he embarked upon what would prove to be an extremely distinguished career. His many appointments, promotions and honours included: SO 2nd Class, Directorate of Operations and Intelligence, 1919; OC, School of Army Co-operation, 1921; Wing Commander, 1921; attended Army Staff College, Camberley, 1923; Directing Staff, Army Staff College, 1925; Deputy Director of Staff Duties, 1928; Group Captain, 1928; Air Attaché, Berlin; SASO, HQ, ADGB, 1931; Air Commodore, 1932; SASO, HQ, Iraq Command, 1934; AOC, British Forces, Aden, 1935; AOC, 11 Group RAF, 1936; Air Vice-Marshal, 1936; CB, 1937; CVO, 1937; Inspector General of the RAF, 1940; Air Marshal, 1940; Air Member for Personnel, 1940; Mentioned in Despatches, *London Gazette* of 11 July 1940; AOC-in-C, Balloon Command, 1941-44; knighted (KCB), 1941; Chief Commandant and Director General of the ATC 1944-46. He lived with his wife and family at 'Abbotswood', Buxted, Sussex. Air Marshal Sir Leslie Gossage died on 8 July 1949.

GOULD, Herbert Ruska

The son of Nathaniel Gould and Mrs Gould, of 'Newhaven', Bedfont, Middlesex, he was born on 23 December 1891. Herbert's father was a famous journalist and a prolific novelist who wrote mainly about horse-racing and gambling. After completing his education, Herbert worked for the Mexican Oil Company in their London offices from 1912 to 1914. Volunteering immediately the war came in 1914, he enlisted as a Trooper into the Middlesex Yeomanry. Picked out for a commission, he was gazetted Second Lieutenant to the RFC on 5 July 1917. His pilot training duly completed, he was confirmed and gazetted Flying Officer on 7 September following. He was sent out to the DH4-equipped 18 Squadron in France soon after qualifying for his 'Wings', achieving six victories between 26 March and 9 August 1918, and attaining the rank of A/Captain and Flight Commander. His MC was announced in the *London Gazette* of 16 September 1918: 'For conspicuous gallantry and devotion to duty. He has carried out twenty-four successful bombing raids, several of which he had led, and twenty-six low reconnaissance and bombing flights, as well as many low flying, harassing and bombing patrols, during which many direct hits have been obtained and severe casualties inflicted. He has destroyed three enemy machines and has shown a very high spirit of zeal throughout'.

By the time the announcement of his MC was published in the *Gazette*, Gould was dead. On 14 August 1918, he and his Observer of the day, Second Lieutenant Ewart F Jinman, from Croydon, in DH4, 'A7903', were shot down and killed, possibly by Vizefeldwebel Georg Staudacher of Jasta 1. Their bodies were never recovered and hence both crewmen are commemorated on the Flying Services Memorial to the Missing, Arras, France.

GOULD, Lionel Thomas Nutcombe

The son of Mr and Mrs L F Gould, of Kenilworth, he was born on 22 November 1893. Educated at Marlborough (1906-11) and at Woolwich. Gazetted Second Lieutenant to the RGA on 19 December 1913. Served in France with the RGA from 6 February 1915. Transferring to the RFC, he was, after training, confirmed and gazetted Flying Officer (Observer) on 9 June 1915. He next trained as a Pilot, gaining his Royal Aero Club Certificate (Number 2623) on 24 March 1916, before going on to formal qualification. Sent out to 23 Squadron in France in his new capacity soon after qualifying for his full 'Wings'. On 28 July 1916, Gould and his Observer of the day, 2 AM F Collinson in FE2b, '6974', were both wounded in the air by shrapnel, whilst escorting a formation of 8 and 12 Squadron bombers intent on raiding the rail junction and bridge at Aubigny-au-Bac. Having recovered within weeks, he was in the air again by 15 September 1916, when he and his Observer, Lieutenant Turnbull, attacked no less than 11 hostile machines over Bapaume, completely destroying one of them. His MC was announced in the *London Gazette* of 18 July 1917: 'For conspicuous gallantry and devotion to duty. He has done consistent, good and valuable work while co-operating with the artillery, often under most difficult conditions. He has always set a splendid example by his exceptional pluck and determination'.

Gould was promoted to A/Major and Squadron Commander in 1917, and would be granted a permanent commission in the RAF after the war. By 1934, he held the rank of Group Captain and was commanding the School of Naval Co-operation at Lee-on-Solent.

GOULD, Robert Gordon

The elder son of Robert Gould, MInstCE and Mrs Gould, of Surrey, he was born on 26 February 1885. Educated at Tonbridge School (1900-02). After leaving school, he became a farmer in the Argentine and was there when war came to Europe in August 1914. Volunteering immediately, he was, on 14 August 1914, numbered amongst the very first of the British Latin American Volunteer contingents which left Argentina bound for the UK. Upon arrival in England on 14 September following, he enlisted as a Trooper in 2 King Edward's Horse. Keen to join the flying service, he learnt to fly at his own expense, gaining his Royal Aero Club Certificate (Number 1190) on 24 April 1915. Accepted into the RFC, he was gazetted Second Lieutenant, via the Special Reserve, on 7 May 1915. His formal pilot training duly completed, he was confirmed and gazetted Flying Officer on 29 June following. Sent out to France at the height of the Fokker 'menace' on 24 September 1915, he served briefly with 3 Squadron, before transferring to the BE2c-equipped 10 Squadron. Heavily committed through the coming months, he acquitted himself well in many, if often inconclusive, engagements with the enemy. He narrowly escaped disaster on 26 April 1916, when he and his Observer, Second Lieutenant J Milner, in BE2c, '2119', were shot down by anti-aircraft fire over Fromelles. John Milner, Durham Light Infantry, from Darlington, was killed in the incident, but the fortunate Gould emerged unscathed from the damaged but repairable BE. Promoted to Captain and Flight Commander, he was next posted to the BE2d-equipped 2 Squadron on 1 July 1916, the first day of the Battle of the Somme. Exactly one week later over Lens, Gould and his Observer, Second Lieutenant L C Chapman, in BE2d, '6231' were attacked by enemy scouts. Despite receiving a machine-gun bullet through the thigh, Gould still managed to bring the BE, and his unharmed Observer, back to his aerodrome. His MC was announced in the *London Gazette* of 19 August 1916: 'For conspicuous gallantry and tenacity. While reconnoitring he was attacked by two enemy machines and, though wounded in the leg, drove one down and the other away. He then continued his work, though heavily fired at by anti-aircraft guns. Finally, he was compelled by weakness to return, and on landing was taken to hospital'.

Once recovered, he was appointed, on 1 January 1917, to the staff of the RE8 Instructional Flight, 13 Squadron, at Dover. Gould assisted 12 Squadron with their training when the unit was re-equipped with RE8s in August 1917. Promoted to A/Major, he was appointed Officer Commanding, 98 Squadron, at Old Sarum, in the UK on 19 December 1917. He next served briefly in Italy from 18 January to 10 March 1918. On this latter date, he accompanied, as Commanding Officer, the RE8-equipped 42 Squadron from their base in Italy, back to the Western Front. Gould returned to the Home Establishment on 20 May 1918. He formed and commanded 225 Squadron, West Coast Anti-Submarine Patrol (2 Flights at Pembroke, 2 Flights at Anglesey and 2 Flights at Luce Bay) before leaving the service, via the Unemployed List, on 18 October 1919.

NB: His medals were advertised for sale by GB Military Antiques on 8 February 2003: MC, 1914-15 Star (Lieut RFC), *British War Medal 1914-20, and Victory Medal 1914-19* (Major, RAF).

GOULDING, Acheson Gosford

From Stoney Mountains, Manitoba, Canada, he was born on 16 May 1893. A law student in Winnipeg from 1910 to 1914, he enlisted into 28 Battalion, Canadian Infantry, in the early weeks of the war and subsequently served with that unit in the trenches on the Ypres Salient. Picked out for a commission, he was gazetted Lieutenant to the Canadian Army on 29 June 1916, immediately afterwards successfully seeking secondment to the RFC. Sent to Egypt to train as a Pilot, he was confirmed and gazetted Flying Officer on 23 February 1917. Posted next to 17 Squadron, then based in Macedonia, he flew BE12s and, later, Nieuports and, later again, SE5As, in that so-called 'side-show'. His MC was announced in the *London Gazette* of 27 October 1917, details in the *Gazette* of 18 March 1918: 'For conspicuous gallantry and devotion to duty. While escorting a bombing squadron, he attacked and drove down a hostile two-seater machine. He showed great determination and gallantry on many other occasions'.

At the turn of the New Year of 1918, SE5As arrived from the UK. On 1 April 1918, 47 Squadron's 'C' Flight became part of the newly formed 150 Squadron, with Goulding appointed as its first Flight Commander. During his combat service in the Balkans, Goulding gained nine victories, five with 17 Squadron, and the remaining four with 150 Squadron. He was awarded the Distinguished Flying Cross in the New Year *London Gazette* of 1 January 1919, and was also Mentioned in Despatches on two occasions, *London Gazettes* of 30 November 1917 and 31 January 1919. The French, too, showed their appreciation of his services with a Croix de Guerre, *London Gazette* of 21 September 1918. Goulding returned to the Home Establishment on 15 November 1918 and, after leaving the RAF early in 1919, returned home to Canada. He served again in the Second World War as a Flight Lieutenant with the Royal Canadian Air Force. Acheson Goulding died in Winnipeg in April 1951.

GOWER, William Edward

From Derby, he was born on 4 April 1891. After completing his education, he worked as a Signals and Telegraph Engineer for the Midland Railway Company, from 1909 to 1914. Gazetted Second Lieutenant to 13 (Reserve) Battalion, Sherwood Foresters on 16 January 1915. He served in the UK throughout 1915 and for most of 1916, before securing a secondment to the RFC. Having trained as an Observer, he was confirmed and gazetted Flying Officer (Observer) on 16 November 1916. He was sent out to the FE2d-equipped 20 Squadron on 7 January 1917. On the same day that he arrived, he went up with Sergeant T T Mottershead in FE2d, 'A39', on an offensive patrol. Mottershead and Gower were engaged in combat at a height of 9,000 feet by two Albatros Scouts. Gower was successful in beating off one of their aggressors, but the other scored hits on the FEs petrol tank which immediately burst into flames. They had been shot up by Leutnant Walter Göttsch of Jasta 8, the fourth of the German's eventual 20 victories. Mottershead, in the Pilot's position nearest to the engine and to the flames, displayed incredible fortitude and courage. He dived the machine away and headed for home, the flames literally licking around him. Gower, in the meantime, did what he could to help by squirting the contents of a fire extinguisher over his Pilot. Ground crews at their home-field were shocked to see the burning FE come into sight from the East. They were amazed, too, when Mottershead circled the landing field in the prescribed manner prior to his approach. As the FE touched down, it over-turned, throwing Gower clear. Mottershead was trapped under the engine and it proved difficult for rescuers, including Gower, to extricate the terribly burned Pilot from the still flaming machine. Mottershead would die in hospital four days later, his incredible courage acknowledged posthumously by the award of a Victoria Cross. For his part in the incident, Gower was given the MC, *London Gazette* of 3 March 1917: 'For conspicuous gallantry in action. When his machine was set on fire, he stood up in his seat and sprayed his pilot with a fire extinguisher, thereby enabling his pilot to regain control of the machine and to make a successful landing'.

Gower had received injuries in the fire and the resultant crash and, after a week in a hospital in France, he returned to England for further treatment. Once recovered, he was sent out, in October 1917, for administration duties to RFC HQ, Middle East and RFC HQ, 40 Wing. Gower returned to the Home Establishment on 4 February 1919, to enjoy some home leave before going back to the Middle East in the following May, this time reporting for duty to the Palestine Brigade, Suez. He was Mentioned in Despatches for his services in Egypt, *London Gazette* of 5 June 1919. On the face of it, therefore, his operational career lasted for just one day, for which he received a MC.

GRACE, Frederick Arthur Darien

From Kingswood, Surrey, he was born on 27 December 1893. Educated at Moncton Coombe School, Somerset (1909-10). After leaving school, he went to work in the Argentine, taking a job in a sugar plantation run by Leach Brothers. His younger brother, Gordon, joined him in Argentina, and the pair, who had a common interest in sailing, shared the ownership of a yacht. (Tragically, Second Lieutenant Alfred Alexander Gordon Grace, 22 TS, RFC, would be killed in a flying accident in Egypt on 26 June 1917). In March 1916, Frederick volunteered for war service, becoming one of the many British Latin American Volunteers to return to the UK. Accepted for a commission in the RFC, he was gazetted Second Lieutenant, via the Special Reserve, on 8 July 1916. After training as a Pilot, he was confirmed and gazetted Flying Officer on 4 January 1917. He married, on 12 February 1917, Sybil May Apperly, at Chipstead Parish Church, Surrey, with whom he had a daughter and a son. He served in Home Defence duties with 50 Squadron, his MC being awarded for an incident that occurred on 7 July 1917, when he and Second Lieutenant George Murray (qv), another volunteer from the Argentine, in an AWFK 8, 'B247', shot down a Gotha over England, *London Gazette* of 18 December 1917: 'His Majesty the King has been pleased to confer the following rewards in recognition of gallantry and distinguished service in connection with anti-aircraft services in the United Kingdom. Awarded the Military Cross – Second Lieutenant Frederick Arthur Darien Grace'.

Grace would eventually receive the insignia of his MC from the hands of the King at an investiture held at Buckingham Palace on 11 September 1918. From '50', he joined 143 HD Squadron, serving with that unit until leaving on 14 February 1918, to become an Instructor with 13 TDS. After a period of ill health, he was obliged to relinquish his commission, with the honorary rank of Lieutenant, on 11 December 1918. Grace and his wife, Sybil, together with their recently-born daughter, Pamela, sailed for the Argentine aboard the SS *Highland Laddie* early in 1919. Their son, Stephen, would be born on 26 August 1923. After spending most of his life in Argentina, living mainly at Mogador, Estefata Nu Pora, Rio Caballos, Providé Cordoba, Grace returned to England and died in October 1987.

GRAHAM, John Benjamin

From Clifton, Bristol, 'Jack' Graham was born on 26 November 1888. He had lived in Yankalilla, South Australia, in the pre-war years, but was in England when he gained his Royal Aero Club Certificate (Number 752) in a Graham-White machine at the eponymous company's School at Hendon on 23 March 1914. Volunteering as soon as the war came, he enlisted as a Private soldier into 22 (Kensington) Battalion, Royal Fusiliers, in August 1914. Picked out for a commission, he was gazetted Second Lieutenant into 16 (Reserve) Battalion, Royal Fusiliers, on 10 March 1915. After services in the trenches with the Fusiliers, he sought secondment to the RFC, which eventually came in the summer of 1916. His formal pilot training duly completed, he was confirmed and gazetted Flying Officer on 22 August following. Sent out to the FE2b-equipped 11 Squadron in France, shortly after qualifying for his 'Wings'. On 22 October 1916, he and his Observer, Lieutenant F D Lutyens, in FE2b '7669', were engaged in combat by Leutnant Hans Imelmann of Jasta 2. Although their FE was damaged in the fight, Graham got it down reasonably intact, apart from two broken propeller blades, behind the British lines. Imelmann, however, later claimed the FE as the second of his eventual six victories. This fight was witnessed from the ground by Gunner W A Franklin, 'B' Battery, 302 Brigade, Royal Field Artillery, who afterwards filed a report: 'On Sunday, October 22nd, I was on air scout duty in the Battery, and in the afternoon I saw 5 FE's come over the Battery and go well over the German lines. About 4.30 I saw 4 of them coming back, and just about over the lines they were attacked by 9 Roland Scouts coming from the south, about 4,000 feet up. They were fighting for about 10 minutes or a quarter of an hour. I saw one FE chasing a Roland down to within a 100 feet from the ground until they disappeared from sight behind some trees. I never saw that Roland get up again. This happened behind the German lines, and the whole time the FE was under heavy rifle and machine-gun fire from the German trenches. Another Roland detached itself from the other fight and followed the FE down, and the FE came back over the lines very low (could not have been more than 150 feet) and landed close to the Battery with the propellor broken (two blades shot away). As soon as they landed the Roland turned to chase a BE, but was stopped by Lewis gun fire from FE which was on the ground. When the two Rolands fell out of the formation the others dispersed and the FE's came back'.

Gunner Franklin saw five FEs crossing into German territory but only four returned. The missing FE2b, '7684', crewed by Second Lieutenant Arthur Lindsay Moore Shepherd, KRRC attached RFC, from Antigua, BWI, and 1 AM N L Brain, was shot down by an enemy machine over Gommecourt. Both men subsequently died of their wounds whilst in German hands. Promoted to Flight Commander and A/Captain on 11 March 1917, John Graham's MC was announced in the *London Gazette* of 18 July 1917: 'For conspicuous gallantry and devotion to duty. He has displayed great skill and courage when leading photographic reconnaissances. On many occasions, although attacked by superior numbers, he, by his courage and determination, has succeeded in completing his reconnaissance'.

Graham was next promoted to A/Major and Squadron Commander on 1 August 1917. He instructed in the UK for the remainder of the war, receiving the Air Force Cross in recognition of his outstanding services in this field, *London Gazette* of 2 November 1918. Graham was granted a permanent commission, and stayed on in the RAF after the war. A Group Captain by 1936, he was appointed Station Commander of Lee-on-Solent, on 1 December 1937. John Graham retired from the RAF, with the rank of Group Captain, in 1939.

GRAN, Jens Herman Tryggve

The son of a shipyard owner, he was born in Bergen, Norway, on 29 January 1888. Educated in Switzerland, at Christiana University, and at the Norwegian Naval Cadet College. He had entertained thoughts of mounting his own Antarctic expedition, but abandoned them when he met Robert Falcon Scott in Norway, in 1910. Scott was so impressed with Gran's skiing ability that he invited him to join him as an Instructor. As well as accompanying the original Scott expedition, Gran would also be part of the group that subsequently found the bodies of Scott, Bowers and Wilson in 1913. An aviation pioneer, Gran secured a French Aviation Certificate Superior, at the Bleriot Flying School at Buc, France, in 1913. He next talked Louis Bleriot into selling him one of his 80hp monoplanes at half-price, going on to use this machine to make a record four and a half hour flight across the North Sea, from Scotland to Norway, in 1914. Unfortunately, largely because of the international situation and the imminence of war, Gran's pioneering flight went largely unheralded. Gran, who had previously served in the Royal Norwegian Naval Reserve, was, by 1916, a Captain in the Royal Norwegian Air Force. Although his country was neutral, he was, for reasons that are still not entirely clear, accepted into the RFC in October 1916. Concerned that his nationality and identity might become known to the Germans with potentially disastrous consequences should he ever be captured, he assumed the nom de guerre, Teddy Grant, and posed as a volunteer from Canada. The subterfuge was not carried out very thoroughly, however, as some contemporary *Army Lists* include in their indices, a 'T. Gran', although, despite providing a page reference, there are no corresponding entries in the body of the publications. When he decided to acquire a Royal Aero Club Certificate (Number 5000) on 2 August 1917, this was duly awarded to 'Tryggve Gran' and not, as might have been expected in the circumstances, to his assumed name of, 'Teddy Grant'. He was, eventually, retrospectively and formally commissioned into the RFC, but it was perhaps fortunate that he never did fall into German hands. His RFC operational career had begun with the HD Squadrons, Gran sharing the dangers and difficulties of night flying against the Zeppelin incursions on Britain. His first overseas posting was to the FE2b-equipped 101 Squadron, arriving for duty in France on 3 September 1917. Although '101' was equipped with the FE2b for night-bombing, Gran himself was given a Sopwith Pup, 'B2188', apparently for independent duties. It was said later that Gran's machine was hangared separately from the rest, and that it had a 'side-car' arrangement attached to the fuselage. The 'side-car', it appears, was intended to carry spies behind the enemy lines. Still, Gran occasionally shared in the raids of 101 Squadron and it was during one of these, on 30 November 1917, in FE2b, 'A5586', with Second Lieutenant G D Shand, acting as his Observer, that he was wounded. After bombing and strafing horse-drawn and mechanised transport near Douai, he received a machine-gun bullet to the left leg. Gran afterwards credited his Observer, Shand, with sustaining him through their combined efforts to get back across the lines. Their under-carriage shot away, Gran was forced to crashland the FE onto an emergency landing ground at Wagonlieu, near to Arras. His MC was announced in the *London Gazette* of 26 March 1918, details in the *Gazette* of 24 August 1918: 'For conspicuous gallantry and devotion to duty. He bombed enemy aeroplanes with great success, and engaged enemy searchlights, transport and other targets with machine-gun fire. He invariably showed the greatest determination and resource'.

Research has unearthed the original recommendation for Gran's MC, which gives more detailed information than does the rather bald, formally published citation: 'T Gran 101 Sqn 31/1/18. For consistent and conspicuous gallantry and devotion to duty on night bomb raids. On 20/9/17 he was detailed to bomb Ledeghem. This duty he carried out with conspicuous success, obtaining direct hits in the centre of the village and on the station. He afterwards engaged searchlights, transport and other targets with machine-gun fire. On 9/10/17 he bombed Ingelmunster in very bad weather. The visibility was so poor that he could not fly over 1,000 feet and in consequence he was heavily engaged by AA fire. On 21/10/17 in spite of adverse weather conditions he bombed Ingelmunster aerodrome with success. The visibility was so bad that the other machines returned without discharging their bombs as they were unable to find the target. Captain Gran however, with the greatest determination at last found his objective and dropped his bombs amongst enemy aeroplanes which were getting off the aerodrome. He afterwards engaged ground targets with machine-gun fire. On 28/10/17 he successfully bombed the billeting areas at Oostniewkerke causing a large fire. As a night flying pilot this Officer is exceptionally good, invariably showing the greatest determination and resource. He was severely wounded on 1st December 1917' [sic].

Once recovered, Gran was posted, in May 1918, for Home Defence duties as a Flight Commander and Second-in-Command, of 78 Squadron, then based at Sutton's Farm. In the following October, Gran was promoted to A/Major and sent out to Archangel to command a squadron of the Allied Intervention Force in Russia. Bad weather precluded any serious flying before Gran's barely healed leg wound started giving him problems, and he was obliged to return to England in the same month that the war on the Western Front ended. He stayed on in the RAF after the war, but, in May 1921, was involved in a serious motor-cycle accident. His left leg was damaged yet again and this decided him to resign his RAF commission and return home to Norway. Later in the decade, having fully regained his fitness, Gran was commissioned into the Royal Norwegian Air Force, his experience no doubt invaluable to his nation's flying service. In 1928, Gran was heavily involved in the famous search for his countryman, Roald Amundsen, who had himself disappeared whilst searching for the crew of the airship, Italia. Gran finally retired from the RNAF in 1935, going to live with his wife and family at Grimstad, near Oslo. Jens Herman Tryggve Gran died at the family home on 8 January 1980.

GRATTAN-BELLEW, William Arthur

The third son of Sir Henry and Lady Sophie Grattan-Bellew, of Mount Bellew, County Galway, Ireland and the nephew of Lord Granard, he was born in 1893. Educated at Downside (1906-11), where he was a member of the OTC, and at Trinity College, Cambridge, where he read Engineering. Gazetted Second Lieutenant to the RFC on 17 January 1915, the same day that he qualified for his Royal Aero Club Certificate (Number 1039). His formal pilot training duly completed, he was confirmed and gazetted Flying Officer on 9 April following. Joining 25 Squadron at Montrose, in September 1915, he subsequently accompanied the unit to France as a 'founder member' on 20 February 1916. On 27 April 1916, Grattan-Bellew was in one of four FEs that countered an incursion of eight Aviatiks, driving a wedge through their formation and forcing them to return east. On 26 June 1916, Grattan-Bellew and his Observer of the day, Lieutenant W Harper, were one of five 25 Squadron FEs returning from a bombing raid on Henin Lietard, when they were attacked by Fokkers. After three of the FEs, including that flown by Captain A W Tedder, had, for one reason or another, been forced out of the fight, the Fokkers turned their full attention on Grattan-Bellew and Harper. Grattan-Bellew engaged one

Fokker and succeeded in driving it off before turning to attack another. Harper fired two drums of ammunition from 30 feet, causing the Fokker to heel over and crash behind the enemy's lines. Suddenly, after a fraught and frantic 15 minutes, the sky was clear and Grattan-Bellew could turn the FE for home. His health impaired, Grattan-Bellew was invalided home shortly after this incident. His MC, with its unusually detailed citation, was announced in the *London Gazette* of 27 July 1916: 'For conspicuous gallantry and skill on several occasions, notably the following:- 1) With three other machines he attacked and drove off eight enemy machines, forcing one to the ground. 2) He attacked four Fokkers, forcing one down to 2,500 feet. Another was seen to crash to the ground during the fight. 3) When on a bombing raid two of the machines got behind owing to the clouds, and were attacked by Fokkers, Captain Grattan-Bellew returned and attacked three Fokkers, one of which his observer shot down, and the others made off'.

Following a recuperative period in the UK, he was promoted to A/Major, formally awarded a permanent commission in the Connaught Rangers, and sent out as CO, 29 Squadron, newly equipped with Nieuport XVIIs. Shortly after his arrival, he crashed, and died of the injuries sustained on 24 March 1917. Major William Grattan-Bellew is buried in Avesnes-le-Comte Communal Cemetery Extension, France.

GRAY, Alexander

Born on 8 September 1896. Gazetted Second Lieutenant to 7 Battalion, Argyll and Sutherland Highlanders (TF), on 10 October 1915. Securing a secondment to the RFC in the summer of 1916, he trained as a Pilot and was confirmed and gazetted Flying Officer on 30 September following. Sent out to France and the BE2e-equipped 9 Squadron soon after he qualified. On 5 November 1916, Gray and his Observer of the day, Second Lieutenant C P Creighton, in BE2e, '6270', narrowly escaped disaster when their machine was hit by anti-aircraft fire over Ginchy. Forced to land, the crew barely had time to reach the shelter of near-by trenches before their BE was shelled to smithereens. His MC was announced in the *London Gazette* of 27 October 1917, details 18 March 1918: 'For conspicuous gallantry and devotion to duty. He took part in many successful operations over the enemy's lines, in over twenty of which he acted as leader. On one occasion, when leading a bombing raid, his formation was heavily attacked by enemy aeroplanes. He shot one of them down, and brought back the whole of his formation safely. He also led a successful raid on an enemy aerodrome, and on several occasions obtained valuable photographs. He has accounted for two enemy aeroplanes with his front gun, and always showed great coolness, ability, and resource'.

Staying on in the RAF after the war, Gray went on to enjoy a distinguished career. He married, in 1922, Leonora Mary, with whom he had two daughters; his wife bringing a step-daughter to the marriage. Gray's many appointments, honours and promotions included: Deputy Air Commander, RAF, Eastern Air Command, South-East Asia Command, 1944; CB, 1944; Director of Flying Training, Air Ministry, 1945; and AOC, Air HQ, Iraq, 1947. He finally retired in 1949 with the rank of Air Vice-Marshal, living in retirement at 8 Greenwood Avenue, Ferndown, Dorset. Air Vice-Marshal Alexander Gray died on 16 May 1980.

GRAY, David Benjamin

The son of Dr E Gray MB, CM, and Mrs Gray, of Regent's Park, London, he was born on 29 July 1884. Educated at King William's College, Isle of Man (1899-1901) and at the Royal Military Academy, Woolwich. Gazetted Second Lieutenant to the Royal Artillery in December 1903, he subsequently transferred to 48 Pioneer Battalion, Indian Army, in October 1905. When war came, Gray would serve with the Indian Expeditionary Force in Mesopotamia from November 1914 to April 1915. Securing a secondment to the RFC in February 1916, he trained as a Pilot in Egypt, and was duly confirmed and gazetted Flying Officer on 16 April following. From Egypt, he was sent home to the UK, reporting for duty with the newly formed 60 Squadron, then based in Gosport, on 10 May 1916. Gray accompanied '60' to France as a 'founder member' on 25 May following. Within weeks, Captain Gray was transferred to the FE2b-equipped 11 Squadron, as a Flight Commander. On 17 September 1916, Gray and his Observer, Lieutenant L B Helder, in FE2b, '7019', were, following an aerial combat, shot down to be taken as prisoners- of-war. Theirs was the dubious distinction of being the 27th of the great German Ace, Hauptmann Oswald Boelcke's eventual 40 victories. Gray, who had been slightly wounded in the Boelcke confrontation, was confined in various prison camps before eventually ending up in Holzminden. In the fullness of time, Gray was to become one of the ten successful escapers from the famous mass tunnel exodus from Holzminden on 23 July 1918, reaching Holland and safety on 5 August following. Gray's part in the escape, along with that of the two others with whom he journeyed to freedom , Caspar Kennard (qv) and Cecil W Blain, is related in great detail in Barry Winchester's book, 'Beyond the Tumult', published in 1971 (Allison and Busby). Relinquishing his Indian Army commission on 30 December 1918, in favour of one in the RAF, Gray went on to serve in North Russia with the Allied Intervention Force from February 1919 to July 1919. His MC was announced in the 'Escapers Gazette', *London Gazette* of 16 December 1919: '....in recognition of gallantry in escaping from captivity whilst Prisoners of War'.

Reversing his earlier decision, Gray returned to the Indian Army in the 1920s, this time serving with 3 Sikh Pioneers, before transferring back to his old regiment, 48 Pioneers. He would, in time, become that regiment's Commanding Officer and be created OBE. Gray finally retired from the Indian Army with the rank of Lieutenant Colonel in 1933, going to live in retirement at Hazel Cottage, Wonstan Sutton, Scotney, Hampshire. As soon as the Second World War came in 1939, he offered to serve in any capacity and was given a commission as a Flight Lieutenant in the RAF. Promoted to Squadron Leader in 1941, he was compulsorily retired because of poor health in 1942. He immediately joined the Home Guard and was promptly given back his true rank of Lieutenant Colonel. In his very first week in this new service, he was run over by a lorry on the Basingstoke road at Micheldever, whilst giving some officers lessons in map-reading. Lieutenant Colonel David Gray is buried in Wonston Churchyard, near Sutton Scotney, Hampshire.

GREEN, Ernest George

From Jesmond, Northumberland, he was born on 2 February 1892. Gazetted Second Lieutenant to Royal Engineers, Signals Service (TF), on 11 December 1915.

Transferring to the RFC, he served with the FE2d-equipped 25 Squadron from the winter of 1916, and was subsequently confirmed as a Flying Officer (Observer) on 14 November 1916. Green was credited, on 6 April 1917, when partnered by his Pilot, Second Lieutenant Alexander Roulstone (qv), with sending a HA down in flames. He was with Roulstone again, on 25 April, when they were attacked by three Albatros Scouts whilst taking photographs. In the event, Green contrived to shoot the wing off one of their attackers and forced the remaining two to withdraw. His MC was announced in the *London Gazette* of 26 May 1917: 'For conspicuous gallantry and devotion to duty as an Observer. He has on several occasions brought down hostile machines, and has carried out many successful photographic reconnaissances. He has at all times set a fine example of courage and initiative'.

Green subsequently trained as a Pilot and, after qualifying, returned to '25' that was, by then, equipped with DH4s. On 3 February 1918, Green and his Observer, Lieutenant Peter Clifford Campbell-Martin (qv), in DH4, 'A7873', were returning from a bombing raid on railway sidings at Melle, when they were attacked over Mariakerke. After a brief fight, they were shot down, the DH's fuel tank shot through and control wires severed. Green was hit in the side by an explosive bullet which fractured his hip. The badly injured Green and his Observer were both taken as prisoners-of-war. The destruction of their DH4 was subsequently claimed as the second of 15 victories by Leutnant Otto Löffler of Jasta 2. Ernest Green would be repatriated to the UK on 2 December 1918. Awarded a short service commission with the Royal Engineers, Green finally left the service on 30 September 1921.

GREEN, John Spencer

From Herne Hill, London SE24, he was born on 29 July 1891. After completing his education, he worked as an Actuarial Clerk with the National Mutual Life Assurance of Australasia Ltd, in Cheapside, London, from January 1911 to 4 August 1914. A pre-war volunteer, he had already enlisted into 21 (County of London) Battalion (The Queen's) (TF) and, along with the rest of the TF, was mobilised as soon as war was declared on 4 August 1914. He accompanied his battalion, with the rank of Corporal, to France on 16 March 1915. After serving in the trenches for more than a year, he was picked out for a commission. He was gazetted Second Lieutenant to the RFC, via the Special Lists, on 5 September 1916. Shortly after qualifying for his 'Wings', he was sent out to the RE8-equipped 13 Squadron in France on 11 April 1917. After completing his tour with '13', he was next promoted to A/Captain and Flight Commander and posted to 59 Squadron, another RE8-equipped artillery observation unit. His MC was announced in the *London Gazette* of 4 March 1918, details in the *Gazette* of 16 August 1918: ' For conspicuous gallantry and devotion to duty. He has proved himself to be a skilful artillery pilot, and has frequently carried out observation at long distance over the enemy's lines under heavy anti-aircraft fire. On one occasion he drove down an enemy two-seater machine and forced it to land in our lines. He has set a splendid example to his Squadron'.

Research has unearthed the original recommendation for the award, which contains more detailed information than does the published citation: 'For gallantry and good service. On 28 December 1917, in the neighbourhood of Monchy-le-Preux, 2/Lt Green saw a hostile two-seater machine returning to its lines at a height of 7,500 feet. He immediately engaged the enemy machine and manoeuvred to obtain a position just below the lines of his tail plane and with such skill and determination was the attack carried out that the EA was forced to the ground and every attempt that he made to regain his own lines was frustrated. The German machine landed in our lines due West of Monchy le Preux, and it was found to be fitted with a new type of camera, the first of its kind to be captured'.

The captured machine was subsequently 're-marked' with British roundels and flown by the RAF. Following a brief stay in hospital in May 1918, Green returned to service with '59', but was soon relieved and ordered home to the UK. He served out the war as an Instructor with 1 and 5 TDS before leaving the RAF, via the Unemployed List, on 16 April 1919, going to live with his wife in Bembridge, Isle of Wight.

NB: His medals were offered for sale by Christie's (lot 128) on 22 July 1986 and then again by Sotheby's (lot 206) on 29 October 1987: MC, 1914-15 Star (Cpl 21/Londons), *British War Medal 1914-20, and Victory Medal 1914-19* (Capt RAF).

GREENWOOD, Herbert John

The son of Mr and Mrs Arthur Greenwood of 'Oakfield', Baildon, North Shipley, Yorkshire, he was born on 3 April 1896. During the early years of the Great War, he was living and working in County Clare, Ireland. Gazetted Second Lieutenant to 2/6 Battalion, West Yorkshire Regiment (TF), on 1 March 1917. Successfully seeking secondment to the RFC, he trained as a Pilot and was sent out to the SE5A-equipped 1 Squadron, by then a unit of the RAF, on 13 April 1918. His MC was announced in the *London Gazette* of 22 June 1918: 'For conspicuous gallantry and devotion to duty. He undertook a long distance reconnaissance under the most adverse conditions and succeeded in returning with the most valuable information. During recent operations his work has often been carried out at extremely low altitudes, and the numerous accurate and complete reports as to hostile movements and dispositions of troops, with which he has returned, prove him to be a most able and determined pilot'.

His operational career was short-lived, as he returned to the Home Establishment in June 1918. He finally left the service, via the Unemployed List, on 11 March 1919. Greenwood would be appointed an officer in the Emergency Reserve in November 1938, obviously anticipating events to come.

GREGORY, William Robert

The only son of the Right Honourable Sir William Gregory, KCMG, and Lady Augusta Gregory, of Coole Park, Gort, County Galway, Ireland, he was born on 20 May 1881. Educated at Harrow (1896-99) and at New College, Oxford, where he boxed at light-weight against Cambridge. He was also a fine cricketer – a right-handed batsman and a leg break and googly bowler – playing for Galway, and for the Gentlemen of Ireland. Gregory was well known in the hunting field, and also rode in many point-to-point races. After Oxford, he studied Art at the Slade School and in Paris, under Blanché. He exhibited at the 'New English' and other art galleries, paintings of West Irish landscapes. Gregory also designed and painted sets in the early days of the Abbey Theatre in Dublin, including those for J M Synge's 'Deirdre of the Sorrows', W B Yeats' 'Shadowy Waters', and for his playwright Mother's 'The Image'. He married Margaret Graham-Parry in 1907, with whom he had a son and two daughters. Gregory was gazetted Second Lieutenant to 4 (Reserve) Battalion, Connaught Rangers on 24 September 1915, transferring to the RFC in January 1916. After training as a Pilot, he was confirmed and gazetted Flying Officer on 19 June 1916. Sent soon afterwards to the newly forming FE8-equipped 40 Squadron in Gosport, he accompanied that unit to France, as a 'founder member', in the following August. Gregory had a narrow escape on 25 September 1916, when the propeller of his FE8, '6383', was shot off by anti-aircraft fire during escort duty. Fortunately, he was able to crashland on the right side of the lines without further mishap or injury. On 30 March 1917, Gregory, now flying a Nieuport XVII, 'A6680', shot down and killed Jasta 11 Pilot, Leutnant Edouard Lübbert from Hamburg, thus registering the first of 40 Squadron's victories in Nieuport Scouts. His MC was announced in the *London Gazette* of 18 July 1917 (the *Gazette*, as, indeed, do the contemporary *Army Lists*, have him as 'Robert' Gregory and NOT, for some unknown reason as 'William Robert Gregory'): 'For conspicuous gallantry and devotion to duty. On many occasions he has, at various altitudes, attacked and destroyed or driven down hostile machines, and has invariable displayed the highest courage and skill'.

The French, too, awarded him the Croix d'Officer, Légion d'Honneur, for, 'many acts of conspicuous bravery', *London Gazette* of 14 July 1917. Promoted to A/Major, he was given command of the Sopwith Camel-equipped 66 Squadron in France, in October 1917, taking that unit to Italy on 22 November following. Gregory was killed returning after a patrol over the Austrian lines on 23 January 1918. William Robert Gregory is buried in Padua Main Cemetery, Italy.

NB: The RAF Museum Hendon has his Légion d'Honneur (France) in its collection.

GRENFELL, Eustace Osborne

From Southend-on-Sea, Essex, he was born on 26 August 1880. A pre-war volunteer, 'Black' Grenfell was gazetted Second Lieutenant into 5 Battalion, Duke of Cornwall's Light Infantry (TF), on 1 March 1914. Mobilised with the rest of the TF on 4 August 1914, he sought secondment to the flying services soon afterwards. Taking flying lessons at his own expense, he gained his Royal Aero Club Certificate (Number 966) on 9 November 1914. Seconded to the RFC, he completed his formal training and was confirmed and gazetted Flying Officer on 22 December following. Sent out to join 1 Squadron in France on 7 March 1915. Grenfell achieved his first victory against an Albatros C on 13 September 1915, and a second against the same type on 7 December 1915. He was Mentioned in Despatches on 1 January 1916. On 17 January 1916, he bagged three Fokkers and one Albatros before breakfast – a feat which, unsurprisingly, gained him the MC, *London Gazette* of 15 March 1916: 'For conspicuous gallantry and skill. He attacked single handed and brought down three Fokker aeroplanes. Captain Grenfell has shown great bravery and initiative at all times'.

Grenfell would recount later how, because he was flying the first Morane Bullet, so similar in profile to the Fokker, the Germans mistook him for one of their own, and he was in amongst them almost before they knew it. He would also recall early bombing raids when 'the bombs were just rolling about in the cockpit and we had to find them with our feet and then drop them over the side'. The early armaments available to air crews consisted of revolvers and rifles with cut down barrels. 'Once', he said, 'I attacked a Zeppelin with a revolver and, running out of ammunition, I just threw it at the airship!'. After a period as an Instructor at the CFS, he was, in September 1916, sent out to 60 Squadron as a Flight Commander. Two more victories followed before he crashed, in almost farcical circumstances, on 11 December 1916, breaking a leg in the process. On this occasion, Grenfell was leading an offensive patrol made up of K L Caldwell (qv), A P V Daly, A D Whitehead, L S Weedon and H Meintjes (qv). The sextet met an unfortunate two-seater Albatros over the British lines and attacked it, en masse. Unsurprisingly, the Germans landed their machine just as quickly as they could. Grenfell delightedly followed the Albatros down, anxious to be the first to claim it. In his haste, he crashed his machine and broke his leg. To add to the farce, the remaining five 60 Squadron machines also landed in the surrounding fields, and three of them also crashed. In the meantime, the German Observer had set the Albatros alight. Just at the moment British Tommies arrived to take the wounded German Pilot and his Observer into captivity, the Albatros blew up, seriously wounding the Observer and a number of the soldiers. Later in the War, Grenfell commanded 23 Squadron and, later again, 1 Squadron, at Tangmere and at Irik. He was awarded an Air Force Cross in the *London Gazette* of 2 November 1918. Staying on in the RAF, he would be awarded a Distinguished Flying Cross for 'distinguished services rendered with the Waziristan Forces between January 1922 and April 1923'., *London Gazette* of 30 May 1924. In 1927, he was a Squadron Leader with 7 Squadron. Again in 1927, he won the RAF Memorial Prize for the 'Laurence Minot (qv) Memorial Trophy'. In 1933, he was promoted to Wing Commander, and appointed to the command of RAF Biggin Hill. Promoted to Group Captain in 1937, he was appointed to the command of RAF Thornaby, in the following year. Group Captain E O Grenfell finally retired from the RAF on 17 February 1942.

GREY-EDWARDS, Henry Bayly Reginald

The only son of Dr Henry Grey-Edwards, MD, and Mrs A H D Grey-Edwards (née Burgess) of 'Bank Place', Bangor, North Wales, and 'The Firs', Rock Ferry, Cheshire, he was born on 2 August 1894. Henry's father was a former Mayor of Bangor. He was educated at Copthorne School, Crawley, at Winchester (1908-13), and at Balliol College, Oxford (1913-14). Interrupting his law studies at Balliol, he was gazetted Second Lieutenant to the Royal Field Artillery on 9 November 1914. Having aspirations to join the flying service, he gained his Royal Aero Club Certificate (Number 995) on 14 December following. Securing a secondment to the RFC in the spring of 1915, he completed his formal training and was confirmed and gazetted Flying Officer on 14 May 1915. Posted out to 6 Squadron in France on 19 May 1915. His MC was announced in the *London Gazette* of 29 October 1915: 'For conspicuous gallantry and skill on 25 September 1915 on the Phalempin-Seclin line when he bombed a train and damaged the track from a height of 400 feet under heavy rifle fire. He was attacked by an enemy aeroplane but drove it off. He brought back a useful reconnaissance. All this was carried out under bad weather conditions'.

He was also Mentioned in Despatches in 1915. Promoted to A/Captain, Grey-Edwards was posted next, on 22 November 1915, to 7 Squadron as a Flight Commander. Wounded on 7 December 1915, he returned to the UK for treatment. Once recovered, he was appointed to instructing duties until 16 November 1917, when he was promoted to A/Major, and given command of the Camel-equipped 70 Squadron. Grey-Edwards led '70' until 6 August 1918, when he returned to the Home Establishment for a rest and to resume his education. Although still officially a member of the Armed Services (he did not relinquish his commission until 1 February 1919), he was allowed to return to his studies at Balliol and, indeed, in the United States. Having gained his BA, he was, in 1919, articled to Messrs Knight and Sons, Solicitors, of Newcastle-under-Lyne. Once qualified as a Solicitor in 1920, he secured a position in the Legal Department of Lever Brothers, working in the Head Office at Port Sunlight, Cheshire, and at the company's US branch in Cambridge, Massachusetts, before transferring to the London offices of the company in the following year. He married, in 1923, Florence May Lee of Beverley Farms, Mass, USA, who he had met during his sojourn in Cambridge, Mass. In 1928, he was appointed Director of Lever House Advertising Services, still working in London, until 1930, when he transferred to the Berlin office. Retiring from Lever Brothers in 1930, he formed his own company, Gloria Products Ltd, in 1932, whilst living at 20 Upper Cheyne Row, Chelsea, London SW3. Henry Grey-Edwards died on 4 February 1975.

GRIBBEN, Edward

From Hollywood, County Down, Ireland, he was born on 10 September 1890. He worked in Belfast as a Motor Engineer after leaving school in 1904, age 14. Already a member of the Belfast Volunteers, Ulster Volunteer Force, Gribben was obviously held in high local esteem, as he was immediately gazetted Second Lieutenant into 8 Battalion, Royal Irish Rifles, on 4 August 1914, the very day that war was declared. Rapid promotion to the rank of Acting Captain was confirmed on 1 December 1914. Having served in the trenches of France with his regiment, he secured a secondment to the RFC in the autumn of 1916, reverting to the rank of Second Lieutenant in the process. After completing his pilot training, he was confirmed and gazetted Flying Officer on 24 December 1916. He served briefly with 46 Squadron in France from 15 February 1917, before joining the Camel-equipped 70 Squadron on 28 March following. Gribben claimed five victories between 17 July and 13 August, for which he received the MC, *London Gazette* of 26 September 1917, details in the *Gazette* of 9 January 1918: 'For conspicuous gallantry and devotion to duty on offensive patrols. In every combat he has been most conspicuous, continually attacking superior numbers of the enemy, destroying some and driving others down out of control. He fights with great dash and skill, and whenever any machine of his formation is in difficulties, he is invariably at hand to render assistance'.

His tour with '70' completed, he returned to the UK on 9 September 1917 and, after a short rest, flew night-fighter Camels with 44 HD Squadron. In 1918, he was posted to Farnborough as a Test Pilot, regaining the rank of Captain he had relinquished when volunteering for the RFC. He also served at an experimental station at Ipswich and at the Air Ministry. On 2 October 1918, he took up his last operational post as a Flight Commander with 41 Squadron. This posting, however, was short-lived, as just two days after his arrival he was shot-up by a Fokker DVII. Wounded in the arm, Gribben was compelled to force-land his SE5A, 'F5494'. After recovering from his wounds, he was engaged on more experimental work from July 1919, before going on to Farnborough again in the following October. He finally left the service, via the Unemployed List, on 24 January 1920. Edward Gribben returned to the RAF just weeks later, receiving a short-service commission which lasted from 20 May 1920 to 10 August 1920. His recall to service may have been related to the so-called, 'Troubles' in Ireland at that time.

GRIMWOOD, Bertie Constantine Ruffell

The son of Herbert Ruffell Grimwood and Amelia Isabel Grimwood, of Villa Thouin, 96 Via Bolognese, Florence, Italy, and 193 Roundhay Road, Leeds, he was born in Richmond, Surrey, on 3 December 1883. Educated at Felsted (1898-1900). He trained as an Engineer and, when war came in August 1914, he was living in Hove, Sussex, and working for the Inspection Staff of the Crown Agents for the Colonies in Whitehall, London. Volunteering immediately, he enlisted as a Trooper (Number 12680) into 18 Hussars on 28 August 1914. He served in France with his regiment from May 1915 to August 1915, before being picked out for a commission and gazetted Second Lieutenant to the Royal Field Artillery on 16 August 1915. Posted to Staff duties, he was formally appointed an ADC (Commands and Staff) in the *London Gazette* of 8 December 1915. On 5 February 1917, he was appointed Staff Officer (Staff Lieutenant 1st Class) to the General Officer Commanding, Royal Artillery and, as such, it became necessary for him to undertake training as an Aerial Observer, attached RFC, as an essential part of his specialised reconnaissance surveillance and reporting duties. He was, following training, subsequently gazetted Flying Officer (Observer) on 16 July 1917. Attached to 4 Squadron, his MC, with its exceptional citation, was won in an incident that occurred on 16 August 1917, when an RE8, 'A3848', crewed by Grimwood and his Pilot, Second Lieutenant Richard Douglas Starley (qv), was hit in mid-air by a shell. The citation for his MC, announced in the *London Gazette* of 26 September 1917, details in the *Gazette* of 9 January 1918, tells the story: 'For conspicuous gallantry and devotion to duty. Having located a strong force of enemy infantry coming up to counter-attack, his machine was immediately afterwards hit by a shell, which wounded him severely and destroyed his wireless apparatus. His machine was obviously so badly damaged that no expert would have believed it could possibly have held together in the air, but in spite of this and of his wounds, he wrote out a message reporting the position of the enemy and dropped it on Divisional Headquarters, who were able to put nine batteries onto the target. His pluck and devotion were worthy of the highest praise'.

Starley, too, received the MC for his gallantry on this occasion. Having recovered from his wounds, Grimwood was up and flying again on 7 November 1917, this time in RE8, 'A3746', with Second Lieutenant A G Grose, in the pilot's seat. They were attacked over Morslede and sent down at about 07.10 by Paul Baümer of Jasta 2, the tenth of the German Ace's eventual 43 victories. Albert Grose from Northampton, was lifted out of the wreckage of the RE8 by German troops, only to die two days later in hospital. Bertie Grimwood's remains, however, have never been recovered and hence he is commemorated on the Flying Services Memorial, Arras, France.

GRINNELL-MILNE, Duncan William

Born in London 6 August 1896 and educated at Cheam School and RN Colleges of Osborne and Dartmouth, then Freiburg University, Germany. Commissioned into the Rifle Brigade in December 1913 he was then gazetted Second Lieutenant to 7 (Extra Reserve) Battalion, Royal Fusiliers, on 15 August 1914. Because he was too young for service in France he was, much to his chagrin, held back in England. Seeking secondment to the RFC, he gained Royal Aero Club Certificate (Number 1609) on 17 August 1915. Having completed his formal pilot training, he was confirmed and gazetted Flying Officer on 29 September following. Almost immediately after qualifying, he was sent out to 16 Squadron in France, flying the ponderous Shorthorns and BEs on reconnaissance sorties over the German lines. He gained the first of his eventual six victories on 28 November 1915, when he and his Observer, Captain C Strong, in BE2c, ' 4086', overcame an Albatros C-type. Three days later, on 1 December, Grinnell-Milne and Strong, again in '4086', hit some very strong head winds just at the moment their engine gave out, with the consequence that the pair were forced to land their BE 2c some eight miles behind the German lines. Grinnell-Milne would, ultimately, become one of the handful of successful escapers from German captivity, crossing back into the Allied lines in April 1918. It was for this outstanding feat that he was subsequently awarded the MC in the 'Escapers Gazette', *London Gazette* of 16 December 1919: '....in recognition of gallantry in escaping from captivity whilst Prisoners of War'.

That was still to come, however, and once back in the war in the spring of 1918, he was determined to return to the front. He was, perhaps surprisingly in view of the German's attitude to escaped prisoners-of-war, allowed to join the SE5A-equipped 56 Squadron for the Final Advance and, in fact, became the squadron's Commander. He claimed one balloon on 5 October, followed by no less than four Fokker DVIIs before the end of the war, his gallantry earning him a Distinguished Flying Cross and Bar, *London Gazettes* of 8 February 1919 and 3 June 1919 respectively. He was also Mentioned in Despatches, *London Gazette* of 15 July 1919. Staying on in the RAF after the war, he served first with 214 Squadron in Egypt in 1919, before transferring to 14 Squadron in 1920. Further postings included a spell as Assistant Air Attaché in the British Embassy in Paris, before he finally retired in 1926, with 2,000 hours on 60 different types of machines under his belt. Inevitably, he served again in the Second World War, flying Wellingtons over Libya in 1940. After a period with the Air Mission in Greece, he was declared unfit for further service with the RAF in 1941, joining the BBC Foreign Service until 1946. Post the Second World War he lived in France, returning the the UK in 1951. An author of some note, he is perhaps best known for his book, 'Wind in the Wires'. Duncan Grinnell-Milne died on 22 November 1973.

GROSVENOR, Robert Arthur

The son of Lord Arthur Grosvenor, his father being the second son of the first son of the Duke of Wellington, and Lady Helen Grosvenor (née Sheffield), he was born on 25 May 1895. Educated at Wellington College (1909-11). After war came, he was initially gazetted Second Lieutenant to the Cheshire Yeomanry (virtually the family regiment) on 14 September 1914. A transfer to 2 Dragoon Guards, The Queen's Bays, was next formally gazetted on 1 November 1915. 'Robin' Grosvenor then decided upon the RFC and, as a preamble, gained his Royal Aero Club Certificate (Number 3513) on 7 September 1916. His pilot training successfully completed, he was confirmed and gazetted Flying Officer on 6 November following. Grosvenor flew first with 18 and 20 Squadrons before joining the FE2d-equipped 57 Squadron in France. However, it was only when he transferred as an A/Captain and Flight

Commander to the SE5A-equipped 84 Squadron in November.1917, that he truly found his niche. No less than 16 victories followed between 6 December 1917 and 18 May 1918, including two 'doubles' on 19 February and 12 April, and a 'treble' on 25 April. His tour with '84' completed, he returned to the Home Establishment in the early Summer of 1918. The announcements of his MC and Bar came in the ensuing weeks – MC, *London Gazette* of 26 July 1918: 'For conspicuous gallantry and devotion to duty as a leader of offensive patrols against hostile aircraft and troops on the ground. On one occasion his patrol was attacked from the rear by five enemy scouts. By skilful piloting he manoeuvred his machine into position behind one of the scouts, which he shot down in flames. He was attacked again, and drove the scout to destruction. On other occasions he has destroyed and driven down out of control at least eight hostile machines'.

Bar to MC, *London Gazette* of 16 September 1918: 'For conspicuous gallantry and devotion to duty in attacking enemy aircraft. He has lately destroyed two machines and driven down four others out of control. He has shown brilliant leadership and dash against heavy odds'.

Robin married, in 1925, Doris May Wignall, with whom he had one son and one daughter. Grosvenor served again briefly in the Second World War, but whilst the spirit was willing, the flesh was weak, and he was invalided out of the RAF in 1940. He lived, in his latter years, at Oak Ash Farm, Chaddleworth near Newbury, Berkshire. Robin Grosvenor died on 12 June 1953.

GRUBB, Richard Raymond de Cruce – **see** Richard Raymond **de CRUCE GRUBB**

GUILFOYLE, William James Yule

The son of Landscape Gardener and Botanist, William Robert Guilfoyle and Mice Guilfoyle (née Darling), of South Yarra, Australia, he was born in Edinburgh, Scotland, on 17 October 1894. His father was Director of the Botanic Gardens in Melbourne. Educated at Trinity College, Melbourne University, where he studied Law. Volunteering immediately war was declared in August 1914, he enlisted as a Trooper in 4 Australian Light Horse. He served in Egypt with the Light Horse, but was soon picked out for a commission and gazetted Second Lieutenant to the Royal Field Artillery on 29 April 1915. Guilfoyle served in Gallipoli with the Gunners, before being evacuated to the UK with sunstroke in July 1915. Recovering his health, he determined upon a transfer to the flying service and, with this end in mind, gained his Royal Aero Club Certificate (Number 1928) on 14 October 1915. His formal training duly completed, he was confirmed and gazetted Flying Officer on 25 November following. Guilfoyle served first with the BE2c-equipped 10 RA Squadron at Farningham. He was injured in a crash whilst taking off in BE2c, '1776', at 1945 on 31 January 1916, in an attempt to respond to a threatened Zeppelin incursion against Liverpool. Once recovered, he was sent out to Egyptian Expeditionary Force, where he flew 14 Squadron Martinsydes over the desert in close co-operation with 1 Squadron, AFC, during the battles of Romani and Gaza. His MC was announced in the *London Gazette* of 3 March 1917: 'For conspicuous gallantry in action. He carried out a daring bombing raid and made a valuable reconnaissance under heavy fire during the same flight. He has at all times set a fine example'.

Guilfoyle returned to the UK in 1917, before going out to Italy to command 28 Squadron in 1918. He stayed on in the RAF after the war and was awarded the OBE in the *London Gazette* of 10 October 1919 ; 'For distinguished service rendered during the war'. Guilfoyle attained the rank of Air Commodore, and served again in the Second World War. Amongst other appointments, he was Commandant, ATC (North West Command), from 1942 to 1946. He was Mentioned in Despatches on no less than six occasions during his career. Air Commodore William Guilfoyle died on 24 April 1948, as a result of an explosion whilst camping. He is buried in Brighton Cemetery, Melbourne, Australia.

(Note: The name of 'Yule' did not appear on his birth certificate and he certainly signed his name, WJG, but despite this, other documents do give Yule as his third forename).

NB: His medals were offered for sale by Christie's (lot 92) on 24 March 1987: OBE (first type, Military Division), MC, 1914-15 Star (Pte 4/LH Regt AIF), *British War Medal, Victory Medal 1914-19 with MID* (Major RAF), *Jubilee Medal 1935, Coronation Medal 1937, 1939-45 Star, Air Crew Europe Star 1939-44, and Africa Star 1940-43. The medals were offered for sale with an inscribed silver trophy won by Wing Commander Guilfoyle in 1930.*

GUNNER, William Henry

The son of Bank Manager, William Henry Gunner and Mrs Louise Jane Gunner, of 'Winfold', Maltravers Street, Arundel, Sussex, he was born on 19 April 1891. Educated at Elmsdale School, Redhill. Before the war he worked as a clerk in the London offices of cigarette manufacturers, W D & H O Wills, whilst lodging with relatives at 'Ravenscroft', Stanley Road, Sutton, Surrey. A pre-war volunteer, he joined 5 Battalion, London Regiment (London Rifle Brigade), as a Private soldier (Number 8916) on 25 March 1909. At the end of his five year engagement with the LRB, he left the volunteer infantry to join the volunteer cavalry. On 6 March 1914, he committed himself, as a Trooper (Number 1037), to a new five-year term with 3 County of London Yeomanry (Sharpshooters). Mobilised in August 1914, he subsequently embarked at Avonmouth on 14 April 1915, bound for Alexandria and the Middle East. From Egypt, he and the Yeomanry Brigade landed in Gallipoli on 14 August 1915. Six weeks later on 24 September 1915, he was admitted to Field Hospital A3, suffering from dysentery. From Gallipoli, Gunner was sent to a military hospital in Alexandria. Failing to respond to treatment, he was sent home on the Hospital Ship *Ebani*, arriving in Cardiff on 13 November 1915. His health restored at last, he was picked out for a commission and gazetted Second Lieutenant to the RFC, via the General List, on 5 September 1916. Gained his Royal Aero Club Certificate (Number 4565) on 3 February 1917. His formal training completed soon afterwards, he was awarded his 'Wings' and sent out to 60 Squadron in France. Before he left for the front, he married Mary Stevens of Radlett, Hertforshire. Gunner enjoyed considerable success with 60 Squadron, being quickly promoted to Acting Flight Commander. On 3 June 1917, Gunner's Nieuport XVII, 'B1618.B3', was shot up during an aerial combat over Vitry, with Leutnant Karl Allmenröder of Jasta 11, and he received a slight head wound. Although Gunner brought his machine back safely, Allmenröder claimed him as the 23rd of his eventual 30 victories. His MC was announced in the *London Gazette* of 18 July 1917: 'For conspicuous gallantry and devotion to duty. While on offensive patrol he engaged and attacked 9 hostile aircraft, two of which were attacking the rear machine of our patrol. Having convoyed the other machine back to the aerodrome, he again returned with his patrol in response to an urgent call for aeroplanes to drive off hostile aircraft. He had been wounded in his previous encounter, but insisted on carrying on, and on numerous other occasions he has shown great skill and courage in offensive work'

In a letter home, one of his contemporaries, Captain W E Molesworth, commends Gunner's efforts: '....every cloud has a silver lining. This time it is in the shape of an MC for one of our flight commanders who thoroughly deserves it. He hasn't managed to get a big bag yet, but there is lots of 'good stuff' in him, in both senses of the word. We are going to have a great 'bust' to-night to commemorate it, and to cheer things up a bit'.

On 29 July 1917, Gunner, on patrol with 60 Squadron in one of the newly received SE5As, 'A8937', was involved in a fight with elements of Jasta 12. He was shot down by Adolf von Tutschek, the 21st of the German Ace's eventual 27 victories. Gunner's death was announced in the *Nord Deutche Allgemeine Zeitung*: 'BE one-seater, Motor Wolesey 700/2233. Occupant burnt. Buried by the German Army with honour'. William Gunner is buried in Cabaret-Rouge Cemetery, France.

GURNEY, Alfred Relf

From Hereford, he was born on 13 December 1894. Educated at Rossall School (1909-12). After leaving school, he trained as a Motor Engineer. Volunteering as soon as the war came, he enlisted in August 1914, as a Private soldier and lorry driver into 47 Company, Army Service Corps, being amongst the relatively few with driving skills in those days. Sent out to France in the same month, he continued to serve there until September 1915, thus earning the 1914 Star. Picked out for a commission, he was gazetted Second Lieutenant into the Motorised Machine Gun Service, RA (the forerunner to the Tank Corps) on 7 October 1915. Posted to the Middle East and the Egyptian Expeditionary Force, he eventually rose to command a Machine Gun Company with the rank of Captain. Having successfully sought secondment to the RFC in August 1917, he trained as an Observer in Egypt before being posted to an operational Squadron in the area. He was Mentioned in General Allenby's Despatches of 14 June 1918 and his MC was announced in the *London Gazette* of 26 July 1918: 'For conspicuous gallantry and devotion to duty. While attacking enemy troops his pilot was wounded and fainted. He connected up the dual-control, but the machine was falling in a spin. However, he got control again at a height of only 500 feet, and got the machine with its occupants safely back. He showed great pluck and determination'.

Returning to the UK, he finally left the service, via the Unemployed List, on 27 March 1919. Alfred Gurney lived, in the immediate post-war years, at Plas Gwyn, Hereford.

H

HACKWILL, George Henry

From Langtree, North Devon, he was born on 22 December 1892. As befitting a Devonian, he had served as a pre-war volunteer in the Royal Naval Volunteer Reserve from 1912 to 1914. When the war came, however, he opted for the Army, joining the Royal North Devon Yeomanry (TF) as a Trooper. Picked out for a commission, he was gazetted Second Lieutenant to 9 Battalion, Somerset Light Infantry on 18 December 1914. Seconded to the RFC in November 1915, he gained his Royal Aero Club Certificate (Number 2292) on 17 December 1915. His formal pilot training duly completed, he was confirmed and gazetted Flying Officer on 21 April 1916. He first flew operationally in FE2b-equipped 22 Squadron, with which unit he accounted for at least two enemy machines. Returning to the Home Establishment in 1917, he acted as an Instructor before going on to 44 HD Squadron towards the end of the year. Hackwill, in Camel 'B2402', in company with colleague, Second Lieutenant C C Banks (qv), brought down one of the dreaded Gothas at Wickford, Essex, on the night of 28/29 January 1918. The award of his MC followed almost immediately, *London Gazette* of 8 February 1918: 'For conspicuous gallantry when he engaged and shot down a Gotha raiding London. During the engagement which lasted a considerable time, they were continually under fire from the enemy machine'.

In the spring of 1918, Hackwill returned to the front, this time as a Flight Commander with the Camel-equipped 54 Squadron. He achieved six further victories between 25 April and 15 September 1918, taking his total to nine. George Hackwill left the RAF, via the Unemployed List, on 15 April 1919, and was last known to be living in Nyasaland in British Central Africa.

HALL, David Sidney

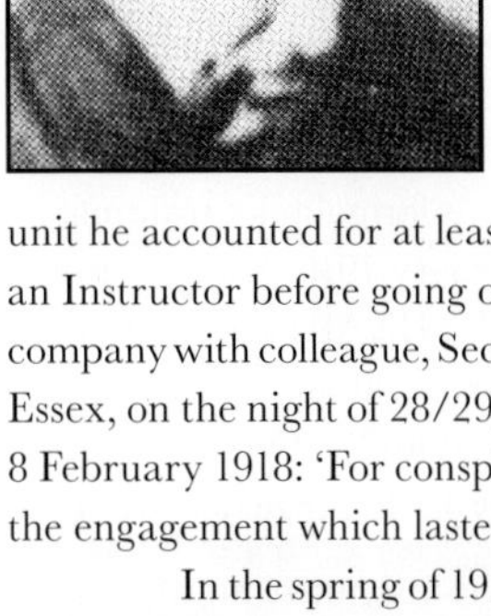

The youngest son of Mr and Mrs William Hall, of Berkfell, Helensburgh, Scotland, he was born in 1892. Educated at Dunoon Grammar School, at the Hermitage School, and at Hillhead High School, where he excelled at Maths and Science. After leaving school, he joined the firm of Paterson and Benzie, Chartered Accountants, of Glasgow. Volunteering his services as soon as the war came, he enlisted as a Private soldier into 17 (Commercial) Battalion, Highland Light Infantry in October 1914. Picked out for a commission, he was gazetted Second Lieutenant to 9 (Dumbartonshire) Battalion, Argyll and Sutherland Highlanders on 17 April 1915. He served in the trenches from July 1915, but secured a transfer to the RFC in the following November. He trained first as an Observer, and was sent out to Vickers FB5-equipped 18 Squadron as a Probationary in December 1915. On 19 December 1915, Hall and his Pilot of the day, Second Lieutenant M LeBlanc-Smith, in Vickers FB5, '5618', 'saw off' an intruding LVG over Ginchy. His tour with '18' completed, he returned to the UK in the summer of 1916, to train as a Pilot. His training duly completed, he was confirmed and gazetted Flying Officer on 22 September following. Sent out to the DH4-equipped 57 Squadron on 10 July 1917, he achieved six victories between 27 July and 28 October, being promoted to A/Captain and Flight Commander on the intervening 31 August. On 20

November 1917, the opening day of the Battle of Cambrai, he and his Observer, Irishman Lieutenant Edward Patrick Hartingan, Royal Munster Fusiliers, in DH4, 'A7586', were posted as 'Missing'. Their machine was later found crashed at Les Alleux, with both crewmen dead. Hall's MC was announced posthumously in the *London Gazette* of 26 November 1917, details in the *Gazette* of 6 April 1918: 'For conspicuous gallantry and devotion to duty. While leading back his formation of five machines from a bombing raid, he was himself attacked on eight different occasions by numerous enemy scouts. He himself shot down one in flames and another out of control, while his observer shot down two in flames. He has at all times completed the task alloted to him, and set a splendid example'.

David Hall is buried in Longuenesse (St Omer) Souvenir Cemetery, France.

HALL, Durham Donald George

The only son of D D G Hall and Mrs Ethel Hall (later Gaskell), of London, he was born on 5 January 1898. Educated at Charterhouse. Gazetted Second Lieutenant to 3 Battalion, Yorkshire Regiment (Green Howards), on 9 May 1915. Seeking secondment to the RFC, he successfully gained his Royal Aero Club Certificate (Number 2052) on 29 October 1915. After completing his formal pilot training, he was confirmed and gazetted Flying Officer on 16 February 1916. Sent out to the BE2e-equipped 9 Squadron in France on 10 March 1916. His MC was announced in the *London Gazette* of 11 December 1916: 'For conspicuous gallantry in action. He has flown in the worst of weather and often at very low altitudes. On one occasion he flew very low under heavy fire from the ground, in order to range our artillery'.

Hall would, subsequently, be presented with the insignia of his MC by the King at an investiture held at Buckingham Palace on 15 January 1918. His tour with '9' ended, he returned to the UK in May 1917, to take up instructing posts at the CFS and with various training squadrons. Promoted Captain and Flight Commander on 27 January 1918, he accompanied, as a 'founder member', the newly formed Camel-equipped 80 Squadron to France. During a patrol on 26 March 1918, Hall's Camel, 'B9179', was shot up over Albert. Badly injured, he was taken to hospital, but died on the following day. Durham Hall is buried in Doullens Communal Cemetery Extension No 1, Somme, France.

HALL, Robert Norwood

Born in Natal, South Africa, on 17 May 1888. A farmer and a pre-war volunteer, he joined the Natal Carabineers in 1909. Promoted to Sergeant on 19 April 1915. After service in South Africa, Hall travelled to England where he enlisted as a Gunner (Number 135726) into the Royal Field Artillery on 2 March 1916. Picked out for a commission, he was gazetted Second Lieutenant to the Royal Field Artillery on 6 August 1916. Securing a secondment to the RFC soon afterwards, he trained as a Pilot and was confirmed and gazetted Flying Officer on 12 February 1917. Sent out to the Nieuport-equipped 40 Squadron on 14 March 1917. He achieved five victories between 24 April and 15 August 1917, including three balloons on the intervening 7 May. His tour with '40' completed, he returned to the UK and, following a short rest, was posted for service with 44 HD Squadron. His MC was announced in the *London Gazette* of 26 September 1917, details in the *Gazette* of 9 January 1918: 'For conspicuous gallantry and devotion to duty. He has shown consistent fearlessness and determination in attacking hostile aircraft at close range, destroying some and bringing others down out of control. On one occasion he attacked three enemy pilots, bringing two down in flames and leaving the third on fire. To accomplish this he crossed the lines at a height of 20 feet, his machine being severely damaged by machine-gun fire from the ground. His gallantry and skill have on all occasions been most noticeable'.

Hall was heavily involved with the counter-incursion work of 44 Squadron. The night of 28/29 January 1918 was particularly frustrating for him as he actually picked up a raiding German 'Giant' bomber east of Woolwich and then followed it all the way to the coast without once being able to clear disabling jams in his guns. Again, during the following night, he got near to another 'Giant' at 11,000 feet above London. His guns gave him trouble once more and, again, he ineffectually pursued the bomber until it disappeared into the haze. He continued to serve with '44' until May 1918, before then going on to 143 HD Squadron as a Flight Commander. Robert Hall finally relinquished his commission on 1 April 1920. After the war he returned to his home farm Arrochar in South Africa, his father having died in 1917. He married in 1919 and owned a farm near Eston with his brother and later a farm at Mooi River. Bob Hall developed Parkinson's Disease soon after his marriage and he spent the rest of his life with this debilitating illness. He died in 1965.

HALL, Robert William Paylor

From Lancaster, he was born on 19 August 1893. Educated at Grant School, Riversdale, California, USA, and at Edinburgh University (1912-14 and 1918-19), where he studied medicine. A pre-war volunteer, he was gazetted Second Lieutenant into 2 West Lancashire Brigade, Royal Field Artillery (TF), on 19 December 1913. Mobilised with the rest of the TF on 4 August 1914, he was obliged to put his studies 'on hold' for the duration of the war. Hall served in France with 276 Brigade, RFA (TF), from September 1915. Securing a secondment to the RFC, he gained his Royal Aero Club Certificate (Number 4559) on 24 October 1916, the same day that he was formally confirmed and gazetted Flying Officer. Sent out to the BE2e-equipped 9 Squadron in France, just a few days after he qualified for his 'Wings'. On Boxing Day 1916, Hall and his Observer of the day, Second Lieutenant E F W Smith, turned the tables on a Halberstadt that had attacked them during a reconnaissance patrol. After their retaliatory machine-gun fire hit and killed the German Pilot, the uncontrolled machine dived to destruction. Hall was Mentioned in Despatches around this time, *London Gazette* of 16 May 1917. Promoted A/Captain and Flight Commander, he was transferred to the RE8-equipped 52 Squadron on 20 April 1917. On 15 July 1917, Hall and his Observer of the day, Captain G Davies, in RE8, 'A4225', were hit by anti-aircraft fire over Nieuport and forced to crashland, fortunately behind British lines. Davies was unscathed in the incident, but Hall received wounds. His MC was announced in the *London Gazette* of 26 September 1917, details in the *Gazette* of 9 January 1918: 'For conspicuous gallantry and devotion to duty during a period of four days. He succeeded in ranging our guns most successfully and causing considerable damage to the enemy, in spite of being engaged by hostile aircraft in considerable numbers, and exposed to heavy anti-aircraft fire. On another occasion, when his machine had been practically destroyed by an anti-aircraft shell and he had been wounded himself, he displayed wonderful skill and coolness in landing safely behind our lines'.

Returning to the Home Establishment on 18 December 1917, he was allowed, under regulations existing at that time, to return to his medical studies at Edinburgh University, from where he subsequently qualified MB in 1919.

HAMERSLEY, Harold Alan

From Guildford, Western Australia, he was born in nearby Swan, on 6 February 1896. He was commissioned Second Lieutenant into the AIF and served in the Gallipoli campaign in 1915. By 1916, he was a Captain in the AIF, but was content to take demotion to be gazetted Second Lieutenant into the RFC on 23 October 1916. His pilot training duly completed, he was confirmed and gazetted Flying Officer on 18 February 1917. Hamersley was posted to the SE5A-equipped 60 Squadron in September 1917. On the 23rd of the same month, he almost fell victim to Werner Voss when he was caught in the early stages of the great German Ace's famous last fight against overwhelming odds. Hamersley's SE5A was actually damaged by Voss' machine guns but, fortunately, he was able to break away and land safely. That Hamersley's demise would have been a great loss to the RFC is evidenced by the fact that he went on to achieve no less than 13 victories by 30 March 1918, including a 'treble' on that latter day. His MC was announced in the *London Gazette* of 22 June 1918: 'For conspicuous gallantry and devotion to duty. On one occasion whilst leading his patrol he attacked a formation of six enemy planes. In the ensuing fight he destroyed two of these machines, one falling in flames and the second crashing to earth, and during the same engagement assisted another officer in destroying a third. In addition to these he has destroyed five hostile machines and driven down three out of control. He is a magnificent pilot, displaying at all times an utter disregard of fear'.

Hamersley stayed on in the RAF after the war, serving again with 60 Squadron in India between 1920-22. He was, for a time, a Test Pilot with the Avro Company, holding an altitude record in a machine powered by an Austin Seven car engine! Promoted to Squadron Leader in March 1935, he was posted to Worthy Down, becoming involved in the development of aviation engineering. Later, he was promoted to Wing Commander. In 1938, he was appointed CO, University of London Air Squadron. Two years later in 1940, he commanded RAF Hullavington, before, later in the war, becoming President of the Aircrew Selection Board in Scotland. He died in December 1967.

HAMILTON, Herbert James

The second son of Jeweller, Arthur Ernest Hamilton and Mrs Hamilton, of 59 Ridge Road, Stroud Green, Middlesex, he was born on 30 April 1895. Educated at the Stationers' Company School, London. A pre-war volunteer, he enlisted as a Private soldier (Number 1238) into 28 Battalion, London Regiment (Artists Rifles). Mobilised on 4 August 1914, he accompanied his battalion to France on 28 October 1914, thus earning the 1914 Star. Picked out for a commission, he was gazetted Second Lieutenant to 1 Battalion, Duke of Cornwall's Light Infantry, on 29 August 1915. Hamilton served on the Somme with the Duke of Cornwall's Light Infantry for nearly six months before securing a secondment to the RFC. Having trained as an Observer, he was sent out as a Probationary to the FE2b-equipped 20 Squadron in March 1916. His 'apprenticeship' satisfactorily completed, he was confirmed and gazetted Flying Officer (Observer) on 4 May 1916. His tour with '20' completed, he subsequently trained as a Pilot and was given his full 'Wings' on 30 August 1916, before going on to instruct at Montrose. Following this spell of instructing, during which time he amassed 500 flying hours, he joined the Nieuport-equipped 1 Squadron at the front in August 1917. Hamilton claimed one victory with '1' on 2 October and was then transferred to 29 Squadron as a Flight Commander. After two more victories flying Nieuport Scouts, he was posted back again to 1 Squadron in March 1918. Now flying SE5As, he took part in many ground-strafing attacks during the German spring offensive, as well as gaining three further victories. On 26 March 1918, he was forced down by a Fokker Triplane, but survived the experience. Returning to the Home Establishment soon after this, he was killed in a flying accident in Sopwith Camel, 'C158', of 68 TDS at Tadcastle, Yorkshire on 13 June 1918, when the port wing broke up at 2,000 feet. His MC was announced posthumously in the *London Gazette* of 26 July 1918: 'For conspicuous gallantry and devotion to duty. He has on many occasions displayed the utmost dash and fearlessness in engaging enemy aircraft at close range, and has succeeded in destroying a considerable number. He also attacked with machine-gun fire, and from low altitudes, enemy formations on the ground, and dropped bombs on points of importance behind the hostile lines. He has invariably shown great determination and a fine offensive spirit'.

Herbert Hamilton is buried in Islington Cemetery, London.

NB: Hamilton's medals were offered for sale by Spink (lot 317) on 8 December 1988: MC (reverse engraved: Capt Herbert J Hamilton RFC. Over Comines 12/10/17 to 26/3/18*), 1914 Star* (Pte No 1238, 28 London Regt)*, British War Medal 1914-20, and Victory Medal 1914-19* (Capt RAF).

HAMILTON, Robert

From Newington, Edinburgh, he was born on 4 July 1895. Gazetted Second Lieutenant into 3 Highland Cyclists Battalion (TF) on 28 May 1915. Seconded to the RFC, he was confirmed and gazetted Flying Officer (Observer) on 27 October 1916. His MC was announced in the *London Gazette* of 11 May 1917: 'For conspicuous gallantry and devotion to duty as an Observer. He carried out a successful artillery observation on a hostile battery in very adverse weather. He worked for two and a half hours at a height of 1,500 and 3,000 feet under very heavy fire. On another occasion, whilst engaged in photography, he drove off three hostile scouts and completed his work'.

Hamilton left the RAF and transferred to the Reserve on 24 October 1922. He enjoyed at least one period of 'hands on' training with 100 Squadron between 3 May and 16 May 1926, before finally relinquishing his commission, with the rank of Flying Officer, on completion of his Reserve services on 24 October 1930.

HAMMOND, Arthur William

From Upton Manor, Essex, he was born in 1890. Gazetted Second Lieutenant to the Royal Engineers on 8 October 1915. Hammond was wounded in France on 3 February 1917. Once recovered, he was seconded to the RFC, and was transferred on 2 May 1917. After training as an Observer, he was sent out to 2 Squadron as a Probationary, before being confirmed and gazetted Flying Officer (Observer) on 10 September following. Despite the poor winter weather, Hammond was soon heavily involved in the photo-reconnaissance work required of his squadron. He was slightly wounded on 3 December 1917, but was soon back in the thick of the action. On 18 February 1918, Hammond and his Pilot, Captain J Allport (qv), earned their MCs when their AWFK8 was attacked by six enemy scouts. Hammond sent one down in flames and another broke up in the air under his fire. His MC was announced in the *London Gazette* of 22 April 1918: 'For conspicuous gallantry and devotion to duty. When acting as observer on photographic work, though his machine was attacked by six enemy machines, he with great coolness shot down two of these. On two later occasions a large number of hostile battery positions were photographed, engaged and successfully silenced, as well as some of our long-range batteries calibrated on hostile targets. The eminently satisfactory manner in which all these tasks were accomplished is due to this officer's keenness, conscientiousness, and devotion to duty'.

On 27 March 1918, for what transpired to be his last operational flight, he was paired with the 19 year old Second Lieutenant Alan A McLeod, from Winnipeg, in AWFK8, 'B5773', part of a 2 Squadron bombing and strafing mission to the east of Albert. On the way out, they accounted for a Fokker Triplane that crossed their path, but later their formation was attacked by a force of eight Fokker Triplanes. Four of the 2 Squadron Big Acks were sent down in this engagement but, especially in the case of McLeod and Hammond, only after a terrific fight. Despite being agonisingly wounded in the body and legs, Hammond fought his gun to such good effect that two of the attacking Fokkers were sent down, one in flames. McLeod, was also wounded in the leg, and now their machine began to burn. The fire destroyed the floor of the cockpit and even their flying boots were burning. The situation in the cockpit became so desperate that both men had to crawl out onto the fuselage. As the 'Big-Ack' descended, McLeod, standing on the wing root, attempted to maintain control whilst, at the same time, doing all he could to keep the flames off a near-fainting Hammond. His Observer was clinging with both hands to the Scarff ring, quite literally for dear life. At last the 'Big-Ack' crashlanded into no-man's land, with McLeod leaping clear as it did so. Despite five bullet wounds, a shrapnel wound and burns to various parts of his body, he returned to the flaming wreckage of AWFK8, its bomb-load still aboard and intact, to extricate the unconscious Hammond. Dragging him clear, McLeod hoisted the comatose Observer onto his back and staggered off towards the friendly trenches. As he did so, he was hit by a splinter from an exploding shell which caused him to drop Hammond. Now he could only crawl, dragging Hammond foot by foot towards a forward trench and safety. 'Babe' McLeod would be awarded the Victoria Cross, *London Gazette* of 1 May 1918, for his great gallantry in this incident. Apart from burns and bullet wounds, both of Hammond's legs were crushed and broken, one so badly that it had to be amputated. Hammond was awarded a Bar to his MC in the *London Gazette* of 26 July 1918: 'For conspicuous gallantry and devotion to duty in aerial fighting. Whilst attacking hostile troops at about 500 feet he was encountered by eight tri-planes, which dived from all directions, firing their front guns. He fired bursts at each machine in turn, shooting three of them down out of control. He was wounded himself six times, but continued the action until his machine caught fire. The Pilot, though wounded five times, with great skill and coolness managed to climb to the left hand bottom plane and controlled the machine from the side of the fuselage, side-slipping to the ground. The machine crashed in no-man's land, and the Pilot managed to extricate himself from the flames and dragged him to a shell-hole, from which they were rescued by the infantry'. They were shot down by Hans Kirchstein of Jasta 6.

After spending some considerable time in a London hospital, Arthur Hammond was obliged, on 10 October 1919, to relinquish his commission due to his continuing ill-health. Later lived in Winnipeg, Canada.

HAMMOND, Henry

From Crediton, Devon. Educated at King's School, Taunton, where he was a member of the OTC. Gazetted Second Lieutenant to a Regular Army battalion of the Devon Regiment on 4 May 1916, with an immediate attachment to 8 Battalion, Duke of Cornwall's Light Infantry. He served in Salonika with the Duke of Cornwall's Light Infantry, before securing a secondment to the RFC in the spring of 1917. Gained his Royal Aero Club Certificate (Number 5128) on 1 June 1917, the same day that he was formally confirmed and gazetted Flying Officer. Posted to the night-bombing, FE2b-equipped 102 Squadron, then in Hingham, on 11 September 1917, he accompanied the unit to France as a 'founder member' just two weeks later. Hammond was badly wounded on 27 November 1917, so badly, in fact, that his left arm had to be amputated. His courage and fortitude on that occasion won him his MC, *London Gazette* of 18 January 1918, details in the *Gazette* of 25 April 1918: 'For conspicuous gallantry and devotion to duty. Having successfully bombed a station behind the enemy lines he was wounded in the arm and fainted. On recovering he again took control, but shortly afterwards lost consciousness once more. His coolness and courage in spite of pain and loss of blood were remarkable. On several occasions he has bombed and derailed trains, and destroyed hangars at hostile aerodromes. He invariably set a fine example of courage and skill'.

Henry Hammond was obliged to relinquish his commission in 1918.

HANDFORD, Leonard Francis

From Willesdon, North London. Gazetted Second Lieutenant to 1/13 (County of London) Battalion, The Kensingtons, on 28 March 1917. Seconded to the RFC in the spring of 1918, he trained as an Observer and was sent out as such to the RE8-equipped 15 Squadron. On 11 April 1918, Handford and his Pilot, Second Lieutenant R G Hart (qv), in RE8, 'B844', were attacked by four enemy Scouts over Contay. Handford used his gun with great effect, shooting down two of the attackers before the RE8's controls were shot away, forcing a crash-landing. Both occupants had been wounded in the air and were further injured in the subsequent crash. The citation for Handford's MC, *London Gazette* of 26 July 1918, graphically describes the events of the day: 'For conspicuous gallantry and devotion to duty. On one occasion, when on patrol, the machine in which he was acting as Observer was attacked from below by four hostile scouts. After he had fired twenty rounds into the nearest scout, the latter burst into flames and crashed in our lines. Despite the fact that he was wounded, and that his gun mounting was put out of action, he continued to fire the remainder of the drum into another hostile scout, which went down out of control, and is confirmed to have crashed in the enemy's lines. The destruction of these two hostile machines was in a great degree due to his gallantry and determination in carrying on with his task under circumstances of great difficulty and danger'.

Hart, too, was also awarded the MC for this action. The wounds Handford received on 11 April 1918 were of such severity that he was obliged to relinquish his commission on 21 December.

HANMAN, John Leo Stanley

From Birmingham, he was born on 19 February 1891. Educated at Cotton Hall School, Oakmoor, North Staffordshire. From August 1913, he worked as an Engineer for Williamson, Balfour and Company, in Conception, Paraguay. Having left his job, he returned to the UK in August 1916, one of the many British Latin American Volunteers. He joined the Inns of Court OTC (Number B/10112) on 4 December 1916, before entering the RFC as a Cadet on 13 March 1917. Gazetted Second Lieutenant to the RFC on 20 April 1917. Having trained as an Observer, he was sent out to an RE8 Squadron as a Probationary on 8 June 1917. His 'apprenticeship' quickly and satisfactorily completed, he was confirmed and gazetted Flying Officer (Observer) on 14 June following. Hanman next trained as a Pilot and, after qualifying for his full 'Wings', was sent out to 12 Squadron, a unit also equipped with RE8s. On 21 March 1918, the first day of the German spring offensive, Hanman and his Observer of the day, Lieutenant C R Cuthbert (qv), on a contact patrol over Croisilles in RE8, 'B833', spotted a large concentration of enemy troops upon whom they were able to bring down the wrath of the Royal Artillery, as the citation for his MC, *London Gazette* of 22 June 1918, testifies: 'For conspicuous gallantry and devotion to duty. While on contact patrol he and his Observer, noticing the enemy massing for an attack, sent down the call to open fire, with the result that the enemy was sent back to their trenches. This was done on two later occasions, until finally the enemy was repulsed, having suffered heavy casualties. A hostile two-seater plane was then attacked, with the result that the latter dived very steeply with smoke issuing from it. His consistent gallantry and good work have proved invaluable'.

Research has unearthed the original recommendation for this award, which provides some further detail: '3rd Brigade HQ, RAF, 1 April 1918 [the first day of the new RAF's existence]. For consistent gallantry and good work during the recent operations, March 21st to March 31st, 1918. Lieutenant Cuthbert, with 2nd Lieutenant Hanman as pilot, has shown the greatest gallantry and skill during the recent battle. They have together completed many successful contact patrols at a very low altitude under heavy fire from rifles and machine guns. On March 24th, while on contact patrol over St Leger and flying at 500 feet, they observed the enemy massed for an attack. An SOS call was sent, which was answered, and the enemy were driven back to their trenches. Ten minutes later another concentration was seen, and another SOS call sent with the same result; fifteen minutes later the enemy massed again and another SOS call was sent, and the enemy heavily engaged by our artillery. They were dispersed with heavy casualties. Both pilot and observer attacked these troops with machine-gun fire from 500 feet, entirely breaking up the enemy attack, which never reached our trenches. Lieutenant Cuthbert and 2nd Lieutenant Hanman then attacked an enemy two-seater which appeared, apparently to do contact patrol with the enemy. After a good burst from Lieutenant Cuthbert's gun the enemy aeroplane dived very steeply, with smoke issuing from the fuselage. He was followed down to 50 feet, and was then lost sight of in the mist, and is believed have crashed near Croisilles'.

Cuthbert, too, was awarded the MC for these actions. John Hanman continued to serve with 12 Squadron until 5 February 1919, when he returned to the UK for subsequent demobilisation.

HANNING, John Edward

From New Brunswick, Canada, he was gazetted Lieutenant to the Canadian Engineers on 23 January 1917. Volunteering for secondment to the RFC, he reported for Observer training in July 1917. Confirmed and gazetted Flying Officer (Observer) on 11 September 1917, he was sent out to the RE8-equipped 59 Squadron in the following month. The incident for which he was awarded his MC occurred on 27 March 1918, when he and his Pilot, Second Lieutenant W L Christian, in RE8, 'B7722', were attacked over Bois D'Aveluy by Leutnant Johann Janzen of Jasta 6. The German's fire shot away the RE8 pilot's controls. Despite being wounded in the leg, Hanning contrived to use a dual control to bring the machine back to the British lines. The citation for Hanning's MC, *London Gazette* of 22 June 1918, not only describes the circumstances of the incident but also credits him with bringing down an enemy machine (whoever Hanning's victim was, it certainly was not Johann Janzen, for, after claiming Christian and Hanning's RE8 as his fourth victory, the German Ace went on to gain a further nine): 'For conspicuous gallantry and devotion to duty. When an observer on patrol he was endeavouring to shoot down a hostile balloon, he was at once attacked by a hostile scout. Although his machine-gun was on two occasions put out of action, and though he himself was wounded in the leg, he succeeded in firing a long burst into the enemy machine, the pilot of which collapsed in his seat, his machine spinning to the ground. The controls of his own machine were so badly damaged that his pilot could not fly it. He therefore fitted a dual control and succeeded in bringing the machine back to our lines and landing it safely. His great courage, skill, and determination undoubtedly saved his pilot's life'.

Following treatment in hospitals in France and in the UK, John Hanning was sent home to Canada on 30 June 1918, for convalescence. He finally relinquished his commission on 31 March 1919.

HARDING, Geoffrey Parker

The son of Mr and Mrs Harding, of 42 Hardy Street, Blackheath, London SE. He was gazetted Second Lieutenant to 1 Battalion, Cheshire Regiment, on 17 February 1915. On the night of 6/7 December 1915, he led a raid on the enemy's trenches south of Mametz, a raid which would subsequently be regarded as a classic of the genre. The raiding party consisted of three officers, two of whom outranked Harding, but nevertheless agreed to be subservient to him for the duration of the raid, and 50 men. Harding led the incursion into the German trenches with great panache, killing a number of the enemy and bringing back a prisoner for interrogation. The Cheshire's casualties were one man seriously wounded (he subsequently died) and seven others slightly wounded. For his gallantry, Harding was awarded the first ever MC won by the 1 Cheshires, *London Gazette* of 22 January 1916. Seconded to the RFC, he was subsequently formally confirmed and gazetted Flying Officer (Observer) on 11 February 1917. Posted to France and 25 Squadron on 30 April 1917, he was unfortunate enough to be shot down and taken prisoner during his first operational flight on the following day. Harding and his Pilot, Lieutenant G S French, in FE2b, 'A815', were shot down in flames by Kurt Wolff, the 29 of the German Ace's eventual 33 victories. On his return from prison camp, Geoffrey Harding recorded the events of the day he was captured: 'We had just pulled off our bombs and were doing a recce of the German positions when we saw another FE, apparently in difficulties with two German machines on its tail. We turned our attention to these machines and engaged them while the other FE got away. Within a few seconds we were surrounded by eight other planes, making ten in all, headed by a red machine which the Germans told us afterwards was piloted by Captain Baron von Richthofen. We were flying at 7,000 feet at the time and the red machine which was well above and behind us, dived at us and put an explosive bullet in our petrol tank which set us on fire. My pilot, although he was getting badly burnt, dived vertically for the ground and made an excellent landing. Both of us got out of the machine safely and were then surrounded by about 2,000 Germans of the 69th Regiment. No Germans approached the machine until it had burnt itself out. My pilot, Lieutenant French, behaved splendidly throughout and it is entirely owing to his presence of mind that we managed to get to earth. My late CO, Lt.Col Cherry, has since told me that the machine we rescued did not belong to 25 Squadron and he thought that it was probably a captured FE2b used by the Germans as a decoy'.

In fact, of course, there is no evidence that the Germans ever used any captured aircraft as 'decoys'. The reference to Manfred von Richthofen is interesting. Every 'red' aeroplane in the Imperial German Air Service was, it seems, piloted by the Red Baron! Von Richthofen was far away from the action on 1 May, on his way home on leave to Germany, in fact. Harding's Pilot, Gerald French, was much more succinct in his recollection of events: 'Shot down in flames by EA, slightly burned. Bomb Raid'.

Harding was, unexceptionally it has to be said, a reluctant prisoner of war, but what was quite exceptional, was that he was able to do something about it. He not only escaped, but also managed to get himself all the way home to England, arriving there on 22 October 1917. Following a lengthy period of leave, Harding returned to the RFC in February 1918, this time to train and qualify as a Pilot. He was not sent overseas again before finally departing the RAF to return to his Cheshire Regiment origins on 19 September 1919. His bravery and ingenuity in escaping his captors was recognised by the award of a Bar to his MC, the announcement of which appeared in the 'Escapers Gazette', the *London Gazette* of 16 December 1919. Harding was also Mentioned in Despatches during his service in the Great War. He wrote of his experiences in 'Escape Fever', published circa 1932 (Hamilton). Geoffrey Harding would subsequently rise to the rank of Brigadier and be awarded the CBE and the DSO. He was also appointed Colonel of his beloved Cheshire Regiment, from 1947 to 1950.

HARDY, Philip

The son of Mr and Mrs Hardy, of 1 Park Lea Road, Roker, Sunderland, he was born on 27 October 1898. Educated at the Bede Collegiate School, Sunderland. After leaving school, he was an apprentice in the Fitting Shop of the Erecting and Drawing Office of the North East Marine Engineering Company, Sunderland. A pre-war part-time member of the Coast Guard, he was, in August 1914, sent to Cornwall as an Admiralty Coast Guard Scout. His request to join the flying service was granted in May 1917 and he was ordered to report to the RFC as an Officer Cadet on 27 June following. Gazetted Second Lieutenant to the RFC, via the General Lists, on 13 September 1917. Having trained as an Observer, he accompanied, as a 'founder member', the newly formed and AWFK8-equipped 82 Squadron to France on 15 November 1917. Hardy was wounded in the foot during a patrol on 29 March 1918, a period when the German spring offensive was still in full swing. His MC was announced in the *London Gazette* of 22 June 1918: 'For conspicuous gallantry and devotion to duty. He carried out a most successful contact patrol under very adverse conditions. Though he was wounded in the foot he continued the reconnaissance and caused many casualties to enemy infantry by his machine-gun fire. He has always set a splendid example of courage and skill'.

His tour completed, he returned to the Home Establishment in June 1918, never again to return to operational flying. Hardy left the RAF, via the Unemployed List, in October 1919 but was, for some unknown reason, offered and accepted a short-lived short service commission later in the same year.

HARKER, Howard Redmayne

The son of Architect, John Dent Harker and Mrs Harker, of Prestwich, Manchester, he was born on 12 May 1891. Educated at Laurence House School, St Annes-on-Sea, at Rossall School (1907-10), and at Manchester University (1910-13), where he was a member of the OTC, and from where he graduated BSc(Eng) with 1st Class Honours. After leaving university, he was employed in the Experimental Department of the Royal Aircraft Factory. Eventually, despite deferment because of important war work, he successfully obtained a commission in the RFC and was consequently gazetted Second Lieutenant, via the General List, on 4 April 1916. Next, on 18 May 1916, he gained his Royal Aero Club Certificate (Number 2945). His formal pilot training duly completed, he was confirmed and gazetted Flying Officer on 22 June following. Harker accompanied, as a 'founder member', the newly formed and FE2d-equipped 57 Squadron to France on 16 December 1916, for fighter reconnaissance duties. On 24 March 1917, he achieved, not only his own, but also 57 Squadron's first victory, in FE2d, 'A1954', with Second Lieutenant V D Fernauld, acting as his Observer. The squadron was re-equipped with DH4s in May 1917 and Harker went on to claim a further four victories between 18 June and 21 August, attaining the rank of A/Captain and Flight Commander in the process. His MC was announced in the *London Gazette* of 9 January 1918: 'For conspicuous gallantry and devotion to duty. For nearly a year he has carried out extremely valuable work in taking aeroplane photographs and leading bombing raids far behind the enemy lines, often in the face of great opposition and trying weather conditions. On a recent occasion while returning from a successful bombing raid his formation was attacked by more than twice its number but by his fine offensive spirit and skilful leadership the enemy were dispersed. He has consistently set a splendid example to his brother officers'.

His tour with '57' completed, he returned to the Home Establishment on 31 August 1917. He was next appointed Acting Squadron Commander of 3 ITS. He also instructed at No 2 School of Navigation and Bomb Dropping, RAF, for which services he would subsequently receive a Mention in Despatches, posthumously announced in the *London Gazette* of 27 May 1919. Harker tragically succumbed to the then raging Spanish 'flu pandemic, dying in Tidworth Barracks Hospital, on 27 February 1919. He is buried in Manchester Southern Cemetery, Lancashire.

NB: His medals were offered for sale by Christie's (lot 169) on 19 July 1988: MC, British War Medal 1914-20, and Victory Medal 1914-19 (Captain, RFC).

HARMAN, Herbert Donald

The son of Mr and Mrs Harman, of 65 Sinclair Road, West Kensington, London W14, he was born on 27 August 1895. He was studying at university when war came in August 1914. Volunteering immediately, he enlisted as a Private soldier into 13 Battalion, Gloucestershire Regiment, and rose quickly to the rank of Sergeant, before being picked out for a commission. Gazetted Second Lieutenant to his own battalion on 19 February 1915. He served in the trenches from March 1916, but then secured a secondment to the RFC in the summer. Gained his Royal Aero Club Certificate (Number 3820) on 25 September 1916, the same day that he was formally confirmed and gazetted Flying Officer. Sent to 100 Squadron at Higham soon after he qualified for his 'Wings', he subsequently accompanied, as a 'founder member', that first night-bombing unit to France on 14 February 1917. His MC was announced in the *London Gazette* of 18 October 1917, details in the *Gazette* of 7 March 1918: 'For conspicuous gallantry and devotion to duty. He has taken part in thirty-eight night bombing raids and has successfully attacked aerodromes, doing considerable damage. He has invariably displayed great gallantry and determination'.

Harman would be presented with the insignia of his MC by the King at an investiture held at Buckingham Palace on 16 March 1918. His tour with '100' completed, he returned to the Home Establishment on 30 December 1917. Following a period of leave, he was posted as an Instructor to 199 (N) TS in February 1918. Harman helped to raise the newly forming SE5-equipped 145 Squadron between March and May 1918, before returning to instructing in the UK. He finally left the RAF, via the Unemployed List, on 17 April 1919, his services as an Instructor recognised by a Mention in Despatches, *London Gazette* of 29 August 1919. Harman was recalled, for some unknown reason, on a short service commission from April 1921 to June 1921.

HARPER, William Eardley

The son of the Reverend Canon James Webber Harper, MA, and Mrs Harper, of The Rectory, Leven, Scotland, he was born in Fife on 17 July 1896. Educated at Glenalmond (1909-14) and at Birmingham University, from where he eventually would, in 1924, graduate LDS. Interrupting his studies as soon as war came, he was gazetted Second Lieutenant to 3 (Reserve) Battalion, Durham Light Infantry, on 15 August 1914. Securing a secondment to the RFC in May 1916, he trained as an Observer and was sent out as a Probationary to the FE2b-equipped 25 Squadron in France on 17 June 1916. Harper was slightly injured on 8 August when his machine crashed in fog, receiving treatment at No 23 Casualty Clearing Station. On 24 August 1916, he was formally confirmed and gazetted Flying Officer (Observer) and, on this same day, Harper and his Pilot, Lieutenant M T Baines, in FE2b, 702', received a direct hit from anti-aircraft fire and were forced down near to Armentières, the wreck being shelled to smithereens. Fortunately, although both men were wounded, they were helped to safety by Tommies, before an artillery barrage descended onto the stricken machine. Harper's MC was announced in the *London Gazette* of 22 September 1916: 'For conspicuous gallantry and skill in many aerial combats and notably, when acting as Gunner/Observer, his machine, with two others, met six hostile aeroplanes. He at once attacked, and shot down one machine. He then attacked and drove down a second one. A thick fog came on and in landing his machine was wrecked and he was badly cut and shaken. He managed to walk two miles to his aerodrome and to deliver his report before collapsing'.

Harper's injuries inhibited a return to active service and hence he was gazetted an Equipment Officer 3rd Class, on 7 May 1917. He was posted to the Air Ministry Staff in April 1918 and subsequently confirmed as a Staff Officer 3rd Class on 1 March 1919. He was Mentioned in Despatches on one occasion during the Great War. Harper finally left the RAF due to ill-health as a result of active service, on 1 May 1920. Taking up his studies again at Birmingham University, he qualified as a Dentist in 1923. William Harper lived, in the 1920s, at Dunimark Castle, Culross, Fife.

HARRISON, Anthony Cecil Boris

Originally from Buckinghamshire, he was living in Wimbledon, when he was gazetted Second Lieutenant from the Royal Military College Camberley to 3 (Reserve) Battalion, Oxfordshire and Buckinghamshire Light Infantry on 16 August 1916. Securing a secondment to the RFC in the early weeks of the New Year of 1917, he trained as a Pilot and was confirmed and gazetted Flying Officer on 3 May 1917. His MC was announced in the *London Gazette* of 18 February 1918, details in the *Gazette* of 18 July 1918: 'For conspicuous gallantry and devotion to duty. He carried out two very successful long-distance photographic reconnaissances under most difficult weather conditions. On one occasion while on patrol he was attacked by two enemy aeroplanes; he drove one of them down in a damaged condition and completed his reconnaissance. He has taken part in many bombing raids and photographic reconnaissances and has set a most valuable example of consistent courage and determination to his squadron'.

Staying on in the RAF after the war, he was granted a permanent commission on 1 August 1919. By the commencement of the Second World War in September 1939, he had attained the rank of Wing Commander. Anthony Harrison served throughout the war, retiring in 1946 with the rank of Group Captain.

HARRISON, Charles Philip

Born in London on 27 July 1888, he was working as a Mining Engineer and Mechanical Draughtsman in South Africa in the years 1910-14. He served with the South African Forces in German West Africa for nine months, before travelling to the UK, where he was gazetted Second Lieutenant to the Royal Engineers on 19 November 1915. Harrison served in France with the Sappers before being seconded to the RFC on 1 November 1917. After training as an Observer, he was sent out to France as a 'founder member' of 98 Squadron (DH9s), in April 1918. Harrison achieved five victories between 21 April and 18 July 1918, thus becoming a Gunner Ace. On the intervening 8 May, Harrison and his Pilot, Second Lieutenant N C Macdonald, in DH9, 'C6108', were involved in a mass 'dog-fight' involving 20 enemy aircraft. After accounting for an Albatros DV down in flames, they were themselves shot up. The Pilot, wounded in the air, was slipping in and out of consciousness. Harrison, despite not having any formal piloting experience, somehow contrived to get the DH9 down reasonably intact. His MC was announced in the *London Gazette* of 16 September 1918: 'For conspicuous gallantry and devotion to duty. This officer was acting as Observer when his pilot was severely wounded. He opened fire and shot down the enemy aeroplane, which fell in flames. He then took control of his own machine, which was very badly damaged, his pilot being *hors de combat*, and not withstanding complete inexperience in piloting a machine he managed to bring it safely back to an aerodrome. His skill and courage undoubtedly saved his pilot's life, and prevented the machine from falling into the hands of the enemy'.

His tour with '98' completed, he returned to the Home Establishment in July 1918, where he saw out the war. His gallantry attracted two further awards in addition to his MC: the French gave him the Croix de Chevalier of the Légion d'Honneur, *London Gazette* of 30 November 1918, and later a Croix de Guerre, *London Gazette* of 21 September 1919. Sent to the Armaments School in Rhodesia in May 1919, he finally left the RAF, via the Unemployed List, on 14 June 1919. Harrison later returned to his mining job in Salisbury, Rhodesia.

HARRISON, William Leeming

The son of Dr and Mrs William Spencer Harrison, of 63 Annette Street, Toronto, Ontario, Canada, he was born 30 December 1897. Educated at St Andrew's College, Toronto (1913-16). He had served as a Home Service volunteer with 9 Mississauga Horse before enlisting, age 19, into 220 York Rangers, Overseas Battalion, on 3 April 1916. Next, on 21 November 1916, he was gazetted Second Lieutenant (on probation) to the RFC, via the Special Reserve, whilst still in Canada. Having trained as a Pilot in England, he was confirmed and gazetted Flying Officer on 7 June 1917. Sent out to France, he joined 'C' Flight, 40 Squadron (Nieuports) on 15 July 1917. Early in 1918, the squadron was re-equipped with SE5As and Harrison blossomed as a consequence. By the spring of the New Year, he had achieved 11 victories and had been promoted to the rank of A/Captain and Flight Commander. In a letter home, he said that the personnel of his squadron had changed three times since he joined and that only himself and an Equipment Officer remained. A transfer to 1 Squadron (SE5As), also as a Flight Commander, came on 10 April 1918. It was with this unit that he achieved what would prove to be his 12th and final victory. On 12 April 1918, Harrison was wounded in an aerial combat, but still managed to get his machine down safely. His MC was announced in the *London Gazette* of 13 May 1918: 'For conspicuous gallantry and devotion to duty in aerial fighting. He destroyed two enemy machines and drove down others out of control. He always showed a splendid spirit of dash, keenness and tenacity, coupled with determination and skill in attacking enemy aircraft'.

He was unable to return to operational flying before the end of the war, and returned home to Canada early in 1919. Bill Harrison died in Canada in 1960.

HARROW-BUNN, Arnold Lawson

The son of Mr and Mrs A Harrow-Bunn, of 'Avenham', College Road, Buxton, Derbyshire, he was born in Chorlton-cum-Hardy, Lancashire, on 11 May 1896. Educated at Repton School (1910-14). Weeks after leaving school, he was gazetted Second Lieutenant to 12 Battalion, Sherwood Foresters (Pioneers), on 20 September 1914. He served in the trenches with his unit from 29 August 1915, before securing a secondment to the RFC in the summer of 1916. Having trained as an Observer, he was sent out as a Probationary to FE2b-equipped 11 Squadron on 20 September 1916. His operational 'apprenticeship' satisfactorily completed, he was formally confirmed and gazetted Flying Officer (Observer) on 15 November following. On 22 November 1916, Harrow-Bunn and his Pilot, Captain Davey, attacked an LVG in the vicinity of Arras. Harrow-Bunn poured 2¼ double drums of Lewis gun ammunition into the enemy machine before it crashed into the British lines near Arras. On the following day, Harrow-Bunn was wounded in the face by anti-aircraft fire during a photo-reconnaissance. Following medical treatment in France, he was sent home to England for further attention. His MC was announced in the *London Gazette* of 10 January 1917: 'For conspicuous gallantry in action. He displayed great courage and determination when acting as Observer to his pilot, and brought down a hostile machine. He has on many previous occasions done fine work'.

Once recovered, Harrow-Bunn served with the Bristol Fighters of 39 HD Squadron, operating out of North Weald, from October 1917 to January 1918. Next, from March to September 1918, he was appointed as an Instructor to the British Aviation Mission in the USA, whose HQ was based at Arcade Buildings, 14th Street and Park Road, Washington DC. Returning to the UK, he formally qualified as a Pilot in September 1918, having had ample opportunity to practise the art during his time at the British Aviation Mission in the US. Harrow-Bunn finally left the RAF in January 1919. He was known to be farming in Nairobi, Kenya, during the 1920s.

HART, Raymond George

From Canterbury, he was born on 28 February 1899. Educated at the Simon Langton School, Canterbury. Gazetted Second Lieutenant to the RFC on 24 May 1917. Having trained as a Pilot, he was duly confirmed and gazetted Flying Officer on 4 December following. Sent out to 15 Squadron (RE8s) in France soon after qualifying for his 'Wings'. On 11 April 1918, Hart and his Observer, Second Lieutenant Handford (qv) in RE8, 'B844', were attacked by four enemy Scouts. Almost as soon as the fight started, the RE8's elevator and aileron controls were shot away. Despite this immense handicap and despite being out-numbered, Hart and his Observer fought back ferociously. Handford hit one of the EA's wings which immediately broke off. By this stage in the action, both RFC men were wounded but continued to fight, forcing another of the enemy machines down out of control. The graphically worded citation for Hart's MC does their desperate fight justice, *London Gazette* of 26 July 1918: 'For conspicuous gallantry and devotion to duty. On one occasion, when on patrol, his machine, of which he was the Pilot, was attacked from below by four hostile scouts. Though he himself was wounded, and his machine seriously damaged by the first burst of fire from the enemy machines, he continued to manoeuvre his machine so skilfully that his Observer was able to send down in flames the nearest hostile scout and to drive down out of control a second enemy machine. Despite the fact that one enemy plane continued to attack him, he succeeded in landing his machine. The destruction of these two hostile machines was in a great degree due to his gallantry and determination in manoeuvring his machine when almost out of control'.

Handford, too, received the MC for his part in this action. Raymond Hart may well have been the youngest recipient of a 'flying' MC during the Great War. Hart's wounds precluded a return to operational flying and he finally left the RAF, via the Unemployed List, on 14 February 1919.

HARVEY, Robert Parsons

The son of Colonel John Robert Harvey, DSO, JP, and Mrs Florence Harvey (née Parsons), of Holmwood, Thorpe Hamlet, Norwich, Norfolk. Robert's father was Mayor of Norwich in 1902-03. A pre-war volunteer, Robert was gazetted Second Lieutenant to 4 Battalion, Norfolk Regiment (TF), on 14 June 1913. Robert's father would, as CO, take the 4 Norfolks to Gallipoli in 1915. Before that happened, however, Robert secured a transfer to 5 Lancers. He then secured a further secondment early in 1916, this time to the RFC. He gained his Royal Aero Club Certificate (Number 2766) on 10 April 1916. Having then completed his formal pilot training, he was confirmed and gazetted Flying Officer on 24 May following. Sent out to France and the reconnaissance and photographic-tasked 11 Squadron, in June 1916. On 20 October 1916, Harvey in FE2b, '7674', with Second Lieutenant George Keith Welsford, acting as his Observer, was attacked by no less an opponent than Hauptmann Oswald Boelcke of Jasta 2, with the almost inevitable outcome. Under the German maestro's relentless assault, Welsford, a 25 year old from Iver Heath, Buckinghamshire, was seen to leap or fall from the 'FE', his remains never to be found. Harvey, wounded in the air, stayed with the stricken machine, which crashed to the ground south of Arras, the 36th of Boelcke's eventual 40 victories. The wounded and injured Harvey was recovered from the wreck by the infantry and carried away for what would prove to be extensive and extended medical treatment. His MC was announced in the *London Gazette* of 14 November 1916: 'For conspicuous gallantry in action. He attacked four hostile machines with great courage and skill, his Observer shooting one of them down. He has on many previous occasions done very fine work'.

Harvey did not return to the RFC, but was, in fact, retained by the Army beyond the cessation of hostilities with the rank of Second Lieutenant and a Half-Pay Officer on the Active List.

HARVEY, William James

Born in Hammersmith, London, on 15 July 1888, his family later moving to Clapham, SW. Educated at Battersea Polytechnic College and at King's College, London. After completing his education, he worked as a journalist, but just prior to the outbreak of the war in August 1914, he was employed as Secretary of the Copenhagen Aerodrome in Denmark. Returning to the UK, he enlisted as a Private soldier (Number 649) into 23 Battalion (1 Sportsmans), Royal Fusiliers, on 9 October 1914. Soon picked out for a commission, he was gazetted Second Lieutenant to 4 (Extra Reserve) Battalion, Royal Dublin Fusiliers, on 14 April 1915. Having secured a secondment to the RFC in June 1917, he trained as an Observer and was eventually sent out for night-bombing with the FE2b-equipped 102 Squadron in France on 27 January 1918. Harvey's MC is one of those awarded for solid and persistent gallantry over a long period, *London Gazette* of 22 June 1918: 'For conspicuous gallantry and devotion to duty. During one night he made five consecutive raids over the enemy's lines, during which period he dropped over a half a ton weight of bombs on his four objectives. In addition he fired during these raids 1,150 rounds of ammunition from 100 to 500 feet on hostile infantry and transport. He has proved himself to be a consistently good Observer, and has performed much successful night-bombing'.

His tour with '102' completed, he returned to the Home Establishment on 27 May 1918 and, following a period of rest and recuperation, was posted for duties with the RAF Administration department. He finally left the RAF, via the Unemployed List, on 1 August 1919. William Harvey would subsequently be deprived of his retired rank of Lieutenant as a consequence of receiving a gaol sentence for obtaining money under false pretences on 233 occasions.

HASLAM, James Alexander Gordon

The third son of Mr and Mrs John Bailey Haslam, of 3 Bilton Road, Rugby, he was born on 24 September 1896. Educated at Rugby (1910-13), at Corpus Christi College, Cambridge (1914-15), and at the Royal Military Academy, Woolwich. Gazetted Second Lieutenant to the Royal Field Artillery, on 19 February 1916. Served in France with 125 Brigade, RFA. Securing a secondment to the flying service in 1918, he trained as an Observer and was sent out to AWFK8-equipped 8 Squadron in the spring. On 22 April 1918, Haslam and his Pilot, Lieutenant F M F West (qv) in AWFK 8, 'C8445', narrowly escaped complete disaster when their machine was hit by anti-aircraft fire and forced to crashland. Both occupants were, fortunately, unscathed. West and Haslam proved to be an outstanding team, their efforts recognised, in the first instance, by the award of an MC to both, the announcements for which appeared in the *London Gazette* of 26 July 1918: 'For conspicuous gallantry and devotion to duty. While on patrol, he, with another officer, observed fifteen motor lorries. As these could not be engaged by artillery by zone call, these officers flew 8,000 yards over the enemy lines, at a height of 3,800 feet, in the face of strong opposition from the ground, and dropped four bombs, obtaining direct hits on the lorries and doing considerable damage to their personnel. They then proceeded to attack them with machine-gun fire as they sought cover. A fortnight later they carried out, at a height of 150 feet, a reconnaissance of their Corps front, on which an attack was expected. Despite the fact that the clouds were at 200 feet, and there was a thick mist, they obtained most valuable information. During this flight they directed and located the fire of our artillery on a concentration of enemy infantry. Throughout the operations their work in co-operation with our artillery was always of the greatest value, and their enterprise in attacking enemy troops and transport with bombs and machine-gun fire was splendid'.

The pair had another close call whilst on tank patrol on 9 August 1918. Their AWFK8, 'D5138', was shot about a little near Caix, and this was followed by a 'hard' landing in fog. Nothing daunted, the pair were up again on the following day, this time in AWFK8, 'C8602', on contact patrol with tanks moving on Roye. Having spent some time assessing the strength and dispositions of the enemy in front of the advancing British troops, they were returning to make their report when they were attacked by at least four enemy Scouts. Almost immediately, 'Freddie' West took five explosive bullets into his left leg, effectively shredding the limb. Whilst Haslam did his best to keep their tormentors at bay with his Lewis gun, West, almost fainting with pain and loss of blood, attempted to apply a tourniquet to quench the flow from the partially severed leg and, at the same time, strove to keep control of the 'Big Ack'. Struggling to lift the remains of his left leg out of the way, he was also hit in the right leg. Now Haslam, too, was wounded, but still managed to discourage the enemy with the judicious use of his machine gun. West at last brought the 'Big-Ack' down to an untidy landing in a field close to some Canadian troops. Both airmen were taken to a nearby Casualty Clearing Station, where West evoked widespread admiration by insisting, despite his terrible injuries, on imparting his intelligence report only to an officer qualified to receive it. Ferdinand Maurice Felix West would be awarded the Victoria Cross for his valour on 10 August 1918, *London Gazette* of 8 November 1918. For his part in this 'VC action', Haslam was awarded the Distinguished Flying Cross, *London Gazette* of 3 December 1918, the citation commenting upon his, 'rare courage and determination'. Haslam stayed on in the RAF after the war. In 1925, he served with the BF2b-equipped 5 Squadron in Waziristan, his service acknowledged with a Mention in Despatches, *London Gazette* of 20 November 1925. Retiring from the RAF on 10 June 1927, he decided to resume his war-interrupted studies at Corpus Christi College, Cambridge, going on to graduate BA in 1930. He entered the Aeronautics Department at Cambridge University in 1933, gained an MA in 1934, and was subsequently elected a Fellow of the Royal Aeronautical Society (FRAeS). Haslam served again in the RAF during the Second World War, before retiring with the rank of Group Captain in December 1945. He took Holy Orders in the 1950s. Group Captain James Haslam died at his home, 9 Cavendish Avenue, Cambridge, on 16 November 1990.

HAY, Roger Bolton

The son of the Rector of Garsdon with Lea and Cleverton, the Reverend Reynell Wreford Hay and Margaret Alice Hay, of Garsdon Rectory, Wiltshire, he was born on 13 April 1895. Educated at Dean's Close School, Cheltenham (1906-08), at Blundell's School, Tiverton (caps for cricket, football and gymnastics, member of the OTC), and intending to go on to Queen's College, Cambridge, when the war intervened. Volunteering soon after the war came, he was gazetted Second Lieutenant to 3 (Reserve) Battalion, West Yorkshire Regiment, on 27 January 1915. Eventually securing a secondment to the RFC at the end of 1916, he trained as a Pilot and was duly confirmed and gazetted Flying Officer on 28 March 1917. Sent, on the very day he qualified, to the BE2b-equipped 48 Squadron in France. Hay achieved five victories and the status of Ace, between 23 April and 12 July 1917. On 17 July 1917, Hay and his Observer, Lieutenant O J Partington, in Brisfit, 'A7166', were attacked over Nieuport by enemy aircraft, including one flown by Vizefeldwebel Werner of Jasta 17, who would later claim the victory. Hay, badly wounded in the fight, was forced to land on a beach just short of the lines. Both crewmen were taken to hospital by German troops. Partington would survive to become a prisoner of war, but Hay died of his severe wounds on the same day he received them. Hay's MC was announced posthumously in the *London Gazette* of 26 July 1917: 'For conspicuous gallantry and devotion to duty. On several occasions he has shown the utmost courage and dash in attacking and dispersing hostile aircraft in superior numbers. His wiliness to undertake the most hazardous duties has at times set a fine example to other pilots and observers of his squadron'.

Roger Bolton Hay is buried in Oostende New Communal Cemetery, Oostende, Belgium.

HAYCOCK, Horace

From Walkley, Sheffield, he was born on 4 October 1891. Educated at Sheffield School. He was a student teacher at the Glasgow Institute for the Deaf, before later attending the City of Leeds Training College, Brocket's Park (1912-14). He enlisted as a Private soldier into 15 West Yorkshire Regiment (1 Leeds 'Pals') in September 1914 but, due to chronic rheumatism, was discharged as unfit in March 1915. Haycock taught at the School for the Deaf, Newcastle-upon-Tyne, before moving to a similar establishment in Northampton in September 1915. Determined to try again, he applied for the flying service and was subsequently accepted as a Cadet in June 1916. Gazetted Second Lieutenant to the RFC, via the Special List, on 1 August 1916. His pilot training duly completed, he was confirmed and gazetted Flying Officer on 6 November following. Sent out to the BE2e-equipped 9 Squadron on 30 December 1916. His tour with '9' ended when he was hospitalised on 3 June 1917, before returning to the Home Establishment on 28 June following. He was still suffering with rheumatism and, after several Medical Boards, it was suggested he be sent to a warmer climate. And so it was that following a brief period of Delivery Pilot duties at the Bristol Aircraft Acceptance Park in July 1917, he was sent out in the following month to the newly formed 113 Squadron, then at Ismailia in Egypt. He soon received a Mention in Despatches from General Allenby, *London Gazette* of 14 June 1918. Haycock's time with '113' ending on 6 April 1918, he was next immediately posted to 142 Squadron. In May 1918, he was detached for a very brief spell with 14 Squadron before returning again to '142'. Wounded in action over Jerusalem on 2 July 1918, his MC was announced in the *London Gazette* of 16 September 1918: 'For conspicuous gallantry and devotion to duty. A hostile aeroplane, escorted by four scouts, was reported to be registering an enemy battery, and as no fighting machines were available to drive off the enemy he went up in an artillery machine and sent down a call to our artillery. No reply being received, he descended to a low height and, in spite of the hostile aeroplanes above him, he attacked the enemy battery, which he silenced with machine-gun fire'.

Once recovered, he served with '142' until 16 September 1918. Haycock left the RAF, via the Unemployed List, on 19 November 1919, but was, for some unknown reason, recalled for 'Special Duties' from 11 April 1921 to 4 June 1921. He was living at that time in Margate.

HAYWARD, George Searle Lomax

The son of James and Kate Hayward, of 96 Brownhill Road, Catford, London SE, he was born in Tunbridge Wells, Kent, on 1 November 1894. Served as a Lance Corporal (Number 21746) in 8 Battalion, Royal West Kent Regiment, before being gazetted Second Lieutenant to the same regiment on 28 September 1916. Transferring to the RFC, he trained as an Observer and was sent to 22 Squadron as a Probationary on 30 June 1917. Hayward proved to be an Observer/Gunner of outstanding merit in 22 Squadron, which had many Ace Pilots and Observers. He is credited with no less than 24 victories between 29 November 1917 and 22 April 1918, making him the third highest scoring Gunner/Ace behind Gass (39) and Fletcher (26). 22 Squadron is credited with making the very first sortie mounted by the new service when the RAF was formed on 1 April 1918. Hayward, himself, became one of the first four men to fly in combat for the RAF. The Squadron Record Book shows ten Bristol Fighters taking off at 08.30, followed 10 minutes later by another six. Captain Weare, with Hayward as his regular Observer, took off first; a second Bristol, crewed by Lieutenants Davison and Morgan, following. The historic photographs taken of members of 22 Squadron following their return from this patrol, were the first ever taken of operational members of the RAF. Hayward's MC was announced in the *London Gazette* of 26 July

1918: 'For conspicuous gallantry and devotion to duty. On three separate occasions when engaged with large hostile formations, he has attacked and sent crashing to earth two hostile machines on each occasion. He has displayed consistent skill, courage and determination in dealing with hostile aircraft'.

Hayward died on 16 August 1924, at Digby, Lincolnshire.

NB: His medals were offered for sale by Dix Noonan Webb (lot 482) on 29 November 1996: MC (engraved: Lt. Roy W Kent R & RFC, Vert Galant, March 1918*), British War Medal 1914-20, and Victory Medal 1914-19* (Lieut., RAF).

HAZELL, Tom Falcon

The eldest son of Mr and Mrs Thomas Hazell, of Roundstone, Clifden, County Galway, Ireland, he was born on 7 August 1892. Educated at Tonbridge School (1906-11), where he was a member of the OTC, and at the City and Guilds College (1911-12), where he studied Electrical Engineering and became a member of the University of London OTC. When war came, he immediately enlisted as a Trooper (Number 1149) into the South Irish Horse (Special Reserve). Quickly picked out for a commission, he was gazetted Second Lieutenant to 7 Battalion, Royal Irish Fusiliers, on 10 October 1914. Sent out to join 2 Battalion of his regiment in France in February 1915, he was appointed Transport and Remount Officer. After more than a year in the trenches, Hazell secured a secondment to the RFC. His pilot training duly completed, he was confirmed and gazetted Flying Officer on 5 June 1916. A naturally gifted Pilot, he was first posted as an Instructor at the CFS. His first overseas posting was aborted when, owing to engine trouble en route for France on 30 June 1916, he attempted to land on his old school's playing fields, but crashed through a hedge and into a hop garden, seriously damaging his machine in the process. The propeller-boss from the damaged machine was eventually presented by him to the School Museum and stood for many years in the school corridor. Hazell finally got to France for operational duty with 1 Squadron on 19 December 1916. Flying Nieuport XVIIs, Hazell accumulated no less than 20 victories between 4 March and 16 August 1917, including five 'doubles' and a 'treble' on single days. His MC was announced in the *London Gazette* of 26 July 1917: 'For conspicuous gallantry and devotion to duty. On several occasions he displayed marked courage in attacking and destroying hostile aircraft'.

His tour with '1' completed, he returned to the CFS and instructing. On 26 June 1918, Hazell returned to operational flying, this time to command 'A' Flight, 24 Squadron (SE5As). A further 23 victories (including ten kite balloons) followed between 4 July and 4 October 1918, with five 'doubles' and a 'treble' coming on single days. On 22 August 1918, Tom Hazell fought an aerial battle with Leutnant Ernst Udet, the highest scoring German Ace (62 victories) to survive the war. Udet would claim Hazell as his 60th victory whereas, in fact, Hazell escaped his attentions, just. His SE5A was riddled from stem to stern, the petrol tank, propellor and two longerons left in tatters. In October 1918, Hazell left '24' to command the Camel-equipped 203 Squadron. A Distinguished Flying Cross and Bar were both announced in the same *London Gazette* of 2 November 1918. He was also awarded the Distinguished Service Order, *London Gazette* of 8 February 1919, and Mentioned in Despatches, *London Gazette* of 11 July 1919. Staying on in the RAF after the war, he was granted a permanent commission in August 1919. Hazell served successively with 1 Canadian Wing and 123 Squadron in 1919, returning to the UK and command of 24 Squadron in 1920. Promoted to Squadron Leader on 30 June 1922, he went on to command 45 Squadron and then 55 Squadron in Iraq in 1922 and 1923. He next commanded 111 Squadron in the UK in 1923. Command of 60 Squadron in India followed from 1925 to 1927. Tom Hazell was placed on the Retirement List at his own request on 20 July 1927, returning to live in his native Ireland until his death at Newport, County Mayo, on 4 September 1946.

NB: His outstanding group of medals was offered for sale by Sotheby's on 17 November 2000: Distinguished Service Order, MC, Distinguished Flying Cross & Bar, 1914-15 Star (2Lt R Innis Fus), *British War Medal 1914-20, and Victory Medal 1914-19 with MID* (Major RAF). *The lot realised £33,000 (hammer price).*

HEAD, Bertram

The son of Mr and Mrs Head, of 125 Second Avenue, Little Ilford, Essex, he was born on 25 April 1891. A pre-war volunteer, he was a Corporal (Number 1754) in 12 (County of London) Battalion, The Rangers, when war came in August 1914. Mobilised immediately, he accompanied his battalion to France on 24 December 1914. Picked out as potential officer material, he was inducted into the Inns of Court OTC (Number 6/3/5756) on 21 August 1915. His experience obviously impressed his Instructors as he was quickly commissioned, being gazetted Second Lieutenant to 1/5 Battalion, Northumberland Fusiliers (TF), on 1 October following. Having served in the trenches with the Northumberlands, he eventually secured secondment to the RFC in July 1917. Following training as an Observer, he was sent out to 52 Squadron (RE8s) as a Probationary in August 1917. His 'apprenticeship' satisfactorily completed, he was confirmed and gazetted Flying Officer (Observer) on 10 September following. Head was slightly wounded in the face on 11 November 1917. His exceptional MC was announced in the *London Gazette* of 22 June 1918: 'For conspicuous gallantry and devotion to duty. Whilst on contact patrol with his pilot he accurately located enemy dispositions from a height of 200 feet. When the machine was forced to land owing to his pilot being severely wounded, he succeeded in destroying the machine and bringing his pilot back to safety. He showed marked courage and resource'.

His tour with '52' completed on 6 June 1918, he returned to the UK for rest and recuperation. Bertram Head finally left the service, via the Unemployed List, on 14 February 1919.

HEAVEN, Archibald Cecil

From Newcastle, Northumberland, he was born on 1 December 1896. After leaving school, he worked as a Motorcycle Mechanic in Davidson's Mains, Midlothian, Scotland. Enlisting on 3 May 1915, he served in France as a Lance Corporal (Number 940) in the newly formed Motorised Machine Gun Service, Royal Artillery. Volunteering for the flying service, he was gazetted Second Lieutenant to the RFC, via the Special List, on 5 August 1916. Having trained as an Observer, he was sent out to 8 Squadron in France early in September. His 'apprenticeship' satisfactorily completed, he was confirmed and gazetted Flying Officer (Observer) on 27 October 1916. On 18 March 1917, Heaven and his Pilot, Captain Charles Holland (qv), in BE2e, '5748', were shot about by anti-aircraft fire. Holland was wounded in the hand and unable to steer. Heaven brought the BE back, crashlanding it into the British front-lines, before dragging Holland from the cockpit and carrying him to the nearest shell crater under fire. For this, and other acts of gallantry, Heaven was awarded his MC, *London Gazette* of 18 June 1917: 'For conspicuous gallantry and devotion to duty when acting as an Observer. On one occasion, when his pilot was wounded, he steered the machine back, and landing in front of our front-lines, he assisted his pilot into a shell-hole, and eventually into our own trenches, under continuous rifle fire'.

Heaven survived the Great War, living afterwards in Airesford, Hampshire, then in Weyhill, near Andover, and finally in Chalfont St Peter, before moving to Canada in 1928.

HEGARTY, Herbert George

From County Galway, Ireland, he was born on 31 October 1887. He worked as a Banker before and after his war service. Gazetted Second Lieutenant to the RFC on June 1917. His pilot training duly completed, he was confirmed and gazetted Flying Officer on 8 September 1917. Posted out to the SE5A-equipped 60 Squadron in France at the turn of the year, he soon established himself an outstanding Scout Pilot in an outstanding squadron. Hegarty achieved eight victories between 28 January and 1 July 1918, being promoted A/Captain and Flight Commander on the intervening 13 June. His MC was announced in the *London Gazette* of 16 September 1918: 'For conspicuous gallantry and devotion to duty on offensive patrols. During recent operations he destroyed four enemy machines and drove down two. He is a bold and fearless pilot and has done splendid work'.

His tour with 60 completed, he returned to the Home Establishment in July 1918, where he saw out the remainder of the war as an Instructor.

NB: His medals were offered for sale by Glendining's (lot 412) on 2 March1988: MC, British War Medal 1914-20, and Victory Medal 1914-19 (Capt RAF).

HENDERSON, Eric Joseph

The son of Robert Hugh Henderson, CMG, MLA, and Mrs Henderson, of Johannesburg, South Africa, he was born in 1897. Eric's father, an Irishman from Armagh, had emigrated to South Africa in 1884, and had become the leading citizen of Kimberley when that town was besieged by the Boers during the South African War 1899-1902. Henderson Senior was created CMG for his services during the siege. Eric was gazetted Second Lieutenant to the RFC, via the Special Reserve, on 13 May 1916. His pilot training duly completed, he was confirmed and gazetted Flying Officer on 14 July following. Sent out to the Sopwith Strutters of 70 Squadron in France on 16 August 1916. On 9 September, Henderson escaped with his life when his Strutter, 'A1911', was shot up over the French lines at Bapaume. Henderson's Observer of the day, Second Lieutenant Guy Newsome Cousans, Royal Inniskilling Fusiliers attached RFC, from Kimbolton, Cambridgeshire, was, however, killed in the air. Again, on 21 October, Henderson and his Observer, Second Lieutenant R D Elliot, in Strutter, 'A892', were reported missing in action but, fortunately, turned up late but safe. Four days later on 25 March 1917, Henderson and his Observer, Second Lieutenant John Moir Sim, Gordon Highlanders attached RFC, from Enzie, Banff, in Strutter, 'A2986', were among the many casualties suffered by 70 Squadron over two consecutive days of reconnaissance above the Hindenburg line. 70 Squadron's experiences over these two days were seen as final proof that the Strutter was no longer a match for the contemporary German Scout planes. Henderson's MC was announced posthumously in the *London Gazette* of 4 June 1917 (no citation). Although no formal citation was published in the *Gazette*, research has unearthed the original recommendation for the award: '70 Squadron: Continuous good work of a very high standard. Ten long reconnaissances. On one occasion completing a reconnaissance over Valenciennes when left with one other machine. He has also taken part and shown great gallantry in many aerial combats'.

Eric Henderson is buried in Achiet-le-Grand Communal Cemetery Extension, France.

HENDERSON, George Lockhart Percy

The son of Lieutenant General Sir Edward Henderson (who served on the Air Council until 1918) and Lady Henderson, of 42 Leinster Gardens, Bayswater, London W. Educated at Eton (1902-07) and at Trinity College, Oxford, from where he graduated BA in 1910. When the war came in August 1914, Henderson, along with other former public school boys, volunteered to serve as motor-cycle despatch riders for the Army in France. Enlisting into the Royal Engineers (Number 28976), he was sent to the Western Front in September 1914, thus earning the 1914 Star. Anxious to join the flying service, he gained his Royal Aero Club Certificate (Number 1143) at the London and Provincial School, Hendon, on 31 March 1915. An obvious candidate for a commission, he was gazetted Second Lieutenant to the RFC, via the Special Reserve, on 23 April 1915. His formal pilot training duly completed, he was confirmed and gazetted Flying Officer on 10 June following. Sent out to 3 Squadron, he served with 'A' Flight and flew the Morane N. On 2 December 1915, Henderson, in Morane N, '5067', was involved in an aerial combat over Don with two German two-seaters. One of the Observers in the German machines was armed only with a rifle, but he used it to great effect, shooting Henderson in the face. Almost blinded by blood and in great pain, Henderson broke off the fight. Although his vision was badly obscured, still he managed a safe landing at Auche. His MC was announced in the *London Gazette* of 22 January 1916: 'For conspicuous gallantry and skill. On 28 November 1915, between La Bassée and Lille, after he had driven down one Albatros, he attacked two other hostile machines and, in spite of heavy fire, put them both to flight. Then under anti-aircraft fire he chased two more machines and drove them off. On 2 December, near Don, when on escort to a bombing expedition, he was hit by a bullet in the head in a fight with a German machine. Though partially stunned and half-blinded, he succeeded in bringing his own machine back to his aerodrome'.

His wound re-arranged his facial features somewhat, but, that aside, he recovered sufficiently to continue flying and, indeed, was appointed to command 66 Squadron in England and in France. The great Ace, James McCudden in his book, 'Flying Fury', mentions Henderson several times. For example, he relates how, during an offensive patrol on 26 July 1917, he and Henderson shared hits on a 'V-Strutter'. Henderson's command of '66' came to an end in November 1917, when he attempted a forced landing in a Sopwith Pup. He crashed heavily and, because he was not strapped in, was flung out through the centre bracing wires to safety as the aircraft burst into flames behind him. He broke his nose, again, but thereafter and forever shunned safety belts, claiming that had he worn one, he would have been burnt to death. Once recovered, he was appointed to various training posts, his services recognised by the award of an Air Force Cross, *London Gazette* of 3 June 1919. Henderson was also Mentioned in Despatches on four occasions, *London Gazettes* of 24 February 1917, 7 November 1917, 14 June 1918, and 22 January 1919. Leaving the RAF after the war, he stayed in aviation and became one of the first Pilots employed by Imperial Airways. Later, he tried his hand at designing and building his own aeroplanes with, it has to be said, little success; one being dubbed, 'The Flying Glasshouse'. He also ran his own airline, often ferrying socialites between France and the UK. On 21 July 1930, Henderson was killed whilst piloting one of his own company's aeroplanes over Kent. He crashed bringing back a party of socialites from a weekend of gambling at Le Touquet and Deauville. All on board were killed.

HENDERSON, Ian Henry David

The son of Captain, later to be Major General, Sir David Henderson, KCB, KCVO, DSO, the Commanding General of the RFC, and Mrs, later Lady, Henderson of 2 Carlyle Mansions, Cheyne Walk, Chelsea, London, he was born on 2 October 1896. Educated at the King-Hall Preparatory School, Elmsworth, at Eton, and at Sandhurst. Gazetted Second Lieutenant to a Regular Army battalion of the Argyll and Sutherland Highlanders on 13 January 1915. Having secured a secondment to the RFC in the early summer of 1915, he trained as a Pilot and was duly confirmed and gazetted Flying Officer on 21 August following. He accompanied the BE12s (fitted with the Vickers interrupter gear) of 19 Squadron to France as a 'founder member' on 30 July 1916. Henderson was heavily involved in a series of aerial combats on 24 and 26 August and again on 3 September 1916, his efforts on these occasions earning him his MC, announced in the *London Gazette* of 20 October 1916: 'For conspicuous gallantry and skill on several occasions. He drove down a machine out of control, and two days later dispersed six enemy machines which were attacking his formation. A few days later again he brought down an enemy bi-plane, the Observer being apparently killed. The week after this he attacked and drove down another machine which had wounded his leader. He has also carried out several excellent contact patrols and attacked retiring artillery and a kite balloon'.

Henderson accumulated a total of seven victories during his time with 19 Squadron. After a period of rest and recuperation in the UK, he was, on 23 February 1917, next posted as A/Captain and Flight Commander to 56 Squadron, then at London Colney. Henderson accompanied '56' (SE5s) to France as a 'founder member' on 8 April 1917, and served there briefly before the unit returned to the UK for Home Defence duties on 20 April following. '56' went again to France in July, destined to become one of the greatest Scout squadrons of the Great War. Henderson left the unit on 10 August 1917, replaced by James McCudden, no less. Back in the UK, Henderson became largely involved with training and associated Staff duties. He also, on the occasion of the memorial service for Albert Ball, represented his distinguished father, who was unable to attend in person. On 21 June 1918, Henderson, with Lieutenant Herbert Redler MC (qv), in DH 9, 'D1018', came to grief in a flying accident at Turnberry in Scotland. He is buried in Girvan (Doune) Cemetery, Ayrshire, Scotland.

NB: The RAF Museum Hendon has his medals in its collection: MC, 1914-15 Star, British War Medal 1914-20, and Victory Medal 1914-19.

HENDERSON, Thomas

Gazetted Second Lieutenant to the Royal Engineers (Tyne Electrical Engineers) (TF) on 6 November 1914. Securing a transfer to the RFC, he trained as an Observer and was sent out as a Probationary to Be2c-equipped 10 Squadron in the autumn of 1915. On 10 October, Henderson, as Observer, with Second Lieutenant Lloyd-Williams in the pilot's seat of BE2c, '1720', narrowly escaped disaster when their machine's fuel tank and propellor were hit and damaged by an attacking Albatros. His 'apprenticeship' satisfactorily completed, he was confirmed and gazetted Flying Officer (Observer) on 22 November 1915. Returning to the UK to train as a Pilot at Catterick Bridge, he gained his Royal Aero Club Certificate (Number 2430) on 10 February 1916, and was gazetted Flying Officer on the same day. Sent out to 14 Squadron in the Middle East, he eventually, as a member of 'C' Flight, became part of the 'Arabian Detachment' designated specifically to assist Colonel T E Lawrence, 'Lawrence of Arabia', with the so-called 'Arab Revolt' against the common enemy, the Turks. His MC was announced in the *London Gazette* of 8 August 1917 (no citation). In 1919, after the war was over, Henderson would help Lawrence again, flying him in a 58 Squadron HP 0/400, 'F301', on one leg of a journey back from Paris to Arabia for high level talks. In 1921, Henderson would also be awarded the Hejaz Order of Nahda (4th Class) for his work in the desert, and for his assisting Lawrence in the Arab cause. Henderson was obliged to leave the RAF in 1927, due to ill-health. He died in his native Tyneside on 21 July 1945.

HERRING, Justin Howard

The son of H H Herring, JP, and Mrs Herring, of Wargrave, Berkshire, he was born on 2 July 1889. Educated at Clifton College (1901-07) and at Christ's College, Cambridge. Herring worked as a Tea Planter in Ceylon from 1911 to 1914. He was, from 1912, a member of the locally raised Ceylon Engineering Volunteers. Mobilised at the outbreak of war, he served in the Middle East with the Ceylon Volunteers, until he was picked out for a commission and gazetted Second Lieutenant to the RFC, via the Special Reserve, on 7 June 1915. He married Honor Harrat de Saint around this time. Herring gained his Royal Aero Club Certificate (Number 1430) on 13 July 1915 and was formally confirmed and gazetted Flying Officer on the same day. Sent out to France for reconnaissance duties with BE2c-equipped 8 Squadron on 22 September 1915. On 14 January 1916, Herring in BE2c, '4087', with Captain R Eskine acting as his Observer, was attacked and shot down by the then Leutnant Oswald Boelcke of FA62, becoming the ninth of the great German Ace's eventual 40 victories. Herring and Erskine, both wounded, were helped away by British troops from the wrecked BE as it came under shell fire. Herring's MC was announced in the Birthday Honours *London Gazette* of 3 June 1916 (no citation). Although no citation was published in the *Gazette*, research has unearthed the original recommendation for the award: 'J H Herring. (8 Sqn) On 14.1.16 on short reconnaissance duty with Captain Erskine he was attacked by a Fokker from behind. After engaging it for a short time, Second Lieutenant Herring was hit twice in the back. The engagement was continued by Captain Erskine keeping up a steady fire; during this period Captain Erskine was hit in the leg and most of the instruments were broken by bullets. Two more Fokkers then joined in the attack. The engine now stopped as the petrol tank was shot through and all the ammunition was expended. Second Lieutenant Herring glided down and landed just W. of our front line of trenches. He and his observer managed to get into a trench. During the fight many of the controls were shot away. On 31.12.15 Second Lieutenant Herring attacked a hostile kite balloon with bombs under a very heavy rocket and anti-aircraft gun fire. (Ralph Erskine MiD)'.

Once recovered, Herring was sent out to the BE2c-equipped 30 Squadron in Mesopotamia on 30 June 1916, serving with that unit with distinction until 4 February 1917. Awarded the Distinguished Service Order in the *London Gazette* of 3 March 1917. Next, he was posted to the command of 17 Squadron in Salonika, before finally returning to the Home Establishment on 5 April 1918. Herring was twice Mentioned in Despatches during the Great War and was also awarded the Croix de Guerre by the French. Staying on in the RAF after the war, his many subsequent appointments included Air Attaché to the British Embassy in Berlin in 1933 and 1934, the years when Adolf Hitler first came to power in Germany. In fact, Herring, in a secret memorandum, provided the Foreign Office with clear evidence that Germany had begun to build aircraft in violation of the Treaty of Versailles. Unfortunately, there were many 'appeasers' in the Government of the day, and the intelligence he offered went unheeded. Following service throughout the Second World War, he finally retired from the RAF with the rank of Group Captain on 29 September 1945. Group Captain Justin Herring lived in his retirement at 84 Bath Hill Court, Bournemouth until his death on 17 February 1974.

HERRING, Robert Samuel

From London, he was born on 29 July 1896. A pre-war volunteer, he enlisted as a Private soldier (Number 1831) into 9 (County of London) Battalion, Queen Victoria's Rifles (TF). When the war came in August 1914, he, along with rest of the TF, was immediately mobilised. Herring landed in France with the QVR on 4 November 1914, thus qualifying for the 1914 Star. After long service in the trenches, he was picked out for a commission and gazetted Second Lieutenant to 20 (County of London) Battalion, (Blackheath and Woolwich) (TF), on 12 March 1917. Securing a secondment to the RFC later in the same year, he trained as an Observer and was posted out to the Bristol Fighter-equipped 48 Squadron early in 1918. On 25 January 1918, over Sequehart, north east of St Quentin, he shot down out of control an Albatros DIII fighter. The Pilot of the German machine was Leutnant Heinrich Kroll, the Staffelführer of Jasta 24, who managed to bring his damaged machine down behind his own lines. Herring gained four further victories before being severely wounded in action on 26 March 1918. His MC was announced in the *London Gazette* of 22 June 1918: 'For conspicuous gallantry and devotion to duty. He carried out a valuable reconnaissance under heavy fire from the ground, obtaining valuable information and engaging enemy troops with machine-gun fire with good effect. On another occasion while on a photo reconnaissance he was attacked by six enemy tri-planes. He drove them all off after a hard fight and returned with his photographs. He has driven four enemy machines out of control and has set a splendid example of determination and resource'.

Following hospital treatment, Herring was transferred to the Administration Branch of the RAF, before finally relinquishing his commission on 15 July 1919, as a direct consequence of ill health brought on by the wounds he had received on 26 March 1918. Despite his unfortunate experiences in the Great War, he was keen to serve again in the Second World War and was gazetted a Pilot Officer in the Administration and Special Duties Branch, RAFVR, on 21 December 1941. Promoted to Flying Officer, he was employed at Air HQ, Far East. Herring later relinquished his temporary commission in the RAFVR, to be appointed to an Army commission on 1 February 1942. He was in Singapore when it fell to the Japanese on 15 February 1942, and was therefore destined to spend the rest of the war in captivity, although it took until the 27 October 1943, for his prisoner-of-war status to be formally confirmed by the Red Cross. Having survived the Japanese camps, he lived until 9 January 1973.

NB: His medals were offered for sale by Christie's (lot 114) on 20 March 1990 : MC, 1914 Star (Pte 1/9 London R)*, British War Medal 1914-20, Victory Medal 1914-19* (Lt RAF)*, 1939-45 Star, Pacific Star 1941-45, and War Medal 1939-45. The First World War medals are officially issued replacements – the originals were lost during the Japanese occupation of Singapore.*

HERVEY, Hamilton Elliot

Born in 1895 in Brighton, Sussex. His parents worked in India and, as a consequence, he was left in the charge of his grandparents who, in turn, sent him to board at Sedbergh School, Yorkshire. Whilst still at school, he developed an interest in aviation. A rubber-driven model aeroplane he designed and built, so impressed *Flight* magazine that they included it as a feature in their 16 October 1914 issue. Early in 1914, Hervey took up a three-year apprenticeship with the British and Colonial Aeroplane Company at Filton. Three months into the Great War, however, Hervey gave up his apprenticeship to enlist into the RFC. In September 1915, 2 AM 'Tim' Hervey (Number 2586), a trained 'Rigger', found himself in France as part of the newly arrived 12 Squadron. By the following March, Hervey had been selected as an Observer/Gunner for the BE2c-equipped squadron. It was not long after this, on 14 June 1916, in fact, that he was gazetted Second Lieutenant to the

RFC, via the Special List. Following a week's leave at home, Hervey was posted to 8 Squadron, which, like his former unit, was equipped with the BE2c. During his service with 8 Squadron, Hervey flew with 'big-hitters' like 'Grid' Caldwell (qv) and Albert Ball (qv), amongst others. His main partner, however, was Captain G A Parker (qv), for whom Hervey had the greatest respect and admiration. Hervey was awarded the MC and Bar in quick succession, both announced in the *London Gazette* of 10 January 1917 – MC: 'For conspicuous gallantry in action. He has done most efficient work in co-operation with artillery, and has displayed great gallantry in numerous aerial combats'.

Bar to MC: 'For conspicuous gallantry in action. He displayed great courage and skill on several occasions as Machine-Gunner, and materially assisted in several successful flights'.

Hervey returned to the UK for pilot training at the end of 1916 and, by March 1917, was a qualified Scout Pilot. A posting to the Nieuport Scout-equipped 60 Squadron, then under the command of Major A J L Scott (qv), came on 29 March 1917. His new Flight Commander was to be Captain W A Bishop (qv). April 1917 – 'Bloody April' – was hardly the most auspicious time to commence a Scout Pilot career, as Hervey was soon to find out. He had a close call on the 5th of the month when his fuel ran out – fortunately, however, this occurred immediately above a friendly aerodrome. On the 7th he was attacked by no less a personage than the Red Baron, himself, who had, just moments before, claimed his 37th victory (George Smart). Hervey, by employing some quite desperate evasive tactics, managed to escape, although his much damaged machine had to be sent off to the Depot for extensive repairs. On the following day, although not required to fly, he insisted on doing so, and was shot down into the German lines for his pains. Confined to Freiburg, there was little for the fertile minds of the inmates to do, other than plan possible escapes. In one attempt, Hervey and two others, managed 80 miles before re-capture. Leefe Robinson, VC, was a member of another trio that followed Hervey's escape from Freiburg, and they got to within four kilometres of the Swiss border before they, too, were re-captured. Failed escapers were sent to Fort Zorndorf, near Berlin, to cool their heels – a sort of Colditz of its day. Seven months later, in March 1918, the policy changed and the prisoners were dispersed to camps around Germany. Hervey, Leefe Robinson and others – including Brian Horrocks of later Rhine crossing fame, and even later TV lecturing fame – were sent to Clausthal in the Harz mountains. Despite further attempts, Hervey remained a prisoner until his repatriation on 17 December 1918. For his activities during captivity, he received a Mention in Despatches, the announcement of which was included in the 'Escapers Gazette', *London Gazette* of 16 December 1919: '.... in recognition of gallantry whilst a Prisoner of War in escaping, or attempting to escape, from captivity, or for valuable services rendered in the Prison Camps of the Enemy'. Hervey wrote a book about his experiences as a prisoner-of-war, which was published in 1940 (Penguin), under the title 'Caged Birds'. For many years after the Great War, Hervey flew commercial aircraft in Australia, before finally returning home in 1936, to take up a job managing the London Gliding Club on Dunstable Downs. When the Second World War came, Hervey joined an Intelligence unit dedicated to helping escaping airmen across Europe and designated, MI9. In 1941, Hervey, by then a Squadron Leader, was appointed to command the Glider TS at Ringway, near Manchester. The GTS moved south to Haddenham, Bucks, in November 1941, and Tim Hervey returned to his duties with MI9, with which unit he saw out the war. He took up ballooning in his mid-seventies, an interest he enjoyed until the age of 90. He was a founder- member of the London Balloon Club. Hamilton Hervey died in May 1990.

HEWETT, Harald

The son of Sir Harald George Hewett, Bart, and Lady Hewett, of Chelworth, Hampshire, and York House, Newbury, Buckinghamshire, he was born on 22 October 1892. Educated at Cheltenham (1906-12) and at the Royal Military College, Sandhurst. Hewett was working in Ceylon when the war came. Returning to England, he passed through Sandhurst before being gazetted Second Lieutenant to a Regular Army battalion of the Royal Berkshire Regiment on 17 February 1915. Seconded to the RFC, he trained as an Observer and was confirmed and gazetted Flying Officer (Observer) on 21 October following. Next he trained as a Pilot, gaining his Royal Aero Club Certificate (Number 2999) on 19 May 1916, being confirmed a Flying Officer on the same day. Sent out to the Middle East, he instructed for a while, before becoming a 'founder member' and Flight Commander of 113 Squadron, formed at Ismailia on 1 August 1917. Hewett and his Observer of the day, Second Lieutenant Alfred Butt, Bedfordshire Regiment, attached RFC, in an RE8 of 113 Squadron, were killed in action at Djenin, Palestine, on 4 January 1918. Hewett's MC was announced posthumously in the *London Gazette* of 18 January 1918, details in the *Gazette* of 25 April 1918: 'For conspicuous gallantry and devotion to duty when co-operating with heavy artillery. He performed gallant and valuable work, which resulted in the partial destruction of an enemy railway bridge'.

Harald Hewett is buried in Jerusalem War Cemetery, Israel.

HIATT, Cuthbert Ambrose Anthony

From North London, he was born on 20 March 1890. Gazetted Second Lieutenant to a Regular Army battalion of the Norfolk Regiment on 17 February 1915. Securing a secondment to the RFC, he gained his Royal Aero Club Certificate (Number 1223) on 5 May 1915, and was duly confirmed and gazetted Flying Officer on the same day. After a period instructing in the UK, he was sent out to 4 Squadron as a Captain and Flight Commander on 29 March 1916. On the first day of the Battle of the Somme, 1 July 1916, Hiatt was entrusted with a special low-level inspection of the German Thiepval trenches, which he conducted at a height of less than 600 feet. Two days later, on 3 July 1916, again over Thiepval, Hiatt and his Observer of the day, Lieutenant G E F Sutton, in BE2c, '2645', had a close call when their machine was shot up and damaged. Hiatt's MC was announced in the New Year *London Gazette* of 1 January 1917 (no citation). Although no citation was published in the *Gazette*, research has revealed that Hiatt was originally recommended for the award by 5 Brigade, RFC, Commander, Brigadier General C A H Longcroft, however, no less a personage than General Trenchard took it upon himself to actually compose the final recommendation, dated 16 October 1916, it reads: 'From September 15 to July 16 he carried out continuous good work and showed exceptional skill and gallantry as a pilot, especially on contact patrol work. He was among the first to set the example of flying low over the enemy's lines to gain information'.

His tour with '4' completed, he was sent next to 66 Squadron on 2 August 1916. After service in France and in the UK with '66', he was promoted to Major and given command of 57 Squadron (DH4s) on 2 November 1917. He eventually returned to the UK late in 1918 to undertake training and related Staff duties. Hiatt finally left the service by relinquishing his commission in October 1919.

HIBBERT, James Edmund

The son of Mr and Mrs C G Hibbert, of London, he was born on 5 June 1891. Educated at Marlborough (1906-08), where he excelled at Hockey (First XI). Before the war, he worked as an Assistant Manager of a rubber plantation on Carley Island, Port Swettenham, Federation of Malay States, from 1910 to 1911, before going on to be the Agency Manager for the rubber trade in the FMS, from 1911 to 1914. Returning to England at his own expense soon after the war came, he was gazetted Second Lieutenant to 8 Battalion, South Lancashire Regiment, on 16 January 1915. Hibbert won the first of his MCs with 8 South Lancs in the trenches at Ploegsteert, *London Gazette* of 3 June 1916. The first Bar to his MC (very belatedly announced in the *London Gazette* of 22 June 1918) was gained during the fighting on the Somme, when he played a significant part in 1 Battalion, South Lancashire's capture of Regina Trench. Securing a transfer to the RFC in the autumn of 1917, he trained as a Pilot and, once qualified, was sent out to France as a 'founder member' with the newly formed AWFK8-equipped 82 Squadron on 20 November 1917. The third of Hibbert's MCs, this one won in the air, was mainly for services and gallantry during the early weeks of the German spring offensive in March and April 1918, and was announced in the *London Gazette* of 22 June 1918: 'For conspicuous gallantry and devotion to duty. During a low flying reconnaissance, in which he met much opposition from machine-gun and rifle fire, he attacked and destroyed enemy transport with bombs and scattered an enemy battalion with fire from his machine-gun. Later, he dropped messages on our batteries, giving them the precise location of hostile bodies and bringing back valuable information. He has by his determination and untiring energy, under adverse conditions, set a magnificent example to his squadron'.

Promoted to Flight Commander in the summer of 1918, his remarkable luck continued when, on 21 July, he and his Observer, Lieutenant L W Edmonds, in AWFK8, 'C8647', were shot down by rifle fire from a low altitude, but still emerged unscathed from the wreck, which was promptly shelled to smithereens by artillery fire. Not only did Hibbert escape injury, but before his machine was obliterated by shelling, he salved some instruments and regained the British lines. He then made a valuable report which was of great help to the advancing infantry. For this and other gallant acts, he was awarded the Distinguished Flying Cross, *London Gazette* of 2 November 1918. Hibbert finally left the service, via the Unemployed List, on 9 January 1919. A Company Director in the post-war years, he lived and worked in London, his offices located at Fairfax House, Fulwood Place, High Holborn, WC1. Died in August 1941.

NB: His remarkable group of medals was offered for sale by Christie's (lot 94) on 30 April 1991: MC & two Bars (engraved: Capt James E Hibbert, MC, Ploegsteert 1915*), Distinguished Flying Cross, 1914-15 Star* (2Lt South Lancs Regt), *British War Medal 1914-20, and Victory Medal 1914-19* (Captain RAF).

HICKS, Ernest Dorland

From Winnipeg, Canada, he was working as a Postal Inspector in his home city, before offering himself for service, and was duly gazetted Lieutenant to 11 Reserve Battalion, Canadian Infantry, on 27 May 1915. Volunteering for attachment to the RFC, he trained as a Pilot, and was duly confirmed and gazetted Flying Officer on 17 June 1916. He first served in France with the FE2b-equipped 23 Squadron from 25 June 1916, and was quickly heavily involved in escort and bombing duties as part of the RFC's contribution to the Battle of the Somme. On 15 July 1916, Hicks and his Observer, 1 AM Fred Libby (qv), in company with Lieutenants Tyler and Turnbull, on escort duty, successfully fought off four Fokkers, two LVGs and another enemy twin-engined machine, sending the latter down in flames. He transferred next, on 1 August 1916, to 27 Squadron (Martinsyde Elephants). During an offensive patrol on 8 August, Hicks, single-handedly, turned back three LVGs attempting to cross over into the British lines. On 8 September following, Hicks in Martinsyde G102, 'A1567', had his fuel tank hit during a bombing raid. Although badly burned by the ignited petrol, he still managed to bring his machine back to the British lines. His MC was announced in the *London Gazette* of 26 September 1916: 'For conspicuous gallantry and skill. He brought down two enemy machines and attacked and drove back over their lines three others. On one occasion he came down to 800 feet and bombed trains. On another he came down to 300 feet and dropped bombs on a station'.

Following extensive treatment to his burns in France and in the UK, he was eventually pronounced permanently unfit on 3 July 1917, and returned home to Canada.

HILL, Geoffrey Terence Roland

From North London, he was born on 29 May 1895. He studied Engineering at University College, London (member of the University of London OTC), from where he graduated BSc in July 1914. Gazetted Second Lieutenant to the RFC, via the Special Reserve, on 3 June 1916. Qualifying as a Pilot, he was sent out to 29 Squadron in France on 18 August 1916. On 21 September 1916, a bad weather day for flying, he attacked a German kite balloon using Buckingham bullets. The balloon was being hastily winched down from 3,000 feet in the area of Comines, when he emptied a drum into it, passing within 20 feet above the flaming mass. His MC was announced in the *London Gazette* of 20 October 1916: 'For conspicuous gallantry and skill. He attacked an enemy kite balloon under very difficult circumstances, and continued firing until he was within twenty feet of it. He was then only a 1,000 feet from the ground and under heavy fire from anti-aircraft and machine guns, but on looking round he saw the burning wreckage of the balloon on the ground'.

Injured and hospitalised on 29 January 1917, he was eventually sent home for treatment. His injuries precluded him from further operational flying, and he spent the remainder of the war testing and reporting on aircraft types. He was Mentioned in Despatches by the Air Ministry for this work, *London Gazette* of 29 August 1919. Hill returned to engineering work in civilian life, and is credited with designing and helping to build the life-size model of the pterodactyl in the Science Museum in London. Geoffrey Hill died in Londonderry, Northern Ireland, on Boxing Day 1955.

HILL, George Alexander

Born in North London in 1893. Educated at Chatham House and abroad. He was in Canada when the war came and subsequently volunteered for the Canadian Infantry. Having once arrived in the UK with the CEF, and given his language skills, he was soon picked out for a commission and gazetted Second Lieutenant to 4 (Extra Reserve) Battalion, Manchester Regiment on 13 May 1915. He spoke Russian, German, French and Bulgarian as an Interpreter and worked on the General Staff, sometimes attached to RFC HQ, France and Flanders. Not content with 'flying a desk', he trained as a Pilot and was duly confirmed and gazetted Flying Officer on 29 May 1917, shortly before being sent out to the Middle East theatre of war on 15 June following. By no means a conventional RFC officer, he served subsequently in Salonika, the Balkans and Russia. Even his MC was announced in a special 'gazetting' which included awards to other 'shadowy' figures including Sydney George Reilly (qv), a known spy, *London Gazette* of 12 February 1919: 'HM the King has been graciously pleased to approve of the undermentioned rewards for distinguished services rendered in connection with military operations in the field. Awarded the MC: Lieutenant Norman Dewhurst, Royal Munster Fusiliers; Lieutenant

George Alexander Hill, 4 Manchester Regiment att. RAF; Second Lieutenant Sydney George Riley, RAF; Lieutenant George Gibson Tomlin [sic], RAF'.

Hill and Reilly, both members of the SIS, were actually in Russia together when the news of their MCs came through on 22 January 1919. A champagne celebration followed that same evening. Hill was awarded an MBE (Military) in the *London Gazette* of 3 April 1919 and was 'Brought to notice for valuable and distinguished service by Major General Poole, North Russia', he was also awarded the Distinguished Service Order, this announced in the *London Gazette* of 27 June 1919. Furthermore, Hill was Mentioned in Despatches on three occasions during this period. Employed by the Foreign Office on the staff of Sir Halford McKinder in 1919 and 1920, he was heavily involved in the Allied Intervention in Russia. This at a time when there was still hope that the 'White' Russian forces would prevail over the 'Red'. That his services were appreciated is evidenced by the awards he received from the 'White' Russians, St Vladimir, 3rd. Class; St Ann, 2nd Class; St Stanilaus 2nd Class, and, from the Rumanians: Star of Rumania 3rd Class; Crown of Rumania, 3rd Class. Although his military service may have been somewhat 'covert', his civilian life was anything but. He lived, at different times, in Russia and Siberia, in Germany, in the USA and in Canada. In 1930 he became the Manager of the Globe Theatre in London and was, for a period, Deputy General Manager to the world-famous Impresario, Charles B Cochran. His book, 'Go Spy the Land', was published in 1932. Two of his plays, 'It is the Law' and 'Release', were performed in London theatres during the 1930s. George Hill lived, in the 1930s, at 63 St James's Street, London SW1.

HILL, Henry Oswald William

The son of Oswald C and Mary Josephine Hill, of 'The Nook', Oughtrington, Lymm, Cheshire, he was born in Davyhulme, Manchester, on 11 February 1888. Educated at St Bede's College, Manchester, and at Manchester University (OTC), where he studied Architecture. Gazetted Second Lieutenant to the RFC via the Special List on 19 March 1916. Having trained as a Pilot, he was confirmed and gazetted Flying Officer on 3 November 1916. Sent out to France and 34 Squadron on 22 November following. Having completed his largely uneventful tour with '34', he was next sent to 52 Squadron as a Flight Commander and A/Captain. On 10 August 1917, Hill and his Observer, Second Lieutenant C E Wharram, in RE8, 'A4666', were shot up in an aerial combat whilst observing for the artillery. Hill, unscathed in the incident, managed to bring the 'Harry Tate' and his wounded Observer down into the trench lines, fortunately on the right side. On 21 October following, he was not so lucky. Hill and his Observer of the day, 2 AM Thomas Cousin Robertson from Kirkcaldy, Fife, in RE8, 'A3540', disappeared without trace during a test flight. Hill's MC was announced after his death in the *London Gazette* of 17 December 1917, details in the *Gazette* of 23 April 1918: 'For conspicuous gallantry and devotion to duty. He carried out artillery observation on a hostile battery for three and a half hours, subjected most of the time to heavy anti-aircraft and machine-gun fire. Nevertheless he directed the shooting most successfully. He has attacked hostile aircraft on twenty-three occasions and driven them off; in one of these attacks he succeeded in driving off five enemy aeroplanes, although his Observer was wounded. He has shown great skill'.

Hill's remains were never recovered and hence he is commemorated on the Flying Services Memorial, Arras, France.

HILL, Richard Frank

The son of Mr and Mrs R F Hill, he was born on 28 April 1899, at Jarvis Bank, Crowborough, his family later moving to Brighton. Educated at Charterhouse (1912-17). As soon as he left school, he was gazetted Second Lieutenant to the RFC, via the General List, on 4 May 1917. Having trained as an Observer, he was, in July 1917, sent out as a Probationary to 20 Squadron in France. His 'apprenticeship' satisfactorily completed, he was confirmed and gazetted Flying Officer (Observer) on 25 August following. The young Hill, he was still only 18, enjoyed immediate success, gaining the status of Observer Ace by claiming seven victories between 19 August and 1 October 1917. His successes were achieved mainly with Captain H G E Luchford (qv) and both men were awarded the MC in the same *London Gazette* of 27 October 1917, details in the *Gazette* of 18 March 1918: 'For conspicuous gallantry and devotion to duty. He has carried out a great deal of useful observation work, and has proved himself an excellent fighting Observer. On one occasion, when acting as observer on a photographic reconnaissance, he and his pilot shot down and destroyed two enemy scouts. He has also destroyed three other hostile machines'.

Hill was amongst the youngest 'Flying MC' holders in the Great War. His tour with '20' completed, he returned to the Home Establishment at the end of October 1917, subsequently serving with 107 Squadron, and with 3 TDS in England. Tragically, Hill died in the Military Hospital, Bovington Camp, Dorset, on 17 September 1918, following two unsuccessful operations on his appendix. Richard Hill is buried in High Hurstwood (Holy Trinity) Churchyard, Sussex.

HILL, Roderic Maxwell

The son of Professor M J M Hill, MA, DSc, FRS, and Mrs Hill, of Hampstead, London, he was born on 1 January 1894. Educated at Bradfield College (1907-11) and at University College, London. He enlisted as a Private soldier into 18 Battalion, (1 Public Schools), Royal Fusiliers, in October 1914, before being commissioned and gazetted Second Lieutenant to 12 Battalion, Northumberland Fusiliers, on 11 December following. Served in the trenches with 12 Northumberland Fusiliers from September 1915, wounded and Mentioned in Despatches. Securing a transfer to the RFC, he trained as a Pilot and was given his 'Wings' and gazetted Flying Officer on 20 June 1916. Shortly after he qualified, Hill was sent to serve with 60 Squadron in France, flying, initially, Morane Bullets. Over the following months, Hill's reputation as a Scout Pilot burgeoned along with that of his squadron. His MC was announced in the *London Gazette* of 14 November 1916: 'For conspicuous skill and gallantry. Under very heavy fire he dived at an enemy balloon and brought it down in flames. On the day before he had dived at a balloon under heavy fire at a low altitude, but had just missed his mark'.

He was also Mentioned in Despatches at this time. Hill was promoted to A/Captain and Flight Commander on 11 December 1916. In 1917, he married Helen Morton, with whom he had two daughters and one son (killed in action 1944). Given his academic abilities and, by now, operational flying experience, he was chosen to head the Experimental Flying Department, RAE, from 1917 to 1923. During this period he would be awarded the Air Force Cross and Bar for experimental flying. A career RAF officer, he next graduated RAF Staff College, Andover in 1924. His many subsequent appointments, honours and promotions during an outstanding career included; Command of 45 Bomber Squadron in Iraq, 1924-26; Technical Staff, Middle-East HQ, Cairo, Egypt, 1926-27; Directing Staff, RAF Staff College, Andover, 1927-30; Chief Instructor, Oxford University Air Squadron, 1930-32; Deputy Director of Repair and Maintenance, Air Ministry, 1932-36; AOC, Palestine and Trans-Jordan, 1936-38 (twice Mentioned in Despatches); Director of Technical Development, Ministry of Aircraft Production, 1938-40; Director General of Research and Development, Ministry of Aircraft Production, 1940-41; CB, 1941; Controller of Technical Services, British Air Commission, Washington DC, USA, 1941-42; Commandant, RAF Staff College, 1942-43; AOC, 12 (Fighter) Group, 1943; Air Marshal Commanding Air Defence of Great Britain, 1943-44; knighted (KCB), 1944; AOC in Chief, Fighter Command, 1944-45; Member of the Air Council for Training, Air Ministry, 1945-46; Member of the Air Council for Technical Services, 1946-48; Principal Air ADC to the King, 1946-48. He finally retired from the RAF in 1948, living at 'Shallows', Woodgaston Lane, Hayling Island, Hampshire. In civilian life, he was appointed Rector of Imperial College of Science and Technology, 1948 to 1954; and was elected Vice-Chancellor of the University of London from 1953 to 1954. His one publication, 'The Baghdad Air Mail', appeared in 1929. Air Chief Marshal Sir Roderic Hill died on 6 October 1954.

HILTON, D'Arcy Fowlis

Born on 17 October 1890, in Toronto, Canada. Accepted as a candidate for the flying service in Canada, he was, upon arrival in the UK, gazetted Second Lieutenant to the RFC, via the Special Reserve, on 21 November 1916. Gained the Royal Aero Club Certificate (Number 4717) on 17 May 1917. After formally qualifying for his 'Wings', he was sent out to join 29 Squadron in the summer of 1917. Flying Nieuport Scouts, he gained eight victories between 31 July and 13 November 1917. His MC was announced in the *London Gazette* of 17 December 1917, details in the *Gazette* of 23 April 1918: :'For conspicuous gallantry and devotion to duty in attacking enemy aircraft and engaging troops on the ground. While on patrol he attacked single-handed six two-seater machines, forcing one down and driving the rest back. He has driven down five other machines'.

His services on the Western Front were further recognised by a Mention in Despatches, *London Gazette* of 24 April 1918. Returning to the Home Establishment on 14 November 1917, he was hospitalised for a period before eventually becoming an Instructor. For his outstanding work as an Instructor, Hilton was again Mentioned in Despatches, *London Gazette* of 22 January 1919, and ultimately awarded the Air Force Cross, *London Gazette* of 3 June 1919. D'Arcy Hilton died in October 1973, in St Catherine's, Ontario.

NB: An MC and Air Force Cross, both unnamed, but attributed to Hilton, were offered for sale by Spink on 6 May 1998.

HIRD, Frederick Leslie

The son of Mr and Mrs F R Hird, of Ridgeway Lodge, Wimbledon, he was born in September 1897. Educated at Uppingham (1907-11) and at Pembroke College, Cambridge. Gazetted Second Lieutenant to 5 Battalion, East Surrey Regiment (TF), on 1 July 1917, he secured a secondment to the RFC shortly afterwards. Having trained as a Pilot, he was duly confirmed and gazetted Flying Officer on 3 November following. Sent out to 3 Squadron (Camel F1s) in France on 28 November 1917. He had a close call on 16 March 1918, when his Camel, 'B9139', was shot up by ground fire during a low-level patrol. Hird accounted for at least one enemy machine, certainly he was responsible for sending one down out of control on 21 March 1918, the opening day of the great German March Offensive. His MC was announced in the *London Gazette* of 22 June 1918: 'For conspicuous gallantry and devotion to duty. Observing a number of troops in a sunken road, he at once attacked them, dropping four bombs, three of which fell in their midst. He then fired 750 rounds into a large body of men marching along a road. By constantly diving and firing on the enemy they were prevented from moving along the road, and suffered extremely heavy casualties. On a later occasion he again attacked a body of enemy troops, dropping two bombs amongst them and firing 330 rounds into them. He has by his great gallantry and skill set a fine example to his squadron'.

His tour with '3' completed, he returned to the Home Establishment in June 1918, where he saw out the remainder of the war as an Instructor. Hird finally left the service on 2 February 1919. Between the World Wars, he worked mainly in the building industry, living at Leigh Mill House, Godstone, Surrey. He served again in the Second World War, this time as a Major in the Royal Army Ordnance Corps. Retiring from the building industry, he lived, post the Second World War, at Limpsfield Court, Oxted, Surrey, where he traded as a Market Gardener.

HOBBS, George Leslie

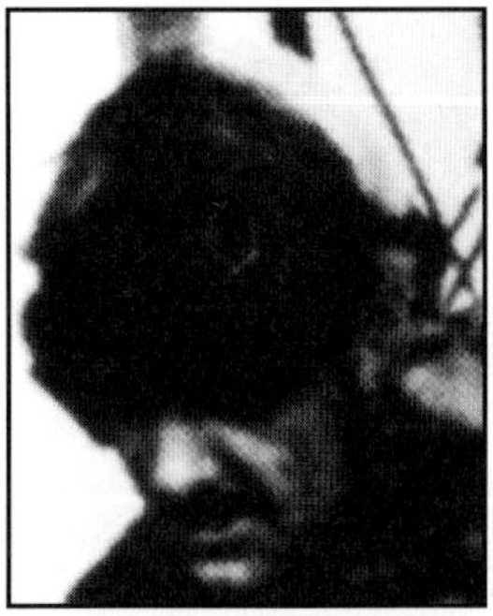

The son of Farmer, George Hobbs and Mrs Ada Hobbs, of Hartfield, East Hendred. Berkshire, he was born on 29 February 1896. Educated at King Alfred's School, Wantage, where he was a member of the OTC from 1910 to 1913, and at Ealing Coaching College. He enlisted as a Private soldier into the Royal Warwickshire Regiment in January 1916. Accepted as a Cadet in March 1917, he was gazetted Second Lieutenant to RFC on 21 June following. Hobbs served first and briefly as an Observer with 12 Squadron (RE8s), before training as a Pilot. Confirmed and gazetted Flying Officer on 27 September 1917, he next joined another RE8-equipped unit, 15 Squadron, on 15 October following. On 25 March 1918, Hobbs and his Observer, Lieutenant H E A Chippindale (qv), were attacked by a formation of enemy Scouts, their numbers variously estimated at seven and eleven. Fighting furiously, they succeeded in sending one of the enemy down in flames, before making good their escape. Both men received the MC for their resource and gallantry on this day, *London Gazette* of 22 June 1918: 'For conspicuous gallantry and devotion to duty. While carrying out a reconnaissance he and his Observer were attacked by eleven hostile scouts. They succeeded in destroying one of them, drove off the remainder, and then completed the reconnaissance. Later, when information was urgently required during an engagement, he and his Observer carried out a most successful reconnaissance, flying at a very low altitude under continuous rifle and machine-gun fire from the ground. They located hostile batteries and enabled very effective counter-battery work to be carried out, and also engaged ground targets with bombs and machine-gun fire. He showed courage and skill'.

Promoted to Flight Commander and A/Captain in October 1918, he went on to serve at RAF HQ, after the war, before finally leaving the service, via the Unemployed List, on 22 September 1919.

HOBBS, Reginald William

Born in Wandsworth, London, on 30 June 1896, his family moving soon afterwards to Cardiff in Wales. He was educated at the County School, Penarth, and was about to take up his studies at University College, Cardiff, when the war intervened. Enlisting as a Private soldier into the Royal Army Medical Corps, he was stationed at No 3 Western General Hospital as a medical orderly from May 1915 to October 1916. Picked out for a commission, he was sent to 10 Officer Cadet Battalion, from whence he successfully graduated, being gazetted Second Lieutenant to 12 Battalion, South Wales Borderers (3 Gwent), on 25 January 1917. Securing a secondment to the RFC in August 1917, he trained as an Observer and was sent out as such to 25 Squadron in the following November. His MC was announced in the *London Gazette* of 26 March 1918, details in the *Gazette* of 24 August 1918: 'For conspicuous gallantry and devotion to duty. He carried out many reconnaissances, always flying a long distance over the enemy's lines or over entirely new country. He invariably obtained successful photographs and brought back valuable information. He showed great keenness and determination at his work'.

Research has unearthed the original recommendation for this award, which provides far more detailed information: 'R W Hobbs 12/SW Bords. 25 Sqn, 9 Wing Feb 1918. For skill and devotion to duty and conspicuous good work during the period 24/11/17 to 5/2/18, especially on the following occasions: On 1/1/18 this Officer carried out a reconnaissance of the hostile aerodromes at St Denis-Westrem, Gontrude and Scheldewindeke. The last named aerodrome had never been photographed till 2/Lt Hobbs succeeded in obtaining photographs of it on this occasion. He located the aerodrome several miles from its reported position. On 2/2/18 he carried out a photographic reconnaissance of the railway line Valenciennes-Aulnoye-Hirson-Wassigny-Busigny and obtained 31 photographs. On 3/2/18 he carried out two important missions. The first was a reconnaissance of the railway line Audenarde-Brussels-Ath. On this occasion he took 54 photographs, all of which were found to contain valuable information. His second journey was a reconnaissance of the railway line Laon-Marle-Vervins-Hirson- Aobentem-Rumigny- Liart-Mont Cornet. He secured 40 photographs including some of a new aerodrome which he located. This Officer has been particularly successful at solo reconnaissance work. Nearly all these reconnaissances have been carried out at a great distance over the enemy's lines, and over entirely new country. He has invariably obtained successful photographs of his pin-points and shown a great aptitude for locating reported aerodromes. He is always anxious to take additional pin-points of places likely to be of value, although this may often entail a much longer course and in consequence staying over the enemy's lines for a much longer period'.

On 26 March 1918, Hobbs and his Pilot, Second Lieutenant C J Fitzgibbon, in DH4, 'A7526', were shot up during a bombing raid, their machine burning to a crisp, fortunately, after they had evacuated their cockpits. Remarkably, Hobbs was unscathed in the incident, although Fitzgibbon was wounded. His tour with '25' completed in May 1918, he returned to the Home Establishment where he saw out the war. Hobbs finally left the service, via the Unemployed List, on 4 February 1919. Returning to his interrupted studies, he subsequently trained as a schoolteacher and was, by the early 1920s, employed at a school in Shipley, Yorkshire.

HOBSON, Frank

The eldest son of Broom Lace Merchant, William Hobson and his wife, Eliza Anne Hobson, of 27 Melton Road, West Bridgford, Nottingham, he was born on 8 October 1894. Gazetted Second Lieutenant to the RFC on 10 May 1917. Having trained as a Pilot, he was confirmed and gazetted Flying Officer on 28 June following. Sent out to 70 Squadron (Camel F1s) in France on 8 September 1917. Hobson fought in the skies above the great battles on the Ypres Salient in the autumn and winter of 1917, and through the German offensive of March 1918. A Camel Pilot of exceptional ability, he amassed no less than 15 victories between 24 September 1917 and 25 March 1918, before returning to the comparative safety of the Home Establishment on 5 May 1918. His MC was announced in the *London Gazette* of 16 August 1918: ' For conspicuous gallantry and devotion to duty. He has destroyed several enemy aeroplanes and driven others down out of control. On one occasion he descended to a height of 100 feet and attacked a party of the enemy with his machine gun, inflicting several casualties on them. He has shown splendid resource and determination on all occasions'.

Following a period of rest and recuperation, he was posted as an Instructor to 72 TS, with which unit he saw out the war, his efforts in this respect being eventually recognised by a Mention in Despatches, *London Gazette* of 3 September 1919. He finally left the RAF, via the Unemployed List, in February 1919. Frank Hobson served again during the Second World War.

NB: His medals were offered for sale by Glendining's (lot 197) on 3 July 1985: MC, British War Medal 1914-20, Victory Medal 1914-19 with MID (Capt RAF), *Defence Medal 1939-45, and War Medal 1939-45.*

HOBSON, Percy Kyme

Born on 20 November 1893, in Fleet, Lincolnshire, he grew up on his father's farm at Stow Park, Bungay, Suffolk. Hobson enlisted as a Driver into the Honourable Artillery Company (TF) on 8 February 1915. He served in France with his regiment until, with the rank of Corporal, he was admitted as a Cadet into the RFC in April 1917. Gazetted Second Lieutenant to the RFC, via the Special Reserve, on 20 June 1917. Having trained as a Pilot, he was duly confirmed and gazetted Flying Officer on 27 September following. Hobson was sent out to join the newly arrived SE5-equipped, 84 Squadron in France, on 7 October 1917. Heavily involved in the intense fighting during the German spring offensive, he achieved seven victories by the end of April 1918. On the intervening 13 March, he shot down an enemy Scout plane in dramatic fashion. The top and bottom planes on the enemy machine broke away, presaging a complete break-up in the air. His MC was announced in the *London Gazette* of 22 June 1918: 'For conspicuous gallantry and devotion to duty. Observing a large body of troops with transport, he descended to within 200 feet, and, despite very severe enemy rifle and machine-gun fire from the ground, dropped four bombs, three of which were direct hits on the transport, causing severe casualties which were increased by the accurate machine-gun fire brought to bear on his targets. On a later occasion, he observed a large body of troops moving across the open, and attacked these with bombs and machine-gun fire, causing many casualties and scattering them in all directions. He has been responsible for the destruction of four enemy machines, and has at all times shown a complete disregard for personal danger'.

His tour with '84' completed, he returned to the Home Establishment on 11 May 1918, and saw out the remainder of the war instructing in the UK. Percy Hobson finally left the RAF on 25 April 1919.

HODGES, Swithan Gane

From Cape Town, South Africa, he was born on 21 April 1892. Gazetted Second Lieutenant to a Regular Army battalion of the Wiltshire Regiment on 24 November 1915, with a secondment to the RFC coming shortly afterwards. Gained his Royal Aero Club Certificate (Number 2309) on 18 January 1916. His formal training completed, he was confirmed and gazetted Flying Officer on 25 March 1916. He was, on 14 October 1916, first sent to 53 Squadron, then in the UK, before accompanying the unit to France as a 'founder member' on 1 January 1917. His squadron was equipped with RE8s in February, and the unit's work of artillery observation began in earnest. Before his tour ended on 14 October 1917, Hodges had been promoted to Flight Commander and A/Captain. His MC was announced in the *London Gazette* of 26 September 1917, details in the *Gazette* of 9 January 1918: 'For conspicuous gallantry and devotion to duty. For many months he has done continuous successful work and photography, and by his skilful observations has been the means of inflicting great damage upon hostile batteries and ammunition dumps. He has consistently displayed great gallantry, frequently working under adverse weather conditions'.

He was next sent out to the Middle East, promoted to A/Major and to the command of 14 Squadron on 5 November 1917. His command of '14' ended on 1 March 1918 and, following a brief rest, he assumed command of 17 Squadron on 2 April 1918. His work on the Salonika front was recognised by a series of awards including a Mention in Despatches, *London Gazette* of 1 November 1918, and an Air Force Cross, *London Gazette* of 1 January 1919. The French gave him a Croix de Guerre avec Palme, *London Gazette* of 15 July 1919, and the Greeks gave him the Medal of Military Merit, 3rd Class, *London Gazette* of 10 October 1919. Hodges finally returned to the Home Establishment on 5 January 1920.

HODGKINSON, Gerard William

The son of W S Hodgkinson, JP, and Mrs Hodgkinson, of Wells, Somerset, he was born in Clifton, Bristol, on 19 December 1883. Educated at Eton (1896-1900) and at Magdalen College, Oxford. Hodgkinson served briefly with the Yeomanry in the South African War 1899-1902. A middle-order batsman of some note, he played as an amateur for his county, Somerset, on 19 occasions between 1903 and 1911. He married, firstly, in 1908, Florence Gladys Mabel Mackenzie-Ashton, who died in 1913, secondly, in 1918, Norah Beryl Record and, thirdly, in 1937, Olive Treloar. Living in East Africa when the war came, he served as a volunteer with the East African Mounted Rifles, a unit of the Nairobi Frontier Force. Returning to England and anxious to get into the war in Europe, he was gazetted Second Lieutenant to 2 County of London Yeomanry (Westminster Dragoons) (TF) on 9 March 1915. Seconded to the RFC, he duly gained his Royal Aero Club Certificate (Number 1896) on 28 September 1915. His formal training completed, he was confirmed and gazetted Flying Officer on 19 January 1916. Engaged largely on Intelligence work, he served again in East Africa, this time attached to 26 Squadron, before, later in the war, going on to 47 Squadron in Salonika. His first MC was announced in the *London Gazette* of 1 February 1917 (no citation), the Bar coming in the New Year *London Gazette* of 1 January 1918 (no citation).

The French, too, gave him a Croix de Guerre avec Palme for his services in Salonika. Returning to the UK in 1918, he served on until leaving the RAF, via the Unemployed List, on 27 March 1920. From 1929 to 1932, Hodgkinson was Master of the Mendip Foxhounds. As soon as the Second World War came, he again volunteered his services, serving in France with the British Expeditionary Force, attached to RAF Intelligence, in 1939 and 1940. Further active service came when he was appointed as Command Security Officer, Balkan Air Force, from 1943 to 1945. For these services, he was rewarded with an OBE in 1944. Hodgkinson retired with the rank of Wing Commander, RAFVR, at the end of the war. He was, post the Second World War, Chairman and Managing Director of Wookey Hole Cave Limited. Gerald Hodgkinson died at his home at Wookey Hole, Somerset, on 6 October 1960.

HODGSON-HORROCKS, Walter James

The son of Mr and Mrs R H Horrocks, of Salkeld Hall, Langwathy, Cumberland, he was born on 2 October 1897. Educated at Harrow (1911-15), where he was a member of the OTC. Gazetted Second Lieutenant to the New Armies on 22 October 1915, with an immediate attachment to the Seaforth Highlanders. Still, however, under-age for active service, he was held for some months at No 1 Young Officers Grouped Companies, Forth Garrison, Kinross, Scotland. Anxious to get involved in the war, he successfully sought a secondment to the RFC, Kite Balloon Service, and was, after training, gazetted a Balloon Officer on 23 September 1916. Sent out to France soon after qualifying, he eventually reached the rank of Lieutenant and Balloon Commander on 30 July 1917. His MC was announced in the *London Gazette* of 17 September 1917: ' For conspicuous gallantry and devotion to duty as a Balloon Observer. Although under accurate hostile shell-fire, he remained in observation in spite of both balloon and basket having been hit by shell splinters, locating the gun which was shelling him, and refusing to descend until darkness made observation impossible. A few moments after he had descended the balloon was brought down by a direct hit. He has always shown remarkable energy and determination whilst engaged in observing'.

Hodgson-Horrocks left the RAF in 1919, returning to his estate in Cumberland. He married, in 1929, Mary Park. He was appointed High Sheriff of Cumberland in 1939. When the Second World War came,

Hodgson-Horrocks served as the local Assistant Group Officer, Royal Observer Corps, from 1939 to 1942. He died on 5 January 1946.

HOIDGE, Reginald Theodore Carlos

From Toronto, Ontario, Canada, he was born on 28 July 1894. Educated at the University of Toronto, from where he graduated Batchelor of Arts and Science (BASc) in 1916. Gazetted Second Lieutenant to the RGA on 11 January 1916, he served in England on the Thames and Medway defences, before securing a secondment to the RFC in the following August. His pilot training duly completed, he was confirmed and gazetted Flying Officer on 15 November following. Posted to 56 Squadron, then at London Colney, shortly after he qualified, he subsequently accompanied the SE5-equipped unit to France as a 'founder member' on 8 April 1917. Yet another outstanding Canadian Ace, the first of his many successes came against an Albatros DIII on 5 May 1917. His tour with '56' ended in November 1917, by which time he had achieved a remarkable 27 victories, latterly flying the improved SE5As. His successes in the period included a 'trio' and four 'doubles' on single days. The first of his MCs was announced in the *London Gazette* of 18 July 1917: 'For conspicuous gallantry and devotion to duty. On many occasions he has attacked and destroyed or driven down hostile machines, and has taken part in twenty-four offensive patrols. In all combats, his bravery and skill have been most marked'.

The Bar to his MC came in the *London Gazette* of 27 October 1917, details in the *Gazette* of 18 March 1918: 'For conspicuous gallantry and devotion to duty in shooting down fourteen enemy aircraft in three and a half months. After attacking a large formation of enemy aircraft, owing to engine trouble, he was driven down 600 feet at least five miles from our lines, but managed to re-cross the lines at a height of 500 feet and so saved his machine'.

The insignia of his MC and Bar were subsequently presented by the King at an investiture held at Buckingham Palace. After a year instructing in the UK, he returned to the front again in the autumn of 1918, this time as a Flight Commander with 1 Squadron (SE5As). The 28th and last of his victories came on 28 October 1918, when he shot down a Fokker DVII, the Pilot of which was seen to bale out, still then quite a rare occurrence. Reginald Hoidge died in New York City, New York, on 1 March 1963.

HOLDEN, Leslie Hubert

The son of Mr and Mrs Hubert William Holden, of 'The Chalet', Winton Street, Warrawee, New South Wales, he was born in East Adelaide, South Australia, on 6 March 1895. After leaving school, he lived and worked as an Assistant Business Manager in Turramurra, NSW. He first enlisted as a Private soldier into the Australian Imperial Force (Infantry) on 26 May 1915, before transferring as a Trooper to the Light Horse on 19 June following. He served in Gallipoli and in Egypt with the Australian Light Horse, before securing a transfer to Australian Flying Corps HQ, also in Egypt, on 5 December 1916. Gazetted Second Lieutenant and Flying Officer on 6 April 1917, he joined 68 Squadron in Heliopolis as a Pilot three days later ('68' would later become 2 Squadron, AFC). From '68' he was sent to France and to 57 Squadron (DH4s) on 26 May 1917, serving with that unit until the following July, when he was posted to 71 (Australian) Squadron, RFC (later 4

Squadron, AFC) then in the UK. After a brief spell with '71', he again joined 68 Squadron (DH5s) that had arrived in France on 21 September 1917. Holden had a number of close calls during his operational career. The first of these occurred on the first day of the Battle of Cambrai, 20 November 1917, when the petrol tank of his DH5, 'A9278', was shot through. He was reported as 'Missing in Action', one of a number of DHs of 68 Squadron lost or damaged on this day, but, happily, he managed to get back to the lines. Three days later on a low-level bombing patrol in DH5, '9326', he was shot up and damaged by an enemy Scout, but managed to land safely. Again on 28 March 1918, by which time '68' had become 2 Squadron, AFC and had been re-equipped with SE5As, Holden, in SE5A, 'B181', was shot up and damaged, but still nursed his machine home to the safety of his own aerodrome. His MC was announced in the *London Gazette* of 4 February 1918, details in the *Gazette* of 5 July 1918: 'For conspicuous gallantry and devotion to duty. Whilst on a special mission he dropped a bomb direct on a support trench full of enemy, causing them to scatter, and another bomb upon a strong point which was holding up our advance. He also bombed a large group of enemy infantry, and turned his machine gun on them from a height of 100 feet. He rendered very valuable service throughout the operations'.

Having achieved four victories during his operational service on the Western Front, Holden returned to the Home Establishment on 8 April 1918, whereupon he was posted as an Instructor to the CFS and the School of Special Flying. Holden's expertise in the instructing field was ultimately recognised by the award of an Air Force Cross, *London Gazette* of 3 June 1919. Returning to Australia on 6 May 1919, he went on to serve with the Citizen's Air Force (CAF), RAAF, in the 1920s. He also began to fly commercially in the 1920s, and was killed in an aeroplane crash near to Bryon Bay, New South Wales, on 18 September 1932.

HOLDER, Frank Douglas)

The son of Mr and Mrs Holder, of 'Lane's End', Springfield, Chelmsford, Essex, he was born in 1898. Educated at Felsted (1910-15), a Scholar, Prefect and Hockey XI. Gazetted Second Lieutenant to a Regular Army battalion of the East Kent Regiment, The Buffs, on 26 January 1916, securing a secondment to the RFC just three months later. His pilot training duly completed, he was confirmed and gazetted Flying Officer on 15 July following. Sent out to the FE2b-equipped 22 Squadron shortly after he qualified. On 31 July, Holden and his Observer, Private Welford, in FE2b, '5242', narrowly escaped complete disaster when their machine was forced down to crash and burn by an enemy Scout. Holder was unscathed but Welford was injured in the crash-landing. Five weeks later on 7 September, Holder again courted disaster when he and Lieutenant E Ambler in FE2b, '4267', were forced down during an aerial combat. Landing on bad and uneven ground, their machine turned over, fortunately without inflicting harm to either occupant. No doubt shaken up by his recent experiences, Holder returned to the UK at the end of 1916, taking up special duties at the Experimental Station, Orfordness. This newly formed unit was meant, as its title suggests, to try out and report on, the many innovations flooding into military aviation at that time. Holder's part was to test machines and various instruments for night-flying. On the evening of 16 June 1917, Holder and his Observer, Sergeant Sidney Ashby (Number 506), in FE2b, 'B401', were ordered up to contact and destroy a Zeppelin (*L38*). Having found no difficulty in locating the airship, Holder and Ashby, after a long, hard climb over the Suffolk farmlands, opened fire on the starboard rear panels of the gigantic envelope. Flames were seen to spread at an amazing pace. Two other Pilots were also attacking the intruder, Captain R H M S Saundby (qv) in a DH2 and Second Lieutenant L P Watkins (qv) in a BE12, and ultimately, Holder and Ashby would share with them, the credit for the destruction of the *L38*. However, one of the two survivors of the wrecked and burnt-out Zeppelin, Machinist's Mate Ellerkamm, said later that the fire had started at the point where Holder and Ashby had launched their attack. Holder's MC and Ashby's Military Medal, were the subjects of a rare joint announcement that appeared in the *London Gazette* of 7 August 1917: 'War Office, 4 August 1917 – His Majesty the King has been graciously pleased to approve the award of the Military Cross and Military Medal respectively, to the under mentioned officer and non-commissioned officer, in recognition of conspicuous gallantry and determination displayed in connection with the destruction of an enemy airship: Second Lieutenant (T/Lieut) Frank Douglas Holder, East Kent Regiment and RFC, Military Cross; Number 506 Sergeant Sidney Ashby, RFC, Military Medal'.

Ashby, a Londoner from Battersea, had been an early entrant into the RFC and had earned a 1914 Star when he crossed to France with the original contingent in August 1914. He was destined to be killed in a flying accident at Martlesham Heath on 16 March 1918. After leaving the RAF in 1919, Holder would go on to build his own manufacturing business and become a prominent personage in his own county of Essex – OBE, DL, JP. He served again in the Second World War, this time as a Squadron Leader in the RAF. His son, J D H Holder, like his father, an Old Festedian, also served as a Meteorologist in the RAF during the Second World War.

HOLLAND, Charles

The son of Mr and Mrs Arthur Charles Holland, of 'Dunedin', King's Road, Horsham, Sussex, he was born in Petworth, Sussex, in 1886. Gazetted Second Lieutenant to the RFC, via the Special Reserve, on 21 January 1916. Gained his Royal Aero Club Certificate (Number 3042) on 8 June 1916. His formal training duly completed, he was confirmed and gazetted Flying Officer on 16 July following. Sent out to BE2c-equipped 8 Squadron just 12 days after qualifying, he was soon heavily involved in reconnaissance duties. Promoted to A/Captain and Flight Commander in December 1916, he appears to have been briefly attached to 60 Squadron around this time. On 18 March 1917, Holland and his Observer, Second Lieutenant A C Heaven (qv), in an 8 Squadron BE2e, '5748', were shot about by ground fire. Holland was wounded in the hand and unable to steer the BE. Fortunately, Heaven was unhurt and somehow managed to bring their machine back, crashing it into the British front lines before dragging Holland clear and carrying him to safety. Heaven received the MC for this act of bravery. Holland's MC was announced in the Birthday Honours *London Gazette* of 4 June 1917 (no citation). Although no citation was published in the *Gazette*, research has unearthed the original recommendation for the award: '4 March 1917, 3/Brigade HQ, RFC – Has done continuous good work especially in artillery co-operation and photography in the course of which he has beaten off hostile machines on several occasions and completed his work'.

Having completed his tour with '8', he returned to the Home Establishment where he was posted as an Instructor. Holland was killed in a flying accident at 5 TDS, on 25 January 1918 and is buried in Horsham (Hills) Cemetery, Sussex.

HOLLAND, Hubert Lee

From Toronto, Ontario, Canada, he was commissioned Lieutenant into the Canadian Reserve Cycling Company, on 13 July 1915. From the Reserve, he was gazetted Lieutenant to the Canadian Divisional Cyclists on 20 May 1916, arriving in the UK just one week later. Following service with the CEF in France, he was seconded to the RFC on 30 June 1917. His pilot training duly completed with 31 TS, 62 TS and 16 TS Infantry and Artillery School, in the UK, he was confirmed and gazetted Flying Officer on 8 December following. Sent out to the Italian front and the RE8-equipped 34 Squadron, 51 Wing, RFC, on 19 January 1918. Promoted to A/Captain and Flight Commander on 18 April 1918, his MC was announced in the *London Gazette* of 16 September 1918: 'For conspicuous gallantry and devotion to duty when working with artillery in carrying out six successful shoots whereby many enemy gun pits were destroyed and explosions caused. In one case he descended to 100 feet and found all pits totally destroyed. He carried out a good low reconnaissance of two suspected hostile batteries and also obtained other very useful information'.

Holland's tour with '34' was completed on 7 October 1918 and he arrived back in the Home Establishment four days later. He served briefly with 27 TDS before going to 123 Squadron, also in the UK. Holland reverted to the rank of Lieutenant from 1 April 1919, with the Canadian Air Force, whilst his unit, 123 Squadron, RAF, became 2 Squadron, Canadian Air Force. Holland served with the CAF and RCAF into the 1920s.

HOLLIDAY, Fred Parkinson

Born in Melbourne, Australia, on 20 February 1888. Educated mainly in England. He was employed by the Swedish General Electric Company in Canada from 1911 to 1914. Holliday enlisted as a Sapper into 2 Field Company, Canadian Engineers, on 23 September 1914. He was gassed in the trenches, whilst serving with the CEF in Flanders during 1915. Once recovered, he was accepted for the flying service and gazetted Second Lieutenant to the RFC, via the Special Lists, on 28 November 1915. He first trained as an Observer and, after completing his probationary period which commenced on 15 December 1915 with 4 Squadron in France, he was confirmed and gazetted Flying Officer (Observer) on 10 March 1916. Almost immediately afterwards, he commenced pilot training and was able to put up his full 'Wings' in April 1916. One of the original 'Brisfit' Pilots, he claimed five victories in 48 Squadron's first month of action in April 1917. Six more victories followed in May, including a 'quartet' on 9th of that month. On 3 June 1917, he shot the tail completely off an Albatros Scout. The last of his eventual 17 victories was achieved on 27 July 1917. His MC was announced in the *London Gazette* of 26 July 1917: 'For conspicuous gallantry and devotion to duty. In company with another pilot he attacked five hostile aircraft, setting one on fire, driving down another out of control, and dispersing the remainder. He has previously done fine work, bringing down eight hostile machines in all'.

His impressive and highly creditable combat career was marked by the award of a gallantry Distinguished Service Order, *London Gazette* of 25 August 1917. He was also Mentioned in Despatches, *London Gazette* of 7 November 1917. Holliday was appointed an Examining Officer in the Midlands in 1918. He briefly commanded 95 Squadron in the UK from 31 October 1918, before being posted as an Instructor to Gosport. He was awarded an Air Force Cross for his outstanding work in this field, *London Gazette* of 3 June 1919. Holliday, by then a Major, toured the USA in 1920, in company with a group of other RAF Aces. Leaving the RAF in the 1920s, he went first to Sweden, before returning to his adopted Canada, eventually becoming President and Managing Director of Swedish Electric. He served again in the Second World War, this time as a Group Captain in the RCAF. Fred Holliday died on 5 March 1980.

HOLLINGHURST, Charles Stanley

The elder son of Mr and Mrs C H Hollinghurst of Brentwood, Essex, he was born on 8 December 1892, in Ilford, Essex. His younger brother Leslie would become, in the fullness of time, Air Chief Marshal Sir Leslie Hollinghurst, GBE, KCB, DFC, etc. Charles trained as a Commercial Artist and was a married man living and working in London when the war came in August 1914. Volunteering for the Armoured Car Section of the RNAS, he won a Distinguished Service Medal with 10 Squadron in the Gallipoli campaign, *London Gazette* of 19 November 1915, and was also Mentioned in Despatches, *London Gazette* of 5 November 1915. Picked out for a commission, he was next gazetted Second Lieutenant to the RFC, via the Special Reserve, on 15 April 1916. Gained his Royal Aero Club Certificate (Number 2962) on 21 May 1916. His formal pilot training duly completed, he was confirmed and gazetted Flying Officer on 21 June following. Sent out to BE2e-equipped 9 Squadron on 12 July 1916. His operational career was short but quite distinguished, and he performed some particularly good contact patrol work during the Battle of the Somme, not least on 21 August 1916, over Guillemont and the Quarry when flying with Second Lieutenant T E Gordon-Scaife (qv). Hollinghurst was wounded in the shoulder by rifle fire from the ground during a low-level reconnaissance on 13 September 1916. The wounds were sufficiently serious to curtail the possibility of further operational flying. His MC was announced in the *London Gazette* of 14 November 1916: 'For conspicuous skill and gallantry on contact patrol work. On one occasion he was attacked first by four and then by three enemy machines, but drove them all off and continued his patrol. On another occasion his Observer was hit, and his machine badly damaged by anti-aircraft fire, but he came back for another machine, and went out again. Two days later he was wounded while flying over the lines at 1,000 feet '

Although he returned again to France in December 1917, he was mainly employed in administration work at the Aeroplane Depots. Charles Hollinghurst finally left the RAF, via the Unemployed List, on 18 April 1919. Died circa 1942.

HOLLINGSWORTH, Percy Collis

The younger son of Mr and Mrs Frederick Joseph Hollingsworth, of Carshalton, Surrey, he was born on 29 June 1893. Educated at Tonbridge School (1906-10). He enlisted as a Private soldier into 1 Battalion, Honourable Artillery Company (Infantry) (TF), in September 1914, being sent out to join his unit in France on 29 December following. Part of 7 Brigade, 3 Division, his battalion was involved in many of the battles that occurred during the early months of 1915, including Neuve Chapelle and the second Battle of Ypres. Hollingsworth was wounded in the trenches on Mount Kemmel on 15 March 1915, receiving a gun shot wound to the leg. Once recovered, he returned again to the front, this time with the rank of Sergeant. Securing a secondment to the flying service in the summer of 1916, he was gazetted Second Lieutenant to the RFC, via the General List, on 26 August 1916. Having trained as an Observer, he was sent out as a Probationary to 6 Squadron in France in the following month. His 'apprenticeship' satisfactorily completed, he was confirmed and gazetted Flying Officer (Observer) on 5 November 1916. On 26 January 1917, Hollingsworth and his Pilot, Captain S.P. Smith, in BE2g, '6278', were, in the course of an Artillery Observation patrol, attacked out of the sun and shot up from behind by Leutnants Brenninger and Ompteda of FAb 3. Hollingsworth was severely wounded in the right arm in the first moments of the attack, but still Smith managed to get them down without further mishap. His MC was announced in the Birthday Honours *London Gazette* of 4 June 1917 (no citation). Although no formal citation was published in the *Gazette*, research has unearthed the original recommendation for the award: '10 March 1917, 2/Brigade HQ, RFC – For gallantry and skill. Lieutenant Hollingsworth has been an observer for five months, during which time he has done much valuable work. On 26 January 1917 whilst engaging a hostile scout he received a wound which resulted in the loss of his right arm'.

His health at least partially restored and despite an empty right tunic sleeve, he returned to Home Service duties on 29 August 1917, with an appointment (Equipment Officer 2nd Class) as an Assistant Instructor at No 1 School of Military Aeronautics. Promoted to A/Captain and Equipment Officer, 1st Class, he was attached to the Air Ministry on 11 January 1918. His last appointment, to the RAF Administration Branch, came later in 1918, and it was from there that he finally left the service, via the Unemployed List, on 6 March 1919. Percy Hollingsworth spent the rest of his business life in the City of London, before retiring to live at 'The Spinney', Langham, Holt, Norfolk.

HOLME, Robert Charles Lyon

The son of Mr and Mrs R F L Holme, he was born in Berkshire, on 10 November 1896. His family moved around considerably, living at various addresses in Somerset and in Barnes, London SW. Educated at Repton (1911-14) and at Sandhurst. Gazetted Second Lieutenant to a Regular Army battalion of the Somerset Light Infantry on 11 November 1914. Kept back in the UK because of his comparative youth, he eventually sought secondment to the flying service, gaining his Royal Aero Club Certificate (Number 1665) on 28 August 1915. Despite holding his pilot's 'ticket', he was first formally trained as an Observer and posted to 16 Squadron as a Probationary on 3 September 1915. His 'apprenticeship' satisfactorily completed, he was confirmed and gazetted Flying Officer (Observer) on 13 January 1916. Subsequently training as a Pilot, he was next posted to Home Defence duties, first reporting to 39 Squadron in Hounslow in the spring of 1916. On the night of 25/26 April 1916, one of Holme's squadron colleagues, Captain A T Harris, became the first to use the new and still experimental Brock explosive bullets against a raiding Zeppelin (LZ97). (Harris would gain undying fame in the Second World War as 'Bomber' Harris). Soon after closing with LZ97, Harris' Lewis gun jammed and whilst he was clearing it, the Zeppelin slipped away into the surrounding gloom. Holme and another colleague spied the same Zeppelin in the distance, coned in the light of searchlights, but it was too far away to be caught. In the summer, Holme transferred to 33 Squadron, then based at Bramham Moor. On the night of 2/3 September 1916 – a significant date in that this was to be when the first Zeppelin was brought down by an aeroplane, famously a BE2c flown by Lieutenant W Leefe Robinson of immortal memory – Holme was unfortunate enough to crash during take-off. His MC was announced in the *London Gazette* of 24 January 1917 (no citation), one of a number awarded for consistent bravery during night-flying Home Defence duties. He was also Mentioned in Despatches at this time. In 1918, he joined the SE5A-equipped 29 Squadron in France as a Flight Commander, claiming five victories between 2 July and 1 August 1918. Staying on in the RAF after the war, he was given a permanent commission in August 1919. Posted out to Mesopotamia, he was killed in a flying accident at Kirkuk on 4 October 1922.

HOLMES, Frank Haddon

From Charlton, Kent. Gazetted Second Lieutenant to 2 Home Counties Field Company, Royal Engineers (TF), on 16 March 1915. He appears to have served only in the UK before eventually securing a secondment to the RFC in January 1917. His training duly completed, he was confirmed and gazetted Flying Officer on 25 April 1917. Sent out to 53 Squadron (RE8s) in France on 9 May 1917. His stint with '53' completed, he returned to the Home Establishment and a training post on 2 December 1917. His MC was announced in the *London Gazette* of 18 January 1918, details in the *Gazette* of 25 April following: 'For conspicuous gallantry and devotion to duty.

He observed for thirty-seven destructive counter battery shoots, and shot down two enemy aeroplanes which attacked him'.

Research has unearthed the original recommendation for the award which gives far more detail than does the formal published citation: 'Posted to his Squadron on 12/5/17, he has been a steady and reliable Artillery Observer to date. He has observed for 37 destructive counter battery shoots during this period, the following being examples: 24th June: Unusually great destructive shoot with 205 RMA 15" Hows, using 106 fuse in billets etc, in Tenbrielen. 90 rounds were observed in two flights lasting 5¾ hours. 20th August: While on artillery observation he was attacked by five enemy aircraft. He drove down one and finished a successful shoot. 3rd September: He shot down one EA while on photography over back areas and brought back nine photographs of counter battery areas. 4th October: During the attack he went up when no other machine was attempting work. Flying at 900 feet for one hour until his observer was ill. He zone-called three active batteries. 11th November: In spite of aggressive enemy aircraft he completed a K.O. shoot with 188 Seige, giving 20 O.Ks. and causing an explosion'.

Promoted to A/Captain in 1918, Holmes eventually left the RAF, via the Unemployed List, on 28 March 1919.

HOME-HAY, Jeffrey Batters

Born in Alloa, Scotland, on 31 January 1890, he emigrated to Canada, along with his widowed mother, three sisters and two brothers, in 1908. He was farming at Wadena, Saskatchewan, when war came in August 1914. Volunteering his services, he enlisted into 32 Battalion, Canadian Infantry, eventually serving in France in the Machine Gun Section of his regiment as part of the first contingent of the CEF. Picked out for a commission, he was gazetted Second Lieutenant to 7 Battalion, Argyll and Sutherland Highlanders (TF), on 23 November 1915. His main ambition, however, was realised when he was allowed a secondment to the RFC. Gained his Royal Aero Club Certificate (Number 3209) on 10 July 1916. His formal training duly completed, he was confirmed and gazetted Flying Officer on 30 July following. Sent to 53 Squadron, then stationed in Catterick, Yorkshire, in August 1916, he eventually accompanied that unit to France as a 'founder member' on 4 January 1917. Promoted to A/Captain and Flight Commander on 7 June 1917, his MC was announced in the *London Gazette* of 26 July following: ' For conspicuous gallantry and devotion to duty. He showed consistent ability and courage in observing for and ranging our artillery upon enemy guns and trenches. His accurate information was of the greatest value to our batteries'.

His tour with '53' completed, he returned to the Home Establishment on 15 December 1917. In May 1918, he was posted to the DH9-equipped 104 Squadron, a element of the newly formed Independent Air Force. He achieved seven victories between 30 June and 15 August 1918, adding a Distinguished Flying Cross to his gallantry awards, *London Gazette* of 21 September 1918. Records at the National Archives show Home-Hay to have been highly regarded by his immediate superiors, one describing his works with '104' as being: 'most valuable and of an inspiring nature' and commenting that: 'he has proved himself to be possessed of exceptional gifts of leadership'. On 22 August 1918, a particularly inauspicious day for '104', Home-Hay and his Observer, Sergeant W T Smith, DCM, MM, were brought down and taken prisoner. Repatriated on 13 December 1918, he returned to Canada, intending to take up farming. In 1920, however, he applied to join the Canadian Air Force. He was offered a captaincy providing he would participate in a proposed CAF transcontinental flight from Halifax, Nova Scotia, to Vancouver, BC, which had never previously been achieved. He duly played his part in the historic Trans-Canada flight, which was successfully completed in October 1920. Home-Hay declined further service in the CAF in 1921, and subsequently became seriously involved in civil aviation. He made regular flights for

Prairie Airways, plying between Winnipeg, Saskatoon, Moose Jaw and Regina. In the fullness of time he became the oldest Pilot flying in the north of Canada, before finally retiring to his farm at Kelington, Saskatchewan, in 1952. Jeffrey Home-Hay died in the summer of 1956.

HOOPER, Geoffrey Herbert

Born in Stanmore, New South Wales, Australia, on 15 April 1891, he was studying Electrical Engineering at London University, where he was a member of the OTC - when the war came. Having once completed his studies, he was gazetted Second Lieutenant to 3 Field Company, Royal Engineers (TF), on 1 November 1915. A transfer to the RFC came in August 1916 and he successfully gained his Royal Aero Club Certificate (Number 3846) on 14 November following. His pilot training duly completed, he was confirmed and gazetted Flying Officer on 2 April 1917. Just ten days later, he was sent out to join 11 Squadron in France. The squadron converted from the FE2b to the BF2b in June 1917, and the first of Hooper's victories came on the 26th of that month. By the time of the award of his MC, he had gained three victories, *London Gazette* of 17 September 1917: 'For conspicuous gallantry and devotion to duty. When leading a patrol of four machines he attacked ten enemy aircraft; during the engagement five of them were destroyed, two by himself. He had previously led a very successful night bombing attack on an aerodrome, in unfavourable weather, dropping bombs from a very low altitude, and doing a great amount of damage. He has invariably displayed great gallantry and skill when engaged in aerial combats'.

His tour with '11' completed, he returned to the Home Establishment in December 1917. After nine months service as an Instructor with 38 TS, he was promoted to A/Captain and Flight Commander and posted out to 20 Squadron in France on 14 September 1918. He developed a devastatingly effective partnership with Lieutenant H L Edwards, the pair accounting for seven Fokker DVIIs between 24 and 29 September 1918. Hooper's 11th and final victory came on the penultimate day of the war – yet another Fokker DVII sent down out of control over Chareloi. The award of a Distinguished Flying Cross was announced in the *London Gazette* of 3 June 1919. Geoffrey Hooper served with the RAAF, until finally he returned to civilian life in 1923.

HOOTON, Lionel Conrad

The son of Mr and Mrs Hooton, of Winchmore Hill, London, he was born in Barnett, Middlesex, on 21 May 1891. Educated at Melville Hall School, Hampstead, London. After leaving school, he emigrated to Canada, working in the Forestry Service and ranching in British Columbia. A pre-war volunteer, he served with 88 Victoria Fusiliers, before transferring to 3 Canadian Pioneers when the war came, eventually crossing to the UK with this unit on 28 March 1915. Hooton was attached briefly to 16 County of London Battalion (TF), Queen's Westministers, going on to attend and train at the School of Signalling. In November 1916, by then a fully qualified signaller, he transferred as a Trooper (Number 430850) to the Fort Garry Horse, a unit of 5 Cavalry Division, CEF, in France. Picked out for a commission, he was gazetted Second Lieutenant to the RFC, via the General List, on 30 May 1917. Having trained as an Observer, he was sent out to 8 Squadron as a Probationary in July 1917. His 'apprenticeship' satisfactorily completed, he was confirmed and gazetted Flying Officer (Observer) on 31 August following. Next, he qualified as a Pilot, continuing to fly with 8 Squadron. He and his Observer, Second Lieutenant H Wisnekowitz (qv), were 'shot up' in their AWFK8s on 23 and 27 March 1918. The first of his MCs was announced in the *London Gazette* of 22 June 1918: 'For conspicuous gallantry and devotion to duty. On one occasion, during a very thick mist, he and his pilot [sic] by flying very low, despite very heavy machine-gun fire, succeeded in locating the enemy's position. Though their machine was hit in all the vital parts, it was flown back to the aerodrome in safety. On a later occasion, when on contact patrol during failing light, they succeeded in locating accurately the position of the enemy. They have shown the utmost gallantry and skill during recent operations, and have carried out their duties with the greatest courage and determination'.

The wording of the citation is, not uniquely, confusing, as it may be taken to imply that Hooton was the Observer on the occasions referred to, whereas, in fact, he was the Pilot. Research has unearthed the original recommendation for the award which is distinctly more explicit: 'HQ, 3 Brigade, RAF: 4 April 1918: For gallantry and good service during the operations, March 21st to March 31st 1918. This officer, together with 2 Lieut Wisnekowitz, as observer, has shown the utmost gallantry and skill throughout the recent operations, during which period they have been flying together. 2 Lieut Hooton has been employed continuously on contact patrol work and he, together with 2 Lieut Wisnekowitz, has brought back information of the greatest value, which has been gained at exceedingly low altitude under heavy machine-gun fire. On March 23rd there was very thick mist which made observation almost impossible. By flying very low over Nerlu, Templeux, La Foose and Buire, in spite of very heavy machine-gun fire from the ground, they were able to locate the enemy's position. 2 Lieut Hooton managed to fly his machine back to the aerodrome, and on examination it was found to have been hit in all vital parts, and had to be written off. On March 27th they did the last contact patrol of the day. The light was so bad that they could not distinguish our infantry from the enemy, but managed to locate the enemy's position by the volume of fire directed at them from the ground. On this occasion also their machine was so riddled with bullets that it necessary to return it to the Depot for repair. These officer have always displayed the utmost courage and determination in carrying out their duties'.

Hooton suffered being shot up yet again on 7 April, this time with Second Lieutenant Eric Irwin Wells (qv), acting as his Observer in AWFK8, 'C3678'. Hooton's good fortune held, as he and Wells escaped unscathed, despite having their petrol tank holed and the Observer having to climb out on the wing to help stabilise the machine. Not the case, however, on 27 May following, when, perhaps inevitably, Hooton was wounded in the air. The Bar to his MC came in the *London Gazette* of 26 July 1918: 'For conspicuous gallantry and devotion to duty. When flying at a 1,000 feet his petrol tank was shot through and immediately afterwards his left aileron control shot away. He tried to turn his machine without success, and it was side-slipping down out of control into the enemy's lines. Realising the danger, his Observer climbed out on the right wing, enabling him to turn and land just within our lines. It was owing to his extraordinary coolness he was able to land the machine in safety. He has also done fine work on reconnaissance and in attacking enemy infantry'.

Hooton was posted to 123 (Canadian) Squadron soon after the war, going on to serve with the Allied Intervention Force in Russia in August 1919,

HOPKINS, Arthur Gorrill

A Methodist Minister before the war, Hopkins was gazetted Second Lieutenant to 5 British West India Regiment on 30 March 1917. Seconded to the RFC, he trained as an Observer and was subsequently confirmed and gazetted Flying Officer (Observer) on 17 July 1917, the same day that he joined 14 Squadron in Palestine. Hopkins recorded, in his diary, his operational experiences and the emotions he experienced during these difficult times: 'Over Gaza we were heavily shelled by Archie, or rather by a heavier type of gun firing a large explosive shell. I don't quite know how to describe the burst of the shell except to say it is like a gigantic matchbox being crushed. If one goes off near the machine, she shakes like anything. One will be sailing along quite nicely, when there will be that sickening 'crunch' and a big ball of black smoke, with a flash in the middle. Then, of course, one dodges or tries to do so. I'm afraid I haven't much of a heroic spirit, for I'm always jolly glad to get on the ground again.

I always imagined Archie fire as rather a joke. On this front it is a very serious proposition indeed'.

He belies his own words, however, when describing the satisfaction and 'buzz' he gets from observing for the artillery: 'It makes one feel good to see the shell bursts getting closer and closer in, and finally, with luck, getting right there'.

Reconnaissance work, too, was satisfying: '....I was up yesterday scouting ahead of our advancing cavalry, when I spotted two big clouds of dust. What was it? Enemy retiring or some of ours? The method of finding out is as follow, come down low over suspected area, and if you get fired on, it's them!'

During the final assault on Umbrella Hill on 2 November 1917, two days after Beersheba fell to British forces, his 14 Squadron machine braved the desperate weather conditions for more than four hours. His Pilot flying at below 1,000 feet, despite heavy fire from the ground, enabled Arthur Hopkins to direct the fire of the Royal Artillery batteries to great effect. It was mainly for this work that Hopkins was awarded his MC, announced in the New Year *London Gazette* of 1 January 1918, the minimal details appearing in the *Gazette* of 11 April 1918: '....military operations culminating in the capture of Jerusalem'.

Hopkin's reaction to news of his award was: '....every man in the infantry deserves it as much as I do'. Arthur Hopkins was able, following its capture by the British, to visit Umbrella Hill and inspect his and the Royal Artillery's handiwork: 'The Turkish trenches are knocked endways, how the poor fellows there stood it all, I don't know. After Umbrella, we went into Gaza. Poor old Gaza! Samson didn't make the mess there our guns did. The place is a complete ruin....'.

These, and other of Arthur Hopkin's thoughts and observations, appeared in a biography written by Leonard T Towers, 'Mr Valiant, The Story of Arthur G Hopkins', MC, published in 1926 (Epworth Press). His tour with 14 Squadron completed on 21 January 1918, he was next posted to the Training Brigade in Egypt, to train as a Pilot. He returned to 14 Squadron for a short period from 18 May to 12 June 1918 as Recording Officer. He was then posted to Base Depot, which generally heralded a return to England. Arthur Hopkins was, however, still rated an Observing Officer in the 1919 *RAF Lists*. A missionary in Trinidad pre-war he returned to the clergy but died of cancer in 1924,

NB: The RAF Museum Hendon has his single MC in its collection.

HORN, Kelham Kirk

Born in Australia on 18 September 1890, he was the son of William A and Penelope E Horn, of South Australia, and of 4 Cornwall Mansions, Kensington, London. His brother, Spencer (qv), also won a 'flying MC'. When the war came in August 1914, Kelham enlisted as a Trooper into King Edward's Horse. Anxious to join the flying service, he obtained his Royal Aero Club Certificate (Number 1171) on 15 April 1915, the same day that he was gazetted Second Lieutenant to the RFC, via the Special Reserve. His formal training duly completed, he was confirmed and gazetted Flying Officer and, on 24 August 1915, was sent to 9 Squadron, then stationed at Brooklands. A transfer to BE2c-equipped 7 Squadron and operational flying in France came in the following month. On 19 December 1915, Horn and his Observer of the day, Lieutenant Moffatt, in BE2c, '2680', attacked an Albatros attempting to cross the lines above Dixmunde. They emptied a drum of ammunition at the enemy machine which dived away. The hunters became the hunted when, successively, they were themselves attacked by five enemy machines. After a running fight, the British machine escaped to safety. Horn was promoted to A/Captain and Flight Commander on 23 January 1916. His tour with '7' completed on 24 May 1916, he subsequently served as a Flight Commander with 56 Squadron in the UK, before taking over the command of 54 Squadron (Sopwith

Pups). His MC was announced in the New Year *London Gazette* of 1 January 1918 (no citation). Although no formal citation was published in the *Gazette*, research has unearthed the original recommendation for the award: 'K K Horn, recommendation dated 4/10/17: A most capable and energetic Squadron Commander. By his good example he has kept his Squadron in a high state of efficiency and morale'.

Horn left the RAF with the rank of Major, via the Unemployed List, on 31 January 1919.

HORN, Spencer Bertram

The son of William A Horn and Penelope E Horn (both natives of South Australia) of 4 Cornwall Mansions, Kensington, London. Spencer's brothers were born in Australia, where the family lived for much of the last decade of the nineteenth century. Exceptionally, Spencer was born in Rebrass, Salisbury, on 18 April 1895, the day after the ship that brought the family to England docked at Southampton. One of Spencer's brothers, Kelham Kirk Horn (qv), also won a 'flying' MC, and went on to command 54 Squadron during 1917. Spencer was educated at Harrow (1909-13) and at Sandhurst. Gazetted to 3 (Prince of Wales's) Dragoon Guards on 1 October 1914, he crossed the Channel with his regiment on 28 October, thus earning the 1914 Star. After serving almost continuously through the latter months of 1914 and all of 1915, Horn, by then a Lieutenant, was transferred to the newly formed 6 Cavalry Machine Gun Squadron on 29 February 1916. Seconded to the RFC at the end of 1916, he trained as a Pilot and was duly confirmed and gazetted Flying Officer on 3 April 1917. Just eleven days later, he was sent to France and 60 Squadron, then equipped with Nieuport Scouts. Over the next six months, this well regarded and popular Pilot gained six victories and was Mentioned in Despatches, *London Gazette* of 11 July 1917. His MC was announced in the *London Gazette* of 18 October 1917, details in the *Gazette* of 7 March 1918: 'For conspicuous gallantry and devotion to duty. He has destroyed several hostile machines and driven down others out of control. On one occasion he attacked along four enemy aircraft, shooting one down completely out of control. He twice co-operated with an infantry attack, diving to a very low altitude. He has shown great skill and gallantry on all occasions'.

With the departure of Billy Bishop, VC, from 60 Squadron, Horn was given command of 'C' Flight. His tour with '60' completed, he returned to the Home Establishment, taking up an instructing post at Ayr. He next received an invitation to renew acquaintance with W A Bishop, VC (qv), who was currently forming 85 Squadron. Horn returned to France in May 1918, as a Flight Commander with '85', taking his victory count up to 13 before the war ended. Reverting to his Army status, Horn eventually retired from active service with the rank of Lieutenant Colonel, 3 Dragoon Guards. Spencer Horn later entered the Indian Army, becoming ADC to the Governor of Bengal in 1924. Renewing an interest in aviation, he took out a flying license in 1937. Spencer Horn was in the Reserve of Officers when the Second War came and went on to serve as a Major with 3 Carabiniers. As a reward for services rendered to Britain's Norwegian allies during the war, Horn was personally presented with the King Haakon VII Liberty Cross by the King of Norway.

HORSFALL, Ewart Douglas

The second son of Howard Douglas Horsfall and Mabel Horsfall (née Smith), of Mere Bank, Liverpool, he was born on 24 May 1892. Educated at Eton (1905-11), where he won the school's Sculling event in 1910 and rowed in the VIII at Henley in 1911, and at Magdalen College, Oxford (College Rowing VIII, 1912, 1913 (Stroke) and 1914), BA, MA. President of the Oxford University Boat Club, 1914-19. Gazetted Second Lieutenant to 9 Battalion, Rifle Brigade, on 12 September 1914. Seeking secondment to the flying service, he next gained his Royal Aero Club Certificate (Number 1032) on 31 December 1914. His formal training completed, he was confirmed and gazetted Flying Officer on 19 February 1915. The start to his operational flying was delayed when, on 31 March 1915, he was hit by a propellor at the very moment of preparing to depart to France. Fortunate, indeed, to survive an encounter with a propellor, it was not until July 1915 before he was fit enough to join the BE2c-equipped 4 Squadron at the front. His MC was announced in the New Year Honours *London Gazette* of 14 January 1916 (no citation). Although no official citation was published, research has unearthed the original recommendation for the award: 'A very gallant and enterprising officer, who has done much good work lately. He particularly distinguished himself on Sept 25th when in very bad weather he attacked and hit a train from 500 feet with a 100lb bomb from a single-seat aeroplane'.

The French, too, showed their appreciation by awarding him the Légion d'Honneur, Croix de Chevalier, *London Gazette* of 24 February 1916. On 19 February 1916, Horsfall and his squadron colleague, Captain J E Tennant (qv), carried out one of the very earliest night bombing raids. Both men were flying the BE2c without Observers in order to maximise their bomb-carrying capacity for their attack on an enemy aerodrome. Tennant's bombs fell on their target, but Horsfall's failed to release, although he did manage to get them away later on to another, secondary, target. As a consequence of this raid, night flying practice in the RFC was considerably increased. Horsfall would go on to command 3 Squadron with the rank of Lieutenant Colonel, from 28 April 1917 to 5 June 1917. After relinquishing his command of 3 Squadron, he would serve out the remainder of the war on the Staff, being twice Mentioned in Despatches. He married, in 1923, Myra Downing of Ballintoy, County Antrim, Ireland, with whom he had two sons and one daughter, living at Sevenhampton Manor, Andoversford, Gloucestershire.

HORSLEY, Clement Flegg

From Fakenham, Norfolk, he was born on 12 February 1895. Educated at the City of Norwich School. He enlisted on 5 August 1914, the day following the outbreak of war, as a Private soldier into 6 Battalion, Norfolk Regiment (TF). Following service in the UK, he was accepted as a Cadet into the Royal Military College, Sandhurst, in January 1916. Graduating from Sandhurst as Prize Cadet on 26 October 1916, he was gazetted Second Lieutenant to a Regular Army battalion of the Norfolk Regiment on the following day. Although an orphan, Horsley was fortunate in that his guardian, Mr F S Wigg, of Mamhurst, Fakenham, Norfolk, undertook to underwrite the expense incurred in fitting him out as an Army officer. Securing an almost immediate secondment to the RFC in November 1916, he trained as a Pilot and was duly confirmed and gazetted Flying Officer on 31 March 1917. Posted out to 18 Squadron in France in April, he gained two victories during a tour which ended in the following November, when he returned to the Home Establishment. On the intervening 24 September, he and his Observer, Lieutenant A Hahn had gallantly fought off no less than eight enemy aircraft that attacked their DH4 during a photographic reconnaissance patrol. More than 700 rounds were expended in their defence, and one of the attackers was driven down out of control. Horsley received his MC as a consequence of this and other actions, *London Gazette* of 27 October 1917, details in the *Gazette* of 18 March 1918: 'For conspicuous gallantry and devotion to duty. While on a photographic reconnaissance he was attacked by eight enemy aeroplanes, and after a fight which lasted over twenty minutes drove down two of the enemy. On another occasion he took part in an encounter between six of our machines and twenty-five enemy machines, in which he displayed great coolness and skill in driving off the attacking enemy. He has led many successful photographic reconnaissances, and on several occasions has been attacked by superior numbers of the enemy'.

His tour with '18' completed, he returned to the Home Establishment, where he spent the remainder of the war as an Instructor with, successively, 9 TS and 51 TDS, being promoted to A/Captain on 13 June 1918. On 17 November 1921, Horsley resigned his Regular Army commission in favour of a permanent commission in the RAF.

HORSLEY, Oswald

The younger son of Sir Victor Horsley, FRS, and Lady Horsley, of 25 Cavendish Square, London, he was born on 14 February 1893. Educated at Bedale's School, Petersfield, (1906-12) and at Christ Church, Oxford (1912-14). Interrupting his studies at Oxford, he enlisted as a Private soldier (Number 1437) into 28 Battalion, London Regiment (Artists Rifles) (TF), as soon as war came. Picked out for a commission, he was gazetted Second Lieutenant to 2 Battalion, Gordon Highlanders, on 15 December 1914. He was wounded on two occasions whilst serving with his battalion in France; firstly on 20 January 1915 and again on 20 July 1915. The first of his MCs, *London Gazette* of 2 October 1916, was won in the trenches at Angle Wood on 18 August 1916, when he led an assault on the German positions and, although wounded (for the third time), continued to direct operations until the objective had been secured. His wounds on this occasion were so severe that he was pronounced unfit for further service with the infantry. Nothing daunted, he, like so many others of this truly remarkable generation, immediately sought further service, this time with the RFC. Training first an Observer, he was subsequently confirmed and gazetted Flying Officer (Observer) on 18 October 1917. Soon after this, he qualified for his full 'Wings' and was sent out to the Nieuport XVII-equipped 40 Squadron on 28 November following. His efforts and successes were rewarded by a Bar to his MC, announced in the *London Gazette* of 22 June 1918: 'For conspicuous gallantry and devotion to duty. He has brought down completely out of control three hostile machines and of two others he engaged one he fought to within a distance of 200 feet from the ground, forcing it to land, the second spinning down to the ground out of control, he being unable to observe it crash owing to the presence of other hostile machines. He has carried out accurate and valuable reconnaissances, and has set a magnificent example of determined gallantry and skill whilst leading low-flying and bombing patrols'.

Horsley was also Mentioned in Despatches around this time. His tour completed, he returned to the Home Establishment in May 1918, and, in July, was sent to Farnborough as a Test Pilot. He and his Observer were both killed near Reading on 19 August 1918, when their machine unaccountably broke up in the air during a test flight. Oswald Horsley is buried in Steep (All Saints) Churchyard, Hampshire.

HOWARD, Bernard Henry Esmé

The only son of Henry Charles Howard, MP, DL, JP, and Lady Mabel Harriet Howard, the second daughter of Captain Mark McDonnell, 5th Earl of Antrim, of Greystoke Castle, Penrith, Cumberland, he was born on 15 September 1880. Developing an interest in aviation, he learnt to fly and gained his Royal Aero Club Certificate (Number 565) by satisfying the examiners in a Bristol machine at the Bristol School of Flying, Brooklands, on 19 July 1913. Commissioned into 3 (Reserve) Battalion, Manchester Regiment on 2 October 1915, he was immediately seconded to the RFC. His formal pilot training duly completed, he was confirmed and gazetted Flying Officer on 11 November 1915, the same day that he was posted to 23 Squadron, then stationed at Gosport. After a brief spell with '23', he transferred to 26 (South African) Squadron on 26 December 1915, accompanying that unit to Mombasa as a 'founder member' in January 1916. He served subsequently with '26' in East Africa and was, for a time, also attached as Liaison Officer to the French forces in the area. His MC was announced in the *London Gazette* of 1 February 1917 (no citation). Howard returned to the UK on 30 March 1917, his health somewhat impaired by the African climate. Bernard Howard finally relinquished his commission, due to ill-health, on 15 January 1919. Returning to live at the family home of Greystoke Castle, Penrith, he married, on 10 February 1934, Glory Evelyn Rollo. Bernard Howard died on 5 October 1949.

HOWARD, Ernest Ford

Originally from Canada, he was gazetted Second Lieutenant to the Royal Field Artillery on 22 August 1917. Seconded to the RFC, he reported to Reading for observer training in the following month. His training completed, he was posted to 98 Squadron, then at Old Sarum in the UK, on 10 December 1917. Next, he was sent out to the FE2b-equipped night-bombing 102 Squadron on 28 December. On 23 May 1918, Howard and his regular Pilot, Lieutenant A B Whiteside (qv), in FE2b, 'A5649', narrowly escaped disaster when shrapnel hit their propellor, causing the engine to stop. Fortunately, Whiteside was able to glide them down in the darkness – it was eleven o'clock at night – to a forced landing at Ficheux. The citation for Howard's MC is both confused and confusing, *London Gazette* of 16 September 1918: 'For conspicuous gallantry and devotion to duty. This officer has taken part in fifty-two night-bombing raids, showing at all times the greatest skill and perseverance in finding his objectives. On one occasion in particular, after having successfully bombed a large ammunition dump which was set on fire and blown up, he proceeded to drop bombs on a town which held large numbers of the enemy, also firing from a low altitude with his machine-gun on the roads leading to it. Returning to his squadron he obtained more bombs and ammunition, and with the same Observer [sic], proceeded to drop bombs on a train behind the enemy's lines. On many occasions his machine was badly damaged by enemy fire from the ground. He has set a fine example of devotion to duty and an entire disregard of danger to the other members of the squadron'.

The wording of the citation gives the impression that Howard was the Pilot during the raid on the 'large ammunition dump'. In fact, Howard acted on this, and on many other raids, as Observer to the previously mentioned fellow Canadian and Pilot, Arthur Barlow Whiteside. Whiteside was given a Bar to his MC for this action in the same *London Gazette* of 16 September 1918, the citation having many similarities with that of Howard. His tour with '102' completed. he returned to the Home Establishment on 10 June 1918. Howard returned to his native Canada on 22 August 1918, subsequently leaving the RAF on returning to a regular unit in Canada, on 19 April 1919.

HOWARD, Harry

The son of Mr and Mrs F A Howard, of Stockton-on-Tees, County Durham, he was born on 27 May 1893. A schoolteacher at Bede College, Durham, he was also a pre-war volunteer, having enlisted as a Private soldier (Number 1957) into 5 Battalion, Durham Light Infantry (TF), on 15 November 1912. Although mobilised with the rest of the TF in August 1914, he would not go to the front, with the rank of Corporal, until 4 November 1915. Picked out soon afterwards for a commission, he was gazetted Second Lieutenant to 29 (Reserve) Battalion (Tyneside Scottish) Northumberland Fusiliers, on 20 January 1916. Following a further stint at the front with the Northumberland Fusiliers, he was seconded to the RFC in the autumn of 1917. After training as an Observer, he accompanied the newly formed night-bombing FE2b-equipped 102 Squadron to France as a Probationary and 'founder member' on 24 September 1917. His 'apprenticeship' satisfactorily completed, he was subsequently confirmed and gazetted Flying Officer (Observer) on 16 November following. His rapidly acquired MC was announced in the *London Gazette* of 18 January 1918, details in the *Gazette* of 25 April 1918: 'For conspicuous gallantry and devotion to duty as Observer. Having successfully bombed a station behind the enemy lines, he took control of the machine on the pilot fainting from a bullet wound in his arm. He managed to keep the machine level, and flew it until his pilot recovered. Shortly afterwards the latter again lost consciousness, and this officer took the control once more, managing to land the machine under very difficult circumstances well behind our lines. This officer has always shown a fine example of courage and skill in the many night bombing raids in which he has taken part'.

His tour with '102' completed, he returned to the UK on 11 February 1918. After seeing out the remainder of the war in a number of training posts, he finally left the RAF, via the Unemployed List, on 6 February 1919.

Howard's life seems to have assumed complications in the immediate post-war years. Firstly, he was accepted for a temporary commission with 4 Battalion, Royal Berkshire Regiment (TF) on 9 April 1921, only to absent himself from duties during the following summer. Next, he enlisted as a Private soldier into the Royal Army Medical Corps in January 1922, after the Air Ministry withdrew permission for him to retain Air Force officer rank. On 6 November 1923, 'Pip' Howard was convicted at Winchester Assizes of bigamy and given nine months hard labour. Howard was discharged from the Army on 21 January 1924, due to a civil power conviction. Apparently, he had married Hilda Maude Dubbin on 24 March 1923, while his lawful wife, Elizabeth, still lived.

HOWARD, Richard Watson

Although born in Sydney, NSW, Australia, on 9 October 1896, he was brought up in Newcastle, NSW. After studying engineering at Hamilton, NSW, he initially enlisted as a Sapper (Number 2765) into the Australian Army Engineers. Picked out for a commission, he was gazetted Second Lieutenant to the AAF on 13 September 1915. He served in France with the Engineers from March to December 1916, before successfully applying for secondment to the RFC. After training, he first joined 68 Squadron on 7 April 1917, before briefly going on to the DH4-equipped 57 Squadron on 26 May following. A return to '68' came in July 1917, by this time also re-equipped with DH5s. The first of his eight victories came on 22 November 1917. The squadron changed to SE5As and was now labelled 2 Australian Flying Corps. Howard would go on to achieve a further seven victories with this new Scout-plane. Promoted to Flight Commander on 22 February 1918, his MC was announced in the *London Gazette* of 4 February 1918, details in the *Gazette* of 5 July 1918: 'For conspicuous gallantry and devotion to duty. Whilst separated from his patrol owing to thick mist he drove down an enemy aeroplane out of control. He then engaged a hostile two-seater, which he forced to land in our lines. On another occasion, though attacked at a height of 400 feet by an enemy two-seater, he manoeuvred, shot the observer, and caused the hostile machine to land, apparently in difficulties, but intact. He has consistently done excellent work at very low altitude'.

On 22 March 1918, Howard was shot down near to Vermond, by Leutnant Hans Böhning, the sixth victory of this eventual 17 victory German Ace, and died of his wounds on the same day. His grave was subsequently lost, and hence he is now commemorated on the Flying Services Memorial, Arras, France.

HOWE, Thomas Sydney Curzon

From Dublin, he was born on 18 January 1895. Gazetted Second Lieutenant to 6 Battalion, Connaught Rangers, via a New Army commission, on 28 August 1915. Seconded to the RFC, he trained as an Observer and was sent out to BE2c-equipped 10 Squadron as a Probationary in February 1916. On 29 February following, Howe and his Pilot, Second Lieutenant E W Leggatt (qv) in BE2c, '1737', fought an enemy machine over the lines at Bois de Biez. The Albatros' engine was hit and the enemy Pilot shot in the leg. Forced to land in the British lines, the German crew was subsequently taken prisoner. Howe and Leggatt both received the MC, *London Gazette* of 30 March 1916: 'For conspicuous gallantry and skill when on patrol. Second Lieutenant Howe and Second

Lieutenant Leggatt attacked a hostile machine and drove it down. They then climbed again and attacked another. Under heavy fire from the machine, by a combination of good flying and shooting, they hit the enemy pilot and damaged his engine, forcing him to descend within our lines. The enemy were made prisoners'.

Research has unearthed the original recommendation for the award which gives just a little more detail: 'For conspicuous gallantry and skill on February 29, 1916, 2/Lt Leggatt and 2/Lt Howe, whilst on patrol in a BE2c, attacked a hostile machine and drove it down in the enemy's lines near La Bassée. Climbing again, they pursued another Albatros towards Lillers. Under heavy fire from the German machine, they got within 150 yards of it and, by a combination of good flying and shooting, hit the pilot and disabled his engine. The Albatros dived, followed by the BE2c firing all the time. The Germans landed, with their machine but little damaged, about a mile south of Merville where they were taken prisoners'.

Howe had won his MC as a Probationary, being confirmed and gazetted Flying Officer (Observer) on 30 May following. He was wounded in the air on 11 December 1916, which meant a return to the UK for medical treatment. Once recovered, he trained and qualified as a Pilot, before joining the Camel-equipped 54 Squadron in France on 17 March 1918. On 17 April 1918, Howe in Sopwith Camel, 'D6583', was shot down and killed during an aerial combat above Outersteene. Thomas Howe's body was never recovered and hence he is commemorated on the Flying Services Memorial, Arras, France.

HOWELL, Cedric Ernest

From Adelaide, South Australia, he was born 17 June 1894. Educated at the Church of England Grammar School, Melbourne. After leaving school, he trained as a Draughtsman. When the war came, his first attempts to volunteer failed, but, in 1915, he was accepted as a Private soldier in the AIF and, following training, sailed for Egypt as part of a contingent intended to reinforce 14 Battalion, AIF. A crack-shot, Howell served in Gallipoli as a sniper before being struck down with malaria. Once recovered, he later served on the Somme with 46 Battalion, AIF. An application for transfer to the flying service was allowed early in 1917, he was one of the 200 men recruited from the AIF and he was gazetted Second Lieutenant to the RFC, via the Special Reserve, on 17 March following. Gained his Royal Aero Club Certificate (Number 4517) on 18 April 1917. His formal pilot training duly completed, he was confirmed and gazetted Flying Officer on 25 July 1917. A posting to France and the Sopwith Camel-equipped 45 Squadron came in October 1917. The CO, 45 Squadron, Major Vaucour (qv), was singularly unimpressed with Howell's sickly pallor, he was still not free from malaria, and sent him back to England to convalesce, and so it was not until November 1917 that he first flew operationally. Soon after he re-joined, '45' was sent to the Italian front. The first of Howell's remarkable total of 19 victories came on 14 January 1918; a total which included a 'quintet' on 12 July, a 'quartet' on 14 May, and three 'doubles', also achieved on single days. Naturally, with this level of success, the honours flowed. His MC was announced in the *London Gazette* of 16 September 1918: 'For conspicuous gallantry and devotion to duty. He bombed an electrical power-house with great skill, obtaining three direct hits from 100 feet. With two other machines he carried out a most dashing attack on a formation of twelve enemy aeroplanes. Although badly hampered by frequent jams in both of his machine guns, he destroyed three and drove down one out of control. He is a most successful and gallant patrol leader, and has destroyed six enemy aeroplanes and shot down one out of control'.

His Distinguished Flying Cross appeared five days later in the *London Gazette* of 21 September 1918, and he was awarded the Distinguished Service Order in the *Gazette* of 2 November 1918. He was also Mentioned in Despatches, *London Gazette* of 6 January 1919. Howell returned to the UK in August 1918 and saw out the remainder of the war instructing at the CFS, Upavon. In March 1919, the Government of Australia, anxious to promote aerial links between the UK and the Antipodes, proposed a competition, with a £10,000 prize, for the first successful flight from Great Britain to Australia. Of particular attraction to the Australian flyers still in the UK after the end of the Great War, many immediately attempted to find 'sponsors'. 'Spike' Howell thought himself extremely fortunate to be nominated by the Martinsyde company to pilot an A1 biplane in the forthcoming race. George Fraser from Coburg, Victoria, was chosen to accompany Howell as Flight Engineer. Their machine, with a wing-span of 43 feet 4 inches and an overall length of 27 feet 5 inches, was powered by a Rolls Royce Falcon engine of 275 hp. Howell and Fraser were the sixth contestants to depart from London on 4 December 1919. The first leg, to Paris, was not without difficulties, but they eventually arrived safely. The following morning, they set off on the next leg to Pisa in Italy. Again, the weather was less than kind, but still they reached their destination as planned. Emergency repairs on a damaged tailskid effected, they took off next for Naples. After Naples, they intended to make for Salerno, but bad weather in the vicinity of Vesuvius, forced them to return to Naples. Their next stop was Taranto, from whence they set out for Athens on 8 December 1919. They were last seen in the semi-darkness over St George's Bay, Corfu, at 8 pm on 10 December 1919. After a prolonged search, the Martinsyde was discovered under about 12 feet of water by an Italian naval search vessel. Howell's body would be washed ashore later, but Fraser's was never found. 'Spike' Howell had married during the war and his wife was aboard the SS *Orsova*, en route for Adelaide, and ready to greet him when he arrived. The news of his death was broken to her by Howell's father, when the ship finally arrived in Australia. Howell's body was taken home and buried with full military honours at Heidelberg Cemetery, Victoria.

NB: His medals were offered for sale by Sotheby's (lot 453) on 11 May 1989: Distinguished Service Order, MC, Distinguished Flying Cross, British War Medal 1914-20, and Victory Medal 1914-19 (Capt RAF).

HOWELL, John Gwynne

The son of Ernest Howell, JP, and Mrs Howell, of Penbigwrn, South Wales, he was born in St Clear, South Wales, on 17 October 1891. Educated at Radley (1906-08), at London University, where he was a member of the OTC, and at Magill University, Montreal, Canada. After completing his education, he worked for an Insurance Company in Montreal from March 1912 to August 1914, whereupon he returned to the UK to volunteer his services. Gazetted Second Lieutenant to the Royal Field Artillery on 23 November 1914. He served in France with the RFA, before being seconded to the RFC in the spring of 1916. After training as an Observer, he was posted to the BE2c-equipped 16 Squadron. On 11 May 1916, Howell and his Pilot, Captain Arthur Reed Tillie, Scottish Rifles attached RFC, were registering for the Royal Arillery in BE2c, '2748', when their machine was struck by anti-aircraft fire. Tillie, from Glasgow, was killed and the BE began to plummet to the ground. Somehow, Howell climbed into the pilot's cockpit and, despite a jammed rudder, managed to land the machine into the British lines, whereupon it immediately came under heavy shell fire. Remarkably, Howell escaped unhurt, his MC being announced within weeks, *London Gazette* of 31 May 1916: 'RFA attached No 16 Squadron, 2 Wing, RFC (it is unusual for a citation to include a squadron number). 'For conspicuous gallantry and skill. When the pilot of his machine was killed, he climbed into the pilot's seat, and, standing in front of him, managed to land the machine in our lines'.

Howell would go on to serve on the Staff of 3 Brigade, RFC, and with the Independent Air Force in 1918, rising to the rank of Major. He married Jessie Elizabeth Preston around this time. He finally left the service, via the Unemployed List, on 28 January 1919. John Howell died on 19 December 1923, at the Vanburgh Nursing Home, Blackheath, London.

HOWSAM, George Robert

From Toronto, Canada, he was born in Post Perry, Ontario, on 21 January 1895. He enlisted as a Private soldier into the CEF in 1916. Picked out for a commission, he was gazetted Second Lieutenant to the RFC in the autumn of 1917. Having trained as a Pilot, he was given his 'Wings' in the November of that year. Sent out to 70 Squadron (Sopwith Camels) soon after he qualified, he gained his first victory on 28 December. Carrying on his successes into the New Year, he went on to claim a further 11, including a 'quartet' of Albatros Scouts on 22 January, and a 'double' on 9 March 1918. His MC was announced in the *London Gazette* of 4 March 1918, details in the *Gazette* of 16 August 1918: ' For conspicuous gallantry and devotion to duty in aerial combats. He has destroyed five enemy machines and driven down others out of control, showing splendid courage and initiative on all occasions'.

Wounded in combat on 24 March 1918, he was returned to the UK for hospital treatment. After recovering, he took up duties in the Home Establishment before returning to the front in October 1918, this time as a Flight Commander with 43 Squadron, recently equipped with the newly introduced Sopwith Snipe. Howsam achieved his last and 13th victory in this new type on 30 October, when he shot a Fokker DVII down in flames over Aulnoye. From the RAF, he joined the Canadian Air Force in 1921. His many subsequent appointments, honours and promotions included: Member of the RCAF Siskin aerobatic team in the 1920s; attended RAF Staff College in 1930 and 1931; attached to the Canadian Army as Air Staff Officer in Toronto, 1932-36; Director of Air Training, 1938-39; 4 Training Command, RCAF; CO, 11 Service Flying Training Command, Yorkton, Saskatchewan; AOC, North West Staging Route; CB, 1945; Legion of Merit (Commander, USA),1946; Order of the White Lion, 3rd Class, Czechoslovakia), 1946; Commander of the Order of the Crown, Belgium), 1948. Howsam retired from the RCAF with the rank of Air Vice-Marshal in 1946. He afterwards became active in Civil Defence and supported the RCAFA. Air Vice-Marshal George Howsam died in Victoria, British Columbia, on 16 April 1988.

HOY, Campbell Alexander

From the North East of England, he was born on 13 February 1893. Gazetted Second Lieutenant to the Northern Cyclist Battalion (TF) on 15 January 1915 and was promoted Lieutenant on 12 July following. Transferring to the RFC, he trained as an Observer and was sent out as a Probationary to FE2d-equipped 20 Squadron in the spring of 1917. On 25 May, he and his Pilot, Second Lieutenant J H Baring-Gould, in FE2d, 'A6366', were in a combat over Irish Farm with Leutnant August Hanko of Jasta 28, becoming the third of the German's eventual five victories. Baring-Gould received a machine-gun bullet in the back and Hoy was injured in the subsequent crash, their machine subsequently being shelled into matchwood. His probationary period satisfactorily completed, he was confirmed and gazetted Flying Officer (Observer) on 17 June 1917, whilst lying in hospital. After recovering his fitness and flying mainly with Lieutenant Richard M Trevethan (qv), he claimed ten victories between 29 June and 9 August 1917, all of them enemy Scout planes. His MC was announced in the *London Gazette* of 17 September 1917: 'For conspicuous gallantry and devotion to duty when acting as Observer on offensive patrols. On four occasions he has shot down hostile scouts, displaying in every instance splendid determination and a very fine offensive spirit'.

Staying on in the RAF after the war, he was, in January 1939, promoted to Wing Commander and, upon his eventual retirement on 15 February 1947, held the rank of Group Captain. Campbell Hoy died on 9 March 1985.

HUBBARD, Thomas O'Brien

From London, he was born on 14 August 1882. In the early years of the century, he worked his way around the world, turning his hand to anything that presented itself, including boundary-riding on a huge sheep station at East Taglai, South Queensland, Australia. As a young man he built his own machine and flew it successfully. Returning to the UK, he gained his Royal Aero Club Certificate (Number 222), satisfying the examiners on a Howard-Wright machine of the Grahame-Wright School at Hendon, on 4 June 1912. When war came in August 1914, Hubbard, who held the rank of T/Captain in the Special Reserve, was immediately mobilised and appointed a Flight Commander and an Instructor in Flying at the CFS. His first fully operational appointment came in November 1915, when he was appointed Commanding Officer of 11 Squadron (mainly equipped with Vickers FB5s) in France. His MC was announced in the Birthday Honours *London Gazette* of 3 June 1916 (no citation). Although no formal citation was published in the *Gazette*, research has unearthed the original recommendation for the award: 'T O'B Hubbard. For exceptionally good work while commanding 11 Squadron from 10th December 1915 to the present date. Has set an example to all his Officers by his energy and by flying different types of machines in bad weather conditions. Has previously done excellent work during the campaign'.

Hubbard would continue to command '11' through the opening weeks of the Battle of the Somme, with Albert Ball as one of his Pilots, before relinquishing the reins in August 1916. He would, later in the war, go on to command the Camel-equipped 73 Squadron at the front, prior to turning his attention to experimental work, a field in which he was credited with exceptional brilliance. It was Hubbard who, in 1918, was largely responsible for ironing out and overcoming the early problems experienced with the Sopwith Snipe, by recommending the fitting of balanced aerilons. For his outstanding work in test and experimental flying, he was awarded the Air Force Cross, *London Gazette* of 1 January 1919. Staying on in the RAF after the war, he eventually retired with the rank of Wing Commander, on 13 September 1931.

HUDSON, Frank

The son of George Matthews Hudson and Rose Crozier Hudson, of Mossel Bay, Cape Town, South Africa, he was born on 1 July 1889. His older brother, Robert James Hudson (qv) also won a 'flying MC' in the Great War. Educated at Repton (1904-07), where he was a member of the OTC, and at the Central Technical College, South Kensington, London (1908-10), from where he obtained a City and Guilds qualification in Engineering. Hudson worked as an Engineer with Messrs J A Fowler and Company of Leeds, before later obtaining a position in the Drawing Office of the Royal Aero Factory, Farnborough. He gained his Royal Aero Club Certificate (Number 507), satisfying the examiners on a Deperdussin monoplane at the Deperdussin School, Hendon, on 3 June 1913. He joined the Inns of Court OTC (Number K/E/1/2288) on 10 December 1914 and was promoted to Corporal before being gazetted Second Lieutenant to the RFC on 9 July 1915. Hudson served with 17 Squadron in Egypt for nine months and in Salonika for a further nine months, being promoted to A/Captain and Flight Commander on the intervening 1 June 1916. His MC was announced in the New Year *London Gazette* of 1 January 1917 (no citation). Hudson contracted malaria in August 1916 and was eventually obliged to return to the UK as a consequence of the disease in May 1917. After treatment in the Euston Square Hospital, London, he returned to duty with 85 Squadron, then at Hounslow, before transferring as a Flight Commander to a training squadron in Dover in January 1918. The lingering effects of his illness appears to have precluded a return to operational flying for the remainder of the war.

HUDSON, Frank Neville

The son of Provision Merchant, Frank Hudson and Mrs Annie M Hudson, of The White House, Oakwood Avenue, Beckenham, Kent, and later Mells Lodge, Halesworth, Suffolk, he was born on 4 November 1897. Educated at Bradfield College (1912-15) and at Sandhurst. Gazetted Second Lieutenant to 1 Battalion, East Kent Regiment (The Buffs), on 15 September 1915, with an immediate secondment to the RFC. Gained his Royal Aero Club Certificate (Number 1830) on 6 October 1915. His formal pilot training duly completed, he was confirmed and gazetted Flying Officer on 10 November following. He accompanied BE2c-equipped 15 Squadron to France as a 'founder member' on 23 December 1915. On 19 January 1916, a bad day for '15', Hudson and his Observer/Gunner, Corporal Edwards, narrowly escaped disaster when, whilst under attack by Fokkers, a spent cartridge case jammed an aileron. Their manoeuverability severely restricted, they were saved only by the propitious intervention of a friendly FE8. Six days later, Hudson and his Observer of the day, 2 AM J A Lathaen (Number 681) in BE2c, '4126', were forced to land when the engine of their machine was hit in a fight with yet more Fokkers. On 21 February 1916, Hudson was wounded in the head by anti-aircraft fire during a reconnaissance flight over the enemy trenches. His MC was announced in the *London Gazette* of 30 March 1916: 'For conspicuous gallantry and skill on several occasions, notably when, although severely wounded in the head, he successfully completed his aerial reconnaissance. After re-crossing the line and landing at an aerodrome, he at once lost consciousness. This young officer is only eighteen years of age, but has many times driven off enemy machines and twice forced them to the ground'.

Fit again for duty by the following 26 June, remarkably, he was again hit in the head from AA fire near Menin. Knocked unconscious, his skull fractured, he came to just as his machine was about to crash and managed not only to regain control, but also regain the British lines. His health and fitness restored, he joined 54 Squadron as an A/Captain and Flight Commander at the turn of the New Year of 1917. Flying the diminutive Sopwith Pup, Hudson achieved six victories between 27 January and 11 July 1917. On 13 July 1917, Hudson in Pup, 'A6240', was wounded in the air when his machine was shot down between Bruges and Ostend by Leutnant Fleckern of Jasta 20. The circumstances were that he had been escorting a reconnaissance machine over Bruges when, surrounded by exploding anti-aircraft shells, his engine cut out. As he glided west, he was attacked by five enemy machines and forced down, crashing onto a beach, his Pup turning over on its back. The wounded and injured Hudson was immediately taken prisoner and committed to hospital. He was repatriated on 19 December 1918, but not before he had made a nuisance of himself to his captors. He was Mentioned in Despatches in the 'Escapers Gazette', *London Gazette* of 16 December 1919: '....for gallantry whilst a Prisoner of War in escaping, or attempting to escape, from captivity, or for valuable services rendered in the Prison Camps of the Enemy'.

Staying on in the RAF after the war, he was killed whilst flying at Suleimaniyeh, Kurdistan, on 6 June 1922.

HUDSON, Harold Byron

Originally from Cobham, Surrey, he was born on 8 December 1898. His family emigrated to Victoria, British Columbia, Canada, in 1912, where his father practised medicine. His education was completed in Canada, where he attended the University School, BC. After leaving school, he was employed as a clerk in Merchant's Bank of Canada. Volunteering for the flying service, he sailed for the UK aboard the SS *Halifax*, on 24 January 1917. Following a period as a Cadet, he was gazetted Second Lieutenant to the RFC on 24 May 1917. His pilot training completed, he was confirmed and gazetted Flying Officer on 31 August following. Hudson was first sent to the Camel-equipped 28 Squadron in France on 8 October 1917, before, very shortly afterwards, accompanying the same unit to the Italian front. Known as 'Steve', he enjoyed accompanying his Flight Commander, Captain William Barker, VC, on balloon 'strafes'. In particular, on 24 January and 12 February 1918, he shared in the destruction of no less than seven balloons. Hudson also accounted for six enemy aircraft. His MC was announced in the *London Gazette* of 16 September 1918: 'For conspicuous gallantry and devotion to duty in destroying four enemy aeroplanes and shooting down two enemy kite balloons in flames'.

His tour with '28' completed, he was, in May 1918, posted to 45 Squadron, also in Italy, but did not add to his victory count with that unit. Further brief post-war service with 30 Squadron came on 1 April 1919, which lasted until he finally left the service, via the Unemployed List, in July 1919. Returning to Canada, he worked in the pulp and paper mill industries in British Columbia, for the rest of his business life. 'Steve' Hudson died in Vancouver in February 1981.

HUDSON, Robert James

Born in Henley, London, on 1 May 1885, he was the son of George Matthews Hudson and Rose Crozier Hudson, of Mossel Bay, Cape Town, South Africa. His younger brother, Frank Hudson (qv), also won a 'flying MC' in the Great War. Educated at the Diocesan College, Rondesbosch, South Africa, and at Caius College, Cambridge, from where he graduated in Law. He was called to the Bar, Middle Temple, in 1909, and practised as a Barrister in Bulawayo, Rhodesia, from 1910 to 1914. Volunteering as soon as the war came in August 1914, he served with 1 Battalion, Rhodesia Regiment, in South West Africa, during the campaigns of 1914 and 1915. Taking ship to the UK at his own expense, he was gazetted Second Lieutenant to 5 (Reserve) Battalion, Royal Fusiliers, on 27 October 1915, with an immediate secondment to the RFC. Gained his Royal Aero Club Certificate (Number 2300) on 18 January 1916. His formal training duly completed, he was confirmed and gazetted Flying Officer on 29 February 1916. Posted out to France and BE2c-equipped 15 Squadron on 6 April 1916. Hudson had two close calls in rapid succession on 23 and 27 August, when, on each occasion, his machines were damaged in the air. During the first of these two incidents, his Observer of the day, Second Lieutenant G S W Wood, was wounded in action. Hudson was promoted to A/Captain and Flight Commander in the following October. On 26 September 1916, Hudson and his Observer, Canadian Lieutenant F G H Manville(qv), descended to very low altitudes on three separate occasions and each time dispersed pockets of enemy infantry with machine-gun fire. His MC announced in the *London Gazette* of 14 November 1916: 'For conspicuous gallantry in action. He carried out artillery reconnaissances with great courage and determination. Later, on three occasions, diving to a low altitude, he engaged parties of infantry with his machine-gun'.

His tour with '15' completed, he returned to the Home Establishment on 8 March 1917. Hudson was duly promoted to Major and appointed to command 93 Squadron in the UK on 4 August 1917. 93 Squadron would remain in the UK, a non-operational unit, until its disbandment in August 1918. Hudson left the RAF, via the Unemployed List, on 14 February 1919, returning to Rhodesia in the following July. He married first in 1920, Constance de Beer, who died, childless, in 1925. Secondly, in 1928, he married Millicent Bruce (née Sutherland), with whom he had one son and one daughter. As his legal and political careers flourished, his various appointments included: Attorney General and Minister of Defence, Southern Rhodesia from 1923 to 1933; Minister of Justice and Defence, 1933; Judge, High Court of Southern Rhodesia from 1933 to 1942; and Chief Justice of Southern Rhodesia from 1943 to 1950. He was created CMG in 1938 and knighted (KCMG) in 1944, . He was also Chairman of the Rhodesian Board of the Standard Bank of South Africa from 1957 to 1962. Sir Robert Hudson died in Salisbury, Southern Rhodesia on 17 June 1963.

HUGHES, Geoffrey Forrest

From Sydney, New South Wales, Australia, he was born on 12 July 1895. He was gazetted Second Lieutenant to the RFC, via the Special Reserve, on 3 June 1916. His pilot training duly completed, he was confirmed and gazetted Flying Officer on the 28 July following. He enjoyed an unusually lengthy spell as an Instructor in the UK, before finally going out to 62 Squadron (Bristol Fighters) in the spring of 1918. Hughes and Captain H Claye proved a formidable Brisfit combination and, by 10 May, had gained 11 victories. Hughes' MC was announced in the *London Gazette* of 13 May 1918: 'For conspicuous gallantry and devotion to duty. While leading his formation over the enemy's lines he was attacked by twelve enemy machines, two of which he shot down. On the following day, when in charge of a patrol, he attacked seven enemy tri-planes, drove down one out of control, and forced three others to land. On another occasion, while in charge of a patrol, he was attacked by a large number of enemy scouts; owing to his skilful flying his Observer succeeded in shooting down one of the enemy machines, which broke up in the air. He always showed the greatest coolness and courage in action, and, as a flight commander, led his formation with splendid courage and determination'.

Hughes and Claye were involved in the fight on 13 March 1918, that saw Lothar von Richthofen quite badly wounded. The following is an extract from the book, 'Under the Guns of the German Aces', published in 1997 (Grub Street): 'On the following day (the 13th of the month!) Lothar von Richthofen was again wounded, this time in a fight with Bristol Fighters from 62 Squadron and Camels from 73 Squadron. The Bristols had been stalking several German fighters for some time but had been unable to manoeuvre themselves into a good position to attack. Just as the leader, Captain G F Hughes, decided to give it up and return to base, he saw two of his crews take it upon themselves to have a go at the enemy. However, the aggressors had not seen reinforcements in the form of several Fokker Tri-planes heading for them at the same height. With no option but to go to the aid of the two errant Bristols, Hughes and the rest of his planes dived into the fray. Lothar von Richthofen singled out Hughes and closed in, but Hughes' observer, Captain H Claye, coolly took careful aim and opened fire as the Fokker tore into them. The top wing of the Tri-plane began to shed fabric and then the whole centre section peeled away, causing Lothar to lose control. At that moment, Hughes and Claye were engaged by Manfred von Richthofen and had their hands full for several minutes before they managed to extricate themselves from what was an extremely fraught situation. Lothar, in the meantime, had crashed, receiving injuries which kept him out of action until the following July. His jaw was badly broken and to his great and evident discomfort, was kept wired-up for months. Hughes, of course, claimed the Triplane but so too, did Captain A H Orlebar (who later captained Britain's Schneider Trophy Team). Orlebar, flying a 73 Squadron Camel, also described his 'kill' as shedding most of its top wing; certainly both British pilots appear to have been credited with this one victory. Lothar was still in hospital when news of his brother's death reached him on 21 April 1918'.

After completing his tour with '62', Hughes returned to instructing duties in the UK. His outstanding services in this field were eventually recognised by the award of an Air Force Cross, *London Gazette* of 3 June

1919. Hughes was also Mentioned in Despatches on two occasions during the Great War, *London Gazettes* of 13 March 1918 and 22 January 1919. Returning to Australia, he became a prominent figure in Sydney's legal and business circles. His brother, Thomas Hughes, became the first Lord Mayor of Sydney. Geoffrey Hughes died of pneumonia on 13 September 1951.

HUNT, Edward Wallis Alleyne

The son of Edward and Sarah Jane Hunt, of Sidcup, Kent, and later 24 Harold Road, Upper Norwood, London, he was born at Melton Mowbray in 1892. Educated at Dover College and at University College London, where he studied Engineering from 1909 to 1913, graduating BSc. Gazetted Second Lieutenant to the RFC on 1 July 1916. His pilot training completed, he was confirmed and gazetted Flying Officer on 24 October following. Sent out to 18 Squadron in France, soon after qualifying. On 1 May 1917, Hunt and his Observer of the day, George Bell Miller, Highland Light Infantry attached RFC, in FE2b, '4968', were reported 'Missing in Action'. Their fate remaining unknown, they were later declared killed in action on that date. After his death, his parents insisted that he had been officially credited with the destruction of four enemy machines. His MC was belatedly announced in the *London Gazette* of 22 April 1918: 'For conspicuous gallantry and devotion to duty. Whilst carrying out a bombing raid on an enemy aerodrome, on being attacked by twenty hostile machines, he engaged a hostile scout at close range and drove it off. On an earlier occasion he attacked and destroyed an enemy scout. He has carried out many most successful night bombing raids, dropping his bombs with good effect on trains and aerodromes and attacking troops and transport with machine-gun fire from low altitudes. He has shown the greatest determination and enterprise under the most difficult conditions'.

His remains were subsequently recovered and he is buried in Neuville-St Remy Churchyard, France.

HUNTER, George Robertson

The son of Farmer, Hector Hunter and his wife, Isobel (née Duncan), of Kirkcaldy, Scotland, he was born on 19 March 1891. Educated at St Leonard's School, Edinburgh. He enlisted as a Private soldier (Number 8682) into Cameron Highlanders on 11 August 1909. After serving in the ranks for 5 years and 126 days, and having attained the rank of Lance Sergeant, he was gazetted Second Lieutenant to 1 Battalion of his regiment on 15 December 1914. Hunter served with 1 Camerons in the trenches during 1914, 1915 and 1916, and was slightly wounded at Albert in 1916. He served through yet another bitter winter in the trenches before being seconded to the RFC in the spring of 1917. Having trained as an Observer, he was confirmed and gazetted Flying Officer (Observer) on 6 May 1917. He flew operationally in the RE8s of 6 Squadron from 15 July 1917 to 17 November 1917. His MC was announced in the *London Gazette* of 25 April 1918: 'For conspicuous gallantry and devotion to duty. After completing four successful bombardment shoots in one flight, giving ninety-six observations, he was attacked by seven enemy aeroplanes but drove them off. On another occasion, though attacked by four enemy aeroplanes, he obtained the information he desired and rendered his report'.

His tour with '6' completed, he returned to the Home Establishment at the end of 1917. He next trained and qualified as a Pilot. He married in 1918, Annie Ingram Legge, with whom he had one son and one daughter. Hunter worked in the Air Ministry in 1918, before going out to the Middle East, where he flew operationally, albeit briefly, with 14 Squadron from 20 September 1918 to 30 September, before returning again to the Home Establishment.

HUNTER, Henry John Francis

The elder son of Henry Charles Vicars Hunter and the Hon Mrs Florence Louise Hunter (only daughter of the twelfth Baron Dormer), of Abermarlais Park, Llangadock, Carmarthenshire, he was born in Chelsea, London, on 29 December 1893. Educated at Roper's School, Bournemouth (1903-07), at Eton (1907-11), and at the Royal Military College, Sandhurst (1912). From Sandhurst he was gazetted Second Lieutenant to 1 Battalion, Rifle Brigade, on 5 February 1913. Hunter served in France with 7 Battalion of his regiment in 1915 and 1916 (wounded). After recovering from his wounds, he was seconded to the RFC. Gained his Royal Aero Club Certificate (Number 2872) on 9 May 1916. His formal pilot training completed, he was confirmed and gazetted Flying Officer on 24 May following. Hunter accompanied BE2c-equipped 34 Squadron to France as a 'founder member' on 15 June 1916. An Artillery co-operation specialist, his MC was announced in the *London Gazette* of 20 October 1916: 'For conspicuous gallantry and skill. He has done fine work for the artillery, and had accounted for many enemy guns. On one occasion, when a heavy storm drove all other machines back to their aerodromes, and the enemy guns took the opportunity to become active, he remained up and did fine work'.

He would, eventually, be presented with the insignia of his MC by the King at an investiture held at Buckingham Palace on 16 March 1918. Hunter would also be Mentioned in Despatches on two occasions during the Great War. He continued to serve in France, employed mainly on Staff duties, but then was promoted to Major and appointed Commanding Officer of 42 Squadron (RE8s) from 16 April 1918 until the end of the war. Hunter married four times, firstly on 11 April 1918, Ethel Elizabeth Lewis, widow of the Hon Francis Geoffrey Pearson; secondly, on 3 February 1927, Una Claire Thurgood; thirdly, in 1935, Kathleen Witts, with whom he had one son and one daughter; and, fourthly, in 1949, Kathleen Kilpatrick (née Morice). Making the RAF his career, he was promoted to Squadron Leader in 1919, going on to serve in Germany with the Army of Occupation in 1921 and 1922. He also served in China and in Iraq between the wars. He was promoted to Wing Commander on 1 January 1926 and to Group Captain on 1 January 1933. Hunter commanded RAF Finningley from 1937 until his retirement on 15 June 1939. Upon the outbreak of war in 1939, he was immediately recalled to command the night bomber station at Driffield. Next, from 1940 to 1942, he was appointed to command RAF Topcliffe, another bomber station in the UK. Created CBE in 1941. On 30 January 1942, he was placed in command of RAF bomber squadrons in Sumatra and Java. Later in the same year, he was appointed AOC, 221 Group (Indris), effectively commanding the RAF bomber squadrons on the Burma Battlefront. He also served in Ceylon, before being appointed to the Staff of Strategic Air Command, South East Asia in 1944, with which command he served until his retirement, with the rank of Air Commodore, in 1946. Hunter was Mentioned in Despatches on two occasions during the Second World War, *London Gazettes* of 2 June 1943 and 14 January 1944. He lived, in retirement, at Little Wareham, Beauford, North Devon. Air Commodore Henry Hunter died at the Royal Devon and Exeter Hospital on 12 September 1966.

NB: His medals are in a private collection: CBE, MC, 1914-15 Star, British War Medal 1914-20, Victory Medal 1914-19 with MID, 1939-45 Star, Pacific Star 1941-45 with clasp, and MID, Burma Star, Defence Medal 1939-45, War Medal 1939-45, Coronation Medal 1953, and Jubilee Medal 1935.

HURR, David Francis

From South Africa, he was born on 22 January 1892. After leaving school in 1908, he worked in the Mohair wool business in the pre-war years. Travelling to the UK, he was gazetted Second Lieutenant to 4 Battalion, Middlesex Regiment, on 5 August 1916. Hurr served with the 'Die-Hards' until October 1917, when he was seconded to the RFC. Having trained as an Observer, he was sent out as a Probationary to the AWFK8s of 35 Squadron on 11 December 1917. On 17 February 1918, Hurr and his Pilot, Second Lieutenant Gilbert McPherson (qv), in a 35 Squadron AWFK8, were sent on a special reconnaissance patrol from which they were extremely fortunate to return. Both men would receive the MC for their gallantry although, not uniquely, there is obvious confusion between the formally published citations. Hurr's, like McPherson's, MC was announced in the *London Gazette* of 22 April 1918: 'For conspicuous gallantry and devotion to duty. While he was on a special reconnaissance his machine was attacked when he was at a height of 5,000 feet over his objective by enemy aeroplanes, which he succeeded in driving off. Having descended to within 1,000 feet of the ground, he was heavily engaged by machine-gun fire, which wounded his Observer [sic], who collapsed. He then descended to within 400 feet of the ground and completed a comprehensive reconnaissance. He has at all times displayed the utmost disregard of danger and great devotion to duty'.

Conversely, McPherson's citation, whilst obviously pertaining to Hurr, reads: 'While acting as Observer on a special reconnaissance, he assisted in driving off an enemy aeroplane when his machine was at 5,000 feet above his objective. Having descended to within 1,000 feet of the ground, he was wounded in the head from machine-gun fire and collapsed. During the period when his pilot was descending still further to within 400 feet of the ground, he revived, and rendered further assistance in the reconnaissance, and on returning to his aerodrome was able to make his report. He has at all times displayed the utmost disregard of danger and great devotion to duty'.

Badly wounded in the action of 17 February 1918, Hurr was still unable to return to operational flying after he left hospital and was, instead, transferred to the Administration Branch. Promoted to A/Captain in February 1919, he finally left the RAF in the following July.

HUSKINSON, Patrick

The son of Colonel C J Huskinson, OBE, TD, and Mrs Huskinson, of Farndon, Newark, Nottinghamshire, he was born on 17 March 1897. Huskinson's father had the unenviable task of commanding the infamous Base Depot at Étaples from 1915 to 1919. Patrick was educated at Harrow (1910-15) and at the Royal Military College, Sandhurst, from where he was gazetted Second Lieutenant to a Regular Army battalion of the Sherwood Foresters on 20 October 1915. Seconded to the RFC, he trained as a Pilot and was confirmed and gazetted Flying Officer on 21 March 1916. Posted to BE2c-equipped 2 Squadron in France in April 1916, he was awarded the first of his MCs in the *London Gazette* of 27 July 1916: 'For conspicuous gallantry and skill. When attacking the enemy's communications, alone and without an Observer, he descended to 800 feet in order to release his bombs on a train and station. He was under continuous fire and his engine and machine were seriously damaged, but he succeeded in flying back at a low altitude and safely landed within our lines. He was again heavily fired at as he crossed the lines'.

His tour with '2' completed, he returned to the Home Establishment. In 1917, he was sent out, as a Flight Commander, to 19 Squadron, flying Spad VIIs as a Scout Pilot. He enjoyed considerable success, claiming 11 victories between 24 October 1917 and 17 March 1918, and winning a Bar to his MC: *London Gazette* of 22 April 1918: 'During a period of six months he had destroyed two hostile machines and driven down seven others out of control. He has also, during an attack, carried out a ground patrol, flying at a very low altitude, during which he engaged a company of the enemy with machine-gun fire. On a later occasion when firing at roads from a low altitude, he received a direct hit from a shell, which carried away a portion of his machine. He, however, regained control, and landing upside down in a shell-hole full of water was suspended in the water until nearly drowned. After his rescue, he remained all day working under shell fire until he salved the engine. He has at all times proved himself to be a very gallant, keen, and able pilot'.

It was widely, if quietly, acknowledged throughout this period that Huskinson was, de facto, 'in command' of 19 Squadron whenever Major Sanday was 'in drink'. Having survived the war, he was given command of 70 Squadron (Sopwith Snipes), then a part of the Army of Occupation in Germany on 1 January 1919. Staying on in the RAF, his various subsequent appointments, honours and promotions included: Staff, Cranwell, 1921; Armament Staff, 1924; Staff, Directorate of Training, 1925; CO, 41 Squadron, February 1930 to September 1931; Wing Commander, 1933; Officer Commanding RAF North Cotes, 1936; Group Captain, 1937; Air Commodore, 1940; Director of Armament Development, Ministry of Aircraft Production, 1940-42; CBE, 1942. Huskinson suffered temporary blindness as a consequence of being injured during an air raid on London in 1941. Despite subsequent problems with his sight, his experience was considered too valuable not to be exploited and he was offered the post of President of the Air Armament Board. He became involved in the development of rockets, medium capacity 'blast bombs', Barnes Wallis' 'Tallboys' and 'Grand Slams', etc. Huskinson, personally, is credited with the invention of the 4,000 lb 'Block-buster' bomb. In 1945, he was appointed an Officer of the Legion of Merit by the Americans. Huskinson finally retired from the RAF in 1946, living at 58 Prices Court, Knightsbridge, London, SW3, and becoming Chairman of a London printing company. He published his autobiography, 'Vision Ahead' in 1949 (Werner Laurie). Air Commodore Patrick Huskinson died on 24 November 1966.

HUSTON, Victor Henry

Born in Ireland on 13 October 1890, Huston was living and working in Vancouver, British Columbia, Canada, when war came in August 1914. Enlisting as a Private soldier into the Canadian Army Service Corps, he crossed over with the CEF in 1915, and was, on 13 September of the same year, gazetted Lieutenant into the CASC. A secondment to the RFC came in the autumn of 1916. After completing his pilot training, he was confirmed and gazetted Flying Officer on 8 December following. Within days of his 'graduation', he was at the front with the FE2b-equipped 18 Squadron. Huston, flying with various Observers, claimed six victories between 15 February 1917 and 27 May 1917. On 17 March 1917, Huston and his Observer of the day, Lieutenant E A Foord, in FE2b, '4990', were fortunate to escape with their lives when their machine was shot up during an aerial combat. Their engine disabled, they were forced to land in the front line trenches at Thiepval. His MC was announced in the *London Gazette* of 16 June 1917; 'For conspicuous gallantry and devotion to duty. He has rendered valuable service when on photographic reconnaissance. He has always shown the greatest skill and courage in leading attacks on hostile machines, and thus enabling valuable photographs to be secured behind the lines'.

His tour with '18' completed, he returned to the Home Establishment on 8 July 1917. Huston subsequently served at Hendon AA Park and at Norwich AA Park, and was promoted to Captain on 20 March 1918. In August 1918, he was loaned to the Chilean government as Chief Instructor to the newly formed Chilean Air Force, the British having given their South American ally, 14 seaplanes and 50 aeroplanes. Victor Huston finally left the RAF in November 1919.

HUXLEY, Frederic George

From Currie, King Island, Tasmania, he was born on 8 August 1891. A Shopkeeper before war came, he volunteered for the AIF, and served with the 26 and 52 Battalions, Australian Infantry, before transferring to the RFC in December 1916. Gazetted Second Lieutenant and Pilot, Australian Flying Corps, he served with 66 Squadron (Sopwith Pups) from April 1917 to August·1917, mainly on Home Defence duties. From '66' he next transferred to 68 Squadron (DH5s) upon that unit's arrival in France from Egypt. '68' then became 2 Squadron, Australian Flying Corps, with Huxley proving himself worthy of that distinguished unit. Indeed, the honour of scoring the squadron's first victory fell to him when, on 22 November 1917, over Bourlon Wood, having just bombed and shot up a column of infantry, he attacked and sent down an Albatros Scout. Huxley's comment on this victory was: 'It was a gift', this because he had expended only 30 rounds at a distance of 50 feet. His MC was announced in the *London Gazette* of 4 February 1918, details in the *Gazette* of 5 July 1918: 'For conspicuous gallantry and devotion to duty. He dropped a bomb upon a gun which was being moved to the rear, damaging it and killing three horses, and another bomb on a wagon, which was blown over, two of the personnel and one of the horses being killed. He then engaged a body of 300 troops marching along a road, and scattered them, causing fourteen casualties. Later, having disorganised a large advance party of enemy infantry with bombs and machine-gun fire, he shot down an enemy scout. He is a very keen and daring pilot'.

In December, '2 AFC' exchanged their DH5s for SE5s. With four victories to his credit, he was promoted to A/Captain and Flight Commander in January 1918. Huxley was hospitalised on 22 February 1918, and this appears to have ended his operational career.

HUXLEY, William Sherrin

The son of Publican, William John Huxley and Mary Huxley (née Sherrin), of the Shard Arms, Old Kent Road, Camberwell, Surrey, he was born on 4 September 1879. A trained Architect, he was employed by the Federation of Malay States Government in Kuala Lumpa from 1913 to 1914. Returning to the UK, he was gazetted Second Lieutenant to 14 (Reserve) Battalion, Royal Fusilier, via a New Armies commission, on 10 November 1915. Seconded to the RFC, he was, following training, confirmed and gazetted Balloon Officer on 25 April 1916. After service with 13 KBS in the UK, Huxley was promoted to A/Captain and gazetted BC Commander, on 13 January 1917. Sent out to France in May 1917, he commanded 12 BC until December 1917, when he returned to Salisbury in the UK. His MC was announced in the New Year *London Gazette* of 1 January 1918 (no citation). Although no formal citation was published in the *London Gazette*, research has unearthed the original recommendation for the award: '5 October 1917. 12 BC. For consistent good work as BC Commander throughout the period. He has set an example of courage and initiative'.

Posted next as Section Commander, 7 Balloon Wing in the UK in February 1918, he eventually returned to France in the same capacity, first to 3 BC, secondly to 19 BC, and thirdly to 12 BC. He was Mentioned in Despatches for his services in France during 1918, *London Gazette* of 11 July 1919. Returning to the Home Establishment on 20 March 1919, Huxley finally left the RAF, via the Unemployed List, on the following day.

HYDE, Frank

From Woodford Green, Essex, he was born in Walthamstow, Essex, on 23 July 1893. Educated at Loughton School and at Burschied School, Germany. After leaving school, he was articled to a firm of Chartered Accountants. A pre-war volunteer, he enlisted as a Trooper into the 1/2 County of London Yeomanry (TF) on 20 February 1913. He served with his regiment in Gallipoli from August 1915, being promoted to Lance Corporal on 7 September following. After the evacuation, he served in Egypt and was promoted to Sergeant at Dabaa on 1 March 1916. Accepted for the flying service, he reported for evaluation to RFC HQ, Aboukir, Egypt. Picked out for a commission, he was gazetted Second Lieutenant to the RFC, via the General List, on 18 February 1917. His pilot training duly completed, he was confirmed and gazetted Flying Officer on 6 May following. Posted next to the Western Front, he reported for duty with 13 Squadron (RE8s) in France on 4 July 1917. Promoted to A/Captain and Flight Commander in March 1918. On 20 April 1918, Hyde and his Observer of the day, Second Lieutenant W T C Blake, in RE8, 'C5086', were shot up during an aerial combat. Fortunately, both crewman suffered no physical harm and Hyde was able to get the damaged 'Harry Tate' back to his own aerodrome. His tour with '13' completed, he returned to the Home Establishment on 5 June 1918. His MC was announced in the *London Gazette* of 16 September 1918: 'For conspicuous gallantry and devotion to duty. He carried out many successful shoots and did valuable reconnaissance work, frequently under heavy anti-aircraft and machine-gun fire and adverse weather conditions. As a Flight Commander his work was splendid, and he set a splendid example of cheerfulness and efficiency to all officers of the squadron'.

Following a short rest, Hyde was posted to 260 Squadron, then based at Westward Ho for anti-submarine work. Frank Hyde was Mentioned in Despatches for his efforts with '260', *London Gazette* of 3 June 1919. He finally left the RAF, via the Unemployed List, on 18 April 1919.

I

INSALL, Gilbert Stuart Martin VC

The elder son of Gilbert Jenkins Insall, an English Dental Surgeon living and practising in Paris, and his wife, Mary Stuart Insall (née Read), he was born at Avenue Mozart in the French capital on 14 May 1894. Educated at the Anglo-Saxon School, Paris, and at Paris University. Gilbert and his younger brother, Algernon, intended following their father into dentistry, but their plans were thwarted by the advent of war. Gilbert enlisted as a Private soldier into 18 Battalion (1 Public Schools), Royal Fusiliers, early in the New Year of 1915. Both boys were keen to join the flying service, and their wishes were granted in March 1915. Gilbert gained his Royal Aero Club Certificate (Number 1110) on 14 March 1915, the same day that he was gazetted Second Lieutenant to the RFC, via the Special Reserve. Upon completion of his formal training, he was confirmed and gazetted Flying Officer on 16 July 1915. A posting to 11 Squadron (Vickers FB5s), then at Netheravon, came on 16 July 1915, and he accompanied that unit to France as a 'founder member', just nine days later. On 7 November 1915, Insall and his Observer/Gunner, 1 AM T H Donald, in Vickers FB5, '5074', on a routine patrol, came across a lone Aviatik and immediately gave chase. It has since been suggested that the enemy machine was a 'decoy', specifically intended to lure unsuspecting Allied aeroplanes to within range of the German anti-aircraft batteries. The truth, one suspects, is rather more prosaic. A German reconnaissance machine, especially if it were nearing the end of its patrol, would, under attack, need no other reason to make haste for the comparative safety of its own lines. Whatever the truth of the matter, Insall continued the chase, diving in as close as he could to allow Donald the opportunity of loosening a whole drum of ammunition at the enemy machine just before it vanished into cloud. When it emerged again into clear sky, the British crew could see that the Aviatik's engine was disabled and they watched it go down to crashland on a ploughed field. Once their machine came to rest, the unscathed German airmen appeared to be preparing to fire up at the circling British machine above them. Before this could happen, Donald opened fire, wounding one of the German crew, before both made good their escape into surrounding trees. Insall then brought the 'Gunbus' around again, this time bombing the abandoned Aviatik to destruction. As they flew back across enemy territory towards their own lines, they were met with a veritable barrage of ground fire. The Vickers was hit a number of times and Insall was eventually forced to land just 500 yards behind the French lines. The disabled 'Gunbus' continued to attract attention from German artillery and so a British recovery team were obliged to await nightfall to make whatever running repairs they could. At dawn, following a fraught take-off over rough ground, Insall and Donald were once again airborne and bound for Bertangles. For this extended exploit, Donald would be awarded the Distinguished Conduct Medal, *London Gazette* of 22 January 1916, and Gilbert Insall the Victoria Cross, *London Gazette* of 23 December 1915. Both men were also Mentioned in Despatches. The formal citation for Insall's VC reads: 'For most conspicuous bravery, skill and determination. He was patrolling in a Vickers fighting machine with First Class Air Mechanic T H Donald as Gunner, when a German machine was sighted, pursued and attacked. The German pilot led the Vickers machine over a rocket battery, but with great skill Lieut Insall dived and got to close range, when Donald fired a drum of cartridges into the German machine, stopping the engine. The German pilot then dived through a cloud, followed by Lieut Insall. Fire was again opened, and the German machine was brought down heavily in a ploughed field. On seeing the Germans scramble out of their machine and prepare to fire, Lieut Insall dived to five hundred feet, thus enabling Donald to open fire upon them. The Germans then fled, one helping the other, who was apparently wounded. Other Germans then commenced heavy fire, but in spite of this Lieut Insall turned again, and an incendiary bomb was dropped on the German machine, which was last seen wreathed in smoke. Lieut Insall then headed west, in order to get back over the German trenches, but as he was only at two thousand feet altitude he dived across them for greater speed, Donald firing into the trenches as he passed over. The German fire, however, damaged the petrol tank, and with great coolness Lieut Insall landed under cover of a wood five hundred yards inside our lines. The Germans fired some one hundred and fifty shells at our machine, but without causing material damage. Much damage had, however, been caused by rifle fire, but during the night it was repaired behind screened lights, and at dawn Lieut Insall flew his machine home with First Class Mechanic T H Donald as passenger'.

The disparity between the awards to the officer and to the other rank, might well jar modern sensibilities, but there it was. On 14 December 1915, before these awards were promulgated, the same crew in the same (repaired) 'Gunbus' were engaged over enemy territory by an enemy two-seater. In the fight, Donald was wounded in the leg and the petrol tank of the FB5 was holed. Insall made a dash for his own lines, but the machine was hit again, this time by anti-aircraft fire. A large fragment of an exploding shell struck Insall in the lower spine. Despite his agony, he made a decent landing, albeit behind the German lines. Both crewmen were taken to hospital and into captivity. Following an operation to remove the shell fragment, Insall was taken to a hospital in Cologne, and later to Fort Prinz Karl, at Ingolstadt. Insall continued to receive excellent medical care, going on to Constance and from there to Heidelberg. Insall was fortunate to be invited to join an escape attempt via a tunnel that had been in preparation for some time prior to his arrival. Insall and two other escapees were at large for five days before they were eventually re-captured in heavy snow, deep in the heart of the Black Forrest. Following a period of punitive solitary confinement, he was moved to Crefeld. Before long, he and another 'inmate' had escaped in a cart in broad daylight. This time they were collared within hours, following, 'a lively chase across fields'. Another spell in solitary preceded yet another transfer, this time to Ströhen, near Hannover. Success came at last in August 1917, when Insall and two companions covered 150 miles on foot over a period of nine days and nights, before crossing into Holland. Two weeks after returning to the UK, Insall was summoned to Buckingham Palace, the King asking for a personal account of the circumstances of his escape, as well as presenting him with his Victoria Cross. Promoted to A/Captain, he returned to instructing duties in the UK, before joining 51 Squadron, a Night Defence Squadron, as a Flight Commander. After the war, he stayed on in the RAF and was, in June 1919, attached to the Inter-Allied Aeronautical Commission of Control in Germany. For his gallantry whilst in captivity, he was awarded the MC in the 'Escapers Gazette', *London Gazette* of 16 December 1919: '....in recognition of gallantry in escaping from captivity whilst Prisoners of war'.

A posting to 6 FTS in Uxbridge came in 1922. In 1926, he married Olwen Scott Yates, with whom he had two sons. The year 1927 saw Insall commanding 70 Squadron in Iraq, where he remained for two years before returning to the UK to take command of 35 Squadron. Insall, who had a life-long interest in archaeology, is credited with the discovery of an important ancient site at Bridge Meadow, Old Lakenham. Whilst flying over the area, he noticed two concentric circles of starkly contrasting green grass. Subsequent detailed examination revealed what had been, in effect, a wooden version of Stonehenge, the huge timbers having long-ago rotted away, but not entirely without trace, at least from the air. This historically significant site is now known as, 'Norwich Woodhenge'. Further service abroad preceded his return to the UK in time for the Battle of Britain in 1940. Insall finally retired with the rank of Group Captain in July 1945. His peaceful and deserved retirement was shattered on 7 October 1969, when his home at Monks Hill, Scrooby, Yorkshire, was broken into and his medals stolen. His great distress at their loss brought on a heart-attack. Happily, to Insall's great delight, the police recovered his complete medal group in the following year. Group Captain Gilbert Insall, VC, MC, died at Bawtry, Yorkshire, on 17 February 1972.

NB: The RAF Museum Hendon has his group of medals in its collection: Victoria Cross, MC, 1914-15 Star (inscription illegible), British War Medal 1914-20, Victory Medal 1914-19 (Capt RAF), General Service Medal 1918-62, with clasp, Iraq and MID (S/L RAF), *Defence Medal 1939-45, War Medal 1939-45, Silver Jubilee Medal 1935, Coronation Medal 1937, and Coronation Medal 1953.*

J

JACKSON, James Lee

The son of the Reverend Canon Jackson, MA, and Mrs Jackson, of The Rectory, Belmullet, County Mayo, Ireland, he was born on 14 May 1895. Educated at Belfast University, where he was a member of the OTC. Gazetted Second Lieutenant to a Regular Army battalion of the Connaught Rangers in April 1913, he was promoted to Lieutenant in July 1914. Having taken his 'Ticket', Royal Aero Club Certificate (Number 744), at the Vickers Flying School, Brooklands, on 26 February 1914, he successfully sought transfer to the RFC when war came in August 1914. His formal pilot training duly completed, he was confirmed and gazetted Flying Officer on 17 November 1914. Promotion to Captain and Flight Commander with 2 Squadron came in May 1915. On 10 May 1915, Jackson was wounded in the face during the Battle of Festubert. He was subsequently Mentioned in Sir John French's Despatches and awarded the MC, announced in the New Year *London Gazette* of 1 January 1916 (no citation). Although no formal citation appeared in the *Gazette*, research has unearthed the original recommendation for the award: '3rd Btn Conn Rangers. Has carried out special missions of bombing a locality having to descend to 300 ft under heavy hostile artillery fire in order to be sure of hitting his mark. On one occasion he was wounded, but managed to return safely to our lines after doing considerable damage to the enemy'.

Once recovered, he was next posted to 12 Squadron in the UK, on 5 July 1915. He served again in France with 3 Squadron, before returning to the UK to take up a post at the CFS in September 1916. Jackson was posted as an Instructor in Canada, before serving with various Reserve Squadrons in the UK during 1917 and 1918. Promoted to Major on the formation of the RAF on 1 April 1918. James Jackson finally left the service, via the Unemployed List, on 11 October 1919.

JAMES, Archibald William Henry

The only son of Mr and Mrs H A James of Hurstmonceux Place, Hurstmonceux, Sussex, he was born in London in 1893. Educated at Eton (1906-11), and at Trinity College, Cambridge. Gazetted Second Lieutenant to 3 (King's Own) Hussars on 23 January 1914. He served with his regiment in France and Flanders from 15 November 1914, through the latter stages of the First Battle of Ypres, thus gaining the 1914 Star, and through the Second Battle of Ypres, before successfully seeking secondment to the flying service. Gained his Royal Aero Club Certificate (Number 1729) on 3 September 1915. His formal pilot training duly completed, he was confirmed and gazetted Flying Officer on 27 October following. Sent out to 5 Squadron (Vickers FB5) soon after qualifying, he was quickly involved in attempting to counter the so-called 'Fokker Scourge'. Promoted to Captain and Flight Commander on 18 April 1916. His MC was announced in the *London Gazette* of 24 June 1916: 'For conspicuous gallantry when making a special reconnaissance. Owing to clouds, he crossed the lines at 1,500 feet, and, seeing signs of movement in the particular locality, he came down to 800 feet in order to get a better view. He re-crossed the lines at 500 feet with very valuable information under heavy fire from rifles, machine-guns, anti-aircraft guns and field guns. His engine and machine were badly damaged by the enemy's fire'.

James would go on to command 6 Squadron, before being appointed to the Staff. A Lieutenant Colonel at the end of the war, he stayed on in the RAF, before finally retiring, with the rank of Wing Commander, in 1926. He married first, in 1919, Bridget Guthrie, with whom he had one son and one daughter, and secondly, in 1940, Eugenia, the widow of Patrick Stirling of Kippendavie, with whom he had two sons. He was elected and served as Unionist Member of Parliament for the Wellingborough Division of Northamptonshire from 1931 to 1945. Appointed Parliamentary Secretary to R A Butler, India Office, and Minister of Labour from 1936 to 1938. An appointment as Honorary First Secretary to the British Embassy, Madrid, Spain, lasted from 1940 to 1941. Returning to the UK, he was next appointed to the Board of Education in 1942. Knighted (KBE), 1945. He lived in retirement at Champions Farm, Thakeham, Pulborough, West Sussex. Sir Archibald James died on 5 May 1980.

JAMES, Baron Trevenen

The eldest son of Dr C A James and Annie Lucy James, of Bradley, Lincolnshire, and later Ebor House, Stamford Hill, he was born in 1889. Educated at Harrow (1903-07), where he was a mathematical scholar and head of his house, and at the Royal Military Academy, Woolwich (1907-09). Gazetted Second Lieutenant to the Royal Engineers in 1909. Gained his Royal Aero Club Certificate (Number 230) on a Howard Wright bi-plane of the Grahame Wright School at Hendon on 4 January 1912, this achieved with just three days of practice. The Official History, 'The War in the Air', records that just before the 1913 Army manoeuvres, James, piloting a BE aeroplane, succeeded in receiving wireless signals with the engine running at full power. In June 1914, D S Lewis (another pioneer of aerial communications) and James flew in company from Netheravon to Bournemouth in BEs each equipped with sending and receiving apparatus. Flying ten miles apart, they kept in close communication throughout the whole journey. When the war came in August 1914, James crossed to France with the original RFC contingent as a Pilot with 'The Wireless Flight', a component of 4 Squadron, thus earning the 1914 Star. When, in September 1914, the HQ Wireless Telegraphy Unit was formed at Fere-en-Tardenois, he was, of course, immediately attached to it, going on to range for the French Army, as well as for the Royal Artillery. His MC was announced in the *London Gazette* of 23 June 1915 (no citation). James was also Mentioned in Despatches on two occasions. He had transferred to 6 Squadron by 13 July 1915, when, on that day, he was flying alone, as was his want, in BE2a, '241'. As he ranged for a Battery, his BE attracted the concerted attention of German ground fire. Hit by a shell, his machine was seen to dive to the ground from a great height. The Germans later dropped a note confirming that he had died where he fell.

One of James' earliest, and historically significant, messages, sent down by wireless from the air, is quoted at length in the Official History:

> 4.2pm A very little short. Fire. Fire.
> 4.4pm Fire again. Fire again.
> 4.12pm A little short; line OK.
> 4.15pm Short. Over, over and a little left.
> 4.20pm You were just between two batteries. Search two hundred yards each side of your last shot Range OK.

4.22pm You have them.
4.26pm Hit Hit, Hit.
4.32pm About 50 yards short and to the right.
4.37pm Your last shot in the middle of three batteries in action; search all round within 300 yards of your last shot and you have them.
4.42pm I am coming home now.

Not only an historic moment in military history, but surely also one of the first recorded instances of the use of the now ubiquitous, 'OK'. Baron Trevenen James' remains were subsequently lost, and hence he is commemorated on the Flying Services Memorial, Arras, France.

JAMESON, Harold

The son of Captain William Storm Jameson and Hannah Margaret Jameson, of 'Ryedale', Chubb Hill, Whitby, Yorkshire, he was born in 1896. Harold's father, then Mate of the SS *Saxon Prince*, was interned by the Germans at Ruhleben, in the early days of the Great War. 'Harry' Jameson was a pre-war direct recruit (Number 1082) into the still comparatively newly formed RFC on 9 February 1914. He was amongst the first RFC contingent to France, crossing the Channel on 12 August 1914, to serve as a 2 AM with RFC HQ, thus earning the 1914 Star. Soon in the thick of things and promoted to 1 AM, he was awarded the Médaille Militaire by the French on 20 September 1914, *London Gazette* of 9 November 1914: '....for gallantry between 21 August and 30 August 1914'. He wrote to his parents soon after learning of the award, 'It seems the Médaille Militaire is very highly prized by the French'. The decoration was presented to him 'in the field' by Brigadier General David Henderson, then commanding the RFC in France. His next award, the Distinguished Conduct Medal, *London Gazette* of 22 June 1915, came as a consequence of his gallantry when flying with 6 Squadron. Again, in a letter to his parents, he explained the circumstances: 'I got it for working the wireless in an aeroplane, over the German lines, when a shell from one of their anti-aircraft guns exploded near us and blew part of our main inlet valve away and cut the pilot's hand. The pilot was Lieutenant Lewis now a Captain, and he was doing some very fine work with the wireless'.

Jameson had impressed his superiors to such a degree that he was gazetted Second Lieutenant to the RFC on 30 October 1915. Subsequently, on 29 January 1916, he was gazetted Assistant Equipment Officer. He also flew as an Observer with 7 Squadron from January 1916, before being posted as an Instructor at the Wireless School. Next, on 21 April 1916, he was posted to 19 Squadron, then at Netheravon. Gained his Royal Aero Club Certificate (Number 3622) on 2 July 1916 and was formally confirmed and gazetted Flying Officer on the same day. Eleven days later, Jameson was posted briefly to 48 Squadron, still forming in the UK. From '48', he reported to 42 Squadron just in time to accompany the unit to France as a 'founder member' on 9 August 1916. His MC was announced in the *London Gazette* of 11 December 1916: 'For conspicuous gallantry in action. He attacked a hostile kite balloon under very heavy fire. Later, his machine descended to 150 feet off the ground, when he got the engine going again and re-crossed our lines at 1,300 feet and returned safely. He has on many occasions done fine work'.

He appears to have been posted to 6 Squadron at the beginning of 1917, because, on fifth day of January, he and his Observer, Lieutenant William Davidson Thomson, from Saskatoon, Princess Patricia's Canadian Light Infantry attached RFC, in BE2g '7190', were shot down in flames over Voormezeele by Vizefeldwebel (later Leutnant) Walter Göttsch of Jasta 8, the third of the German Ace's eventual 20 victories. The redoubtable Harry Jameson is buried in Lijssenthoek Military Cemetery, Poperinghe, West-Vlaanderen, Belgium.

NB: The RAF Museum Hendon has his group of medals in its collection, donated by his sister in 1972: MC, Distinguished Conduct Medal (Cpl, Number 1082, RFC)*, 1914 Star with Bar, British War Medal 1914-20, Victory Medal 1914-19, and Médaille Militaire (France).*

JARDINE, Douglas Graeme Burness

The son of Major William Jardine and Mrs M H N Jardine, of 'Applegarth', Sir Lowry's Pass, Cape of Good Hope, South Africa, he was born in 1894. Jardine arrived in England in 1915, armed with a letter from the GOC, South African Forces, recommending him for a Cadetship at Sandhurst. From Sandhurst, he was gazetted Second Lieutenant to a Regular Army battalion of the Highland Light Infantry on 22 December 1915. Keen to join the flying service, he gained his Royal Aero Club Certificate (Number 2551) on 9 March 1916. His formal pilot training completed, he was confirmed and gazetted Flying Officer on 17 May following. Jardine flew the FEs of 25 Squadron in France and, later in 1917, the newly arrived DH4s. His MC was announced in the *London Gazette* of 22 April 1918: 'For conspicuous gallantry and devotion to duty. On two occasions when his formation was attacked by larger bodies of enemy scouts, he and his Observer sent one of the enemy down in flames and two others completely out of control. During a period of three months he carried out two exceptionally long reconnaissances, during which he took a large number of photographs, containing most valuable information. His personal efforts and example are of the highest value to the other pilots of the squadron'.

Following a rest from operational flying, Jardine was employed as an Instructor in the UK. On the morning of 5 August 1918, he arrived for duty at 4 Group, RAF, Yarmouth. That same evening, although unfamiliar with local conditions, he took off in the dark at 8.55 pm in DH9, 'D5802' on an anti-Zeppelin patrol, accompanied by his Observer, Lieutenant Edward Richard Munday, from Toronto, Canada. They and others from Great Yarmouth were in the air to counter a five-strong Zeppelin attack on England, the last to be launched against the UK in the Great War. Their DH9 was reported missing over the North Sea and Jardine's body was subsequently washed ashore in Jutland. Munday's body was never recovered. Douglas Jardine is buried in Vederso Churchyard, Denmark.

JARVIS, Ralph Hensworth

The son of Edmund M Jarvis and Mrs Jarvis, of Toronto, he was born on 22 October 1890. Educated at the Model School and Jarvis Street Collegiate Institute, Toronto, at University College (1907-08), and at Toronto University (1908-12), from where he graduated BASc (Civil Engineering with Honours). After graduating he embarked upon a career as a Civil Engineer and married his fiancée, Evelyn Mary. The war, however, intervened. Crossing the Atlantic, he was gazetted Second Lieutenant to the RFC via the Special Reserve on 7 December 1915. He had initially taken up flying at the Curtiss School in Canada, but eventually gained his Royal Aero Club Certificate (Number 2400) in England, on 1 February 1916. His formal pilot training completed, he was confirmed and gazetted Flying Officer on 16 April 1916. He was sent out first to the BE2c-equipped 4 Squadron in May 1916. On 22 August 1916, Jarvis and his Observer of the day, Second Lieutenant F deB Collenette engaged a LVG over Courcellete, during the course of an artillery patrol. They emptied two drums of ammunition into the enemy machine, sending it down to crash north west of High Wood. Jarvis was obliged to immediately turn for home, as two flying wires on the BE2c had been shot through in the course of the combat with the LVG. Jarvis was promoted to A/Captain and Flight Commander and posted to 5 Squadron in the September following. His MC was announced in the *London Gazette* of 14 November 1916: 'For conspicuous gallantry and devotion to duty in driving off three enemy machines, after which he returned to complete his work of observation and for carrying out later a reconnaissance in a strong gale'.

His tour with '5' completed, he returned to the UK in March 1917, subsequently serving at Brooklands until July 1917, when he returned again to the front. A tour over the Ypres Salient with the RE8s of 7 Squadron, ended in February 1918. For this stint, he received the Croix de Guerre from the Belgians, *London Gazette* of 15 April 1918. A recommendation for this award, sent to RFC HQ on 6 January 1918, reads: 'For continuous good work as a counter-battery observer, from 30 July 1917 to 5 January 1918. He has set a high standard of skill to his flight, and an inspiring example of working under all conditions'. Jarvis was also Mentioned in Despatches on two occasions during the Great War. Returning to England in January 1918, he was promoted to the rank of A/Major and appointed as a Senior Instructor at Grantham. He was killed in an accident whilst flying with a pupil on 27 February 1918. Ralph Jarvis is buried in Walton and Weybridge Cemetery, Surrey.

JENKIN, Louis Fleeming

The son of Austin Fleeming Jenkin and Elizabeth Jane Jenkin of 93 Iverna Court, Kensington, London, he was born on 22 August 1895. Educated at Dulwich College, where he gained a Senior Mathematical Scholarship and was in the Cricket First XI, the Rugby Third XV, and a Sergeant in the OTC. He earned a scholarship to Trinity College, Cambridge, but the outbreak of war intervened and he enlisted instead as a Private soldier into 18 Battalion (1 Public Schools), Royal Fusiliers. He was soon picked out for a commission and gazetted Second Lieutenant to 9 Battalion, Loyal North Lancashire Regiment, on 17 October 1914. Jenkin accompanied his battalion to France on 26 September 1915 and served in the trenches until badly wounded near Vimy Ridge, in April 1916. Once recovered, he was seconded to the RFC in December 1916. He next trained as a Pilot and was duly confirmed and gazetted Flying Officer on 19 April 1917. Sent out to 1 Squadron (Nieuport Scouts) in France soon after qualifying, he achieved a remarkable 22 victories between 23 May and 11 September 1917. Promoted to A/Captain and Flight Commander in July 1917, the first of his MCs was announced in the *London Gazette* of 16 August 1917: 'For conspicuous gallantry and devotion to duty. Whilst on offensive patrol has continuously shown the greatest dash and determination in attacking enemy aircraft in superior numbers, destroying some and bringing others down out of control'.

On one occasion, Jenkin strafed the German aerodrome at Herseaux, setting fire to one of six Scout planes lined up there. He was killed in action on 11 September 1917, the same day that he achieved his 22nd victory. Flying Nieuport XVII, 'B3648, he sent down, out of control, an Albatros DV, at 08.35 hours. Later in the same afternoon, in the same machine, he fell to his death during an aerial dual with Oberleutnant Otto Schmidt of Jasta 29, the eighth of the German Ace's eventual 20 victories. The great French Ace, Georges Guynemer, was also killed on this day. A Bar to Jenkin's MC was announced posthumously in the *London Gazette* of 17 September 1917: 'For conspicuous gallantry and devotion to duty in continually attacking hostile aircraft at close range, destroying some and driving others down out of control. His dash and offensive spirit have at all times been admirable'.

Louis Jenkin's remains were never recovered and hence he is commemorated on the Flying Services Memorial, Arras, France.

JENKINS, Frederick Howard

Originally from Essex, England, he was born on 10 November 1886. Educated at Denstone College (1900-05), where he was in the Rugby First XV. A Civil Engineer, he worked in Kissimee, Florida, from 1906 until war came in 1914, when he returned to the UK to volunteer his services. He enlisted as a Gunner into the newly formed Motor Machine Gun Service, Royal Artillery, in 1914. Picked out for commission, he was gazetted Second Lieutenant to the RFC, via the Special Reserve, on 27 November 1914. Posted early in 1915 to 14 Squadron, then forming at Shoreham with the BE2c. Next he gained his Royal Aero Club Certificate (Number 1450) on 26 February 1915. His formal pilot training duly completed, he was confirmed and gazetted Flying Officer on 23 April following. Promoted to A/Captain and Flight Commander on 6 November 1915, he accompanied '14' to the Middle East as a 'founder member', aboard the Australian Blue Funnel liner, SS *Anchises*, on the following day. Jenkins commanded a small detachment of '14' (two BE2c aircraft) at Mersa Metruh in the Western Desert, before returning to duties in support of the army. His MC was announced in the *London Gazette* of 25 November 1916: 'For conspicuous gallantry in action. He flew 150 miles at night and bombed an enemy aerodrome, descending to 500 feet under heavy fire. He has throughout done excellent work in reconnaissance'.

After service with '14', Jenkins was posted to Staff duties. Promotions to Major and then Lieutenant Colonel, came by the end of the war. He was twice Mentioned in Despatches during the Great War and also appointed OBE in the *London Gazette* of 3 June 1919. In 1919, Jenkins left the RAF to return to live and work in Micomi, Florida, USA.

JENKINS, Leoline

The son of Leo and Maud Jenkins of Ecclesfield, Ashford, Middlesex, he was born on 3 May 1891. Educated at Durlston Court, Swanage, and at St Bee's (1905-10), where he was in the Cricket XI, the Rugby XV, Honorary Secretary of Games and a Sergeant in the OTC. A good shot, he won the Dixon Shooting Cup, three years in succession. After leaving school in 1910, he returned to Durlston Court School, Swanage, this time as a Master. A pre-war volunteer, he was gazetted Second Lieutenant to 3 Company (Portland), Dorsetshire Garrison, RGA (TF). Mobilised with the rest of the TF as soon as war came on 4 August 1914. Jenkins had been promoted to Captain by the time his application for secondment to the RFC was granted in June 1915. Gained his Royal Aero Club Certificate (Number 1423) on 6 July 1915, the same day that he was confirmed and gazetted Flying Officer. Joined 15 Squadron, then at Dover, on 4 November 1915. Proceeded to France as a Flight Commander and 'founder member' with BE2c-equipped 15 Squadron on 23 December following. The first of his distinctions, an MC, was announced in the Birthday Honours *London Gazette* of 3 June 1916 (no citation). Although no formal citation was published in the *Gazette*, research has unearthed the original and detailed recommendation for the award: ' For exceptional good work as a Flight Commander. Has shown great gallantry and skill on many Army reconnaissances and he has had several fights with hostile aircraft. On 7th Feby 1916, he attacked two Aviatiks over Poperinghe and chased one down over the lines at a height of under 3,000 feet. On 13th Feby he had combats single-handed with three hostile aircraft and drove them severally back over the lines. On 29th Feby, while taking photographs he had to drive off enemy machines twice and took all his photographs required. He has been with the Expeditionary Force since 23rd December 1915'.

A Bar to his MC came in the *London Gazette* of 22 September 1916: 'For conspicuous gallantry and skill. He has done much fine work for the artillery often under most difficult circumstances. On one occasion he flew for a long time at a very low altitude under continual machine-gun and artillery fire'.

Two days before this latter *Gazette* announcement, Jenkins had been appointed Commanding Officer of BE2e-equipped 6 Squadron. His squadron did much fine work for the Royal Artillery, before he was promoted to a position with the Staff. He served briefly with 29 Wing, RFC, before being promoted to Lieutenant Colonel and to the command of 39 Wing, RFC, on 23 November 1917. He was Mentioned in Despatches in the *London Gazette* of 11 December 1917. Jenkins was awarded the Distinguished Service Order in the New Year *London Gazette* of 1 January 1918. He was placed in charge of a new aerodrome at Brandon, and for his subsequent success in that post, he was appointed 1st Class Staff Officer, 1 Area. Jenkins was taken ill soon after the end of the Great War and tragically died of pneumonia in Millbank Hospital, on 20 November 1918. Lieutenant Colonel Leoline Jenkins was buried with full military honours in Acton Cemetery, Middlesex.

JENNINGS, Montague Righton Nevill

The youngest son of Mr and Mrs F A M Jennings of 'Fair Lawn', Forest Hill, London SE23, he was born in the Isle of Wight, on 14 August 1890. His eldest brother, Frank, would win an MC and a Croix de Guerre with the RFA, and would also later be appointed CBE. Montague was educated at Uppingham (1905-09). Having developed an interest in aviation, he gained an early Royal Aero Club Certificate (Number 223), satisfying the examiners on a Bristol machine at the Bristol School, Salisbury Plain, on 4 June 1912. Gazetted Second Lieutenant to the RFC, via the Special Reserve, on 23 February 1916. His formal pilot training duly completed, he was confirmed and gazetted Flying Officer on 20 May following. Jennings was first mainly employed as an Instructor, indeed, he was gazetted a Captain whilst acting as a Wing Instructor in Gunnery (graded as equivalent to Flight Commander, RFC, Military Wing) on 4 October 1916. He did, however, eventually serve with an operational squadron on the Western Front, joining 19 Squadron (Spad VIIs) in France on 22 September 1917. On 26 October 1917, during the Cambrai operations, Jennings strafed a battery of German machine gunners, effectively silencing them with no less than 700 rounds from 600 feet. Although not quite achieving Ace status, he was credited with several victories and his expertise at ground strafing was widely acknowledged. Having flown through the dangerous and busy days of the German March Offensive, he completed his tour with '19' on 5 May 1918 and returned to the UK. His MC was announced in the *London Gazette* of 16 September 1918: 'For conspicuous gallantry and devotion to duty. He has carried out many low flying patrols and reconnaissances, engaging troops, transports, etc., with machine-gun fire. On one occasion he engaged and silenced a machine-gun battery; on other occasions he personally completely destroyed three enemy machines'.

Following a short rest, he was appointed to instruct at the BEF No 2 School of Navigation and Bombing, in June 1918. His outstanding work in this field was marked by the award of an Air Force Cross, *London Gazette* of 3 June 1919. Jennings finally left the RAF, with the rank of Major, in November 1919. When the Second World War came in 1939, he was living at Longshott Manor, Horley, Surrey. He was accepted for the RAFVR on 5 June 1940, serving as a Flight Lieutenant. Later in life, Montague Jennings lived in retirement at Easton House, Easton Lane, Freshwater Bay, Isle of Wight.

JENSEN, Harold Drewett

From Worthing, he was born on 22 March 1879. He was working in the Straits Settlement, Penang, when the war came in August 1914. Returning to the UK, he was gazetted Second Lieutenant to 9 (Reserve) Battalion, Royal Scots Fusiliers, on 31 May 1915. Volunteering for the RFC Balloon Service, he was ordered to report to the Kite Balloon School, Roehampton, on 29 November 1915. His training duly completed, he was gazetted Balloon Officer on 29 December following. He served with 9 and 4 Kite Balloon Sections in France, before returning to the Home Establishment on 18 June 1916. He was next posted as an Instructor to the Kite Balloon Training Battalion, on 20 September 1916. Gazetted Captain and Company Commander (graded as Flight Commander), RFC (Balloons), on 24 October 1916, the same day that he was appointed to command 17 KBS in Salonika. His MC was announced in the Birthday Honours *London Gazette* of 4 June 1917 (no citation). His tour with 17 KBS completed, he returned again to the Home Establishment on 18 September 1917. After a further stint as an Instructor at the Balloon Training Wing, he was posted to Mesopotamia and to the command of 23 KBS in November 1917. Jensen was Mentioned in Despatches, *London Gazette* of 27 August 1918. Promoted to Major, he was sent to 2 Balloon Training Wing, Middle East, on 8 December 1918. Major Harold Jensen returned to the UK and finally left the RAF, via the Unemployed List, on 4 March 1919.

JILLINGS, David Samuel

The son of Mr and Mrs Alfred Jillings of Hanley Place, Brook Street, Brentwood, Essex, he was born on 11 June 1881. After leaving school, he worked as a clerk until, age 18, he enlisted as a Private soldier (Number 8410), into 3 Battalion, Grenadier Guards on 11 November 1899. He progressed steadily through the ranks: Lance Corporal, 1901; Corporal, 1902; Lance Sergeant, 1905; and Sergeant, 1907. On the staff of the Tower of London in 1908, he re-engaged for a further 21 years Regular Army service. Selected to infuse discipline and smartness into the ranks of the RFC, he transferred to the recently formed Corps with the rank of Flight Sergeant on 21 January 1913 (RFC Number 9). Jillings was gazetted Sergeant Major on 11 August 1914, the day before proceeding to France with the original contingent of the RFC. He became the first RFC man to be wounded in action, when, on 22 August 1914, he and his Pilot, Second Lieutenant W M Noel, King's (Liverpool Regiment) attached RFC, on patrol over Ath, Belgium, in a 2 Squadron BE, were shot up by ground fire. Jillings was hit at the top of his thigh and when Noel brought them down to a safe landing, 2 AM George Alderton drove him to a Paris hospital in his lorry. He had recovered and was back on strength by the following October. For his gallant work as an Observer, Jillings was initially recommended for the Victoria Cross, but this was down-graded by Army HQ, to a proposed Distinguished Conduct Medal. When, however, the MC was introduced for Warrant Officers and Subalterns, he was amongst the first listed recipients in the *London Gazette* of 1 January 1915 (no citation). Before this announcement, he had been recommended for a commission and was duly gazetted Second Lieutenant to the West Yorkshire Regiment, with an immediate secondment to the RFC, on 11 December 1914. Jilling was also Mentioned in Despatches on four occasions during the Great War, *London Gazette*s of 8 October 1914, 4 December 1914, 1 January 1915, and 4 August 1915. Keen to progress to piloting, he gained his Royal Aero Club Certificate (Number 1178) on 15 April 1915. His formal pilot training duly completed, he was confirmed and gazetted Flying Officer on 2 July following. He served with 14 Squadron in the UK, but, age 34, was probably considered a little old for operational flying and was subsequently appointed Adjutant to 2 Reserve Aeroplane Squadron in November 1915. Jillings held this position until January 1918, before serving out the remainder of the war in various Administration posts as A/Major. Staying on after the war, he was granted a permanent commission in the RAF in August 1919. David Jillings finally retired with the rank of Squadron Leader on 1

October 1926. He served again in the Second World War, a member of Personnel Staff, 2 (Bomber) Group HQ, Andover, Hampshire. For his services at this time, he was awarded the MBE.

JOHNSON, George Owen

The son of Mr and Mrs George Edward Johnson of Woodstock, Ontario, Canada, he was born on 24 January 1896. Educated at Woodstock School, Ontario. A full-time school teacher in Alberta and a part-time pre-war volunteer, he was a Lieutenant in the local volunteers from 1913 to 1916. Granted a commission as a Probationary Sub-Lieutenant, RNAS, in Canada, on 24 April 1917, he crossed the Atlantic only to be accepted as a Cadet in the RFC. Gazetted Second Lieutenant on 27 September 1917, the same day that he was confirmed and gazetted Flying Officer. Posted to 84 Squadron (SE5As) on 22 October 1917, he achieved six victories between 16 February and 12 April 1918. Promotion to Flight Commander and a posting to 24 Squadron (also SE5As) followed on 18 April, with Johnson going on to gain five further victories. The last of these, on 17 June 1918, was a share in the forcing down of Leutnant Kurt Wusthoff, a 27 victory German Ace, who, wounded in both legs, was duly taken prisoner by the French Army. He was awarded the Croix de Guerre avec Palme, by the French, although this would not be formally promulgated until the *London Gazette* of 29 March 1927. His MC was announced in the *London Gazette* of 22 June 1918: 'For conspicuous gallantry and devotion to duty. Observing a large body of the enemy on a road, he descended to a low altitude and dropped four bombs, which exploded amongst them, causing the most severe casualties. He then attacked the enemy with machine-gun fire from a height of 20 feet, causing many more casualties and scattering them in all directions. On a later occasion, he secured four direct hits on a column of horse transport, and diving down to 50 feet, by his persistent attacks held up an enemy advance for a considerable period. He has destroyed two hostile machines, has driven down two others out of control, and has always displayed the greatest courage and coolness in the most difficult situations'.

His tour with '24' completed on 19 June 1918, he served as an Instructor at Cranwell, Hooton and Shotworth, before joining 1 Squadron, Canadian Air Force, on 29 November 1918 and embarking upon what would prove to be a distinguished career. His many subsequent appointments, promotions and honours, included: OC, War Trophy Party, Canada, 1919-20; participation in the Trans-Canada Flight of 1920; command of Station Winnipeg, 1925-27; RAF Staff College; Assistant Director of Civil Government Operations; Acting Senior Air Officer, RCAF, 1933; Command of Station Trenton, 1935-36; Imperial Defence College; CO, Western Air Command, 1938; Air Member for Organisation and Training, 1939; Deputy Chief of Air Staff, 1940; AOC, 1 Training Command, 1942; AOC, Eastern Air Command, 1943; CB, 1943; and AOC, RCAF Overseas, 1945-46. He finally retired with the rank of Air Marshal in 1947. Married, first, Jean Eleanor (née McKay) (died 1968) of Pembroke, Ontario, with whom he had two daughters, and secondly, in 1968, Sarah Jane (née Roberts) who died in 1977. The Johnson family lived at 6688 Ash Street, Vancouver, British Columbia. Air Marshal George Owen Johnson died in Vancouver on 28 March 1980.

JOHNSTONE, Robert

From Edinburgh, he was born on 8 May 1895. After completing his education, he was articled to a firm of Chartered Accountants in George Street, Edinburgh, from October 1913 to August 1914, when war intervened. He enlisted as a Private soldier (Number 3136) into 28 London Regiment (Artists Rifles) (TF). Picked out for a commission, he was gazetted Second Lieutenant to 4 (City of London) Battalion, Royal Fusiliers (TF), on 2 July 1915, with an immediate secondment to the RFC. Having trained as an Observer, he joined 9 Squadron as a Probationary in April 1916. His 'apprenticeship' satisfactorily completed, he was confirmed and gazetted Flying Officer (Observer) on 9 May 1916. Flying with Second Lieutenant F A Coward, the pair enjoyed an excellent rapport with their Royal Artillery counterparts. He was twice Mentioned in Despatches through this period, *London Gazettes* of 11 December 1916 and 4 January 1917. Research has unearthed a previously unpublished recommendation for the first of these: '9 Sqd 10 October 1916: For excellent artillery observation work from 10 May till 30 September 1916. Lieut Johnstone has shown great quickness in turning batteries on to bodies of infantry. On 12 July, on his own initiative, he called for a barrage near Trones Wood and stopped an attempted counter attack'. His MC was announced in the *London Gazette* of 11 December 1916: 'For conspicuous gallantry in action. He has shown marked courage and initiative in turning our artillery on to columns of enemy infantry. On one occasion he carried out counter battery work in cloud and mist at 800 feet under heavy fire from the ground'.

The 'occasion' referred to in the citation occurred on 17 October 1916, near to Le Transloy and the infamous ridge. After completing his tour with '9', Johnstone decided upon pilot training. He next gained his Royal Aero Club Certificate (Number 4677) on 19 May 1917 and, after formally qualifying for his full 'Wings', was employed as an Instructor in the UK. He was Mentioned in Despatches again, this time for his work as an Instructor, *London Gazette* of 4 November 1917. Johnstone joined 10 Squadron (AWFK8s) at the front on 25 June 1918, before transferring as a Flight Commander to 82 Squadron (also AWFK8s), on 2 October 1918. On 17 October, Johnstone and his Observer, Second Lieutenant R Alcock, in AWFK8, 'F7413', were both wounded in the air, Johnstone seriously, whilst attacking an ammunition dump. He was quite fortunate to survive, and was rated 'seriously ill' from November 1918 to January 1919. Recovering somewhat, he was finally demobilised on 25 September 1919.

JOLLEY, Samuel

From Newtown, Wigan, he was born on 21 June 1891. Educated at St Marks School, Newtown. After leaving school, he worked as a mechanic and electrician until enlisting as a Gunner into the Royal Horse Artillery, on 21 December 1914. On 21 February 1915, he transferred to the RFC with the rank of 2 AM (Number 4264) and was sent to 2 Aircraft Depot, BEF, on 27 March following. Progressing steadily through the ranks, he was promoted to 1 AM in September 1915; Corporal in March 1916; and Sergeant in May 1916. Picked out for a commission, he was gazetted Second Lieutenant to the RFC, via the Special Lists, on 10 October 1916. After completing his training, he was confirmed and gazetted Balloon Officer, RFC, on 13 March 1917. He served in France in kite balloons from 1 May 1917 until 4 April 1918, when he returned to the UK. He was recorded as having had to parachute from balloons whilst under attack, on five occasions during 97 hours of observation duty. His MC was announced in the *London Gazette* of 26 September 1917, its exceptional citation appearing in the *Gazette* of 9 January 1918: 'For conspicuous gallantry and devotion to duty when being heavily shelled in his balloon. Although under fire for two hours from guns in four different positions, he engaged them in his balloon and silenced three. The shelling was accurate and his balloon was punctured, but he continued to remain up for another two hours and reported the enemy's movements'.

The insignia of his MC was presented to him by the King at an investiture held in Buckingham Palace, on 15 January 1918. Jolley was posted to instructing duties in the UK before finally leaving the RAF, via the Unemployed List, in April 1919. During the Second World War, Jolley, re-engaging as a Flying Officer, RAF, ran the RAF Recruiting Office in Northampton throughout 1939 and 1940. Samuel Jolley died on 4 August 1977.

JONES, Allan Murray

From Caulfield, Melbourne, Australia, he was born on 25 February 1895 and became a Pharmacist in civilian life. Jones trained on the second Pilot's course at Point Cook in 1915, gaining his Royal Aero Club Certificate (Number 1416) at the CFS, Werribee, Australia, on 10 May following. Gazetted Second Lieutenant to the Australian Flying Corps on 2 November 1915. A 'founder member' of 67 Squadron, RFC, formed in Heliopolis, Egypt, in June 1916, which immediately transmuted itself into 1 Squadron, Australian Flying Corps. Became one of the main-stay Pilots and personalities of the Australian Flying Corps, always heavily involved with Number 1 Squadron's operations until subsequently commanding 2 Squadron, AFC. His MC was announced in the *London Gazette* of 26 April 1917: 'For conspicuous gallantry and devotion to duty. When carrying out a raid on a hostile aerodrome he descended to a height of 200 feet under very heavy fire and destroyed two hangars. On another occasion he flew for a total of nine hours and twenty minutes in search of two officers who were lost'.

Flying a Martinsyde G100 on 16 May 1917, near to Galjun, he was wounded during an aerial combat with the noted German Pilot, Oberleutnant Felmy, of FAb300. Murray Jones was Mentioned in Despatches on three occasions during the Great War, *London Gazettes* of 6 July 1917, 26 September 1917 (both Egypt) and 3 June 1918 (Palestine). He was also awarded one of the first Distinguished Flying Crosses announced in the very first gazetting, *London Gazette* of 3 June 1918. A Bar to his Distinguished Flying Cross, for his fine leadership as a Squadron Commander in France, followed in the *London Gazette* of 8 February 1919. In 1929, Murray Jones joined the Civilian Air Board of Australia as Superintendent of Flying Operations. Two years later in 1931, he left the CAB to take up a position as General Manager (and later, Chairman) of De Havilland, Australia.

JONES, Ernest James

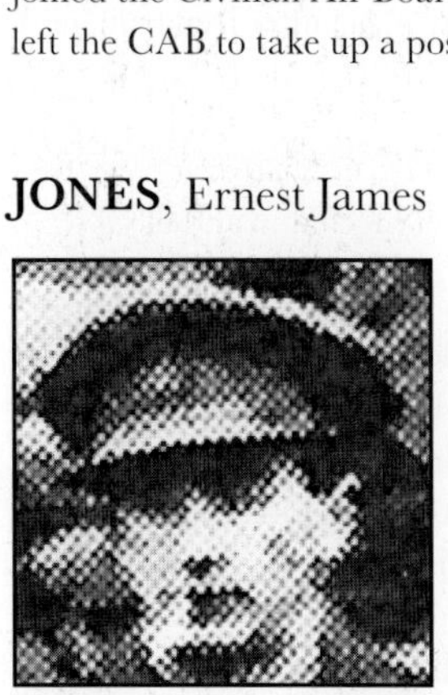

Born on 1 June 1892, in Abbotsford, Victoria, Australia, he lived later with his widowed mother at the Newbridge Hotel, Toorak Road, South Yarra, Victoria. After leaving school, he worked on the railway as a surveyor and draughtsman. He enlisted into the AIF on 3 March 1915. Following the completion of his basic training, Jones embarked at Melbourne aboard the SS *Euripides* with 'D' Company, 23 Battalion, Australian Infantry, bound for Alexandria, Egypt. Once in Heliopolis, Egypt, he was transferred to 5 Field Company, Australian Engineers, on 13 August 1915. He landed in Gallipoli on 3 September 1915, but was soon wounded in action. Promoted to Corporal on 14 September and to Sergeant on 27 November 1915. Having recovered from his wounds, he was sent to France, arriving there on 26 March 1916. Subsequently accepted as a candidate for the flying service, he reported to the School of Military

Aeronautics on 5 December 1916. His training duly completed, he was gazetted Pilot and Second Lieutenant to the Australian Flying Corps, on 8 June 1917. Although initially intended to await the arrival of 68 Squadron from Egypt, soon to be re-designated 2 Squadron, AFC, he was ordered instead to report to 3 Squadron (RE8s), AFC, on 29 October 1917. Promoted to Captain and Flight Commander on 22 January 1918. He fought through the great German spring offensive with 3 Squadron, AFC until, on 20 May 1918, Jones and his Observer, Lieutenant A L D Taylor, in RE8, 'B8876', whilst observing the fire of 22 Siege Battery, RGA, were badly shot about by a Fokker DRI, one of a formation of six that attacked the '3' AFC machine. Albert Taylor, from Williamstown, Melbourne, was killed in the air. Although the wounded Jones got them back to their home field, he crashed the already badly damaged 'Harry Tate' on landing. Once recovered, he was sent, on 18 July 1918, to 7 TS as an Instructor before going on to the Artillery and Infantry School, Winchester, on 10 August 1918. Jones was awarded the newly introduced Distinguished Flying Cross in its very first gazetting on 3 June 1918. Unusually, and possibly uniquely, the announcement of his MC came later in the year in the *London Gazette* of 16 September 1918: 'For conspicuous gallantry and devotion to duty. Whilst co-operating with artillery, he was attacked by three tri-planes. He was wounded and the controls of his machine damaged. He out-manoeuvred the enemy, reported his observation to his battery by wireless, and returned to his aerodrome. On landing, owing to the damage of his machine, he crashed but although much weakened by loss of blood, extricated his Observer [this was, of course, 21-year-old Lieutenant A L D Taylor] from the wreckage. On another occasion while on photography he was attacked by six tri-planes. One of these his Observer shot down out of control, while the remainder were forced to withdraw. He then continued his work. At all times he has set a fine example of courage and determination'.

Jones was next sent to 1 Wing HQ on 17 September 1918, before returning again to 3 Squadron, AFC, now re-equipped with Bristol Fighters, in October 1918. On 9 October 1918, Jones dropped his bombs on a retreating column of enemy transport on the Le Cateau-Catillon road, which caused them to break up in total confusion. On 30 October, Jones and his Observer of the day, Lieutenant A D Cherry, were charged with finding an enemy observation post thought to be located in the Forest of Mormal. After a careful and painstaking reconnaissance above tree-top level, a girder type tower of timber, four times the height of the surrounding trees and painted a dark grey colour, was found and its location reported. Jones' appointment terminated on 20 June 1919 and he returned to Australia. He joined the Australian Air Corps (the pre-runner to the Australian Air Force) in March 1920, serving at the CFS, Point Cook. In August 1920, Jones flew the Prince of Wales' mail from South Australia to Sydney, during the Royal Visit to Australia. He also flew the inaugural Geraldton to Derby Western Australia mail run in November 1921. Appointed member of the Air Accidents Committee in 1927 and Deputy Controller of Civilian Aviation circa 1929. Ernest Jones joined the Aviation Department of Shell Oil of Australia in 1929.

JONES, Henry Albert

The second of the three sons of Horse Keeper, Josiah G Jones and Annie Jones, of 18 Whitmore Road, St Leonard's, Shoreditch, he was born on 6 August 1893. Educated at the Grocers School, London, where he was a member of the Cadet Force for five years, three as a Private and two as an officer. A gifted linguist, he was particularly fluent in French and German. Jones worked in a secretarial capacity for the Red Cross in France from January 1915 to August 1915. Next, he was gazetted Second Lieutenant to 8 (Reserve) Battalion, Wiltshire Regiment, on 9 October 1915. Seconded to the RFC in the first weeks of 1917, he was, after the requisite training, confirmed and gazetted Flying Officer (Observer) on 30 April 1917. He served with 47 Squadron in Salonika and subsequently wrote the squadron history, 'Over the Balkans and South Russia, 1917-1919', which was published in 1923. On 20 August 1917, Jones and his Pilot, Lieutenant F W H Thomas (qv), in AWFK8, 'A1466', were the 'rearguard' covering the withdrawal of a formation following a bombing raid on Prilep. The subsequent events are graphically described by Jones, himself, in the 47 Squadron history. The RFC machines were fiercely attacked by several German Albatroses. Second Lieutenant J L Bamford, 17 Squadron, was sent down to his death by Leutnant Gerhard Fieseler of Jasta 25. Next the Germans turned their attentions to Thomas and Jones. Thomas was wounded in the back early in the fight. A spent bullet hit Jones' Sam Browne belt, inflicting no harm, but then he was hit in the mouth and received an explosive bullet in the left hand, which fractured his thumb and index finger. Thomas, in the meantime, had fainted twice due to loss of blood, the AWFK inevitably hurtling towards the ground. Just 200 feet from the ground, Thomas, with a supreme effort, regained control and managed, despite intense pain, to get them home. Thomas would return to the UK, only to die of his painful and crippling wounds months later. For their gallantry in this fight, Jones, like Thomas, would be awarded the MC, *London Gazette* of 17 December 1917, details in the *Gazette* of 7 March 1918: 'For conspicuous gallantry and devotion to duty. When returning from a bombing raid the machine in which he was Observer was attacked by four enemy aeroplanes. One was driven down, and though his pilot was severely wounded he continued the fight until his gun was put out of action by enemy fire. He showed great courage and determination'.

Sent to No 33 Stationary Hospital, Salonika, and then to No 28 Stationary Hospital, Salonika, for treatment to his wounds, further complications in the form of malaria set in, and he was invalided out of the area and sent home on 7 November 1917. He would, subsequently, be presented with the insignia of his MC by the King at an investiture held at Buckingham Palace on 9 March 1918. Jones also received the Croix de Guerre avec Palme from the French, *London Gazette* of 22 August 1917, and was also made Officer of the Légion d'Honneur. The still recuperating Henry Jones was appointed to the Historical Section of the Committee of Imperial Defence in 1918, with an advance to Director of the Air Branch of that organisation following in 1920. When, in 1922, the final decision was made to prepare Official Histories of the Great War, Jones was appointed Official Air Historian, eventually writing six volumes of 'The War in the Air'. In 1939, he was a member of the Air Staff Secretariat. He was subsequently appointed Senior Administration Officer, UK Air Liaison Mission, in Ottawa, and was a member of the RAF delegation in Washington, DC. Created CMG, 1943. Henry Jones died on 27 March 1945.

JONES, Hubert Wilson Godfrey

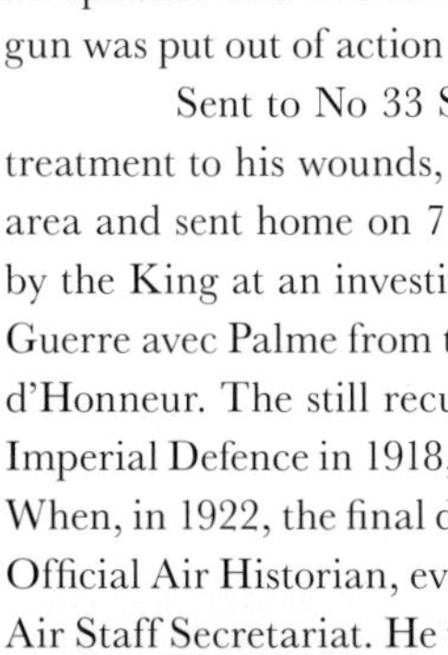

A pre-war volunteer, he was gazetted Second Lieutenant to 4 Battalion, Welsh Regiment (TF), on 17 April 1913. Mobilised as soon war came on 4 August 1914, he would eventually accompany his battalion, with the rank of Lieutenant, to Gallipoli on 9 August 1915. Jones was listed as wounded amongst the 14 officers and 272 other ranks of 4 Welsh Regiment killed or wounded in the five days following the landing at Suvla Bay. After returning to the UK and recovering from his wounds, he gained the Royal Aero Club Certificate (Number 2747) on 17 April 1916, as a preliminary to securing a secondment to the flying service. His formal training duly completed, he was confirmed and gazetted Flying Officer on 22 July following. Sent out to the DH2s of 32 Squadron shortly after qualifying for his 'Wings', he was soon in the thick of the action, gaining the first of his seven victories, against a Fokker E, on 11 August 1916. On 1 October 1916, in DH2, 'A2533', he was involved in a fierce aerial combat over the tiny hamlet of Flers, on the Somme front. Shot down, he crashed very heavily into a shell hole, but, amazingly, was able to scramble, unhurt, away from his doomed machine. His adversary in this combat was the peerless Hauptmann Oswald Boelcke, Jones becoming the 30th of the great German Ace's eventual 40 victories. On 15 February 1917, in DH2, 'A2535', Jones was again shot up in an aerial combat and this time slightly wounded. His MC was announced in the *London Gazette* of 26 March 1917: 'For conspicuous gallantry in action. With a patrol of three scouts he attacked a hostile formation of ten enemy machines. Although wounded he continued the combat and drove down an enemy machine. Later, although again wounded, he remained with his patrol until the enemy retired'.

Once recovered, the undaunted Jones was transferred, on 11 March 1917, as a Flight Commander, to 24 Squadron (Nieuport XVIIs). Just ten days later, Jones, in Nieuport XVII, 'A305', was seen, during an aerial combat over Roupy, to be spinning down out of control to the ground. Although initially reported as missing in action, happily, he was subsequently found wounded (again), but alive. His victorious adversaries on this occasion were Leutnants W Olsen and W Hilf of Fliegerabteilung 23. Having recovered from these latest wounds, he was not required to fly operationally again but, was, for the remainder of the war, employed as an Instructor at the CFS. In November 1918, with the rank of Major, he assumed command of 19 Squadron. Staying on in the RAF after the war, he would again command 19 Squadron from 1925 to 1928.

JONES, James Ira Thomas

From St Clears, near Carmarthen, South Wales, he was born on 18 April 1896. A pre-war volunteer member of the TF, he first enlisted in 1913. When the war came, he was training as a civilian wireless operator, a 'reserved occupation' at that time, and it was therefore some months before, with his newly acquired skills, he was accepted into the RFC as a 1st Class Air Mechanic (Number 6326). After training, he was posted to 10 Squadron in the UK on wireless duties. Jones and '10' crossed to France late in July 1915, by which time he was a Probationary Observer. In May 1916, whilst working on liaison duties with a ground-based wireless receiving station in the front lines, he rescued two Royal Artillery Gunners whose Battery had come under an intense counter-barrage. For his gallantry on this occasion, Jones received the Military Medal, *London Gazette* of 10 August 1916, and, from the Czar of Russia, the Medal of St George, 4th Class, *London Gazette* of 15 February 1917. His Observer status was confirmed in October 1916, and he was then able to put up his Brevet. Sent home for pilot training and commissioning in May 1917, he must have stood out head and shoulders above his fellow 'greenhorn' novitiates. Jones was sent out to 74 Squadron (SE5As) early in 1918 and at once struck up a friendship with his Flight Commander, Captain Edward 'Mick' Mannock, with whom he shared many experiences. Despite a propensity to crash on landing (an essential skill he often confessed to never having quite mastered) his fighting qualities soon had him scoring victories, not to mention the award of the MC, its unusually detailed and graphic citation appearing in the *London Gazette* of 16 September 1918: 'For conspicuous gallantry and devotion to duty. This officer, one of an offensive patrol, engaged and shot down in flames a two-seater which fell to earth. Ten days later, on offensive patrol, he shot down a Hanover two-seater, which crashed. The next day, when patrolling, he pursued, overtook and shot down an Albatros two-seater. During the same flight he met a Halberstadt two-seater and killed the Observer, who either jumped or fell overboard, but had to break off as his ammunition was finished. The next day he shot a balloon down in flames. Three days later he got a good burst with both guns on a Pfalz scout, both wings coming off. He has driven two others down out of control'.

In June 1918, he was promoted to A/Captain and Flight Commander, while his victories continued to mount, evidenced by the award of a Distinguished Flying Cross, *London Gazette* of 3 August 1918, for destroying six enemy aircraft in eleven days. On 30 July, he had managed to shoot down an LVG whilst flying a badly damaged SE5A – so badly damaged in fact that it collapsed when he landed it. A gallantry Distinguished Service Order, *London Gazette* of 2 November 1918, a Bar to his Distinguished Flying Cross, *London Gazette* of 21 September 1918, and a Mention in Despatches, *London Gazette* of 31 December 1918, capped his operational career, not to mention credit for no less than a remarkable 37 victories. Soon after the Armistice, he was appointed to the command of 74 Squadron until its disbandment in 1919. He next volunteered for the Intervention Forces, serving with the

Allies on the Archangel front. He married, around this time, Olive Gwynedd Edmund-Davies. A keen Rugby footballer, Jones played at different times for the RAF, London Welsh, Richmond, Bristol and Northampton. Securing a permanent commission with the RAF, he served continuously until 1936, his many appointments and postings including: Signal Duties in Iraq, 1923-25 and in Egypt, 1925-27; OC, Home Communication Flight, 1928-29; Experimental Section, Farnborough, 1930-31; Signal Staff Duties, 1 Air Defence HQ, 1932-35; and Air Ministry, 1935-36. When the Second World War came, Jones was recalled from the Reserve with the rank of Group Captain and charged with the operational training of Fighter Pilots. Strictly against orders, he unofficially flew Spitfires in a number of sweeps across enemy-occupied Europe. Once, during the Battle of Britain, he engaged a Junkers JU 88 whilst flying an unarmed Hawker Henley target-tower. In the absence of machine guns, he fired the Henley's Very pistol at the enemy machine – without success it should be added. Jones wrote three books, one of which, a biography of Edward Mannock, 'King of Air Fighters', has achieved the status of an aviation classic. Another of his books, 'Tiger Squadron', the story of his beloved 74 Squadron, can similarly claim classic status. Ira Jones died on 29 August 1960, at Morrison Hospital, Glamorgan. He had fallen off a ladder at his home at Tangnefedd, New Quay, Cardiganshire – yet another bad landing.

NB: The RAF Museum Hendon has his medals in its collection: Distinguished Service Order (end of Cross engraved: Capt Ira Jones RAF*), MC (reverse engraved:* Capt Ira Jones RAF*), Distinguished Flying Cross & Bar, Military Medal* (6326 1/CL AM, JIT Jones, RFC)*, 1914-15 Star* (6326 2 AM RFC)*, British War Medal 1914-20, Victory Medal 1914-19 with MID* (Capt., RAF)*, India General Service Medal 1908-35 (naming erased), War Medal 1939-45, Medal of St George (Russia, Silver, Number 901640, impressed:* 6326 1AM JIT Jones RFC*).*

JONES, James Sidney

From West Hampstead, London, he was born on 8 November 1888. Educated at Clifton College (1901-06), Shooting VIII and Rugby XV, and at Pembroke College, Cambridge, Rugby XV, where he studied French in 1907, and Law in 1909. After leaving Cambridge, he left the UK to ranch in Knutsford, British Columbia, Canada. He enlisted into the British Columbia Horse on 14 August 1914, before transferring to Lord Strathcona's Horse, 1 Canadian Cavalry, one month later. He served in France with the first contingent of the CEF until October 1916, when he was accepted for a commission in the British Army. Gazetted Second Lieutenant to the RGA, via the Special Reserve, on 13 November 1916. Jones continued to serve in France with the RGA, until transferring to the RFC in October 1917. Having trained as an Observer, he was sent out as such to 47 Squadron in Salonika. He was injured in a flying accident on 29 January 1918, but soon recovered and went on to win the MC, *London Gazette* of 26 March 1918, details in the *Gazette* of 24 August 1918: 'For conspicuous gallantry and devotion to duty. Over an extended period he has displayed a marked and consistent daring and enterprise when on reconnaissance and escort duty, and on six separate occasions has attacked hostile aircraft. On one occasion, after a most determined encounter at close range with a hostile machine, he shot it down in flames, this severe combat proving his initiative, resource and skill to be of the highest order'.

He was also Mentioned in Despatches during this period, *London Gazette* of 11 June 1918. Returning to the UK, he was granted special leave and allowed to return to Canada for 12 weeks from 8 July 1918. Following his sojourn in Canada, his fitness precluded a return to operational flying and he was eventually forced to relinquish his commission, due to ill-health, on 12 February 1919, before returning once again to British Columbia.

JONES, Lionel Baker

The son of Mr and Mrs Jones of 'Brynfield', Reynoldston, Glamorgan, South Wales, he was born on 25 July 1895. Educated at Christ College, Brecon, and at Edinburgh University, where he studied Medicine and was a member of the OTC. He interrupted his studies to enter the Inns of Court OTC, on 31 May 1915 (Number 4/3854). After training, he was gazetted Second Lieutenant to 6 (Glamorgan) Battalion, Welsh Regiment (TF), on 16 September 1915. Secondment to the RFC followed in the summer of 1916 and, after training as an Observer, he was confirmed and gazetted Flying Officer (Observer) on 7 August 1916. Sent out to 12 Squadron in France in December 1916. His MC was announced in the *London Gazette* of 26 May 1917: 'For conspicuous gallantry and devotion to duty when acting as an Observer. He has on many occasions assisted in beating off hostile machines. He has done exceptionally fine work in artillery observation'.

Jones returned to the UK in June 1917, never to fly operationally again. Sent out next to Egypt, he was appointed an Assistant Instructor at No 3 School of Military Aeronautics, from 21 May 1918. Lionel Jones finally left the RAF, via the Unemployed List, on 31 July 1919, returning to live in Reynoldston, South Wales.

JONES, Richard Neville Kenward

The son of R A Jones and Mrs Helen Mildred Jones, of 48 Bridge Street Row (West), Chester, he was born 4 July 1895. His father was a Master Draper in Chester, owning a large store on the charming shopping 'Rows' of that beautiful city. Educated at St Bee's, Cumbria (1909-14), from which school's OTC he was directly gazetted Second Lieutenant to the Army Service Corps on 19 September 1914. Jones saw service in France with the Army Service Corps, before successfully applying for secondment to the flying service. Having trained as an Observer, he was gazetted Flying Officer (Observer) on 24 July 1916. He was next ordered to report to 60 Squadron as a replacement Observer just six days later. Shortly after his arrival, his Morane Biplane, '5162', piloted by Roderic Hill, crashed on take-off at St André. Although relatively unharmed, he was obliged to leave '60' within days of the crash, the unit having been re-equipped with single-seater Morane Bullets and Nieuports and hence the Observers had become redundant. Posted next to the Morane Parasol-equipped 3 Squadron, then at La Houssoye, he became something of a specialist in photographic reconnaissance work, as the award of his MC testifies, *London Gazette* of 18 July 1917: 'For conspicuous gallantry and devotion to duty. He has done consistent good work in the taking of photographs under very adverse weather conditions, by his perseverance and determination he has set a very high standard of efficiency in the photographic work of his Squadron'.

Jones was also Mentioned in Despatches in the *London Gazette* of 15 May 1917. Leaving '3' upon the completion of his tour, he next joined No 5 School of Military Aeronautics on 7 September 1917. Seven months later on 7 April 1918, Jones joined 16 Squadron (RE8s) at the front and only nine days later he was wounded in the air, suffering burns to his hands. Following hospital treatment and a spell of recuperative leave in the UK, Jones re-joined '16' in June 1918. On 18 October 1918, Jones' RE8 was hit by machine-gun fire from the ground and he was wounded in the right arm, the bullet fracturing his humerus. After treatment at various hospitals in France and in England, he was finally discharged and placed on the Unemployed List on 22 February 1919. Returning to the family business in Chester, he married Nasli Mary, taking up residence at 'The Nook', Quarry Lane, Kelsall, Cheshire. He would eventually take up arms once again in anticipation of the forthcoming war with Germany, enlisting into 290 Anti-Aircraft Battery, Royal Artillery (TA), on 8 April 1939. He was mobilised with his unit when war broke out on 3 September 1939 and, soon afterwards, was promoted to Sergeant. He served as a No 1 on a Heavy Anti-Aircraft Battery throughout the Blitz on nearby Liverpool. Given a commission as a Lieutenant in the Emergency Reserve, he assisted with the formation and training of various mixed units of anti-aircraft batteries, eventually reaching the rank of Captain. He died of pulmonary TB in Moston Hall Military Hospital, Chester, on 9 April 1942, and was buried at Helsington, near Kelsall.

JONES, Sidney Stevenson – see Sidney **STEVENSON-JONES**

JONES, William Walter

From London, he enlisted as a Private soldier (Number 4991) into 14 Battalion, London Regiment, the London Scottish. He served with 'B' Company on the first day of the Battle of the Somme, 1 July 1916 and, although wounded, he survived that terrible day. Having recovered from his wounds, he was gazetted Second Lieutenant into the London Scottish on 26 April 1917. A secondment to the flying service followed later in the year and, after training as an Observer, he joined 35 Squadron (AWFK8) as a Probationary on 12 January 1918. On 24 March 1918, during the desperate days of the German spring offensive, the by-then experienced and confirmed Flying Officer (Observer), Bill Jones, was lucky to escape with his life. He and his Pilot, Second Lieutenant Evan Pybus (qv), in AWFK8, 'C3549' were, during a photo-reconnaissance patrol, forced to land their machine before flames totally engulfed them. Both crewmen survived to win the MC. Jones' award was announced in the *London Gazette* of 22 June 1918: 'For conspicuous gallantry and devotion to duty. On one occasion he attacked enemy transport, dropping eight bombs and firing 300 rounds into its midst, with the result that several limbers were completely destroyed and severe casualties inflicted on the enemy. Later in the same day, he again attacked enemy transport, causing a stampede amongst the horses and inflicted many casualties. Whilst returning to his aerodrome, he attacked with machine-gun fire two hostile batteries in action, firing 400 rounds into their midst, his pluck and determination were beyond all praise'.

His tour with '35' completed on 16 May 1918, he was, following a short rest, sent as an Instructor to No 1 School of Aviation, where he saw out the remainder of the war. He was also Mentioned in Despatches on one occasion during the Great War. Bill Jones left the service, via the Unemployed List, early in 1919. He is noted in the London Scottish Journal as having attended a regimental re-union in 1952.

JONES-WILLIAMS, Arthur Gordon

The son of Mr and Mrs A H Jones-Williams, of Cwy Park, Talybont-on-Usk, Breconshire, South Wales, he was born on 6 October 1898. Educated at Haileybury (1912-15) and at Sandhurst (1916). Gazetted Second Lieutenant to a Regular Army battalion of the Welsh Regiment on 16 August 1916, with an immediate secondment to the RFC. Following training and service with 66 Squadron in the UK, he was posted to the Nieuport Scout-equipped 29 Squadron at the front on 22 March 1917. He enjoyed almost immediate success and, by the following May, had achieved three victories, was promoted to A/Captain and Flight Commander, and awarded the first of his two MCs, announced in the *London Gazette* of 18 July 1917: 'For conspicuous gallantry and devotion to duty. He has continuously shown the utmost dash and gallantry in attacking superior numbers of hostile machines. On one occasion he attacked twelve hostile scouts and succeeded in destroying one and driving down another'.

In July 1917, he was briefly hospitalised before being posted to the Home Establishment. He could claim the status of Ace by this time, having gained six victories. A Bar to his MC came in the *London Gazette* of 17

September 1917: 'For conspicuous gallantry and devotion to duty when engaged in combat with hostile aircraft. On several occasions he attacked enemy formations although they were in superior numbers, fighting them in more than one instance single-handed, and showing the finest offensive spirit. He drove several machines down completely out of control, fighting until his ammunition was expended'.

In the early autumn of 1918, Jones-Williams returned to the front as a Flight Commander with 65 Squadron (Sopwith Camels), achieving a further five victories before the end of the war. The French, too, showed their appreciation of his services with the award of a Croix de Guerre avec Palme, *London Gazette* of 5 April 1919. Jones-Williams was given a permanent commission in the RAF after the war, his next operational posting being to the Kurdistan campaign of 1923 (DH9s). In April 1929, Squadron Leader Jones-Williams, with Flight Lieutenant N H Jenkins, flew a record-breaking non-stop 50-hour flight from Cranwell to India, a distance of 4,130 miles. Later in the same year, the two airmen were planning another record-breaking flight to South Africa when their Fairey Monoplane crashed in Tunisia on 17 December 1929. Both men were killed.

JUNOR, Kenneth William

The son of William and Alice E Junor, of 106 Jameson Avenue, Toronto, Canada, he was born on 3 August 1894. Educated at Queen Victoria Public School, Toronto, at St Andrew's College (1908-12), and at University College, Toronto (1912-15). He had served as a Home Service volunteer with 9 Mississauga Horse and 4 Mounted Rifles, before enlisting, on 24 July 1915, into a machine-gun unit with the CEF. Crossing to England in March 1916, he was gazetted Lieutenant to the Canadian Machine Corps on 29 of that month and posted to 11 Machine Gun Company. Junor accompanied his unit to France in July 1916, serving first at St Eloi and later on the Somme. An application to transfer to the RFC was granted on 24 April 1917, when he was ordered to report to Reading. His pilot training duly completed, he was confirmed and gazetted Flying Officer on 28 July 1917 and sent out to France and the SE5A-equipped 56 Squadron on 15 December 1917. He served with '56' over the Third, Fourth and Fifth Army fronts from St Quentin to Arras, achieving eight victories and the status of Ace. He had a narrow escape on 22 March 1918, when his SE5A, 'B536', was shot up and damaged during a fight with Leutnant Hans Böhning of Jasta 79. On 23 April 1918, Junor was reported missing at Bray-sur-Somme, the second of the eventual nine victories of Leutnant Egon Koepsch of Jasta 4. Junor's MC was announced posthumously in the *London Gazette* of 13 May 1918: 'For conspicuous gallantry and devotion to duty in aerial fighting. He destroyed two enemy machines and drove down two others out of control, which crashed on landing. He always showed the greatest courage, skill and resource'.

Kenneth Junor's remains were never recovered and hence he is commemorated on the Flying Services Memorial, Arras, France.

K

KEEN, Arthur Willan

The eldest son of Arthur Thomas Keen and Charlotte Keen, of Harborne Park, Birmingham, he was born on 20 March 1895. His father was Chairman of the internationally known engineering firm, Guest, Keen and Nettlefold, 'GKN'. Educated at Rugby (1909-13) and at Trinity College, Cambridge. Gazetted Second Lieutenant to the Army Service Corps, via the Special Lists, on 24 May 1915. He was employed, initially, with the Explosives Department of the War Office, but soon sought secondment to the RFC, which was granted late in 1915. He achieved his 'ticket' on 17 January 1916 (Royal Aero Club Certificate Number 2298). His formal pilot training duly completed, he was confirmed and gazetted Flying Officer on 15 February following. Keen was awarded the Royal Humane Society's Bronze Medal at Montrose, in Scotland, in June 1916. His CO gave the following account of the exploit: 'On 17 June 1916, a BE X belonging to this Squadron fell into the sea about 150 yards out. The occupants were badly damaged and the machine was in a sinking position. One of my officers, 2 Lt A W Keen, whilst flying over the wreck, realised the plight they were in. He returned to the aerodrome, got into his car and rushed across to the shore. He went straight into the water in his clothes and heavy field boots without hesitating for a moment, swam out to the wreck and managed to reach one of the officers (Lieutenant Macbeth), just as the latter was drowning. Lieutenant Macbeth was nearly unconscious and clutched 2 Lt Keen by the throat and struggled so violently as nearly to drown his rescuer. The latter managed to free himself and just succeeded in bringing Lieutenant Macbeth to the shore. I consider that 2 Lt Keen's action showed remarkable bravery and coolness and is worthy of very high praise'.

Flying operationally for the first time with the Sopwith Strutters of 70 Squadron, he achieved that unit's first victory on 28 August 1916, sending an Albatros down out of control over Bapaume. From December 1916 to April 1917, he was instructing in England. Promoted to A/Captain, he was next posted to 40 Squadron as a Flight Commander. Keen enjoyed considerable success with that unit's Nieuport Scouts, claiming a further 11 victories. His MC was announced in the *London Gazette* of 16 August 1917: 'For conspicuous gallantry and devotion to duty. He has shown the greatest gallantry and skill in aerial fighting, and his daring in leading offensive patrols into favourable positions for attack has been the means of many hostile aircraft being destroyed and driven down'.

From November 1917 to June 1918, he commanded a training squadron at the CFS, being promoted to Major in March. He returned again to 40 Squadron (SE5As), this time to succeed the late Major Dallas, who had recently been killed in action. Two more victories followed before he was severely burned when his SE5A, 'D6122', stalled and crashed in flames at Bruay aerodrome on 15 August 1918. A brother officer writing to his parents, said: 'His total combats while serving with this Squadron were eleven, nine of which were certain crashes or in flames'. Major Arthur Willan Keen died of his injuries on 12 September 1918, and is buried in Terlincthun British Cemetery, Wimille, France.

KEEP, Arthur Stuart

Born of English parents in Sydney, NSW, Australia, on 15 July 1891. After the death of his father, he and his mother returned to live in Balsall Heath, Birmingham. Educated at King Edward's School, Birmingham (1904-08). After leaving school, he trained as a Metallurgist and was working as such when war came in August 1914. He enlisted as a Private soldier into 14 Battalion, Royal Warwickshire Regiment (1 Birmingham 'Pals'), on 10 September 1914. Keep had achieved the rank of Sergeant by 9 March 1915, when he was recommended for a commission. Gazetted Second Lieutenant to his own battalion of the Royal Warwicks on 1 April 1915. He accompanied 1 Birmingham 'Pals' to France on 21 November 1915, commanding XIV Platoon, 'D' Company, and serving in the trenches until March 1916, when he contracted a foot infection, probably 'trench foot'. After hospital treatment in the UK, he was pronounced fit for further service and successfully applied for secondment to the RFC on 21 August 1916. Gained his Royal Aero Club Certificate (Number 7207) on 27 October 1916, the same day that he was formally confirmed and gazetted Flying Officer. He served in France with 55 Squadron (DH4s) from 23 April 1917. Keep and his Observer of the day, Second Lieutenant W R Patey, were credited with driving two enemy machines down out of control during the period 13 to 19 May 1918. On 20 July 1918, during a 55 Squadron bombing raid on Oberndorf munitions works, the RAF machines were attacked over the target by a large formation of German Scouts. Keep and his Observer, Second Lieutenant James Ferguson Pollock, in DH4, 'A7427', were shot down, their machine wrecked. Keep was wounded in the action, Pollock killed. Keep's MC was announced in the *London Gazette* of 16 September 1918. 'For conspicuous gallantry and devotion to duty on long-distance bombing raids. He showed great skill and determination while raiding enemy towns. One day, with his oil-feed pipe broken, he reached his objective, and disposed of an enemy machine on his way back. His work was splendid'.

After leaving the RAF after the war, he continued his aviation career, becoming a Test Pilot. In the Air Ministry Trials of 1920, Keep won the First Prize of £7,500 in a Westland 'Limousine'. Unfortunately, however, he suffered a very bad crash at the Bristol Flying School in a Bristol Fighter on 31 May 1923 and so was unable to continue flying. Subsequently, he became a Director and the General Manager of Westland Aircraft in the 1930s.

KELLER, Roderick Leopold

The son of Leopold Ernest Keller and Evelyn Keller, of 'New Mount', Windsor Terrace, Hampstead, London, and later of 'Wairora', Hadley Wood, Middlesex, he was born on 12 September 1892. After completing his education, he worked as a Pearl Merchant in his father's company at Hatton Garden, London. Volunteering as soon as war came, he was gazetted Second Lieutenant to 4 (Extra Reserve) Battalion, Royal Warwickshire Regiment, on 15 August 1914. After serving in France with his regiment, he was seconded to the flying service in January 1916. His pilot training duly completed, he was confirmed and gazetted Flying Officer on 1 June following. Sent out to France and 23 Squadron on 6 December 1916. Flying Spads, Keller gained four victories between April and June 1917. He was promoted to A/Captain and Flight Commander in July 1917, just immediately prior to completing his tour with '23', and returning to the UK. His MC was announced in the *London Gazette* of 17 September 1917: 'For conspicuous gallantry and devotion to duty in attacking hostile aircraft, destroying one, and driving down others out of control. His dash and offensive spirit on all occasions have been splendid'.

Keller held various instructing posts in the UK before being sent, in July 1918, to 41 TDS. He was killed in a flying accident at London Colney aerodrome on 15 August 1918. Roderick Keller was buried with full military honours in Shenley (St Botolph) Churchyard, Hertfordshire.

KELLY, Augustine Patrick

From Dublin, Ireland, he was born on 1 September 1894. Educated at Dublin University (1912-14). Volunteering as soon as war came, he was gazetted Second Lieutenant to the Army Service Corps on 24 October 1914. He served in France with the Army Service Corps, before securing a secondment to the flying service in April 1916. Having trained as an Observer, he was sent out as a Probationary to 4 Squadron in June. His 'apprenticeship' satisfactorily completed, he was confirmed and gazetted Flying Officer (Observer) on 27 July 1916. Two days later, Kelly and his Pilot of the day, Captain C J MacKay, in BE2c, '2491', on a photo-reconnaissance patrol, survived an attack by two LVGs over Courcellette, sending down one of their attackers. Kelly eventually trained as a Pilot and, once qualified, was sent out to the RE8-equipped 59 Squadron on 10 January 1918. On 21 March 1918, the first day of the German spring offensive, Kelly and his Observer, Second Lieutenant R Hegan, in RE8, 'B6517', were hit by ground fire. Kelly, though wounded, completed the low-level reconnaissance before bringing the 'Harry Tate' safely back to base. After preliminary medical treatment in France, Kelly was returned to the Home Establishment on 24 March following. His MC was announced in the *London Gazette* of 22 June 1918: 'For conspicuous gallantry and devotion to duty. When information was urgently needed as to the enemy's position during an action, he carried out a reconnaissance at a low altitude under heavy machine-gun fire. Though wounded he completed his patrol, located the enemy's position and brought back most valuable information. He showed splendid courage and skill throughout the operations'.

Once recovered, Kelly would, before the end of the war, serve with the DH9s of 49 Squadron, before finally leaving the service, via the Unemployed List, in 1919. Kelly would serve again with the Royal Army Service Corps during the Second World War.

KENNARD, Casper

Originally from Frith Hall, East Farleigh, Kent. Educated at Felsted (1906-07). After leaving school, Casper and his brother, Leonard, travelled to the family ranch at Estancia, La Constancia, FCCA, in the Argentine. Leonard, too, would be awarded the MC in the Great War whilst serving as a Lieutenant, Army Service Corps, attached Royal West Kent Regiment. One of the many British Latin American Volunteers of the Great War, Casper returned to the UK to be gazetted Second Lieutenant to the RFC, via the Special Reserve, on 17 June 1916. After training as a Pilot, he was duly confirmed and gazetted Flying Officer on 22 September following. Just six days after qualifying for his 'Wings', he was sent out to BE2c-equipped 16 Squadron in France. On 9 October, Kennard and his Observer/Gunner, 1 AM B C Digby, in BE2c,'4494', on a patrol from Bruay to Bethune to Houdin and back to Bruay, were forced to land behind German lines and were taken prisoners-of-war. They explained afterwards that they had become lost in bad weather and, on coming down low in an attempt to re-orientate themselves, had come under intense ground fire which wounded Kennard and brought their BE down. Kennard was first held at Clausthal before being moved to Holzminden. He became one of the successful escapers who gained their freedom through the famous tunnel at Holzminden in August 1918. The story of Kennard and his 'co-escapees', C W Blain and D B Gray (qv), is told in Barry Winchester's book, 'Beyond the Tumult', published in 1971 (Allinson and Busby Ltd). After reaching the UK, Kennard was posted to the School of Technical Training in October 1918, where he saw out the remainder of the war. He was awarded his MC in the 'Escapers Gazette', *London Gazette* of 16 December 1919: '....in recognition of gallantry in escaping from captivity whilst Prisoners of War'.

He returned to Argentina in 1919 and was killed there in a shooting accident on 7 May 1935. Casper Kennard is buried in the British Cemetery, Buenos Aires, Argentina.

KENNEDY, Douglas Stewart

The son of James S and Mary F Kennedy, of 'St Katherine's', Broughty Ferry, Forfarshire, Scotland, he was born on 8 September 1887. After completing his early education in Scotland, he studied engineering at Leeds University. From university, he served a pupilage with an engineering company in the UK, before gaining a position as an assistant engineer with the Madras and Southern Mahratta Railway in India, with responsibilities for 110 miles of main line. Kennedy was elected an Associate Member of the Institute of Civil Engineers in January 1915. He married around this time and he and his wife, Kathleen Mary, bought 'Craigmore', a house in their home town of Broughty Ferry. As the war dragged on, Kennedy decided he had to do his share and gave up his work in India, before returning to the UK. After arriving in England, he was gazetted Second Lieutenant to the RFC, via the Special Lists, on 17 June 1916. His pilot training duly completed he was confirmed and gazetted Flying Officer on 15 November following. He was sent out to the FE2b-equipped 11 Squadron in France soon after qualifying. On 6 April 1917, Kennedy and his Observer/Gunner, 2 AM J F Carr, in FE2b, 'A5500', were extremely fortunate to escape injury or worse, when their machine was shot down by Leutnant Wilhelm Frankl of Jasta 4, the 18th of the German Ace's eventual 20 victories, and the third of the four he would achieve on that particular day. Kennedy's MC was announced in the *London Gazette* of 18 July 1917: 'For conspicuous gallantry and devotion to duty. While on a close patrol he attacked three hostile scouts and succeeded in dispersing them. A second formation of four enemy machines then attacked but were also dispersed, two of them being driven down. The results of these combats were largely due to his skill and determination'.

Following a spell in the UK instructing, Kennedy was promoted to A/Captain and Flight Commander in time to accompany the Bristol F2b-equipped 62 Squadron to France as a 'founder member', on 23 January 1918. On 12 March following, Kennedy and his Observer of the day, Lieutenant H G Gill, West Yorkshire Regiment attached RFC, in BF2b, 'B1247', were part of a 62 Squadron offensive sweep from Cambrai to Caudry and Le Catelet. The British formation were unfortunate enough to run into the veritable 'Flying Circus' of enemy aeroplanes, led by the Red Baron himself. '62' lost four machines in the ensuing battle; one to Manfred von Richthofen, two to his brother, Lothar, and the fourth fell to Werner Steinhauser. Kennedy and Hugh Gill fell to Lothar von Richthofen at 11.00 over Maretz, and both were killed. Douglas Kennedy is buried in Honnechy British Cemetery, Nord, France.

KERNOT, Charles Henry

An Exceptional Service, not a flying, award

Kernot joined the RFC as a Disciplinarian (RFC Number 1717) and A/Sergeant Major, on 12 September 1914. Promoted to Warrant Officer (D) on 12 March 1915. His MC was announced in the New Year London Gazette of 1 January 1917 (no citation). Although no formal citation appeared in the Gazette, research has unearthed the original recommendation for the award: 'Sgt Maj C H Kernot. For exceptional service and devotion to duty as Sergeant Major since 12-3-15. He has always performed his duties in the most highly efficient manner. His personal example and the influence he has had on those under him has contributed in no small degree to the efficiency of his unit'.

On 1 April 1918, Kernot transferred to the RAF, with the rank of Sergeant Major, Class 1.

KIDD, Leonard Cameron

The second son of Dr Cameron Kidd, MB, FRCS, and Mrs Clara Louisa Kidd, of New Road, Bromsgrove, Worcestershire, he was born on 22 June 1893. Educated at Bromsgrove School (1905-10). On leaving school, he worked as a motor engineer at the Austin Motor Company, Longridge Works, Birmingham, whilst living at Oak Cottage, Bromsgrove. A keen aviator, he obtained his Royal Aero Club Certificate (Number 655) at Hendon on 22 October 1913, before going out to Ceylon as a Tea Planter. Returning to England as soon as he was able to relinquish his responsibilities in Ceylon, he was gazetted Second Lieutenant to the RFC, via the Special Reserve, on 25 August 1915. His formal pilot training duly completed, he was confirmed and gazetted Flying Officer on 4 January 1916. Sent out to 3 Squadron in the following month, he was soon heavily involved in contact patrolling. Typically, during a contact patrol on 3 September 1916, he and his Observer, Lieutenant F E S Phillips, spotted enemy troops massing in trenches opposite British infantry who were still in the process of preparing their positions. Contact was made with the Royal Artillery, who immediately obliged with some excellent shooting which undoubtedly thwarted the enemy's intentions. On 10 October 1916, Kidd and Phillips were forced to land amongst shell holes between Pozières and Contalmaison on the Somme. Kidd's promotion to Lieutenant came just two days later on 12 October 1916. On that day, Kidd and his Observer, Lieutenant Fenton Ellis Stanley Phillips (qv), in Morane BB, '5178', were on a routine dawn contact patrol when they were hit by 'friendly fire' which severed a wing on their machine and sent them down to their deaths. Devonian 'Pip' Phillips was well known to C A Lewis (qv), who mentions his, and Kidd's, passing with deep regret in his classic, 'Sagittarius Rising'. Kidd's MC was announced posthumously in the *London Gazette* of 14 November 1916: 'For conspicuous skill and gallantry on contact patrol work. On one occasion he carried out three contact patrol flights, each one 1,000 feet, and obtained valuable information under heavy fire. He also attacked enemy reinforcements with a machine-gun from a height of 500 feet'

Leonard Kidd's remains were never recovered and hence he is commemorated on the Flying Services Memorial, Arras, France.

KING, Cecil Frederick

The first son of Frederick Hamilton King and Nora King, of Springfield Dukes, Chelmsford and later, 'Lingwood', East Liss, Hampshire, he was born on 19 February 1899. Educated at Charterhouse. Gazetted Second Lieutenant to the RFC on 10 May 1917. His pilot training duly completed, he was confirmed and gazetted Flying Officer on 18 July following. Sent out to 43 Squadron (Camel F1s) in France late in 1917. By September 1918, and despite being wounded on 28 March, King had achieved a remarkable 22 victories and the award of the MC, the citation of which is testimony to his reckless courage, *London Gazette* of 22 April 1918 : 'For conspicuous gallantry and devotion to duty. On five occasions during a period of three months he has sent down four enemy machines completely out of control and has destroyed one other. Later, under very adverse weather conditions, he carried out a low reconnaissance, during which he engaged troops in a station, causing several casualties, fired into a body of the enemy entering a village from a height of 50 feet, attacked four gun limbers, causing the teams to stampede, and finally dived into a parade of troops, who scattered in all directions. He has displayed exceptional daring and skill, which, combined with a splendid dash and initiative, have set a fine example to his squadron'.

King's last three victories – he was, by then, a Flight Commander – were gained in the newly introduced Sopwith Snipe. A Distinguished Flying Cross followed in the *London Gazette* of 3 August 1918, its citation extolling his leadership qualities. The French, too, weighed in with a Croix de Guerre avec Palme in recognition of his work during the Second Battle of the Marne. Having survived the Great War, King returned home for a well deserved rest. On 24 January 1919, he was flying at Sedgeford, Norfolk, when he was killed by a colliding aircraft. He was posthumously Mentioned in Despatches, *London Gazette* of 3 June 1919. Cecil King is buried in Docking (St Mary) Churchyard, Norfolk.

NB: The RAF Museum Hendon has his MC and Distinguished Flying Cross in its collection.

KING, Charles Ley

The son of George Ley King and Georgina L King, of 129 McGregor Avenue, Sault Ste Marie, Ontario, Canada, he was born on 17 February 1891. An Electrician by trade, he enlisted as a Private soldier (Number 1003557) into 227 Battalion, Canadian Infantry, on 1 July 1916. He served in Hamilton, Ontario, until 3 April 1917, when, as a Corporal, he was struck off the strength of the Canadian Army and allowed to join the RFC. Gazetted Second Lieutenant to the RFC on 23 July 1917. His pilot training completed, he was confirmed and gazetted Flying Officer on 31 August following. In the following month, King was sent out to 12 Squadron (RE8s) in France. His MC was announced in the *London Gazette* of 16 September 1918: 'For conspicuous gallantry and devotion to duty when working with artillery in carrying out 13 successful shoots, by which numerous enemy gun pits were destroyed and fires and explosions caused. He also carried out two very good long distance reconnaissances, taking excellent photographs and obtaining valuable information'.

On 27 October 1918, King landed his damaged aircraft safely in enemy territory, subsequently evaded capture and rejoined his unit on 4 November following. A Distinguished Flying Cross for, amongst other things, 'excellent work both on reconnaissance duty and in co-operation with our artillery', followed in the *London Gazette* of 2 November 1918. Staying on in the RAF after the war, his many subsequent appointments, honours and promotions, included: Staff, School of Army Co-operation, 1921; Flight Commander, 4 Squadron,1924, and 70 Squadron, 1925; Mentioned in Despatches: '....for distinguished services in operations against the Ikhwan in the southern desert, Iraq, during the period, November 1927, May 1928'; OC, 502 (Ulster) Squadron, Royal Auxiliary Air Force, 1928; Personnel Staff, HQ Inland Area, 1932; OC, 3 APC, Sutton Brigade, 1935; Wing Commander, 1935; Air Staff, HQ, Iraq Command, 1935; Group Captain, 1938; SASO, HQ, Technical Training Command, 1940; 8 Air Gunner School, 1942. He was awarded the Air Force Cross in the *London Gazette* of 1 January 1942. Charles King finally retired from the RAF on 17 February 1944 with the rank of Air Commodore. He died in Bourne County, Ontario, Canada, on 22 April 1956.

KING, Ebenezer

The son of Ebenezer and Catherine King of 'Roseau', Anwoth Villas, Corstophine, Midlothian, Scotland, he was born in 1892. Gazetted Second Lieutenant, via the Special Reserve, to 3 (Reserve) Battalion, King's Own Scottish Borderers, on 11 June 1915. In January 1916, he was sent out to Egypt to the depleted and exhausted 1 Battalion of his regiment, still then recovering from the rigours of the Gallipoli campaign. He was one, as the battalion's War Diary wearily states, of the, 'Officers who came thick and fast', at that time. Seconded to the RFC, he trained as an Observer in Egypt and was eventually confirmed and gazetted Flying Officer (Observer) on 5 April 1916. Apparently, he was next sent to 58 Squadron, a training unit in the UK, in 1917. He was further transferred to 37 RS at Lincoln and pilot training then followed. On 17 March 1917, King was piloting an RE8, 'A3440', with 2 AM Ernest Alfred Harris (Number 45670) from Southend in the rear seat, when it crashed. Both men were killed. King's MC was announced in the Birthday Honours *London Gazette* of 4 June 1917, (no citation). Unfortunately, despite considerable research, the reasons for the award remain unclear. Ebenezer King is buried in Lincoln (Newport) Cemetery, Lincolnshire.

KINGSFORD-SMITH, Charles Edward

Born in Hamilton, Brisbane, Australia, on 9 February 1897. Educated in Vancouver, at St Andrews, Sydney, and at Sydney Technical High School. At the time of the Great War, he was living in Neutral Bay, Sydney, and indentured to an Electrical Engineering company in that city. Interrupting his apprenticeship, he enlisted into the Signals Section, Australian Engineers. He was one of a number of Australian volunteers accepted for transfer as Cadets to the flying service at the end of 1916. Gazetted Second Lieutenant to the RFC, via the Special Reserve, on 17 March 1917. His pilot training completed, he was confirmed and gazetted Flying Officer on 13 May following. He was sent to serve in France with the Spad VIIs of 23 Squadron in June 1917. On 31 July 1917, the first day of the Third Battle of Ypres, Kingsford-Smith fired 50 rounds into a number of German lorries north east of Houlthulst Forest from 600 feet. On 10 August, he attacked and destroyed a two-seater DFW. Four days later on 14 August, Kingsford-Smith was wounded in the foot during an aerial combat over Boesinghe with Oberleutnant Wilhelm Reinhard of Jasta 11, the German Ace claiming him as the fourth of his eventual 20 victories. His MC was announced in the *London Gazette* of 26 September 1917, details in the *Gazette* of 9 January 1918: 'For conspicuous gallantry and devotion to duty. He has himself brought down four machines during his first month at the front, and has done most valuable work in attacking ground targets and hostile balloons. Of the latter he forced at least nine to be hauled down by his persistent attacks, during which he was repeatedly attacked himself by large hostile formations, and by his efforts undoubtedly stopped all hostile balloon observation during a critical period. His efforts and fine offensive spirit and disregard of danger have set a fine example'.

As a consequence of the wound inflicted by Reinhard, Kingsford-Smith returned to the UK for medical treatment and, once recovered, saw out the remainder of the war in a series of instructing posts. After the war, he carved out a career as one of the truly great aviation pioneers. Some of his most noteworthy achievements included piloting the Southern Cross in the first trans-Pacific flight in June 1928, for which feat he was awarded the Air Force Cross. Next, in the September of the same year of 1928, he made the first return flight from Australia to New Zealand. In 1929, he made a record-breaking flight, again in the Southern Cross, from Australia to England. He flew from Ireland to America in 1930 and then flew across the USA to deliver the Southern Cross to Oakland, California. Returning to England, he broke the record previously held by Squadron Leader Hinkler by flying from England to Australia in 10½ days in October 1930. In December 1931, he made the first all-Australian air mail flight to England and back again. He next set up a new record by flying from England to Australia in 7 days, 4 hours and 50 minutes in 1933. He married in 1930, Mary Powell, with whom he had one son. Air Commodore Kingsford-Smith was knighted (KBE), 1932. His book, 'The Old Bus', was published in 1932. He lived, in 1935, at 27 Greenoaks Avenue, Darling Point, Sydney, NSW, Sir Charles Kingsford-Smith was lost in a flight over the Bay of Bengal on 7 November 1935.

KINGSLEY, Shirley George

Born in Golders Green, London, on 20 January 1893. Educated at Framlingham College (1910-11), where he was a member of the OTC. He was one of a body of Cadets paraded at Windsor Castle during the Coronation ceremonies of 1911. He trained as a Motor Engineer at Hendon in 1911, before leaving to work in Uruguay and Argentina between 1912 and 1914. Returning to the UK as one of the many British Latin American Volunteers, he was gazetted Second Lieutenant to 11 (Reserve) Battalion, York and Lancaster Regiment, via a New Armies commission, on 21 January 1915. Seconded to the flying service, he gained his Royal Aero Club Certificate (Number 3294) on 3 April 1916. His formal pilot training duly completed, he was confirmed and gazetted Flying Officer on 24 May following. Sent out to 20 Reserve Wing, RFC, in Alexandria, Egypt, in July 1916, he was posted on to 14 Squadron on 5 September following. On 11 January 1917, Kingsley was flying alone in a BE12, when he rashly decided to attack three enemy machines, although his MC citation accuses the three enemies of attacking him. Out-gunned, he was wounded in two places, including the left calf, and his petrol tank was pierced. Putting down the nose of his BE, he managed to evade the enemy trio and made for the coast. En route, he randomly dropped his bomb load onto an enemy encampment. As he arrived over the sea, his petrol-starved engine stopped. Putting his machine down gently on the sea, just north of Rafah, he staggered ashore and was doing his best to bind up his wounds, before setting off on the long walk to the British lines, when he was seized and stripped naked by a many Arabs. Luckily, at that blackest of moments, an Australian cavalry patrol arrived just in time to rescue the naked and exhausted Kingsley and to deal with his captors. His MC was announced in the *London Gazette* of 3 March 1917: 'For conspicuous gallantry in action. He was attacked by three hostile machines and shot down. To ensure that his machine would not be destroyed, he deliberately landed in the sea at great risk to himself, as he had been wounded, and only with difficulty swam ashore'.

Kingsley was also Mentioned in Despatches at this time, *London Gazette* of 18 March 1917. Restored to 14 Squadron after recovering from his wounds, he was promoted to A/Captain and Flight Commander on 1 March 1917. His tour with '14' completed on 23 July 1917, he was posted to RFC HQ, Egypt, for a period of rest and recuperation. Kingsley next served briefly with 111 Squadron, before returning to the UK in October 1917. He finally left the RAF in 1919 with the rank of Major. Kingsley returned to live again in the Argentine for a time, before returning to London. A keen motorist, he was caught speeding twice in rapid succession, in Hayes, Middlesex, on 14 December 1935, and again shortly afterwards, in Ricksmanworth, quite rare events in those days. On 10 March 1936, Major S G Kingsley MC, was fined £1 and had his license endorsed for these offences. Kingsley died at his home at Flat 18, 35 Bryanston Square, London W1, on 4 July 1971.

KINKAID, Herbert Rae

His surname seems to have caused some confusion, being given as 'Kincaid' in some sources. From Ottawa, he was born on 19 May 1894. Gazetted Lieutenant to 21 Battalion, Canadian Infantry, on 23 August 1916. He transferred to the RFC in July 1917 and, after training as an Observer, was sent to the Bristol Fighter-equipped 11 Squadron as a Probationary on 20 November of that year. He gained a victory flying with Second Lieutenant J S Chick (qv) on the first day of the New Year of 1918, shooting down an enemy Scout out of control. His 'apprenticeship' satisfactorily completed, he was confirmed and gazetted Flying Officer (Observer) on 8 January 1918. He was successful again on 9 March, this time in company with Second Lieutenant D C M Brooks (qv). Kinkaid and Brooks carried out a valuable long-range reconnaissance in poor weather conditions, shooting down an enemy machine in the process. Again, on 16 May, the same pair dived on a large formation of enemy tri-planes, sending one down to crash into a field north west of Mametz. On the following day, however, Kinkaid was wounded in action, wounds which necessitated him being sent to the UK for medical treatment four days later. His MC was announced in the *London Gazette* of 22 June 1918: 'For conspicuous gallantry and devotion to duty. On one occasion he succeeded in completing a very long reconnaissance over the enemy's lines under the most difficult conditions, and returned with information of the greatest value. He has performed most efficient work on photographic reconnaissance during the recent operations, the work being carried out on several occasions at very low altitudes'

Once recovered, he was posted to an instructing post on 8 August 1918. Herbert Kinkaid left the RAF, via the Unemployed List, on 21 May 1919, returning to Canada soon afterwards.

KINNEAR, Albert Marlow

The son of Mr and Mrs Albert Kinnear, he was born 17 November 1893, at Kinnear's Mills, Quebec, Canada. Educated at Quebec High School (1905-11). He secured a position with the Canadian Bank of Commerce on 1 March 1912, after brief service in a similar capacity with the Eastern Townships Bank. Kinnear worked at the Sherbrooke branch of the bank, and it was from there that he was accepted into the RFC as a Cadet, in December 1916. Gazetted Second Lieutenant to the RFC, via the Special Reserve, on 13 April 1917. His pilot training duly completed, he was confirmed and gazetted Flying Officer on 31 August following. Within weeks of qualifying, he was sent out to the AWFK8s of 8 Squadron. On 30 November 1917, Kinnear and his Observer of the day, Lieutenant A A Browne, in AWFK8, 'B308', were shot up during an aerial combat over Masnières. Their 'Big-Ack' was damaged and Browne was wounded. Despite this trauma, Kinnear was up again on the following day, this time with Lieutenant M A O'Callaghan acting as his Observer in AWFK8, 'B314'. On this occasion, machine-gun fire from the ground at Mericourt shot through their fuel pipe and Kinnear was wounded in the scalp. Both of these incidents are described in the citation to Kinnear's MC, announced in the *London Gazette* of 4 February 1918, details in the *Gazette* of 5 July 1918: 'For conspicuous gallantry and devotion to duty. This officer, on one occasion, while on patrol was attacked by six enemy aircraft, his elevator controls shot away and his observer wounded, but he drove them off. The following day he was wounded in the head and both his petrol tanks were shot through but he brought his machine back. This gallant officer has shown great determination and initiative and on previous occasions has done very valuable work'.

Research has unearthed the original recommendation for this award: 'HQ, 3 Brigade, RFC: For skill and gallantry. On November 30th he carried out a successful contact patrol at low altitude owing to clouds. In the course of this flight he was attacked by six enemy aeroplanes, his observer being wounded in the hand and the elevator controls on one side shot through. He succeeded in beating off the enemy aircraft and returned with very valuable information. On December 1st he carried out a contact patrol in very different weather under very heavy rifle and machine-gun fire from Banteaux Ravine, at a height of 200 feet. His observer returned the fire with his Lewis gun, but at this point the pilot was hit in the head by a bullet which dazed him, and both petrol tanks were shot through. 2nd Lieutenant Kinnear, however, succeeded in bringing his machine back to our lines and made a forced landing. This officer has been untiring in his efforts to obtain information by contact patrols, and has brought back valuable reports, in spite of the weather being at times almost impossible for flying'.

Kinnear's own version of the events of 1 December 1917, where contained in a letter home: '....I had 110 holes in the bus and one in my head. All the petrol tanks were shot through, but fortunately I got over our lines instead of crashing in Hunland. I had come down low to ascertain certain things, and 'Umpteen' machine-guns started to shoot the bus to pieces. I was hit on the head and faded away, and when I came to, my observer was pushing a flask down my throat and the bus was diving for the earth. I had enough sense to pull her up and managed to steer west. When I crossed our lines the engine died, so I planted her in a field and once more passed away'.

After recovering, he returned again to 8 Squadron, serving through the very difficult days of the German spring offensive. His tour with '8' completed, he returned to the Home Establishment to take up instructing duties on 29 July 1918 and was promoted Captain in the following month. Demobilised in August 1919, Albert Kinnear returned to his job with the Canadian Bank of Commerce.

KINNEAR, John Lawson

The son of the Reverend Henry Kinnear and Mrs Frances Kinnear, of The Rectory, Copgrove, Yorkshire, he was born on 9 February 1890. Educated at Stubbington School, Farnham (1903-05), at Knaresborough, Yorkshire (1905-06), and at West Wrathing Park, Cambridgeshire (1907). Gazetted Second Lieutenant to 1 Battalion, King's (Liverpool Regiment) in 1910. Seconded to the RFC, he gained his Royal Aero Club Certificate (Number 884) on 31 August 1914. His formal pilot training duly completed, he was confirmed and gazetted Flying Officer on 3 October following. He served with 6 Squadron in France from the spring of 1915. As was usual in those early days, he was frequently involved in generally inconclusive confrontations with enemy aircraft. On 21 September 1915, Kinnear and his Observer in FE2a, '2864', were reconnoitring for the artillery near Hooge at 08.25, when they sighted a large two-engined enemy machine escorted by a Scout. The two main adversaries started a scrap that would last for no less than 35 minutes. Pass after pass was made with no tangible effect, whilst the escorting Scout kept nipping in to lend a hand to its heavy-weight partner, firing down vertically onto the BE. Finally, the two Germans broke off the engagement and headed for home. As they did so, yet another enemy aircraft hove up, fired a burst of 50 rounds or so at the RFC machine and then promptly turned tail and flew east. The gunners of 10 Anti-Aircraft Section, RA, were sufficiently impressed by what they had witnessed, to send the following telegram to 6 Squadron: 'A British FE remained over the German lines for ¾ hours and succeeded in driving off four [sic] German patrolling planes one of which was a twin engine tractor, after a stiff fight'. Kinnear would receive his MC as a direct consequence of this action, announced in the New Year *London Gazette* of 1 January 1916 (no citation). Although no formal citation appeared in the *Gazette*, research has unearthed the original recommendation for the award: '6 Sqd. On 21st Sept., when doing artillery observation attacked a large twin engined machine and persisted in the attack until the enemy was driven off, the engagement lasting 35 minutes. In the encounter, the two machines approached eight times within 60 yards of each other. Drove off two other machines after which the reconnaissance was completed successfully. A telegram was received from our anti aircraft guns with information of this encounter. Always shows great determination in carrying out any work allocated'.

Kinnear continued to be involved in many inconclusive confrontations for the remainder of 1915. He was particularly fortunate on 14 December, when flying Bristol Scout '4680'. Having fought an aerial combat with a Fokker at 5,000 feet over Poelcappelle, which petered out without resolution, he was immediately confronted by an Aviatik at 4,000 feet. Again, this was inconclusive, although his machine did receive a number of hits. When he landed it was found that a bullet had gone through the back of his seat, fortunately without hitting him. After a rest in the UK, Kinnear was promoted to Major and, on 1 June 1916, was sent to command 42 Squadron, an artillery observation unit, then still forming at Filton. Kinnear took eight BE2d and ten BE2e of 42 Squadron to France on 8 August 1916, and was operationally ready at Bailleul as part 2 Wing, II Brigade, RFC, one week later. He commanded '42' throughout the remainder of the Battle of the Somme in 1916 and on through most of the great battles of 1917, before returning to the Home Establishment on 8 December in that year. For his services as a Commanding Officer, he was awarded a Distinguished Service Order, *London Gazette* of 1 January 1918, and was twice Mentioned in Despatches. He was presented with the insignia of the Distinguished Service Order by the King at an investiture held at Buckingham Palace on 13 April 1918. Just

15 days later, on 28 April 1918, Kinnear, in Camel 'B9234', was killed when his machine stalled and plunged to the ground at 1 TS, Beaulieu. Major John Lawson Kinnear, DSO, MC is buried in nearby East Boldre (St Paul) Churchyard, Hampshire.

KIRK, James

From Denistoun, Glasgow, he was born on 24 April 1891. Educated at Glasgow University. Gazetted Second Lieutenant to 1 Battalion, Royal Highlanders (Black Watch), on 23 August 1914, later becoming attached to 5 (Renfrewshire) Battalion, Argyll and Sutherland Highlanders (TF). He served as an Observer with 14 Squadron in Mesopotamia from 27 April 1917 to 21 January 1918. His MC was announced in the *London Gazette* of 11 April 1918 (no citation), awarded for: '....military operations culminating in the capture of Jerusalem'.

His tour with '14' completed, Kirk was next posted as an Instructor to the Artillery Observers School in Egypt in November 1918. Next, he trained as a Pilot at Training Brigade, Egypt. After qualifying for his full 'Wings', he joined 113 Squadron in Palestine in 1919, before going on to serve with 208 Squadron in Ismailia, from February 1920. James Kirk finally left the service with the rank of Lieutenant on 13 August 1920.

KIRKMAN, Robert Kirby

The third son and youngest child of the seven children of Farmer, John William Kirkman and Annie Elizabeth Kirkman, of Broughton Astley, Leicester, he was born in 1891. Enlisted as a Private soldier (Number 3896) into 12 (Service) Battalion, Hampshire Regiment, and subsequently accompanied that unit to France in September 1915. Picked out for a commission, he was gazetted Second Lieutenant into 7 Battalion, Leicestershire Regiment, on 12 December 1915. He served in the trenches with 7 Leicesters, before being seconded to the RFC late in 1916. His pilot training duly completed, he was confirmed and gazetted Flying Officer on 14 February 1917. Posted to 20 Squadron in the summer of 1917, he really came into his own when '20' was re-equipped with Bristol Fighters in the following September. With the aid of several Observers, he gained eight victories between 11 September 1917 and 23 March 1918, having been promoted to A/Captain and Flight Commander on the intervening 18 December 1917. Kirkman's seventh and eighth victories were achieved on 23 March 1918 when, with Ace Gunner, Captain J H Hedley, he shot down two Albatros Scouts. Four days later, however, Kirkman and Hedley in BF2b, 'B1156', were themselves shot down by Leutnant Karl Gallwitz of Jasta 2 (Boelcke), the ninth of the German Ace's ten victories. Forced to bring their Brisfit down smack in front of the first wave of an enemy infantry advance, they were shot at by some of the oncoming German troops. Fortunately, they were not hit, but were subsequently taken prisoner by some of the advancing rear echelon troops. Kirkman's MC was announced in the *London Gazette* of 26 March 1918, details in the *Gazette* of 24 August 1918: 'For conspicuous gallantry and devotion to duty. He led a patrol of eleven aeroplanes, and through his skilful manoeuvring and leadership the patrol destroyed four enemy scouts and drove down three more out of control. On several other occasions he has driven down and destroyed hostile machines, and has always set a fine example of courage and determination'.

Research has unearthed the original recommendation for the award, which gives a little more detail than does the formal citation: 'R K Kirkman. On the 25th January 1918, this Officer led a patrol of 11 Bristol Fighters, and, through his skilful manoeuvring and leadership, this patrol destroyed four enemy scouts and drove down three more out of control, only one Bristol Fighter being lost. This patrol worked over the lines for an hour and a half, attacking five separate enemy formations, going over as far as Thielt to find two of them. Captain Kirkman himself destroyed one scout. In addition to the above he:

:

Destroyed one Albatros Scout on 11/9/17, over Menin.
Drove down out of control one Albatros Scout on 21/9/17, over Roulers.
Drove down out of control one Albatros Scout on 13/11/17, over Tenbrielen.
Drove down out of control one Albatros Scout on 5/12/17, over Oostniewkerke

He has on all occasions set a fine example of bravery and tenacity. Offensive Patrols led by him have been characterised by a thoroughly offensive spirit'.

Both Hedley and Kirkman would be repatriated to the UK on the same day – 17 December 1918.

KITTO, Francis Mansel

The son of Bank Accountant, Joseph Bice Kitto and Annie Mary Kitto (née Dawkin), of 78 Plasturton Avenue, Cardiff, Glamorgan, Wales, he was born in Aberystwyth on 1 January 1897. Educated at Aberystwyth Grammar School, at Llandovery College, and at the University of Wales, where he was a member of the OTC. Kitto had a pupilage as an apprentice Electrical Engineer with the Chiswick Electricity Supply Company (Aberystwyth Branch), prior to volunteering for military service. Gazetted Second Lieutenant into 23 Battalion, Welsh Regiment (Welsh Pioneers), on 29 October 1915. A secondment to the RFC was granted in June 1916 and, after the appropriate pilot training, he was confirmed and gazetted Flying Officer on 9 November following. A 'founder member' of the Sopwith Strutter-equipped 43 Squadron, he accompanied that unit to France on 17 January 1917. Kitto gained a victory in each of the months of March and April, before he was himself wounded and forced to return to the UK for medical treatment. On 8 April 1917, Kitto and his Observer, 1 AM (Number 77690) A W Cant, came under attack by five Albatros Scouts and managed to send one of them down, although they continued to be hard pressed by the remaining four. They were rescued by the timely arrival of the aerial cavalry in the form of Nieuport Scouts from 40 Squadron. (Cant, from Uppingham, would later be awarded the Distinguished Conduct Medal, *London Gazette* of 26 January 1918). Kitto re-joined '43' in the summer of 1917, and he and Cant, in 'A8224', claimed the last Strutter victory on 17 August 1917, before the squadron was re-equipped with Camels. Kitto was promoted to A/Captain and posted to the Camels of 54 Squadron as a Flight Commander early in 1918. Six further victories followed, including a 'double' on 24 March 1918. His MC was announced in the *London Gazette* of 22 June 1918: 'For conspicuous gallantry and devotion to duty. While engaged in attacking ground targets with machine-gun fire and bombs he observed a large party of troops, amongst whom he dropped the remainder of his bombs with the most excellent results. On a later occasion he attacked a formation of enemy scouts and, having caused one of these to crash to the ground, he pursued another and attacked it eleven miles behind the enemy's lines, bringing it to the ground and destroying it. In addition to these he has shot down two other hostile machines, and has shown throughout the greatest determination and dash'.

Kitto would also serve as a Flight Commander with the DH9-equipped 49 Squadron in 1919.

KNIGHT, Arthur Gerald

The son of Arthur Cecil Knight and Mrs Knight of Inchfield House, Holly Walk, Leamington, he was born in Bedford, on 30 July 1895. Spending some of his formative years in Canada, his later education was at Upper Canada College and at Toronto University, where he studied Applied Science until 1915, when he returned to England to seek a commission in the RFC. Gained his Royal Aero Club Certificate (Number 2063) on 11 November 1915 and was gazetted Second Lieutenant to the RFC, via the Special Reserve, on 20 November following. His formal training duly completed, he was confirmed and gazetted Flying Officer on 4 February 1916. Sent out to the BEs of 4 Squadron in France soon after qualifying. Four months later, he was transferred to the DH2-equipped 24 Squadron, then under the distinguished command of Major Lanoe Hawker VC, DSO, and was soon heavily involved in the aerial operations in support of the Somme offensive. On 28 October 1916, Knight and a colleague, Alfred McKay, were indirectly involved with the accidental death of Oswald Boelcke. In manoeuvring to attack Knight and McKay's DH2s, Boelcke and Erwin Böhme's machines collided. Although the latter's machine was relatively unscathed, Boelcke's upper wing broke away and he fell to his death. Knight gained eight victories between 22 June and 16 December 1918. His MC was announced in the *London Gazette* of 14 November 1916: 'For conspicuous gallantry and skill. He has shown great pluck in fights with enemy machines, and has accounted for several. On one occasion, when a hostile machine was interfering with a reconnaissance, he attacked at very close range, and brought down the machine in flames'

As the Battle of the Somme came to a close in November 1916, Knight was transferred as a Flight Commander to 29 Squadron, another DH2 unit. The announcement of his gallantry Distinguished Service Order came in the *London Gazette* of 11 December 1916. Just nine days later, Knight, in DH2, '7927', on offensive patrol with squadron colleagues, became embroiled in an aerial battle with elements of Jasta 2. The five enemy machines involved included one flown by Manfred von Richthofen, who had, by then, already achieved 12victories. Von Richthofen's post-combat report gives his version of events; 'About 11.30 I attacked, together with four planes and at 3,000 metres altitude, enemy one-seater squadron above Menchy (Monchy) After some curve fighting I managed to press adversary down to 1,500 metres, where I attacked him at closest range (plane length). I saw immediately that I had hit the enemy; first he went down in curves, then he dashed to the ground. I pursued him until 100 metres above the ground. This plane had only been attacked by me'.

Thus Knight became the 13th of the Red Baron's eventual 80 victories. Arthur Knight is buried in Douchy-les-Ayette British Cemetery, France.

KNIGHT, Geoffrey

From Godalming, Surrey, he was born 13 February 1889. Educated at Victoria Park School and at Owens College, Manchester. He studied Mechanical Engineering for six years with the International Correspondence Schools, whilst at the same time working in a sugar plantation in the Argentine. Once qualified, he worked as a Mechanical Engineer in San Pedro de Jujuy, Argentina, until September 1914. He returned home to the UK and enlisted as a Trooper into the City of London Yeomanry (Rough Riders) (TF) on 27 October 1914. Knight accompanied his regiment to Egypt on 15 August 1915 and was with them when they landed in Galliopli as a dismounted unit, just three days later. Falling ill, he became, on 28 October 1915, one of the many soldiers invalided from Suvla Bay with enteric fever. He was hospitalised in Egypt and underwent medical care, until the spring of 1916. Once recovered, he was accepted as a candidate for the flying service and was duly gazetted Second Lieutenant to the RFC, via the General List, on 27 May 1916. Gained his Royal Aero Club Certificate (Number 3245) on 13 July 1916. His formal pilot training duly completed, he was confirmed and gazetted Flying Officer on 12

August following. Sent out to BE2e-equipped 6 Squadron in France just four days after qualifying. Knight was promoted to A/Captain and Flight Commander on 23 May 1917. His MC was announced in the *London Gazette* of 26 July 1917: 'For conspicuous gallantry and devotion to duty. He showed great dash and promptness in diving to the assistance of one of his squadron, who had been attacked by five hostile scouts and dispersing them. His assistance to our artillery in engaging hostile batteries from a low altitude was of the greatest value'.

His tour with '6' completed, he returned to the Home Establishment on 4 January 1918. Following a brief rest, he was next posted to instructing duties in the UK. The Belgians showed their appreciation of his services at this time with an award of the Croix de Guerre, *London Gazette* of 15 May 1918. Promotion to A/Major followed on 5 June 1918. His last operational posting, from 3 November 1918 until 4 April 1919, was with 5 Squadron (RE8s). Geoffrey Knight finally left the RAF, via the Unemployed List, on 6 April 1919.

KNIGHT, Gerald Featherstone

Born in Stanmore, Torquay, Devon, on 18 September 1894. Educated at Toronto University (1912-13). Having already returned to the UK, he joined the Inns of Court OTC (Number A/1334) on 26 September 1914. From the ranks of the OTC, he was gazetted Second Lieutenant to 3 (Reserve) Battalion, Devon Regiment, on 4 November 1914, with an immediate detachment to the Gloucestershire Regiment. Seconded to the RFC in November 1915, he trained as an Observer and was sent out to 5 Squadron as a Probationary in January 1916. His 'apprenticeship' satisfactorily completed, he was confirmed and gazetted Flying Officer (Observer) on 29 April 1916. Returning to the Home Establishment in June 1916, he trained next as a Pilot, gaining his Royal Aero Club Certificate (Number 3344) on 27 July 1916. Further service and training with 35 Squadron, then in Thetford, followed, before, having formally qualified for his full 'Wings', he was sent out to BE2c-equipped 12 Squadron in France, on 15 October 1916. On 9 November following, Knight, in BE2c, '2502', was involved, along with others of his squadron, in a combat against elements of Jasta 2. His engine disabled, probably by the guns of Leutnant Hans Imelmann, he was forced to crashland behind German lines and was duly taken prisoner of war. Knight somehow contrived to escape from captivity and into Switzerland, before being returned to England on 16 September 1917. His book, 'Brother Boche', which relates the circumstances of his escape, was subsequently published in 1919 (Heinemann). Knight's health, however, was not good, but, despite this, he was promoted to Captain and posted as an Instructor to 27 TDS on 1 August 1918. He suffered a relapse in July 1919 and was admitted to Eaton Square Hospital, London, classified as dangerously ill. Gerald Knight subsequently died at 10.40am in the Eaton Square Hospital on 30 October 1919. The announcement of his MC appeared posthumously in the 'Escapers Gazette', *London Gazette* of 16 December 1919: '....in recognition of gallantry in escaping from captivity whilst Prisoners of War'.

KNIGHT, Osbert Richmond

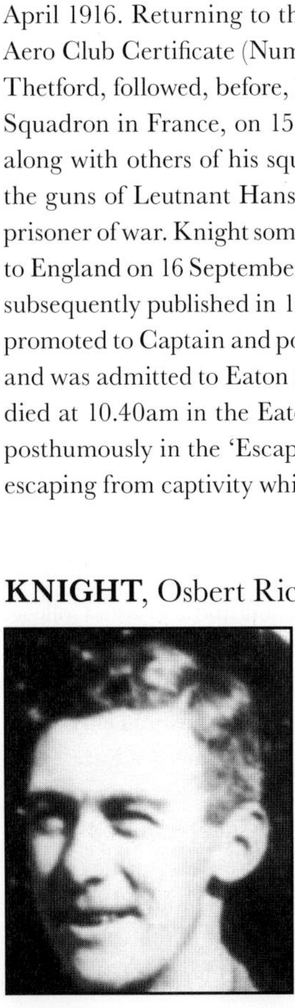

The son of William T Knight and Margaret S Knight, of 12 Albany Road, St Leonard's-on-Sea, Sussex, he was born on 4 December 1889. Educated at Clifton College (1905-06). By the time the war came in 1914, he had emigrated and was living and working in Pine Lake, Alberta, Canada. He returned to England as a member of 5 Battalion, Canadian Infantry, part of the first CEF contingent, before crossing to France in February 1915. He served in the trenches for nine months, during which time he was wounded at Festubert. Picked out for a commission, he was gazetted Second Lieutenant to 4 Battalion, Royal West Surrey Regiment (TF), on 21 November 1915, before being seconded to the RFC in the following June. Gained his Royal Aero Club Certificate (Number 4009) on 21 August 1916, the same day that he was confirmed and gazetted Flying Officer. His first job was as an Instructor at Salisbury Plain, but he was eventually sent out to France and BE2e-equipped 16 Squadron in February 1917. Knight was slightly wounded twice in quite rapid succession; firstly on 6 March and secondly on 28 March 1917. On 6 April 1917, Bloody April, Knight and his Observer, Second Lieutenant Ubalde Hormisdas Seguin from Ottawa, in BE2e, '6823', on artillery observation patrol over Thelus, were both killed when their machine was sent down in flames during an aerial combat. Knight's MC was announced posthumously shortly afterwards in the *London Gazette* of 17 April 1917: 'For conspicuous gallantry and devotion to duty when attacked by two hostile machines. Although wounded, he succeeded in driving the two machines away, and continued to observe for his batteries. Later, he again drove off an enemy machine and continued his observations'.

Research has unearthed the original recommendation for the award, which gives a little more specific detail of the circumstances: '1st Brigade, RFC. For gallantry and devotion to duty. On 6th March 1917, whilst on Artillery Observation, he was attacked near Neuville St Vaast by two hostile machines simultaneously. Although slightly wounded in the arm at the outset, he managed to drive the two machines away, and continued to observe for his battery. An hour later he was again attacked at close quarters by a hostile scout. He drove this machine away, and although his own machine was much shot about, he continued his observation until his petrol had run out. This officer has done excellent work on other occasions'.

Osbert Knight is buried in Thelus Military Cemetery, France.

NB: An auction house in the West Country offered for sale his incomplete group in March 2002: MC, 1914-15 Star (Pte CEF), *Victory Medal 1914-19, and Canadian Memorial Cross (the British War Medal 1914-20 was missing).*

KNOWLES, Robert Millington

The son of Andrew Knowles, JP, and Mrs Knowles, of Taverham Hall, Norwich, he was born on 10 July 1893. Educated at Dulwich College (1906-12), Rugby XV, Rowing VIII, and at Trinity Hall, Cambridge. Robert's brother, Second Lieutenant Andrew Brooks Knowles, 17 Cavalry, Indian Army, was killed in action near to Luckhomo in German East Africa, on 11 June 1916. Volunteering as soon as the war came, Robert was gazetted Second Lieutenant to 3 (Reserve) Battalion, Norfolk Regiment, on 15 August 1914. Seconded to the RFC, he trained as an Observer and accompanied 60 Squadron to France as a 'founder member' on 20 May 1916. The Observers of '60' became redundant when the squadron was equipped exclusively with Scout planes early in 1917 and Knowles was, soon afterwards, next sent to FE2d-equipped 20 Squadron. On 3 February 1917, Knowles, flying with Second Lieutenant C Gordon-Davies, engaged seven hostiles over Wervicq, sending one of them down out of control. His MC was announced in the *London Gazette* of 12 March 1917: 'For conspicuous gallantry and devotion to duty when acting as an Observer. He showed throughout the greatest courage in the face of very superior forces, and a high standard of marksmanship'.

On 5 April 1917, Knowles, this time on patrol with Captain G J Mahoney-Jones, helped squadron colleagues to send down and destroy two Halberstadts. On 24 April 1917 – Bloody April – Captain Knowles and his Pilot, Lieutenant N L Robertson, in FE2d, 'A5144', came down in flames following a combat with Leutnant Walter von Bülow-Bothkamp of Jasta 18, the 12th of the German Ace's eventual 28 victories. Both Knowles and Robertson suffered wounds and burns in this incident. Knowles, however, was sufficiently recovered by 2 June 1917 to marry his fiancée, Olive Marjory Berners. Knowles did not fly operationally again before finally leaving the service, via the Unemployed List, on 3 January 1919. He was Mentioned in Despatches on one occasion during the Great War. Robert Knowles lived, post-war, at Gissing Hall, Diss, Norfolk.

KOCH, Alfred

From Grandbunten, Switzerland, he was born on 25 January 1894. When he was four years old, his family emigrated to Canada, settling in Edmonton, Alberta. Amongst the first to volunteer when war came, he enlisted as a Trooper into 19 Alberta Dragoons as a trumpeter, crossing to England with 1 Cavalry Division, CEF, in October 1914, before going to France with the first Canadian contingent early in 1915. Accepted as a candidate for the RFC, he trained as an Observer/Gunner and flew operationally with 1 Squadron from May 1916 to June 1916. Picked out for a commission, he was gazetted Second Lieutenant to the RFC, via the Special Lists, on 3 August 1916, and confirmed and gazetted Flying Officer (Observer) in the *Gazette* of the following day. Sent out next to 6 Squadron, he was wounded in action on 22 October 1916, when his BE2d was shot up in the air and he was hit by a bullet in the back. After recovering his health and fitness in an English hospital and enjoying a brief leave in Canada, he trained next as a Pilot. Sent out in that capacity to 70 Squadron in France, he flew his first combat patrol in a Camel on 6 October 1917. Claiming the first of his victories on 18 October 1917, he went on to gain a further nine by 23 March 1918. On 27 March, with the German spring offensive in full swing, he was on a low-flying patrol in Sopwith Camel, 'C8297', when he and his machine were hit by machine-gun fire from the ground over Pozières. Fortunately, he was able to get the Camel safely down, whereupon he was whisked off to hospital. His MC was announced in the *London Gazette* of 22 June 1918: 'For conspicuous gallantry and devotion to duty. During ten days' operations, he carried out eleven reconnaissances at low altitudes. He continually attacked and disorganised enemy troops and transport, and on one occasion, he dispersed a battalion of enemy infantry, which was marching along a road. On a later occasion, after he had completed a reconnaissance and bombed an enemy position, he was attacked by an enemy patrol. Though his tanks were pierced and he was wounded, he succeeded in flying his machine back to the aerodrome. He showed splendid courage and initiative'.

Research has unearthed the original recommendation for this award, which provides more detail than does the formal citation: 'HQ 3 Brigade, RAF, 8 April 1918 : For continued good service and gallantry during the battle, March 21st to March 31st. 2nd Lieut Koch, during the period mentioned above, fired 4,850 rounds and dropped 32 bombs in the course of eleven patrols. All these patrols were undertaken at very low altitudes and the salient features of which were as follows:

> On 24 March 1918 he did three low flying patrols, during which he reconnoitred the Le-Transloy-Guedecourt area and brought back much valuable information. He also obtained a direct hit with a bomb on a transport near Le Transloy, and disorganised with bombs and machine-gun fire transport west of Rocquigny.
>
> On 25 March 1918 this officer again did three patrols. In the morning he dispersed a battalion of infantry, marching in column from Petit Miraumont to Irles. Later in the day he scattered a party of infantry marching west from Bapaume and Avesnes, a second party which he attacked in the same neighbourhood scattered and then re-formed, on which he attacked them again.
>
> On 26 March 1918 this officer bombed a column of infantry north of Beaumont Hamel, with such success that it broke and turned back.
>
> On 27 March 1918 after this officer had reconnoitred the position and dropped his bombs near Pozières, he was attacked by a patrol of Albatros Scouts and Triplanes. His tanks were pierced and he was wounded, but in spite of this, he managed to fly his machine back to his aerodrome.

2nd Lieut Koch has up to date driven down six enemy aircraft out of control. Since joining 70 Squadron on 6 October 1917 he has done the most excellent work, and is not only willing to, but actually undertakes, any difficult or dangerous operation. He is now in hospital suffering from a wound which he sustained on 27 March 1918'.

Once recovered from his wounds, he was posted to serve with 50 HD Squadron on 19 September 1918, with which unit he saw out the remainder of the war. A Lawyer in civilian life, he became, in the fullness of time, a Judicial Officer. In 1984, age 90, he attended a veteran Canadian fliers reunion. Alfred Koch died in Vancouver, Canada, later in the 1980s.

KOZAKOV, Aleksandr Alexandrovich

Born on 15 January 1889, in Kherson Province, Russia. He first joined the Russian Army as a cavalryman in 1908. A transfer to the Air Service came in 1913 and, in 1914, when the war came, he flew operationally in Poland. He tried, unsuccessfully it has to be said, a series of bizarre methods in order to bring down enemy machines, including employing grappling hooks and trailing explosives beneath his machine. In the spring of 1915, he finally achieved his first victory, of a sort, by ramming an opponent! Kozakov was given command of 19 Corps Air Detachment in September 1915, before moving, in August 1916, to take charge of 1 CAG. 1 CAG was sent to Roumania in February 1917 and Kozakov continued to achieve victories on that front, before being wounded in action on 27 June 1917. With 20 victories, he was the leading Russian Ace of the Great War and had, amongst many other honours, been awarded the MC by the British. A life-long royalist, Kozakov was shaken to the core by the onset of the Russian Revolution, which came in the following November. He fought with the White Russian forces until he was able to ally himself with the Allied Intervention Force by joining the British Military Mission in Murmansk in June 1918. Given the rank of Major, RAF, he was posted to the command of the Slavo-British Squadron at Benezniky. Wounded in action in January 1919, it was three months before he could return to active duty. The failure of the Allied Intervention and the end of the White Russian counter-revolution dismayed Kozakov and, having declined an invitation to attend a farewell dinner for the departing British airmen, to be held on 1 August 1919, he instead took off in a Camel, only to crash minutes later. Contemporary opinion was that the crash was a deliberate act and that he took his own life.

L

LALLY, Conrad Tolendal

Born in Toronto, Ontario, Canada, on 3 April 1888. At the time of his enlistment into the Canadian Army, he was the relatively youthful Mayor of Wainwright, Alberta. Transferred into the RFC whilst still in Canada, he was, upon his arrival in the UK, gazetted Second Lieutenant to the RFC, via the Special Reserve, on 1 January 1916. His pilot training duly completed, he was confirmed and gazetted Flying Officer on 27 June 1916. Served briefly with 28 TS in England, before he was sent out to France and the FE2d-equipped 25 Squadron. Obviously because of his maturity and experience of life in general, he had, by this time, already been promoted to A/Captain. Lally claimed five victories between 7 June and 3 September 1917, the first two in the FE2d, the latter three in the DH4. On 8 December 1917, Lally and his Observer, Lieutenant J E Cole, in DH4, 'A7605', were engaged in a combat which damaged their machine and caused them to crash on landing. Both men were slightly wounded, Lally being hit in the back by a spent bullet. He returned to England ten days later, his MC having already been announced in the *London Gazette* of 1 December 1917, details in the *Gazette* of 25 April 1918: 'For conspicuous gallantry and devotion to duty in many bomb raids and photographic and long-distance reconnaissances, many of which he has led most successfully. He has taken part in numerous combats and has destroyed three hostile positions. When ordered to bomb a position he spent 1½ hours looking for it, then returned for more petrol and at the second attempt dropped a bomb on it, with another set a dump on fire, under most difficult weather conditions'.

A Bar to his MC followed in the *London Gazette* of 4 February 1918, details in the *Gazette* of 5 July 1918: 'For conspicuous gallantry and devotion to duty. Flying through and above the clouds, he released his bombs over his objective, well behind the enemy lines, at a height of 500 feet under very heavy fire. On two later occasions he carried out photographic reconnaissances of hostile aerodromes under very bad weather conditions, on account of which several other machines had to give up the journey. He has shown himself to be a most determined and successful leader, his example of courage and skill being of great advantage to his squadron'.

After returning to the Home Establishment in 1918, he was appointed to various training stations and was injured in an aeroplane accident whilst giving instruction on 13 September 1918. For his outstanding services in the field of training, he was awarded the Air Force Cross, *London Gazette* of 2 November 1918. Lally returned to Canada after the war only to die quite soon afterwards.

LANCASHIRE, Arthur Edward

Born in Bath on 31 March 1892, his family moving later to Manchester. After completing his education and trade apprenticeship, he was employed as a Printer at the Co-operative Wholesale Society Paper Works, Longsight, Manchester, from May 1913 to August 1914. He volunteered as soon as the war came in August 1914, enlisting as a Driver (Number T/576) into the Army Service Corps. Accompanied the Transport and Supply Columns, 42 (East Lancashire) Division to Egypt on 10 September 1914. After service in Gallipoli and in Egypt, he was gazetted Second Lieutenant to a Regular Army battalion of the Lancashire Fusiliers on 26 April 1917. Seconded to the RFC, he trained as an Observer and was eventually sent out to 35 Squadron as a Probationary on 13 November 1917. On 24 March 1918, Lancashire and his Pilot, Lieutenant R M C MacFarlane (qv) in AWFK8, 'C3534', were heavily involved with others of the squadron in vital reconnaissance work on what was one of the most difficult days of the German spring offensive. Indeed, both men were awarded the MC for their work on this day. Lancashire's MC was announced in the *London Gazette* of 22 June 1918: 'For conspicuous gallantry and devotion to duty. During a flight, lasting for over two hours, carried out at a height of 700 feet, he performed a very accurate contact patrol at a very critical period, obtaining the most valuable information concerning the enemy's dispositions. He also engaged many batteries and infantry with machine-gun fire, and throughout, by his courage and keenness, he set a fine example to all ranks'.

On 3 April 1918, Lancashire and MacFarlane, in AWFK8, 'C3682', on photographic reconnaissance over Blagny-Tronville, were attacked and shot down by Leutnant Viktor von Pressentin of Jasta 3, the second of the German Ace's eventual 15 victories. Both crewmen were wounded and their machine burnt and wrecked. Neither would again serve operationally during the Great War. Arthur Lancashire finally left the service, via the Unemployed List, in May 1919.

LANDER, Thomas Eaton

The son of Major T E Lander, Highland Light Infantry and Mrs Lander of Pollok Castle, Newton Mearns, Renfrewshire, he was born on 18 October 1893. Educated at Uppingham (1908-12) and at Trinity College Cambridge. Gazetted Second Lieutenant to 3 (Reserve) Battalion, Highland Light Infantry, on 14 October 1914. He served in the trenches with 1 Battalion of his regiment in 1915. Gained Royal Aero Club Certificate (Number 1889) on 14 October 1915, which resulted in him being seconded to the RFC in January 1916. His formal pilot training duly completed, he was confirmed and gazetted Flying Officer on 25 May 1916. Sent out to the Middle East, he arrived for service with 30 Squadron in Egypt on 6 July 1916. Accompanying '30' to the Mesopotamian front, Lander and his Observer, Lieutenant E N D Barr (qv), in a BE2c, gained the first British victory in that theatre of war on 13 August 1916. A colleague, Lieutenant the Hon J H B Rodowney, also in a 30 Squadron BE2c, was under attack from a Pfalz monoplane over Shumran airfield, when Lander and Barr intervened, sending the enemy machine down. Both men were awarded the MC for this, *London Gazette* of 14 November 1916: 'For conspicuous gallantry and skill in an encounter with an enemy machine. By skilful manoeuvring, Lieutenant Lander and Second Lieutenant Barr drove the enemy machine behind the enemy's lines in a damaged condition'.

On 6 May 1917, Lander's Martinsyde G100, '7466', was sent down during an aerial combat with a Halberstadt Scout, flown by Sergeant Pomerich. Pomerich's fire hit the water jacket on the Martinsyde and pierced one of the cylinders. Lander himself was also hit by a machine-gun bullet in the left leg, which caused it to fracture. He crashlanded on an island in the Tigris, near to Tekrit, and was taken prisoner by the Turks. He remained in Turkish hands until his repatriation on 27 November 1918. Lander finally left the service, via the Unemployed List, in April 1919, returning to his profession as a Motor Engineer. By 1931, Lander was living at The Old Rectory, Harpenden. He was a founder member of the British Gliding Association and was amongst the first in the country to hold a glider pilot's certificate. Ironically, on 8 March 1931, he also became the first to die in a gliding accident in Britain. The Coroner heard that Lander was experimenting with a launching device powered by a motor car engine. Unfortunately, the attempt ended in disastrous failure, the glider smashing into the ground. Lander's skull was fractured and he was killed outright.

LANE, William Ivor Emms

The son of Draper, William Lane and Rose Alice Lane (née Emms), of 84-86 Stapleton Road, Bristol, he was born in 1899. Educated at the Merchant Venturers College, Bristol, and at Bristol University, where he was a member of the OTC. A Draper in his father's shop in civilian life, he joined the flying service as a Cadet in April 1917. Gazetted Second Lieutenant to the RFC on 5 July 1917, he duly trained as an Observer and was subsequently sent out as a Probationary to the RE8s of 52 Squadron. On 10 April 1918, Lane and his Pilot, Second Lieutenant H L Taylor, in RE8, 'B6641', on reconnaissance patrol, were attacked by a formation of nine Fokker DRIs over Amiens. Although severely wounded in the leg, Taylor put up a great fight, shooting down one of the enemy machines before he and Taylor were themselves sent down to a forced landing by Leutnant Walter Göttsch of Jasta 19, the last of the German Ace's 20 victories. However, just as Göttsch administered the coup de grace to his RE8, Taylor retaliated with a burst into the German Tri-plane, which sent it down to crash near Gontelles behind the British lines. When British Tommies arrived at the wrecked Drl, Göttsch was found to be dead. Lane's MC was announced in the *London Gazette* of 26 July 1918: 'For conspicuous gallantry and devotion to duty. While on artillery patrol, he was attacked by nine hostile tri-planes. He at once opened fire, shot one down, which fell in the enemy's lines. Although seriously wounded in the leg, he continued, with the greatest gallantry to engage the enemy, shooting down a second scout, which fell in our lines. Throughout the fight he displayed exceptional skill in handling his machine, and a magnificent determination to get at close quarters with his opponents'.

Lane did not return to operational flying before the end of the war and finally left the RAF, via the Unemployed List, on 27 February 1919.

LARKIN, Reginald Stanley

Born in Adelaide, living later in Esendon and in St Kilda, Victoria, Australia. Gazetted Second Lieutenant to the RFC, via the Special Reserve, on 3 June 1916. His pilot training duly completed, Larkin was confirmed and gazetted Flying Officer on 17 September 1916. He served with 5 Squadron in 1916 and early in 1917, before joining the FE2b-equipped 101 Squadron, later in the same year. His MC was announced in the *London Gazette* of 26 March 1918, details in the *Gazette* of 24 August 1918: 'For conspicuous gallantry and devotion to duty on long-distance bomb raids. He successfully bombed enemy aerodromes and railway communications on several occasions, and his skill and determination in reaching his objectives, frequently under adverse weather conditions, were a splendid example to the squadron. On one occasion, though his machine was partially disabled by anti-aircraft fire, he reached his objective and obtained a direct hit'.

Research has unearthed the original recommendation for this award which provides more detail than does the formal citation: 'R S Larkin, 101 Sqn 29/1/18. For gallantry and devotion to duty when carrying out night bomb raids, notably on the following occasions: On 30/11/17 this Officer made two trips in one night to bomb Douai station. He obtained direct hits on the station and fired many rounds from very low altitude. On 3/12/17 his objective was Sains-les-Marquoin. He made two trips in one night, diving down to a very low altitude. He dropped his bombs, afterwards firing into enemy troops and other objectives. On 17/12/17, on crossing the lines to bomb Rumbeke aerodrome, this Officer's machine was hit by AA fire, carrying away a portion of the bottom right-hand plane and breaking the main spar and aileron. He nevertheless proceeded to his objective and succeeded in obtaining one direct hit. He returned to the aerodrome and made a good landing. On 21/1/18, although the sky was completely clouded over, this Officer set out for his objective (Rumbeke aerodrome). Just after he crossed the lines he had trouble with his engine, so returned and crossed the lines again. He was successful in getting his engine to run better, so re-crossed the lines, and though he could not get above 1,200 feet, he proceeded to his objective and dropped his bombs with success. This Officer has carried out many bomb raids at a very low altitude and although in many cases the weather has been most unfavourable he has done some very successful work and has always shown the greatest determination'.

Larkin was presented with his MC by the King at an investiture held at Buckingham Palace on 9 March 1918 and left the RAF, via the Unemployed List, in May 1919.

LASCELLES, John Frederick

The fourth son of Lieutenant Colonel Henry Arthur Lascelles, MVO, and Caroline Maria Lascelles (née Gore), of Woolbeding, Midhurst, Sussex, he was born on 13 November 1895. One of his brothers, Francis, a Captain in the Royal Sussex Regiment, would also win an MC in the Great War. John was educated at Winchester (1909-14) and at Sandhurst, from where he was gazetted Second Lieutenant to the Rifle Brigade on 16 December 1914. Seconded immediately to the RFC, he was sent, four days later, to 4 Squadron in France. On 17 April 1915, Lascelles and his Pilot, Captain R M Vaughan (qv), in BE2c, '1669', on a reconnaissance patrol to Bruges, met a German Albatros over Boesinghe. Aerial combat was almost an unknown concept in those early days, but Lascelles did carry a rifle in his cockpit. Aiming and firing from varying ranges fluctuating down to 80 yards, he eventually, after 25 rounds, hit the German Pilot in the head, killing him outright. The enemy Observer contrived to bring the Albatros down reasonably intact behind the French lines near to Elverdinge, whereupon he was immediately taken prisoner. John Lascelles and Ralph Vaughan were Mentioned in Despatches and awarded MCs, both announced in the *London Gazette* of 23 June 1915 (no citation).

Lascelles narrowly escaped death on 15 June 1915, when he and his Pilot, Lieutenant W G S Mitchell (qv), in BE2b, '746', had a shell pass through their wings before exploding above their heads. Again, just fives days later, Lascelles and his Pilot, Captain Macdonnell, in a Voisin LAS, '5028', were forced to make a hurried descent when their engine was hit by anti-aircraft fire. His luck finally ran out on 31 July 1915, when he was killed in action. John Frederick Lascelles is buried in Beauval Communal Cemetery, Somme, France.

NB: The RAF Museum Hendon has his medals in its collection, donated by the aviation historian Neal W. O'Connor: MC, 1914-15 Star, British War Medal 1914-20, Victory Medal 1914-19, and Next of Kin Memorial Plaque.

LATIMER, Dennis

The son of hotel proprietor, James D Latimer and Ida L Latimer, of the Corbett Arms Hotel, Corbett Square, Towyn, Merioneth, he was born in Stretford, Lancashire, on 31 August 1895. Educated at Manchester University (1912-14). A School Master, he was deferred from military service until being accepted as a Cadet to the flying service in November 1916. Gazetted Second Lieutenant to the RFC on 26 January 1917. His pilot training duly completed, he was confirmed and gazetted Flying Officer on 27 April following. He joined BF2b-equipped 20 Squadron early in 1918, gaining the first of his 28 victories on 13 March. In the following May, Latimer with Lieutenant Thomas Cecil Noel, King's Own Scottish Borderers attached RFC (qv), acting as his Observer, claimed no less than 13 victories, both being awarded the MC as a consequence. Latimer's award was announced in the *London Gazette* of 16 September 1918: 'For conspicuous gallantry and devotion to duty on offensive patrol. He and his Observer in four days' fighting destroyed seven enemy machines and drove down three. They did magnificent service'.

Latimer was promoted to A/Captain and Flight Commander and the partnership continued to chalk up successes against the enemy. In August 1918, Latimer flew with the talented Sergeant Arthur Newland (Number 67162), from Enfield Wash, who would be rewarded with a Distinguished Flying Medal and Bar. This new pairing took Latimer's victory total to 28. On 22 August, Latimer, flying again with Tom Noel in Bristol BF2b, 'D7993', was shot down by Leutnant Willi Nebgen of Jasta 7. Latimer's luck continued to hold, for he survived the encounter and was taken prisoner. However, Old Etonian Tom Noel (qv), the recipient of an MC and Bar, was tragically killed in the encounter. The announcement of a Distinguished Flying Cross, awarded to Latimer for his repeated victories over enemy machines, came in the *London Gazette* of 21 September 1918. Dennis Latimer was repatriated on 23 December 1918 and finally left the RAF, via the Unemployed List, in the following April.

LATTA, James Douglas

Originally from Hendon, London, he was born on 13 May 1897. He spent two years as an Apprentice Engineer in Glasgow. Gazetted Second Lieutenant to the RFC, via the Special Reserve, on 9 February 1915. Gained his Royal Aero Club Certificate (Number 2067) on 16 November 1915. His pilot training duly completed, he was confirmed and gazetted Flying Officer on 24 February 1916. Sent out to the Nieuport XVII-equipped 1 Squadron as a Scout Pilot on 13 April 1916, he would gain three victories over the coming weeks. His MC was announced in the *London Gazette* of 27 July 1916: 'For conspicuous gallantry and skill. On two occasions he attacked enemy kite balloons, and each time he brought a kite down in flames. He has often driven off enemy aircraft and his own machine has been badly hit'.

Promoted to A/Captain, he was sent next to 60 Squadron (Nieuport XVIIs) as a Flight Commander on 18 August 1916. Two further victories followed and he was Mentioned in Despatches, *London Gazette* of 13 November 1916. Research has unearthed the original recommendation for this 'Mention': '17 October 1916: 'For consistent good service. Since November 1915 this Officer has set a fine example of initiative and devotion to duty'.

On 9 November 1916, Latta, in Nieuport XVII, 'A272', was involved in an aerial combat with Leutnant Wortmann of Jasta 2. The German optimistically claimed the Nieuport as a victory whereas, in fact, Latta was able to return safely, although his machine was damaged. His tour with '60' completed, he was sent home for a rest on 5 December 1916. Suitably refreshed, Latta was sent out again as a Flight Commander to the Sopwith Pup-equipped 66 Squadron in May 1917. His service with 66 was brief as, on 8 June, he was shot down and wounded in a fight with Oberleutnant von Voight of Jasta 8. This action effectively brought Jim Latta's combat career to an end. He was again Mentioned in Despatches, this announced in the *London Gazette* of 29 August 1919. After the war, he became an active member of the Royal Auxiliary Air Force, until eventually resigning his commission on 6 May 1927, when acting as CO, 602 Squadron, Royal Auxiliary Air Force.

LAURENCE, Frederic Hope

The son of Solicitor, Gerald Bixby Laurence and Georgina Hope Alice Laurence, of 22 Orsett Terrace, Paddington, London, and Milbourne Lodge, Esher, Surrey, he was born on 9 March 1896. Educated at Repton School (1909-12). A pre-war Militia officer, he was gazetted Second Lieutenant to 2 Battalion, Worcester Regiment, as soon as war came in August 1914. Sent out to 2 Battalion of his regiment in France in December 1914. Promoted to Captain on 24 August 1915, he was wounded in the trenches just south of the La Bassée Canal in April 1916. Once recovered, he sought secondment to the RFC, which was granted in September 1916. Having trained as a Pilot, he was duly confirmed and gazetted Flying Officer on 23 May 1917. Sent out to 70 Squadron, the first RFC unit to fly the Sopwith Camel, in the summer of 1917, he was soon promoted to Flight Commander, he already held the rank of Captain, of course. Laurence achieved five victories and the status of Ace, between 28 July and 27 October 1917. His MC was announced in the *London Gazette* of 26 November 1917, details in the *Gazette* of 6 April 1918: 'For conspicuous gallantry and devotion to duty. While leading a patrol of eight scouts, which were protecting a number of bombing machines, he attacked ten enemy machines, driving one down in flames and preventing the bombing machines being interfered with. On another occasion he attacked five enemy scouts, bringing one down in flames. He has brought down two other machines, and has at all times shown the greatest coolness and courage'.

Given a permanent commission in 1919, Laurence stayed on in the RAF after the war, eventually attaining the rank of Group Captain.

LAVARACK, Philip James Vaughan

The son of Mr and Mrs Hamlet Lavarack, of Hendon, Middlesex, he was born in 1890. Educated at Aldenham (1903-06). After leaving school, he entered the Inland Revenue, becoming a Valuer in the Valuation Department of that organisation. Appointed Temporary Inspector of Works, Royal Engineer Services, with the honorary rank of Lieutenant on 22 December 1914. Sent out to France as an Inspector of Works, early in 1916, he sought secondment to the flying service which was granted in the July of that year. His pilot training duly completed, he was confirmed and gazetted Flying Officer on 5 November 1916. Joined BE2e-equipped 12 Squadron in France soon after qualifying. On 23 April 1917, Lavarack and his Observer of the day, Lieutenant Budgett, in BE2e, 7099, were fortunate to escape with their lives when a main spar was shot through and broke, forcing them down to a crash landing. Budgett was injured in the incident, but Lavarack emerged unscathed. The first of his two MCs was announced in the *London Gazette* of 26 May 1917: 'For conspicuous gallantry and devotion to duty. While on a photographic patrol he shot down and destroyed a hostile machine. He has done consistently good work in artillery observation and photography throughout the operations'.

The Bar to his MC came in the *London Gazette* of 18 October 1917, details in the *Gazette* of 7 March 1918: 'For conspicuous gallantry and devotion to duty. When attacked on artillery patrol by eight enemy aircraft he succeeded in driving down one machine, the rest being driven off east. Later, he drove off three scouts badly hit, which could not be followed owing to the clouds. In the last month he has fought and driven off enemy aircraft on seven occasions, and afterwards completed his work'.

Returning to the UK late in 1917, he was posted as an Instructor and promoted to Major. He married Lillian Gladys, and set up home at 7 Wycombe Gardens, Golders Green, London. Killed in a flying accident at Cramlington Aerodrome, Northumberland, on 15 May 1918, whilst serving with 120 Squadron, Philip Lavarack is buried in Newcastle-upon-Tyne (St Andrews and Jesmond) Cemetery.

LEACH, Anthony

Born on 25 August 1896, he was a volunteer in the West Indian Local Forces, before being gazetted Second Lieutenant to the British West India Regiment, on 30 March 1917. Seconded to the RFC on 1 February 1918, he trained as an Observer and was, in the following month, sent out as a Probationary to 57 Squadron (DH4s). On 27 March, Leach and his Pilot, Lieutenant Powell, in DH4, 'A2155', narrowly escaped disaster when their machine was hit by anti-aircraft fire over Bapaume. Just five days later on 1 April 1918, the day the RAF came into being, Leach was wounded in the air and awarded the MC for his gallantry on that occasion, *London Gazette* of 26 July 1918: 'For conspicuous gallantry and devotion to duty. As an Observer, whilst engaged on photographic work, he was attacked by five hostile tri-planes. After he had fired a burst of 30 rounds at a range of 100 yards, one of the enemy planes went down in flames. Though the remaining hostile planes were reinforced by another ten machines, and though he himself was wounded, he fired a drum at a range of 150 yards, which resulted in another of the enemy machines rolling over on its side and falling to pieces. By his skill and coolness he undoubtedly saved his pilot and the machine'.

Leach stayed on in the RAF after the war. He served throughout the Second World War, attaining the rank of T/Group Captain on 1 March 1941, before finally retiring as a Wing Commander, with the honorary rank of Group Captain, on 9 June 1946.

LEACROFT, John

The son of Dr John William Leacroft and Mrs Leacroft, of Derby, he was born on 4 November 1888. Educated at Aldenham (1902-07) and at Pembroke College, Cambridge (1907-10). A Regular Army officer with the Army Service Corps when the war came, he was gazetted Captain on 6 January 1915. Seconded to the RFC, he trained as an Observer and served as such with 14 Squadron in Egypt, late in 1915 and in 1916. Next, he trained as a Pilot and, after qualifying, joined 19 Squadron (Spads) in France, in the early summer of 1917. After two highly successful tours with the unit, he achieved a total of 22 victories and was awarded the MC and Bar. The first of his MCs was announced in the *London Gazette* of 27 October 1917, details in the *Gazette* of 18 March 1918: 'For conspicuous gallantry and devotion to duty. On one occasion he flew at a very low altitude in extremely bad weather and successfully engaged enemy troops with machine-gun fire, and on another occasion carried out a most valuable reconnaissance and engaged enemy troops from a height of 100 feet. He destroyed two hostile machines, and has proved himself a courageous and determined pilot'.

The Bar to his MC came in the *London Gazette* of 22 June 1918: 'For conspicuous gallantry and devotion to duty. During a period of six months he has destroyed four and has brought down completely out of control six hostile machines. In all he has destroyed eight enemy machines and driven down thirteen out of control. On one occasion, when leading an offensive patrol, his formation destroyed six enemy planes and drove another down out of control without suffering any damage itself. He has displayed exceptional qualities as a leader, and his patrols have always been characterised by vigour and dash'.

He was shot down on two occasions, each time walking away from his crashed machine virtually unscathed. Leacroft stayed on in the RAF after the war, serving in Iraq from 1922 to 1924. He represented the RAF at both Polo and Cricket. He married in 1926, having one son and one daughter. Leacroft retired with the rank of Group Captain, in December 1937. He returned to the RAF in 1939, to serve again in the Second World

War, his appointments including President of the Air Crew Selection Board at Cardington. After the Second World War, he finally retired to his home at 20 Carlton Court, Bexhill-on-Sea, where he died on 26 August 1971.

NB: The RAF Museum Hendon has his medals in its collection: MC & Bar, 1914-15 Star (Capt ASC), *British War Medal 1914-20, Victory Medal 1914-19* (Capt RAF), *Silver Jubilee Medal 1935, General Service Medal 1918-62, with clasp, Kurdistan* (F/Lt RAF).

LEAKE, Eric Gilbert

The son of James Medley Leake and Florence Leake, of 'Ardencraig', 129 Hale Road, Hale, Altrincham, Cheshire, he was born on 26 January 1893. Educated at Sedbergh (1906-10), the second oldest of four brothers all educated there. Emigrating to Canada, he worked as a clerk in the Royal Bank of Canada in Toronto, from 1913 to 1914. He volunteered for the Canadian Infantry and was wounded in France in the summer of 1915, when serving with the CEF. Once recovered, he was given a commission in the British Army and gazetted Second Lieutenant to 7 Battalion, Manchester Regiment (TF), on 28 November 1915. Seconded to the RFC in December 1916, he gained his Royal Aero Club Certificate (Number 4072) on 5 January 1917. His formal pilot training duly completed, he was confirmed and gazetted Flying Officer on 19 March following. Sent out to 59 Squadron (RE8s) in France within days of qualifying. On 8 April 1917, Leake and his Observer, Lieutenant P L Hogan, in RE8, 'A3418', were involved in a combat with an enemy Scout over Etaing. Although their machine was shot up and Hogan wounded, still Leake got them back safely. Leake himself was slightly wounded when his RE8 was caught by anti-aircraft fire on 4 May following. On 5 June, he was again wounded, this time in the shoulder and a little more seriously. Following a period of hospitalisation and recuperation, he was sent back to '59' and France, just in time for the German Spring offensive. On 26 March 1918, Leake and his Observer, Second Lieutenant T H Upfill (qv), in RE8, 'B6656', narrowly escaped with their lives when their machine was shot up and damaged over Loupart Wood. The same crew were fortunate again on 28 March, when their RE8, 'D4686', was hit by machine-gun fire and forced down to crash land near to Collincamp. Both men were unscathed and even managed to salvage their instruments and other equipment, before destroying the remains of their machine. For this, Leake and Upfill would be awarded the MC. Leake's award was announced in the *London Gazette* of 22 June 1918: 'For conspicuous gallantry and devotion to duty. On one occasion, observing a hostile scout, he at once attacked and fired 1,000 rounds at close range. The hostile machine went down in a steep glide and crashed to earth. Later, when on contact patrol, his machine was damaged, and forced to land just behind our lines. Although under heavy shell fire, he, assisted by another officer, succeeded in salving all the instruments and equipment on the machine before destroying it. He has set a very high example of courage and devotion to duty throughout the operations'.

Leake's remarkable luck finally ran out on 24 July 1918, when his RE8 was shot down by anti-aircraft fire and he was mortally wounded. Carried off to hospital, he died exactly one week later on 31 July 1918. Eric Leake is buried in Bagneux British Cemetery, Gezaincourt, Somme, France.

LEARMOUNT, Leonard Wright

The son of Mr and Mrs R K Learmount, of 5 Collingwood Terrace, Jesmond, Newcastle-on-Tyne, he was born in Gateshead, Durham, on 21 October 1889. Educated at the Royal Grammar School, Newcastle (1899-1905). He was working in the Straits Settlements, Malaya, when the war came in August 1914. Although a volunteer with a locally raised unit, the Penang Volunteers, he nevertheless decided to return to the UK to offer his services. Gazetted Second Lieutenant to the RFC, via the Special Reserve, on 2 April 1915, the same day that he qualified for his Royal Aero Club Certificate (Number 1146). His formal pilot training duly completed, he was confirmed and gazetted Flying Officer on 7 June following. Sent out to 7 Squadron in France just four days after qualifying. On 31 July 1915, he and his Observer, Second Lieutenant H H Watkins, in Voisin LAS, '5028', were involved in two skirmishes with enemy aircraft during a reconnaissance patrol over Flanders. On this same day, a 7 Squadron colleague, Lieutenant J A Liddell, earned a posthumous Victoria Cross. 7 Squadron planes and personnel were heavily involved during the Battle of Loos which started on 25 September 1915. His tour with '7' completed, he returned to the Home Establishment on 8 May 1916. His MC was announced in the Birthday Honours *London Gazette* of 3 June 1916 (no citation). Although no formal citation appeared in the *Gazette*, research has unearthed the original recommendation for the award: 'L W Learmount. Consistent good work, done most gallantly and conscientiously from 13.6.15 to present time. This Officer bombed and hit one half of a train on 26.9.15, coming down to 500 feet immediately after Lieut. D A C Symington [qv] had bombed the other half'.

Learmount's next significant posting came on 25 January 1917, when he was promoted to Major and appointed Commanding Officer of 22 Squadron in France. Although COs were discouraged from participating in operational flying, Learmount was slightly wounded in action flying FE2b, '7703' on 10 May 1917. For his outstanding work as a Commanding Officer of an operational squadron and for gallantry on 19 May 1917 over the Hindenburg line, Learmount was awarded the Distinguished Service Order, *London Gazette* of 18 July 1917. The French, too, awarded him a Croix de Guerre avec Palme, *London Gazette* of 14 July 1917. He was also Mentioned in Despatches later in the same year, *London Gazette* of 11 December 1917. Learmount was wounded again on 9 March 1918, this time when piloting a Bristol Fighter. On this occasion Learmount attacked an enemy artillery reconnaissance machine, but was quite badly wounded in the ensuing combat. Losing blood at an alarming rate, he barely made it back to land safely on his home field. Learmount finally left the RAF, via the Unemployed List, in February 1919. Even after his departure he was again Mentioned in Despatches, *London Gazette* of 29 August 1919. Post war he was in shipping in the Far East and formed flying clubs in Singapore and Kuala Lumpur. Returning to England he became a Farmer and was the first to introduce battery farming. He became Commodore of the Lymington Yacht Club but was lost sailing in the Channel on 12 July 1957, the Royal Navy recovering his body. It was assumed he had been swept overboard and was unable to regain the boat. His home was in Hordle, Hants.

LEASK, Kenneth Malise St Clair Graeme

The son of Dr John Leask MB, CM, and Mrs Leask, of Boardhouse, Birsay, Orkney, Scotland, and 40 Bath Street, Jersey, he was born on 30 October 1896. Educated at St Bees, Cumberland (1910-11) and at Victoria College, Jersey (1911-14). He entered the employment of Vickers Maxim and Company, before being gazetted Second Lieutenant to 8 Battalion, Devonshire Regiment, on 19 November 1914. Having first trained as a Machine-Gun Officer with his regiment in 1915, he soon sought secondment to the flying service, which was allowed in May 1916. Gained his Royal Aero Club Certificate (Number 3673) on 20 July 1916 and was confirmed and gazetted Flying Officer on the same day. He was first posted for artillery observation with 42 Squadron in France, before going on to 41 Squadron as a Flight Commander on 10 January 1917. Leask flew the FE8s of 41 Squadron until returning to the UK as an Instructor in May 1917. A 'founder member' of 84 Squadron, he took out 'A' Flight's SE5As to France in September 1917. Leask flew more than 100 combat patrols and gained eight victories before 23 March 1918, although, in fact, he was generally regarded as more of a specialist in ground strafing. His MC was announced in the *London Gazette* of 26 March 1918, with details appearing in the *Gazette* of 24 August 1918: 'For conspicuous gallantry and devotion to duty in leading offensive patrols against superior numbers of the enemy. His patrol twice engaged more than double their own numbers and drove away the enemy back into their own lines. He drove down three enemy machines, which were seen to be destroyed, and accounted for eleven in all. He showed splendid determination and initiative.'.

The Bar to his MC came in the *London Gazette* of 22 June 1918: 'For conspicuous gallantry and devotion to duty. He attacked a formation of five enemy scouts, one of which he destroyed. Later, he carried out a very valuable reconnaissance at a height of 100 feet in order to locate the enemy's position. While thus engaged he observed a large column of enemy troops advancing along a road. He dived down to a height of about 30 feet and attacked and scattered them, and held up their advance for a considerable time. He has done splendid work in attacking enemy troops from a low altitude, showing great courage and determination under heavy fire. '

Leask stayed on in the RAF with a permanent commission after the war, eventually achieving high rank. He married, in 1923, Lydia Alexandrovna Modestoff with whom he had a daughter. His many appointments, promotions and honours included: Staff, HQ, RAF Southern Area and Inland Area, 1919-20; Flight Commander with 208 Squadron in Egypt and Turkey, 1921-23; Directorate of Air Intelligence, Air Ministry 1923-26; Squadron Leader, 1925; Senior Officers Course at Sheerness, 1926; Officers Long Engineering Course, 1926-28, and qualified MIMechE; Chief Technical Officer, 4 Apprentices Wing, Halton, 1928-29; CTO, Aircraft Depot, Karachi, India, 1929-32; OC, 60 Squadron, Kohat, 1932-33; Wing Commander, 1933; Senior Engineer Staff Officer, HQ, RAF India, 1933-34; Senior Engineer Officer, HQ ADGB and Bomber Command, 1935-40; Mentioned in Despatches; Group Captain, 1938; AOC, 43 Group as Acting Air Commodore, 1940 and as Acting Air Vice-Marshal 1942; Air Commodore and Air Vice-Marshal, 1946; AOC, 24 Group, RAF, 1944-47; CB, 1945; Director General of Engineering, Air Ministry, 1947-49. He lived in retirement at 'Per Ardua', Vache Lane, Chalfont St Giles, Buckinghamshire. Tragically, Kenneth Leask and his wife were killed in a car crash on 24 April 1974.

LEATHLEY, Forde

From Trillick, Dunboyne, Ireland, he was born on 17 February 1896. Gazetted Second Lieutenant to 1 Battalion, Royal Inniskilling Fusiliers on 16 June 1915. Served in Gallipoli, Egypt and France with the 'Skins'. Seconded to the RFC early in 1917, he trained as an Observer before being sent out to the FE2d-equipped 57 Squadron. He claimed one victory in an FE2d on 30 April and seven further victories in the recently acquired DH4s between 28 July and 20 August 1917. His MC was announced in the *London Gazette* of 9 January 1918: 'For conspicuous gallantry and devotion to duty in making photographic reconnaissance and in fighting enemy aircraft. Since April he has taken part in numerous combats, during which seven hostile machines have been driven down and destroyed either by him or his pilot, and although attacked by superior numbers of the enemy, his skill and offensive spirit have enabled him to carry out photographic reconnaissances'.

Leathley later trained as a Pilot, gaining his Royal Aero Club Certificate (Number 5455) on 26 November 1917, formally qualifying for his 'Wings' on the same day. He appears not to have flown operationally as a Pilot. Forde Leathley retired from the RAF, with the rank of Flight Lieutenant, on 27 January 1925.

LEE, Arthur Stanley Gould

The son of Mr and Mrs Arthur Lee of Nottinghamshire, he was born on 31 August 1894. After attending University of Nottingham (OTC), he worked as a journalist. Gazetted Second Lieutenant to 13 (Reserve) Battalion, Sherwood Foresters, on 23 February 1915. He married, first, in 1916, Gwyneth Lewis (died 1951) with whom he had one daughter, and, secondly, in 1953, Fay, widow of S/Ldr A R Atkinson. Seconded to the RFC in 1916, his pilot training was severely delayed when he broke a leg. He was, however, eventually confirmed and gazetted Flying Officer on 10 January 1917. Because of lingering doubts regarding his fitness, he was made to remain in the UK longer than normally would have been the case. One positive aspect of this, was that he was able to amass considerably more flying hours than most novitiates, before finally crossing the Channel to join 46 Squadron (Sopwith Pups, later Camels) at the front in May 1917. An eventful few months followed, during which he was shot down by ground fire in the Battle of Cambrai, was reported 'Missing' on no less than four occasions, attained the status of a Flight Commander, gained seven victories, and was awarded the MC, announced in the *London Gazette* of 5 July 1918: 'For conspicuous gallantry and devotion to duty. He bombed an enemy battery and fired on the gunners with his machine-gun, and then attacked and drove off the enemy machines. While flying in very low clouds he lost his way, and could not steady his compass, and after flying for some distance, in what he believed to be the direction of our lines, he landed in open country, and was at once attacked and fired upon by enemy cavalry. He had kept his engine running and succeeded in getting off, and, having fired on the enemy, found his position and returned to our lines. On another occasion he made a flight in a very thick mist, drove down an enemy machine, bombed an enemy position, and assisted the infantry to repel an enemy attack. He has shown splendid courage and initiative'.

The main incident referred to in the citation occurred on 20 November 1917, the opening day of the Battle of Cambrai. Lee's experiences on this day are extensively quoted in the Official History, 'The War in the Air, Volume VI'. Cambrai was significant in that it was the first occasion when tanks were employed on a massive scale. Lee recalls flying so low that he had 'to rise to pass over tanks moving through the thick haze of smoke towards the German defences'. He remembered 'little groups of infantry behind each tank, trudging forward with cigarettes alight, of flames leaping from disabled tanks with small helpless groups of infantry standing around, of the ludicrous expressions of amazement on the upturned faces of German troops as we passed a few feet above their trenches'.

Staying on in the RAF after the war, his many appointments, promotions and honours included: Staff, General HQ, Iraq, 1925-27; psa, 1928; commanded 10 (B) Squadron, 1929-30; Staff, Air Ministry 1931-34; idc, 1935; commanded RAF Hornchurch (54, 65 and 74 Fighter Squadrons), 1935-37; Group Captain, 1938; Chief Instructor, Turkish Air Force Staff College, 1937-40; SASO, British Air Forces, Greece, 1941 (Mentioned in Despatches, Order of King George I of Greece with Crossed Swords); Deputy SASO, Middle East HQ, 1941-42; Air Commodore, 1942; SASO, 12 Group, Fighter Command, 1943-44 (Mentioned in Despatches); Chief of Air Section, British Armistice Control Commission, Roumania, 1944; Chief of Military Air Mission to Marshal Tito of Yugoslavia, 1945; Air Vice-Marshal, 1945; Retired 1946. In civilian life he was appointed Chairman of the Anglo-Turkish Society 1958-62 and Vice-President in 1962. He was awarded the Order of the Partisan Star, Yugoslavia in 1970. Lee was responsible for many publications, including, 'No Parachute', 1968 and 'Open Cockpit', 1969, and some fiction. He lived in retirement at 52 Queens Gate Terrace, London SW7. Air Vice-Marshal Lee succeeded W J F Harvey as President of the Cross and Cockade Society, an honoured position he held until his death on 21 May 1975.

LEE, Oliver Mathew

The son of Mr and Mrs George Lee of Mole Creek, Tasmania, he was born on 22 June 1888. A foreman carpenter, he enlisted into the AIF on 28 August 1914. He married his fiancée, Bessie, shortly before proceeding overseas. Promoted to Sergeant, he embarked from Hobart on 19 October 1914, aboard the SS *Katuna*, bound for the Middle East with 'C' Company, 3 Light Horse Regiment. Disembarked in Alexandria on 8 December 1914, before going on to camp Maadi in Egypt. He served in Gallipoli from late May '15. Evacuated from the Peninsula in December 1915, his unit was posted to Tel el Kebir in Egypt. Lee was next sent to 1 Double Squadron, Australian Light Horse, as Sergeant Major, on 1 July 1916. Next, he joined 4 Camel Regiment, Australian Light Horse, on 2 November 1916. Picked out for a commission, he was gazetted Second Lieutenant, AIF, on 1 January 1917. A posting to 18 Company, Imperial Camel Corps, came on 15 February 1917, with promotion to Lieutenant following on 15 May. Seconded to the flying service, he was attached to 67 Squadron, AFC, on 4 July 1917. He attended the RFC Aerial Gunnery School from 12 to 27 August 1917. His formal training completed, he was confirmed and gazetted Flying Officer (Observer) on 3 December 1917. Lee flew operationally above Jordania and the River Jordan with 1 Squadron, AFC, in RE8s and later in Bristol Fighters. On 19 March 1918, Lee and his Pilot, Captain R A Austin (qv), in BF2b, 'B1128', were escorting four Martinsydes returning from a bombing raid. One of the Martinsydes, 'A3960' flown by Captain A J Evans, was forced to land due to engine failure. Austin and Lee landed their Brisfit close to Evans with the intention of rescuing him. Unfortunately, the Bristol broke a wheel as they landed and they found themselves as helpless as Evans. The grounded trio set fire to both machines, which were blazing away as a group of Arabs arrived to take them in charge prior to handing them over to the Turks. The Turks paid T£5 for every captured British officer. Lee's MC (noted as being for Jerusalem operations) was announced in the *London Gazette* of 11 April 1918 (no citation) and he was also Mentioned in Despatches. Lee would remain a captive of the Turks in Constantinople until his repatriation in November 1918. Returning to Australia, he finally left the AFC on 28 April 1919. During the Second World War, he served with 1 Battalion, Volunteer Defence Corps, from 23 January 1942 to 4 March 1943. Oliver Lee, living at 54 Water Street, Ulverstone, Tasmania, died on 27 September 1966.

LEES, George Martin

The son of Mr and Mrs George Murray Lees, of Dublin, Ireland, he was born on 14 April 1898. Educated at St Andrew's College, Dublin, at the Royal Military Academy, Woolwich, at the Royal School of Mines, and at Vienna University. Gazetted Second Lieutenant to the RGA on 19 February 1916. Seconded to the RFC at the end of 1916, he trained as an Observer and was sent out to 6 Squadron as a Probationary before being confirmed and gazetted Flying Officer (Observer) on 21 February 1917. Official records say this of him at this time: 'During the period 31 May to 3 June in four flights....he successfully ranged and observed fire for effect of 14 Batteries on different trench targets. On 18 June 1917 while on photographic escort, his machine was attacked by nine Albatros Scouts over Zandvoorde. He shot one EA down, the wings falling off in the air. On 8 August 1917, while on photographic reconnaissance, his formation was attacked by 10 enemy Scouts. The enemy were driven off and 24 successful exposures were brought back'. This would form the basis of a recommendation for his MC, which was announced in the *London Gazette* of 26 September 1917, details in the *Gazette* of 9 January 1918: 'For conspicuous gallantry and devotion to duty on numerous occasions. His work has been invaluable both when engaged in ranging batteries on hostile trenches and in making daring and invaluable reconnaissances at low altitudes over the enemy's trenches. On at least two occasions whilst on photographic duty he was attacked by superior numbers of the enemy, one of whom he shot down and dispersed the remainder, returning from his flight with a number of successful exposures. All his work has been of a high order'.

He next trained as a Pilot, and having qualified, he joined 72 Squadron in Netheravon on 3 January 1918, just three months prior to that unit's departure to Mesopotamia. Lees subsequently accompanied '72' to the Middle East on 18 March 1918, as a Flight Commander. The 72 Squadron War Diary records the following regarding his involvement: 'Lieut Lees on Bristol Mono attacked with machine-gun fire the Aerodrome and Camp at Altun Keupri from 1000 feet. He came under heavy AA fire but was not hit. 12/5/18: Lieut Lees on Bristol Mono attacked camps, aerodrome, bivouacs and transport on roads with mg fire, firing 300 rounds from 100 to 500 feet. 13/5/18: Lieut Lees on Bristol Mono, fired 200 rounds into a camel convoy of 50 camels, also transport, camps and AA gun in the Altun Kupri area; Several camels were killed and remainder stampeded and AA gun crew scattered. 16/10/18: Lt Lees, 'C' Flight carried out an offensive patrol over Kirkuk. Two EA on the aerodrome were attacked from 1000 feet. Bullets seen to hit machines. 18/10/18: Lt Lees sighted an EA Scout above him. He at once took off and climbed after the EA which appeared slightly faster and Lt Lees could not overtake it. It flew over Taza to Kirkuk aerodrome, Lt Lees just managing to keep it in sight. Over Kirkuk aerodrome it commenced to glide down and was overtaken when at about 500 feet....Lt Lees dived and fired a good burst at about 50 feet range, EA did a flat turn and dived steeply and landed, the pilot did not leave the machine and was probably wounded'.

For his services on this front, he was awarded the Distinguished Flying Cross, *London Gazette* of 1 January 1919. Lees transferred to 63 Squadron, also stationed in Mesopotamia, in June 1919. Leaving the RAF, he secured a position in 1920 as an Assistant Political Officer in the Civil Administration of Iraq, serving mainly in Kurdistan. He joined the Anglo-Iranian Oil Company as Assistant Geologist in 1921, and spent the following three years assisting with survey work in the Middle East. Lees also took part in survey of Oman in 1925, and was awarded a Doctorate of Philosophy from the University of Vienna for his thesis on Oman's geology. Appointed and served as Chief Geologist with Anglo-Iranian Oil from 1931 to 1953. During the Second World War, he was seconded to the Petroleum Division, Ministry of Fuel and Power, from 1939 to 1945. He was elected as Fellow of the Royal Society in 1948. Appointed President of the Geological Society, 1951-53. He was also a Fellow of the Institute of Petroleum. Other appointments and honours included: Member, Geological Survey Board; Member, Colonial Geological Survey Board; Geological Adviser to Anglo-Iranian Oil Co Ltd and Iraq Petroleum Ltd;

Bigsby Medallist, Geological Society, 1943; Sidney Powers Gold Medalist, American Association of Petroleum Geologists, 1954. He lived at The White House, Ongar, Essex. Doctor George Lees died on 25 January 1955.

NB: His medals were offered for sale by Christie's (lot 170) on 24 July 1990: MC, Distinguished Flying Cross, British War Medal 1914-20, and Victory Medal 1914-19 (Lieut RAF).

LEGGATT, Edward Wilmer

The eldest son of Mr and Mrs Edward Owen Every Leggatt, he was born in Bareilly, United Provinces, India, on 12 February 1892. Educated at Rugby (1906-08). He was in Canada working as a Fruit Farmer when war came in 1914. He immediately enlisted into 1 British Columbia Battalion, Canadian Infantry, and crossed the Atlantic with the original contingent of the CEF. Picked out for a commission, he was gazetted Second Lieutenant to a Regular Army battalion of the Wiltshire Regiment on 12 May 1915. Seconded to the RFC within weeks, he first trained as an Observer and was sent out as such to 6 Squadron as a Probationary in July 1915. His 'apprenticeship' satisfactorily completed, he was subsequently confirmed and gazetted Flying Officer (Observer) on 21 October following. He next trained as a Pilot, gaining his Royal Aero Club Certificate (Number 2124) on 2 December 1915. Once qualified as a Pilot, Leggatt was sent out to the BE2c-equipped 10 Squadron at the front. On 29 February 1916, Leggatt and his Observer, Second Lieutenant T S C Howe (qv), Connaught Rangers attached RFC, in BE2c, '1737', were twice involved in combats with Albatroses and, in the second fight, wounded the enemy Pilot in the leg, sending him and his Observer, down into captivity. His MC was announced in the *London Gazette* of 30 March 1916: 'For conspicuous gallantry and skill when on patrol. Second Lieutenant Howe and Second Lieutenant Leggatt attacked a hostile machine and drove it down. They then climbed again and attacked another. Under heavy fire from the machine, by a combination of good flying and shooting, they hit the enemy pilot and damaged his engine, forcing him to descend within our lines. The enemy were made prisoners'.

Research has unearthed the original recommendation for the award, which gives a little more detail: 'For conspicuous gallantry and skill on February 29, 1916, 2/Lt Leggatt and 2/Lt Howe, whilst on patrol in a BE2c, attacked a hostile machine and drove it down in the enemy's lines near La Bassée. Climbing again, they pursued another Albatros towards Lillers. Under heavy fire from the German machine, they got within 150 yards of it and, by a combination of good flying and shooting, hit the pilot and disabled his engine. The Albatros dived, followed by the BE2c firing all the time. The Germans landed with their machine but little damaged, about a mile south of Merville where they were taken prisoners'.

On 13 May 1916, Leggatt was promoted to A/Captain and sent to 2 Squadron as a Flight Commander. On 9 August following, he was flying alone in BE2d, '5741', when he was forced to land behind enemy lines, with the inevitable consequence of being taken prisoner of war. Leggatt would earn a second MC by being amongst those brave souls who, in August 1918, escaped from Holzminden via the famous tunnel. His Bar was announced in the 'Escapers Gazette', *London Gazette* of 16 December 1919: '....in recognition of gallantry in escaping from captivity whilst Prisoners of War'.

After the war, Leggatt transferred to the Royal Australian Air Force, serving at 1 Station, RAAF, Point Cook, Victoria, Australia, whilst retaining his home in England, Nutwood Cottage, Hindhead Road, Godalming, Surrey.

LEHMANN, Henry Maurice Talbot

The son of Caroline Lehmann, of Ramsbury Road, St Albans, Hertfordshire, he was born on 3 November 1897, in Paddington, London. He was actually christened, 'Heinz', but subsequently preferred to be known as 'Henry', probably because of the prevailing anti-German sentiments of the time. Educated at Clifton College (1909-13) and at the Royal Military College, Sandhurst, which establishment he entered at just 16 years of age. Once the war started, however, he was 'held back' somewhat because of his extreme youth and not gazetted Second Lieutenant to a Regular Army battalion of the Essex Regiment until 16 June 1915. Seconded to the RFC in November 1915, he gained his Royal Aero Club Certificate (Number 2226) on 17 December following. His formal pilot training duly completed, he was confirmed and gazetted Flying Officer on 28 March 1916. His MC was won in France in the summer of 1916 with Be2c-equipped 2 Squadron, *London Gazette* of 27 July 1916: 'For conspicuous gallantry and skill. When attacking the enemy's communications, alone and without an Observer, he dived down to 1,000 feet under heavy fire, released his bombs on a railway station with great effect and successfully brought his machine back to his aerodrome'.

Transferred to 56 Squadron (SE5s), he accompanied that unit to France as a 'founder member' in April 1917. One year later in April 1918, Lehmann was shot down by anti-aircraft fire into the British lines. Badly concussed, he was invalided back to the UK. He finally relinquished his commission due to ill-health on 16 April 1919. After the war, he worked with a flying circus as a wing walker and, in the 1930s, became an advisor to the Chinese Nationalist Air Force. Later he emigrated to Canada, served in the RCAF, and then became a commercial Pilot. Henry Lehmann was known to be living in Vancouver, BC, Canada, in the 1950s and he died in 1956.

LEIGH, John Walker Dickinson

The son of Dr John Dickinson Leigh, MD, the Tuberculosis Medical Officer for Sunderland, and Helena Ann Leigh (née Walker), of 7 Avenue Road, Scarborough, Yorkshire, he was born in Brotton in Cleveland in 1893. Gazetted Second Lieutenant to the Northern Cyclist Battalion (TF) on 17 June 1915. Seconded to the RFC in May 1916, he gained his Royal Aero Club Certificate (Number 3465) on 10 August 1916. His formal pilot training duly completed, he was confirmed and gazetted Flying Officer on 9 September following. A Training and Delivery Pilot of exceptional ability, he was subsequently Mentioned in Despatches, *London Gazette* of 21 July 1917. Posted to 17 Squadron in Salonika he won the French Croix de Guerre, *London Gazette* of 17 December 1917, and awarded the MC in the New Year *London Gazette* of 1 January 1918 (no citation). He left the services, via the Unemployed List, on 28 June 1919, but was subsequently, on 1 August 1919, granted a permanent commission in the RAF.

LEIGH-PEMBERTON, Robert Douglas

The son of Mr and Mrs Robert Leigh-Pemberton, of Torry Hill, Sittingbourne, Kent, he was born on 27 April 1896. Educated at Eton. Gazetted Second Lieutenant to the Grenadier Guards on 17 March 1915. He served in the trenches with 4 Battalion of his regiment from 15 August 1915, surviving the Battle of Loos, in the following month. Following further service with the Guards Machine Gun Regiment in 1916 and 1917, he was seconded to the RFC in May 1917. His pilot training completed, he was gazetted Flying Officer on 7 November following.

Sent out to the Bristol Fighter-equipped 20 Squadron at the front in January 1918. On the sixth day of the German spring offensive, 26 March 1918, Leigh-Pemberton and his Observer, Captain N W Taylor, in BF2b, 'B1196', were shot about over Albert. Leigh-Pemberton, wounded in the air, brought the Brisfit down safely with Taylor unscathed. They landed, however, in what they thought was British territory but what had, by then, been overrun by German infantry. Their machine was already a write-off and so the intrepid pair set off, successfully it transpired, to find the British front lines. His MC was announced in the *London Gazette* of 22 June 1918: 'For conspicuous gallantry and devotion to duty. On one occasion he bombed enemy infantry from a height of 500 feet, and attacking them continuously with machine-gun fire scattering them. While he was returning for a fresh supply of bombs and ammunition, both his petrol tanks were shot through and he was forced to land some distance in the rear of the enemy's advance lines. He, together with his Observer, successfully evaded the enemy's patrols and eventually reached our infantry. He has also destroyed one hostile scout and has sent down another out of control. Throughout the operations he set a very fine example of dash and gallantry'.

The injured Leigh-Pemberton was sent home for treatment on 30 March 1918 and was subsequently invalided out of the service. However, in the best traditions of that exceptional generation, Leigh-Pemberton would not call it a day and, somehow, in October 1918, managed to inveigle himself back to his old army unit, 4 Battalion, Grenadier Guards, just in time to actively participate in the final advance to victory.

LEIGHTON, John Burgh Talbot

The elder son of Sir Bryan Baldwin Mawddwy Leighton, 9th Baronet, TD, and Margaret Lady Leighton, of Loton Park, Shrewsbury, Shropshire, and South Wellington Court, Knightsbridge, London SW, he was born on 9 February 1892. His younger brother, Richard Tihel Leighton, Westmorland and Cumberland Yeomanry (who would, in time, become the 10th Baronet), also served in the RFC as a Scout Pilot with 56 Squadron, wounded and taken prisoner on 17 August 1917. John was educated at Eton (1905-09) and at the Royal Military College, Sandhurst, from where he was gazetted Second Lieutenant to the Scots Guards in 1912. Developing an interest in aviation, he obtained his Royal Aero Club Certificate (Number 790) on 20 May 1914 and, having completed his formal training, was subsequently confirmed and gazetted Flying Officer on 12 September following. When the war came in August 1914, he was permanently seconded to the RFC. In November 1914, he flew to France and served there for nine months before being sent out to Egypt with 14 Squadron. Leighton flew with '14' until 12 February 1916, when he returned to the UK. His MC was announced in the *London Gazette* of 31 May 1916: 'Scots Guards, attached 14 Sqd, RFC. For conspicuous gallantry and skill. He took photographs at a height of 200 feet while his Observer engaged the enemy with rifle fire. On other occasions he has done fine and gallant work'.

Promoted to Major, he was given command of 23 Squadron in France, taking over on 17 January 1917. He was thrice Mentioned in Despatches before being severely injured in an aero accident at Baisieux, France, on 7 March 1917. Major John Leighton would die of those injuries exactly two months later on 7 May 1917. He is buried in Varennes Military Cemetery, Somme, France.

LEITCH, Alfred Alexander

From Manitoba, Canada, he was born on 5 February 1894. Following service with the Canadian Army, he was accepted as a candidate for the flying service and subsequently gazetted Second Lieutenant to the RFC on 1 September 1917. Given his forename initials, he was known, inevitably and henceforth, as 'Ack-Ack' Leitch. His pilot training completed, he was sent to 1 ASD in October 1917, where he had the opportunity of amassing more flying time. A posting to 43 Squadron (Sopwith Camels) at the front followed in the December of the same year and he served with that unit for two months without attaining particular distinction. His next posting to 65 Squadron, also equipped with Camels, was much more eventful. In all, despite a crippled foot, the tall and gangling Alfred Leitch achieved seven victories between 5 February and 26 June 1918 including, on 25 May, forcing down into the Allied lines, a Jasta 76 Pilot, Vizefeldwebel Karl Keller. His MC was announced in the *London Gazette* of 16 September 1918: 'For conspicuous gallantry and devotion to duty while on fighting patrols. During recent operations he displayed great courage and determination in attacking superior forces of enemy aircraft, and engaging with machine-gun fire enemy troops and transport on the ground. He did splendid work, and set a most inspiring example'.

He was also awarded a Distinguished Flying Cross in the *London Gazette* of 2 November 1918. About to return to the UK for a well-earned rest, he crashed, on 24 August 1918, a Sopwith Salamander he was testing and was taken to hospital. By the time he recovered, the war was over and he was next posted to the Allied Intervention Force in Russia. He also became involved in the experimental deck landings onto HMS *Argus*, an early aircraft carrier, on 30 July 1919. 'Ack-Ack' Leitch returned to Canada and transferred to the newly formed RCAF. He participated in the Hudson Straits Expedition in 1927-28 and became a Squadron Leader in the 1930s.

LEITH, James Leith

The son of Frederick W and Helen M Leith, of 99 Addison Road, London, he was born in Southampton on 20 December 1896. Joined the Inns of Court OTC (Number F/1867) on 16 October 1914, and was subsequently gazetted Second Lieutenant to 2/9 (Cyclist) Battalion, Hampshire Regiment (TF) on 27 February 1915. Seconded to the RFC in February 1916, he gained his Royal Aero Club Certificate (Number 3278) on 30 July 1916. His formal pilot training duly completed, he was confirmed and gazetted Flying Officer on 13 August following. Sent out to FE2b-equipped 25 Squadron in France, five days after qualifying, he gained his first victory on 22 October 1916. By the time he was promoted to Flight Commander in February 1917, he had a further three victories to his credit. His tour with '25' ended on 22 May 1917 and he returned to the UK for rest and recuperation with his victory total standing at eight. His MC had already been announced in the *London Gazette* of 17 April 1917: 'For conspicuous gallantry and devotion to duty. When leading a formation of five machines he drove down one of eleven hostile scouts which attacked his patrol. He completed his reconnaissance, and, although again attacked, succeeded in leading his patrol safely back to our lines. On previous occasions he has brought down three hostile machines'.

Following a lengthy period instructing in the UK, Leith returned to France once more, joining the Camels of 46 Squadron as a Flight Commander in September 1918. He added one more victory to his total when, on 2 October 1918, he helped to send a Fokker DVII down out of control. Leith returned to the UK on 2 February 1919, finally leaving the service, via the Unemployed List, just three days later.

LE JEUNE, Hubert Edmond

A Staff, not a flying, award

The son of Baron and Baroness Le Jeune of Paris, he was born in France on 10 October 1882. He was living in south west London when the war came in August 1914. Volunteering for service with the British Forces, he was gazetted Second Lieutenant to the Royal Marine Light Infantry on 24 October 1914. Subsequently, he transferred to the RFC, via the Special Reserve, being gazetted an Assistant Equipment Officer on 15 April 1915. A photographic specialist, he was first attached to 2 Wing HQ, RFC, in France, before falling ill and spending a period in hospital. Once recovered, he was sent again to France in November 1915, this time to 5 Brigade, RFC, HQ. His MC was announced in the *London Gazette* of 1 July 1916 (no citation): Although no formal citation was published, research has unearthed the original recommendation for the award: 'H Le Jeune. For consistent good work as a photographic Officer. His skill and attention to his duties have done much to bring this highly important work to its present state of efficiency'.

From May 1918, he was employed in training other photographic specialists at the Air Ministry (Records) in London. Hubert Le Jeune finally left the RAF, via the Unemployment List, on 21 April 1919.

LEMAN, Cyril Mountain

The son of Plain and Fancy Box Maker, Degoulyhan Ernest Leman and Mary Ann Leman (née Slater), of 70 Hamlet Court Road, Prittlewell, Southend-on-Sea, Essex, he was born in Hackney, London, in 1892. Gazetted Second Lieutenant to 3 Company (Southend), Essex and Suffolk Brigade, RGA (TF), on 11 August 1914. Cyril's two brothers, 24 year old William Ernest Leman and 23 year old Reginald Leslie Leman, were also gazetted Second Lieutenants to the same Company on this day. Cyril was seconded to the RFC in the summer of 1915 and gained his Royal Aero Club Certificate (Number 1405) at the Military School, Birmingham, on 3 July 1915. His formal pilot training duly completed, he was confirmed and gazetted Flying Officer on 12 October following and immediately sent out to join 3 Squadron. On 22 August 1916, he was responsible for calling fire down upon an enemy battery with devastating effect. Seven direct hits exploded the battery's ammunition, completely destroying the emplacement. He received a Mention in Despatches, which was posted in the *London Gazette* of 2 January 1917. Research has unearthed the original recommendation for this 'Mention' which, in effect, summarises his work over the period: '3 Sqd. For very good artillery work from 17 October 1915 to 30 September 1916. Lieut Leman is an excellent pilot and has not hesitated to fly in the worst of weathers'.

After a period of rest and recuperation, Leman instructed for a while in the UK, before again joining 3 Squadron, now equipped with Camels, in the early weeks of 1918. During the frenetic aerial activity on the first day of the German spring offensive, 21 March 1918, Leman, in Sopwith Camel 'B9155', was shot down, possibly by Leutnant W von Manteuffel-Szoge of Jasta 35. Fortunately, Leman emerged unscathed from the wreckage of his Camel and made his way back to the British lines. Again on 4 April, his Camel, 'C1653', was shot up and damaged. Leman nursed his machine home and again escaped hurt. His MC was announced in the *London Gazette* of 22 June 1918: 'For conspicuous gallantry and devotion to duty. While on a low level flying bombing patrol, he, by a direct hit from a bomb put out of action a hostile battery and silenced another by machine-gun fire. The enemy fire was so intense that he was forced to land in front of the enemy's advanced line, whence he returned to make his report after leaving his machine a total wreck. He has on many occasions created great havoc as a result of bombing and attacking with machine-gun fire batteries in action, enemy transport and infantry, inflicting very heavy casualties on them. His skill and gallantry have been most marked'.

He was also awarded a Distinguished Flying Cross in the Birthday Honours *London Gazette* of 3 June 1919. Leman was promoted to Major and appointed to command 80 Squadron (Sopwith Snipes) in Egypt from February 1919 to its disbandment one year later.

LeROYER, Joseph Achille

From Quebec, Canada, he was born on 28 January 1890. He worked as a Civil Engineer in Montreal in 1914 and 1915. Gazetted Lieutenant to 163 Battalion, Canadian Infantry, in 1915, he was subsequently promoted to Captain on 26 May 1916. Seconded to the RFC in February 1917, he trained as an Observer and was sent out as a Probationary to FE2b-equipped 11 Squadron on 18 March following. His status quickly confirmed, he was gazetted Flying Officer (Observer) just one week later on 25 March 1917. He gained his first victory with Second Lieutenant G A Exley on 14 April 1917. On the evening of 27 April, LeRoyer and Second Lieutenant D S Kennedy (qv) drove down an enemy plane in flames and then proceeded to destroy a second over Vitry before, soon afterwards, sending a third down out of control. He was wounded in the air on 5 July 1917 and returned to the UK for treatment. His MC was announced in the *London Gazette* of 18 July 1917: 'For conspicuous gallantry and devotion to duty. He has constantly shown great skill and courage when acting as an Observer. His accurate shooting and coolness under fire have largely contributed to his successful aerial combats against superior numbers'.

He next trained as a Pilot, qualifying in February 1918, and was sent to 33 Squadron in the UK in the following month. LeRoyer returned to France on 1 May 1918, joining FE2b-equipped 102 Night Bombing Squadron, as a Pilot. His tour with '102' completed in the following September, he returned to Canada on the 5th of that month before finally relinquishing his commission shortly afterwards. Once back in Canada, he joined the RCAF. He helped the Americans on a pioneering flight to Alaska in 1920. LeRoyer was severely injured in a flying accident at Camp Borden on 1 April 1921, when he stalled an Avro 504K and crashed into the ground from 200 feet. LeRoyer suffered internal injuries and, despite the best efforts of the doctors, he died four days later on 5 April 1921. Joseph LeRoyer is buried in Notre Dame Cemetery, Ottawa.

LETTS, John Herbert Towne

The only son of Walter John Letts and Charlotte Helen Letts, of Steep Hill House, Lincoln, he was born on 10 June 1897. Educated at Lancing College (1911-15) and at the Royal Military College, Sandhurst (1915). Gazetted Second Lieutenant in a Regular Army Battalion of the Lincolnshire Regiment on 26 January 1916, with an immediate secondment to the RFC. Gained his Royal Aero Club Certificate (Number 2618) on 24 March 1916. His formal training duly completed, he was confirmed and gazetted Flying Officer on 4 May 1916. He first flew operationally with the 'Flying Elephants' of 27 Squadron, before being ordered, in March 1917, to join 48 Squadron, then about to leave for France equipped with the first Bristol Fighters. Took over as Flight Commander on 5 April 1917, when Leefe Robinson VC was shot down on his first patrol with the unit. Four days later on 9 April, Letts and his Observer, Lieutenant H G Collins, in BF2b, 'A3315', were shot about during a combat over Arras. Letts was unhurt but Harold Collins from Croydon was killed in the air. Letts was himself shot down and wounded when flying with Second Lieutenant J Jameson in BF2b, 'A7104', on 11 May 1917. Theirs was one of four Brisfits shot down by elements of Jasta 11. Fortunately, Letts was only slightly wounded and his Observer/Gunner Jameson was virtually unscathed in the incident. Letts was up and flying again just 13 days later on 24 May. On this occasion, he escaped unhurt when his Bristol Fighter, 'A3350', was shot up during an aerial combat. However, his Observer of the day, Lieutenant L W Allen, was not so fortunate and was wounded in the action. Letts, an energetic and aggressive Pilot, was again involved in a fraught situation on 22 August 1917. Flying with Second Lieutenant H R Power, Royal Irish Rifles, attached RFC, in BF2b, 'A7219', he gave chase to a Gotha bomber making its way out to sea. In the ensuing pursuit, Henry Power was shot and killed in the air. As the Gotha's machine-gun bullets struck him, Power involuntarily struck Letts in the head with his Lewis gun. Despite his head injury and the resultant concussion, Letts nursed the stricken Brisfit back to base. Letts accumulated no less than 13 victories between 9 April and 15 September 1917. Soon after achieving his 13th victory, Letts returned to England for rest and recuperation. His MC had already been announced in the *London Gazette* of 16 August 1917: 'For conspicuous gallantry and devotion to duty. He attacked four large two-seaters, driving two down out of control and forcing the remaining two down. He has helped to destroy eight machines, and throughout has set a splendid example'.

A year later, he was again despatched to France, originally intended as a Flight Commander for 64 Squadron but, in the event, was ordered to report to 87 Squadron (Dolphins). On 11 October 1918, he took off in an SE5A, 'C6484', belonging, oddly enough, to 32 Squadron. Immediately after take-off, and still close to the ground, he attempted to roll the aircraft with disastrous results. The SE5A crashed to the ground, killing its occupant outright. John Letts is buried in Bac-du-Sud British Cemetery, Bailleulval, France.

LEWIS, Cecil Arthur

From Birkenhead, he was born on 29 March 1898. Educated at Dulwich College, at University College School, Hampstead (1910-12), and at Oundle (1912-15). Gazetted Second Lieutenant to the RFC, via the Special Reserve, on 13 December 1915. At six foot, four inches tall, he suffered some discomfort in fitting into the diminutive cockpits of Great War aeroplanes. Despite these difficulties, he completed his pilot training and was confirmed and gazetted Flying Officer on 17 February 1916. He first served operationally with the Morane Parasols of 3 Squadron from May 1916, on through a large part of the Battle of the Somme until the following September, when he returned to the UK. His MC was announced in the *London Gazette* of 14 November 1916: 'For conspicuous skill and gallantry. He has done fine work in photography, with artillery and on contact patrols. On one occasion he came down very low and attacked a column of horse limbers, causing casualties and scattering the limbers'.

He next went to the front in April 1917, this time as a 'founder member' of the SE5-equipped 56 Squadron, going on to achieve eight victories between 5 May and 17 June 1917. Completing his tour with '56', Lewis returned to the UK to serve, successively, with 44 and 51 HD Squadrons, flying many sorties against Zeppelin and Gotha attacks upon British soil. His last active posting came when, again as a 'founder member', he accompanied the newly formed and Camel F1-equipped 152 Squadron, a night-flying fighter unit, to France on 18 October 1918. The war, however, came to an end on 11 November, before '152' could actually go into action. Lewis was twice Mentioned in Despatches during the Great War. After leaving the RAF in 1919, he first formed a 'flying circus' with two other Pilots, touring Britain and giving joy rides in clapped-out Avro 504Ks. The venture was unsuccessful, and he was obliged to get a 'proper' job, becoming the manager of the embryonic Civil Aviation division of Vickers Ltd. Next, he took himself off to China, one of a number of Flying Instructors employed by a Chinese Government anxious not to be left behind in the development of military and civil aviation. After nearly two years in China, he returned to London in 1922, just in time to become one of the four founding members of the British Broadcasting Corporation. It is hard to imagine a more disparate contrast between the swashbuckling, devil-may-care personality of Cecil Lewis and the stolid, straitlaced, albeit intellectually brilliant, John Charles Walsham Reith, the senior of the four-man panel. Reith had, of course, served in the Great War, going to the front with the Scottish Rifles in 1914 and being wounded with the Royal Engineers in 1915. However diverse the experience and chemistry of the four men, they went on to lay the foundations of what became a universally renowned institution. After four years with the BBC, Lewis moved on, writing and lecturing around the world. His book about his wartime experiences as a Scout Pilot, 'Sagittarius Rising', published in 1936, quickly became, and remains to this day, a classic of the genre. He was jointly responsible for adapting two of George Bernard Shaw's plays for the screen. Indeed, he and his co-writers, W P Limscomb and Ian Dalrymple, were awarded an Oscar in 1938 (best adaption) for their script for the Hollywood production of Pygmalion, starring Leslie Howard as Professor Higgins and Wendy Hiller as Eliza Doolittle. Lewis served again in the RAF throughout the Second World War (1939-45). After that war, he founded a quasi-religious community in South Africa and, at the same time, tried his hand at sheep farming (1947-50). When that palled, he joined the United Nations Secretariat, New York, as an advisor on radio and television (1953-55). Next, he returned to London to work in Commercial TV (1955-56). Lewis then worked for the *Daily Mail* as a columnist and commentator from 1956, also helping to organise that newspaper's annual Ideal Home Exhibition, until he finally retired to Corfu in 1966. Perhaps, 'semi-retired' would be more apt, for he continued with his writing on into an extremely spritely old age. He married first, in Peking in 1921, Eudoxia Horvath, daughter of the White Russian leader, General Horvath (dissolved in 1940); secondly, in 1942, Olga Burnett (dissolved in 1950); and, thirdly, Fanny, in 1960. Cecil Lewis died in January 1997.

LEWIS, Thomas Archibald Metford Stuart

The son of Arthur Smart Lewis and Mable Grace Lewis (née Tracy), of 26 York Road, Worthing, West Sussex, he was born in Whitley Bay, Northumberland, on 26 June 1894. Gazetted Second Lieutenant to a Regular Army Battalion of the Royal West Kent Regiment on 5 August 1916, with a secondment to the RFC coming in the following October. Having trained as an observer, he was sent out to FE2d-equipped 20 Squadron as a Probationary in the spring of 1917. His 'apprenticeship' satisfactorily completed, he was confirmed and gazetted Flying Officer (Observer) in April 1917. Lewis claimed six victories between 29 April and 27 July 1917, including one of particular distinction. On 5 June 1917, Lewis, with Lieutenant H L Satchell in FE2d, 'A6469', shot down Leutnant Karl Emil Schäfer, the Commander of Jasta 28, and an outstanding Ace with no less than 30 victories to his credit. In another fight on 27 July 1917, Lewis and his Pilot, Lieutenant G T W Burkett, were both wounded during the course of a massive dog fight. Lewis, hit in the leg by a phosphorus bullet, continued to engage the attacking enemy machine from a supine position. Treated afterwards in No 53 Casualty Clearing Station, the doctors decided his badly mashed-up leg would have to be amputated. His MC was announced in the *London Gazette* of 9 January 1918: 'For conspicuous gallantry and devotion to duty. While acting as Observer his patrol engaged a superior force of enemy scouts. His pilot was wounded, but they continued to fight, destroying one enemy machine. He was then severely wounded, but continued to work his gun lying on his back. By this means they were able to destroy a second enemy machine. Afterwards, when returning to our lines with their machine badly damaged, he and his pilot drove off two machines which were pursuing them, having displayed the greatest gallantry and presence of minds'.

Staying on in the RAF despite his infirmity, Lewis became an Administration Officer attached to the Air Ministry, before finally leaving the RAF on 1 August 1920. After the war, he preferred to be known as T Stuart Lewis. During the 1930s, he lived at 54 Brockhill Road, Hythe, Kent, and was a Director of the local Cinque Ports Flying Club. A Flight Lieutenant in the RAFVR, in 1941, he helped with the general administration of the war-time ATC. T Stuart Lewis died on 21 June 1961.

LIBBY, Frederick

From Sterling, Colorado, USA, he was born on 15 July 1891. Soon after the Great War broke out in August 1914, Libby travelled north and enlisted into the Canadian Army. Arriving in the UK in 1915, he soon sought transfer to the flying service. Having trained as an Observer/Gunner, he was sent out to the FE2b-equipped 23 Squadron in the summer of 1916. On his very first operational flight on 15 July 1916, he and his Pilot, Lieutenant E D Hicks (qv), helped to shoot down an enemy machine in flames. Picked out for a commission, he was gazetted Second Lieutenant to the RFC, via the Special Lists, on 4 August 1916, and was promptly sent out, still rated a Probationary, to 11 Squadron. Flying mainly with Captain Stephen Price, he was immediately effective. The pair shared a 'trio' of victories on 22 August, and achieved another just two days later. Thus Libby became the first ever American to claim the status of Ace. His 'apprenticeship' more than satisfactorily completed, he was duly confirmed and gazetted Flying Officer (Observer) on 26 September following. His MC was announced in the *London Gazette* of 14 November 1916: 'For conspicuous gallantry in action. As an Observer, he, with his pilot, attacked four hostile machines and shot down one. He has previously shot down four enemy machines'.

A further five victories would follow by 20 October, just before his tour with '11' ended and he returned to the UK for pilot training. On 7 March 1917, duly qualified, he joined 43 Squadron to fly Sopwith Strutters. Two further victories came with '43', before he transferred yet again, this time to the DH4-equipped 25 Squadron. Yet two more victories came with '25', giving him a total of 14, before, on 15 September 1917, he took his skill and extensive experience to the United States Air Service. Employed occasionally to raise funds for the American war effort, via the Liberty Loans drive, he was mainly used in a training and tactical role but, because of serious illness, never flew operationally again. Libby related his experiences in his book, 'Horses Don't Fly – The True Story of the Cowboy Who Became a World 1 Hero and America's First Ace'. Fred Libby died in Los Angeles, California, on 9 January 1970.

LINDLEY, Bryant Lutellus

The son of J Bryant Lindley and Mary Eveline Lindley, of Barkly House, Claremount, Cape Province, South Africa, he was born on 10 November 1898. He travelled to the UK at his own expense and was gazetted Second Lieutenant to the RFC on 2 August 1917. His pilot training duly completed, he was confirmed and gazetted Flying Officer on 17 October following. Sent out to 25 Squadron (DH4s) in France on 30 December 1917. On 25 March 1918, Lindley and his Observer, Sergeant A Remington (Number 58887), in DH4, 'A7535', were fortunate to survive when a shell hit and broke the axle between their landing wheels. Lindley, despite the obvious difficulties, managed to crashland the DH4 without injury to his Observer or himself. Sergeant Remington, from Colne, Lancashire, would be awarded a Military Medal later in the war. Lindley was not so fortunate during a photo-reconnaissance over Bruges on 29 June, when, with Second Lieutenant D Boe acting as his Observer in DH4, 'A7913', he was forced down behind enemy lines. Lindley was killed, whilst Boe was taken prisoner. Lindley's MC was announced posthumously in the *London Gazette* of 16 September 1918: 'For conspicuous gallantry and devotion to duty during recent operations. He carried out several very successful long-distance reconnaissances and bomb-raids under adverse weather conditions, and during low bombing and machine-gunning actions he did most brilliant work. Throughout he showed great gallantry and skill'.

Bryant Lindley is buried in Larch Wood (Railway Cutting) Cemetery, Ypres, West-Vlaanderen, Belgium.

LINDUP, Ernest

From South Africa. After travelling to the UK, he was gazetted Second Lieutenant to the RFC on 24 May 1917. His pilot training duly completed, he was confirmed and gazetted Flying Officer on 3 October 1917. Just two weeks later on 17 October, he was sent out to the Camel FI-equipped 70 Squadron. Transferring to the Bristol Fighters of 20 Squadron on 26 January 1918, he achieved five victories and the status of Ace between 2 February and 31 May 1918. His MC was announced in the *London Gazette* of 22 June 1918: 'For conspicuous gallantry and devotion to duty. During the recent operations, when bombing troops on the road from low altitudes, he was attacked by three hostile tri-planes, one of which he shot down, finally driving off the remaining two. Though his lateral controls were shot away, he succeeded in landing his machine at his aerodrome. On a later occasion, whilst on photographic work, when his machine was badly damaged by anti-aircraft fire, he succeeded in landing it behind our lines. He has destroyed one enemy machine and shot down out of control four others. His services have been characterised by gallantry and determination'.

Lindup was hospitalised on 3 June 1918 and did not, subsequently, return to operational flying.

LINES, George Frederick

The son of Mechanical Engineer Frederick G Lines and Edith Mary Lines (née Davies), of 40 Ellington Street, Islington, London, he was born on 11 July 1890, the family living later in Kentish Town. Educated at the British Schools, Kentish Town. Although trained as an Electrical and Mechanical Engineer, he worked, pre-war, as a Lorry Driver with the Construction Department of South African Railways, before returning to the UK to enlist as a Private soldier (later Corporal) into the Army Service Corps (Mechanical Transport). Picked out for a commission, he was gazetted Second Lieutenant to the RFC, via the Special List, on 17 June 1916. His pilot training duly completed, he was confirmed and gazetted Flying Officer on 19 August following. The following is an extract from 'The First War in the Air': 'It is, however, of especial interest to note that this officer was one of the SURVIVORS of BLOODY APRIL, for he was still gallantly flying as an 'artillery spotter' in August and September 1917. Only one Combat Report submitted by Lines survived, during Bloody April, and in the BEs which, more often than not, proved to be death-traps for the men who flew in them. Richthofen himself was always happiest when he was on the tail of a BE, and much preferred this comparatively 'easy meat' to an encounter with, say one of our Naval Tri-planes'. His MC was announced in the *London Gazette* of 16 August 1917: 'For conspicuous gallantry and devotion to duty. He rendered valuable assistance to our artillery by locating a hostile battery, descending to a very low altitude. On his return he attacked hostile infantry, inflicting many casualties. On many other occasions he displayed similar fearlessness in attacking and bombing hostile wiring parties, infantry and ammunition dumps'.

Lines was also awarded the Croix de Guerre avec Palmes by the Belgians, *London Gazette* of 25 July 1918. Staying on in the RAF after the war, he would subsequently serve in Waziristan in the early 1920s.

NB: His medals were offered for sale by Glendining's (lot 293) on 13 December 1989: MC (named on reverse: Lt RFC*), British War Medal 1914-20, Victory Medal 1914-19* (Lt RFC)*, India General Service Medal 1908-35, with clasp, Waziristan 1921-24* (F/O RAF)*, and Croix de Guerre avec Palmes (Belgium).*

LLOYD, George Lawrence

From South Africa, hence his nickname 'Zulu'. When the war came in August 1914, he enlisted as a Private soldier (Number 68) into 1 Battalion, Rhodesia Regiment and served with his unit in the German South West Africa campaign. Eventually making his way to the UK, he was gazetted Second Lieutenant to the Staffordshire Yeomanry (TF) on 19 November 1915. Seconded to the flying service late in 1916, he trained as a Pilot and was duly confirmed and gazetted Flying Officer on 28 February 1917. Lloyd served first with 60 Squadron, achieving four victories between 22 April and 7 July 1917. Promoted to A/Captain, he was posted next as a Flight Commander to the Nieuport-equipped 40 Squadron, gaining a further four victories before October 1917. The announcement of his MC came in the *London Gazette* of 19 November 1917, details in the *Gazette* of 22 March 1918: 'For conspicuous gallantry and devotion to duty. Single-handed, he attacked three enemy machines, one of which he brought down out of control. On another occasion he attacked four enemy machines, one of which he brought down in a steep dive. He has brought down many other enemy machines and taken part in numerous combats, displaying magnificent gallantry and skill on all occasions'.

Returning to the Home Establishment on 4 December 1917, he was appointed to a series of training posts, his outstanding service in this field being recognised by promotion to Major and the award of the Air Force Cross, *London Gazette* of 3 June 1919. Lloyd was later married to Martha Boswell, one of the singing Boswell Sisters, a well-known singing trio of the 1930s. In 1935 he was working for Aero Insurance Underwriters in New York. He died in 1955.

LLOYD, Hugh Pughe

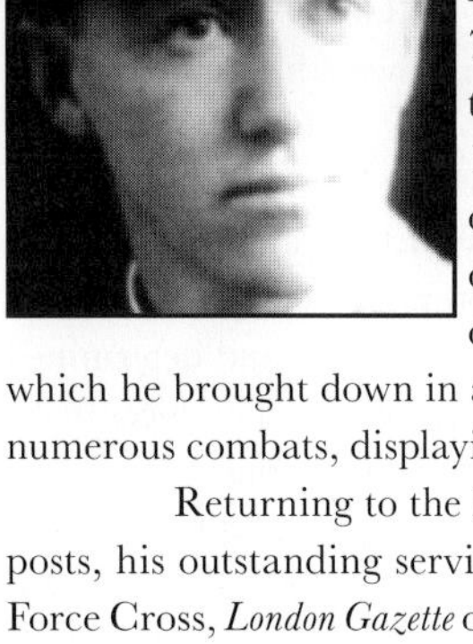

The second son of Mr and Mrs Llewellyn T Lloyd, of Alfrick, Worcester, he was born on 12 December 1894. All four sons of the Lloyds served in the RFC/RAF. Hugh worked as a Clerk at the Malvern Post Office, before enlisting as a despatch rider into the Royal Engineers in 1914. He was twice wounded in France in the early weeks of the war, before subsequently serving in Gallipoli and Egypt, again as a despatch rider. Eventually picked out for a commission, he was gazetted Second Lieutenant to the RFC on 26 April 1917. His pilot training duly completed, he was confirmed and gazetted Flying Officer on 30 November following. Sent out to France in January 1918, he served with the BE2e-equipped 52 Squadron. Lloyd was decorated for his gallantry and work during the German spring offensive in the March and April of 1918. His MC was announced in the *London Gazette* of 22 June 1918: 'For conspicuous gallantry and devotion to duty. During an offensive patrol he dropped bombs on motor transport, one lorry being completely destroyed and others damaged. Enemy troops advancing to the attack were then engaged with machine-gun fire, which inflicted numerous casualties on them. Later, he bombed an enemy battery coming into action, the horses of which bolted, a great number of the gun detachments being killed. He has on all occasions shown the greatest pluck and determination in carrying out any task allotted to him'.

The French, too, awarded him the Croix de Guerre, *London Gazette* of 21 September 1918, the official citation for which commends the skill and courage he displayed whilst keeping in touch with the French infantry. During one flight in particular he determinedly provided the French Army with accurate and valuable information, in spite of the fact that many hostile machines were flying above him. Lloyd was also awarded the Distinguished Flying Cross for his services during the final weeks of the Great War, *London Gazette* of 8 February

1919. Staying on in the RAF after the war, he embarked upon what would prove to be a truly remarkable career, particularly so for a man who lacked any of the privileges usually associated with the attainment of high rank – from Post Office Clerk to Air Chief Marshal of the RAF. His many appointments, honours and promotions included: Flight Commander, 28 Squadron, 1920; Flight Commander, 16 Squadron, 1924; RAF Staff College, 1925; Air Staff, HQ, 23 Group; CFI, 2 FTS, 1930; Squadron Leader, 1931; Army Staff College, Quetta, 1931; Staff, HQ, 1 (Indian) Group; RAF Instructor, Army Staff College, Camberley, 1936; Wing Commander, 1936; OC, 9 Squadron, 1939; OC, RAF, Marham, 1939; Staff, HQ, 3 Group, 1939; SASO, HQ, 3 Group, 1940; Group Captain, 1940; Air ADC to King George VI, 1940-41; Air Commodore, 1941; CBE, 1941; AOC, Malta, 1941-42; CB, 1942; Commander, Allied Coastal Air Forces, Mediterranean, 1943-44; Order of the Legion of Merit (USA), 1944; Officier Légion d'Honneur (France), 1944; Commander, Commonwealth Bomber Forces, Okinawa, 1944-45; Air Vice-Marshal, 1946; Senior Instructor, Imperial Defence College, 1946-47; C-in-C, Air Command, Far East, 1947-49; Air Marshal, 1948; AOC-in-C, Bomber Command Far East, 1947-49; AOC-in-C, Bomber Command, 1950-53; Air Chief Marsal, 1951; KCB, 1951; Honorary LLD (Wales); GBE, 1953. Lloyd married Kathleen Meadows, with whom he had one daughter. He will be forever remembered as AOC in Malta during the great assault by the Axis forces on that gallant island. Lloyd's brilliant and determined leadership during that period undoubtedly helped to break the siege. He wrote of some of his experiences in his book, 'Briefed to Attack', published in 1949. Sir Hugh Lloyd retired from the RAF in 1953, living thereafter at Peterley Manor Farm, Great Missenden, Buckinghamshire. He died on 13 July 1981.

LOMAX, Alan

The son of Colliery Manager, Thomas Lomax and Sarah Lomax, of 363 Wigan Road, Ashton-in-Makerfield, Lancashire, he was born on 27 September 1896. He enlisted first as a Driver (Number 42982) into the Royal Field Artillery, before being picked out for a commission and gazetted Second Lieutenant to the same regiment on 5 August 1915. After service at the front with the Gunners, he was seconded to the RFC in September 1917. Having trained as an Observer, he was sent out as a Probationary to 53 Squadron (RE8s) in the following November. On 25 April 1918, over Kemmel, Lomax and his Pilot, Captain H M Gibbs, in RE8, 'B6615', were both wounded in the air and sent down by Leutnant Karl Fritz Schattauer of Jasta 16, the sixth of the German Ace's eventual nine victories. Lomax's MC was announced in the *London Gazette* of 26 July 1918: 'For conspicuous gallantry and devotion to duty on many occasions in bringing back accurate and detailed reports. He carried out five low reconnaissances over the enemy's lines in thick weather, in which most of the flying had to be done at under 500 feet. On four occasions his machine was badly shot about by machine-gun fire from the ground. He also carried out three offensive patrols, using bombs and machine-gun fire against enemy troops'.

Hospitalised for a time after his wounding, he did not again return to operational flying and finally left the service, via the Unemployed List, in June 1919. When the Second World War came in 1939, Lomax was living in Hatfield, Hertfordshire. On 10 June 1940, he successfully applied for a commission in the RAFVR.

LONG, Selden Herbert

The only son of Major General Sidney Selden Long, CB, and Augusta Elizabeth Long (née Glover), of Doannce, Bebington, Cheshire, he was born in Aldershot on 6 October 1895. Educated at Stubbington House School, Fareham, at the Imperial Services College, and at Sandhurst. Gazetted Second Lieutenant to a Regular Army battalion of the Durham Light Infantry on 23 December 1914. Seconded to the RFC, he gained his Royal Aero Club Certificate (Number 1046) on 25 January 1915, at Brooklands. His formal pilot training duly completed, he was confirmed and gazetted Flying Officer on 26 March 1915. Long served with the RFC in France from 26 April 1915, his MC being announced in the *London Gazette* of 29 October 1915: 'For conspicuous gallantry on several occasions, notably the following: On 10 September he went out to attack an observation balloon shed with a 100 lb bomb, but, being heavily fired at by an anti-aircraft battery, he silenced the guns with this bomb and returned for another one, with which he attacked the balloon, he only narrowly missed it as it was being deflated beside the shed. On 23 September he made two determined attacks on trains from 500 feet, breaking the rails in two places. On the first occasion he returned to the attack three times, and finally climbed to 1,000 feet in order to make better use of his bomb sight; on the second occasion he made most of his return journey at 1,000 feet in order to better examine villages, roads, etc. On 25 September he attacked a train at 500 feet under heavy rifle fire and damaged the line. Late in the afternoon of 25 September he heard that trains were moving at 25 miles distance, and in spite of darkness and bad weather, he volunteered to attack them. Heavy rain prevented him from reaching them, so he turned to attack Peronne Station, descending to 500 feet under heavy anti-aircraft gun fire. The fire prevented him from reaching the station, but he climbed to 1,500 feet and attacked a 'Rocket' battery, silencing one of its guns'.

The first of his eventual five Mentions in Despatches also appeared in the *London Gazette* of 29 October 1915. Long gained his first victory flying a 29 Squadron DH2, '7915', on 6 August 1916, when he sent a Fokker E down out of control over the Ypres Salient. He transferred shortly after this to 24 Squadron (also DH2s), gaining the second of his victories with that unit on 16 November following. Promoted to A/Captain and Flight Commander early in 1917, he took his total of victories to nine by 6 March 1917. He was awarded a Distinguished Service Order in the *London Gazette* of 12 March 1917, for gallantry at Morval. Returning to the Home Establishment soon after this, 'Tubby' Long served with 46 Squadron (Sopwith Pups) at Sutton's Farm on Home Defence duties, before returning to France with that unit as acting CO on 30 August 1917. Within days, he was posted back to the UK to instruct, briefly, at 28 TS. Next, he was appointed to command No 1 Africa Survey Party, which was charged with selecting aerodromes to be used later on the Cape Town to Cairo air route. Finally, travelling to the Middle East with the rank of Major, he commanded 111 Squadron in Mesopotamia from September 1918 to February 1919. Returning to the UK, he resigned his commission with the rank of Major on 31 July 1919. He wrote of his wartime experiences in his book, 'In the Blue', published in 1920. Long married, in 1937, Marian Beatrice Smith from Whalley, Lancashire. He served again in the Second World War, rejoining the RAF as Squadron Leader on 1 June 1940. Serving in North Africa, he was promoted to Wing Commander on 15 September 1942. He retired from the RAF for a second time in 1945. Wing Commander Selden ' Tubby' Long died in Cape Town, South Africa, on 12 December 1952.

NB: The RAF Museum Hendon has his medals in its collection: Distinguished Service Order, MC (engraved: S H Long, RFC, Presented by HM The King March 11th 1916, France October 4th 1915*), 1914-15 Star* (2 Lt DLI), *British War Medal 1914-20, Victory Medal 1914-19* (Major, RAF), *1939-45 Star, Africa Star 1940-43, Defence Medal 1939-45, and War Medal 1939-45.*

LORAINE, Robert

The son of actor Henry Loraine and Ellen Loraine (née Bayliss), of Mersey Terrace, New Brighton, Wirral, Cheshire, he was born on 4 January 1876. Educated at New Brighton High School. He left school age 14 to join his Shakespearean actor father's stock company. His first stage appearance was made in a Liverpool back street theatre, The Adelphi, which he later described as a 'sailors' dive'. He travelled the country appearing in all manner of plays, sometimes as many as half a dozen a week. He married first, in 1897, the actress and former New York journalist, Julie Opp. By then a successful stage actor, he did not hesitate to volunteer his services when the South African war came in 1899. Enlisting as a Trooper into the Montgomeryshire Yeomanry (TF), he trained at that regiment's depot in Welshpool before leaving for South Africa on 13 March 1900. His service in the second Boer War took in the actions and campaigns at Slobbert's Nek, Rieteff's Nek, Wonderboon, Pyramids, Waterval, Peinaars River and Warm Baths. During these operations, he gained experience on the unit's mobile Colt machine gun, mounted on a Dundonald galloping carriage. A knowledge of machine guns would prove useful in the years yet to come. Like so many others in the South African War, he became a casualty of disease and had to be invalided home. For his services, he received the Queen's South Africa Medal 1899-1902, with three clasps, Wittebergen, Cape Colony and Transvaal. Having recovered his health, he accepted an offer of a contract from impresario Daniel Frohman, to act in the USA. After a slow start, his career progressed satisfactorily. He secured the American rights of George Bernard Shaw's 'Man and Superman', which he produced and starred in to critical acclaim. Returning to England in 1907, his fame and reputation continued to blossom. His first marriage had, by this time, failed. Suddenly gripped by the aviation bug, Loraine learnt to fly at the Bleriot School in Pau and at the Farman School at Mourmelons, gaining his Royal Aero Club Certificate (Number Fr 126) on 21 June 1910. Entering flying competitions as soon as he qualified, he broke new ground when he flew across the Irish Sea from Holyhead, breaking the existing record for an 'oversea' flight. Volunteering for the RFC when war came, he was, initially, accepted only as an Observer, despite his qualifications. The reason for this was that he was 38 years old and a spectacles-wearer. He crossed to France on 3 September 1914, thus earning the 1914 Star. After flying as an Observer for a time, he was duly appointed a Pilot, but was soon sent back to an observing role following complaints from a gunnery major concerning his short-sightedness. Loraine was wounded in the air by ground-fire above Fromelles on 22 November 1914, a piece of shrapnel hitting him in the back, penetrating a lung and exiting through his collar bone. His injuries were so severe that he was not expected to live and was sent back to England for intensive medical treatment. His hair turned white and his weight, quite literally, halved from 182 lbs to 91 lbs. Despite the gloomy prognostications, he slowly recovered and, before long, was agitating to get back into operational flying. By July 1915 and with only one functioning lung, he was piloting a 5 Squadron BE2c on artillery observation duties from Abeele. His age and infirmity were acknowledged to the extent that he was allowed home on leave every seven weeks, but apart from that concession, he took his chance along with the rest. On 1 September he was promoted to Captain and Flight Commander, taking charge of 'B' Flight, which had been newly equipped with the FB5 'Gunbus', probably the first exclusively 'fighter' unit to be employed on the Allied side of the Western Front. He was Mentioned in Despatches for this work on 11 October 1915. His MC was announced in the *London Gazette* of 6 November 1915: 'For conspicuous gallantry and devotion to duty. On 26 October he attacked an Albatros, getting within 15 yards of it. When it dived, he dived after it, and followed it from 9,000 feet to 600 feet. The enemy pilot was hit, and his camera and wireless transmitter were subsequently found to have bullet-holes through them. The Albatros fell in our lines'.

His Observer on this occasion, the Hon Eric Fox Pitt Lubbock (qv), also received the MC for the action, graphically describing the events in a letter home. Recalled to England on 11 March 1916, Loraine was given command of 40 Squadron and eventually accompanied that unit, as a 'founder member', to France on

2 August. In February 1917, Loraine returned to England before going out to France again to command, with the rank of Lieutenant Colonel, 14 Wing RFC. His Wing was made up of 22 and 24 Squadrons, RFC, and 1 and 6 Naval Squadrons, RNAS. Loraine's health and mental state began to deteriorate as the stress and strain increased through the trials and tribulations of 'Bloody April' and beyond. He was withdrawn from the front and awarded the Distinguished Service Order in the Birthday Honours *London Gazette* of 4 June 1917. Following some rest and recuperation, he was next appointed Wing Commander of 36 Training Wing at Andover. Here he gained a reputation as a martinet and was universally disliked. He defended his harshness by saying that he knew only too well what awaited the young trainees under his command and it would do them no favours to molly coddle them beforehand. In 1918, reverting to the rank of Major, he took command of 211 Squadron (DH9s), a day-bombing unit of the Independent Air Force. He had been at the front in every year of the war and, despite the stress and strain, he still flew occasionally in an observing capacity. On 20 July 1918, he and his Pilot, Captain Harold Mervyn Ireland, in DH9, 'B7624', were returning from a bombing raid on Bruges docks when they were attacked by a German seaplane. Loraine shot that machine down, but they immediately came under attack from a second seaplane. In the course of the ensuing fight, Loraine was hit by a machine-gun bullet in the left knee, which shattered the bone. Harold Ireland, who would later be awarded the Distinguished Flying Cross for other reasons, was unscathed and landed the DH9 safely at La Paune. Even after the attentions of several of the most eminent surgeons in the land, still Loraine could not bend his leg and was frequently in pain. He finally relinquished his commission on 10 December 1918, declared permanently unfit for further service. Returning to acting, he travelled the world with his own theatre company. In 1921, he met and married Winifred Lydia Strangman, the daughter of the Adjutant General of Bombay, with whom he would have three daughters. His wife occasionally appeared with him on the stage and, although untrained, showed an outstanding talent for set design. Loraine made his first film in England in 1922, and would, later, make a further five films in Hollywood. In 1927 he took out a five-year lease on the Apollo Theatre, Shaftesbury Avenue, London, and took up residence at 36 James Street, Westminster, London. The timing, to say the least, was inopportune as it coincided with the onset of the great depression that came with the end of the 'Roaring Twenties'. Robert Loraine died at Golden Square Hospital, Golden Square, London, on 23 December 1935, and is buried in Putney Vale Cemetery, London.

LOWCOCK, Reginald John

The son of Edward Charles Lowcock and Mary V Lowcock, of 'Oakwood', Haydock Road, Liscard, Wirral, Cheshire, he was born on 27 August 1896. Reginald's father died whilst he was still quite young and he was sent out to Coquimbo, Chile, to be looked after by his uncle, John J McAuliffe. When he was eight, his uncle sent him to be educated in England. Three years later, he entered King William's College, Isle of Man (1907-14), Rugby XV, Cricket XI. When the war came in August 1914, he enlisted as a Private soldier into 18 (1 Public Schools) Battalion, Royal Fusiliers. Picked out as potential officer material, he was allowed to enter Sandhurst in November 1914. Passing out from the Royal Military College, he was gazetted Second Lieutenant to a Regular Army battalion of the Sherwood Foresters on 17 April 1915. Seconded to the RFC in October 1915, he gained his Royal Aero Club Certificate (Number 1900), satisfying the examiners in a Maurice Farnham biplane at the Military School, Birmingham, on 5 November 1915. His formal pilot training duly completed, he was gazetted Flying Officer on 28 January 1916. Joining BE2e-equipped 34 Squadron in the UK, he accompanied that unit to France as a 'founder member' on 15 June 1916. Lowcock served on artillery observation duties throughout the summer, autumn and winter of 1916. On 4 December 1916, his ranging of 75 Siege Battery, RGA, was particularly successful, resulting in seven direct hits on a hostile battery. His MC was announced in the *London Gazette* of 11 December 1916: 'For conspicuous gallantry in action. He beat off an attack by four enemy machines and continued his ranging. Later, he flew under 1,000 feet, in a zone full of our shells, in order to silence hostile batteries'.

On 22 December 1916, he was promoted to A/Captain and Flight Commander and posted to 9 Squadron (also equipped with the BE2e). On 26 April 1917, Lowcock was shot up and wounded in the shoulder during a reconnaissance patrol. His wounds healed, Lowcock was next posted, again as a Flight Commander, to the RE8s of 52 Squadron. On 20 July, he and his Observer, Lieutenant Manley, in an RE8, were shot up during a combat with five enemy Albatros Ds over Westende. Lowcock, who was wounded in the leg, managed to bring the 'Harry Tate' down comparatively intact onto 3 Naval Squadron's aerodrome. Fortunately, Manley emerged from the incident unscathed. Lowcock was awarded the Distinguished Service Order for his gallantry on this occasion, *London Gazette* of 26 September 1917, details in the *Gazette* of 9 January 1918. He received the insignia of the Distinguished Service Order from the hands of the King at an investiture held at Buckingham Palace on 7 November 1917. Once fully recovered, he was promoted to Major and given command of the Army and Infantry Co-operation School. He was killed on 22 July 1918, whilst flying a Bristol Fighter, 'C861, over Bournemouth, the machine crashing near to Tilshead. Fortunately, the Observer, Captain Bridgewood, escaped serious injury. Major Reginald Lowcock, DSO, MC, was buried in a Commonwealth War Grave plot in the north-east part of Figheldean (St Michael) Churchyard, Wiltshire.

LOWE, Cyril Nelson

The son of the Reverend Charles William Nelson Lowe, MA, and Mrs Lowe, of Highfield School, Trinity Road, Wandsworth Common, London, he was born in Holbeach, Lincolnshire, on 7 October 1891. Educated at Dulwich (1905-11) Rugby XV, Cricket XI, Captain of Sports, and at Pembroke College, Cambridge, from where he graduated BA. He was a Rugby Blue at Cambridge in 1911, 1912 and 1913. Lowe first played Rugby for England against South Africa in 1913 and subsequently gained 25 International Caps for his country. An Assistant Master at Rossall School in 1914, he immediately volunteered when war came in the August of that year. Gazetted Second Lieutenant to the Army Service Corps on 31 August 1914. He served in France with the Army Service Corps in 1914 (earning the 1914 Star), 1915 and 1916, before transferring to the RFC, with the rank of Captain, in the summer. Having trained as a Pilot, he was confirmed and gazetted Flying Officer on 30 September 1916. Sent out to FE2b-equipped 11 Squadron in France in October following. Lowe achieved two victories in March 1917, being slightly injured during the course of the first of these on 24.March. A promotion to Flight Commander and a posting to 24 Squadron (SE5As) came early in 1918. Seven more victories were achieved by the following July. On the intervening 20 May 1918, Lowe in SE5A, 'D275', and Lieutenant R T Mark, MC (qv), in SE5A, 'C5367', were involved in a combat with a number of enemy Scouts. Both were shot up in the course of the fight, each coming to the other's aid and eventual rescue, as the citation to Lowe's MC makes clear, *London Gazette* of 16 September 1918: 'For conspicuous gallantry and devotion to duty. This officer and another pilot were escorting a formation of machines engaged on a bombing raid when seven enemy scouts attacked the bombers. They both attacked these scouts, but at the outset this officer's machine was set on fire, and the other pilot's right hand top plane broke. During the fight that ensued each came to the rescue of the other. The other pilot first caused Captain Lowe's pursuer to break off his attack, and then Captain Lowe shot down the scout attacking his comrade. The action of both these officers, in practicably un-manoeuvrable machines, in coming to the rescue of each other in turn, showed courage and self-sacrifice of a very high order'.

Lowe was also awarded the Distinguished Flying Cross for gallantry as a Scout Pilot in the *London Gazette* of 3 August 1918, a date, surprisingly, earlier than the award of his MC (above). It appears that this, too, was originally intended to have been an MC award but was amended to the newer RAF award. Odd, then, that his later announced MC was not also changed. Lowe stayed on in the RAF after the war, representing the service as a wing three-quarter in the Rugby XV in 1924 and 1925. He commanded both 1 and 6 Squadrons in Iraq in 1926 and 1927. He also commanded RAF Station, Amman, TransJordan He married Ethel Mary Watson, with whom he had one son and two daughters. From 1927 to 1930, he commanded 43 Squadron and was, as a consequence of this command, involved in the organisation of the early Hendon Air Pageants. In 1930, he was appointed CFI, at 2 FTS and promoted to the rank of Wing Commander three years later. A Group Captain in 1938, he served through most of the Second World War before retiring in 1944. He lived, in retirement, at Little Brook, Burrow Hill, Chobham, Surrey. Group Captain Cyril 'Kit' Lowe died in 1985. He was supposedly the inspiration for Captain W E John's hero, 'Biggles'.

LOWE, Thomas Cleland

Born in Scotland on 28 May 1892. He trained as an Electrical Engineer and was employed as such with Archibald Russell, Coal Masters, Burabank, Scotland, from 1910 to 1914. Gazetted Second Lieutenant to the Royal Engineers on 12 March 1916. Seconded to the RFC late in 1916, he trained as an Observer and was sent out to BE2e-equipped 9 Squadron as a Probationary in January 1917. On 23 January 1917, Lowe and his Pilot, Second Lieutenant J G Kidd, engaged on artillery observation duties, were attacked by a hostile machine that they succeeded in sending down in flames into the British lines. His 'apprenticeship' satisfactorily completed, he was confirmed and gazetted Flying Officer (Observer) on 1 April 1917. His tour with '9' completed, he returned to the UK on 18 June 1917. Lowe trained as a Pilot at No 2 Flying School and, once qualified, was sent next to Italy on 19 January 1918, where he flew as an A/Captain and Flight Commander ('Z' Flight, with the BF2b) with 34 Squadron. On 4 April 1918, Lowe and his Observer of the day, Lieutenant H V N Bankes, Royal Engineers attached RFC, in BF2b, 'B1214', gained 'Z' Flight's first victory against an Albatros DV, sending it down out of control. Bankes was wounded in this action. Lowe was himself injured in an aero accident in Italy on 9 June 1918. His MC was announced in the *London Gazette* of 16 September 1918: 'For conspicuous gallantry and devotion to duty in carrying out numerous successful reconnaissances and taking a large number of successful photographs, on several occasions driving off enemy aircraft. He has repeatedly carried out long reconnaissances, showing great determination in overcoming difficulties and completing his duty. When attacked by seven enemy aeroplanes he and his Observer engaged them and drove one down out of control'.

After recovering, Lowe would see out the remainder of the war as an Instructor, before finally leaving the RAF, via the Unemployed List, on 10 April 1919. A Flying Officer in the Reserve of Officers in the mid-1920s, he trained annually at a civilian flying school, thus 'keeping his hand in'. He lived with his wife during this period, firstly in Cambuslang, Lanarkshire and later in Ormiston, East Lothian. He finally relinquished his commission in the Reserve of Officers, due to ill-health, on 7 October 1925.

LUBBOCK, The Honourable Eric Fox Pitt

The fifth son of Lord and Lady Avebury of Windsor, and of High Elms, Farnborough, Kent, he was born in 1893. Educated at Eton (1905-12) and at Balliol College, Oxford, where he read Biology. A keen rower, he had trials with both the University Four and the Eight in 1913. His attempts to join up as soon as the war came were frustrated when he was refused on medical grounds. Following a spell of voluntary patrolling in a motor car, he enlisted as a Private in the Army Service Corps and was first sent to France in September 1914, thus qualifying for the 1914 Star. About six weeks later, he was tasked to assist the head of the Division Post Office in his own car and, during this time, had many adventures, once helping to remove the wounded from a hospital that was under heavy shell fire. After this period of duty in France, he was gazetted Second Lieutenant to the Army Service Corps, on 27 January 1915. A transfer to the RFC followed and, after the appropriate training, he joined 5 Squadron (Vickers FB5s) as an Observer in August 1915. He flew with, amongst others, Robert Loraine (qv), the famous actor. His MC, won with Loraine, was announced in the *London Gazette* of 6 November 1915: 'For conspicuous gallantry and skill on 26 October 1915, when he attacked a German Albatros machine at a height of 9,000 feet with machine-gun fire. The hostile pilot was shot and the aeroplane brought to the ground within our lines. The attack finished at a height of only 600 feet, and during an almost vertical dive, when the pilot was fully occupied, Lieutenant Lubbock fired deliberately and with great effect'.

Lubbock recounted the events of this day in a letter home, which was later published in the *Eton College Chronicle*: 'Yesterday Loraine and I had an exciting adventure. We sighted a German about two miles off and attacked. We both opened fire at about 50 yards. I fired again at about 25, firing 26 rounds, and then my gun jammed. From that moment I knew nothing except that I was working desperately at my gun. I heard Loraine give a great shout, but felt neither fear nor triumph. Then our machine turned downwards. As I fired my last shot I had seen the German turn down. I knew that if he got below us my machine-gun was the only one that could fire at him. We were diving, I was standing almost on the front of the body. Then we turned level. I finished my gun but there was no German! Well, the luckless Boche fell 20 yards behind our front line trench. The pilot was shot through the stomach – the observer, a boy of 17 – just grazed in the head. On the machine was found an odd machine gun. It had been taken from the Canadians months ago and has now come back to them. It is absolutely unfit for aeroplane work, being three times as heavy as the one we used and having lots of other technical drawbacks. There was a camera with a Zeiss lens, which will be most valuable to us, although the camera was pierced by two bullets. There were some plates which are being developed at the moment. The camera is heavy and clumsy, not a patch on ours. It is such that you cannot take a vertical photograph. There was a carbine, a very nice weapon. There was a pistol for firing coloured lights, which had been hit by us and spoiled. There was a priceless pair of binoculars, magnifying 18 times, I am to take all these things myself to GHQ, which makes me very shy'.

RFC Communiqué No 17 is given over entirely to the interrogation report on the young, 17 year old, Observer, Leutnant Buchholz, brought down by Loraine and Lubbock and subsequently captured. Young Buchholz, a former infantry officer, had already won an Iron Cross, 2nd Class, in the trenches, before training as an Observer. The Communiqué makes fascinating reading. Lubbock continued to be heavily involved in 5 Squadron's operations throughout November and December 1915, before returning to the UK early in 1916. Next, he trained as a Pilot and, after qualifying, joined 45 Squadron, then stationed at Gosport, as a Flight Commander (gazetted as such on 1 July 1916). Equipped with Sopwith Strutters, '45' went to France on 12 October 1916, Lubbock accompanying the unit as a 'founder member'. Here again, Lubbock was heavily involved in operations, surviving near misses on a number of occasions as well as enjoying some successes. On 11 March 1917, Lubbock and his Observer, Lieutenant John Thompson, in Strutter, 'A1082', were killed in action when their machine was shot down into Railway Wood, near Ypres, by Leutnant Paul Strähle of Jasta 18, the second of the German Ace's eventual 15 victories. Eric Lubbock was twice Mentioned in Despatches during his service in the Great War. He is buried in Ljssenthoek Military Cemetery, Poperinghe, West-Vlaaderen, Belgium.

LUCHFORD, Harry George Ernest

The son of Company Quarter Master Sergeant (later a civil servant) George James Luchford, East Lancashire Regiment, and his wife, Helena Elizabeth Luchford, of 'Walmer', Quernmore Road, Bromley, Kent, he was born on 28 October 1894. Harry's brother, Lieutenant C G Luchford, Northumberland Fusiliers, would also win an MC in the Great War. A Bank Clerk, pre-war, Harry enlisted as a Private soldier into the Norfolk Regiment as soon as war came in August 1914. Picked out for a commission, he was gazetted Second Lieutenant to the Army Service Corps on 26 September 1914. He saw active service at the front with 433 Company, Army Service Corps, mainly attached to the Indian Cavalry Division, until January 1916, when he returned to the UK. Transferring to the flying service on 30 October 1916, he trained as a Pilot and was duly confirmed and gazetted Flying Officer on 17 May following. Sent out in the same month to FE2d-equipped 20 Squadron, he went on to achieve 11 victories between 18 June and 17 August, flying FEs, and a further 13 victories between 9 September and 21 October 1917, flying Bristol Fighters. Although he flew with several different Observers, his partnership with Lieutenant V R S White (qv), was particularly successful, with both men being awarded the MC and Bar. Luchford's MC was announced in the *London Gazette* of 27 October 1917, details in the *Gazette* of 18 March 1918: 'For conspicuous gallantry and devotion to duty. He has carried out a great deal of extremely useful work, and has proved himself a capable and determined leader. On one occasion when on photographic reconnaissance he and his observer shot down and destroyed two enemy scouts. He has destroyed five other hostile machines'.

The Bar to his MC was in the *London Gazette* of 26 November 1917, details in the *Gazette* of 6 April 1918: 'For conspicuous gallantry and devotion to duty. When engaged on patrol he and his observer encountered about 15 hostile machines and shot one of them down in flames. Later, when engaged on a reconnaissance with three other machines he encountered 8 hostile aeroplanes and shot one of them down. On another occasion he destroyed one of the 3 hostile scouts which were attacking one of our machines and also shot down a hostile two-seater'.

On 2 December 1917, Luchford and his Observer of the day, Captain J E Johnson, in BF2b, 'A7270', were shot down near Becelaere by Leutnant Walter von Bülow-Bothkamp of Jasta 36, the 28th and last of the German Ace's victories. Luchford was killed but Johnson survived to be taken prisoner of war. George Luchford's remains were lost and hence he is commemorated on the Flying Services Memorial to the Missing, Arras, France.

NB: His medals were offered for sale by Glendining's (lot 348) on 28 March 1990: MC & Bar, 1915 Star (2Lt ASC), *British War Medal 1914-20, and Victory Medal 1914-19* (Capt RFC). *They are now in the collection of the RAF Museum Hendon.*

LUDLOW-HEWITT, Edgar Rainey

The son of the Reverend Thomas Arthur Ludlow-Hewitt of Clancoole, Bandon, County Cork, Ireland, and Vicar of Minety, Wiltshire, and Mrs Ludlow-Hewitt, he was born in 1886. Educated at Radley (1909-11) and at Sandhurst. Gazetted Second Lieutenant to 1 Battalion, Royal Irish Rifles, in 1905. Developing an interest in aviation, he gained his Royal Aero Club Certificate (Number 887) on 19 August 1914 and immediately secured a secondment to the RFC. Sent out to 1 Squadron in France, he was promoted to Flight Commander on 14 November 1914. Heavily involved in aerial operations over the front from March 1915, he was in no small way responsible for improving communications between aerial observation machines and the artillery on the ground. Promoted to Major, he was appointed to command 3 Squadron early in November 1915. His MC was announced in the New Year *London*

Gazette of 1 January 1916 (no citation). By the opening day of the Battle of the Somme, 1 July 1916, Ludlow-Hewitt, promoted to Lieutenant Colonel, had advanced to the command of Third (Corps) Wing, consisting of 3, 4, 9 and 15 Squadrons, RFC, and 1 Kite Balloon Squadron, RFC. Other distinctions included: Brevet of Major, Royal Irish Rifles, *London Gazette* of 1 January 1917; Distinguished Service Order, *London Gazette* of 1 January 1918; Chevalier, Légion d'Honneur (France), *London Gazette* of 14 July 1917; and six Mentions in Despatches during the Great War, *London Gazettes* of 22 June 1915, 1 January 1916, 4 January 1917, 11 December 1917, 31 December 1918 and 11 July 1919. He commanded 10 Brigade, RFC, in 1918, and was Chief Staff Officer in France, RAF HQ, in 1918 and 1919. Created CMG in 1919. He married, in 1923, Albinia Mary, née Evans-Loome, and widow of Captain Francis W T Cleke, Grenadier Guards (killed in action on 26 September 1916), who died in 1972. Not surprisingly, he remained in the RAF after the war, going on to carve out an extremely distinguished career, his many appointments and distinctions included: Air ADC to the King, 1921-23; CB, 1928; Commandant RAF Staff College, 1926-30; AOC, Iraq Command, 1930-32. Director of Operations and Intelligence, Air Ministry, 1933-35; KCB, 1933; AOC, RAF India, 1935-37; AOC-in-C, Bomber Command, 1937-40; Principal Air ADC to the King, 1943-45; GBE, 1943; Inspector General of the RAF, 1940-45. Ludlow-Hewitt retired from the RAF with the rank of Air Chief Marshal. In civilian life, he became Chairman of the Board of Governors, College of Aeronautics, 1945-53; President of the Southern Area of the British Legion, 1946-51; and Deputy Lieutenant of Wiltshire, 1953. He lived in retirement at Westbrook House, Bronham, Chippenham, Wiltshire. Air Chief Marshal Sir Edgar Ludlow-Hewitt died on 15 August 1973.

NB: The RAF Museum Hendon has his group of medals in its collection: Distinguished Service Order, MC, 1914-15 Star (Capt Rir Rif att RFC)*, British War Medal 1914-20, Victory Medal 1914-19 with MID* (Brig Gen RAF)*, Africa Star 1940-43, France and Germany Star 1944-45, Defence Medal 1939-45, War Medal 1939-45, Silver Jubilee Medal 1935, Coronation Medal 1937, Order of the Légion d'Honneur (Chevalier, France), and King Feisal War Medal with clasp (Iraq).*

LUKE, Thomas Carlyon

The son of Gents Outfitter and Tailor, Epenetus Ernest Luke and Ida Mary Luke (née Mabley), of 24 Leigham Street, Plymouth, Devon, he was born on 21 July 1891. By the time the war came in August 1914, he was working as a Clerk in the City of London. He enlisted as a despatch rider into the Royal Engineers (Number 32062) and, eventually, with the rank of Corporal, was sent out to France as such on 3 June 1915. Picked out for a commission, he was gazetted Second Lieutenant to the Royal Engineers on 26 March 1916. Securing a secondment to the flying service at the end of 1916, he gained his Royal Aero Club Certificate (Number 7740) on 4 January 1917, and was, on the same day, formally confirmed and gazetted Flying Officer. 'Sammy' Luke first flew operationally with 66 Squadron (Sopwith Pups), gaining four victories between 23 May and 28 July 1917. On the same day that he achieved his fourth victory, he and his Sopwith Pup were shot up. Although wounded, he managed to land safety and then had to return to the UK for medical treatment. His MC was announced in the *London Gazette* of 25 August 1917: 'For conspicuous gallantry and devotion to duty in aerial combat. On several occasions he attacked hostile formations and dispersed them, although they were in superior numbers, showing great dash and fearlessness in engaging them at close range. He has taken part in 35 offensive patrols, at all times setting a fine example of courage and devotion to duty'.

Returning again to the front in the summer of 1918, this time as a Flight Commander with 209 Squadron (Sopwith Camels), he claimed two further victories before the end of the war. Remaining in the RAF, he was given command of 18 Squadron in 1934, and was awarded the Air Force Cross, *London Gazette* of 3 June 1935, shortly before his death in Princess Mary's RAF Hospital, Halton, Buckinghamshire, on 1 July 1935. He is buried in Halton Churchyard.

NB: His medals were offered for sale by Spink (lot 191) on 20 May 1991: MC, Air Force Cross, 1914-15 Star (Cpl RE), *British War Medal 1914-20, and Victory Medal 1914-19* (Capt RAF).

M

MacDONALD, Alexander Lindsay

From Hyde Park, London. Gazetted Second Lieutenant to a Regular Army battalion of the Royal Highlanders (Black Watch) on 11 August 1915, with an almost immediate secondment to the RFC. Gained his Royal Aero Club Certificate (Number 1761) on 17 September 1915. His formal training duly completed, he was confirmed and gazetted Flying Officer on 10 November following. MacDonald joined 9 Squadron in Dover, before accompanying the unit to France on its return to the front on 19 December 1915. Promoted to A/Captain and Flight Commander on 14 September 1916. His MC was announced in the *London Gazette* of 22 September 1916: 'For conspicuous gallantry and skill when carrying out artillery and patrol work at low altitudes and under heavy fire. On one occasion he dispersed a large body of infantry by machine-gun fire from 1200 feet and then at once turned a battery on to another advancing battalion causing many casualties'.

His tour with '9' completed, he returned to the Home Establishment on 25 November 1916. MacDonald then served with a succession of Reserve Squadrons in the UK, specifically, 13, 31 and 65, before joining 83 Squadron in Montrose, Scotland. He went to France again on 17 August 1917, this time to join the RE8s of 9 Squadron. Just nine days later on 26 August 1917, MacDonald and his Observer, Second Lieutenant F J A Wodehouse, Duke of Corwall's Light Infantry attached RFC, on artillery observation duties in RE8, 'A4390', were shot down over Langemarck by Oberleutnant Wilhelm Reinhard of Jasta 11, the fifth of the German Ace's eventual 20 victories. Both MacDonald and Wodehouse were killed. Alex MacDonald is buried in Mendinghem Military Cemetery, Poperinghe, Belgium.

MacFARLANE, Ruthven Montgomerie Chase

The son of Ruthven and Rose MacFarlane of South Kensington, London. Educated at Eastbourne College (1910-14). Gazetted Second Lieutenant to the Royal Field Artillery on 22 April 1915, he served with the Gunners in the Middle East in 1915 and 1916. Transferring to the RFC in the summer of 1916, he trained as an Observer and was sent out as a Probationary to 30 Squadron in Mesopotamia on 19 September following. His tour with '30' ended on 4 April 1917 and, following a rest, he undertook pilot training. Having qualified, he was sent next to 35 Squadron (AWFK8s) on the Western Front on 5 November 1917. He narrowly missed disaster on 24 March 1918, but emerged unscathed from a potentially calamitous situation. Indeed, the work he and his Observer, Second Lieutenant A E Lancashire (qv), did on that most difficult day of the German spring offensive earned them both the MC. However, on 3 April following, MacFarlane with Arthur Lancashire again acting as his Observer in AWFK8, 'C3682', were shot down over Blangy-Tronville by Leutnant Viktor von Pressentin of Jasta 3, the second of the German Ace's eventual 15 victories. Both crewmen were wounded and their machine burnt and wrecked. Neither would serve operationally again during the Great War. MacFarlane's MC was announced in the *London Gazette* of 22 June 1918: 'For conspicuous gallantry and devotion to duty. During a flight lasting over two hours, carried out at a height of 700 feet, he performed a very accurate contact patrol at a critical period, obtaining the most valuable information concerning the enemy's dispositions. He also engaged many batteries and infantry with machine-gun fire, and throughout by his courage and keenness he set a fine example to all ranks'.

He was also Mentioned in Despatches on one occasion during the Great War. Staying on in the RAF, he held the rank of Wing Commander when the Second World War came in September 1939. He had, by this time, married and was living with his wife, Edith Muriel, at their home, Hough House, Hough-on-the-Hill, Grantham, Lincolnshire. Their son, 19 year old Pilot Officer Ruthven Arnold MacFarlane, a Beaufort Pilot with 22 Squadron, was killed in action in air operations against the enemy over France on 18 September 1940 (buried in Bayeux War Cemetery). Wing Commander Ruthven MacFarlane died on active service on 10 March 1943, and is buried in Hough-on-the-Hill (All Saints) Churchyard, Lincolnshire.

NB: His medals were offered for sale by Sotheby's (lot 167) on 30 June 1988: MC, 1914-15 Star (2Lt RFA), *British War Medal 1914-20, and Victory Medal 1914-19 with MID* (Lt RAF).

MacKAY, Charles Joseph

The son of Solicitor, John Mackay and Mrs Mackay, of Priorland, Dundalk, Ireland, he was born in Morte, Athlone, West Meath, on 30 October 1895. Educated at Ampleforth College, where he was a member of the OTC, at Yorks College, at Engelberg College, Switzerland, and at Trinity College, Dublin (1912-13). Gazetted, pre-war, from the Militia to 5 (Extra Reserve) Battalion, Prince of Wales's Leinster Regiment on 1 June 1914. Mobilised on 5 August 1914, he eventually joined 1 Battalion of his regiment at the front on 5 March 1915. Suffered a slight bayonet wound to his right heel on 22 April, but then contracted a bout of German measles which kept him out of the trenches for a while. He had requested a transfer to the flying service in December 1914 and now, at last, he was seconded to the RFC. Gained his Royal Aero Club Certificate (Number 1895) on 25 September 1915, at the Military Flying School, Shoreham. His formal pilot training duly completed, he was confirmed and gazetted Flying Officer on 18 November following. Sent out to BE2c-equipped 2 Squadron at the front shortly after qualifying. He would be wounded in the air on 27 May 1916, when his BE2c, '6232', was shot up. Within weeks he had recovered and was posted as a Flight Commander to 4 Squadron (also equipped with the BE2c) on 1 July 1916, and was soon again in the thick of the action. He was especially active during the closing days of July, when hardly a day went by without his photo-reconnaissance patrols over the Somme battlefields being challenged by enemy aircraft. His MC was announced in the *London Gazette* of 11 December 1916: 'For conspicuous gallantry in action. In very unfavourable weather he obtained most valuable photographs of the enemy's position. He fought four hostile machines for ten minutes until assistance arrived and they were driven off; afterwards he continued his work with the artillery'.

Charles Mackay was promoted Major, and appointed to the command of 59 Squadron (RE8s) from 23 December 1917 to December 1918. He would go on to receive two further awards for his service in the Great War; the Distinguished Flying Cross in the New Year *London Gazette* of 1 January 1919 and, from the French, the Croix de Guerre, *London Gazette* of 18 April 1918.

MacKENZIE, William George

From Vancouver, British Columbia, Canada, he was born on 24 November 1898. Attended the Royal Military College, Kingston, Ontario, from August 1916 to June 1917 and was offered, and accepted, a commission in the flying service. Having crossed the Atlantic, he was gazetted Second Lieutenant to the RFC on 19 August 1917. His pilot training duly completed, he was confirmed and gazetted Flying Officer on 29 September 1917. Joining 82 Squadron (AWFK8s) in the UK, he accompanied that unit to France as a 'founder member' on 20 November 1917. On 20 February 1918, MacKenzie and his Observer of the day, Second Lieutenant E H S Morris, in AWFK8, 'B5815', on a photo-reconnaissance patrol, escaped with their lives when their machine was shot up by a Fokker DRI. Forced to land, MacKenzie contrived to hit a mole hill which badly damaged his undercarriage. He fought through the troubled days of the German spring offensive, winning his MC in the process, announced in the *London Gazette* of 22 June 1918: 'For conspicuous gallantry and devotion to duty. While on a contact patrol he saw the enemy launch an attack in force. He dropped on the enemy's reserves, causing many casualties. He then attacked the advancing enemy, flying just above their heads and killing a large number of them. When his ammunition was exhausted, he returned and made a valuable report. He showed magnificent courage and determination throughout the operations'.

Having survived his tour with '82', he returned to the Home Establishment on 20 July 1918. MacKenzie spent the remainder of the war in various instructing posts at 12 Group, and later at 44 TS.

MacKIE, Douglas Runnels

From Ladywood Vicarage, Birmingham, he was born on 26 January 1889. A Civil Engineer by training (AIMechE), he was employed pre-war by the Crown Agents for the Colonies. Enlisted as a Sapper (Number 255439) into the Royal Engineers in 1915. Picked out for a commission, he was gazetted Second Lieutenant to the Royal Engineers on 28 August 1915. Seconded to the RFC, he trained as a Pilot and was duly confirmed and gazetted Flying Officer on 17 July 1917. He served in Palestine and the Middle East in 1917 and 1918, firstly, for just two days, with 111 Squadron, before going on to join 14 Squadron in August 1917. His MC was announced in the *London Gazette* of 11 April 1918 (no citation): '....military operations culminating in the capture of Jerusalem'.

Promoted to A/Captain on 10 August 1918, he was posted as an Instructor to RAF HQ (Training Brigade), Egypt, in the same month. He returned briefly to 14 Squadron on 25 October 1918, but only for four days. Returning to the UK in December 1918, he finally left the RAF, via the Unemployed List, on 9 April 1919.

MacLAREN, Archibald Stuart Charles

Born on 15 May 1892 in Reading, Berkshire. After leaving school he took on a series of jobs, including working on a rubber plantation in Malaya and growing fruit in Canada. Returning to the UK, he first gained his Royal Aero Club Certificate (Number 1310) on 4 June 1915. Next, he was gazetted Second Lieutenant to 3 (Reserve) Battalion, King's Own Scottish Borderers on 12 July 1915, with an immediate secondment to the RFC. Having completed his formal pilot training, he was duly confirmed and gazetted Flying Officer on 25 September 1915. Sent to 14 Squadron, then stationed at Shoreham, immediately after qualifying, he accompanied that unit to the Middle East as a 'founder member' on 4 November 1915. On 18 June 1916, a combined force of '14' and 17 Squadron machines mounted a surprise raid on the German airfield at El Arish. The first BE2c, armed with a 100lb bomb, to arrive over the target was flown by Archie MacLaren. He came down to 100 feet and dropped his weapon directly onto an enemy aeroplane, blowing it to pieces and wounding two Pilots of FA300. MacLaren was awarded the first of his two MCs for this raid, *London Gazette* of 27 July 1916: 'For conspicuous gallantry. On approaching an aerodrome he observed a hostile aeroplane on the ground preparing to start, with pilot and observer in their seats and mechanics holding on to the wings. He descended to 100 feet dropped a bomb squarely into the machine and blew it up, together with the pilot, observer and mechanics. He then attacked and set fire to a Fokker, which was in a hangar'.

On 2 August 1916, MacLaren and his Observer of the day, Lieutenant T J West, in DH1A, '4609', scored the first Allied victory on the Egyptian front when they sent a Fokker down near to Salmana. The enemy crew, Leutnant H Henkel and Oblt Stalter, were taken prisoner. His first tour with '14' ended on 9 October 1916, the award of a Bar to his MC coming in the *London Gazette* of 25 November 1916: 'For conspicuous gallantry and devotion to duty. He attacked and brought down an enemy machine from a height of 5,000 feet. He has on many previous occasions done very fine work'.

MacLaren was also Mentioned in Despatches (Kantara), *London Gazette* of 1 December 1916. Turning next to a training role, his success in that field is evidenced by the awards of an Air Force Cross (Egypt), *London Gazette* of 3 December 1918, and an OBE (Military Division), *London Gazette* of 22 December 1919. MacLaren flew for a total of 1,500 hours during the Great War, no mean feat in itself. Staying on in the RAF, MacLaren, by then a Squadron Leader, attempted a pioneering round-the-world flight in a Vickers Vulture amphibius bi-plane (G-EBHO) in 1924. Sharing the flying with Flight Lieutenant William Noble Plenderleith and with Sergeant W H Andrews acting as Flight Engineer, MacLaren hoped to circumnavigate the world, inititally via France, Italy and the Mediterranean to Cairo. From Cairo they would then cross India, Burma and China and continue on through Japan and Russia, via the Aleutian Islands, to Alaska. They would then cross Canada and Newfoundland, before flying the Atlantic to Portugal, Spain and back through France to their starting point in Southampton. King George V gave the enterprise his blessing and support. The attempt, sadly, was beset by bad weather and plagued by mishaps. In Civitavecchia, Italy, they struck some surface driftwood, which resulted in damage to the plane. Engine failure forced an unplanned landing in Lake Korissia, Greece, and they were obliged to replace the engine with another sent out from England. The replaced engine later failed, and they had to make an emergency landing at Kornra/Parlu, India, to await a second replacement engine. Further problems with a radiator were experienced in Allahabad, India. Severe weather forced them to land on Akyab Island, Burma. Seconds after take off from Akyab, they crashed into the harbour, destroying their machine. A replacement Vulture (G-EBGO) was shipped out to them and, on June 25, 1924, they resumed their attempt. Bad weather and poor luck continued to beset their efforts and, next, Sergeant Andrews was taken ill in Shanghai. Lieutenant Bryant took over Andrews' duties until the latter was fit enough to re-join at Kasumigaura Naval Station, in Tokyo. They then turned north, flying across the largely unchartered and desolate Russian coast with no advance meteorological weather information to help them. They soon lost radio contact and the weather closed in. MacLaren and Andrews fell ill and were feverish, but still they persevered. They left West Kamchatka on August 4, 1924 and, once near to Bering Island, fog finally brought their round-the-world attempt to an end, when Plenderleith was forced to land on the sea. Surviving the forced landing, they beached the Vulture and were subsequently rescued by a Russian ship.

MacLAREN, Donald Roderick

The son of Mr and Mrs Robert James MacLaren, he was born in Ottawa on 28 May 1893, his family moving to Calgary six years later. He entered McGill University to study Electrical Engineering in 1912, but had to leave because of ill-health early in 1914. He worked thereafter in the family fur-trading post in the remote hinterland of Alberta. Joined the RFC as a Cadet on 8 May 1917, before being gazetted Second Lieutenant on 19 August 1917. He trained as a Pilot in Canada and was duly confirmed and gazetted Flying Officer on 10 October following. He had shown natural ability as a Pilot and was kept back for a while to instruct at Camp Borden, Ontario. Posted to the UK, he was sent to the front and the Camel-equipped 46 Squadron on the 23 November 1917. MacLaren gained an amazing 54 victories, including six balloons, between 6 March and 9 October 1918. Not surprisingly, he rose to command his squadron with the rank of Major and collected a veritable plethora of gallantry awards. The first of his two MCs was announced in the *London Gazette* of 22 June 1918: 'For conspicuous gallantry and devotion to duty. On one occasion, when on low bombing work, he bombed a long-range enemy gun 9,000 yards behind the lines, obtaining from a height of 200 feet two direct hits on the gun truck and two on the railway track alongside. When returning to our lines he encountered a hostile two-seater machine, which he shot down crashing to earth. He then attacked a balloon, which burst into flames, and finally, observing another enemy two-seater plane, he engaged it and eventually succeeded in crashing it to earth. He has set an excellent example of gallantry and skill to his squadron'.

The Bar to his MC followed in the *London Gazette* of 16 September 1918: 'For conspicuous gallantry and devotion to duty as a fighting pilot. He has recently destroyed no less than nine enemy machines, and proved himself a brilliant fighting pilot against enemy aircraft often far superior in number. He has done magnificent service and set a splendid example to his patrol'.

On 10 October 1918, still at the height of his powers, he broke a leg whilst indulging in horseplay with one of his friends, an event which effectively ended his operational career in the Great War. His outstanding services continued to be recognised, a Distinguished Flying Cross came in the *London Gazette* of 21 September 1918, followed by a gallantry Distinguished Service Order announced in the *London Gazette* of 8 February 1919. The French awarded him a Croix de Guerre avec Palme and made him a Chevalier of the Légion d'Honneur, both appearing in *London Gazette* of 15 July 1919. He married Verna Harrison in 1919. After the war he was appointed to the British Air Board and sent as an Attaché to Canada to help with the formation of the Royal Canadian Air Force. He was subsequently appointed Director of Air Services, RCAF. In 1921 he resigned his commission to make a successful career in civilian aviation, eventually becoming executive assistant to the President of Trans-Canadian Airways. He retired in 1958 and was subsequently appointed President of the Air Cadet League of Canada. Don MacLaren died in July 1989.

NB: The Canadian War Museum has his medals in its collection.

MacMILLAN, Norman

The second son of John Campbell MacMillan and Jeannie Hamilton Macmillan, of Carsphairn, Kirkcudbrightshire, Scotland, he was born in Glasgow on 9 August 1892. Educated at Allen Glen's School and at the Royal Technical College. He enlisted as a Private soldier into the Highland Light Infantry when war came in 1914, and served in the trenches in 1914 (earning the 1914 Star) and in 1915. Picked out for a commission, he was gazetted Second Lieutenant to the RFC on 26 September 1916. Having trained as a Pilot, he was confirmed and gazetted Flying Officer on 27 February 1917. Perhaps surprisingly, he subsequently gained his Royal Aero Club Certificate (Number 7823) on 28 March following. Sent out to 45 Squadron, he achieved two victories in Sopwith Strutters, before the unit was re-equipped with Camel FIs in the following August. A further seven victories were claimed by MacMillan between 25 August and 20 October 1917, this last on the Italian front, to where '45' had re-located. However, two of his claims, both supposedly occurring on 11 September 1917, are now known to have been overly optimistic. The two claims involved Fokker Tri-planes, but, in point of fact, it was actually the same machine, a prototype flown, on each occasion, by no less a personage than Werner Voss. The German Ace managed to escape, not without considerable difficulty, on both occasions and lived to tell the tale. MacMillan was injured on 6 January 1918 and was invalided home, never again to return to operational flying during the Great War. His MC was announced in the *London Gazette* of 18 July 1918: 'For conspicuous gallantry and devotion to duty. He has shot down in flames three enemy planes, and has driven down out of control six other machines. He has by his skill and courage afforded a magnificent example to all ranks with whom he has come into contact'.

Once recovered from his injuries, he was posted for duty as an Instructor, for which services he would eventually receive the Air Force Cross, *London Gazette* of 3 June 1919. He had the distinction of commanding Special Mobile Flight, RAF, in 1921. He married around this time, Gladys Mary Peterkin, of Dundee. After leaving the RAF in the early 1920s, he worked as an Air Ministry approved Test Pilot, becoming the first airman to fly from London to Sweden in a single day. In 1922, his attempt to fly around the world, the first attempt ever, ended in the Bay of Bengal, due to engine failure. During a visit to South America in 1931, he became the first Pilot to fly over the Andes. His many successes, appointments and qualifications included: Instructor to Spanish Military and Naval schools in 1922; winner of various aviation speed races; FRAeS, 1928; MRAeS, 1973; founder member and Warden of Guild of Air Pilots, 1929-34; National League of Airmen, 1935-38; FRSA, 1936-57; Special Air and Aviation Correspondent, *Daily Mail*, 1935-39; service in the Second World War in the RAFVR, 1939-45; Official War Correspondent during the Second World War; founder member of the Circle of Aviation Writers, 1941; Command of the ATC Wing in Cornwall; Deputy Lieutenant of Cornwall; OBE, 1956; Operational flights during the Malayan Emergency, 1958; President RAF Association, 1961-73; UK Special Correspondent, Aircraft, Melbourne, Australia. Wing Commander MacMillan was also a prolific writer who contributed to numerous publications, national and international. His many books included what has become a recognised classic of the genre, 'Into the Blue', published in 1929. He lived with his wife at Trecara Lodge, 2 Edward Street, Truro, Cornwall. Norman MacMillan died at the Royal Cornwall Hospital, on 5 August 1976.

MacRAE, John Finlay Noel

The son of J F MacRae and Mildred A MacRae, of 'Tigh na Bruaich', Warlingham, Surrey, he was born on Christmas Day, 1891. After leaving school, he was employed as an Actuarial Clerk with Commercial Union of London, from 1909 to 1914. When war came in August 1914, he enlisted as a Private soldier into a TF battalion of the Cameron Highlanders. Picked out for a commission, he was gazetted Second Lieutenant to 11 (Reserve)

Battalion, Royal Highlanders (Black Watch), via a New Army commission, on 15 February 1915. Served in the trenches and fought through the Battles of Festubert and Loos, being slightly wounded and gassed. Returning to duty, he was wounded again on 14 August 1916, during an attack by 9 Black Watch on 'The Elbow', a strong-point near Contalmaison, on the Somme. He was actually recommended for the MC because of his gallantry on this occasion, but had to be content with a Mention in Despatches, *London Gazette* of 5 January 1917. Once recovered, he sought secondment to the RFC, which came in December 1916. His pilot training duly completed, he was confirmed and gazetted Flying Officer on 5 February 1917. His health was still not good following his last wounding and it was not until 8 August 1917, that he could join 23 Squadron (Spads) at the front. MacRae achieved three victories between 18 November 1917 and 9 March 1918 and a further two on 21 March, the first day of the German spring offensive. His tour with '23' completed on 23 March 1918, he returned to the Home Establishment. His MC was announced in the *London Gazette* of 13 May 1918: 'For conspicuous gallantry and devotion to duty. While on an offensive patrol he attacked an enemy machine and drove it down damaged. On the same day he took part in a bombing raid at a low altitude on an enemy aerodrome and secured a direct hit on one of the hangars. While returning he engaged enemy troops and transport on a road, causing casualties and confusion. He then climbed and attacked an enemy kite balloon and in spite of intense fire, succeeded in forcing it down damaged. He showed splendid courage and initiative'.

MacRae next served with 92 Squadron in the UK, before moving on to, successively, 42 and 63 TS, receiving a further Mention in Despatches for his expertise in this field. John MacRae finally left the service, via the Unemployed List, on 28 May 1919.

MADDOCKS, Henry Hollindrake

The second of the three sons of Solicitor, Henry Maddocks and Elsie May Maddocks (née Anslow), of 'Witheford', Stoke Green, Coventry, Warwickshire, he was born on 7 August 1898. Educated at Berkhampstead School, where he was a Sergeant in the OTC. Went straight from school to be gazetted Second Lieutenant to the RFC, via the Special List, on 5 August 1916. His pilot training duly completed, he was confirmed and gazetted Flying Officer on 26 December following. Sent out to the Sopwith Pup-equipped 54 Squadron at the front on 2 June 1917. He achieved four victories on Pups, before the squadron re-equipped to Camels in the winter. Promoted to A/Captain and Flight Commander on 3 January 1918, he celebrated by gaining his first victory in a newly issued Camel. Maddocks took his victories to seven on 3 February, including the notable scalp of Leutnant Karl Stock, CO, Jasta 48. Maddock's well merited MC was announced in the *London Gazette* of 17 December 1917, details in the *Gazette* of 23 April 1918: 'For conspicuous gallantry and devotion to duty. Whilst attacking two hostile aeroplanes he saw an enemy machine attacking one of his patrols. He at once attacked the enemy machine, which was seen to crash. On one occasion during a fight between seven enemy machines and a patrol of our scouts, he engaged one of the enemy machines causing it to drop from 6,000 feet to 1,000 feet, where it caught fire and dived vertically down. On two other occasions he drove down an enemy machine after a short fight. He has done consistent and continual good work'.

His tour with '54' completed, he returned to the UK in March 1918, where he saw out the remainder of the war in various training posts, before finally leaving the RAF, via the Unemployed List, in May 1919. Maddocks was fleetingly recalled from the Reserve to the RAF early in April 1921, before reverting to his civilian status just two months later. Died Harrow, Middlesex, 11 July 1969.

MADDOX, Ernest Reynolds

The son of Dr E E Maddox and Mrs Maddox, of Bournemouth, Hampshire, he was born on 30 October 1898. He was gazetted Second Lieutenant to a Regular Army battalion of the Hampshire Regiment on 5 July 1917, with immediate secondment to the RFC. Gained his Royal Aero Club Certificate (Number 5052) on 6 August 1917. His pilot training duly completed, he was confirmed and gazetted Flying Officer in the following September. Posted out to the Camel FI-equipped 3 Squadron on 24 November 1917, he was heavily involved during the frenetic days of the German spring offensive that commenced on 21 March 1918. Maddox achieved his first victory on 6 April 1918, sending an enemy machine down to crash in flames. His MC was announced in the *London Gazette* of 22 June 1918: 'For conspicuous gallantry and devotion to duty. During an enemy attack he repeatedly dived to a very low altitude and engaged the enemy troops with bombs and machine-gun fire. The enemy were in massed formation, and sustained very heavy casualties. On numerous occasions during the recent operations he has inflicted very heavy casualties, and caused the greatest panic among enemy troops and transport by the daring manner in which he employed his bombs. His gallantry and skill have been most praiseworthy'.

His tour with '3' completed, he returned to the Home Establishment on 13 June 1918 and was posted to instructing duties in the following month. Although Maddox returned to his army unit, Hampshire Regiment, at the end of the war, he is nevertheless noted as attending, as a Flying Officer, 2 TDS for a Refresher Course on Sopwith Snipes, in March and April 1924.

MAGOUN, Francis Peabody

The son of Francis Peabody Magoun and Jeanne Magoun (née Bartholow), of Cambridge, Massachusetts, USA, he was born in New York City on 6 January 1895. Educated at the Noble and Greenough School, Boston, and at Harvard College, from where he graduated in 1916. In February 1916, he joined the American Ambulance Field Service and sailed for Europe. He was first employed as a volunteer driver with SSU, No 1, from 3 March to 3 August 1916. The work of this unit was acknowledged by the French with a citation that was published in the French Divisional Orders of 15 July 1916. Magoun returned to the US and, in the following February, again proceeded overseas, this time to London. In March 1917, Magoun enlisted into the RFC. He first attended the School of Military Aeronautics at Oxford and was trained in elementary flying at the RNAS School, Vendome, France. Next he was sent to Catterick, Yorkshire, for lessons in advanced flying, and also attended the School of Aerial Gunnery, at Turnberry in Scotland. He was gazetted Second Lieutenant to the RFC on 4 July 1917. His pilot training duly completed, he was confirmed and gazetted Flying Officer on 3 September following. Sent out to France on 15 November 1917, he was attached to 1 Squadron (Nieuport XVIIs), a single-seater fighter unit. '1' converted to SE5As soon after Magoun arrived in France, and it was in this machine that he achieved four victories between 2 February and 28 March 1918. His MC was won on 9 April 1918 and announced in the *London Gazette* of 22 June 1918: 'For conspicuous gallantry and devotion to duty. When engaged on bombing work, he attacked and shot down an enemy machine, with the result that it crashed to earth. He also engaged massed enemy troops and transport with machine-gun fire from low altitudes, throwing the enemy into the utmost confusion and inflicting heavy casualties. His work has been carried out with consistent keenness and tenacity'.

On 10 April 1918, Magoun was again flying low and strafing enemy infantry when he and his machine were hit by ground fire. Although wounded, he managed to bring the damaged SE5A down safely. In the summer of 1918, after a spell in hospital, he returned to the US on leave. Returning again to France on 9 October, he rejoined his squadron and claimed one more victory before the end of the war. He was demobilised in Folkestone on 10 January 1919 and immediately enrolled for post-graduate work at Trinity College, Cambridge. In the summer of 1919, Magoun returned to his home in the United States. He later became a Professor of English at Harvard University, specialising in Finnish Studies, his magnus opus being a translation of a great Finnish epic, 'The Kalevala'. He was honoured by the Government of Finland in 1964 with the Order of the Lion. Frank Magoun died in Cambridge, Massachusetts, on 5 June 1979.

MAGUIRE, Matthew Laurence

The son of James Maguire JP and Mrs Dora Maguire, of Tomgar, Ballycanew, Gorey, County Wexford, Ireland. He worked for the Irish Civil Service prior to entering the Royal Military College, Sandhurst in August 1915. Maguire was gazetted Second Lieutenant to 1 Battalion, Connaught Rangers, on 22 December 1915, with an almost immediate secondment to the RFC. Gained his Royal Aero Club Certificate (Number 2364) on 30 January 1916. His formal pilot training duly completed, he was confirmed and gazetted Flying Officer on 1 April following. Sent out to the Middle East, he joined 30 Squadron in Mesopotamia on 6 September 1916. On 22 April 1917, Maguire achieved his first and only victory, sending a Halberstadt D down to crash near Istabulat. The combat occurred during the final assault on Samarra and was in full view of the attacking British and Empire troops, who roared their encouragement. Six days later, on 28 April, Maguire was himself shot down in an aerial combat above the Tigris River, by Hauptmann Hans Schuz of FAb2, the ninth of the German Ace's eventual 11 victories. Initial reports suggested that he was wounded and had been taken prisoner, only to die sometime in the following May. The facts, however, were impossible to ascertain and so now he is recorded a having been killed in action on the day he was shot down. His MC was announced posthumously in the *London Gazette* of 26 May 1917, details in the *Gazette* of 26 July 1917: 'For conspicuous gallantry. With great courage and skill he attacked and completely destroyed an enemy aeroplane, which crashed to the ground from 4,000 feet'.

His remains never recovered, Matthew Maguire is commemorated on the Basra Memorial, Iraq.

MAINGOT, Joseph Henry

The son of Solicitor, Alexander Maingot and Mrs Maingot, he was born in Trinidad, on 18 June 1893. His father was employed on Government service in Port of Spain, Trinidad, and Joseph was brought up in the West Indies. His brother, Captain P S Maingot, also won an MC with 9 East Surreys. Joseph enlisted as a Private soldier (Number 5019) into 28 Battalion, London Regiment (Artists Rifles) (TF), before being gazetted Second Lieutenant to 2 Battalion, British West India Regiment, on 7 July 1916. Seconded immediately to the RFC, he trained as an Observer and was sent out as such to serve with BE2e-equipped 14 Squadron in Arabia on 2 July 1917. Maingot completed his tour with '14' on 20 March 1918, by then the squadron was in Palestine. His MC was announced in the *London Gazette* of 11 April 1918 (no citation). Maingot finally left the RAF, via the Unemployed List, in August 1919.

MAKEPEACE, Reginald Milburn

The third son of compositor, John Pattinson Makepeace and Mary Anne Makepeace, of 52 Oakfield Road, Anfield, Liverpool, he was born in Darlington on 27 December 1891. He was living and working in Montreal, Canada, when war came in August 1914. He promptly enlisted into the Canadian Army and crossed the Atlantic to fight with the CEF in France in 1915. Picked out for a commission, he was gazetted Second Lieutenant to the RFC, via the Special Reserve, on 17 November 1916. His pilot training duly completed, he was confirmed and gazetted Flying Officer on 29 May 1917. Sent out to FE2d-equipped 20 Squadron in France soon after qualifying, he achieved the first of what would prove to be 17 victories on 29 June 1917. On 27 July, he and his Observer, Private S E Pilbrow, claimed three Albatros DIII Scouts shot down on the one day. Makepeace was given the MC for this remarkable feat, *London Gazette* of 26 September 1917, details in the *Gazette* of 9 January 1918: 'For conspicuous gallantry and devotion to duty whilst on an offensive patrol. He and his gunner shot down three enemy aircraft in quick succession, having attacked a large hostile formation, about 20 in number, with great dash and determination'.

Private Stanley Edward Pilbrow (Number 44340), Manchester Regiment, from Chelsea, London, was awarded the Military Medal, *London Gazette* of 28 September 1917. Pilbrow would be killed in action before he could accept the Military Medal. On 15 August following, his and Second Lieutenant C H Cameron's FE2b, 'A5152', was shot down by Werner Voss, the German Ace's 36th victory. After Makepeace had gained eight victories, 20 Squadron took delivery of Bristol Fighters. Makepeace was able to double his 'score' in the new Brisfits until, in January 1918, he was promoted to A/Captain and Flight Commander and posted to 11 Squadron (also equipped with the BF2b). Oddly, he claimed his 17th and last victory on 28 January 1918, whilst acting as Observer to Lieutenant John Chick (qv). Returning to the UK to take up an instructing post, he was killed in a flying accident at No 1 School of Aerial Fighting and Gunnery, Turnberry, Ayrshire, Scotland, on 28 May 1918. Reginald Makepeace was buried with full military honours in Anfield Cemetery, Liverpool, on 31 May 1918.

MALCOLM, Reginald George

From Owen Sound, Ontario, Canada, he was born on 14 January 1891. After completing his education in 1907, he secured a position as a Clerk and subsequently Deputy Manager, with the Prudential Life Assurance Company in Montreal, where he met and married his wife. When the Great War came, he was intent on joining the flying service and, with this in end in mind, he gained the North American version of the Royal Aero Club Certificate (Number AM440) on 21 March 1916. Crossing to England soon afterwards, he was accepted into the RFC with the rank of Sergeant and sent to 45 Squadron, then stationed at Gosport. Next, he joined FE2d-equipped 25 Squadron in France in November 1916. Picked out for a commission, he was gazetted Second Lieutenant to the RFC on 24 February 1917, the same day that he was confirmed and gazetted Flying Officer. Flying and fighting throughout the fraught and dangerous days of 'Bloody April', Malcolm achieved eight victories between 4 March and 1 May 1917. His tour with '25' completed, he returned to the Home Establishment on 18 June 1917. His MC was announced in the *London Gazette* of 18 July 1917: 'For conspicuous gallantry and devotion to duty. He has shown exceptional skill and courage in aerial fighting. He has several times been attacked by superior numbers, on each occasion he has accounted for more than one of the hostile machines and effected a safe landing himself'.

Research has unearthed the original recommendation for this award, which is a little more detailed than is the formal citation: 'HQ 1st Brigade, RFC. For exceptional skill and courage in aerial fighting on many occasions, particularly the following: On 1st May 1917 he was one of a formation of six which was attacked by 15 hostile scouts. He attacked one which he shot down and destroyed near Izel. A little later he was attacked by five scouts, one of which he drove down damaged. This machine was seen to land just west of Lens. Again, on the same patrol, he drove off two scouts which were attacking one of our artillery machines. Later in the same day, whilst on a bomb raid, he was attacked by a red scout, which damaged his engine. He immediately dived, and his observer shot down the hostile machine, which fell in flames near Bois Bernard. 2nd Lieutenant Malcolm managed to land on our side of the lines. On other occasions he has done exceptionally fine work, and has destroyed in all six hostile machines'.

He was posted next to No 2 School of Aerial Gunnery as an Instructor, in July 1917. Malcolm served with that unit until December 1917, when he was sent home to Canada, again as an Instructor, eventually being appointed to the command of 2 Aerial Fighting Squadron, Beamsville, before leaving the RAF in 1919.

MALLEY, Garnet Francis

The son of Mr and Mrs F Malley of 'Elowera', Harbour Street, Mosman, New South Wales, Australia, he was born on 2 November 1893. He was working as a mechanic when war came in 1914. He enlisted as a Gunner (Number 5883) into the AIF in Sydney, on 12 October 1915, and was sent to train at Camp Liverpool. On 9 November 1915, he embarked aboard the SS *Wandilla* in Sydney Harbour as part of 12 Reinforcements Group for 1 Field Artillery Brigade in Egypt. Following a number of transfers around the Middle East, he and 1 Field Artillery Brigade were sent to France and Flanders on 15 May 1916. Transferring to the Australian Flying Corps on 30 April 1917, he was, after training, sent to 30 TS as a 2 AM on 15 June following. Next, he was sent to AIF HQ on 6 July 1917, before going on to 29 TS on 11 August and 34 TS on 31 August 1917. Picked out for a commission, he was gazetted Second Lieutenant on 9 October 1917. Sent to France and Flanders on 6 November 1917, he joined 71 Squadron which would become 4 Squadron (Sopwith Camels), AFC on 19 January 1918. Malley would go on to achieve six victories between 16 March and 1 June 1918. He would also be promoted to Flight Commander and A/Captain on the intervening 26 March 1918. Malley was slightly wounded on 18 May 1918, when his Camel, 'C8261', was hit by anti-aircraft fire. His MC was announced in the *London Gazette* of 22 June 1918: 'For conspicuous gallantry and devotion to duty. When on offensive and low-flying patrol, he attacked one of two hostile scouts, which eventually turned over and fell out of control, being seen to crash by another pilot. Later, a general engagement ensued with four enemy scouts, one of which he attacked, with the result that it fell completely out of control and crashed. Prior to this occasion he had also shot down out of control another hostile machine. His courage and able leadership have resulted in his patrol carrying out excellent work under the most adverse conditions'.

His tour with '4' AFC completed, Malley returned to the Home Establishment on 3 August 1918 and then embarked upon a successful period as a Flying Instructor. After a spell with 5 TS, he went on to the School of Flying, Gosport, in October 1918. His outstanding efforts in this field were rewarded with an Air Force Cross, announced in the *London Gazette* of 3 June 1919. Returning home to Australia, his appointment with the AFC was finally terminated on 4 October 1919. He joined the Citizen Air Force, RAAF Richmond, as a Flight Lieutenant on 19 June 1925, being promoted to Squadron Leader on 1 January 1928, before being posted to the RAAF Reserve in 1930. In 1931, he went to China to act as aviation advisor to General Chiang Kai-Shek, a post he held until 1940. Malley subsequently observed and reported on the Chino-Japanese conflict. During the Second World War, he served with the RAAF on a part-time duty basis before being discharged on 9 January 1943. In the post-war years, Malley showed another aspect of his varied talents when he wrote a play during a period of residence in Fiji, circa 1957, entitled 'The Scented Hibiscus'.

MALONE, James Joseph

A Technical, not a flying, award

The son of Mr and Mrs Peter Malone, of Lismore, New South Wales, Australia, he was born on 5 August 1883. A Telegraph Engineer with the Post Office in civilian life. He enlisted into the AIF on 14 August 1916 and was quickly gazetted Second Lieutenant on 1 September following. Accepted into the embryonic Australian Flying Corps as an Equipment Officer, he embarked, on 17 January 1917, aboard the Royal Mail Ship *Omrah* in Melbourne harbour, bound for the Middle East as part of HW Flight, 4 Squadron, AFC. He would subsequently serve with 3 Squadron, AFC, from 2 March to 5 November 1918, essentially as a Wireless Officer. His MC was announced in the *London Gazette* of 1 January 1919 (no citation); it was for outstanding work in the development of wireless telegraphy in aircraft.. Discharged in England on 19 March 1920, he returned to Australia and to his job in the Post Office. He would rise to become the Deputy Director Post Master by the time the Second World War came in 1939, and would be created OBE, Civil, for his services in this field. He lived in retirement with his wife, Kate, in Linfield, New South Wales. James Malone died on 6 May 1967.

MANN, Arthur

From Leeds, he was born on 12 January 1895. He worked as an engineer in Leeds from 1911 to 1914. Gazetted Second Lieutenant to the Army Service Corps on 21 October 1914. He served in France with the Army Service Corps from October 1915, before securing a secondment to the RFC in August 1916. Having trained as a Pilot, he was confirmed and gazetted Flying Officer on 4 January 1917. Sent out to BE2g-equipped 12 Squadron in March 1917, he survived the rigours of 'Bloody April' and continued to serve for a full year at the front, attaining the rank of Captain and Flight Commander, before returning to the Home Establishment in March 1918. His MC was announced in the *London Gazette* of 18 January 1918, details in the *Gazette* of 25 April 1918: 'For conspicuous gallantry and devotion to duty. He successfully took photographs though attacked by several enemy aeroplanes, one of which he drove down. On another occasion, though attacked by four Albatros scouts and driven down from 9,500 feet to 4,000 feet, he drove off the enemy and completed his task'.

Posted next to 120 Squadron (DH9s) in 1918, he flew specialised communication flights for the remainder of the war. Mann finally left the RAF, via the Unemployed List, on 7 January 1919. His services in the last year of the war were recognised by the award of the Air Force Cross, which was announced in the Birthday Honours *London Gazette* of 3 June 1919.

MANN, John (sometimes Ian) Anderson

The first son of Sir John Mann, KBE, and Lady Margaret Mann (née Henderson), of 'Duncryne', Woldingham, Surrey, he was born in Glasgow in 1895. Educated at Charterhouse School, Rowing VIII, and at Trinity College, Cambridge. Interrupting his studies at Cambridge as soon as war came, he volunteered his services and was gazetted Second Lieutenant to 5 Battalion, Cameronians (Scottish Rifles) (TF), on 27 August 1914. The 5 Cameronians were one of the first TF battalions to go over to France and Mann was part of the original contingent that landed on 5 November 1914, thus earning a 1914 Star. Mann was one of three battalion members who transferred to the flying service, the others being Lieutenants C S Workman (qv) and Graham Nelson. Sadly, all three would be killed in action. Seconded to the RFC in March 1916, Mann trained as an Observer and was sent out as a Probationary to FE2b-equipped 25 Squadron soon afterwards. His 'apprenticeship' satisfactorily completed, he was confirmed and gazetted Flying Officer (Observer) on 12 June following. His MC was announced in the *London Gazette* of 24 June 1916, although the composer of the citation confused the roles of Mann (Observer) and G R M Reid (Pilot) (qv): 'For consistent gallantry and skill. In the course of seven days Sec Lieuts Mann as pilot [sic] and Reid as Observer [sic] attacked no less than eight enemy aeroplanes. They drove down four, three of which were seriously damaged. The remainder were driven off, one escaping by getting into a cloud'.

On 9 August 1916, Mann and his Pilot on the day, Londoner Lieutenant Clifford John Hart, in FE2b, '6996', were shot down in flames and both men killed. John Mann is buried in Rue-Petillon Military Cemetery, Fleurbaix, France.

MANN, Leslie John – later Douglas-Mann by deed poll

The son of Solicitor, F J Mann and Mrs Mann, of 17 Essex Street, Strand, London WC, he was born on 14 September 1894. Educated at Highgate School (1905-10). After leaving school, he was articled to his father's law practice in London. A pre-war volunteer in the Honourable Artillery Company (Infantry) (TF), he was mobilised as soon as war broke out on 4 August 1914. He served as a Private soldier in the trenches with the HAC from September 1914 to January 1915, thus earning the 1914 Star. Picked out for a commission, he was gazetted Second Lieutenant to the Army Service Corps on 15 February 1915. Successfully seeking secondment to the RFC, he gained his Royal Aero Club Certificate (Number 1920) on 16 October 1915. His formal pilot training duly completed, he was confirmed and gazetted Flying Officer on 6 January 1916. Joined 31 Squadron in India (the first RFC unit to go to the sub-continent) in February 1916 and served on the North West Frontier. He served next at RFC HQ, Egypt, from October 1916 until January 1917, when he returned again to '31' at Risalpur, India. In October 1917, he transferred to the newly formed 114 Squadron (Henri Farman's), subsequently serving in Aden and Arabia. On 23 January 1918, he was forced to land after his Henri Farman was shot up. Mann was unscathed in the incident but his Observer of the day, Lieutenant J S Owden, was wounded. He was, however, wounded over the Turkish lines near Aden on 8 May following. His MC, possibly unique to this unit, was announced in the *London Gazette* of 16 September 1918: 'For conspicuous gallantry and devotion to duty in skilfully bombing enemy munition and supply depots, in spite of heavy shell and machine-gun fire, which had seriously damaged his plane. On many occasions he has set a fine example of courage, especially on one, when he endeavoured to assist the occupants of an aeroplane which had been brought down in the enemy's lines'.

Mann was also twice Mentioned in Despatches during the Great War. He returned to the UK in August 1918 and was promoted to Captain the following December. Leaving the RAF in February 1919, he duly qualified as a Solicitor. In November 1920, and for some unknown reason, he changed his surname by deed poll to Douglas-Mann. He became a partner in the practice of Barnard, Taylor and Douglas-Mann, Solicitors, Lincoln's Inn Fields, London WC2. In the Second World War, he was appointed Legal Advisor to the British Air Mission in the USA, from 1940 to 1944. He also served on the Joint British/US Patents Committee from 1943 to 1944, and as Legal and Economic Consultant, Combined Production and Resources Board, in the USA, from 1941 to 1945.

MANNING, Edye Rolleston

The son of Solicitor, William Alexander Manning and Marion Manning, of Sydney, New South Wales, Australia, he was born on 14 February 1889. Educated at the Church of England Grammar School, Sydney, and at Edinburgh University (1913-14), where he studied Medicine. As soon as war came in August 1914, he interrupted his medical studies to volunteer as a Trooper into the Lothian and Border Horse Yeomanry (TF). Picked out for a commission, he was gazetted Second Lieutenant to 15 Hussars on 9 September 1914, with an immediate attachment to 14 Reserve Regiment of Cavalry. After a period in the UK, Manning served with 15 Hussars in France and Belgium from March 1915, until he was wounded in the following August. Once recovered, he sought secondment to the flying service and with this in mind, gained his Royal Aero Club Certificate (Number 2253) on 9 January 1916. His formal pilot training duly completed, he was confirmed and gazetted Flying Officer on 27 June following. Sent out to FE2b-equipped 23 Squadron within days of qualifying, he was wounded during an aerial combat with an enemy aircraft on 19 July 1916. He and his Observer, Second Lieutenant C V J Borton, in FE2b, '5235', were both wounded and their machine shot up and damaged. In February 1917, Manning was promoted to A/Captain and Flight Commander and sent to 11 Squadron (also equipped with the FE2b). On 22 April, 11 Squadron were charged with reconnoitring the Drocourt-Queant line. They were met, morning and afternoon, with fierce and unrelenting opposition by elements of the Imperial German Air Service, including Jasta 11. FE2b aircraft in various states of damage limped back to their field, wounded Pilots and Observers in almost every machine, four of which subsequently crashlanded. Manning and his Observer of the day, Corporal R E Tollerfield (Number 1197), in FE2b, 'A810', were amongst those who crashlanded. Tollerfield was wounded in the air, but Manning escaped unscathed. (Tollerfield, a direct entrant into the RFC and a 1914 Star holder, would be awarded the Military Medal in the *London Gazette* of 9 July 1917.) On 20 May 1917, Manning and his Observer, Second Lieutenant A M West, in 'A5517' achieved 11 Squadron's last victory in the FE2b, against an Albatros DIII over the Sensée Canal, before the squadron was re-equipped with Bristol Fighters. His MC was announced in the *London Gazette* of 18 July 1917: 'For conspicuous gallantry and devotion to duty when conducting photographic reconnaissances. On one occasion he obtained successful photographs though attacked by eight hostile machines, and he has on all occasions displayed the utmost pluck and gallantry'.

Promoted to A/Major in September 1917. Staying on in the RAF after the war, he served in Iraq and Kurdistan from 1922-24 and was awarded the Distinguished Service Order in 1924. In 1928, he attempted a flight from England to Australia in a Westland Wigeon. Following a serious of set-backs, he was obliged to finally abandon the attempt when he crashed, writing off the Wigeon, in Tripoli, North Africa. He married, in 1930, Phyllis Mary Louise Deganhardt, with whom he had one son and two daughters. Manning retired from the RAF for the first time on 10 August 1935, after commanding RAF Manston, returning to Australia and joining the Sydney Stock Exchange. Recalled to the Active List when the Second World War came in 1939, he served in Malaya, Burma, India, and in the UK. Promoted to A/Air Commodore in 1942, he was created CBE in 1943. He finally reverted to the Retired List at the end of the war in 1945, with the rank of Air Commodore. Returning to live in Australia, he took up residence at Turramurra, New South Wales. Air Commodore Edye Manning died in Sydney, NSW, on 26 April 1957.

MANNOCK, Edward VC

The son of Corporal Edward Mannock, 2 Dragoons, and Mrs Julia Mannock, of Preston Cavalry Barracks, Brighton, he was born on 24 May 1887. Educated at the Army School, India, and at St Thomas School, Canterbury. Leaving school age 13, he became, successively, a Greengrocer's Boy, a Barber's Assistant and a Clerk with the National Telephone Company, before exchanging the office environment to become a Linesman with NTC. He was also a peace-time volunteer, serving with the Home Counties (TF) Company, Royal Army Medical Corps. Sent out to Turkey, he became a District Inspector for the English Telephone Company's new expansion into that country. When war came and Turkey allied itself to Germany, Mannock was immediately interned as an enemy alien. His health was not good and so the Turks had few qualms in allowing his repatriation on the assumption that he would not be fit enough to serve in the British Armed Forces. He eventually arrived back in England on 1 April 1915 and promptly presented himself to his old Royal Army Medical Corps TF unit, then based at Ashford in Kent. Promoted to Sergeant, he was posted next to the 2/3 Home Counties Field Ambulance Unit (TF) at Halton Park. Picked out for a commission, he was gazetted Second Lieutenant to the Royal Engineers on 1 April 1916. Originally intending to become a tunneller with the RE, these aspirations went by the board when he was accepted into the RFC in August 1916. His pilot training duly completed, he was given his 'Wings' in April 1917 and sent out to the Nieuport XVII-equipped 40 Squadron. After a hesitant start, when some even suspected a lack of 'bottle' (how wrong could they be?), he achieved the first of his amazing 61 victories against a balloon at Quierry la Motte on 7 May 1917. Exactly one month later on 7 June, he sent his first enemy aircraft, an Albatros DIII, down out of control over north Lille. He finally got into his stride in July 1917 and from then on could only be described as 'prolific'. The first of his many gallantry awards came with the announcement of an MC in the *London Gazette* of 17 September 1917: 'For conspicuous gallantry and devotion to duty. In the course of many combats he has driven off a large number of enemy machines, and has forced down three balloons, showing a very fine offensive spirit and great fearlessness in attacking the enemy at close range and low altitudes under heavy fire from the ground'.

He had 15 victories in Nieuport Scouts by 25 September 1917 and then the unit converted to SE5As, with Mannock achieving his 16th victory in this new type on 1 January 1918. Bar to MC, *London Gazette*, 18 October 1917, details in *London Gazette,* 7 March 1918: 'He has destroyed several hostile machines and driven others down out of control. On one occasion he attacked a formation of five enemy machines single-handed, and shot one down out of control. On another occasion, while engaged with an enemy machine, he was attacked by two others, one of which he forced to the ground. He has consistently shown great courage and initiative'.

A Distinguished Service Order and Bar followed in May, both *London Gazette,* 16 September 1918, 2nd Bar, *London Gazette,* 3 August 1918, after being made a Flight Commander with the new 74 Squadron in 1918. Just why the *Gazette* dates are out of sequence is unclear. He added more victories to his tally and then was given command of 85 Squadron in June. Killed in action on 26 July 1918 by ground fire, with a score of at least 60, he has no known grave. In 1919 came the announcement of the Victoria Cross for this supreme air fighter, *London Gazette,* 18 July: 'On the 17th June, 1918, he attacked a Halberstadt machine near Armentières and destroyed it from a height of 8,000 feet. On the 7th July 1918, near Doulieu, he attacked and destroyed one Fokker (red-bodied) machine, which went down vertically into the ground from a height of 1,500 feet. Shortly afterwards he ascended 1,000 feet and attacked another Fokker biplane, firing 60 rounds into it which produced an immediate spin, resulting, it is believed, in a crash. On the 14th July, 1918, near Merville, he fired 80 rounds into an Albatros two-seater, which went into the ground in flames. On the 20th July, 1918, East of La Bassée, he attacked and crashed an enemy two-seater from a height of 10,000 feet. About an hour afterwards he attacked at 8,000 feet a Fokker biplane near Steenwercke and drove it down out of control, emitting smoke. On the 22nd

July, 1918, near Armentières he destroyed an enemy Triplane from a height of 10,000 feet. Major Mannock was awarded the undermentioned distinctions for his previous combats in the air in France and Flanders: MC, gazetted 17th September, 1917; Bar to MC, gazetted 18th October, 1917; Distinguished Service Order, gazetted 16th September, 1918; Bar to Distinguished Service Order (1st), gazetted 16th September 1918; Bar to Distinguished Service Order (2nd), gazetted 3rd August 1918. This highly distinguished officer during the whole of his career in the RAF, was an outstanding example of fearless courage, remarkable skill, devotion to duty and self sacrifice, which has never been surpassed. The total number of machines definitely accounted for by Major Mannock up to the date of his death in France (26th July, 1918) is 50 – the total specified in the *Gazette* of 3rd August, 1918, was incorrectly given as 48 instead of 41'.

Mannock has no known grave but his name is engraved on the Arras Flying Services Memorial.

MANVILLE, Frederick George Herbert

From Leask, Saskatchewan, he was born on 22 March 1893. After completing his education, he worked first as an Engineer in Chicago, USA, from February 1912 to June 1913. Returning home, he next worked as a Rancher in Prince Albert, Saskatchewan, from June to August 1914, when he enlisted as a Private soldier into the Canadian Infantry. Picked out for a commission, he was gazetted Lieutenant to 28 Battalion, Canadian Infantry, on 29 May 1915. Seeking a transfer to the RFC, he trained as an Observer and was subsequently sent out to 15 Squadron as a Probationary on 16 March 1916. His 'apprenticeship' satisfactorily completed, he was confirmed and gazetted Flying Officer (Observer) on 16 July 1916. On 26 September 1916, Manville and his Pilot, Second Lieutenant R J Hudson (qv), on three separate occasions, descended to very low altitudes and dispersed bodies of enemy infantry with machine-gun fire. Hudson would receive the MC for these actions, *London Gazette* of 14 November 1916. Manville's own MC was announced in the *London Gazette* of 10 January 1917: 'For conspicuous gallantry in action. He has done exceptionally brilliant work, often under most difficult conditions. On one occasion he flew for three hours at a low altitude far over the lines, ranging on active enemy batteries'.

His tour with '15' completed, he returned to the Home Establishment on 17 November 1916. Manville subsequently served as an Instructor at the CFS, Reading, and at the School of Bombing. Transferring to the Technical Section of the CAF in March 1919, he was promoted to Captain (Administration) on 15 May following.

MARCHANT, Cecil James

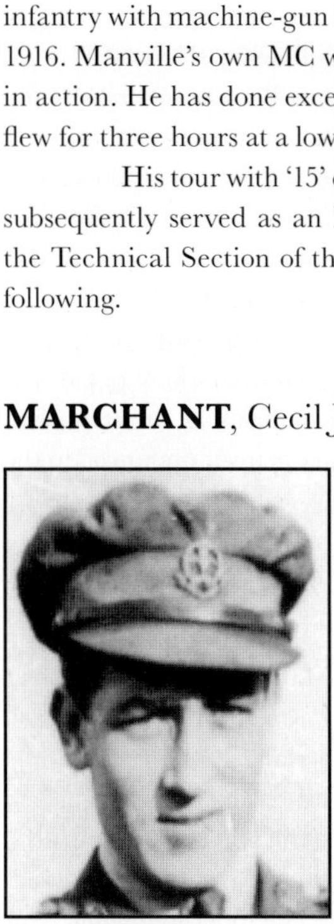

The son of Ice Merchant, James Marchant and Lucy Marchant, of 39 Erskine Road, Walthamstow, Essex, he was born on 15 July 1895. He enlisted as a Private soldier (Number 2120) into 1/2 City of London Regiment (Royal Fusiliers) in the early weeks of the war. His unit was first sent to Malta on 14 September 1914. Just over three months later, 2 Londons sailed for France, arriving in Marseilles on 6 January 1915. Following service in the trenches, Marchant was picked out for commission and gazetted Second Lieutenant to 14 (Reserve) Battalion, Middlesex Regiment, on 22 July 1915. Seconded to the RFC on 9 May 1916, he gained his Royal Aero Club Certificate (Number 3971) on 1 August 1916, the same day that he was confirmed and gazetted Flying Officer. Posted to the Sopwith Pup-equipped 46 Squadron on 4 April 1917, he completed his first tour of operational duty on 19 June following. He next served in the UK with 44 and 78 HD Squadrons from late in 1917 to February 1918. On 14 February 1918, 'Chips' Marchant returned to '46' at the front, this time as Flight Commander and A/Captain. On this tour, flying Sopwith Camels, he was outstanding, gaining no less than nine victories between

22 March and 6 May 1918. His MC was announced in the *London Gazette* of 22 June 1918: 'For conspicuous gallantry and devotion to duty. He, with two other pilots of his squadron, bombed a freight train from a height of 50 feet, three trucks being de-railed. Again, on a later occasion, he, with five other pilots, bombed and fired at a column of enemy transport with such good effect that three-quarters of the personnel became casualties and most of the vehicles were destroyed. Whilst on a low-bombing reconnaissance during the recent operations, he brought down two hostile two-seater machines out of control and shot down a third in flames. He has at all times displayed marked gallantry and resource'.

He was wounded in action on 2 July 1918, wounds which effectively ended his combat career. After the war, Marchant entered his family's business in London. An active member of his old Squadron Association, he helped to organise many of its reunions. Cecil Marchant died during the 1960s.

MARE-MONTEMBAULT, Maximilien John Jules Gabriel

The only son of French Teachers, Charles Maximilien I Mare-Montembault and Constance Gabrielle Mare-Montembault (née Girerd), of 43 Waddon Road, Croydon, and later the ward of the Honourable Mrs Cook of 'Baynords', Cranleigh, Surrey. Educated at Whitgift Grammar School. He joined the Inns of Court OTC (Number Sq/3054) on 15 March 1915, and was duly gazetted Second Lieutenant to the North Somerset Yeomanry on 25 June following. Seconded to the RFC in the early summer of 1916, he trained as a Pilot and was confirmed and gazetted Flying Officer on 3 August following. He was sent out to 32 Squadron in France just one week later on 10 August 1916. Mare-Montembault claimed his first victory on 15 September 1916, but was himself, on 10 October following, shot down by the legendary Oswald Boelcke – the German Ace's 34th victory. Boelcke sat on 'Monte's tail for almost the whole length of the Bapaume-Albert road before sending him down, physically unscathed, into the British lines. That this experience did not affect his nerve is evidenced by the fact that he achieved five more victories before, on 6 March 1917, his DH2, '7882', was sent down into enemy lines by yet another German Ace, Adolf von Tutschek. Mare-Montembault was wounded and taken prisoner. Although originally recommended for the Distinguished Service Order, he was actually awarded the MC in the Birthday Honours *London Gazette* of 4 June 1917 (no citation). Mare-Montembault remained a prisoner of war until repatriated in January 1919. It seems that he was a less than model prisoner from the German point of view, as he later received a Mention in Despatches for: '....gallantry whilst a Prisoner of War in escaping, or attempting to escape, from captivity, or for valuable services rendered in the Prison Camps of the Enemy'.announced in the 'Escapers Gazette', *London Gazette* of 16 December 1919.

MARK, Ronald Turnbull

The son of Hide, Skin, Wool and Tallow Broker, John Mark and his wife, Ellen Mark (née Turnbull), of 17 Highbury, Jesmond, Newcastle-upon-Tyne, he was born in 1898. Educated at the Royal Grammar School, Newcastle-on-Tyne (1906-13). Ronald's brother, Captain A W D Mark, Northumberland Fusiliers, would be recommended for the Victoria Cross during the Great War but, in the event, would receive a Distinguished Service Order as well as an MC and Bar. Ronald was gazetted Second Lieutenant to the RFC on 5 April 1917. Whilst under training, he was injured in a crash with 85 Squadron in the UK, on 7 June 1917. Once recovered, he completed his training and was duly confirmed and gazetted Flying Officer on 20 October following. Sent out to the SE5A-equipped 24 Squadron on 10 January 1918, he gained no less than 14 victories between 18 February and 3 May 1918. On 21 May 1918, he dived on an enemy only to find his top plane cracking under the strain. Diving now for cover with an enemy Scout on his tail, Mark was rescued by Captain C N Lowe (qv) who shot down his attacker. Mark's SE5A burst into flames on landing, but, fortunately, he was able to scramble clear, relatively unscathed. Ronald Mark would receive a Bar to his MC for this action. His tour with '24' ended one week after this close call, whereupon he returned to the Home Establishment and was appointed to instructing duties with, successively, 38 TDS and 21 TDS, where he saw out the war. The first of his MCs was announced in the *London Gazette* of 22 June 1918: 'For conspicuous gallantry and devotion to duty. He showed great determination and resource during operations in attacking enemy troops and transport with machine-gun fire. Observing some enemy transport in a village, he attacked it repeatedly and caused it to stampede. While on an offensive patrol he attacked and destroyed an enemy two-seater machine. He has destroyed one other enemy machine and driven down others out of control'.

The Bar to his MC came in the *London Gazette* of 16 September 1918: 'For conspicuous gallantry and devotion to duty. This officer and another pilot were escorting a formation of machines engaged on bombing a village, when seven enemy scouts attacked the bombers. They both attacked these scouts, but at the outset the other pilot's machine was set on fire, and Second Lieutenant Mark's right-hand top plane broke. During the fight that ensued each came to the rescue of the other. Second Lieutenant Mark first caused the other pilot's pursuer to break off his attack, then the other pilot shot down the scout attacking Second Lieutenant Mark. The action of both these officers, in practically unmanoeuvrable machines, in coming to the rescue of each other in turn, showed courage and self-sacrifice of a very high order'.

He finally left the RAF, via the Unemployed List, on 9 April 1919. Mark would go into business after the war, eventually becoming a Director of the Scots Gap Company and living at 'Ettrick', Grove Road, Gosforth, Newcatle-upon-Tyne.

MARTIN-MASSEY, Herbert

Born 19 January 1898, the son of Mr and Mrs E Martin-Massey, of Hilton, Derbyshire. Educated at Oundle (1912-15) and at the Royal Military College, Sandhurst. From Sandhurst, he was gazetted Second Lieutenant into a Regular Army battalion of the Nottinghamshire and Derbyshire Regiment (Sherwood Foresters) on 7 April 1916, with an immediate secondment to the RFC. His pilot training duly completed, he was confirmed and gazetted Flying Officer on 7 July following. Sent out to BE2c-equipped 16 Squadron in France soon after qualifying. On 2 August 1916, his BE2c, '2688', was damaged by anti-aircraft fire during a long-range bombing raid on the Brussels airship sheds. Fortunately, Martin-Massey and his Observer of the day, Second Lieutenant G Westcott, were unscathed and returned safely. He was, however, injured on 22 October during a combat with an enemy monoplane. On 4 February 1917, he and his Observer, Second Lieutenant N M H Vernham, in BE2d, '5927', were engaged on an artillery observation sortie when they were attacked by two German Scout planes. Within minutes, their BE was in flames and plummeting down to crash inside the British lines near Givenchy. Noel Vernham, a Londoner, was killed in the air but Martin-Massey, painfully burnt around the head and face, managed to pull back on the controls and somehow contrived to arrest, slightly, the speed of the descent and hence he survived the impact. They had been shot down by Werner Voss, the fifth of the great German Ace's eventual 48 victories. Martin-Massey's MC was announced in the Birthday Honours *London Gazette* of 4 June 1917 (no citation). Although no citation was published in the *Gazette*, research has unearthed the original recommendation for the award: '9 March 1917. As a pilot in No 16 Squadron from 2 September 1916 to 4 February 1917, when he was severely wounded, this officer distinguished himself by the skill, gallantry and determination with which he carried out his duties in Artillery Observation and Reconnaissances'.

He was also Mentioned in Despatches at this time, *London Gazette* of 4 June 1917. Martin-Massey stayed on in the RAF after the war. On 13 September 1920, he injured his head playing football at HQ, 3 Group, RAF Spittlehead, Lincolnshire. His ill luck continued on 29 October 1922, when he suffered severe concussion whilst hunting with hounds. During service with 8 Squadron in Iraq, he broke his right leg whilst roller skating in Baghdad on 11 March 1923. The injury-prone Martin-Massey was promoted Squadron Leader and appointed Commanding Officer of 6 Squadron on 10 January 1934. In the *London Gazette* of 6 November 1936, he was awarded the Distinguished Service Order: '....for gallant and distinguished services rendered in connection with the emergency operations in Palestine during the period 15 April 1936 to 14 September 1936'. In fact, what happened was that, on 3 September 1936, Martin-Massey had taken part in a 6 Squadron operation to rescue a detachment of the Lincolnshire Regiment, who were pinned down on the Nalbus to Tulkham road in Palestine. In the course of the rescue attempt, one Hawker Hart was lost and the crew killed. Martin-Massey in his Hart was wounded by ground fire but still managed to land safely at Tulkham. In July 1937, after being promoted to Wing Commander, he was given command of 5 Bomber Group. A further promotion to Group Captain came in 1940. Shortly before he was due to be posted to the USA for liaison duties, he rashly insisted on accompanying a 7 Squadron bombing mission to Essen on the night of 1/2 June 1942. His Stirling bomber, 'N3750', piloted by Flight Lieutenant N E Winch, was shot down during the raid, with the whole crew successfully baling out. The acutely accident-prone Martin-Massey, however, suffered severe injuries to his foot in the subsequent parachute landing. Following a lengthy spell in a German hospital, he was sent as Senior British Officer (SBO) to Stalag Luft III and was acting as such when the so-called 'Great Escape' occurred in March 1944. (The actor James Donald, assuming the name 'Ramsey', played the role of the SBO in the fanciful, but highly successful 1963 Hollywood film version of 'The Great Escape'). It was Martin-Massey who first received the dreadful news that 50 of the escapers had been re-captured and summarily executed by the Gestapo, on the orders of Adolf Hitler himself. Martin-Massey, in poor health, was repatriated from Germany in May 1944, the Germans making the fairly safe assumption that he would not see active service again. Martin-Massey retired with the rank of Air Commodore on 21 June 1950 and was created CBE in the same year. He lived in retirement at 5 Dormers, Austen Wood, Gerrards Cross, Buckinghamshire, and died in the 1970s.

MARTYN, Rutter Barry

Born on 28 September 1887. Educated at Shrewsbury and at Sandhurst. Gazetted Second Lieutenant to a Regular Army battalion of the Wiltshire Regiment on 19 August 1908. Seeking secondment to the RFC, he gained his Royal Aero Club Certificate (Number Fr1032) in France on a Bleriot Monoplane at the Bleriot School on 17 September 1912. He accompanied 2 Squadron to France as part of the original RFC contingent in August 1914, thus earning the 1914 Star. Martyn commanded 'D' Group, RFC, during the Battle of Neuve Chapelle which commenced on 10 March 1915. He was awarded the Order of St Anne with Swords, 3rd Class, by the Czar of Russia, *London Gazette* of 14 April 1916. Promoted to Major, he took 22 Squadron to France on 1 April 1916 and commanded it through the Battle of the Somme which started on 1 July following. His MC was announced in the New Year *London Gazette* of 1 January 1917 (no citation). Although no citation was published in the *Gazette*, research has unearthed the original recommendation for the award: 'T/Maj R B Martyn. (22 Sqn) For remarkably good work in the command of 22 Squadron RFC. Shortly before the operations of July, 1916, Major Martyn brought out a new Squadron; under his command it has done a great deal of hard fighting to keep German machines away from the Army Front. The squadron has also done excellent photography and reconnaissance work'.

Martyn was also Mentioned in Despatches on two occasions during the Great War. He was advanced to a Staff position in 1917 and was promoted to the rank of Lieutenant Colonel in the newly formed RAF on 1 April 1918. Martyn attempted to rejoin the RAFVR as a Pilot Officer in 1939, but his age and health prevented him doing so.

MARTYN, Thomas John Clement

The son of Mr and Mrs Martyn, of Greenhayes, Manchester, he was born on 2 January 1894. His family emigrated to Canada in the early years of the century and, by the advent of the Great War, his widowed mother had re-married, become Mrs N M Vavasour, and was living with her husband in Salmon Arm, British Columbia. Thomas was a part-time volunteer with 102 Regiment of Canadian Militia and was working as a clerk in a Bank. He enlisted into the CEF in Victoria, BC, on 3 March 1915. After service with the CEF in France, he was picked out for a commission and gazetted Second Lieutenant to 3 (City of London) Battalion, London Regiment (Royal Fusiliers) (TF), on 11 November 1915, with an immediate secondment to the RFC. Gained his Royal Aero Club Certificate (Number 3800) on 14 July 1916. Subsequently appointed Flying Officer, he was posted to FE2b-equipped 101 Squadron, then stationed at Farnborough. Martyn accompanied '101' to France as a 'founder member' on 25 July 1917. On 27 September 1917, Martyn and his Observer of the day, Second Lieutenant H W Steele, in FE2b, 'A5526', were fortunate to escape with their lives when their machine's fuel tank was shot through and they were forced to land. He was promoted to A/Captain and Flight Commander on 10 December 1917. His MC was announced in the *London Gazette* of 22 April 1918: 'For conspicuous gallantry and devotion to duty. On numerous occasions during a period of five months he has reached his objectives and released his bombs with marked effect and with the most excellent results. His work has invariably been characterised by the greatest keenness, determination and devotion to duty'.

After completing his tour with '101' in France on 31 March 1918, Martyn commanded 'C' Flight, 51 Squadron, on Home Defence duties. On the night of 5/6 August 1918, he climbed to the then incredible height of 19,300 feet over the North Sea, in the vain pursuit of a Zeppelin. He became disorientated and only with great difficult contrived to land at North Coates, some 65 miles north of his own base at Marham, with barely a cup full of petrol left in his tank. Martyn received serious injuries in a crash on 18 September 1918, which caused him to be hospitalised for some weeks. He was awarded the Air Force Cross in the *London Gazette* of 1 January 1919. Once recovered, Martyn went on to serve, in 1919, with 112, 39 and 143 Squadrons in the UK. He finally left the RAF, via the Unemployed List, on 1 November 1919. He was living in Santa Caterina, Brazil, in 1972.

MATHESON, William Drummond

From New Glasgow, Nova Scotia, he was born on 7 August 1890. Educated at St Andrew's College, Toronto (1905-10). He trained and worked as a mechanical engineer in his home town. Matheson took a flying course in Georgia, USA, and then at the Wright School, gaining the North American version of the Royal Aero Club Certificate (Number AM425) on 6 March 1916. Accepted for the flying service, first as a 1 AM (Number 25582), he was promoted to Sergeant in the following September. Picked out for a commission, he was gazetted Second Lieutenant to the RFC, via the Special Lists, on 12 November 1916. He first trained as an Observer and was sent out to FE2b-equipped 25 Squadron late in 1916. On 24 January 1917, he and his Pilot, Second Lieutenant J L Leith (qv), engaged and drove down out of control an enemy machine which had just sent a British machine down into the German lines. Matheson next trained as a Pilot and, once qualified, continued to serve with 25 Squadron. On 16 March 1917, Matheson and his Observer of the day, Sergeant G Goodman, in FE2b, 'A780', were badly shot up over Bailleul-sur-Scarpe, both crewmen being wounded in the air. Matheson received a gunshot to his left foot which necessitated its amputation through the ankle joint. His MC was announced in the *London Gazette* of 11 May 1917: 'For conspicuous gallantry and devotion to duty in leading a formation of eight machines against sixteen of the enemy. He drove down one hostile machine and eventually succeeded in landing his machine safely in spite of being attacked by several enemy machines. On other occasions he has brought down four hostile machines'.

After the appropriate hospital treatment in the UK and in Canada, he served again with the RFC in Canada in 1918 and 1919. In fact, he was brought to the notice of the Secretary of State for Air in respect of valuable service, Air Ministry List dated 29 August 1919: 'For services in Canada'.

MATHIAS, Frederick William

The son of Mr and Mrs F W Mathias of 'Brynteg', Station Road, Radnyr, Glamorganshire, he was born in Nelson, near Cardiff, on 7 August 1898. Educated at Clifton College (1914-16), Cricket XI and Rugby XV, and, post-war, at Caius College, Cambridge, from where he graduated BA. Gazetted Second Lieutenant to the RFC, via the Special Lists, on 12 August 1916. Gained his Royal Aero Club Certificate (Number 4132) on 5 January 1917. His formal pilot training duly completed, he was confirmed and gazetted Flying Officer on 22 March following. Sent out just six days later to the RE8-equipped 34 Squadron in France. Later in the year, '34' moved its operational front to Italy, arriving in Milan on 14 November 1917. After being hospitalised on 16 January 1918, Mathias returned to the UK where he was posted to various training depots. His MC was announced in the *London Gazette* of 16 September 1918: 'For conspicuous gallantry and devotion to duty. He carried out several successful shoots, doing considerable damage; he took a large number of successful photographs, and completed several long reconnaissances, obtaining valuable information'.

Mathias finally left the RAF, via the Unemployed List, on 14 February 1919, to enter Caius College, Cambridge, to read for a degree. An exceptional cricketer, middle order right hand batsman and slow right-arm bowler, he played 28 times for Glamorgan between 1922 and 1930 and once, in 1926, represented Wales. A self-employed Stockbroker with his own firm, he was a member of the Cardiff Stock Exchange for many years. Holding a civilian flying licence, he also enjoyed membership of the Cardiff Aero Club. He married, between the wars, Eileen Anne, with whom he had four sons. He served as a Captain in the Home Guard during the Second World War. Frederick Mathias died on 19 April 1955.

MAUDUIT, Ronald Frank Strickland

The son of Major F S Mauduit and Mrs Mauduit, he was born in India on 30 October 1895. Educated at Wellington College (1908-12), Rugby XV, where he was a member of the OTC, and at the Royal Military College, Sandhurst. Ronald's brother, H C E Mauduit, King's Royal Rifle Corps and 13 Londons, also won an MC in the Great War. Ronald was gazetted Second Lieutenant to 7 (Princess Royal's) Dragoon Guards on 4 August 1914, the very day that war broke out. He joined his regiment in France on 26 December 1915 and was posted to serve with 'B' Squadron. Seconded to the RFC on 29 September 1916, he gained his Royal Aero Club Certificate (Number 4271) on 24 February 1917. His formal training duly completed, he was confirmed and gazetted Flying Officer on 25 April following. Sent out to FE2b-equipped 11 Squadron on 3 June 1917. Flying with various Gunners, he gained nine victories between 12 July and 21 October 1917. Indeed, he gained three victories on the one day, 21 October 1917, when he and his Gunner/Observer, Corporal J Mason (Number 13911), from Everton, Liverpool, combined to shoot down one in flames and one out of control with the front gun and sent down another to crash with the rear gun. Mason, who also had other successes with other Pilots, was awarded the Military Medal, *London Gazette* of 19 November 1917. Mauduit's MC was announced in the *London Gazette* of 4 February 1918, the details appearing later in the *London Gazette* of 5 July 1918: 'For conspicuous gallantry and devotion to duty. He carried out a most valuable single machine reconnaissance at a height of 500 feet, searching enemy roads and railways, and obtaining important information. On another occasion, while on a photographic reconnaissance, he encountered twenty hostile scouts, and drove two of them down out of control. He has destroyed ten enemy machines and shown the greatest determination at his work'.

He finally left the RAF in 1919 to rejoin his regiment, 7 Dragoon Guards, and married Irene Helen in the same year. Ronald Mauduit died in Sialkot, India, on 13 March 1928.

MAWBEY, Lawrence Walter

The son of Mr and Mrs P C Mawbey of Acock's Green, Birmingham, he was born on 23 March 1899. Educated at Cambridge House School, Edgbaston. Gazetted Second Lieutenant to the RFC on 5 July 1917. His pilot training duly completed, he was confirmed and gazetted Flying Officer on 27 September following. Mawbey went on to serve with 'A' Flight, 1 Squadron, from 7 November 1917 to 8 June 1918, and was particularly active during the fraught and dangerous days of the great German spring offensive. His MC was announced in the *London Gazette* of 26 July 1918: 'For conspicuous gallantry and devotion to duty while engaged on low-flying and bombing attacks over the hostile lines, when, on many occasions, he dropped bombs on the enemy personnel, horses, transport camps and engaged enemy troops with his machine-gun fire from very low altitudes. At all times he displayed a fine fighting spirit and a determination to get to close quarters with his opponents which was deserving of the highest praise'.

Although he had intended to make a career in the RAF, he was, in fact, obliged to relinquish his commission due to ill-health on 8 January 1921.

NB: The RAF Museum Hendon has his MC, British War Medal 1914-20, and Victory Medal 1914-19 in its collection.

MAXWELL, Gerald Joseph Constable

The son of the Honourable Bernard Constable Maxwell (son of the 15th Baron Herries) and the Honourable Alice Fraser (daughter of the 13th Baron Lovat), he was born 8 September 1895. Educated at Downside College (1905-13). Gazetted Second Lieutenant to 1 Lovat Scouts (TF) on 29 August 1914, he served with the family regiment in Gallipoli and in Egypt, before securing a secondment to the RFC in September 1916. Possessing a natural flying talent, he received only 22 minutes of two-seater instruction before 'solo-ing' for the first time on 11 December 1916. His pilot training duly completed, he was confirmed and gazetted Flying Officer in March 1917. Sent to 56 Squadron (SE5s) then at London Colney, he accompanied that unit to France on 8 April 1917, as a member of Albert Ball's 'A' Flight. Maxwell achieved a remarkable 20 victories between 24 April 1917 (his first patrol) and 30 September 1917, being appointed Flight Commander on 26 July intervening.

His MC was announced in the *London Gazette* of 18 October 1917, details in the *Gazette* of 7 March 1918: 'For conspicuous gallantry and devotion to duty. He has taken part in 43 offensive patrols, in 14 of which he acted as leader. He has destroyed at least three enemy aircraft, and driven down nine others completely out of control. He has consistently shown great skill in aerial combats, and his fearlessness and fine offensive spirit have been a splendid example to others'.

His tour with '56' completed on 21 October 1917, he returned to the UK and was posted to instruct at the School of Aerial Fighting at Turnberry. He returned to the front and to 56 Squadron in the summer of 1918, and proceeded to add a further six victories to his 'score' between 16 June and 5 July. Maxwell was awarded a Distinguished Flying Cross in the *London Gazette* of 3 August 1918. He returned to an instructing role in the final months of the war and his outstanding services in this field were recognised by the award of an Air Force Cross in the Birthday Honours *London Gazette* of 3 June 1919. After leaving the RAF with the rank of Major in 1922, he embarked upon a career as a Broker in the London Stock Exchange. He married, in 1920, Carolyn Carden of Dallas, Texas, with whom he had two sons and four daughters (one of his sons being killed in the RAF in 1950). When the Second World War came in 1939, he returned to the RAF, attaining the rank of Wing Commander, Mentioned in Despatches and awarded the Air Efficiency Award. His appointments included a position in the 'Tactics' department of Fighter Command in 1940, before he went on to command the Night Fighter Station at Ford, Sussex, from 1941 to 1945. His younger brother, Michael, became an Ace in the Second World War. In civilian life Gerald Maxwell was appointed a Director of several Public Companies. He was elected Prime Warden to the Fishmongers Company in 1956 and 1957, and was Third Warden in 1958. The Queen appointed him Deputy Lieutenant to the City of Southampton in 1957. He was a member of the Royal Company of Archers (the Queen's Body Guard for Scotland). Maxwell's other honours included Knight of Malta and, as a devout Roman Catholic, he was made a Papal Chamberlain by Rome. He lived at Old Alresford House, Alresford, Hampshire. Gerald Maxwell died on 18 December 1959.

MAXWELL, Reginald Stuart

The son of Mr and Mrs J A Maxwell, of 8 Rosslyn Mansions, London NW6, he was born on 20 July 1894. Educated at Haileybury (1908-12). Gazetted Second Lieutenant to 8 Battalion, East Yorkshire Regiment, on 22 September 1914, before transferring to the Army Cyclist Corps in the following year. Gained his Royal Aero Club Certificate (Number 1375) on 30 June 1915 and was again transferred, this time to the RFC. His formal pilot training duly completed, he was confirmed and gazetted Flying Officer on 11 September 1915. Maxwell flew Home Defence sorties with 17 (Reserve) Squadron in the UK, before going on to, firstly, 25 Squadron and then to 20 Squadron, where he arrived in the summer of 1916. In December 1916, with, by then, four victories to his name, he was appointed to command the FE2b-equipped 18 Squadron. His MC was announced in the *London Gazette* of 1 January 1917 (no citation). Although no citation was published in the *Gazette*, research has unearthed the original recommendation for the award: 'R S Maxwell. Conspicuous gallantry and devotion to duty since February 1916, during which time he has fought some twenty combats in the air. By his keenness in his duties as a Flight Commander and by his courage in the air, he has set a fine example to all ranks in his squadron'.

Maxwell returned to the Home Establishment in March 1917, where he took up instructing and associated Staff duties. 'George' Maxwell married first, in 1917, Sylvia Marion Norton and secondly, in 1936, Margery Jackson. His next command came in 1918, taking over the Camel-equipped 54 Squadron. He accrued five more victories during the course of the last year of the war, and added a Distinguished Flying Cross to his decorations, *London Gazette* of 8 February 1919. Staying on in the RAF after the war, he served with 55 Squadron in the Middle East, including Mesopotamia and, when that country changed its name to Iraq, he received a Bar to his Distinguished Flying Cross, announced in the *London Gazette* of 28 October 1921. The main reason for this award was for his gallantry when, having landed in hostile territory due to engine failure, and after his attempts to remedy the fault under fire had failed, he took advantage of a rescue offer made by a colleague who had landed nearby. This could only be effected by him lying prone on the lower plane of the rescuing DH9a, whilst it took off and carried him to safety. His next command appointment was to 47 Squadron in Egypt from 1925 to 1927. Maxwell was awarded the Air Force Cross in April 1929. In 1931, he was promoted to Wing Commander and then, in 1936, he was appointed to command RAF Mildenhall with the rank of Group Captain. He finally retired from the RAF in 1941. Perhaps surprisingly, he was accepted into the Royal Navy (A) and served as a Commander from 1941 to 1945. Reginald Maxwell died in Sydney, Australia, on 1 July 1960.

MAXWELL-SCOTT, Thomas

From Edgecliffe, Sydney, New South Wales, Australia, he was born in Sydney on 10 October 1893. Educated at Brokesbury School, and at Sydney Grammar School. Although trained as an Architect and Surveyor, he worked, pre-war, on a sheep station. As a young Cadet, he had attended the Coronation of King George V in 1911, as part of the Australian contingent. When the war came in 1914, he volunteered for the Australian Imperial Force. With ambitions to join the flying service, he gained, at his own expense, his Royal Aero Club Certificate (Number 1603) on 17 August 1915. Accepted for the RFC, he was gazetted Second Lieutenant, via the Special Reserve, on 1 September 1915. His formal pilot training duly completed, he was gazetted Flying Officer on 4 November following. He served with the BE2c-equipped 4 Squadron in France, his MC announced in the *London Gazette* of 25 November 1916: 'For conspicuous gallantry in action. He carried out artillery reconnaissances with great courage and determination. Later, diving to a low altitude, he attacked an enemy communication trench with his machine-gun'.

Promoted to Major, Maxwell-Scott would go on to command 103 Squadron in the UK in 1917, 28 Squadron in Italy in 1918, and 119 Squadron in the UK in 1918 and 1919.

MAY, Clacy William Patrick

The son of William C and Edith A May, of 21 Wellington Road, Wanstead, Essex, he was born in 1896. Keen to join the flying service, he gained his Royal Aero Club Certificate (Number 1690) on 30 August 1915. Subsequently gazetted Second Lieutenant to 4 Battalion, Royal Irish Rifles, on 23 September 1915, he was almost immediately seconded to the RFC. His formal pilot training duly completed, he was confirmed and gazetted Flying Officer on 7 March 1916. Served in France with 1AD, from February 1916, transferring to 2AD, in the following March. On 25 June 1916, there was an orchestrated and concerted assault on the enemy's kite balloons along much of the front. Of the 23 enemy balloons that were up and observing on the day, 15 were attacked and six brought down. May, of 2AD, in a Nieuport Scout, was one of the successful Pilots. His MC was announced in the *London Gazette* of 27 July 1916: 'For conspicuous gallantry and skill. He dived low over the enemy lines under heavy fire to attack a kite balloon. He succeeded in hitting it and bringing it down to the ground in flames'.

May was hospitalised on 2 October 1916 and appears not have regained his fitness as he was forced to relinquish his commission, due to ill health, on 12 June 1918.

MAYBERY, Richard Aveline

The only son of Major H O Aveline Maybery and Mrs Lucy Powys Maybery, of The Priory, Brecon, Powys, he was born on 4 January 1896. Educated at Connaught House, Weymouth, at Wellington College (1908-12), Rugby XV, and at Sandhurst (Prize Cadetship), from where he passed out fifth. Gazetted Second Lieutenant to 21 (Empress of India's) Lancers on 17 September 1913. He joined his regiment in India and served there through much of the fighting on the Frontier, where, for a time, he was ADC to the commanding General. Maybery was dangerously wounded in the action at Shrabkadr on 15 September 1915. Once recovered from his wounds, he decided to apply for the flying service. He served briefly in India as an Observer with 31 Squadron, before being sent to RFC HQ, Egypt, where he completed his pilot training and was duly confirmed and gazetted Flying Officer on 26 May 1917. Sent to England in June, he accompanied 56 Squadron (SE5As) to France, when that unit returned to the Western Front for the second time on 5 July 1917. Just two days after arriving in France, Maybery brought down an Albatros DV, the first of an eventual 21 victories achieved by 19 December following. Widely acknowledged as an aggressive and skilful Scout Pilot of the first rank, he was, nevertheless, perhaps too brave and too reckless for his own good. The first of his two MCs was announced in the *London Gazette* of 26 September 1917, details in the *Gazette* of 9 January 1918: 'For conspicuous gallantry and devotion to duty. After attacking two aeroplanes in succession at very low altitudes, and inflicting considerable damage, he attacked and dispersed a number of mounted men and then attacked a goods train. He next attacked and shot down a hostile machine at 500 feet, and before returning attacked a passenger train. On numerous occasions he has attacked, single handed, large hostile formations and set a fine example by his gallantry and determination'.

The Bar to his MC came in the *London Gazette* of 17 December 1917, details in the *Gazette* of 23 April 1918: 'For conspicuous gallantry and devotion to duty as leader of offensive patrols for three months, during which he personally destroyed nine enemy aeroplanes and drove down three out of control. On one occasion, having lost his patrol, he attacked a formation of eight enemy aeroplanes. One was seen to crash and two others went down out of control, the formation being completely broken up'.

On 19 December 1917, Maybery in SE5A, 'B3585', achieved his 21st and last victory over Bourlon Wood, sending an Albatros DV down in flames. Minutes later, Maybery, was himself sent down, whether by Vizefeldwebel Artur Weber of Jasta 5 or by the anti-aircraft guns of K-Batterie Nr 108 is still a matter of conjecture. Maybery's SE5A certainly crashed to earth near to the battery's emplacement and Maybery's remains were buried with full military honours under the supervision of the Artillery Unit's Commanding Officer. Confirmation of his death was delivered in a note dropped by a German machine just a few days later. Richard Maybery's remains were eventually re-interred in Flesquires Hill British Cemetery, Nord, France.

McBAIN, William Robert Brown

Born in Shanghai, China. Gazetted Second Lieutenant to 'B' Battery, 13 County of London, 5 London Brigade, Royal Field Artillery (TF), on 20 August 1915. Seeking secondment to the flying service, he gained his Royal Aero Club Certificate (Number 1979) at the Ruffy Baumann School, Hendon, on 29 October 1915. Transferred to the RFC in May 1916, he trained formally as a Pilot and was duly confirmed and gazetted Flying Officer on 31 July following. Posted first to 43 Squadron in the UK, he was next sent overseas to the Middle East on 24 January 1917, arriving for duty with 17 Squadron on 11 February following. His promotion to Captain and Flight Commander on 26 July 1917 coincided with a posting to RFC HQ, Egypt. His MC was announced in the New Year *London Gazette* of 1 January 1918 (no citation). McBain served in Salonika with 47 Squadron from

January 1918 and with 150 Squadron from 11 April 1918. He was Mentioned in Despatches on three occasions during the Great War, *London Gazettes* of 11 June 1918, 14 August 1918 and 9 March 1919, all awarded for services in Salonika. The French, too, weighed in with the award of a Croix de Guerre, *London Gazette* of 21 September 1918. McBain returned to the UK on 9 March 1919, before finally leaving the RAF, via the Unemployed List, on 6 April 1919. The further award of an Air Force Cross, again for services in Salonika, was announced, post his retirement, in the Birthday Honours *London Gazette* of 3 June 1919. In later life, McBain was created OBE (Civil) in the *London Gazette* of 11 June 1966.

McCALL, Frederick Robert Gordon

From Vernon, British Columbia, Canada, he was born on 4 December 1896. Enlisted into 175 Overseas Battalion, Alberta Regiment, in February 1916. Crossed the Atlantic with the rank of Sergeant in October 1916. Gazetted Lieutenant to the Canadian Local Forces on 24 February 1917 and immediately sought secondment to the flying service. Once accepted, he trained as a Pilot and was duly gazetted Flying Officer on 22 November 1917. Sent out to the Western Front, he joined the RE8-equipped 13 Squadron in December 1917. Teaming up with Lieutenant F C Farrington (qv), the aggressive pair gained three victories even on these plodding reconnaissance machines between 6 January and 27 March 1918. His talents recognised, McCall was posted to the SE5As of 41 Squadron, where he found his niche. Yet another brilliant Canadian Pilot, he gained a further 32 victories before the end of the war. Remarkably, five of these victories came on a single day, 30 June 1918, four in the morning and another in the evening. Just two days earlier, he had achieved a 'quartet' against various types of German machines. His first MC, for services as a Reconnaissance Pilot with 13 Squadron, was announced in the *London Gazette* of 4 March 1918, details in the *Gazette* of 16 August 1918: 'For conspicuous gallantry and devotion to duty. While observing artillery fire he attacked an enemy scout and destroyed it. He has set a fine example of courage and determination on all occasions, and has rendered most valuable services'.

The Bar to his MC came in the *London Gazette* of 22 June 1918: 'For conspicuous gallantry and devotion to duty. Whilst engaged on photographic work, he observed a hostile scout, on which he dived and fired a burst from his machine-gun. The enemy machine went down in a steep dive out of control. On a later occasion he engaged two hostile two-seater planes which immediately turned East. Though a steady rate of fire was kept up against him, he continued the attack, during which the observer of one of the machines collapsed in the cockpit, other observers reporting that this machine crashed to earth in the enemy lines. He has always displayed the greatest gallantry and determination in carrying out his work, and has set a very high example to his squadron'.

The decorations he received continued to reflect his outstanding service, with a Distinguished Flying Cross and a Distinguished Service Order announced in the same *London Gazette* of 3 August 1918. He was also Mentioned in Despatches, *London Gazette* of 31 December 1918. McCall fell ill and was sent to recuperate first in England and then back home in Canada, by which time the war was over. Having returned to civilian life, McCall decided to make a career in aviation and entered upon a series of ventures ranging from stunt and exhibition flying to the carriage of freight and passengers. He formed his own company, McCall Aero Corporation Ltd, which enjoyed moderate success. When the Second World War came in 1939, he served again as a Squadron Leader in the RCAF. Frederick McCall died in Calgary on 2 January 1949.

McCALLUM, Kenneth Campbell

From Victoria, British Columbia, Canada, he was born on 11 July 1891. A pre-war volunteer, he served from 1912, with 8 Canadian Garrison Artillery, Victoria, whilst earning his living in real estate. Offering his full commitment as soon as the Great War came, he served initially with 1 Depot Battery, 1 Artillery Brigade, Canadian Artillery, from 2 September 1914. Interestingly, he was medically examined by Major John McCrae, CAMC, of later 'In Flanders Fields' fame. McCallum served with the CEF as a Gunner with 5 Canadian Garrison Artillery, before being picked out for a commission. Gazetted Second Lieutenant to 4 (Extra Reserve) Battalion, Argyll and Sutherland Highlanders, on 9 April 1915. Gained his Royal Aero Club Certificate (Number 3166) on 12 June 1916. Seconded to the RFC, he trained formally as a Pilot and was confirmed and gazetted Flying Officer on 16 July following. Sent out to 23 Squadron in France as a Scout Pilot on 18 November 1916, he flew Spad VIIs. On 6 April 1917, McCallum, in Spad VII, 'A6709', achieved 23 Squadron's first victory since the unit had been re-equipped with Spads. On 22 April following, he was escorting an 18 Squadron bombing raid when he ran into a formation of enemy Scouts. The citation for his MC, announced in the *London Gazette* of 18 July 1917, relates the circumstances: 'For conspicuous gallantry and devotion to duty. When engaged in escorting a formation of bombing machines, he attacked four hostile aircraft, bringing down two of them. While fighting these he was attacked by a large hostile formation which completely surrounded him. Although badly wounded in the foot he succeeded in effecting a safe landing behind our own lines'.

So severe was the injury to McCallum's right foot, caused by an explosive bullet, that it had to be amputated at the ankle. Later, a further four inches had to be cut off from his leg and he was fitted with an artificial lower limb. He was finally forced to relinquish his commission on being declared unfit for further service on 28 October 1918. Settling in the UK, Kenneth McCallum became a licensee in the pub trade after the war, running the Victoria Hotel in Wells Road, Holkham, Norfolk, from 1921, before moving to the Bell Hotel in Bridge Street, Thetford, Norfolk, in 1926.

McCHESNEY, Frederick William

Born in Buenos Aires, Argentina, on 26 September 1895, he lived, pre-war, with his father in South America. He worked as a locomotive draughtsman with Buenos Aires Railway Company, Argentina. Returning to the UK, he was gazetted Second Lieutenant to the RFC on 30 August 1917. His pilot training duly completed, he was confirmed and gazetted Flying Officer on 6 November 1917. Sent out to France and 4 Squadron (RE8s) on 30 December 1917. After six months with '4', he was promoted to A/Captain and sent to 10 Squadron (AWFK8s) as a Flight Commander. McChesney was wounded in action on 18 July 1918 and invalided back to the UK two days later. His MC was announced in the *London Gazette* of 16 September 1918: 'For conspicuous gallantry and devotion to duty. He succeeded in getting valuable photographs of the enemy's system, his machine being damaged by machine-gun fire from the trenches. On six occasions he carried out low reconnaissance flights, bringing back valuable information, though his machine was badly damaged by machine-gun fire from the ground'.

McChesney's wounds were sufficiently serious to force him to relinquish his commission, with the honorary rank of Captain on 21 December 1918. Frederick McChesney died in Buenos Aires in 1936.

McCLATCHIE, William Arthur

From Dublin, he was born on 21 February 1889. He worked as a Civil Servant with the Board of Ireland, Dublin, from July 1911 to September 1914. Gazetted Second Lieutenant to the RFC, via the Special List, on 5 August 1916. Gained his Royal Aero Club Certificate (Number 3839) on 14 November 1916. His formal training duly completed, he was confirmed and gazetted Flying Officer on 23 January 1917. Sent out to 43 Squadron (Sopwith Strutters) at the front, he was promoted to A/ Captain and Flight Commander in the following April. His MC was announced in the *London Gazette* of 26 September 1917, details in the *Gazette* of January 1918: 'For conspicuous gallantry and devotion to duty in aerial fighting and reconnaissances on many occasions. He has shown great dash and fearlessness in engaging enemy infantry and taking photographs at very low altitudes, on one occasion after inflicting heavy casualties bringing his machine back, although it was very badly shot about, and crossing the lines under very heavy fire at 200 feet. On another occasion he attacked a hostile machine and drove it down, and although attacked by three enemy scouts on his way back he successfully drove them off'.

On 13 September 1917, during the squadron's transition from Strutters to Camels, McClatchie was injured when he crashed his newly acquired Camel, 'B2352'. William McClatchie finally left the RAF, via the Unemployed List, on 11 February 1919.

McCLAUGHRY, Wilfred Ashton

The son of James and Charlotte McClaughry of 45 Melbourbe Street, North Adelaide, South Australia, he was born on 26 November 1894, in Knightsbridge, South Australia. Educated at Queen's College, North Adelaide, at Adelaide University, and at Adelaide School of Mines. He was articled to a law firm when he enlisted into the Light Horse Regiment in 1914. Picked out for a commission, he was gazetted Second Lieutenant to the AIF, on 16 January 1915, with an immediate attachment to 9 (Victoria and South Australia) Light Horse Regiment. He embarked at Melbourne on 12 February 1915, bound for the Middle East with 2 Reinforcement Group for 9 Light Horse Regiment, aboard the transport, SS *Armadale* (A26). McClaughry served in Gallipoli from 20 May to 11 August 1915 and was twice wounded in action. Having recovered in a Military Hospital in Egypt, he sought transfer to the RFC, gaining his Royal Aero Club Certificate (Number 2368) on 1 April 1916. His formal pilot training duly completed in the UK, he was confirmed and gazetted Flying Officer on 21 June following. Sent first to 50 HD Squadron, then at Dover, he flew day and night patrols against the Zeppelin raids over the south coast. Next, he was sent to 100 (Night Bombing) Squadron, accompanying that unit to France as a 'founder member' and Flight Commander on 28 March 1917. His MC was announced in the *London Gazette* of 18 July 1917: 'For conspicuous gallantry and devotion. On many occasions he has displayed the highest courage and skill in successfully bombing stations and trains, often at very low altitudes, and has always given a fine example of energy and determination.

He would, on 16 March 1918, receive his MC from the hands of the King at an investiture held at Buckingham Palace. From '100', he was posted to 2 Squadron, Australian Flying Corps, again as a Flight Commander. In 1918, McClaughry was promoted to A/Major, and appointed to the command of 4 Squadron, AFC, a position he continued to hold beyond the end of the war. A Distinguished Flying Cross came to him in the *London Gazette* of 2 November 1918 and a Distinguished Service Order in the *Gazette* of 8 February 1919. He was also Mentioned in Despatches on three occasions during the Great War. Returning to the UK on 1

December 1918, he was placed in command of 8 TS, AFC, six days later. A permanent commission in the RAF was offered and accepted, McClaughry next taking command of No 2 School of Navigation and Bomb Dropping on 20 February 1919. He married Angela, from St John's Wood, London, at this time. His subsequent honours and appointments included: CO, 8 (Bomber) Squadron, Iraq, Aden and Somaliland; Graduate of the Imperial Defence College and of the RAF Staff College; AOC, British Forces in Aden, 1936-38; Director of Training, Air Ministry, 1938-40; Group Captain in command of 109 Fighter Group in the early months of the Second World War; Group Captain in the Chief of Air Staff's Department, Air Ministry; CB, 1942; Air Vice-Marshal and AOC, Egypt from 1942. Air Vice-Marshal Wilfred McClaughry died on active service on 4 January 1943 and is buried in Heliopolis War Cemetery, Egypt.

NB: An odd situation exists in that Wilfred had an equally distinguished younger brother who also rose to high rank and distinction in the RAF, Air Vice-Marshal Edgar James Kingston-McCloughry, CB, CBE, DSO, DFC and Bar, AFRAeS, who insisted not only upon a 'double-barrelled' surname, but also upon spelling his last name with an 'o' rather than, as in Wilfred's case, with an 'a'. The reasons for these inconsistencies remain unclear.

McCLINTOCK, Ronald St Clair

Born on 13 June 1898, he was living and working in Ceylon when the war came in August 1914. Despite his extreme youth, he enlisted as a Rifleman (Number 2176) into the Ceylon Planters Rifles and arrived in Egypt with that unit on 17 November 1914. Almost immediately upon arrival, he was picked out as officer material and gazetted Second Lieutenant to 'A' Battery, 3 West Lancashire Brigade, Royal Field Artillery (TF), on 28 November 1914. After service in the Middle East with the RFA, he was seconded to the RFC at the end of 1915. His pilot training duly completed, he was confirmed and gazetted Flying Officer on 4 April 1916. McClintock served at the front with 64 Squadron (DH5s) before joining 3 Squadron (Camels) early in 1918. His MC was announced in the *London Gazette* of 22 June 1918: 'For conspicuous gallantry and devotion to duty. On one occasion he shot down two enemy machines, and on the following day he attacked and shot down a hostile two-seater machine at a height of 100 feet. He has led upwards of forty patrols and has performed much valuable work on low-flying reconnaissance and bombing patrols. As a flight commander he has been untiring in his care of personnel and machines, and as a patrol leader he has displayed the greatest courage and resource'. McClintock would be promoted to A/Major, and go on to command 3 Squadron before the end of the war.

McCONKEY, Thomas William

The son of Grain Merchant, Lewis J McConkey and Mrs McConkey, he was born on 23 May 1890, at Bradford, Ontario, Canada. Educated at Bradford High School. Obtained a position as a clerk with the Canadian Bank of Commerce in October 1912. He left his job in the Fort Rouge, Winnipeg, branch of the bank in December 1915 and was gazetted as a Lieutenant into 100 Winnipeg Grenadiers. After service with the CEF in the Manitoba Regiment, he was seconded to the RFC in January 1917 and trained as an Observer. Sent to France and the RE8s of 59 Squadron on 20 March 1917. On 11 May 1917, McConkey and his Pilot, Captain F D Pemberton, also from Canada, in RE8, 'A3472', were wounded in action when their machine was shot up in a fight with enemy aircraft. McConkey was awarded the MC for his part in this incident, *London Gazette* of 26 July 1917: 'For conspicuous gallantry and devotion to duty. He was attacked by several hostile machines and was wounded in three places. He continued to work his machine guns, driving off the hostile machines. His courage and determination undoubtedly saved his pilot and machine'.

The wounds he received were machine-gun bullets to the thigh, shoulder and face. In the following September, McConkey described the events of that day in a letter home: '....while photographing about 9,000 yards into Hunland, we were attacked by five Albatros Scouts which broke up our formation. My pilot, Captain Pemberton from BC manoeuvred the machine in a most excellent fashion, evading the five Huns as much as possible and giving me every opportunity to bring my Lewis gun into play. He received a spent bullet in the back, necessitating his spending a week in the casualty clearing station. I came off less fortunately, with four bullets in the right thigh, one in the shoulder and one in the face – all flesh wounds. At present I am spending a quiet holiday in Weybridge-on-the-Thames'. Following further service with various units in the UK, McConkey was demobilised on 24 January 1919, returning to work at the Canadian Bank of Commerce on 8 February 1919.

McCONNELL, Horace Lincoln Cyril

The son of the Reverend Charles James McConnell and Commissioner Beatrice H J McConnell, of Pylle Rectory, Pylle, Somerset, he was born on 10 June 1892. Educated at Lancing College (1907-1909). Gazetted Second Lieutenant to a battalion of Sappers and Miners, Indian Army Reserve of Officers, on 27 November 1914. Whilst serving in Mesopotamia, he was seconded to the RFC. After pilot training in Egypt, he was confirmed and gazetted Flying Officer on 19 July 1917 and posted for active service with 14 Squadron on the same day. He subsequently served in India, Egypt and Palestine. On 10 November 1917, McConnell volunteered to help in an attack on a single-span cantilever bridge over the Wadi es Surar which, if successful, would cut two branch lines to Jerusalem and Bathsheba. The plan called for him to follow Lieutenant Henry Hanmer down to 500 feet in their respective BE2e and drop two 100lb bombs each onto the bridge. In fact, not only was the bomb-load too much for the BEs, but there was nobody available with sufficient knowledge to properly fuse and arm them. The help of a young Gunner Officer was enlisted and, after he thought that he had managed to arm them correctly, the pair took-off. In the event, none of the bombs exploded and, furthermore, McConnell was brought down by ground fire over the target. Fortunately, Hanmer, although slightly wounded, escaped with his life. Horace McConnell, a prisoner of the Turks, died as a consequence of his wounds in a Damascus hospital 12 days later on 22 November 1917. He is buried in Damascus Commonwealth War Cemetery, Syria. The award of the MC was announced posthumously in the *London Gazette* of 11 April 1918 (no citation). There appears to be little doubt that the award was for his gallantry in the attack on the bridge at Wadi es Surar.

McCREARY, Frank Leonard

The younger son of Umbrella and Corset Warehouse Manager, Frederick L McCreary and Emmeline H McCreary, of 52 Somerset Road, Walthamstow, Essex, he was born on 8 September 1897. Educated at St Peter's School, Eaton Square, London. Gazetted Second Lieutenant to 10 (Reserve) Battalion, South Lancashire Regiment, on 12 May 1915. McCreary was sent to France for the first time in December 1916, detached to a battalion of the South Staffordshire Regiment. After services in the trenches, he was seconded to the RFC in May 1917. He trained as an Observer and was sent out to 6 Squadron (RE8s) as a Probationary in July 1917. His 'apprenticeship' satisfactorily completed, he was formally confirmed and gazetted Flying Officer (Observer) on 1 August following. On 15 September 1917, McCreary and his Pilot, Lieutenant G A S Nicholson, in RE8,

'A4630', narrowly escaped disaster when their machine was shot up and the fuel tank set on fire. They were forced to crashland, but emerged from the wreck unscathed. Ten days later, McCreary and his Pilot of the day, Lieutenant John Worstenholm, in RE8, 'A4216', were attacked in the air. Worstenholm, from Darlington, County Durham, was killed immediately and McCreary, although wounded himself, was forced to attempt to land the machine. He managed to get the 'Harry Tate' down to 200 feet, but then lost control, the machine spinning in to a heavy crash-landing. The impact added injuries to the wounds he had already received in the air but, despite this, he struggled his way to Headquarters to make his report, before collapsing. He was awarded the MC for his bravery in this action, *London Gazette* of 27 October 1917, details in the *Gazette* of 18 March 1918: 'For conspicuous gallantry and devotion to duty. When his machine was attacked by a hostile scout in a thick mist the pilot was killed instantly, and the machine started going down with the enemy machine still following. Though wounded in the hand he drove the enemy machine off with his machine-gun and got the machine under control. He brought it to within 200 feet of the ground when it crashed within a mile of his aerodrome. Although wounded and much shaken he proceeded to his corps headquarters and made his report. He showed great coolness and skill'.

McCreary appears not to have fully recovered from the wounds and injuries he received in his MC action. He was allowed to leave the RAF, via the Unemployed List, in January 1919.

McCRINDLE, John Ronald

The son of surgeon, Dr James R McCrindle and Elizabeth P McCrindle, of Southfield Road, Middlesborough, Yorkshire, he was born in 1895. Gazetted Second Lieutenant to 1/7 Battalion, Gordon Highlanders (Deeside Highland) (TF), on 26 August 1914. Gained his Royal Aero Club Certificate (Number 1056) on 28 January 1915. Securing a transfer to the RFC, he trained formally as a Pilot and was confirmed and gazetted Flying Officer on 14 May 1915. Sent out to 30 Squadron in Mesopotamia, he arrived for duty on 10 December 1915. For his efforts during the attempts to relieve the besieged garrison at Kut-al-Amara, McCrindle was Mentioned in Despatches in April 1916. His MC was announced in the *London Gazette* of 22 December 1916, general citation, 'for services in Mesopotamia'. His tour with '30' completed on 23 December 1916, McCrindle was posted to RFC HQ, Egypt.

McCUDDEN, James Thomas Byford VC

The third of the six children of Quarter Master Sergeant William T H McCudden, Royal Engineers, and Amelie Emma McCudden (née Byford), he was born on 28 March 1895, in Gillingham, Kent. Educated at the RE School, Brompton Barracks, Gillingham, Kent. Leaving school age 14, he briefly became a telegraph boy with the Post Office before enlisting as a boy entrant into the Royal Engineers on 26 April 1910. He went overseas for the first time, by then a trained Bugler, in 1911, being stationed with the Garrison at Gibralter. Returning to the UK in the following year, he immediately applied for transfer to the newly forming RFC. His wish was fulfilled in April 1913, when he became Number 892 Air Mechanic 2nd Class, J T B McCudden and was posted to Farnborough as an engine fitter. The two McCuddens, his brother Bill was also in the RFC, enjoyed varied and spasmodic flying experiences in the months leading to the outbreak of war. Once the war came, James travelled with the original RFC contingent to France on 12 August 1914 as a member of 3 Squadron, thus earning the 1914 Star.

As Corporal-in-Charge of engines, his task was to run and warm-up every engine of every machine, every day before dawn, so that they were always primed and ready for take-off. A promotion to Flight Sergeant and overall responsibility for the engines and motors of the squadron came on 1 April 1915. Tragically, his brother Bill was killed in an accident during take-off in a Bleriot monoplane on 2 May 1915. James began to fly on an occasional basis as a Gunner/Observer, and was eventually recommended for pilot training. The French awarded him the Croix de Guerre on 21 January 1916, the medal being pinned to his tunic by General Joffre himself at Lillers on the same day. He subsequently qualified as a First Class Pilot of the Military Wing, RFC, on 25 June 1916. Just 13 days later, he was posted back to France and the FE2b-equipped 20 Squadron, the first step in an extraordinary career that would see him becoming one of the leading British Aces of the Great War. After a brief spell with '20', he was transferred to the single-seater DH2s of 29 Squadron on 7 August 1916. On 6 September following, he achieved the first of his eventual total of 57 victories against an Albatros, over Gheluwe. The second of his many gallantry awards came in the form of a Military Medal, *London Gazette* of 1 October 1916, for his, 'gallantry, courage and dash'. Picked out for a commission, he was gazetted Second Lieutenant to the RFC on 1 January 1917, going on to win all of the gallantry awards open to British Army officers, two of them twice over. He left '29' with six victories in July 1917 for rest and recuperation at home. He was next posted to 66 Squadron in France, on attachment for a Fighting Instructors course. During this period, he managed two further victories as a 'guest' of 56 and 66 Squadrons respectively. His first MC was announced in the *London Gazette* of 12 March 1917: 'For conspicuous gallantry in action. He followed a hostile machine down to a height of 300 feet and drove it to the ground. He has shown marked skill on many previous occasions, and has destroyed two hostile machines and driven another one down out of control'.

His instructing course completed, he was posted, as a Flight Commander, to the newly arrived SE5s of 56 Squadron, with which unit his victories accumulated at an astonishing rate. One of his many significant combats came on 23 September 1917, when he witnessed Werner Voss' extraordinary last fight against overwhelming odds. The Bar to his MC came in the *London Gazette* of 27 October 1917, details in the *Gazette* of 18 March 1918: 'For conspicuous gallantry and devotion to duty. He took part in many offensive patrols, over thirty of which he led. He destroyed five enemy machines and drove down three others out of control. He showed the greatest gallantry, dash and skill'.

McCudden adopted almost a scientific approach to his air fighting and gunnery, taking great pains over the alignment of his guns and their sights. He was described by Geoffrey Bowman (qv), no mean hand himself, as a 'shooting genius'. He was awarded the Distinguished Service Order, announced in the *London Gazette* of 14 December 1917, to which was added a Bar in the *London Gazette* of 3 January 1918. He finally left '56' in March 1918, having amassed a total of 57 victories. McCudden arrived in England to be greeted by the news that his brother, John Anthony (qv), a Pilot with 84 Squadron, was reported 'Missing', later to be sadly confirmed as killed in action on 18 March 1918. As to how to mark James McCudden's remarkable achievements, there seemed no other accolade left to the authorities, other than the ultimate award itself. His Victoria Cross was announced in the *London Gazette* of 2 April 1918, the details of which, having taken some time to compile, appeared later: 'For conspicuous bravery, exceptional perseverance, and a very high devotion to duty. Captain McCudden has at the present time accounted for 54 enemy aeroplanes. Of these, 42 have been definitely destroyed, 19 of them on our side of the lines. Only 12 of the 54 have been driven out of control. On two occasions he has totally destroyed four two-seater enemy machines on the same day, and on the last occasion all four machines were destroyed in the space of one hour and thirty minutes. While in his present squadron he has participated in 78 offensive patrols, and in nearly every case has been the leader. On at least 30 other occasions, whilst with the same squadron, he has crossed the lines alone, either in pursuit or in quest of enemy machines. The following incidents are examples of the work he has done recently: On 23 December 1917, when leading his patrol, eight enemy machines were attacked between 2.30pm and 3.50pm. Of these, two were shot down by Captain McCudden in our lines. On the morning of the same day he left the ground at 10.50, and encountered four enemy aeroplanes; of these he shot down two. On 30 January 1918, he single-handed, attacked five enemy scouts, as a result of which, two were destroyed. On this occasion he only returned home when the enemy scouts had been driven far east; his Lewis gun ammunition was all finished, and the belt of his Vickers gun had broken. As a patrol leader, he has at all times shown the utmost gallantry and skill, not only in the manner in which he has attacked and destroyed the enemy, but in the way he has during several aerial fights protected the newer members of his flight, thus keeping down their casualties to a minimum. This officer is considered, by the record he has made, by his fearlessness, and by the great service he has rendered to his country, deserving of the very highest honour'.

After his leave, he was posted as an Instructor to Ayr in Scotland. By popular demand, he wrote his book around this time, handing the manuscript, hand-written in a number of service notebooks, to his publisher. Published after his death as, 'Five Years in the Royal Flying Corps', it also appeared later as, 'Flying Fury'. The Aero Club of America announced that their Medal of Honour and Merit was to be made to the newly promoted Major J T B McCudden. Sent out again to France, this time to command 60 Squadron, McCudden landed his SE5A, 'C1126', by mistake at 8 Squadron's aerodrome at Auxi-le-Château, on 9 July 1918. After making enquiries, he took off again and was at no more than 70 feet, when he appeared to attempt to turn back. The attempt failed and he flew full tilt into a small wood nearby. When rescuers reached him, he was still alive, but only just, his skull badly fractured. Carried to the near-by No 21 Casualty Clearing Station, he died there three hours after arriving. Major James McCudden, VC, is buried in Wavans British Cemetery, France.

McCUDDEN, John Anthony

The son of Sergeant Major William T H McCudden, Royal Engineers, and Amelie Emma McCudden (née Byford), and brother of James McCudden VC, he was born on 14 June 1897. Like his brothers, he joined the Royal Engineers as a Boy Entrant in 1912. When he was old enough, he was sent to France as a despatch rider in May 1916. No doubt using some family influence and connections, he was allowed to transfer to the RFC. After pilot training, he was given his 'Wings' and commissioned. In September 1917, he was sent out to 25 Squadron to fly DH4 bombers. He gained two victories in DH4s before, ever anxious to emulate his famous brother, he secured a transfer to SE5A-equipped 84 Squadron early in 1918. James considered his younger brother far too impetuous and tried hard to rein him in with sound and practical advice. Still, his aggressive brother gained six more victories with '84', between 30 January and 19 February 1918. On 18 March 1918, McCudden in SE5A, 'B172', fought his last battle with elements of the Red Baron's 'Flying Circus', JGI, over Busigny. He was shot down and killed by Leutnant Hans Joachin Wolff of Jasta 11, the first of the German Ace's eventual ten victories. J A McCudden's MC was announced posthumously in the *London Gazette* of 6 April 1918, details in the *Gazette* of 22 April 1918: 'While on patrol he attacked single-handed two enemy tri-planes, causing one to dive down steeply out of control and the other to crash to the ground. On the day previous to this he destroyed a hostile two-seater, besides which he has driven down one other machine, which was observed to be destroyed and four others completely out of control. He has always displayed great courage and determination'.

The McCudden parents would lose three sons and a son-in-law in the Great War, and Mrs McCudden would also lose her husband shortly after the war. J A McCudden is buried in St Souplet British Cemetery, France.

McDONALD, Ian Donald Roy

The son of Mr and Mrs Donald McDonald, of 57 Harvard Road, Gunnersbury, London W4, he was born in St John's, Antigua, British West Indies, on 9 September 1898. His father was a Member of the Legislative Council of the Leeward Islands in the British West Indies and hence he was brought up mainly in Antigua. Educated at King's College, Antigua, and at Denstone College (1913-16), where he was a member of the OTC. Entering the flying service as a Cadet late in 1916, he was gazetted Second Lieutenant to the RFC, via the Special List, on 27 February 1917. His pilot training duly completed, he was confirmed and gazetted Flying Officer on 26 April following. Sent out to 24 Squadron's 'A' Flight (DH5s) on 11 July, he achieved the first of his eventual 20 victories under the tutelage of Captain B P G Beanlands (qv), against an Albatros DIII, on 15 November 1917. Two further victories came in the DH5, before his squadron re-equipped with SE5As early in 1918. McDonald's squadron was opposed along a front stretching from Havrincourt to La Fère, by Jagdstraffel 12, led by the German Ace, Adolf von Tutschek. Still, despite the quality of his opponents, McDonald continued to accumulate successes and was promoted to A/Captain and Flight Commander, the youngest in the squadron, in March 1918. His dog, 'Jock', was adopted as the squadron mascot, and he had the words, Antigua B W I painted on the side of his SE5A. On his last flight over the Western Front on 17 June 1918, McDonald helped to force down into captivity, the 27 victories German Ace and Blue Max recipient, Leutnant Kurt Wusthoff. McDonald sent a stream of machine-gun bullets into Wusthoff and his machine and, along with squadron colleagues, Johnson and Barton, proceeded to shepherd the badly wounded Wusthoff down into the French lines. The French cut out Wusthoff's skull and crossbones motif from the canvas of his crashed Fokker DVII (2469/18), and duly presented it to McDonald, to his great delight. This was to be the last, albeit shared, of his 20 victories and he returned to the Home Establishment for a rest and less exacting duties. His understandably proud father wrote of his son's achievements in an article in the *New York Post*, entitled, 'He's 19, a Captain, and 'Did In' 20 Enemy Aircraft', it went on to relate a number of close shaves Ian had experienced. One example quoted was when, with his engine stalling, he was driven down to below 200 feet by enemy Scouts: 'I thought I was going to be taken prisoner and was dodging this way and that. The engine would give no power and then, in a most unaccountable way, it picked up without me doing anything....and we zoomed up'. The *New York Post* was delighted with the newly coined, 'zoomed', and thought it quite the best word, etymologically speaking, to have come out of the Great War. McDonald was awarded a Distinguished Flying Cross in the *London Gazette* of 2 July 1918, surprisingly in advance of his MC, which was announced later in the *London Gazette* of 16 September 1918: 'For conspicuous gallantry & devotion to duty. With seven scouts he attacked eighteen enemy machines, of which three were destroyed and one driven down completely out of control. When driven down to within 200 feet of the ground by two enemy machines owing to a choked engine, he turned on them and drove one down. He has in all destroyed eleven enemy aircraft and carried out valuable work in attacking enemy troops on the ground'.

After the war, he returned to live in Antigua, but life in 'paradise' soon palled and after a while he successfully applied for a permanent commission in the RAF. Following a period training new Pilots at Cranwell, he was sent overseas to 84 Squadron, then based at that perennial trouble-spot, Mesopotamia, soon to be re-named Iraq. On 22 September 1920, Flying Officer Charles Bocket-Pugh with, unusually, Ian McDonald acting his Observer, were shot down by ground fire whilst dropping supplies to HMS *Greenfly*, then stranded and under siege up the Samawahon River. The sailors on the British ship clearly saw McDonald swim from his crashed machine to the safety of the riverbank, only to be taken prisoner. It may have been better had he been killed in the crash. Days later, the Air Ministry revealed that they had received a report that he had been murdered at Dangatora. Ian McDonald's remains were never recovered, and hence he is commemorated on the Basra Memorial, Iraq.

NB: The RAF Museum Hendon has his medals in its collection: MC (engraved May 9, 1918*), Distinguished Flying Cross, British War Medal 1914-20, Victory Medal 1914-19* (Capt RAF), *and General Service Medal 1918-62, with clasp, Iraq* (F/O IDR McDonald, RAF).

McDOUGALL, Peter Aitken

The son of Major and Mrs McDougall, of Scallaway, Shetland Islands, he was born on 11 August 1898. After leaving school, he secured a position in the Union Bank of Scotland Ltd, working in the Lerwick branch of that organisation. When he was old enough, he enlisted as a Private soldier (Number 756043) into 28 London Regiment (Artists Rifles), a unit which was, in effect, an Officers Training Corps. Picked out for a commission, he was gazetted Second Lieutenant to the RFC on 21 June 1917. His pilot training duly completed, he was confirmed and gazetted Flying Officer on 22 August following. Sent out to the DH5-equipped 24 Squadron soon after he qualified, he was slightly wounded on 24 October 1917. Returning to duty, he achieved the first of his eventual seven victories, against an Albatros DIII, on 15 November 1917. His squadron re-equipped with SE5As early in 1918 and McDougall went on to gain a further six victories before being wounded in action on 12 March 1918. During a combat on that day, the propeller of his SE5A, 'B891', was shot off and his machine broke in half in the subsequent crash-landing. His MC was announced in the *London Gazette* of 13 May 1918: 'For conspicuous gallantry and devotion to duty. He always showed great initiative and skill in attacking enemy aircraft, and drove down or destroyed several enemy machines. On one occasion while on patrol he encountered three enemy two-seater machines, and though his engine was giving trouble he attacked them single-handed and drove one of them down out of control, having shot the observer. On another occasion, after driving down an enemy machine, he attacked and silenced a battery of six guns which were firing on our machines. His example of pluck and determination was of the utmost value to the squadron'.

Once recovered, McDougall was posted to 91 Squadron in the UK in November 1918. The Armistice intervened and neither he, nor '91', would go on to fly operationally in the Great War. Peter McDougall finally left the RAF, via the Unemployed List, on 29 April 1919.

McELROY, George Edward Henry

The son of Samuel McElroy, BA, Head Master of Donnybrook School, Dublin, and Ellen McElroy, he was born on 14 May 1893. George was of Scottish descent, his ancestors having migrated to the West of Ireland and settled near Boyle. One of his ancestors fought under General Wolfe at Quebec. Educated at the Educational Institution, Dundalk, and at Mountjoy School, Dublin. From school, he entered the Civil Service as a Second Division Clerk, serving first with the Inland Revenue and afterwards with the National Health Insurance Office, in Dublin. When war came in August 1914, he enlisted into the Royal Engineers and served as a despatch rider in France from 1 October 1914, thus earning a 1914 Star. Picked out for a commission, he was gazetted Second Lieutenant to the Royal Irish Regiment on 9 May 1915. Just one week later he was sent to 1 Battalion of his regiment, then in the trenches at Sanctuary Wood. Gassed later in the year, he was returned to the UK for treatment and convalescence. Once recovered, McElroy was posted to the Royal Irish Regimental Depot in Dublin. In April 1916, the Easter Rebellion broke out and McElroy was involved in the heavy street-to-street fighting before the insurrectionists were subdued. Deciding upon a career in the Army, he entered the Royal Military Academy at Woolwich, in pursuit of a permanent commission. A keen sportsman, he played at scrum-half in the Woolwich Rugby XV that defeated Sandhurst in November 1916. His course at Woolwich successfully completed, he was gazetted Second Lieutenant to the RGA in February 1917, with an immediate secondment to the RFC. His pilot training duly completed, he was confirmed and gazetted Flying Officer on 28 June 1917. His first operational posting came in September 1917, being sent to 40 Squadron (Nieuport Scouts) in France. His squadron was subsequently re-equipped with SE5As and McElroy achieved the first of an astonishing 47 victories against an LVG C on 28 December 1917. Nine further victories came with 40 Squadron, before he was promoted to A/Captain and Flight Commander and transferred to 24 Squadron in February 1918. The first of his MCs was announced in the *London Gazette* of 26 March 1918, details in the *Gazette* of 24 August 1918: 'For conspicuous gallantry and devotion to duty. He has shown a splendid offensive spirit in dealing with enemy aircraft. He destroyed at least two enemy machines and has always set a magnificent example of courage and initiative'.

A Bar to his MC followed in the *London Gazette* of 22 April 1918: 'When on offensive patrol, observing a hostile scout diving on one of our aeroplanes, he opened fire, and sent down the enemy machine in an irregular spin out of control, when it finally crashed completely. Later in the same day he sent down another enemy machine in flames. On another occasion, when on offensive patrol, he singled one out of four enemy machines, and sent it down crashing to earth. On the same day he attacked another enemy machine, and, after firing 200 rounds, it burst into flames. On a later occasion he opened fire on an enemy scout at 400 yards range, and finally sent it down in a slow spin out of control. In addition this officer has brought down two other enemy machines completely out of control, his skill and determination being most praiseworthy'.

These, the first two of his MCs, were no doubt awarded for his prowess and successes with 40 Squadron. As his victory total continued to accrue, so did his gallantry awards, with yet a second Bar to his MC coming in the *London Gazette* of 26 July 1918: 'For conspicuous gallantry and devotion to duty. While flying at 2,000 feet, he observed a patrol of five enemy aircraft patrolling behind the lines. After climbing into the clouds, he dived to the attack, shot down and crashed one of them. Later, observing a two-seater, he engaged and shot it down out of control. On another occasion he shot down an enemy scout which was attacking our positions with machine-gun fire. He has carried out most enterprising work in attacking enemy troops and transport and in the course of a month has shot down six enemy aircraft, which were seen to crash and five others out of control'.

McElroy, or 'McIrish' as he was known by his colleagues, was injured in a landing on 7 April 1918, crashing his machine into a tree, before afterwards returning to the Home Establishment for treatment and a brief rest. In June he returned again to 40 Squadron and proceeded to win two of the newly introduced Distinguished Flying Crosses, each announced posthumously in the *London Gazettes* of 3 August 1918 and 21 September 1918 respectively. On 31 July 1918, McElroy in SE5A, 'E1310', was patrolling alone when he was brought down in the vicinity of Armentières, possibly by Vizefeldwebel Gullman of Jasta 56. George McElroy is buried in Laventie Military Cemetery, France.

NB: The RAF Museum Hendon has his extraordinary group of medals in its collection: MC & two Bars, Distinguished Flying Cross & Bar, 1914 Star, British War Medal 1914-20, and Victory Medal 1914-19.

McEWEN, Basil Charles

The younger son of Mercantile Clerk, John P McEwen and Charlotte McEwen, of 1 North Brook Road, Lewisham, he was born on 27 October 1888. He was employed as a Science Professor in Hydrabad, India, from 1909 to 1915, when he returned to the UK to volunteer his services. Gained his Royal Aero Club Certificate (Number 1275) on 28 May 1915, the same day that he was gazetted Second Lieutenant to the RFC, via the Special Reserve. His formal pilot training duly completed, he was sent out to BE2c-equipped 16 Squadron on 30 September following. He served with '16' on reconnaissance duties, being promoted to A/Captain and Flight Commander on 13 February 1916, until June 1916, when he returned to the Home Establishment. His MC was announced in the Birthday Honours *London Gazette* of 3 June 1916 (no citation). Although no formal citation was published in the *Gazette*, research has unearthed the original recommendation for the award: 'For conspicuous gallantry and skill. 2/Lt (T/Captain) McEwen has done excellent work as a pilot and flight commander; notably on February 22nd 1916, he carried out an important three hours patrol, in snow and sleet, and under a very heavy fire'.

After rest and recuperation in the UK, McEwen served briefly again in France as CO, 55 Squadron, September-October 1916, and was again in France from 15 January 1917 until 19 February 1917, when he returned to the UK and administration duties. Left the service 2 August 1919.

NB: The RAF Museum Hendon has his single MC in its collection

McEWEN, Clifford Mackay

From Griswold, Manitoba, he was born on 2 July 1897. A graduate of the University of Saskatchewan, he joined the Canadian Army in 1916. Picked out for a commission, he was gazetted Lieutenant to the Canadian Local Forces on 28 April 1917. Transferring to the RFC in June 1917, he trained as a Pilot and was duly confirmed and gazetted Flying Officer on 19 October following. A 'founder member' of 28 Squadron (Sopwith Camels), he accompanied the unit to Italy, via a brief sojourn in France. An aggressive Fighter Pilot, he gained 27 victories over the Italian Front between 30 December 1917 and 4 October 1918. His MC was announced in the *London Gazette* of 16 September 1918: 'For conspicuous gallantry and devotion to duty in destroying six enemy aeroplanes. A most gallant pilot and patrol leader'.

He was also awarded one of the first newly instituted Distinguished Flying Crosses, *London Gazette* of 2 July 1918 and, later, a Bar to his Distinguished Flying Cross, *London Gazette* of 3 December 1918. The Italians, too, showed their appreciation of his skill and gallantry with the award of their Bronze Medaglia al Valore Militare, *London Gazette* of 2 November 1918. After the war, 'Black Mike', as he was known, returned to Canada and obtained a permanent commission in the newly formed Royal Canadian Air Force. By the time of the Second World War, McEwen had attained the rank of Air Vice-Marshal and served as AOC, 6 (RCAF) Bomber Group, the largest overseas formation in the RCAF. He was created CB for his services in this command. In 1948, McEwen was conferred with an Honorary Doctorate of Laws by his old alma mater, the University of Saskatchewan. Clifford McEwen died in Toronto on 6 August 1967 and is buried in Pointe Claire, Quebec. In a special ceremony held on 6 August 2003 at 15 Wing, RCAF, Airfield, at Moose Jaw, Saskatchewan, the aerodrome was dedicated to the memory of Air Vice- Marshal Clifford Mackay McEwen, CB, MC, DFC and Bar, and it was announced that, henceforth, it would be known as the Air Vice-Marshal C M McEwen Airfield.

McGLASHAN, Alan Fleming

The younger son of physician and surgeon, Captain James McGlashan, Royal Army Medical Corps, and Marian K McGlashan, of Newtown, Bedworth, Warwickshire, he was born in Nottingham on 22 June 1898. Educated at Epsom College (1910-16), Rugby XV, and, post-war, at Clare College, Cambridge, BA, and St George's Hospital. Accepted as a Cadet into the flying service in December 1916, he was duly gazetted Second Lieutenant to the RFC, via the Special List, on 13 April 1917. Gained his Royal Aero Club Certificate (Number 4639) on 13 May 1917, the same day that he was formally confirmed and gazetted Flying Officer. Served with 2 Squadron (AWFK8s) in 1917 until 21 May 1918, when he returned to the Home Establishment. McGlashan received a Croix de Guerre from the French, *London Gazette* of 17 August 1918, and was Mentioned in Despatches on two occasions during the Great War. His MC was announced in the *London Gazette* of 16 September 1918: 'For conspicuous gallantry and devotion to duty on contact patrol, reconnaissance, day and night bombing, and in aerial fighting, especially in dropping eighteen bombs on a village, from only 900 feet owing to bad weather, six days excellent photographic work during heavy fighting, frequent contact patrols resulting in good information, and also firing many rounds at the infantry on the ground from low altitudes. His work and example for ten months have been splendid'.

Posted as an Instructor to the School of Photography in the summer of 1918, McGlashan remained there until leaving the RAF, via the Unemployed List, on 22 July 1919. Continuing his education, he duly graduated MRCS and LRCP from St George's Hospital in London in 1924. While training at St George's, he worked as a drama critic for *The Observer* and *The News Chronicle.* He next worked briefly as a ship's surgeon on a tramp steamer, then as a general medical practitioner, before settling into a career as a consulting psychiatrist. For recreation, he took up ballooning and gliding. Awarded a DPM degree in 1940. On 2 March 1940, Alan's father, Dr James McGlashan, was killed whilst employed as a ship's doctor aboard the passenger ship, MV *Domala*. The *Domala* was bombed, but not sunk, by a Heinkel bomber in the English Channel, when bound for Calcutta via Antwerp. The Heinkel dropped four bombs on the ship before sweeping her decks with machine-gun fire, the combined effects of which caused heavy casualties amongst the passengers and crew. The ship's captain, Captain William A Fitt, and 99 others were killed. Alan McGlashan also wrote poetry, 'St George and the Dragon', 1931, and was author of 'The Savage and Beautiful Country' published in 1966. He served in the Second World War from 1939 to 1945, as a Major in the Royal Army Medical Corps and lived, post-the Second World War, at 16 Montpelier Square, London SW7. Predeceased by his first wife, Robin, his second wife, Sasha, was left a widow when he died on 6 May 1997.

McGOUN, David Mackay

From Montreal, Canada, he was born on 4 December 1892. After leaving school, he secured a position as a Clerk with the Bank of Montreal. A volunteer with the Westmount Rifles, he first went to France with 24 Battalion, CEF. After serving in the trenches, he volunteered for the flying service and was accepted as a Cadet in October 1916. Gazetted Second Lieutenant to the RFC on 27 February 1917. His pilot training duly completed, he was confirmed and gazetted Flying Officer on 11 July following. Sent out to BF2b-equipped 20 Squadron, he achieved five victories between 27 October 1917 and 17 February 1918. Promotion to A/Captain and Flight Commander, with a transfer to 22 Squadron (also Bristol Fighters) came in March 1918. Four more victories accrued to him during the hectic days of the German spring offensive. His MC was announced in the *London Gazette* of 26 July 1918: 'For conspicuous gallantry and devotion to duty as a leader of offensive patrols. It is entirely due to his determination and skill that his patrol has destroyed many enemy machines. His consistent keenness, his gallantry, and untiring energy have at all times set a magnificent example to all the pilots and observers in his squadron. He has personally destroyed many hostile machines, never hesitating to attack, and on all occasions displayed fighting spirit which has earned the admiration of all those in contact with him'.

His tour with '22' completed, he returned to the Home Establishment on 29 April 1918, where he was appointed to a series of instructing posts before returning to Canada on 21 August 1918. McGoun finally left the RAF, via the Unemployed List, on 29 April 1919.

McGREGOR, Douglas Urchart

From Waterdown, Ontario, Canada, he was born in March 1895. A student in 1916, he was commissioned Lieutenant into the Hamilton Militia, before being accepted as a candidate for the flying service. Crossing the Atlantic on the SS *Corsican*, on 25 September 1916, he was, after arriving in the UK, duly gazetted Second Lieutenant to the RFC on 10 October following. His pilot training completed, he was confirmed and gazetted Flying Officer on 28 February 1917. McGregor was first posted to France and 23 Squadron (Spads) in April 1917, going on to achieve 12 victories between 13 May and 26 September 1917. He was particularly adept in ground strafing attacks, notably a daring dawn raid on a German airfield on the morning of 6 June 1917. His MC was announced in the *London Gazette* of 26 September 1917, details in the *Gazette* of 9 January 1918: 'For conspicuous gallantry and devotion to duty in leading patrols against hostile formations. He has attacked and driven down enemy aircraft on several occasions, in spite of their being in superior numbers, displaying in every instance splendid dash and determination to get to close range'.

Promoted to A/Captain and Flight Commander in September 1917. His tour with '23' completed, McGregor returned to England on 5 October 1917, and was later sent home to Canada for duties as an Instructor. He studied medicine after the war, eventually becoming a well-known surgeon. Douglas McGregor died of a heart seizure in 1953.

McKAY, Evans Alexander

Born in Toronto, Canada, he was born on 3 May 1896. Educated at the James Collegiate Institute, Toronto (1910-14). Accepted as a candidate for the flying service whilst still in Canada, he crossed the Atlantic early in 1916. Gained his Royal Aero Club Certificate (Number 2870) on 9 May 1916, the same day that he was gazetted Second Lieutenant to the RFC, via the Special List. His formal pilot training duly completed, he was confirmed and gazetted Flying Officer on 21 June following. He was posted first to Farnborough for duties as a Ferry Pilot. In November 1916, he flew a Mr Williamson, a journalist with a Toronto newspaper, across the Channel to France. He also flew from London to Glasgow, a distance of 450 miles, in just four hours and twenty minutes. After a short rest, he returned to London, completing the return leg in four hours and ten minutes, quite remarkable times for those days. It was the following December before he was sent to the front and 6 Squadron, charged with artillery observation and reconnaissance duties. McKay was promoted to A/Captain and Flight Commander in June 1917, his MC being announced in the *London Gazette* of 16 August 1917: 'For conspicuous gallantry and devotion to duty in making valuable photographic reconnaissances under heavy hostile fire. His work whilst engaged on reconnaissance and patrolling has at all times shown a fine offensive spirit, notably in flying at low altitudes and engaging hostile troops with his machine gun'.

McKay subsequently served with 42 Squadron, before returning to the Home Establishment on 15 October 1917. He returned to France on 19 May 1918, this time as a Flight Commander and 'founder member' of 104 Squadron (DH9s), part of the recently formed 'Independent Force'. On 22 August 1918, McKay and his Observer, Lieutenant R A C Brie, in DH9, 'D2812', were forced to land in enemy territory after their machine was damaged during an aerial combat. Both crewmen were taken prisoner. The announcement of the award of a Distinguished Flying Cross to McKay, for leading a highly effective raid upon an enemy railway station, came in the *London Gazette* of 21 September 1918. Repatriated to the UK on 8 December 1918, he was finally demobilised and able to return to Canada on 7 March 1919.

McKEEVER, Andrew Edward

From Listowel, Ontario, he was born on 21 August 1895. Educated at the Central College, Toronto. When the war came he left his job as a bank clerk and enlisted into the Queen's Own Rifles of Canada. Served in the trenches with the CEF, gaining a reputation as a expert marksman. After volunteering for the flying service, he was gazetted Second Lieutenant to the RFC on 5 December 1916. His formal pilot training duly completed, he was confirmed and gazetted Flying Officer 19 April 1917. Sent out to 11 Squadron in May 1917, just as the unit was being re-equipped with the BF2b, which was, to say the least, providential, as he was to become the leading Brisfit Ace of the Great War. His first successes came on 26 June 1917, when he sent down two Albatroses DVs on the same day. He was successful with a number of Observers but worked best with Second Lieutenant L A Powell (qv), with whom he shared 17 victories. The first of McKeever's MCs was announced in the *London Gazette* of 17 September 1917: 'For conspicuous gallantry and devotion to duty, particularly when on offensive patrol. He attacked eight enemy aircraft single-handed at close range, and by his splendid dash and determination destroyed one and drove five down completely out of control. He has previously shown exceptional fearlessness in attacking the enemy when in superior numbers, and in the space of three weeks he destroyed eight hostile machines, setting a fine example to his squadron'.

The Bar to his MC came in the *London Gazette* of 27 October 1917, details in the *Gazette* of 18 March 1918 : 'For conspicuous gallantry and devotion to duty in aerial combats. He has recently destroyed five enemy aeroplanes and driven down six out of control. On one occasion he encountered five enemy scouts and drove two down out of control. Later, when leading a patrol, he engaged nine enemy scouts. He destroyed two, drove down one out of control, and dispersed the remainder. His dash and determination have been a fine example to his squadron'.

McKeever fought the enemy for the last time on 30 November 1917 and gained, with Second Lieutenant L A Powell, no less than four victories on that one day. His victory total now standing at 30, McKeever returned to the Home Establishment, where he was appointed to a number of instructing posts, before being sent to Canada to continue this work. Mentioned in Despatches, *London Gazette* of 20 May 1918. His outstanding achievements were further acknowledged when he was awarded the Distinguished Service Order, announced in the *London Gazette* of 4 February 1918, details in the *Gazette* of 5 July 1918. Once in Canada, he assisted Lieutenant Colonel W A Bishop, VC, in the organising of the newly evolving Royal Canadian Air Force and was appointed as the first Commanding Officer of the Sopwith Dolphin-equipped 1 Squadron, RCAF. Perhaps surprisingly, he left the RCAF in 1919, to take up the offer of a position as an aerodrome manager of the Mineola Field in the USA. On 3 September 1919, he was badly injured in an automobile accident. Despite the best of care, he died on the following Christmas Day and is buried in his hometown of Listowel, Ontario.

McKENZIE, Robert William

From Adelaide, Victoria, Australia, he was born in June 1895. A chemist by training, he volunteered for the Australian Army Medical Corps in 1914. After service in the Middle East, he sought transfer to the Australian Flying Corps, which came on 2 December 1916. His pilot training duly completed, he was gazetted Lieutenant and Pilot, AFC, on 24 April 1917. McKenzie first served with 41 Squadron as an Observer, before joining 68 Squadron (DH5s), in September 1917. He gained his first victory against an Albatros DV on 1 December 1917. 68 Squadron was re-designated as 2 Squadron, AFC, and equipped with SE5As in January 1918. McKenzie went on to achieve five further victories between 19 February and 23 March 1918. His MC was announced in the *London Gazette* of 13 May 1918: 'For conspicuous gallantry and devotion to duty. As a result of engaging hostile aircraft during four months, he on four occasions has destroyed a total of four hostile machines. He has also carried out numerous low-flying reconnaissances, in which he has bombed and engaged with machine-gun fire enemy formations. He has at all times displayed marked determination and devotion to duty'. McKenzie left the service in 1919, returning to Australia. He died in a boating accident in 1945.

McLEAN, James Younger

The son of the Reverend D McLean and Mrs McLean of Ramsay Lodge, The Mound, Edinburgh, he was born on 17 August 1889. Educated at Edinburgh Academy (1903-08) and at Edinburgh University (1909-1912), where he was a member of the OTC. Gazetted Second Lieutenant to the Royal Field Artillery, 4 Northumberland Brigade (TF) on 8 October 1914. Transferring to the Balloon Section, RFC, he served in France in 1915 and 1916. Gazetted Flight Commander on 5 December 1916, he commanded 22 BC in Salonika in 1917. He was Mentioned in Despatches in July 1915 and again in November 1917. His MC was announced in the *London Gazette* of 1 January 1918 (no citation). He was demobilised in 1919 and went into the brewing industry.James McLean married in 1921, Roberta Catherine Proctor of Alloa, setting up home at Bedford House, in that Scottish town.

McLEAN, Louden James

The son of L F McLean, CIE, and Mrs McLean, of Ealing, London, he was born on 1 February 1893. Educated at Fettes (1907-09), at the Royal Military Academy, Woolwich, and later at Cambridge University, from where he graduated BA in 1927. His elder brother, Lachlan Loudon McLean, served in the Gurkhas and in the RFC/RAF. Loudon was gazetted Second Lieutenant to 57 Field Company, Royal Engineers, on 1 April 1914. He served with the Royal Engineers in the first weeks of the war, thus earning the 1914 Star. The first of his two MCs was won for gallantry whilst supervising the erection of a bridge across the Yser Canal, near to Boesinghe, under heavy fire during the nights of 25 to 31 August 1915 and was announced in the *London Gazette* of 2 October 1915. Anxious to join the flying service, he gained his Royal Aero Club Certificate (Number 4376) on 13 March 1917. Accepted for formal pilot training, he duly qualified and was confirmed and gazetted Flying Officer on 6 May following. Sent out to 41 Squadron (FE8s) in France soon after qualifying. '41' was re-equipped with DH5s in July 1917 and re-equipped with SE5As in the following November, by which time McLean had been promoted to Captain and Flight Commander. Employing the SE5A to considerable effect, he proceeded to achieve five victories and the status of Ace between 29 November 1917 and 13 February 1918. His tour with '41' completed, he returned to the Home Establishment in February 1918. The Bar to his MC was announced in the same month, *London Gazette* of 4 February 1918: 'For conspicuous gallantry and devotion to duty. While leading a patrol he attacked and drove down an enemy two-seater machine and destroyed an enemy scout. He showed the greatest determination in leading patrols and splendid coolness and courage, most of his work being done under very difficult conditions'.

McLean was also Mentioned in Despatches on one occasion during the Great War. Staying on in the RAF after the war, he served with 85 Squadron in December 1918, and subsequently with 43 Squadron. He attained the rank of Squadron Leader in 1927, the same year that he graduated BA at Cambridge. In 1932 he was appointed to instruct at No 1 School of Tactical Training, at Halton Camp, Buckinghamshire.

McLEAN, William Elser

From Belfast, he was born on 25 September 1892. His family later moved to Wolverhampton and he was educated at the Grammar School in that town. After leaving school, he trained as a motor engineer. McLean enlisted as a Trooper (Number 3405) in 2 Life Guards in October 1914. After service with the Life Guards in France, he entered the flying service as a Cadet in April 1917 and was subsequently gazetted Second Lieutenant to the RFC on 30 August 1917. Having trained as an Observer, he was sent out to 42 Squadron (RE8s) as a Probationary in the October following. Served with '42' in Italy, from November 1917 to March 1918, when the unit returned to France and the Western Front, just in time to confront the great German spring offensive. He was wounded in action on 13 April 1918, sustaining a skull fracture and a flesh bullet wound to the right hand, and invalided home to the UK four days later. His MC was announced in the *London Gazette* of 26 July 1918: 'For conspicuous gallantry and devotion to duty. During recent operations this officer carried a contact patrol in a thick mist at a height of only 150 feet under heavy machine-gun and rifle fire, and flew daily during the misty weather at low altitudes, bringing back much useful information about the enemy, and harassing them with machine-gun and bombs. It was greatly due to his magnificent work that headquarters were kept informed of the enemy's movements during the difficult phases of the battle. By his gallant and cheerful spirit at a time when the squadron was suffering heavy casualties he set a splendid example to the others'.

William McLean finally left the RAF, via the Unemployed List, in July 1919.

McNAUGHTON, Norman George

The son of barrister, D Norman McNaughton and his wife, Christina, of 4 Grenville Place, Cornwall Gardens, South Kensington, London, he was born in May 1890. Educated at Loretto School (1904-09). After leaving Loretto, he secured a position on a cattle ranch in the Argentine. One of the many British Latin American Volunteers, he returned to the UK to offer his services. Gazetted Second Lieutenant to the RFC, via the Special Reserve, on 21 July 1915, the same day that he gained his Royal Aero Club Certificate (Number 1453). His formal pilot training duly completed, he was confirmed and gazetted Flying Officer on 1 December following. McNaughton accompanied FE2b-equipped 20 Squadron to France as a 'founder member' on 14 January 1916. On 21 April 1916, McNaughton and his Observer/Gunner of the day, 1 AM S Catton, in FE2b, '6332', were attacked by two enemy machines over Zonnebeke. Catton was unscathed in the engagement, but McNaughton was wounded in the leg. Despite his wound, still McNaughton managed to land his machine at Abeele without further mishap. Once recovered, he returned to the front with FE2d-equipped 57 Squadron as an A/Captain and Flight Commander. With '57', a fighter/reconnaissance unit, he went on to account for five hostiles, including two out-of-controls between Gommecourt and Sailly on 4 March 1917 and, on 29 April 1917, one destroyed over Noyelles, the unfortunate enemy Pilot falling from his machine. His MC was announced in the *London Gazette* of 1 June 1917: 'For conspicuous gallantry and devotion to duty when acting as a patrol leader in numerous combats. On one occasion he led his formation against an enemy patrol and himself drove down two hostile machines. He has set a fine example of courage and skilful leadership'.

On 24 June 1917, McNaughton and his Observer of the day, Lieutenant Angus H Mearns from Montrose, in one of the newly acquired DH4s, 'A7473', had the extreme misfortune to fall under the guns of Baron Manfred von Richthofen of JG1, becoming the 55th of the Red Baron's eventual 80 victories. Their remains were never found and, hence, they are both commemorated on the Flying Services Memorial, Arras.

McPHERSON, Gilbert

From Paisley, Scotland, he was born on 27 November 1898. Gained his Royal Aero Club Certificate (Number 3339) at his own expense on 11 August 1916 and was, as a consequence, admitted as a Cadet into the RFC. Subsequently gazetted Second Lieutenant on 27 February 1917. His formal pilot training duly completed, he was confirmed and gazetted Flying Officer on 10 May following. Sent out 35 Squadron (AWFK8s) on 24 May 1917. On 17 February 1918, McPherson and his Observer, Second Lieutenant D F Hurr (qv), were sent on a special reconnaissance from which they were extremely fortunate to return, Hurr being wounded in the incident. Both men would receive the MC for their gallantry. Not uniquely, there is obvious confusion between the formally published citations. McPherson's MC, like Hurr's, was announced in the *London Gazette* of 22 April 1918: McPherson's citation, obviously intended for Hurr's award, reads: 'For conspicuous gallantry and devotion to duty. While acting as Observer on a special reconnaissance, he assisted in driving off an enemy aeroplane when his machine was at 5,000 feet above his objective. Having descended to within 1,000 feet off the ground, he was wounded in the head from machine-gun fire, and collapsed. During the period when his pilot was descending still further to within 400 feet of the ground, he revived, and rendered further assistance in the reconnaissance, and on returning to his aerodrome was able to make his report. He has at all times displayed the utmost disregard of danger and great devotion to duty'.

Conversely, Hurr's citation was intended for McPherson's award: 'For conspicuous gallantry and devotion to duty. While he was on a special reconnaissance his machine was attacked when he was at a height of 5,000 feet over his objective by enemy aeroplanes, which he succeeded in driving off. Having descended to within 1,000 feet of the ground, he was heavily engaged by machine-gun fire, which wounded his Observer, who collapsed. He then descended to within 400 feet of the ground and completed a comprehensive reconnaissance. He has at all times displayed the utmost disregard of danger and great devotion to duty'.

His tour with '35' completed, he returned to the Home Establishment on 26 April 1918. Next, he was posted as an Instructor to the School of Special Flying on 1 July following, where he saw out the remainder of the war. He was Mentioned in Despatches, *London Gazette* of 22 January 1919, for his services as an Instructor. McPherson finally left the RAF, via the Unemployed List, on 14 April 1919.

MEAD, John

A Technical, not a flying, award

The older of the two sons of Farm Foreman, George Mead and his wife, Elizabeth, of Grange Dairy House, Steeple Entire, Dorset, he was born in South Tyneham, Dorset, on 1 June 1885. He enlisted into the newly formed RFC (Number 270) on 18 July 1912, being attached to 2 Squadron. Promoted to Sergeant, he gained his Royal Aero Club Certificate (Number 475) in a Maurice Farman at Montrose on 2 May 1913. Crossing to France with the original RFC contingent, he served in the Aircraft Park from 16 August 1914, thus earning the 1914 Star. Promoted to Sergeant Major (Warrant Officer, Class 1), he was Mentioned in Despatches for his work, *London Gazette* of 22 June 1915. He was next gazetted Lieutenant Quartermaster (Equipment Officer), via the Special Lists, on 13 August 1915. A hard working 'back-room boy', he organised the maintenance of the RFC's aeroplanes throughout the Battle of the Somme in 1916. His MC was announced in the New Year *London Gazette* of 1 January 1917 (no citation). Although no formal citation was published in the *Gazette*, research has unearthed the original recommendation for the award: 'J Mead. Honorary Lt & Qr Mr, T/Maj. Has commanded the Aircraft Repair Section, 2 Air Depot since 16 Apl 1916, and is responsible for repairing aeroplanes damaged during the battle on the Somme. Besides continuing his work by day, he has worked through many nights in order to get machines ready for issue. His work under high pressure is of an excellently high quality, and it is due in no small degree to his capacity for work that squadrons at the front have been supplied'.

Mead also received a second Mention in Despatches for his work, this one a direct recommendation from Major General Trenchard, himself: '15 March 1916. A most valuable technical officer who has been employed for six months in the Aeroplane Repair Section. He possesses technical knowledge of a high order. His work often necessitates long hours, but it is invariably characterised by energy and thoroughness'.

Mead was promoted to Major (Technical), when the RAF came into being on 1 April 1918. Staying on after the war, he was further promoted to Wing Commander in 1921 and was created CBE. John Mead eventually retired from the RAF on 14 March 1923.

MEALING, Maurice Edmund

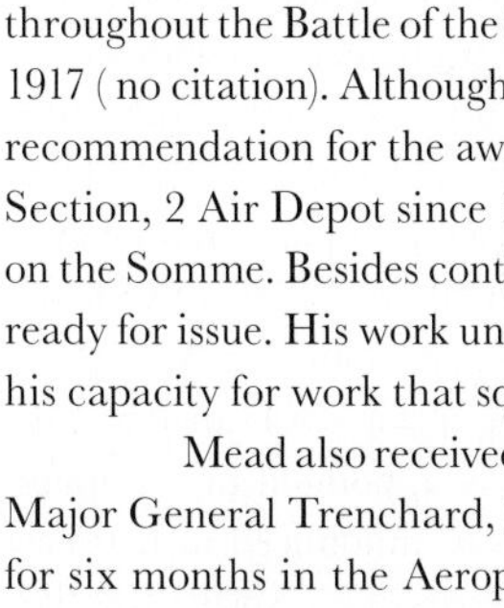

The son of Arthur and Rosa Mealing, of 143 Abercrombie Avenue, Higher Wycombe, Buckinghamshire, he was born on 21 July 1893. Gazetted Second Lieutenant to a Regular Army battalion of the King's Shropshire Light Infantry on 7 May 1916. Seconded to the RFC, he trained as an Observer and was sent out to BE2e-equipped 15 Squadron as a Probationary on 1 August 1916. His 'apprenticeship' satisfactorily and quickly completed, he was confirmed and gazetted Flying Officer (Observer) just six days later. On 2 April 1917, Mealing and his Pilot of the day, Second Lieutenant J H de Conway, in BE2e, 'A3161', narrowly escaped disaster when their machine was hit by anti-aircraft fire and they were forced to crash land. In May 1917, Mealing was sent back to the UK to train as a Pilot, returning to France in this new capacity to join 56 Squadron (SE5As) on 18 October following. After a somewhat slow start, he achieved the first of what proved to be a total of 14 victories on 30 November 1917. On 24 March 1918, three days into the German spring offensive, Mealing in SE5A, 'B182', had just gained his 14th victory and was in pursuit of another in the form of a German two-seater, when he was brought down. Quite what brought him down, either ground fire or, indeed, the machine gun of the FAb245 two-seater he was chasing, is unclear. The abiding mystery is that despite Mealing being spotted by an airborne squadron colleague waving merrily alongside his grounded SE5A, he then disappeared, never to be seen again. Perhaps he was caught up in the advance of the German infantry, still rampant and unchecked at that time. His MC was posthumously announced in the *London Gazette* of 13 May

1918: 'For conspicuous gallantry and devotion to duty in aerial fighting. He destroyed three enemy machines and drove three down out of control. He also drove down an enemy balloon in flames. He always showed a splendid spirit of courage, keenness and determination'.

Maurice Mealing's remains were never recovered and hence he is commemorated on the Flying Services Memorial to the Missing, Arras, France.

MEDHURST, Charles Edward Hastings

The second son of the Reverend C E Medhurst and Mrs Medhurst, of Collingham, he was born on 12 December 1896. Educated at St Peter's, York, at Rossall, and at Sandhurst. Gazetted Second Lieutenant to a Regular Army battalion of the Royal Inniskilling Fusiliers on 16 June 1915, with an almost immediate secondment to the RFC. Gained his Royal Aero Club Certificate (Number 1437) on 13 July 1915. His formal pilot training duly completed, he was confirmed and gazetted Flying Officer on 20 August following. Sent out to BE2c-equipped 13 Squadron soon after qualifying, he survived a forced and heavy landing in BE2c, '4079', after being shot up over Peronne on 8 December 1915. Medhurst was promoted to A/Captain and Flight Commander on 16 April 1916 and, following service in France in 1915 and 1916, he was sent out to Egypt and was eventually appointed to command 14 Squadron in Palestine in October 1917. His MC was announced in the New Year *London Gazette* of 1 January 1918, details in the *Gazette* of 25 April 1918: 'For conspicuous gallantry and devotion to duty. He successfully bombed from a low altitude batteries which were in action and silenced their fire'.

Medhurst was Mentioned in Despatches at this time and was also created an OBE, *London Gazette* of 1 January1919. He married, in 1919, Christobel Elizabeth Guy, with whom he had one son (Flying Officer (Pilot) Richard Edward Hastings Medhurst, 271 Squadron, RAFVR, who was killed in action age 19, on 19 September 1944, and is buried in Arnhem Oosterbeek War Cemetery, Holland) and two daughters. Staying on in the RAF after the war, he served again in Palestine and in Egypt in 1919 and 1920. His many honours, appointments and promotions during a long and distinguished career included: psa, 1926; idc, 1929; served Iraq, 1926-28; Instructor RAF Staff College, 1931-33; Deputy Director of Intelligence, 1934-37; Air Attaché in Rome, in Berne and in Athens, 1937-40; Assistant Chief of Air Staff (Intelligence), 1941; Assistant Chief of Air Staff (Policy), 1942; CB, 1942; Commandant RAF Staff College, 1943-44; KCB, 1945; Air Commander-in-Chief RAF, Mediterranean Middle-East, 1945-48; retired 1950. Air Chief Marshal Sir Charles Medhurst died on 18 October 1954, at the Lymington Hospital, Hampshire.

NB: His medals were offered for sale by C J & A J Dixon in 2004: Order of the Bath (Military Division, second class KCB, neck badge and breast star), OBE (first type, Brittania in obverse centre), Military Cross, 1914-15 Star (2Lt R Innis Fus), *British War Medal 1914-20, Victory Medal 1914-19 with MID* (Major RAF), *General Service Medal 1918-62 (GV), with two clasps, Southern Desert, Iraq, Palestine* (S/L RAF), *1939-45 Star, Africa Star 1940-43, Defence Medal 1939-45, War Medal 1939-45, Coronation Medal 1937, King Feisal War Medal (Iraq), and Legion of Merit (USA, Commander, neck badge in gilt and enamels).*

MEGGITT, William Geoffrey

From Monmouthshire, he was born in 1894. Gazetted Second Lieutenant to 3 (Reserve) Battalion, Welsh Regiment, on 31 March 1915. He was attached to and served with, the Monmouthshire Regiment, before securing a secondment to the RFC. Meggitt trained as an Observer and was sent out to FE2b-equipped 25 Squadron as a Probationary in September 1916. Flying with various Pilots, he achieved four victories between 22 October 1916 and 15 February 1917. His 'apprenticeship' more than satisfactorily completed, he was confirmed and gazetted Flying Officer (Observer) on the intervening 28 October 1916. His MC was announced in the *London Gazette* of 17 April 1917: 'For conspicuous gallantry and devotion to duty whilst one of a patrol engaging five hostile machines. He drove down one enemy machine and then attacked another, which was seen to go down vertically. He has previously brought down three hostile machines'.

Returning to the UK, he trained as a Pilot, going back to France in that new capacity to join 22 Squadron, a Bristol Fighter unit, in September 1917. He claimed two further victories on 10 and 11 October 1917, with Captain F A Durrad, Army Service Corps attached RFC, acting as his Observer, before he and Durrad were themselves shot down on 8 November 1917. On offensive patrol above Moorslede, their BF2b, 'B1123', was sent spinning down out of control by Leutnant Heinrich Bongartz of Jasta 36, the 21st of the German Ace's eventual 33 victories. Francis Durrad, from Oadby, was killed, Meggitt wounded and taken prisoner. Meggitt was subsequently repatriated on 2 June 1918, long before the end of the war, presumably because of poor health He stayed on in the RAF after the war and, by 1931, was a Flight Lieutenant and living with his wife, Lydia Bertha Elizabeth, at 171 Everine Road, Stoke Newington, Middlesex. He died in Croydon General Hospital on 28 January 1927 from injuries sustained in an aeroplane accident.

MEINTJES, Henry

From Colesburg, South Africa, he was born on 25 December 1892. Travelling to the UK at his own expense, he was gazetted Second Lieutenant to the RFC, via the Special Lists, on 8 November 1915. Gained his Royal Aero Club Certificate (Number 2385) on 2 January 1916. His formal pilot training duly completed, he was confirmed and gazetted Flying Officer on 17 May following. Sent out to 60 Squadron, he flew Nieuport Scouts to some effect, achieving four victories between 22 October 1916 and 29 January 1917. His MC was announced in the Birthday Honours *London Gazette* of 4 June 1917 (no citation). Although no formal citation appeared in the *Gazette*, research has unearthed the original recommendation for the award: '4 March 1917, 3/Brigade HQ, RFC: For continuous good work in attacking hostile machines in which he has had considerable success. He has always shown great determination and frequently descended to very low altitudes over the enemy's lines'.

In April 1917, 'Duke' Meintjes was promoted to A/Captain and sent out again to France as a Flight Commander and 'founder member' of the SE5-equipped 56 Squadron. He had added four further victories to his credit when, on 7 May 1917, in SE5, 'A8900', during the same evening patrol when the peerless Albert Ball was killed, he was wounded in the wrist by machine-gun fire from a Jasta 11 Albatros DIII. After recovering from his wounds, he was sent next as an Instructor to the CFS, then under the command his old 60 Squadron CO, Jack Scott (qv). For his outstanding work in this capacity, Meintjes was subsequently awarded the Air Force Cross, *London Gazette* of 3 June 1919. Returning to South Africa after the war, he later served with the South Africa Air Force, attaining the rank of Major.

MENENDEZ, Frank Tremar Silby

From Midford, Bath, he was born on 26 January 1896. Educated at Wycliffe School and at Cambridge. He interrupted his studies at Cambridge to volunteer his services and was gazetted Second Lieutenant to 11 (Reserve) Battalion, York and Lancaster Regiment, on 19 March 1915. Transferring to the Gloucestershire Regiment in September 1915, he served in the trenches with that unit until allowed a secondment to the RFC in May 1917, having already attained the rank of A/Captain. He trained as an Observer and was duly confirmed and gazetted Flying Officer (Observer) on 28 May following. Sent out to France, he joined the DH4-equipped 57 Squadron, achieving six victories between 18 August and 12 November 1917, in company with his usual Pilot, Australian Lieutenant A T Drinkwater. His tour with '57' completed, he returned to the Home Establishment in January 1918. His MC was announced in the *London Gazette* of 18 March 1918: 'For conspicuous gallantry and devotion to duty in carrying out photographic reconnaissances and bombing raids far behind the enemy lines. On one occasion, when attacked by five enemy scouts, he drove three of them down and the other two then withdrew. On two other occasions he has driven down enemy machines out of control'.

Menendez would subsequently receive the insignia of his award from the hands of the King at an investiture held at Buckingham Palace. Reverting to a training role in the UK, he was subsequently seriously injured in a flying accident on 1 August 1918. Menendez relinquished his commission due to ill-health on 5 June 1919.

MERTON, Gerald

From London, he was born on 21 January 1893. Graduated BA (Science Tripos) from Trinity College, Cambridge, in 1914. Anxious to serve with the RFC and with the help of his father's £60 added to his own more modest contribution of £15, he learnt to fly as a pupil with the Beatty School of Flying at Hendon Aerodrome. He qualified for his Royal Aero Club Certificate (Number 1059) in one of the Beatty-Wright trainers on 29 January 1915. Armed with his 'ticket', Merton presented himself as a candidate for direct entry to the RFC. After a brief appraisal at Brooklands, he was gazetted Second Lieutenant, via the Special Reserve, to the Military Wing, RFC on 25 March 1915. His formal training duly completed at Upavon, he was confirmed and gazetted Flying Officer on 14 May 1915. Posted as an Instructor to 9 Squadron at Swingate Downs, near Dover, he flew a wide variety of aircraft over the next two months. On 28 July 1915, he crossed the Channel in a Bristol Scout C, '4667', landing at St Omer. From St Omer, he was sent to Major Hugh Dowding's BE2c-equipped 16 Squadron on 5 August 1915. The daily grind of reconnaissance duties included, for a while, providing day-long air cover above a military hospital at Aire wherein King George V was recovering from a heavy fall from his horse during a visit to the front. He was, however, quite frequently involved in brushes with the enemy, including one on 25 January 1916, in Bristol Scout C, '4670', he almost certainly wounded an Observer in one of two Albatroses he had engaged in combat. Merton returned to England in February 1916 and, following a rest, he left Plymouth for India in March. From India, he travelled to Mesopotamia to join 30 Squadron, arriving on 16 April 1916. Within two weeks Merton had taken ill and was on his way back to India. Returning to Basra and 30 Squadron at the end of September 1916, Merton flew mainly artillery observations in Henry Farmans. He received the news of the award of his MC in a letter from the C-in-C, Lieutenant General G S Maude, who also offered his condolences for the death of Merton's wife, Rena. His MC was announced in the *London Gazette* of 3 March 1917: 'For conspicuous gallantry in action. Whilst on reconnaissance he attacked and drove down a hostile machine. Later, although his machine was badly damaged, he succeeded in regaining our lines'.

Merton was promoted to A/Captain and Flight Commander on 1 March 1917 and was also Mentioned in Despatches on three occasions, *London Gazette*s of 11 February 1917, 15 August 1917 and 15 April 1918. Merton's squadron played their part in the recapture of Kut and in the advance upon, and eventual capture of, Baghdad. Better aeroplanes in the form of Bristol Scouts and Martinsydes arrived from Egypt and they were reinforced by the newly arrived 63 Squadron. On 26 September 1917, Merton and Lieutenant Stranger were on a low flying cavalry support patrol, when a bullet fired from the ground glanced off both of Merton's knees. Despite the pain, he contrived to get the machine back safely and was taken to hospital. He returned to 30 Squadron and operational flying on 26 October, his work now mainly photo-reconnaissance. On 17 January 1918, Merton and his Observer of the day, Lieutenant D Craik, in an RE8, were shot up over the Euphrates River and both men slightly wounded. In February 1918, Merton, after 346 operational flying hours with 30 Squadron, was allowed to go to Egypt, not only to take a well earned rest, but also to attend a series of courses in aerial fighting, aerial gunnery and artillery observation. On 23 August 1918, he was promoted to Major and given command of No 3 School of Navigation and Bomb Dropping at Helwan. The Armistice was announced during his journey home and so he was able to leave the RAF on 19 January 1919. Merton returned to his interrupted studies at Cambridge, gaining a Masters Degree, before adding a PhD in Astronomy in 1927. Subsequently, whilst owning and flying his own Gipsy Moth, he became Honorary Treasurer of the Astronomical Society, a Fellow of the Royal Aeronautical Society, President of the British Astronomical Association and Chairman of the Air League. When the Second World War came, he joined the Air Transport Auxiliary as a Pilot, flying more than a dozen different types of aircraft before later taking up a post with the Accident Investigation Section. After that war, he joined the Air Safety Committee of BAOC. Merton died in Oxford on 4 May 1983.

MICHELL-CLARKE, Alfred John

The son of Lieutenant Colonel John Michell-Clarke, MA, MD, FRCP, and Mrs Michell Clarke, of Kensington, London, he was born on 26 April 1895. Educated at Clifton College (1909-13), at Caius College, Cambridge, and at Sandhurst. Gazetted Second Lieutenant to 2 Battalion, Gloucestershire Regiment, on 22 August 1914, serving later with 7 Battalion. Seconded to the RFC in the Spring of 1915, he gained his Royal Aero Club Certificate (Number 1285) on 30 May 1915. His formal pilot training duly completed, he was confirmed and gazetted Flying Officer on 20 November 1915. Sent out to 10 Squadron in France on 20 December 1915, he was subsequently promoted to A/Captain and Flight Commander on 8 August 1916. His tour with '10' completed, he returned to the Home Establishment on 15 August 1916, being posted as Flight Commander to the newly formed 62 Squadron, then stationed at Filton in the UK. After the stint with '62', he was posted, again as a Flight Commander, this time to 40 RS. After a period instructing in the UK, he joined the 'Flying Elephants' of 27 Squadron (Martinsyde G100s) in France on 15 March 1917. On 6 April 1917, the day the USA entered the Great War, Michell-Clarke, with the help of two of his colleagues, Lieutenant W H S Wedderspoon and Second Lieutenant E W Kirby, was instrumental in sending down two Halberstadts of Jasta 30, part of an enemy formation attacking six 'Elephants' as they returned from a bombing raid on Aulnoye railway station. His tour completed, a no-doubt exhausted Michell-Clarke returned to the UK on 27 July 1917, never again to return to operational flying. His MC was announced in the *London Gazette* of 17 September 1917; 'For conspicuous gallantry and devotion to duty. He has led fourteen bomb raids, the majority of them against distant objectives, and his gallantry and skill have inspired the greatest confidence. Although continually heavily attacked by enemy aircraft, he has successfully inflicted considerable damage upon his opponents, as well as upon his objectives'.

Clarke was promoted to A/Major and to the command of 205 Squadron, before eventually resigning his RAF commission on 14 April 1920, with the intention of reverting to the Gloucestershire Regiment. After leaving the services altogether, he became a Director of Dickinson and Company (Manchester) Ltd. He married and lived with his wife and daughter at 79 Chesterfield House, London W1. During the Second World War, Michell-Clarke served with his local Home Guard.

MICHIE, John Smith

Michie enlisted as a Gunner (Number 667) into 14 Motor Machine Gun Section, Royal Field Artillery, going to the front with that unit for the first time on 17 July 1915. Subsequently picked out for a commission, he was gazetted Second Lieutenant to the RFC on 15 September 1916. His formal pilot training duly completed, he was confirmed and gazetted Flying Officer (Observer) on 30 September following. After service as an Observer, Michie returned to the UK for pilot training, joining 70 Squadron (Sopwith Camels) in that capacity on 15 September 1917. On 20 October 1917, 22 Wing, including 70 Squadron, launched a successful mass attack on Rumbeke aerodrome. Michie dropped three 25lb bombs on machines lined up ready for take-off, blowing one to smithereens. He then joined with his colleagues in shooting up the enemy field. His MC, awarded largely for this action, was announced in the *London Gazette* of 6 April 1918: 'For conspicuous gallantry and devotion to duty. On one occasion he attacked a hostile two-seater machine while it was leaving the ground, and forced it to dive. He then from a height of 150 feet dropped his bombs on the machines on the aerodrome, destroying one. His machine was hit in the petrol tank and touched the ground, but he recovered and led his patrol back safely. On another occasion he attacked three hostile scouts, bringing one of them down. He has also carried out numerous actions on enemy troops and led many patrols with great success'.

On the night of 3/4 November 1917, he became disorientated in fog and subsequently crashed his Sopwith Camel, 'B2318'. He lost some of his sharpness after this, but, following a brief rest, was promoted to A/Captain and Flight Commander and posted to the Camel F1-equipped 3 Squadron on 5 December 1917. His health was badly impaired, however, and his career with '3' curtailed when he was taken into hospital on 2 February 1918. The 21 year old Michie, pronounced as permanently unfit for further service, was forced to relinquish his commission and leave the RAF on 8 April 1919.

MIDDLETON, John Archibald

The son of Mr and Mrs A T Middleton, of 'The Homestead', Lostock, near Bolton, he was born on 17 July 1893, in Leyland, Lancashire. Educated at Marlborough (1907-08). He was apprenticed as a Pupil Engineer in Manchester when the war came in August 1914. Volunteering immediately, he was gazetted Second Lieutenant into 'C' Battery, 3 East Lancashire Brigade (Bolton Artillery), Royal Field Artillery (TF), on 29 August 1914. He served in Gallipoli and later in Egypt with 42 East Lancashire Divisional Artillery in 1915 and 1916. Securing a secondment to the RFC in October 1916, he trained as a Pilot and was confirmed and gazetted Flying Officer on 12 November following. Middleton accompanied FE2b-equipped 101 (Night-Bombing) Squadron to France as a 'founder member' on 25 July 1917. His MC was announced in the *London Gazette* of 22 April 1918: 'For conspicuous gallantry and devotion to duty. On one occasion he made two successive attacks on an enemy aerodrome, and, despite a mist and the intense activity of hostile aircraft, dropped his bombs, obtaining two direct hits on the hangars. On a later occasion, during a gale, he made two journeys to bomb enemy rest billets, obtaining several direct hits on his objectives and attacking hostile transport on the roads with machine-gun fire. He has at all times shown great courage and skill, and has set an example which has been of great value to his squadron'.

On the night of 22/23 April 1918, Middleton and his Observer, Captain R E Smith, Northumberland Hussars attached RFC, in FE2b, 'A6408', were involved in a crash on the outward leg of a bombing raid. Middleton was injured, but Ralph Smith, from Newcastle-upon-Tyne, was killed, their grounded machine shelled to matchwood. Middleton finally left the RAF, via the Unemployed List, on 18 April 1919. In 1925, he was living in Ashton-on-Ribble, Preston. A Flying Officer in the Reserve, Middleton was obliged to resign because of ill health on 28 June 1927.

MIDDLETON, John Edwin Matthew

The third of the four sons of Coachbuilder, George Middleton and his wife, Jessie M, of 16 Fanthorpe Street, Putney, London, he was born in Chelsea in 1896. He enlisted as a Private soldier (Number 06919) into the Army Service Corps on 19 October 1914, before proceeding to France just nine days later to join the Army Service Corps detachment, 1 Cavalry Division, thus earning the 1914 Star. Middleton served in France with the Army Service Corps until eventually being transferred as a Cadet to the flying service late in 1916. Gazetted Second Lieutenant to the RFC on 2 January 1917. Having trained as an Observer, he served with 10 Squadron in France as a Probationary, before being formally gazetted Flying Officer (Observer) on 21 January 1917. He next returned to the UK to train as a Pilot and was duly awarded his full 'Wings' on 30 September 1917, shortly before re-joining 10 Squadron as an RE8 Pilot later in 1917. Promoted to A/Captain in the spring of 1918, his tour with '10' was completed in May 1918. His MC was announced in the *London Gazette* of 26 July 1918: 'For conspicuous gallantry and devotion to duty. He has carried some extremely good contact patrols in thick weather, flying at 200 to 500 feet. He made two flights on one day. On one, his machine was so badly damaged by machine-gun fire that he had to return. On the other, he made a good report of the situation. On several other occasions he made good reports, and also bombed and machine-gunned the enemy'.

His next posting, on 29 May 1918, was as a Flight Commander to the RE8-equipped 7 Squadron. Hospitalised on 10 July 1918, he was returned to the UK for further treatment just eight days later, his operational service days over. Middleton finally left the RAF, via the Unemployed List, on 7 January 1919.

MILES, Charles Cleaver

From Bristol, he was born on 6 June 1887. Enlisted as a Trooper (Number 1755) into the City of London Yeomanry (TF). Gained his Royal Aero Club Certificate (Number 1185) on 21 April 1915, the same day that he was gazetted Second Lieutenant to the RFC, via the Special Reserve. His formal pilot training duly completed, he was gazetted Flying Officer on 16 July following. Sent out to 1 Squadron on 22 July 1915, he flew Avro 504As through the dark days of the 'Fokker Scourge'. On 2 October 1915, Miles and his Observer of the day, Captain L Prickett, in Avro 504A, '773', somehow survived a three-pronged attack from behind by two Albatroses and an LVG, west of Lille. He was not so fortunate on 10 November following, when both he and his Observer, Second Lieutenant L J Baily, were wounded in the air. Once recovered, he was sent out in the summer of 1916 to 3 Squadron (Moranes). On 25 August, he was again wounded whilst strafing the enemy trenches at low level in the vicinity of Delville Wood, hit by a rifle bullet fired from the ground. His MC was announced in the *London Gazette* of 20 October 1916: 'For conspicuous gallantry and skill. He has shown great dash in contact patrol work. On one occasion he reconnoitred an enemy trench at 500 feet altitude, under heavy fire, which severely damaged his machine. Five days later, while working at 600 feet, he was severely wounded'.

Having once again recovered from his wounds, Miles was promoted to A/Major and appointed to the command of 43 Squadron (Camel F1s) in 1918. Staying on in the RAF after the war, he became a Squadron Leader in 1919 and was promoted to Wing Commander in 1924. Charles Miles served as an Air Staff Officer at RAF HQ, Mediterranean, in the 1930s.

MILLMAN, Norman Craig

From Toronto, Canada, he was born on 30 March 1890. Educated at the University of Toronto, from where he graduated BASc in 1913. When the war came in 1914, he enlisted as a Sapper into 2 Field Company, Canadian Engineers. Accepted as a volunteer in the flying service, he was gazetted Second Lieutenant to the RFC, via the Special Reserve, on 7 December 1915. Gained his Royal Aero Club Certificate (Number 2392) on 27 January 1916. His formal pilot training duly completed, he was confirmed and gazetted Flying Officer on 27 May following. His first posting was as an Instructor at Brooklands. In the autumn of 1916, he was sent out to 1 AD, St Omer, as a Test Pilot. Next, he joined the newly forming 48 Squadron, the first to be equipped with Bristol Fighters in the UK, and accompanied the unit to France as a 'founder member' in March 1917. Yet another Canadian Ace, Millman would achieve six victories between 11 November 1917 and 8 March 1918. He was promoted to A/Captain and Flight Commander on 22 January 1918, serving over the Salient as well as the IV and V Army fronts from Cambrai to Laon. Millman's tour with '48', which unit he had, on occasions, commanded, ended in May 1918, and he returned to the UK for rest and recuperation. His MC, along with that of his Observer, H A Cooper's (qv), was announced in the *London Gazette* of 22 June 1918: 'For conspicuous gallantry and devotion to duty. Whilst on offensive patrol, he encountered a hostile formation of twelve machines. He led his patrol in such brilliant fashion that five of the enemy machines were shot down either in flames or out of control, two of these being accounted for by himself and his Observer. Previous to this, he had carried out voluntarily a reconnaissance from which he succeeded in returning with the most valuable information, despite the fact that he had been engaged by machine-gun fire during the greater part of the flight. Later, he commanded a formation on one flank of the attack during a daylight-bombing raid on a hostile aerodrome, and carried out his task in a most dashing and successful manner. He has at all times displayed powers of leadership of the highest order'.

Millman's next posting was as an Instructor to 33 TDS, his outstanding services in this capacity being marked by the award of an Air Force Cross, *London Gazette* of 3 June 1919. Millman left the RAF, via the Unemployed List, on 20 May 1919, and returned to Canada. He died on 27 July 1981.

MILLS, Reginald Percy

The youngest son of William Henry Mills, JP, and Mrs Mills, of Parkstone, Dorset, he was born in Lincolnshire on 7 December 1885. Educated at Felsted (1900-04). Gazetted Second Lieutenant to a Regular Army battalion of the Royal Fusiliers in 1909. Developing an interest in aviation, he gained his Royal Aero Club Certificate (Number 377) on a Bristol machine at the Bristol School, Brooklands, on 17 December 1912. Securing a secondment to the RFC in 1913, he accompanied the original contingent to France in August 1914 as a Flying Officer with 4 Squadron, although, oddly enough, he was not officially confirmed and gazetted Flying Officer until 26 September 1914. In the early months of the war, aeroplanes on both sides operated singly or, at most, in pairs, but on 22 January 1915, as a harbinger of things to come, a formation of 12 German machines came in from over the sea and proceeded to bomb Dunkirk. A motley collection of British, French and Belgian aeroplanes took off to counter the incursion. Mills, flying a BE2c, engaged an Albatros with a rifle as, indeed, did his 4 Squadron colleague, Captain F V Holt, from his BE. A rifle bullet hit and stopped the enemy machine's engine which caused it to glide down to a landing and eventual capture. Whether the bullet was fired by Mills or Holt has never been satisfactorily established. Mills would serve as a Flight Commander with 7 Squadron later in 1915 and, early in 1916, his MC was announced in the *London Gazette* of 30 March 1916: 'For co-operating with the artillery in operations resulting in the capture of the enemy's position'.

Promoted to Major, Mills commanded 6 Squadron at Abeele during the Battle of the Somme. After further advancement to A/Lieutenant Colonel, he would go on to command 14 Wing, RFC, in France, and 51 Wing in Italy in 1917 and 1918. He was Mentioned in Despatches on two occasions during the Great War, *London Gazettes* of 22 June 1915 and 31 May 1918 (Italy). His service in Italy was also marked by the award of the Italian Order of St Maurice and St Lazarus (Chevalier), *London Gazette* of 2 November 1918. The French weighed in with the Croix d'Officier, Légion d'Honneur, and a Croix de Guerre. Mills also received the Air Force Cross in the Birthday Honours *London Gazette* of 3 June 1919. He married, in 1919, Helen Bulpett, with whom he had one daughter (marriage dissolved in 1936). Staying on in the RAF after the war, his many appointments, honours and promotions thereafter included: Deputy Director Air Ministry, 1922-26; Chief Staff Officer, RAF in India, 1926-31; CB, 1930; Director of Organisation and Staff Duties, Air Ministry, 1931-33; AOC, Oxford Bombing Area, 1933-34; Director of Postings, Air Ministry, 1934-35. Mills retired from the RAF with the rank of Air Vice-Marshal in 1936. During the Second World War, Mills was re-employed as a Group Captain in 1939 and as an Air Vice-Marshal between 1941-42. He lived, post the Second World War, at 50 Proctors Road, Hobart, Tasmania. Reginald Mills died in Hobart on 4 July 1968.

MILNE, John Theobald

The son of Mr and Mrs John Alexander Milne, of Brook House, Sutton Courtney, and of 24 Half Moon Street, London W, he was born on 20 August 1895. Educated at Radley (1909-12). Gazetted Second Lieutenant to 6 Battalion, Oxfordshire and Buckinghamshire Light Infantry, on 9 September 1914. He served in the trenches from August 1915, until he secured a secondment to the RFC in the spring of 1916. Milne married, around this time, Joan Florence Hamer. Gained his Royal Aero Club Certificate (Number 3084) on 29 May 1916. His formal pilot training duly completed, he was confirmed and gazetted Flying Officer on 24 June following. Sent to 48 Squadron, the first to be equipped with Bristol Fighters, he accompanied the unit to France as a 'founder member' on 8 March 1917. Milne achieved nine victories between 6 July and 28 September 1917, he was also promoted A/Captain and Flight Commander during this period. His MC was announced in the *London Gazette* of 17 September 1917: 'For conspicuous gallantry and devotion to duty whilst leading offensive patrols. He has shown great determination and courage in attacking hostile formations, although in superior numbers, at close range. He has also done long and arduous reconnaissances and secured good photographs under very adverse conditions and heavy fire, displaying throughout an admirable spirit of fearlessness and energy'.

On 24 October 1917, Milne and his Observer, Lieutenant Stanley Wright MC, Royal Engineers attached RFC, in BF2b, 'B1117', were both killed during a combat with Leutnant Fritz Kieckhafer of Jasta 29, the sixth of the German Ace's eventual eight victories. After Milne's death, fellow Flight Commander Keith Park, delivered his personal effects to his widow, Joan. During the course of this visit, Park was introduced to Joan Milne's cousin, who he eventually married. John Milne's remains were never recovered and hence he is commemorated on the Flying Services Memorial, Arras, France.

MILNE, William

The youngest son of James Milne and Henrietta Milne (née Traquir), of Mary Island, British Columbia, Canada, he was born in Baberton, Juniper Green, Midlothian, Scotland, on 31 December 1888. Educated at Edinburgh Academy, in Heidelberg, Germany, and at the Royal Military College, Sandhurst. Gazetted Second Lieutenant to 2 Battalion, Loyal North Lancashire Regiment, on 6 February 1909. Served with the Loyals in Mauritius and in Poona, India. Returning to the UK in 1912, he resigned his commission to join his father who was then working and living in British Columbia, Canada. As soon as he was able to do so, after war came, he returned to the UK and sought a commission in his old regiment. The War Office allowed his application and he was gazetted T/Captain to 8 (Service) Battalion, Loyal North Lancashire Regiment, on 26 November 1914, with an almost immediate secondment to the RFC. Training at Chelmsford, he was badly hurt in a flying accident on 22 December 1914. His fitness restored, he returned to duty and training in March 1915. Milne was sent out as an Observer to BE2c-equipped 2 Squadron in France, in May 1915. On 26 July 1915, Milne and his Pilot, Captain T W C Carthew, DSO, Bedfordshire Regiment attached RFC, in BE2c, '1669', were involved in a combat over Tournai. Although inconclusive, the combat was significant in that it was the RFC's first recorded encounter with a Fokker Eindecker. On 11 August, Milne and his Pilot of the day, Captain J G Hearson, in BE2c, '1703', would again be involved with an Eindecker over Armentières, suffering some damage to their machine. During August 1915, Milne, as well as fulfilling his observing duties, attended the Flying School at Le Crotoy, where he qualified for his Royal Aero Club Certificate (Number 1735) on 11 September 1915. Returning to the UK, he completed his formal pilot training at Montrose, at Newcastle and at Thetford. In February 1916, he was again sent to the front, this time as a Pilot, a Flight Commander and a 'founder member' of FE2b-equipped 25 Squadron. On 17 May 1916, Milne and his Observer, Second Lieutenant E R Davies, in FE2b, '5238', were involved in a combat over the La Bassée Canal. Although Davies was unscathed, Milne was wounded in an engagement and afterwards invalided to the UK. His MC was announced in the *London Gazette* of 27 June 1916: 'For conspicuous gallantry and skill. When attacked by two hostile aeroplanes he drove off one, and though slightly wounded in the face, drove the other vertically to the ground. He then at once attacked another and drove it down, this time being shot through the hand. Despite his wounds, he landed his machine safely in his own aerodrome'.

He was also Mentioned in Despatches for 'gallant and distinguished service in the field' on one occasion during the Great War. In August 1916, he was made Liaison Officer between Adastra House and the Horse Guards and, in October, was given command of 77 HD Squadron, based in Edinburgh. William Milne was killed in an aeroplane accident on 13 April 1917, near Reston, County Berwick. He is buried in Edinburgh (Grange) Cemetery.

MILNES, William Henry Goodenough

Gazetted Second Lieutenant to a Regular Army battalion of the Royal Warwickshire Regiment on 1 May 1917 with an immediate secondment to the RFC. His pilot training duly completed, he was gazetted Flying Officer on 19 August following. Sent out to 25 Squadron (DH4s) on 29 September 1917, he served with that unit through to 19 June 1918, when he returned to the Home Establishment. His MC was announced in the *London Gazette* of 22 June 1918: 'For conspicuous gallantry and devotion to duty. When on a bombing raid at a height of 800 feet, he was attacked by four enemy two-seater machines, and by skilful manoeuvring enabled his Observer to destroy one of them. In the course of five days' operations he dropped nearly a ton of bombs on enemy troops, camps and railways from a low altitude, and also used his machine-gun with good effect. He did excellent photographic work, and carried out several valuable long-distance reconnaissances. He always showed great courage and resource'.

Milnes finally left the RAF, via the Unemployed List, on 10 September 1919.

MINCHIN, Frederick Frank Reilly

The son of Major General Frederick Falkiner Minchin and Margery Minchin, of Annagh, Borrisokane, County Tipperary, Ireland, he was born in Madras, India, on 16 June 1890. Acquiring an early interest in aviation, he gained his Royal Aero Club Certificate (Number 419) on an Eastbourne Aviation Company Bristol machine, at Eastbourne aerodrome on 18 February 1913. In Canada when the war came, he immediately volunteered and was gazetted Lieutenant to Princess Patricia's Canadian Light Infantry on 22 September 1914. After service with Princess Patricia's Canadian Light Infantry, he was seconded to the RFC in March 1915. His formal pilot training completed, he was duly confirmed and gazetted Flying Officer on 5 October following. Minchin accompanied 14 Squadron to the Middle East as a 'founder member' on 4 November 1915. For his work over the Eastern Desert, Minchin's first MC was announced in the *London Gazette* of 31 May 1916: 'For conspicuous gallantry and skill on many occasions notably when leading a successful bomb and machine-gun raid on a force of the enemy which he had located overnight. Next day he took part in two other raids. During these operations he flew for thirteen hours over enemy country'.

Minchin was promoted to A/Captain and Flight Commander on 15 May 1916. By November 1916, the British advance on Palestine had progressed sufficiently to allow the RFC and AFC machines in the area to operate over the Western Desert. The Bar to Minchin's MC came in the *London Gazette* of 25 November 1916: ' For conspicuous gallantry in action. He flew 150 miles at night to bomb an enemy aerodrome, descending to 500 feet, and doing serious damage. On another occasion he landed 45 miles from our line to pick up the pilot of a damaged machine in a hostile country'.

The practice of landing to rescue downed colleagues, although not by any means routine, was nonetheless, not uncommon. Indeed, Minchin himself had been the beneficiary of just such a rescue on 2 November 1916, when, after his fuel tank had been holed in a combat with an enemy machine, he had been forced to land in the desert. His 14 Squadron colleague, Captain Russell Freeman (qv), landed his Martinsyde G100 alongside Minchin's downed machine. Minchin climbed aboard the Martinsyde to sit on the cowl and, in this precarious position, was flown to safety by Freeman. Minchin was next promoted to Major and appointed to the command of 47 Squadron in Salonika from 1 January 1917. His services as CO, 47 Squadron, were subsequently recognised by the award of the Distinguished Service Order, *London Gazette* of 1 January 1918. He was also Mentioned in Despatches on three occasions during the Great War. Minchin returned to the UK on 13 March 1918, completing his service in a series of Staff and technical posts. His post-war work in aviation was recognised by the award of the CBE in July 1920. Minchin, by then a senior Pilot with Imperial Airways, made, in partnership with Mr Leslie Hamilton, DFC, an attempt on a non-stop trans-Atlantic flight from Baldonnel Airport, near Dublin, to Ottawa, in a Fokker 7a, powered by a Bristol Jupiter 450hp radial engine. The attempt failed and both men were lost without trace on 26 June 1927.

NB: The RAF Museum Hendon has his medals in its collection: CBE, Distinguished Service Order, and MC.

MINOT, Laurence

The son of John Edward and Ada Minot, of 30 Beaulah Hill, Upper Norwood, London, he was born in 1897. Educated at Dulwich College (1909-15), Rugby XV. On leaving school, he immediately entered Hall's Flying School, Hendon, and, at his own expense, gained his Royal Aero Club Certificate (Number 1409) on 8 July 1915. The 'ticket' ensured his desired entry into the RFC and, accordingly, he was gazetted Second Lieutenant, via the Special Reserve, on 28 October following. His formal pilot training duly completed, he was confirmed and gazetted Flying Officer on 1 February 1916. He was sent out to 16 Squadron in France within days of qualifying. In July 1916, he was promoted to A/Captain and Flight Commander and transferred as such to 7 Squadron. On 9 August, Minot and his Observer, Second Lieutenant G H Wood (qv), in BE2d, '5792', narrowly escaped death when their machine was shot up over Pozières. His tour with '7' completed, he returned to the Home Establishment in December 1916. Following a spell of instructing in the UK, he was next sent out to 57 Squadron, taking over 'B' Flight from the late Captain N G McNaughton MC (qv), who had recently been killed in action. Minot achieved six victories in DH4s of 57 Squadron between 3 July and 27 July 1917, including, on 3 July, the machine flown by the15-victory Ace and Commander of Jasta 10, Oberleutnant Albert Dossenbach. On 27 July 1917, Minot and his Observer, Lieutenant A F Britton, in DH4, 'B3963', were involved in a combat with Albatros DVs. Britton received a bullet wound in his calf, but Minot was, fortunately, unscathed in the action. On the following day, however, disaster struck. Minot and his Observer, Second Lieutenant Sydney John Leete, Worcestershire Regiment attached RFC, in DH4, 'A7540', were shot down and killed over Oostroosebeke by Leutnant Hans Ritter von Adam of Jasta 6. Minot's MC was announced posthumously in the *London Gazette* of 22 April 1918: 'For conspicuous gallantry and devotion to duty. When leading a formation of five machines he attacked a hostile formation of 20 machines and in the ensuing fight himself drove down two enemy machines completely OOC whilst his Observer destroyed another. Another four of the enemy formation were driven down completely out of control and, as a result of his gallant leadership and determined action, his formation succeeded in getting back with the loss of but one machine. On a previous occasion he, in company with two other machines, attacked four of the enemy, who were reinforced later by thirteen scouts and after heavy fighting drove down one of the enemy out of control; his formation returning safely'.

Laurence is buried in the Harlebeke New British Cemetery, Harlebeke, Belgium.

MITCHELL, Erik Harrison

The son of Mr and Mrs H B Mitchell, of 68 Bensham Manor Road, Thornton Heath. Educated at Whitgift Grammar School. A pre-war volunteer, he was gazetted Second Lieutenant to 4 Kent Howitzer Battery, 4 Home Counties (Howitzer) Brigade, Royal Field Artillery (TF), on 29 July 1913. He was, of course, mobilised with the rest of the TF immediately upon the outbreak of war on 4 August 1914. Seeking secondment to the RFC, he gained his Royal Aero Club Certificate (Number 972) on 17 November 1914. His formal pilot training duly completed, he was confirmed and gazetted Flying Officer on 4 February 1915. He was sent out to 4 Squadron in France, immediately after qualifying. On 26 September following, Mitchell and his Observer of the day, Lieutenant F E Hellyer, were both wounded when their BE2c, '1726', was shot through by three shells. He was Mentioned in Despatches in the same *Gazette* that announced the award of his MC, New Year *London Gazette* of 1 January 1916 (no citation). Although no formal citation was published in the *Gazette*, research has unearthed the original recommendation for the award: '4 Sqd and RA. Great gallantry and devotion to duty in the field since last February. Always exceptionally determined in face of AA gun fire and has frequently returned from a successful reconnaissance with his aircraft badly damaged by shell fire. A very fine pilot and quite regardless of weather. Bombed railway near Aubigny with success from a height of 400 feet under heavy rifle fire on Sept 26th; on his return journey he was wounded and his aeroplane very severely damaged by a high explosive shell, but in spite of the machine being almost out of control, he effected a good landing on his own aerodrome'.

Once recovered, 'Bim' Mitchell was sent next as a Flight Commander to 15 Squadron, then at Dover, on 15 October 1915. From '15', Mitchell was posted to 24 Squadron, then stationed at Hounslow, on 12 November 1915. Mitchell accompanied 24 Squadron, a single-seater fighter unit equipped with DH2s, to France as a 'founder member' on 2 February 1916. Unfortunately, he was killed in a flying accident on 29 April following, and is buried in Terlincthun British Cemetery, Wimille, France.

MITCHELL, James Hart

The only son of Coal Factor, Amos Mitchell and Mrs Mitchell, of Todmorden, Yorkshire, he was born in Hereford on 8 May 1899. Educated at Clyde House School, at Boys House School, Hereford, and, post-war, at Cambridge from where he graduated with Second Class Honours. Gazetted Second Lieutenant to the RFC on 5 September 1916. His formal pilot training duly completed, he was confirmed and gazetted Flying Officer on 5 June 1917. Sent to 28 Squadron (Sopwith Camels) then forming in Gosport, he eventually accompanied that unit to France as a 'founder member' on 8 October 1917. On 20 October following, whilst engaged on escorting Camels of 70 Squadron on an aerodrome strafe, he shot down an Albatros Scout that was in the act of attacking W G Barker, who would later win a VC. Mitchell's squadron was posted to Italy in November 1917, whereupon he was promoted to A/Captain and Flight Commander. In addition to three victories gained in France, Mitchell achieved a further eight in Italy, including an AEG bomber. His MC was announced in the *London Gazette* of 18 February 1918, details in the *Gazette* of 18 July 1918: 'For conspicuous gallantry and devotion to duty. When on patrol work on four separate occasions he has shot down five enemy planes, three of which were observed to burst into flames, one being a large three-seater. On two of these occasions his formation was attacked by superior formations of the enemy. His magnificent work has been marked by great dash and fearlessness'.

His tour with '28' completed, he returned to the Home Establishment in July 1918. He was awarded a Distinguished Flying Cross in the *London Gazette* of 2 July 1918, details in the *Gazette* of 21 September 1918, for: '....destroying five enemy aeroplanes'. The Italians also showed their appreciation of his services with a Bronze Medaglia al Valore Militare, *London Gazette* of 2 November 1918. Mitchell would leave the RAF in 1919 and go on to Cambridge to pursue his studies.

MITCHELL, William Gore Sutherland

The son of Mr and Mrs W B Mitchell, of Sydney, Australia, he was born on 8 March 1888. Educated at Wellington College (1902-06) and at Sandhurst. Gazetted Second Lieutenant to a Regular Army battalion of the Highland Light Infantry in 1909. Acquiring an interest in aviation, he gained his Royal Aero Club Certificate (Number 483) on a Vickers machine at the Vickers School, Brooklands, on 17 May 1913. Seconded to the RFC, he completed his formal pilot training and was duly confirmed and gazetted Flying Officer on 17 December following. Mitchell accompanied the original RFC contingent to France in August 1914 as a Flying Officer with 4 Squadron, thus earning a 1914 Star. On 30 September 1914, Mitchell and his Observer, Captain D LeG Pitcher, in BE2a, '314', suffered the indignity of having the fuselage of their machine shot up by 'friendly fire', in this instance the French being the offenders. Fortunately, neither man was wounded. On 8 November following, BE2a, '314', having been repaired, was again damaged by shrapnel, forcing Mitchell to crashland. Fortunately, he and his Observer, Captain H H Hughes-Hallett, were unscathed. Again on 19 November, the unlucky '314' was damaged by shell fire at 2,800 feet. On this occasion, Hughes-Hallett was wounded, although Mitchell again escaped injury. Mitchell's good fortune continued into the summer of 1915, when, on 15 June 1915, a shell penetrated the planes of his BE2b, '746', and exploded in the air immediately above the machine. Mitchell and his Observer of the day, Lieutenant J F Lascelles (qv), were shaken but unhurt. Mitchell was appointed to the command of 10 Squadron on 2 June 1916, leading his unit from its base at Chocques, throughout the Battle of the Somme. His MC was announced in the New Year *London Gazette* of 1 January 1917 (no citation). Although no formal citation appeared in the *Gazette*, research has unearthed the original recommendation for the award: 'T/Maj W G S Mitchell. For continued good service as a Pilot and Flight Commander both in the retreat and afterwards. Latterly as Officer Commanding an Artillery Squadron since 2-6-16, he has both by his personal example and his devotion to duty succeeded in raising his unit to a high state of efficiency in their work of co-operating with the artillery'.

There is also a recommendation for the award of the Russian 3rd Class Order of St Stanislaus, but no firm record of it having been acted upon. Mitchell went on to command 12 Wing, RFC, in 1917 and 1918, with the rank of A/Lieutenant Colonel, and was duly awarded the Distinguished Service Order in the *London Gazette* of 1 January 1918. He was also Mentioned in Despatches on three occasions during the Great War, *London Gazettes* of 8 October 1914, 1 January 1916, and 7 November 1917. The final accolade for this particular phase of his career was the award of the Air Force Cross, announced in the Birthday Honours *London Gazette* of 3 June 1919. He married in 1919, Essy Plant. Staying on in the RAF after the war, he went on to carve out a highly distinguished career. His many honours and appointments included: CO, 1 Wing, Waziristan campaigns, 1919-20 and 1922-23 (Mentioned in Despatches); CBE, 1924; Commander, British Forces in Aden, 1928; Director of Training, Air Ministry, 1929-33; Commandant, RAF College, Cranwell, 1933-35; CB, 1935; AOC, British Forces in Iraq, 1935-37; Air Member for Personnel on Air Council, 1937-39; knighted (KCB), 1938; Air Officer

C-in-C RAF, Middle East, 1939-40; and Inspector General of the RAF, 1940-41. His health generally declining, he passed into partial retirement and was appointed Gentleman Usher of Black Rod in 1941 and Commandant of the London Command ATC in 1942. He lived at 14 Eresby House, Rutland Gate, London SW. Air Chief Marshal Sir William Mitchell died on 15 August 1944.

MOLESWORTH, William Earle

The son of Colonel W Molesworth, CIE, CBE, of the Indian Medical Service, and Mrs Molesworth, he was born in the Andaman Islands on 14 March 1894. Educated at Marlborough College (1908-12) and at Sandhurst. Gazetted Second Lieutenant to 2 Battalion, Royal Munster Fusiliers, on 8 August 1914. Served with his regiment in France from October 1914 to March 1916, being wounded at Festubert on 22 December 1914, after a 60-hour running battle with German infantry. Seconded to the RFC in March 1916, he subsequently graduated at Upavon and was confirmed and gazetted Flying Officer on 26 December following. Sent out to 60 Squadron, he served in Albert Ball's Flight in April 1917. Flying, firstly, Nieuport XVIIs and, later, SE5As, he claimed six victories between 22 April and 9 August 1917. Returning to the UK, he instructed at Dover and then later at the Special School for Advanced Flying at Gosport. The first of his MCs was announced in the *London Gazette* of 26 September 1917, details in the *Gazette* of 9 January 1918: 'For conspicuous gallantry and devotion to duty on offensive patrol. He has frequently led his patrol against superior numbers of the enemy, destroying some and dispersing others. He has also brought down two balloons, and has proved himself to be a dashing and fearless pilot of great skill and determination'.

He journeyed to France again on 20 October 1917, this time to join 29 Squadron. Once again flying Nieuport Scouts, Molesworth achieved a further 12 victories between 8 November 1917 and 18 March 1918. The announcement of a Bar to his MC came in the *London Gazette* of 26 March 1918, details in the *Gazette* of 24 August 1918: 'For conspicuous gallantry and devotion to duty. He has done excellent work as patrol leader, handling his formations with great skill and courage. He has destroyed four enemy machines and driven down several out of control'.

He was also awarded the Italian Silver Medaglia al Valore Militare at this time. Transferred to the Home Establishment, he took up a position as an Instructor at the CFS. On 1 April 1918, upon the formation of the RAF, 'Moley' Molesworth was promoted to A/Major, and given the responsibility of forming the entirely new 158 Squadron at Upper Heyford, in Oxfordshire. After a brief period commanding '158', Molesworth reverted to his Regular Army commission and the Royal Munster Fusiliers. Following the disbandment of the Munsters after Irish independence in 1922, he transferred to the Tank Corps, with which unit he continued to serve into the 1930s.

NB: His medals were offered for sale by Wallis and Wallis (lot 2) on 12 October 2004: MC and Bar, 1914 Star with Bar, British War Medal 1914-20, Victory Medal 1914-19, and Silver Medaglia al Valore Militare (Italy).

MOLLER, Francis Steele

From Sioux City, Iowa, USA, he was born in November 1891. Educated at Felsted (1908-09). After leaving school in the UK, he returned to the USA and later worked as, amongst other things, a 'Cow-Puncher' on a Texas cattle ranch, before formally training as an Engineer. Travelling to the UK and offering his services in 1915, he was gazetted Second Lieutenant to the New Armies on 20 September, with an immediate secondment to the RFC. He first trained as an Observer, and was sent out as such to FE2b-equipped 20 Squadron. However, he very quickly requested a change of role to Pilot, having already gained his Royal Aero Club Certificate (Number 2259) at the Military School, Shoreham, on 9 January 1916. His formal pilot training duly completed, he was confirmed and gazetted Flying Officer on 20 May 1916 and sent out to FE2b-equipped 25 Squadron in France shortly afterwards. On 23 November 1916, Moller, in FE2b, '7683', was wounded in the back during an action with about 20 hostile scouts, although his Observer of the day, Sergeant C Butler, was unscathed. Despite his wounds, he continued the fight until his radiator was hit and his engine seized up. Still, he managed to land his machine reasonably intact near to St Eloi. His MC was announced in the *London Gazette* of 14 November 1916: 'For conspicuous gallantry and devotion to duty. During a raid he dived 1,500 feet and dropped his bombs on an ammunition train. He then chased three other trains, and attacked them with great courage and skill'.

Once recovered from his wounds in 1917, Moller was appointed to the staff of the Special Aviation Mission to Roumania before, later in 1918, being promoted to Major and accompanying the same organisation to Russia as part of the Allied Intervention Force. For a period, he commanded the RAF contingent on the Archangel front, receiving, for his services, the Distinguished Flying Cross, *London Gazette* of 5 April 1919 (Murmansk). Additionally, he received a number of foreign awards, including: Chevalier, Star of Roumania with Swords and Officer, Crown of Roumania with Swords, both *London Gazette* of 23 August 1919, and the Russian Order of St Anne, 2nd Class. After the Allied Intervention collapsed and failed, Moller returned to the UK and left the RAF. He settled in the Essex area, becoming, in the fullness of time, Managing Director of Hooper Struve Ltd and, in 1931, Worshipful Master of the Felsted Lodge. Also in 1931, he edited the 6th edition of 'Alumni Felstedienes' for his old school. In 1938, Moller retired to the Seychelles Islands. He died at Mahe Colony, Seychelles Island, ten years later on 19 January 1948, from injuries received when the verandah of his home, on which he was sitting, collapsed.

MOLONEY, Peter Joseph

From Ennismore, Ontario, Canada, he was born on 21 August 1893. He enlisted into the Canadian Army MGC in 1916, but subsequently volunteered for, and was accepted into, the RFC. Gazetted Second Lieutenant to Military Wing, RFC, on 5 December 1916. His pilot training duly completed, he was confirmed and gazetted Flying Officer on 7 May 1917. Sent to 84 Squadron (SE5As), then stationed at Beaulieu, and accompanied that unit to France as a 'founder member', on 23 September 1917. On 22 November 1917, Moloney in SE5A, 'B4866', on patrol over Cambrai, was attacked by six enemy machines. Despite being severely wounded in the initial pass, Moloney fought on, inflicting damage upon his opponents before being forced to land near to Bus. He received his MC for his gallantry on this occasion, announced in the *London Gazette* of 18 January 1918, details in the *Gazette* of 25 April 1918: 'For conspicuous gallantry and devotion to duty. When on patrol, he was attacked by six hostile aeroplanes which dived at him out of the clouds. In the first burst of fire he received a severe wound, his control wires were very badly cut, and several of his flying wires were shot away. Despite this he attacked four of the enemy aeroplanes, one of whom disappeared, another crashing down out of control. Feeling very faint from loss of blood, he then made for our lines through the nearest clouds. Though the fog was very thick, he succeeded in landing his machine undamaged behind our lines. On another occasion, when on patrol, he engaged the leader of a hostile formation and drove him down. Though he suffered from engine trouble, he finally succeeded in driving off another enemy scout which had attacked him. This officer's tenacity and pluck are worthy of the highest praise'.

Moloney did not return to operational flying and was demobilised from the RAF on 5 May 1919, returning then to Canada.

MONTGOMERY, Kenneth Barbour

The only son of Mr and Mrs James Montgomery, of West Knowle, Bidston Road, Oxton, Birkenhead, he was born on 22 October 1898. Educated at Rugby (1912-16). Gazetted Second Lieutenant to the RFC on 13 April 1917. His pilot training duly completed, he was confirmed and gazetted Flying Officer on 29 May following. Sent out to 45 Squadron in France, he achieved four victories in Sopwith Strutters between 13 July and 23 August 1917. The squadron having been re-equipped with Camels, Montgomery went on to gain a further six victories between 20 September 1917 and 15 November 1917. His squadron was transferred to the Italian front on 17 November 1917 and he gained his 11th victory there on 3 January following. Immediately after this victory, Montgomery was promoted to Captain and Flight Commander, and posted to 66 Squadron (also Camels) on the same front. His MC was announced in the *London Gazette* of 18 January 1918, details in the *Gazette* of 18 July 1918: 'For conspicuous gallantry and devotion to duty. He has on several occasions, during a period of three months, shot down in flames four hostile machines, three of which were large high-powered two-seaters, and has driven down out of control six enemy planes. He is a most determined scout pilot, his skill and courage being of a very high order'.

He gained his 12th and final victory on 12 January 1918, but was himself shot down and taken prisoner of war on 22 February following. Montgomery was repatriated on 20 November 1918. The Italians also showed their appreciation of his services on their behalf, with an award of the Croce di Guerra, *London Gazette* of 8 February 1919. After leaving the RAF in 1919, he returned to work as a Merchant in Liverpool's commercial centre, whilst taking up residence at 'Leighton Croft', Neston, Cheshire.

MOODY, Henry Michael

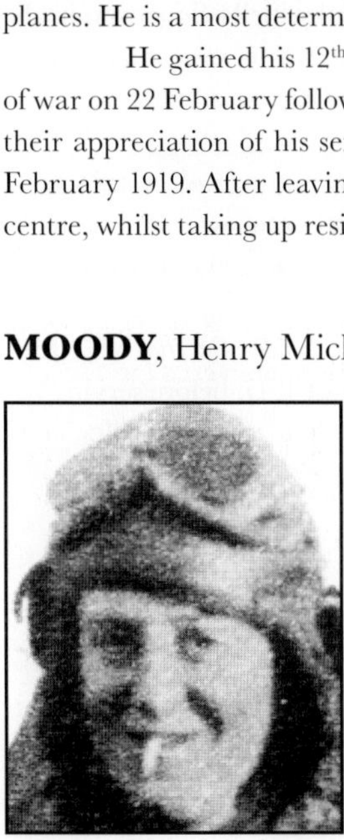

The twin son of Prebendary R H Moody and Mrs Moody, of Welshampton Vicarage, Ellesmere, Shropshire, he was born in 1898. Educated at King William's College, Isle of Man (1912-16). His twin brother, Charles Angelo, a Nieuport XXIII Pilot with 1 Squadron, RFC, was shot down and killed in action by Leutnant Fritz Loerzer of Jasta 26 on 21 August 1917, the fourth of the German Ace's eventual 11 victories. Henry joined the RFC as a Mechanic in December 1916. Picked out for a commission, he was subsequently gazetted Second Lieutenant to the RFC on 13 April 1917. His pilot training duly completed, he was confirmed and gazetted Flying Officer on 21 June following. Posted to 45 Squadron (Camels) in France, he achieved four victories between 4 September and 13 November 1917, one of which was an armoured Junkers J1. His squadron was posted to the Italian front in November 1917, where Moody gained a further four victories, and was promoted to A/Captain and Flight Commander. Moody's tour with '45' completed, he returned to the Home Establishment in June 1918. His MC was announced in the *London Gazette* of 16 September 1918: 'For conspicuous gallantry and devotion to duty in leading patrols. He has destroyed four enemy aircraft and shot down three out of control. He has further carried out very successfully a number of low-flying patrols, photographic reconnaissances and escorts, and has on all occasions shown a very fine spirit of dash and determination'.

Staying on in the RAF after the war, he instructed at Cranwell for a short time before being sent to India and 31 Squadron at Dardoni on the North West Frontier. Returning to the UK, he was posted to Winchester and then back to an instructing role at Cranwell. He married, in 1922, Austin Robina Hall from Canterbury, with whom he had one son and one daughter. From Cranwell, he was posted to Uxbridge in February 1931. Just one month later, on 23 March 1931, he was killed in a mid-air collision over Seahurst Park, Sussex, when flying his AOC, Air Vice-Marshal F M Vesey-Holy, in a DH Gipsy Moth, 'K1838', of 24 Communications Squadron, from RAF Northolt. Moody's Gipsy Moth collided with a Siskin, the left-hand machine of a welcoming diving salute formation staged for the Air Vice-Marshal by a flight of 43 Squadron. The Siskin Pilot, Sergeant C G Wareham, survived, his machine only slightly damaged in the collision but the Gipsy Moth turned over before diving to the ground. TheAir Vice-Marshal exited the Moth in the air, his parachute opening but too close to the ground to save him. Moody was still in the machine when it struck the ground.

MOORE, Alfred Garnet

Born in Hackney, London, on 21 September 1882. He served in the South African War with the Manchester Regiment, earning the Queen's South Africa Medal 1899-1902. Gazetted Captain to 4 (Extra Reserve) Battalion, Manchester Regiment, on 22 April 1905, having previously served as a Staff Officer. Moore worked in Malaya as a Rubber Planter in 1911 and 1912. Developing an interest in aviation, he gained his Royal Aero Club Certificate (Number 788) on a Graham White at the Graham White School, Hendon, on 19 May 1914. Embodied from the Militia when the war came, he successfully sought secondment to the RFC. His formal pilot training duly completed, he was confirmed and gazetted Flying Officer on 2 July 1915. He served with 14 Squadron in the Middle East from 4 November 1915 to 5 February 1916. Returning to the UK, he was next sent as a Flight Commander to 34 Squadron for Home Defence duties on 18 April 1916. His first MC was announced in the Birthday Honours *London Gazette* of 3 June 1916 (no citation).

From '34', he was sent to 24 Squadron in France, the Bar to his MC coming in the *London Gazette* of 20 October 1916: 'For conspicuous gallantry and skill. While fighting he had several wires shot away and his main spar damaged. His machine went into a spinning nose-dive. Nevertheless he finally managed to get some sort of control, and landed safely in an aerodrome'.

He was also Mentioned in Despatches on two occasions around this time, *London Gazette*s of 21 June 1916 and 20 October 1916. Moore returned to the Home Establishment on 24 August 1917, before serving out the remainder of the war in various training and Staff posts. He lived, in the immediate post-war years, at 47 Knightsbridge, Hyde Park Corner, London, SW1.

MOORE, Beaufoi John Warwick Montressor

The only son of Barrister at Law, Beaufoi Moore and Mrs Cecelia Moore, of 4 Pump Court, Temple, London, he was born in London on 25 January 1885. Educated privately, at King's College, London (1901-02) and at the Polytechnic School of Engineering, London (1902 05). After completing his apprenticeship as an Electrical Engineer (Associate Member of the Institution of Electrical Engineers, 1912), he was employed as a Chief Draughtsman by his grandfather's firm, J C Fuller & Company of London. Over the next few years, he travelled to Egypt and to Canada for his firm, and was in Winnipeg, Canada, shortly before war broke out in 1914. Returning to England, he tried to get a commission via the London University OTC, but was refused entry on medical grounds. Undeterred, he travelled to Avonmouth to enlist in the RFC. His technical abilities apparent, he was immediately promoted to 1st Class Mechanic. Next, he qualified for his 'ticket', gaining the Royal Aero Certificate (Number 931) at his own expense, on 10 October 1914. He was accepted as a Cadet in February 1915 and was eventually gazetted Second Lieutenant to the RFC, via the Special Reserve, on 23 August following. After completing his formal pilot training at the CFS and elsewhere, he was confirmed and gazetted Flying Officer on 28 October 1915. Posted out to 1 Squadron (Nieuport XVIIs), then at Bailleul, on 11 February 1916, he was soon in the thick of the fighting. On 25 June 1916, Moore and others were involved in a concerted attack on the German balloon line stretching along the Somme front. In the area above Albert and Bapaume, Moore sent a German kite balloon down in flames in just ten seconds. His MC was announced in the *London Gazette* of 27 July 1916: 'For conspicuous gallantry and skill. He has destroyed two enemy kite balloons, one of which was being guarded by an enemy aeroplane. He has repeatedly attacked hostile aircraft, on one occasion attacking a flight of four, all of which he drove down and two of which he followed to 2,000 feet, one being apparently hard hit'.

Moore and his squadron continued to be heavily involved in the Somme fighting over the following months. On 30 September 1916, he was appointed Flight Commander and given the rank of A/Captain. His tour with '1' completed, he returned to the Home Establishment on 27 December 1916. Following a short leave, he joined 81 Squadron at Scampton, Lincolnshire. A transfer to 1 RS at Gosforth came on 3 May 1917. On 10 June 1917, he was instructing a pupil and, as their machine ascended, control was suddenly lost and they crashed to the ground. Beau Moore is buried in Gosport (Ann's Hill) Cemetery, Hampshire.

MOORE, Guy Boothwick

From Mattawa, Ontario, Canada, he was born on 28 May 1895. Educated at the University of British Columbia. He enlisted into 11 Fusiliers, Royal Irish, of Canada in 1916, but soon transferred to the RFC as a Cadet, travelling to the UK in January 1917. Gazetted Second Lieutenant to the RFC on 27 February 1917. His pilot training duly completed, he was gazetted Flying Officer on 9 June following. Sent out to 1 Squadron on 16 August 1917, he achieved ten victories between 2 October 1917 and 28 March 1918, the first seven in Nieuport Scouts, the remaining three in SE5As – yet another Canadian Ace. On 7 April 1918, Moore, in SE5A, 'C1083', was seen to explode in flames at 2,000 feet above Hollebeke, Belgium, probably as a consequence of a direct hit from an anti-aircraft shell. His MC was announced posthumously in the *London Gazette* of 13 May 1918: 'For conspicuous gallantry and devotion to duty. He led a patrol to attack hostile balloons. The patrol drove down three balloons in a collapsed position, one of which he accounted for himself. He has also destroyed three enemy aeroplanes and driven down three others out of control. He has always shown splendid courage and resource'.

Guy Moore's remains were never recovered and hence he is commemorated on the Flying Services Memorial, Arras, France.

MOORE, Guy Murton

From Claygate, Surrey, he was born in March 1896. Gazetted Second Lieutenant to the Special Reserve of the Princess Charlotte of Wales's (Royal Berkshire Regiment) on 5 November 1913. Embodied as soon as war came, he embarked for France with 1 Battalion, Royal Berkshire Regiment, on 12 August 1914, thus earning the 1914 Star. Moore was blown up and shell-shocked during the Battle of the Aisne on 15 September 1914, and was invalided back to the UK for treatment. Following a four-month recuperative home leave, he returned to France in April 1915. Just one month later, he was sent back to the UK. Seconded to the RFC in September 1915, he trained as an Observer and was sent first to 9 Squadron, then at Dover, in the winter of 1915. Going to France, he was injured in a flying accident on 22 April 1916, dislocating his right shoulder. Once recovered, he joined 15 Squadron as a Probationary and, his 'apprenticeship' satisfactorily completed, was duly confirmed and gazetted Flying Officer (Observer) on 27 October 1916. On 16 November following, Moore and his Pilot, Lieutenant Acland, opened fire with their Lewis guns on trenches thickly populated by enemy troops. Their fire scattered the infantry, forcing many of them back down into their underground dug-outs. His MC was announced in the *London Gazette* of 10 January 1917: 'For conspicuous gallantry in action. He brought in much valuable information by flying at 500 feet over the enemy's trenches. On another occasion he engaged enemy troops with his machine-gun and scattered them'.

He next trained as a Pilot and, once qualified, returned to 15 Squadron in that capacity in the winter of 1916-17. On 1 February 1917, Moore in a BE2e was wounded when his machine was hit by ground fire from the trenches, his fibula fractured by a machine-gun bullet. Continuing to experience difficulties with his badly injured leg, foot and ankle, Moore does not appear to have returned to operational flying during the remainder of the Great War.

MOORE, Joseph Michael John

From Burton-on-Trent, Staffordshire, he was born on 3 October 1889. Having previously served with the Staffordshire Yeomanry pre-war, he was given Sergeant's stripes in the same unit when he re-enlisted on 19 October 1914. Picked out for a commission, he was subsequently gazetted Second Lieutenant to the Cavalry Special Reserve on 7 October 1915, with an attachment to the South Irish Horse coming on 26 May 1916. He served in France with the South Irish Horse from August 1916. Seconded to the RFC on 20 August 1917, he trained as an Observer and was sent out as a Probationary to BF2b-equipped 48 Squadron on 8 October following. His 'apprenticeship' duly completed, he was confirmed and gazetted Flying Officer (Observer) on 31 January 1918, with his seniority backdated to 22 November 1917. On 21 March 1918, the first day of the German spring offensive, Moore and his Pilot, Second Lieutenant C G D Napier (qv), in BF2b, 'B1187', were forced to land after being hit by machine-gun fire from the ground. Six days later on 27 March, Moore and Napier shot down an enemy two-seater which crashed to the ground near to the River Avre, south west of Roye. On 27 April 1918, Moore was admitted to hospital and subsequently invalided back to England. His MC was announced in the *London Gazette* of 26 July 1918: 'For conspicuous gallantry and devotion to duty. When on a special reconnaissance, under poor climatic conditions, he flew below the clouds in the face of exceptionally heavy shell and machine-gun fire. He completed his task, and returned with intelligence of the greatest value. On a previous occasion, while on reconnaissance, he attacked four hostile machines and succeeded in destroying one and sending another down completely out of control. His work throughout has been carried out in the most courageous and dashing manner'.

Moore finally left the service, via the Unemployed List, on 10 April 1919.

MOORE-BRABAZON, John Theodore Cuthbert

A Staff, not a flying, award

The son of Lieutenant Colonel J A H Moore-Brabazon and Mrs Moore-Brabazon, of Tara Hall, County Meath, Ireland, he was born in London on 8 February 1884. Educated at Harrow and at Trinity College, Cambridge. He married, in 1906, Hilda Mary Krabbe, with whom he had two sons. A pioneer motorist as well as aviator, he won the Circuit des Ardennes motor race in 1907. Credited as the first British aviator, he gained the Royal Aero Club Certificate (Number 1) at Shellbeach in a Short machine on 8 March 1910, although the first four certificates were given to established Pilots before any set test had been agreed. Henry Farman was, in fact, the first Englishman to become a Pilot, but still the Society deemed it appropriate to give Moore-Brabazon the abiding distinction of receiving their first Certificate. Moore-Brabazon won the *Daily Mail*'s £1,000 prize for flying a circular mile in an all-English-made machine in 1909. He also won the first British Empire Michelin Cup in 1910. When war came, he first volunteered his services to the Red Cross, crossing to France in September 1914, at the wheel of his mother-in-law's four-cylinder Napier motorcar, thus earning the 1914 Star. Pulling strings, he decided to try for a commission in the flying service and was gazetted Second Lieutenant to the RFC on 2 December 1914, before being appointed and gazetted Equipment Officer on 31 March 1915. Moore-Brabazon was largely responsible for the RFC Photographic Section during the war, and for the development of aerial photography generally. His MC was announced in the *London Gazette* of 15 February 1917 (no citation). Although no formal citation appeared in the *Gazette*, research has unearthed the original recommendation for the award: 'T/Maj J T C Moore-Brabazon. Is employed on the Staff at Headquarters, RFC, and is responsible in the first instance for the great expansion of photography carried out by the Royal Flying Corps during the preparations for, and during the battle of the Somme. His technical knowledge and foresight have been invaluable and his assistance to the Brigades carrying out the work has been of much value'.

The French gave him the Croix de Chevalier, Légion d'Honneur, *London Gazette* of 24 February 1916. He was also Mentioned in Despatches on three occasions during the Great War. Leaving the RAF with the rank of Lieutenant Colonel after the war, Moore-Brabazon embarked upon an outstanding and multi-faceted career of which politics was the mainstay. His many honours and appointments included: Unionist MP for the Chatham Division of Rochester, 1918-29: MP for Wallasey, Cheshire, 1931-42; Privy Counsellor, 1940; 1st Baron Brabazon of Tara, created 1942; Parliamentary Secretary to Ministry of Transport, 1923- 27; Minister of Transport 1940-41; Minister of Aircraft Production, 1941-42; GBE, 1953; Member of the original Civil Aviation Committee; Chairman of the Air Mails Committee, 1923; Assessor in the R 101 Enquiry, 1930-31; President, Royal Aeronautical Society, 1935; President, Royal Aero Club, 1943-64; President Royal Institution, 1948-63; Member London County Council, St George's Division, Westminster, 1931-32; President of the English Golf Union, 1938; Captain of the Royal and Ancient (St Andrews), 1952-53; President, Professional Golfers Association, 1954; Winner of the Curzon Cup, St Moritz, 1920, 1922, 1927; Chairman ACV; Director of Kodak; Director of EMI; Director, David Brown Corporation Ltd; Director, Leyland Motors;. Chairman, Committee on Post-war Civil Aircraft; Chairman, Air Registration Board; Chairman, Air Safety Board; President, Radio Industry

Council; Gold Medal, Royal Aero Club, 1959; Wakefield Gold Medal (RAeS), 1963; Honorary LLD, St Andrews University, 1959. His publications included: 'The Brabazon Story' 1956 and 'Glastonbury, A Legend' (play) 1963. He lived at 20 Berkeley Square, London. Lord Brabazon of Tara died on 17 May 1964.

NB: The RAF Museum Hendon has his medals in its collection: MC, 1914 Star (JTC Moore-Brabazon, BRCS & O St J), *British War Medal 1914-20, Victory Medal 1914-19* (Major, RFC), *and Coronation Medal 1937.*

MORGAN, Josiah Lewis

The only son of Mr and Mrs Morgan, of 121 Commercial Street, Eglwysilan, Glamorgan, he was born in Porth, Glamorgan, in 1893. Gazetted Second Lieutenant to a Regular Army Battalion of the South Wales Borderers on 26 September 1916. In February 1917, Morgan led a small patrol into the enemy trenches and, on finding them empty, held the position for a full day, only withdrawing because the area was about to be bombarded by the Royal Artillery in advance of an attack by the British 86 Brigade. Seconded to the RFC on 10 October 1917, he trained as an Observer and was posted to the Bristol Fighter-equipped 22 Squadron on 13 January 1918. Aggressive and skilful, he claimed 12 victories between 6 March and 29 May 1918, all but one with Lieutenant H F Davison (qv), before returning to the Home Establishment on the 4 April following. His MC was announced in the *London Gazette* of 26 July 1918: 'For conspicuous gallantry and devotion to duty when carrying out many low-flying and offensive patrols, and engaging enemy troops, transports, etc., with machine-gun fire, and inflicting heavy casualties. On many occasions he attacked and destroyed, or drove down out of control, hostile machines, and he invariably displayed a dash and determination worthy of the highest praise'.

Morgan saw out the war instructing, latterly with No 6 School of Aviation, prior to finally leaving the RAF on 11 April 1919.

MORGAN, Lewis Langharne

The son of William Langharne and Alice Emily Morgan, of Underwood, Mumbles, Swansea, Glamorgan, and later 10 Kingsbury Street, Marlborough, Wiltshire, he was born on 11 December 1896. Educated at Llanyre Hall Preparatory School, Radnorshire and at Highgate School, London (1911-13), where he gained his colours with the Rugby XV. On the second day of the war, he volunteered to serve as a motor-cycle despatch rider. Picked out for a commission, he was gazetted Second Lieutenant to 6 (Glamorgan) Battalion, Welsh Regiment (TF), on 6 August 1916. Seeking secondment to the RFC, he gained his Royal Aero Club Certificate (Number 4148) on 17 January 1917. His formal pilot training duly completed, he was confirmed and gazetted Flying Officer on 15 March 1917. Within days of being awarded his 'Wings', he was sent out to join 40 Squadron (Nieuport XVIIs) in France. He was Mentioned in Despatches for his part in a surprise attack on enemy balloons. Having crossed the lines at 100 feet, members of 40 Squadron brought five balloons down in flames. The Commander-in-Chief of the BEF, Sir Douglas Haig, no less, sent the following signal to the squadron CO: 'A very fine performance. Please congratulate those that carried out the attack on the great success of their efforts'. His MC was announced in the *London Gazette* of 18 July 1917: 'For conspicuous gallantry and devotion to duty. He crossed the lines at a height of under 100 feet, and destroyed a hostile kite balloon. Previously he attacked a hostile scout at close range and brought it down in flames. He has shown great gallantry in many combats'.

The squadron's Chaplain wrote a congratulatory note to Morgan's parents: '....his work has been characterised not only by brilliancy but also by steadiness. He got his balloon in the first of the two special balloon attacks although when he went up in his machine he found that only eight of his nine cylinders were working – to have still gone on and carried out his job successfully under these conditions was a splendid and brilliant achievement. Although he was not 'down' to take part in the second balloon expedition, he would not be out of it, but went off and got a balloon on his own in magnificent style. One typical story I must tell you – when he got his balloon the German Observer descended in his parachute, and when someone asked your son if he had shot him as he came down, he said, 'No, I couldn't shoot at the poor chap when he was like that, I just flew close past him and made a face at him'. So typical of his chivalrous and generous spirit. Never was the MC more deservedly awarded than in the case of your son'. By the time his MC was announced, however, Morgan had already been seriously wounded. He had acquired a reputation as a lone 'trouble shooter' and was given the nom de guerre, 'Air Hog'. On the evening of 24 May 1917, he was stooging around in Nieuport XVII, 'B1642', looking for trouble, when, either his machine was hit by a shell or he was shot down by the German Ace, Oberleutnant Max Müller. Certainly Müller claimed a Nieuport going down in the British lines in the area of St Eloi, at 20.35 German time, a place and time which appears fairly conclusive. The consensus on the British side, however, favoured, for obvious reasons, the random shell theory. A version of the events of 24 May 1917 were reported in the *Daily Telegraph* as follows: 'A still more wonderful experience has just come to a British pilot who, while flying at four thousand feet across the lines, was hit by an artillery shell! The shell crashed through the body of his machine, but did not explode until it struck the engine. It tore away two cylinders and smashed the engine bearers. Hit by splinters, the pilot's right leg was fractured in two places. Despite this, however, he brought the machine down in his own lines....'. After he was extricated from a hole in the side of the machine, his right leg was found to be shattered below the knee and had to be amputated – again below the knee. A mere two hours later he found the strength to write a reassuring letter to his parents: 'I made certain I was killed, so to find that after all I was only a foot missing, hardly seems any punishment at all....My leg gives me very little pain, I hardly notice it'. A contemporary book entitled 'An Airman's Wife' makes several allusions to Lewis Morgan: 'I haven't told you about the 'Air Hog'. He is simply crazy to get Huns. After going up a few times he developed a habit of going up and tearing about the sky all alone. At last he was put on a 'Roving Commission Game', and since then he has spent at least eight hours a day in the air'. And, later on in the same book: 'The 'Air Hog' had to lose one leg just below the knee. I don't think many people so well deserved an MC'. Fitted with an artificial limb, Morgan re-joined in March 1918, being posted to 50 Squadron, then in Bekesbourne, Kent. Appointed Aerial Fighting Instructor to the squadron, he was accidentally killed in a side-slip and sudden nose-dive at a low altitude on 26 April 1918. The engine of his SE5, 'C5342', spluttered and coughed on take-off and he 'did a McCudden', turning back at 125 feet, but hit a railway embankment north of the airfield. Lewis Morgan is buried in Canterbury Cemetery, Kent.

MORGAN, Whitworth Archibald Cecil

From Clifton, Bristol, he was born on 13 May 1894. Educated at Lancing College (1908-11). He was working as a Tea Planter in Ceylon when war came in 1914. Returning to the UK, he entered the Royal Military College, Camberley, and was subsequently gazetted Second Lieutenant to a Regular Army battalion of the Welsh Regiment on 11 August 1915, with an immediate secondment to the RFC. Gained his Royal Aero Club Certificate (Number 1950) on 7 October 1915. His formal pilot training duly completed, he was confirmed and gazetted Flying Officer on 28 October following. Posted to 24 Squadron (DH2s), then forming at Hounslow, he accompanied it, the first single-seater Scout unit, to France as a 'founder member' on 7 February 1916. On 18 June 1916, Morgan, in company with Captain J A H Crook (qv), 11 Squadron, engaged an enemy formation in the neighbourhood of Arras, driving one of them down near Terre Mesnil, east of Doullens. The enemy machine hit the ground left wing first and the crew were taken prisoner. Morgan and Crook each received the MC, Morgan's was announced in the *London Gazette* of 27 July 1916: 'For conspicuous gallantry and skill. With other pilots he attacked an enemy reconnaissance of nine machines. Under heavy machine-gun fire he got within twenty yards of one of them, shot the Observer and brought the machine down in our lines'.

Morgan's tour with '24' ended early in 1917, whereupon he returned to the Home Establishment to take up a training post. In February 1918, he returned to France as a 'founder member' and Flight Commander of 79 Squadron, newly equipped with Sopwith Dolphins. He flew with '79' through the dark days of the German spring offensive and was wounded in action on 31 May 1918. Morgan did not return to operationally flying before the end of the war, but did receive a permanent commission in the RAF on 1 August 1919. He rose to the rank of Group Captain by 1 January 1939, but was obliged to retire on 13 July 1940.

MORICE, Charles Stewart

The son of Stock Jobber, William Morice and Laura Morice, of 25 Exbury Road, Catford, London, he was born on 28 May 1890. Gazetted as a Supplementary Reserve Officer into the Worcestershire Regiment on 1 October 1913, attached to 6 (Militia) Battalion. Embodied and posted to France by 14 August 1914, he witnessed the first shots of the war fired in the area of Mons. Wounded near the Aisne in December 1914, he returned to the UK for medical treatment, before going back to serve with the BEF in May 1915, only to be wounded again at St Eloi on 19 August following. Once recovered, he successfully sought secondment to the RFC in February 1916. Gained his Royal Aero Club Certificate (Number 3940) on 24 September 1916, the same day that he was formally confirmed and gazetted Flying Officer. Sent out to FE2d-equipped 57 Squadron in France soon after he qualified. On 30 April 1917, Morice and his Observer, Lieutenant F Leathley (qv), in FE2d, 'A1966', were one of a quartet of 57 Squadron FEs that fell foul of elements of von Richthofen's 'Flying Circus' over Douai. Sent down and crashing heavily, Morice and Leathley were extremely fortunate to escape relatively unscathed. His MC was announced in the *London Gazette* of 1 January 1918 (no citation). Although no formal citation appeared in the *Gazette*, research has uncovered the original recommendation for the award: 'T/Capt C S Morice. Worcs Rgt 6/10/17: For exceptional skill and valuable work in the taking of aeroplane photographs, often under most difficult weather conditions from April 1917-September 1917. At all times his excellent example and spirit have inspired those around him'.

His tour with '57' completed, he returned to the Home Establishment in September 1917, where he saw out the remainder of the war. Staying on in the RAF after the war, he served at the Air Ministry and in Iraq until his retirement (at his own request) with the rank of Squadron Leader on 3 June 1925. In 1927, Morice joined the Dunlop Rubber Company as the technical expert on the tyre performance of the buses belonging to the London General Omnibus Company. He was also the Transport Service Supervisor on the tyre side of Dunlop's Albany Street Depot, London, until he was recalled to the RAF in 1939. He was first sent to France as a Censor with the Advanced Striking Force in 1939-40, before serving next as the Operational Controller at RAF Wittering, throughout the Battle of Britain. Morice then helped to form 121 Wing of the Tactical Air Force in May 1943. By that time, he had flown every type of operational aircraft and it was he who actually led the Wing into Normandy after the landings in 1944. Landing six days after D Day, he had his rocket-firing Typhoons in action just two days later. For his outstanding services, he was awarded the Distinguished Service Order in September 1944. He finally handed over command of 121 Wing in December 1944. Group Captain Morice's contribution to the invasion of Europe was recognised by the Dutch with the award of the Commander of the Order of Orange Nassau, the insignia of which was presented to him personally by Queen Wilhelmina. After the war, he joined Dunlop again, this time as Sales Manager of their Aviation Division, based firstly at Foleshill, Coventry, and later in London. Morice retired from Dunlop in 1956 and moved with his wife to Tangmere, near Chichester. Over the years he had played cricket for the RAF, the MCC, and for Hertfordshire. An accomplished golfer, he was Captain of the Aero Golfing Society in 1954, Chairman and Captain of the Dunlop (London) Golfing Society, and a member of East Brighton Golf Club. Group Captain Charles Morice died at the RAFA Home, Storrington, Sussex, on 5 February 1969.

MORRIS, James (also known as J Fitz Morris)

His birth certificate gives only the name, James Morris, although, perhaps significantly, his father's name is J F Morris. The 'Fitz' seems to appear only after he was promoted to Captain and had received the first of his MCs. He was born in Falkirk, Scotland, on 6 April 1897 (although he gave his birth year as 1895 when he enlisted under-age). Educated at Polmont School, Polmont, Scotland. A motor engineer by profession. He enlisted as a Sapper (Number 32208) into the Royal Engineers in 1914 and was sent to France, with the rank of Corporal, in June 1915, serving there as a motor-cycle despatch rider with the Indian Division. Picked out for a commission, he was gazetted Second Lieutenant to the Highland Light Infantry, via the General List, on 18 November 1915, with an immediate secondment to the RFC. Having trained as an Observer, he served at the front with the Vickers FB5-equipped 11 Squadron from December following. He next trained as a Pilot in the UK and was duly confirmed and gazetted Flying Officer on 12 July 1916. Returning again to 11 Squadron in this new capacity, he suffered two accidents during practice flights on 20 and 26 July 1916, incurring minor injuries. Sent next to 1 Squadron, his operational career was soon curtailed when he was injured yet again in a flying accident on 5 August 1916, this time fracturing his nose and suffering severe concussion. Once recovered, he was sent to the DH4-equipped 25 Squadron on 1 July 1917. Striking up an effective partnership with Canadian, Lieutenant D L Burgess (qv), the pair achieved seven victories between 7 July and 25 August 1917, each receiving the MC for their efforts, announced in the *London Gazette* of 26 September 1917, details in the *Gazette* of 9 January 1918: 'For conspicuous gallantry and devotion to duty on photographic and offensive patrols. On at least four occasions he has displayed great dash and courage in attacking hostile machines, two of which he completely destroyed, and has driven others down out of control'.

Research has unearthed the original recommendation for this award, which provides more detailed information: 'HQ, 1st Brigade, RFC. 12 September 1917. For courage and skill in aerial fighting, and for good leadership on Photographic Reconnaissance and Offensive Patrols:- On August 8th 1917, in very bad weather, he successfully led a formation to bomb Courrières. During this raid he encountered three hostile machines and forced one to land near Seclin. On August 5th 1917, after bombing Mouveaux Aerodrome, he attacked one of three hostile scouts. About 300 rounds were fired from both guns, and the enemy machine fell in flames near Perenchies. On July 22 1917, whilst on photography east of Lille, his machine was twice attacked by four enemy scouts. During the second fight, one of the enemy machines was shot down in flames. This was confirmed by anti-aircraft observers. On 11th July 1917, whilst bombing Derignies Aerodrome, nine hostile scouts attempted to cut him off from the lines. By skilful handling of his machine, the leading scout was shot down completely out of control'.

Early in 1918, Morris was promoted to A/Captain and sent to Spad XIII-equipped 23 Squadron as a Flight Commander. With '23', he accounted for a further seven enemy machines between 1 March and 24 March 1918, on which latter date he himself was shot down and slightly wounded. He was soon in the air again, however, and suffered being shot down again on 30 March, when his propellor was destroyed by anti-aircraft fire over Villers Bretonneaux. The Bar to his MC came in the *London Gazette* of 22 June 1918: 'For conspicuous gallantry and devotion to duty. During operations he carried out many reconnaissances at at a low altitude and obtained valuable information. On one occasion, while on a bombing patrol, he saw an enemy machine attacking our troops with machine-gun fire from about 500 feet, and at once attacked it and drove it to the ground. He then attacked seven enemy scouts, one of which he drove down in flames inside our lines. He has also destroyed five other enemy machines and driven down two others out of control. He has always set a magnificent example of dash and determination'.

Morris, an Ace of distinction and the holder of the MC and Bar, was sent out to the British War Mission in Washington, DC, to serve as an Instructor to the USAS. Oddly, although incorrectly, he is shown in the records of that organisation as a holder of the Distinguished Service Order as well as his undoubted MC and Bar. He was killed in a flying accident in Camel, 'F1341', at Indianapolis, on 14 August 1918, the exact cause ofwhich could not established by a subsequent Court of Enquiry. It appears that his father had great difficulty in persuading the authorities to return his body to Scotland. However, by dint of perseverance, he succeeded and hence James Morris is buried in Polment churchyard, Stirlingshire. He was 21.

MORRIS, Robert Kay

From Brondesbury, North West London, he was born on 14 January 1893. He enlisted as a Private soldier (Number 2782) into 14 Battalion, London Regiment, the London Scottish, on 1 September 1914. Morris served as a Lance Corporal in the trenches, before being picked out for a commission and gazetted Second Lieutenant to 21 (Reserve) Battalion, Durham Light Infantry, on 8 December 1915. Seconded to the RFC in the early summer of 1916, he trained as a Pilot and was duly confirmed and gazetted Flying Officer on 25 September following. Sent out to 30 Squadron in Mesopotamia on 31 December 1916. Morris was Mentioned in Despatches in the *London Gazette* of 12 March 1918. His tour with '30' completed on 11 April 1918, he next reported to RAF HQ, Egypt for duties as an Instructor. He next served with the RAF Palestine Brigade in February 1919 and with BE2e-equipped 113 Squadron from the following month. He was promoted to A/Captain in April 1919, before returning to the UK in the following month. The very late announcement of his MC appeared in the *London Gazette* of 11 January 1919 (Mesopotamia): 'For conspicuous gallantry and devotion to duty. He fought a number of battles in the air with great skill and daring, and on one occasion brought down an enemy machine behind our lines'.

Morris relinquished his commission in the RAF in September 1921, retaining the rank of Flight Lieutenant. He died on 15 December 1969.

MORTON, Allen Handfield

The only son of Major Philip Francis Morton and Mrs Morton, of 15 Ashley Place, London, SW1, he was born on 16 February 1890. Educated at Rugby School (1904-08) and at the Royal Military Academy, Woolwich. Gazetted Second Lieutenant to the Royal Field Artillery in 1910. He served on the Brigade Staff, 40 Brigade, RFA, in 1914 and 1915. Seconded to the RFC in the spring of 1915, he gained his Royal Aero Club Certificate (Number 1274) on 29 May following. His formal pilot training duly completed, he was confirmed and gazetted Flying Officer on 20 July following. Sent to 13 Squadron, then stationed in Gosport, on 9 August 1915, he accompanied the unit to France as a 'founder member' on 19 October following. He was next promoted to A/Captain and Flight Commander and transferred to 8 Squadron on 14 January 1916. On 13 March 1916, Morton and his Observer of the day, Lieutenant Robinson, were part of an 8 Squadron patrol that was engaged in combat by three Fokkers. Two of the BE2c were sent down, although Morton and Robinson in BE2c, '4180', managed to get away – not, however, before they had witnessed BE2c, '4151' (Second Lieutenant M A J Orde and 1 AM P Shaw) being chased down to ground level by two of the Fokkers, one of which landed alongside the disabled British machine. His MC was announced in the New Year *London Gazette* of 1 January 1917 (no citation). Although no formal citation was published in the *Gazette*, research has unearthed the original recommendation for the award: 'A H Morton: From March to July 1916 he carried out successful and gallant work in co-operation with artillery, often at low heights and in bad weather. On the 28th June '16 he went out twice over the trenches at Gommecourt and reconnoitred the state of the German wire at 1,000 feet and 500 feet, handing in a most valuable report. On the 18th March '16 he successfully carried out a special mission over the lines at night. His example to the pilots and observers of his squadron was most valuable'.

The Russians, too, awarded him the Order of St Stanislaus, 2nd Class, and he was Mentioned in Despatches on two occasions around this time, *London Gazette*s of 15 June 1916 and 25 January 1917. His tour with '8' completed on 17 July 1916, he was next promoted to A/Major and appointed to the command of 34 Squadron (RE8s) from 23 March 1917. His command of '34' ended on 11 July 1917, when he returned to the Home Establishment. Morton reverted to the Royal Artillery at the end of the war and was an Instructor in Gunnery at the School of Artillery, Larkhill, Salisbury Plain, from 1920 to 1924.

MUIR, Stanley Keith

The son of Mr and Mrs J F Muir, of 28 Jolimont Street, Jolimont, Victoria, Australia, he was born in 1892. Educated at Scotch College, Melbourne. After leaving school, he became a Sheep Station Overseer. When the war came, he enlisted into the AIF in Melbourne on 19 October 1914 and was sent to the training camp at Broadmeadows. A member of 'A' Squadron, 4 Light Horse Regiment, he embarked at Melbourne aboard the SS *Wiltshire* (Transport A18), bound for Alexandria. Arriving in Egypt, he was sent to Camp Mena, from where he and his unit were sent to Gallipoli on 22 May 1915. Promoted to Corporal on 13 August 1915. Sent next to England as a candidate for a commission, he was gazetted Second Lieutenant to the New Armies on 18 November 1915, with an immediate attachment to 20 Battalion, King's Royal Rifle Corps. He soon successfully sought secondment to the RFC, gaining his Royal Aero Club Certificate (Number 2942) on 11 May 1916. His formal pilot training duly completed, he was confirmed and gazetted Flying Officer on 10 June following. Sent out again to the Middle East, he joined 67 Squadron (later 1 Squadron, Australian Flying Corps). On 24 November 1916, he and Captain R H Freeman (qv), of 14 Squadron, both flying Martinsydes, conducted a daring long-range bombing raid on the Hejaz railway on the far side of the Dead Sea. His MC was announced in the *London Gazette* of 3 March 1917: 'For conspicuous gallantry in action. He carried out a daring bombing raid and was largely instrumental in shooting down a hostile machine. On another occasion he pursued two enemy machines and succeeded in bringing one of them down'.

His tour with '67' completed, he returned to the UK and was posted as an Instructor. On 12 September 1917, he was killed in a flying accident and is buried nearby in Harlaxton (SS Mary and Peter) Churchyard, Lincolnshire.

MULCAHY-MORGAN, Thomas Westropp

Gazetted Second Lieutenant to a Regular Army battalion of the Royal Irish Fusiliers in 1912. Developing an interest in aviation, he gained his Royal Aero Club Certificate (Number 457) on a Bristol machine at the Bristol School, Brooklands, on 12 April 1913. Soon afterwards seconded to the RFC, he was formally gazetted a Flight Commander on 13 August 1913. Mulcahy-Morgan accompanied, as a Flying Officer with 4 Squadron, the original RFC contingent to France in August 1914, thus earning a 1914 Star. After completing his tour with '4', Mulcahy-Morgan was posted later in 1915 to 6 Squadron as a Flight Commander. On 10 September 1915, Mulcahy-Morgan, in a Martinsyde S1, '1601', successfully engaged an Albatros over Wieltse, sending it down to crash. On 13 September 1915, Mulcahy-Morgan in BE2c, '1680', made the first ever attempt to drop a spy behind enemy lines. The plan was to land in a field near Courtrai, which bordered upon a dense wood, so chosen to allow the secret-service agent to disappear into its depths as soon as they came to a halt. In the event, the landing ground was a bad choice, narrow and small. Mulcahy-Morgan was unable to avoid a collision with a tree and consequently his BE2c was badly damaged. French civilians were helpful in taking away various sensitive documents and the cage of carrier pigeons they carried, before German troops arrived on the scene. They could do little, however, for Mulcahy-Morgan and his passenger, both of whom were badly injured and subsequently taken to Courtrai hospital and into captivity. The first of his two MCs was belatedly announced in the *London Gazette* of 8 August 1917 (no citation). Although no formal citation was published in the *Gazette*, it is reasonable to assume that it was awarded for his failed attempt to deliver a spy behind the lines. Remarkably, Mulcahy-Morgan subsequently escaped from a German prison camp and made his way back to the UK in April 1917. This achievement was acknowledged by the award of a Bar to his MC, announced in the 'Escapers Gazette', *London Gazette* of 16 December 1919: 'His Majesty the King has been pleased to approve the award of a Bar to the MC to Lieut/Temp Captain (now Sqd Ldr) Thomas Westropp Mulcahy-Morgan, MC (R Ir Fus), in recognition of gallantry in escaping whilst Prisoners of War.'

MURLIS GREEN, Gilbert Ware

Born in Bridgwater on 24 January 1895, his family later moving to live in London. Pre-war, Murlis Green worked for Bradley's, a firm of Furriers in London. When the war came, he enlisted as a Private soldier (Number 1863) in 2/16 Battalion, London Regiment, Queen's Westminster Rifles. Picked out for a commission, he was originally gazetted Second Lieutenant to 7 Battalion, South Staffordshire Regiment, on 9 September 1914, but was soon transferred to the Army Cyclist Corps and, by early 1915, was serving in France with the Cyclists. An opportunity for a further transfer to the RFC was offered and accepted. Having trained as an Observer, he was sent back to France as a Probationary with 5 Squadron (Vickers FB5s), then stationed at Abeele. Employed mainly on photo-reconnaissance whilst sitting in the front seat of a Vickers Pusher high above the enemy trenches on the Ypres Salient, he complained in a letter home, that, 'one's hand became intensely cold and occasionally a slide is dropped and blown back through the propeller, a performance which immediately brings forth a shower of curses and grimaces from the pilot!'. After eight months service as an Observer, he was sent back to England for pilot training. Following qualification on 1 April 1916, he was given a further short course on flying instruction before being posted to 17 Squadron (BE12s) in Macedonia. Despite the short-comings of the BE12 (a fairly unsuccessful up-dated conversation of the by-then obsolete BE 2), Murlis Green soon gained a number of victories. His first was against a DFW two-seater on 13 December 1916; the second coming on the following day when he forced an Albatros two-seater to crashland. His first MC was announced in the New Year *London Gazette* of 1 January 1917 (no citation).

A Bar to his MC came soon afterwards in the *London Gazette* of 13 February 1917: 'For conspicuous gallantry in action. He brought down two enemy machines on successive days under adverse circumstances. He has displayed great dash and courage at every opportunity'.

The leading enemy Ace on this front was Leutnant Rudolf von Eschwege, 'The Eagle of The Aegean'. On 18 February 1917, 'Todger' Murlis Green and a colleague, Lieutenant J C F Owen (qv), decided to confront and challenge von Eschwege and so they waited for him above his home field. Obligingly, the German Ace soon climbed to engage his challengers. Unfortunately, Murlis Green's guns jammed at a crucial moment and, whilst he struggled to correct the fault, von Eschwege shot Owen down to a crash-landing. Unable to free his gun, Murlis Green turned for home, while the downed Owen set fire to his machine before enemy troops took him captive. Three more victories followed, before, on 18 March 1917, Murlis Green in BE12a, 'A4007, performed a coup de main by bringing down two twin-engined Friedrikschafen bombers in the same combat. These newly-arrived enemy machines had been greeted with some trepidation by the Anglo-French air forces in the Macedonian theatre of war, and so, following his successes against them, Murlis Green found himself appointed to command a squadron newly-formed specifically to combat their menace. Because the new enemy bombers were invariably given umbrella fighter cover, Murlis Green decided that they should be attacked from below and, putting his theory into practice, he shot one down into no-man's land on his first patrol with his new command. Shortly afterwards, he attacked yet another Friedrikschafen and, after emptying three drums into it, saw it fall away with petrol pouring out of its punctured fuel tanks, a crew member slumped dead or unconscious over the side of the cockpit. Murlis Green achieved two more victories in the Greek skies, before being ordered home to the UK in the summer of 1917. For his services during this period, he was awarded the Distinguished Service Order, to which, subsequently, he would also add a Bar, *London Gazette* of 18 December 1917. Back in England, he was given command of the Camel-equipped 44 Squadron, a unit which became one of the first night-fighter squadrons employed against the increasing Gotha bombing raids over home territory. On 18 December 1917, the day he received a Bar to his Distinguished Service Order, Murlis Green, in Sopwith Camel, 'B5192', became one of the first Pilots to shoot down a Gotha. He spotted the bomber's exhaust flames in the night sky over

Goodmayes in Essex and, helped by a searchlight which caught and fixed the giant machine in its beam, Murlis Green attacked, 'taking out' one of the Gotha's engines. Despite the loss of an engine, the German fliers showed great courage by continuing on to their target, dropping bombs on Bermondsey some ten minutes later. Soon afterwards, however, the Gotha started to lose altitude, especially when a second engine failed and eventually it fell into the sea off Folkestone. A passing trawler took the floating Gotha in tow, with the crew still aboard, but soon afterwards an explosion destroyed the machine and killed the Pilot, although the Observer and Gunner survived to be taken prisoner. For this feat Murlis Green received a second Bar to his MC, *London Gazette* of 7 January 1918: 'Whilst flying at night on patrol duty, he encountered an enemy aeroplane, which he attacked with great determination and skill, and although there was very little light he succeeded in hitting one of the engines of the machine, which, by reason of damage, was forced to come down in the sea off a south coast port, where two of the occupants were made prisoners'.

Considering the great range of decorations showered upon Murlis Green, the total of his victories numbered no more than eight, in stark contrast to many other fliers with more confirmed successes, who received absolutely nothing. Only two men have ever received this combination of five gallantry awards, Murlis Green's being unique to the RFC. His other awards included: Chevalier, Légion d'Honneur; Croix de Guerre (France); Serbian Order of the White Eagle 4th Class (with swords); and Croix de Guerre (Belgium). Murlis Green briefly commanded 151 and 112 Squadrons in the UK, before going to France in August 1918, to take charge of a badly mauled and dispirited 70 Squadron, restoring that unit's confidence and leading it through to the end of the war. Staying on in the RAF, he eventually rose to the rank of Group Captain and also served throughout the Second World War. Died on 26 August 1958 at Kitale, Kenya.

NB: The RAF Museum Hendon has his medals in its collection: Distinguished Service Order & Bar, MC & two Bars, 1914-15 Star (2Lt A Cyc Corps), *British War Medal 1914-20, Victory Medal 1914-19 with MID* (Major, RAF), *Silver Jubilee Medal 1935, Coronation Medal 1937, Africa Star 1940-43, War Medal 1939-45, Légion d'Honneur (Chevalier, France), Order of the White Eagle (Civil Companion, Badge, Serbia), Croix de Guerre with bronze laurel (France), and Croix de Guerre 1914-18 (Belgium). His 1939-45 Star is missing.*

MURPHY, Cyril Francis De Sales

The son of Mr and Mrs Jerome Murphy, of Ashton, County Cork, Ireland, he was born on 17 May 1882. Educated at Beaumont School and at Sandhurst. Gazetted Second Lieutenant to 2 Battalion, Royal Berkshire Regiment in 1902. He served with the Berkshires until 1910, when he was seconded to the Army Gymnastics Staff. Developing an interest in aviation, he gained his Royal Aero Club Certificate (Number 599) on a Bristol machine at the Bristol School, Brooklands, Salisbury Plain, on 20 August 1913. Seconded to the RFC, he was formally confirmed and gazetted Flying Officer on 30 June 1914. He served with 4 Squadron operationally in the spring and summer of 1915, before being appointed Commanding Officer of 2 Squadron on 2 November 1915. His MC was announced in the Birthday Honours *London Gazette* of 3 June 1916 (no citation). Although no formal citation was published in the *Gazette*, research has unearthed the original recommendation for the award: 'C F deS Murphy. For conspicuous ability and good work. Major Murphy has commanded 2 Squadron RFC from November 3rd, 1915 to March 1916 with marked skill, particularly in co-operations with the artillery; he has induced in his Squadron a fighting spirit of a very high order'.

By the opening of the Battle of the Somme on 1 July 1916, Murphy had been promoted to Lieutenant Colonel and given command of the Thirteenth Army Wing, III Brigade, at Foufflin-Ricametz. For his work on the Somme, Murphy was awarded the Distinguished Service Order in the *London Gazette* of 1 January 1917. He had also been Mentioned in Despatches on three occasions and the Belgians conferred upon him the Officier l'Ordre de la Coruone, *London Gazette* of 24 September 1917. Returning to the Home Establishment early in 1917, he was, after a period of rest and recuperation, sent next to command 6 Wing, RFC, in the December following. From 6 March 1918, Murphy commanded an RFC Brigade in France. He finally resigned his commission, retaining the honorary rank of Brigadier General, on 17 September 1919. His brother, Cuthbert Morgan Murphy, was also a senior Staff Officer in the RAF. Having returned to Ireland to farm the family estates, Cyril married, in 1926, Marguerita Nagle. He lectured at the National Institute of Agricultural Botany, Cambridge, from 1922 to 1927 and again between 1944-47. Murphy owned residences at 3 Chesham Street, London SW1, and at 'The Bridge', Banagher, Southern Ireland. When the Second World War came, he returned to the RAF and served at the Air Ministry from 1939 until 1944. Cyril Murphy retired to his estate in Ireland in 1947 and died there on 7 January 1961.

MURRAY, Eric Mackay

The son of Colonel R D Murray, MB, Indian Medical Service, and Mrs Murray, he was born on 24 September 1886. Educated at Clifton College (1899-1904) and at Sandhurst. His brother, Robin George Hamilton Murray (RAeC Certificate Number 320) won an MC with 1/9 Gurkha Rifles in March 1915, before transferring to the RFC and serving subsequently as a Flight Commander in France from 1915 to 1917; commanding a HD Squadron in the UK and a squadron in India in 1917, and serving as a Wing Commander in Palestine in 1918. Eric was gazetted Second Lieutenant to the Royal Highlanders, Black Watch, in 1906, and subsequently served in India (India General Service Medal 1908-35, with clasp, North West Frontier 1908), before transferring into the Queen Victoria's Own Corps of Guides Frontier Force (Cavalry), Indian Army, in 1909. Developing an interest in aviation, he gained an early Royal Aero Club Certificate (Number 177) on a Bristol machine at the Bristol School, Salisbury Plain, on 30 January 1912. He was eventually seconded to the RFC in September 1914 and, having completed his formal training, was confirmed and gazetted Flying Officer on 19 November following. He subsequently served in France, Egypt and in Mesopotamia, joining 30 Squadron in Basra on 20 November 1915. For his services during the attempts to relieve the besieged garrison at Kut-al-Amara, he was awarded his MC, announced in the *London Gazette* of 15 April 1916: 'For conspicuous gallantry and determination. He has flown continually in all winds and weathers, and carried out many daring reconnaissances with great skill'.

His tour with '30' completed on 15 August 1916, he was posted next to RFC HQ, Egypt. He married around this time, Vivien Woodruff, with whom he had three daughters. Promoted to A/Major and given command of a squadron, his efforts in this regard were acknowledged when he was awarded the Distinguished Service Order, *London Gazette* of 2 December 1918. He was also Mentioned in Despatches on one occasion during the Great War. Staying on in the RAF after the war, his subsequent appointments included: Assistant Commandant RAF College, Cranwell, 1924-29; Director of Staff, RAF Staff College, 1929-30; and President, Air Crew Selection Board, 1939. Group Captain Eric Murray lived in retirement at 'Inches', Battledown, Cheltenham.

MURRAY, George

From Hampstead, London, he was born on 20 February 1891. His father was in business in Buenos Aires, Argentina, and, consequently, George spent much of his boyhood and youth in that country. He was a trained architect and fluent in French, Italian and Spanish. Travelling to the UK as one of the many British Latin American Volunteers, he enlisted as a Private soldier (Number 7442) into 28 Battalion, London Regiment (Artists Rifles) (TF). Picked out for a commission, he was first sent to the flying service as a Cadet on 11 November 1916, before being gazetted Second Lieutenant to the RFC on 26 January 1917. Having trained as an Observer, he was posted to 50 Squadron for Home Defence duties in the UK. On 7 July 1917, Murray and his Pilot, Second Lieutenant F A D Grace (qv), another volunteer from the Argentine, in AWFK8, 'B247', intercepted a formation of Gothas at 16,000 feet north of Girdler. The enemy had already been attacked by a RNAS tri-plane, which had turned away. Now Grace dived onto three of the enemy machines, which immediately responded with retaliatory fire. Next he turned his attention to another Gotha, which was trailing behind the trio he had just attacked. Within moments, the enemy bomber was on fire, smoke pouring from its centre section. Grace and Murray followed the stricken German machine down and watched it hit the sea. As the wreckage started to sink, two of the crew climbed out onto the port upper wing. Grace and Murray could do nothing to help the men, except to fire flares in the hope of attracting a nearby ship to the scene. His MC was announced in the *London Gazette* of 18 December 1917: 'His Majesty the King has been pleased to confer the following rewards in recognition of gallantry and distinguished service in connection with anti-aircraft services in the United Kingdom. Awarded the Military Cross – Second Lieutenant George Murray'

Murray and his Pilot, Fred Grace, both received their Crosses from the hands of the King at an investiture held at Buckingham Palace on 20 July 1917, quite some time before the formal announcement appeared in the *London Gazette*. Murray would go on to serve, successively, with 143 HD Squadron from 14 February 1918; with 141 HD Squadron later in 1918; with 166 Squadron from February 1919; with 5 Communication Squadron later in 1919; and, finally, with 274 Squadron from July 1919. He finally left the RAF, via the Unemployed List, on 27 September 1919. George Murray sailed for Argentina aboard the SS *Almonzora* on 5 June 1920. For his work as an interpreter for the Spanish government in the winter of 1919-20, he was awarded the Spanish Order of Military Merit, Class 1, in the *London Gazette* of 23 November 1920.

MURRAY, George Scott

From Nelson, New Zealand, he was born on 10 April 1892. Coming to the UK, he was accepted for a commission and gazetted Second Lieutenant to the New Armies, attached 30 (Reserve) Battalion, Royal Fusiliers, on 22 August 1915. Subsequently transferring to the RFC, he gained his Royal Aero Club Certificate (Number 4876) on 13 August 1916 and was formally confirmed and gazetted Flying Officer on the same day. Sent to 26 Squadron on 27 August 1916, he served with that unit in East Africa from 13 October 1916 until 22 August 1917. His MC was announced in the New Year *London Gazette* of 1 January 1918 (no citation).

Murray was allowed home on leave in New Zealand from April 1918, returning to the UK in the following October. He left for New Zealand for the last time on 16 May 1919, leaving the RAF, via the Unemployed List, with the rank of Captain on 22 June 1919.

MURRAY, Keith Day Pearce

The son of Mr Charles Henry Murray (died 1901) and Mrs Murray, of Auckland, New Zealand, and the stepson of New Zealand Senate member, Dr William Chisolm Wilson McDowell, MD, of Edinburgh, Remuera, Auckland, New Zealand and of Somerville House, Finchley Lane, Hendon, London NW4, he was born on 5 July 1892. Educated at King's College, Auckland, New Zealand, at Mill Hill School, London (1906-07), and at the Architectural Association, School of Architecture, from where he qualified ARIBA. He practised as an Architectural Draughtsman in Auckland from 1911 to 1914. Journeying to England, he gained his Royal Aero Club Certificate (Number 1290) on 1 June 1915 and was duly gazetted Second Lieutenant (on probation) to the RFC on the same day. After formally qualifying for his 'Wings', he was sent out to the BE2c-equipped 2 Squadron in France in the late summer of 1915. Promoted to A/Captain and Flight Commander on 1 March 1916. His tour with '2' completed, he was sent back to the UK to instruct, serving with 15RS from 4 June 1916. Joining 52 Squadron, then at Hounslow, on 22 October 1916, he accompanied that unit, the first to be equipped with RE8s, as a 'founder member' and Flight Commander, to France on 21 November following. His MC was announced in the *London Gazette* of 26 September 1917, details in the *Gazette* of 9 January 1918: 'For conspicuous gallantry and devotion to duty on numerous occasions. He has displayed the utmost skill and fearlessness in ranging our batteries on hostile battery positions. Most of this work he had to carry out at a very low altitude and under very heavy fire, owing to the fact that the target was very well camouflaged, but, in spite of being repeatedly attacked and his machine several times damaged by anti-aircraft and machine-gun fire, he was invariably successful'.

Murray would go on to command 10 Squadron in the field in 1917 and in 1918, and be Mentioned in Despatches on no less than five occasions during the Great War, *London Gazettes* of 1 June 1915, 30 April 1916, 15 May 1917, 20 May 1918 and 8 November 1918. The Belgians also gave him their Croix de Guerre, *London Gazette* of 5 July 1919. After leaving the RAF with the rank of Major in 1919, Murray remained in the UK, working for a firm of Architects and carving out an impressive reputation for himself as an Architect, Designer and Artist. Amongst other notable achievements, he designed the BEA Engineering Base at Heathrow Airport and the Hong Kong Air Terminal. He also worked as a Designer and Artist in pottery and glass for Wedgewood, at their factory at Barlaston, and in silver for Mappin and Webb in London. Awarded the Gold Medal at the 5th Triennale of Milan in 1933. Practised in partnership with C S White from 1936. RDI, 1936, and FRIBA, 1939. When the Second World War came, he served again in the RAF from 1939 to 1941, for which he was Mentioned in Despatches. Appointed Master of the Faculty of Royal Designers for Industry from 1945 to 1947. In 1948, he married Mary Beatrice de Cararet Hayes, with whom he had one daughter. He lived in retirement at 'Stephouse', Tarrant Gunville, Blandford, Dorset. Keith Murray died on 16 May 1981.

MURRAY JONES, Allan – see Allan Murray **JONES**

MUSPRATT, Keith Knox

The son of Dr Charles Drummond Muspratt and Mabel Muspratt (née Knox), of 11 Madeira Road, Tantallon, Bournemouth, he was born on 22 December 1897. Educated at Sherbourne School (1911-16). He gained his Royal Aero Club Certificate (Number 2789), at his own expense, on 27 April 1916, whilst still a pupil at Sherbourne. As soon as he left school, he was gazetted Second Lieutenant to the Dorset Regiment, via the Special List, on 8 August 1916, with an immediate secondment to the RFC. His formal pilot training duly completed, he was confirmed and gazetted Flying Officer on 2 November following. After qualifying as a Pilot, he acted as an Instructor for a while, one of his pupils being Arthur Rhys Davids (qv), later one of the most successfully 56 Squadron Pilots. Muspratt himself subsequently served with the SE5-equipped 56 Squadron in France, achieving eight victories between 24 May 1917 and 31 October 1917. His MC was announced in the *London Gazette* of 18 October 1917, details in the *Gazette* of 7 March 1918: 'He showed great initiative throughout the offensive operations, and seldom failed to become engaged with enemy aircraft when on offensive patrol. He destroyed several hostile machines. He took part in over 40 offensive patrols, the majority of which entailed very severe fighting at low altitudes under heavy fire, and he set a magnificent example by his skill, gallantry and initiative'.

His tour with '56' completed, he was posted as a Test Pilot at Martlesham Heath, Suffolk, where he was killed in a crash that occurred on 16 March 1918. Keith Muspratt is buried in Bournemouth (Wimbourne Road) Cemetery, Hampshire.

NB: The RAF Museum Hendon has his medals in its collection: MC (engraved: 2Lt K K Muspratt, RFC, 1918), *British War Medal 1914-20, and Victory Medal 1914-19* (2Lt).

N

NAPIER, Charles Georges Douglas

The son of Commercial Clerk, George Charles Napier and Mrs Napier, of 34 Aldbourne Road, Shepherd's Bush, London, he was born in 1892. When war came in 1914, he enlisted as a Private soldier (Number 269, later 13028) into 47 Division Cyclist Company (TF). Going to France with the Cyclists on 16 March 1915, he won the Distinguished Conduct Medal in the trenches at Givenchy on 25/26 May 1915, *London Gazette* of 5 August 1915. He was also awarded the Médaille Militaire by the French. Picked out for a commission, he was gazetted Second Lieutenant to the RFC on 2 August 1917. His formal pilot training duly completed, he was confirmed and gazetted Flying Officer on 23 September following. He served first with the BF2b-equipped 20 Squadron late in 1917, before joining 48 Squadron, also equipped with Brisfits, as a Flight Commander early in 1918. Napier achieved nine victories between 7 February and 9 May 1918. On this later date, Napier and his Observer/Gunner Sergeant W Beales, in BF2b, 'C4750', after claiming a victory of their own, were shot up and damaged in a fight with Vizefeldwebel Robert Heibert of Jasta 46. The British pair returned safely to base but still Heibert, optimistically, claimed them as a victory. Just six days later on 15 May, Napier with Sergeant Patrick Murphy, in BF2b, 'B1337', were shot down in flames over Lamotte during a combat with Leutnant Hans Kirschstein of Jasta 6, the tenth of the German Ace's eventual 27 victories. His MC was announced posthumously in the *London Gazette* of 22 June 1918: 'For conspicuous gallantry and devotion to duty. On one occasion during a low-flying bomb attack he descended to a height of 100 feet and dropped four bombs amongst a body of enemy troops, causing heavy casualties and scattering the enemy in all directions. Later, whilst on offensive patrols, he observed an enemy two-seater and two scouts. He fired twenty rounds at the two-seater, with the result that it crashed, and then attacked one of the scouts, which turned over completely, and finally went down in a vertical nose dive. In all he has to his credit two enemy machines crashed and four driven down out of control. He has displayed great judgment, determination and daring'.

Charles Napier's remains were never recovered and hence he is commemorated on the Flying Services Memorial, Arras, France.

NAPIER, Ian Patrick Robert

The younger son of Henry Melvill Napier JP, and Margaret Agnes Napier (née Muter), of Milton House, Bowling, Dumbartonshire, he was born on 24 July 1895. Educated at Summer Fields (1905-09), and at Eton, Rowing XIII, 1912, 1913 and 1914). Gazetted Second Lieutenant to 9 (Dumbartonshire) Battalion, Argyll and Sutherland Highlanders (TF), on 2 September 1914. Seconded to the RFC in June 1916, he gained his Royal Aero Club Certificate (Number 3269) on 18 July following. His formal pilot training duly completed, he was confirmed and gazetted Flying Officer on 4 August 1916. Sent out to 40 Squadron (Nieuport Scouts), he achieved 12 victories between 14 April 1917 and 4 July 1918. Interspersed with his operational duties, Napier, an accomplished linguist, was detached to the French Air Force and Army as a Liaison Officer. The French showed their appreciation of his work with the awards of the Croix de Chevalier, Légion d'Honneur and the Croix de Guerre,

London Gazette of 17 December 1917. On 29 April 1918, 'Old Naps' as he was known to his squadron colleagues, forced an enemy two-seater of FA7 down into the British lines, both occupants being taken prisoner. His MC was announced in the *London Gazette* of 16 September 1918: 'For conspicuous gallantry and devotion to duty. This officer has carried out many reconnaissances, and flying at low altitudes has engaged massed enemy troops with bombs and machine-gun fire, inflicting heavy casualties. He has brought down seven enemy machines'.

He finally left the RAF, via the Unemployed List, on 18 April 1919, and entered the family ship-building and ship-owning businesses. He married, firstly in 1927, the Hon Frieda Essenson, with whom he had two sons (dissolved 1940) and, secondly, in 1942, Nora Moore, with whom he had one son. He held various Directorships over the ensuing years, including Burns and Lairds Line Ltd; Eagle Star Insurance Co (West End Board); Brush Power Engineering Ltd; Napier & Millers Ltd, 1925-34; the Hudson's Bay Company, 1934-68; Coast Lines Ltd 1949-66; and was Chairman of David MacBrayne Ltd, 1953-66. Other honours and appointments included: Governor, Cutty Sark Society 1954-75; Member of the Canadian Chamber of Commerce in GB; Member of the Scottish Transport Council, 1951-63; Member of the Royal Company of Archers (The Sovereign's Body Guard for Scotland); Member of the Institute of Hammerman and Freeman of the City of Glasgow. He also received the Order of St John. He lived at 169 Queen's Gate, London SW7, and died on 9 May 1977.

NAPIER, Kenneth Russel

The son of the Reverend J A Napier and Mrs Napier, of Old Windsor, Berkshire, he was born on 15 November 1892. After leaving school, he worked as a Rancher in Alberta, Canada, from 1910 to 1914. Enlisting as a Trooper into Lord Strathcona's Horse, he served with the first contingent of the CEF in France, before being accepted into the RFC, first serving as an Observer with 4 Squadron from 1 September 1916. Picked out for a commission, he was gazetted Second Lieutenant to the RFC on 14 October 1916. Transferring to 3 Squadron, he completed his 'apprenticeship' satisfactorily, and was duly confirmed and gazetted Flying Officer (Observer) in March 1917. He next trained as a Pilot and, after formally qualifying in October 1917, served with 53 Squadron (RE8s) from 1 November 1917 to 31 July 1918. His MC was announced in the *London Gazette* of 16 September 1918: 'For conspicuous gallantry and devotion to duty during recent operations. He carried out several successful reconnaissances under heavy machine-gun fire from the ground, dropping bombs on troops and machine-gunning them, while attacked himself by enemy aircraft. Under very trying weather conditions he brought back most valuable information. He did very fine work'.

Research has also unearthed the original recommendation for this award, which provides a little more detail: '2 Brigade, RAF. For conspicuous gallantry and devotion to duty, during the period 21 March 1918 to 24 March 1918 and 10 April 1918 to 30 April 1918. During the period 21 March 1918 to 24 March 1918 he carried out on 24th a special reconnaissance of the bridges at Peronne under heavy machine-gun fire from the ground, dropping four bombs on troops in Peronne, and on 21st, 22nd, 23rd, he bombed and machine-gunned the enemy from low altitudes, although on each occasion he was attacked by enemy aeroplanes. During the period 10 April 1918 to 30 April 1918, this officer, with Captain O'Leary [qv] as Observer, carried out twelve reconnaissances on the enemy's lines at a low altitude under very trying weather conditions. He brought back much valuable information, noticeably from the 11th, 15th, 16th and 30th ultimo, when he accurately located enemy's positions by flying at a low altitude, under heavy machine-gun fire from the ground, his machine being hit in many places'.

His tour with '53' completed, he served, after a brief rest, with the School of Special Flying from 12 August to 18 September 1918, and later instructed at 33 TDS. Returning to Canada, he was demobilised in that country on 6 March 1919.

NATHAN, Cecil Frederick

From Port Elizabeth, South Africa, he was born on 29 September 1897. Travelling to the UK, he was sent as a Cadet to the flying service before being gazetted Second Lieutenant to the RFC on 13 August 1917. Having next trained as an Observer, he was sent out to the RE8-equipped 59 Squadron later in 1917. His MC was announced in the *London Gazette* of 18 January 1918, details in the *Gazette* of 25 April 1918: 'For conspicuous gallantry and devotion to duty as Observer. When information was urgently required during an attack, and several attempts to obtain it had been unsuccessful, owing to exceptionally bad weather conditions, he went out with his pilot and succeeded in gaining the necessary information, flying at a height of about 50 feet under heavy rifle and machine-gun fire. He had already made flight under similar conditions on the same day. He showed great courage and determination'.

From '59', Nathan was transferred to 6 Squadron, also equipped with RE8s, on 21 February 1918. His operational service over, he returned to the Home Establishment in the summer of 1918, where he was posted to instructing duties. Nathan finally left the RAF, via the Unemployed List, on 5 August 1919.

NEALE, Albert Leslie

From Wales, he was born on 28 January 1894. A medical student at London University (where he was a member of the OTC) and at St Thomas' Hospital, London. He interrupted his studies to volunteer his services and was gazetted Second Lieutenant to a Regular Army battalion of the Lincolnshire Regiment on 16 June 1915, with an almost immediate secondment to the RFC. Gained his Royal Aero Club Certificate (Number 1383) on 1 July 1915. Posted out to 11 Squadron (Vickers FB5s) in August 1915, soon after qualifying for his 'Wings', he survived the 'Fokker Scourge' on the Western Front despite often being involved in aerial combats. Slightly wounded in April 1916, he returned to the Home Establishment. After rest and recuperation, Neale returned to France and 11 Squadron in January 1917. His MC was announced in the *London Gazette* of 26 May 1917: 'For conspicuous gallantry and devotion to duty on many occasions. He carried out two successful contact patrols, flying for a considerable period very low and on our barrage, rendering very complete reports on each occasion. He has rendered particularly good service in observing for siege batteries'.

Promoted to A/Captain and Flight Commander on 1 July 1917, he returned to the UK shortly afterwards. Neale was next posted as an Instructor in the UK until October 1918, when he was sent out to Italy to command 66 Squadron from 1 November and continued to serve in that theatre until the following April. Staying on in the RAF after the war, he commanded 31 Squadron in India in 1920-21.

NEVILLE, Roger Henry Gartside

The son of Mr and Mrs E G Neville of Minster Road, Cricklewood, London, he was born on 8 March 1895. Educated at Highgate School, London (1910-13) and at Sandhurst. Gazetted Second Lieutenant to the Duke of Cornwall's Light Infantry on 14 July 1915, with an almost immediate secondment to the RFC. His formal pilot training duly completed, he was confirmed and gazetted Flying Officer on 18 November following. Sent out to France, he joined the BE12-equipped 21 Squadron late in 1915, going to France in January. In just under a year of operational flying with '21', he claimed just one victory before being wounded on 21 September 1916, by which time he was a flight commander. His MC was announced in the *London Gazette* of 14 November 1916: 'For conspicuous gallantry. He is a fine leader of patrol work, and has done much to keep enemy machines away from our lines. On one occasion, flying in a rainstorm, after nearly colliding with an enemy machine, he pursued it and brought it down half a mile from an enemy aerodrome'.

After regaining his fitness and health, Neville served at home with 83 Squadron, before joining 35 Squadron in France in March 1917. Transferred to 23 Squadron (Spad VIIs) in June 1917, as an A/Captain and Flight Commander. Four further victories followed in July 1917 allowing Neville to claim the status of an Ace. On 19 August 1917, however, he had the misfortune to be burnt and injured when a Very flare, he was carrying, exploded. A posting to 81 Squadron at Scampton in February 1918 was followed by instructional posts till the end of the war. Staying on in the RAF after the war, he was awarded the OBE in 1931. He served as a Group Captain in the RAF during the Second World War, Mentioned in Despatches, before finally retiring in 1946.

NOEL, Tom Cecil

The son of Cecil and Edith Noel, of Cottesmore, Oakham, Rutland, he was born on 12 December 1897. Educated at Eton College, Windsor. Gazetted Second Lieutenant to 3 (Reserve) Battalion, King's Own Scottish Borderers, in August 1914. Posted to 1 Battalion of his regiment, he served in the trenches on the Western Front. Noel led no less than three patrols into enemy territory during the first days of July 1917. 1 King's Own Scottish Borderers was, at the time, preparing jumping off trenches in the area of Boesinghe/Wieltje for the great offensive that was to follow on 31 July 1917 – the opening day of the Third Battle of Ypres. The ribbon of the first of Noel's two MCs, announced in the *London Gazette* of 9 January 1918, was presented to him by the General Officer Commanding, Lord Cavan, at an 'Honours Parade' near the front lines on 3 September 1917. He was later presented with the insignia of the award by the King at Buckingham Palace on 16 March 1918. Transferring to the RFC late in 1917, he trained as an Observer and was sent out as such to the Bristol Fighter-equipped 20 Squadron. A 'top gun', indeed, he shared in no less than 24 victories with several Pilots between 19 January and 19 July 1918. On 22 August 1918, Noel, flying with Captain Dennis Latimer (qv), in BF2b, 'C 987', were engaged in combat by Leutnant Willi Negben of Jasta 7. Negben sent the RAF machine down into German held Flanders territory near to Westroosbeke. Latimer survived to be taken prisoner, but Tom Noel was killed in the action. A posthumous announcement of a Bar to his MC came in the *London Gazette* of 16 September 1918: 'For conspicuous gallantry and devotion to duty. In four days he and his pilot destroyed seven enemy machines and drove down three out of control. His courage and skill are of the first order, and of inestimable value to his squadron'. Tom Noel is buried in Perth Cemetery (China Wall), Ypres, West-Vlaanderen, Belgium 20.

NORTON, John Hamilton

The son of John and Annie Norton, of Plumboro Mount, Hockley, Essex, he was born in Southend, Essex, on 10 October 1896. After leaving school, he worked as an Insurance Broker at Lloyds of London from January 1913 to August 1914. As soon as war came, he enlisted as a Trooper (Number 1105) into the Essex Yeomanry (TF). Picked out for a commission, he was gazetted Second Lieutenant to 7 Reserve Regiment of Cavalry, via the Special List, on 16 November 1914. Norton served with the Essex Yeomanry in the UK before being seconded to the RFC early in 1916. Gained his Royal Aero Club Certificate (Number 2456) on 10 February 1916. His formal training duly completed, he was confirmed and gazetted Flying Officer on 23 June following. Sent out to 12 Squadron on 5 July 1916, his first operational tour was interrupted when he was confined to hospital on 24 October following. Once recovered, he was sent out to 13 Squadron as a Flight Commander on 18 March 1917. On 9 April 1917, the first day of the Battle of Arras, Norton and his Observer of the day, Captain T L Tibbs, in BE2e 'A2878', came close to disaster when their machine was hit by shellfire and forced to crashland. Norton and Tibbs were unscathed but the wreckage of their machine was subsequently shelled to smithereens. Norton's MC was announced in the *London Gazette* of 27 May 1917: 'For conspicuous gallantry and devotion to duty. He reconnoitred the enemy's wire at a height of 300 feet and brought back most valuable information. He has at all times displayed great courage and skill'.

Returning to the Home Establishment, he next instructed at the CFS for some months before accompanying the BF2b-equipped 62 Squadron to France as a Flight Commander and 'founder member' on 23 January 1918. The Bar to his MC came in the *London Gazette* of 22 April 1918: 'For conspicuous gallantry and devotion to duty. While he was carrying out observation for an artillery shoot, two hostile aeroplanes endeavoured to interfere. These he at once attacked and drove off, afterwards continuing his observations for the shoot, during which two hostile emplacements were destroyed. His dash and determination contributed greatly to the success of the operation'.

From '62', Norton was sent out to 142 Squadron in Palestine. He was wounded in the left foot on 29 July 1918, when carrying out a shoot against two anti-aircraft gunpits. Despite his wound, he continued to call down the fire of the Royal Artillery onto the enemy gunpits, completely destroying them. For this action he was awarded the Distinguished Flying Cross in the *London Gazette* of 8 February 1919. Norton was hospitalised in Egypt until recovering sufficiently to be sent next to 111 Squadron. He appears to have suffered some difficulties as a consequence of discrepancies relating to mess chits, which resulted in the AOC, Middle East, calling upon him to resign his commission in December 1919.

NOSS, Arthur Rex Hurdon

The son of Arthur Alfred and Laura Maude Noss, of 'Banavie', Beltinge Road, Herne Bay, Kent, he was born in 1897. Enlisted and served as a Gunner (Number 6250, later 521869) in 'B' Battery, Honourable Artillery Company (TF). Picked out for a commission, he was gazetted Second Lieutenant to the RFC, via the General List, on 4 April 1917. Having trained as an Observer, he was confirmed and gazetted Flying Officer (Observer) 16 May following. Noss flew operationally with BF2b-equipped 48 Squadron from June 1917, often acting as Observer to Captain K R Park, MC (qv). He achieved nine victories between 26 May to 25 August 1917, including no less than four Albatros DVs on 17 August, for which feat he was recommended for the MC, announced in the *London Gazette* of 26 September 1917, details in the *Gazette* of 9 January 1918: 'For conspicuous gallantry and devotion to duty. During an engagement with several large hostile formations, the two machines with which he was patrolling were put out of action. In spite, however, of being left alone he continued to attack, and engaged the enemy in so determined a manner that he and his pilot between them destroyed one and drove three others down completely out of control. He has performed several other fine feats, and has at all times set a most inspiring example by his dash and tenacity'.

This citation is virtually identical to that of his Pilot, Second Lieutenant K R Park. Research has unearthed the original recommendation for the award, which is rather more informative: 'A R Noss (joint reco with his Pilot, K R Park, 48 Sqn, 19/8/17) These two officers were on a special High patrol near Middlekerke on the 17th August in company with two other Bristols, when several large formations of EA were seen and immediately attacked. Early in the engagement the Observer of one Bristol was killed and the pilot wounded thereby putting this machine out of action which returned to the lines. Shortly afterwards a second Bristol was forced down and compelled to retire. In spite of being left alone, Lt Park continued to attack and engage the enemy in so determined a manner that he and his Observer between them destroyed one of the enemy machines which was seen to crash; shortly afterwards Lt Park's gun jammed and his Observer continued the engagement until Lt Park managed to clear the jam and immediately brought his front gun into action again; between them they succeeded in driving down two other machines completely out of control, following the first down to 3,500 feet, and when they were absolutely certain this machine could not recover they left him and started to engage another which they also succeeded in driving down completely out of control. They were unable to watch the machine crash as they were again attacked by another hostile aircraft. This they engaged and drove off and they were only compelled to return owing to lack of ammunition. Lt Park has performed several other fine feats and has at all times set a most inspiring example by his dash and tenacity'.

Sadly, Noss received mortal injuries in a landing accident which occurred on 15 September 1917, in Brisfit, 'A7217', flown by Second Lieutenant E B Corry. Arthur Noss is buried in Zuydcoote Military Cemetery, France.

NUTTALL, Frank

The son of W T and Mrs H C Nuttall, of 39 Beresford Street, New Brighton, Christchurch, New Zealand, he was born on 16 November 1887. Gazetted Second Lieutenant to the RFC, via the Special Lists, on 6 April 1916. Gained his Royal Aero Club Certificate (Number 2803) on 28 April 1916. His formal pilot training duly completed, he was confirmed and gazetted Flying Officer on 1 June following. Nuttall instructed in the UK for a period before being sent to RFC HQ, Egypt, in the same capacity. His first operational posting, to 30 Squadron, came on 5 April 1917. He served with '30' in Mesopotamia, during which time he was promoted to A/Captain and Flight Commander. On 25 January 1918, Nuttall and his Observer, Lieutenant R B-B Sievier (qv), in a DH4, were, due to engine failure, forced to land in the desert near to Quara Tepe. Having burnt their machine, the pair walked 24 miles across the desert, carrying two Lewis guns and a quantity of ammunition, before reaching the British lines. His MC, awarded for another descent to the floor of the desert, was announced in the *London Gazette* of 26 March 1918, details in the *Gazette* of 24 August 1918: 'For conspicuous gallantry and devotion to duty. Seeing another machine driven down by hostile fire in the enemy's line, he glided to the ground under heavy fire and dispersed the enemy with his machine gun. He took the stranded Pilot on board and got safely away. By his prompt and courageous action he saved his comrade from being taken prisoner' (Palestine).

The Pilot he rescued on this occasion was Second Lieutenant A P Adams, also of 30 Squadron. On 27 April 1918, Nuttall's Martinsyde was shot up during a low-level bombing run near Kirkuk and Nuttall was wounded. For this and other gallantry with 30 Squadron, he was, rather belatedly, awarded the Distinguished Flying Cross in the *London Gazette* of 15 July 1919. After recovering from his wounds, he spent some time in Egypt, before being posted out again to Mesopotamia in June 1919, this time to 63 Squadron. Three months later in September 1919, Nuttall was posted back to Egypt, before returning to the UK shortly afterwards. An Air Force Cross was added to his honours in the *London Gazette* of 10 October 1919. Nuttall was also Mentioned in Despatches on one occasion during the Great War, *London Gazette* of 5 June 1919 (Mesopotamia). Having acquired a permanent commission in the RAF, he again returned to the Middle East in January 1920, reporting for duty initially with 63 Squadron, before joining 30 Squadron in Persia (Iran) as a Flight Commander on 29 February following. Frank Nuttall was killed in a flying accident in RE8, 'D4698', on 18 September 1920, and is buried in Tehran War Cemetery, Iran.

O

O'BRIEN, Patrick Alva

From Momence, Illinois, USA, he was born in December 1891. After completing his education in 1909, he left home for California, where he and a friend built and flew their own aeroplane. O'Brien was, at this time, employed as a locomotive engineer with the Santa Fe railroad. In 1916, he joined the United States Air Service, spending about eight months at the Army Flying School in San Diego, before resigning and travelling to Victoria, British Columbia, to volunteer for the RFC. After training at Camp Borden, Toronto, O'Brien embarked aboard the SS *Megantic* with 17 other aspiring 'fledglings', half of them Americans, bound for England. He gained his Royal Aero Club Certificate (Number 5297) on 16 June 1917, before formally qualifying for his 'Wings' shortly afterwards. Sent out to 66 Squadron (Sopwith Pups) on 28 July 1917, his short operational career ended less than three weeks later when, on 17 August, he was shot down in Sopwith Pup, 'B1732'. Taken prisoner of war, he was confined in a prison in Courtrai for several weeks before being put on a train with other prisoners bound for confinement in Germany. Determined to escape before the train got too far into Europe, O'Brien leapt out into the night. Travelling mainly during darkness, he worked his way back towards Belgium, spending nine days in Luxembourg on the way. Once in Belgium, he headed for the neutral Dutch border, until, after 72 days and many adventures and hardships, he succeeded in crossing into Holland and freedom on 19 November 1917. From Holland he was allowed to return to England where, on 7 December 1917, he was invited to Buckingham Palace to tell his story to the King. O'Brien was given leave to go home for Christmas and released from the service of the Crown with the Sovereign's grateful thanks. Formally, for purposes of record, he relinquished his commission due to ill-health on 21 March 1918. Returning to Illinois, O'Brien recorded his experiences and the details of his escape in a book which enjoyed some moderate success, 'Outwitting the Hun', was published in New York in March 1918. He travelled around the US giving lectures and exhibition flights, once crashing down from 2,000 feet onto Kelley Field, San Antonio, Texas, but escaping with nothing more than a broken nose. The award of his MC, '....in recognition of gallantry in escaping from captivity whilst Prisoner of War', was announced in the 'Escapers Gazette', *London Gazette* of 16 December 1919. It would be interesting to know how, and even if, the insignia of the award was ever actually delivered to O'Brien. In the Summer of 1920, O'Brien was engaged on film work in Washington DC, when he met and married a former newspaper women, Virginia Dale, aka Virginia Dare. The marriage soon ran into trouble, largely, it appears, due to the intervention of another woman, but not in the conventional sense. When, in the following December, Mrs O'Brien invited the other woman into their home to the exclusion of her husband, Pat O'Brien, after penning a final note to his wife, shot himself in a New York hotel room. O'Brien's sister, Mrs Clara Clegg, always refused to believe that her brother had actually taken his own life and remained convinced that he had been murdered and that the so-called 'suicide' note was a forgery. The truly dramatic story of Pat O'Brien's life and death seems to have been overlooked by Hollywood.

O'GRADY, Standish Conn

From Dublin, Ireland, he was born on 4 January 1888. Educated at Trinity College, Dublin, from where he graduated BA in 1910. An Engineer by training, he left Ireland to work in Ottawa, Canada, in 1911. Returning to the UK in 1916, he was gazetted Second Lieutenant to the RFC, via the Special Reserve, on 26 July following. His pilot training duly completed, he was confirmed and gazetted Flying Officer on 31 October 1916. He worked as an Instructor at the CFS through the winter of 1916-17, before eventually being sent to 23 Squadron (Spad VIIs) in France on 23 April 1917. O'Grady achieved nine victories and the status of Ace between 30 April and 26 August 1917, being promoted to A/Captain and Flight Commander in the process. His tour with '23' completed, he returned to the Home Establishment in September 1917 and would there see out the war in a series of instructing and Staff posts. His MC was announced in the *London Gazette* of 26 September 1917, details in the *Gazette* of 9 January 1918 (his name appears as Conn Standish O'Grady and, indeed, in the *Army List* as C S O'Grady): 'For conspicuous gallantry and devotion to duty in leading fighting patrols against superior numbers of enemy aircraft. He has himself brought down three enemy machines completely out of control, and others were seen to be destroyed, and his dash and determination when outnumbered by the enemy has continually won the highest praise'.

He was also Mentioned in Despatches on one occasion during the Great War, *London Gazette* of 29 August 1917. After leaving the RAF in 1919, O'Grady entered academia and, by the mid-1930s, had achieved a professorship. He became an established Glider Pilot and in 1938 flew 70 miles in two and a half hours.

O'HANLON, Sydney Esmond

The son of William Sydney and Isobel O'Hanlon, of Windyridge Farm, Dean Row, Wilmslow, Cheshire, he was born on 31 August 1894, in nearby Hale. Educated at Leys School (1908-12), where he was a member of the OTC. Fond of mechanical contrivances and of shooting, he was too small to gain distinction in games. In 1911, he shot in the Bisley VIII for his school. After leaving Leys, he studied wireless telegraphy, obtaining a certificate of special skill in this field. When the war came, he first tried to enlist as a despatch rider but, due to the huge numbers with the same intention, was not accepted. He was, however, gazetted Second Lieutenant to 15 Battalion (1 Salfords) Lancashire Fusiliers on 5 October 1914, a 'Bantams Battalion'. He accompanied his unit to France in November 1915, as the battalion's Machine-Gun Officer. In April 1916, he was seconded to the RFC and, following training as an Observer, was sent to 4 Squadron as a Probationary. His 'apprenticeship' satisfactorily completed, he was formally confirmed and gazetted Flying Officer (Observer) on 30 May following. Working with a number of different Pilots, O'Hanlon was particularly successful co-operating with 65 Siege Battery (12-inch howitzers). His MC was announced in the *London Gazette* of 14 November 1916: 'For conspicuous gallantry in action. As Observer, on many occasions, he has rendered most valuable reports, displaying great courage and determination throughout'.

His tour with '4' completed at the end of 1916, he returned to England and qualified as a Pilot. Working as a Ferry Pilot and as an Instructor throughout 1917, he was severely injured on 28 January 1918, when, whilst instructing a pupil, he was involved in an aerial collision. Taken to the Australian Hospital, Joyce Green, Dartford, Kent, he lingered for five days before dying as bravely as he had lived on 3 February 1918. Esmond O'Hanlon, as he was known, was cremated in Manchester Crematorium on 3 February 1918.

O'LEARY, Edward Launce

From Richibucto, New Brunswick, Canada. When the war came in August 1914, he immediately enlisted as a Gunner into Canadian Field Artillery and fought with the CEF in France from February 1915. Gazetted Lieutenant to the Canadian Field Artillery in January 1916. Seconded to the RFC in the summer of 1917, he trained as an Observer and was gazetted as such on 31 August following. He served in France with 53 Squadron (RE8s) from 20 November 1917. His MC was announced in the *London Gazette* of 16 September 1918: 'For conspicuous gallantry and devotion to duty. When on bombing duty, he successfully drove off three enemy aeroplanes, and when on escort duty, and attacked by six enemy aeroplanes, he brought down one out of control. He made twelve successful reconnaissance flights during a fortnight of bad weather conditions at low altitude, his machine being hit in many places'.

Research has unearthed the original recommendation for the award, which provides more detailed information: 'For conspicuous gallantry and devotion to duty, during the period 21 March 1918 to 24 March 1918. On 22 March 1918 this officer when on bombing with Lieutenant Quinn [qv] as pilot, successfully drove off a determined attack by three enemy aircraft, and on 23 March 1918 when on escort duty with the same pilot, being attacked by six enemy aircraft, he brought one down out of control, the machine being seen and pinpointed on the ground. During the period 10 April 1918 to 30 April 1918, this officer, with Captain Napier [qv] as pilot, carried out twelve reconnaissances on the enemy's lines at a low altitude under very trying weather conditions. He brought back much valuable information, noticeably from the 11th, 15th, 16th and 30th ultimo, when he accurately located enemy positions by flying at a low altitude, under heavy machine-gun fire from the ground, on the 30th ultimo his machine being hit in many places'.

His tour with '53' completed, he returned to the Home Establishment on 30 May 1918. O'Leary returned to Canada on 12 November 1918 and finally relinquished his commission on 18 March 1919. He served as Administration Officer in the RCAF during the Second World War.

O'NEILL, William Hickley Lovell

Born 7 February 1890, he became a regular army officer in September 1909. In January 1911, he was commissioned into the Indian Army and by September 1915 was a Captain with 51 Sikhs. Transferred into the RFC and, on 30 February 1917, was posted to 30 Squadron as a Probationary Observer. He served in this capacity in Mesopotamia till 18 June when he became the Adjutant to 31 Wing. Trained as a pilot in Egypt in October 1917. The award of the Military Cross was gazetted on 8 March 1918 (but dated 1 January), and he was also Mentioned in Despatches on the 12th of that month. Post-war he remained in the RAF and, between August 1925 and September 1927, commanded 24 Squadron in England. He was killed in the *R101* Airship disaster on 5 October 1930, on his way to take up an appointment in India.

OADES, Sidney Arthur

The son of Plumber, Frederick T Oades and Mary J Oades, of 2 Oglander Road, Camberwell, London, he was born in Lambeth, London, on 27 September 1890. He had his own Ladies and Gents Tailoring business in New Cross Gate from 1907 to 1915, marrying his wife, Mildred from Greenwich, on 28 June 1915. Able to drive petrol-driven vehicles, he enlisted as a Sapper (Number 109448) into the Royal Engineers on 14 September 1915, before going to the Front for the first time in January 1916. He served with 276 Field Company, RE, from April 1916 until transferring to the 53 RC, RE, in the following July. Oades was Mentioned in Despatches in September 1916, for his outstanding services with the Royal Engineers. Picked out for a commission, he was gazetted Second Lieutenant to the RFC on 15 May 1917. His pilot training duly completed, he was confirmed and gazetted Flying Officer on 22 June following. He served briefly as a Flying Officer with the Middle East Brigade, RFC, before being sent out to BF2b-equipped 22 Squadron on the Western Front, on 23 September 1917. Oades achieved 11 victories between 27 October 1917 and 5 March 1918. On this latter day, Oades and his Observer, Second Lieutenant S W Bunting, in BF2b, 'B1168', were both slightly wounded in the air when their machine was shot up and their propellor shot off in the course of gaining the 11th of Oades', and the seventh of Bunting's, victories. His MC was announced in the *London Gazette* of 22 April 1918: 'For conspicuous gallantry and devotion to duty. On six different occasions during four months he has driven down three enemy machines which crashed on reaching the ground and has destroyed two others causing them to descend in flames. A sixth machine, after he had fired eight rounds into it, turned over and went spinning down out of control but owing to bad visibility it was not observed to crash. In addition to these he has brought down another three hostile machines out of control and has always shown the most magnificent dash, gallantry and determination'.

Oades was injured in a crash on 13 March 1918, which effectively put an end to his combat flying. He left the RAF, via the Unemployed List, on 11 April 1919. Once recovered, Oades was briefly returned to the Active List for temporary duty between 10 April 1921 and 5 June 1921.

NB: His medals were offered for sale by Sotheby's (lot 546) on 4 March 1982 : MC, British War Medal 1914-20, and Victory Medal 1914-19 (Lt RAF).

OLIVER, Douglas Harold

From Kent, he was born on 30 May 1998. Educated at Christ's Hospital. After leaving school, he worked as an insurance clerk in Dublin from April 1914 until August 1915. Gazetted Second Lieutenant to the RFC in April 1917, he trained as a Pilot and was sent out to 59 Squadron (RE8s) later in the same year. On the 21 March 1918, the first day of the German spring offensive, Oliver and Second Lieutenant W H Leighton in RE8, 'B6547', were credited with being the first to discover the scale of the German advance into the British Third Army front. They established and were able to report that the enemy was within reach of Vaulx-Vracourt in a wide swath of advance between Bullecourt and Doignies. As they flew low over Lagnicourt, a shell passed straight through their fuselage and, although both men were unscathed, it curtailed their reconnaissance more than somewhat. Oliver's MC was announced in the *London Gazette* of 22 June 1918: 'For conspicuous gallantry and devotion to duty He carried out a most successful reconnaissance, flying at a height of 500 feet under heavy fire. Despite the fact that his machine had received a direct hit from a shell he succeeded in landing it at the aerodrome and brought back information of the greatest value. On the following day he carried out a low altitude patrol under heavy machine-gun and rifle fire and obtained valuable information. His gallantry and determination have been most marked'.

His tour with '59' completed, he returned to the Home Establishment on 13 May 1918, never to return to operational flying. Oliver left the RAF, via the Unemployed List, on 28 May 1919. He was known to be living, in the 1930s, in Chandlers Ford, Hampshire.

ORTON, John Overton Cone

From Marylebone, London, he was born on 30 August 1889. A Regular Army officer, he was gazetted, pre-war, to 2 Battalion, Norfolk Regiment. By the time the war came, he was a married man, his wife living in Retford, whilst he was with his regiment in India. Orton accompanied the 2 Norfolks to Mesopotamia from their base in India on 3 November 1914. He was wounded in a bayonet charge against the Turkish trenches north of Barjisiyeh, on 14 April 1915. Once recovered, he successfully sought secondment to the RFC late in 1915. Having trained as an Observer in Egypt, he was formally gazetted Flying Officer (Observer) on 1 January 1916. He subsequently served operationally in Mesopotamia with 30 Squadron. He was Mentioned in Despatches for a successful operation on 24 August 1916, *London Gazette* of 19 October 1916, and was also awarded the Order of the Karageorge, 4th Class with Swords, by the Serbs, *London Gazette* of 15 February 1917. His MC was belatedly announced in the *London Gazette* of 2 December 1917 (Mesopotamia): 'For conspicuous gallantry and devotion to duty during three months' operations. He showed splendid qualities as an Observer and rendered most valuable service. His intimate knowledge of the country enabled his reports to be most accurate throughout. He was three times in action against enemy aircraft, and on the last occasion returned with 20 bullet holes in his machine, after 1½ drums of ammunition from a Lewis gun had been emptied at the adversary'.

Returning to the UK, he trained as a Pilot, gaining his Royal Aero Club Certificate (Number 4552) on 30 April 1917 and being confirmed Flying Officer on the same day. Soon after qualifying, Orton joined BE2e-equipped 39 HD Squadron at Hainault. Later in the summer of 1917, Orton was sent to 76 HD Squadron as a Flight Commander. In May 1918, he was promoted to A/Major and given command of 199 TS. His efforts with '199' were eventually recognised by the award of an Air Force Cross, *London Gazette* of 3 June 1919. He subsequently decided to revert to his old regiment, the Norfolks, on 31 December 1919. John Orton died on 23 May 1962 in St Peter's Hospital, London.

ORTWEILER, Frederick John

The son of Leather Goods Manufacturer, Simon Ortweiler and Mrs Matilda Ortweiler, of 13 Cavendish Road, Brondesbury, London NW6, Frederick was born on 25 February 1898. He was educated at Brondesbury Preparatory School and at St Paul's, Westminster (1911-16). Ortweiler's parents were both German born, coming to England in 1886, before being 'naturalised' on 27 February 1897, the year before Frederick's birth. A note in Ortweiler's personal file – now held in the National Archives – suggests that British Intelligence officers were satisfied that the senior Ortweilers were British 'sympathisers'. On leaving St Paul's in December 1916, he volunteered for service with the RFC, being accepted as a Cadet in March 1917 and sent to Oxford for training in the following month. Gazetted Second Lieutenant to the RFC on 3 May 1917. Gained the RAC Certificate (Number 4681) on 19 May following. His formal pilot training duly completed, he was confirmed and gazetted Flying Officer on 11 August 1917. He served with both 69 and 81 Squadrons in the UK, before being sent out to join 29 Squadron (Nieuport XVIIs) in France on 29 September 1917. Less than three weeks later, on 16 October, he was forced down by Erwin Böhme - the German Ace's 20th victory. Ortweiler's Nieuport XVII, 'B3598', was captured virtually intact and undamaged by the German infantry. Following his capture, he was first taken to Lendelede for interrogation before going on to a series of camps including Karlsruhe and Bruf, before finally arriving at Halle on 16 December 1917. His first break for freedom came on 7 January 1918, but was short-lived as he was re-captured at the Dutch border on the following day. He was detained at Aachen for three days, before being sent to Halle civil prison where he was kept for a further three days. From Halle he was shuttled to Fort Zorndorf and then on to Causthal, the scene of his second failed escape bid in April 1918. Not surprisingly, he was sent to Holzminden in the following July and then on to Stralsund in August. His third escape attempt, on 12 October 1918, was entirely successful and for this he was eventually awarded the MC, the announcement appearing in the 'Escapers Gazette', the *London Gazette* of 16 December 1919: '....in recognition of gallantry in escaping from captivity whilst Prisoners of War'. After completing his war service in April 1919, he took a shortened degree course at King's College, Cambridge, gaining a BA in 1920. Deciding upon a career in aviation, he became Chief Pilot at the Cambridge School of Flying. He flew an SE5A in the 1921 Derby aerial display and also represented the de Havilland Company, travelling to Spain for the aeroplane manufacturer on a number of occasions. On 14 February 1922, he was a passenger in a Bristol machine that crashed at Cuatro Vientos aerodrome near Madrid. Onlookers said that the Bristol appeared to stall in a steep turn over the airfield. Ortweiler and two other men were killed, one of whom, Herbert Brian Richardson (qv), was also a Flying MC winner. Ortweiler's body was returned home for burial; he was just 11 days short of his 23rd birthday.

NB: The RAF Museum Hendon has his medals in its collection: MC, British War Medal 1914-20, and Victory Medal 1914-19.

OWEN, James Collins Farish

From Annapolis Royal, Nova Scotia, Canada. Gazetted Lieutenant to the Canadian Army Service Corps on 8 December 1914. After service with the CEF, he was seconded to the RFC in June 1916. Gained his Royal Aero Club Certificate (Number 3429) on 23 August 1916. His formal pilot training duly completed, he was confirmed and gazetted Flying Officer on 6 September following. Sent out to 17 Squadron in Salonika in the same month that he qualified for his 'Wings'. On 18 February 1917, Owen in BE12a, 'A589', together with a colleague, Gilbert Murlis Green (qv), decided to challenge the leading German aviator in the sector, Leutnant R von Eschwege, and so waited for him directly above his home field. Obligingly, the German Ace soon climbed to engage his challengers. Unfortunately, Murlis Green's guns jammed at a crucial moment and whilst he struggled to correct the fault, von Eschwege shot Owen down to a crash-landing. Unable to free his gun, Murlis Green turned for home whilst the downed Owen set fire to his machine before enemy troops took him into captivity and eventual incarceration in Bulgaria. His MC was announced in the Birthday Honours *London Gazette* of 4 June 1917 (no citation).

Owen returned from captivity in Bulgaria on 16 October 1918, going home to Canada soon afterwards. He finally and formally left the RAF on 30 April 1919. It appears that he was hardly a model prisoner during his incarceration, as he was subsequently Mentioned in Despatches in the 'Escapers Gazette', *London Gazette* of 16 December 1919: '....for gallantry whilst a Prisoner of War in escaping, or attempting to escape, from captivity, or for valuable services rendered in the Prison Camps of the Enemy'.

OWEN, Tom

From Welshpool. Gazetted Second Lieutenant to a Regular Army battalion of the South Staffordshire Regiment on 26 July 1915, with an almost immediate attachment to 2/10 Battalion, Middlesex Regiment. He served in Gallipoli from August 1915, until evacuated to Egypt in the following December. Transferring to the RFC whilst still in Egypt, he trained there as a Pilot and was duly gazetted Flying Officer on 16 March 1917. Owen was then sent to France to serve with 4 Squadron (RE8s) and survived a close call on 21 September 1917, when he and his Observer, Second Lieutenant L V W Clark, in RE8, 'A4298', eventually extricated themselves and got home safely following a fraught combat with five enemy machines above Polygon Wood. Sent out to 14 Squadron in Palestine, he was wounded in action during a photo-reconnaissance patrol on 9 January 1918. Owen returned to the Home Establishment for the last time on 4 June 1918. His MC was announced in the *London Gazette* of 26 July 1918: 'For conspicuous gallantry and devotion to duty. He has carried out many successful low reconnaissances, bringing back good reports. When on artillery patrol, he succeeded in completely disorganising the traffic on a main road, getting direct hits on troops and transport by artillery. On this occasion it is estimated that forty lorries were destroyed. He also attacked enemy troops and transport with bombs and machine-guns with success'.

Tom Owen finally left the RAF, via the Unemployed List, on 27 May 1919.

OWEN-HOLDSWORTH, James Philip

The son of Herbert Lacy Owen-Holdsworth and Winifred Owen-Holdsworth, of Jewell House, Marden, Kent and, later, of Thurlow Cottage, Westfield, Battle, Sussex, he was born in 1898. Admitted as a Cadet into the flying service in September 1916, he was subsequently gazetted Second Lieutenant to the RFC on 12 February 1917. Gained his Royal Aero Club Certificate (Number 4425) on 25 March 1917. His formal pilot training duly completed, he was confirmed and gazetted Flying Officer on 12 June following. Accompanying FE2b-equipped 101 Squadron to France as a 'founder member' on 25 July 1917, he participated in no less than 52 bombing raids. Many of these raids occurred during the massive German spring offensive which commenced on 21 March 1918. On 12 April 1918, Owen-Holdsworth and his Observer, Second Lieutenant H J Collins, in FE2b, 'A5728', were shot down, very possibly by so-called 'friendly fire' in the form of a French anti-aircraft battery. Collins was injured in the crash but Owen-Holdsworth was killed. His MC was announced, posthumously, in the *London Gazette* of 26 July 1918: 'For conspicuous gallantry and devotion to duty. During the last six months he has carried out fifty-two bombing raids on the enemy lines of communication, their aerodromes and their rest billets, often flying in very bad weather. Descending to a low altitude he has obtained several direct hits, both on their hangars and their billets. On several occasions he has returned with his machine riddled with bullets. He has set a fine example of courage and determination'.

James Owen-Holdsworth is buried in St Pierre Cemetery, Amiens, Somme, France.

OWLES, Ernest Tafford

From Weald, Essex, he was born on 24 August 1889. Educated at Felsted School (1905-06) and privately by the Reverend T J Sewell, MA, at The Vicarage, Lynsted, Kent. After completing his education, he worked as a clerk in the City of London. When war came in August 1914, he immediately enlisted as a Private soldier into 10 Battalion, Royal Fusiliers (Stockbrokers). Picked out for a commission, he was gazetted Second Lieutenant to 3 (Reserve) Battalion, Royal Irish Fusiliers on 17 March 1915. He served in the trenches with his regiment, and was wounded in the right thigh on 5 August 1915. Once recovered, he successfully sought secondment to the RFC in May 1916. He trained as an Observer and was formally confirmed and gazetted Flying Officer (Observer) on 4 October 1916, before joining 16 Squadron at the front immediately afterwards. His tour with '16' was short-lived, as he was forced to return to the Home Establishment due to ill-health in the following November. Having recovered his fitness, he next trained as a Pilot and was duly given his full 'Wings' on 3 May 1917. Sent out to 12 Squadron just two days later on 5 May, he was eventually promoted to A/Captain and Flight Commander on 5 December following. On 21 March 1918, the first day of the German spring offensive, he was badly wounded in the mouth and jaw. His MC was announced in the *London Gazette* of 25 April 1918: 'For conspicuous gallantry and devotion to duty. He made a successful wire reconnaissance along a corps front at a height of 300 to 800 feet under heavy machine-gun and rifle fire. On another occasion while on reconnoitring patrol he had four encounters with enemy aeroplanes, in one of which he was attacked at 800 feet by five enemy scouts. By his clever manoeuvring, the enemy machines were driven off, and he completed a valuable reconnaissance. He showed the greatest keenness and determination at his work'.

His wounds were so severe that they kept him in hospital throughout the remainder of 1918 and all of 1919, before he was eventually obliged to relinquish his commission due to ill-health on 23 January 1920. After leaving the RAF, he went to live in Africa. He married in England in 1923, before returning to Kenya with his new bride. His wounds continued to trouble him and he spent many years attempting to secure a pension to compensate him for his disabilities. He was still living in Kenya in the 1960s, but returned to live in retirement in Tunbridge Wells. Ernest Owles died on 11 September 1974.

OXENHAM, Herbert Anselm

A Technical, not a flying, award

Born on 7 April 1876. A wireless expert, he worked in the USA for the Federal Telegraph Company in San Francisco from June 1912 to April 1915. Returning to the UK, he was gazetted Second Lieutenant to the RFC, via the Special Reserve, on 1 June 1915. His appointment as an Assistant Equipment Officer was confirmed in the *London Gazette* of 18 July following. Oxenham worked briefly with 19 Squadron in the UK, before going out to instruct at the Wireless School and at RFC HQ, France. Research has unearthed a recommendation for a Mention in Despatches: '12 March 1916. For excellent work as Wing Wireless Officer. Combines great technical skill and a marked devotion to duty. He has served with the BEF since 27 July 1915'. His MC was announced in the New Year *London Gazette* of 1 January 1917 (no citation). Although no formal citation appeared in the *Gazette*, again research has unearthed the original recommendation for the award: 'H A Oxenham. For very valuable work in charge of the wireless telegraphy of the 3rd Wing RFC from April 1st to the end of September, 1916. Captain Oxenham organised the wireless stations of the whole of the artillery of the Fourth Army during the battle of the Somme'.

Oxenham finally left the RAF, via the Unemployed List, in December 1919. By 1921, he had returned to the USA and was working in Honolulu, Hawaii, for the Radio Corporation of America (RCA).

OXSPRING, Robert

The son of Farmer Joseph E Oxspring and Mary Oxspring, of Wardsend House, Ecclesfield, Yorkshire, he was born on 20 June 1892. After completing his education, he farmed in the Sheffield, Yorkshire, area from 1910 to 1914. Gazetted Second Lieutenant to 3 (Reserve) Battalion, King's Own Yorkshire Light Infantry on 15 August 1915, he was sent to serve in the trenches shortly afterwards. He was awarded the first of his MCs in the *London Gazette* of 14 January 1916, (no citation). Securing a secondment to the RFC in the spring of 1916, he was, following training, confirmed and gazetted Flying Officer (Observer) on 31 May 1916. Oxspring served as an Observer in the UK with 43 Squadron, then a HD unit, before training as a Pilot later in the year. Once qualified for his full 'Wings', he accompanied 54 Squadron (Sopwith Pups) to France as a 'founder member', on 24 December 1916. Promoted to A/Captain, he was next posted to 66 Squadron (also Pups) as a Flight Commander on 6 April 1917. On 24 April 1917, Oxspring's Sopwith Pup 'A7305', was shot up and damaged during a long-distance reconnaissance but, fortunately, he was unscathed in the incident. On 30 April following, however, he was involved in a collision, which resulted in two broken legs. A Bar to his MC came in the *London Gazette* of 26

May 1917: 'For conspicuous gallantry and devotion to duty on several occasions. He has brought down three hostile machines, and in addition has forced several others to land. He has at all times set a splendid example of courage and initiative'.

Oxspring finally left the RAF in 1919 to return to farming in Yorkshire. In the Second World War, his son, Squadron Leader Robert Wardlow Oxspring, DFC and Bar, fought in the Battle of Britain with 66 Squadron and, later in the war, with 72 Squadron, becoming an Ace.

P

PALETHORPE, John

From Dudley, Worcestershire, he was born on 17 August 1883. Educated at Tettenhall College. A Director of the famous family sausage-making firm, he was working and living in Birmingham when the war came in 1914. He enlisted as a Trooper (Number 2363) into the Worcestershire Yeomanry and subsequently served in Gallipoli from 14 August 1915. He was taken ill in September, receiving treatment at No 14 Casualty Clearing Station, before being returned to the UK in a Hospital Ship in October 1915. Once recovered, he reported for duty as a motor cyclist (Lance Corporal) with 4 Provincial Worcester Brigade Yeomanry in March 1916. Anxious to join the flying service, he gained, at his own expense, a Royal Aero Club Certificate (Number 2519) on 1 March 1916. His success in acquiring a 'ticket' no doubt expedited his ambitions and he was gazetted Second Lieutenant to the RFC, via the Special Lists, on 27 May 1916. His formal pilot training duly completed, he was confirmed and gazetted Flying Officer on 28 July following. Sent to serve at the Testing Station at Martlesham Heath, it seemed unlikely that he would see much action. In the event, however, as the citation for his MC makes clear, he would see his share. His MC was announced in the *London Gazette* of 17 July 1917 : 'During a recent hostile air raid Captain Palethorpe, with 1st Class Air Mechanic J O Jessop, RFC, as gunner, was engaged in an endurance trial from a testing station. When about three miles from the coast a formation of seventeen enemy aeroplanes was sighted. Captain Palethorpe at once attacked with great courage and determination, under very heavy fire until the gunner was killed. He then landed, and having procured another gunner, endeavoured to renew the attack'.

This action had taken place just 13 days earlier on 4 July 1917, when Palethorpe and his Gunner/ Observer, 1 AM James Oliver Jessop, were endurance testing a Royal Aircraft Factory-engined DH4 when they ran into 17 or 18 Gothas, intent on bombing Harwich and Felixstowe. Palethorpe immediately attacked the centre machine of the formation. His own gun jammed, but Jessop's weapon hammered its way through a full drum before the unfortunate Gunner was struck in the heart by retaliatory fire from one of the several Gothas firing at the DH4. Palethorpe broke away and made good his escape. Number 25501 1 AM James Oliver Jessop, RFC, a 24 year old from Forest Hill, London, is buried in Lewisham (Ladywell) Cemetery, London. He was posthumously Mentioned in Despatches, *London Gazette* of 17 July 1917: '....for his gallant and distinguished service in connection with recent enemy air raids'. After landing and overseeing the removal of Jessop's body, Palethorpe demanded the services of another Gunner and took off again in vain pursuit of the Gothas. He was in action again just three days later. Flying the same DH4, he attacked the starboard aircraft in a formation of Gothas making their way across Essex. His own gun failed again, but he was able to make a series of passes which allowed his Gunner, James, to fire off all seven of his drums. During the final pass, the Gothas' retaliatory fire struck home, wounding Palethorpe in the right buttock. The blood-soaked Palethorpe broke off the action and nursed his bullet-riddled machine down to a safe landing at Rochford. For his aircraft testing work at Martlesham Heath, Palethorpe was awarded the Air Force Cross, *London Gazette* of 2 November 1918.

PALING, Leslie George

From Nottingham, he was born on 20 January 1895. Gazetted Second Lieutenant to 4 (Extra Reserve) Battalion, Sherwood Foresters (Nottinghamshire and Derbyshire Regiment), on 7 May 1915. Securing a secondment to the RFC in September 1916, he gained his Royal Aero Club Certificate (Number 4071) on 27 December 1916. His formal pilot training duly completed, he was confirmed and gazetted Flying Officer on 2 May 1917. Sent out to 35 Squadron (AWFK8s) on 21 June following. On 23 November 1917, Paling and his Observer of the day, Second Lieutenant D O Duthie, in 'B5767', narrowly escaped disaster when their 'Big Ack' was shot up by ground fire over Longavesnes. Duthie was wounded in the action but, fortunately, Paling got him back safely for medical treatment. On 24 March 1918, three days into the German spring offensive, Paling and his Observer, Captain J R Fasson, in 'C3631', were forced down near to Mons during a combat with enemy machines. After setting fire to the remains of their 'Big Ack', Paling sought out the local Infantry Brigade HQ and passed on the information he and Fasson had gathered during their patrol. For his courage on this and other occasions, he would be awarded the MC, announced in the *London Gazette* of 22 June 1918: 'For conspicuous gallantry and devotion to duty. While on contact patrol he engaged a hostile battalion moving to the attack with bombs and machine-gun fire, inflicting heavy casualties. On his return he was attacked by ten enemy scouts, all of which he succeeded in driving off after a hard fight, but was forced to land in front of our lines. Having destroyed his machine, he gave information as to the dispositions of the enemy and the nearest hostile field batteries. His exceptional courage, dash and capacity for hard work have proved invaluable.

His tour with '35' completed on 17 April 1918, he returned to the Home Establishment where he saw out the remainder of the war and beyond as an Instructor. He finally left the RAF, via the Unemployed List, on 30 October 1919, to return to his home in Ousebridge, Carlton, Notts.

PALMER, Frank Bacon

A ground based Gallantry, not a flying, award

Originally from farming stock in North Walsham, Norfolk, he was born on 8 January 1891. Before the war came in 1914, he was working for the family business, the Palmer Realtory Company, in Manitoba, Canada. He enlisted as a Trooper at Valcartier into Fort Garry Horse Reserve Regiment on 4 October 1914. He served subsequently with 6 Battalion, CEF, in France. Volunteering for the flying service, he was gazetted Second Lieutenant to the RFC, via the Special Lists, on 13 November 1916. Palmer was gazetted Equipment Officer, 3rd Class, on 24 July 1917, on the same day that he was posted to 48 Squadron. Hospitalised on 16 June 1918, due to sickness. He was back with '48' in the following August when, unexpectedly, he won the MC. Palmer's MC was announced in a special gazetting of awards relating to gallantry displayed following a devastating hostile air-raid on Bertangles, the 48 Squadron aerodrome. Fires destroyed five hangars containing the unit's Bristol Fighters, many of which were burnt to a crisp. Hits also occurred on stores, dumps and billets. Fifteen flying personnel were wounded or suffered burns, with two dying later. Palmer was the only officer honoured but, remarkably, no less than 18 Military Medals were awarded to RAF other ranks. London Gazette of 8 November 1918: 'War Office, 8 November 1918. His Majesty the King has approved of the under-mentioned rewards in recognition of bravery in the field. Awarded the Military Cross: Second Lieutenant (Acting Lieutenant) Frank Bacon Palmer, RAF. On the night of 24 August 1918, this officer performed very gallant and meritorious service. In an attack on one of our aerodromes by hostile aircraft, a hangar full of machines was set on fire, illuminating the whole camp, making the aerodrome an easy mark for the raiders, who continued dropping bombs for fifteen minutes. Great confusion ensued, and twenty officers and men were wounded. Lieutenant Palmer was blown over by the explosion of a bomb, and although badly shaken he exhibited coolness and courage of a high order, and by his promptitude succeeded in collecting the wounded, placing them in comparative safety, and also managed to remove the machines and transport from the burning hangars and shelters notwithstanding the continual dropping of the enemy's bombs in the area'.

The announcement goes on to name 18 RAF other ranks who were to receive the Military Medal. The squadron was pulled out of Bertangles and sent to Boisdinghem to be re-equipped. Remarkably, the unit was again putting up patrols over the front just two days later. After a period of rest and recuperation in the UK, Palmer returned again to 48 Squadron on 7 November 1918.

PARIS, Darell Kilburn

From Goring-on-Thames, Middlesex. A pre-war volunteer, he served as a Driver (Number 378) in the Honourable Artillery Company (TF). On 4 August 1914, Paris, along with the entire TF, was mobilised, serving subsequently in France with the HAC from 21 April 1915. Picked out for a commission, he was gazetted Second Lieutenant to the Royal Artillery, via the Special Lists, on 26 February 1916. Immediately seconded to the RFC, he trained as an Observer and was sent out to 14 Squadron in the Middle East as a Probationary on 13 April 1916. His 'apprenticeship' satisfactorily completed, he was confirmed and gazetted Flying Officer (Observer) on 1 June following. On 18 June 1916, elements of 14 and 17 Squadrons mounted a retaliatory attack on El Arish aerodrome as a response to enemy bombing raids on two British garrisons. One of the BE2c of 17 Squadron, '2691', flown by South African Captain H A van Ryneveld (qv), its engine having been stopped by a rifle bullet in the oil sump, was brought down in the desert. Van Ryneveld's predicament was observed by Paris, flying in BE2c, '2700', with Captain Stuart Grant-Dalton, Yorkshire Regiment, attached RFC. Grant-Dalton brought his BE down alongside the stranded van Ryneveld and, following a number of unsuccessful attempts to take off from the surrounding soft sand, the three men dragged and pulled the machine onto firmer ground, from where they got airborne, having destroyed the abandoned BE. Grant-Dalton, who would go on to high rank in the RNZAF, received the first of his two Distinguished Service Orders for this incident. Paris' MC was announced in the *London Gazette* of 27 July 1916: 'For conspicuous gallantry and resource. When Observer with Captain Grant-Dalton as pilot, he observed far within the enemy's country one of our machines on the ground, damaged by hostile fire. They landed, destroyed the machine, which was past repair, and brought back the pilot ninety miles to their own aerodrome. It was due to 2nd Lieutenant Paris' keen observation and Captain Grant-Dalton's skill that the pilot was rescued'.

Paris was also Mentioned in Despatches on two occasions during the Great War, Sir Archibald Murray's Despatches of 27 July 1916 and 1 December 1916. He completed his tour with 14 Squadron on 19 July 1916, going on to train as a Pilot but was seriously injured on 13 August 1916. Once recovered, he gained his full 'Wings' and was sent out to 15 Squadron in France on 26 March 1917. On 30 April following, Paris and his Observer of the day, Second Lieutenant Fereman, in BE2e, '7060', were reported as missing during an artillery observation patrol. It was subsequently reported that both men had been taken as prisoners of war. Paris was eventually repatriated on 1 January 1919. He decided to revert to his Royal Artillery commission on 14 April 1919.

PARK, Keith Rodney

The son of Professor James L and Mrs Frances Park, of Thames, near Auckland, New Zealand, he was born on 15 June 1892. Educated at King's College, Auckland, and at Ortago Bay Boys School, Dunedin. Joined the Union Steam Ship Company as a Purser in 1911 till December 1914. He enlisted and served as a Gunner with the New Zealand Artillery in Egypt and in Gallipoli, before being selected for a commission in July 1915. He was then attached to the British Army for some months before being formally gazetted Second Lieutenant to Royal Field Artillery on 4 May 1916. Sent to serve in France, he was wounded on 21 October 1916, wounds which were of sufficient severity to have him invalided out of the Army. Despite this, he persisted in his attempts to be accepted into the flying service. At last admitted to the RFC, he trained as a Pilot and was duly confirmed and gazetted Flying Officer on 23 May 1917. Showing great natural ability, he was initially selected to remain as an Instructor in the UK, a delay which meant his practical flying experience increased from 35 to 100 hours, before he left to join the Bristol Fighter-equipped 48 Squadron at the front on 7 July 1917. An extremely successful combat career followed, as is evidenced by no less than 20 victories achieved between 24 July 1917 and 25 June 1918. The first of his MCs was announced in the *London Gazette* of 26 September 1917, details in the *Gazette* of 9 January 1918: 'For conspicuous gallantry and devotion to duty. During an engagement with several large hostile formations, the two machines with which he was patrolling were put out of action. In spite, however, of being left alone, he continued to attack, and engaged the enemy machines in so determined a manner that he and his Observer between them destroyed one and drove three others down completely out of control. He has performed several other fine feats, and has at all times set a most inspiring example by his dash and tenacity'.

The Observer referred to in the citation was A R H Noss (qv), whose own citation for his MC is virtually identical to that of Park. Research has unearthed the original recommendation for their awards which is rather more informative: 'A R Noss (joint reco with his Pilot, K R Park, 48 Sqn, 19/8/17) These two officers were on a special High patrol near Middlekerke on the 17th August in company with two other Bristols, when several large formations of EA were seen and immediately attacked. Early in the engagement the Observer of one Bristol was killed and the Pilot wounded thereby putting this machine out of action which returned to the lines. Shortly afterwards a second Bristol was forced down and compelled to retire. In spite of being left alone, Lt Park continued to attack and engage the enemy in so determined a manner that he and his Observer between them destroyed one of the enemy machines which was seen to crash; shortly afterwards Lt Park's gun jammed and his Observer continued the engagement until Lt Park managed to clear the jam and immediately brought his front gun into action again; between them they succeeded in driving down two other machines completely out of control, following the first down to 3,500 feet, and when they were absolutely certain this machine could not recover they left him and started to engage another which they also succeeded in driving down completely out of control. They were unable to watch the machine crash as they were again attacked by another hostile aircraft. This they engaged and drove off and they were only compelled to return owing to lack of ammunition. Lt Park has performed several other fine feats and has at all times set a most inspiriting example by his dash and tenacity'.

The Bar to Park's MC came in the *London Gazette* of 27 October 1917: 'For conspicuous gallantry and devotion to duty in accounting for nine enemy aircraft, three of which were completely destroyed and six driven down out of control'.

Not all was plain-sailing for the brilliant Kiwi, however, as he was shot down on two occasions, once by anti-aircraft fire and again, on 3 January 1918, by the then aspiring German Ace, Unteroffizier Kurt Ungewitter of SchlachtStaffel 5, although, happily, he emerged unscathed from both experiences. Ungewitter would go on to achieve seven victories. Promoted to A/Major, Park was appointed to command '48' on 10 April 1918. The

French showed their appreciation by awarding him the Croix de Guerre at this time, *London Gazette* of 18 April 1918. Park would also receive the Distinguished Flying Cross in the Birthday Honours *London Gazette* of 3 June 1919.

He married in 1918, Dorothy Margarita Parish (died 1971), with whom he had two sons, one being killed on active service in 1951. Staying on in the RAF after the Great War, he would go on to command 25 and then 111 Squadrons in the 1920s. By 1935 he was a Group Captain and Air Attaché in the British Embassy in the Argentinian Capital, Buenos Aires. His outstanding career was capped by his huge contribution to the winning of the Battle of Britain in 1940, when he commanded 11 Fighter Group. His many honours and appointments included: AOC, RAF, Egypt; AOC, RAF, Malta, 1942-43; AOC-in-C, Middle East, 1944; Allied Air C-in-C South-East Asia, 1945-46; CB, 1940; KBE, 1942; KCB, 1945; and GCB, 1946. He lived in retirement at 'Blue Waters', Lucerne Road, Remuera, Auckland, New Zealand. Air Chief Marshal Sir Keith Park died on 5 February 1975. A biography, 'Sir Keith Park', by Vincent Orange, was published in 1984.

PARK, Walter Henry

Park served as a Corporal in the Auckland Mounted Rifles in Egypt and then in Gallipoli, where he was wounded in action. Once recovered, he was picked out for a commission and was gazetted Second Lieutenant to a Regular Army battalion of the Royal Irish Rifles on 20 June 1916, serving later with 6 Battalion of his regiment in Macedonia. Seconded to the RFC, he trained as a Pilot and was formally gazetted Flying Officer on 17 May 1917. Sent out to FE2b-equipped 11 Squadron soon after qualifying, he had been promoted to Captain and Flight Commander by the time his MC was announced in the *London Gazette* of 22 June 1918: 'For conspicuous gallantry and devotion to duty. He undertook a long distance reconnaissance under the most adverse conditions, and though several other machines were compelled to abandon the attempt by his persistence completed his task and returned with valuable information. He is a patrol leader of the highest order, and his consistent gallantry and valuable services cannot be too highly praised'.

Staying on in the RAF after the war, he went on to command a seaplane squadron in Murmansk during the Allied Intervention in Russia. For his services during the operations with 'Syren Force' in North Russia, he was awarded the Distinguished Flying Cross, *London Gazette* of 18 November 1919. He later served in Egypt and in Iraq. Park was in charge of the successful evacuation of Sulimani, Kurdistan, in 1922, for which he received a Bar to the Distinguished Flying Cross, *London Gazette* of 19 December 1922. In 1927, Park was a married man and a Squadron Leader on Sir John Salmond's Staff at the HQ, Air Defence of Great Britain. In the following year he was appointed to command the RAF Station at Hawkinge. Unfortunately, he was taken ill and during an operation to correct matters, he died in Shorecliff Military Hospital, on 19 October 1928. His widow, Edith Mary, and his long-term friend and colleague, Flight Lieutenant John Stanley Chick, MC, AFC (qv), were appointed joint executors of his estate.

PARKER, Aubrey Hastings

The son of Commander Phillip Reginald Hastings Parker, RN, and Mrs Hastings, of Cheltenham, he was born in India on 1 October 1873. Educated as a day boy at Cheltenham 1887-88, at Melbourne University, and at King's College, Cambridge Passed for Royal Military Academy, Woolwich, but did not go there. Passed the examination for entry into the Indian Civil Service in 1896. Employed at the India Office, Whitehall, before going out to India with an appointment as Assistant Commissioner, Punjab, in 1897. Served later as a District and Sessions Judge and as a Judge in the Punjab. Came over as a volunteer with the Indian Division, landing in France on 7 December 1914. Gazetted Lieutenant to the Special Lists on 6 January 1915, with an immediate detachment to the Balloon Service, RFC. Served in France until 6 July 1915, when he was wounded. Once recovered, he returned to duty and was promoted to Captain and Balloon Commander on 18 December 1915. Served again in France with 7 KBS, his MC was announced in the *London Gazette* of 14 January 1916 (no citation). Parker was later recommended for a Bar to his MC by Major General H M Trenchard on 16 October 1916 but, in the event, this was reduced to a Mention in Despatches. Research has unearthed Trenchard's recommendation for this latter award: 'From March to August 1916 he carried out successful and consistent good work in command of a Kite Balloon Section. He invariably displayed great energy and trained his officers admirably. His work has been most valuable. On the 5th August his balloon was brought down by shell fire. He displayed great coolness and resource in assisting his observer to make a parachute descent before doing so himself'.

Parker served on the Staff with 7 Balloon Wing in 1917 and was involved in a kite balloon training post in the UK in 1918. He left the UK in March 1919, to be repatriated to India where he was seconded to the Air Board Department, Government of India. He retired from this post in 1924.

PARKER, Charles Allen

From Longford, Tasmania, Australia, he was born on 3 December 1898, in Park Nook, Lake River. He was living and working in Charleville, Queensland, when the war came. Enlisting into the AIF early in the war, he was picked out for a commission and subsequently gazetted Second Lieutenant, at a very early age, to the Royal Field Artillery on 22 November 1915. Kept back in the UK, he eventually succeeded in securing a secondment to the RFC in August 1916. His pilot training duly completed, he was confirmed and gazetted Flying Officer on 6 January 1917. Sent out to FE2b-equipped11 Squadron in France just 11 days after qualifying. On 22 April 1917, Parker and his Observer, Second Lieutenant J E B Hesketh, in FE2b, 'A820', were shot down by Leutnant Karl Emil Schäfer, one of the many 'stars' of Jasta 11, the 21st of the German Ace's eventual 30 victories. James Hesketh from Altrincham, Cheshire, was shot and mortally wounded early on in the confrontation. Parker desperately held on to his unfortunate and largely unconscious Observer who was in danger of falling out, whilst at the same time wrestling with badly damaged controls in his attempts to effect a reasonable landing. As they crashlanded, the FE burst into flames and also came under shell fire from the enemy artillery. Young Parker lifted the inert Hesketh onto his shoulder and carried him away from the wreckage and the shelling. Sadly, his efforts were in vain as Hesketh died soon afterwards. Parker's well-deserved MC was announced in the *London Gazette* of 18 July 1917: 'For conspicuous gallantry and devotion to duty. When on a photographic reconnaissance, he was attacked by hostile scouts, and his Observer was severely wounded. He effected a landing near our front line, and carried his Observer clear of the machine, which was heavily shelled the entire time, and had burst into flames'.

Parker was himself wounded whilst low-strafing the German infantry in the trenches of the Hindenburg line on 20 May 1917. Once recovered, he reported for duty with the Home Establishment on 15 October 1917, before being sent to the Middle East as an Instructor with 23 TS in the following month. Charles Parker was killed in a flying accident in Mesopotamia on 18 February 1918 and is buried in Basra War Cemetery, Iraq.

PARKER, Egbert John

An Exceptional Service, not a flying, award

From Tring in Hertfordshire, he was born on 6 March 1881. A soldier of the Regular Army, he was a Lance Sergeant (Number 8308) in 1 Battalion, Grenadier Guards, when he transferred to the RFC in the second year of the Corps' existence on 2 April 1913. Promoted rapidly, he was Sergeant Major (Number 808) at Gosport from 3 September 1913. Parker accompanied 5 Squadron to France in August 1914, as part of the original RFC contingent, thus earning the 1914 Star. Mentioned in Despatches in the *London Gazette* of 8 October 1914. His MC was amongst the very first listed in the New Year *London Gazette* of 1 January 1915 (no citation). A total of 99 MCs were given in this first gazetting, including 27 to Warrant Officers, three of whom, Parker, Ramsey and Jilling, belonged to the RFC. Selected for a QM commission, Parker was gazetted Lieutenant and Quartermaster on 1 June 1915. His other decorations included the Merite Agricole from the French and, from the Sovereign, King George V, the Royal Victorian Medal. Parker subsequently relinquished his RAF commission (A/Major) on 1 April 1920 and returned to the Army. In 1921, he was living with his wife in the garrison town of Caterham, Surrey.

PARKER, George Alec

The son of Lewis Jacques Parker and Emily Parker, of 26 Castle Street, Salisbury, he was born on 19 December 1892. Educated at Dean Close School (1907-1909). Gained his Royal Aero Club Certificate (Number 347) in a Bristol machine at the Bristol School, Salisbury Plain, on 29 October 1912. Although he would have liked direct entry into the flying service, he had to be content with being gazetted Second Lieutenant to the Northamptonshire Regiment from the Special Reserve on 24 March 1913. He was serving in Alexandria, Egypt, with 2 Battalion of his regiment when war broke out and was soon accompanying 'The Steelbacks' on their return to England, before subsequently landing with them in France on 6 November 1914, thus earning the 1914 Star. Parker spent an unpleasant winter in the trenches and was at one time in charge of the Brigade bombing contingent. Tragically, in the Battle of Neuve Chapelle between 10th and 12th March 1915, 2 Northants was virtually annihilated. Only three officers emerged apparently unscathed from the battle, and of those, Parker and another subaltern subsequently collapsed and were taken to hospital suffering from the debilitating effects of standing waist-deep in water for four consecutive days and nights. Once recovered, he successfully sought secondment to the RFC. Training first as an Observer, he joined 6 Squadron in France, flying often with Captain L A Strange (qv) in one of the unit's newly acquired FE2a. Next, he underwent formal training as a Pilot and was duly confirmed and gazetted Flying Officer on 16 December 1915. Sent out to BE2c-equipped 13 Squadron on 31 March 1916, he was soon heavily involved with that unit's work. Promoted to Captain, he next transferred to 8 Squadron as a Flight Commander on 2 June 1916. His tour with '8' completed, he returned to the Home Establishment for rest, recuperation and, eventually, training on single-seater scouts. Returning again to the front, he joined the Nieuport XVII-equipped 60 Squadron, as a Flight Commander. On 27 November 1916, Parker in Nieuport XVII, 'A281/A1', was killed in aerial combat with Werner Voss, the first of the German Ace's eventual 48 victories. Parker was, posthumously, awarded the Distinguished Service Order and awarded the MC in the same *London Gazette* of 10 January 1917, the citation for his Distinguished Service Order speaking of his gallantry in aerial combat, his MC awarded: 'For conspicuous gallantry in action. He attacked a hostile scout machine and forced it to land after a long combat. He displayed great courage and skill in out-manoeuvring this machine'.

He was also twice Mentioned in Despatches around this time, *London Gazettes* of 9 April 1917 and 15 May 1917. George Parker's remains were never recovered and hence he is commemorated on the Flying Services Memorial, Arras, France.

PATTINSON, Lawrence Arthur

The son of H L Pattinson and Mrs H P R Pattinson, of Lowlynn, Beal, Northumberland, he was born on 8 October 1890. Educated at Rugby, at Wesley College, Melbourne, Australia, and at Jesus College, Cambridge (MA, 2nd Class Honours, History Tripos, LLB). A pre war volunteer, he was gazetted Second Lieutenant to 5 Battalion, Durham Light Infantry (TF), on 11 January 1914. Mobilised with the rest of the TF on 4 August 1914, he was subsequently seconded to the RFC in the spring of 1915. Gained his Royal Aero Club Certificate (Number 12142) on 30 April 1915. His formal pilot training duly completed, he was confirmed and gazetted Flying Officer on 5 July following. In the meantime, Pattinson had been awarded a permanent commission in the Royal Fusiliers (City of London) Regiment. He accompanied 11 Squadron (FB5s), the first British two-seater fighter unit on the Western Front, to France as a 'founder member' on 25 July 1915. Promoted to A/Captain and Flight Commander in October 1915, he was continuously involved in much of the largely inconclusive aerial skirmishing of the period. On 30 April 1916, however, Pattinson in one of the newly acquired Nieuport XVIs, 'A117', shot down an Albatros Scout in the Ecurie-Douai sector, thus registering the first victory for this marque. His MC was announced in the Birthday Honours *London Gazette* of 3 June 1916 (no citation). Although no formal citation was published in the *Gazette*, research has unearthed the original recommendation for the award: 'L A Pattinson. (R Fus – City of London Rgt) 11 Sqn. For continuous good work as a flying officer and flight commander from August 1915 to the present date. Has invariably shown great gallantry and determination while on patrol duty notably on the 19.12.15 when he drove off two hostile double fuselage machines and finished his photographic duty, and on 25.1.16 when he attacked and drove down a hostile kite balloon under heave anti-aircraft gun fire'.

His tour with '11' completed, he returned to the UK where he was promoted to A/Major and placed in command of FE2d-equipped 57 Squadron then at Copmanthorpe. Pattinson led '57' to France on 16 December 1916, serving continuously until returning to the Home Establishment in November 1917. His next command, from May 1918, was of the DH9-equipped 99 Squadron, Independent Air Force, firstly at St Omer, then at Tantonville, and finally at Azelot. Awarded the Distinguished Flying Cross in the *London Gazette* of 2 November 1918 for 'exceptional leadership of bombing formations' amongst other attributes. He was also Mentioned in Despatches around this time. After promotion to A/Lieutenant Colonel, he was given command of 41 Wing, IF, in October 1918. Awarded the Distinguished Service Order in the Birthday Honours *London Gazette* of 3 June 1919. Staying in the RAF, he commanded a Squadron in India in 1919. He married, in 1923, Mabel Copeland (née Capper) with whom he had one son and one daughter. His various appointments, promotions and honours in what would prove a extremely distinguished career, included: Wing Commander, 1922; Staff College Camberley, 1922; Air Staff HQ, RAF India, 1926-30; Group Captain, 1930; ADC to the King, 1933-34; Deputy Director of Organisation, Air Ministry, 1930-34; Air Commodore, 1934; AOC, Armament Group, Eastchurch, 1934-37; AOC, 23 (Training) Group, 1937-40; CB, 1938; and AOC-in-Chief, Flying Training Command, 1940-41. He retired in 1941, only to be recalled to the Active List in October 1942, as Head of the RAF Training Mission to the Chinese Air Force. Knighted (KBE), 1945. He finally retired with the rank of Air Marshal and lived at Salkeld Hall, Little Salkeld, Penrith, Cumberland. He wrote and published 'The History of 99 Squadron, RAF' in 1920. Air Marshal Sir Lawrence Pattinson died on 28 March 1958.

PAWSON, George St Vincent

The fourth son of William Hargrave Pawson and Mrs Pawson (later the Honourable Mrs John Howard), of Sibton Park, Lyminge, Kent, he was born on 7 October 1890, in Lymington, Hampshire. Educated at Marlborough College (1904-07). Gazetted Second Lieutenant to the Westmorland and Cumberland Yeomanry on 5 May 1915, he was seconded to the RFC in the following November. Having trained as an Observer, he was sent to 26 Squadron, then in Netheravon, on 23 December 1915. Pawson accompanied '26' to Mombasa as a 'founder member' on 31 January 1916 and was later formally confirmed and gazetted Flying Officer (Observer) on 15 February following. Served in East Africa with '26' until 17 May 1918, his MC announced in the *London Gazette* of 1 February 1917 (no citation). After a period of rest and recuperation, Pawson returned to '26' in time to accompany the unit back to England for its eventual disbandment on 8 July 1918. Pawson died of septic pneumonia following influenza, whilst on leave at his home in Lyminge on 6 November 1918, just five days before the Armistice. He is buried in Lyminge (SS Mary & Ethelburga) Churchyard, Kent.

PAYNE, Ernest William John

A Technical, not a flying, award

From Neasden, London. Gazetted Second Lieutenant to the RFC, via the Special Reserve, on 21 June 1915. Subsequently gazetted Assistant Equipment Officer on 1 July 1915. Posted to photographic operations, his MC was announced in the New Year *London Gazette* of 1 January 1917 (no citation). Although no formal citation was published in the *Gazette*, research has unearthed the original recommendation for the award: 'E W J Payne. (3rd Brigade) Has done most valuable work as photographic officer from April to October 1916. He has great technical ability and has shown untiring energy in his work. The results he has obtained have been very good'.

Payne finally left the RAF, via the Unemployed List, on 29 November 1919, to return to his wife and home in Neasdon.

PAYNE, James Dennis

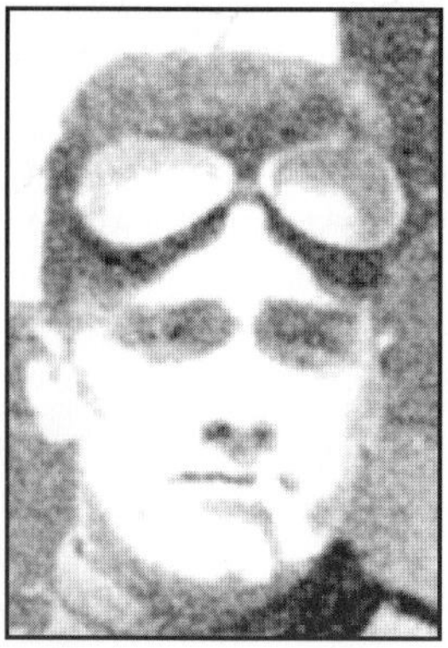

From Leamington Spa, he was born on 22 July 1887. Enlisted (Number 923) into the RFC in the second year of its existence on 10 October 1913. He served as a 2nd Class Air Mechanic with 6 Squadron in France, from 2 March 1915. Whilst still an NCO, he gained his RAC Certificate (Number 1415) on 10 July 1915. Eventually, he was gazetted Second Lieutenant (extra regimentally employed), attached RFC, on 30 October 1916. His formal pilot training duly completed, he was confirmed and gazetted Flying Officer on 3 March 1917. He was first sent to 41 Squadron in France on 12 June 1917, but was soon transferred to 29 Squadron (Nieuport XVIIs), arriving on 6 August following. Soon afterwards, on 10 August 1917, Payne in Nieuport XVII, 'B1687', was injured and rendered temporarily unconscious in the resultant crash-landing, after he lost a propellor during an aerial combat. Amazingly, the damaged Nieuport's instruments were stolen before Payne had regained consciousness. That he quickly recovered is evidenced by the fact that he gained the first of his victories just two days later on 12 August. In fact, Payne went on to achieve no fewer than 14 victories between 12 August

1917 and 9 January 1918, and was also promoted to A/Captain and Flight Commander. His MC was announced in the *London Gazette* of 26 November 1917, details in the *Gazette* of 6 April 1918: 'For conspicuous gallantry and devotion to duty. While on patrol with two other scouts he attacked a formation of seven two-seaters, bringing down two himself while the two scouts brought down two more. Besides these, he has accounted for five other machines, and at all times shown the greatest gallantry'.

His tour with '29' completed, he returned to the Home Establishment on 9 January 1918, where he saw out the war in various training capacities. Payne finally left the RAF after relinquishing his commission on 17 September 1919.

PAYNE, Kenneth Willie

The son of K and Mrs E Payne, of Kenilworth, Newport, Monmouthshire, he was born on 11 February 1891. After completing his education, he emigrated to Australia. Starting as a 'Jackeroo', he worked his way up from Station Hand to an Under Manager in a sheep station in Ivanhoe and Hay, New South Wales, in the years from 1910 to 1914. From his home at Kilfera Station, Ivanhoe, NSW, he enlisted as a Private soldier (Number 2545) into the AIF on 1 September 1914, being assigned to 1 Division Ammunition Column. On 18 October 1914, he embarked aboard the SS *Argyllshire* (Transport A8) at Sydney, part of 1 Section, 1 DAC, bound for the Middle East. Arriving in Egypt, he trained as a Driver with the Brigade Ammunition Column. Next, he was posted to 1 Field Artillery, AIF, on 24 February 1915. After more than two years as an Artilleryman, he was accepted as a volunteer for the flying service and transferred to No 3 School of Aeronautics on 26 January 1917. Gazetted Second Lieutenant to the RFC, via the Special Reserve, on 17 March 1917. His formal pilot training duly completed, he was confirmed and gazetted Flying Officer on 13 June following. After service with 33 and 78 HD Squadrons, he accompanied the night-bombing FE2b-equipped 83 Squadron to France as a 'founder member' on 8 March 1918. His MC was announced in the *London Gazette* of 16 September 1918: 'For conspicuous gallantry and devotion to duty. This officer has shown great skill in carrying out night bombing raids on back areas under adverse weather conditions. On one occasion observing a train in motion fifty miles behind the enemy's lines, he descended to within 800 feet of the ground and dropped a bomb, obtaining a direct hit; he then dropped three bombs on a brilliantly lighted building with good effect. After this he returned to the train, which his Observer attacked with machine-gun fire. On another occasion, when on a bombing raid, his machine caught fire, but with great coolness he brought it safely to earth. He has taken part in over thirty raids, always showing great determination in reaching his objective'.

His tour with '83' completed, he returned to the Home Establishment on 8 September 1918, where he was posted to instructing duties. Payne finally left the RAF on 24 February 1919, returning to his home in Ivanhoe, NSW. He later lived (circa 1922) at 'Booranda', Mullaby, NSW, and later again (circa 1938) was a Stock and Station Agent at Coonabarabran, NSW.

PAYNE, Leonard Allan

The son of Alfred Harold Payne and Sarah Payne, of 'Casa Bonnefoi', Little Hill, Pulborough, Sussex, he was born in Barberton, Transvaal, South Africa, on 15 July 1894. Educated at Barberton Public School in the Transvaal. After completing his education, he was employed as a Revenue Clerk in the Swaziland Administration from May 1913 to October 1916. He enlisted (Number 60100) into the RFC in Pretoria in January 1917, recruited by Captain A L Miller, who would, later in the war, achieve further recruiting 'fame' in Canada, as Major Miller. Once in the UK, Payne was gazetted Second Lieutenant to the RFC, via the General List, on 11 May 1917. Soon after qualifying for his 'Wings', he was sent out, on 5 September 1917, to BF2b-equipped 48 Squadron in France. A highly effective Brisfit Pilot, he accumulated ten victories between 29 October 1917 and 30 May 1918, being promoted A/Captain and Flight Commander on the intervening 25 April. His MC was announced in the *London Gazette* of 26 July 1918: 'For conspicuous gallantry and devotion to duty. Volunteering to proceed on a special reconnaissance under adverse weather conditions, he penetrated for a distance of nine miles behind the enemy's lines, flying at an altitude of 200 feet, despite the most intense machine-gun and rifle fire. He returned later, his machine riddled with bullets, with the required information. Previous to this he had bombed and engaged with machine-gun fire bodies of hostile infantry with the most effective results. He has destroyed one hostile plane and driven down two others out of control. He has at all times displayed the greatest fearlessness and dash'.

His tour with '48' completed, he returned to the Home Establishment on 8 June 1918. Following a rest and some brief duties as an Instructor, he went out again to '48' on 21 October 1918, gaining his 11th victory on 4 November. After the war, Payne was stationed with the Amy of Occupation in Germany and was killed in a flying accident on 18 February 1919, possibly whilst piloting a German machine. He was Mentioned in Despatches posthumously in the *London Gazette* of 1 July 1919. Leonard Payne is buried in Cologne Southern Cemetery, Germany.

NB: His medals are in the hands of a private collector in South Africa: MC, British War Medal 1914-20, and Victory Medal 1914-19 with MID.

PAYNE, Lionel Guy Stanhope

Born 2 October 1894. ADC to the Governor of Ceylon, 1913-14. Gazetted Second Lieutenant to 3 (Reserve) Battalion, Suffolk Regiment, on 23 August 1914. Served in the trenches with 1 Battalion of his regiment from 15 January 1915. Seconded to the RFC at the end of 1915. Gained his Royal Aero Club Certificate (Number 4874) on 1 March 1916. His formal pilot training duly completed, he was confirmed and gazetted Flying Officer on 22 April following. Payne served at HQ, 6 Brigade, RFC, before eventually being sent, in the summer of 1917, to the newly forming night-bombing FE2b-equipped 101 Squadron at Farnborough. Accompanied '101' to France as a 'founder member' on 25 July 1917. On 28 September 1917, Payne and his Observer of the day, Lieutenant F P Worthington, in FE2b, 'A5686', narrowly escaped disaster when their machine was shot up and badly damaged. His MC was announced in the *London Gazette* of 18 February 1918: 'For conspicuous gallantry and devotion to duty. On four occasions he bombed important enemy railway stations, obtaining direct hits on each occasion. He also carried out a long distance raid on an enemy aerodrome, which he bombed from 1,100 feet making the return journey at a height of 800 feet with his machine damaged. He has taken part in many night bombing raids, always at a low altitude, and has set a fine example of determination to all ranks of his squadron'.

After completing his tour with '101', Payne returned to the UK to take up a succession of instructing posts. His efforts were rewarded with a Mention in Despatches, *London Gazette* of 22 January 1919, and the award of an Air Force Cross, announced in the *London Gazette* of 3 June 1919. Payne stayed on in the RAF after the war, eventually retiring as a Group Captain on 1 July 1937. Became the Air Correspondent for the *Daily Telegraph* before being recalled to the RAF when the Second World War came in September 1939. He subsequently became the Director of Air Intelligence in the Air Ministry, with the rank of Air Commodore, for which services he was created CBE. Was again Air Correspondent to the *Daily Telegraph* post the Second World War. Died 11 February 1965.

PEACOCK, Ernest Frederic Woodham

From Montreal, Canada, he was born on 23 June 1893. He trained and worked as an Electrical Engineer in his home city from 1912 to 1914, before volunteering for the Canadian Infantry when the war came. Peacock served in France with 26 (New Brunswick) Battalion, Canadian Infantry. Keen to join the flying service, he gained his Royal Aero Club Certificate (Number 5174) on 3 March 1917. Subsequently accepted, he was gazetted Second Lieutenant to the RFC on 2 August 1917. His formal pilot training duly completed, he was confirmed and gazetted Flying Officer on 21 October following. Sent out to 1 Aeroplane Supply Depot on 14 November 1917, he joined 65 Squadron (Sopwith Camels) just two days later. His MC was announced in the *London Gazette* of 28 May 1918, details in the *Gazette* of 16 September 1918: 'For conspicuous gallantry and devotion to duty while on fighting patrols. He showed great determination and courage in attacking superior numbers of enemy aircraft, and carried out fine work in engaging enemy troops and transport on the ground with machine-gun fire'.

His tour with '65' completed on 29 August 1918, he returned to the Home Establishment and an instructing post with No 3 Fighting School, Bircham Newton. Peacock was seriously injured in a flying accident on 5 September 1918, when his Camel, 'C185', sideslipped into the ground. He was able to return again to France in February 1919, being briefly attached to 2 AD. Peacock finally left the RAF, via the Unemployed List, on 17 April 1919.

PEARSON, Harold Aubrey

Gazetted Second Lieutenant to the Royal Field Artillery on 26 February 1915, serving in the Ypres Salient with 10 Battery, North & West Riding Brigade, RFA, in the same year. Seconded to the RFC in the summer of 1916, he trained as an Observer and was sent out as a Probationary to BE2e-equipped 34 Squadron shortly afterwards. His 'apprenticeship' satisfactorily completed, he was formally gazetted Flying Officer (Observer) on 21 October 1916. On 22 October 1916, Pearson and his Pilot of the day, Lieutenant J H C Minchin, in BE2e, '5855', crashlanded into a shell hole following a combat with an enemy machine. Fortunately both crewmen emerged unscathed. His MC was announced in the *London Gazette* of 11 December 1916: 'For conspicuous gallantry in action. He flew with another officer under 1,000 feet in our shell zone in order to silence hostile batteries. He has rendered the most valuable services throughout as an artillery observer'.

After returning to the UK early in 1917, he decided to train as a Pilot, obtaining his Royal Aero Club Certificate (Number 4697) on 26 May 1917 and formally qualified for his full 'Wings' on the same day. Pearson accompanied, as a Pilot, the RE8-equipped 34 Squadron to Italy on 13 November 1917. On 15 June 1918, Pearson and his Observer, Second Lieutenant R B Carey, in RE8, 'C5077', were badly shot up by ground fire. Although Pearson was unhurt, Carey was wounded in the action. The day before this incident, Pearson had completed a very successful photo-reconnaissance in advance of an Austrian offensive. He would be awarded a Distinguished Flying Cross for this and other fine work, *London Gazette* of 3 December 1918 (Italy).

PEARSON, Kenneth Noble

The son of the Reverend Alfred Pearson and Mrs Caroline Doncaster Pearson, of Melbourne Avenue, Eccleshall Bierlow, Yorkshire, he was born in Brighton, Sussex, on 14 August 1889. He studied Practical Structural Steel Engineering at Sheffield University and worked later as an Improver and Engineer in Worksop and London. Gazetted Second Lieutenant to the Royal Engineers on 1 October 1914. Gained his Royal Aero Club Certificate (Number 1621) on 20 August 1915. His formal pilot training duly completed, he was confirmed and gazetted Flying Officer on 3 November following. Flew first with 21 Squadron before joining 27 Squadron (G100 Elephants) as a Flight Commander and A/Captain in June 1916. His MC was announced in the *London Gazette* of 20 October 1916: 'For conspicuous gallantry and skill. With one other pilot he attacked ten hostile aeroplanes. The other pilot had his controls cut and had to return, but Captain Pearson fought on till all the enemy aeroplanes were dispersed. On another occasion he bombed trains from a low altitude. He has done other fine work'.

His tour with '27' completed in October 1916, he returned to the Home Establishment to take up instructing duties. Joined 110 Squadron, then at Rendcombe, in November 1917, flying various types in the UK. Tried by Court Martial and found guilty on 8 April 1919. Finally left the RAF, via the Unemployed List, in October 1919.

PEARSON, Thomas Sydney

The son of Mr and Mrs Sydney James Pearson, he was born in Richmond, Yorkshire, on 16 November 1896. Educated at Lancing College (1911-12). Gazetted Second Lieutenant to the Royal Field Artillery on 19 February 1916. Seconded to the RFC, he trained as an Observer and accompanied BE2e-equipped 34 Squadron to France as a Probationary and a 'founder member', on 15 June 1916. His 'apprenticeship' satisfactorily completed, Pearson was confirmed and gazetted Flying Officer (Observer) on 10 July 1916. On 22 July 1916, Pearson and his Pilot, Captain C H B Blount (qv), despite poor weather, completed an extremely valuable patrol on a line from Bazentin-le-Petit to High Wood, spotting and plotting a new and previously unknown elaborate enemy trench system. Their discovery caused alterations to be made to the upcoming second phase Somme Offensive in the British sector. His MC was announced in the *London Gazette* of 14 November 1916: 'For conspicuous skill and gallantry. He has done fine contact patrol work. On one occasion, with another officer as pilot, he flew for a long time at 500 feet under heavy rifle fire, in order to locate a lost battalion'.

After the war, he was posted to the Air Historical Branch of the War Cabinet Office in March 1919, before eventually reverting to the Army and the Royal Artillery in May 1920.

PECK, Arthur Hicks

The son of Lieutenant Colonel F S Peck, Indian Medical Service, and Mrs Peck, he was born in India on 25 April 1889. Educated at Clifton College (1903-06) and at Christ's College, Cambridge. After completing his education, he lived and worked in Australia from 1908 until 1914. Returning to the UK when the war came, he enlisted as a Private soldier into the Devonshire Regiment. Soon picked out for a commission, he was gazetted Second Lieutenant to 10 Battalion, Devonshire Regiment, on 7 December 1914. Seconded to the RFC in the summer of

1916, he trained as a Pilot and was gazetted Flying Officer on 4 October following. Posted first as an Instructor with 22 Training School in the Middle East, he was later sent out to 'C' Flight, 111 Squadron, in Palestine, as a Flight Commander. Peck went on to achieve eight victories, the first three in Brisfits, the remainder in SE5As, between 30 October 1917 and 23 March 1918. The first of his MCs was announced in the *London Gazette* of 18 January 1918, details in the *Gazette* of 25 April 1918: 'For conspicuous gallantry and devotion to duty. He engaged single handed three enemy aeroplanes, though they had superior height. He drove them back over their lines and prevented them from carrying out their reconnaissance'.

Next, he was awarded the Distinguished Service Order in the *London Gazette* of 4 March 1918, details in the *Gazette* of 16 August 1918. The Bar to his MC came in the *London Gazette* of 26 July 1918: 'For conspicuous gallantry and devotion to duty. While patrolling at a height of 14,000 feet he observed a formation of five enemy aircraft attempting a reconnaissance. He attacked the top machine, a scout, and drove it down out of control. He then attacked the second scout, which he also drove down out of control. He finally attacked a two-seater, and so quickly that he got to close quarters and opened fire with both guns. That, too, he sent down out of control. His performance was a splendid one, besides being costly for the enemy'.

Peck was also Mentioned in Despatches on one occasion during the Great War. He married Marjorie Amy Smith of Clifton, with whom he had one son and one daughter. Staying on in the RAF after the war, he subsequently served again in Egypt, commanding 25 Squadron in the Middle East in 1923 and, in 1928, served in Iraq (Mentioned in Despatches) before eventually attaining the rank of Group Captain in 1935. Brought back for duty as a Group Captain when the Second World War came in 1939, he eventually and finally retired, still with the rank of Group Captain on 8 September 1944.

PENDER, William Gordon

The eldest son of John and Annie Catherine Bennet Pender, of Great Brookham, Surrey, he was born in 1887. After completing his education, he went to live and work in Rhodesia, and it was from there that he returned to England to volunteer his services when war came. Gazetted Second Lieutenant to the RFC, via the Special Reserve, on 30 August 1915, the same day that he gained his Royal Aero Club Certificate (Number 1668). His formal pilot training duly completed, he was confirmed and gazetted Flying Officer on 11 January 1916. Sent first to 1 Squadron, he soon afterwards transferred to BE2d-equipped 5 Squadron in June 1916. On 10 July following, Pender was wounded in action when his BE2d, '5824', was shot up and damaged. He was wounded again on 29 August, but soon recovered. Promoted to A/Captain and Flight Commander, he was sent to 15 Squadron in that capacity on 16 October 1916. His MC was announced in the *London Gazette* of 10 January 1917: 'For conspicuous gallantry in action. On three occasions he flew over the enemy's trenches for long periods at a height of 500 feet, enabling his Observer to gain valuable information'.

His tour with '15' completed, Pender returned to the Home Establishment on 1 January 1917. Following a short leave, he served with 54RS for several months before going out to France again on 1 August 1917, this time to join the Nieuport XVII-equipped 40 Squadron. Just two weeks later on 15 August, he was killed in action when his Nieuport XVII, 'B1682' was shot down by Oberleutnant Hans Bethge of Jasta 30, the 11th of the German Ace's eventual 20 victories. William Pender's remains were never recovered and hence he is commemorated on the Flying Services Memorial, Arras, France.

PENNY, Arthur Robert

From Loughborough, Leicestershire, he was born on 8 March 1890. Educated at Bromsgrove School, leaving in 1907. Before the war came, he was living and working as a School Master in Tonbridge Wells. He enlisted as a Private soldier (Number 6106) into 19 (2 Public Schools) Battalion, Royal Fusiliers, on 21 January 1915, serving in the trenches with that unit from 14 November 1915 to 12 April 1916, when it was disbanded, with most of its members being subsequently commissioned. Gazetted Second Lieutenant to the RFC, via the Special Lists, on 26 September 1916. His formal pilot training duly completed, he was confirmed and gazetted Flying Officer on 24 March 1917. Sent out to 60 Squadron (Nieuport Scouts) soon after qualifying. In May 1917, the left lower plane of his Nieuport came off while he was diving on an enemy. Despite this, he managed to fly the machine back to an RFC aerodrome. This was one of a series of failures caused, it was said, by badly seasoned wood being used in the construction of the Nieuports by the French manufacturers. In the following month, he was initially reported as having 'gone west' by his Flight Commander, but, in the event, somehow managed, with great difficulty, to get his badly damaged machine back to his home field. When he landed, the machine turned over and crashed but he was able to crawl out from the wreckage unhurt. On 5 August 1917, when flying apparently with 29 Squadron, his Nieuport XXIII, 'B1609', was badly shot up and damaged by Vizefeldwebel Kurt Wüsthoff of Jasta 4, the German Ace over optimistically claiming Penny as the seventh of his eventual 27 victories. In fact, Penny, despite wounds in his wrist and ankle and one of his controls being shot away, nursed his battered Nieuport back to his home aerodrome. Penny was promoted to A/Captain and Flight Commander on 6 October 1917. His MC was announced in the New Year *London Gazette* of 1 January 1918 (no citation). Although no formal citation was published in the *Gazette*, research has unearthed the original recommendation for the award: 'T/Capt A R Penny. 6/10/17 This Officer during four months took part in over 30 aerial combats, and three attacks on hostile balloons, in one of these successfully bringing down his balloon. On August 5th 1917, whilst engaging single-handed four enemy aircraft, he was wounded in the wrist and ankle. Despite this and the fact that one of his controls had been shot away, he flew his machine back to his aerodrome. He has always shown the greatest bravery'.

Arthur Penny survived the war to return to Tonbridge Wells.

PENTLAND, Alexander Augustus Norman Dudley

From Terrigal, New South Wales, Australia, he was born on 5 August 1894 in Maitland, NSW. An early volunteer into the AIF, he served in Egypt, in Gallipoli and in Egypt again with 12 Light Horse Regiment from 1914 to 1916. Picked out for a commission, he was gazetted Second Lieutenant to the RFC, via the Special Lists, on 22 February 1916. His formal pilot training duly completed, he was confirmed and gazetted Flying Officer on 27 May following. Sent out to France and BE2c-equipped 16 Squadron, he gained the first of his eventual 23 victories on 9 June 1916. A transfer to the DH2s of 29 Squadron followed later in the same year. He broke his leg playing rugby, which forced a return to England and, upon recovery, spent some time instructing. In July 1917, he again went out to France, this time joining the Spad-equipped 19 Squadron. On one memorable occasion he took on, single-handedly, ten Albatros Scouts, and managed to eventually fight them all off. When he returned to base, his shot-about Spad was pronounced a write-off. His flying suit had four bullet holes through it, but the projectiles had all missed him personally. On 16 August 1917, he was the subject of a slightly over-enthusiastic claim by Oberflugmeister Kurt Schönfelder of Jasta 7, who thought that he destroyed Pentland's machine. His MC was announced in the *London Gazette* of 26 September 1917, details in the *Gazette* of 9 January 1918: 'For conspicuous gallantry and devotion to duty. On a recent occasion he flew to an aerodrome 15 miles behind the enemy lines, descended to within 20 feet of the ground, and fired into eight hostile machines. On his return journey he attacked a train with considerable effect from a low altitude. He has in addition brought down several enemy machines, and has always set a splendid example of fearlessness and devotion to duty in attacking enemy balloons and troops on the ground'.

On the same day that his MC was announced (by which time he had ten victories) Pentland, in Spad VII, 'B3620', was brought down when his machine was hit by an artillery shell, causing him facial and other injuries. Recovering from his injuries, he again returned to instructing duties for a time before going to the front on 26 April 1918 as a Flight Commander and 'founder member' of the newly formed 87 Squadron. By the end of August 1918, Pentland had increased his victory total to 23 and added a Distinguished Flying Cross, *London Gazette* of 3 August 1918, to his MC. On 25 August, Pentland and his Sopwith Dolphin were shot down by elements of Jasta 57 and he was wounded in the foot. After the war he served for a time with the RAAF, but then left to seek his fortune in the goldfields of New Guinea. In 1930, he became a Pilot with Australian National Airways. When the Second World War came, he took charge of an RAAF Air Sea Rescue unit in the Pacific, with the rank of Squadron Leader, receiving an Air Force Cross in recognition of his efforts. His biography, 'Australian Air Ace, The Exploits of 'Jerry' Pentland MC,DFC,AFC', written by Charles Schaedel, was published in 1979. 'Jerry' Pentland died in a war veterans home in Bayview, NSW, on 3 November 1983. His wife Madge had died 18 months earlier.

PERKINS, Alan Christopher Temple

The son of the Reverend J Perkins and Mrs Perkins, of Dean's Yard, Westminster Abbey, London, SW1, he was born on 15 June 1897. Educated at King's College, Westminster (1910-15). Gazetted Second Lieutenant to the RGA on 27 November 1915. Served in France as a Gunnery Officer from May 1916 until October 1916, when he was wounded and invalided home for treatment. Seconded to the RFC in the spring of 1917, he trained as an Observer and was sent out to 35 Squadron (AWFK8s) on 22 July 1917, being formally gazetted Flying Officer (Observer) on the following day, 23 July 1917. His MC was announced in the *London Gazette* of 18 October 1917, details in the *Gazette* of 7 March 1918: 'For conspicuous gallantry and devotion to duty. The machine in which he was an observer came into collision with another when he was at a height of 4,000 feet, and had its right-hand bottom plane so badly damaged that it got into a spinning nose dive. Seeing, this, he immediately climbed to the outer bay of the left-hand plane, and by his weight there enabled his pilot to right his machine and to land without further damage'.

Perkins was wounded in action on 23 November 1917. Following recuperation in the UK, Perkins returned to the front in September 1918, this time to serve with BF2b-equipped 20 Squadron. He was injured again in a crash after the war on 18 January 1919. Perkins finally left the service, via the Unemployed List, on 26 February 1919. Alan Perkins died at his home, 1 Park Lane, Britford, Salisbury, on 15 November 1971.

PETER, Leslie Hurst

The third of the four sons of solicitor Claude H Peter and Matilda L B Peter, of 'Craigmore', Launceston, Cornwall, he was born in 1892. Gazetted Second Lieutenant to the Falmouth, Cornwall, Lights No 1 Company, Royal Engineers (TF), on 11 October 1914. After service with the BEF in France and Flanders, he was seconded to the RFC early in 1916. His pilot training duly completed, he was confirmed and gazetted Flying Officer on 5 July 1916. Accompanied 'C' Flight, 70 Squadron (Strutters), to France as a 'founder member' on 30 July 1916. On 24 March 1917, Peter and his Observer of the day, Lieutenant B Balfour, in Sopwith Strutter, 'A2983', were shot up over Cambrai during an encounter with a formation of 12 hostile aircraft. Although Balfour escaped unscathed, Peter was injured in the resultant crash-landing. His MC was announced in the *London Gazette* of 18 July 1917: 'For conspicuous gallantry and devotion to duty. When leading a reconnaissance his party was attacked by hostile scouts. He kept his machines together and carried out a successful photograph reconnaissance despite a strong attack. To his leadership and initiative were largely due the success of his patrol'.

Peter was promoted to A/Major in 1918. He was Mentioned in Despatches in the *London Gazette* of 14 June 1918. An award of an Air Force Cross came under a general citation in the *London Gazette* of 2 November 1918: '....in recognition of valuable flying services performed in their various capacities, Flying Instructor, test, ferry and experimental pilots, etc'.

NB: His medals were offered for sale by Spink (lot 641) on 9 June 1992: MC, Air Force Cross, British War Medal 1914-20, and Victory Medal 1914-19 (Capt RFC).

PETRE, Henry Aloysius

The eldest son of Sebastian Henry Petre and Elise Petre (née Sibeth), of Essex, he was born on 12 June 1884. Educated at Mount St Mary's College, Chesterfield. Petre was admitted a Solicitor in 1905. He took up aviation in 1910, gaining his Royal Aero Certificate (Number 128) in a Hanriot monoplane at the Hanriot School at Brooklands on 12 September 1911. In 1912, he took part in various trials of military machines with men like Tommy Sopwith and Colonel Cody. He was selected, along with Mr E Harrison, in December 1912, to go to Australia to found the Australian Flying Corps. Henry, who was known as 'Petre the Monk', had a brother, Edward, known as 'Petre the Painter', who was also an aviation pioneer. In the same month that Henry set sail for Australia, Edward was killed on Christmas Eve when his Martin-Handasyde monoplane crashed in bad weather near to Marske-by-the-Sea, Yorkshire, during an attempt to fly non-stop from Brooklands to Edinburgh. Arriving in Australia early in 1913, Henry Petre set about forming a flying school for the Australian Government at Point Cook, near Melbourne. Petre and Harrison were given honorary commissions as Flying Instructors and supplied with five machines. In response to a plea for help from the Government of India in February 1915, the Australian Government provided a small aviation unit for service in Mesopotamia. Known as the Mesopotamian Half Flight, it was commanded by Henry Petre. Petre also served with 30 Squadron in Mesopotamia from 14 May 1915 to 22 May 1916. For his services in this theatre of war, Petre was awarded the MC in the *London Gazette* of 14 January 1916 (no citation) and was awarded the Distinguished Service Order in the *London Gazette* of 22 December 1916. He was also Mentioned in Despatches on no less than five occasions during the Great War. Petre subsequently served in Staff capacities in the UK in 1916, 1917 and 1918. He went out to Egypt in 1918 and served there until finally retiring from the service in 1919. Petre returned to his profession, becoming a partner in the firm of Blount, Petre and Company, Solicitors, in London. He achieved the British Glider Duration record with a flight of three hours, 28 minutes, five seconds, on 24 May 1931. Petre used his expertise in gliding during the Second World War, when he became a Gliding Instructor to the ATC. He lived, in later life, at 38 South Lodge, Grove End Road, London NW8. Henry Petre died in University College Hospital, St Pancras, London, on 24 April 1962.

PETT, Henry Basil

The son of Brickworks Manager, Richard Pett and Maria Pett, of Common Side, Bradfield, West Riding, Yorkshire, he was born in Bolsterstone, Yorkshire, on 14 February 1888. His family moved to South Wales and he received most of his education at the County School, Aberdare, Glamorgan. Moving back to Sheffield, he completed, in 1910, a five-year apprenticeship as a Mechanical Engineer, Fitter and Tool Maker, with the Yorkshire Silica Company, Sheffield. By the time the Great War came in August 1914, he was living and working in Coventry. He enlisted, on 2 September 1914, as a Sapper (Number 46011) into the Royal Engineers Signal Depot at Dunstable. Soon promoted to Sergeant, he served in France with 17 and 71 Brigades, Royal Engineers. Picked out for a commission, he was gazetted Second Lieutenant to the RFC on 27 February 1917. His pilot training duly completed, he was confirmed and gazetted Flying Officer on 27 June following. Sent out to join the RE8-equipped 15 Squadron at the front. Subsequently promoted to A/Captain and Flight Commander, he was next posted to the Bristol Fighters of 11 Squadron. His MC was announced in the *London Gazette* of 22 June 1918: 'For conspicuous gallantry and devotion to duty. He showed great courage and skill while engaged on reconnaissance and contact patrols during operations, flying at very low altitudes under heavy rifle and machine-gun fire. On many occasions he located the enemy's line by deliberately drawing their fire from the ground. On one occasion he made a reconnaissance of a whole corps front in very bad weather, which made it necessary for him to fly at a height of 350 feet. He was continuously under very heavy fire, but completed his reconnaissance and obtained valuable information'.

Pett survived the Great War, leaving the RAF in 1919.

NB: The RAF Museum Hendon has his medals in its collection: MC, 1914-15 Star (46011, Sgt, RE), *British War Medal 1914-20, and Victory Medal 1914-19* (Capt RAF).

PHILIPPI, George

The second son of Merchant, Otto Ernst Philippi and Mrs Philippi of Largs, Ayrshire, he was born on 27 January 1890. Educated first at Exeter College (entered 1909) and later privately. Gazetted Second Lieutenant to 1 (Royal) Dragoons on 14 October 1914. Seconded to the RFC in September 1915, he gained his Royal Aero Club Certificate (Number 2604) on 24 March 1916. His formal pilot training duly completed, he was confirmed and gazetted Flying Officer on 9 June following. Sent out 60 Squadron (Nieuport XVIIs) in France soon after qualifying for his 'Wings'. On 26 September 1916, he was wounded in the head when his Nieuport XVII, 'A201 A2', was hit by shrapnel from an anti-aircraft shell over Bapaume during a successful balloon strafe. His MC was announced in the *London Gazette* of 14 November 1916: 'For conspicuous skill and gallantry. He dived at a hostile balloon under heavy fire, and brought it down in flames. Though wounded in the head, he brought the machine back at a low altitude, and landed safely in his aerodrome'.

Once recovered, he was posted to duty in the offices of the Secretary of State, Air Board, at the Air Ministry in London. Mentioned in Despatches in 1918. Promoted to T/Lieutenant Colonel, he was sent to the British Aviation Mission in the USA on 5 June 1918. Philippi finally left the RAF, via the Unemployed List, on 13 January 1919.

PHILLIPS, Fenton Ellis Stanley (also known as F E Stanley-Phillips)

The son of the Rector of Bow, Edward Stanley Phillips and his wife, Gertrude Elizabeth Phillips, of The Rectory, Bow, Devonshire, he was born at Pembroke House, Broad Lane, Hampton, Middlesex, on 4 July 1895. He enlisted as a Private soldier (Number 2678) into 2/28 Battalion, London Regiment (Artists Rifles), on 15 September 1914, and later served in the trenches with 1/28. Picked out for a commission, he was gazetted Second Lieutenant to 3 (Reserve) Battalion, Devonshire Regiment on 13 January 1915. Seconded to the RFC, he trained as an Observer and was sent out to 3 Squadron (Morane Parasols) on 10 May 1916, just in time to participate in the Battle of the Somme. He flew for much of his time as Cecil Lewis' (qv) Observer and he is mentioned many times under his nickname 'Pip' in Lewis' classic, 'Sagittarius Rising'. During a contact patrol on 3 September 1916, he and his Pilot of the day, Lieutenant L C Kidd (qv), spotted enemy troops massing in trenches opposite British infantry who were still in the process of preparing their positions. Contact was made with the Royal Artillery and the Gunners immediately obliged with some excellent shooting which thwarted the enemy's intentions. On 10 October 1916, Kidd and Phillips were forced to land amongst shell holes between Pozières and Contalmaison, on the Somme. On 12 October 1916, Phillips, again flying with Kidd, in Morane BB, '5178', was on a routine dawn contact patrol when their machine was hit by 'friendly fire' which severed a wing and sent them to their deaths. C A Lewis mentions the death of Phillips and Kidd with deep regret in 'Sagittarius Rising'. Phillip's MC was announced eight days after his death in the *London Gazette* of 20 October 1916: 'For conspicuous gallantry and skill. He has done fine contact patrol work. On one occasion he came down to a low altitude while making a report, and his machine was much damaged by rifle and machine-gun fire, but he carried on and successfully put our artillery on to the enemy, who were massing for a counter-attack'

Phillip's remains were never recovered and hence he is commemorated on the Flying Services Memorial, Arras, France.

PHILLIPS, Roy Cecil

The son of William Hargreave Phillips and Mrs Cecil Phillips, of Sydney, New South Wales, Australia, he was born on 1 March 1892. An Accountant by profession, he was living in Perth, Western Australia, when he volunteered for the AIF Infantry, being commissioned into 28 Battalion (Western Australia). He served in the trenches in France, until wounded in the leg during the first trench raid mounted by the Australian Infantry on the Western Front. Although one of his legs remained partially paralysed, he managed, in May 1917, to wangle a transfer into the Australian Flying Corps. Qualifying as a Pilot, he initially joined 2 Squadron, AFC, which became 68 Squadron RFC. In the summer of 1917, Phillips was attached to 32 Squadron (DH5s), RFC, in the Ypres Salient, to gain experience with a fighting-scout unit. Just three days later, on 7 August 1917, he survived a crash-landing forced upon him when his DH5, 'A9372', was hit by anti-aircraft fire. He returned to 68 Squadron (DH5s) in September 1917, with an appointment as Flight Commander. He gained the first of his eventual 15 victories on 22 November

1917, when he forced an enemy Scout to land. At the turn of the New Year, '68' was re-designated as 2 Squadron, Australian Flying Corps, and shortly after that was re-equipped with SE5As. Phillips' first MC was announced in the *London Gazette* of 4 February 1918: 'For conspicuous gallantry and devotion to duty. He has performed continuous gallant work at very low altitudes in almost impossible weather. Whilst flying alone in a mist he forced an enemy aeroplane to land. On two occasions, flying at an altitude of 200 feet he made very valuable reconnaissances, and his reports on the ground situation were of the greatest value. His leadership is excellent, and he has set a high example to his flight'. He was presented with his Cross by the King in an investiture held at Buckingham Palace on 9 March 1918. A brave and aggressive Scout Pilot, he was heavily engaged during the dark days of the German spring offensive, his victory count accumulating steadily. The Bar to his MC came in the *London Gazette* of 22 June 1918, details in the *Gazette* of 5 July 1918: 'For conspicuous gallantry and devotion to duty. Whilst engaged with hostile aircraft during the recent operations he has destroyed three enemy machines, and has in addition brought down two hostiles out of control. He has also brought back accurate and valuable information regarding hostile movements under the most adverse conditions, particularly on one occasion, when he flew through a heavy barrage at a low altitude behind the enemy's lines. He has shown conspicuous skill and determination when escorting low-flying bombing patrols'.

The award of a Distinguished Flying Cross was next announced in the *London Gazette* of 3 August 1918, this in recognition of his continuing success in aerial combats and for his outstanding work in attacking enemy troops and transports. Given a well-earned rest, he was next promoted to Major and appointed to the command of 6 TS in the UK. In the 1920s and 1930s Phillips farmed in Eastern Australia. He was married to Ellen Hillmand from Toowoomba by the time of the Second World War, when he rejoined the RAAF and was given command of No 2 Elementary FTS in Archerfield, with the rank of Squadron Leader. Roy Phillips was killed in a night-flying accident on 21 May 1941 and is commemorated on the Queensland Cremation Memorial, Brisbane, Queensland, Australia.

PHILPOTT, John Reginald

The son of the Reverend Canon John Nigel Philpott and Mary Florence Philpott, of Southchurch Rectory, Southend-on-Sea, Essex (later Cole Orton Rectory, Leicester), he was born in Stoke Albany, Northamptonshire, on 12 July 1883. Educated at Marlborough (1907-12) and at Magdalen College, Oxford. Volunteering as soon as the war came, he was gazetted Second Lieutenant to 7 Battalion, Suffolk Regiment on 1 September 1914. Seconded to the RFC, he gained his Royal Aero Club Certificate (Number 1536) on 5 August 1915. His formal pilot training duly completed, he was confirmed and gazetted Flying Officer on 4 December following. Sent out to 12 Squadron soon after qualifying. On 21 July 1916, Philpott's BE2d, '5795', was damaged by rifle fire from the ground during a bombing raid on a railway junction and bridge at Aubigny-au-Bac. It is said that he was recommended for a Victoria Cross for his bravery on this occasion but, in the event, was awarded the MC, which was announced in the *London Gazette* of 20 October 1916: 'For conspicuous gallantry and skill in descending to about 300 feet, under heavy fire of all descriptions, in order to bomb a train. Finding that Capt Tyson [qv] had wrecked the train, he dropped his bombs on a station and then assisted him to beat off hostile machines. He then, with Capt Tyson, attacked a machine which was endeavouring to leave the ground. He has previously displayed great gallantry'.

Again, on 30 July 1916, the same BE2d was damaged by anti-aircraft fire over St Leger. Fortunately, Philpott was again unscathed. Philpott was promoted to A/Captain and Flight Commander in October 1916, his tour with '12' coming to an end on 9 January 1917, when he was hospitalised. Once recovered, Philpott accompanied 63 Squadron (RE8s) as a Flight Commander to Mesopotamia, arriving there in September 1917. On the 25th of that month, two RE8s were lost on the unit's very first reconnaissance patrol. An RE8 was crewed by Lieutenant M G Begg MC (qv) and Lieutenant L N Baillon, were involved in a combat with a Halberstadt over Tekrit. A wing folded under the pressure of a dive during the fight and the machine crashed. Both occupants, shaken but unhurt, were taken prisoner by the Turks. Philpott and Corporal Oliver William Arthur Grant (Number 46448), in the other RE8, had witnessed these happenings from on high, when, suddenly, they found themselves in exactly the same situation as their colleagues, when the engine of their 'Harry Tate' packed up. The four men received mixed treatment from their captors over the following weeks as they journeyed to eventual confinement in Turkey. Unfortunately, 'Rex' Philpott was taken seriously ill and, after a long illness, died of dysentery in hospital at Afion-karahissar on 15 January 1918. He is buried in Baghdad (North Gate) Cemetery, Iraq.

PICKERING, Albert Edward

From Lancaster, Lancashire, he was born on 19 June 1892. He was a bank employee living and working in Gradview, Manitoba, Canada, when he enlisted as a Private soldier into 7 Battalion, Canadian Infantry, on 24 September 1914. Picked out for a commission, he was gazetted Lieutenant to 1 Canadian Infantry Battalion (Ontario Regiment) on 10 July 1915. Pickering served with the CEF in France, until being seconded to the RFC in March 1917. Having trained as an Observer, he was sent out as a Probationary to 43 Squadron (Sopwith Strutters) on 5 April 1917. His 'apprenticeship' satisfactorily completed, he was confirmed and gazetted Flying Officer (Observer) on 18 May 1917. On 7 June following, Pickering and his Pilot of the day, Second Lieutenant the Honourable S H A D'Arcy, in Strutter, 'A8248', were shot up by ground fire during a low-level attack on enemy troops and transport. They subsequently crashed in Ploegsteert Wood and although D'Arcy was wounded, Pickering emerged relatively unscathed. His MC was announced in the *London Gazette* of 26 July 1917: 'For conspicuous gallantry and devotion to duty when acting as observer, in making reconnaissances at very low altitudes, and attacking hostile infantry, transport and machines, with great courage and determination. In conjunction with his pilot, he was instrumental in destroying several hostile machines, and in rendering valuable information to our artillery'.

Samuel D'Arcy, Pickering's Pilot in 7 June 1917 crash, would become the youngest recipient of the Distinguished Service Order. (Tragically, D'Arcy, still then only 19 years old, was killed in a flying accident in the UK on 8 June 1918.) Pickering's tour with '43' completed on 24 August 1917, he next trained as a Pilot and, once qualified on 25 February 1918, went on to serve with 15 Squadron (RE8s) in France and with 48 TDS in the UK. Pickering finally relinquished his commission on 30 April 1919.

PICKTHORN, Charles Edward Murray

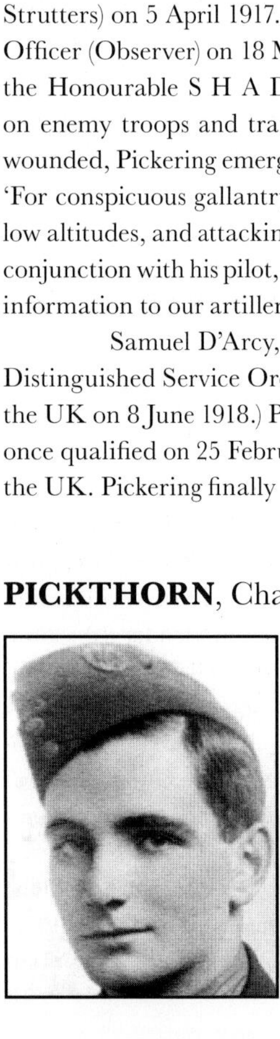

The younger son of Master Mariner, Charles Wright Pickthorn and Mrs Pickthorn of Suffolk, he was born on 20 September 1896. Educated at Aldenham (1910-11). His elder brother, Kenneth, would serve in the Great War with 15 London Regiment and with the RFC in France and Macedonia. An Observer with 17 Squadron, Kenneth was wounded in action on 10 May 1917, during a combat with Leutnant Rudolph von Eschwege of FAb30. In later life, he became a Barrister of note, subsequently being created a Baronet in 1959. Charles was gazetted Second Lieutenant to the Army Service Corps, via the Special Reserve, on 8 February 1915. Seconded to the RFC in December 1915, he trained as an Observer and was sent out as a Probationary to 8 Squadron. His 'apprenticeship' satisfactorily completed, he was confirmed and gazetted Flying Officer (Observer) on 25 June 1916. On 29 June 1916, whilst over enemy lines, his BE2, '5763', was attacked by three Fokkers that appeared suddenly out of a cloud. Pickthorn's Pilot, Second Lieutenant A H Vaisey, was wounded and lost consciousness. Pickthorn climbed out of his seat and managed to rouse his Pilot sufficiently to allow the two of them to make a safe return. During the descent, Pickthorn used his Morse key to request a doctor and ambulance be standing-by to attend to his wounded Pilot, probably one of the first occasions such a message was sent ahead. Pickthorn was Mentioned in Despatches at this time, *London Gazette* of 13 November 1916. Research has unearthed the original recommendation for this 'Mention': 'ASC/RFC 8 October 1916. 8 Sqd. Has done most successful and gallant work in Artillery Co-operation and infantry liaison work, from April to August 1916, frequently at low altitudes. Has always shown the utmost coolness and determination'.

Pickthorn next trained as a Pilot and, once qualified, was sent as such to the DH2-equipped 32 Squadron at the end of 1916. On 6 March 1917, Pickthorn in DH2, '7938', was very slightly wounded in the head and face in a fight, but still contrived to bring his adversary down for his first victory. Five days later, again in '7898', he engaged, over Bapaume, an Albatros Scout sporting a skull and crossbones motif on its fuselage. His persistent and sustained attacks forced the enemy Pilot to land his machine down into the British lines. Pickthorn's machine was also shot up in the fight and he, too, was forced to crashland, the DH2 turning over in the process. Pickthorn, unscathed, was delighted to learn that his downed, and by now, mortally wounded (by ground troops while trying to escape) opponent was no less a personage than Prince Friedrich Karl of Prussia, a second cousin to the Kaiser. His MC was announced in the *London Gazette* of 26 April 1917: 'For conspicuous gallantry and devotion to duty in attacking hostile aircraft, and in carrying out difficult reconnaissances. On one occasion, although wounded, he continued his combat and brought down a hostile machine. On two other occasions he brought down hostile machines in flames'.

His tour with '32' ended on 13 May 1917, when he returned to the UK to take up various training posts. Pickthorn actually received the MC after achieving four victories but, subsequently, would go on to gain a fifth – and the status of Ace – on the penultimate day of the war, 10 November 1918, just six days after he had taken over command of 84 Squadron with the rank of Major. Pickthorn finally left the RAF, via the Unemployed List, on 1 May 1919. In the early 1920s, using his aviation expertise, he helped to form the Chilean Air Force and, for his efforts, was awarded the Chilean Order Al Merits 2nd Class, announced in the *London Gazette* of 27 February 1925: 'In recognition of services rendered to the Chilean Government'. Charles Pickthorn married his wife, Hilda Margaret, and took up farming at Richmond Farm, Orford, Suffolk, but died on 3 March 1938.

PICOT, Michael Henry

A Swiss national, his widowed mother lived in Paris during the Great War years. Admitted as a Cadet to the flying service in June 1917, he was gazetted Second Lieutenant to the RFC on 13 August 1917. He trained as an Observer and was sent out as a Probationary to 8 Squadron (AWFK8s) on 16 September 1917. On 22 December 1917, Picot and his Pilot, Lieutenant A M Kinnear (qv), in 'B3321', were involved in an aerial combat with enemy scouts over Havrincourt Wood. Their machine was badly shot about and they were obliged to force-land onto bad ground, which inevitably resulted in yet more damage to the 'Big-Ack', but not, fortunately, to Picot and Kinnear. Picot's 'apprenticeship' satisfactorily completed, he was confirmed and gazetted Flying Officer (Observer) on 8 January 1918. On 22 March 1918, Picot and his Pilot of the day, Second Lieutenant R Grice, were again extremely lucky to escape unharmed after their AWFK8, 'B3376', was struck by an artillery shell over Péronne. They landed safely but the machine had to be abandoned, being judged beyond repair. His MC was announced in the *London Gazette* of 22 June 1918: 'For conspicuous gallantry and devotion to duty. The information which he has brought back has been accurate and of the greatest value. In order to obtain such information he has been compelled to fly at very low altitudes, where he has been subjected to intense machine-gun and rifle fire. On one occasion, when the situation on the corps front was very obscure, he gained most valuable information by flying very low, but was compelled to return on account of his machine being riddled with bullets. He at once went up in another machine and completed his reconnaissance. His courage, persistence and good service have been most marked'.

His tour with '8' completed, he returned to the Home Establishment in May 1918, never to return to operational flying. Michael Picot finally left the RAF, via the Unemployed List, on 16 February 1919.

PIERCE, Walter Maurice

The younger son of Commercial Clerk, Timothy G Pierce and Mary A Pierce, of Stanmore Villa, Hughenden Road, High Wycombe, Buckinghamshire, he was born on 6 August 1893. Gazetted Second Lieutenant to 18 (1 Public Works Pioneers) Battalion, Middlesex Regiment, on 7 January 1915. Transferring to the RFC late in 1916, he trained as an Observer and was eventually confirmed and gazetted Flying Officer (Observer) on 7 March 1917. Sent out to France and 3 Squadron on 15 May 1917. On 9 August 1917, Pierce and his Pilot of the day, Lieutenant D King, in Morane P, 'A6700', were both wounded during an aerial combat. For his gallantry on this and other occasions, he was awarded the MC, announced in the *London Gazette* of 18 October 1917, details in the *Gazette* of 7 March 1918: 'For conspicuous gallantry and devotion to duty. Whilst on artillery patrol his machine was attacked by a hostile scout. Although he was wounded by the first burst of hostile fire, he continued to work his gun, and succeeded in driving off the enemy machine, which is believed to have been severely damaged. When taken to the Casualty Clearing Station he insisted on being sent to his squadron, in order to make a reconnaissance report on movement behind the enemy's lines. After doing this he was taken back to the Casualty Clearing Station where he was operated on and the bullet extracted. This officer has proved himself a most reliable Observer. He has done consistent good work, and many of his reports have been of the greatest value'.

Walter Pierce did not fly operationally again, but instead worked in a number of administrative posts in the UK, until leaving the RAF, via the Unemployed List, on 12 February 1919. Still living in High Wycombe when the Second World War came, he applied for service with the RAFVR on 26 September 1939.

PILDITCH, Gerald

From Pretoria, South Africa, he was born on 27 October 1892. A Cattle Farmer in the pre-war years. He was gazetted Second Lieutenant to the RFC on 30 August 1917. His pilot training duly completed, he was confirmed and gazetted Flying Officer on 29 October 1917. Sent out to the Sopwith Camel-equipped 73 Squadron, he gained five victories between 22 March and 11 June 1918. On 26 March 1918, with the German spring offensive in full swing, he narrowly escaped with his life when his low-flying Sopwith Camel, 'C1619', was struck by ground fire. Forced to land near Albert, he was obliged to abandon his machine to the mercies of the artillery on both sides of the lines. His MC was announced in the *London Gazette* of 22 April 1918, details in the *Gazette* of 22 June 1918: 'For conspicuous gallantry and devotion to duty. He engaged the enemy massed ready for an attack from a height of 300 feet using up all his ammunition and scattering the enemy in all directions, inflicting very heavy casualties. Previously to this he had dived and fired on a hostile battery until he had silenced it and had also destroyed an enemy tri-plane and a two-seater machine. His work has been of the highest order, and he has shown the greatest courage and energy in attacking ground targets'.

On 11 June 1918, Pilditch's bravery and prompt action undoubtedly saved his squadron colleague, Lieutenant J H Ackermann, USAS, who was wounded during a dog-fight with six enemy Scouts. Ackermann later reported that Pilditch had shot down one, or possibly two, of the enemy aircraft attacking his tail-end. Pilditch left the RAF, via the Unemployed List, on 16 June 1919, returning to South Africa immediately. In the Second World War, he served as a Captain in the Union of South Africa Defence Forces from March 1941.

PIRIE, George Clark

Born on 28 July 1896. Educated at St Andrews University. Gazetted Second Lieutenant to 3 (Reserve) Battalion, Cameronians (Scottish Rifles) on 12 March 1915. Seconded to the RFC, he trained as an Observer and was sent out to 2 Squadron as a Probationary early in 1916. His 'apprenticeship' satisfactorily completed, he was confirmed and gazetted Flying Officer (Observer) on 4 May 1916. Next he trained as a Pilot and, having qualified for his full 'Wings', was sent out to the RE8-equipped 34 Squadron. On 13 August 1917, he and his Observer, Second Lieutenant W C Thompson, were fortunate to survive when their RE8, 'A4268', was shot up and damaged by anti-aircraft fire. His MC was announced in the *London Gazette* of 23 August 1917: 'For conspicuous gallantry and devotion to duty. On two successive occasions whilst doing a shoot he was attacked by hostile scouts in large superior numbers, all of whom he dispersed and continued his work. On another occasion, having by means of the artillery knocked out three guns of a hostile battery, he descended to 500 feet and dispersed with his machine-gun a party of the enemy who were endeavouring to remove the remaining guns'.

Research has unearthed the original recommendation for this award which gives a little more detail of the circumstances, as well as, interestingly, a version of his middle name, not seen elsewhere: 'Capt George de Chierri Pirie, 3 Scot Rif, 25/6/17, 4th Bde. This Officer has done exceptionally fine artillery work and he sets a fine example of thoroughness to the other pilots. On 1st May while carrying out a shoot he was attacked by five hostile scouts which he drove off, continuing and completing his shoot. On 29 April while shooting at an enemy battery, he KO'd three of the guns which were in the open; seeing a lorry coming up to try and drag the remaining gun away he attempted to switch a battery on to it, but his wireless failed; he thereupon came down to 800 feet and drove the men off with his machine gun'.

Pirie accompanied '34' to Italy in November 1917 and was awarded Medaglia al Valore Militare by the Italians. He was also given a Croix de Guerre by the French. Staying on in the RAF after the war, he went on to serve as a Flight Commander in Palestine and Mesopotamia, earning a Distinguished Flying Cross, *London Gazette* of 28 October 1921: 'For great gallantry and good work....during operations in the relief of Diwaniyah and during our retirement to Hillah'. Pirie then embarked upon what would prove to be a brilliant career in the RAF. As well as graduating LLD and becoming a Barrister at Law, his many honours and appointments included: RAF Staff College, Andover, Hampshire, 1925; service in Iraq, 1928; Wing Commander, 1932; Air Staff Officer, Directorate of Operations and Intelligence, Department of the Chief of the Air Staff, Air Ministry, 1934-37; Group Captain, 1937; Air Attaché, Washington DC, USA, 1937-40; served in the Second World War, 1939-45; AOC, Northern Ireland, 1941; Air Officer in Charge of Administration, Middle East, 1941-943; CBE, 1942; CB, 1943; Director General, War Organisation, Air Ministry, 1943-45; Deputy Allied Air Commander-in-Chief, South East Asia, 1945-46; created KBE, 1946; Allied Air Commander-in-Chief, South East Asia, 1946-47; Inspector General, RAF, 1948; Member, Air Council for Supply and Organisation, 1948-50; Air Chief Marshal, 1949; Head of Air Force Staff, British Joint Services Mission to the USA, 1950-51; retired, 1951; KCB, 1951; and Chairman, Air League of the British Empire, 1955-58. Sir George lived in retirement at Cottage13, Headbourne Worthy, Winchester. He died on 21 January 1980.

PIXLEY, Reginald George Hewett

The second son of Major Stewart Aitken Pixley OBE, VD, and Patricia Hindle Pixley, of Maybury Knowle, Woking, Surrey, he was born in 1893. Educated at Stratheden House, Blackheath, and at Eton (1907-12), where he was the captain of the Shooting VIII. In 1911, he was chosen to represent a combined English Schools rifle team in Canada, and liked the country so much that he returned there as soon as he left school in 1912. An accident precipitated his return home to England but, after recovering from his injuries, he successfully passed examinations which allowed him to enter the Imperial College of Science and Technology (Royal School of Mines), which institution he was attending when war broke out. Following the example of his elder brother, he volunteered and was gazetted Second Lieutenant to 7 Ammunition Column, 7 London Brigade, Royal Field Artillery (TF), on 27 September 1914. Seconded to the RFC in 1916, he trained as a Pilot and was subsequently gazetted Flying Officer on 15 October following. Sent to join 54 Squadron at the front, he narrowly escaped death on 10 May 1917, when a wing on his Sopwith Pup, 'A668', buckled after being shot up. Pixley was injured in the consequent forced landing which culminated in a shell-hole in the front lines. Having recovered, he was in the air again on 4 June, this time in Pup, 'B2151', when he had the extreme misfortune to encounter the great German Ace, Oberleutnant Werner Voss of Jasta 5. Pixley had taken off at 07.10 as part of an escort conducting some FEs on an intelligence-gathering patrol, when the entire formation was attacked by a formation of German Scouts south-east of Douai. In the ensuing melée, his Pup was seen to be under attack, but was then soon lost to sight. A British AA unit later raised the hopes of his comrades when they reported seeing a Pup forced-landing behind the enemy lines. Unfortunately, however, German troops found Pixley dead when they reached the crashed machine, although it was to be almost another two years before his family knew, for certain, of his demise. Pixley's grave was discovered in 1919, by a friend who had gone to France at the behest of the family for that express purpose. He was claimed as the 32nd victory of Werner Voss. Pixley's MC was posthumously announced in the *London Gazette* of 27 July 1917, although he was still then officially listed as missing in action: 'For conspicuous gallantry and devotion to duty. He attacked a hostile balloon with three other pilots and, remaining after they had left, finally sent it down in flames. He has assisted in bringing down several hostile machines and has done good work throughout'.

Reginald Pixley's remains were re-interned by the Imperial War Graves Commission in Prospect Hill Cemetery, Guoy, France.

PLAYFAIR, Patrick Henry Lyon

The son of Dr John Playfair, MD, FRCPE, and Mrs Playfair, he was born in Edinburgh on 22 November 1889. Educated at Cheltenham College (1903-08) and at the Royal Military Academy, Woolwich. Gazetted Second Lieutenant to the Royal Field Artillery in 1910. Developing an interest in aviation, he gained his Royal Aero Club Certificate (Number 283) in a Bristol machine at the Bristol School, Brooklands, on 3 September 1912. Seconded to the RFC, he first joined 2 Squadron before transferring to 4 Squadron in November 1912. When the war came in August 1914, Playfair accompanied '4' to France as part of the original RFC contingent. Following service over the Western Front in the closing months of 1914, he was sent back in January 1915 to the UK and Netheravon where 11 Squadron was forming up. Playfair next accompanied '11' to France as a 'founder member' and Flight Commander on 25 July 1915. Equipped with FB5s, '11' was the first dedicated two-seater fighter squadron on the Western Front. The next few months saw Playfair heavily engaged in the evolving 'war in the air'. His MC was announced in the *London Gazette* of 14 January 1916 (no citation). Although no formal citation was published in the *Gazette*, research has unearthed the original recommendation for the award: 'Capt P H L Playfair 11 Sqd and RA: For exceptionally good work as a Flight Commander. Has been successful in 6 fights with hostile aircraft during the past 2 months, and has shown great courage and determination on all occasions'.

Promotion to Major and command of 8 Squadron came on 12 January 1916. His squadron was deployed as part of 12 (Corps) Wing, III Brigade, RFC, for the Battle of the Somme which commenced on 1 July 1916.

Further promotion to Lieutenant Colonel and command of 13 (Army) Wing, RFC, came on 28 August 1916. Playfair was Mentioned in Despatches on two occasions during the Great War and was also awarded the Order of St Stanilaus by the Russians. The Russians also conferred the Order of St George, 4th Class, upon him, *London Gazette* of 15 February 1917. In January 1919, Playfair was appointed Commandant of the CFS. Staying on in the RAF with a permanent commission, he went on to enjoy a highly distinguished career, his many subsequent honours, promotions and appointments included: OC, Netheravon Flying School, 1919; CSO, HQ, Coastal Area, 1925; OC, RAF Transjordan and Palestine, 1928; Deputy AOC, RAF Transjordan and Palestine, 1929; SASO, HQ, RAF India, 1930; CB, 1930; AOC, 23 Group, 1932; AOC, Wessex Bombing Area, 1933; AOC, Western Area, 1933; CVO, 1935; AOC, 3 Group, 1936; AOC, 1 Group, 1938; AOC, Advanced Air Striking Force, 1939; AOC, Air Forces in India, 1940; KBE, 1940; retired, 1942; Distinguished Service Medal (USA); and Légion d'Honneur (France). He married, in 1937, Kate Strudwick, with whom he had one adopted son. Lived in retirement at St Mary's House, 56 Whiting Street, Bury St Edmund's, Suffolk. Air Marshal Sir Patrick Playfair died one day after his 85th birthday on 23 November 1974.

NB: The RAF Museum Hendon has his medals in its collection: Sealed in a glazed display case in four rows, no naming available: Top – Silver Jubilee Medal 1977, RVO (Commander, Badge), KBE (Military, Badge), CB (Badge), and Coronation Medal 1937; Second – British War Medal 1914-20, KCBE (Star), and War Medal 1939-45; Third – Victory Medal 1914-19 with MID, MC, Distinguished Service Medal (USA), and 1939-45 Star; Fourth – 1914 Star with Bar, Croix de Guerre avec Palme (France), Légion d'Honneur (Commandeur, France), Order of St Stanislav (Imperial Russia, missing eagle in lower left corner), and France and Germany Star 1944-45.

POLAND, Thomas George

The elder son of Journeyman Joiner, Thomas H Poland and Ann J Poland, of 19 Elm Grove, Edge Hill, Liverpool, he was born on 5 March 1892. A Civil Servant with the GPO telephone service from 1908, he was living and working in London when the war came in August 1914. Gazetted Second Lieutenant to 14 (Reserve) Battalion, East Surrey Regiment in 1915. Seconded to the RFC in August 1916, he trained as a Pilot in the CFS and was duly confirmed and gazetted Flying Officer on 27 December following. Sent out originally to FE2d-equipped 57 Squadron on 30 December 1916, he soon transferred to the BE2e-equipped 15 Squadron. On 5 May 1917, he was wounded in the leg by machine-gun fire from the ground. His MC was announced in the *London Gazette* of 18 June 1917: 'For conspicuous gallantry and devotion to duty. He has frequently shown great courage and initiative in attacking the enemy on the ground with machine-gun fire. To carry out this work, he has often flown at very low altitudes, and his machine has been under very heavy machine-gun and rifle fire'.

Once recovered, Poland served again in France with the DH9s of 108 Squadron before returning to the Home Establishment to instruct with 14 TDS. Poland finally left the RAF on 10 March 1920.

POLLAK, Edmond Robert Harris

Born in New York on 22 October 1896. Pollak was living and working in the City of London when war came in August 1914. Enlisting as a Private soldier (Number 1493) into the Honourable Artillery Company (Infantry) (TF), he accompanied his regiment to France on 18 September 1914, thus earning the 1914 Star. Picked out for a commission, he was gazetted Second Lieutenant to 4 South Midland Brigade, Royal Field Artillery (TF), on 10 March 1915. Following further service with the Gunners in France, he was seconded to the RFC in the spring of 1916. Gained his Royal Aero Club Certificate (Number 3295) on 3 May 1916. His formal pilot training duly completed, he was confirmed and gazetted Flying Officer on 27 June following. Sent out to join the BE2c-equipped 9 Squadron on 12 July 1916, he was soon in the thick of things. On 25 July, Pollak and his Observer, Second Lieutenant C P Creighton, in BE2c, '2615', narrowly escaped disaster when their machine was shot up and damaged. Pollak returned to the Home Establishment, his tour with '9' completed, on 28 April 1917. Following some rest and recuperation in the UK, he returned to France as a Flight Commander and 'founder member' of the AWFK8-equipped 82 Squadron on 15 November 1917. On 1 March 1918, Pollak and his Observer of the day, Second Lieutenant J A Moore, in 'B5837', were fortunate to escape with their lives when they were attacked by two Fokker DRIs over Flavy. Their gun jammed and they were forced to spiral down to a crash-landing with the machine on fire. Moore was wounded in the action but Pollak emerged relatively unscathed. The first of his MCs was announced in the *London Gazette* of 22 April 1918: 'For conspicuous gallantry and devotion to duty. Whilst observing a shoot on a hostile battery, he was attacked by two enemy tri-planes, one of which he engaged and succeeded in driving it off. On the second machine attacking him, his observer being wounded and his forward machine gun being out of action, he put his machine into a spin down to within 500 feet of the ground, during which time flames began to come out of the engine. These ceased, however, when his machine was once again on a level keel, and on their breaking out again he landed his machine, and was partially successful in extinguishing them. He has always shown great coolness and determination under the most trying circumstances'.

The Bar to his MC came in the *London Gazette* of 26 July 1918: 'For conspicuous gallantry and devotion to duty in reconnaissance work during a flight lasting three and a half hours. Throughout he scarcely flew at a height greater than 200 feet; he attacked enemy infantry and dropped messages on ourbatteries which enabled them to shoot with good effect on the enemy as they advanced; he also shot down one machine out of control. On returning to the aerodrome it was found that his own machine was riddled with bullets'.

The French also awarded him a Croix de Guerre. His tour with '82' completed on 13 September 1918, Pollak returned to the Home Establishment where he saw out the remainder of the war. Between the wars, Pollak lived mainly in Austria. A world-class bridge player, he was a member of the Austrian team that won the European Bridge Championships in 1932, 1933 and 1936. When the Nazis marched into Austria in March 1938, and Pollak realised that there was not going to be any serious opposition to Anschluss with Germany, he wisely decided that, as a Jew, he had better leave. Within days, he arrived in England a penniless refugee. Joining the RAF when the Second World War came in 1939, he served mainly in Washington DC. After the war, he became a very successful businessman, living at Loxwood Chase, Loxwood, Sussex. Edmond Pollak died on 19 October 1964.

PORTAL, Charles Frederick Algernon

The third of the six sons of Edward Robert Portal, former Master of the Craven Hounds, and Ellinor Portal, née Hill, of Sulham, Pangbourne, he was born on 21 May 1893. Educated at Winchester (1906-12) and at Christ Church, Oxford. Represented Christ Church in the Cricket XI at Lords in 1912. All six of the Portal boys would serve in the Great War. As soon as the war came, he, in common with dozens of other Public School boys, enlisted into the Royal Engineers (Number 28029), specifically to serve in France as a motor-cycle despatch rider with the rank of Corporal, thus earning a 1914 Star. Very quickly picked out for a commission, he was gazetted Second Lieutenant to the Motor Cyclist Section, Royal Engineers, Special Reserve, on 27 September 1914. After services as Motor Cyclist Officer, HQ Signal Company, 1 Corps, he was seconded to the RFC in June 1915. Served as an Observer with 3 Squadron from 22 July 1915, being confirmed and gazetted Flying Officer (Observer) on 22 November following. Next, he trained as a Pilot, gaining his Royal Aero Club Certificate (Number 2543) on 9 March 1916. His formal training duly completed, he was given his full 'Wings' on 27 April 1916. Sent to 60 Squadron (Morane Bullets and Morane Bi-planes) on 3 May 1916, he accompanied the unit to France as a 'founder member'. Rapid promotion to A/Captain and a posting as a Flight Commander to 3 Squadron came on 16 July following. His MC was announced in the *London Gazette* of 10 January 1917: 'For conspicuous gallantry in action. He has done excellent artillery work in the air, often in bad weather and at low altitudes; he has always set his flight the best of examples. On one occasion he shot down an enemy machine'.

On 16 June 1917, Portal was appointed Officer Commanding 16 Squadron (RE8s). He was awarded the Distinguished Service Order in the *London Gazette* of 18 July 1917. Portal's next posting was to the command of 24 (Training) Wing in the UK. A Bar to his Distinguished Service Order came in the *London Gazette* of 26 July 1918. Portal was Mentioned in Despatches on three occasions during the Great War. During 1919, he successively commanded 1 Wing and 15 Wing in France, and then 59 (Training) Wing back in the UK. He married in 1919, Joan Margaret Welby, with whom he had two daughters. Given a permanent commission with the rank of Major on 1 August 1919, he embarked upon what would prove to be a brilliant career. His many honours, promotions and appointments included: CFI at RAF College, Cranwell, 1919; RAF Staff College, 1922; Air Staff, Flying Operations (Home), 1923; OC, 7 Squadron, 1927-29; attended Imperial Defence College, 1929; Deputy Director of Plans, Directorate of Operations and Intelligence, 1930; OC, Aden Command, 1934; Directing Staff, Imperial Defence College, 1936; Director of Organisation, 1937; Air Member for Personnel, 1939; CB, 1939; AOC in C, Bomber Command, 1940; Chief of the Air Staff, 1940; KCB, 1940; GCB, 1942; 1st Baron Hungerford, created 1945; Portal of Hungerford, 1st Viscount, created 1946; KG, 1946; OM, 1946. Marshal of the RAF Lord Portal of Hungerford retired in December 1945, after five years as Chief of Air Staff, only Lord Trenchard had held that post longer. His many foreign awards included: Grand Cross of the Légion d'Honneur, Polonia Restituta, St Olaf of Norway; Distinguished Service Medal (USA) and others. His civil decorations were also many and various, including: Honorary DCL Oxford, Durham and Belfast; Honorary DSc, Reading; Freeman of the City of London; Controller, Atomic Energy, Ministry of Supply, 1946-51. He also held a number of directorships including Barclay's Bank DCO, 1946-69; Director, Barclay's Bank Ltd, 1947-69; Director, Portals Holdings Ltd; Whitbread Investment Co, 1962-71. Other appointments included: Chairman, King Edward VII Hospital, Midhurst, 1950-68 and President of the MCC, 1958-59. Portal lived in retirement at West Ashling House, Chichester, Sussex. Marshal of the RAF Lord Portal died on 22 April 1971.

NB: The RAF Museum Hendon has his medals in its collection: Distinguished Service Order & Bar (suspender bar engraved: Capt CFA Portal, RE & RFC May 11th 1917*), MC (engraved:* Captain CFA Portal, RE & RFC, Dec 10th 1916*),*

1914 Star with Bar (28029 Cpl RE), *British War Medal 1914-20, Victory Medal 1914-19* (Major RAF), *Defence Medal 1939-45, War Medal 1939-45, Silver Jubilee Medal 1935, Coronation Medal 1937, Coronation Medal 1953, Distinguished Service Medal, Army (USA), Croix de Guerre 1939-40 (France), and Croix de Guerre 1939-45 avec Palme (Belgium).*

POWELL, Frederick James

The son of Frederick Henry Powell and Florence Catherine N Powell (née Prior), of 20 Moor Lane, Great Crosby, Liverpool, he was born in Patricroft, Lancashire, in August 1895. He later lived with relatives at The Vicarage, South Shore, Blackpool. A Railway Clerk pre-war, he was also a volunteer trooper in the Duke of Lancaster's Own Yeomanry, from 6 November 1913. Gazetted Second Lieutenant to 18 Battalion (3 City 'Pals'), Manchester Regiment, on 21 September 1914. Seconded to the RFC, he gained his Royal Aero Club Certificate (Number 1130) on 2 March 1915. His formal pilot training duly completed, he was confirmed and gazetted Flying Officer on 25 May following. Sent out to the Vickers FB5-equipped 5 Squadron, he became heavily involved in the increasingly intensive air war and in countering the Fokker menace. His MC was announced in the New Year *London Gazette* of 1 January 1916 (no citation). Although no formal citation was published in the *Gazette*, research has unearthed the original recommendation for the award: 'F J Powell & AM J Shaw (recommended for the Distinguished Conduct Medal): 'On 19 Sept attacked four armed enemy machines. One of these – a large double-engined machine – was seen to dive to earth. A report by agent was received, stating pilot and observer killed. During these four fights, both pilot and passenger showed great initiative and pluck. 5 Sqd'.

He was also Mentioned in Despatches at this time, *London Gazette* of 1 January 1916. On 17 January 1916, by then 'B' Flight Commander and A/Captain, Fred Powell, in a newly arrived FE8, '7457', shot down an Aviatik over Becelaere. Three days later, he was himself forced down in '7457', following engine failure after some damage inflicted by an Aviatik. Fortunately, Powell was unhurt in the subsequent crash-landing. His FE8 duly repaired and fully functioning, he claimed two more victories on 5 February 1916. Transferring to 40 Squadron late in 1916, he became one of the original Flight Commanders of that unit. Promoted to A/Major on 16 May 1917, he was next appointed Commanding Officer of 41 Squadron on 2 August following. On 2 February 1918, Powell, in SE5A, 'B8273', came off worse in a combat with Leutnant Kühn of Jasta 10 over Auberchicourt. Wounded in the air, Powell was taken prisoner as soon as his damaged machine crashlanded. Powell was repatriated in December 1918. Staying on in the RAF after the war, he served with 28 Squadron in India. He lived in Dorset in his retirement and was subsequently awarded the OBE. Fred Powell died in the 1980s

POWELL, Henry Stewart

The son of Mr and Mrs H E Powell of Stalheim, Basingstoke, he was born in 1894. Educated at Sherborne School (1907-1911), where he was a member of the OTC. He was living and working in Ceylon when the Great War came in 1914 and was subsequently gazetted Second Lieutenant to the Ceylon Rifles, via the Special Lists, on 19 April 1915. Seconded to the RFC, he was confirmed and gazetted Flying Officer on 14 December following. Posted to Home Defence duties, he served with BE2c-equipped 19 Reserve Aeroplane Squadron flying out of Suttons Farm. On the night of 31 March/1 April 1916, Powell was involved in an attempt to counter a Zeppelin raid. Flying at 6,000 feet, he witnessed his colleague, Alfred deBathe Brandon's (qv) attack on *L15*, but was still climbing towards the airship when it disappeared from view. Promoted to A/Captain and Flight Commander on 1 May 1916. On 1 August 1916, the night of a Zeppelin raid, he was serving with 51 HD Squadron when he crashed and suffered severe facial injuries and a badly damaged left leg. Such were his facial injuries that he lost his left eye. His MC was announced in the *London Gazette* of 24 January 1917 (no citation).

Powell was also Mentioned in Despatches on one occasion during the Great War. Staying on in the RAF after the war, he subsequently commanded 31 Squadron in India between 1924-25. Graduating from the Staff College, he had attained the rank of Wing Commander by 1935.

POWELL, Leslie Archibald

From Redland, Bristol, he was born on 27 June 1896. Educated at the Merchant Venturers School, Bristol, and at Bristol University. A journalist with the *Western Daily Press* in 1913-14. A volunteer with the Royal Naval Volunteer Reserve, he embarked for Gallipoli on 1 March 1915 as a Corporal in the Royal Naval Division. After service in the Dardanelles, he was picked out for a commission and gazetted Second Lieutenant to 8 Battalion, Gloucestershire Regiment on 5 August 1916. Following service with 8 and 13 Battalions, Gloucesters, he was seconded to the RFC and trained as an Observer. His training duly completed, he was confirmed and gazetted Flying Officer (Observer) on 15 May 1917. Sent out to FE2b-equipped 11 Squadron in France in the following July, he became a hugely successful Observer Ace. Teaming up with Andrew McKeever (qv), he shared all but one of his subsequent 19 victories with the great Canadian Ace. The first of his MCs was announced in the *London Gazette* of 26 September 1917, details in the *Gazette* of 9 January 1918: 'For conspicuous gallantry and devotion to duty on several occasions in attacking enemy aircraft in superior numbers at close range, destroying some and driving down others out of control. He had also done excellent work on photographic reconnaissances, and has in every instance displayed the greatest gallantry and splendid offensive spirit'.

A Bar to his MC rapidly followed in the *London Gazette* of 17 December 1917, details in the *Gazette* of 23 April 1918: 'For conspicuous gallantry and devotion to duty. Since his name was last brought to notice he has destroyed eight hostile machines. On one occasion, with his pilot, he engaged eleven enemy aeroplanes, his pilot bringing down one. On another six Albatros scouts and two two-seaters were encountered, two being brought down and three others engaged with indecisive results'. The full recommendation is as follows: 'For skill and gallantry. While flying with Lieutenant McKeever as his Pilot, 11 EA were engaged on 31/10/17 during a patrol over Fressie, his pilot bringing one down completely out of control. 2/Lt Powell fired 100 rounds at 1 EA at 75 yards range, the EA stalled, nose dived and burst into flames. He immediately turned his gun on another EA, which went into a spin and then turned over and over completely out of control, but was not seen to crash owing to thick clouds.

Previously on 16/16/17 near Brebières, 6 Albatros Scouts and 2 two-seaters were encountered. 2/Lt Powell's machine was attacked from the rear. He fired 50 rounds at 50 yards range and the EA fluttered down and was seen to crash. On this occasion his pilot attacked another EA which was crashed. Three other EA were also attacked with indecisive results.

Since this Officer's name was last brought to the notice of the Army Commander, he has destroyed 8 hostile machines of which 2 were in flames and 2 crashed. His pluck and determination have been a fine example to his squadron'.

Powell returned to the Home Establishment in January 1918, where he saw out the remainder of the war. Reverting to the Army in 1920, Powell obtained a Regular Army commission in the Gloucestershire Regiment. From 1926-30, he was Adjutant, 6 Battalion, Gloucesters, and from 1932-35, he was Adjutant of the Kedah Volunteers in Malaya. He retired in 1935, but was recalled for service during the Second World War. He finally retired from the Reserve of Officers with the rank of Honorary Colonel in 1946. Colonel 'Pip' Powell died at his home at 46 Ladydell Road, Worthing, where he lived with his wife, Mary, on 6 February 1961.

POWELL-WHITAKER, John Tudor – see John Tudor WHITAKER

PRESTON, Ian Polson Harvey

The second son of James H Preston and Mary H Preston, of 14 Eliot Vale, Lewisham, London, he was born on 4 April 1893. Educated at Blackheath Preparatory School (1904-07) and at Framlingham College (1907-09), where he was a member of the OTC. When the war came, he was living in Blackheath, London, and working as a Bank Clerk with the Bank of Scotland. Enlisting into the Honourable Artillery Company, he served as a Driver with 'A' Battery, HAC, attached Ammunition Column, 4 London Mounted Brigade, at Walsham, from 27 August 1914 to 27 February 1915. Picked out for a commission, he was gazetted Second Lieutenant to the Royal Field Artillery on 27 February 1915. Seconded to the RFC in the autumn, he trained for kite balloons and was formally gazetted Balloon Officer on 29 December 1915. Preston served with 49 KBS, Mediterranean Expeditionary Force, his MC announced in the *London Gazette* of 11 April 1918, for (no citation): '....military operations culminating in the capture of Jerusalem'. Promoted to Major, he stayed on in the RAF after the war, serving as an Instructor to the Egyptian Army in the 1920s.

PRESTON, Overton Inett

A Technical, not a flying, award

The son of Mr and Mrs Martin Inett Preston, of Derby Road, Nottingham, he was born on 22 May 1894. Educated at Sedburgh School (1909-12). A pre-war volunteer, he was gazetted Second Lieutenant to 7 (Robin Hood) Battalion, Sherwood Foresters, Nottinghamshire and Derbyshire Regiment (TF), on 16 May 1912. However, when the war came in August 1914, Preston was working on a ranch in the Argentine. One of the many British Latin American Volunteers, he returned to the UK in 1916, and was given a Captaincy in the Sherwood Foresters. Seconded to the RFC, he was gazetted Equipment Officer, 3rd Class, on 17 July 1916. Subsequently served in France as Equipment Officer (photographic) with 18 and 16 Wings, RFC, and later from May 1918 to March 1919 with 3 Brigade HQ. His MC was announced in the New Year *London Gazette* of 1 January 1918 (no citation).

Preston was Mentioned in Despatches on three occasions during the Great War, *London Gazettes* of 6 December 1916, 28 November 1917 and 3 June 1919. He was also awarded a Croix de Guerre by the French. After the war, Preston reverted to his Army roots, serving again as a part-time volunteer with the 'Robin Hoods', 7 Battalion, Sherwood Foresters.

PRICE, Stephen William

The third of the four sons of Solicitor, Samuel Hugh Price and Annie Sarah Price (née Poley), of 6 Gloucester Road, Stoke Newington, London, he was born in South Hornsey, on 28 November 1893. Gazetted Second Lieutenant to 10 (Reserve) Battalion, Leicestershire Regiment, on 19 September 1914. Served in France with 8 Battalion of his regiment from 29 July 1915, before being seconded to the RFC in the September following. Gained his Royal Aero Club Certificate (Number 1970) on 27 October 1915. His formal pilot training duly completed, he was confirmed and gazetted Flying Officer on 1 April 1916. Served first with the FE2b-equipped 23 Squadron, where he formed a formidable team with the American-born Gunner, Lieutenant Fred Libby (qv). Although not positively confirmed, it is probable that Price and Libby gained three victories with '23' before being posted in tandem to 11 Squadron, also equipped with the FE2b. Seven confirmed victories, achieved between the 22 August and 20 October 1916, were marked with awards of MCs to both men. Price's MC was announced in the *London Gazette* of 25 November 1916, the citation, not uniquely, incorrect in describing his function: 'For conspicuous gallantry in action. During a reconnaissance he was attacked by a large number of enemy machines. He manoeuvred his machine with great skill, and fought down a hostile machine. On four previous occasions he and his pilot [sic] have accounted for enemy machines'.

His tour with '11' completed on 30 October 1916, he returned to the UK where he served as a Flight Commander with 33 Squadron on Home Defence duties. Promoted to A/Major, he was next given command of 36 Squadron, again a HD unit, on 1 January 1918. Price returned to the front to take command of 83 (Night Bombing) Squadron on 27 July 1918. He was Mentioned in Despatches in the *London Gazette* of 8 November 1918. He finally left the RAF, via the Unemployed List, to resume his Law studies on 31 January 1919. Later, he qualified and practised as a Barrister-at-Law. Stephen Price died in Leamington Spa on 17 January 1982.

PRICE, William Thomas

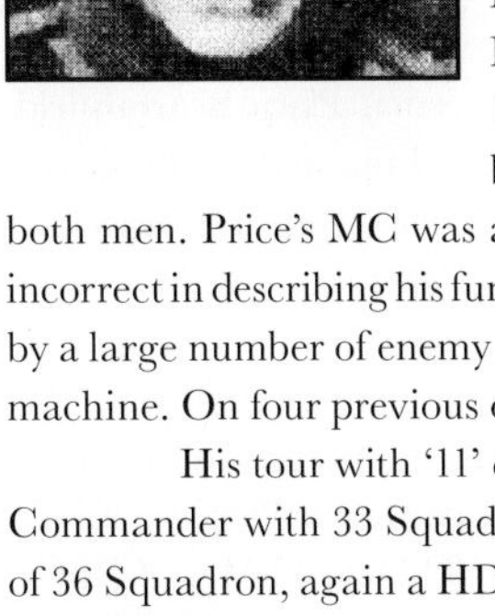

The son of Mr and Mrs Price, of 12 Ridbourne Ave, Finchley, London, he was born on 15 November 1895. Educated at Christ College, London, and at Reading University, from where he graduated BSc. Almost directly from university, he was gazetted Second Lieutenant to 13 Battalion, Royal Warwickshire Regiment, on 26 August 1915. Seconded to the RFC, he gained his Royal Aero Club Certificate (Number 4121) on 28 November 1916, the same day that he was formally confirmed and gazetted Flying Officer. Price accompanied the BF2b-equipped 48 Squadron to the front as a 'founder member' on 8 March 1917. He quickly achieved seven victories between 6 April and 9 May 1917. On the very day of his last victory, he and his Observer, Second Lieutenant Charles Geoffrey Claye in BF2b, 'A7110', were themselves wounded and forced down to a crash-landing by the great German Ace, Lothar von Richtofen. Lothar, brother of 'The Red Baron', was also a supreme Fighter Pilot in his own right, eventually gaining 40 victories. William Price's MC, announced in the *London Gazette* of 18 July 1917, was, in part at least, a reward for his pluck and skill in the fight with Lothar von Richthofen: 'For conspicuous gallantry and devotion to duty. His machine being disabled by hostile fire, and his gun out of action, he managed by skilful handling to effect a safe landing, thus saving the machine and his passenger from capture. He has previously done fine work against hostile aircraft'.

Price was presented with the insignia of his MC by the King at an investiture held at Buckingham Palace on 9 March 1918. After leaving the RAF following the end of the war, he flew for a time with a civilian aviation company, giving joyrides to holiday-makers in Blackpool. His career-path changed dramatically when he became a Lecturer in Dairy Husbandry at the Staffordshire Farm Institute from 1920 to 1922, before going on to lecture on Estate Management at the Harper Agricultural College from 1922 to 1924. He married in 1923, Fanny Louise Dale. In 1926, he was appointed Organiser of Agricultural Education, a position he held until 1946, when he was made Principal of the Harper Adams Agricultural College. In 1960, Price was awarded the CBE for his contribution to British agriculture, retiring two years later. Price worked for the BBC as an agricultural correspondent, as well as writing books and articles on his particular expertise, the breeding and care of pigs. He lived in retirement at 'Eversleigh', 2 Clarendon Place, Leamington Spa, Warwickshire, and died there on 17 January 1982.

PRITCHARD, Thomas Bradley

The son of Matthew John and Susannah Pritchard, of 5 Freeman Place, Beaconsfield, Cape Province, South Africa, he was born on 1 April 1893. Educated locally, he was a member of his school's Cadet Corps (1906-09). After leaving school, he trained and worked as an Engineer (fitter and turner) in the UK. As soon as the war came, he enlisted as a Private soldier (Number MS/2209) into 70 Company (Motor Transport), Army Service Corps, on 10 August 1914. He proceeded to France with his unit in September 1914, thus earning the 1914 Star. Pritchard later served in France with 52 Motor Transport Company, Royal Army Service Corps. Picked out for a commission, he was gazetted Second Lieutenant to the RFC on 30 May 1917. His pilot training duly completed, he was confirmed and gazetted Flying Officer on 23 July 1917. Posted to 39 HD Squadron at North Weald. On the night of 19/20 October 1917, there was a full scale alert when a large force of Zeppelins targeted Northern England. In the event, the weather created great difficulties for the German airships and they experienced their worst single day's disaster of the war, losing five of their machines. Tom Pritchard played his part by relentlessly pursuing one of the Zeppelins, *L45* (Kapitänleutnant M von Freudenreich). Although he could never match the *L45*'s ceiling, his constant harassment from below forced the Zeppelin higher and higher and into the teeth of a gale which swept it off course and eventually sent it down to destruction near Sisteron in France. Pritchard, in the meantime, found himself well out to sea and running short of fuel. Using his flares in the stygian darkness, Pritchard cautiously worked his way down and over land before stalling and coming down hard. Luckily, he escaped from his badly damaged BE2e with little more than a cut above his left eye and some concussion. His MC was announced in the *London Gazette* of 18 December 1917: 'HM the King has been pleased to confer the following rewards in recognition of gallantry and distinguished service with Anti-Aircraft services in the United Kingdom. Awarded the MC, Second Lieutenant Frederick Arthur Darien Grace [qv]: Second Lieutenant George Murray [qv], RFC; Second Lieutenant Thomas Bradley Pritchard'.

Tom Pritchard was subsequently killed in a flying accident, while his squadron was changing from the BE to the BF2b on 5 December 1917, and is buried in Hendon Cemetery, Middlesex.

PRITT, Walbanke Ashby

From Leamington Spa, Worcestershire, he was born on 31 October 1897. Educated at St Olave's, York, and at St Peter's School, York. Pritt lived in Clifton, York, with his guardians, the Misses J A L and B N Pritt. While still a schoolboy at St Peter's in the summer of 1916, he tried to get a direct commission into the RFC. He was, at the time, undergoing flying lessons at the Bournemouth Aviation Company. Although 18 years old, he was very small and boyish-looking, weighing just 108 pounds. Pritt's application was refused because, they said, 'the RFC was full-up! Was a Private in the West Yorkshire Regiment. His privately funded flying lessons came good when he gained his Royal Aero Club Certificate (Number 3564) on 16 September 1916. Persisting with his application, he was finally accepted and gazetted Second Lieutenant to the RFC on 16 March 1917. His formal pilot training duly completed, he was confirmed and gazetted Flying Officer on 2 June 1917. Sent out to the Sopwith Pup-equipped 66 Squadron within days of qualifying, he proved himself a very aggressive Pilot, despite his youthful appearance. On 16 August 1917, he was strafing an enemy airfield when a resident Albatros took off to confront him. As it climbed to meet him, he used his height advantage to great effect, swooping down to send the enemy machine down to crash. As he triumphantly climbed up and away, he spotted yet another enemy scout attempting to take off and promptly shot that one down also. On another occasion, he had actually run out of ammunition and was returning to his home field when he saw an open-topped German Staff car below him. He dived down low in a token attack, only to be greeted by pistol shots aimed at him by one of the occupants. Frustrated, he looked around his cockpit and spotted his Very pistol. Turning back for another pass at the speeding vehicle, he shot a flare into it. Pritt claimed five victories and the status of Ace, between 28 July and 30 September 1917. His MC was announced in the *London Gazette* of 26 September 1917, details in the *Gazette* of 9 January 1918: 'For conspicuous gallantry and devotion to duty in attacking a hostile aerodrome with exceptional dash and determination. Having reached his objective and dropped bombs from a very low altitude, he then attacked and destroyed two hostile machines almost as soon as they left the ground. A machine-gun then opened upon him from the aerodrome, which he immediately attacked,. Both on his outward and homeward journey he was under very heavy machine-gun and anti-aircraft fire. On another occasion, he attacked a motor-car, and shot one of the occupants from about 50 feet, afterwards attacking infantry on the march and inflicting severe casualties upon them. He has at all times shown consistent gallantry and fine offensive spirit'. His tour with '66' completed in the autumn of 1917, he returned to the Home Establishment and subsequently served with 44 HD Squadron. On 15 February 1918, he was injured when his Camel, 'B7332', crashed due to engine failure. Post-war he was a Commercial Artist and involved in poultry farming, but was killed in an auto accident near Bagby, West. Yorkshire on 27 January 1928.

PROCTOR, Andrew Frederick Weatherby Beauchamp VC

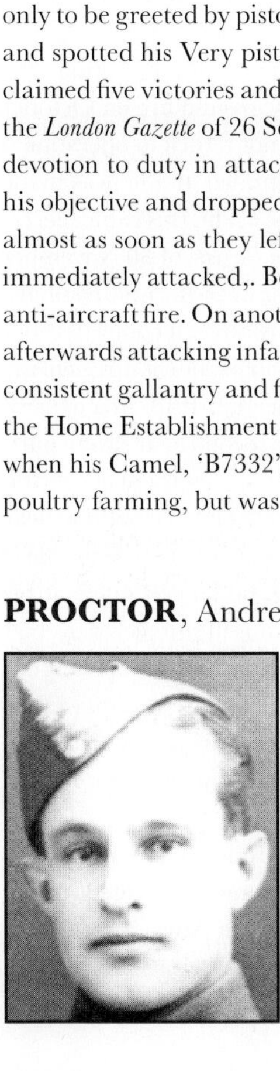

The younger son of Mr and Mrs John J Proctor, he was born in Mossel Bay, Cape Province, South Africa, on 4 September 1894. Educated at George School, Mafeking, and at Old South African College, Capetown (later to be known as the University of Capetown), where he studied engineering from 1912. Two years later he gained a second year pass in his Engineering Diploma, shortly before the war intervened. Volunteering on 1 October 1914, he enlisted as a Signaller into the Duke of Edinburgh's Own Rifles (SAI) on 1 October 1914. He fought in the South West Africa campaign against the Germans, before later being transferred to the South African Field Telegraph and Postal Corps. Released from his commitment by the South Africa Government in August 1915, he returned to his studies in Capetown. After completing his third year of study, he was recruited by Major A M Miller DSO, who had been sent to South Africa by the War Office to find likely candidates for the RFC. The diminutive Beauchamp Proctor attested as a Third Class Air Mechanic and sailed for the UK in March 1917 (reputedly, his father told him to add 'Beauchamp' to his name to impress the English!) On arrival two weeks later, he was sent first to an Officer Cadet Battalion, and then to the School of Military Aeronautics at Oxford. His flying training began at Castle Bromwich with 5 RS and continued at Netheravon, and finally at the CFS, Upavon, where he was confirmed and gazetted Flying Officer on 29 July 1917. Beauchamp Proctor accompanied the SE5A-equipped 84 Squadron to France as a 'founder member' on 21 September 1917. His first victory came on 3 January 1918, the first of what was to become a monumental total of 54 over the next ten months. The first of his two MCs was announced in the *London Gazette* of 22 June 1918: 'For conspicuous gallantry and devotion to duty. While on offensive patrol he observed an enemy two-seater plane attempting to cross our lines. He engaged it and opened fire, with the result that it fell over on its side and crashed to earth. On a later occasion, when on patrol, he observed three enemy scouts attacking one of our bombing machines. He attacked one of these, after firing 100 rounds into it, it fell over on its back and was seen to descend in that position from 5,000 ft. He then attacked another group of hostile scouts, one of which he shot down completely out of control, and another crumpled up and crashed to earth. In addition to these, he destroyed another hostile machine, and shot down three completely out of control. He has at all times displayed the utmost dash and initiative, and is a patrol leader of great merit and courage'.

The Bar to his MC came in the *London Gazette* of 16 September 1918: 'For conspicuous gallantry and devotion to duty when leading offensive patrols. He has lately destroyed three enemy machines, driven down one other completely out of control, and carried out valuable work in attacking enemy troops and transport on the ground from low altitudes. He has done splendid service'.

A Distinguished Flying Cross, awarded for his continuing success and brilliance at air fighting, was announced in the *London Gazette* of 2 July 1918. Beauchamp Proctor was shot down by ground fire on October 1918, receiving a wound in the arm. His subsequent hospitalisation meant that he did not return to operational flying before the end of the war. Profound appreciation of his services, however, continued and he was made Companion of the Distinguished Order in the *London Gazette* of 2 November 1918. In the event, this came merely as a precursor to the ultimate accolade of the Victoria Cross announced in the *London Gazette* of 30 November 1918: 'Between August 8th, 1918 and October 8th, 1918, this officer proved himself victor in 26 decisive combats, destroying 12 enemy kite balloons, 10 enemy aircraft, and diving down four other enemy aircraft completely out of control. Between October 1st, 1918 and October 5th. 1918, he destroyed two enemy scouts, burnt three enemy kite balloons, and drove down one enemy scout completely out of control. On October 1st. 1918, in a general engagement with about 28 machines, he crashed one Fokker biplane near Fontaine and a second near Ramicourt; on October 2nd he burnt a hostile balloon near Selvigny; on October 3rd he drove down, completely out of control, an enemy scout near Mont d'Origny, and burnt a hostile balloon; on October 5th the third hostile balloon near Bohain. On October 8th 1918, while flying home at a low altitude, after destroying an enemy two-seater near Maretz, he was painfully wounded in the arm by machine-gun fire, but, continuing, he landed safely at his aerodrome, and after making his report was admitted to hospital. In all he has proved himself conqueror over 54 foes, destroying 22 enemy machines, 16 enemy kite balloons, and driving down 16 enemy aircraft completely out of control. Captain Beauchamp Proctor's work in attacking enemy troops on the ground and in reconnaissance during the withdrawal following on the battle of St Quentin from March 1st, 1918 and during the victorious advance of our armies on August 8th, has been unsurpassed in its brilliancy and as such has made an impression on those serving in his Squadron and those around him that will not be easily forgotten'.

After leaving hospital in March 1919, he made a four-month lecture tour of the United States. Returning to England he was, unsurprisingly, given a permanent commission as a Flight Lieutenant in the RAF in the summer of 1919. The investiture of his Victoria Cross was held at Buckingham Palace in November 1919, a full year after its announcement. He was then allowed to return to South Africa, partly for a prolonged leave, and partly to finish his Engineering studies. Armed with his BSc, he returned to England late in 1920. Sir

Hugh Trenchard had conceived the idea of an annual RAF Pageant, the first had been held in 1920, and now Beauchamp Proctor was invited to take part in the 1921 event. It was while practising for the Pageant on 21 June 1921, the day before the show was due to take place, that his Sopwith Snipe fell away from a loop into an inverted spin before crashing at Enford, killing its Pilot. His body was first buried, with full military honours, at Upavon. However, South Africa laid claim to their hero's remains and he were taken there aboard the SS *Balmoral Castle* for a state funeral at Mafeking.

PUGH, John Edwards

The second of the three sons of retired Farmer, Thomas Edwards Pugh and Annie Esther Pugh (née Leigh), of 117 Upper Canning Street, Liverpool, he was born in Shotwick, Cheshire, on 29 April 1890. He emigrated to Canada in 1913, becoming a civil servant in the Department of Indian Affairs, and was living in Alberta when war came in the following year. He trained with 9 (Reserve) Battalion, Alberta Regiment, before being gazetted Lieutenant into 49 Battalion, Canadian Infantry, on 10 July 1916. Served in France with 19 Alberta Dragoons, CEF, being wounded on the Somme on 16 September 1916. Once recovered in May 1917, he volunteered for service with the RFC and, following pilot training, was confirmed and gazetted Flying Officer on 26 July 1917. Sent out to 25 Squadron (DH4s) on 27 September 1917. Although '25' was a daylight bombing unit, Pugh managed to gain five victories with various Observers between 13 January and 5 June 1918. His MC was announced in the *London Gazette* of 22 June 1918: 'For conspicuous gallantry and devotion to duty. He carried out twenty successful bombing raids and fifteen long-distance photographic reconnaissances showing great determination in carrying out his work, in spite of strong opposition by enemy aircraft. In two days he took 108 photographs in the course of long-distance flights. During a period of five days he dropped three-quarters of a ton of bombs on enemy troops and transport, and engaged ground targets with machine-gun fire from a low altitude. On one occasion whilst on a bombing raid he was attacked by five enemy machines, one of which he destroyed. He set a splendid example of skill and resource'.

Pugh was promoted to A/Captain and Flight Commander in April 1918. His tour with '25' ending on 12 June 1918, he returned to the Home Establishment where he saw out the remainder of the war. He returned to Canada in December 1918. Pugh would rise to a senior position in the Department of Indian Affairs. He died from an aneurysm on 28 May 1966.

PURDOM, Thomas Laurence

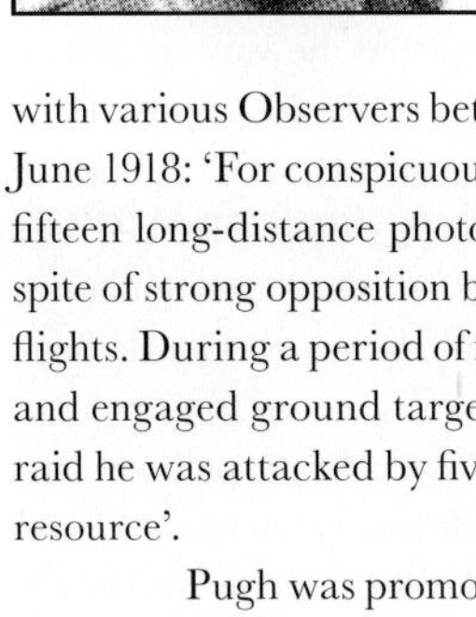

The son of Solicitor, John Ritchie Purdom and Mrs Purdom, of Langheugh, Hawick, North Berwick, he was born on 24 June 1892. Educated at Edinburgh Academy (1907-09). He was living and working in London when the war came in August 1914 and he immediately enlisted as a Private soldier into 12 Battalion, Middlesex Regiment. Picked out for a commission, he was gazetted Second Lieutenant to 4 Battalion, King's Own Scottish Borderers (TF), on 14 October 1914. Seconded to the RFC in the autumn of 1915, he gained his Royal Aero Club Certificate (Number 1873) on 11 October 1915. His formal pilot training duly completed, he was confirmed and gazetted Flying Officer on 18 January 1916. Sent out to the BE2-equipped 15 Squadron on 6 April 1916, he flew many sorties over the next months until returning to the Home Establishment on 10 January 1917. Purdom returned briefly to France on

19 January 1918, but was recalled to Biggin Hill to attend a Radio course in March. Over to France again on 1 April 1918, the actual birthday of the RAF, this time as an A/Captain and Flight Commander with the Bristol Fighter-equipped 62 Squadron. Hugely successful in Brisfits, Purdom claimed 13 victories between 21 March and 19 May 1918, the first 12 of which were with Second Lieutenant P V G Chambers acting as his Observer. His MC was announced in the *London Gazette* of 22 June 1918: 'For conspicuous gallantry and devotion to duty. He attacked and shot down a hostile scout, and when himself attacked by a second scout, he shot the latter down out of control, also. He has in addition to these destroyed four enemy machines within a month. He has shown the most exceptional gallantry and daring in engaging enemy aircraft'.

Surviving the exigencies of the Western Front in 1918, he finally left the RAF, via the Unemployed List, on 19 February 1919.

PURSER, Philip Charles

The younger son of Civil Engineer and Surveyor, Walter Bishop Purser and Eva Arabella Purser (née Phillips), of 31 Bedford Road, Horsham, West Sussex, he was born in Swinton, Manchester, on 4 January 1896. Educated at King's School, Grantham, where he was a member of the OTC. Gazetted Second Lieutenant to the Wessex Divisional Train, Army Service Corps (TF), on 21 October 1914. Seconded to the RFC in January 1916, he trained as an Observer and was sent out to France in that capacity. His 'apprenticeship' satisfactorily completed, he was confirmed and gazetted Flying Officer (Observer) in September 1916. On 9 November 1916, Purser returned to the Home Establishment for pilot training. He was Mentioned in Despatches, *London Gazette* of 14 November 1916, at this time. His MC was announced in the *London Gazette* of 16 November 1916: 'For conspicuous gallantry in action. Twice he carried out long reconnaissances, obtaining valuable information. He has previously done fine work on offensive patrols'.

Purser would instruct in the UK before being sent out again in April 1918 for a brief spell with the DH9s of 99 Squadron, Independent Air Force, which lasted until the following June. He finally left the RAF, via the Unemployed List, on 8 November 1919. Phillip Purser served again with the RAFVR in the Second World War, being recommissioned in 1940, having applied as soon as war broke out in September 1939.

PURVES, Stanley Stewart Beatie

From Kirkcaldy, Fife, Scotland. Gazetted Second Lieutenant to the Scottish Horse Yeomanry on 27 December 1915. Seconded to the RFC in July 1916, he trained as a Pilot and was duly confirmed and gazetted Flying Officer on 21 October following. Sent out to 19 Squadron on 27 December 1916. '19' was the first squadron to be equipped with the French Spad VIIs and, on 19 March 1917, Purves was unfortunate enough to become the first RFC casualty flying this type. He was attacked in 'A6633' near Le Catelet, and shot down to be taken prisoner of war by either Hauptmann Paul von Osterroht of Jasta 12 or by Leutnant Kurt Schneider of Jasta 5, each of them receiving credit for this one victory. Purves was one of the successful escapers via the famous tunnel from the notorious Holzminden camp, reaching England on 16 August 1918. His MC was announced in the 'Escapers Gazette', *London Gazette* of 16 December 1919: '....in recognition of gallantry in escaping from captivity whilst Prisoners of War'.

Purves finally left the RAF, via the Unemployed List, on 13 April 1919, with the rank of Lieutenant. He was twice presented to the King of England, George V in 1919, no doubt to talk about his escape, and again in 1948, this time to George VI. While the exact reason for the second meeting is unclear, the surviving members of the Holzminden escapers held reunions in London in 1938, 1943, and 1948.

PYBUS, Evan

The younger son of Solicitor, John Pybus and Dora M Pybus, of Eastfield House, Corbridge, Northumberland, he was born in Newcastle-upon-Tyne, on 13 November 1895. Educated at Oundle School (1908-12), where he was a member of the OTC. Enlisting into the Royal Engineers when the war came, he rose to the rank of Sergeant (Number 54019) whilst serving with 14 Signal Company, Royal Engineers. Picked out for a commission, he was accepted as a Cadet to the flying service on 12 April 1917 and was subsequently gazetted Second Lieutenant to the RFC on 17 May following. His formal pilot training duly completed, he was confirmed and gazetted Flying Officer on 10 July 1917. Sent out to 35 Squadron (AWFK8s) on 16 August 1917. On 24 March 1918, at the height of the German spring offensive, 35 Squadron had a number of machines lost and damaged. Pybus and his Observer of the day, Second Lieutenant W W Jones, in 'C3549', were forced to land following an aerial combat over Bethancourt. They burnt their damaged Big-Ack before making their way to safety. Promoted to A/Captain and Flight Commander on 17 April 1918, his MC was announced in the *London Gazette* of 13 May 1918: 'For conspicuous gallantry and devotion to duty. He carried out valuable photographic reconnaissances of enemy areas. Though on one occasion he was attacked by twelve enemy machines, he succeeded in taking the required photographs. On three occasions, in the course of flights lasting four hours or more, he ranged a siege battery most effectively on hostile batteries, with the result that several gun pits were destroyed and three explosions were caused. He showed splendid determination and initiative'.

Pybus was also Mentioned in Despatches in the *London Gazette* of 20 June 1918. His tour with '35' completed, he returned to the Home Establishment on 1 August 1918, where he saw out the remainder of the war. Pybus finally left the RAF, via the Unemployed List, on 8 February 1919. He lived at Lakenham Farm, Chobham, Woking, Surrey, and died there on 19 January 1974.

Q

QUESTED, John Bowley

The son of Mr and Mrs J E Quested, of 'The Firs', Cheriton, Folkestone, Kent, he was born on 14 December 1893. Educated at St Edward's School, Oxford, where he was a member of the OTC. He was sheep farming in East Anglia when war came in August 1914. Gazetted Second Lieutenant to the Army Service Corps on 11 November 1914. Seconded to the RFC in the spring of 1915, he trained as an Observer and was sent to 11 Squadron, then in Netheravon, in April 1915. He accompanied '11' (VFB5s) to France as a 'founder member' when that unit went to the front as the first two-seater fighter squadron, on 25 July following. After an intensive stint as an Observer, Quested returned to the UK to train as a Pilot. Confirmed and gazetted Flying Officer on 6 July 1916, he returned to 11 Squadron to fly the FE2b at the front shortly afterwards. On 27 December 1916, he and his Observer of the day, Second Lieutenant H J H Dicksee, in FE2b, '7666', ran into Jasta 1 near to Cherisy. Following a successful combat victory over Leutnant Gustav Leffers, an Ace with nine victories to his credit, Quested and Dicksee were themselves forced down behind British lines at Wancourt by Vizefeldwebel Wilhelm Cymera, also of Jasta 1, the first of the German's five victories. Although Dicksee was slightly wounded, Quested, fortunately, was unhurt. In all, Quested gained eight victories between 16 August 1916 and 25 January 1917. His MC was announced in the *London Gazette* of 13 February 1917: 'For conspicuous gallantry in action. He manoeuvred his machine with great skill, and thereby enabled his Observer to bring down a hostile machine. He has on many previous occasions displayed great courage and ability'.

He was also awarded the Croix de Guerre by the French, *London Gazette* of 1 May 1917. Quested, after a rest, joined 40 Squadron in July 1917, but was, shortly afterwards, injured in a crash which effectively curtailed his flying career. In October 1917, he was working again, this time as CO, 1 Aerial Gunnery Range, in France. Injured yet again, he was sent back to the UK for hospital treatment in February 1918. Regaining his health, he was given command of Number 2 Aeroplane Supply Depot, where he saw out the war. Staying on for a period after the war, Quested commanded 79 Squadron in 1919, serving in both Germany and in India with 48 Squadron. He finally left the RAF to take up farming in East Anglia. John Quested died at 41 Grimstone Avenue, Folkestone, Kent, on 11 March 1948.

QUIGLEY, Francis Grainger

The son of Robert John and Annie Primrose Quigley, of Toronto, Canada, he was born on 10 July 1894. Educated at St Andrew's, Aurora (1907-09) and entered Queen's University, Kingston, Ontario, in September 1913, and was still studying there when he decided to enlist into the Canadian Engineers in January 1915. Crossing to England in May 1915, he soon afterwards accompanied his unit to France to serve with the CEF. Picked out for a commission, he was gazetted Second Lieutenant to the RFC on 10 May 1917. His pilot training duly completed, he was confirmed and gazetted Flying Officer on 16 July following. Sent out to the Sopwith Camel F1-equipped 70 Squadron in France on 12 September 1917. Quigley proved to be a Camel Pilot of exceptional bravery and skill, achieving no less than 33 victories between 10 October 1917 and 23 March 1918, including two 'quartets', two 'trios' and three 'doubles' on single days. The first of his MCs was announced in the *London Gazette* of 18 February 1918, details in the *Gazette* of 18 July 1918: 'For conspicuous gallantry and devotion to duty when engaging hostile aircraft. On one occasion, while on patrol, he attacked an enemy two-seater which, after close fighting and skilful manoeuvring, he crashed to the ground. He has, within a short period, destroyed or driven down out of control, seven other enemy machines, and on all occasions has displayed high courage and fine fighting spirit'.

On 27 March 1918, he was wounded during a combat, his ankle shattered. The Bar to his MC came in the *London Gazette* of 13 May 1918: 'For conspicuous gallantry and devotion to duty in aerial combats. He destroyed five enemy machines and one balloon, and drove down four enemy machines out of control. He showed splendid courage and initiative'.

Soon afterwards, Quigley was awarded the Distinguished Service Order, *London Gazette* of 22 June 1918. He was also Mentioned in Despatches on several occasions. Following medical treatment to his badly damaged ankle, he had recovered sufficiently to be sent home to Canada to take up an instructing post at Armour Heights. Unfortunately, he was one of the many millions infected in the influenza pandemic raging across the world and, after a short illness, died on 20 October 1918, shortly after returning to England. Francis Quigley is buried in Toronto (Mount Pleasant) Cemetery, Ontario, Canada.

QUINE, Sylvester Lindsay

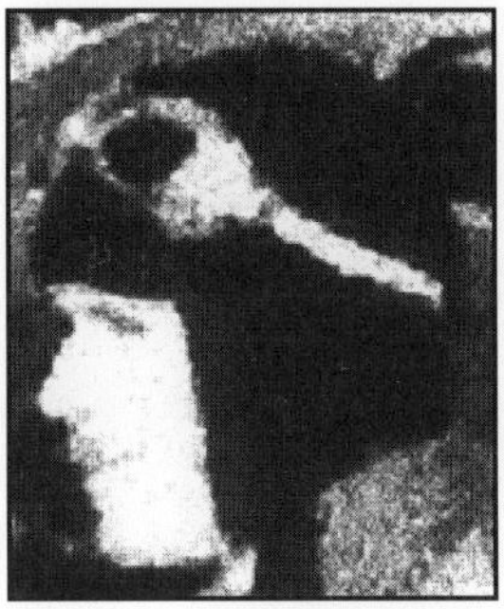

The son of the Reverend Canon J Quine and Mrs Quine, of Lonan Vicarage, Isle of Man, he was born on 25 January 1894. Educated as a day boy at King William's College, Isle of Man (1909-11), Rugby XV. Volunteering as soon as the war came, he enlisted as a Private soldier into 7 Battalion, King's Liverpool Regiment (TF). Quine was promoted to Lance Corporal, before being picked out for a commission and gazetted Second Lieutenant to 16 (Reserve) Battalion, King's Liverpool Regiment, on 9 March 1915, with an immediate transfer to 3 (Reserve) Battalion, Cheshire Regiment. Served in Salonika with 2 Battalion, Cheshire Regiment, from January 1916 until the following November, when he transferred to the RFC. He trained as a Pilot at RFC HQ, Egypt, being duly confirmed and gazetted Flying Officer on 30 April 1917. Sent to serve on the Western Front with 21 Squadron in May 1917, his MC was announced in the *London Gazette* of 8 January 1918, details in the *Gazette* of 25 April 1918: 'For conspicuous gallantry and devotion to duty. He went out in exceptionally rough and stormy weather during an attack, and, flying very low over the enemy's batteries, reported and located those which were in action. By his courageous and determined efforts he assisted materially in clearing up the situation and enabled effective fire to be brought to bear on the enemy's batteries'.

Quine was also Mentioned in Despatches on one occasion during the Great War. Returning to the Home Establishment in December 1917, he next took up a series of training posts. Staying on in the RAF after the war, he subsequently qualified as a Signals Officer, before going on to instruct at the Electrical and Wireless School in 1920 and 1921. He served in Iraq from 1921 to 1923 and in Palestine from 1924 to 1925, later becoming Air Staff Signals Officer, Wessex Bombing Area, RAF. Sylvester Quine had risen to the rank of Wing Commander by 1937, retiring as a Group Captain with the Engineering Branch. Died 31 January 1945.

QUINN, James John

From Ottawa, Canada, he was born on 18 December 1896. Educated at St Patrick's School, Ottawa (1901-09), and at Ottawa University (1909-10 and again, 1911-13). After working as a Clerk and a Chainman with survey parties, he became an Articled Pupil with the Dominion Land Survey organisation. He was next employed by the Topographical Surveys Branch of the Department of the Interior from May 1916 until December 1916. Joining the RFC as a Cadet in April 1917, he was gazetted Second Lieutenant on 24 May following. His pilot training duly completed, he was confirmed and gazetted Flying Officer on 18 September 1917. Sent out to 53 Squadron with artillery observation duties on 6 October 1917. Taken ill in April 1918, he returned to the UK for treatment. His health restored, he again went to the front, this time to fly the Bristol Fighters of 20 Squadron. His MC was announced in the *London Gazette* of 26 July 1918: 'For conspicuous gallantry and devotion to duty. He carried out five low reconnaissances over the enemy's lines, bringing back valuable information, his machine on three occasions being badly shot about by machine-gun fire from the ground. He carried out one offensive patrol and one escort, attacking with bombs and machine-gun fire from a low altitude. On both occasions be was attacked by enemy aeroplane formations, his Observer driving one down out of control, and his own machine being much shot about'.

On 2 August 1918, Quinn and his Observer of the day, Probationer K Penrose, in BF2b, 'B1168', were both wounded in action when their machine was shot up over Aire and they were obliged to force land. Quinn finally left the RAF, via the Unemployed List, on 12 July 1919, when he returned to his native Canada.

R

RABAGLIATI, Cuthbert Euen Charles

From Bradford, Yorkshire, he was born on 1 January 1892. Educated at Loretto (1907-09) and at Sandhurst. Gazetted Second Lieutenant to a Regular Army battalion of the King's Own Yorkshire Light Infantry on 14 February 1912. Developing an interest in aviation, he gained his Royal Aero Club Certificate (Number 779) in a Bristol machine at the Bristol School, Brooklands, on 11 May 1914. Seconded to the RFC, he completed his formal pilot training and was duly confirmed and gazetted Flying Officer on 12 August 1914. Rabagliati accompanied the original RFC contingent to France in August 1914, as a member of 5 Squadron, thus earning the 1914 Star. 5 Squadron's ammunition and bomb lorry in France had been requisitioned from a leading sauce manufacturer in the UK and was painted in the company's livery, bright red with gold lettering that proclaimed, The World's Appetiser! The first aerial victory of all time, on 25 August 1914, was credited to Lieutenants H D Harvey-Kelly and W H C Mansfield. However, one of 5 Squadron's Pilots, Second Lieutenant C W Wilson, later claimed that the credit for the victory should have gone to his Observer, Lieutenant C E C Rabagliati and his hunting rifle. Wilson's diary entry for 29 August 1914 reads: 'Lunched at hotel in Compiègne, many pilots of the RFC collected. Harvey-Kelly (Lieutenant of 2 Squadron) posing as successful warrior, relating his method of downing Huns and showing small plaque taken from machine downed by Rab and 398 [the number of his and Rab's machine]. Stopped him in full career and claimed first Hun for 398. He had landed beside our prey and attended to its burning! H-K handed the plaque gracefully to me, with the words, "Your bird, I think" '. On 5 November 1914, Rabagliati was acting as Observer to Lieutenant R M Vaughan as the pair patrolled above Hollebeke. Vaughan was wounded when their machine was hit by fire from the ground. Rabagliati contrived to take over the controls and managed to land the machine safely at Ypres. Rabagliati's MC was announced in the *London Gazette* of 4 November 1915: 'For conspicuous gallantry and skill on 28 September 1915, when, accompanied by Second Lieutenant Vaucour [qv], they carried out a reconnaissance over Valenciennes and Douai. They had to fly in thick cloud for nearly the whole distance, and several times their aeroplane got into a 'spin'. The pilot, however, succeeded each time in righting his machine, and they reached their objective and carried out the reconnaissance at 2,800 feet under very heavy fire'.

He was also Mentioned in Despatches on three occasions during the Great War, *London Gazettes* of 8 October 1914, 22 June 1915 and 1 January 1919. Rabagliati would go on to serve with 10 Squadron before being promoted to Major and appointed to the command of 24 Squadron from November 1916 until March 1917. Promoted next to Lieutenant Colonel and Wing Commander in 1917, he commanded the RFC in Ireland in 1918 and represented the RAF at the Armistice Commission. Awarded an Air Force Cross in the Birthday Honours *London Gazette* of 3 June 1919. The French, too, showed their appreciation by appointing him Chevalier, Légion d'Honneur. Rabagliati finally left the RAF with the rank of Lieutenant Colonel in 1919. Subsequently becoming an underwriter at Lloyds, he specialised in aviation insurance with the Aviation Insurance Company in the City of London, whilst living at Tatmore Place, Hitchin, Hertfordshire.

RAMSEY, James Robert

Not a flying award

From Martlesham, he was born on 16 November 1872. Served in the Royal Artillery when he was a youngster, but bought himself out for £10 and took up his trade as a Sign-Writer and Painter. This lifestyle seems to have palled as, on 3 July 1897, he re-enlisted as a Sapper (Number 1015) into the Royal Engineers at Woolwich. Ramsey served in South Africa during the Boer War, earning a Queen's South Africa Medal 1899-1902, with four clasps, Cape Colony, Orange Free State, Transvaal, and South Africa 1901, and later in Malta and in Gibralter. Transferred to the Air Battalion, Royal Engineers, he earned his promotion from Corporal to Sergeant by saving the airship, *Nulli Secundas*, when it broke away from its mooring mast during a storm at Crystal Palace on 10 October 1907. Ramsay at first tried to deflate the airship by opening the appropriate valves, but finding that too slow, he split the fabric using a sharp knife on the end of a long pole. On 1 April 1910, he transferred to 2 BC, Balloon School, and was promoted to Company Sergeant Major on 30 September of the same year. Next he transferred from Air Balloons, Royal Engineers, to the newly formed RFC, on 13 May 1912. A keen motor cyclist and a contemporary of James McCudden, Ramsey is mentioned in the great Ace's biography, 'Flying Fury'. He crossed to France with the original contingent of the RFC as a member of 3 Squadron, thus earning the 1914 Star. His MC, amongst the first RFC recipients of the award, was announced in the New Year *London Gazette* of 1 January 1915 (no citation). He was also Mentioned in Despatches on three occasions during the Great War, *London Gazettes* of 19 October 1914, 1 January 1915 and 1 January 1916. Picked out for a QM commission, he was gazetted Lieutenant and Quarter Master on 1 March 1915. Ramsey served with 6 Wing, RFC, in the UK and in France, in 1915 and 1916 and was subsequently promoted to Captain and Quarter Master in 1918.

RAYMOND-BARKER, Richard

The son of Edward and Rose Raymond-Barker, of 'Paulmead', Bisley, Gloucestershire, he was born on 6 May 1894. Educated at Wimbledon College, and at Mount St Mary's College. After completing his education, he assisted in the laying of submarine cable from Sydney to Auckland aboard the telegraph steamer, Silverton and, later, was involved in other cable-laying projects on the west and south-east African coasts. Just prior to the Great War, he went to Canada to take up farming but, when the war came, he immediately returned to the UK to enlist as a Private soldier in the Middlesex Regiment. Within three months he had been promoted to Sergeant, and was then gazetted Second Lieutenant into 5 Battalion, Northumberland Fusiliers, on 30 November 1914. Gained his Royal Aero Club Certificate (Number 1460) on 18 July 1915, prior to his secondment to the RFC on 6 August following. His formal pilot training duly completed, he was confirmed and gazetted Flying Officer on 19 October 1915. Sent out to France on 22 November 1915, he flew with 6 and 16 Squadrons over the next 13 months, before promotion to A/Captain and Flight Commander and a posting to the Bristol Fighter-equipped 48 Squadron came on 12 May 1917. On 2 July 1917, he was posted to 11 Squadron, yet another 'Brisfit' unit. By that time, Raymond-Barker had achieved six victories. His MC was announced in the *London Gazette* of 17 September 1917: 'For conspicuous gallantry and devotion to duty when leading a fighting patrol. He attacked a large hostile formation, destroying two of them. He has also done excellent work in leading distant photographic reconnaissances, notably upon two occasions when his skilful leadership enabled photographs to be taken of all the required hostile area in spite of repeated attacks from enemy aircraft. He has helped to destroy seven hostile machines and has at all times displayed conspicuous skill and gallantry'.

Raymond-Barker was presented with the insignia of his MC by the King at an investiture held at Buckingham Palace in the spring of 1918. In the same month of the announcement of his MC, he was promoted to Major and given command of 3 Squadron. On 20 April 1918, Dick Raymond-Barker became Baron Manfred von Richthofen's penultimate and 79th victory when his Sopwith Camel, 'D6439' was shot down during a dog-fight. The Red Baron's combat report stated, 'With six planes of Jasta 11, I attacked a large enemy Squadron. During the fight, I observed that a Tri-plane was attacked and shot at from below by a Camel. I put myself behind the adversary and brought him down, burning, with only a few shots. The enemy plane crashed down near the forest of Hamel where it burned further on the ground'. Raymond-Barker's remains were never recovered and hence he is commemorated on the Flying Services Memorial, Arras, France.

READ, William Ronald

Born in Hampstead, London, on 17 May 1885. A Regular Army officer pre-war, he was gazetted Second Lieutenant to 1 (King's) Dragoon Guards in 1912. Developing an interest in aviation, he gained his Royal Aero Club Certificate (Number 463) on a Bristol machine at Salisbury Plain on 12 April 1913. Seconded to the RFC, he duly completed his formal pilot training and was confirmed and gazetted Flying Officer on 28 April 1914. Attached to 3 Squadron, he accompanied the original RFC contingent to France in August 1914, thus earning the 1914 Star. Read was wounded on 3 November 1914, returning afterwards to the UK for treatment. Read later served as a Flight Commander with 5 Squadron flying Bristol Scouts and frequently becoming involved in the largely inconclusive aerial combats which were the order of the day prior to the advent of the Fokker menace late in 1915. His MC was announced in the *London Gazette* of 14 January 1916 (no citation). Although no formal citation was published in the *Gazette*, research has unearthed the original, if somewhat terse, recommendation for the award: '1/Drag Gds, 5 Sqd. General Service. A fine example. Has never returned without carrying through his allotted task'.

Promoted to A/Major, he was next, in April 1916, appointed to the command of 45 Squadron, then stationed at Gosport. Read led the Strutter-equipped '45' to France on 15 October 1916, landing at Fienvillers Aerodrome during the closing days of the Battle of the Somme. For some non-apparent reason, Read temporarily reverted to his parent regiment, 1 Dragoon Guards, in April 1917. However, he did return to the RAF as Commanding Officer of 216 Squadron, Independent Force, taking over the unit on the last day of the war, 11 November 1918. He was awarded the Distinguished Flying Cross in the Birthday Honours *London Gazette* of 3 June 1919. Staying on in the RAF, he was at the Flying Wing of the RAF College, Cranwell, with the rank of Squadron Leader in April 1922, and later at No 1 School of Technical Training (Boys) at RAF, Halton, in May 1923. Remarkably, Read would receive the Air Force Cross and two Bars during the course of his career. 'Willie' Read retired from the RAF with the rank of Wing Commander, on 17 May 1932. In anticipation of the outbreak of the Second World War, he was recalled to the service on 28 August 1939 and served again before finally retiring on 1 February 1941.

REDLER, Herbert Bolton

The son of Daniel Bolton Redler and Anne Pethick Redler, of Boschbeek, Newlands, Cape Town, South Africa, he was born in West Moncton, Somerset, in 1897. Living and working in London at the time, he enlisted as a Private soldier (Number 7596) into 28 Battalion, London Regiment (Artist Rifles). Picked out for a commission, he was gazetted Second Lieutenant to the RFC on 27 January 1917. His formal pilot training duly completed, he was confirmed and gazetted Flying Officer on 9 April following. Posted to 40 Squadron (Nieuport Scouts), he claimed three victories between 7 May and 14 July 1917. Redler next transferred to the SE5A-equipped 24 Squadron early in 1918, gaining a further seven victories before the end of April 1918, including, on 15 March 1918, sending down to his death the great German fighter Ace, Adolf von Tutschek. Redler returned to the UK for a well deserved rest, but was tragically killed in an aeroplane accident at Turnberry, Ayr, Scotland, on 21 June 1918, flying with Captain I H D Henderson MC (qv) in a DH9, 'D1018'. Redler's MC was announced in the *London Gazette* of 22 June 1918, the day after he was killed: 'For conspicuous gallantry and devotion to duty. He encountered four enemy two-seater machines, and attacking the lowest drove it to the ground with its engine damaged. Later, he attacked, one of five two-seater enemy machines and drove it down out of control. He has destroyed in all three enemy machines and driven three others down out of control. He continually attacked enemy troops and transport from a low altitude during operations, and showed splendid qualities of courage and determination throughout'.

Herbert Redler is buried in West Monkton (St Augustine) Churchyard, Somerset.

REES, Lionel Wilmot Brabazon VC

The son of Colonel Charles H Rees and Leonora Rees, of Caernarvon, North Wales, he was born on 31 July 1884. Educated at Colvall, at Eastbourne College (1898-01) and at the Royal Military Academy, Woolwich. Gazetted Second Lieutenant to the RGA on 23 December 1903. He was seconded to the Native Mountain Artillery, Sierra Leone in 1911, before returning to the UK. Next, he took flying lessons at his own expense, gaining his Royal Aero Club Certificate (Number 392) on a Bristol machine at the Bristol School, Larkhill, on 7 January 1913. He served again after this with the RGA in West Africa in 1913, this time being seconded to an artillery unit attached to the Nigeria Regiment, West African Frontier Force. Upon his return to the UK, he was seconded to the RFC on 10 August 1914. Promoted to Captain, Rees was posted to the CFS, Upavon, as an Instructor. He served later with 7 Squadron in the UK and with 11 Squadron (VFB5s). Rees accompanied '11' to France as a 'founder member' on 25 July 1915. Within days of his arrival on 28 July 1915, Rees and his Observer, Flight Sergeant J M Hargreaves, in FB5, '1649', were involved in a combat with a Fokker. On 31 August, an unusual incident occurred when Rees and his Observer, Flight Sergeant Hargreaves, fought an LVG, but then lost it in cloud as their engine spluttered. Rees immediately landed, re-fuelled, and not only took-off again, but actually succeeded in relocating the LVG they had fought and damaged earlier. This time they finished off the intruder, sending it spiralling down. Rees and Hargreaves continued to be heavily involved in various aerial skirmishing. On 21 September, the pair, in '1649', successfully confronted a large twin-nacelled machine, sending it down, 'smoking'. On 30 September, the pair, again in '1649', shot the wing off a Albatros C-type, sending it down into the British lines. Flight Sergeant Hargreaves received the Distinguished Conduct Medal, *London Gazette* of 16 November 1915. Rees' MC, with an almost identical citation to Hargreave's Distinguished Conduct Medal, was announced in the *London Gazette* of 29 November 1915: 'For conspicuous gallantry and skill on several occasions, notably the following:- On September 21, when flying a machine with one machine-gun, accompanied by Flight-Sergeant Hargreaves, he sighted a large German biplane with two machine-guns 2,000 feet below him. He spiralled down and dived at the enemy, who, having the faster machine, manoeuvred to get him broadside on and then opened heavy fire. In spite of this Captain Rees pressed his attack and apparently succeeding in hitting the enemy's engine, for the machine made a quick turn, glided some distance, and finally fell just inside the German lines near Herbecourt. On July 28 he attacked and drove down a hostile monoplane in spite of the fact that the main spar of his machine had been shot through and the rear spar shattered. On August 31, accompanied by Flight Sergeant Hargreaves, he fought a German machine more powerful than his own for three-quarters of an hour, then returned for more ammunition, and went out to attack again, finally bringing the enemy's machine down apparently wrecked'.

In November 1915, Rees returned to the UK to be promoted to Major, and appointed to the command of the CFS. This proved a short-lived appointment, as he was next, on 12 January 1916, ordered to the command of 32 Squadron (DH2s) then forming at Netheravon. Rees led '32' to France on 28 May 1916, and was subsequently credited with a total of eight victories between 28 July 1915 and 1 July 1916. On 1 July 1916, the opening day of the Battle of the Somme, Lionel Rees in DH2, '6015', was wounded in an unequal combat against a superior number of enemy machines, winning his Victoria Cross in the process. The citation for his VC, in the *London Gazette* of 5 August 1916, graphically describes the circumstances: 'For conspicuous gallantry and devotion to duty. While on flying duties Major Rees sighted what he thought to be a bombing party of our own machines returning home. He went up to escort them, but on getting nearer found they were a party of enemy machines, about ten in all. Major Rees was immediately attacked by one of them, and after a short encounter it disappeared behind the enemy lines damaged. Five others then attacked him at long range, but these he dispersed on coming to close quarters, after seriously damaging two. Seeing two others going westwards he gave chase, but on coming nearer he was seriously wounded in the thigh, causing him temporarily to lose control of his machine. He soon righted it, and immediately closed with the enemy, firing at close range of only a few yards, until all his ammunition was used up. He then returned home, landing his machine safely in our lines'.

Once recovered from his wounds, Rees was sent to represent the RFC at the British War Mission in the USA. On arrival in America, he was attached for duty to the aviation division of the Signal Corps of the American Army, as British Liaison Officer. He was awarded the Air Force Cross in the *London Gazette* of 2 November 1918 and, subsequently, appointed OBE in the Birthday Honours *London Gazette* of 3 June 1919. Rees was also honoured with the Freedom of the Borough of Caernarvon in 1919. Awarded Brevet of Lieutenant Colonel, he stayed on in the RAF after the war. Appointed ADC to King George V from 1925, he retired with the rank of Group Captain in 1931. Rees was re-employed during the Second World War, serving in Africa in 1941 and 1942. Lionel Rees VC, died on 28 September 1955.

REEVES, Archibald Charles

The younger son of Building Contractor, Charles R Reeves and Lucy Reeves (née Thompson), of 18 North Street, Wellingborough, Northamptonshire, he was born on 6 August 1895. Educated at Wellingborough Grammar School. After leaving school, he worked as a Slag Contractor's Assistant at the Wellingborough Iron Company Ltd. Gazetted Second Lieutenant to the RFC, via the Special Reserve, on 3 June 1916, he gained his Royal Aero Club Certificate (Number 3442) on 23 August following. His formal pilot training duly completed, he was confirmed and gazetted Flying Officer on 23 November 1916. Sent out to 4 Squadron just six days after putting up his 'Wings'. Reeves was Mentioned in Despatches in the *London Gazette* of 9 December 1916. His MC was announced in the *London Gazette* of 17 September 1917: 'For conspicuous gallantry and devotion to duty in artillery observation, contact patrols and reconnaissances. He has continually done very daring and excellent work at low altitudes with a fine disregard of hostile fire and adverse weather conditions, and has contributed information of the greatest value by his enterprise and fearlessness on all occasions'.

His tour with '4' ending on 18 September 1917, he returned to the Home Establishment to take up a series of instructing posts. Reeves received the insignia of his MC from the hand of the King at an investiture held at Buckingham Palace on 9 March 1918. He did not return to operational flying before the end of the war.

REEVES, James Heath

The son of Dr Alexander Reeves and Mrs Reeves, of Alvercote, near Tamworth, Staffordshire, he was born in Mount Pleasant, Liverpool, on 22 September 1897. Educated at Tamworth Grammar School until 1913. Articled as an Engineering Pupil with Messrs Thornewill and Warham, Burton on Trent, in 1913, he soon progressed to the Drawing Office in that firm. He enlisted as a Private soldier (Number 28582) into the Oxfordshire and Buckinghamshire Light Infantry in 1915. Picked out for a commission, he was gazetted Second Lieutenant to the RFC on 7 June 1917. His pilot training completed unusually quickly, he was confirmed and gazetted Flying Officer on 17 July following. Sent out to 52 Squadron (RE8s) in July 1917. He was wounded in action on 21 March 1918, the first day of the German spring offensive. His MC was announced in the *London Gazette* of 22 June 1918: 'For conspicuous gallantry and devotion to duty, in attacking enemy troops on the ground and in carrying out contact patrol work during operations. On one occasion he flew for two hours at a very low altitude, sometimes at only 50 feet, attacking enemy troops and transport. He was eventually severely wounded, but brought his machine back safely. He consistently showed great coolness and resource'.

Reeves would not return again to operational flying being demobilised from the RAF with the rank of Lieutenant on 20 September 1919.

REID, George Ranold Macfarlane

The son of successful gold prospector, George Macfarlane Reid and Gertrude Macquiston Reid of Prestwich, Ayrshire, Scotland, he was born in Largs on 25 October 1893. Educated at Routenburn and at Malvern College (1908-10). Although gazetted Second Lieutenant to 4 (Extra Reserve) Battalion, Argyll and Sutherland Highlanders on 15 August 1914, he actually served with 2 Battalion, Black Watch. Seconded to the RFC, he gained his Royal Aero Club Certificate (1900) on 16 October 1915. His formal pilot training duly completed, he was confirmed and gazetted Flying Officer on 15 November following. Reid accompanied FE2b-equipped 25 Squadron to France as a 'founder member' on 20 February 1916. Reid, flying with Lieutenant J A 'Ian' Mann, enjoyed a number of successes against enemy machines for which they both received the MC, announced in the *London Gazette* of 24 June 1916, although the composer of the citation completely confused the protagonists: 'For conspicuous gallantry and skill. In the course of seven days, 2nd Lts Mann [qv] as pilot [sic] and Reid as Observer [sic], attacked no less than eight enemy aeroplanes. They drove down four, three of which were seriously damaged. The remainder were driven off, one escaping by getting into a cloud'.

Reid served with '25' until August 1916, before transferring to 20 Squadron as a Flight Commander in the same month. The Bar to his MC came in the *London Gazette* of 25 November 1916: 'For conspicuous gallantry in action. He with his Observer pursued a hostile aeroplane for some six miles into the enemy's territory, and there shot it down. He has on many previous occasions done very fine work'.

The Observer referred to as Second Lieutenant was Londoner, Second Lieutenant L H Scott (qv), who also received the MC. Reid would eventually be presented with the insignia of his MC and Bar by the King at an investiture held at Buckingham Palace on 9 March 1918.

His tour with '20' completed in February 1917, he was, very briefly, placed in command of 9 Squadron (RE8s). Reid returned to the UK and was posted to the School of Special Flying, Gosport, where he was one of the first to use 'the Gosport Tube' method of communication between pupil and Instructor. Next, late in March 1917, he was appointed to the command of 18 Squadron. Reid's command of '18' extended to the following November, when he returned to the Home Establishment. In June 1918, Reid commanded 206 Squadron, a DH9-equipped day bombing unit based at Dunkirk, principally employed in bombing Bruges docks. He then took over command of 211 Squadron, another DH4 outfit. For his services as a Commanding Officer, he was awarded the Distinguished Service Order in the New Year *London Gazette* of 1 January 1919. He was also Mentioned in Despatches on three occasions during the Great War. Staying on in the RAF, his subsequent service, honours and appointments included: service with 206 and 47 Squadrons in Egypt; command of 99 Squadron, a home-based bomber unit, 1924; service in the Sudan from 1927 to 1929; RAF Staff College, 1930; Imperial Defence College, 1932; Air Attaché, British Embassy, Washington, USA, from 1933 to 1935; AOC, Air Apprentice School, Halton, from 1936 to 1938; AOC, British Forces, Aden, 1938-41; CB, 1941; Air Officer Administration, Flying Training Command; AOC, 54 Group RAF; AOC, West Africa, 1944-45. He married, in 1934, Leslie Livermore Washburne Wright of Washington, DC, with whom he had one son and one daughter. Reid was knighted (KCB), 1945, retiring from the RAF with the rank of Air Vice-Marshal in 1946. He was appointed Gentleman Usher to King George VI in 1952. After the King's death, he was appointed in the same capacity to Queen Elizabeth II. He became a Director of several gold mining companies in Australia. Sir Ranold later retired to Perth in Western Australia, dying there on 19 May 1991.

REID, Guy Patrick Spence

The son of Thomas Miller Reid and Lisette Reid (née Livings), of Puerto Orotava, Tenerife, Canary Islands, he was born on 18 May 1897. Educated at Borlase School. Gazetted Second Lieutenant to a Regular Army battalion of the Seaforth Highlanders on 11 August 1915, with an immediate secondment to the RFC. Gained his Royal Aero Club Certificate (Number 1693) on 4 September 1915. His formal pilot training duly completed, he was confirmed and gazetted Flying Officer on 21 October following. Accompanied the FE2b-equipped 20 Squadron to France as a 'founder member' on 23 January 1916. Gained five victories between 7 February and 6 September 1916, his first was also the first for 20 Squadron. His MC was announced in the *London Gazette* of 26 September 1916: 'For conspicuous skill and gallantry on many occasions. Captain Dixon-Spain [qv], with 2 Lt Reid as pilot, attacked and drove back a hostile machine. A few minutes later four hostile machines were seen, three of which were attacked one after another and driven back, the fourth being accounted for by another patrol. Another time they attacked two hostile machines, shot one down and drove the other back'.

On 11 November 1916, Reid, with his Gunner/Observer, 1 AM A M Alexander, came near to death when they were engaged by a number of enemy scouts. Alexander was wounded twice but Reid was unharmed, although badly shaken. His tour with '20' completed, Reid returned to the UK to take up a series of instructing posts. He was killed in a flying accident on 16 October 1917 and is buried in Lincoln (Newport) Cemetery, Lincolnshire. A memorial to Guy Reid can be seen in All Saints' Church, Tenerife.

REID, Robert Wolstenholme

The son of Mr and Mrs Reid, of 'The Deane', Stanmore, Middlesex, he was born on 22 February 1898. Educated at Mill Hill School (1911-16), where he was a member of the OTC. Admitted to the School of Instruction, Reading, straight from school, he was subsequently gazetted Second Lieutenant to the RFC, via the Special Reserve, on 15 July 1916. His pilot training duly completed, he was confirmed and gazetted Flying Officer on 19 October following. Sent out to FE2b-equipped 18 Squadron in France soon after qualifying for his 'Wings'. On 29 April 1917, Reid and his Observer, Second Lieutenant R C Doughty, in FE2b, 'A5466', on a photo-reconnaissance patrol, were attacked at 10,000 feet over Marquion-Barelle by four red enemy aircraft. By diving into a convenient cloud, Reid shook off all but one of his attackers, who persisted in chasing them down to 3,000 feet. Doughty managed just one shot at their tormentor before being wounded himself. Reid, still unscathed, eventually managed to escape the enemy machine's attentions and was able to steer the FE safely back to his home field. Reid's MC was announced in the *London Gazette* of 26 July 1917: 'For conspicuous gallantry and devotion to duty. He has done fine work in taking aeroplane photographs. His work has been carried out while flying at very low altitudes and often under very heavy machine-gun fire'.

Robert Reid survived the Great War.

REILLY, Sydney George (also known as Siegfried Rosenblum)

A shadowy figure who, apparently, started life as an American citizen by the name of 'Siegfried Rosenblum'. He lived with his wife at 120 Broadway, New York, before taking her previous married name, 'Reilly', as his own. It seems that Reilly worked for the British Secret Service before the Great War, and that his covert activities came to a temporary halt when the war came. In the early months of the war, a firm of international bankers invited him first to Japan and then to the USA as their Representative. Acting on behalf of the Imperial Russian Government, he was hired at an enormous salary to purchase the raw materials necessary to manufacture explosives. He spent only a short time in Japan before becoming established in New York (the USA still being a neutral country, of course) where he was kept busy buying the necessary scarce commodities in direct competition with the Germans. At this time, he set up his own intelligence network to monitor the commercial and political activities of the Germans in the US. It was not long before he was reapproached by British Intelligence to re-establish old links. Although happy to oblige on an occasional basis, his main commitment was to the locating, purchasing and shipping of essential materials to Russia. Reilly was said to be successful in uncovering and thwarting, a number of sabotage plots instigated by German agents within the borders of the USA. It has to be said that the British had an ambivalent attitude to such acts of sabotage, knowing, as they did, that incidents of this nature could help sway American opinion to the Allied cause. It has even been suggested by some conspiracy theorists, that not all the information Reilly may have uncovered was passed on to the American authorities in advance of sabotage attacks. The relatively large numbers of Americans joining the Canadian and British colours at this time, was indicative of the broad sympathies of the American people towards the Allied cause. Reilly, perhaps deciding that he had stood on the sidelines for too long, joined the RFC in Canada, although, in fact, his first posting was to Military Intelligence, Department 1c. He finally arrived in England with the rank of Acting Captain early in 1917. Following the uprising in Russia and the imminent consequent collapse of the Eastern Front, the Allies – and Britain in particular – were anxious to keep Russia in the War. Support in many forms was offered to the White Russian cause in the still ongoing and unresolved revolution, although, in the event, nothing could prevent the collapse of the front. Early in 1918, Reilly was sent to Russia with the code name, 'ST 1', to help pave the way for the planned Allied intervention. Such was the effectiveness of his 'cover', that at one point Reilly was arrested by the Royal Navy and locked up in the brig of HMS *Glory* then docked at Murmansk. Reilly spent nine months travelling around Russia, collecting intelligence in advance of the proposed Intervention. War Office records state that he was employed by them in conjunction with Foreign Office Special Missions from March 1918. He was also employed by the Foreign Office from December 1918 to April 1919. A 'Protection Certificate' for Russia was issued by the Foreign Office. He was recommended for the Distinguished Service Order but, in the event, received the MC. Actually, it is very surprising in view of the nature of his work, that any award was publically acknowledged and announced. Such was his perceived effectiveness, that a sentence of death was said to have been passed upon him by the Bolsheviks in 1918. The announcement of Reilly's award and of other special recipients of the MC was made in the *London Gazette* of 12 February 1919: 'HM the King has been graciously pleased to approve of the undermentioned rewards for distinguished services rendered in connection with military operations in the field. Awarded the MC: Lieutenant Norman Dewhurst, Royal Munster Fusiliers; Lieutenant George Alexander Hill, 4/Manchester Regiment att RAF; Second Lieutenant Sydney George Reilly, RAF; Lieutenant George Gibson Tomlin, RAF'.

Reilly left the RAF, via the Unemployed List, on 24 April 1920, still only ranked as a Second Lieutenant. Quite how he spent the next few years is not clear, but he was killed on 28 September 1925, near the village of Allekul, Russia, by OGPU (State Security) troops. So much of his life was shrouded in mystery, it is perhaps unsurprising that so, too, were the circumstances of his death. This, and some of his supposed exploits, were portrayed in the TV series 'Reilly, Ace of Spies'.

RHYS DAVIDS, Arthur Percival Foley

The son of Professor Thomas William Rhys Davids, FBA, and Caroline Augusta Rhys Davids (née Foley), D.Lit, of Middleshaws, Chipstead, near Redhill, Surrey, he was born on 26 September 1897. Educated at Ashton-upon-Mersey High School for Boys, at Summer Fields and at Eton (1911-16), where he was King's Scholar and Captain of the School. Academically gifted, he enjoyed great success throughout, and was awarded the prestigious Newcastle Scholarship in the spring of 1916. He was elected to a Domus Exhibition in Classics scholarship at Balliol College, Oxford, in December 1915, but instead of going up, he went into the Army, being gazetted Second Lieutenant (on probation) to the RFC on 28 August 1916. His pilot training duly completed, he was confirmed and gazetted Flying Officer on 2 January 1917. A Scout Pilot course at Turnberry was followed in March 1917 by a posting to the newly forming 56 Squadron, then at London Colney. Commanded by Major R G Blomfield, and with Flight Commanders of the calibre of Albert Ball (qv), E L 'Feet' Foot (qv) and Ian H D Henderson (qv), the SE5-equipped '56' was obviously destined for great things. Arthur accompanied 56 Squadron to France as a 'founder member' on 7 April 1917. Rhys Davids' brilliant and reckless courage and his 25 victories achieved between 23 May and 11 October 1917, including two 'trios', and three 'doubles' on single days, earned him repeated distinctions. On 23 September 1917, he was involved in one of the greatest aerial combats of all time when a galaxy of Aces, including McCudden, Bowman, Hoidge, and Maybery, fought the brilliant German Ace, Werner Voss, who, single-handedly, dealt out as good as he got until finally falling to Rhys Davids' fire. In the same engagement, Rhys Davids also shot down another German Ace, Leutnant Karl Menckhoff, who had come to Voss' aid. The first of his MCs was announced in the *London Gazette* of 18 July 1917: 'For conspicuous gallantry and devotion. On many occasions he has shot down hostile machines and put others out of action, frequently pursuing to low altitudes. On all occasions his fearlessness and dash have been most marked'.

The Bar to his MC came in the *London Gazette* of 17 September 1917: 'For conspicuous gallantry and devotion to duty while on offensive patrols. He has in all destroyed four enemy aircraft, and driven down many others out of control. In all his combats his gallantry and skill have been most marked, and on one occasion he shot down an enemy pilot who had accounted for twenty-nine Allied machines. His offensive spirit and initiative have set a magnificent example to all'.

He was also Mentioned in Despatches and awarded the Distinguished Service Order, in the *London Gazette* of 27 October 1917, details in the *Gazette* of 18 March 1918. In early October 1917, Arthur was singled out by General Trenchard and his aide, Maurice Baring, for yet another, entirely unexpected, distinction, he was to have his portrait painted by the war artist, Major, later Sir William Orpen, RA. On 27 October 1917, Rhys Davids in SE5A, 'B31', during a routine patrol, was shot down and killed during an aerial combat over Polterrjebrug by Leutnant Karl Gallwitz of Jasta 2, the fifth of the German Ace's eventual ten victories. In a flash of prescience, Rhys Davids had foretold of his death to Maurice Baring at their last meeting around the time of the Orpen portrait sitting. Arthur Rhys Davids' remains were never recovered and, hence, he is commemorated on the Flying Services Memorial, Arras, France.

RICE, Bernard Curtis

The eldest of the three sons of Dr Edward Rice and Mrs Rice of 'Gable Ends', Allesley, near Coventry, he was born in 1891 at St Giles, Oxford. Educated privately. Along with his younger brother, Edward (qv), with whom he had been apprenticed to the Daimler Motor Company, he enlisted as a Private soldier (Number MS-3068) into the Army Service Corps on 8 August 1914, just four days into the war. Both boys were able to drive cars and ride motor cycles, comparatively rare skills in those days, and were almost immediately employed transporting supplies and messages for the British Expeditionary Force in France and Flanders, thus earning the 1914 Star. Bernard actually served with the BEF as an Army Service Corps motor cyclist from15 August 1914 to 26 August 1915. Picked out for a commission, he was gazetted Second Lieutenant to the RFC, via the Special Lists, on 27 August 1915. He trained as an Observer and was sent out as a Probationary to the BE2c-equipped 2 Squadron in September 1915, just in time to face the Fokker menace. His 'apprenticeship' satisfactorily completed, he was formally confirmed and gazetted Flying Officer (Observer) on 22 November 1915. Having been constantly and heavily involved with 2 Squadron's operations over the Western Front, he next decided to train as a Pilot, gaining his Royal Aero Club Certificate (Number 2698) on 2 April 1916. He flew as a Pilot with BE2e-equipped 8 Squadron in 1917, sometimes with Second Lieutenant A C Heaven (qv) acting as his Observer. Rice's MC was announced in the *London Gazette* of 18 June 1917: 'For conspicuous gallantry and devotion to duty. While flying at a low altitude he located several enemy batteries. He was attacked by enemy machines and, although under heavy fire from the ground, succeeded in driving them off. He has on numerous occasions obtained the most valuable information'.

Bernard and Edward Rice were subsequently presented with the insignia of their MCs by the King at an investiture held at Buckingham Palace on 9 March 1918. He was also Mentioned in Despatches on one occasion during the Great War. Having survived the war, Bernard returned to the Motor Trade, becoming a dealer in his own right.

NB: The RAF Museum Hendon has his medals in its collection: MC, 1914 Star with Bar (MS-3068 Pte B C Rice ASC), *British War Medal 1914-20, and Victory Medal 1914-19 with MID* (Capt RFC).

RICE, Edward Arthur Beckton

The middle of the three sons of Dr Edward Rice and Mrs Rice, of 'Gable Ends', Allesley, near Coventry, he was born on 19 December 1893 in Oxford. Educated privately. Along with his elder brother, Bernard (qv), with whom he had been apprenticed to the Daimler Motor Company, he enlisted as a Private soldier into the Army Service Corps on 8 August 1914, just four days into the war. Both boys were able to drive cars and ride motor cycles, comparatively rare skills in those days and were almost immediately employed transporting supplies and messages for the British Expeditionary Force in France and Flanders, thus earning the 1914 Star. Eddie Rice injured his leg carrying despatches on a motor-cycle in November 1914 and was returned to the UK for treatment. Upon recovery, he was gazetted Second Lieutenant to the RFC, via the Special Reserve, on 8 June 1915, having gained his Royal Aero Club Certificate (Number 1308) on the same day. His formal pilot training duly completed, he was confirmed and gazetted Flying Officer on 23 August following. Rice accompanied 21 Squadron (RE7s) to France as a 'founder member' on 23 January 1916. On 8 June following, Rice and his Observer, Lieutenant W Russell, in RE7, '2375', were attacked by an enemy machine whilst returning from an aborted patrol due to their engine misfiring and generally 'acting up'. Both Russell and the faulty engine were struck by machine-gun bullets and Rice was obliged to glide into a forced landing. A steady and reliable Reconnaissance Pilot, Rice had been promoted to A/Captain and Flight Commander by the time his MC was announced in the *London Gazette* of 18 July 1917: 'For conspicuous gallantry and devotion to duty when leading photographic reconnaissances. Though repeatedly attacked, he led the formation to its objective on every occasion with the utmost skill and determination, and has set a very fine example of leadership in no less than eleven successful operations'.

Edward and Bernard Rice were subsequently presented with the insignia of their MCs by the King at an investiture held at Buckingham Palace on 9 March 1918. He married, in 1917, Dora Marguette Harman-Brown (later OBE) with whom he had one daughter. Staying on in the RAF after the war, he would serve in Germany with the Army of Occupation in 1919. Carving out a distinguished career, his many honours, appointments and promotions included: service in Iraq, 1920 to 1922; Wing Commander, 1928; service in Egypt and Iraq, including command of 216 Squadron, 1929 -34; OC, RAF Training at Calshot, in 1934; Group Captain, 1934; Air Commodore, 1940; AOC, West Africa, 1941-42; Air Vice-Marshal, 1943; AOC, 1 Group, Bomber Command, 1942 to 1945; CB 1944; knighted (KBE), 1946. Having retired from the RAF in 1946, he subsequently became the Deputy Director of Civil Aviation in India. Air Vice-Marshal Edward Rice lived at Highweek, South Devon, and died there on 14 April 1948.

RICHARDS, Cecil Roy

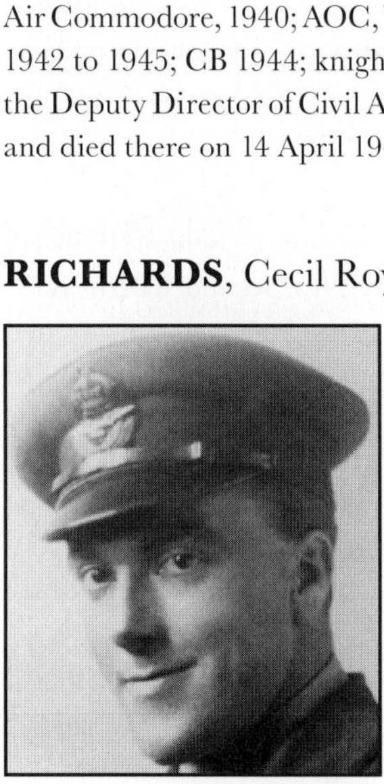

From Garvoc, Victoria, Australia, he was born on 24 July 1893 in North Carlton, Melboune. He volunteered for, and served with, the AIF in Egypt, in Gallipoli and in France, before being accepted as a Cadet into the flying service in the closing weeks of 1916. Gazetted Second Lieutenant to the RFC, via the Special Reserve, on 17 March 1917. His formal pilot training duly completed, he was confirmed and gazetted Flying Officer on 22 May following. Sent out to FE2d-equipped 20 Squadron shortly after qualifying for his 'Wings', he gained 12 victories between 14 June and 16 August 1917, including a 'quartet' on 17 July. On the intervening 6 July 1917, Richards and his Observer, Second Lieutenant A E Wear, in FE2d, 'A6448', were involved in a combat with up to 40 enemy machines. In this fight, Manfred von Richthofen, the Red Baron himself, was hit in the head and lost consciousness, barely recovering in time to land his red Albatros. On 19 August 1917, Richards and his Observer, Second Lieutenant S F Thompson, in FE2d, 'B1890', were wounded and their machine shot down over Le Quesnoy by Leutnant Ernst Hess of Jasta 28, the ninth of the German Ace's eventual 17 victories. Both injured men were taken to hospital by their German captors. Richards' MC was announced in the *London Gazette* of 17 September 1917: 'For conspicuous gallantry and devotion to duty when on offensive patrols in attacking and shooting down hostile machines. On one occasion he shot down four in one day, displaying great dash and a fine offensive spirit'.

Richards would be repatriated on 2 January 1919, after which he was able to return to Australia. Joined Shell Oil Co in Australia in 1920 and later became Manager of Shell in Adelaide. Cecil Richards died on 28 March 1973 in Gleneig, South Australia.

RICHARDSON, Herbert Brian

The third of the three sons of Brewer and Maltster, Walter M Richardson and Ellen Richardson, of Eastholme House, Ashford, Kent, he was born on 27 May 1898. Educated at Oxford High School (1910-14). After service as a Trooper with the Queen's Own Oxfordshire Hussars (TF), he was gazetted Second Lieutenant to the RFC on 21 June 1917. His formal pilot training duly completed, he was confirmed and gazetted Flying Officer on 17 September following. Sent out to 24 Squadron (SE5As) in France on 14 November 1917. After a slow start, he went on to achieve no less than 15 victories between 18 February and 4 April 1918, including three Pfalz DIIIs sent down on 21 March 1918, the first day of the great German spring offensive. His MC was announced in the *London Gazette* of 22 June 1918: 'For conspicuous gallantry and devotion to duty. While on patrol he attacked a formation of eight enemy, one of which he destroyed. On another occasion he engaged two enemy two-seater machines, and destroyed one of them. He has destroyed six enemy machines and driven down five others out of control, and has done valuable work in attacking enemy troops on the ground. He has consistently displayed great courage and skill'.

After the war, he was awarded a short-service commission in the RAF, which lasted until 1921. Next, he was appointed a Flying Instructor to the Spanish Government. A married man by this time, he was killed on 14 February 1922 in the same air crash at Cuatro Vientos, Madrid, in which F J Ortweiler, MC (qv) also died.

RICHARDSON, James Temple

From Bishop Auckland, Durham, he was born in 1895. Educated at North Eastern Counties School (1908-11). Gazetted Second Lieutenant to 6 Battalion, Durham Light Infantry (TF), on 20 July 1915. Seconded to the RFC on 10 October 1917, he trained as an Observer and, following probationary service, was confirmed and gazetted Flying Officer (Observer) on 18 December 1917. Sent out to France and FE2b-equipped 102 Squadron on 18 January 1918. His intensive tour with '102', a night-bombing squadron, completed, he returned to the Home Establishment on 6 April 1918. His MC was announced in the *London Gazette* of 22 June 1918: 'For conspicuous gallantry and devotion to duty. During one night he made three successive flights over the enemy's lines, dropping a large number of bombs on transport and attacking ground targets with machine-gun fire. He has carried out upwards of sixty night-bombing raids, and has himself dropped over five tons of bombs. By his keenness and skill as an observer he has been of the greatest assistance to the pilots with whom he has flown'.

Richardson was subsequently injured in a flying accident on Martlesham Heath on 6 August 1918 and this may well have precluded him from returning to the front before the end of the war. He finally left the service, via the Unemployed List, on 20 February 1919.

RICHARDSON, Lancelot Lytton

From Bereen Barrara, New South Wales, Australia, he was born on 18 October 1895. Gazetted Second Lieutenant to the RFC, via the Special Lists, on 28 December 1915. Gained his Royal Aero Club Certificate (Number 2363) on 30 January 1916. His formal pilot training duly completed, he was confirmed and gazetted Flying Officer on 16 May 1916. Served fleetingly with 18 Squadron from 18 May 1916, before transferring to FE2b equipped 25 Squadron on 3 June following. Richardson proceeded to achieve five victories between 17 June and 20 July 1916. Later on the day of his fifth victory, Richardson and his Observer, 1 AM Leslie Simpson Court, in FE2b, '6932', were involved in a combat with two enemy machines. Their FE was shot up and Richardson was wounded, although he managed to get down safely. Court would subsequently become an 'Ace Gunner', achieving five victories and receiving the Médaille Militaire from the French, *London Gazette* of 1 May 1917. He would also be commissioned but, sadly, died on 10 December 1918, whilst serving with 26 Training Depot Station in the UK. Richardson returned to duty with '25' on 24 January 1917 and was soon promoted to A/Captain and Flight Commander. He added two further victories to his 'score' before, on 13 April 1917, Bloody April, he and his Observer of the day, Second Lieutenant Douglas Clark Wollen, were shot down and killed by Oberleutnant Hans Klein of Jasta 4 – the seventh of the German Ace's eventual 22 victories. Richardson's MC was announced posthumously in the *London Gazette* of 11 May 1917: 'For conspicuous gallantry and devotion to duty. He attacked a formation of five hostile scouts, and brought two of them down. On another occasion, although himself wounded, he destroyed two hostile machines, and drove down, damaged, at least two others'.

Lance Richardson is buried in Bois-Carre British cemetery, Thelus, France.

RICKARDS, Gilbert Braithwaite

The son of Mr and Mrs W H Rickards, of Carlton Lodge, Whalley Range, he was born in Manchester in April 1869. Educated at Uppingham (1882-84). Gazetted Second Lieutenant to a Regular Army battalion of the Royal Munster Fusiliers on 10 November 1888. He later served with the Royal Dublin Fusiliers, before relinquishing his commission in the 1890s. When the South African War came in 1899, Rickards volunteered and was given a Captaincy in 42 (Hertfordshire) Company, 12 Battalion, Imperial Yeomanry. Arriving in South Africa early in 1900, he was wounded in action near Johannesburg on 31 August following. Returning to civilian life after the Boer War, he developed an interest in aviation and gained his Royal Aero Club Certificate (Number 400) on a Bristol machine at the Bristol School on 21 January 1913. Despite his advanced years, he was gazetted Second Lieutenant to the RFC, via the Special Reserve, on 5 August 1914. His formal pilot training duly completed, he was confirmed and gazetted Flying Officer on 1 December following. Sent out to Egypt on 12 December 1914, he subsequently served with 30 Squadron in Mesopotamia. His MC was announced in the *London Gazette* of 29 October 1915 (no citation), surely, at 46, the oldest recipient of a 'Flying MC'.

His tour with '30' ended on 20 May 1916 and he was next promoted to A/Major and appointed to the command of 21 RS on 26 May 1916. During his period as CO, 21 RS, he was, in July 1916, given temporary command of 20 Reserve Wing. His tour with 21 RS coming to an end on 8 April 1917, he reverted to Staff duties for the remainder of the war. Gilbert Rickards died in October 1922.

RIDLEY, Claude Alward

The son of Solicitor, Louis C Ridley and Mrs Ridley, of Newcastle-upon-Tyne and Holland Park, London, he was born in Sunderland on 15 November 1897. Educated at Dr Roscoe's School, Harrogate, at Colet Court, at St Paul's, London (1911-13), and, subsequently, at Sandhurst. Worked, pe-war, at the Napier Motor Works. Ridley received a temporary commission in the RFC in 1914, but resigned it when offered a place at the Royal Military College. From Sandhurst he was gazetted Second Lieutenant to the Royal Fusiliers on 17 April 1915. Seconded to the RFC, he gained his Royal Aero Club Certificate (Number 1458) on 9 July 1915. His formal pilot training duly completed, he was confirmed and gazetted Flying Officer on 7 August 1915. Sent out to 3 Squadron in France soon after qualifying for his 'Wings', he was soon involved in a number of aerial combats. On 5 September 1915, Ridley and his Observer of the day, Second Lieutenant C T Cleaver (qv), in Morane L, '1863', narrowly escaped death when they were left virtually defenceless after their machine gun failed during a combat with two Aviatiks over Lille. One of the Aviatiks relentlessly pursued the Morane, which received between 40 and 50 hits into its fuselage and wings. Ridley was wounded in the foot, but was still able to guide his stricken machine safely down. Cleaver, who would later go on to win an MC and Bar, also a Distinguished Flying Cross, was, amazingly, unscathed, despite the hail of lead to which they had been subjected. After recovering from his wound in the UK, Ridley was next posted for Home Defence service with 19 Reserve Aeroplane Squadron, his flight operating out of Joyce Green aerodrome. On the night of 31 March/1 April 1916, the German Imperial Navy launched a five-strong Zeppelin attack on targets in London and in East Anglia. One of the Zeppelins, *L15*, was seen first by Ridley at 2136 hours, its vast shape caught in the beam of searchlights. Striving to gain height and close the considerable distance between them, Claude Ridley fired 20 rounds from extreme range before the airship slipped the beam of the searchlights and disappeared into stygian darkness. *L15* would also be attacked by Kiwi Alfred deBathe Brandon (qv), but would eventually be brought down into the sea off Margate by anti-aircraft guns based at Purfleet. For his efforts in this incident, Ridley was awarded the MC, announced in the *London Gazette* of 16 May 1916: 'For conspicuous gallantry and good work during Zeppelin raids'.

For their part in the destruction of *L15*, Ridley and Brandon would also be presented with a Gold Medal, and the thanks of the citizens of London, by the Lord Mayor of the capital city. Ridley went next to France in July 1916, this time as a 'founder member' of the newly formed 60 Squadron. On 3 August following, Ridley, in Morane LA, 'A143', was on a spy-dropping mission when his engine failed over Cambrai. Forced to land near to Douai, Ridley was provided with civilian clothes by the French spy he was carrying, and advised to try to evade capture! After first taking note of the area surrounding Douai aerodrome, including watching young German aviators taking flying lessons and, remarkably, witnessing a BE brought down in the vicinity and its British crew marched off to captivity, he set out for the Dutch frontier. Unable to speak either French or German, he assumed the role of a deaf mute. He did occasionally take a chance by revealing himself as a British officer to potentially friendly Frenchmen, before enlisting their help. His luck held, the subterfuge worked, and so he was able to slip across the Dutch frontier on 8 October, a little more than two months after his crash-landing. Following an exhaustive and valuable de-briefing, he was sent home for a private audience with King George V at Buckingham Palace. Back in France within days, he was decorated in the field with the Distinguished Service Order by General Haig, the formal announcement of which appeared in the *London Gazette* of 14 November 1916. Ridley was also Mentioned in Despatches on five occasions during the Great War. Granted a permanent commission in the RAF after the war, he had attained the rank of Squadron Leader by the time of his retirement on 19 December 1928. He married, in 1925, Lillias Elizabeth McAlpine, with whom he had one son and two daughters. An all-round sportsman, he won the lightweight title in the RAF boxing championships in India for three years in succession. He was also a brilliant amateur rider and racehorse trainer, good enough, in fact, to ride in the Grand National. Ridley lived and trained horses at Bleak House, de Warrenne Road, Lewes, Sussex. Recalled for service with the RAF in 1939, he was, for a time, personal assistant to Air Chief Marshal Sir Arthur Tedder. In January 1941, he formed the Leeds University Air Squadron and became its first Commanding Officer. Ridley was promoted to the rank of Wing Commander shortly before he died, at the Dorchester Hotel, Park Lane, London, on 27 June 1942. Wing Commander Claude Ridley is buried in Stow Maries (SS Mary and Margaret) Churchyard, Essex.

RIGBY, Harry Alexander

From Melbourne, Victoria, Australia, he was born on 2 November 1897, at St Kilda. Educated at Wesley College (1910-15), where he was a Sergeant in the school's Cadet Force. Having travelled to the UK with the express purpose of joining the flying service, he gained his Royal Aero Club Certificate (Number 2651) at his own expense on 1 April 1916. Admitted a Cadet almost immediately, he was subsequently gazetted Second Lieutenant to the RFC on 27 May 1916. His formal pilot training duly completed, he was confirmed and gazetted Flying Officer on 15 July following. Posted to the FE8-equipped 40 Squadron then at Gosport, he accompanied the unit to France as a 'founder member' on 2 August 1916. After just a month's service at the front, he was taken ill and forced to return to the UK for medical treatment. Following a prolonged absence, he joined 1 Squadron at the front on 31 January 1918, with promotion to A/Captain and Flight Commander following on 11 April 1918. Coming into his own at last, he achieved six victories between 13 March and 11 May 1918, before again falling ill and being invalided back to the UK on 21 May as a consequence. His MC was announced in the *London Gazette* of 22 June 1918: 'For conspicuous gallantry and devotion to duty. He has carried out many low-flying bombing raids, obtaining direct hits on enemy troops, hutments and camps. On one occasion, after attacking a large column of enemy infantry on a road with machine-gun fire, he attacked and shot down in flames, a hostile scout. His work has always been carried out with the utmost keenness and determination'.

Rigby finally left the RAF, via the Unemployed List, in June 1919.

RILEY, George Raby

The son of Mr and G W Riley, of 114 West Side, Clapham Common, London, he was born on 23 February 1899. Educated at the City of London School. Accepted as a Cadet into the flying service straight from school, he was subsequently gazetted Second Lieutenant to the RFC on 14 August 1917. Gained his Royal Aero Club Certificate (Number 5205) on 7 September 1917. His formal pilot training duly completed, he was confirmed and gazetted Flying Officer on 12 December following. Earmarked as the best at a course for aspirants to single-seater Scout Squadrons, he was sent to France and the Sopwith Camel-equipped 3 Squadron commanded by Major R Raymond-Barker (qv) on his 19 birthday, 23 February 1918. Riley quickly proved a brave and determined Pilot, being especially aggressive in attacking ground targets. On 22 March 1918, he claimed his first victory, an Albatros DV, out of control near Havrincourt Wood. Four days later he destroyed an LVG.C, and, on 12 April, an Albatros north of Pozières. On 8 April 1918, he opened his account as a top 'balloon buster', sending one down in flames over Mory, the first of five such victories against those heavily defended and thus most hazardous of targets. On 20 April, '3' was engaged by von Richtofen's 'Flying Circus'. After a confused melée, 3 Squadron's CO, Major

Richard Raymond-Barker MC, and Riley's colleague, Second Lieutenant D G 'Babe' Lewis, were shot down by the Red Baron himself, for what proved to be the Maestro's penultimate and final victories. Riley, meanwhile, was himself shot about and wounded in the arm and shoulder by Leutnant Hans Weiss of Jasta 11, but still managed to regain his base and crashland. On the following day, 21 April 1918, Riley was sent home to recover and Manfred von Richthofen was killed by a single bullet through the chest, fired, almost certainly, by an Australian machine gunner on the ground. When Riley returned to the front, he shared his tented accommodation and flew in company with a recently joined American Pilot, Albert McManus, who enjoyed the squadron identification 'U'. As Riley's identification was 'S', McManus delighted in telling his mother in letters home, that he enjoyed flying with Riley because when they did, they spelt, 'US'. McManus' diary includes several mentions of Riley, including: '18 July, Riley and I chased a Hun two-seater clear to his aerodrome and then didn't get him.... We went for a balloon on our way back and deflated it, but couldn't set it on fire. The Observers jumped out in their parachutes'. And, on 1 August: 'About 70 machines went 18 miles into Hunland and blew up one of the largest aerodromes the Huns have. I was the first machine on the leader's left and Riley was on his right. We each had four 25lb bombs and we dropped them on hangars and sheds, destroying and setting fire to the buildings. We bombed and machine-gunned the Hun from 100 feet and just about ruined him'.

Riley's MC was announced in the *London Gazette* of 16 September 1918: 'For conspicuous gallantry and devotion to duty. He obtained four direct hits on a long line of enemy transport and afterwards caused havoc amongst them with his machine-gun. Several times he attacked troops and transport from low altitude, also he brought down one enemy machine and drove another down out of control'.

Riley continued to add to his personal tally, including, on 21 August 1918, sending down a Fokker DVII into the Allied lines. Following a spell of leave, he returned to France and, on 27 September 1918, claimed three balloons destroyed on the same day – an achievement equalled by only two other RFC/RAF Pilots. On the following day, he achieved his 13th and final victory, his combat report described the circumstances, thus: 'Whilst on low bombing, I saw eight EA below at 3,000 feet, I dropped my bombs and attacked. Picking out a Fokker, I dived at him and he spiralled down. He pulled out at 2,000 feet, I got under his tail and fired a good burst of 100 rounds at very close range. EA immediately cart wheeled and began falling out of control. I last saw him diving vertically'.

Promoted to A/Captain and Flight Commander on 14 October 1918, he ended the war in command of 'C' Flight. George Riley was awarded the Distinguished Flying Cross in the *London Gazette* of 8 February 1919, mainly for his balloon busting exploits. Riley finally left the RAF, via the Unemployed List, in April 1919. He was known to be living in Croydon in 1964.

NB: His medals were offered for sale in Spink Numismatic Circular, *June 1999: MC (engraved:* Lt George Raby Riley, 3 Sqd RFC 27/3/1918*), Distinguished Flying Cross, British War Medal 1914-20, and Victory Medal 1914-19* (Capt RAF).

ROBARTS, Geoffrey Ward

From Durban, South Africa, he was born on 17 April 1889. Living and working in the UK when war came on 4 August 1914, he enlisted as a Trooper into King Edward's Horse just four days later. Picked out for a commission, he was gazetted Second Lieutenant to the Royal Horse Artillery, via the Special Reserve, on 28 April 1915. Seconded to the RFC in July 1915, he gained his Royal Aero Club Certificate (Number 1948) on 17 September following. His formal pilot training duly completed, he was confirmed and gazetted Flying Officer on 2 December 1915. Robarts accompanied FE2b-equipped 22 Squadron to France as a 'founder member' on 1 April 1916. On 24 September 1916, Robarts and his Observer of the day, Canadian Second Lieutenant John Scott Williams (qv), brought down two enemy machines in quick succession. Both men received the MC, announced in the *London Gazette* of 14 November 1916: 'For conspicuous skill and gallantry when attacking hostile machines. On one occasion, when on offensive patrol, he brought down two machines'.

His tour with '22' completed, he returned to the Home Establishment to take up instructing duties. On 24 March 1917, Robarts, promoted to A/Captain and Flight Commander, returned to the front as a 'founder member' of 66 Squadron (Sopwith Pups). On 8 April 1917, Robarts and his colleagues, C C S Montgomery and A J Lucas, broke up a patrol of six Halberstadt Scouts, driving three of them down out of control. On either 7 or 8 July 1917, Robarts in Pup, 'B1758', on offensive patrol over the Somme valley, was shot up, badly wounded and forced to crashland at Bailleul. Robarts was hit in the lower jaw, which was badly fractured, and in the right eye, which severely impaired his sight. He was also wounded in the right thigh, but that was much more of a routine injury. The severely disfigured Robarts embarked upon a long course of medical treatment. By 1920, he was able to take up some light duties at the Air Ministry and even attempted to return to flying, but in vain. He finally relinquished his commission, with the rank of Captain, on 1 April 1920.

ROBB, Hugh Anselm Boulton

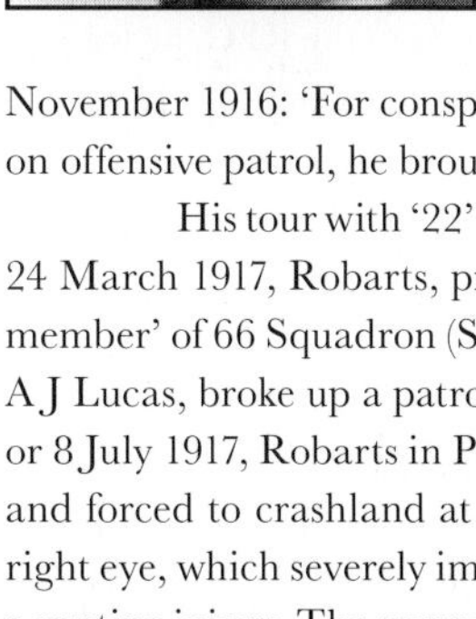

The son of John Montague C Robb and Florence Robb (née Boughton), of Chitty Place, Bramshott, Hampshire, he was born in Liphook, Hampshire, on 8 February 1897. Educated at Eton (1910-15). He learnt to fly at his parent's expense at the Beatty School, on Maurice Farman Shorthorns, gaining his Royal Aero Club Certificate (Number 1565) on 29 July 1915. The acquisition of his 'ticket' secured his acceptance into the flying service and he was gazetted Second Lieutenant to the RFC, via the Special Reserve, on 4 September 1915. His formal pilot training duly completed, he was confirmed and gazetted Flying Officer on 15 December following. After enjoying a short leave, he was sent out for artillery observation duties to 3 Squadron on 29 December 1915. Once he had familiarised himself with his duties and with the Morane Parasol, Robb would be kept extremely busy for the rest of the year, particularly prior to, and then during, the Battle of the Somme which commenced on 1 July 1916. His MC was announced in the *London Gazette* of 14 November 1916: 'For conspicuous gallantry and devotion to duty. He has done fine artillery work in all weathers. On one occasion, while flying a new type of machine, his engine failed, but he glided it back over the lines under heavy fire, and landed his machine without damage on ground pitted with holes'.

His long tour with '3' completed, he had accumulated 331 hours, 50 minutes flying time, he returned to the Home Establishment on 8 March 1917. Next, he was tasked with testing new and repaired machines in aircraft acceptance parks and training squadrons before, in August 1917, being promoted to A/Major and posted over to Canada in a similar capacity. After the war, he was awarded the Air Force Cross, *London Gazette* of 1 January 1919, for his work in the hazardous and exacting aircraft testing field. Returning to the UK in March 1919, he commanded the CFS at Upavon for two months before finally leaving the RAF.

ROBBINS, Charles Robinson

The youngest of the four sons of Dr Tom Wiltshire Robbins, MD, and Evangeline Annie Robbins (née Corke), of 142 St Albans Road, Watford, he was born in Maidstone, Kent, in 1897. Educated at Watford Grammar School (1907-10) and at Framlingham (1911-14), where he sub-edited *The Framlinghamian*, won various prizes for Maths, Science and Modern Languages, and was a member of the OTC (Sergeant). Robbins enlisted as a Private soldier into 18 Battalion (University and Public Schools) Royal Fusiliers, in 1914. Picked out for a commission, he was gazetted Second Lieutenant to the Royal Field Artillery on 27 October 1915. Seconded to the RFC, he trained as an Observer and was sent out as a Probationary to the BE2c-equipped 15 Squadron in December 1915. On 19 January 1916, Robbins and his Pilot, Captain P C Maltby, in BE2c, '2694', were extremely fortunate to survive a combat with a Fokker, two Aviatiks and two Albatroses. On 25 April 1916, Robbins and his Pilot of the day, Lieutenant A B Adams, in a BE2c, spotted, for the first time, an elaborate and formidable Third Line trench system constructed by the Germans along a line through Ablainzevelle-Irles-Le Sars-Flers. Their reconnaissance was completed unhindered, thanks to the cover given by their escorts from their own and from 24 Squadron. Robbins' probationary period satisfactorily completed, he was confirmed and gazetted Flying Officer (Observer) on 1 May 1916. His MC was announced in the New Year *London Gazette* of 1 January 1917 (no citation). Although no formal citation was published in the *Gazette*, research has unearthed the original recommendation for the award: 'C R Robbins. From December 1915 to July 1916 he was employed as an observer in a Corps squadron. He invariably showed conspicuous ability in carrying out his duties in co-operation with artillery'.

Robbins next trained as a Pilot and was subsequently awarded a Distinguished Flying Cross in the *London Gazette* of 8 February 1919 for, amongst other things, 'flying at a very low altitude in face of intense hostile fire, and dispersing a body of enemy infantry, his machine riddled with bullets'.

ROBERTS, Elmer Peter

The son of Poultry Farmer, William H S Roberts and Mrs Roberts, of Little London, Waldron, East Sussex, he was born in Uckfield, Sussex, in 1892. Roberts enlisted into the RFC in August 1914 (Number 1689), having learnt to fly at his own expense and gained his Royal Aero Club Certificate (Number 889) on 29 August 1914. He accompanied the original RFC contingent to France in August 1914, thus earning the 1914 Star. Despite holding a 'ticket', Roberts was used as a Gunner/Observer and, by the summer of 1915, was flying as such with the rank of Corporal, with 3 Squadron. Whilst patrolling during an intense artillery bombardment on 25 September 1915 – the opening day of the Battle of Loos – Roberts reported actually seeing a shell travelling through the air close to his Morane (RFC Communiqué No 14, 10 October 1915). The advent of the Fokker menace had started to shift the nature of aerial combat from the largely inconclusive to the deadly conclusive. On 10 October 1915, Roberts and his Pilot of the day, Lieutenant Harold Richard Johnson, West Kent Yeomanry, attached RFC, in Morane L, '1874', were attacked from behind whilst engrossed in taking photographs over Hulluch. Roberts, armed only with a rifle, was hit in three places but, fortunately, Johnson retained control over the Morane and was able to bring it back to base. Johnson, from Tunbridge Wells, Kent, lucky on this occasion, would be killed in a flying accident three months later on 19 January 1916. The wounded Roberts' efforts were recognised by the award of a Distinguished Conduct Medal, *London Gazette* of 11 March 1916, for, among other things, 'taking photographs under heavy fire'. His long-overdue commissioning came on 23 October 1915, when he was gazetted Second Lieutenant to a Regular Army battalion of the Royal Sussex Regiment, with an immediate secondment to the RFC. His wounds healed and his formal pilot training duly completed, he was confirmed and gazetted Flying Officer on 21 May 1916. Perhaps a little surprisingly, as non-commissioned officers rarely returned to the same unit once commissioned, he was again posted to 3 Squadron. The demand for aerial photographs by the Staff, especially through the Battle of the Somme which commenced on 1 July 1916, ensured a busy schedule for Roberts and 3 Squadron as a whole. On 22 November 1916, Roberts and his Observer of the day, Captain G L Watson, were both wounded when their Morane LA, 'A248', was attacked by the German Ace, Erwin Böhme, the seventh of his 24 victories. Although German frontline Observers, watching the Morane's dive into British lines, assumed its destruction, in fact, Roberts was able to bring the machine down comparatively gently. Amongst other injuries, Roberts sustained a badly broken leg. His MC was announced in the *London Gazette* of 3 March 1917: 'For conspicuous gallantry in action, he three times dispersed an enemy working party with bombs and machine-gun fire from a height of 1,000 feet. On another occasion, he shot down an enemy machine. He has shown great determination on many occasions in taking photographss under most difficult and trying conditions'.

Staying on in the RAF after the war, he went on to win a Distinguished Flying Cross in the Iraqi campaign of 1924, *London Gazette* of 28 May 1926.

NB: His unique medal group was offered for sale by Christie's (lot 237a) on 13 April 1983: MC, Distinguished Flying Cross, Distinguished Conduct Medal, 1914 Star with Bar, British War Medal 1914-20, Victory Medal 1914-19, and General Service Medal 1918-62, with clasp, Kurdistan.

ROBERTSON, Albert Ernest

From Prahran, Melbourne, Victoria, Australia, he was born on 19 December 1892. A qualified Electrical Engineer, he had married Rebecca Gertrude and was living at 90 Edgecliffe Road, Woolaha, New South Wales, when he enlisted as a Private soldier (Number 937, later V358759) from 6 Infantry Regiment (Militia) into the Australian Flying Corps, AIF, on 5 September 1916. Robertson embarked from Melbourne aboard the Royal Mail Steamer *Omrah* on 17 January 1917, bound for the UK, as a 2 AM with HQ, 4 Flight, AFC. Picked out for a commission and to train as a Pilot, he was eventually gazetted Second Lieutenant on 12 November 1917, the same day that he was awarded his 'Wings' and formally gazetted,Pilot, Australian Flying Corps. Sent out to France and 4 AFC on 27 January 1918. Robertson gained the first of his victories on 21 March 1918, the opening day of the great German spring offensive. He was also extremely effective on low-level bombing and strafing patrols, creating havoc amongst the advancing German troops. On 23 March, he shot down three enemy machines in rapid succession, a feat for which he received the MC, announced in the *London Gazette* of 22 June 1918: 'For conspicuous gallantry and devotion to duty. When carrying out a low-flying bombing patrol, he observed a hostile tri-plane, accompanied by three scouts. He fired a burst of 30 rounds at very close range, and the hostile plane turned over on its side and crashed. Then, seeing an enemy scout below him, he fired 20 rounds in to its cockpit, and it fell down vertically out of control. In addition to these, he has shot down one other enemy machine, which finally crashed to earth. His dash and daring have been at all times most marked'.

His intensive tour with 4 AFC completed, he returned to the UK on 25 April 1918 to take up instructing duties. He returned to Melbourne in September 1919, his appointment terminated on 19 October following. Robertson served in the Volunteer Defence Corps during the Second World War.

ROBERTSON, Hector Murdoch Maxwell

A Royal Artillery Liaison Work, not a flying, award

The son of Colonel H Maxwell Robertson and Mrs Robertson, of Eastbourne, he was born on 27 May 1888. Educated at Wellington College (1902-05), Rugby XV (Captain 04), and at the Royal Military Academy, Woolwich. Gazetted Second Lieutenant to the RFC in 1907. Served with the RA in various capacities and postings in the pre-war years. When the war came in August 1914, he was attached as ADC to the GOC, RA, 2 Division, in France, thus earning the 1914 Star. Wounded in action at Ypres in the following November. Having recovered, he served from March 1915 with 118 Brigade, RFA, attached to 1 Canadian Division, until he was invalided home due to ill health in the following November. His health restored in March 1916, he was appointed to the command of A/184 Battery, RFA, 39 Division. Late in 1916, he was attached to 15 Wing, RFC, as RA Liaison Officer. His MC was announced in the New Year *London Gazette* of 1 January 1918 (no citation). Although no formal citation appeared in the *Gazette*, research has unearthed the original recommendation for the award: '6 October 1917, Royal Artillery, attached 15 Wing RFC: As Royal Artillery Liaison Officer with the 15 Wing, Captain Robertson has carried out invaluable work for more than twelve months. By his knowledge, capability and keenness he has succeeded in developing a firm liaison between the RFC and Royal Artillery and has assisted both sides with the greatest skill, in their co-operation'.

For the remainder of the war, Robertson continued performing Staff and Liaison duties with the RAF in France and, in 1919, in Germany. His work in this field was further marked with an appointment as OBE (Military Division) announced in the *London Gazette* of 3 June 1919. He married, in 1919, Emilie Marie Edouard Gilland of Liège, Belgium, with whom he had one son and three daughters, living at Moorland House, Westmount Road, Eltham. Served with the Royal Artillery on the North West Frontier of India in 1930-31. Awarded Brevet of Lieutenant Colonel in 1932. Appointed Member of the Royal Artillery Committee in 1938. Brigadier in command of Royal Artillery, Western Command, in 1939. Robertson retired in 1942, and was subsequently appointed to the executive branch of the Ministry of Food from 1942 to 1947. Brigadier Hector Robertson died at his home, 'Maronan', Long Lane, Newbury, Berkshire, on 6 February 1953.

ROBESON, Vyvyan Arthur Hemming

The son of Captain Arthur Hemming Robeson and Mrs Robeson, of Governor's House, HM Prison, Galway, Ireland, he was born on 11 February 1894. Educated at Cheltenham College (1907-11). He trained as a Mechanical Engineer (AMICE) with Pontifax and Sons of Birmingham and London. Gained his Royal Aero Club Certificate (Number 1040) on 18 January 1915, the same day that he was gazetted Second Lieutenant to the Military Wing, RFC. His formal pilot training duly completed, he was confirmed and gazetted Flying Officer on 30 April 1915. Kept back in the UK as an Instructor, he eventually accompanied BE2c-equipped 9 Squadron to France as a 'founder member' on 20 December 1915. Robeson was Mentioned in Despatches on 4 January 1917 and research has unearthed the original recommendation for this: '16 October 1916: From 1 July 1916 he has performed consistent good work in co-operation with artillery and on reconnaissance. He set a fine example of determination and skill'. Robeson would, in 1917, serve with 10 Squadron as a Flight Commander. His MC was announced in the *London Gazette* of 4 February 1918, details in the *Gazette* of 5 July 1918: 'For conspicuous gallantry and devotion to duty. In the course of three flights, which he carried out in one day in very bad weather, he bombed an enemy battery and fired 250 rounds on it from his machine-gun and bombed and fired on enemy infantry. He also carried out a valuable reconnaissance. On the following day, in the course of two flights he attacked enemy infantry with bombs and machine-gun fire. He showed the greatest skill, courage and judgment'.

Promoted to A/Major, he briefly commanded 46 Squadron, before, in February 1918, going on to command 24 Squadron (SE5As) for the next 12 months. '24' would be credited with destroying 99 enemy machines in March and April 1918. He was awarded the Croix de Guerre by the French, and was Mentioned in Despatches on two further occasions. Granted a permanent commission in the RAF in 1919, he was also elected a Fellow of the Royal Aeronautical Society. Robeson was commanding the RAF Experimental Station and living at The Abbey Cottage, Tewkesbury, Gloucestershire, when he died on 17 October 1923.

ROBINSON, Harry Noel Cornforth

The son of Mr and Mrs H Robinson, of Abbotsleigh, West Hartlepool, he was born on Christmas Day 1898. Educated at Durham School (1914-17). In April 1917, he was accepted straight from school as a Cadet into the RFC. Gazetted Second Lieutenant to the RFC on 10 May 1917. His formal pilot training duly completed, he was confirmed and gazetted Flying Officer on 12 July following. He was sent to France and the Sopwith Pup-equipped 46 Squadron within days of qualifying for his 'Wings'. He became a specialist in low-flying ground attacks, especially during the Battle of Cambrai, by which time '46' were re-equipped with Camels. The Camel evidently suited Robinson very well, as he achieved eight victories between 28 December 1917 and 24 March 1918 in that nimble machine. His MC was announced in the *London Gazette* of 28 March 1918, details in the *Gazette* of 13 May 1918: 'For conspicuous gallantry and devotion to duty. While on an offensive patrol he had trouble with his petrol pressure and was forced to turn back towards our lines. On his way back he saw seven enemy scouts attacking two of our artillery machines. He immediately dived on to the enemy and drove one of them down. During this operation one of his guns jammed. The enemy still continued the attack and he again dived on them, but his remaining gun also jammed. Though both his guns were out of action and he had very little petrol left, he continued to dive on the enemy repeatedly and eventually drove them away. He showed splendid courage and resource'.

Following a short leave, Robinson transferred to 70 Squadron, another Camel unit, gaining a further two victories by 15 May 1918. He was awarded the Croix de Guerre by the French. Granted a permanent commission in the RAF after the war, he served for two years as a Flight Commander in Mesopotamia and was awarded the Distinguished Flying Cross, *London Gazette* of 28 October 1921, for gallantry in operations round Samawah and Nasiriyeh. Returning to the UK, he was appointed a Lecturer and Instructor in Gunnery at Eastchurch. Harry Robinson died at Mundesley Sanatorium, Gimingham, Norfolk, on 2 June 1926 and is buried in Henley-on-Arden.

ROBINSON, Percy Dickson

The elder son of Farmer, Thomas Robinson and Elizabeth Robinson, of 'Prospect', Distington, Cumberland, he was born in Transvaal, South Africa, in 1893. Educated at St Bees (1904-05). Gained his Royal Aero Club Certificate (Number 843) on a Graham White machine at the Graham White School, Hendon, on 16 July 1914. Gazetted Second Lieutenant to the RFC, via the Special Reserve, on 6 April 1915. His formal pilot training duly completed, he was confirmed and gazetted Flying Officer on 24 June 1915. Robinson instructed in the UK until going out to the DH4-equipped day-bombing 57 Squadron on 31 October 1917. His MC was announced in the *London Gazette* of 4 March 1918, details in the *Gazette* of 16 August 1918: 'For conspicuous gallantry and devotion to duty. While on a photographic reconnaissance he was attacked by ten enemy aeroplanes. He handled his machine with such skill that his Observer shot down two enemy machines and dispersed the remainder. Although his machine was damaged and almost unmanageable, he continued to take photographs, and finally brought his machine back safely. He has taken part in a large number of photographic reconnaissances and over 70 bomb raids, and has shown the greatest courage and determination on all occasions'.

His Observer on this occasion was 1 AM H Doran from Belfast, who received the Military Medal, *London Gazette* of 14 January 1918. On 31 March 1918, the last day of the existence of the RFC, Robinson and his Observer of the day, Second Lieutenant John Quinton Frederick Walker from Apsley Guise, Bedfordshire, in DH4, 'A7674', failed to return and were, at first, reported as *missing*, but their machine was afterwards found shot down and burned near Beugnatre-Ecoust. Robinson's remains were never recovered and hence he is commemorated on the Flying Services Memorial, Arras, France.

ROBSON, Charles Crichton

From Edinburgh, he was born on 22 November 1895. He enlisted on 7 November 1914, as a Private soldier (Number 2560) into 9 Battalion, Royal Scots (TF). Robson accompanied the original contingent of the 'Dandy Ninth' (so-called because they were the only kilted battalion of the Royal Scots) to France on 26 February 1915. Robson suffered a gunshot wound to the buttock in the trenches at Sanctuary Wood on 17 May 1915. Once recovered, he was picked out for a commission and gazetted Second Lieutenant to 12 Battalion of his own regiment on 6 August 1915. Seconded to the RFC in September 1917, he trained as an Observer before being sent out as a Probationary to BF2b-equipped 11 Squadron on 19 December following. Striking up a formidable partnership with Lieutenant H W Sellars, he achieved eight victories between 12 March and 15 May 1918. One of these, on 21 March, the first day of the great German spring offensive, was particularly notable as it was over Leutnant Ludwig Hanstein, an accomplished Ace with 16 victories and CO, Jasta 35. On 15 May 1918, Robson and Sellars were themselves claimed by another German Ace, Leutnant Josef Mai, of Jasta 5, the 12th of his eventual 30 victories. The British pair in BF2b, 'C845', were intercepted and shot down over Contalmaison during the afternoon, with Robson surviving to be taken prisoner of war, but Herbert Sellars of Hoylake, Cheshire, being killed outright in the incident. Robson's MC was announced in the *London Gazette* of 22 June 1918: 'For conspicuous gallantry and devotion to duty. He completed a long distance reconnaissance under very trying weather conditions, and succeeded in returning with most valuable information. He has shown himself to be very cool and resourceful under all conditions'.

It was strange that Sellars, who had shared so much with Robson, was not awarded an MC after his death. Robson was incarcerated at Karlsruhe, amongst other places, before being repatriated in December 1918. He finally left the RAF, via the Unemployed List, on 28 February 1919.

RODNEY, The Honourable James Henry Bertie

A son of the 7th Baron Rodney, he was born in Grosvenor Street, Westminster W1 on 29 March 1893. Served with the Rifle Brigade, Special Reserve, and was in France by 15 August 1914. Transferred to the RFC in March 1915 and was posted to Mesopotamia for observer duties in May but was wounded in the right forearm on 23 June. He was not away from his duties for very long and continued to serve in the area till mid-November 1916, at which time he was sent to Palestine. By May 1916 he had become a pilot and joined 30 Squadron. He was wounded in the leg during an air fight with a Fokker on 13 August, flying BE2, '4141', and returned to England.His work brought him the Military Cross, *London Gazette* of 25 August 1917, to be dated 3 June 1917 (no citation).Promoted to T/Captain he returned to Palestine in August but was wounded by a bomb splinter to the abdomen on 29 November, presumably during an air attack on his base and, while in hospital, went down with dysentery which necessitated a return to England in early January 1918. He was promoted to T/Major. He left the service in March 1919. His MC was sent to him by post on 20 February 1922. In 1928 he married Frances, the American fashion editor with *Vogue*. They were guests of the wealthy L J McCormick of Chicago, in his Whitchurch, Hampshire, manor house in December 1933, where the chief guest was the French Duke, Prince Louis de la Trémoilles. A fire broke out in the early hours of the 9th in which the Duke was burnt to death and Rodney and his wife became trapped in an upstairs bedroom. Rodney smashed a window although in doing so he severely gashed his arms. He managed to get his wife out, but she was injured in the fall. He too then jumped but died in the Royal Hants Hospital in Winchester from loss of blood and other injuries.

ROGERS, George Clarence

From Envermere, British Columbia, Canada. After service in the trenches of the Ypres Salient with the Canadian Infantry, he was gazetted Lieutenant to 30 Reserve Battalion, Canadian Infantry, on 5 February 1916. Transferring to the RFC, he trained as a Pilot and was subsequently confirmed and gazetted Flying Officer on 13 September 1916. Sent to 52 Squadron in Hounslow on 4 October 1916, he accompanied the unit, the first to be equipped with RE8s, to France as a 'founder member' on 22 November following. Promoted to A/Captain and Flight Commander on 31 August 1917. His MC was announced in the *London Gazette* of 26 September 1917, details in the *Gazette* of 9 January 1918: 'For conspicuous gallantry and devotion to duty on several occasions. He has rendered valuable service to the artillery in ranging them on hostile batteries. In order to carry out the shoots successfully he has flown long distances over the line under very heavy anti-aircraft fire, returning in nearly every case with his machine badly damaged by pieces of shell: and although frequently attacked by hostile aircraft, he engaged and drove them off with scarcely any interruption to the shoot'.

On 27 October 1917, Rogers and his Observer of the day, Second Lieutenant E G Henderson, were fortunate to escape with their lives when they were attacked by four Albatros DVs over Nieuport during an artillery observation patrol. Vizefeldwebel Franz Hemer of Jasta 6, somewhat optimistically, claimed Rogers and Henderson as the first of his eventual 18 victories, for, whilst their RE8 was badly shot up and Rogers severely wounded, the pair were able to return to their base. Unfortunately, however, Rogers died of his wounds just three days later on 30 October 1917. He is buried in Zuydcoote Military Cemetery, Belgium.

ROGERS, William Wendell

From Alberton, Prince Edward Island, Canada, he was born on 10 November 1896. Educated at the University of Toronto, where he was a member of the COTC. Gazetted Lieutenant to 37 Battery, Canadian Field Artillery in November 1915. A later application for transfer to the flying service was approved and he was gazetted Second Lieutenant to the RFC, vià the Special Reserve, on 19 December 1916. His formal pilot training duly completed, he was confirmed and gazetted Flying Officer on 25 April 1917. Sent out to 1 Squadron (Nieuport Scouts) in France in the following month, he achieved nine victories between 12 July and 18 December 1917. Notable amongst these was the destruction of a Gotha bomber of Boghohl 1, north of Frelingien, on 12 December. Rogers saw service over a wide variety of fronts including Messines, Ypres, Passchendaele, Armentières and Houlthulst before his MC was announced in the *London Gazette* of 4 February 1918, details in the *Gazette* of 5 July 1918: 'For conspicuous gallantry and devotion to duty in shooting down seven enemy aeroplanes, and on two occasions attacking enemy troops with machine-gun fire from very low altitudes. He proved himself a daring patrol leader'.

Returning to Canada as an Instructor in February 1918, he was given command of 92 Canadian TS, Borden, in the following August. Released from the RAF, Rogers took up his interrupted studies at the University of Toronto late in 1918. In civilian life, he owned and ran an automobile business in St John, New Brunswick, and, for recreation, flew with the St John Flying Club, of which he became a life member. Bill Rogers died on 11 January 1967, at St Johns, New Brunswick.

ROSENBLUM, Siegfried – see Sydney George **REILLY**

ROSS, James Hector

The son of the Honourable J H Ross and Mrs Ross, of Montreal, his father being a Member of the Senate at Montreal. Educated at the University of Toronto, where he was a member of the Canadian OTC. Accepted as a candidate for the flying service, he crossed to the UK and was gazetted Second Lieutenant to the RFC, via the Special Reserve, on 30 April 1915. His pilot training duly completed, he was confirmed and gazetted Flying Officer on 20 November following. Sent to BE2c-equipped 4 Squadron in France on 4 May 1916, his operational career was to last just over two months. On 7 July 1916, his BE2c, ' 2638', was shot up during a morning patrol over Forceville. Although his Observer, Lieutenant G E F Sutton, was unharmed, Ross, having already been wounded in the air, suffered further serious injuries in the subsequent crash. His MC was announced in the *London Gazette* of 25 August 1916: 'For conspicuous gallantry when on two occasions he carried out reconnaissances at very low altitude to determine the general situation. His machine was repeatedly hit by rifle fire, and he was severely wounded in the arm. His reports were most valuable'.

Never able to recover his health, he was finally demobilised as 'permanently unfit' on 6 January 1918, whereupon he returned home to Canada, to resume his interrupted studies at the University of Toronto.

ROSS-HUME, Percy Gilbert

The second son of James Alexander Ross-Hume and Frances Isobel Ross-Hume (née Innes), of Ninewells, Chirnside, Berwickshire, Scotland, he was born on 13 September 1888. Educated at Rugby (1902-06), and at Corpus Christi College, Oxford, from where he graduated BA. He trained as a Chartered Accountant and passed ACA in 1914. Volunteering his services as soon as the war came, he was gazetted Second Lieutenant to 6 Battalion, King's Own Scottish Borderers, on 29 August 1914. Seeking secondment to the flying service, he gained his Royal Aero Club Certificate (Number 1021) at his own expense on 24 December 1914. Transferring to the RFC, he completed his formal pilot training and was duly confirmed and gazetted Flying Officer on 22 April following. Sent out first to 4 Squadron in France on 15 June 1915, he transferred to 12 Squadron on 27 August following. Promoted to A/Captain and Flight Commander on 23 January 1916. He was transferred again, this time briefly, to 8 Squadron, before returning to the Home Establishment on 9 September 1916. His MC was announced in the New Year *London Gazette* of.1 January 1917 (no citation). Although no formal citation was published in the *Gazette*, research has unearthed General Trenchard's original recommendation for the award: '16 October 1916, RFC HQ: 'From March to August 1916 he carried out very consistent, skilful and gallant work in co-operation with artillery, and in leading bombing raids'.

Following promotion to A/Major, Ross-Hume worked in various posts in the UK, before returning to France on 21 August 1918 as CO, 2 Squadron. His command of '2' at an end, he returned to the Home Establishment on 25 February 1919, before finally leaving the service, via the Unemployed List, on 10 April following.

ROULSTONE, Alexander

The son of Mr and Mrs Frederick Roulstone, of 120 Egypt Road, Basford, Nottingham, he was born on 10 October 1890. Gazetted Second Lieutenant to 12 Battalion (Pioneers), Sherwood Foresters, on 7 April 1915, he accompanied his unit to the front on 4 November following. After service in the trenches, he was seconded to the RFC in August 1916. His pilot training duly completed, he was confirmed and gazetted Flying Officer on 2 February 1917. Sent out to the FE2s of 25 Squadron on 21 February 1917, he was promoted to A/Captain and Flight Commander on 17 July following. Roulstone achieved six victories with '25', three in the FE2b and three in the DH4. His MC was announced in the *London Gazette* of 17 September 1917: 'For conspicuous gallantry and devotion to duty when engaged in aerial fighting and in photographic reconnaissances. In spite of continual hostile attacks he has proved most successful in securing photographs, and on several occasions he shot down enemy machines out of control, displaying skilful manoeuvring and great determination'.

His tour with '25' ended on 4 September 1917, Roulstone returned to the Home Establishment. After a period instructing, he returned to the front as a Flight Commander with 57 Squadron, another DH 4 unit, on 27 February 1918. Roulstone gained another two victories with '57', the second of which, on 17 March 1918, was over Oberleutnant Hans Bethge, CO, Jasta 30, an Ace with 20 victories, who was killed in the action. However, Roulstone, too, was hit and wounded in the fight, although he managed to get down his machine and his wounded Observer, Second Lieutenant W C Venmore, without further mishap. Staying on in the RAF after the war, he served with 110 Squadron in July 1919, before, in March 1920, being posted to 100 Squadron, then attached to HQ, 12 Irish Group. Very shortly after this, on 18 March 1920, Roulstone finally left the RAF, via the Unemployed List, and was known to be living in Loughborough later in the 1920s. He then took up business in East Leake, becoming a well-known figure in the village; acting for a time as Chairman of the Parish Council and donating the land upon which the Catholic Church is built. He eventually retired to the Isle of Wight, where his daughter lived. Alex Roulstone died in 1965 and is buried in East Leake Churchyard.

ROWDEN, Cuthbert Roger

The only son of Arthur Roger Rowden and Blanche Mary Rowden, of Hillend, Eastnor, Ledbury, Herefordshire, he was born on 26 December 1896. Educated at Rugby (1911-14) and at Sandhurst. Gazetted Second Lieutenant to 5 (Reserve) Battalion, Worcestershire Regiment, on 11 November 1914. Seconded to the RFC, he was still training as an Observer when he and a Pilot, Lieutenant A M Read, were given a 2 RA Squadron Shorthorn 343, and placed on standby at Lydd on 20 December 1914, just six days short of his 18th birthday. The RFC, aware of possible enemy raids over Christmas, had strategically stationed stand-by units along and around the coast. All remained quiet, however, and so Rowden was sent to France early in the New Year. At the battle of Neuve Chapelle in March 1915, he was brought down and slightly wounded. Once recovered, he took flying lessons, gaining his Royal Aero Club Certificate (Number 1256) on 7 May 1915. His formal pilot training duly completed, he was confirmed and gazetted Flying Officer on 2 July following. Rowden was next sent to 14 Squadron in Egypt on 25 February 1916. His MC was announced soon afterwards in the *London Gazette* of 28 March 1916: 'War Office: HM the King has been graciously pleased to confer the undermentioned rewards for gallant and distinguished service in the field, in connection with the engagement at Sollum, Egypt, 14 to 17 March 1916. DSO, the Duke of Westminster. Awarded the MC Lieutenant Cuthbert Roger Rowden, Worcestershire Regiment and RFC'.

The award was given for service and gallantry during the Sennusi Campaign. Rowden then took part in the fighting on the east of the Nile, a Half-Flight of 14 Squadron having been sent to Port Said to counter the persistent German bombing of that city. He was slightly injured on 25 April 1916, but soon recovered. On 3 May 1916, he was more seriously wounded when his BE2c was shot about during a combat with an enemy machine. Rowden was one of the party who had bombed the Turks out of Katia and, after being severely wounded in the leg, flew his machine the 65 miles back to base. He was Mentioned in Despatches on two occasions around this time, *London Gazettes* of 1 July 1916 and 25 September 1916. His injuries were such that he was invalided home on 14 May 1916. Having regained his fitness in 1917, he was promoted to Captain and Flight Commander with 50 HD Squadron. Later in 1917, and despite still not being 21years old, he was given further promotion to A/Major and appointed to the command of 78 HD Squadron. He married, on 12 September 1917, Frances Lilias Maud Jobson of Hill Croft, Rottingdean. Cuthbert Rowden was accidentally killed while flying near to his home at Coventry House, Emerson Park, Hornchurch, Essex, on 20 April 1918. He is buried in Rottingdean (St Margaret) Churchyard, Sussex.

ROYLE, Leopold Victor Arnold

The son of Arnold B Royle, CB, and Jennie Royle, of Albany Lodge, Esher, Surrey, he was born on 9 April 1882. After completing his education, Royle secured a position with the Egyptian Coast Guard Service in 1900. On 30 November 1914, he was attached to 30 Squadron, RFC, for special duties as an Observer – his intimate knowledge of the largely unmapped desert territory the squadron would overfly, it was reasoned, could prove inestimable. He had been in Egypt since the turn of the century and had once spent a full year in the desert wilderness, before successfully tracking down and apprehending a notorious smuggler. 30 Squadron was, late in 1914, in the process of forming-up and Royle became only the fifth member to join the embryonic unit. Records show him being involved in a crash on 15 December 1914 and also being involved in an unusually long practice endurance flight which lasted four hours and forty-five minutes. In March 1915, Royle was the Observer in a BE2a machine – one specially fitted with a large, non-standard, petrol tank – that made a long-range reconnaissance over enemy territory. He and his Pilot, Captain H L Reilly, covered 176 miles in three hours, 28 minutes, bombing, in the process, 207 tents and 300 Turkish infantrymen, despite heavy countering fire from the ground. Thanks to the fine research conducted by Wing Commander Jim Routledge (*OMRS Journal*, Autumn 1977) it has been established that it was for this and other good work with 30 Squadron, that Royle was awarded the MC, announced in the *London Gazette* of 29 October 1915 (no citation).

It was also around this time that Royle left the squadron to return, overtly at least, to the Egyptian Coastguard Service. Royle, who shared many characteristics with Colonel T E Lawrence, returned to Intelligence work on behalf of the Egyptian Government and the British Army, including, at one stage, guiding the Duke of Westminster's Armoured Car Squadron through the desert to secure the freedom of the Tara and Moorina prisoners from their Sennusi captors. He was Mentioned in Despatches, *London Gazette* of 21 June 1916, for his part in this successful enterprise. Moreover, he was Mentioned in Despatches on four further occasions during the Great War. He was also presented with the Medaglia al Valore Militare by the Italians, *London Gazette* of 31 August 1917, and with the Order of the Nile, 4th Class, by the Egyptians, *London Gazette* of 21 August 1917. Royle appears not to have shaken off the attraction of aviation, however, and was allowed, at his own request, to re-enter the RFC at the end of 1917. He trained as a Pilot and was duly confirmed and gazetted Flying Officer on 3 February 1918, serving first with 21 RS, Egyptian Expeditionary Force. He then joined 111 Squadron on 10 April 1918 and was killed some months later on 17 August, when his aircraft, for no apparent reason, broke up in the air. Leopold Royle is buried in Ramleh War Cemetery, Israel.

RUSHFORTH, Henry Philip

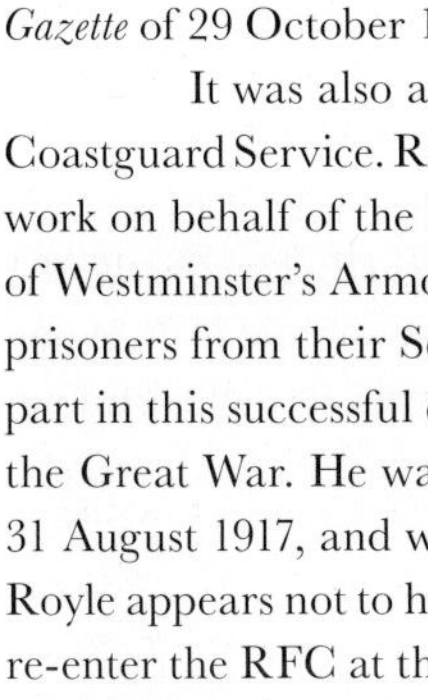

The son of Solicitor, Robert Henry Rushforth and Kate Elizabeth Rushforth (née Mulloney), of High Street, Amersham, Buckinghamshire, he was born on 31 March 1896. Gazetted Second Lieutenant to the RFC, via the Special Lists, on 5 August 1916. His formal pilot training duly completed, he was confirmed and gazetted Flying Officer on 28 November following. Sent out to the 'Flying Elephants' of 27 Squadron on 7 February 1917, he was promoted to A/Captain and Flight Commander in the following summer. His MC was announced in the *London Gazette* of 17 September 1917: 'For conspicuous gallantry and devotion to duty in leading bombing raids, the majority of which have been on distant objectives. Notably on one occasion, he led a most successful raid under extremely adverse weather conditions, in spite of which the objective was reached and bombed from a low altitude, after which the whole formation of eight machines returned in safety, after a total flight of over five hours. The success of the operation was due to his determination and fine leadership'.

The raids referred to were mainly against enemy airfields or railways junctions and sidings. After completing his tour with '27', he served, briefly, in the UK with 85 Squadron, before going out again to France in March 1918, this time as a Flight Commander of the Sopwith Dolphin-equipped 79 Squadron. On 20 May 1918, Rushforth was wounded when his Dolphin, 'C3901', was shot up and its fuel tank pierced during a combat with three enemy aircraft. Again on 7 September 1918, having recovered his fitness, he was wounded again when his Dolphin was struck by anti-aircraft fire. Rushforth finally left the RAF, via the Unemployed List, in May 1920.

RUTLEDGE, Thomas Forster

From Warrnambool, Victoria, he was born, one of a family of seven children, on 21 March 1887. Educated at the Church of England School, Geelong. He lived and worked as a Sharebroker in Melbourne, as well as owning a sheep station outside the city. He learnt to fly at his own expense, gaining his Royal Aero Club Certificate (Number 841) on 30 June 1914. Accepted for a commission, he was gazetted Second Lieutenant to the RFC, via the Special Reserve, on 12 August 1914. He travelled to the UK and having completed his formal pilot training, he was confirmed and gazetted Flying Officer on 17 November 1914. After a period at the CFS, he was struck down with ill health, suffering with both influenza and appendicitis. Once recovered, he was sent to 7 Squadron in Netheravon, and accompanied that unit to France as a 'founder member' on 8 April 1915. His tour with '7' completed in July 1915, he returned to the UK. Next, he was promoted to A/Major and sent out to the Middle East to assume command of 1 Squadron, Australian Flying Corps. Rutledge spent 13 months in Egypt, but bouts of jaundice curtailed his operational flying. His MC was announced in the New Year *London Gazette* of 1 January 1918 (no citation). Promoted to A/Lieutenant Colonel, he was appointed to the command of 26 Wing, RFC. Rutledge resigned his commission in the RAF on 30 April 1918, in order to transfer to the Australian Flying Corps on a permanent basis.

RUTTER, Donald Campbell

The son of Hugh Rutter, JP, and Hilda Rutter, of White House, Pilt Down, Uckfield, Sussex, he was born on 1 April 1897. Mr Rutter Senior was, throughout the Great War, Chairman of Merton Urban Council. Donald was educated at Shrewsbury (1911-14). Gazetted Second Lieutenant to 3 (Reserve) Battalion, Sussex Regiment, on 18 November 1914, with a brief and temporary attachment to the Gloucestershire Regiment. Served in the trenches with the Sussex Regiment before being seconded to the RFC later in 1915. He first trained as an Observer and was sent out as such to BE2c-equipped 8 Squadron before the year's end. He next trained as a Pilot, and was duly confirmed and gazetted Flying Officer on 8 February 1916. Promoted to A/Captain and Flight Commander, he completed his tour with '8' and was posted to the CFS in the following August. He returned to the front as a Flight Commander and 'founder member' of the Sopwith Strutter-equipped 43 Squadron on 25 January 1917. His MC was announced in the *London Gazette* of 11 May 1917: 'For conspicuous gallantry and devotion to duty. He completed a valuable reconnaissance alone and at very low altitude and in the face of heavy fire which riddled his machine. On another occasion he single-handedly succeeded in driving off three hostile machines'.

On 7 June 1917, Rutter and his Observer, Second Lieutenant John Bell Jackson, Royal Scots, in Strutter, 'A8221', were shot down and killed during a low-level ground strafing patrol over Messines. The squadron history describes his last flight, thus: 'Capt Rutter, first away at 0410 hours, with his observer 2Lt Jackson, was never seen again. Almost certainly their aircraft must have received a direct hit from a heavy shell as they flew towards their targets. Capt Rutter who had seen service in the front-line trenches of the Royal Sussex Regiment and the back cockpits of 8 Sqd's BE2's was the only surviving Flight Cdr, the sole surviving pilot in fact excepting Major Dore of the original Northolt contingent. He had been in the forefront from the beginning. His aircraft was riddled and his observer killed in the first engagement with the enemy in far off February and through all the trials and tribulation of the heavy casualties that followed he had been a tower of strength. A fearless leader with the most gallant and distinguished record; the thoroughness with which he did his work was beyond praise'.

Donald Rutter is buried in Tyne Cot Cemetery, Belgium.

RYAN, Charles Edmund

Born on 10 August 1890. A pre-war Regular Army officer, he was gazetted Second Lieutenant to the Royal Artillery on 23 December 1910. Served in France with 67 Brigade, Royal Field Artillery, from 20 December 1914. Sent out to 6 Squadron in France in the summer of 1915, his experience as an artillery officer obviously invaluable to a reconnaissance unit. On 19 September 1915, Ryan and his Pilot, Lieutenant A A Somervail (qv), in BE2c, '1740', brought down a large two-engined tractor machine which fell at Biffeghem. For this feat, the two would receive the MC, announced in the *London Gazette* of 14 January 1916 (no citation). Although no formal citation was published in the *Gazette*, research has unearthed the original recommendation for the award: '6 Sqd and RFA. Continued excellence of work as an observer. As passenger attacked a large twin engined tractor. With great pluck and determination, pursued the enemy till out of range. He then attacked another which nose-dived out of sight. Information was later received through an agent that a machine had fallen at Biffeghem. This is believed to be the second machine he attacked'.

On 4 November 1915, Ryan and his Pilot of the day, Second Lieutenant H Bright, in BE2c, '2031', were attacked in the air by several enemy machines. Ryan was twice wounded in the right arm and their BE was badly shot-up, the fuel tank pierced, the rudder jammed and useless. Fortunately, they were rescued by 6 Squadron colleagues, Second Lieutenant C H Kelway-Bamber and Lieutenant H J Payne, in BE2c, '5644', who fought off the German machines, allowing the unscathed Bright to bring his machine in without further mishap. Having recovered from his wounds, Ryan next served briefly with 2 Squadron from 6 March 1916, until going to the CFS on 14 April following. Ryan left the CFS on 24 May 1916 and reverted back to the Royal Artillery, attaining the rank of Major in 1918. He was Mentioned in Despatches on two occasions during the Great War, *London Gazettes* of 1 January 1916 and 20 May 1918. He served as a Staff Captain, RA, in India from 1 August 1920 to 10 May 1922 and again from 1 February 1925 to 22 May 1925. He was appointed DAAG, India, from 28 May 1925 to 28 May 1929. He served as a GSO II at the War Office from 1 October 1930 to 31 October 1934, and as a GSO I from 1 February 1938 to 31 July 1939. His promotions included: Brevet of Lieutenant Colonel, 1 July 1932; substantive Lieutenant Colonel, 1 May 1937; Colonel, 1 February 1938; T/Brigadier, 1 August 1939. Ryan commanded 2 Corps, RA, in France in 1940. He had retired as Brigadier in 1945 and was on the RA Reserve of Officers.

S

SANDAY, William Douglas Stock

The son of Corn Merchant, Samuel Sanday and Mrs Sanday, of Knolle Park, Woolton, Liverpool, and of Paddington Hall, Cheshire, he was born on 25 May 1883. Educated at Bilton Grange (1892-97) and at Uppingham (1897-98). He married, in 1905, Mary Brodrick, also of Liverpool. After completing his education he worked for some years with Hull Pacific as a Corn Merchant. When the war came in August 1914, Sanday served in France and Flanders as a volunteer with the British Red Cross. Keen to join the flying service, he gained his Royal Aero Club Certificate (Number 1295) on 2 June 1915, the same day that he was gazetted Second Lieutenant to the Military Wing, RFC. His formal pilot training duly completed, he was confirmed and gazetted Flying Officer on 7 August following. Sent out to BE2c-equipped 2 Squadron soon after qualifying for his 'Wings'. On 11 October 1915, Sanday and his Observer, Lieutenant Ellison, in a BE2c, shared, with two other machines, a victory over an Albatros 'C' type, which force-landed in the British lines. Exactly one month later on 11 November, Sanday and his Observer of the day, Sergeant Hodgson, in BE2c, '1730', fought an inconclusive combat with an enemy LVG over Mazingarbe. The British pair used a rifle in the confrontation as there were no machine guns available when they took-off, all were already in use. On 2 January 1916, Sanday was injured in a crash and this event effectively ended his tour with '2'. His MC was announced in the *London Gazette* of 22 January 1916: 'For conspicuous gallantry and skill near Hulloch on 1 January 1916. He went out in a very high wind to observe the fire of a battery, and, owing to the clouds, was forced to fly at a height of between 800 and 900 feet. Although continually subjected to very heavy rifle fire from the German trenches, he enabled our batteries to obtain several direct hits'.

Once recovered, he was promoted to A/Captain and Flight Commander and accompanied the Sopwith Strutter-equipped 70 Squadron to France as a 'founder member' in the summer of 1916. On 6 August 1916, Sanday led a patrol which completely frustrated a ten-strong enemy bomb raid. Sanday and his Observer, Lieutenant Clifford Westly Busk (qv), accounted for two of the raiders before running out of ammunition. The remaining eight enemy machines were forced to retreat by other members of his patrol, with not one bomb dropped. On 6 September 1916, the same pair, in Sopwith Strutter, 'A3431', sent down a Roland CII in flames near to Elincourt. Sanday was awarded the Distinguished Service Order in the *London Gazette* of 20 October 1916. He was also Mentioned in Despatches on two occasions during the Great War. In January 1917, following the death of Major G H Harvey-Kelly, he was appointed to the command of 19 Squadron. Although Commanding Officers were generally discouraged from operational flying, Sanday was a 'hands-on' type, and would go on to claim his fifth and last victory, thus attaining the status of Ace, over an Albatros on 13 July 1917. His command of '19' relinquished early in 1918, he returned to the Home Establishment to take up a number of Staff and instructing duties, attaining the rank of Lieutenant Colonel before finally leaving the RAF in 1919. He lived, in the 1920s, at 39 Hyde Park Gardens, London, SW7, and in the 1930s, at York House, Kensington, London. However, he was living at 223 East 61st Street, New York, when he died on 30 March 1952.

SANSOM, George Samuel

The son of Samuel G C Sansom and Annie Sansom, of East Grinstead, Sussex, he was born in London on 7 August 1888. Educated at Wellington College (1903-05) and at University College, London, (1908-14), where he studied Medicine and was a Zoological Research Student, graduating BSc in 1911, and a Derby Scholar, Zoology, 1912. Sansom planned and took part in many new difficult rock climbs in Cumberland, including Scafell Central Buttress in1914. Gazetted Second Lieutenant (Balloon Officer) to the Military Wing, RFC, on 5 September 1915, with a posting to 5 KBS on the same day. He gained his Aeronauts Certificate (Number 43) on 30 September following. Sent to France in March 1916, he was later posted to 7 KBS as a Flight Commander and A/Captain on 22 August 1916. His MC was announced in the *London Gazette* of 18 June 1917: 'For conspicuous gallantry and devotion to duty. Although attacked three times by hostile aircraft, he remained in the air with his balloon at its maximum height, and completed his task. He has on many previous occasions done fine works'.

Returning to the Home Establishment on 22 November 1917, he was given command of No 1 Balloon School, two days later. Sent again to France on 7 June 1918, this time as Squadron Commander, 13 BC, with the rank of T/Major. Awarded the Distinguished Flying Cross in the *London Gazette* of 3 December 1918 for, amongst other things: '....completing almost 600 hours of balloon observation'. Sansom finally left the RAF, via the Unemployed List, in the spring of 1919, to return to his research studies in the Department of Embryology at University College, London. He married, in 1921, Dorothy Vivien Dodgson (died 1973) with whom he had three sons, living at Kennel Moor, Godalming, Surrey. He was subsequently elected to a Fellowship at UCL in 1930. Dr George Sansom died on 21 March 1980.

SAUNDBY, Robert Henry Magnus Spencer

The son of Dr Robert Saundby, MD, LLD, FRCP, Lieutenant Colonel, Royal Army Medical Corps; and Professor of Medicine at Birmingham University, and Mary Edith Saundby (née Spencer), of The Tower House, Harrow-on-the-Hill, he was born on 26 April 1896. Educated at King Edward's School, Birmingham (1910-14). A pre-war volunteer, he was gazetted Second Lieutenant to 5 Battalion, Royal Warwickshire Regiment (TF), on 15 June 1914. He was working as a 'Probationer' in the Traffic Department at the Kenilworth depot of the London and North Western Railway Company, when he was mobilised with the rest of the TF as soon as war broke out on 4 August 1914. Saundby suffered a period of ill health, before being seconded to the RFC in January 1916. Having trained as a Pilot, he was duly confirmed and gazetted Flying Officer on 17 June 1916, although his physique – he was six foot, three inches tall and weighed 13 stones – was hardly compatible with the cubic capacity of the average aeroplane cockpits of the day. Despite this, he was sent out to the DH2-equipped 24 Squadron soon after qualifying. On 31 July 1916, Saundby in DH2, '5998', was wounded during an aerial combat on the Fourth Army front. Having recovered, he was, later in the year, involved in Lanoe Hawker VC's last flight on 23 November 1916, when the revered British Ace was shot down and killed by Manfred von Richthofen. In fact, Saundby it was who rescued the Flight Commander on that occasion, chasing away a German Scout from the threatened J O Andrews' (qv) tail. His tour with '24' completed, he returned to the Home Establishment for a period before briefly joining 41 Squadron (FE8s) on 26 January 1917, with which unit he gained his fourth victory. His next posting, in April 1917, was to the Experimental Station at Orfordness, where Home Defence duties were part of his role. On the night of 16/17 July 1917, Saundby, on his first ever night flight, in DH2, 'A5058', shared, with Captain L P Watkins (qv), in the destruction of Zeppelin *Z48*, which was brought down in flames to destruction in East Anglia. In a letter home, Saundby said, 'I had never been up at night before, but it was a fine experience, the Zep burnt beautifully'. His and Watkins' MCs were announced in the *London Gazette* of 5 July 1917: 'In recognition of their conspicuous gallantry in attacking and destroying an enemy airship'

Research has unearthed the original recommendation for this award, which is a little more detailed: 'For conspicuous gallantry in attacking and destroying an enemy airship. At about 2am two airships came a short distance inland, one crossing the East Anglian coast, made an attack on a coast town of East Anglia at about 2.30am She was heavily shelled by the guns of the anti-aircraft defences, and was driven off. Shortly afterwards this raider, after dropping a number of bombs in open places, was engaged and brought down in flames by a pilot of the RFC. The airship was destroyed. No casualties or damage were caused in East Anglia'.

Saundby would see out the remainder of the war in a series of instructing posts. He married, around this time, Joyce Mary Rees-Webbe, with whom he had one son and two daughters. His biographical book, 'Flying Colours', was published in December 1918. He took a seaplane course at Lee-on-Solent, and studied at the RAF and Naval Cooperation School at Calshot. Awarded an Air Force Cross in the *London Gazette* of 1 January 1919. Given a permanent commission in 1919, he embarked upon what would prove to be an illustrious career. His many honours, appointments and promotions included: Iraq, Aden and Egypt , 1922-26, DFC for gallant services 'in the Hinterland of Aden', *London Gazette* of 26 January 1926; RAF Staff College course, 1928: Air Staff, HQ, Wessex Bombing Area, 1929-30; Air Staff, Air Ministry, 1931-32;. idc course, 1933; Instructor at RAF Staff College, 1934-36; Deputy Director of Air Ops, Air Ministry, 1937; Director of Operational Requirements, Air Ministry, 1938-39; Assistant Chief of Air Staff (T), 1940; SASO, Bomber Command, 1941-42; CB, 1942; Deputy AOC-in-C, Bomber Command, RAF, 1943-45, Second in Command to 'Bomber' Harris (Mentioned in Despatches on three occasions); KBE, 1944; Commander, Legion of Merit ,USA, 1946; Grand Officer, Order of Leopold II, Belgium; Croix de Guerre avec Palme, Belgium, 1947; Retired 1946. His civilian honours and appointments post-retirement, included: Life Vice-President RAF Association; Chairman, National Council, 1945-58; DL Berkshire; President, Metropolitan Area British Legion, 1947-62, Patron, 1962; KCB, 1956. He lived in retirement at Oxleas, Burghclere, near Newbury, Berkshire. Air Marshal Sir Robert Saundby died on 25 September 1971.

SAUNDERS, Franklin Geoffrey

The elder of the two sons of Metal Merchant, Franklin Stokes Saunders and Lucy Matilda Saunders (née Redford), of 'The Wilderness', Tadley Entire, Southampton, he was born in Mumbles, Glamorgan, on 3 June 1891. A trained Motor Engineer, he was a Director of the Motor Supply Company Ltd, Park Lane, London, from 1910 to 1912. A pre-war Naval volunteer, he was gazetted Sub-Lieutenant to the RNVR, training for sea gunnery at Whale Island and at HMS *Vernon*. Developing an interest in aviation, he learnt to fly and gained his Royal Aero Club Certificate (Number 721) in a Bristol machine at the Bristol School, Brooklands, on 1 January 1914. His engagement with the RNVR had expired by the time the war came in August 1914 and he then sought, and was given, a commission in the cavalry, being gazetted Second Lieutenant to 4 Reserve Regiment of Cavalry on 9 September 1914, subsequently transferring to 7 (Princess Royal's) Dragoon Guards. Saunders joined 7 Dragoon Guards at the front on 4 February 1916, but left shortly afterwards on secondment to the RFC. His formal pilot training duly completed, he was confirmed and gazetted Flying Officer on 27 May 1916. Sent out to 17 Squadron in Salonika early in 1917. Although forced to fly the dreadful BE12, he gained four victories between 14 January and 25 June 1917, despite having been wounded in an aerial combat on the intervening 8 April. The first of his MCs was announced in the Birthday Honours *London Gazette* of 4 June 1917 (no citation).

In January 1918, part of 17 Squadron combined with elements of 47 Squadron, the new unit being designated 150 Squadron and equipped with SE5As. Saunders was posted as a Flight Commander to the new squadron and went on to add four more victories to his tally during the first two months of the New Year. The Bar to his MC came in the *London Gazette* of 26 March 1918, details in the *Gazette* of 24 August 1918: 'For conspicuous gallantry and devotion to duty. On three separate occasions during a month, he has fought a hostile machine, pursued it over the enemy's lines and driven it down to earth where it was completely wrecked. He has shown the most consistent gallantry and skill in action'.

Staying on in the RAF for a while after the war, he finally left the service, via the Unemployed List, on 4 June 1921. Saunders rejoined the RAF in 1939, with the rank of Flight Lieutenant.

SAUNDERS, Hugh William Lumsden

The son of Frederick William Saunders and Mrs Saunders, of Transvaal, South Africa, he was born on 24 August 1894. Educated at Marist Brothers' School, Johannesburg. When the war came in August 1914, he immediately enlisted, serving first with the Witwatersrand Rifles and later in the South Africa Horse (Number 5456, Lance Corporal). Because of his extravagant bravery, he was known to his comrades as 'Dingbat'. Awarded the Military Medal for bravery, *London Gazette* of 12 March 1917. Picked out for a commission, he was gazetted Second Lieutenant to the RFC on 2 August 1917. His formal pilot training duly completed, he was confirmed and gazetted Flying Officer on 19 October following. Sent out to the SE5A-equipped 84 Squadron in November 1917, he would ultimately achieve 15 victories, including two kite balloons between 25 January and 29 July 1918. He was also promoted to A/Captain and Flight Commander in the intervening April. His MC was announced in the *London Gazette* of 16 September 1918: 'For conspicuous gallantry and devotion to duty. During recent operations he destroyed five enemy machines and shot down four out of control. He showed great courage and skill in engaging enemy aircraft, and did splendid service'.

The first of his Distinguished Flying Crosses followed in the *London Gazette* of 2 November 1918. Staying on in the RAF with a permanent commission, he served again with 84 Squadron in Iraq from 1920 to 1923, receiving a Bar to his Distinguished Flying Cross, *London Gazette* of 28 October 1921 for, amongst other things, 'dropping food and supplies to the garrison at Samawah and the gunboat, 'Greenfly' '. He married, in 1923, Phyllis Margaret Mabbett (died 1980), with whom he had two daughters. Saunders was appointed to a number of Staff jobs following his stint in Iraq, until he was given command of 45 Squadron in Egypt from 1931 to 1934. His many subsequent honours, appointments and promotions included: Group Captain, 1939: Chief of Air Staff, NZ, 1939-41; Air Commodore, 1941: AOC, 11 Group, Fighter Command, 1942-44; CB, 1943; T/Air Vice-Marshal, 1942; Director General of Postings, Air Ministry, 1944-45; KBE, 1945; Air Marshal Commanding RAF Burma 1945-46; Air Marshal, 1947; AOC-in-C, Bomber Command, 1947; Air Counsel Member for Personnel, 1947-49; Inspector General of the RAF, 1949-50; Air Chief Marshal, 1950; KCB, 1950; C-in-C Air Forces Western Europe, January-April 1951; Air Deputy to Supreme Allied Commander, Europe, 1951-53; GCB, 1953. After retiring as Marshal of the RAF in 1953, his various subsequent civilian appointments included: Special Air Advisor to Royal Danish Air Force, 1954-56; Chief Co-ordinator of Anglo-American hospitality activities in UK, 1956-59; Vice-Chairman, National Savings Committee, 1956-70. His many foreign awards included: Order of Polonia Restituta, 2nd Class (Poland); Commander Order of Merit, (USA); Officier Légion d'Honneur (France); Grand Cross of Dannebrog (Denmark). Marshal of the RAF Sir Hugh Saunders died on 8 May 1987.

SAUNDERS, Reginald Arthur

The son of Arthur and Annie Saunders, of 10 Regent's Park Road, Gloucester Gate, London, he was born in 1894. A pre-war volunteer, he joined the Inns of Court OTC (Number C/644) on 18 June 1912, before being gazetted Second Lieutenant to 20 County of London Battery, Royal Field Artillery (TF), later in the same year. Mobilised with the rest of the TF as soon as war came on 4 August 1914. Anxious to join the flying service, he gained his Royal Aero Club certificate (Number 1182) on 16 April 1915. The acquisition of his 'ticket' assured his acceptance into the RFC and, upon completion of his formal pilot training, he was confirmed and gazetted Flying Officer on 30 June 1915. He was sent out to 3 Squadron (Moranes) on 3 July 1915. On 25 September 1915, Saunders and his Observer, Lieutenant A J Evans (qv), whilst directing the fire of 8 Siege Battery on a bridge over the Haute Duele canal, were persistently attacked for more than 20 minutes by a hostile machine armed with a machine gun. The British pair, armed only with a pistol, used this to great effect. Their well-directed fire not only kept the enemy machine at bay, but also slightly wounded both the German Pilot and Observer in the process. Both men received the MC, Saunders' was announced in the New Year *London Gazette* of 1 January 1916 (no citation). Although no formal citation was published in the *Gazette*, research has unearthed the original recommendation for the award: 'R A Saunders. Lt Saunders did consistently good work from July 3rd to October 10th. On September 25th he was the pilot with Lt Evans. His skill and coolness greatly contributed to the successful result of the combat that took place over Pont á Vendin'.

Saunders transferred, on the last day of 1915, to 1 Squadron, another Morane-equipped unit. These were dangerous days over the Western Front, and Saunders was kept very busy. Not untypically, on 29 February 1916, Saunders and his Observer, Second Lieutenant J B Joske, in Morane LA, '5119', fought a long, albeit largely inconclusive, combat with four Aviatiks over Passchendaele. On 14 March following, Saunders, alone in Morane LA, '5107', was attacked during a photo-reconnaissance patrol over La Clytte by three Fokkers. Although giving a good account of himself, Saunders was badly wounded in the stomach. He dived steeply away and brought the Morane down largely under control, but hit the ground first with his left wing. He died of his wounds and injuries soon afterwards. By coincidence, he was Mentioned in Despatches on the day of his death, *London Gazette* of 14 March 1916. Reginald Saunders is buried in La Clytte Military Cemetery, Heuvelland, West-Vlaanderen, Belgium.

SAVAGE, Douglas Alfred

The eldest of the four sons of Bookseller and Stationer, Alfred Savage and Kezia Marian Savage (née De La Mare), of 155 Iffley Road, Cowley St John, Oxford, he was born on 20 February 1892. Educated at City of Oxford High School (1902-1907), leaving in July 1907 at the same time as fellow student, T E Lawrence (Lawrence of Arabia). He worked as a Stationer in Oxford before the war came in 1914. Gazetted Second Lieutenant to the New Armies on 19 March 1915, with a transfer to a Trench Mortar Battery coming on 23 April 1916. Seconded to the RFC late in 1917, he trained as a Pilot and, having qualified, accompanied, as a 'founder member', the BF2b-equipped 62 Squadron to France on 23 January 1918. By 21 April 1918, the day the Red Baron was killed, he had achieved five victories but on that day, he and his Observer, Second Lieutenant L M Thompson, in 'B1234', were both injured when their machine was hit by anti-aircraft fire and he was forced to crashland near to Armentières. Once recovered, Savage went on to achieve two further victories by 2 June 1918, shortly before returning to the Home Establishment at the end of his tour with '62'. His MC was announced in the *London Gazette* of 26 July 1918: 'For conspicuous gallantry and devotion to duty, especially on the following occasions. When on patrol attacked a formation of enemy aeroplanes, crashing one, while another fell to pieces in the air after a short combat. Attacked an Albatros, which he set on fire, and drove another down out of control. Attacked many ground targets from low altitudes'.

Savage was posted to instructing duties for the remainder of the war, eventually leaving the RAF, via the Unemployed List, on 15 June 1919.

SCAIFE, Thomas Earle Gordon (also known as T E Gordon-Scaife)

The son of Thomas Earle Scaife and Carla Scaife, MICE, of Burnholme, Robertson, Cape Province, South Africa, he was born in 1892. Coming to the UK, Scaife was gazetted Second Lieutenant to 6 Dragoon Guards (Carabiniers) on 15 September 1915, with an immediate secondment to the RFC. He gained his Royal Aero Club Certificate (Number 2181) on 22 October 1915. Despite the acquisition of his 'ticket', Scaife actually trained as an Observer and was eventually sent out as a Probationary to BE2c-equipped 9 Squadron on 6 January 1916. His 'apprenticeship' satisfactorily completed, he was confirmed and gazetted Flying Officer (Observer) on 25 May 1916. On 1 July 1916 - the first day of the Battle of the Somme, Scaife and his Pilot, Captain J T (Powell) Whitaker (qv), in BE2c, '2689', arrived over the devastation at 10.00am. Most of the casualties on that terrible day, 20,000 dead and 40,000 wounded on the British side, had already occurred by that time. Some of the infantry carried mirrors on their backs and, by this device, airmen were able to spot some who had moved forward into the German positions. Whitaker and Scaife came down to 700 feet and strafed a machine-gun position in Bernafay Wood. Flying along the lines, the pair saw the men of 18 Division, mainly Liverpool and Manchester 'Pals', advancing near Montauban, the one successful point of attack. The airmen celebrated this singular success by wagging their wings as they skimmed the British troops, who, in turn, reciprocated with wildly waving arms. Their BE2c was then hit by anti-aircraft fire, but the pair escaped unscathed and managed to bring their damaged machine back safely. Just six days later, the same pair, in BE2d, '6236', were again hit by anti-aircraft fire over Montauban but, once again, got back safely without harm. On 16 July, Scaife and his Pilot, Lieutenant Bernard Tarrant Coller from Norwich, in BE2c, '4189', were attacked in the air, their machine damaged, but again the crew were unhurt. The same crew on 20 July, this time in '2507', sent down a Fokker in flames over Bazentin-le-Petit. Just three days later, Scaife and Coller, in BE2d, '5807', were shot up during a contact patrol, but once again emerged unscathed. His MC was announced in the *London Gazette* of 22 September 1916: 'For conspicuous gallantry and skill when on contact patrol work during active operations, often flying low under heavy fire. On one occasion, when flying at 1,000 feet, his petrol tanks were pierced by shell fire. He managed to stop the holes and enabled his pilot to bring the machine home'.

Yet again, on 9 September, BE2c, '2507', was shot up, the pilot's seat struck by machine-gun bullets, but Scaife and Coller still escaped injury. Their luck, however, finally ran out on 26 September 1916, when their BE2e, '7079', was hit by anti-aircraft fire over Lesboeffs. Their remains were never recovered and hence they are commemorated on the Flying Services Memorial, Arras, France.

SCALES, Herbert James

The son of Alfred and Elgener Scales of 35 Kenilworth Road, Penge, London SE, he was born in 1888. As soon as war came in August 1914, he enlisted as a Trooper (Number 2290) into 1 City of London Yeomanry (Roughriders) (TF). He accompanied his regiment to Egypt in April 1915, as a Corporal motor-cycle despatch rider. In August 1915, the Roughriders landed at Suvla Bay, Gallipoli, as a dismounted infantry unit. After the Gallipoli fiasco, the Roughriders returned to Egypt. Picked out for a commission, he was gazetted Second Lieutenant on 24 May 1916 to 11 Battalion, Worcestershire Regiment, then stationed in Salonika. Seconded to the RFC in the autumn of 1916, he trained as a Pilot in Egypt and was duly confirmed and gazetted Flying Officer on 9 February 1917. Sent out to 47 Squadron in Salonika, Scales soon made a reputation as a skilled and brave Pilot. He was Mentioned in Despatches in the *London Gazette* of 28 November 1917 and his MC was announced in the New Year *London Gazette* of 1 January 1918 (no citation). Promoted to A/Captain and Flight Commander in February 1918. Coinciding with the formation of the RAF on 1 April 1918, a new squadron was raised in Salonika from one flight of 17 Squadron and one flight of 47 Squadron and designated 150 Squadron, RAF. A third flight, 'C' Flight, was added in the first days of May and Scales was appointed to command it. Unfortunately, Scales was killed as a result of a flying accident on 12 June 1918. His colleague and fellow MC recipient, Captain H A Jones (qv), pays him this compliment in his book, 'Over the Balkans and South Russia, 1917-1919': 'His loss was keenly felt by all those in '47' who had flown with him. Tall, always immaculate, generous to a degree, and a keen flier who sought the most dangerous jobs, Captain Scales was a loss to the Air Force'. Herbert Scales is buried in Sarigol Military Cemetery, Kriston, Greece.

SCHOLTE, Owen John Frederick

The son of Frederick Petros Scholte and Emma Scholte, of 'Sunnyfield', West Heath, Hampstead, London, he was born on 22 June 1896. Educated at Mill Hill School (1909-12). When the war came in August 1914, Scholte, like many other Public School boys, immediately enlisted into the Royal Engineers as a motor-cycle despatch rider. Picked out for a commission, he was gazetted Second Lieutenant to the New Armies, with an attachment to the Bedfordshire Regiment on 20 March 1915. Seconded to the RFC later in the same year, he trained as an Observer and was sent out to 18 Squadron (Vickers FB5s). On 19 December 1915, Scholte and his Pilot, Lieutenant M Henderson, in FB5, '5476', successfully 'saw off' a DFW over Laventie. On 20 February 1916, the same pair in FB5, '5476', were shot down in flames by anti-aircraft fire. Scholte was able to extricate himself from the wreckage but his Pilot, Lieutenant M Henderson, was trapped, his leg having been struck by an AA shell. Scholte was forced to complete the amputation of the partly severed limb in order to free his Pilot and then to carry him away from the flames to safety. Scholte next trained as a Pilot and was duly confirmed and gazetted Flying Officer on 5 June 1916. He flew with 51 HD Squadron, before accompanying, as a 'founder member', 48 Squadron, the first to be equipped with Bristol Fighters, to France on 8 March 1917. Scholte achieved six victories between 2 May and 5 September 1917, his MC being announced in the *London Gazette* of 17 September 1917: 'For conspicuous gallantry and devotion to duty. On 2 July 1917, when on special patrol far out to sea off Ostend and at a height of 20,000 feet, this officer spotted five Gotha machines returning from a raid on England. He immediately fired a signal and dived to attack the enemy. As a result of his vigilance and promptitude one of the enemy aeroplanes was destroyed. On 13 July, over Snaeskirk-Slype, whilst on patrol with a formation he attacked seven hostile aeroplanes which were driven off, one of them driven out of control. This officer has destroyed three enemy aeroplanes, and has driven down three others completely out of control'.

Following a period instructing in the UK, he was sent out in the spring of 1918 to join 60 Squadron as a Flight Commander – this time flying SE5As. Two further victories followed on 15 and 19 May. Tragically, he was killed in a motor accident on 29 July 1918, when returning from a party at a neighbouring squadron, the crashed car driven by another MC winner, C M Crowe (qv). Owen Scholte is buried in St Riquier British Cemetery, Somme, France.

NB: The RAF Museum Hendon has his medals in its collection: MC, 1914-15 Star (2Lt RFC)*, British War Medal 1914-20, and Victory Medal 1914-19* (Capt RAF).

SCLANDERS, Gerald

From Pollackshields, Glasgow, he was born on 23 November 1893. Educated at Glasgow Academy. When the war came in 1914, he immediately enlisted as a Private soldier (Number 2407) into 1/9 Battalion, Highland Light Infantry (TF), and accompanied the original contingent to France on 5 November 1914, thus earning the 1914 Star. Served in the trenches in France and Flanders in 1914 and 1915. Picked out for a commission, he was gazetted Second Lieutenant to the New Armies on 27 March 1916, with an attachment to the Army Cycling Corps coming on 1 July following. He transferred to the RFC at the end of 1916 and, having successfully trained as a Pilot, was duly confirmed and gazetted Flying Officer on 13 March 1917. Sent out to 14 Squadron in the Middle East within days of qualifying for his 'Wings', he was rapidly promoted to A/Captain and Flight Commander in the following month of April 1917. His MC was announced in the *London Gazette* of 18 January 1918, details in the *Gazette* of 25 April 1918: 'For conspicuous gallantry and devotion to duty. He carried out two most important photographic reconnaissances of the enemy's position under intense anti-aircraft fire'.

He was also Mentioned in Despatches on two occasions during the Great War. Sclanders finally left the RAF, via the Unemployed List, in May 1919.

SCOTT, Alan John Lance

From Christchurch, New Zealand, he was born on 29 June 1884. He was living and practising as a Barrister in London in the years immediately preceding the outbreak of war. He was also a pre-war volunteer, having been gazetted Second Lieutenant to the Sussex Yeomanry (TF) in 1911. Mobilised with the rest of the TF on 4 August 1914, he took flying lessons to enhance his chances of transferring to the RFC. Gained his Royal Aero Club Certificate (Number 975) on 20 November 1914. His formal pilot training duly completed, he was confirmed and gazetted Flying Officer on 1 February 1915. Whilst building up his flying experience in the UK, he crashed and broke both his legs. The bones did not knit well and he could walk only with the aid of sticks, and had to be helped in and out of the cockpit of his machine. In 1917, he flew Sopwith Strutters with 43 Squadron before, later in the same year, being given command of 60 Squadron. Never regarded as a particularly good Pilot, he was certainly enthusiastic and aggressive. Given to flying off alone looking for trouble, he more than once ran into difficulties, not least when he confronted the German Ace Leutnant Karl Allmenroder of Jasta 11 and was forced down near to Monchy-le-Preux. This encounter, if nothing else, provided Scott with further pieces of his wrecked or shot-up machine, with which he delighted in decorating his office. Scott achieved five victories between 31 March and

10 July 1917, receiving a wound in the arm on the day he gained his fifth, an Albatros DIII down in flames. His MC was announced in the *London Gazette* of 26 July 1917: 'For conspicuous gallantry and devotion to duty. He has on several occasions attacked and destroyed enemy aircraft, and taken successful photographs under heavy fire. He has constantly shown the greatest courage in attacking numerous hostile machines single-handed, during which on two occasions his own machine was considerably damaged. His great coolness, dash, and resource have set an excellent example to his squadron'.

Having relinquished his command of '60', he served on the Staff at 11 Wing HQ, before being given command of the CFS at Upavon. He was awarded the Air Force Cross, *London Gazette* of 1 January 1919, and promoted to Lieutenant Colonel. In the following year, he was created a CB and confirmed in the rank of Group Captain, RAF. Scott wrote a history of 60 Squadron, which has become a classic of the genre. 'Jack' Scott died at 26 Chester Street, London, as a consequence of double pneumonia on 16 January 1922.

SCOTT, David Harden

The son of Station Master, Matthew Scott and Elizabeth Scott, of 11 Dufferin Avenue, Bangor, County Down, Ireland, he was born on 24 November 1895. Educated at the Municipal Technical Institute and the Belfast Trade Preparatory School. Worked as a Weaver in the linen trade, living in Ballynahinch, County Down. Served in the Ulster Volunteer Force and Queen's University OTC, from August 1914, when the war came. He enlisted as a Private soldier into the Ulster Division in October 1914. Gazetted Second Lieutenant to 16 Battalion, Royal Irish Rifles (2 County Down Pioneers), on 28 January 1915. Scott subsequently served with the Army Cyclist Corps in France, before being seconded to the RFC in the summer of 1916. Having trained as an Observer, he was sent out as a Probationary to FE2b-equipped 11 Squadron in France. On 28 August 1916, Scott and his Pilot, Second Lieutenant H H Turk (qv), in FE2b, '4926', confronted a formation of seven enemy machines over Montauban. After accounting for one of the enemy, their rudder was damaged and Turk was forced to crashland the spiralling FE. Fortunately, although their machine was wrecked, the crew were unhurt. Scott and Turk each received the MC for this incident, announced in the *London Gazette* of 20 October 1916: 'For conspicuous gallantry and skill. With Second Lieutenant Turk [qv] as pilot, he attacked seven hostile machines flying in formation, and brought down one as a wreck'.

Scott's 'apprenticeship' satisfactorily completed, he was confirmed and gazetted Flying Officer (Observer) on 18 October 1916. His tour with '11' completed, he returned to the UK to undertake pilot training. Once qualified, he accompanied the Sopwith Camel F1-equipped 65 Squadron to France on 27 October 1917. On 27 November 1917, Scott's Camel, 'B2417', appears to have been struck by a shell during an offensive patrol over German occupied territory. His body was originally buried by the Germans, but is now in the Commonwealth War Graves cemetery at Pont-du-Hem, La Gorgue, France.

SCOTT, Francis James

The son of Mr and Mrs R C Scott, of Gorree Station, Widgiewa Siding, New South Wales, Australia, he was born in Kurrumburra, Victoria, on 27 July 1895. After completing his education, he worked as a grazier from 1912 to 1916. He enlisted into the AIF on 11 September 1916 and, his basic training completed, he embarked from Melbourne aboard SS *Ulysses*, (Transport A38), bound for the UK, on 25 October 1916. Scott was, by this time, an Acting Sergeant with 'C' Flight, 2 Squadron, Australian Flying Corps. He was demoted to 2 AM on 28 December 1916, but this appears to have been a temporary aberration as he was next gazetted Second Lieutenant and Pilot, Australian Flying Corps, on 8 September 1917. Scott served with 4 Squadron, AFC, from early in the New Year of 1918, claiming his first victory against a Rumpler over Lens on 6 March 1918. He fought through the fraught and dangerous days of the German Spring offensive that commenced on 21 March 1918. Two of his own reports for 26 March 1918, give insights into the work of Scout Pilots in those anxious days: 'Dropped two bombs, one on village of Gommecourt and one on village of Achiet-le-Grand from 1,000 feet (11.25am). Fired 600 rounds at troops and transport on road Bihucourt-Sapignies from 800 feet. Observed number fall and remainder seek cover. Bomb dropped on Gommecourt exploded amongst vehicles and guns'.

'Dropped two bombs on park of transport at Gueudecourt from 1,000 feet (3.45pm). Fired 550 rounds at troops and billets along road Le Sars-Gueudecourt from 800 feet'.

On 28 March 1918, he shot down an enemy machine which turned over on to its back and then spun full tilt into the ground. Scott was hospitalised on 2 May 1918, his operational career curtailed. His MC was announced in the *London Gazette* of 22 June 1918: 'For conspicuous gallantry and devotion to duty. After carrying out a bombing attack, he observed an enemy plane, into which he fired 80 rounds. The hostile plane turned on its back and crashed to earth. Four days previous to this he had destroyed an enemy two-seater machine and had sent down out of control a hostile scout. In addition to these, he had destroyed another hostile two-seater machine. He had displayed marked courage and determination'.

Obviously determined to return home as soon as possible, he arrived back in Melbourne aboard the SS *Niagara*, on 19 September 1918, having travelled at his own expense. His appointment with the AIF terminated on 10 October 1918.

SCOTT, James Stanley

The son of Colonel B A Scott and Mrs Scott, of Quebec, Canada, he was born on 18 February 1889. Educated at Quebec High School and privately. He worked in the family's lumber and paper mills prior to volunteering his services when the Great War came. Gazetted Lieutenant to the Canadian Field Artillery on 30 December 1914. He crossed to England with 26 Battery, Canadian Field Artillery, arriving on 10 August 1915. Once in the UK, he tried for the flying service, gaining his Royal Aero Club Certificate (Number 1988) at the Military School, Birmingham, on 5 November 1915. His formal pilot training duly completed, he was confirmed and gazetted Flying Officer on 21 March 1916. Sent out to BE2c-equipped 5 Squadron on 20 April following. On 3 July 1916, his BE2c, '2752', was shot up and damaged by fire from the ground as he was bombing a train near to Cambrai. He received an immediate MC for this incident, announced in the *London Gazette* of 27 July 1916: 'For conspicuous gallantry and skill. He descended to 1,000 feet to attack a train well behind the enemy's line, and though his engine was much damaged, his tank pierced, and his flying wires carried away by hostile fire, he succeeded in landing his machine safely within our lines'.

On 20 July 1916, he was promoted to A/Captain and Flight Commander and sent to 6 Squadron. Scott was injured in a crash in the following August which necessitated his return to the UK for medical treatment. Once recovered, he was posted to instructing duties in the UK. In 1918, Scott was promoted to A/Major and sent to North America to instruct in Texas, and at Camp Borden, Ontario, Canada. Further advancement to the rank of Lieutenant Colonel was followed by the award of the Air Force Cross for his services in the training field, *London Gazette* of 1 January 1919. Scott left the RAF to revert to the Canadian Army, on 30 March 1919. Scott was appointed Superintendent, Certificates Branch, Canadian Air Board, on 4 November 1919. Soon afterwards the title of this post was changed to Controller of Civil Aviation in Canada. In 1922, he was a Wing Commander and CO at Camp Borden. He next took the RAF Staff course at Andover, becoming the first Canadian officer to qualify as psa. Promoted to Group Captain in 1925, he was also appointed Honorary ADC to the Governor General of Canada. He left the RCAF between the wars, but returned to service when the Second World War came in 1939. Following service in various training commands, Scott finally retired in

February 1945, with the honorary rank of Air Commodore. Air Commodore James Scott died in Halifax, Nova Scotia, on 19 July 1975.

NB: The Canadian War Museum has his medals in its collection: MC, Air Force Cross, British War Medal 1914-20, Victory Medal 1914-19, Canada Voluntary Service Medal 1939-47, War Medal 1939-45, Jubilee Medal 1935, and Efficiency Decoration.

SCOTT, Laurence Henry

The son of Henry and Ada Augusta Scott (née Gibbons), of 88 Drakefield Road, Streatham, London, he was born in Forest Gate, Essex, on 9 March 1896. Educated at the City of London School (1908-13) and at the University of Paris (1913-14). Gazetted Second Lieutenant to 8 Battalion, Middlesex Regiment (TF), on 26 February 1915. Sent out to join his battalion in the Ypres Salient on 2 April 1915, just in time to participate in the Battle of St Julien, later in the same month. Seconded to the RFC in the early summer of 1916, he trained as an Observer and was sent out as a Probationary to 20 Squadron in France. Striking up an excellent partnership with Captain G R M Reid (qv), Scott achieved six victories between 29 July and 21 October 1916. His MC was announced in the *London Gazette* of 25 November 1916: 'For conspicuous gallantry in action. He and his pilot pursued a hostile aeroplane for some six miles into the enemy's territory and there shot it down. He has on many previous occasions done very fine work'.

Scott was also Mentioned in Despatches inn the *London Gazette* of 25 November 1916. His tour with '20' completed on 26 November 1916, he returned to the Home Establishment for a short rest. In 1917, he was promoted to A/Captain and posted to No 1 School of Air Gunnery as an Instructor, never again to return to operational flying. He finally left the service, via the Unemployed List, on 20 April 1919. Laurence Scott died on 4 September 1982.

SCOTT, Maurice Douglas Guest

The second son of Mr and Mrs P W G Scott, of 'Oakwood', Sananita Road, Westcliffe-on-Sea, he was born on 13 August 1895 in Felixstowe. Educated at Charterhouse (1909-10). Gazetted Second Lieutenant to 3 (Reserve) Battalion, Loyal North Lancashire Regiment on 14 November 1914. Seconded to the RFC in January 1916, he trained as an Observer and was sent out to 18 Squadron as a Probationary in the following month. On 3 April 1916, Scott and his Pilot, Lieutenant A L Findlay, attacked and damaged an Albatros, which was then finished off by colleagues, Captain D M Rawcliffe and Sergeant Woodfield, who sent it down into the British lines south of Souchez. Both German crew members were killed in the subsequent crash and the German artillery afterwards pounded the wreck of the Albatros into smithereens. His 'apprenticeship' satisfactorily completed, Scott was formally confirmed and gazetted Flying Officer (Observer) on 25 May 1916. Scott next trained as a Pilot and, once qualified, flew Sopwith Pups with 54 Squadron during the spring of 1917, gaining four victories between 5 April and 1 June. Promoted to A/Captain and Flight Commander, he was posted next to 46 Squadron- a unit also equipped with Sopwith Pups. Seven further victories followed in the month of September, taking his tally to 12. His tour completed, he returned to the Home Establishment on 3 October 1917, the announcement of his MC coming in the *London Gazette* of 27 October 1917: 'For conspicuous gallantry and devotion to duty in aerial combats. On one occasion his patrol encountered seven enemy machines, two of which he drove down out of control. He has destroyed eleven enemy aeroplanes, and proved himself a dashing patrol leader'.

Scott was serving with 91 Squadron in the UK in 1918, when he was critically injured in a flying accident at Shoreham on 17 March 1918, dying later that day in Brighton Hospital, Brighton. Maurice Scott is buried in Ockbrook (All Saints) Churchyard, Derbyshire, near to his widowed mother's home at 72 Wilson Street, Derby.

SCOTT, Walter Somerville

The son of Mr and Mrs W Scott, of Lyngarth, Disley, Cheshire, he was born in November 1895. Educated at Uppingham (1910-13). Volunteering as soon as war came, he was gazetted Second Lieutenant to 7 Battalion, Lancashire Fusiliers (TF). He served in Gallipoli and in Egypt with his battalion, before gaining his Royal Aero Club Certificate (Number 2780) on 25 April 1916. His formal pilot training duly completed at RFC HQ, Egypt, he was confirmed and gazetted Flying Officer on 31 August following. Sent out to 17 Squadron in Salonika soon after qualifying for his 'Wings'. On 10 December 1916, Scott in a BE2c, accompanied by a Greek Army officer, was on a special patrol looking for a likely location to drop a spy on a future mission. Intent on scanning the landscape, they were surprised by an enemy machine which had taken off from Drama aerodrome to challenge their intrusion. After a brief fight, Scott sent the enemy machine down out of control. The first of his MCs was announced in the *London Gazette* of 3 March 1917: 'For conspicuous gallantry and devotion to duty. On several occasions he displayed great skill and daring in carrying out his orders under dangerous conditions'.

On 10 May following, Scott and his Observer of the day, Captain K W M Pickthorn, in a BE2c, were attacked near Vorna, west of Tahinos Lake, by the German Ace, Leutnant Rudolf von Eschwege of FAb30. Rather optimistically, von Eschwege claimed the British pair as the seventh of his eventual 20 victories. In fact, Scott got their shot-up BE back to safety, although Pickthorn, a future MP and Baronet, was wounded in the air. Scott was Mentioned in Despatches for Salonika in the *London Gazette* of 18 July 1917. A Bar to his MC was announced in the New Year *London Gazette* of 1 January 1918 (no citation). Following his exertions with 17 Squadron, he was withdrawn from operational flying to instructing duties – duties he performed to such a high standard that he was awarded the Air Force Cross in recognition, *London Gazette* of 1 January 1919. The Greeks, too, showed their appreciation with the award of the Greek Military Cross, 3rd Class, *London Gazette* of 16 December 1919. By 1931, Scott had married and was living with his wife, Helen Edith, at their home at 'Minden', Eshe Road North, Blundellsands, Liverpool. Walter Scott died on 15 June 1931 at the Rose and Crown Hotel, Evesham, Worcester.

SCUTT, George Howard Homer (also known as G H Homer-Scutt)

The son of Brewer Master, George Decimus Homer Scutt and Mrs Scutt, of Greywelt, New Ross, County Wexford, Ireland, he was born on 5 May 1898. Educated at the John Ivon School, New Ross (1908-11), at Cheltenham (1912-15), where he was a member of the OTC, and at Sandhurst. Gazetted Second Lieutenant to a Regular Army battalion of the King's (Liverpool Regiment) on 7 April 1916, Colonel Tripp of the KLR was an uncle. Serving with 1 Battalion of his regiment, Scutt received a shrapnel wound to his right arm during a successful trench raid at Serre, on the Somme, on 15 September 1916, and was invalided to the UK as a consequence. Once recovered, he trained as an Observer and was sent out as such to the F2b-equipped 48 Squadron in France. He enjoyed success with various Pilots, including Captain L A Payne (qv), his MC announced in the *London Gazette* of 22 June 1918: 'For conspicuous gallantry and devotion to duty. He has destroyed one hostile machine, and driven down three others out of control. He carried out an important single-machine reconnaissance, frequently descending to a height of 100 feet under heavy rifle and machine-gun-fire. While returning, he attacked five enemy machines, and ably assisted his pilot in driving them back over their lines. He has carried out many successful photographic reconnaissances, and has at all times proved himself to be a keen and daring officer'.

Staying on in the RAF after the war, he was a Flight Lieutenant when he was killed whilst flying over Hawkings Aerodrome, Folkestone, Kent, on 15 February 1924.

SELBY, James Geoffrey

The son of Mr and Mrs H T Selby, Northfield, Bromley, Kent, he was born on 28 February 1895. Educated at Haileybury (1909-12). Volunteering immediately the war came, he was gazetted Second Lieutenant to the Royal Field Artillery on 11 August 1914. After service in France with the RFA, he was seconded to the RFC in the late summer of 1915. He served first as an Observer, being confirmed and gazetted Flying Officer (Observer) on 21 October 1915. Having already begun flying lessons, he gained his Royal Aero Club Certificate (Number 1927) on 23 October 1915, but still Selby was sent out to Egypt as an Observer with 14 Squadron, serving operationally from 5 February to 11 June 1916. His formal pilot training eventually completed, he was given his full 'Wings' on the intervening 9 June 1916. He returned first to the UK before being sent out to 6 Squadron in France as an A/Captain and Flight Commander on 22 December 1916. His MC was announced in the *London Gazette* of 26 July 1917: 'For conspicuous gallantry and devotion to duty. During a photographic reconnaissance he was attacked by five hostile scouts, whom he put to flight, continuing his work with complete success. He afterwards attacked and put to flight an enemy battery. His work at all times has been marked by the greatest courage and ability'.

His tour with '6' completed, he returned to the Home Establishment on 28 July 1917 and was posted to instructing duties. Selby received his MC from the hands of the King at an investiture held at Buckingham Palace on 16 March 1918. After the war, he reverted to his commission with the Royal Artillery. He married, in 1929, Auvigny Scudmore. In the Second World War, Selby was promoted to Brigadier and served as Chief Instructor at the School of Artillery from 1941 to 1942. Further service in India and in Italy followed during 1943 and 1945. Selby retired from the Army with the rank of Brigadier in 1948. In civilian life he held a position with the International Refugee Organisation from 1948 to 1950. James Selby subsequently became Managing Director of the family firm, H & E Selby Ltd, Wine Merchants, living at 'Fairfield', Coombe Hill, East Grinstead, Sussex.

SELLARS, Herbert Whiteley

The son of Mr and Mrs Frank Sellars, of 'Wentworth', Meols Drive, Hoylake, Wirral, Cheshire, he was born in Liverpool on 11 June 1896. His brother, Eric Francis Sellars, also won an MC with 12 Battalion, Cheshire Regiment, before he was killed in action in Salonika on 18 September 1918. Herbert was educated at The Leas, Hoylake, at Loretto (1910-15), where he was a Corporal in the OTC, and was entered for Caius College, Cambridge, when the war intervened. Anxious to join the flying service, he gained, at his own expense, his Royal Aero Club Certificate (Number 2852) on 10 May 1916. The acquisition of his 'ticket' no doubt helped his cause, as he was gazetted Second Lieutenant to the RFC, via the Special Reserve, on 3 June following. His formal pilot training duly completed, he was confirmed and gazetted Flying Officer on 20 July 1916. Sent out to the FEs of 25 Squadron in the same month that he qualified for his 'Wings'. His stint with '25' was cut short when he was injured in a crash and hospitalised on 16 September 1916. Once fully recovered, Sellars joined the Bristol Fighter-equipped 11 Squadron on 6 October 1917. Teaming up with Lieutenant C C Robson (qv), the pair became a formidable partnership, achieving eight victories between 12 March and 15 May 1918. One of their two victories on 21 March 1918, the first day of the great German spring offensive, was particularly notable as it was over Leutnant Ludwig Hanstein, an Ace with 16 victories to his credit and also the Commanding Officer of Jasta 35. Sellars was slightly wounded on 14 April 1918, but quickly recovered. On 15 May 1918, Sellars and Robson fell victim to Leutnant Josef Mai of Jasta 5, becoming the 12th of the German Ace's eventual 30 victories. The British pair in F2b, 'C845', were intercepted and shot down over Contalmaison, with Robson surviving to be taken prisoner of war, but Herbert Sellars being killed outright in the incident. His MC, mainly for his successes on 21 March 1918, was posthumously announced in the *London Gazette* of 22 June 1918: 'For conspicuous gallantry and devotion to duty. Whilst on offensive patrol, he attacked a hostile two-seater machine which dived vertically and eventually crashed. Having attacked another two-seater machine, which dived down over the enemy's lines, he engaged three hostile scouts, at the nearest of which his Observer fired two bursts at 75 yards range, causing the enemy machine to crash down in flames. His skill and gallantry have been most marked'.

Sellars' body was never recovered and hence he is commemorated on the Flying Services Memorial, Arras, France.

SELOUS, Frederick Hatherley Bruce

The eldest son of Captain Frederick Courtney Selous, DSO, and Marie Catherine Gladys Selous (née Maddy), of 'Heatherside', Worplesdon, Surrey, he was born on 21 April 1898. Educated at Rugby (1912-15) Rugby XV, Rowing VIII, 1st Athletic Cup, 1915, and at Sandhurst. Gazetted Second Lieutenant to a Regular Army battalion of the Queen's, Royal West Surrey Regiment, on 7 April 1916, with an immediate secondment to the RFC. Gained his Royal Aero Club Certificate (Number 2844) on 3 May 1916. His formal pilot training duly completed, he was confirmed and gazetted Flying Officer on 9 July following. Accompanied 19 Squadron, newly equipped with BE12s fitted with Vickers interrupter gear, to France as a 'founder member' on 30 July 1916. On 25 September 1916, Selous' BE12, '6553', was shot up during a contact patrol, but despite the damage inflicted, he managed to get the machine back to his own aerodrome. His tour with '19' completed, he returned to the Home Establishment on 28 April 1917 and was posted to instruct at the CFS, Upavon. In May 1917, the Italians awarded him the Silver Medaglia al Valore Militare, *London Gazette* of 26 May 1917. His MC was announced in the *London Gazette* of 4 June 1917 (no citation). Although no formal citation was published, research has unearthed the original recommendation for the award: '19 Squadron. Has attacked HA on many occasions and has set a fine example by his courage and bold tactics. He has done very useful contact patrol work at low altitudes'.

Promoted to A/Captain and Flight Commander, Selous was next sent out to 60 Squadron on 4 September 1917. Although his victories were few, he gained a sound reputation as a brave and resourceful Flight Commander. On 4 January 1918, Selous in SE5A, 'C5334, dived at some enemy machines several thousand feet below him. In the middle of his dive, at a speed estimated at 300 mph, the wings of his machine stripped completely off. By an amazing coincidence, Selous' father, Captain F C Selous, DSO, a famous explorer and elephant hunter, had been killed in action in East Africa on 4 January 1917, precisely one year earlier. In a letter to Frederick's mother, a brother officer wrote: 'I was up at 15,000 feet over the German lines on 4 January in company with my Squadron Leader, Captain Selous. All at once both wings of his aeroplane suddenly collapsed and the machine fell like a stone to the earth. We are terribly upset at this, as he was idolised by us all'. His body was never recovered and hence he is commemorated on the Flying Services Memorial, Arras.

SESSIONS, Donald Humphrey

The son of Mr and Mrs Herbert Sessions, of Quedgeley Court, Gloucester, he was born on 21 February 1897. Educated, as were his three brothers, at Radley College (1911-14). One brother, Herbert, won an MC with 5 Gloucesters and another brother, Reginald, served as a Pilot in the RFC. The third brother, Lionel, a Solicitor, lost his leg above the knee while serving with the British Red Cross in Italy. Donald worked as a Clerk with the family firm, Sessions and Sons of Gloucester, from September 1914 until January 1916. As soon as he was old enough, he enlisted as a Private soldier (Number 7517) into 28 London Regiment (Artist Rifles). Picked out for a commission, he was gazetted Second Lieutenant to the RFC, via the General List, on 27 January 1917. His formal pilot training duly completed, he was confirmed and gazetted Flying Officer on 24 April 1917. Sent out to 21 Squadron (RE8s) in France on 28 April 1917. On 26 September 1917, Sessions and his Observer, Second Lieutenant D Alexander, were attacked by three enemy aircraft. Sessions sent his machine into a dive and fired upwards into one of his attackers from below, shooting its wing straight off. His tour with '21' completed on 29 November 1917, he returned to the UK and was posted to training duties. His MC was announced in the *London Gazette* of 8 January 1918, details in the *Gazette* of 25 April 1918: 'For conspicuous gallantry and devotion to duty. During two months he did 111 hours flying on artillery work, often under heavy anti-aircraft fire. He constantly observed most successfully for the artillery, causing direct hits on gun pits, fires and explosions'.

Attached to No 2 School of Aerial Gunnery and instructing with 48 TS in Kent, he was killed in a flying accident over New Romney on 20 June 1918. Donald Sessions is buried in Quedgeley (St James) Churchyard, Gloucestershire.

SEWARD, William Eric Louis

From London, he was born on 6 July 1891. He worked as an Articled Clerk in the City of London from 1910 to 1914. Anxious to join the flying service, he took lessons at his own expense, gaining his Royal Aero Club Certificate (Number 1975) at the Hall Aviation Company School, Hendon, on 29 October 1915. No doubt the acquisition of his 'ticket' helped his cause, and he was gazetted Second Lieutenant to the RFC, via the Special List, on 15 April 1916. His formal pilot training duly completed, he was confirmed and gazetted Flying Officer on 6 July 1916. Sent out to the Middle East and 14 Squadron, he commenced his operational flying on 27 August 1916 and was soon promoted to Flight Commander. On 24 March 1917, flying a Martinsyde G100, he came under anti-aircraft fire over Ramleh which hit his petrol tank. He succeeded in reaching the coast just four miles north of Ascalon, but his engine failed and he was forced to land in the sea. Seventeen miles behind the Turkish lines and treading water just 200 yards from a Turkish post, it seemed that matters could not get worse for Seward, but then a shore-based machine gun opened fire upon him. He swam away from the shore as quickly as he could before, becoming exhausted, he floated on the surface, partly to catch his breath and partly in the hope that the Turks would assume him dead. The ruse appeared to work, as the machine gunners left him alone. Seward gradually stripped off his clothes and swam steadily south for four hours before, exhausted again and feeling the cold, he waded ashore just before dusk. After resting in nearby sandhills, he set off along the shoreline. Skirting Gaza as best he could, he was occasionally forced to take cover to avoid Turkish patrols. After walking for 13 miles, he reached Wadi Guzzeh and safety. His tour with '14' completed on 9 October 1917, he was posted back to Egypt and instructing duties there. His MC was announced in the New Year *London Gazette* of 1 January 1918 (no citation). He was also Mentioned in Despatches in the *London Gazette* of 12 January 1918. William Seward died on 11 October 1975.

SHAKESPEARE, William Harold Nelson

The son of Mr and Mrs William Shakespeare of Chatsworth, Barbourne, Worcester, he was born on 24 August 1893. Educated at the Royal Grammar School, Worcester. A fine cricketer for the Grammar School and later as Captain of the Barbourne XI. When the war came, he immediately enlisted into 8 Battalion, Worcestershire Regiment (TF), and subsequently accompanied the unit to France on 31 March 1918. After serving in the trenches for twelve months, he was picked out as officer material and sent to 9 OTC at Gailies. Gazetted Second Lieutenant to the RFC, via the Special Lists, on 7 July 1916. He next gained his Royal Aero Club Certificate (Number 3548) on 7 September 1916. His formal pilot training duly completed, he was confirmed and gazetted Flying Officer on 3 November following. Posted on the following day to the AWFK8-equipped 35 Squadron, then at Thetford, he eventually accompanied the unit to France as a 'founder member' on 26 January 1917. His service with '35' was interrupted when he was hospitalised on 7 April 1917. His health restored, he re-joined '35' on 19 June 1917 and was subsequently promoted to Captain and Flight Commander on 14 September following. His tour completed, he returned to the Home Establishment and a posting to instructing duties on 5 December 1917. His MC was announced in the *London Gazette* of 4 February 1918, details in the *Gazette* of 5 July 1918: 'For conspicuous gallantry and devotion to duty. He carried out a most successful contact patrol in very bad weather at a height of 400 feet and brought back very valuable information. Later, he carried out another successful contact patrol at a low altitude, his machine being subjected to intense rifle and machine-gun fire. He is a gallant and determined pilot and has set a fine example to his squadron'.

His work as an Instructor was duly acknowledged with the award of an Air Force Cross, announced in the *London Gazette* of 2 November 1918. After leaving the RAF, Shakespeare became a journalist in London, working as a reporter and foreign correspondent for a number of newspapers. Later in life, Shakespeare returned to live in Worcester, becoming an Alderman and a Justice of the Peace. He died on 10 July 1976.

SHARP, Jonathan Gumersal

From Toronto, he was born in 1894. He was studying Divinity at the University of Toronto when the war came in 1914. He proceeded overseas in December 1915 and, after arriving in the UK, was gazetted Second Lieutenant to the RGA on 11 January 1916. A secondment to the RFC came later in the same year and, after training as an Observer, he was appointed a Balloon Officer on 22 February 1917. He joined 4 Balloon Wing on 20 March 1917, but soon afterwards changed tack and, following the appropriate training, was gazetted Flying Officer (Observer) on 1 June 1917. Sent out to the RE8-equipped 34 Squadron, he mainly flew operationally over Herbecourt, Epehy, Marcoin, St Quentin and Nieuport, and it was near this latter place that he won his MC in unusual circumstances on 5 August 1917. One version of the incident states that Sharp, flying with Second Lieutenant A W Little, in RE8, 'A4709', on an afternoon patrol, were hit by anti-aircraft fire and fell into the sea. Their machine sank, forcing the uninjured Sharp and his wounded Pilot to swim to the shore and to safety behind Allied lines. However, the formal citation of his MC tells a different story, *London Gazette* of 26 September 1917, details in the *Gazette* of 9 January 1918: 'For conspicuous gallantry and devotion to duty. When on patrol his machine was brought down by an anti-aircraft gun and turned completely over on landing, pinning the pilot underneath. Second Lieutenant Sharp who had been thrown clear, immediately went to his assistance and pulled him out. They then ran towards the canal, which they swam, and reached our lines in safety. From the moment their machine was hit until they reached our lines they were under continual fire, but both escaped unwounded'.

He next accompanied his squadron to Italy in December 1917 and was subsequently wounded in the air over Piave on 31 March 1918. Eventually returning home to Canada, he again took up his studies at the University of Toronto, graduating BA in 1920.

SHAW-LAWRENCE, Lawrence Ernest

From Wye, Kent, he was born on 1 June 1888. He was a qualified Mechanical Engineer living with his wife in Norbiton, London SW, and working for the P & O Steam Navigation Company, London EC, when the war came in August 1914. He immediately enlisted as a Private soldier into 4 Battalion, East Kent Regiment (TF), subsequently serving with the Buffs in India and in Aden. Gazetted Second Lieutenant into his own unit in 1916, he returned to the UK for secondment to the RFC. Having trained as an Observer, he was sent to France on 16 July 1917, with a posting as a Probationary to the RE8-equipped 59 Squadron coming just six days later. His 'apprenticeship' satisfactorily completed, he was confirmed and gazetted Flying Officer on 11 September 1917. His tour with '59' completed on 11 February 1918, he returned to the Home Establishment and a posting to instructing duties. His MC was announced in the *London Gazette* of 4 February 1918, details in the *Gazette* of 5 July 1918: 'For conspicuous gallantry and devotion to duty. He carried out thirteen successful contact patrols and reconnaissances, many of them at a very low altitude and in very bad weather under heavy rifle and machine-gun fire. On one occasion during an enemy attack he carried out three patrols in one day at a low altitude under heavy fire and brought back valuable information. In the course of one patrol he attacked a large party of the enemy from a height of 100 feet and dispersed them with machine-gun fire. He showed the greatest determination and initiative'.

Shaw-Lawrence finally left the RAF, via the Unemployed List, on 14 April 1919.

SHEPHARD, Gordon Strachey

The second son of Sir Horatio and Lady Shephard, of 58 Montagu Square, London W, he was born in Madras, India, on 9 July 1885, and named for General Gordon, killed in Khartoum in the same year. Educated at Summer Fields, at Eton (1898-1903), and at Sandhurst. Gazetted Second Lieutenant to a Regular Army battalion of the Royal Fusiliers on 28 January 1905. He was an outstanding yachtsman and is thought to have 'spied' on strategic places around the German seaboard in the manner of the heroes of Erskine Childers' fictional novel, 'The Riddle of the Sands', published in 1903. In point of fact, Shephard had, indeed, met Erskine Childers and knew him well. Shephard's covert operations came to an abrupt halt when he and a companion were briefly detained by the German authorities at Emden, after injudiciously taking graphs in a sensitive area. Released without charge, Shephard returned to the UK and, after receiving lessons at the Bristol School, Brooklands, gained his Royal Aero Club Certificate (Number 215) on a Bristol machine on 14 May 1912. Attached to the RFC from July 1912, he at first concentrated on the use of airships for military purposes, but soon turned his attentions to aeroplanes. On 13 August 1914, as a Flight Commander with 4 Squadron, he accompanied the original RFC contingent to France, personally piloting a BE2 to the front. On 22 August 1914, Shephard landed at Beaumont, about 12 miles east of Maubeuge, for petrol and there received first hand accounts of the fighting in the vicinity from French cavalry units falling back from the Sambre canal. Shephard made an immediate and significant impact on events when, on 24 August 1914, he and his Observer, Lieutenant I M Bonham-Carter, brought back conclusive evidence to the Staff, that von Kluck's Right Wing would swamp the British Army unless the retreat was continued. On 4 November 1914, Shephard narrowly escaped disaster when the longeron of his BE2b, '487', was shot through. He was, around this time, appointed Chevalier of the Légion d'Honneur by the French. His MC was announced in the *London Gazette* of 18 February 1915: 'For services in connection with operations in the field'.

After a brief return to the UK, Shephard crossed again to France on 4 March 1915, this time to command 6 Squadron. Shephard led '6' through the great battles of 1915, before returning to England in December to command Eighth Wing, RFC, with the rank of Lieutenant Colonel. He returned to France again in the New Year of 1916, this time to command 12 Corps, RFC, which comprised 8, 12 and 13 Squadrons. His command was engaged mainly on counter-battery work from 1 July 1916, the opening day of the Battle of the Somme, through to the battle's end in the following November. In January 1917, Shephard took over temporary command of III Brigade RFC, and, on 8 February following, was appointed to the command of I Brigade, RFC, with the rank of Brigadier General. After the fighting in and around Arras in the following April, Shephard was awarded the Distinguished Service Order, *London Gazette* of 4 June 1917: '....for distinguished service in the field'. Shephard was also Mentioned in Despatches on no less than six occasions during the Great War, *London Gazettes* of 20 November 1914, 15 October 1915, 13 November 1916, 9 April 1917, 7 November 1917 and 7 April 1918. Research has unearthed an original recommendation for one of his 'Mentions', specifically that which appeared in the *London Gazette* of 13 November 1916: '8 October 1916: Has shown great energy and ability in command of the Corps Wing from April to October 1916. He has extensive knowledge of Artillery co-operation and has superintended the work of his squadrons admirably. His work has been very valuable'.

On 19 January 1918, Shephard decided to visit the aerodrome at Auchel, where three of his squadrons were stationed. His Nieuport Scout, 'B3610', for no obvious reason, suddenly spun into the ground. Barely alive, he was lifted from the wreckage and taken to hospital, where he died within hours, the highest ranking officer of the flying services to be killed in a theatre of war during the Great War. Brigadier Gordon Shephard is buried in Lapugnoy Military Cemetery, France.

A biography written by Shane Leslie,'The Memoirs of Gordon Shephard', was privately published in 1924

SHEPHERD, Alfred Seymour

From New South Wales, Australia, born in Nowra, on 13 April 1893. When he enlisted into the Australian Army he was living in Peterham. Served as an officer in 30 and 46 Infantry Battalions before transferring to the RFC on 23 October 1916. Having trained as a pilot he joined 29 Squadron on 25 April 1917 and flying Nieuport Scouts began scoring in May and brought his score to ten by the end of June. He was awarded the Military Cross, *London Gazette* of 17 September: 'While on balloon attack he came under heavy fire from a rocket battery. He attacked this battery from a low altitude, silencing it, and dispersing the gunners. He then returned to the attack on a balloon and fired all his ammunition, and though his machine was badly hit, crossed the lines at 100 feet.' He became a Flight Commander on 13 July but on the 20th he was shot down by Alfred Neiderhoff of Jasta 11 and killed. It was the German's sixth victory, but after gaining one further victory, he was himself shot down and killed by a pilot from 29 Squadron on the 28th. Shepherd's award of the Distinguished Service Order was gazetted on 16 August 1917: 'For conspicuous gallantry in combat with hostile aircraft. Though surrounded by enemy machines. He continued to fight for nearly an hour with the utmost gallantry and determination against two hostile formations, finally bringing down one of the enemy out of control. Within a month he brought down seven hostile machines completely out of control.' Shepherd has no known grave and his name appears on the Arras Memorial.

SHERREN, Percy Clark

The son of William Douglas Sherren and Florence Sherren (née Carrier), of Charlottetown, Prince Edward Island, Canada. When the war came in 1914, he was working as a Bank Clerk with the Bank of Nova Scotia in St John, New Brunswick. A volunteer with 62 Canadian Regiment, St John's Fusiliers, in 1914, he was later gazetted Lieutenant to 12 Battalion, Canadian Infantry, on 15 June 1915. Leaving for the CEF in France in October 1915, he served in the trenches with 26 Canadian Infantry until being wounded during a patrol early in 1916. Following treatment in a London hospital, he was accepted for service with the RFC, gaining his Royal Aero Club Certificate (Number 3281) on 6 July 1916. His formal pilot training duly completed, he was confirmed and gazetted Flying Officer on 30 July following. Sent out to France and the 'Flying Elephants' of 27 Squadron, shortly after qualifying for his 'Wings'. He narrowly escaped disaster on 19 August 1916, when his Martinsyde G100, '7464', was shot up in a combat with an enemy machine. His engine hit and malfunctioning, Sherren was forced to land, but escaped the incident physically unscathed. The first of his MCs was announced in the *London Gazette* of 23 November 1916: 'For conspicuous gallantry in action. He led a successful bomb raid, collecting and landing his formation with great skill. Later, he dropped bombs on an ammunition train from 500 feet, causing much damage'.

Research has unearthed the original recommendation for this award, which gives a more detailed description of the circumstances: 'P C Sherren. 23/10/16, 26 Can Rgt, 27 Sq. On October 20th led a bomb raid to Aulnoye. The formation descended through clouds and dropped their bombs under heavy fire. He collected the formation afterwards, and all landed together. On September 15th he dropped bombs before dawn on Bourlon Château, and in the afternoon dropped one bomb on an ammunition train from 500 feet, causing several coaches to explode, and the other bomb on a large group of men. On September 6th he dropped his bombs at Aulnoye from 700 feet and damaged a train in the sidings'.

The Bar to his MC came in the Birthday Honours *London Gazette* of 4 June 1917 (no citation).

Sherren was also Mentioned in Despatches on three occasions during the Great War. A highly respected and mature Flight Commander with 27 Squadron, he was later promoted to Major, going on to command 98 and 108 Squadrons. Given a permanent commission in the RAF in 1919, he commanded 60 Squadron on the North West Frontier of India at Risalpur from 1920 to 1922, receiving the Indian General Service Medal 1908, with clasp, Waziristan. He served later at the RAF Depot at Uxbridge and at the Home Aircraft Depot at Henslow He married and set up home with his wife, Joyce, at Marine Drive, Scarborough, Yorkshire. Promoted to Wing Commander on 1 January 1930. Commanded 10 (Bomber) Squadron at Upper Heyford and Boscombe Down from 1930 to March 1933. In March 1934, he was confirmed in the command of No 1 Armament Training Camp at Catfoss, near Hull. Later in 1934, he was sent to the Home Aircraft Depot at Henlow for administration duties. Wing Commander Sherren was placed on the Retired List in June 1936. In 1937, Sherren and his friend and colleague, Wing Commander E G Hilton, entered as competitors in the King's Cup Air Race. On 11 September 1937, competitors were obliged to fly low over the Castle Hill, Scarborough, turning point in order to be identified by the ground Observers. The wind was stiff and in a northerly direction. Hilton, who was piloting the machine, took a slightly different course from the other competitors. Flying very close to the cliff edge, their machine was suddenly flung 50 feet upwards, with Sherren being catapulted through the air, before falling out of the sight of the more than 1,000 spectators present. The aeroplane then crashed to the ground and was smashed to pieces, killing Wing Commander Hilton, whose body was picked up 20 yards from the wrecked machine. Sherren's body was found on the beach at the bottom of a 200-foot cliff. Wing Commander Percy Sherren was buried with full military honours in Ipswich Cemetery, Suffolk.

SHIELD, Horace Scott

The elder son of Branch Insurance Office Manager, William Sanderson Shield and Isabel Harriet Shield (née Scott), of Palace Road, East Moseley, Surrey, he was born in Newcastle-upon-Tyne on 14 February 1895. He was a sickly child, suffering from diptheria from 1906 to 1907. His younger brother, Second Lieutenant William James Shield, 6 Battalion, King's (Liverpool Regiment), was killed in action in Flanders on 2 March 1917. His father having died, his widowed mother married a Mr Roberts and went to live with her new husband at 32, St Mathew's Avenue, Surbiton, Surrey, during the Great War years. Horace was gazetted Second Lieutenant to the North Staffordshire Regiment on 22 September 1914, becoming attached to 14 Battalion, Durham Light Infantry, early in 1915. His application for transfer to the RFC was allowed in the spring of 1915, and he gained his Royal Aero Club Certificate (Number 1211) on 2 May following. His formal pilot training duly completed, he was confirmed and gazetted Flying Officer on 10 July 1915. Sent out to 16 Squadron in France soon after he qualified for his 'Wings'. On 13 September 1915, Shield and his Observer, Corporal T Bennett (Number 448), attacked an Albatros over the Bois de Biez. Bennett fired two drums into the enemy machine, bringing it down into the British lines. The enemy Pilot, Fleiger Josef Suwelak, FA24, attached XIXth (Saxon) Corps, and the Observer, Leutnant Oskar Teichmann, 2 Photographic Section, were both killed by bullets in the air. Three cameras were found in the wrecked Albatros. On 28 September 1915, Shield and the same Observer, Corporal Bennett, in BE2c, '2037', during a inconclusive combat with an enemy Albatros north west of Wavrin, passed so close to their opponent that the faces of the crewmen could clearly be seen. Shield's MC was announced in the *London Gazette* of 2 October 1915: 'For conspicuous gallantry and devotion to duty. When on patrol with Corporal T Bennett on 13 September over Bois de Biez, at about 10,000 feet, he sighted an Albatros and attacked it though subject to heavy anti-aircraft gunfire. The German Albatros used a machine gun, very conveniently mounted, but Corporal Bennett disabled the German machine, which side-slipped and then nose-dived to the ground in our lines. This was the climax of various other gallant acts'.

The gallant Corporal Bennett received the Distinguished Conduct Medal for this action, *London Gazette* of 9 October 1915. Shield was also Mentioned in Despatches on two occasions around this time, *London Gazettes* of 15 October 1915 and 1 January 1916. He was promoted to A/Captain and Flight Commander on 24 January 1916. His tour with '16' completed early in 1916, he returned to the Home Establishment and a series of instructing posts. He was promoted to Major in 1917 and stayed on in the RAF after the war. In 1935 he was living in Germany.

SHIRLEY, Frank Lawrence James

The son of Government School Teacher, Archibald James Shirley and Sarah Jane Shirley, of 4 Oxford Road, Abingdon, Berkshire, he was born on 31 May 1896. Gazetted Second Lieutenant to a Regular Army battalion of the Yorkshire Regiment on 22 December 1915. Seconded to the RFC, he gained his Royal Aero Club Certificate (Number 2770) on 21 April 1916. His formal pilot training duly completed, he was confirmed and gazetted Flying Officer on 19 May following. He accompanied BE2e-equipped 34 Squadron to France as a 'founder member' on 15 June 1916. By 12 April 1917, Shirley had been promoted to A/Captain and Flight Commander and 34 Squadron had recently acquired the RE8. On that day, Shirley and his Observer of the day, Lieutenant L T Smith, in RE8, 'A104', were shot up during an aerial combat with a black-painted Albatros DV trailing streamers, which usually denoted a patrol leader. Although Smith survived the resultant forced-landing unscathed, Shirley was severely wounded in the stomach in the air. Their wrecked RE8 immediately became the target for artillery and the two only just got clear before it suffered a direct hit. Shirley's MC was announced in the *London Gazette* of 26 May 1917: 'For conspicuous gallantry and devotion to duty. He displayed great courage and skill on many occasions in photographing the enemy's position. On one occasion, although severely wounded, he completed his work and succeeded in landing his machine safely'. Shirley did not return to operational flying. He married on 16 September 1919 and settled in Rugby.

SHORT, Cuthbert William

The only surviving son of John Short, MVO, Secretary to the Rangoon Municipality, and Mrs Catherine Short (née Bowen), he was born in Bangalore, India, on 25 March 1886. Educated at Daniel Steart's College, Edinburgh. He trained as a Mechanical and Electrical Engineer and was living and working in Rangoon when the war came in August 1914. He volunteered immediately, attempting to secure a commission in the Indian Army. He was eventually gazetted Second Lieutenant to the Durham Light Infantry on 10 January 1915. Subsequently transferring to 10 Lancers (Hodgson's Horse), Indian Army, then stationed at Ambala, he proceeded to France with this unit in August 1915, as part of 6 Cavalry Brigade. Transferring to the RFC in December 1915, he trained as an Observer and was sent out as such to 3 Squadron. On 23 February 1916, Short, with his Pilot, Second Lieutenant F E Goodrich, in Morane LA, '5120', were fortunate to survive when their rudder was shot away by anti-aircraft fire over La Bassée. Short's 'apprenticeship' satisfactorily completed, he was confirmed and gazetted Flying Officer (Observer) on 1 July 1916. His MC was announced in the *London Gazette* of 22 September 1916: 'For conspicuous gallantry and skill. On one occasion, when our cavalry were held up by machine-gun fire, he, with Captain Miller as pilot, came close to the ground and flew several times along the line of hostile machine guns, drawing their fire, and engaged them with his Lewis gun, thus preventing the cavalry from advancing into ambush'.

Next, he returned to the UK for pilot training and, having qualified for his full 'Wings', duly rejoined 3 Squadron in France. On 6 March 1917, Short and his Observer of the day, Lieutenant S McK Fraser, in Morane P, 'A268', on an Artillery Observation patrol over Ligny, were shot down by Offizierstellvertreter Edmund Nathanael of Jasta 5, the first of the German Ace's 15 victories. Both Short and Fraser were wounded in the incident but Short mortally so, dying of his wounds later the same day. Cuthbert Short is buried in Heilly Station Cemetery, Mericourt-L'Abbe, Somme, France.

SHORT, Leonard Highton

The son of Inland Revenue Officer, James Andrew Short and Sarah Ruth Short (née Highton), of 11 Rothwell Road, South Gosforth, Northumberland, he was born in Earsdon, Northumberland, on 29 May 1897. Educated at the Royal Grammar School, Newcastle-upon-Tyne (1910 -11). Short studied Engineering in Lincoln from March 1914 to 31 May 1915, when he enlisted into the Inns of Court OTC (Number 1/3884). Gazetted Second Lieutenant to 3/7 Battalion, Durham Light Infantry (TF), on 8 October 1915. His application to transfer to the RFC was eventually allowed at the end of 1916. Having trained as an Observer, he was confirmed and gazetted as such on 15 January 1917. Served at the front with 5 Squadron (RE8s) on artillery observation from 18 July to 16 September 1917. Returning to the UK, he next trained as a Pilot, qualifying for his 'Wings' at 50 TS in January 1918. Sent out again to the front on 2 March 1918, this time as a Pilot with 10 Squadron (AWFK8s). On 30 May 1918, Short and Probationary Observer, Second Lieutenant

A C Clinton, in AWFK8, 'C8522', on an artillery observation patrol, were hit by a shell and forced to land. Both crewmen were wounded in this incident. Short's MC was announced in the *London Gazette* of 26 July 1918: 'For conspicuous gallantry and devotion to duty in bringing in many excellent and accurate contact patrol reports, and, owing to adverse weather conditions, having to fly very low. On one occasion his Observer was wounded from the ground, and he was attacked by three enemy aeroplanes, but he brought him safely back. On another occasion his Observer was wounded when bombing enemy troops from 1,000 feet'.

Having recovered from his wounds, Short was flying operationally again in AWFK8, 'F7410', on 2 October 1918, this time accompanied by Lieutenant F C Peacock, when their 'Big Ack' was hit by machine-gun fire. Both men were badly shaken and taken to hospital after landing. Short finally left the RAF, via the Unemployed List, on 1 September 1919, living first at 6 Victoria Parade, Ashton-on-Ribble, Preston, Lancashire, before returning to his family home at 6 Norbury Court Road, Norbury, London SW16.

SIEVIER, Robert Brudenell-Bruce

The son of Robert Standish Sievier and Mrs Sievier, of 31 St James Place, London, SW, he was born in Paris on 13 October 1894. His father was an Actor, Playwright, Journalist and Author, who had served in the Kaffir, Zulu and Basuto Wars of the 1870s,and who, later in life, would become one of the most successful race horse owners of all time. He also founded the extremely successful racing newspaper *The Winning Post*. Robert junior was educated at Uppingham (1907-12) and at the Cambourne School of Mines. Volunteering as soon as the war came and, despite giving his occupation as 'Aviator', he was gazetted Second Lieutenant to the Royal Field Artillery on 9 October 1914. He served with 209 Battery, Royal Field Artillery, 66 Division, in the UK and in Egypt, from June 1915. Wounded in action on 3 February 1917. Once recovered, he was seconded to HQ, RFC Baghdad, on 3 June 1917. Having trained as an Observer, he was sent in the following July to 30 Squadron, also in Mesopotamia. On 25 January 1918, Sievier and his Pilot, New Zealander Captain Frank Nuttall (qv), in a DH4, were forced to land in the desert near to Quara Tepe because of an engine fire. They burnt their disabled machine and set off to walk back to safety, carrying both Lewis guns and as much of the ammunition as they could manage. Navigating by the stars, they walked for two days and nights before running into a British patrol which guided them back to the lines. Theirs was the second of the only two DH4s in Mesoptamia to be lost within a week. Sievier would be wounded in action on 21 May 1918. His MC was announced belatedly in the *London Gazette* of 11 January 1919: '(Mesopotamia) RFA and RAF: For conspicuous gallantry and devotion to duty. He carried out particularly difficult artillery co-operation with great success, displaying skill and coolness. On one occasion, when flying at night, after having landed behind the enemy's lines in flames, he got back 24 miles into his own lines, carrying a Lewis gun'.

Sievier was also Mentioned in Despatches on two occasions during the Great War. After leaving the RAF on 12 March 1919, he, like his father, became a prolific author, writing under a number of different nom de plumes including Bruce Sievier, Kathleen Egan, etc. He lived at 4 Corfton Road, Ealing, London, W3. Robert Sievier died on 16 April 1953.

SILLY, Benjamin James

The son of George and Lucy Silly, of Sydney, New South Wales, Australia, he was born in 1893. He worked in Switzerland from 1909 to 1911, but was living and working in London when the war came in August 1914. He enlisted as a Private soldier (Number 885) into 19 Battalion, Royal Fusiliers (2 Public Schools) and proceeded to France with his unit on 12 November 1915. His battalion was one of those which was disbanded in France in April 1916, with most of the members returning to the UK to be commissioned. Silly was gazetted Second Lieutenant to the Royal Field Artillery, via the Special Lists, on 4 September 1916, with a secondment to the RFC coming on the following day. His formal pilot training duly completed, he was confirmed and gazetted Flying Officer on 4 April 1917. Sent out to the DH4-equipped 55 Squadron soon after he qualified for his 'Wings'. On 4 May 1917, Silly and his Observer, Lieutenant R K Abram, in DH4, 'A2157', were attacked during a photo-reconnaissance patrol over Valenciennes. Their machine was shot up and Abram wounded but Silly, who was obliged to make a forced landing, escaped unscathed. Promoted to A/Captain and Flight Commander on 29 November 1917. His MC was announced in the *London Gazette* of 4 March 1918, details in the *Gazette* of 16 August 1918: 'For conspicuous gallantry and devotion to duty. He led several successful bomb raids and carried out many long distance reconnaissances. By his skill and determination he has invariably set a fine example to his Squadron'.

Silly, promoted to Major, would go on to command 55 Squadron, then part of the IAF, from 20 September 1918. The award of a Distinguished Flying Cross for his leadership and gallantry, was announced in the *London Gazette* of the following day, 21 September 1918. Given a permanent commission in 1919, he went on to enjoy a distinguished career, his many appointments, honours and promotions included: Staff position at RAF HQ, Middle East, 1925; RAF Staff College, 1927; Air Staff, HQ, Iraq Command, 1934; Wing Commander, 1935; attended Imperial Defence College, 1936; Group Captain, 1938; OC, RAF Pembroke Dock, 1938; Air Staff, HQ, RAF Far East, 1939; SASO, HQ, RAF Far East, 1940; Air Commodore, 1942; and AOC, Rear Base, Batavia, 1942. Captured by the Japanese, Air Commodore Ben Silly died in captivity on 7 December 1943 and is buried in the Sai Wan War Cemetery, China.

SIMPSON, George Kenneth

The son of Henry John and Emily Simpson, of 'South Haven', Stanley Road, Lymington, Hampshire, he was born on 5 January 1891, in Hoylake, Cheshire. Educated at Dulwich College (1904-05). He emigrated to Vancouver, Canada, in 1910, taking up residence at 1076 Denman Street in that city and purchasing land at Fort George. When the war came, he enlisted for 2 Canadian Contingent in September 1914, but then, in the following November, asked to be discharged so that he could travel to the UK, so as to get into the fight earlier. Soon after arriving in the UK, he was gazetted Second Lieutenant to the RGA on 26 March 1915. Seconded to the KBS in October 1915, he trained as an Observer and was subsequently gazetted Balloon Officer on 3 April 1916. Sent out to the front on 25 May 1916, he served with 14 KBS, 4 Balloon Wing, throughout the Battle of the Somme. Promoted and gazetted Balloon Commander in February 1917. Just days later on 1 March, his balloon came under attack and was set alight. Simpson waited until the Air Mechanic who was aloft with him, was well clear of the balloon before he himself jumped. Seconds later, the flaming balloon suddenly dropped and enveloped Simpson and his parachute, the whole lot falling blazing to the ground. After lingering for a few days, he died on 7 March 1917, at Bray-sur-Somme. His MC was posthumously announced in the *London Gazette* of 17 April 1917: 'For conspicuous gallantry and devotion to duty whilst observing from a balloon which was set on fire. He went to the assistance of his fellow Observer, and would not leave the balloon himself until he had seen the other Observer clear. He was severely burnt'. The German Pilot was Leutnant Renatus Theiller of Jasta 5, his ninth of 12 victories, who was himself killed before the month was out.

George Simpson is buried in Bray Military Cemetery, Bray-sur-Somme, Somme, France.

SISON, Herbert Martin

From Bayswater, London, he was born on 11 November 1895. Educated at Elstow School, where he was a member of the OTC. After leaving school, he secured a pupilage as an Engineering Engraver at the Daimler Car Company in 1912. When the war came, he immediately volunteered and was gazetted Second Lieutenant to the Army Service Corps on 7 October 1914. Following service at the front with the Army Service Corps, he was seconded to the RFC in January 1915, gaining his Royal Aero Club Certificate (Number Fr 1908) on 29 April 1915, whilst still in France. His formal pilot training duly completed, he was confirmed and gazetted Flying Officer on 10 June following. He accompanied 10 Squadron to France as a 'founder member' on 25 July 1915. On 14 December 1915, Sison and his Observer of the day, Second Lieutenant A R Goodson, in BE2c, '2671', sent down an Albatros over Pont à Vendin, but were then attacked themselves by a twin-engined enemy machine over Lille. The 10 Squadron pair were rescued by the intervention of escorting colleagues, Captains Mitchell and Bruce. His MC was announced in the New Year *London Gazette* of 1 January 1916 (no citation). Although no formal citation appeared in the *Gazette*, research has unearthed the original recommendation for the award: 'H M Sison On September 29th a reconnaissance was urgently required over a certain railway centre (Douai). Lt Sison with great skill and daring found his way there in thick clouds and came down over the railway at a low altitude under heavy fire'.

Following a return to the Home Establishment and a spell of instructing, he went again to the front, this time joining 19 Squadron as an A/Captain and Flight Commander. His tour with '19' completed in the spring of 1917, he returned to the UK and to instructional duties there. Sison's third operational tour, again as Flight Commander, came when he joined the SE5A-equipped 1 Squadron at the front on 4 June 1918. He narrowly escaped disaster on 4 July 1918, when his SE5A, 'D6894', was struck by anti-aircraft fire and he was forced to crashland. His tour with '1' ended on 3 August 1918, when he was hospitalised and sent home to the UK for treatment. Sison finally left the RAF, via the Unemployed List, in April 1919.

SKINNER, Alfred Ernest Lionel

The first son of Mr and Mrs Alfred Ernest Skinner, of Aylesbury, Buckinghamshire, and of London W1, he was born on 25 October 1897. Educated at Charterhouse. Although barely old enough, he was gazetted Second Lieutenant to the Norfolk Yeomanry (TF) on 7 June 1915. At 18 years old, Skinner was considered too young to accompany the Norfolk Yeomanry to Gallipoli in August 1915, but he was allowed to join his regiment in Egypt in the following year. A subsequent application to join the RFC was rewarded with a posting to 21 RS at Heliopolis on the outskirts of Cairo. With eight hours dual and 24 and a half hours of solo flying, he graduated and was duly confirmed and gazetted Flying Officer on 9 November 1916. After a couple of postings within Egypt, he was sent to 30 Squadron, then stationed at Basra, Mesopotamia, in December 1916. Skinner flew operationally in support of the advancing British Army for more than 15 months before leaving for Egypt, via Bombay, in April 1918. He was Mentioned in Despatches in the *London Gazette* of 12 March 1918. In July 1918, he was ordered back to England where, upon arrival, he was given a month's leave. Following an Instructor's course at Gosport, he was sent to 45 TDS at Rencomb in Gloucestershire. On 4 November 1918, he was again sent out to Egypt as an Instructor to the Special School of Flying, HQ, Middle East Training Brigade. A posting to 19 TDS came one week later and he instructed with that unit for four months. His MC, awarded for his service with 30 Squadron in Mesopotamia, was announced very belatedly in the *London Gazette* of 11 January 1919: 'For conspicuous gallantry and devotion to duty. He carried out many long-distance reconnaissances alone, bringing back most valuable information. He fought many battles in the air, and succeeded in bringing down an enemy machine behind our lines. He did fine work'.

His final flight in Egypt was on 14 May 1919, whereupon he returned home, before finally leaving the service on 20 June 1919. Skinner returned to the family business, becoming the Senior Partner in Skinner & Company, Court Jewellers, a high-class jewellery firm in Old Bond Street, London. He married, in 1922, Elsie Sturridge. Skinner was recalled to the RAF in 1941 as a Squadron Leader, RAFVR, and was employed thereafter to initiate RAF and Polish airmen into the art of flying.

SLATER, James Anderson

The son of John and Rose Slater, of 4 Polsham Park, Paignton, Devonshire, he was born on 27 November 1896. He was living and working in Brighton, Sussex, when war came in August 1914. Slater enlisted as a Private soldier (Number 3060) into the Sussex Regiment on 10 September following. Gazetted Second Lieutenant to the New Armies soon afterwards on 29 September 1914, with an initial attachment to the Royal Irish Rifles, but then to his preferred county regiment, the Royal Sussex. Seconded to the RFC, he trained as an Observer and was sent out as such to 18 Squadron (Vickers FB5s) in November 1915. Next, he trained as a Pilot and was duly confirmed and gazetted Flying Officer on 30 June 1916. Sent out to France and the Nieuport Scout-equipped 1 Squadron in August 1916, he achieved two victories before returning to the UK to instruct in May 1917. Promoted to Captain and Flight Commander, he accompanied the newly formed DH5-equipped 64 Squadron to France as a 'founder member' in October 1917, gaining a further victory with that unit. On 13 December 1917, Slater was presented with his MC by no less a luminary than General Trenchard, the award subsequently announced in the *London Gazette* of 4 February 1918, details in the *Gazette* of 5 July 1918: 'For conspicuous gallantry and devotion to duty. When returning from a patrol he attacked enemy infantry, silenced a field gun and fired on transport. On another occasion he silenced a battery in very difficult weather conditions, fired on ammunition wagons and enemy infantry, and brought back his patrol safely. He also led a patrol of 12 machines in very bad weather to attack a wood held by the enemy. His patrol dropped over 30 bombs, fired 3,000 rounds and drove the enemy from the wood with heavy casualties. In the course of this flight six enemy scouts were engaged and driven off. Later, he led a similar patrol with great success. He showed splendid courage and determination'.

'64' was re-equipped with SE5As early in 1918, and Slater's success rate soared as a consequence. Between 8 March and 31 May 1918, he added a further 21 victories. The Bar to his MC came in the *London Gazette* of 22 June 1918: 'For conspicuous gallantry and devotion to duty. On one occasion during the recent operations he attacked a large formation of hostile scouts, one of which he drove down in flames. Later, during the same flight, he took part in a general engagement, in which he drove down another enemy machine completely out of control. Two days later he attacked two enemy scouts, causing one of them to crash to earth. In 18 days he has engaged in 25 combats at close quarters, shooting down eight hostile machines. His great gallantry and fine offensive spirit have inspired all ranks to a very high degree'.

One of the newly instituted Distinguished Flying Crosses came next, *London Gazette* of 2 July 1918, this for his skill, leadership and determination. Returning to the UK in July 1918, Slater saw out the remainder of the war as an Instructor. One of his trademark 'stunts' during this period was flying through the hangar at Sedgeford aerodrome. He was asked, on one occasion, to give an aerobatic display before Queen Alexandra, during a visit to Sedgeford aerodrome from nearby Sandringham. After watching him for a few moments, the Queen turned to his CO and said, 'Order that young man down immediately, before he kills himself'. Staying on in the RAF after the war, Slater continued to instruct in the UK and in the Middle East. During one of his postings to the CFS, he was killed in a flying accident on 26 November 1925.

SLESSOR, John Cotesworth

The son of Major Arthur Kerr Slessor, Sherwood Foresters, and Mrs Slessor, of Christ Church, Oxford, he was born in Rhanikhet, India on 3 June 1897. Educated at the Dragon School, Oxford, and at Haileybury (1911-14). Gazetted Second Lieutenant (on probation) to the RFC on 6 July 1915, the same day that he gained his Royal Aero Club Certificate (Number 1447). His formal pilot training duly completed, he was confirmed and gazetted Flying Officer on 9 September following. Posted first to 17 Squadron, he was soon detached to 23 Squadron, then on Home Defence duties and operating from Sutton's Farm. On the night of 13/14 October 1915, he spotted Zeppelin *L15*, illuminated by searchlights. He attempted to follow and intercept it, but cloud obscured his view and he lost the giant airship in the darkness. Sent out to the Middle East as a 'founder member' of 17 Squadron early in 1916, he subsequently served in Egypt and in the Darfur Campaign in the Sudan (Khedive's Sudan Medal 1910, with two clasps, Darfur 1916 and Fasher). During a reconnaissance patrol on 23 May 1916, Slessor, in BE2c, '5413', attacked and shot up some cavalry before bombing and machine-gunning infantry in the vicinity of El Fasher. Subjected to concerted volleys from the ground, Slessor was hit in the thigh by a rifle bullet, but still managed to get his machine back to safety. This one tiny incident was later credited with breaking the spirit of the dissident Sultan's forces. Such was the panic created by Slessor's aerial assault, that British and Egyptian forces were able to enter El Fasher virtually unopposed on the following day. His MC was announced in the New Year *London Gazette* of 1 January 1917 (no citation). Sent back to the UK for treatment to his leg, he was, upon recovery, posted out to France as a Flight Commander with 5 Squadron (RE8s), observing for XIII Corps and the Canadian Corps. After a year with '5', Slessor returned to the Home Establishment and an appointment as Second-in-Command at the CFS, where he saw out the remainder of the war. He was Mentioned in Despatches on one occasion during the Great War. Staying on in the RAF after the war, Slessor embarked upon what would prove to be an outstandingly distinguished career. He married first, on 8 May 1923, Hermione Grace Carter (died 1970), the widow of his friend, Lieutenant Colonel Herbert Carter, King's Own Yorkshire Light Infantry, who died in Vladivostok in 1919, during the Allied intervention in the Russian revolution, with whom he had one son and one daughter. Secondly, in 1971, he married Marcella Florence, widow of Brigadier R T Priest. Slessor's many subsequent honours, appointments and promotions included: Served in India, 1921-23; RAF Staff College, 1924-25; commanded 4 Squadron, 1925-28; Air Staff, Air Ministry, 1928-30; Wing Commander, 1932; Instructor, Staff College, Camberley, 1931-34; Commanded 3 Indian Wing, Quetta, 1935; Waziristan Operations, 1936-37; DSO; Mentioned in Despatches; Indian General Service Medal 1936-39, with clasp, North West Frontier 1936-37; Director of Plans, Air Ministry, 1937-41; ADC to the King, 1938; Air Commodore, 1939; Air Representative, Anglo-French Conversations, 1939, and Anglo-American (ABC) Staff Conversations, 1941; AOC, 5 (Bomber)

Group, 1941; Air Vice-Marshal, 1941; CB, 1942; ACAS (Policy), 1942-43 (Casablanca Conference); AOC-in-C, Coastal Command, 1943; KCB, 1943; Air Marshal, 1943; C-in-C, RAF, Mediterranean and Middle East, 1944-45; Member of Air Council for Personnel, 1945-47; Air Chief Marshal, 1946; GCB, 1948; Commandant Imperial Defence College, 1948-49; Principal Air ADC to the King, 1948-50; Marshal of the RAF, 1950; Chief of the Air Staff, 1950-52; Representative, British Chiefs of Staff, NATO Conferences in Brussels, Rome, Lisbon, Paris and Washington; Member, UK Delegations, Commonwealth Relations Conferences, 1954 and 1959; His many foreign orders and decorations include: Order of Leopold, Belgium; Légion d'Honneur, France; Order of Phoenix, Greece; Order of St Olaf, Norway; Legion of Merit, USA; Order of the Sword, Sweden; Partisan Star, Yugoslavia. His civil appointments included: President, The Victory Services Club; Chairman, Star and Garter Home, 1953-67; Vice-President, Institute of Strategic Studies; Governor, Haileybury, Sherborne, King's (Bruton); JP and CC, Somerset, 1963-74; High Sheriff, Somerset, 1965; Deputy Lieutenant, Somerset, 1969. His publications included: 'Air Power and Armies', 1936; 'Strategy for the West', 1954; 'The Central Blue' (his autobiography), 1956; 'The Great Deterrent', 1959; 'What Price Co-Existence', 1961; 'These Remain', 1969. He lived at Rimpton Manor, Yeovil, Somerset. Marshal of the RAF, Sir John Slessor, died on 12 July 1979.

NB: The RAF Museum Hendon has his medals, but not all his orders, in its collection: Distinguished Service Order, MC, 1914-15 Star, British War Medal 1914-20, Victory Medal 1914-19 with MID, India General Service Medal 1936-39, with clasp, North West Frontier 1936-37, 1939-45 Star, Italy Star 1943-45, Defence Medal 1939-45, War Medal 1939-45 with MID, Jubilee Medal 1935, Coronation Medal 1953, Jubilee Medal 1977, Order of Leopold I (5th Class, Belgium), Croix de Guerre 1939-45 avec Palme (Belgium), Légion d'Honneur (Officier, France), and Khedive's Sudan Medal 1910-22, with clasps, Darfur 1916, Fasher.

SMART, Charles Douglas

The son of Cotton and Hemp Dealer, Arthur Smart, and Edith Smart (née Orme), of Church Road, Urmston, Lancashire, he was born on 20 October 1884. Educated at Bicton House School, Southport. After leaving school, he worked for, and was eventually made a Director of, the family cotton manufacturing firm, The Cotton Mill Company Ltd, of Manchester. When war came, he enlisted as a Private soldier into 19 (2 Public Schools) Battalion, Royal Fusiliers, on 9 September 1914. Promoted to Sergeant on 1 May 1915, he accompanied his unit to France on 27 November 1915. The 19 Royal Fusiliers was one of those units disbanded in France in April 1916, with most of its members then returning to the UK to be subsequently commissioned. Smart was gazetted Second Lieutenant to the RFC, via the Special Lists, on 7 July 1916. His formal pilot training duly completed, he was confirmed and gazetted Flying Officer on 17 November 1916. He served with 5 Squadron in France, his MC announced in the *London Gazette* of 17 September 1917: 'For conspicuous gallantry and devotion to duty when acting as pilot to another officer. They faced a violent thunderstorm, accompanied by a gale of wind and blinding rain, which had compelled all other machines to return to their aerodromes or to make forced landings, in order to locate the position of our infantry in the front line. This they successfully did, having spent one and a half hours in the air under fearful conditions, and returned with a valuable and accurate report to Headquarters'.

Smart later served with 99 Squadron in the UK, but was diagnosed as suffering from stress in the early weeks of 1918 and this appears to have curtailed his operational flying. Served in an Administration capacity, before finally leaving the RAF in 1919.

SMITH, Allen Higson

The son of John Higson Smith and Annie Elizabeth Smith, of Cromwell House, Grimsby, he was born in 1894. Educated at Manchester University (1912-16), where he was a member of the OTC, and from where he graduated BSc (Engineering). Although he actually graduated in 1916, he was, in fact, first commissioned into 10 Battalion, Lincolnshire Regiment, 'The Grimsby Chums', on 9 September 1914. His 'take-up' apparently deferred, he developed an interest in aviation whilst still studying at University and gained his Royal Aero Club Certificate (Number 1514) on 6 August 1915. His formal pilot training duly completed, he was confirmed and gazetted Flying Officer on 2 November following. Served on corps reconnaissance work with 4 Squadron in 1916. His MC was announced in the *London Gazette* of 25 August 1916: 'For most gallant and skilful work in connection with artillery. In one instance flying at 1,000 feet under heavy fire his information led to the destruction of two enemy batteries. On another occasion he flew under clouds for two hours at 600 feet, sending down information. His machine was repeatedly hit. He has set a fine example'.

Because of his engineering and combat experience, he was kept back from the front for a time as an Instructor, serving for a period as Acting Commandant of the Aerial Gunnery School. Sent out again to 21 Squadron (RE8s), as A/Captain and Flight Commander, in the summer of 1917. On 21 August 1917, Smith and his Observer of the day, 2 AM Christopher Hallam (Number 77450), from Heckmondwike, Yorkshire, in RE8, 'A3622', were on an Artillery Observation patrol over the Frezenberg ridge, when they were attacked and sent down in flames by Leutnant Ernst Hess of Jasta 28, the 11th of the German Ace's eventual 17 victories. Allen Smith's remains were never recovered and hence he is commemorated on the Flying Services Memorial, Arras, France.

SMITH, Bernard Valentine Seymour

The son of Joseph Stewart Smith and Annie Ely Smith, of Bermuda, he was born on that Atlantic island on 9 March 1898. Educated at Blundells School, Tiverton, Devon (1914-15). Gazetted Second Lieutenant to a Regular Army battalion of the Royal Warwickshire Regiment on 26 January 1916, with an immediate secondment to the RFC. Gained his Royal Aero Club Certificate (Number 2646) on 31 March 1916. His formal pilot training duly completed, he was confirmed and gazetted Flying Officer on 17 May following. Sent out to the 'Flying Elephants' of 27 Squadron on 15 June 1916. On 27 September 1916, a formation of 27 Squadron Martinsyde G100s were attacked by five of Oswald Boelcke's Jasta 2. Three of the Martinsydes were badly knocked about and two sent down to destruction. Smith, in 'A1562, although wounded, escaped with his life and managed to bring his machine safely home. His MC was announced in the *London Gazette* of 20 October 1916: 'For conspicuous gallantry and determination on several occasions when dropping bombs from a low altitude on points behind the enemy's lines'.

Once recovered, he joined 49 Squadron (RE7s), then stationed at Dover, on 10 May 1917. From '49', he was sent to Redcar as an Instructor and there saw out the remainder of the war. His outstanding services in the instructing field were formally recognised by an award of an Air Force Cross, *London Gazette* of 1 January 1919. Smith was a Flying Officer with 24 Squadron, then stationed at Kenley, when he resigned his commission on 30 October 1920.

SMITH, Gordon Keith

The son of George and Anna Maria Smith, of 131 Harrow Road, Paddington, London, he was born on 8 April 1891. Although not a pupil at the school, he was a member of Merchant Taylor's OTC. After completing his education, he worked in the City of London as a Stockbrokers Clerk. He enlisted as a Private soldier (Number 845) in 1 Battalion (Infantry) Honourable Artillery Company (TF), on the day war broke out, 4 August 1914. Smith accompanied his battalion to France on 18 September 1914, thus earning the 1914 Star. Subsequently promoted to Corporal on 28 June 1915 and Lance Sergeant on 22 August 1915. Picked out for a commission, he was gazetted Second Lieutenant to 13 Battalion, Yorkshire Regiment (Green Howards), on 7 September 1915. Seconded to the RFC early in 1917, he qualified as a Pilot and was sent out as such in the following April to the 'Flying Elephants' of 27 Squadron. On 21 August 1917, Smith in Martinsyde G102, 'A6259', came under attack from a number of Albatros Scouts. Smith was thought to have collided with a squadron colleague, Second Lieutenant Derek Percy Cox, in Martinsyde, 'A3992', but was, in fact, the subject of a claim by Leutnant Hans Bethge of Jasta 30, the 14th of the German Ace's eventual 20 victories. Carried from the wreckage of his machine, Smith died shortly afterwards in hospital. His MC was announced posthumously in the *London Gazette* of 26 September 1917, details in the *Gazette* of 9 January 1918: 'For conspicuous gallantry and devotion to duty. When on long-distance bombing raids during a period of four months he has consistently shown great dash and determination – on two occasions attacking aeroplanes from low altitudes in spite of anti-aircraft fire, and bringing back valuable information'.

Gordon Smith is buried in Y Farm Military Cemetery, Bois-Grenier, France.

SMITH, Harry Augustus

Smith enlisted as a Private soldier into the Coldstream Guards, and served in the trenches in 1915. Picked out for a commission, he was gazetted Second Lieutenant to 10 Battalion, Middlesex Regiment, on 24 September 1915. Seconded to the RFC, he trained as a Pilot and was confirmed and gazetted Flying Officer on 27 April 1917. Promoted to A/Captain and Flight Commander on 31 October 1917. His MC was announced in the *London Gazette* of 18 February 1918, details in the *Gazette* of 18 July 1918: 'For conspicuous gallantry and devotion to duty. On five separate occasions during raids on points beyond the enemy lines he has found his objectives although on more than one occasion he was badly hampered by adverse conditions. He drove down one enemy plane out of control and engaged two others with indecisive results owing to the clouds. He has taken part in many bombing raids and his example of energy and determination had been of the utmost value to his Squadron'.

Smith stayed on in the RAF after the war, subsequently serving in Iraq in 1928.

NB: His medals were offered for sale by Buckland Dix & Webb (lot 547) on 27 September 1994: MC, 1914-15 Star (Pte C Gds), *British War Medal 1914-20, Victory Medal 1914-19* (Capt RFC), *General Service Medal 1918-62, with clasp, Southern Desert Iraq* (F/L RAF), *and Coronation Medal 1937.*

SMITH, Ross Macpherson

From Adelaide, Australia, he was born on 4 December 1892. Educated at Queen's School, Adelaide, and at Warriston School, Moffat, Scotland. Commissioned into 3 Regiment (South Australia and Tasmania), Australian Light Horse when the war came, he served in Gallipoli and Sinai, before transferring to the Australian Flying Corps early in 1917. He flew first as an Observer with 67 (Australian) Squadron in Egypt and Palestine, and quickly made his mark. The first of his MCs was gazetted in the *London Gazette* of 11 May 1917: 'For conspicuous gallantry and devotion to duty when his pilot (R F Ballieu) [qv] descended to the rescue of an officer who had been forced to land. On landing he held the enemy at bay with his revolver, thus enabling his pilot to rescue the officer and safely fly away his machine'.

He then trained as a Pilot and was duly formally confirmed and gazetted as such to the AFC on 3 July 1917. An aggressive and fearless Pilot, he gained the first of his eventual 11 victories in a BE2e on 1 September 1917. 67 (Australian) Squadron, RFC, was, on 6 February 1918, re-designated 1 Squadron, Australian Flying Corps. The Bar to his MC came in the *London Gazette* of 26 March 1918: 'For conspicuous gallantry and devotion to duty. He was one of two pilots who carried out a remarkable series of photographs in one flight, completely covering an important area of 45 square miles. On a later occasion he successfully bombed an important bridgehead from low altitude, and his work throughout, as well as his photography, has been invaluable and characterised by the most consistent gallantry'.

His next ten victories, coming between 7 May and 19 October 1918, were all achieved in BF2b, 'B1229'. The last of these victories, on 19 October 1918, was particularly audacious, in that having forced an enemy machine to land behind its own lines, he promptly landed alongside it. Covered by the machine guns of his Observer, Lieutenant A V McCann, he sauntered over to the enemy machine and, having ordered the two-man crew to dismount, set it alight before taking off again. Astonishingly, 'Hadji' Smith was awarded no less than three Distinguished Flying Crosses in the *London Gazette* of 8 February 1919, the third of which was for his audacity on 19 October 1918. Smith made the first flight from Cairo to Calcutta in 1918, for which feat an Air Force Cross was awarded, Birthday Honours *London Gazette* of 3 June 1919. In 1919, the Australian Prime Minister, Billy Hughes, announced an Air Race with a £10,000 prize to be given to the first aeroplane to fly from London to Australia in 30 days or less. Ross Smith and his brother, Keith, who was also an RAF Pilot, successfully petitioned the Vickers company to supply them with a Vickers Vimy bomber for their attempt on the record. Enlisting the help of mechanics, Sergeants W H Shiers and J M Bennett, the four intrepid airmen eventually landed in Darwin on 10 December 1919, just 27 days and 20 hours after leaving London. The four men shared the £10,000 prize and the two Smith brothers were knighted (KBE, Civil Division), *London Gazette* of 26 December 1919. On 14 April 1922, Sir Ross Smith and Sergeant J M Bennett were killed in an accident whilst flying a Vickers Viking during preparation for an attempt on a round the world flight.

SMITH, Stephen Berthold

From London, he was born in 1890, and became an Engineer in civilian life. Gazetted Second Lieutenant to 8 Battalion, South Staffordshire Regiment, on 2 February 1915, with an immediate transfer to 10 Battalion of the same regiment. Posted to the Hampshire Aircraft Parks, South Farnborough, on 23 December 1915, he was then formally seconded to the RFC on 27 March 1916. His formal pilot training duly completed, he was confirmed and gazetted Flying Officer on 7 July following, with an immediate posting to 40 Squadron, then at Gosport. On 22 August following, Smith was appointed to the RFC Mission to Imperial Russia under the command of Major James Valentine. Re-classified from Flying Officer to Equipment Officer 2nd Class in the *London Gazette* of 23 January 1917, Smith proceeded to Russia in a technical capacity on 22 February following, with the rank of Captain. Major Valentine, a pre-war aviation pioneer (RAeC Number 47), had been placed in command of an RFC detachment sent to Russia to teach Russian Pilots to fly British and French machines. Although the Revolution was still to come, the morale of the Russian forces was already beginning to disintegrate and they were falling back in the face of a determined German offensive. In July 1917, with the help of some men and vehicles from Commander Locker Lampson's British Armoured Car Squadron, Valentine's detachment salved large amounts of aeroplane gear, not to mention five new machines from their aerodrome at Denisof, before the advancing Germans arrived. The gear and aeroplanes were loaded onto railway trucks and sent back deeper into Russia. Valentine continued to command the detachment in its retirement as far as Proskuroff. Unfortunately, however, Valentine, who was awarded the Distinguished Service Order in June 1917, suffered a break down in his health under the stress of recent events and he died after an operation on 7 August 1917. Smith, no doubt involved in all of this, was awarded his MC in the New Year *London Gazette* of 1 January 1918 (no citation). He was also awarded the Croix de Guerre by the French. Smith finally left the RAF, via the Unemployed List, on 11 March 1919. He served again in the Second World War, being given a Lieutenancy in the Pioneer Corps on 8 February 1940.

SMITH, Tom Vincent

A Technical, not a flying, award

The son of Printer, Henry Smith and Mrs Smith, of Northwood, Middlesex, he was born in 1872. Educated privately at Margate, at Eastbourne, and at Leipzig. He studied in Germany as a church organist and composed sacred music whilst still a very young man. Always interested in wireless telephony, this subject soon took over his life and he became a leading pioneer in wireless research. He joined the Amalgamated Radio Telegraph Company in 1906 and was also, at one time, a Director of the British Radio Telegraph Company. When the war came, he was given the rank of T/Captain when gazetted, via the Special Lists, as an Equipment Officer in the RFC on 30 June 1915. He was posted first to 9 Squadron, then at Dover, as Equipment Officer, Wireless, and sent next to 1 Aircraft Depot, France, in February 1916. Promoted to A/Major on 18 May 1916. His MC was announced in the Birthday Honours *London Gazette* of 3 June 1916 (no citation). Although no formal citation was published in the *Gazette*, research has unearthed the original recommendation for the award: 'T V Smith. This officer has been responsible for the progress made in wireless in the Brigades, RFC, working with the Armies. In pursuance of his duties, which he has always carried out efficiently and courageously, he has repeatedly visited receiving stations at the front under heavy fire'.

He was also Mentioned in Despatches on two occasions, *London Gazette*s of 1 January 1916 and 3 June 1919. Smith served next as Aircraft Park Commander from 13 October 1916 to 1 December 1916, before reporting for duties with RFC HQ, France. Smith was also created Cavaliere of the Order of St Maurice and St Lazarus by the Italians, *London Gazette* of 26 May 1917. While serving in France as Senior Wireless Officer, he was gassed. When the Independent Air force was formed in 1918, he was appointed to a special technical post with 97 Squadron, then stationed at Waddington. Following a brief sojourn with '97', he was posted to the Air Ministry in London, in charge of wireless for all theatres of war, and remained there until leaving the RAF, via the Unemployed List, on 3 April 1919. In the post-war years he was constantly recalled as a consultant to the Air Ministry, and also wrote on wireless matters for *The Times*. Smith was a Member of the Wireless Section of the Institute of Electrical Engineers, and also of the Radio Society of Great Britain. He rose to high rank in Masonry and was a keen and gifted yachtsman. Unmarried, he lived at 29 Holland Way, Kensington, London. T Vincent Smith died on the way to St Bartholomew's Hospital, London, on 5 September 1927.

SMITH, William

From Ilford, Essex, born 28 June 1894, he joined the regular army and was commissioned into the 10th London Regiment (Hackney Rifles) on 21 September 1914. In November 1916, he transferred to the RFC and, after pilot training, was sent to 27 Squadron in March 1917, equipped with Martinsyde G100s and then DH4s. Captain Smith flew a number of bombing sorties, including one on 30 July, the eve of the Third Battle of Ypres. His target was a German airfield near Courtrai, the home of Jasta 4. Completing his tour of duty he returned to the Home Establishment in September. His MC was gazetted on 27 October, with this citation in the *Gazette* of 25 April 1918: 'For conspicuous gallantry and devotion to duty in thirty-two long distance bomb raids, many of which were carried out under very unfavourable weather conditions.' He served again very briefly as a Flight Lieutenant in 1921.

SNOW, Wilfred Rippon

From Adelaide, South Australia, he was born on 9 June 1893. Educated at the Prince Alfred College, South Australia, and at Adelaide University, from where he graduated Bachelor of Engineering in 1915. During his undergraduate years at Adelaide University, he was a Lieutenant of Senior Cadets of the Commonwealth Military Forces. Armed with a letter of introduction from Sir George Reid, KC, High Commissioner for Australia, Snow travelled at his own expense to the UK, hoping to join the RFC. Once arrived, he took up temporary residence in Wallington, Surrey. Taking flying lessons, again at his own expense, he gained his Royal Aero Club Certificate (Number 2359) at the L & P Aviation School, Hendon, on 28 January 1916. The course of flying tuition cost him £100, a relatively huge sum at that time, but, fortunately, once he joined the RFC, they refunded him with £75 of the cost. His commission granted, he was gazetted Second Lieutenant to the RFC on 23 February 1916. His formal pilot training duly completed, he was confirmed and gazetted Flying Officer on 18 May following. Sent out to France and 10 Squadron on 25 May 1916. On 8 June following, Snow, together with Lieutenant C O Fairbairn, normally a Pilot but on this occasion acting as his Observer, successfully directed the fire of 118 Heavy Battery, RGA, onto a train at Salome, using the 'GF' (Greeting target) signal. Six shells fell on the train, setting it alight, the resultant fire spreading to a nearby shed. Promoted to A/Captain and Flight Commander on 1 January 1917. His MC was announced in the *London Gazette* of 26 March 1917: 'For conspicuous gallantry in action. He successfully bombed a hostile aerodrome from a height of 1,000 feet. Later, in another machine, he again bombed the hostile aerodrome from a low altitude. On another occasion he made two very daring trench reconnaissances'.

On 22 July 1917, Snow's AWFK8 was struck by anti-aircraft fire and he received a wound in the leg. Soon recovered, Snow was promoted to A/Major and appointed to the command of 2 Squadron, equipped with the BE2e and AWFK8, on 12 August 1917. Snow was Mentioned in Despatches on two occasions during the Great War, *London Gazettes* of 11 December 1917 and 20 May 1918. Research has uncovered the original recommendation for first of these Mentions: '5/10/17: Has shown continuous keenness and devotion to duty, both as a Flight Commander and a Squadron Commander (2 Sqd)'.

Snow's gallantry and leadership were further recognised by the award of a Distinguished Service Order, *London Gazette* of 22 April 1918. His command of '2' came to an end in August 1918, when Snow was hospitalised and forced to return to the UK. Staying on in the RAF after the war, he finally left the service, via the Unemployed List, on 3 January 1920.

SOAMES, Arthur Henry Leslie

The eldest son of Brewer, Frederick William Soames and Mrs Soames, of Bryn Estyn, Wrexham, Denbighshire, North Wales, he was born in 1887. Educated at St Neots, Eversley, at Eton (1901-02), abroad, and at Sandhurst. Gazetted Second Lieutenant to 3 (King's Own) Hussars in 1909. Served with his regiment in South Africa in 1911. On returning to the UK, he developed an interest in aviation, gaining his Royal Aero Club Certificate (Number 369) on a Vickers monoplane at the Vickers School, Brooklands, on 26 November 1912. Seconded to the RFC in 1913, he instructed at the CFS. He accompanied the original RFC contingent to France as an A/ Captain and Flight Commander with 4 Squadron. Soames flew some of the first aerial reconnaissance patrols in the history of warfare, including one, on 31 August 1914, when he spotted a huge column of enemy infantry and cavalry 'stretching from Roye to Chevincourt'. He was Mentioned in Despatches, *London Gazette* of 19 October 1914, and became the very first airman to be listed as a MC winner in the New Year *London Gazette* of 1 January 1915 (no citation). Recalled to the CFS for experimental work, he was killed in the air on 7 July 1915, whilst practising bomb throwing during a flight over the range at Netheravon, Wiltshire. Arthur Soames is buried near his parents' home in Gresford (All Saints) Churchyard, Denbighshire.

SOLOMON, Jerrold Bernard

From London, he was born on 4 April 1888. A Chemist working in London, he was also a pre-war volunteer (Number 375) with 28 London Regiment (Artists Rifles) and had attained the rank of Sergeant by the time the war came in August 1914. Picked out for a commission, he was gazetted Second Lieutenant to 2 Battalion, Oxfordshire and Buckinghamshire Light Infantry, on 27 January 1915. Sent out to France, he joined his unit in the trenches on 17 February 1915, but was released just two months later on 18 April 1915 to allow his secondment to the RFC. Having trained as an Observer, he served at the front for more than six months with 5 Squadron during 1915, before taking up a Staff position as Wing Adjutant. He received a Mention in Despatches in the *London Gazette* of 30 April 1916. Research has unearthed the recommendation for this 'Mention': 'March 1916, HQ 2/Brigade: During the twelve months, seven as an observer, and five as a Wing Adjutant, he has carried out his duties in a zealous and energetic manner'. He was next graded as a Staff Officer 2nd Class to the Military Wing, RFC, on 6 July 1916. Returning to active duty, he trained as a Pilot and was granted his full 'Wings' in the summer of 1917. Because of his seniority and experience, he was sent out to 15 Squadron (RE8s) as an A/Captain and Flight Commander on 16 August 1917. His MC, largely for his gallantry on 20 and 24 November 1917, was announced in the *London Gazette* of 25 April 1918: 'For conspicuous gallantry and devotion to duty. He carried out a patrol lasting nearly three hours in a very high wind and low clouds, flying at an average height of 500 feet and brought back a valuable report. During the flight he attacked and drove down an enemy two-seater machine under heavy rifle and machine-gun fire from the ground. He also made a valuable reconnaissance in very bad weather, flying at an average height of 100 feet under heavy rifle and machine-gun fire, in the course of which he engaged a hostile battery with his machine gun. He set a splendid example of courage and determination'.

Promoted to A/Major, he was next appointed to the command of 82 Squadron (AWFK8s) on 9 April 1918, and served as such until 6 January 1919. Awarded the Croix de Guerre avec Palme by the French and the Croix de Guerre by the Belgians. He was also Mentioned in Despatches for a second time, before finally leaving the RAF in 1919.

SOMERVAIL, Alexander Alastair

From Kelso, Scotland, he was born on 22 June 1887. Educated at Loretto (1902-06) and at the University of Edinburgh (1907-09). His younger brother, William Fulton Somervail, won a Distinguished Service Order and an MC with the Cameronians and was killed in action as a Brigade Major on 4 October 1918. Alexander, after completing his education, became a Farmer in the area of Broomdykes, Chirnside, from 1910. A pre-war volunteer, he was commissioned into 4 Battalion, King's Own Scottish Borderers (TF), and was mobilised immediately upon the outbreak of war on 4 August 1914. Seconded to the RFC, he gained his Royal Aero Club Certificate (Number 1198) at the Military School, Farnborough, on 24 April 1915. His formal training duly completed, he was confirmed and gazetted Flying Officer on 3 July following. Sent out to 6 Squadron in France soon after he qualified for his 'Wings'. On 19 September 1915, Somervail and his Observer of the day, Lieutenant C E Ryan (qv), in BE2c, '1740', brought down a large two-engined tractor machine which fell at Biffeghem. For this feat, the two would receive the MC, announced, in Somervail's case, in the New Year *London Gazette* of 1 January 1916 (no citation). Although no formal citation was published in the *Gazette*, research has unearthed the original recommendation for Somervail's award: 'On 19th September, attacked a large twin engined tractor machine. With great pluck and determination pursued the enemy till out of range. He then turned on another which nose dived out of sight. Information was later received through an agent that a machine had fallen at Biffeghem. This was believed to be the second machine he attacked. On the 30th Sept when on a bombing raid to Deynze had an engine failure over the German lines. Though shot in the wrist and both legs, manoeuvred the machine so as to land inside our lines. He passed over the German trenches at immediate risk at a very low altitude, regardless of the wounds he had already received'.

He was also Mentioned in Despatches in the *London Gazette* of 1 January 1916. Badly wounded in the incident of 30 September 1915, it was some time before he recovered sufficiently to return to operational flying. He served for a time as a Flight Commander with the DH4s of 57 Squadron in 1917, before being promoted to A/Major and appointed to the command of 77 HD Squadron on 1 January 1918. Eventually, after the war, he moved to the command of 36 Squadron, also in the UK, from 2 December 1918. Awarded the Air Force Cross in the *London Gazette* of 2 November 1918. Somervail finally relinquished his commission on 7 September 1920, returning to farming in Scotland. Alexander Somervail died in 1943.

SORSOLEIL, Jack Victor

From Toronto, Ontario, Canada, he was born on 2 June 1898. Crossing the Atlantic as a volunteer for the flying service, he was gazetted Second Lieutenant to the RFC on 19 August 1917. His training duly completed, he was confirmed and gazetted Flying Officer on 13 October following. Yet another Canadian Ace to be, he was sent out to 84 Squadron (SE5As) in November 1917, going on to achieve 14 victories between 13 January and 27 June 1918 and becoming a Flight Commander in the process. His MC was announced in the *London Gazette* of 22 April 1918: 'For conspicuous gallantry and devotion to duty. While on patrol with three other scouts he engaged a hostile formation of ten scouts, driving one of these down. While climbing to rejoin his patrol he was attacked by an enemy scout, upon which he opened fire at close range, bringing it down spinning, with the result that it crashed to earth. He has also driven down one enemy machine in flames, and sent another crashing to earth, where it was destroyed. His gallantry and skill have been most conspicuous'.

His tour with '84' completed, he returned to the Home Establishment in July 1918, where he saw out the remainder of the war as an Instructor. Returning to Canada after the war, he became a successful businessman in Toronto. He served again during the Second World War, this time as a Squadron Leader in the Royal Canadian Air Force. Jack Sorsoleil died in 1946.

SOWREY, Frederick

The second son of the Deputy Chief Inspector of the Inland Revenue at Somerset House, John Sowrey, and Mrs Susan Sowrey (née Chambers), of Yeoveney Manor, Staines, he was born in Gloucestershire, on 25 August 1893. Educated at King's College School, Wimbledon, at King's College, London University, and at Caius College, Cambridge, from where he graduated BSc in 1910. He was one of three brothers who all flew with the RFC/RAF in the Great War; one brother, William, attaining the rank of Air Commodore, CBE, DFC, AFC. When the war came in August 1914, Frederick enlisted as a Private soldier into 18 (Public Schools) Battalion, Royal Fusiliers. Picked out for a commission, he was gazetted Second Lieutenant to the Northumberland Fusiliers on 23 November 1914, with an immediate detachment to the Royal Fusiliers. He served in the trenches with the Royal Fusiliers from July to December 1915 and was slightly wounded and gassed during the Battle of Loos in the intervening September. Seconded to the RFC in January 1916, he gained his Royal Aero Club Certificate (Number 2838) on 23 April 1916. His formal training duly completed, he was confirmed and gazetted Flying Officer on 17 June following. Sent to BE2c-equipped 39 HD Squadron at Sutton Farm on Home Defence duties soon after he qualified for his 'Wings'. On the night of 23/24 September 1916, Sowrey, in BE2c, '4112', spotted the search-light illuminated Zeppelin *L32*, 10 miles south of the Thames on her way home after dropping her bombs on South Ockenden. Following a 25 minute pursuit, Sowrey caught up with the giant machine at a height of 13,000 feet. Despite coming under heavy fire from the gondola, he pressed home his attack. His first two drums of ammunition seemed to have little effect, but the third caused flames to burst from several points along the hull. Within minutes, the airship was ablaze from end to end, and fell spectacularly to the ground near to Billericay at 01.20. For this feat, only the second Zeppelin to be destroyed, Sowrey was awarded the Distinguished Service Order, *London Gazette* of 4 October 1916. He was Mentioned in Despatches around this time, *London Gazette* of 25 January 1917. He next joined another HD unit, 37 Squadron, before being sent to France on liaison duties. Soon afterwards, on 14 June 1917, he joined the Spad-equipped 19 Squadron as a Flight Commander. Sowrey went on to achieve a further 12 victories between 17 June and 15 October 1917. His MC was announced in the *London Gazette* of 26 November 1917, details in the *Gazette* of 6 April 1918: "For conspicuous gallantry and devotion to duty in shooting down in less than two months two Albatros Scouts and a Rumpler two-seater and a Fokker Scout, and in two engagements flying very low and engaging and scattering hostile infantry'.

His tour with '19' completed in October 1917, he returned to Home Defence duties, being promoted to A/Major and appointed to the command of 143 HD Squadron (SE5As). On the night of 20 May 1918, Sowrey attacked a Gotha returning home after dropping its bombs. It seems likely that he wounded the Pilot during an inconclusive engagement and was therefore instrumental in its eventual downfall when it shortly afterwards fell under the guns of Lieutenants Turner and Barwise in a 141 HD Squadron Brisfit. Thus Sowrey joined the exclusive club of those who had shot down both a Zeppelin and a Gotha. Staying on in the RAF after the war, he went on to command 100 Squadron in Ireland, 8 Squadron in Iraq and 41 Squadron at Northolt. He married, in 1921, Margarita Beatrice White, with whom he had one son and one daughter. His son would, in the fullness of time, attain the rank of Air Marshal, RAF. Promoted to Group Captain in 1934, Frederick retired finally in 1940. He had homes at 1 Priory Court, Eastbourne, Sussex, and at Brookfields, Warsash, Hampshire. Group Captain Frederick Sowrey died on 21 October 1968.

St CLAIR, Alexander Hugh

The son of Alexander St Clair and Annie Reid St Clair, of South Africa, he was born in 1895. Educated at Blundell's School (1907-13). Gazetted Second Lieutenant to 11 Battalion, Argyll and Sutherland Highlanders on 29 December 1914. Served in the trenches from July 1915, until he was seriously wounded on 25 September 1915, the first day of the Battle of Loos. Once recovered, he was seconded to the RFC and, after training, was gazetted Balloon Officer on 10 June 1916. Served as an Air Balloon Observation Officer with the Egyptian Expeditionary Force. His MC was announced in the *London Gazette* of 11 April 1918: 'For distinguished services in the field in connection with military operations culminating in the capture of Jerusalem'.

Late in 1917 and in 1918, HQ, Middle East, RFC/RAF deployed 33 Caquot Balloon Officers on detachment to the Army. St Clair left the service in 1919, and returned to South Africa. Volunteering again in 1940, he served with 'Q Branch' in Mombasa, before being seconded to the British Forces for civilian relief work in Greece and in the Balkans. He was Mentioned in Despatches for his services in the Mediterranean Theatre in 1946. Joined the UN Refugee Relief Agency in 1946.

NB: His medals were offered for sale by Glendining's (lot 266) on 22 June 1988: MC, British War Medal 1914-20, Victory Medal 1914-19 (Lt RAF), *1939-45 Star, Africa Star 1940-43, Italy Star 1943-45, Defence Medal 1939-35, War Medal 1939-45 with Oakleaf, and Africa Service Medal 1939-45* (61976 A H St Clair).

STAFFORD, William George

The son of Grocer, William Stafford and Lettie Stafford, of 'Hugos', Kea, Cornwall, he was born on 22 November 1879. He enlisted as a Sapper (Number 1939) into the Royal Engineers in 1898. Stafford served in 1900, with 4 Balloon Section, Royal Engineers, in China, during the Third China War, receiving the China Medal 1900, no clasp. By 1910, Stafford was a 2nd Corporal with 2 BC (Dismounted), becoming, soon afterwards, a 'founder member' of the Air Battalion, Royal Engineers. When the RFC came into being in 1912, Stafford was co-opted as an original member with the rank of Sergeant and the Number '22'. He took flying lessons and eventually gained his Royal Aero Club Certificate (Number 438) in a CFS Maurice Farman on Salisbury Plain on 18 March 1913, so becoming one of a small number of NCOs who were qualified Pilots at this time. In November 1915, Stafford was sent out to the Middle East as a 'founder member' of 14 Squadron. Promoted to Flight Sergeant, his engineering skills rather than his piloting expertise appeared to be in demand as he was awarded a Distinguished Conduct Medal, *London Gazette* of 31 May 1917, with the surprising citation: 'For consistent good work in connection with the care and repair of aeroplanes'. The late gazetting of this award followed some months after his commissioning, which had come on 12 October 1916, when he was gazetted as an Extra Regimentally employed Second Lieutenant on detachment to the RFC. Towards the end of 1916, air support for the Arab forces under Sherif Feisal and Captain T E Lawrence, 'Lawrence of Arabia', was provided by 'C' Flight, 14 Squadron, under the command of Major A J Ross, Intelligence Department. Known as the Arabian Detachment, this famous Flight, comprising four rather elderly BEs and a handful of officers, including Stafford, played an important part in the so-called, Revolt in the Desert. Stafford's involvement in the Hedjaz Mission and his personal links with the historical figure of Lawrence is reflected to some extent by the timing of the award of his MC, which appeared in the same *Gazette* as the CB to Major Lawrence and the Bar to Major Ross' Distinguished Service Order, *London Gazette* of 8 August 1917 (no citation). Stafford was fortunate to survive the Hedjaz operations, particularly when he and a mechanic, 1 AM Porter, almost died after they and their Crossley tender became lost in the desert. It was the height of the summer, with temperatures in the order of 112 degrees Fahrenheit.

Obviously affected by the heat, Stafford and Porter left their vehicle and wandered off into the desert. Stafford left a message for possible rescuers which said: 'We have no water. We have gone on to west into next wadi. Going to keep west when possible. Hurry after us if you see this. Cannot last long. W G Stafford, 22 6 17'.

When the note was found, there was no sign of either man but, by sheer good fortune, the two exhausted men ran into a band of friendly Bedouins who gave them food and water and led them to safety. After the war, Stafford was attached to the Marine and Armament Experimental Establishment of the RAF, on the Isle of Grain. Belatedly awarded the Order of El Nahda, 4th Class, for his service in the Hedjaz operations, *London Gazette* of 2 September 1924: 'Awarded by the King of the Hedjaz to Lieutenant (now Flying Officer) William George Stafford, MC, DCM'. He retired from the service in 1927, with the rank of Flight Lieutenant, RAF. William Stafford of the White Hart Hotel, Naylands, Suffolk, at the Essex County Nursing Home, Beverley Road, Colchester, just one year after retiring from the RAF.

NB: His unique medal group was offered for sale by Christie's (lot 135) on 22 March 1988: MC (engraved: Lt W G Stafford, RFC 3/6/17), *Distinguished Conduct Medal* (22 Flt Sergeant, No 14 Sqd, RFC), *China Medal 1900, no clasp* (Sapper RE), *1914-15 Star* (S.Mjr RFC), *British War Medal 1914-20, Victory Medal 1914-19 with MID* (Lt RAF), *Army Long Service & Good Conduct Medal* (22 Sjt RFC), *and Order of El Nahda (Hedjaz, Fourth Class, Neck Badge in silver and enamels).*

STANES, Eric Henry

The son of Tea Planter, Thomas Stanes and Mrs Stanes, of Streatham, London SW, he was born in Coonor, India, on 4 April 1897. Educated at Moncton Coombe School, Bath (1909-15), where he was a member of the OTC, at Birmingham University, and eventually matriculating, post-war, at the University of London. Gazetted Second Lieutenant to 3 (Reserve) Battalion, Manchester Regiment, on 26 September 1916. Seconded to the RFC in the summer of 1917, he trained as an Observer and was sent out as a Probationary to BF2b-equipped 48 Squadron in the July following. His 'apprenticeship' satisfactorily completed, he was confirmed and gazetted Flying Officer (Observer) on 23 September 1917. On 24 March 1918, Stanes and his Pilot, Captain C R Steele, in BF2b, 'C4710', were lucky to escape disaster when the engine of their machine was hit and disabled by ground fire. His tour with '48' completed in May 1918, Stanes returned to the Home Establishment and instructing duties. His MC was announced in the *London Gazette* of 26 July 1918: 'For conspicuous gallantry and devotion to duty. On one occasion he carried out at an altitude of between 500 and 700 feet, despite hostile machine-gun and rifle fire, a very comprehensive reconnaissance of railways, roads, dumps, and aerodromes behind the enemy's lines, obtaining information of inestimable value. On a later occasion, while on a photographic reconnaissance, being attacked most persistently by hostile aircraft, he repeatedly drove off the enemy machines, and only returned to his aerodrome when he obtained the photographs required. His courage and determination were of the highest quality, and the services he has rendered of exceptional merit'.

Stanes relinquished his commission due to ill-health on 14 October 1919, subsequently working as a Tea Planter with the family firm, T Stanes and Company, in Coimbatore, India. He retired in 1964, going to live at Down House, Broadmayne, near Dorchester, Dorset. Eric Stanes died on 29 April 1970.

STANGER, Stanley

An Investment Broker from Montreal, Canada, he was born on 10 July 1894. After serving for two and a half years as a despatch rider with the Canadian infantry, he was accepted as Cadet for the flying service early in 1917. Gazetted Second Lieutenant to the RFC, via the General List, on 10 May 1917. Within days of qualifying for his 'Wings', he was posted to 66 Squadron (Camel F1s) in France on 18 October 1917. Accompanying '66' to Italy on 22 November 1917, he achieved three victories between 14 December 1917 and 17 April 1918. A transfer to the Camel-equipped 28 Squadron, as an A/Captain and Flight Commander, came on 27 April 1918. Stanger gained a further ten victories between 2 May and 4 October on the Italian front. Wounded and put out of action by anti-aircraft fire on 23 August 1918, he recovered and was flying again within weeks. His MC was announced in the *London Gazette* of 16 September 1918: 'For conspicuous gallantry and devotion to duty in destroying six enemy aeroplanes. He did splendid service'.

One day in October, feeling quite unwell, he landed on what he assumed to be a friendly aerodrome. Having switched off his engine, he alighted only to realise he had landed on an Austrian airfield. Whipping off his flying boots, he used them as chocks as he swung the propellor to get his machine going again. Leaping into the cockpit, he took off before the Austrians could intervene. He was awarded a Distinguished Flying Cross in the *London Gazette* of 3 December 1918, for his gallantry and outstanding leadership. Returning to Canada after the war, he joined the family business, The Guardian Trust Company of Montreal, becoming President in 1939. Stan Stanger died on 10 September 1967.

STANLEY-CLARKE, Arthur Ramsey

The son of Quarter Master Sergeant Arthur Clarke, 3 Battalion, Devonshire Regiment, and Helen Clarke, of 6 Wesley Terrace, Plymouth, he was born in Alexandria, Egypt, on 17 June 1891. A pre-war Regular Army officer, he assumed the surname 'Stanley-Clarke' and was gazetted Second Lieutenant to the Dorsetshire Regiment in 1913. He accompanied 1 Battalion of his regiment to France on 14 August 1914, thus qualifying for the 1914 Star. Stanley-Clarke was gassed on 5 May 1915 in the Salient trenches during the closing days of the Second Battle of Ypres. Once recovered, he secured a secondment to the RFC, gaining his Royal Aero Club Certificate (Number 1627) on 23 August 1915. His formal training duly completed, he was confirmed and gazetted Flying Officer on 14 December following. Sent out to the BE2c-equipped 8 Squadron on 1 February 1916, he was eventually promoted to A/Captain and Flight Commander on 8 July 1916. His MC was announced in the *London Gazette* of 13 February 1917: 'For conspicuous gallantry in action. He carried out successfully and quickly some artillery registration that was urgently needed. He has previously on very many occasions shown great courage and skill'.

His tour with '8' completed, Stanley-Clarke returned to the Home Establishment where he was promoted to A/Major on 1 May 1917 and given command of 61 TS. He would also go on to command the dedicated mail-carrying 120 Squadron (DH9s) from June 1918. Although granted a permanent commission on 1 August 1919, Stanley-Clarke was medically downgraded and, as a consequence, resigned from the RAF on 4 February 1920, to revert to the Army.

STARLEY, Richard Douglas

The son of R and Mrs M H Starley of Barr's Hill House, Coventry, Warwickshire, he was born on 7 September 1891. Educated at Mill Hill School, London (1905-07), where he was a member of the OTC. He had trained as a Civil Engineer and was living and working in Edmondton, Canada, when the war came in August 1914. He immediately enlisted as a Private soldier (Number 18688) into 4 Battalion, 101 Fusiliers, on 10 August 1914. Subsequently, he served in 9 Canadian Infantry with the CEF in France before being accepted as a Cadet for the flying service in November 1916. Gazetted Second Lieutenant to the RFC on 27 February 1917. His formal training duly completed, he was confirmed and gazetted Flying Officer on 10 May following. Posted to 4 Squadron (RE8s) in France soon after qualifying for his 'Wings'. On 16 August 1917, Starley and his Observer, Lieutenant B C R Grimwood (qv), in RE8, 'A3848', were about to transmit news of enemy troops massing in preparation for a counterattack, when their machine was struck by a shell. Their wireless set was smashed in the explosion and Grimwood was wounded. Despite their predicament, Starley handwrote a message which he placed in a weighted bag and dropped it on Divisional HQ. Starley then got the 'Harry Tate' and the injured Grimwood back to their base and medical treatment. His, and Grimwood's, MCs were announced in the *London Gazette* of 26 September 1917, details in the *Gazette* of 9 January 1918: 'For conspicuous gallantry and devotion to duty. When he had located a large force of the enemy infantry who were about to counter-attack, his machine was immediately afterwards hit by a shell, which destroyed the wireless, and so prevented his reporting what he had seen. His machine was obviously so badly damaged that no expert would have believed that it could possibly hold together in the air. In spite of this he went down and dropped a message on Divisional Headquarters, who were able to put nine batteries on to the counter-attack. He then managed to get his machine back to the aerodrome and confirmed the message by telephone. Throughout the operations he has on all occasions shown the same spirit of pluck and determination'.

Starley subsequently served as a Flight Lieutenant, RAF, at the Aircraft Depot, Aboukir, Egypt. He lived, post-war, in Leamington, Warwickshire. By 1938 he was a Wing Commander and later a Group Captain.

STATON, William Ernest

The son of an Under Manager of a Gypsum Mine, William Newton Staton and Ada Staton (née Walkerdine), of Oak Villas, Hatton Road, Hatton (Entire), Derbyshire, he was born on 27 August 1898. He enlisted as a Private soldier (Number 765057) into 28 Battalion, London Regiment (Artists Rifles) (TF), as soon as he was old enough to do so, late in 1916. Picked out for a commission, he was gazetted Second Lieutenant to the RFC on 4 May 1917. His training duly completed, he was confirmed and gazetted Flying Officer on 21 September following. Sent to the BF2b-equipped 62 Squadron then at Filton, he accompanied the unit to France as a 'founder member' on 23 January 1918. Staton proved to be an Ace (in every sense of the word) exponent in the use of the formidable Bristol Fighter as a fighting machine. He achieved no less than 26 victories between 13 March and 24 September 1918. He was particularly effective when flying with Aussie J R Gordon (qv), the two sharing 15 successes. Staton was promoted to A/Captain and Flight Commander in the same month that his MC was announced, *London Gazette* of 22 June 1918: 'For conspicuous gallantry and devotion to duty. On one occasion when on offensive patrol, he, by the skilful handling of his machine and accurate shooting, destroyed two enemy aeroplanes and brought down a third out of control. In addition, during the nine-days previous to this, he had destroyed five other enemy machines, two of these being tri-planes. The services which he has rendered have been exceptionally brilliant, and his skill and determination are deserving of the highest praise'.

An award of the recently instituted Distinguished Flying Cross came in the *London Gazette* of 21 September 1918, for his continuing success as a Fighter Pilot. His luck ran out to some extent on the day of his last and 26th victory, 24 September 1918, when his Brisfit was shot up during a dogfight involving more than 30 enemy machines. Although getting his Observer, Second Lieutenant L E Mitchell, down safely, Staton himself was wounded in the air, wounds which effectively ended his operational flying in the Great War. A Bar to his Distinguished Flying Cross, yet further recognition of his effectiveness, was subsequently announced in the *London Gazette* of 3 December 1918. He was subsequently granted a permanent commission in the RAF on 1 August 1919. An expert rifle and pistol shot, he represented the RAF at Bisley. His subsequent appointments, honours and promotions during a distinguished career, included: Pilot, 20 Squadron, 1920; Staff, RAF Base, Calshott, 1927; Pilot, 205 Squadron, 1931; Adjutant/QFI, 501 (County of Gloucester) Squadron Auxiliary Air Force; CFI, 3 FTS, 1935; Squadron Leader, 1935; Flight Commander/Conversion Training, 76 Squadron (Whitley), 1938; OC, 10 Squadron (Whitleys), 1938; Wing Commander, 1938; OC, RAF Leeming, 1940; appointed ADC to the King, 1940; DSO, *London Gazette* of 20 February 1940; Bar to DSO, *London Gazette* of 7 July 1940; Mentioned in Despatches, *London Gazette* of 20 February 1940; SASO, HQ, RAF Far East, 1941; Group Captain, 1942; Prisoner of War, 1942; AOC, 46 (Transport) Group, 1945; Commandant, Central Bomber Establishment, RAF Marham, 1947; CB, 1947; Air Commodore, 1947; AOA, HQ, Technical Training Command, 1949; Air Vice-Marshal, 1950.

'Bull' Staton was a larger than life character in many ways, he even later acquired the additional nickname of 'King Kong' because of his size and physical presence. During the early bombing operations in the Second World War, he was amongst the first to realise that by marking targets in advance with flares and Very lights, accuracy would improve. Remarkably, he was awarded a Distinguished Service Order and Bar for his leadership and gallantry in 1940, the citation for the Bar relating how, despite his aircraft being hit by six shells during a low level attack on the oil depot at Bremen, he still manged to bring it home. Posted next to the Far East, he was captured by the Japanese in Java in 1942. He suffered badly at the hands of his Japanese captors, at one time having all his teeth removed as a punishment for his 'lack of co-operation'. He was Mentioned in Despatches for his leadership while in Japanese captivity, *London Gazette* of 1 October 1946. Staton married, firstly, in 1919, Norah Carina Workman, with whom he had two sons, and secondly, in 1973 (after Norah's death in 1969), Jean Patricia Primrose. He retired from the RAF on 12 November 1952. Air Vice-Marshal William Staton died on 22 July 1983, in Elmsworth, Hampshire.

STEELE, Thomas Lancaster

The son of Farmer Adam William Steele and Mrs Steele, of Christchurch, Canterbury, New Zealand, he was born on 31 August 1890. Educated at Christchurch College, at Waitaki High School, and at Lincoln College. He enlisted as a Private soldier into the New Zealand Mounted Rifles in February 1915, and was, soon afterwards, promoted Lance Corporal with the Machine Gun Squadron. After service in the Middle East with the Kiwis, he was accepted as a Cadet into the flying service in April 1917. Gazetted Second Lieutenant to the RFC on 7 August 1917. His training duly completed at RFC HQ, Egypt, he was confirmed and gazetted Flying Officer on 17 September following. Posted to 14 Squadron, then still in Arabia, on 8 October 1917, he was wounded in action just four days later on 12 October. His MC was announced in the *London Gazette* of 26 March 1918, details in the *Gazette* of 24 August 1918: 'For conspicuous gallantry and devotion to duty. When instructed to attack a hostile concentration he encountered heavy machine-gun and rifle fire, his petrol tank being pierced. Despite the risk of his tank catching fire, he continued to his objective, where he obtained excellent results from bombs dropped from 400 feet. On a later occasion, though shot through his arm, he continued to his objective and obtained excellent results. His courage and determination were most praiseworthy'.

Once recovered, he reported to 111 Squadron, a single-seater fighter unit, on 2 January 1918. On 10 April 1918, Steele, in Nieuport, 'B3594', completely disappeared without trace. His remains were never recovered and hence he is commemorated on the Jerusalem Memorial, Israel.

STENT, Frederick William

Born in Cyprus in 1890. Gazetted Second Lieutenant to the Military Wing, RFC, via the Special Reserve, on 1 May 1915. Gained his Royal Aero Club Certificate (Number 2748) on 31 August 1915. His formal pilot training duly completed, he was confirmed and gazetted Flying Officer on 7 October following. Posted first to 77 HD Squadron at Turnhouse, before accompanying 17 Squadron to the Middle East. A fluent Arabic speaker, he was next appointed as Second in Command of the Arabian Detachment of 14 Squadron. After nine months in an unexplored and torrid land with an alien culture, the ordinary dangers of warfare seemed slight, and the Detachment was relieved to re-join the rest of 14 Squadron at Deir el Balah, south of Gaza, early in August 1917. On 26 August, Stent and three of his Pilots flew 100 miles south to a roughly prepared landing ground at El Quntilla. Two days later they took off to attack and bomb a railway station and troop concentrations 65 miles east at Ma'an. The surprise worked perfectly, as T E Lawrence confirms in 'Seven Pillars of Wisdom': '....two bombs into the barracks killed thirty-five men and wounded fifty. Eight struck the engine shed, heavily damaging the plant and stock. A bomb in the General's kitchen finished his cook and his breakfast. Four fell on the aerodrome....'. On the following day, they took off again to bomb and strafe the huge camp at Abu el Lissan. Horses stampeded into the Turkish tents, causing great confusion. Although the machines were struck by ground fire on both days, none were brought down and the occupants were unscathed. Arriving back at Deir el Balah on 30 August, they were told to prepare themselves for permanent detachment to Prince Feisal's forces at Akaba. Stent was appointed CO of the designated 'X' Flight, which arrived for business at Akaba on 9 September 1917. By the end of 1917, the Flight had assisted the Arab forces in their 100 mile advance along the Hedjaz railway. Stent's MC was announced in the *London Gazette* of 22 June 1918: 'For conspicuous gallantry and devotion to duty. He attacked and brought down a hostile two-seater, the observer of which was in a position to give the enemy valuable information of our movements. On another occasion he encountered and brought down an enemy two-seater, wounding both pilot and observer, who were made prisoners. On both occasions he showed great gallantry and ability'.

He was also Mentioned in Despatches on two occasions during the Great War. Promoted to A/Major, he was given command of 111 Squadron from November 1917 to July 1918. Stent was subsequently awarded the Order of the Rising Sun by the Japanese and the Order of al Nahda of the Kingdom of Hedjaz. Staying on in the RAF after the war, he had attained the rank of Wing Commander by the time he retired from the RAF in January 1936. He lived, following his retirement, with his wife, Gladys Emily, at Sessay Pond Lane, Sonning, Berkshire. On 28 June 1938, Stent, flying from Reading to Martlesham and an entrant in the forthcoming King's Cup Air Race, was killed in a crash at Harefield, near Uxbridge, whilst practising for the event in a Miles Monarch machine.

STEPHENSON, William Samuel

The son of Victor and Christina Stephenson, of Winnipeg, Canada, he was born on 11 January 1896 in Point Douglas, Manitoba. Educated locally, he showed an early propensity for engineering. When the war came in 1914, he enlisted into the Canadian Engineers and served with the CEF with the rank of Sergeant. Apparently commissioned Lieutenant in the field (although the contemporary *Army Lists* do not appear to record the event), he was subsequently gassed on more than one occasion and, in 1916, was returned to the UK for medical treatment. Once recovered, he was successful in applying for a Cadetship in the flying service and was subsequently gazetted Second Lieutenant to the RFC in the late summer of 1917. His pilot training duly completed, he qualified for his 'Wings' in October 1917. Sent to the Camel F1-equipped 73 Squadron, then at Upavon, he accompanied the unit to France as a 'founder member' on 9 January 1918. Stephenson achieved 12 victories between 22 March and 28 July 1918. His MC was announced in the *London Gazette* of 22 June 1918: For conspicuous gallantry and devotion to duty. When flying low and observing an open staff car on the road, he attacked it with such success that later it was seen lying in a ditch upside down. During the same flight he caused a stampede amongst some enemy transport horses on the road. Previous to this he had destroyed a hostile scout and a two-seater plane. His work has been of the highest order, and he has shown the highest courage and energy in engaging every kind of target'.

On 28 July 1918, Stephenson, in Sopwith Camel, 'C8296', was involved in a combat with up to seven Fokker DVIIIs over Fére-en-Tardenois. He claimed one of the enemy down in flames, but was himself shot down, probably by Leutnant Justus Grassmann of Jasta 10, the third of the German Ace's eventual ten victories. Initially posted as missing in action, Stephenson was later reported as having been made prisoner by the Germans. Some sources say that after some months in captivity, he contrived to escape and make his way back to the British lines, but contemporary records kept by Cox & Co, his Bankers, less dramatically show him to have been repatriated in the usual way after the war on 30 December 1918. Certainly, his name was not amongst those honoured for escaping in the so-called 'Escapers Gazette', *London Gazette* of 16 December 1919. His prowess in the air prior to his capture was, however, further recognised by the award of a Distinguished Flying Cross, announced in the *London Gazette* of 21 September 1918, this mainly for his courage and tenacity in the low-level strafing of ground targets. Again, some sources erroneously credit him with winning a Distinguished Flying Cross and two Bars and others with having gained, variously, a total of 26 or 27 victories. After the war, Stephenson returned to Canada and set about building up his father's business with outstanding success. He married, in 1924, Mary Simmons (died 1978), with whom he had one adopted daughter. Whilst a prisoner of war in Germany, he had been impressed by the ingenious design of a can-opener used in the camp. Bringing one home with him, he discovered, post-war, that it was patented only in Germany. Adding one or two slight modifications, he patented the kitchen tool worldwide and proceeded to make a veritable fortune with it. He also set up manufacturing processes for other household goods and invested heavily in steel.

Alert to the new threat posed by Hitler and Nazi Germany, Stephenson renewed earlier acquaintances with British Intelligence and offered his services in liaising with the US intelligence branch, the OSS, from his New York office. When the war came in 1939, Stephenson was appointed head of SIS (MI6) operations in the US, working from Room 3603 in the RCA Building. His war work was acknowledged when he was created Knight Bachelor on 13 February 1945 at Buckingham Palace. In 1946, General W J Donovan, US Army, presented Stephenson with the Presidential Medal for Merit, the first non-American to receive the honour. Sir William settled in Jamaica in 1946, but continued to act as a consultant on security matters, particularly to the Canadian Government. In 1980, Sir William was invested Companion of the Order of Canada (CC) by the Governor

General of Canada in a special ceremony in Bermuda. He also held many honorary appointments, including: Patron, CDF Intelligence Branch; Honorary Life Member Royal Military Institute, Canada; Fellow, Bermuda College, Bermuda, 1986; Honorary Member Canadian Security Intelligence Service, 1986; Honorary DSc University of the West Indies, 1950; Honorary DSc Military, Royal Military College; Honorary LLD, Winnipeg; Honorary DSc, Manitoba, 1979, Winnipeg, 1980, and Windsor, Ontario 1985. Scholarships were established in his name at the University of the West Indies, Jamaica, at the University of Winnipeg and at Bermuda College. Appointed GCSJ, 1986. Honorary Citizen of Winnipeg, 1984. General Donovan Award, Veterans of OSS, 1983. Chief Hunter, Order of Buffalo Hunt, Province of Manitoba, 1985. Croix de Guerre avec Palmes (France). His biography, 'The Quiet Canadian' by H H Hyde was published in 1962. Two other books about Stephenson, 'A Man Called Intrepid' and 'Intrepid's Last Case' by William Stevenson, were published in 1977 and 1984 respectively. He had moved from Jamaica to Paget, Bermuda, in the 1960s, and he died there on 31 January 1989. After his death, *The Times* credited Stephenson with being a genuine intelligence hero but added that some of his background and accomplishments had been of his own invention.

STEVENS, Cecil Alfred

The son of Mr and Mrs Alfred Stevens, of Putney, London, he was born on 31 October 1898. Educated at the Emmanuel School and at Sandhurst. Gazetted Second Lieutenant to a Regular Army battalion of the Duke of Wellington's (West Rdiing) Regiment on 16 August 1916, with an immediate secondment to the RFC. His formal training duly completed, he was confirmed and gazetted Flying Officer on 14 March 1917. Sent out almost immediately to 55 Squadron (DH4s), a unit which had only very recently gone to France for the first time. On 10 May 1917, a bad day for the squadron, Stevens and his Observer, Lieutenant F L Oliver, in DH4, 'A2150', were fortunate to survive after being shot up during a photo-reconnaissance over Neuvilly. Three other DH4s of 55 Squadron were shot down, with five of the six occupants killed in action and the sixth wounded. On 14 August, Stevens and his Observer of the day, Second Lieutenant B F Sandy, in DH4, 'A7470', were again shot up during an aerial combat. Although Sandy was wounded in the incident, the unscathed Stevens got them safely back to base. The first of his MCs was announced in the *London Gazette* of 27 October 1917, details in the *Gazette* of 18 March 1918: 'For conspicuous gallantry and devotion to duty. He took part in over thirty successful operations over the enemy's lines, including long-distance photographic reconnaissances and bombing raids. On one occasion he was heavily attacked by enemy aeroplanes, one of which he destroyed and returned with excellent photographs and with his machine badly shot about. On another occasion, when leading a bombing raid, the formation was heavily attacked by enemy aeroplanes. He skilfully kept the formation together and led it back to the aerodrome. He consistently set a fine example by his skill and determination'.

The Bar to his MC followed in the *London Gazette* of 18 February 1918, details in the *Gazette* of 18 July 1918: 'For conspicuous gallantry and devotion to duty as a leader of numerous bombing raids. On one occasion he led ten machines a distance of 130 miles from his aerodrome, obtaining good results. During all the raids in which he has acted as leader he has lost only one machine, and he has invariably given a splendid example of skill and courage. His skill and determination have had an admirable influence in his squadron'.

Staying on in the RAF after the war, his many subsequent appointments, honours and promotions included: India, 1924-30, India General Service Medal 1908-35, with clasp, Waziristan 1925, and Mentioned in Despatches, *London Gazette* of 20 November 1925; Wing Commander, 1936; SASO, Aden 1937-41; Group Captain, 1939; Air Commodore, 1941; Mentioned in Despatches, *London Gazette* of 24 September 1941; AOA, Burma, 1944-45; CBE, 1944; AOC, Allied Air Forces, Netherlands East Indies, 1945-46, General Service Medal 1918-62, with clasp, SE Asia 1945-46; CB, (Military) 1947; AOC, 28 Group, 1947-49; AOC, 62 (S) Group, 1949-51; Air Vice-Marshal, 1951; and SASO, Home Command, 1951-54. Stevens married, 1946, Naterlie Pratt (née Koltsoff). Air Vice-Marshal Stevens retired in November 1954, going to live in Bexhill-on-Sea, East Sussex and was later appointed Deputy Lieutenant, of Somerset in 1957. He died on 30 November 1958.

NB: Hiss medals were offered for sale by Spink on 6 May 1998: CB (Military Division), CBE (Military Division), MC & Bar, British War Medal 1914-20, Victory Medal 1914-19, India General Service Medal 1908-35, with clasp, Waziristan 1925, and MID, 1939 45 Star, Burma Star 1941 45, Defence Medal 1939 45, War Medal 1939-45, General Service Medal 1918-62, with clasp, S.E. Asia 1945-46, and Coronation Medal 1953.

STEVENSON, Donald Fasken

The son of Lieutenant Colonel John Stevenson and Mrs Stevenson, he was born on 7 April 1895. Gazetted Second Lieutenant to the Nottinghamshire Yeomanry (Sherwood Rangers) (TF) on 22 November 1915. At the time of his commissioning, his regiment was away in Gallipoli and about to be evacuated to Egypt, but Stevenson was destined not to join it, as he was successful in applying for a secondment to the RFC, which came in the late summer of 1916. His formal training duly completed, he was confirmed and gazetted Flying Officer on 13 November 1916. Sent out immediately to 12 Squadron (equipped with the BE2c and BE2e) in France. A steady and reliable officer, he was promoted to A/Captain and Flight Commander in the summer of 1917, the first of his MCs announced in the *London Gazette* of 17 September 1917: 'For conspicuous gallantry and devotion to duty in carrying out three contact patrols in one day in bad weather, and at low altitudes. Although attacked by enemy machines in superior numbers, he drove them off, and by his fine reconnaissance work brought back valuable information. He has at all times displayed indomitable pluck and initiative'.

The announcement of the Bar to his MC soon followed in the *London Gazette* of 18 October 1917, details in the *Gazette* of 7 March 1918: 'For conspicuous gallantry and devotion to duty in obtaining photographs of a raid carried out by our troops which necessitated his flying through our barrage at a height of less than 1,000 feet. On another occasion he brought down a hostile machine. He was under heavy fire from the ground the whole time, and was eventually forced to land behind our lines owing to his petrol tank being shot through'.

He married, in 1917, Janet Mary Hull, with whom he had one son and one daughter. Stevenson was awarded the Distinguished Service Order in the *London Gazette* of 26 July 1918. Promoted to A/Major, he was appointed to the command of 35 Squadron in France on 8 September 1918. Mentioned in Despatches in the *London Gazette* of 31 December 1918. Staying on in the RAF after the war, his many subsequent appointments, honours and promotions, included: OC, 5 Squadron in Germany and at Bicester from 2 March 1919; Instructor, RAF College, 1919; Instructor, School of Army Co-operation, 1921; Staff College, 1923; Air Staff, HQ, Iraq Command, 1924; OC, 6 Squadron, Mosul, 1925; Naval Staff College, 1927; Imperial Defence College, 1929; OC, 12 Squadron, Andover; SASO, HQ, Transjordan and Palestine, 1933-36; OBE, 1937; Deputy Director of Operations (Home), 1938; Director of Operations (Home); ADC to the King, 1939-40; AOC, 2 (Bomber) Group; AOC, 221 Group, RAF Burma, 1941; AOC, AHQ, Bengal, 1942; CBE, 1942; Mentioned in Despatches, *London Gazette* of 1 January 1943; AOC, RAF, Northern Ireland, 1943; AOC, 9 Group, 1943; Head of British Military Mission, High Commissioner, Romania, 1944. CB, 1946. He retired from the RAF on 10 February 1948, going to live in York, Toronto, Canada. Air Vice-Marshal Stevenson died on 10 July 1964.

STEVENSON, John Affleck

The son of Lieutenant Colonel John Stevenson, Royal Army Medical Corps, and Mrs Stevenson, of 2 Bay Terrace, Berwick-on-Tweed, Northumberland, he was born in Simla, India, on 20 July 1888. Educated at Hulme, Berwick, and Doncaster Grammar Schools, before entering Edinburgh University where he graduated both BSc and MA in 1912. Stevenson lived and worked in Germany and Austria in 1912 and 1913. He next gained a position as a Maths Master at Haverfordwest Grammar School in 1913 and was still there when war came in August 1914. Although a married man by this time, he enlisted as a Gunner into the Royal Field Artillery in December 1914. Gazetted Second Lieutenant to the RFA very soon afterwards on 4 January 1915. Promoted Lieutenant on 31 January 1916, he shortly afterwards transferred to the RFC. After training as a Balloon Officer in the UK, he was sent to 8 BC in France in March 1916 and was subsequently formally appointed a Balloon Officer on 26 June following. His MC, for services with 17 KB Company, was announced in the *London Gazette* of 26 September 1917, details in the *Gazette* of 9 January 1918: 'For conspicuous gallantry and devotion to duty as a balloon observer. Working under very great difficulties owing to a high and gusty wind, he has furnished invaluable information to our artillery, continually ranging them on hostile batteries with complete accuracy and success in spite of the difficulties with which he had to contend. He has at all times set a very fine example of pluck and determination'.

Stevenson was presented with the insignia of his MC by the King at an investiture held at Buckingham Palace on 16 March 1918. He was promoted to Captain and BC Commander (equivalent to Flight Commander) in February 1918. Stevenson survived the Great War.

STEVENSON-JONES, Sidney

The son of Mr and Mrs R Stephenson-Jones, of 'Castlerigg', 12 Prospect Road, Prenton, Birkenhead, he was born on 21 April 1892, in Sefton Park, Liverpool. Educated at Greenbank School (1902-06), privately until 1910, and at Liverpool University, from where he graduated with Honours in Architecture. Practised as an Architect in Liverpool from September 1912 until March 1915. Gazetted Second Lieutenant to 3 (Reserve) Battalion, South Lancashire Regiment on 3 March 1915, with an immediate attachment to 2 Battalion. Served in the trenches on the Western Front with 2 South Lancs and was awarded the first of his MCs in the New Year *London Gazette* of 1 January 1917 (no citation). Seconded to the RFC in March 1917, he trained as an Observer and was sent out as a Probationary to the DH4-equipped 55 Squadron in June 1917. The Bar to his MC was announced in the *London Gazette* of 13 May 1918: 'For conspicuous gallantry and devotion to duty as an Observer. He took part in long-distance bombing raids and in raids on enemy aerodromes. He carried out several long-distance reconnaissances over the enemy's lines, taking a large number of photographs, from which valuable information was obtained. On one occasion, when his machine caught fire, at a height of 4,000 feet, and was wrecked on landing, he showed great promptitude and presence of mind in extricating the pilot and extinguishing his clothes, which were on fire. He has always showed great skill and gallantry, and set an excellent example to the Observers of his squadron'.

He next trained as a Pilot, and, once qualified, served with the Sopwith Camel F1-equipped 70 Squadron on the Western Front. Stevenson-Jones survived the Great War.

STEWART, David Arthur

The son of an Irish father, he was born in Hull on 8 March 1890. Educated at the National School, Day Street, Hull. Became an Engineer in civilian life. Having enlisted into the RFC on 11 January 1915, 1 AM Stewart flew as a Gunner/Observer in the FE2d-equipped 20 Squadron from 23 May 1916. On 1 August 1916, Stewart, with Second Lieutenant D H Dabbs in the pilot's seat of A13, brought a Fokker EIII down into a ploughed field near to Moorslede. Three days later while carrying out a height test, Stewart and Captain R S Maxwell (qv) spotted an enemy machine over Ypres. Their attack lasted more than ten minutes with 12 drums of ammunition expended in the process. The hostile machine was eventually forced down and crashed into a field near to Gheluwe. Returning to the UK, Stewart gained his Royal Aero Club Certificate (Number 3958) on 7 December 1916, whilst still a Corporal. His formal pilot training duly completed, he was promoted to Sergeant and rated NCO Pilot on 23 February 1917. Unsurprisingly picked out for a commission, Stewart was gazetted Second Lieutenant to the RFC, via the General List, on 29 May 1917, the same day that he was formally confirmed Flying Officer. Posted to the DH4-equipped 18 Squadron in the autumn of 1917, he achieved a further 14 victories between 6 January and 17 June 1918, an astonishing feat for a Bomber Pilot. He had survived a close call on 23 November 1917, when, flying with Second Lieutenant H W MacKay as his Observer in DH4, 'A7501', the pair were forced to land after their machine was hit by anti-aircraft fire over Bapaume. More seriously, on 6 March 1918, Stewart and his Observer of the day, Aberdonian Second Lieutenant H W M Mackay, Gordon Highlanders attached RFC, in DH4, 'A7797', after claiming no less than three enemy aircraft down out of control and one destroyed on that one day over Lens-Pont à Vendin, were themselves sent down due to damaged controls. Despite a heavy crash-landing, Stewart emerged unscathed from the wreckage, but the 20 year old Harry Mackay died of his wounds and injuries later on the same day. Stewart was promoted to A/Captain and Flight Commander on 25 March 1918, The first of his MCs was announced in the *London Gazette* of 22 April 1918: 'For conspicuous gallantry and devotion to duty. On one occasion, when returning from bombing an enemy dump, he was intercepted by a formation of 30 hostile machines. He attacked the leader and shot his machine down out of control, whilst his Observer shot down another enemy scout. He then fired a burst at another large scout, which dived down vertically out of control. On his Observer being hit while engaged with another four machines, he spun down to 4,000 feet and dived for our lines. Later, when on photographic duty, he was attacked by five enemy scouts, three of which were accounted for by his Observer and himself. In the face of heavy odds, his courage, skill and fine fighting spirit have been most conspicuous'.

The Bar to his MC came along soon afterwards in the *London Gazette* of 22 June 1918: 'For conspicuous gallantry and devotion to duty. During the past month, when engaged with superior numbers of enemy aircraft, he has destroyed four hostile machines, all of which were seen to crash by other observers. He has in addition carried out nine successful reconnaissances, as a result of which he has returned with information of the greatest value. He has displayed the greatest courage and determination at all times on his many low flying and bombing attacks on hostile troops and transports'.

He was also awarded a Distinguished Flying Cross, *London Gazette* of 2 November 1918, mainly for his leadership and gallantry in bombing raids, reconnaissances and photographic flights, frequently at very low altitudes. David Stewart survived the Great War and won an Air Force Cross in 1921 opening the route between Cairo and Baghdad. Left the RAF in 1933.

STEWART, Douglas

A pre-war volunteer, he was gazetted Second Lieutenant, 4 Company, Tynemouth Battery, RGA (TF), on 16 September 1911. Mobilised with the rest of the TF as soon as war came on 4 August 1914, he subsequently served in France and Flanders with his unit in 1915. Seconded to the RFC, he trained as an Observer and was sent out as such to the Sopwith Strutter-equipped 70 Squadron in the summer of 1916. On 2 September 1916, Stewart and his Pilot, Captain H G Salmond, in Strutter, 'A888', were shot down during a low-level combat with enemy machines over Bourlon Wood. Both men were taken prisoner, with Salmond wounded in the engagement. Remarkably, Stewart contrived to escape from captivity in April 1917. He next trained as a Pilot, and was sent out again to 18 Squadron (DH4s) in the spring of 1918. He claimed at least two victories in June 1918, shortly after being promoted to A/Captain and Flight Commander. His tour with '18' completed, he returned to the Home Establishment and instructing duties. His outstanding services as an Instructor were acknowledged with the award of an Air Force Cross, *London Gazette* of 3 June 1919. Stewart's remarkable feat in escaping from captivity was rewarded with the MC, announced in the 'Escapers Gazette', *London Gazette* of 16 December 1919: '....in recognition of gallantry in escaping from captivity whilst Prisoners of War'.

STEWART, Oliver

From London, he was born on 26 November 1895. Educated at Copethorne School at Bradfield (1909-12) and at the Royal College of Music. He was studying at the RCM when the war came in August 1914. He enlisted as a Private soldier (Number 2289) into 28 London Regiment (Artists Rifles), before, soon afterwards, on 27 October 1914, being gazetted Second Lieutenant to 9 Battalion, Middlesex Regiment. Seconded to the RFC, he gained his Royal Aero Club Certificate (Number 2630) on 30 March 1916. His formal pilot training duly completed, he was confirmed and gazetted Flying Officer on 24 May following. Stewart served briefly with 22 Squadron in France, before joining the Sopwith Pup-equipped 54 Squadron early in 1917. He achieved five victories between 6 April and 25 September 1917. The first of these, on 6 April, was against a particularly accomplished Scout Pilot who attacked the numerically superior 54 Squadron with aplomb, but soon regretted his rash intervention. Promoted to A/Captain and Flight Commander, Stewart's MC was announced in the *London Gazette* of 17 September 1917: 'For conspicuous gallantry and devotion to duty. He has done consistent good work for six months, both on escorts and offensive patrols, and has displayed great fearlessness and skill during severe fighting at close range with enemy machines, successfully holding his own, although on several occasions outnumbered by them'.

His tour with '54' completed, he returned to the Home Establishment and, in June 1918, upon his appointment to the command of the Aeroplane and Armament Experimental Establishment at Orfordness and Martlesham Heath, was promoted to Major. For his outstanding services with this unit, Stewart received the Air Force Cross, *London Gazette* of 2 November 1918. He married, in 1921, Odette Suzanne Le Lay, with whom he had one daughter. Retiring from the RAF in 1921, he became a well-known writer, broadcaster and commentator on aviation matters including: Aeronautical Correspondent for the *Morning Post*, 1924-37, *The Times*, 1939, *Evening Standard*, 1940, and *Manchester Guardian*, 1941-58. He also edited *The Motor*, 1937 and the *Aeronautics Magazine*, 1939-62. Stewart was also the official commentator at the Farnborough Air Show from 1948 to 1962. His publications included: 'Aerobatics', 1928; 'Aeolus, or the Future of the Flying Machine'; 'Cross Country Flying', 1931; (with L Bridgman) 'The Clouds Remember', 1936; 2nd edition 1972; 'Air Power and the Expanding Community', 1944; 'First Flights', 1957; 'Danger in the Air', 1958; 'Of Flight and Flyers', 1964; 'Aviation, the Creative Ideas', 1966; 'Bad Sailing Made Good', 1971. His autobiography, 'Words and Music of a Mechanical

Man', was published shortly before his death. He lived, in retirement, at Seaview, Osborne, Isle of Wight. Oliver Stewart died on 22 December 1976.

NB: His medals were offered for sale by Spink on 6 May 1998: MC, Air Force Cross, British War Medal 1914-20, and Victory Medal 1914-19.

STOCK, Ewart Elliot

The son of Mr and Mrs E Stock of 'Wastdale', Radlett, Hertfordshire, he was born on 20 December 1897. Joined the Inns of Court OTC (Number B/10555) on 19 January 1917. Gazetted Second Lieutenant to the RFC on 20 April 1917. His formal pilot training duly completed, he was confirmed and gazetted Flying Officer on 26 July following. Sent out to 54 Squadron, then equipped with Sopwith Pups, on 23 October 1917. '54' were re-equipped with Camels in December 1917 and Stock had mastered the tricky, if highly effective, little Scout plane by the onset of the great German spring offensive which commenced on 21 March 1918. By then credited with three victories, he was wounded in action on 1 April 1918, an event which effectively ended his operational flying. His MC was announced in the *London Gazette* of 22 April 1918, details in the *Gazette* of 22 June 1918: 'For conspicuous gallantry and devotion to duty. During an engagement he bombed enemy troops who were approaching a bridge and caused great confusion among them. He then attacked, with machine-gun fire from a very low altitude, the troops, who were endeavouring to cross the bridge. Diving on to several parties of the enemy who remained on the bridge in a state of indecision, he almost completely annihilated them. His action undoubtedly hampered the enemy by making the bridge impassable for half an hour. On numerous other occasions he disorganised and hindered the enemy's advance by his attacks on troops and transport. He has destroyed three hostile machines, and has always set an excellent example of courage and enterprise'.

Leaving the RAF early in 1919, he returned to live in Radlett, Hertfordshire.

STOOKES, Valentine Alexander

The son of Surgeon Dr Alexander Stookes, MB, CM Edinburgh, FRCS, and Mrs Stookes, of 4 Gambier Terrace, Hope Street, Liverpool, he was born in Formby on 25 November 1893. Educated at Liverpool College, at the Liverpool Institute, at Merchant Taylor's School, Crosby, at St Andrew's University (from where he graduated BSc in 1915), and at Edinburgh University, where he had just started studying medicine as the war came. Even before his graduation in 1915, Stookes had already received a commission, via the Special Reserve, in the Royal Scots Greys (Second Dragoons), almost as soon as the war started, being gazetted Second Lieutenant to the only Scottish cavalry regiment on 15 August 1914. Seconded to the RFC, he trained as an Observer and was posted as such on 25 February 1915 to 14 Squadron, equipped with the BE2c, then forming at Shoreham. He accompanied '14' to the Middle East as a 'founder member' in November 1915, serving with the unit in Egypt until 28 April 1916. His MC was announced in the *London Gazette* of 31 May 1916: 'For conspicuous gallantry and skill. He engaged the enemy with rifle fire and shot two while his pilot was photographing at 200 feet altitude. On other occasions he has done fine work'.

He was wounded in the back by a rifle bullet during the incident which won him his MC, and subsequently returned to the UK for medical treatment. Formal recognition of his status came when he was confirmed and gazetted Flying Officer (Observer) on 1 August 1916. Once recovered, Stookes trained as a Pilot, subsequently joining 60 Squadron at the front on 13 September 1916. His tour with '60', during which he was promoted to A/Captain and Flight Commander, ended on 11 March 1917. Stookes was allowed to leave the service on 16 October 1917, under special provisions that permitted medical students to return to their studies, as there was a great shortage of qualified doctors at this time. A married man with a wife in Liverpool, Valentine Stookes returned to Edinburgh University to resume his studies. Although he had ceased active service in 1917, Stookes still retained his commission in the Scots Greys and, perhaps surprisingly, he returned to his regiment in 1919, before finally resigning his commission whilst stationed in the Straits Settlements, Singapore, in 1920.

STOUT, George Ronald Yorston

The younger son of George and Margaret Paterson Wingate Stout, of 11 Princes Gardens, Glasgow, he was born in January 1897. Educated at Kelvinside Academy, Glasgow, and at Fettes College, Edinburgh (1910-13). George's brother, Thomas, a Lieutenant in the RNVR, died of illness contracted during service in the Far East in the Great War. After completing his education, George entered his father's ship-broking firm, Messrs Geo Stout & Company, of Glasgow. Gazetted Second Lieutenant to 8 Battalion, Argyll and Sutherland Highlanders (TF), on 10 July 1915. Seconded to the RFC in the summer of 1916, he trained as an Observer and, after being formally confirmed and gazetted Flying Officer (Observer) on 21 October 1916, was sent out to 16 Squadron on 4 January 1917. On 30 April 1917, Stout and his Pilot of the day, Second Lieutenant Norman Alan Lawrence from Brighton, in BE2g, 'A2942', were sent down in flames to their deaths south east of Vimy by Leutnant Lothar von Richthofen of Jasta 11, the 15th of the German Ace's eventual 40 victories. Lothar, a great Ace in his own right, was, of course, the younger brother of Manfred von Richthofen, the Red Baron himself. Stout's gallantry during the earlier battles to capture Vimy Ridge was acknowledged with the award of an MC posthumously announced in the *London Gazette* of 26 May 1917: 'For conspicuous gallantry and devotion to duty. When on infantry contact patrol he flew twice for periods of two hours at very low altitude and, on each occasion, brought a very complete and detailed report on the situation of the attack. He has at all times displayed great courage and skill'.

The original recommendation for Stout's MC, dated 13 April 1917 and sanctioned by Brigadier G S Shephard MC (qv), commanding 1 Brigade, is specific in detailing the low level operations occurring near Thelus on 9 April 1917 and in the area of Farbus on the following day during a particularly heavy snow storm. On both occasions Stout's machine was damaged by ground fire from rifles and machine guns. George Stout is buried in Lieven Communal Cemetery Extension, France.

NB: His medals were offered for sale by Sotheby's (lot 534) on 25 July 1991: MC, British War Medal 1914-20, Victory Medal 1914-19, and Next of Kin Memorial Plaque.

STRANGE, Louis Arbon

The son of Mr and Mrs W J Strange, of Blandford, Dorset, he was born in 1891. Educated at St Edward's School, Oxford (1905-07). Louis' younger brother, 19 year old Captain Gilbert John 'Ben' Strange, Dorset Regiment and 40 Squadron, RAF, an Ace with seven victories, was shot down in flames over Cambrai on 24 September 1918 by Leutnant Martin Dehmisch of Jasta 58, the tenth and last of the German Ace's victories. Dehmisch was himself shot down almost immediately afterwards by Lieutenant J S Smith, a colleague of Ben's from 40 Squadron. Louis, a pre-war volunteer originally commissioned into the Dorset Yeomanry (TF), developed an interest in aviation and was duly accepted into the RFC after gaining his Royal Aero Club Certificate (Number 575) on a Cauldron at the Ewen School at Hendon on 5 August 1913. He participated in many of the early cross-country air races. On one occasion in June 1914, his Bleriot was leading the field in the London-Manchester-London cross-country handicap race. As he landed at the half-way point, the Lord Mayor of Manchester, in his anxiety to be the first to congratulate Louis, clambered on to his machine, using the flying wires as a ladder. His Worship's not inconsiderable bulk apparently imposed a strain which the wires were not designed to withstand, for as Strange took off again on the next leg, the stressed wire snapped, the released and now untethered end flying into the propellor, which, in turn, promptly disintegrated.. Fortunately, Louis was unscathed in the incident. W L Brock from the USA, in a Morane-Saulnier, went on to win the race at an average speed of 69 mph. Strange was formally confirmed and gazetted Flying Officer on 16 September 1914, although, in fact, he had, by then, already flown to France a month earlier as a Pilot with 5 Squadron, part of the original RFC contingent to the Western Front. On 22 August 1914, the day before the serious fighting began on the ground, an airborne German aircraft was seen for the very first time by the RFC over Maubeuge aerodrome at about 14.25. Three machines took off to intercept, one, manned by Strange and his Observer, Lieutenant Leslie Da Costa Penn-Gaskell, Norfolk Regiment and RFC, carried a Lewis gun, unofficially smuggled aboard by Louis. The weight of the gun and its ammunition dampened the Farman 341's already limited performance more than somewhat and, although Penn-Gaskell was able to loose off a few ineffectual rounds after the departing German machine, the pair were ordered to remove the offending gun and take a rifle next time. At least, Strange could claim to be ahead of his time. Nothing if not persistent, Strange had the forbidden Lewis gun mounted onto a Avro 504 when, on 22 November 1914, he and his Observer, Lieutenant F G Small, managed to shoot down an enemy machine. Small was wounded in the finger during the engagement, when the enemy crew fired back at them with a pistol. Promoted to A/Captain and Flight Commander, he was posted next to 6 Squadron. On 10 March 1915, the first day of the Battle of Neuve Chapelle, Strange in a BE2c, despite heavy opposing fire from the ground, dropped bombs from a very low level onto an enemy train with devastating effect, causing many casualties. His MC was announced in the *London Gazette* of 27 March 1915: 'For gallantry and ability on reconnaissance and other duties on numerous occasions, especially on the occasion when he dropped three bombs from a height of only 200 feet on the railway junction at Courtrai, whilst being assailed by heavy rifle fire'.

Always heavily involved with 6 Squadron's operations over the front, he experienced a novel form of attack on 30 April 1915, when an enemy machine attempted to snag and break the propellor of his Martinsyde S1, '2449', by means of a weighty ball dangled on the end of a copper cable! On 10 May 1915, again in '2449', Strange was apparently thrown out of his cockpit during a combat with an enemy machine, but still managed to clamber back in and subsequently land safely. On 6 June following, Strange and his Observer, Lieutenant G A Parker (qv), fought the first ever recorded combat in a newly issued FE2a, '4228'. His busy tour with '6' completed, he returned to the Home Establishment where he was eventually promoted to A/Major and briefly given command of 12 Squadron, before going on to command 23 Squadron, then at Gosport, in September 1915. Following a period in hospital, Strange was posted to the School of Air Gunnery at the CFS. Promoted to Lieutenant Colonel in 1918, he was given the command of 80 Wing, RAF. On 30 October 1918, the heaviest day of fighting in the entire war, the whole of 80 Wing was deployed to attack Rebaix aerodrome, north of Ath. The raid was led, inevitably perhaps, by Lieutenant Colonel Louis Strange, in his personal Sopwith Camel, 'D1943'. The raid left three hangars burning and many enemy aircraft smashed and wrecked on the ground. The first of his Distinguished Flying Crosses came in the *London Gazette* of 2 November 1918, this for his fine leadership and meticulous planning of successful bombing raids. He was also awarded the Distinguished Service Order in the *London Gazette* of 8 February 1919 for, amongst other attributes, 'brilliant leadership'. He was also Mentioned in Despatches on two occasions during the Great War, *London Gazettes* of 17 February 1915 and 15 July 1919.

After leaving the RAF, he stayed on in aviation, becoming a Director of Spartan Aircraft Ltd, making his home at 'High Ground', The Drive, Rickmansworth, Herts. When the Second World War came in 1939, he immediately rejoined via the RAFVR, adding a Bar to his Distinguished Flying Cross, *London Gazette* of 21 June 1940. The lowly ranked Pilot Officer Strange's citation for this award is worth repeating: 'Pilot Officer Strange was detailed to proceed from Hendon to Merville to act as Ground Control Officer during the arrival and departure of various aircraft carrying food supplies. He displayed great skill and determination whilst under heavy bombing attacks and machine-gun fire at Merville, where he was responsible for the repair and successful despatch of two aircraft to England. In the last remaining aircraft, which was repaired under his supervision, he returned to Hendon, in spite of being repeatedly attacked by Messerschmitts until well out to sea. He had no guns in action and had never flown this type of aircraft previously, but his brilliant piloting enabled him to return with this much needed aircraft'. Appointed an OBE in 1945, he left the service with the rank of Group Captain. His book, 'Recollections of an Airman', was published in 1933. Louis Strange died on 15 November 1966.

STREATFEILD, Geoffrey Hugh Benbow

The second son of Major Hugh Sidney Streatfeild and Mrs Eleveen Streatfeild (née Booth), of Ryhope Hall, County Durham, he was born on 28 July 1897. Educated at Rugby (1911-14). Gazetted Second Lieutenant to 4 (Extra Reserve) Battalion, Durham Light Infantry, on 3 October 1914. Seconded to the RFC early in 1916, he gained his Royal Aero Club Certificate (Number 2490) on 21 February 1916. His formal pilot training duly completed, he was confirmed and gazetted Flying Officer on 6 May following. He served with BE2e-equipped 9 Squadron before later going on to 16 Squadron as a Flight Commander. On 30 March 1918, Streatfeild and his Observer, Lieutenant B W Sims, were both wounded, Streatfeild very badly, when their RE8 was brought down. His MC was announced in the *London Gazette* of 22 April 1918: 'For conspicuous gallantry and devotion to duty. When on photographic work, accompanied by one other machine, he attacked and drove off seven hostile scouts, finally securing some very valuable photographs. On a previous occasion, while on the same duty, he drove off a patrol of five hostile aeroplanes and then continued and completed his photography. On four other successive occasions he successfully drove off numerous enemy aeroplanes, which attempted to interfere with his work. He showed splendid pluck and devotion to duty'.

Streatfeild, after prolonged medical treatment, left the RAF, via the Unemployed List, on 13 September 1919, returning to the study of law. He married, on 11 December 1919, Marjorie Booth. Streatfeild was called to the Bar, Inner Temple, in 1921, North-Eastern Circuit. He lived, at this time, at 13 Gloucester Terrace, Hyde Park, London W2. His legal career progressed through a series of important appointments which included: Recorder of Rotherham, 1932-34; and of Huddersfield, 1934-43; King's Counsel (KC), 1938; Solicitor-General and Attorney-General of the County Palatine of Durham, 1939-47; High Court Judge, Queen's Bench Division, 1942-66. When the Second World War came, he became extra-regimentally employed from 31 May 1940, rising to the rank of Lieutenant Colonel. He was employed on the Judge Advocates Staff on 31 May 1940 and as Assistant Judge Advocate-General (graded AAG) on 2 May 1942. He finally left the service in 1947 and was knighted in the same year. Sir Geoffrey Streatfeild died on 7 October 1979.

STRUGNELL, William Victor

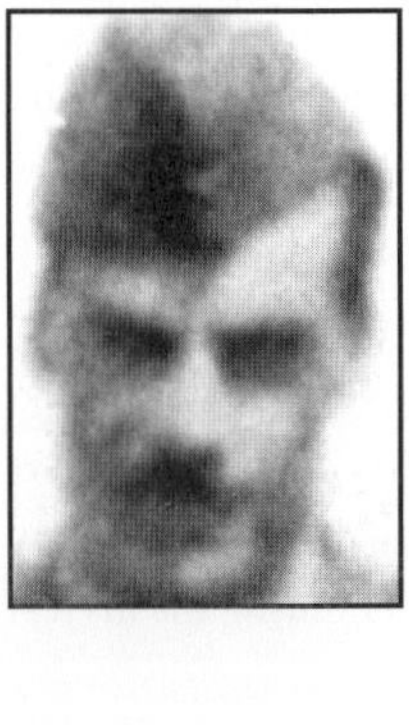

From Southampton, he was born the scion of a military family on 23 July 1892. Educated locally, in fact, at the same school as was the great Ace to be, James T B McCudden. Served first with the Air Battalion, Royal Engineers, before being amongst the earliest entrants to the newly formed RFC in 1912 (Number 71). Gained his Royal Aero Club Certificate (Number 253) as an Air Mechanic 1st Class on a Bristol of the CFS on Salisbury Plain on 24 July 1912, the third NCO to qualify for a 'ticket' and thus acquiring the rank of 1 AM (Pilot). Strugnell crossed to France with the original RFC contingent in August 1914. He served with 3 Squadron as a Sergeant Pilot in the early months of 1915. Picked out for a commission, he was gazetted Second Lieutenant to a Regular Army battalion of the Hampshire Regiment (his county regiment) on 27 June 1915, with immediate detachment to 1 Squadron, RFC. Formally confirmed and gazetted Flying Officer in the *London Gazette* of 24 August 1915, he was patrolling the Western Front within days. On 5 February 1916, he gained his first victory over an LVG over Armentières, probably hitting both enemy crewmen in the process. The first of his MCs was announced in the Birthday Honours *London Gazette* of 3 June 1916 (no citation). Although no formal citation was published in the *Gazette*, research has unearthed the original recommendation for the award: 'W V Strugnell. For constant good work and efficiency. On numerous occasions has showed great initiative and pluck in engaging hostile aircraft, often in superior numbers, never leaving them until driven down behind their own lines'.

His tour with '1' completed. he spent the next few months instructing in the UK before returning to France as a Flight Commander and 'founder member' of the Sopwith Pup-equipped 54 Squadron on 24 December 1916. Strugnell gained a further five victories between 19 March and 11 May 1917. A Bar to his MC came in the *London Gazette* of 26 July 1917: 'For conspicuous gallantry and devotion to duty. Whilst leading an offensive patrol he attacked and brought down a hostile machine, later on the same patrol he brought down a second machine'.

Strugnell was promoted to Major in September 1917 and employed in various instructing duties for the remainder of the war. Staying on in the RAF, he held a series of appointments including, in 1928, Officer Commanding, 1 Armoured Car Company, RAF, in Mosul, Iraq. A Group Captain in 1934, he went on to command RAF Manston, 24 (Training) Group, in 1935. He was awarded the Silver Jubilee Medal 1935 and, two years later, the Coronation Medal 1937. Undertaking general duties throughout the Second World War, he finally retired on 7 June 1945. 'Struggy' Strugnell enjoyed a long association with the ATC near to his retirement home in Cornwall, before he died in 1977.

STUART-WORTLEY, Rothesay Nicholas Montague

The son of Major General the Honourable Edward James Montague Stuart-Wortley, CB, CMG, DSO, MVO, and his wife, Violet (née Guthrie), CBE, of Highcliffe Castle, Christchurch, Hampshire, and 10 Bryanston Street, London, W, he was born on 9 January 1892. Educated at Eton (1904-09) and at Balliol College, Oxford, from where he graduated with an Honours degree in History. A pre-war volunteer, he was gazetted Second Lieutenant to the Hampshire Yeomanry (TF) in the summer of 1914. Mobilised on 4 August 1914 with the rest of the TF, he was, on the following day, gazetted an Aide-de-Camp and subsequently served as a Staff Officer with an Infantry Brigade commanded by his father in Egypt. Seconded to the RFC in the spring of 1917, he trained as a Pilot and was duly confirmed and gazetted Flying Officer on 12 June following. Posted out to 22 Squadron, he achieved six victories in Bristol Fighters between 6 September 1917 and 28 January 1918, being promoted to A/Captain and Flight Commander on 25 October intervening. His MC was announced in the *London Gazette* of 6 April 1918, details in the *Gazette* of 22 April 1918: 'For conspicuous gallantry and devotion to duty. On each of three occasions when on offensive patrol, he has attacked and brought down in flames one enemy aeroplane, in addition to which he has sent down out of control three other hostile machines. He has displayed great courage and determination as a patrol leader'.

His tour with '22' completed, he returned to the UK, where he was promoted to Major and appointed to the command of 44 HD Squadron. He was Mentioned in Despatches on two occasions during the Great War. Returning to France in September 1918, he commanded BF2b-equipped 88 Squadron until the end of the war. Leaving the RAF in 1919, he went to live in the South of France marrying Madame Edvina, a celebrated prima donna. He became ill with diabetes and died there in the mid-1920s.

STYRAN, Arthur John Graham

From Londonderry, Ireland, he was born on 28 July 1890. A boy soldier, he joined the Royal Field Artillery in 1904, age 14 years, two months. He served with the Gunners in India from January 1911 until August 1914, when he went to the Western Front with the original British Army contingents, thus earning the 1914 Star. He had risen to the rank of Sergeant when he was picked out for a commission and gazetted Second Lieutenant to the Royal Artillery on 27 August 1915, with a secondment to the RFC following shortly afterwards. He trained as an Observer and was sent out to France with BE2e-equipped 9 Squadron as a Probationary and 'founder member' on 20 December 1915. His 'apprenticeship' satisfactorily completed, he was confirmed and gazetted Flying Officer (Observer) on 1 May 1916. His MC was announced in the *London Gazette* of 14 November 1916: 'For conspicuous gallantry and devotion to duty. He has done fine work with artillery for a long time, often in bad weather and under heavy fire. On one occasion he directed the fire of nine batteries on the enemy's trenches, and obtained a large number of direct hits'.

His tour with '9' completed, he returned to England, learnt to fly and was posted to Mesopotamia, where he served with 63 Squadron. Returning to the Home Establishment he took up a succession of instructing posts. His outstanding efforts in this field were recognised by the award of an Air Force Cross, announced in the *London Gazette* of 10 October 1919. He was living in Rushall, Marlborough, Wiltshire, in 1922 and, although leaving the service in January 1923, he retained his reserve commission in the RAFO. Arthur Styran was killed in a flying accident on 1 October 1933.

SUMMERS, John Kenneth

The son of John Alexander Summers, sometime Professor of English at the Chinese College at Canton, and Mrs Summers, of 76 Stanhope Avenue, Church End, Finchley, London N3, he was born on 22 December 1894. Educated at Denstone College (1908-12) and at Birmingham University (1912-14). Gazetted Second Lieutenant to a New Army battalion of the Royal Warwickshire Regiment on 25 January 1915. Seconded to the RFC in April 1915, he trained as an Observer and was sent out as a Probationary to 3 Squadron the following month. His 'apprenticeship' satisfacorily completed, he was confirmed and gazetted Flying Officer (Observer) on 21 October 1915. Typically, on 3 July 1915, Summers and his Pilot, Second Lieutenant A Payze, in a Morane L, '1875', fought an inconclusive battle with an Aviatik over Don. Payze received slight wounds in the incident. After five months of operational flying he returned to Castle Bromwich for pilot training. Having gained his Royal Aero Club Certificate (Number 2154) on 13 December 1915 Summers re-joined 3 Squadron in France as a Pilot in June 1916. He was fortunate on 25 September 1916, when a grenade exploded in Morane LA, 'A140', unsurprisingly compelling him and his Observer of the day, Second Lieutenant L Reynolds, to a forced landing and safety. His tour with '3' ended in October 1916, when he returned to the Home Establishment. He undertook some Staff work, including serving with 1 Brigade, RFC HQ, as a Liaison Officer. Summers returned to the front in June 1918 as a Flight Commander with 209 Squadron (Sopwith Camels). An accomplished Camel Pilot, he achieved eight victories between 23 June and 11 August 1918. On 8 July 1918, he was wounded in action when his Camel, 'D9607', was hit by ground fire. His MC was announced in the *London Gazette* of 18 July 1918, almost certainly a belated gazetting and relating to his work with 3 Squadron in 1916: 'For conspicuous gallantry and devotion to duty. He has continuously performed valuable work in co-operating with artillery. He has on many occasions flown at a very low altitude in order to give information to the infantry, which has proved of the utmost value'.

Summers was also Mentioned in Despatches around this time. On 12 August 1918, Summers and his Camel, 'D9668', were shot down by Lothar von Richthofen of Jasta 11, the 40th and last of the Red Baron's brother's victories. Taken prisoner by the Germans, Summers would remain in captivity until repatriation came on 23 December 1918. He decided to make the RAF his career and was given a permanent commission in August 1919. His subsequent career included appointments and postings: CO, 45 Squadron, Iraq, 1925; Squadron Leader, 1926; and service with HQ, Air Defence of Great Britain and with Bomber Command. In 1940 he became CO, Blenheim Operational Training Unit. His last posting was to Rhodesia, where he formed the Combined Air Observers' School. Summers retired to farming in Rhodesia in 1943.

SUMMERS, William Assheton

The son of Frank Bright Summers and his wife, Constance, of Froyle Place, Froyle, Hampshire, he was born in 1896. Educated at Eton (1908-12) and at Sandhurst. Gazetted Second Lieutenant to 18 (Queen Mary's Own) Hussars on 25 February 1914. He accompanied his regiment to France on 15 August 1914, thus earning the 1914 Star. Seconded to the RFC in May 1915, he gained his Royal Aero Club Certificate (Number 1732) on 9 September 1915. His formal pilot training duly completed, he was confirmed and gazetted Flying Officer on 7 October following. Sent out to FE2b-equipped 22 Squadron in France soon after he qualified. On 8 July 1916, Summers and his Observer, Second Lieutenant C M Chaworth-Musters, were fortunate to escape unscathed when their FE2b, '6375', was forced to land after a combat with three enemy machines over Frement. Their crashed and abandoned machine was subsequently shelled to smithereens. His MC was announced in the *London Gazette* of 27 July 1916, and is, unusually, a joint citation: 'Captain William Assheton Summers and Lieutenant William Owen Tudor Tudor-Hart [qv]. 'For conspicuous gallantry and skill. Captain Summers, as pilot, and Lieut Tudor-Hart, as Observer, attacked a flight of ten enemy aeroplanes, completely breaking up their formation. They were quite unsupported, but only broke off the engagement when all their ammunition was expended many miles over the enemy's lines. Their machine was under constant heavy fire from as many as four hostile machines at once, and was badly damaged'.

Five days after his MC was announced, Summers and his Observer of the day, Londoner Flight Sergeant Norman Thomas Clarkson (Number 1565), in FE2b, '4278', were shot down in flames after being hit by anti-aircraft fire south west of Bapaume, on the Somme. The remains of their burnt-out aircraft was found inside the British lines later that day. Their bodies, however, were never recovered. William Summers, like his Observer, is commemorated on the Flying Services memorial, Arras, France.

SUNDY, Charles Anthony

The son of Railway Goods Guard, William Anthony Sundy and Rebecca Emily Sundy (née Harris), of 16 Rose Street, Newport, Monmouthshire, he was born on 20 November 1894. He was working as a clerk when he enlisted as a Private soldier into 12 Reserve Cavalry Regiment, then stationed at Aldershot, in September 1914. Sent out subsequently as a reinforcement to 13 Hussars in France, he was taken ill suffering with varicoceles and hospitalised in September 1915. Once recovered, he was picked out for a commission and gazetted Second Lieutenant to 10 Battalion, South Wales Borderers (1 Gwent), on 25 October 1916. Seconded to the RFC in November 1917, he trained as an Observer and was sent out to 25 Squadron (DH4s) as such, on 3 January 1918. He flew with '25' throughout the fraught days of the German spring offensive and beyond, returning to the

Home Establishment and instructing duties on 20 June 1918. His MC was announced in the *London Gazette* of 16 September 1918: 'For conspicuous gallantry and devotion to duty during recent operations. When attacked by seven enemy aircraft, he opened fire and sent one to the ground. He showed great brilliance at long-distance photography and reconnaissance, and located a number of new hostile aerodromes and brought back much valuable information. He carried out his work with remarkable coolness and determination'.

Sundy finally left the service, via the Unemployed List, in May 1919. He lived and worked in London in the 1920s and, later still, in Cambridge.

SUTHERLAND, Leslie William

From Murrumbeena, Melbourne, he was born on 17 December 1892. A Carpenter by trade, he volunteered for the Australian Signal Service, Australian Infantry (holding the personal Number 4), and was soon attached to a Light Horse regiment in Egypt. As a signaller, he was Mentioned in Despatches, *London Gazette* of 6 September 1916, and also awarded the Distinguished Conduct Medal, *London Gazette* of 20 October 1916. Picked out for a commission, he was transferred to the Australian Flying Corps and gazetted Recording Officer and Acting Adjutant on 1 November 1917. Next, he trained as an Observer and served as such with 1 Squadron, AFC, achieving eight victories (including, with R A Austin (qv), the squadron's first ever) between 3 January and 28 September 1918. His MC was announced in the *London Gazette* of 18 July 1918: 'For conspicuous gallantry and devotion to duty. He continually carried out difficult reconnaissances and brought in most valuable reports, though he was often attacked by hostile aeroplanes. He showed the greatest initiative and determination'.

Returning to Australia after the war, he eventually became a Pilot in the RAAF. His book, 'Aces and Kings', 1937, an unofficial history of 1 Squadron, AFC, is a classic of the genre. Sutherland died on 24 October 1967.

SUTTON, Bertine Entwisle

The oldest son of the Reverend Canon Alfred Sutton, Vicar of Bridekirk, Cockermouth, Cumberland, and Mrs Sutton, he was born in 1886. Educated at Summer Fields, at Eton (1900-04), and at University College, Oxford, from where he graduated BA. Gazetted Second Lieutenant to the Westmorland and Cumberland Yeomanry (TF) on 19 October 1914. Seconded to the RFC late in 1915, he trained as an Observer and was sent out as such to 15 Squadron as a Probationary. His 'apprenticeship' satisfactorily completed, he was confirmed and gazetted Flying Officer (Observer) on 2 February 1916. He was also used in a Staff capacity as Wing Adjutant during this period. His MC was announced in the New Year *London Gazette* of 1 January 1917 (no citation). Although no formal citation appeared in the *Gazette*, research has unearthed the original recommendation for the award: 'B E Sutton. For continuous hard work and untiring energy in carrying out his duties as Wing Adjutant, from May to September 1916. This officer has previously carried out most valuable work as an Observer Flying Officer'.

He next trained as a Pilot, gaining his Royal Aero Club Certificate (Number 4018) on 16 February 1917, the same day that he was formally given his full 'Wings', and continued to serve with '15' in this new capacity. From '15', he was sent to the RE8s of 9 Squadron. Awarded the Distinguished Service Order in the *London Gazette* of 26 September 1917, this specifically for his consistent gallantry in operations between Langemarck and Bosinghe during July and August 1917. Sutton was also Mentioned in Despatches on three occasions during the Great War and awarded the Croix de Guerre by the Belgians. Sutton was wounded on 5 September 1917, during an inconclusive combat with an enemy machine. Once recovered, he was promoted to Major and posted to Staff duties, for which services he received an OBE (Military) in 1919. Staying on in the RAF after the war, he embarked upon what would become a highly distinguished career. His many appointments, honours and promotions included; Group Captain, Instructor at Imperial Defence College, 1929,; Operations against Upper Mohmands 1933, whilst CO, 7 Squadron (Mentioned in Despatches); Instructor at Imperial Defence College, 1929-32; commanded 1 Indian Group, RAF, Peshawar, 1932-34; SASO, RAF India, 1934-36; AOC, 22 Group, 1936-39; Air Vice-Marshal, 1937; CB, 1939; AOC, 23 Group, 1939-40; AOC, 24 Group, 1940; Commandant, RAF Staff College, 1941; KBE, 1942; Air Member for Personnel 1942-45. He married, in 1928, Margaret Griselda Wedderburn, widow of Stuary de la Rue, with whom he had two sons. Air Marshal Sir Bertine Sutton finally retired from the RAF in 1945 and lived, in retirement, at Little Pink Farm, Crookham, Newbury. He died on 28 September 1946.

SUTTON, George Ernest Frederick

Born in England, he was living in Saskatoon, Saskatchewan, Canada, when war came in August 1914. Gazetted Lieutenant to 28 (North West) Battalion, Canadian Infantry, on 19 October 1914. After service with the CEF in France, he was accepted into the RFC in the spring of 1916. Having trained as an Observer, he was sent out as a Probationary to the BE2c-equipped 4 Squadron in July 1916. On 3 July 1916, very soon after he arrived, Sutton and his Pilot, Captain C A A Hiatt (qv), in BE2c, '2645', were fortunate to escape with their lives when their machine was shot up over Thiepval. Again, just four days later, this time with Second Lieutenant J H Ross (qv), as his Pilot in BE2c, '2638', Sutton emerged unscathed from potential disaster when their machine was shot up over Forceville. Ross, who was wounded in the air, was forced to land, the BE being completely wrecked in the process. The unfortunate Ross, a fellow Canadian, suffered further injuries in the crash. The two men received the MC, announced in the *London Gazette* of 25 August 1916: 'For conspicuous gallantry when, as observer with 2Lt Ross [qv], he carried out two reconnaissances at very low altitude. Their machine was repeatedly hit by bullets, and the pilot was severely wounded in the arm. The reports rendered were most valuable'.

His 'apprenticeship' more than satisfactorily completed, he was confirmed and gazetted Flying Officer (Observer) on 13 July 1916. He next trained as a Pilot, gaining his Royal Aero Club Certificate (Number 4018) on 15 December 1916, before eventually qualifying for his full 'Wings' in February 1917. Posted to 5 TDS early in 1918, he saw out the war as an Instructor before finally returning to Canada on 16 December 1918.

SUTTON, Oliver Manners

The fourth son of Algernon Charles Sutton and Winifred Alice Sutton, of 'Woodcroft', Sandhurst Road, Tunbridge Wells, Kent, he was born on 13 March 1896. Educated at Tonbridge (1910-13) and at the Central Technical College, South Kensington, London (1913-14). He enlisted as a Private soldier into 19 (2 Public Schools) Battalion, Royal Fusiliers, in September 1914. Picked out for a commission, he was gazetted Second Lieutenant to 3 (Reserve) Battalion, South Lancashire Regiment on 6 February 1915. Seconded to 1 Battalion, Loyal North Lancashire Regiment, then part of 2 Brigade, 1 Division, he served in the trenches from 20 May 1915. Gassed and wounded by a machine-gun bullet in the leg on 25 September 1915 during the first day of the Battle of Loos. After treatment in France, he was evacuated to the UK for further medical care on 10 October 1915. Once recovered, he successfully sought transfer to the RFC, which came on 15 July 1916. Having trained as a Pilot, he was duly confirmed and gazetted Flying Officer on 23 September following. Sent out to France and 21 Squadron on 9 October 1916, he acted on occasions as an Observer with this unit. Sent next to the Sopwith Pup-equipped 54 Squadron, he achieved six victories as a Pilot between 2 April and 6 June 1917. On the intervening 24 May 1917, Sutton, in Pup 'A6183', collided with an Albatros, taking a foot off his starboard top wing. Despite the damage, Sutton returned safely to base. This incident sparked off a ridiculous rumour in the Imperial German Air Service to the effect that RFC Pilots were deliberately employing ramming tactics! His MC was announced in the *London Gazette* of 26 July 1917: 'For conspicuous gallantry and devotion to duty. On at least eight separate occasions he showed great determination in attacking hostile aircraft destroying them or driving them down out of control, and he has also done very good work in other flights by preventing hostile aircraft from getting on the tails of other machines. On one occasion, though his gun jammed, he dived three times and drove off an enemy machine'.

His tour with '54' completed on 16 June 1917, he returned to the UK and instructing duties with, successively, 91 and 93 Squadrons. During the summer of 1918, he was posted out to 28 Squadron (Sopwith Camels), 14 Wing, then at Piave, Italy, as a Captain and Flight Commander. Sutton claimed his seventh victory on 15 August 1918, before being wounded on 3 November 1918. Once recovered, he served for almost a year on the Inter-Allied Commission of Control in Germany. He was granted a permanent commission in the RAF with the rank of Captain, on 21 August 1919. Sutton returned as a Test Pilot to Martlesham Heath and was killed there in a flying accident on 16 August 1921. Oliver Sutton is buried in Withyham (St Michael) Churchyard, Sussex.

SWART, Jacob Guy

From Johannesburg, South Africa, he was born on 28 June 1893. He had been a volunteer Cadet in the Transvaal Horse Artillery for seven years prior to the war. When war came, he made his way to the UK to seek a commission. He was duly accepted and gazetted Second Lieutenant to the Royal Field Artillery on 29 November 1914. Seconded to the RFC in December 1914, he gained his Royal Aero Club Certificate (Number 1084) on 25 January 1915. His formal pilot training completed, he was confirmed and gazetted Flying Officer on 1 April following. Sent out to 5 Squadron in France on 7 June 1915, he was quickly into the action. On 16 June, his Avro 504, '4228', was shot up and damaged, although he and his Observer, Lieutenant Andrews, were unscathed in the incident. Again, on 26 October 1915, Swart and his Observer of the day, Captain Simpson, in BE2c, '1736', miraculously survived successive attacks by a Fokker, an Aviatik and an Albatros over Langemarck. His tour with 5 Squadron completed, he returned briefly to the UK before going out again on 1 April 1916, this time as an A/Captain and Flight Commander and 'founder member' of 22 Squadron (FE2b). On 15 July 1916, Swart and his Observer, Captain H E F Wyncoll (qv), in company with squadron colleagues, Lieutenants Bowen and Mansell, descended to 2,000 feet to attack German infantry with their machine guns on the Flers-Longueval road. Their three passes caused a number of casualties and scattered the column. Subsequently, they attacked some wagons and a gun limber, killing one of the animals and scattering the drivers. Swart and Wyncoll each received MCs for this action. Swart's tour with '22' came to an end on 22 September 1916, coincidently, the same day that his MC was announced in the *London Gazette*: 'For conspicuous gallantry and skill in attacking troops on the ground from a low altitude, his machine being frequently subjected to very heavy machine-gun and rifle fire from the ground'.

Following a period in the UK instructing, he next commanded 24 Squadron (DH5s) with the rank of A/Major, from 22 August 1917 until 6 February 1918, when he was obliged to stand down due to stress. Jacob Swart finally left the RAF, via the Unemployed List, 8 April 1919, living, in the immediate post-war years, at 55

Trentham Road, Longton, Staffordshire. In the Second World War, he served as a Major in the Union Defence Forces in South Africa in 1941.

SWEENEY, Leo John

From Vancouver, British Columbia, Canada. Served with the Canadian Infantry in France from November 1916, before being picked out for a commission and gazetted Lieutenant on 28 April 1917. Seconded to the RFC in June 1917, he trained as a Pilot and was confirmed and gazetted Flying Officer on 11 November 1917. Sent out to 4 Squadron in France on 29 December 1917. On 8 March 1918, accompanied by Lieutenant H G Burgess in an RE8, he gained a victory, no mean feat for a Bomber and Reconnaissance Pilot and Observer. Sweeney was killed in action on 30 April 1918. His MC was posthumously announced in the *London Gazette* of 26 July 1918: 'For conspicuous gallantry and devotion to duty. When leading a bombing raid this officer attacked enemy troops and transport with bombs and machine-gun fire from 500 feet, causing a great many casualties. Although his Observer was wounded and his machine badly damaged, he succeeded in landing behind our lines. During two subsequent low flights he caused many casualties, his Observer being again wounded and his machine badly damaged'.

Leo John Sweeney is buried in Longuenesse (St Omer) Souvenir Cemetery, France.

SYMINGTON, Douglas Archibald Colquhoan

The son of Mr and Mrs Archibald Colquhoan Symington, of Auchentoshan House, Dalmuir, Dumbartonshire, he was born on 13 April 1896. Educated at Rugby (1913-15). Gazetted Second Lieutenant to the RFC, Military Wing, on 11 May 1915, the same day that he gained his Royal Aero Club Certificate (Number 1227). His formal pilot training duly completed, he was confirmed and gazetted Flying Officer on 7 August following. He was sent out five days later to BE2c-equipped 7 Squadron in France and soon became heavily involved in aerial combats, many inconclusive, over the Western Front. On 26 September 1915, Symington bombed a train on the Lille-Valenciennes line from 500 feet. His bombs fell with devastating effect, completely wrecking the front of the train and causing chaos on the enemy rail system. His MC was announced in the *London Gazette* of 29 October 1915: 'For conspicuous gallantry and devotion to duty. On 26 September, he demolished part of a train moving towards St Amand by bombs from 500 feet. A large portion of the train was completely wrecked. The remainder of the train was unable to proceed'.

Lieutenant L W Learmount (qv) was also involved in this action. On 16 March 1916, Symington and his Observer, Corporal Hunt, carried out what a later Communiqué described as a 'very successful special shoot', when they brought down the combined fire of 1 Canadian Battery, 53, 35 and 21 Siege Batteries, RGA, onto a concentration of German anti-aircraft guns firing from emplacements and from motor lorries. Not only were the enemy guns silenced, but the proceedings were crowned with a great spurt of flame and a cloud of smoke, obviously an ammunition dump exploding. Posted next to 1 Squadron on 18 April 1916, he was promoted to A/Captain and Flight Commander on 30 April following. His brief tour with '1' completed, he was withdrawn to the Home Establishment on 23 May 1916. Symington was seriously injured in a crash on 29 July 1916 and ,despite extensive medical treatment, was obliged to retire due to ill health on 26 February 1918.

SYMONDSON, Francis Stanley

The son of S V Symondson and Mrs J K Symondson, of Northwall, East Chiltington, near Lewes, Sussex, he was born in March 1897. Educated at Uppingham (1911-13). His elder brother, Captain Vernon Francis Symondson, 13 Hussars and 210 Squadron, RAF, was accidentally killed in France on 13 November 1918. Francis was gazetted Second Lieutenant to 25 (County of London) Cyclist Battalion, London Regiment (TF), on 18 March 1915. After service with the Cyclists and, later, with 5 Battalion, East Kent Regiment (TF), in the UK, he was seconded to the RFC at the end of 1916. His pilot training duly completed, he was confirmed and gazetted Flying Officer on 29 May 1917. Sent out to France and his first operational unit, 29 Squadron, on 4 September 1917, he proceeded to crash three Nieuports in just over a fortnight. Not surprisingly, he was sent home for further training. This done, he was next sent out to 66 Squadron in Italy, where he found his 'touch' in no uncertain manner, claiming 13 victories between 7 March and 15 September 1918, including a 'double' on 17 April and a 'treble' on 6 May. His MC was announced in the *London Gazette* of 16 September 1918: 'For conspicuous gallantry and devotion to duty. In two months he destroyed five enemy machines and one enemy kite balloon'.

The Italians, too, showed their appreciation of his expertise and gallantry with the award of a Silver Medaglia al Valore Militare. After leaving the RAF in 1919, he kept up his interest in flying, owning and piloting many light aircraft between the wars. In May 1935, he flew a Gypsy Moth as part of an Air Display celebrating the Jubilee of King George V. He served again in the Second World War as a Code and Cypher Officer at Andover, and later in the Middle East. He lived, post the Second World War, at 'Wooley', Uplyme, Lyme Regis, Dorset. Francis Symondson died on 1 May 1975.

NB: His medals were offered for sale by Glendining's (lot 638) on 17 September 1990: MC, British War Medal 1914-20, Victory Medal 1914-19 (Lieutenant, RAF)*, 1939-45 Star, Africa Star 1940-43, Defence Medal 1939-45, War Medal 1939-45, and Silver Medaglia al Valore Militare (Italy).*

T

TANSLEY, Herbert Edwin

Born 1 September 1887, he saw service with 4 Battalion, King's Royal Rifle Corps as an NCO (Number 8006) and was in France by late December 1914, for which he became entitled to the 1915 Star. He was attached to the RFC and became a Flying Officer on 9 June 1917, effective from 14 September 1916, serving in the Balkans with 47 Squadron; believed to be an Observer. He received the MC, *London Gazette* of 10 January 1917: 'For conspicuous gallantry and enterprise during a bomb attack by aircraft on an important enemy railway bridge. A subsequent reconnaissance showed that the whole of the centre section of the bridge had collapsed into the river, thereby interrupting important enemy communications.' The date of this attack was 15 October 1916. By the spring of 1918, he had become a pilot and was flying with 211 Squadron on the Western Front, but on 21 May, in DH9 'B7661', he and his observer, Second Lieutenant N B Harris, were shot down off Mariakerke, the 11th victory of Oberleutnant sur See Gerhard Sachsenberg of MFJ 1, and both became prisoners of war. He continued his service post-war and was serving in Palestine as a Flight Lieutenant (Stores) in 1924 and in Palestine and in the early 1930s. By 1 January 1938, he was a Wing Commander in the Equipment Branch of the RAF and retired with the rank of Group Captain in September 1944. He died on 29 January 1980.

TAYLER, St Cyprian Churchill

The son of John Frederic Jenner Tayler and Minnie Ruth Tayler ,of 'The Haven', Boshoffs Road, Natal, South Africa. He was born in Winchester, in the UK, on 26 February 1896 but when war came he was living in Swaziland. Gazetted Second Lieutenant to a Regular Army battalion of the Royal Sussex Regiment on 16 August 1916, with an immediate secondment to the RFC. His pilot training duly completed, he was confirmed and gazetted Flying Officer on 6 February 1917. Sent out to 32 Squadron, he mainly flew DH5s, achieving six victories before, on 31 July 1917, he was wounded in the side and arm by ground fire. His MC was announced in the *London Gazette* of 26 September 1917, details in the *Gazette* of 9 January 1918: 'For conspicuous gallantry and devotion to duty in leading offensive patrols against enemy aircraft. On five occasions at least he and his patrol have attacked and brought down hostile machines. These successes were almost entirely due to his very skilful piloting'.

Once recovered, he was promoted to Captain and Flight Commander, before accompanying the Sopwith Camel-equipped 80 Squadron to France as a 'founder member' on 27 January 1918. Tayler added three more victories to his total before he himself was shot down and killed. On 17 March 1918, Tayler, in Camel, 'B9209', in the course of a morning offensive patrol was shot down over Cambrai by Oberleutnant Heinrich Kroll of Jasta 24, the 21st of the German Ace's eventual 33 victories. Tayler's remains were never recovered and hence he is commemorated on the Flying Services Memorial, Arras, France.

TAYLOR, Frank Harold

From Toronto, Canada, he was born on 11 August 1896. Educated at the University of Toronto, to where he returned after the war to take his degree in Applied Science (1918-21). Gazetted Lieutenant to 109 Battalion, Canadian Infantry, on 26 September 1916, he duly transferred to 204 Battalion, before successfully seeking secondment to the RFC, which came in the summer of 1917. His pilot training completed, he was confirmed and gazetted Flying Officer on 10 September 1917. Sent out to 41 Squadron soon after qualifying for his 'Wings', he achieved one victory in a DH5 on 30 November 1917, before, shortly afterwards, the unit was re-equipped with SE5As. Yet another Canadian Ace, he went on to achieve seven victories in the SE5As of '41' between 23 January and 24 March 1918. His MC was announced in the *London Gazette* of 22 June 1918: 'For conspicuous gallantry and devotion to duty. On one occasion, whilst on offensive patrol, he shot down a hostile scout in flames and a second out of control. On the following day he shot down an enemy triplane, which finally crashed to earth. During the recent operations he has carried out many successful attacks on enemy infantry from low altitudes, and has taken part in over 80 offensive patrols. His gallantry and good service merit the highest praise'.

After a spell training new Pilots in the UK, he returned to the front as a Captain and Flight Commander with 84 Squadron (SE5As) on 26 September 1918, gaining two more victories, including one against a Fokker DVII at 10.00 on the penultimate day of the Great War, 10 November 1918. The war over, he immediately returned home to Canada and took up his studies in Applied Science at the University of Toronto, graduating in 1921. Frank Taylor died at Long Island, New York, USA, on 7 June 1985.

TAYLOR, Henry

From Birmingham, he was born in 1889. A Mechanic by trade, he emigrated to Australia whilst still in his early twenties. When the war came, he enlisted, age 25 years and four months, as a Private soldier (Number 1489) into the Australian Army Service Corps at Victoria Barracks, Sydney, on 17 September 1914. Served in Gallipoli and in Egypt, being promoted Corporal on 24 December 1915. His Military Medal, announced in the *London Gazette* of 27 October 1916, was for gallantry during his service in Egypt. From the Middle East, he was sent, on 15 November 1916, to 1 Division's Ammunition Sub Park in France. His request for transfer to the Australian Flying Corps was granted in December 1916. His flying training duly completed, he was gazetted Second Lieutenant and Pilot, AFC, on 8 May 1917. He was posted first to 43 TS in the UK, before going on to 2 Squadron, AFC, then at Harlaxton. Next Taylor was sent to France and 41 Squadron, RFC, to gain experience. '41' was, at the time, changing from FE8s to DH5s. Taylor spent eight days with '41' before returning to 2 AFC. He accompanied 2 AFC (DH5s) to France on 21 September 1917. His MC, for quite exceptional gallantry in unusual circumstances in the Cambrai area in December 1917, was announced in the *London Gazette* of 4 February 1918, details in the *Gazette* of 5 July 1918: 'For conspicuous gallantry and devotion to duty. Whilst he was engaging enemy troops his machine was shot down and crashed in the open. On crawling out of his machine he was fired upon by enemy snipers, whom he engaged with a rifle, which he had picked up. He eventually made his way back to one of our patrols, carrying a badly wounded man whom he had discovered on the way. On a later occasion, when flying at 1,500 feet, he engaged an enemy two-seater, which dived steeply to the ground and crashed. He is a clever and daring pilot, and is always ready to perform any kind of duty'.

On 3 January 1918, he crashed 'B74' after landing in deep snow at the edge of the aerodrome. A deeply cut forehead and concussion caused him to be admitted to No 56 Casualty Clearing Station. He had, by then, completed 29 hours of operational flying. Taylor returned to his squadron, but after a short while it became obvious that he had not fully recovered after the crash. Next, he was posted to the UK on 19 January 1918, to take up duties as an Instructor. Still patently unwell, he was admitted to Central Hospital in Hampstead, London, where his injuries were, at last, properly diagnosed. Taylor was found to have sustained a fracture at the base of the skull and was still suffering from severe concussion, in fact, his medical notes contained the words, 'Should be dead. Wounded. Concussion severe'. Released from hospital at last in July 1918, he was posted to 8 (Training) Squadron, AFC, where he took up an instructing post. He served for one month in this capacity before he was killed on 18 August 1918, whilst flying a Sopwith Pup (D4170) and engaging in a mock dogfight with Lieutenant Douglas Ferguson, in a Camel, over the village church at Shipton Moyne. A service was taking place in the church when the aeroplanes were heard to collide. Both Pilots were killed. Harry Taylor, MC, MM, was buried five days later with full military honours, in Birmingham (Lodge Hill) Cemetery, Warwickshire.

TAYLOR, Henry Arthur

The first son of Frederick Henry Taylor and Agnes Mundell Taylor, of Vineyard Hill, Wimbledon, London, he was born on 3 January 1898. A great nephew of General Sir John Aitchison, Scots Guards, he was educated at Charterhouse and at Sandhurst. Gazetted Second Lieutenant to a Regular Army battalion of the Royal West Kent Regiment on 24 November 1915 (age 17) with an immediate secondment to the RFC. Gained his Royal Aero Club Certificate (Number 2306) on 18 January 1916. His formal pilot training duly completed, he was confirmed and gazetted Flying Officer on 1 April following. Sent out to the 'Flying Elephants' of 27 Squadron, he proved a gallant and effective Pilot, achieving several victories and being promoted to A/Captain and Flight Commander whilst still only 18 years old. His MC was announced in the *London Gazette* of 19 August 1916: 'For conspicuous gallantry when on a bombing raid in unfavourable weather with Lieutenant Boyd and two other pilots. He descended to less than 1,000 feet and bombed a train, derailing several trucks'.

The Lieutenant Boyd referred to in the citation was, of course, O T Boyd (qv). Taylor was also Mentioned in Despatches at this time. On 27 September 1916, six 27 Squadron 'Elephants' were attacked by four Albatros DIIs of Jasta 2, led by Oswald Boelcke. Taylor in Martinsyde G102, 'A1568', was unfortunate enough to be attacked by Boelcke himself. The almost inevitable outcome was described by Boelcke in a letter home to his parents, after a brief fight, he wrote, the Martinsyde 'fell like a sack'. This was the 29th of the German Ace's eventual 40 victories. The grave dug by the Germans for Taylor was discovered during the British advances in May 1917. He was subsequently re-interned and is now buried in Mory Abbey Military Cemetery, Mory, France.

TAYLOR, Patrick Gordon GC

From Mosman, Sydney, Australia, he was born on 20 October 1896. Gazetted Second Lieutenant to the RFC, via the Special Reserve, on 12 August 1916. His formal pilot training duly completed, he was confirmed and gazetted Flying Officer on 5 December following. Served with the Sopwith Pups of 66 Squadron, he claimed at least one victory when he sent a Rumpler down in flames into the British lines, two miles north west of Ypres, on 20 August 1917. His MC was announced in the *London Gazette* of 26 July 1917: 'For conspicuous gallantry and devotion to duty. He has taken part in over forty offensive patrols at low altitudes and under heavy fire from the ground. He has always shown exceptional dash and gallantry in attacking large formations of enemy machines, setting a fine example to all his comrades'.

Taylor later served with 94 and 88 Squadrons in the UK and in France. Taylor wrote of his experiences during this part of his life in 'Sopwith Scout 7309', published by Cassell in 1966. Taylor became, in the years between the World Wars, a world famous aviator; most notably in 1934 for his cross-Pacific flight, Australia to the USA, when acting as Navigator and Relief Pilot to Charles Kingsford-Smith in the first single-engined crossing of the Pacific. In the following year, Taylor saved his own and Kingsford-Smith's lives, as well as the aeroplane 'Southern Cross', during an airmail flight from Australia to New Zealand. For his exceptional gallantry on this occasion, Taylor was awarded the Empire Gallantry Medal in the *London Gazette* of 9 July 1937, the citation for which gives a graphic account of the circumstances: 'On 15 May 1935, the monoplane Southern Cross piloted by Sir Charles Kingsford-Smith, with Captain Taylor as Navigator, left Sydney for an airmail flight across the Tasman Sea. About 600 miles from Sydney the starboard engine failed and the pilot had to turn back. The strain on the other two engines began to tell and the port engine began to use too much oil. Fuel and cargo were jettisoned but the aircraft lost height and at times was only a few feet above the water. It was in these hazardous conditions that Captain Taylor, six times at intervals of 35 minutes, climbed out of the cockpit, carrying oil by means of a vacuum flask to the overheating port engine. This almost incredible feat, and the skilful handling of the crippled aircraft by its pilot, resulted in the plane arriving safely back at the airport after 16 hours in the air'.

(Taylor, like every other living recipient of the Empire Gallantry Medal, would, in 1940, be required to return that medal and exchange it for the newly instituted George Cross.)

He made other significant and pioneering flights including, in 1939, the first crossing of the Indian Ocean whilst surveying the air route for the British and Australian governments. During the Second World War, he served as a Squadron Leader in the RAAF until 1944 and then with RAF Transport Command for the remainder of the war. In 1944, Taylor made the first crossing of the central Pacific, formally surveying the route for the RAF. Returning to civilian life in 1945, he went on to make the first crossing of the South Pacific, Australia to Chile, in 1951. He married first, in 1938, Eileen J Broadwood (died 1950) with whom he had two daughters and secondly, in 1951, Joyce A Kennington, with whom he had one son and two daughters. He was living, at this time, at 141 York Street, Sydney. He also wrote, over the years: 'Pacific Flight', 'VH-UXX', 'Call to the Winds', 'Forgotten Island', 'Frigate Bird', 'The Sky Beyond' and 'Bird of the Islands'. He was knighted (KBE), 1954. Sir Gordon Taylor died on 14 December 1966 in Honolulu, Hawaii.

TAYLOR, Stanley Wedgewood

From farming stock in Natal, South Africa, he was born on 11 January 1890. Gazetted Second Lieutenant to the RFC, via the Special Reserve, on 6 May 1916. His formal pilot training duly completed, he was confirmed and gazetted Flying Officer on 8 August following. Accompanied the FE8 equipped 41 Squadron to France as a 'founder member' on 16 October 1916. Taylor was promoted to A/Captain and Flight Commander on 2 May 1917. His tour with '41' completed, he returned to the UK and instructing duties on 25 June 1917. His MC was announced in the *London Gazette* of 26 July 1917: 'He has at all times shown the greatest fearlessness, especially in volunteering for any duty entailing special risk. His dash and determination in engaging hostile machine guns, transport and bodies of troops from a very low altitude have been most marked'.

After a short rest, Taylor was posted as an Instructor to No 1 School of Air Fighting where he remained for the remainder of the war. His skill and expertise in this field were duly recognised by the award of an Air Force Cross, *London Gazette* of 2 November 1918. Taylor finally left the RAF, via the Unemployed List, on 1 August 1919.

TEMPEST, Edmund Roger

The third son of William F Tempest and Florence Helen O'Rourke Tempest, of Ackworth Grange, Ackworth, Yorkshire, he was born on 30 October 1894, in Pontefract, Yorkshire. Edmund and his brother, Wulston (qv), were both farming in Saskatchewan, Canada, when the war came. Both returned home and each was gazetted Second Lieutenant to 6 Battalion, King's Own Yorkshire Light Infantry, on 30 November 1914. After a brief period with the 6 King's Own Yorkshire Light Infantry in the UK, Edmund successfully sought secondment to the RFC, gaining his Royal Aero Club Certificate (Number 1604) on 18 August 1915. His formal pilot training duly completed, he was confirmed and gazetted Flying Officer on 3 November following. Joined BE2c-equipped 6 Squadron in France soon after qualifying for his 'Wings'. In August 1916, Tempest was posted briefly to 29 Squadron, before yet a further posting to 15 Squadron. On 1 July 1917, he was sent to the DH 5-equipped 64 Squadron. He gained his first victory on 30 November 1917 in a DH5, but, when early in 1918, the unit was re-equipped with SE5As, he really came into his own. Between 8 March and 14 August 1918, he accumulated a further 16 victories, the great majority of which were scout planes. In the process of these achievements, he was promoted A/Captain and Flight Commander, receiving both the MC and the Distinguished Flying Cross. His MC was announced in the *London Gazette* of 13 May 1918: 'For conspicuous gallantry and devotion to duty. He attacked a formation of seven enemy machines, firing on one from a distance of only a few feet and destroying it. On another occasion with his patrol he engaged 13 enemy machines. Though both of his guns were out of action, he continued fighting for 15 minutes in order to enable the rest of his patrol to keep up the fight. Having driven off the enemy, he brought his patrol back safely. He showed splendid courage and initiative'.

His Distinguished Flying Cross, *London Gazette* of 2 November 1918, was awarded for, among other things, 'his brilliant leadership'.

TEMPEST, Wulston Joseph

The second son of William F Tempest and Florence Helen O'Rourke Tempest, of Ackworth Grange, Ackworth, Yorkshire, he was born on 22 January 1890. Educated at Stonyhurst. Wulston and his brother, Edmund (qv), were both farming in Saskatchewan, Canada, when the war came. Both returned home and each was gazetted Second Lieutenant to 6 Battalion, King's Own Yorkshire Light Infantry, on 30 November 1914. Wolstan accompanied 6 King's Own Yorkshire Light Infantry to France on 21 May 1915, serving in the trenches during the battles of Hooge and Loos. Following Edmund's example who was already in the RFC, Wulston sought secondment to the flying service, which came in the spring of 1916. He gained his Royal Aero Club Certificate (Number 2965) on 22 March 1916. His formal pilot training duly completed, he was confirmed and gazetted Flying Officer on 17 June following. Posted first to 'A' Flight, 39 HD Squadron, then stationed at North Weald. On the night of 1/2 October 1916, Tempest was, despite a faulty petrol pressure pump and having to fly through a blanket of 'friendly' anti-aircraft fire, responsible for shooting down Zeppelin *L31*, commanded by Kapitänleutnant Heinrich Mathy. Getting up to point-blank range, he emptied a drum into the huge craft with spectacular effect. The hull 'began to go red inside like an enormous Chinese lantern'. Tempest described later how he had to put his BE2c, '4577', into a spin to avoid being enveloped by the flaming airship as it fell. For this feat, he was awarded the Distinguished Service Order in the *London Gazette* of 13 October 1916. He was also Mentioned in Despatches in the *London Gazette* of 25 January 1917, for other Home Defence duties admirably performed. Sent out to France as a Flight Commander with 100 Squadron in the spring of 1917. On the night of 15/16 August 1917, Tempest and his Observer of the day, Lieutenant R S Greenslade, spotted a great deal of rail traffic on the brightly illuminated Gares de Fives. The pair dropped one large and five smaller bombs into the centre of the target and then raked the station with their machine guns. His MC was announced in the *London Gazette* of 18 October 1917, details in the *Gazette* of 7 March 1918: 'For conspicuous gallantry and devotion to duty on many occasions. He has successfully bombed railway sidings and aerodromes, often in misty and cloudy weather, at a low altitude, causing much damage to his objectives. On one occasion he descended to a very low altitude and dropped bombs on two moving trains, causing them both to be derailed. This officer has taken part in thirty-four night bombing raids'.

Promoted to Major, he commanded 100 Squadron from 11 December 1917 to 12 June 1918. Tempest left the RAF in 1919. He married, in 1923, Ethel Fernandes, with whom he had one son, whilst living at Badsworth House, Newbury.

TENNANT, John Edward)

The eldest son Francis John and Annie Geraldine Tennant, of Innes House, Elgin, Morayshire, Scotland, he was born on 12 October 1890. Educated at Hoddleston Preparatory School (1901-03) and at the Royal Naval Colleges, Osborne and Dartmouth, from where he emerged Midshipman in 1908. Unfortunately, his Naval career came to an end when he was obliged to leave the service due to sickness and ill-health in February 1910. His health restored, he was gazetted Second Lieutenant to the Scots Guards on 1 February 1912. Developing an interest in aviation, he gained his Royal Aero Club Certificate (Number 811) on a Vickers machine at Brooklands on 9 June 1914. Seconded to the RFC, he completed his formal pilot training and was duly confirmed and gazetted Flying Officer (Military Wing) on 12 September

1914. He served with 4 Squadron in France from December 1915. Notably, on the night of 19/20 February 1916, Tennant and Captain E D Horsfall (qv), each flying a BE2c without an Observer, mounted a moon lit bombing raid on Cambrai aerodrome. Tennant dropped his full load of seven 20lb Hales bombs directly onto the sheds from a height of 30 feet. The fabric on the wings of his BE was torn and rent by the splinters erupting from the explosions. Horfall was less successful, his bombs failing to release from their racks. Despite Horfall's disappointment, General Trenchard was impressed with Tennant's efforts and urged all Brigades to take every opportunity to mount night bombing raids. His MC was announced in the *London Gazette* of 30 March 1916: 'For conspicuous gallantry and skill. During the night he bombed the sheds of an enemy aeroplane, descending to 30 feet to do so. He shut off his engine in order to avoid giving warning, although there was risk of not being able to start it again. His machine was much damaged by the explosion of his own bombs at so low a height. On his return he requested permission to take another machine and repeat the operation'.

Tennant was also Mentioned in Despatches on five occasions during the Great War. Research has unearthed the original recommendation for one of these 'Mentions': '4 Sqd 12 March 1916: He has done consistent good work as a Flight Commander and set an excellent example and shown great devotion to duty on many occasions. He on two occasions led bombing raids on hostile aerodromes, on 14 and 28 December 1915. On the night of 29/30 January, he went up in a pursuit of a Zeppelin and being unable to see the ground owing to thick fog flew into the wall around the aerodrome on attempting to land. On the evening of 22 February when a heavy bombardment was opened on our trenches at Fricourt he made a most gallant attempt in spite of the darkness and stormy weather to observe for counter batteries. He has recently been awarded the MC for a night attack on Cambrai aerodrome on the night of 19/20 February. Has been with the Expeditionary Force since December 1915'.

Promoted to A/Major, he was next sent out to command 30 Squadron in Mesopotamia from 7 August 1916. Tennant was soon in action, leading a flight of bombing planes over Shumran aerodrome. All three machines returned safely but were heavily shot up by ground fire. Promoted to A/Lieutenant Colonel, he was given command of 3 Wing, RFC, from 11 January 1917 to 17 April 1917. He continued to be part of the RFC planning and operational Staff into the New Year of 1918. On 25 March 1918, Tennant and Major P C S Hobart, took off in a DH4 to observe for themselves the Baghdad positions that were to be attacked on the following day. Their machine was hit by anti-aircraft fire and Tennant was forced to land. No doubt the Turks were surprised at the high ranks of their prisoners and, after initial interrogation, they were taken to Ana for onward transportation to Aleppo. Two days later, Ana was taken by British forces, including an Armoured Car Squadron. After establishing the fate of the two senior RFC officers, eight armoured cars were sent after them, hopefully to secure their release. On the following day, after a 32 mile race across rough terrain, the cars caught up with the Turkish detachment and forced the release of Tennant and Hobart. Tennant was awarded the Distinguished Service Order for his service in Mesopotamia, *London Gazette* of 3 August 1918. He was ordered back to the UK but was then redirected to India, where he served as Director of Aeronautics in 1918 and 1919. The French created him Chevalier Légion d'Honneur before he resigned his commission on 10 July 1919. He married first, in 1918, Georgina Helen Kirkpatrick (divorced 1925), with whom he had one son, and, secondly, Victoria Maud Veronica Duff, with whom he had two sons and one daughter. His book, 'In the Clouds Above Baghdad', was published in 1920. He became a partner in the firm of Hohler and Company, banking agents and a director of C Tennant, Son and Company Ltd and of Caledonian Associated Cinemas. He contested Moray and Nairn for the Liberals in the General Election of 1929. Tennant carried out the Shirkar expeditions up the White Nile, in India, and the Sinai Peninsula. He was a member of the Oxford University Arctic Expedition to North East Land in 1924. Lived Innes House, Elgin, Morayshire and at 10a Lansdowne House, Berkeley Square, London W 1. When the Second World War came in 1939, he served again as a Wing Commander in the RAFVR, joining the Intelligence Staff at the Air Ministry. Appointed Personal Air Secretary to the Chief of Air Staff, Sir Charles Portal from 1940-41. In 1941, he was made Commandant of the Scotland ATC. Group Captain John Tennant died on 7 August 1941 and is buried in Innes House Private Burial Ground, Moray.

THAYRE, Frederic James Harry

From London, he was born on 20 October 1893, the family moving later to Littlehampton. He enlisted as a Private soldier (Number 2522) into the Honourable Artillery Company (Infantry) on 28 September 1914. He was allowed leave from the HAC to take flying lessons at the Brooklands School of Aviation. Picked out for a commission, he was gazetted Second Lieutenant to the RFC, via the Special Reserve, on 29 July 1915, the same day that he gained his Royal Aero Club Certificate (Number 1478). His formal pilot training duly completed, he was confirmed and gazetted Flying Officer on 10 November following. Sent out to 16 Squadron in France on 8 January 1916, he had been flying operationally for only a short time when, on 27 February 1916, he suffered an embarrassment he was not allowed to forget. During a bombing mission, he found himself involved in a fight with a number of hostile machines. His bomb release mechanism jammed and he was unable to release his bombs. During the course of the violent evasion tactics he employed whilst avoiding the attentions of his attackers, his map and compass were thrown out of his cockpit. When he finally broke clear after a long-running fight, he found himself alone, over the sea and lost. With his fuel almost gone, he at last spotted land and immediately came down, immensely relieved and believing himself to be in neutral Holland. He had, in fact, landed at Herne Bay in Kent. His initial attempts to converse in broken English with a born-and-bred and puzzled local inhabitant failed and Thayre began to realise his error. His machine topped up with fuel, he flew back to his base on the following day, aghast at the thought of explaining the circumstances of his disappearance to his CO. Predictably perhaps, the next issue of the 16 Squadron 'house magazine', *The* Beaupre *Gift Book*, contained the following limerick:

There was a young pilot called Thayre
Who went for a ride in the air
When his petrol was spent
He landed in Kent
And surrendered at once to the Mayor

Thayre was Mentioned in Despatches at this time and research has unearthed the original recommendation for the award, which, it has to be said, presents a much more positive 'spin' to his adventure on 27 February: '16 Sqd. For conspicuous gallantry and continued good work as a pilot from 8 January till March 1916. On 27 February when flying over the clouds he was driven out to sea; he came down through the mist to about twenty feet, and found himself near the Goodwin Light Ship. He succeeded in landing at Sheerness, and immediately went into the air again, although the weather was very bad, in order to get his machine safely housed at an aerodrome'.

Despite this inauspicious start, Thayre would go on to be a 20-victory Ace with two MCs to his name. The first of his victories came when he was still with '16' on 18 March 1916. He and Lieutenant C R Davidson, in BE2c, '4077', were attacked by three enemy machines. A drum of ammunition emptied into the second of their attackers, settled for him, whilst the remaining two shied away. He was promoted to A/Captain and Flight Commander on 10 July 1916. His tour with '16' completed, he returned to the Home Establishment and instructing duties before going out again to FE2d-equipped 20 Squadron where he teamed up with Francis Cubbon (qv) to form a formidable partnership. Thayre and Cubbon gained no less than 19 victories between 29 April and 7 June 1917. On the intervening 3 May, soon after forcing down a two-seater, they and four others of their Squadron had a titanic battle with no less than twenty-seven Albatros Scouts, shooting two down and driving off the rest. By the end of this particular battle, they had, unsurprisingly, expended every round of their machine-gun ammunition and were reduced to firing their pistols at the retreating enemy. On 9 June 1917,

Thayre and his usual Observer, Captain Francis Richard Cubbon (qv), in FE 2d, 'A6430', were both killed in action when their machine received a direct hit from the German Anti-Aircraft Battery, K Flak 60, near to Warneton. Both of Thayre's MCs were announced posthumously in the same *London Gazette* of 18 July 1917 – MC: 'For conspicuous gallantry and devotion to duty. He has consistently displayed great dash and skill when acting as a pilot in bombing raids. His fine offensive spirit and determination to close with the enemy has set a splendid example to his squadron'.

Bar to MC: 'For conspicuous gallantry and devotion to duty. When in command of an offensive patrol he showed fine leadership and skill being personally responsible for bringing down three hostile machines. His coolness and courage enabled his small command to inflict severe losses on numerically superior forces'.

Frederic Thayre's body was never recovered and hence he is commemorated on the Flying Services Memorial, Arras, France.

THOMAS, Frank William Henry

The son of William Elliot Thomas and Ellen Prynn Thomas (née Poultney), of Dryden, Plumtree, South Rhodesia, he was born at Zeerust, Transvaal, South Africa, in 1896. He worked as a professional Big Game Hunter prior to travelling to the UK to offer his services. Gazetted Second Lieutenant to the Staffordshire Yeomanry (TF) on 7 December 1915. Seconded to the RFC, he trained as a Pilot and was duly confirmed and gazetted Flying Officer on 23 October 1916. Posted out to Salonika and 47 Squadron, he was kept busy with bombing raids and observation duties. Claimed, in April 1917, at least one victory. On 20 August 1917, Thomas and his Observer, Second Lieutenant H A Jones (qv), in AWFK8, 'A1466', were the rearguard of a formation returning from a bombing raid on a German aerodrome and billets, when they were attacked by four Albatros DIIIs over Prilep. Jones sent down one enemy machine as they positioned themselves to continue to cover the rear of their raiding party. The 'Big-Ack' bore the brunt of the enemy's attack and was heavily shot up. Thomas received a serious wound in the back in the first moments of the attack, while Jones was slightly wounded in the stomach – the offending bullet having largely expended its energy on the thick leather of his Sam Browne belt. The onslaught continued and now Jones was hit in the mouth and by an explosive bullet in the left hand. Thomas passed out twice with the shock and pain of his back injuries and from loss of blood but, each time, with the encouragement of his Observer, he recovered sufficiently to coach the damaged machine back across the lines and to land perfectly, some 50 minutes after they had been attacked. His MC was announced in the *London Gazette* of 18 October 1917, details in the *Gazette* of 7 March 1918: 'For conspicuous gallantry and devotion to duty. Whilst returning from a bombing raid he was attacked by four hostile machines, one of which he succeeded in bringing down. He was then severely wounded and on two occasions lost consciousness. He nevertheless successfully brought his machine back and landed it undamaged on his aerodrome. His pluck and determination were worthy of the highest praise'.

The French, too, acknowledged his services with the Croix de Guerre avec Palme, *London Gazette* of 17 December 1917. Thomas' wounds, painful in the extreme, would have rendered him a cripple had he lived. However, after undergoing an agonising journey from Serbia, via Salonika and Malta, to a London hospital, he died four and a half months later on 5 January 1918. He is buried in Brookwood Military Cemetery, Surrey.

THOMAS, William

A Technical, not a flying, award

From Godalming, Surrey, he was born on 31 October 1883. He enlisted in his youth into the Royal Engineers (Number 21613) and had reached the rank of Staff Sergeant when, on 13 May 1912, he became one of the earliest (Number 7) entrants into the newly formed RFC. One of the small number of NCOs taught to fly, he gained his Royal Aero Club Certificate (Number 276) in a Short machine on Salisbury Plain on 3 September 1912. On 25 November 1912, he was promoted to Sergeant Major and, in the following year, was rated Sergeant Major (Pilot), and stationed at Farnborough. By then a married man, he was one of four RFC Sergeant Majors living in married quarters at Farnborough Common. When the war came, he crossed to France on 12 August 1914, a member of 4 Squadron and part of the original RFC contingent, thus earning the 1914 Star. There is no evidence that he flew operationally in France and appears to have been mainly employed in the repair and maintenance of aeroplanes. Gazetted Lieutenant and Quartermaster, RFC, on 29 August 1915. His MC was announced in the New Year *London Gazette* of 1 January 1917 (no citation). Although no formal citation appeared in the *Gazette*, research has unearthed the original recommendation for the award: 'W Thomas. Honorary Lt/Qr Mr. From May 16 until the present time he has shown continuing zeal, initiative and ability in charge of the metal workers in the Aircraft Repair Section, 2 Air Depot. He has had to work at great pressure for long hours, and he has never failed to complete the work required'.

Thomas was also Mentioned in Despatches in the same *London Gazette*. Promoted to Captain when the RAF came into being on 1 April 1918. Staying on in the RAF after the war, he was promoted to Squadron Leader on 1 November 1919, whilst stationed at the CFS, Upavon. Continued to serve in the RAF into the late 1920s.

THOMPSON, Samuel Frederick Henry

The son of Samuel Whitell Thompson and Florence Augusta Jane Thompson, of 44 Vanbrugh Hill, Blackheath, London, he was born on 30 August 1890. Educated at East London College, Finsbury, at the Sir John Cass Technical Institute, and at the University of London, where he was a member of the OTC. A Civil and Mechanical Engineer, he was employed for two years in Northern Nigeria before returning to England in 1910, to take up a job in a machine shop in Erith, working on turbine engines. A pre-war volunteer, he enlisted as a Private soldier in the Army Service Corps (TF) in 1910. Picked out for a commission, he was gazetted Second Lieutenant to the Army Service Corps on 22 March 1915. Served in Egypt and Salonika with the Army Service Corps before successfully seeking secondment to the RFC in January 1917. His formal pilot training duly completed, he was confirmed and gazetted Flying Officer on 7 June following. He joined BF2d-equipped 20 Squadron later in 1917 but was injured in a crash on 20 October. Once recovered, he was next sent to 22 Squadron, also equipped with Brisfits. An aggressive Pilot, he gained no less than 30 victories, including two 'trios' and seven 'doubles' on single days, between 22 April and 27 September 1918. His most effective partnership was with Sergeant Ronald Malcolm Fletcher (Number P22398), who would ultimately receive the Distinguished Flying Medal, *London Gazette* of 2 November 1918. Thompson was, after Andrew McKeever (qv), the second most successful Bristol Fighter Pilot. His MC was announced in the *London Gazette* of 16 September 1918: 'For conspicuous gallantry and devotion to duty as a fighting pilot. During recent operations he destroyed five enemy machines. He showed great courage and skill, and by his keenness and dash set a fine example to all'.

On 27 September 1918, Thompson and his Observer of the day, Second Lieutenant Clifford John Tolman from the Isle of Wight, in BF2b, 'E2477', were seen, shortly after destroying a Halberstadt 'C', going east into enemy territory over Cambrai. They were never seen again. Thompson's Distinguished Flying Cross, awarded for, amongst other things, 'his boldness in attack', was posthumously announced in the *London Gazette* of 2 November 1918. 'Siffy' Thompson is commemorated on the Flying Services Memorial, Arras, France.

THOMSON, Arthur Ashford Benjamin

The son of Colonel and Mrs T G Thomson, he was born in Dinapore, India, on 2 April 1895. Educated at Wellington College (1907-11). Developing an interest in aviation, he gained his Royal Aero Club Certificate (Number 452) on a Bristol machine of the Eastbourne Aviation Company at Eastbourne aerodrome on 1 April 1913. Gazetted Second Lieutenant to the Royal Warwickshire Regiment on 30 June 1914, with an immediate attachment to the Military Wing, RFC. His formal pilot training duly completed, he was confirmed and gazetted Flying Officer on 16 September 1914. In fact, this was a month after he had already accompanied 5 Squadron to France as a Pilot, part of the original RFC contingent, on 14 August 1914. Thomson also served with 1 Squadron in 1914 before, promoted to Captain, joining 16 Squadron as a Flight Commander in the late summer of 1915. On 18 September 1915, Thomson, in a Bristol Scout with a Lewis gun mounted on the rear spar of the top plane, challenged, in succession, three enemy machines, driving each of them back to their lines. Three days later, this time armed only with a rifle, Thomson in a Maurice Farman, challenged an Albatros crossing into the British lines at 8,500 feet. The enemy machine turned for home, with Thomson in hot pursuit. Thomson kept firing, expending a total of 45 rounds, until, over Wytschaete with his machine hit by ground fire, he was forced to give up the chase. These actions were, in many ways, typical of the many inconclusive combats of those days. Thomson also gained a reputation for flying low over the enemy trenches, firing at the Germans occupants with a rifle or a pistol. His MC was announced in the *London Gazette* of 2 October 1915: 'For conspicuous gallantry and determination on August 29th 1915, near Neuve Chapelle. When ranging a heavy gun on the German trenches he stayed up for over two hours in heavy rain with clouds at about 500 feet. At one time he found himself in a cloud on the far side of the German trenches; but after coming back under heavy fire, he continued to observe with the greatest bravery and skill, only returning when too dark for more work. His gallant conduct resulted in 10 direct hits on the enemy's parapet'.

His tour with '16' completed, he returned to the Home Establishment, serving first with 15 RA Squadron at Doncaster, on Home Defence duties. He survived a quite serious crash on the night of 3/4 April 1916, but continued to be heavily involved in anti–Zeppelin operations. A Bar to his MC came in the *London Gazette* of 9 September 1916: 'For conspicuous gallantry and good work during Zeppelin raids'.

'Ack Ack Beer', as he was known because of his initials, was promoted to Major and given command of 33 Squadron in 1917. Later in the same year, he was promoted to A/Lieutenant Colonel and given command of a Wing, whilst still only 22 years old. He was given an Air Force Cross in the very first gazetting of the new decoration, Birthday Honours *London Gazette* of 3 June 1918. He was also Mentioned in Despatches on four occasions, *London Gazettes* of 1 January 1916, 25 January 1917, 20 December 1917 and 22 January 1922. He was given a permanent commission in the RAF, and decided to specialise in armament. Between 1920-27, he served on RAF Missions to Austria and Hungary, and at RAF HQ, Iraq. From 1930 to 1933, he served as Assistant Director (Armaments) at the Air Ministry. Promoted to Air Commodore in 1938, the youngest in the service, he was given command of 3 Bomber Group. On 28 August 1939, just six days before the outbreak of the Second World War, Thomson landed a Wellington bomber at Boscombe Down. He had been conducting bomb trials and came down to investigate a problem with the bomb release mechanism. After making some adjustments to the controls in the bomb bay, he stood back to inspect his work, only to walk into an idling propeller. Terribly injured, he died in an ambulance on the way to hospital. Thomson was living, at this time, with his wife at 'The Limes', Mildenhall, Suffolk.

THOMSON, David Norrie

From Airdrie, Scotland, he was born on 31 January 1891. After completing his education, he worked as a Stockbroker with Messrs R Easton and Company of Glasgow from 1911 to 1914. Gazetted Second Lieutenant to the Queen's Own Glasgow Yeomanry (TF) on 26 July 1915. Seconded to the RFC in the summer of 1916, he trained as an Observer and was sent out as such to 14 Squadron in Arabia. Formally confirmed and gazetted Flying Officer (Observer) on 3 September 1916. His tour with '14' completed, he was next posted to No 3 School of Air Gunnery in Egypt on 2 August 1917. His MC was announced in the *London Gazette* of 8 August 1917 (no citation). He was also Mentioned in Despatches, *London Gazette* of 17 September 1917, and awarded the Order of the Nile, 4th Class, by His Highness, the Sultan of Egypt, *London Gazette* of 18 November 1917. Promoted accordingly, he was posted to RFC HQ, Middle East, as a Staff Captain, serving there until July 1919, when he was sent for service with the Palestine Brigade, RFC. Thomson returned to the UK in December 1919, leaving the RAF, via the Unemployed List, in the same month. For his services in the desert in 1917, Thomson was awarded the Order of El Nahda by HM the King of Hedjaz, *London Gazette* of 2 September 1924.

THOMSON, George Edwin

The son of James and Ellen Thomson of Glenfuccan, Helensburgh, Dumbartonshire, Scotland, he was born on 19 September 1897. Gazetted Second Lieutenant to a Regular Army battalion of the King's Own Scottish Borderers on 11 November 1915. Seconded to the RFC in September 1916, he trained as a Pilot and was duly confirmed and gazetted Flying Officer on 30 December following. Badly injured in a crash which resulted in his face being permanently scarred, his departure to the front was delayed as a consequence. Substantially recovered, he was sent out to France and 46 Squadron in June 1917. Gained his first victory in a Sopwith Pup on 25 September, shortly before the unit converted to Camels. Thomson and the Camel proved a formidable combination, and he went on to gain a further 20 victories between 30 November 1917 and 23 March 1918, including one 'quartet', one 'trio', and three 'doubles' on single days. His MC was announced in the *London Gazette* of 22 April 1918: 'On one occasion when testing his machine he observed a hostile two-seater machine between himself and the lines. He dived on it and fired 60 rounds at a close range, rendering the Observer insensible. He then pulled up under the tail of the enemy machine, fired another 30 rounds, and observed it going down in a slow spin. He has accounted for six enemy machines, and has rendered continuous gallant and valuable service'.

His tour with '46' completed, he returned to the Home Establishment at the end of March 1918 and was posted to 7 Training Depot Station at Feltwell. On 23 May 1918, he was taking off from Port Meadow, Oxford, when his machine burst into flames and Thomson was killed. His Distinguished Service Order was posthumously announced in the *London Gazette* of 22 June 1918. George Thomson is buried in Oxford (Wolvercote) Cemetery, Oxfordshire.

THOMSON, William McKenzie

From Lachine, Province of Quebec, he was born on 15 September 1898, although his family moved afterwards to Toronto, where he was raised and educated. Came to the UK and was gazetted Second Lieutenant to the RFC on 1 November 1917. He obviously already had flying experience, as he was confirmed and gazetted Flying Officer just six days later on 7 November 1917. Sent out to the Bristol Fighter-equipped 20 Squadron early in 1918, he amassed a remarkable 26 victories between 9 May and 16 September 1918, including two 'trios' and five 'doubles' on single days. He enjoyed success with several Observers but, in particular, with Lieutenants G H Kemp and H L Edwards. However, on 1 June 1918, Thomson and his Observer of the day, Londoner George Hubert Kemp, were attacked by four enemy machines after losing touch with the rest of their patrol. Thomson accounted for one of the enemy after expending 200 rounds, whilst Kemp sent another down with a burst from point-blank range. But then an Albatros swooped down on them from above and Kemp was killed. Thomson dived to below 2,000 feet before turning to confront the Albatros which had followed him down. After a further exchange, the German machine turned east and away from the fight. Thomson was able to bring his dead Observer home without further mishap to himself or his machine. His MC was announced in the *London Gazette* of 5 June 1918, details in the *Gazette* of 16 September 1918: 'For conspicuous gallantry and devotion to duty on offensive patrols. In five days he destroyed many enemy machines. He showed fine determination to close with the enemy, and set a splendid example of enterprise and gallantry'.

A Distinguished Flying Cross came in the *London Gazette* of 2 November 1918, this, for amongst other things, 'invariably displaying courage, determination and skill'. Thomson left the RAF to return home to Canada in 1919. He served again in the Second World War, this time with the Royal Canadian Air Force. William Mackenzie Thomson died on 9 July 1987.

THORNTON, Thomas George

From Northallerton, Yorkshire, he was born on 7 March 1890. After completing his education, he worked for a timber importer, Messrs Calder Dixon and Company, in their Edinburgh office from 1906 to 1914. Volunteering as soon as war came, he was gazetted Second Lieutenant to 4 Battalion, Yorkshire Regiment (Green Howards) (TF) on 5 September 1914. Accompanied his battalion to France on 17 April 1915. Wounded in the trenches during the Battle of Flers in September 1916, he was returned to the UK for medical treatment soon afterwards. Once recovered, he was seconded to the RFC in February 1917. Having trained as a Balloon Officer, he was sent out to 2 Balloon Section in France. Returning to the Home Establishment on 15 June 1917, he was posted to the Balloon Training Wing, where he was promoted to A/Captain and gazetted BC Commander on 30 August following. Sent out to 21 BC in Palestine, on 10 October 1917. His MC was announced in the *London Gazette* of 11 April 1918 (no citation) for: '....military operations culminating in the capture of Jerusalem'.

Posted next to 50 Balloon Section on 1 April 1918 and subsequently to 21 Balloon Section on 18 July 1918. Awarded a Distinguished Flying Cross in the New Year *London Gazette* of 1 January 1919, for services in Jerusalem. Returned to the UK and left the RAF, via the Unemployed List, on 7 August 1919. Tom Thornton died on 7 August 1961 at his home, Mayo Farm, Shaftesbury, Dorset.

TIDMARSH, David Mary

The second son of Mr and Mrs Tidmarsh of Lota, Limerick, Ireland, he was born on 28 January 1892. Educated in Ireland and at Stonyhurst (1905-09). Gazetted Second Lieutenant to 4 (Extra Reserve) Battalion, Royal Irish Regiment on 23 April 1915, with an immediate secondment to the RFC. Gained his Royal Aero Club Certificate (Number 1833) on 7 October 1915. His pilot training duly completed, he was confirmed and gazetted Flying Officer on 13 January 1916. Accompanied 24 Squadron (DH2s) to France as a 'founder member' on 7 February 1916. On 2 April 1916, Tidmarsh, in DH2, '5924', and squadron colleague, Second Lieutenant S J Sibley, in '5948', shared in what was, in fact, the first victory of 24 Squadron over an enemy machine, which fell near to Grandcourt. On 21 April, Tidmarsh had a miraculous escape when the nacelle of his DH2, '5929', was pierced by a shell. On 30 April, Tidmarsh, in '5965', gained another success, this time in unusual circumstances, albeit against a dreaded Fokker. The Official History, 'The War in the Air', relates it thus: 'Second Lieutenant Tidmarsh left some FE2b's he was escorting and attacked a Fokker which dived so steeply to avoid him that it crashed on the roof of a building in Bapaume and fell to pieces before the De Haviland Pilot had got close enough to fire a shot'. Leutnant Otto Schmedes of FA32 was the unfortunate German Pilot involved in this incident. Tidmarsh's MC was announced in the *London Gazette* of 31 May 1916: 'For conspicuous gallantry and skill when attacking hostile aircraft on several occasions, notably on one occasion when he dived on an enemy machine and drove it down wrecked upon the ground'.

His tour with '24' completed, he returned to the UK in October 1916, to take up an instructing post at the School of Air Gunnery. Tidmarsh was invested with the insignia of his MC by the King at Buckingham Palace. He returned to France in March 1917, this time as a Flight Commander with the newly formed and Bristol Fighter-equipped 48 Squadron. Four further victories followed in rapid succession in the four days from 8 to 11 April 1917, before he was himself, along with his Observer, Second Lieutenant Cator Barclay Holland, in BF2a, 'A3338', shot down by Kurt Wolff, the ninth of the great German Ace's eventual 33 victories. After returning from captivity at the end of the war, Tidmarsh related how his patrol of three machines was attacked by seven German Scouts. Despite having one of their number brought down in the first attack, the enemy machines regrouped and launched a second assault. In this, Holland was wounded and the Brisfit's engine hit and stopped by machine-gun fire. Tidmarsh glided the Brisfit down to a safe and intact landing behind the German lines, whereupon he and Holland were immediately taken as prisoners. Their still relatively new Bristol F2A was, no doubt, of great interest to the Imperial German Air Service. Repatriated in December 1918, Tidmarsh finally left the RAF on 28 October 1919. Tidmarsh served again in the Second World War. Having joined the RAFVR in May 1939, he subsequently worked in the Administration and Special Duties Branch and was promoted to Squadron Leader in 1942. Tidmarsh relinquished his commission in January 1944, on grounds of ill health. He died on 27 November 1944.

TILNEY, Leonard Arthur

The elder son of Colonel R H Tilney, DSO and Daisey F M Tilney, of Millbank House, Tattenhall, Cheshire, and 8 Onslow Crescent, South Kensington, London, he was born in 1895. Educated at Eversley, Windfield, and at Eton (1908-14). When the war came, he was, coincidently, actually in camp with the Eton College OTC. Gazetted Second Lieutenant to his father's regiment, the Duke of Lancaster's Own Yeomanry (TF), on 29 August 1914. He transferred briefly to the Royal Horse Guards, Household Cavalry, before a further secondment to the RFC came in January 1915. Gained his Royal Aero Club Certificate (Number 1445) on 2 March 1915. His formal training duly completed, he was confirmed and gazetted Flying Officer on 12 April following. Accompanied 11 Squadron (VFB5s) to France on 25 July 1915. After six months with '11', during which he was promoted to A/Captain and Flight Commander, he returned to the Home Establishment early in 1916. After a period in the UK, Tilney was promoted to A/Major and appointed to the command of the newly formed 40 Squadron, which unit he led to France at the turn of the year. Created Officier de l'Ordre de la Couroune by the Belgians, *London Gazette* of 24 September 1917. His MC was announced in the New Year *London Gazette* of 1 January 1918 (no citation). Although no formal citation was published in the *Gazette*, research has unearthed the original recommendation for the award: 'L A Tilney. 40 Sqn. As a squadron commander he has succeeded by his personal example and unsparing efforts, in raising his unit to a high state of efficiency'.

Tilney was presented with his MC during the same investiture at Buckingham Palace as that at which his father received the Distinguished Service Order from the King. The Belgians, too, added their appreciation, awarding the Croix de Guerre, *London Gazette* of 11 March 1918. He was also Mentioned in Despatches on one occasion. On 9 March 1918, Tilney in SE5A, 'C9538', was said by RFC Observers to have broken up in the air whilst diving upon an opponent. However, he was the subject of a claim over Noyelle-Vion by Leutnant Paul Billik of Jasta 52 – the ninth of the German Ace's 31 victories. Leonard Tilney is buried in Cabaret Rouge British Cemetery, France.

NB: His medals were offered for sale by Spink on 17 December 1997: MC, 1915 Star (2Lt D of LOY), *British War Medal 1914-20, Victory Medal 1914-19* (Major), *Order of the Crown (Belgium), and Croix de Guerre (Belgium).*

TODD, John

From Southport, Lancashire, he was born on 29 September 1898. He was a Student of Medicine at Edinburgh University in 1916 and 1917, where he was a member of the OTC. Joined the flying service as a Cadet in April 1917. Gazetted Second Lieutenant to the RFC on 2 August 1917, he qualified for his 'Wings' and was sent out to 70 Squadron (Camels) late in 1917. Todd achieved 18 victories between 22 January and 1 July 1918, including four 'doubles' on single days. He was also promoted to A/Captain and Flight Commander at this time. Again, unusually, the announcement of the award of a Distinguished Flying Cross, *London Gazette* of 3 August 1918, came in advance of the announcement of his MC, *London Gazette* of 16 September 1918: 'For conspicuous gallantry and devotion to duty. During recent operations he destroyed three enemy aircraft, forced one to land in our lines, and drove four down out of control. He did very fine work'.

His Distinguished Flying Cross was, of course, given for his continuing success as a free-scoring Scout Pilot. His tour with '70' completed, he served out the war as an Air Fighting

Instructor with 204 TS. After leaving the RAF early in 1919, he returned to his medical studies at Edinburgh University.

TOMLING, George Gibson

The son of Professor of Music, George Tomling, and Lilian C Tomling, of 4 Whellock Road, Acton, Middlesex, he was born in Moscow, Russia, on 2 August 1897. Educated at West Ealing College, London, whilst living at Gerrards Cross. He enlisted as a Private soldier (Number 8056) into 28 Battalion, London Regiment (Artists Rifles), in 1916. Picked out for a commission, he was gazetted Second Lieutenant to the RFC on 26 January 1917. His pilot training duly completed, he was confirmed and gazetted Flying Officer on 23 July 1917. Fluent in the language, he was selected to accompany the Russian Mission to that country on 12 September 1917. The nature of his work is not clear, but it was rewarded with the award of an MC in the *London Gazette* of 12 February 1919 (no citation). The announcement simply states that: 'The King is graciously pleased to approve of the undermentioned rewards for distinguished services rendered in connection with Military operations in the Field'. Interestingly, as well as Tomling, amongst the others named are: Lieutenant George Alexander Hill qv), 4 Manchester Regiment attached RAF and Second Lieutenant Sidney George Reilly (qv), RAF. We can deduce from what we know of Reilly's activities, that the nature of the work performed by these officers can almost certainly be classified as 'covert'. His tour with the Russian Mission completed, he returned to the UK in 1919. Tomling married, on 18 March 1920, a Russian lady, Lubov Shingardelova, in Novorossisk. An RAF Chaplain married the couple, with two fellow RAF officers acting as witnesses. A daughter of this union, Irena Lilian, was born on 19 April 1921, when the couple were living in Wandsworth, South London, Tomling working at this time as an Engineers Storeman. He married again, as a widower, on 16 July 1955, Winifred Elizabeth, whilst living at Stafford; he was 57 years old, his bride 38. Living later in Tettenhall, Wolverhampton, he was admitted to the New Cross Hospital in that town, suffering with coronary and asthma complications. George Tomling died soon afterwards on 13 December 1977.

TOMLINSON, Hugh

The fourth and youngest son of George William Tomlinson, FSA, and Charlotte Tomlinson, of 65 Iverna Court, Kensington, London, he was born in Huddersfield, Yorkshire, on 20 June 1882. Educated at Charterhouse (1896-99). In the pre-war years, Tomlinson farmed and traded as a Chinchona Tree Planter in South America. (The Chinchona tree yields Peruvian bark, the source of quinine.) When the war came, he first served in France as a Motor Ambulance Driver with the French Red Cross. Wishing next to join the flying service, he gained, at his own expense, his Royal Aero Club Certificate (Number 1548) on 9 August 1915 and was duly gazetted Second Lieutenant to the RFC on the same day. His formal pilot training completed, he was confirmed and gazetted Flying Officer on 1 November following. He had joined 17 RA Squadron, then stationed at Wimbledon Common on Home Defence duties, and it was with this unit that he suffered, on 31 January, the first of two accidents he would endure in 1916. Once recovered, he was sent next, in April 1916, to 39 Squadron, again on Home Defence duties. In the following month, Tomlinson would again be involved in a flying accident. He was promoted to A/Captain and Flight Commander on 24 June 1916, his MC announced in the *London Gazette* of the same day, details in the *Gazette* of 27 July 1916: 'For conspicuous gallantry and devotion to duty. Capt Tomlinson has taken part in several raids. On two occasions he has had serious accidents at night flying. But he has not been in the least discouraged, and has continued to do most valuable work'.

Tomlinson was also Mentioned in Despatches. Sent next to FE2d-equipped 57 Squadron then at Copmanthorpe, York, he accompanied that unit to France as a Flight Commander and 'founder member' on 16 December 1916. On 2 April 1917, Hugh Tomlinson and his Observer of the day, Lieutenant N C Denison, FE2d, 'A5151', were shot down during a combat over Bapaume by Leutnant Krefft of Jasta 11. Both crewmen were wounded and were carried by their German captors to a Field Hospital at Orgnies. Unfortunately, Hugh Tomlinson died later that same day and is buried in Cabaret-Rouge British Cemetery, Souchez, France.

TREADWELL, Robert Naylor

The son of Dr Oliver Fereira Naylor Treadwell and Mrs Treadwell, of 189 Belgrave Road, London SW1, he was born on 26 March 1893. Educated at Birkhampstead School, where he was a member of the OTC for four years. After completing his education, he worked in Wanarajah, Dickoya, Ceylon. Returning to the UK as soon as war came, he joined the Inns of Court OTC (Number A/2068) on 12 November 1914. Gazetted Second Lieutenant to 7 Battalion, Berkshire Regiment, on 2 December 1914, subsequently transferring to 9 Battalion, Essex Regiment. Accompanied 9 Essex to France on 31 May 1915. He was seriously wounded in the face and legs as a consequence of a grenade accident on 14 March 1916. Scarred but otherwise recovered, he next successfully sought secondment to the RFC early in 1917. Given his 'Wings', he was sent out to the BF2b-equipped 22 Squadron in the summer. On 11 August 1917, his Brisfit was badly shot up and he was severely wounded. Despite what proved to be mortal injuries, he brought his machine and his Observer back to safety. Too badly injured to be moved, Treadwell subsequently died of his wounds at No 42 Casualty Clearing Station on 9 September 1917. His MC was posthumously announced in the *London Gazette* of 26 September 1917, details in the *Gazette* of 9 January 1918: 'Although very severely wounded during a combat, he succeeded in bringing back his machine against a very strong wind to his aerodrome, saving both machine and Observer by his great pluck and determination. When lifted out of his machine he was utterly exhausted. He has been concerned in many successful patrols and bomb raids, showing on all occasions conspicuous dash and devotion to duty'.

Robert Treadwell is buried in Aubigny Communal Cemetery Extension, France.

TREVETHAN, Richard Michael

A member of an old family from Falmouth, Devon, he was born in Park City, USA, on 24 January 1895. Returning to the UK as a boy, he was educated at Falmouth Grammar School, at Portsmouth Grammar School, and at the Imperial College of Science, London. In 1913, he was nominated for the Paymaster Branch of the Royal Navy, but was still awaiting acceptance into the Senior Service when war came in August 1914. Volunteering immediately, he was gazetted Second Lieutenant to 6 Battalion, South Lancashire Regiment, on 29 September 1914. Trevethan accompanied his battalion to Gallipoli, landing at Anzac Cove on 4 August 1915, one of his brother officers being Captain C R Attlee, the future Labour Prime Minister. Following service in the Middle East, he returned to the UK at the end of 1916, after volunteering for secondment to the RFC. His formal pilot training duly completed, he was confirmed and gazetted Flying Officer on 14 May 1917. Sent out to France and FE2d-equipped 20 Squadron he claimed 12 victories between 2 June and 9 August 1917, all of them against enemy Scouts. He was accompanied by Lieutenant C A Hoy (qv) for nine of these successes. Trevethan was actually presented with the ribbon of his MC in the field by General Sir Herbert Plumer on 17 August 1917, although the announcement appeared later in the *London Gazette* of 17 September 1917: 'For conspicuous gallantry and devotion to duty when on offensive patrols. He has continuously displayed the greatest dash and determination in attacking enemy formations, regardless of their superiority in numbers, and has shot down at least four, driving down others out of control'.

One of Trevethan's combat reports suggests that he was convinced that, on one occasion, at least, he was involved in a dog-fight with the Red Baron. Later, on 18 September 1917, flying one of the new two-seater Bristol fighters with which '20' had recently been re-equipped, he received wounds which effectively brought his combat career to an end. He returned to England to recover from his wounds and did not fly operationally again for the duration of the war. In 1919, however, he served in North Russia as part of the combined British Syren Force, being Mentioned in Despatches, *London Gazette* of 22 December 1919 (North Russia) and also awarded the Order of St Anne, 2nd Class with Swords, by the White Russians, for services with Syren Force, the award conferred by Major General Skobe Itzin, commanding troops in the Murmansk district. Staying on in the RAF, he specialised in meteorology, becoming Senior Meteorological Officer, Iraq, 1926-29. From 1930-33, he commanded the Reconnaissance Squadron, Far East, HMS *Hermes*, and then commanded the Flying and Parachute Test Squadron, Home Aircraft Depot, 1934-35. In 1937 he left the RAF, having been appointed Air Advisor to the Kwantung Government in China. Perhaps surprisingly, he was attached to the Admiralty during the Second World War, serving as mate and second officer in RN small ships. Wing Commander Trevethan held the speed record in service aircraft for a non-stop flight from Scotland to the South Coast for 11 years and was also the unbeaten wrestling champion of all three Forces, as well as boxing champion of the RAF for a time. He became a Fellow of the Royal Meteorological Society, a Fellow of the Royal Geographical Society, and for many years was Superintendent of Falmouth Observatory. He died at the Royal Cornwall Hospital, Treliske, in 1971.

NB: His medals were offered for sale by Dix Noonan and Webb (lot 407) on 18 June 1997: MC (engraved: R M Trevethan RFC 20 Sqd July 1917*), 1914-15 Star* (2Lt S Lancs R)*, British War Medal 1914-20, Victory Medal 1914-19 with MID* (Lt RAF)*, and Order of St Anne (Russia, 2nd Class neck badge with Swords).*

TROLLOPE, John Lightfoot

The son of Mr and Mrs H W Trollope, of Green Hayes, Banstead, Surrey, he was born in Wallington, Surrey, on 30 May 1897. Educated at Malvern College (1911-14). Enlisted as a Sapper into the Royal Engineers and subsequently served as a Corporal motor-cycle despatch rider. Picked out for a commission, he was gazetted Second Lieutenant to the RFC, via the Special Lists, on 17 June 1916. Gained his Royal Aero Club Certificate (Number 3772) on 1 August 1916. His formal pilot training duly completed, he was confirmed and gazetted Flying Officer on 2 September following. Sent out to 70 Squadron (Sopwith Strutters) shortly after qualifying for his 'Wings'. After completing a fairly unremarkable tour comprising mainly reconnaissance duties and during which he was promoted to A/Captain and Flight Commander, he returned to the Home Establishment in the summer of 1917. Later in the same year, he was next sent out as a Flight Commander to the Camel-equipped 43 Squadron with remarkable results. Trollope claimed no less than 18 victories between 19 January and 28 March 1918, including seven whilst flying Camel, 'C8270', in the morning and afternoon patrols of 24 March. Four days later, on 28 March, five 43 Squadron Camels, out of a patrol of nine, were shot down in a clash with a formation of Albatros DVs. Trollope, in Camel, 'C8270', was actually given credit for two of the enemy and a balloon, on that same day, before he was himself shot down by Leutnant Paul Billik of Jasta 52, the 12th of the German Ace's eventual 31 victories. Badly wounded in the engagement, he crashed-landed on the German side of the lines and was taken prisoner. Trollope's left hand was subsequently amputated by German doctors. The first of his MCs was announced in the *London Gazette* of 13 May 1918: 'For conspicuous gallantry and devotion to duty. During a period of three months he has engaged and brought down completely out of control four hostile machines, and has sent down crashing to earth three others. On all occasions he has displayed the greatest courage, determination and skill, and it is largely due to his fine leadership that the flight under his command has contributed so much to the marked success of the squadron'.

The Bar to his MC followed shortly afterwards in the *London Gazette* of 22 June 1918: 'For conspicuous gallantry and devotion to duty. On one occasion during the recent operations, while on offensive patrol, he encountered three enemy machines, two of which he completely destroyed. He then attacked a scout, and after firing 100 rounds into it, the enemy machine went down completely out of control, eventually crashing. Later in the same day, on his flight encountering four enemy two-seater planes, he sent three of them down crashing to earth. Within a month previous to this he fought two hostile formations, numbering 12 machines in all, single-handed, and did not break off the engagement until he had driven off all of them towards the East. He has accounted for 14 enemy machines, and has rendered exceptionally brilliant service by his gallantry and determination'.

Trollope was also recommended for a gallantry Distinguished Service Order but, in the event, this was not awarded. Because of his injuries and incapacities, Trollope was exchanged back from captivity in June 1918, the remainder of his left arm being amputated by British surgeons later. Leaving the RAF in 1919, he became a Chartered Surveyor and practised as an Estate Agent whilst living at The Cottage, Banstead, Surrey.

TUDHOPE, John Henry

The only son of chartered accountant turned farmer, Francis Selwyn Tudhope and Mrs Tudhope, of Johannesburg, South Africa, he was born on 17 April 1891. Educated at the Diocesan College, Cape Town, at St John's College, Johannesburg, and at Tonbridge School (1906-10), Rugby XV and Rowing IV. After completing his education, he returned to South Africa and took employment as a Fitter in the gold mines of the Transvaal. When the war came, he enlisted as a Trooper into 1 Imperial Light Horse, South African Defence Forces, on 20 August 1914. A trained machine gunner, he served in South Africa, including participation in quelling the Rebellion, from 10 September to 1 December 1914, before going on to serve in German South West Africa until 30 August 1915. He travelled to the UK at his own expense in 1916, married Jessie Graham Elizabeth Jackson from Hinton St Mary, Dorset, and enlisted as a Private soldier (Number 27400) into the Dorset Regiment. Picked out for a commission, he was first accepted as an Officer Cadet on 1 February 1917, before being gazetted Second Lieutenant to the RFC, via the General List, on 13 April following. His pilot training duly completed, he was confirmed and gazetted Flying Officer on 29 May 1917. Sent out to 40 Squadron (Nieuport Scouts) on 7 July 1917, it was not long before he narrowly escaped with his life following a bruising encounter with Oberleutnant Adolf von Tutschek and Jasta 12. On 28 July, Tudhope in company with squadron colleagues, Lieutenants E Mannock and H A Kennedy, encountered seven German Albatroses. A hard and prolonged fight ensued and, although heavily outnumbered by experienced and battle-hardened opponents, the RFC trio managed to extricate themselves and return, barely intact and somewhat chastened, to their base. Their arrival was witnessed by a squadron colleague, Lieutenant W 'Mac' MacLanachan, who described the aftermath in his book, 'Fighter Pilot', published in 1936: 'Tud's machine was in such a condition that it might have been sent to a flying school to act as an inspiration and a warning to budding fighters. An explosive bullet had burnt through his main spar a few inches from the 'V' strut, one of the top planes had been cut to ribbons by bullets, every one of his instruments were smashed, and a bullet had passed through his coat collar. Tud's face was a study, it depicted a combination of cynicism and amusement. He had certainly been very close to death that morning'. In fact, the great Ace, von

Tutschek, actually, if somewhat optimistically, claimed Tudhope as the 20th of his eventual 27 victories. As though to assert his unblemished effectiveness, Tudhope went on to claim ten victories between 22 September 1917 and 11 April 1918, the first two in Nieuports and the remaining eight in SE5As. He was promoted to A/Captain and Flight Commander on the intervening 18 November 1917. His MC was announced in the *London Gazette* of 26 March 1918, details in the *Gazette* of 24 August 1918 'For conspicuous gallantry and devotion to duty. He showed a splendid offensive spirit in continually attacking enemy aeroplanes. He has destroyed three enemy machines and has driven others down out of control, and always set a splendid example of courage and initiative'.

The Bar to his MC also came in the *London Gazette* of 24 August 1918: 'For conspicuous gallantry and devotion to duty in fighting with exceptional dash and skill over a period of nine months, when he carried out numerous reconnaissances, flying low and engaging with bombs and machine-gun fire enemy troops, guns and transport. He obtained many direct hits and inflicted heavy casualties, often flying under very difficult weather conditions. He has crashed three enemy aeroplanes and shot down two others out of control. His determination and courage have been a brilliant example to the pilots of the flight he has been leading'.

His tour with '40' completed, he returned to the Home Establishment on 25 April 1918. After a months leave he served with 90 Squadron in the UK from 20 June 1918, before going on to 51 TDS; serving with that unit until 31 August 1919. He finally left the RAF, via the Unemployed List, on 13 November 1919. Going next to Canada, he joined the RCAF, securing a position with the Air Board, HQ, in 1920. Later, during his career with the civil aviation authorities, he surveyed and planned the transcontinental air routes across Canada. He personally flew many pioneering airmail flights, delivering mail from trans-Atlantic Ocean liners to ports in the Gulf of St Lawrence. He was inducted into Canada's Aviation Hall of Fame in 1973. 'Tud' Tudhope died in London, Ontario, on 12 October 1956. At his own request, his ashes were scattered over the Rocky Mountains from an aeroplane.

TUDOR-HART, William Owen Tudor

Born in England on 20 February 1884, he lived later in Canada. A married man by 1914, his wife was living in Holland Park, London, when he joined the Inns of Court OTC (Number E/1506) on 1 October 1914. Gazetted Second Lieutenant to 19 Battalion (2 Tyneside Pioneers), Northumberland Fusiliers, on 16 December 1914. Seconded to the RFC at the beginning of 1916, he trained as an Observer and accompanied FE2b-equipped 22 Squadron to France as a 'founder member' and Probationary on 1 April following. On an unidentified day in June, Tudor-Hart and his Pilot of the day, Captain W A Summers, 18 Hussars, took it upon themselves to attack an enemy formation of ten machines and only broke off their attack when they found themselves miles over the German lines, their machine riddled with bullets. Their recklessness earned them both the MC, unusually announced with a joint citation in the *London Gazette* of 27 July 1916: 'Captain William Assheton Summers and Lieutenant William Owen Tudor Tudor-Hart. 'For conspicuous gallantry and skill. Captain Summers, as pilot, and Lieut Tudor-Hart, as Observer, attacked a flight of ten enemy aeroplanes, completely breaking up their formation. They were quite unsupported, but only broke off the engagement when all their ammunition was expended many miles over the enemy's lines. Their machine was under constant heavy fire from as many as four hostile machines at once, and was badly damaged'.

Tudor-Hart's 'apprenticeship' satisfactorily completed, he was confirmed and gazetted Flying Officer (Observer) on 25 June 1916. On 1 July 1916, the opening day of the Battle of the Somme, Tudor-Hart and his Pilot, Ulsterman Captain Gilbert Watson Webb, Royal Irish Rifles, in FE2b, '6928', were on offensive patrol duty between Douchy and Miraumont in company with another 22 Squadron FE. Both machines were shot down, becoming the first casualties suffered by '22'. Webb was killed in the air and Tudor-Hart wounded and taken prisoner when the wreckage of their machine fell into enemy lines. A fascinating glimpse into the circumstances of this incident is given in an extract of a letter written by Tudor-Hart on 25 July 1916, which was, subsequently, included in RFC Communiqué No 60: 'I was with Capt Webb and we went about 4 or 5 miles over the German lines in his machine on 1st July at 11am. We saw eight Germans approaching from the south-west, they were higher than us, and we flew towards them to attack. Two passed over our heads together about 300 yards or so apart, and I opened fire on one. They both replied together. I gave the signal to Webb to turn so that I could fire at the other machine behind us, but he put the machine's head down. I turned to see what was the matter, and he pointed to his abdomen and collapsed over the 'joy stick'. He died in a few seconds I think, but his last thought was to save his machine.

The machine at once began turning towards the German side, and I had to get back to my machine gun to fire at a machine diving at us. This happened again and again, but my fire would always prevent them finishing the dive. Other machines fired from above all the time. I had only time to get the machine pointing towards our lines when I had to get back to the gun. I never got the chance to pull Webb out of the pilot's seat, so had to steer with my hand over the windscreen. I didn't expect to get off alive, but tried to put up as good a fight as possible, and tried all the time to keep her towards our lines, but having to man the gun so often made it impossible to make progress, but the erratic course the machine flew probably saved it. At last, still being fired at, I got right down near the ground and proceeded to make a landing, as it was all I could do. I saw a lot of men with rifles, and realised that I might get shot before I could set fire to the machine, so I, at the last minute, put her nose down in order to crash.

One wing tip hit first, the whole machine was destroyed, I was hurled out and escaped with a bruised and paralysed side and broken ankle and rib. All right now, but the ankle, I was very kindly treated, and the German pilots acted like sportsmen and gentlemen....'.

Repatriated on 22 November 1918, Tudor-Hart left the RAF in 1919.

TULLIS, Jack Kiel

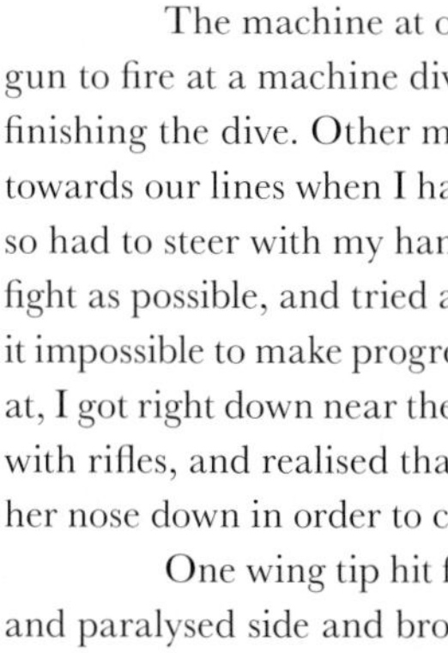

From Glasgow, Scotland, he was born on 26 October 1894. Enlisted as a trooper into the Scottish Horse Yeomanry (TF) in 1915. Picked out for a commission, he was gazetted Second Lieutenant to 2 South Midland Brigade, Royal Field Artillery (TF), on 20 December 1915. Seconded to the RFC in the spring of 1916, he gained his Royal Aero Club Certificate (Number 3136) at the Military School, South Ruislip, on 8 June 1916. His formal pilot training duly completed, he was confirmed and gazetted Flying Officer on 6 July following. Accompanied 70 Squadron (Sopwith Strutters) to France as a 'founder member' on 30 July 1916. On 6 September 1916, Tullis and his Observer of the day, Second Lieutenant J C Taylor, in Strutter, 'A886', were shot down during a combat with three enemy machines south of Cambrai. Both crewmen were taken prisoner and, although Tullis was unhurt, Taylor suffered wounds to the face and other injuries. After almost a year in incarceration i, successively, in Gutersloh, Clausthal (where he attempted to escape but failed), Strohen and finally Holzminden, Tullis was to be one of those who escaped via the famous tunnel on 25 August 1918, getting into Holland 14 days later. Tullis finally left the RAF, via the Unemployed List, on 5 February 1919. His MC was announced in the 'Escapers Gazette', *London Gazette* of 16 December 1919: '....in recognition of gallantry in escaping from captivity whilst Prisoners of War'.

TUNBRIDGE, John Vincent)

From Ballarat, Victoria, Australia, he was born on 13 February 1894. After completing his education, he worked as a warehouseman whilst living at 1437 Sturt Street, Ballarat. Enlisted into the AIF (Numbers 155 and, subsequently, 251590) on 1 February 1916, and was almost immediately promoted to Lance Corporal. Embarked at Melbourne on 16 March 1916 as part of 1 Squadron, AFC, aboard Transport *A67*, the SS *Orsova*, bound for the Middle East. Gazetted Second Lieutenant to the Commonwealth Military Forces on 16 June 1916. Having trained as a Pilot, he was confirmed as such in the *London Gazette* of 24 October 1916. Served with 67 (Australian) Squadron in Palestine. On 7 March 1917, anti-aircraft fire over Tel el Sheria hit Tunbridge's machine and he was forced to land at Rafa. Shocked after his ordeal, he set out to walk home through a land populated by Arabs of uncertain loyalty. Some time later he was picked up in an exhausted state by Squadron colleagues Lieutenants P W Snell and J A Morgan, King's Shropshire Light Infantry, attached RFC, who landed their BE in the desert to pick him up. Londoner Joseph Anthony Morgan would himself be killed in action on 30 May 1917 following. On 11 May 1917, Tunbridge in a Martinsyde G100 was involved in a combat with a Fokker near to Tel el Sheria, Beersheba. During the course of the fight, a bullet from the enemy machine struck a Very-light cartridge in Tunbridge's cockpit. The resultant explosion set the cockpit and Tunbridge's flying suit alight, forcing him to descend immediately. He made a good landing in the circumstances but was so badly burned that he was invalided back home to Australia on 11 July following. He was claimed as a victory by Leutnant F Schleiff and Oberleutnant Daum of FA300. His MC was gazetted on 1 January 1918 (no citation). Tunbridge served again in the Second World War, this time as a Wing Commander in the RAAF, being appointed Deputy Director of Manning. Discharged finally from the RAAF on 11 October 1945.

TURK, Herbert Henry

The son of George and Alice Turk, of North Area, NC Line, Queensland, Australia, he was born in 1889. Enlisted, initially, into 17 Battalion, AIF, but was allowed release in order to travel to the UK to seek a commission in the flying service. Gazetted Second Lieutenant to the RFC, via the Special Reserve, on 3 January 1916. Gained his Royal Aero Club Certificate (Number 2835) on 5 April 1916. His formal pilot training duly completed, he was confirmed and gazetted Flying Officer on 17 June following. Sent out to FE2b-equipped 11 Squadron in France just four days after qualifying for his 'Wings', in time to be involved in the heavy aerial activity precipitated by the Battle of the Somme. On 28 August 1916, Turk and his Observer of the day, Lieutenant D H Scott (qv), in FE2b, '4926', were involved in an aerial combat with superior numbers of enemy machines. During the course of the fight, the FE's rudder was badly damaged and Turk had a tremendous battle with the controls to get the machine, his Observer, and himself, down safely. His MC was announced in the *London Gazette* of 20 October 1916: 'For conspicuous gallantry and skill. With Lieutenant Scott as Observer he attacked seven machines flying in formation. One was brought down as a wreck. When turning to meet another machine his rudder controls were shot away, and his machine got into a spinning nose-dive. After falling 5,000 feet he partially regained control, and, though his machine kept turning, he managed to land safely. The machine was badly damaged, but, thanks to his skill, neither he nor his Observer were hurt'.

On 3 November 1916, Turk and his Observer of the day, Scots/Canadian John Allan, suffered a crash. Turk died immediately, whilst Allan died of his injuries on the following day. Herbert Turk is buried in Avesnes-le-Comte Communal Cemetery, France.

TURNER, Francis McDougall Charlewood

The son of the Right Reverend Bishop of Islington and Mrs Turner, he was born in Clapham, South London, on 17 March 1897. Educated at Marlborough College (1910-15) and, subsequently, at Magdalen College, Cambridge, where he gained his MA in 1920. Gazetted Second Lieutenant to the RFC, via the Special Reserve, on 3 January 1916. His formal pilot training duly completed, he was confirmed and gazetted Flying Officer on 17 June following. Posted first to Home Defence duties with the BE2c-equipped 36 Squadron. On the night of 27/28 November 1916, Turner was positioning himself to attack Zeppelin *L34* over Hartlepool when a Squadron colleague, Second Lieutenant I V Pyott, beat him to the punch and sent the giant machine down in flames into the sea one mile off the mouth of the River Tees. Posted to 55 Squadron (DH4s) in France in the summer of 1917, he claimed two victories on 13 August, before transferring to 57 Squadron, also equipped with DH4s, in the following month. The intrepid leader of many photo-operational and reconnaissance flights, his MC was announced in the *London Gazette* of 26 September 1917, details in the *Gazette* of 9 January 1918: 'For conspicuous gallantry and devotion to duty as leader of long distance bombing raids and on photographic reconnaissances. He has taken part in many successful operations, in 24 of which he acted as leader, and by his skill and determination has invariably done good work in spite of very adverse weather, and though more than once attacked by enemy formations in greatly superior numbers to his own. He was the first officer to carry out a single machine long distance reconnaissance successfully, and has more than once been congratulated for the excellence of his photographic work'.

Turner went on to gain a further five victories with '57' between 1 April and 8 August 1918 and, almost inevitably, the award of the Distinguished Flying Cross came in the *London Gazette* of 2 November 1918, this mainly for leading an outstandingly successful raid into enemy territory. He was also Mentioned in Despatches on two occasions during the Great War, *London Gazettes* of 25 January 1917 and 2 November 1918. On 8 August 1918, Turner and his Observer, Canadian Second Lieutenant H S Musgrove, in DH4, 'D8398', were attacked by a DVII over Moislains. In the ensuing scrap, Turner received very slight injuries whilst Musgrove escaped unscathed. Despite this, on the following day, Turner was sufficiently recovered to take Lieutenant H E W Bryning up in DH4, 'D8428', for some dual instruction. The landing was a disaster, the machine hitting a tree and putting both crewmen into hospital. Turner subsequently relinquished his commission in 1920, due to ill-health. Returning to his studies at Magdalen College, Cambridge, he would, in time, become Director of Music Studies there. When the Second War came in September 1939, he immediately applied to serve in the RAFVR.

TWIST, Thomas Kenyon

The son of Ironfounder Joseph Theakestone Twist and Mrs Twist, of Heaton Terrace, Glasgow, Scotland, and later of 10 Eden Mount, Carlisle, he was born 26 August 1895. Educated at Carlisle Grammar School (1908-10) and at Shrewsbury (1910-14), Cricket XI. After completing his education, he worked in the Grain Trade before being gazetted Second Lieutenant to the New Armies on 15 March 1915, with an immediate attachment to 14 Battalion, Durham Light Infantry. Accompanying his unit to France on 11 September 1915, he served in the trenches before being seconded to the RFC in the autumn of 1916. Having trained as an Observer, he was confirmed and gazetted Flying Officer (Observer) on 16 October 1916. He next trained as a Pilot, gaining his Royal Aero Club Certificate (Number 4608) on 27 April 1917, and was given his full 'Wings' and confirmed Flying Officer on the same day. Twist served on the RE8s of 16 Squadron from 23 June 1917, until completing his tour on 3 April 1918, before returning to the Home Establishment, where he saw out the war. His MC was announced in the *London Gazette* of 22 June 1918: 'For conspicuous gallantry and devotion to duty. On several occasions he has successfully carried out observations on hostile batteries, has under the most adverse weather conditions bombed and engaged with machine-gun fire hostile troops and transport, and has on twelve occasions, fought and driven away superior numbers of enemy machines, two of which he succeeded in bringing down out of control. He has at all times set a most magnificent example of dash and daring, and has accomplished most valuable and successful work'.

He was also Mentioned in Despatches, *London Gazette* of 20 May 1918. Twist finally left the RAF, via the Unemployed List, on 10 February 1919. He returned to the Grain Trade, which took him, in time, to Argentina, before going to live and work as a Coffee Planter at Kitumamba, Kiambu, Kenya. Twist served again in the Second World War as a Flight Lieutenant, RAFVR, with postings to Egypt, Madagascar and other parts of East Africa, for which he was Mentioned in Despatches, *London Gazette* of 14 January 1944. He resigned his commission, retaining his rank of Flight Lieutenant, on 8 September 1945. Twist later served as a Police Inspector during the Mau Mau campaign in Kenya, receiving the African General Service Medal 1899-1956, with clasp, Kenya. He was also awarded the Efficiency Service Medal, with clasp, Kenya in July 1955.

NB: His medals were offered for sale by Spink in July 2000.

TYLER, Alfred John

The youngest son of Commercial Traveller, Alfred Tyler and Annie L Tyler, of 3 Aldborough Gardens, Ilford, Essex, he was born on 25 March 1897. Educated in London, including Trinity College, London (1908-13). Gazetted Second Lieutenant to the Royal Field Artillery on 28 September 1915. Seconded to the RFC early in 1917, he trained as an Observer and was formally gazetted Flying Officer (Observer) on 12 May 1917. Served with the RE of 6 Squadron in France. On 9 October 1917, he and his Pilot, Lieutenant N W Wadham, in RE8, 'A3675', narrowly escaped with their lives when their machine was hit in mid-air by a British shell. Forced to land near to Hooge, Wadham managed to get them down without further mishap. Tyler, luckily, was unscathed in the incident. His tour with '6' completed, he returned to the Home Establishment in December 1917, where he saw out the war as an Instructor. His solid, if unspectacular, work was acknowledged with the award of an MC, announced in the *London Gazette* of 18 January 1918, details in the *Gazette* of 25 April 1918: 'For conspicuous gallantry and devotion to duty. He took an active part in several engagements. He went up in all weathers and located many enemy batteries. He showed splendid determination and resource when under heavy fire'.

Tyler finally left the RAF, via the Unemployed List, in March 1919.

TYRRELL, Walter Alexander

One of the three sons of Alderman John Tyrrell, High Sheriff of Belfast, and Mrs Tyrrell, of Ballyholme, County Down, Ireland, he was born in Belfast on 28 August 1898. Educated at the College of St Columbia, Dublin, and at the Municipal Technical Institute, Belfast, where he studied Motor Engineering. Walter's brother, William, became Air Vice-Marshal Sir William Tyrrell, KBE, DSO, MC, etc., who served in the Great War as Regimental Medical Officer of a battalion of the Lancashire Fusiliers, before later transferring to the Medical Branch of the RAF. His other brother, John Marcus, was killed in a flying accident at 1 ASD on 20 June 1918. Walter served first as a Petty Officer Mechanic, RNAS, in Commander Sansom's Armoured Car Squadron, from 26 November 1914 until 24 November 1915. Picked out for a commission, he was gazetted Second Lieutenant to the RFC on 21 June 1917. His formal training duly completed, he was confirmed and gazetted Flying Officer on 30 August following. Sent out to the DH5-equipped 32 Squadron in France soon after qualifying, he gained five victories between 30 October and 5 December 1917. In the New Year of 1918, '32' re-equipped with SE5As, which machine obviously suited Tyrrell very well, as he gained a further 12 victories, including three 'trios' on single days, between 7 April and 6 June 1918. On 9 June 1918, Tyrrell, in SE5A, 'B8391.B', was returning from a patrol when his machine rolled and, inexplicably, dived into the ground. It was suggested afterwards that he may have been hit by machine-gun fire from the ground. His MC was posthumously announced in the *London Gazette* of 16 September 1918: 'For conspicuous gallantry and devotion to duty. On one day this officer attacked two enemy triplanes destroying one and driving down the other out of control. After this he was attacked by two other machines, one of which he forced to land, taking the occupants prisoners. On various other occasions he has destroyed or driven down out of control enemy machines'.

Walter Tyrrell is buried in Beauvais Communal Cemetery, Oise, France.

TYSON, Eric James

The only son of Joseph and Annie Tyson, of 4 Balham Park Road, Balham, Surrey, he was born on 17 March 1892. Educated at Westminster School (1905-10). After leaving school he trained as a Motor Engineer. When war came in August 1914, he immediately enlisted as a Private soldier into the Army Service Corps (Motor Transport). After service in France with the Army Service Corps, he was picked out for a commission and gazetted Second Lieutenant to the RFC, via the General List, on 5 August 1915. Gained his Royal Aero Club Certificate (Number 1710) on 9 September 1915. His formal training duly completed, he was confirmed and gazetted Flying Officer on 25 November following. Sent out to 12 Squadron in France on 28 December 1915, he specialised in photo-reconnaissance. Promoted to A/Captain and Flight Commander on 23 June 1916. On 7 September 1916, Tyson led a highly successful bombing raid on the enemy aerodromes at Valenciennes and La Briquette. Heavy cloud totally obscured the ground for much of the way, yet, despite this considerable difficulty, Tyson still led his formation, purely by compass, straight to the targets. His MC was announced in the *London Gazette* of 20 October 1916: 'For conspicuous gallantry and skill during bombing raids. Descending to about 300 feet under heavy fire of all descriptions, he succeeded in wrecking a train. Whilst doing this he was attacked by other hostile machines, which he beat off with the assistance of Lieutenant Philpott [qv] in another machine. Although wounded and with the engine severely damaged he attacked with Lieutenant Philpott, a group of men who were endeavouring to start a hostile machine, and scattered them in all directions. His machine was riddled with bullets'.

In November 1916, his tour with '12' completed, he returned to the Home Establishment and a succession of instructing posts. Promoted to A/Major, he was next sent to command 5 Squadron in France on 16 May 1917. For his outstanding leadership, Tyson was awarded the Distinguished Service Order in the *London Gazette* of 26 September 1917, details in the *Gazette* of 9 January 1918. He was also Mentioned in Despatches on one occasion. He married around this time, Cora Florence Gladys Davies. On 11 March 1918, Tyson and his Observer of the day, Second Lieutenant B Bidmead, Sherwood Foresters attached RFC, in RE8, 'C5096', were attacked and shot up during an artillery observation patrol over Arras, probably by Gottfried Sielemann of Jasta 57. Forced down to a crash-landing, Tyson died of his wounds later on the same day. Bidmead, although wounded and injured, fortunately survived. Major Eric Tyson is buried in Maroeuil British Cemetery, France.

TYSSEN, John Hugh Samuel

The son of Hugh S Tyssen and Mrs Tyssen, of Hylsbroke, Langford, near Bristol, he was born on 20 June 1889. Educated at Wellington College (1903-08). He married in 1914, Sydney Mary Gill, with whom he had one son. A pre-war volunteer, he had been commissioned into the North Somerset Yeomanry by the time war came in August 1914. Mobilised immediately, he accompanied his regiment to France on 3 November 1914, thus earning the 1914 Star. Seconded to the RFC in the spring of 1915, he trained as an Observer and was sent out as such to 3 Squadron in France. On 5 May 1915, Tyssen and his Pilot of the day, Captain G F Pretyman, in Morane L, '1849', forced down what they described as a Fokker Parasol (actually a two-seater A111) into a ploughed field near to Lille. On 29 August following, he was hit in the leg by shrapnel whilst flying over the same area of Lille. Once recovered, he took flying lessons, gaining his Royal Aero Club Certificate (Number 1624) on 20 August 1915. His formal training duly completed, he was confirmed and gazetted Flying Officer on 16 September following. On 1 April 1916, Tyssen accompanied FE2b-equipped 22 Squadron to France as a 'founder member' and Flight Commander. On 25 August, Tyssen and his Observer, Lieutenant S H Clarke (qv), in FE2b, '4289', were forced to land after their fuel tank was holed during a combat with two Fokkers over Combles. Fortunately, neither crewman was injured. His MC was announced in the *London Gazette* of 14 November 1916: 'For conspicuous skill and gallantry. He has done fine work in photography, often fighting against odds in order to get his work done. On one occasion, when five enemy machines interfered with our patrol, he with another officer, dived at one and brought it down'.

The action referred to in his MC citation is noted in the Official History, 'The War in the Air' : 'Five FE's of 22 Sqd were fighting an equal enemy formation at the same time over Bus, south of Bertincourt with greater success. Without loss to themselves they shot down one which crashed into a telegraph line, another which fell and overturned near the wood of St Pierre Vaast and two others were last seen in steep dives close to the ground'.

His tour with '22' completed, he returned to the Home Establishment in October 1916. Promoted to A/Major, he was next appointed to the command of 58 Squadron, eventually taking that FE2b-equipped night bombing unit to France on 10 January 1918. He remained in command of '58' until July 1918 when he returned to the UK and Staff duties. Staying on in the RAF after the war, his many appointments, postings and honours included : command of 20 Squadron in India, 1920-23.; Wing Commander, 1923; SAFO, HMS *Argus*, 1928-30; Group Captain, 1931; in command at Gosport, 1931-35; SASO, HQ, Fighting Area, 1935-36; Air Commodore, 1935; AOC, 12 Group, 1937; AOA, Iraq, 1937; Air Vice-Marshal, 1938; AOC, British Forces in Iraq, 1938-39; AOC, 16 Group, RAF, Chatham, 1940-41; CB, 1941. Tyssen retired from the RAF in 1942. Appointed to take charge of North East Civil Defence Region, 1942-45. Lived in retirement at Petertavy Lodge, Near Tavistock, Devon. Air Vice-Marshal Tyssen died on 4 January 1953.

NB: Tyssen's medals were offered for sale by Christie's (lot 132) on 22 March 1988: CB (Military Division), MC (engraved: Capt J H S Tyssen, RFC photography, The Somme 1916, North Somerset Yeomanry*), 1914 Star with Bar* (Capt N Som Yeo)*, British War Medal 1914-20, Victory Medal 1914-19* (Major RAF)*, India General Service Medal 1908-35, with clasp, Waziristan 1919-21* (S/L RAF)*, Defence Medal 1939-45, War Medal 1939-45 with MID, Jubilee Medal 1935, and Coronation Medal 1937.*

U

UMNEY, John Howard

The only son of Mr and Mrs John Charles Umney, of 27a Sloane Square, Chelsea, London, he was born on 11 April 1898. Umney's father was an important figure in the Pharmaceutical world and Director of a number of leading Pharmaceutical companies, Silver Medallist of the Royal Society of Arts, Fellow of the Royal Chemical Society, Fellow of the Royal Horticultural Society, and Fellow of the Society of Public Analysts. John junior was educated at Charterhouse. A research chemist, he was a married man and living at 35 Northcourt Road, Reading, when he was gazetted Second Lieutenant to the RFC, via the General List, on 3 January 1918. Having trained as an Observer, he was sent out as such to the Bristol F2b-equipped 22 Squadron in France on 11 April 1918. A highly successful Observer/Ace, he achieved no less than 13 victories between 6 May and 25 August 1918, including two 'doubles' on single days. On 20 May 1918, Umney and his Pilot, Second Lieutenant C H Dunster, in BF2b, 'C4747', narrowly escaped death when their machine was forced to crash after being hit by anti-aircraft fire. His MC was announced in the *London Gazette* of 16 September 1918: 'For conspicuous gallantry and devotion to duty. During recent operations he destroyed five enemy machines. By his untiring energy and keenness, both in the air and on the ground, he set a splendid example to other Observers in the squadron, and greatly helped his pilot in successful encounters'.

After suffering a period of ill health, he returned to the Home Establishment on 5 September 1918, where he saw out the remaining weeks of the war. He finally left the RAF on 17 January 1919. John Umney died in Reading on 14 August 1934. He left a widow, Maude Louise, and two children; a third child was born soon after his death.

UPFILL, Thomas Henry

The son of Bank Manager John Marsall Howey Upfill and Una Grace Upfill, of 88a Cromwell Road, London SW, and later of 'Pasturehill', Luscastes Avenue, Hayward's Heath, Sussex, he was born on 16 July 1897. Educated at Repton School (1912-14). Gazetted Second Lieutenant to the Royal Field Artillery, via the Special Reserve, on 11 May 1916. Seconded to the RFC early in 1917, he trained as an Observer and was subsequently confirmed and gazetted Flying Officer (Observer) on 16 March following. Sent out to 59 Squadron (RE8s) on 8 May 1917. On 27 March 1918, Upfill and his Pilot, Lieutenant E G Leake (qv), were attacked by an enemy Scout. Their robust response, including more than 100 rounds being fired into the enemy machine, disabled its engine and caused it to crash south of Serre. The same crew were fortunate on 28 March, when their RE8, 'D4686', was hit by machine-gun fire and forced down to crashland near to Collincamp. Both men were unscathed and even managed to salvage their instruments and other equipment before destroying the remains of their machine. Upfill's MC was announced in the *London Gazette* of 22 June 1918: 'On one occasion, observing a hostile scout, he at once attacked and fired 1,000 rounds at close range. The hostile plane went down in a steep glide and crashed to earth. Later, when on contact patrol, his machine was damaged and forced to land just behind our lines. Although under heavy shell fire, he, assisted by another officer, succeed in salving all the instruments and equipment on the machine before destroying it. He has set a very high example of courage and devotion to duty during the recent operations'.

He next trained as a Pilot and returned to '59' as such on 12 October 1918, only to be killed just six days later. On 18 October 1918, Upfill and his Observer of the day, Lieutenant John Cyril Walker from Hull, in RE8, 'D4909', were shot down and killed in action over Solesnes by Leutnant Heinrich Henkel of Jasta 37, the sixth of the German Ace's eventual eight victories. Thomas Upfill is buried in Caudry British Cemetery, France.

USHER, Robert Howell Craster

The son of the Reverend Robert Usher and Alice Mabel Usher (née Edwards), of 2 Church Hill, East Knoyle, Wiltshire, he was born in Wareham, Dorset, in 1896. Educated at Shrewsbury (1910-14). Gazetted Second Lieutenant to 3 (Reserve) Battalion, Wiltshire Regiment, on 15 August 1914. Seconded to the RFC early in 1916, he trained as a Pilot and was duly confirmed and gazetted Flying Officer on 10 May following. Sent out to 27 Squadron (Martinsyde G100s) in France shortly after qualifying for his 'Wings'. Soon involved with 27 Squadron's heavy schedule of bombing raids into enemy territory. On 31 July 1916, Usher, in Martinsyde '7282', was embarked upon a raid on Marcoing when he became separated from his squadron colleagues. His retrospective report gives a detailed account of what happened next: 'The patrol seemed to break up just as we were crossing the Lines. As I didn't see any signals to return, and as I had a Sopwith [70 Squadron Sopwith Strutter as escort] with me, I went on to Marcoing and dropped my bombs, both of which fell in the village. I turned quickly round and almost ran into an LVG. I gave him a drum (of Lewis gun ammunition) and he went down under me. I saw the Sopwith take him on and whilst I was changing drums I was attacked in front by a Roland. I gave him a drum and at the same time heard a machine gun behind me, looked around and saw three Rolands on my tail. I was hit in the leg almost immediately but managed to give him a drum of my side gun and they went away. My engine started spluttering and I saw a hole in my petrol tank, my engine stopped so I started gliding down thinking I should have to land. Petrol was flowing all over my left leg so I put my left knee over the hole in the petrol tank. It struck me that by pumping I might be able to get up a little pressure. By this time I was about 200 feet up, the engine started and I was 15 miles from our Lines. I kept pumping hard all the time and managed to keep just enough engine going. I thought I would have to land, but my engine picked up in time three or four times. I came back to the lines for about 15 miles at an average height of 50 feet. I had lost myself and was so low that I could see very little of the country. I then picked up a (Farman) French biplane that was flying low and followed him and eventually landed at Moreuill aerodrome, crashing the machine on landing, I was feeling very weak as I had lost a lot of blood and was exhausted by having to pump for so long. After having engaged the first (enemy) machine I did not see anything of the Sopwith. During the time that I was flying low I was subjected to a lot of rifle and machine-gun fire'. His MC was announced in the *London Gazette* of 25 August 1916: 'For conspicuous gallantry and devotion to duty in attacking three hostile machines and driving them off. On another occasion he fought five hostile machines, and although hit in the leg, continued to fight till his engine stopped. He succeeded under great difficulties in reaching an aerodrome, where he collapsed through loss of blood'.

Once recovered, he was mainly employed as an Instructor and Test Pilot in the UK. His efforts in these fields were recognised by the award of an Air Force Cross, *London Gazette* of 2 November 1918. Usher represented England in Rugby Union International matches. He was killed on 5 June 1924 at Northolt aerodrome, whilst testing a de Haviland Dormouse (J7005),

V

VACHELL, Charles Theodore

The son of Mr and Mrs T Vachell, of St Gwnlliw, Newport, Monmouthshire, he was born on 21 March 1896. His brother John (qv) also won an MC with the RFC. Educated at Repton School (1909-13). Both brothers volunteered their services on the same day. Charles was gazetted Second Lieutenant to 1 Battalion, Monmouthshire Regiment (TF), on 29 August 1914. Served in the trenches with 1/1 Monmouths from 13 February 1915, before eventually being seconded to the RFC in the autumn of 1916. His pilot training duly completed, he was confirmed and gazetted Flying Officer on 31 January 1917. Joined 4 Squadron in France on 14 March 1917, his tour extending to 16 December following, being promoted to A/Captain and Flight Commander on the intervening 3 July. His MC was announced in the *London Gazette* of 26 October 1917, details in the *Gazette* of 7 March 1918: 'He performed continuous good work on contact patrols and reconnaissance, flying at a low altitude. On one occasion in a very strong gale, flying low, he obtained information of the greatest importance'.

Returning to the UK at the end of 1917, subsequently served with 106 Squadron (RE8s) at Andover and in Ireland. One blot only occurred on his record when he was severely censured by the GOC, South West Area, on 24 October 1918, for a badly conducted Court Martial for which he was responsible. He was, however, subsequently Mentioned in Despatches in the *London Gazette* of 29 August 1919. A trained engineer, he lived post-war at Rockmount, Weston-super-Mare.

VACHELL, John Lyne (later Group Captain, RAF)

The son of Mr and Mrs T Vachell of St Gwnlliw, Newport, Monmouthshire, he was born on 12 June 1892. Educated at Repton School (1905-09). His brother, Charles (qv), also won an MC with the RFC. John was gazetted Second Lieutenant to 2 Monmouthshire Battery, Royal Field Artillery (TF), on 29 August 1914, the brothers having volunteered on the same day. After service with the Gunners in France and Flanders during 1915 and 1916, he was seconded to the RFC in August 1916. His formal pilot training duly completed, he was confirmed and gazetted Flying Officer on 27 November following. Flew with 15 Squadron (BE2c), being promoted to A/Captain and Flight Commander in July 1917. His MC was announced in the *London Gazette* of 25 April 1918: 'For conspicuous gallantry and devotion to duty. He did excellent work on many occasions, continually locating and engaging successfully enemy heavy batteries'.

Staying on in the RAF after the war, he commanded 5 Squadron briefly in 1919 and subsequently served in Waziristan 1919-20; attended the Staff College, Quetta, 1921; RAF Staff College, 1930-33; and served on the Air Staff in Iraq as a Wing Commander in 1933. Became a Group Captain on 1 January 1938.

Van der BEN, Reginald Charles

The son of Mercantile Clerk, Charles K Van der Ben and Lydia M Van der Ben, of 62 Cunard Road, Hammersmith, London. He enlisted as a Private soldier (105531) into the Army Ordnance Corps in 1914. He served subsequently with the AOC in the Middle East, with the rank of Sergeant. Picked out for a commission, he was gazetted Second Lieutenant to the RFC late in 1917. He trained as an Observer at RFC HQ, Egypt, and was sent out as such to 142 Squadron in the Eastern Mediterranean. Attached to 14 Squadron, Van der Ben was wounded in action on 4 May 1918, during his operations in Palestine. His MC was announced in the *London Gazette* of 24 September 1918: 'For conspicuous gallantry and devotion to duty. When on contact patrol this officer was severely wounded in the leg from the ground. Notwithstanding this, he continued his offensive action, machine-gunning the enemy troops, and told his pilot to carry on, thus enabling him to complete his reconnaissance'.

Once recovered, he returned to operational duties with '142' in February 1918. His Distinguished Flying Cross, was announced in the *London Gazette* of 8 February 1919 (Egypt), in recognition of invaluable reconnaissance work and his readiness 'to volunteer for any service requiring quick initiative and daring'.

Van der SPUY, Kenneth Reid

From Pretoria, South Africa, he was born in Stellenbosch, on 18 March 1892. As a boy he watched as the British marched into Pretoria under Field Marshal Lord Roberts VC. He first learnt to fly at Kimberley, South Africa, in 1913. When the South African Defence Forces decided to form an aviation section, he responded to an advertisement seeking volunteer 'officer aviators' and subsequently reported to the Paterson Aviation Syndicate's airfield at Kimberley. The rather dodgy machine used to teach the men to fly, the Paterson Bi-Plane, played only a brief part in the embryonic airmen's education before, with Paterson himself and Van der Spuy aboard, going into an uncontrollable side-slip and dashing itself into fragments. Fortunately, the occupants were unhurt. Travelling to the UK, he next gained his Royal Aero Club Certificate (Number 803) on a Maurice Farman at the CFS, Upavon, on 2 June 1914. Attached to the RFC, he accompanied the original contingent to France in August 1914 as a Pilot with 2 Squadron. Meanwhile, in South Africa, Generals Botha and Smuts planned to invade German West Africa in order to neutralise the ports of Walvis Bay and Swakopmund, as well as take out a number of enemy wireless stations. The South African airmen were recalled and a South African Aviation Corps formed. By May 1915, they were organised and operational and playing their part in forcing the German surrender which came in July 1915. Van der Spuy and his fellow Springboks next returned to the UK, there forming 26 Squadron. However, it was not long before they were needed in Africa and consequently were ordered next to German East, in the area of Kilimanjaro, landing at Mombasa in January 1916, before going up-country. The detachment operated from a strip in the wilds of Africa known as 'Daniels Den' because of the large number of lions that roamed in the area. His MC was announced in the *London Gazette* of 20 October 1916 (South African Contingent): 'For conspicuous gallantry and skill. He flew for 4½ hours under dangerous climatic conditions, and brought back information of great value'.

He was also Mentioned in Despatches at this time. In 1917, Van der Spuy returned to the UK and was given command of 77 Squadron, a HD unit charged with guarding Edinburgh and the surrounding area. He next commanded Training Wings at Castle Bromwich and at Shoreham. As the war drew to a conclusion, Van der Spuy was appointed to command an air wing of an expeditionary force sent, initially, to north Russia to fight alongside the White Russians and the Czechs in preventing the Germans establishing submarine bases at Archangel and Murmansk. The war with Germany over, the expeditionary force remained to aid the White Russian cause against the Bolsheviks. On 14 April 1919, The engine of Van der Spuy's Camel gave up over the Viga River and he was obliged to crashland. After a difficult time attempting to get back to his own lines, he was taken captive by the Reds on 26 April. Taken to Moscow, he was imprisoned and treated like a common criminal, expecting to be executed at any time. In 1920, after 15 months of captivity and following a prisoner exchange, he was able to return to South Africa. He married Una, with whom he had three sons. In 1921, he was appointed Chief SO of the new SAAF, going on to hold various senior appointments until 1938, when he was posted to the South African High Commission in London as Military Advisor. Returning to South Africa in 1941, he became the Director of Technical Services, SAAF, until retiring at the end of the war with the rank of Major General. Awarded the CBE in 1946. Settling on his farm, 'Old Nectar', at Jonkershoek, he wrote poetry and a number of books, including an autobiography, 'Chasing the Wind' in 1960. Major General Kenneth Van der Spuy died on 26 May 1991.

Van RYNEVELD, Helperus Andrias

The son of D J Van Ryneveld JP and Mrs Van Ryneveld, of Theunnissen, Orange Free State, South Africa, he was born on 2 May 1891. Educated at Grey College School at Grey University College, South Africa, from where he graduated BA, and Imperial College, London, from where he graduated BSc (Eng). Gazetted Second Lieutenant to 7 Loyal North Lancashire Regiment on 9 September 1914. Seconded to the RFC in April 1915, he gained his Royal Aero Club Certificate (Number 1318) on 21 June following. His formal pilot training duly completed, he was confirmed and gazetted Flying Officer on 16 July 1915. Sent out to RFC HQ, Egypt in October 1915, he was eventually sent on to 17 Squadron. Van Ryneveld's MC was announced in the Birthday Honours *London Gazette* of 3 June 1916 (no citation).

The Egyptians also bestowed the Order of the Nile, 4th Class, upon him at this time. On 18 June 1916, Van Ryneveld in BE2c, '2691', was forced to land on a beach after his engine had been damaged by ground fire. Squadron colleagues Captain S Grant-Dalton and Lieutenant D K Paris (qv) in BE2c, '2700', brought their BE down alongside the stranded van Ryneveld. Following a number of unsuccessful attempts to take off from the surrounding soft sand, the three men hauled the machine on to firmer ground, from where they eventually got airborne, having first destroyed the abandoned BE. Grant-Dalton, who would go on to high rank in the RNZAF, received the first of his two Distinguished Service Orders for this incident. Paris received the MC. Van Ryneveld accompanied '17' to Salonika at the end of June 1916, serving on this front until the following November when he returned to the UK. Promoted to A/Major, Van Ryneveld was sent out to France to command 45 Squadron in April 1917. On 18 August 1917, Van Ryneveld in Sopwith Camel, 'B3871', was himself shot up and wounded in the head whilst attacking an enemy two-seater. This, in fact, was the first casualty suffered by the squadron since it had acquired Camels. He was Mentioned in Despatches on no less than six occasions during the Great War and, interestingly, research has unearthed the original recommendation for one of these: '(MID Oct 1917): Joined the BEF in April 1917 after considerable flying service in the East, and took command of a Squadron which had suffered severely in the Battle of the Somme. His personal skill and daring soon raised his Squadron to the very first rank of fighter squadrons. A very strong personality combined with sound knowledge make him a very valuable officer who has done excellent service. On 18 August 1917 he was severely wounded in combat with enemy aircraft'.

His leadership qualities were further acknowledged when he was awarded the Distinguished Service Order, *London Gazette* of 1 January 1919. He was also honoured by the French with the Chevalier, Légion d'Honneur and by the Belgians with the Croix d'Officier de l'Ordre de Leopold and the Croix de Guerre. After service in Germany with the Army of Occupation, Van Ryneveld, by then a Lieutenant Colonel, acted as Liaison Officer between the SAAF and the RAF. He also made a number of pioneering flights at this time, including, in 1920, London to Cape Town via Cairo. His subsequent honours, postings and appointments included: KBE (Military Division), 1920, knighted for his flight to Cape Town with Sir Joseph Quintin Brand (qv), DSO, MC, DFC and adopting the preferred name, 'Sir Pierre'; Colonel and Director, South African Air Force from 1921; Director, Union of South African Air Force, Pretoria; Commandant SA Military College; OC Troops, Robert's Heights, 1929; Chairman, Civil Air Board, South Africa; and Fellow, Imperial College of Science. Lived in retirement at Spitzkop, Bronkhorstspruit, Transvaal, South Africa. Brigadier General Sir Pierre Van Ryneveld died on 2 December 1972.

VARLEY, Eric Ralph

The youngest of the three sons of Accountant, Jesse Varley and Katherine Jane Varley (née McKee), of 'Longleat', Paget Road, Wolverhampton, Staffordshire, he was born on 19 January 1899. Gazetted Second Lieutenant to the RFC on 19 July 1917. Gained his Royal Aero Club Certificate (Number 5660) on 26 September 1917 and was confirmed and gazetted Flying Officer just two days later on 28 September. Sent out to 23 Squadron on 31 October 1917. On 24 March 1918, at the height of the German spring offensive, Varley was slightly wounded in the shoulder. Despite this, he was in the air again on 29 March, this time, in Spad VII, 'B6731', when his engine was shot up and, following a hurried landing, his aircraft was burnt. Just eight days later, his Spad XIII, 'B6878', was hit by anti-aircraft fire over Domart, forcing him to land, wounded in the arm, south of Amiens. His MC was announced in the *London Gazette* of 22 June 1918: 'For conspicuous gallantry and devotion to duty. Observing two enemy two-seater machines, he, by skilful piloting, obtained a position under the tail of one and opened fire at close range, with the result that the hostile machine fell out of control and crashed. On two later occasions he attacked and destroyed two other hostile machines, the pilot of one being taken prisoner. He has also shown great dash in attacking enemy balloons and hostile troops on the march, and has displayed marked gallantry throughout'.

His wounds were such that he was obliged to relinquish his commission, with the rank of Lieutenant, on 22 October 1918. Varley was known to be living in Sheffield in 1922. When the Second World War came, he applied for service in the RAFVR on 1 June 1940. He was living at that time in Girvan, Ayrshire, Scotland.

VAUCOUR, Awry Morris

The only son of the Reverend H M Vaucour and Mrs Vaucour, of 71 Belverede Road, Norwood, London SE, he was born at Topcliffe, Yorkshire, on 8 March 1890. Educated at City and Guilds College and was a member of the University of London OTC. Gazetted Second Lieutenant to the Royal Field Artillery on 24 March 1915. Seconded to the RFC, he trained as an Observer and was sent out as such to BE2c-equipped 10 Squadron in the autumn of 1915. Flying mainly with Captain R G Gould (qv), he was kept busy throughout the fraught days of the Fokker menace, although the first of his MCs was won in company with Captain Rabagliati (qv), *London Gazette* of 4 November 1915: 'For conspicuous gallantry and skill on 28 Sept 1915, when, accompanied by Capt Rabagliati, they carried out a reconnaissance over Valenciennes and Douai. They had to fly in thick cloud for nearly the whole distance, and several times their aeroplane got into a 'spin'. The Pilot, however, succeeded each time in righting his machine and they reached their objective and carried out the reconnaissance at 2,800 feet under heavy fire'.

Vaucour next trained as a Pilot, gaining his Royal Aero Club Certificate (Number 2765) on 10 April 1916. His formal training duly completed, he was confirmed and gazetted Flying Officer on 6 May following. Accompanied 70 Squadron (Sopwith Strutters) to France in the summer of 1916. On 24 August 1916, Vaucour and his Observer of the day, Lieutenant A J Bott (qv), in Strutter, 'A890', were on patrol south west of Cambrai when their machine was hit by anti-aircraft fire. Part of the fuselage was set alight and Bott tore at it with his hands to quench the flames before the fire could spread. To add to their woes they were attacked on the way home by three enemy machines but Bott performed wonders in keeping them at bay before they were forced to land short of their base. Bott duly received the MC for his bravery and skill. Perhaps a shade optimistically, Offizierstellvertreter Leopold Rudolf Reimann claimed Vaucour's Strutter as the first of his eventual five victories. On the following day, Vaucour took an Observer with him, 1 AM Henry Percy Warminger, a near Geordie from Jarrow-on-Tyne, to recover the crash-landed Strutter. After effecting some repairs, the pair took off. The jinxed Strutter was hit again by anti-aircraft fire and Warminger was mortally wounded. Vaucour somehow managed to nurse the damaged machine home where his desperately wounded passenger was lifted out and taken to hospital, dying later that same evening. On 2 September following, Vaucour and Bott claimed two Fokker Es on the same day. The same pair claimed another Fokker on 15 September. The Bar to Vaucour's MC came in the *London Gazette* of 25 November 1916: 'For conspicuous gallantry in action. He attacked ten hostile machines and completely scattered their formation. Previous, while returning with a perforated petrol tank, he shot down an enemy machine. Later, he shot down a hostile machine, being engaged with eight altogether. On another occasion, he and his observer shot down two hostile machines'.

His tour with '70' completed in January 1917, he returned to the Home Establishment and an instructing post at the CFS. By now a hugely experienced combat airman, Vaucour was promoted to Major and sent to command the Camel F1-equipped 45 Squadron in France on 22 August 1917. Three months later, on 17 November 1917, Vaucour led his squadron to the Italian front. Despite his status as a CO, Vaucour continued to involve himself in combat duties, adding a further four victories to his 'score' between 27 February and 25 June 1918. Vaucour was awarded the newly instituted Distinguished Flying Cross in the Birthday Honours *London Gazette* of 3 June 1918. On 16 July 1918, Vaucour in Camel, 'D8102', was shot down and killed in a 'friendly fire' incident when Lieutenant Alberto Moresco of the Italian Aviation Corps, mistook him for an enemy. With the blunt candour of the day, a letter from the Air Ministry, dated 1 August 1918, describing the circumstances of Vaucour's death, was sent to his mother: 'With reference to the death of your son who was reported from this office to have been killed in action in Italy on 16 July, I am writing to say that the particulars of his death have now reached this office under a covering letter sent by the direction of the OC, Italian Aviation. It appears that on the date mentioned, Alberto Moresco of the Italian Aviation was piloting a flying machine belonging to the 78 Squadron and was making a patrol. At about 9am when flying at high altitude, he saw approaching him in opposite direction but slightly higher, a machine of foreign make; as the sun was in his eyes he imagined he could distinctly see the black cross painted on the machine. Feeling certain that he encountered an enemy machine and was unobserved by the pilot, Lieutenant Moresco flew over the machine and making a right hand turn came down within 60 metres of the tail of the machine from whence he fired five rounds into it. The machine instantaneously looped and it was during the actual moment of looping that Lieut Moresco observed the English markings and realised his mistake. It appears that your son was fatally wounded and the machine dived and crashed to the ground. Lieutenant Moresco immediately reported his terrible mistake to his CO who communicated it to the GOC for transmission to the CO of the English troops in Italy. I have given you the information as nearly as possible verbatim as it has been received, leaving out only the names of the places. I think I need hardly say how deeply the loss of your son is felt by all concerned in Italy, more especially in view of the tragic circumstances under which it occurred. For political and other reasons, which I am sure you will appreciate, in sending you these details I would ask you to treat them as quite confidential, and not to communicate them in any way to other than members of your family, and may I myself, add an expression of deep sympathy in the loss you have sustained. Yours sincerely, W W Warner, Brigadier General'.

By way of gratitude and no doubt some contrition, the Italians awarded him the Silver Medaglia al Valore Militare, *London Gazette* of 2 November 1918, and the Gold Medal, Lega Area Nazionale, 1918. Awry Vacour is buried in Montecchio Precalcino Communal Cemetery Extension, Italy.

NB: His medals were offered for sale by Glendining's (lot 388) on 19 September 1989: MC & Bar, Distinguished Flying Cross, 1915 Star (2Lt RFA), *British War Medal 1914-20, Victory Medal 1914-19 with MID* (Major, RAF), *Medaglia al Valore Militare (Italy, reverse engraved:* Piave, Tretitino Inverno 1917-18 - Vaucour Awdry Morris*), Leega Area Nazionale Gold Medal (Italy,* Al Major RFC Awdry M Vaucour Valoroso Difensore Del Cielo D'Italia, 1918*).*

VAUGHAN, Ralph Montgomery

From County Down, Ireland, he was born on 24 September 1890. A Regular Army officer, he was gazetted Second Lieutenant to 2 Battalion, Royal Inniskilling Fusiliers in 1912. Developing an interest in aviation, he gained his Royal Aero Club Certificate (Number 417) on a Bristol machine at the Bristol School, Salisbury Plain, on 18 February 1913. Seconded to the RFC, he completed his formal training and was duly confirmed and gazetted Flying Officer on 18 December following. Accompanied the original RFC contingent to France in August 1914 as a member of 5 Squadron. When he arrived in France for the first time, it was via a forced landing near to Boulogne, well short of his intended destination. He was promptly arrested by the French police and imprisoned for five days, suspected of being a German spy. On 30 October 1914, Vaughan was acting as Observer to Major J F A Higgins, Royal Field Artillery and RFC, during a reconnaissance over Hollebeke- Houthem when Higgins was wounded by rifle fire from the ground. Fortunately, they were able to land safely. Just two days later on 1 November, Vaughan was the Pilot in MFSH, '633', with Lieutenant C E C Rabagliati (qv) in the observer's seat on a reconnaissance flight in the area of Oostlaverne-Hollebeke, when they were shot up and Vaughan was wounded. Rabagliati took over the controls and flew them home to a forced landing. Recovered, Vaughan was flying again with 4 Squadron when, on 17 April 1915, in BE2c, '1669', with Second Lieutenant J F Lascelles (qv) as Observer, they encountered an enemy Aviatik during a reconnaissance flight to Bruges. The Official History, 'War in the Air', describes events, thus: 'The officers were on their way to reconnoitre as far as Bruges when they met their enemy. The Observer fired twenty-four shots from an average range of eighty yards and the Aviatik fell in the French lines near Elvindinghe. The German pilot was found to be dead, but the observer, unwounded, was made prisoner. Vaughan waited over the area long enough to watch the German aeroplane crash, and then went on to Bruges'. Both men were Mentioned in Despatches, *London Gazette* of 22 June 1915, and awarded the MC in the *London Gazette* of 23 June 1915 (no citation). Vaughan, promoted to Major, would go on to command 5 Squadron (ten of the BE2c and two of the BE2d) at Droglandt during the Battle of the Somme in 1916. Returning to the Home Establishment, he next commanded 33 HD, 5 and 7 Squadrons from 5 October 1916 until November 1916. He left the RFC to revert to his regiment, the 'Skins', on 7 September 1917. Ralph Vaughan died on 9 September 1976.

VERNON, Leslie Gottfried Harcourt

The son of a Merchant, C J Vernon, and Mrs Vernon of Drenham, South Wales, he was born in Colobra, Bombay, India, on 19 April 1898. Gazetted Second Lieutenant to a Regular Army battalion of the Royal Welsh Fusiliers on 22 December 1915. Seconded to the RFC, he trained as an Observer and was duly sent out as a Probationary to FE2b-equipped 23 Squadron in France. His 'apprenticeship' satisfactorily completed, he was confirmed and gazetted Flying Officer (Observer) on 26 July 1916. On the following day, the formal announcement of his MC was announced in the *London Gazette*: 'For conspicuous gallantry and skill. With Captain Adams [qv] as pilot he attacked a flight of six enemy machines within their lines. They brought down one in flames, and, after being joined by a second British machine, drove off the remainder, one falling out of control. He has previously done fine work'.

On 11 September, Vernon, with his Pilot, Second Lieutenant Godfrey Benjamin Joseph Firbank from Wrington, Somerset, in FE2b, '4851', left their formation to dive upon an enemy machine but were then lost from sight, forever, as it transpired. Leslie Vernon's remains were never found and hence he is commemorated on the Flying Services Memorial, Arras, France.

VICKERS, Stephen Wynne

The son of Mr and Mrs Joseph Vickers of 'Ivy Nook', Bramhall Moor Lane, Hazel Grove, Stockport, Cheshire, he was born in Leeds in 1895. Educated at Stockport Grammar School and at Manchester University, where he was a member of the OTC. Gazetted Second Lieutenant to 11 Battalion, Cheshire Regiment, on 17 September 1914, with promotion to A/Lieutenant in the following month. Vickers was a 'founding member' of the 11 Cheshires whose combined efforts helped, despite great difficulties, in getting the battalion into shape. At the beginning, they had no proper uniforms, no washing facilities and poor quarters, yet, despite all this the unit was moulded into a fighting unit, able to be sent to France on 26 September 1915. Following service in the trenches, Vickers was seconded to the RFC in September 1916. Gained his Royal Aero Club Certificate (Number 6632) on 1 January 1917 and was formally gazetted Flying Officer on the same day. Accompanied the night bombing FE2b-equipped 101 Squadron to France on 25 July 1917. Despite suffering an injury on 1 October 1917, Vickers safely completed his exacting, if unspectacular tour, with '101' and returned to the Home Establishment on 31 May 1918. An award of the newly instituted Distinguished Flying Cross was announced in the Birthday Honours *London Gazette* of 3 June 1918. Vickers' MC was announced in the *London Gazette* of 22 June 1918: 'For conspicuous gallantry and devotion to duty. He has taken part in fifty-three night bombing raids on enemy aerodromes, billets and communications, flying at times in most unfavourable weather and in the face of intense rifle and machine-gun fire. On two occasions he made three flights in one night, reaching his objective on each occasion and doing considerable damage with direct hits. He has set a splendid example of courage and determination to the rest of the squadron'.

Following a period of instructing in the UK, Vickers fell victim to the influenza pandemic raging around the world at this time and died at No 4 General Military Hospital, Lincoln, on 18 February 1919. Stephen Vickers is buried in Norbury (St Thomas) Churchyard, Cheshire.

W

WALD, Alexander

The son of Mr and Mrs Alec Wald, of Hannay Street, Largs Bay, South Australia, he was born in Peterburg, South Australia, on 19 June 1893. A Railway Engineer and Surveyor with the South Australia Railway Depot, Adelaide, from June 1911, he had recently secured a position as a Draftsman with the Australian Defence Department when he enlisted into the AIF on 9 August 1914. Because of his occupation, he was discharged from the Divisional Ammunition Column to which he had been assigned and sent back to the Defence Department just a month later on 10 September. Nothing daunted, he re-enlisted on 10 December 1914. This time he accompanied, as a Gunner, 8 Australian Army Service Corps, 17 Divisional Ammunition Park, 301 Motor Transport Company, when they embarked on 22 December 1914 at Melbourne, boarding the SS *Ceramic* (Transport A 40), bound for the Middle East. Wald was subsequently wounded in action in Gallipoli on 28 June 1915. Once recovered, he was posted to ANZAC HQ on 23 October 1915. Following the evacuation, Wald was posted to 1 Division HQ on 21 April 1916. A volunteer for the flying service, he was gazetted Second Lieutenant to the RFC, via the Special Reserve, on 17 March 1917. His pilot training duly completed, he was confirmed and gazetted Flying Officer on 14 June following. Sent out to the night-bombing 100 Squadron in France on 10 July 1917. His MC was announced in the *London Gazette* of 4 March 1918, details in the *Gazette* of 16 August 1918: 'For conspicuous gallantry and devotion to duty. He carried out a large number of night bomb raids on enemy headquarters, aerodromes and railways with great success. Many of these flights were carried out in bad weather and at very low altitudes. On one occasion, though he had engine trouble and his radiator burst when he was over the enemy's lines, he continued his flight and bombed a railway station from 1,500 feet. He set a fine example of determination to his squadron'.

His tour with '100' completed on 31 March 1918, he returned to the UK and Home Defence duties with 36 Squadron. Wald suffered injuries in a flying accident that occurred on 3 July 1918. Having recovered, he was flying again on 11 August 1918, but was killed in yet another flying accident on that day. Alexander Wald is buried in Newcastle-upon-Tyne (St Andrew's and Jesmond Cemetery), Northumberland.

WALKER, Gerald Gladstone

From Dunham Massey, Altrincham, Cheshire, he was born on 10 May 1898. Educated at Bowden College, Cheshire (1911-15). Joined the Inns of Court OTC (Number 4/3/4688) on 8 July 1915, age 17. Picked out as an exceptional candidate, he was discharged for further training and assessment at the Royal Military College, Sandhurst, on 29 August 1916. Gazetted Second Lieutenant to the Loyal North Lancashire Regiment on 1 May 1917, with an immediate attachment to the RFC. His pilot training duly completed, he was confirmed and gazetted Flying Officer on 17 July following. Sent out to 35 Squadron on 22 September 1917, he served with that unit until returning to the Home Establishment on 1 August 1918, having been promoted A/Captain and Flight Commander on the intervening 26 April. He was Mentioned in Despatches in the *London Gazette* of 20 May 1918. His MC was announced in the *London Gazette* of 22 June 1918: 'On one occasion he assisted in an attack on enemy transport, dropping eight bombs and firing 300 rounds into its midst with the result that several limbers were completely destroyed and severe casualties inflicted on the enemy. Later in the same day he again attacked enemy transport, causing a stampede amongst the horses and inflicting many casualties. While returning to his aerodrome he attacked with machine-gun fire two hostile batteries in action, firing 400 rounds into their midst. His pluck and determination were beyond all praise'.

Walker finally resigned his commission on 1 August 1919. Lived in Margate during the 1930s and, by the time war came again in September 1939, he was a Wing Commander in the RAFVR. Served again before eventually retiring with the rank of Group Captain. Lived, post the Second World War, at 'Glenferry', Regent Road, Altrincham. Gerald Walker died on 5 November 1963.

WALKER, Henry Edward

The son of Dr and Mrs Walker of Leyton, Essex, he was born in Buenos Aires, Argentina, on 23 April 1897. Enlisted as a Private soldier (Number 762920) into 28 Battalion, London Regiment (Artists Rifles), before being gazetted Second Lieutenant to the RFC, via the General Lists, on 10 April 1917. His formal pilot training duly completed, he was confirmed and gazetted Flying Officer on 14 July following. Sent out to the newly formed 111 Squadron in Palestine. His MC, awarded for his gallantry at Kefr Saba Dier Ballut between 19 March and 10 April 1918, was announced in the *London Gazette* of 16 September 1918: 'For conspicuous gallantry and devotion to duty during many flights and encounters in the air, when often single-handed he was most successful in bringing down enemy machines, and invariably displayed the utmost skill and resolution. He has been engaged in 14 combats, which have either been decisive or have resulted in enemy aircraft being driven down to a low height, and he has on occasions gone up as many as five times in one day'.

Walker was also awarded the Distinguished Flying Cross in the *London Gazette* of 8 February 1919 (Egypt), this for outstanding service on this front for 12 months during which time he brought down several enemy machines and bombed targets with great accuracy. Staying on in the RAF after the war, he served as a Flight Lieutenant with the RAF Armoured Cars in Transjordan in the 1920s. He later served with 45 Squadron at Helwan in 1930 and as a Squadron Leader with 502 Squadron in 1933. Joined the Air Staff at the Air Ministry and was promoted to Wing Commander in 1937. Served as a Group Captain throughout the Second World War, before finally retiring from the RAF with the rank of Air Commodore on 1 March 1951.

WALKER, Robert Verschoyle

From Fort View, Cootehill, County Cavan, Ireland, he was born on 18 December 1893. Gazetted Second Lieutenanr to the New Armies on 6 November 1915, with an immediate attachment to 6 Battalion, Connaught Rangers. Seconded to the RFC, he trained as an Observer and accompanied 25 Squadron to France as a Probationary in March 1916. Flew mainly as Observer to fellow Irishman, Lord Doune (qv). On 29 April 1916, Doune and Walker in FE2b, '5209', fought a successful combat above Hulluch against a Fokker, sending the enemy machine down to destruction. On 4 June following, the Irishmen's FE2b, '6938', was hit by anti-aircraft fire over Bethune and forced down at Essars. Although Doune escaped unscathed, Walker suffered wounds to his face. The pair were awarded a joint MC in the *London Gazette* of 31 May 1916: 'For conspicuous gallantry and skill. When on patrol duty with Second Lieut Lord Doune, he sighted a Fokker machine 1,000 feet below them. Second Lieut Lord Doune at once dived, and, when within 60 yards, Second Lieut Walker opened fire. Lord Doune then headed straight for the Fokker, which had to rise steeply to avoid a collision. Second Lieuts Walker and Lord Doune then both opened fire and shot away one wing of the Fokker, which fell behind our lines'.

Walker's 'apprenticeship' more than satisfactorily completed, he was confirmed and gazetted Flying Officer (Observer) on 12 June 1916. Once recovered from his wounds, Walker was posted to instructing duties, only to subsequently suffer another misfortune when he was injured at 42 TS in the UK on 31 October 1917. Walker finally left the RAF, via the Unemployed List, on 17 April 1919.

WALKERDINE, Harold John

The son of Building Contractor, William Walkerdine and Sarah A Walkerdine, of Glen Thorn House, Thornhill Road, Derby, he was born on 13 January 1899. Gazetted Second Lieutenant to the RFC on 7 June 1917. His pilot training duly completed, he was confirmed and gazetted Flying Officer on 31 August following. He was sent out to 56 Squadron (SE5As) on 2 November 1917. Achieved seven victories with '56' between 29 November 1917 and 27 March 1918, including two Pfalz Scouts in one fight on 18 March. His combat report for this day reads, in part: '....on patrol with 'B' Flight under Capt McCudden we met 3 EA two-seaters. Capt McCudden engaged the foremost and I engaged the second – the machine went down in a steep dive, practically vertical – at 12 o'clock we met four EA scouts, I fired a drum of Lewis and about 50 Vickers at one EA Scout which dived down – the Camels crossed the line west of Bullecourt. About 10 EA scouts dived on the Camels from 5,000 feet. We were about 4,000 feet and we dived on them....one Scout went down and crashed, the second I fired at went down in a spin....I fired at a third but had to leave it as I had emptied my drum of Lewis and had a stoppage in my Vickers....we attacked 6 Enemy Scouts,,,,I followed this machine down and saw it crash. I fired at a second machine but had to leave it because 2 EA were on my tail firing at me'. His MC, awarded for the fight on 18 March, was announced in the *London Gazette* of 13 May 1918: 'For conspicuous gallantry and devotion to duty. Whilst escorting machines of another squadron who were engaged on low bombing work, he encountered ten hostile scouts two of which he succeeded in crashing to earth. He has at all times, by conspicuous skill and gallantry, set an excellent example to his squadron'.

He was also Mentioned in Despatches on one occasion. His tour with '56' ended when he was wounded in the head on 11 April 1918. Once recovered, he was posted to instructing duties. In October 1918, Walkerdine was seriously injured in a crash in Scotland and left the RAF early in 1919. He died on 18 June 1966.

NB: His medals were offered for sale by Christie's (lot 75) on 17 November 1987: MC (engraved: For bravery in the air – March 1918*), British War Medal 1914-20, and Victory Medal 1914-19 with MID.*

WALL, Anthony Herbert William

From London, he was born on 17 June 1888. After completing his education, he became a journalist working for the *Daily Mail* from 1911. Before the war came, he travelled extensively in Europe, Africa and North America. When war broke out in August 1914, he served for six months with the Belgian Army. Came to the RFC after service in France from 18 November 1915, with 17 Battalion, Middlesex Regiment. Having trained as an Observer, he was sent out as such to the BF2b-equipped 48 Squadron where he formed a formidable partnership with Captain Fred Holliday (qv) with whom he shared no less than 16 victories between 6 April and 3 July 1917. His MC was announced in the *London Gazette* of 18 July 1917: 'For conspicuous gallantry and devotion to duty. As an Observer he has on several occasions assisted to bring down hostile machines. His coolness and accurate shooting have helped very largely in aerial combats'.

The Bar to his MC appeared in the *London Gazette* of 25 August 1917: 'By his initiative and skilful manoeuvring he led six hostile machines to an encounter with our own formations, during which five out of the six hostile machines were destroyed and driven down. He had been equally successful the day before in misleading hostile aircraft and his originality and fearless example were of the greatest value to his squadron'.

Returning to the UK in the late summer of 1917, he was subsequently promoted to Major and appointed to the Committee of Imperial Defence in the Air Ministry, with special responsibilities for setting up the formal recording of RFC/RAF history. He was awarded the OBE (Military Division) in the New Year *London Gazette* of 1 January 1919 for services in this regard. Wall finally left the service on 18 October 1919.

WALLACE, William

The son of Mr and Mrs W Wallace, of 1 Sefton Grove, Lark Lane, Liverpool, he was born on 1 December 1894. Educated at Lawrence Road Council School, Liverpool. His education completed, he secured a position in the Export Department of Lever Brothers, Liver Buildings, Liverpool. A pre-war volunteer with 10 (Scottish) Battalion, King's (Liverpool Regiment) (TF), the Liverpool Scottish, he was mobilised immediately war broke out on 4 August 1914. Accompanied the original contingent of the Liverpool Scottish to France on 1 November 1914, thus earning the 1914 Star. Wallace was often referred to by the battalion's Medical Officer, the immortal Captain Noel Chavasse VC, as, 'the lad who never missed a trench'. After serving through the hard fighting of 1914 and 1915, he was gazetted Second Lieutenant to the New Armies, via the General Lists, on 4 December 1915, with an immediate attachment to the Cheshire Regiment, On 30 May 1916, he was transferred to a Trench Mortar Battery. A further transfer to the RFC followed and Wallace duly trained as an Observer, serving first on Home Defence duties at Orfordness. His 'apprenticeship' satisfactorily completed, he was confirmed and gazetted Flying Officer (Observer) 13 November 1916. Sent out to France and BE2c-equipped 4 Squadron on 25 February 1917. Wallace and his Pilot, Second Lieutenant R M H Young, in BE2c, '2532', narrowly escaped disaster when their machine was hit by anti-aircraft fire on 3 April 1917. Shortly after this, Wallace transferred to the Strutters of 45 Squadron and was wounded in action by anti-aircraft fire on 18 May 1917. Whilst observing over the enemy lines, he was hit in the shoulder, which rendered his right arm useless, but, despite this, he continued working the wireless with his left hand until the observation was finished. His MC was announced in the *London Gazette* of 26 September 1917, details in the *Gazette* of 9 January 1918: 'For conspicuous gallantry and devotion to duty when co-operating with artillery. He has consistently shown great skill as an observer, ranging siege batteries on hostile batteries with such accuracy that very severe damage was inflicted on the enemy. He has been responsible for the destruction of at least two hostile batteries and has carried out most valuable work for a very long period'.

His Commanding Officer, in a letter of congratulations regarding his MC, wrote: 'You thoroughly earned it'. Once recovered, he was sent to Reading for flying instruction on 24 August 1917. Having qualified as a Pilot, he instructed at various training squadrons in 1918, before he was injured in an aeroplane accident on 21 September. William Wallace finally left the RAF, via the Unemployed List, on 15 April 1919.

WALLAGE, Stanley Harry

The son of Foreman Flour Miller, Christopher Harry Wallage and Mary Eliza Wallage (née Swann), of 21 Philip Road, Ipswich, Suffolk, he was born on 24 July 1895. Educated at Ipswich Municipal Secondary School and at the Ipswich Technical School, where he studied Draftsmanship, Engineering and Survey. Enlisted as a Private soldier (Number 9369) into 7 Battalion, Suffolk Regiment, with an almost immediate promotion to Corporal. Accompanying his battalion to France on 30 May 1915, he served in the trenches until wounded on 16 October 1916. Once recovered, he was picked out for a commission and gazetted Second Lieutenant to the RFC on 3 May 1917. His pilot training duly completed, he was confirmed and gazetted Flying Officer on 6 July following. Sent out to BF2b-equipped 22 Squadron early in 1918, he gained nine victories, shared with various Observers, between 18 February and 26 May 1918. He was promoted to A/Captain and Flight Commander in June, his MC being announced in the *London Gazette* of 16 September 1918: 'For conspicuous gallantry and devotion to duty during recent operations. He personally destroyed seven enemy machines. He showed a fine spirit of dash and tenacity, and his skill and success as a fighting pilot was a fine example to others in his Squadron'.

Following a rest in the UK, he returned to the front again, claiming his tenth and final victory on 4 November 1918. Wallage finally left the RAF in 1919.

NB: His medals were offered for sale by Glendining's (lot 289) on 24 March 1993: MC, 1914-15 Star (Cpl, Suffolk Regt), *British War Medal 1914-20, and Victory Medal 1914-19* (Capt RAF).

WALLER, Albert Gregory

Originally from Banagher, Ireland, he attended Blackheath Preparatory School, London (1903-05). A Regular Army officer, he was gazetted pre-war to the Army Service Corps. Served in France with the Army Service Corps from 6 November 1914, thus earning the 1914 Star. Seconded to the RFC on 4 September 1916, he gained his Royal Aero Club Certificate (Number 4015) on 3 December following. His formal training duly completed, he was confirmed and gazetted Flying Officer on 10 February 1917. Sent out to 1 AD in France on 21 February 1917. Joined 55 Squadron on 15 November 1917 for a relatively brief tour which ended on 12 February 1918, when he returned to the UK. Sent out again in the following month as a Flight Commander with 18 Squadron (DH4s), he achieved 11 victories between 6 March and 30 May 1918 as well as completing many successful bombing raids and reconnaissance sorties. His MC was announced in the *London Gazette* of 16 September 1918: 'For conspicuous gallantry and devotion to duty. He has led fifteen successful bombing raids. twenty-two low-bombing and reconnaissance flights and eight successful photographic flights. In addition he has destroyed five enemy machines. As a flight-commander he has shown initiative and enterprise both in the air and on the ground, and the excellent work done by the flight under his command is entirely due to his fine example and untiring energy'.

Following his service with '18', Waller returned to the Home Establishment on 26 June 1918. After a short rest, he became a Communications Pilot for the Air Ministry during the late summer of 1918, before, in October 1918, being promoted to A/Major and appointed as second in command of 22 TDS. He finally left the Service, via the Unemployed List, on 3 February 1919.

WALLER, John Thomas

Born on 1 September 1889 (or 30 August 1889). Educated at Dean Close School (1902-07). A Regular Army officer, he was, pre-war, gazetted Second Lieutenant to 1 Battalion, Leicestershire Regiment. Accompanied his battalion to France on 8 September 1914, thus earning the 1914 Star. Received the congratulations of the General Officer Commanding I Corps on his valuable patrol work during the retreat from Mons. Wounded in the area of Rue de Bois-La Boutillerie on 30 October 1914, during the final days of the retreat. It was after this date that trench warfare really began in earnest. Once recovered and by then a Captain, Waller rejoined his battalion at the front only to be wounded again in June 1915, this time on the Ypres Salient near Wieltje. Having again recovered from his wounds, Waller sought secondment to the RFC, which was allowed in the early summer of 1916. Gained his Royal Aero Club Certificate (Number 3182) on 21 June 1916. His formal pilot training duly completed, he was confirmed and gazetted Flying Officer on 1 August following. Posted to 26 (South Africa) Squadron in East Africa on 23 December 1916. His MC was announced in the *London Gazette* of 26 May 1917: 'For conspicuous gallantry and devotion to duty. He has consistently carried out with unfailing success long reconnaissances and daring bombing raids'.

He was also Mentioned in Despatches on one occasion during the Great War. The effect of the wounds he had received earlier in the war and the climatic conditions of East Africa, combined to adversely affect his health and consequently he was invalided home on 4 January 1918. John Waller died at his home, 'Farthings', Bromyard, Herefordshire, on 4 October 1961.

NB: The RAF Museum Hendon has his medals in its collection: MC, 1914 Star and Bar (Lieut J T Waller, Leics Regt), *British War Medal 1914-20, and Victory Medal 1914-19 with MID.*

WALLWORK, John Wilson

The son of Assistant Workhouse Manager, James Wallwork and Marion Stuart Wallwork (née Wilson), of 100 Cross Lane, Radcliffe. Lancashire, he was born on 6 May 1898. Educated at Stand Grammar School. After completing his education, he was employed as a Bank Clerk in London. Wallwork enlisted as a Private soldier (Number 765096) into 2/28 Battalion, London Regiment (Artists Rifles). Picked out for a commission, he was gazetted Second Lieutenant to the RFC on 20 April 1917. His formal pilot training duly completed, he was confirmed and gazetted Flying Officer on 15 July following. Sent out to the SE5A-equipped 40 Squadron early in 1918, he claimed five victories between 6 March and 12 April 1918. His MC was announced in the *London Gazette* of 26 July 1918: 'For conspicuous gallantry and devotion to duty. During recent operations he participated in many offensive low-flying and bombing attacks, and carried them out with great courage and determination. From very low altitudes he bombed enemy troops and transport, inflicting heavy casualties. He caused while on offensive patrol more than one enemy machine to crash, and brought down others out of control. He set a magnificent example of courage and skill'.

John Wallwork survived the Great War, but died of injuries received in a flying accident on 18 December 1922.

WALMSLEY, Hugh Sydney Porter

The third son of Mr and Mrs James Walmsley of Broughton, near Preston, Lancashire, he was born on 6 June 1898. Educated at Old College, Windermere, and at Dover College. Gazetted Second Lieutenant to 4 Battalion, Loyal North Lancashire Regiment (TF) on 15 January 1916. Seconded to the RFC late in 1916, he trained as a Pilot and was duly confirmed and gazetted Flying Officer on 10 June 1917. Sent out to the DH4-equipped 55 Squadron in France in September 1917. His intensive, if unspectacular, tour with '55' completed, he returned to the Home Establishment in July 1918. His MC was announced in the *London Gazette* of 16 September 1918: 'For conspicuous gallantry and devotion to duty on long-distance bomb raids. In four of these he acted as leader and displayed great skill and tenacity in getting the better of the enemy. He has carried out twelve raids into the enemy's country, and his work throughout has been consistently of a high order'.

Staying on in the RAF after the war, he represented the service in the Inter-Services Athletics in 1919, 1924 and 1926. He married, in 1928, Audrey Maude Seaford, with whom he had three sons. The many postings, promotions, appointments and honours of his highly successful career included: Flight Lieutenant, 1921; Iraq, 1921-23, awarded the Distinguished Flying Cross, *London Gazette* of 10 October 1922: '....for distinguished service rendered during active operations in Iraq during 1920-21' ; Squadron Leader 1931; OC, 33 Squadron, Bicester 1933-34: 8 Squadron, Aden, 1935-37; Wing Commander 1937; OBE, 1937; Group Captain 1939; OC, 71 Wing, AASF, 1939-40; OC, RAF Station, Scampton, 1940-41; Air Commodore, 1942; HQ, Bomber Command 41-42; AOC, 91 Group, 1942-43; Air Vice-Marshal, 1943; CBE, 1943; SASO, HQ Bomber Command, 1944-45; CB, 1944; and AOC, 4 Group, Transport Command, 1945-46; Walmsley was Mentioned in Despatches on five occasions during the Second World War; AOC, Transport Command, South East Asia, 1946; AOC-in-Command, Air HQ, India, 1946-47; A/Air Marshal, 1947-48; Air Marshal, 1949; Deputy Chief of the Air Staff, 1948-50; AOC-in-Command, Flying Training Command, 1950-52. KCB, 1952. Air Marshal Sir Hugh Walmsley retired from the Active List in 1952. In civilian life he was Managing Director of Air Service Training Ltd from 1952-59, later becoming the Principal of College of Air Training in 1960, before resigning in the same year. Lived at 'Upwood', Tiptoe, Lymington, Hampshire. Air Marshal Sir Hugh Walmsley died on 2 September 1985.

WALMSLEY, Lionel (also known as Leo Walmsley)

The son of Landscape Painter, James Ulric Walmsley and Jeanie Walmsley, of King Street, Fylingdales, Yorkshire, he was born on 28 September 1892. His family moved to Robin Hood Bay, also in Yorkshire, whilst he was still quite young. After completing his education, he took up a position as a Teacher at the Old Wesleyan School, Robin Hood Bay, in 1913. When the war came in 1914, he enlisted as a Private soldier into the Royal Army Medical Corps. Picked out for a commission, he was gazetted Second Lieutenant to 3 (Reserve) Battalion, East Yorkshire Regiment, on 13 April 1915, with a secondment to the RFC following later in the same year. Having trained as an Observer, he was sent to 26 Squadron as a Probationary on 23 December 1915. '26', known as the 'South African' Squadron, was sent to Mombasa to fight in the East African campaign, arriving there on 31 January 1916. Walmsley was duly confirmed and gazetted Flying Officer (Observer) on 14 February following. He spent the best part of the next two years in the operations to drive the brilliant German commander, Colonel von Lettow-Vorbec and his forces, out of British East Africa, through German East Africa, and eventually across Portuguese Africa and on into the area around Lake Nyasa. His MC was announced in the *London Gazette* of 26 October 1917, details in the *Gazette* of 7 March 1918: 'While acting as observer during a flight over enemy lines the petrol pipe burst. With great coolness he attempted to stop the leak in spite of great danger from fire, eventually enabling the pilot to land safely in our own lines. He has consistently done very fine work throughout'.

Walmsley, who was destined to become an author of note, wrote of his experiences in East Africa in his book, 'Flying and Sport in East Africa', published in 1920 (Blackwood). After suffering a particularly heavy crash, his unusually extended tour with '26' came to an end on 8 January 1918. Returning to the UK in March 1918, he was used as an Instructor until being sent out to Aden in the following June. A victim of the influenza pandemic, Walmsley was invalided back to the UK on 20 December 1918. He finally left the service, via the Unemployed List, on 30 May 1919. Using the nom de plume, Leo Walmsley, he would enjoy success as an author, particularly well known for his 'Bramblewick' books. A Walmsley Society exists for devotees. Leo Walmsley died on 8 June 1966.

WALSER, Andre Adolphe (also known as Andrew Adolphus Walser)

From London, he was born on 8 April 1889. A pre-war volunteer, he was gazetted Second Lieutenant to 10 (County of London) Battalion, London Regiment (Hackney Rifles) (TF). He held the rank of Captain when his unit was mobilised on the outbreak of war on 4 August 1914. He had been taking flying lessons and was able to gain his Royal Aero Club Certificate (Number 892) on 2 September 1914, although he choose to remain with the Hackney Rifles for the time being. Accompanied his battalion to Gallipoli on 11 August 1915. After the evacuation from the accursed Peninsula, he successfully sought secondment to the RFC. His formal pilot training duly completed, he was confirmed and gazetted Flying Officer on 26 April 1916. Served with 4 Squadron on the Western Front in the summer of 1916, with a swift advancement to Flight Commander coming on 25 August 1916. Walser, a qualified Artillery Instructor, proved also an extremely capable Artillery Ranging Pilot with many outstanding successes, mainly working in conjunction with 13 Siege Battery, RGA, and its 9.2inch howitzers. His MC was announced in the *London Gazette* of 14 November 1916: 'For conspicuous gallantry in action. He carried out a most valuable artillery reconnaissance under very heavy fire, displaying great courage and determination. He has, on many occasions, done fine work'.

Walser, still holding a TF commission, was now rewarded with a permanent commission, being gazetted Captain to a Regular Army battalion of Alexandra, Princess of Wales's Own (Yorkshire Regiment) (Green Howards), on 27 December 1916. Promoted to A/Major, he was next sent out as Commanding Officer of the RE8-equipped 52 Squadron. He would also go on to command 21 Squadron from 6 September 1918. Awarded the Distinguished Flying Cross, *London Gazette* of 8 February 1919, for his brilliant and exceptional ability as a squadron commander. He was also Mentioned in Despatches on two occasions during the Great War and research has unearthed an original recommendation for one of these: 'T/Major A A Walser MC 52 Sqd. 'For good work while in command of 52 Squadron RFC. He is an expert Artillery Observer himself, and has trained his Squadron to a very high standard'. The French, too, weighed in with an award of a Croix de Guerre, *London Gazette* of 18 April 1918. Staying on after the cessation of hostilities, he was awarded a permanent commission as a Major in the RAF on 1 August 1919. Walser's many appointments, honours and postings during a long and distinguished career included: Staff, Directorate of Training and Organisation, 1920; attended RAF Staff College, 1924; CO, 31 Squadron, 1924; Wing Commander, 1924; OC, 1 (Indian) Wing, 1924; Air Staff, RAF Halton, 1929; Group Captain, 1931; Deputy Director of Staff Duties, 1931; Directing Staff, RAF Staff College, 1932; Air Commodore, 1935; SASO, HQ, RAF Middle East, 1936; AOA, HQ, RAF Middle East, 1937; A/Air Vice-Marshal, 1939; Acting AOC, RAF Middle East, 1939; AOC, 32 (Balloon Barrage) Group UK, 1940; relinquished rank of Air Commodore and re-employed as Group Captain, 1942; A/Air Commodore, 1942. Reverted to the Retired List on 6 November 1945. Lived in retirement at Park House, Cholderton, near Salisbury, Wiltshire. Air Commodore Walser died at St Andrew's Hospital, Northampton, on 26 February 1966.

WANKLYN, Frederic Angus

From Montreal, Canada, he was born on 14 August 1888. A professional soldier, he was gazetted, pre-war, to the Royal Field Artillery. An aviation pioneer, he gained his Royal Aero Club Certificate (Number 284) on a Bristol machine at the Bristol School, Brooklands, on 3 September 1912. Seconded to the RFC, he was appointed to instruct at the CFS from October 1913. His MC was announced in the *London Gazette* of 23 June 1915 (no citation). He was also Mentioned in Despatches at this time, *London Gazette* of 22 June 1915.

Served subsequently with 2 RA Squadron from September 1915 and, from November 1915, with 9 Squadron. Flew next with 37 Squadron on Home Defence duties in the UK. From March 1917, Wanklyn instructed at the CFS before being sent to Canada in the same capacity in the following July, promoted to Major. Returned, eventually, to the UK with the rank of Acting Lieutenant Colonel. 37 Brigade, RFA, Ipswich, 24 June 1919, and relinquished his commission as a Major.

WARD, George Bernard

The eldest son of brewer David Ward and Mrs Ward of Lower Hall, Foxearth, Long Melford, Suffolk, he was born in 1891. Educated at Sudbury Grammar School, Malvern College (1907-08), and at the Birmingham School of Brewing, where he secured his Diploma. Enlisted as a Private soldier into the Royal Engineers as a motor-cycle despatch rider. Picked out for a commission, he was gazetted Second Lieutenant to the New Armies, with an immediate attachment to 9 Battalion, North Staffordshire Regiment, on 9 April 1915. Seconded to the RFC, he took lessons at his own expense at a private school at Hendon, where he gained, in a record of nine days, his Royal Aero Club Certificate (Number 1590) on 13 August 1915. His formal training duly completed, he was confirmed and gazetted Flying Officer on 10 November following. Sent out to 2 Squadron on 19 February 1916, he proved a highly successful ranging officer and promotion to A/Captain and Flight Commander soon followed on 7 May 1916. The first of his MCs was announced in the *London Gazette* of 25 November 1916: 'For conspicuous gallantry in action. He flew over the enemy's lines at a height of 1,000 feet, under heavy fire and carried out a very successful artillery reconnaissance. He has previously done very fine work'.

His tour with '2' completed, he instructed for a while in the UK, before he was promoted to A/Major and sent out to command 10 Squadron (AWFK8s) in France early in 1917. On 20 August 1917, Ward and his Observer of the day, Second Lieutenant E Wilson, successfully repulsed a determined attack on their flight of three 'Big-Acks', shooting down one of the enemy machines in the process. Just a month later on 21 September, Ward and his Observer, Second Lieutenant William Archibald Campbell, 1/7 West Yorkshire Regiment, from Headingley, Leeds, in AWFK8, 'B270', were attacked during a photographic reconnaissance by four enemy machines and sent down. Ward was killed and Campbell mortally wounded, their 'Big-Ack' completely wrecked in the crash. The Bar to Ward's MC came posthumously in the *London Gazette* of 26 September 1917, details in the *Gazette* of 9 January 1918: 'For conspicuous gallantry and devotion to duty. When in one of three machines engaged on photographic reconnaissance they were attacked by a formation of nine hostile scouts. A determined resistance was offered to this attack, which was beaten off, and the photographs were then taken. While returning to the aerodrome this officer turned back alone to take some further photographs, and observing six hostile machines approaching he promptly attacked them at close range, and after a sharp fight brought one down and drove off the remainder. He then completed his photography'.

George Ward is buried in Chocques Military Cemetery, France.

WARDEN, William Edwin

The son of Corn Merchant William Warden and Mrs Warden, of 4 Wellington Road, Oxton, Birkenhead, he was born on 24 December 1896. Warden was living and working in the Argentine when the war came. Returning to the UK as one of the many British Latin American Volunteers, he enlisted as a Private soldier into 2/A Battery, Honourable Artillery Company (TF) on 10 February 1915. Accepted as a Cadet into the flying service in October 1916, he was subsequently gazetted Second Lieutenant to the RFC on 27 February 1917. His formal pilot training duly completed, he was confirmed and gazetted Flying Officer on 31 May following. Sent out to 40 Squadron (Nieuport Scouts) on 26 September 1917, the unit re-equipped with SE5s in the following month. Warden fought through the fraught days of the German spring offensive which started on 21 March 1918 and was credited with at least two victories. His MC was announced in the *London Gazette* of 22 June 1918: 'When on a low-flying patrol he attacked seven scouts, one of which he succeeded in sending crashing to earth. Previous to this he had attacked and sent down out of control another hostile scout. He has also brought back accurate and valuable information regarding hostile movements, and has flown at very low altitudes in order to engage enemy troops and transport. His skill, determination and courage have been most marked'.

His tour with '40' completed, he returned to the Home Establishment on 26 June 1918. Following a brief rest, he instructed, successively, at No 2 and No 3 Fighting Schools. Warden finally left the RAF, via the Unemployed List, on 12 August 1919. He returned to live and work in the Argentine and, in 1932, was known to be living at Cordova 838, Buenos Aires, Argentina.

WARMAN, Clive Wilson

The son of Ralph and Jessie Warman, of Lower Lodge, Bedington, Horsham, Sussex, he was born in Norfolk, Virginia, USA, on 30 June 1892. Following service with the Canadian infantry, he was gazetted Second Lieutenant to the RFC on 18 August 1916. Gained his Royal Aero Club Certificate (Number 5395) on 1 April 1917 and was confirmed and gazetted Flying Officer on the same day. Joined the Spad VII-equipped 23 Squadron in France in the early Summer of 1917 and made an immediate impact. Claimed 12 victories between 6 July and 18 August 1917, but was then quite badly wounded in the shoulder during an offensive patrol combat on 20 August 1917. The wound would preclude him from returning to combat flying. Just four days before this, on 16 August 1917, he shot down a enemy two-seater and a balloon in rapid succession before engaging three German scouts. In the middle of this fight, his machine gun jammed and, when he could not free it up, in sheer frustration he threw his gun mallet at the nearest enemy machine. Next he snatched his Very pistol from its bracket and, firing a succession of cartridges at his adversaries, fought himself clear of the mélee and back to his aerodrome, although, in the process, his Spad XXIII was badly shot about. For this and other gallantry he was awarded the Distinguished Service Order, *London Gazette* of 26 September 1917, details in the *Gazette* of 9 January 1918. In precisely the same Gazettes, his MC was also announced: 'For conspicuous gallantry and devotion to duty. He has on all occasions proved himself to be an exceptionally skilled and gallant pilot, having in the space of six weeks brought down six machines and destroyed a hostile balloon. He has also driven down at least five other enemy machines, displaying a consistent determination to attack at close range regardless of personal danger'.

Warman was presented with the insignia of both his awards by the King at Buckingham Palace during an investiture held on 13 April 1918. Once fully recovered, he was posted to 81 Squadron in the UK and was subsequently badly injured in a flying accident at Chingford, Essex, on 8 May 1919, dying four days later at the Royal Military Hospital, Edmondton, Middlesex. Clive Warman is buried in Brookwood Military Cemetery, Surrey.

WASEY, Cyril Walter Carleton

The son of George Kindersley Wasey and Sidney Jane Wasey, of Leigh Hall House, Savernake Forest, Marlborough, Wiltshire, he was born in 1893. Educated at Eton (1907-11). Entered Sandhurst in December 1911. Gazetted Second Lieutenant to a Regular Army battalion of the Royal Warwickshire Regiment in March 1913. Accompanied 1 Battalion, Royal Warwickshire Regiment, to France on 22 August 1914, thus earning the 1914 Star. Fought through the retreat from Mons and in subsequent engagements. Awarded Croix de Chevalier, Légion d'Honneur, by the French and was Mentioned in Despatches by Sir John French. Continued to serve on the Western Front for the next three years, apart for a period when he was in England recovering from the effects of a broken jaw. Seconded to the RFC in the summer of 1917, he trained as an Observer and was sent out as such to 16 Squadron (RE8s) in September. On 28 October 1917, Wasey and his Pilot, Lieutenant Edward Hugh Keir, King's Own (Royal Lancaster Regiment), from Lancaster, in RE8, 'A4426', were engaged on an artilleryobservation patrol, despite quite heavy fog over the battlefields. Over Mont St Eloi, they fell victim to Leutnant Julius Buckler of Jasta 17, the 20th of the German Ace's 36 victories. Apparently, Wasey fired 250 rounds at Buckler before he was shot in the head and killed outright. Despite the heavy damage inflicted by Buckler, Keir managed to maintain control of the RE8 for most of the forced descent. However, he lost control when, within a couple of hundred of feet from the ground, the machine crashed heavily, bursting into flames near to Carency. Keir appeared to have been slowly strangled to death by shot-through wires that wrapped themselves around his neck as he descended. Wasey's MC was announced posthumously in the New Year *London Gazette* of 1 January 1918 (no citation). Cyril Wasey is buried alongside his Pilot in Aubigny Communal Cemetery Extension, France.

NB: His medals were offered for sale by Bosleys on 15 September 2004: MC, 1914 Star, British War Medal 1914-20, Victory Medal 1914-19, and Légion d'Honneur (Chevalier, France).

WATERLOW, Eric

The son of Wholesale Stationer, Herbert J Waterlow and Marian Waterlow, of 154 Gloucester Terrace, Paddington, London, he was born on 4 November 1893. He was married to Alice Mabel and farming in Regina, Saskatchewan, Canada, when the war came in August 1914. On 29 December 1914, he enlisted as a Private soldier into the Canadian Army and served in France with 10 Battalion, Canadian Mounted Rifles, 3 Cavalry Division. Accepted as a volunteer to the flying service, he was gazetted Second Lieutenant to the RFC on 17 March 1917. Gained his Royal Aero Club Certificate (Number 4776) on 8 June 1917. His formal training duly completed, he was confirmed and gazetted Flying Officer on 21 July following. Sent out to 25 Squadron (DH4s) soon after qualifying for his 'Wings'. Promoted to Captain and Flight Commander in the early summer of 1918, he was Mentioned in Despatches in the *London Gazette* of 20 May 1918. Research has unearthed the recommendation for this Mention: 'This officer has distinguished himself as a pilot, especially setting a fine example to his squadron when it was experiencing great difficulty with its machines, and has done much to make the BHP engine a success'. His MC was announced in the *London Gazette* of 22 June 1918: 'For conspicuous gallantry and devotion to duty. He carried out two long reconnaissances, flying at very low altitude, and brought back most valuable information. During one of these flights he was attacked by a hostile scout, which he destroyed. He carried out four exceptionally long flights, during each of which he took a great number of photographs. He has always undertaken himself the longest and most arduous operations given to his flight, and by his skill, gallantry and determination has on each occasion completed his task with the greatest success'.

On 16 July 1918, Waterlow and his Observer of the day, Canadian Lieutenant James Mathew Mackie DCM, Manitoba Regiment, in DH4, 'D8380', on a photo-reconnaissance patrol, were attacked over Pilckem and sent down to their deaths by Leutnant Franz Piechulek of Jasta 56, the ninth of the German Ace's eventual 14 victories. An award of a Distinguished Flying Cross to Waterlow was announced posthumously in the *London Gazette* of 21 September 1918, this in recognition of, amongst other things: '....thirty-three bombing raids and over forty solo photographic and long distance reconnaissances'. Waterlow is buried in Ypres Reservoir Cemetery, Ypres, West-Vlaanderen, Belgium.

WATKINS, Loudon Pierce

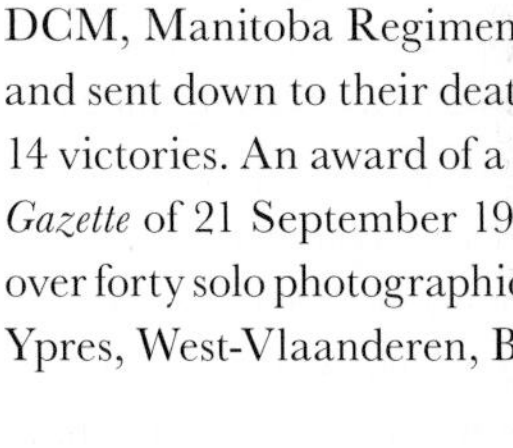

The son of Edward James and Elizabeth Watkins, of Toronto, Canada, he was born in 1897. Gazetted Lieutenant to the Canadian Militia early in the war. Loudon and his brother, Edward, after taking some lessons at the Curtis Flying School, applied for transfer to the flying service and were duly gazetted Second Lieutenants to the RFC on 7 December 1915. Loudon gained his Royal Aero Club Certificate (Number 2532) on 12 February 1916. His formal training completed, he was confirmed and gazetted Flying Officer on 3 May following. Served with 21 Squadron in France until 30 November 1916, when he returned to the Home Establishment. Following a short rest, he was posted to Home Defence duties with 37 HD Squadron (BE12s), stationed at Goldhanger, in December 1916. Kept very busy in countering interminable real and, sometimes, imagined, daylight and night raids by Zepps and Gothas. On the night of 16/17 June 1917, Watkins, in BE12, '6610', shared, with Captain R H M S Saundby (qv), in the destruction of Zeppelin *Z48*, which was brought down in flames in East Anglia. His, and Saundby's, MCs were announced in the *London Gazette* of 5 July 1917: 'In recognition of their conspicuous gallantry in attacking and destroying an enemy airship' – Captain Robert Henry Saundby, R Warwicks Regiment and RFC; Second Lieutenant Loudon Pierce Watkins, Canadian Local Forces and RFC'.

Research has unearthed the original recommendation for this award: 'For conspicuous gallantry in attacking and destroying an enemy airship. At about 2am two airships came a short distance inland, one crossing the East Anglian coast, made an attack on a coast town of East Anglia at about 2.30am She was heavily shelled by the guns of the anti-aircraft defences, and was driven off. Shortly afterwards this raider, after dropping a number of bombs in open places, was engaged and brought down in flames by a pilot of the RFC. The airship was destroyed. No casualties or damage were caused in East Anglia'.

Watkins later served with 38 HD Squadron, commanding 'B' Flight out of Buckminster, before eventually accompanying the night-bombing FE2b-equipped 148 Squadron to France as a 'founder member' and Senior Flight Commander on 26 April 1918. He had completed 16 bombing raids and five reconnaissance missions by the night of 1 July 1918 when he crashed near to Ostreville due to engine problems when returning from a raid. He suffered a broken neck in the crash and died shortly afterwards. Loudon Watkins is buried in Ligny-St Flochel British Cemetery, Averdoingt, France.

WEARE, Frank Gerald Craven

The son of Director of Brickworks, Frank Weare and Mary Loise Weare (née Smith), of Berkeley Lodge, Ferndale, Tunbridge Wells, Kent, he was born in 1897. Educated at Kent House, Eastbourne, Charterhouse School and Sandhurst. Gazetted Second Lieutenant to 1 Battalion, East Kent Regiment (The Buffs,, on 20 October 1915, with an immediate secondment to 2 Battalion, Queen's, Royal West Surrey Regiment. Weare was present with 2 Royal West Surreys when they attacked High Wood on 14 July 1916, during the Battle of the Somme. On 1 September 1916, he led two platoons of 'C' Company on a bombing attack along the eastern edge of Delville Wood. However, the trench they were to travel along had all but been obliterated by shell-fire and hence they were badly exposed to enemy fire. Weare was wounded by the machine-gun fire that eventually brought his entire party to a halt. He was hit in the left thigh, the wound leaving a sizable indentation. He was also struck by shrapnel splinters in the nose and right cheek. His gallantry would probably have attracted the award of the MC had he been one of the Royal West Surrey's own and not merely on detachment from the Buffs. Once recovered, he successfully sought transfer to the RFC in the spring of 1917. His pilot training duly completed, he was confirmed and gazetted Flying Officer on 11 July 1917. Sent out eventually to France and the Bristol Fighters of 22 Squadron, he achieved 15 victories, including one 'trio' and four 'doubles' on single days between 13 March and 22 April 1918. His MC was announced in the *London Gazette* of 22 June 1918: 'In the course of eight days' operations he destroyed two enemy machines, drove down one out of control and enabled his observer to destroy two others. During an earlier engagement he carried out two valuable reconnaissances at a low altitude. He showed a splendid fighting spirit and displayed great skill and judgement in leading his formation'.

Offered a permanent commission on 1 August 1919, Weare eventually retired with the rank of Lieutenant Colonel, becoming a Justice of the Peace and a member of Tunbridge Wells Council. He died on 6 July 1971.

WEBB, Noel William Ward

The youngest son of William Trego Webb and Isobel Mary Webb, of 7 Scarsdale Villas, Kensington, London, he was born in Margate on 12 December 1896. Educated at The Briary, Westgate-on-Sea, and St Paul's School, London, where he played three-quarter for the First Rugby XV. Gazetted Second Lieutenant to the RFC, via the General List, on 15 March 1916. Gained his Royal Aero Club Certificate (Number 3059) on 29 May 1916. His formal pilot training duly completed, he was confirmed and gazetted Flying Officer on the 3 July following. Sent out to FE2b-equipped 25 Squadron in France the day after qualifying for his 'Wings', he achieved five victories between 19 July and 15 September 1916, before being invalided home in October. Promoted to A/Captain, he instructed in England, where he also gained experience as a stand-in Squadron Commander. The first of his MCs was announced in the New Year *London Gazette* of 1 January 1917, for which there was no formal citation other than: '....for service performed under most perilous conditions'. Research, however, has unearthed the original recommendation for the award: 'N W (W) Webb 25 Sqn recommendation 5/9/16 by OC 1 Bde. For conspicuous gallantry. On September 1st while on patrol over the Loos salient he crossed the lines under heavy fire at 2,000 feet and attacked two hostile balloons near Sallaumines at very close quarters with machine-gun fire, many hits being scored. On the balloons being pulled down he then dropped bombs on them, but just failed to hit them. He returned with his machine badly shot about and the petrol tank pierced, crossing the lines at 1,200 feet. In addition this Officer has on different occasions successfully engaged several hostile aeroplanes, including a Fokker over its own aerodrome at Provin on July 19. The Fokker had a wing shot off and fell, a complete wreck, in front of its own sheds'.

Webb returned to the front as an A/Captain and Flight Commander with 70 Squadron (Sopwith Camels) on 21 June 1917. Picking up where he left off, he gained a further nine victories between 12 July and 13 August 1917. Amongst these victories was the first ever by an RFC Pilot flying a Camel. On 12 July 1917, whilst flying an air test, Webb stumbled upon a German two-seater, promptly sending it down into the British lines, wounding both the Pilot and Observer in the process. On 16 August 1917, however, Webb, in Camel, 'B3756', in company with another 70 Squadron Camel, attempted to fight off a superior force of German Scouts which were attacking some FE2s. The leader of the German Scouts, the great Ace, Oberleutnant Werner Voss, claimed Webb as his 37th victory, the Englishman and his machine vanishing into thin air. The Bar to Webb's MC was announced posthumously in the *London Gazette* of 26 September 1917, details in the *Gazette* of 9 January 1918: 'For conspicuous gallantry and devotion to duty in aerial combats. He has destroyed three hostile machines and driven down four others completely out of control. By his spirit and gallantry he has set a fine example which has inspired the pilots of his flight to successfully attack formations many times more numerous than their own'.

Noel Webb's remains were never recovered and hence he is commemorated on the Flying Services Memorial, Arras, France.

WELLESLEY, Lord George

The son of the fourth Duke of Wellington, KG, and the Duchess of Wellington, of Apsley House, Hyde Park, London, he was born on 29 July 1889. Educated at Wellington College (1902-05). Gazetted Second Lieutenant to the Grenadier Guards in 1909. Awarded the Royal Humane Society Medal for Saving Life in 1910. Developing an interest in aviation, he gained his Royal Aero Club Certificate (Number 605) on a Bristol machine at the Bristol School, Salisbury Plain, on 28 August 1913. Seconded to the RFC, he accompanied the original contingent to France as a Pilot with 5 Squadron, thus earning the 1914 Star. He returned to the UK and to service at the CFS in December 1914. He next served with 12 Squadron at Netheravon from May 1915 and with 17 Squadron at Gosport from November 1915. Promoted to Major, he was placed in command of 1 RS in May 1916. His MC was announced in the Birthday Honours *London Gazette* of 3 June 1916 (no citation). He was also Mentioned in Despatches at this time, *London Gazette* of 21 June 1916. Appointed to the Staff, HQ, 43 Wing in July 1916, before being posted to 65 Squadron, then at Wyton, in the following October. Sent to Canada in February 1917, he was promoted to Lieutenant Colonel in October. Wellesley returned to the UK in 1918 and finally relinquished his commission due to ill-health on 3 September 1919. He married firstly in 1917, Nesta, daughter of Sir Maurice Fitzgerald Bt, with whom he had one son and secondly, in 1955, Jean McGillivray. Subsequently became Managing Director of Coxeter and Company Ltd from 1923 to 1940. Rejoined the service as an RAFVR Squadron Leader in 1940, working in the Ministry of Aircraft Production until the end of the war in 1945. He lived, when in London, at Flat 5, Woodsford, 14 Melbury Rd W14 and, when in New York City, at 40 West 84th Street. Lord George died on 31 July 1967, age78.

WELLS, Eric Irwin

The son of Mr and Mrs Wells of 19a Charleville Road, West Kensington, London W14, and of Eastbourne, he was born on 29 March 1895. Gazetted Second Lieutenant to a Regular Army battalion of the Rifle Brigade on 21 November 1916. Seconded to the RFC in November 1917, he trained as an Observer and was sent out as such to France in the following month. Joined 8 Squadron (AWFK8s) in February 1918. On 14 March 1918, Wells and his Pilot, Second Lieutenant A M Kinnear, in AWFK8, 'A2732', had their controls shot away during a special reconnaissance but still landed safely. On 7 April 1918, Wells and his Pilot of the day, Second Lieutenant L C Hooton (qv), in 'C3678', were shot up over Buire and their fuel tank hit. The Big-Ack was damaged in the subsequent forced landing, but, again, he and his Pilot were unscathed. His MC was announced in the *London Gazette* of 22 June 1918: 'For conspicuous gallantry and devotion to duty. While he was flying over the enemy's lines the petrol tank of his machine was shot through and immediately afterwards the left aileron was shot away. The machine was side-slipping out of control towards the enemy's position, and the pilot tried in vain to turn it back to our lines. With great presence of mind he climbed out on to the right wing and brought the machine to an even keel, enabling the pilot to land it 100 yards behind our front line. But for his great coolness and resource the machine would undoubtedly have crashed to earth in the enemy's lines. He has done excellent work on many occasions, and has obtained much valuable and accurate information'.

His tour with 8 Squadron completed in July 1918, he returned to the Home Establishment and was thereafter posted to instructing duties. Wells finally left the RAF, via the Unemployed List, on 14 April 1919. He was known to be still living in West Kensington, London, in the 1930s.

WELLS, George Alfred

The son of Mr and Mrs M Wells, of Seacombe, Victoria, Australia, he was born in Surrey Hills, Victoria, on 14 March 1894. Worked on his father's farm before enlisting as a Private soldier into the AIF on 23 November 1914. Posted to 3 Light Horse Battalion, on 8 December 1914. Embarked aboard the SS *Chilka* (Transport A51) at Melbourne on 2 February 1915, as part of 12 Australian Army Service Corps Company, 3 Light Horse Battalion Train, bound for the Middle East. Transferred to 46 Battalion, AIF, he enjoyed rapid promotion and was Acting Quarter Master Sergeant by 28 May 1916. Wounded in action on 11 August 1916. Once recovered, he sought secondment to the flying service and was gazetted Second Lieutenant to the RFC, via the Special Reserve, on 17 March 1917. Sent to 65 Squadron in the UK, he completed his formal pilot training and was duly confirmed and gazetted Flying Officer on 19 May 1917. Sent out to 32 Squadron (DH5s) in France on 26 May 1917. On 11 August 1917, Wells was wounded thrice in the same arm by retaliatory fire whilst attacking ground targets. After receiving treatment in France, he was returned to the UK for hospitalisation on 19 August following. His MC was announced in the *London Gazette* of 26 September 1917, details in the *Gazette* of 9 January 1918: 'For conspicuous gallantry and devotion to duty in engaging enemy infantry with machine-gun fire from low altitudes and attacking enemy aircraft. On one occasion, whilst attacking enemy strong points his machine was so badly shot about that he was forced to return to his aerodrome. He resumed his patrol, however, as soon as he had obtained another machine, and on the following day he attacked a series of strong points with machine-gun fire, flying at a very low altitude for 40 minutes under intense machine-gun fire and field-gun barrage. He was eventually wounded in three places in the arm, but in spite of this he returned to his aerodrome and landed his machine safely'.

He was also Mentioned in Despatches at this time. Once recovered, Wells was sent to 67 TS as an Instructor on 9 January 1918. Sent out again to France on 23 August 1918, this time as a Flight Commander with 92 Squadron (SE5As). On 5 September 1918, Wells in SE5A, 'B8428', was involved in a combat over

Cambrai and shot down into captivity. Two German Aces, Hauptmann Bruno Loerzer, JGIII, and Lieutnant Georg Meyer of Jasta 37, laid claim to an SE5A victory at this time and it remains uncertain to this day, who actually was Wells' conqueror. Wells was repatriated on 9 December 1918 and finally left the RAF, via the Unemployed List, on 20 August 1919. Returning to Australia soon afterwards, Wells joined the RAAF. Flight Lieutenant Wells flew in the 1928 Essendon (Melbourne) Aerial Derby in modified DH9A and sustained severe head injuries when his machine struck high tension wires and crashed. George Wells served part-time with the RAAF during the Second World War.

WELLS, Thomas Ralph

The son of Dr D R Wells and Mrs Wells of Cuckfield, Sussex, he was born on 11 March 1887. After attending Sandhurst in 1905, he was gazetted Second Lieutenant to 33 Punjabis, Indian Army, in 1906. Developing an interest in aviation whilst in the UK, he gained his Royal Aero Club Certificate (Number 851) on a Vickers machine at the Vickers School, Brooklands, on 21 July 1914. Eventually seconded to the RFC in Egypt in March 1915, he duly completed his formal pilot training and was confirmed and gazetted Flying Officer to the Military Wing on 7 June following. Served in Mesopotamia with 30 Squadron and was promoted to Captain in October 1915, to take effect from the previous August. Twice Mentioned in Despatches during this period, *London Gazettes* of 26 June 1915 (Mesopotamia) and 25 July 1915 (Euphrates). Wounded in action on 18 December 1915. His MC was announced in the *London Gazette* of 17 April 1916 (no citation). Captured by the Turks following the fall and surrender of the Kut-al-Amara Garrison on 28 April 1916. Wells was repatriated on 11 November 1918 and finally left the service on 15 October 1919. He was Mentioned in Despatches in the 'Escapers Gazette', *London Gazette* of 16 December 1919: '....for gallantry whilst a Prisoner of War in escaping, or attempting to escape, from captivity, or for valuable services rendered in the Prison Camps of the Enemy'.

WELLS, William Lewis

The son of Surveyor of Taxes William Wells and his wife, Emily Elizabeth Wells, of 14 Staines Road, Hounslow, Middlesex, he was born in 1894. Enlisted as a Private soldier into 1/15 (County of London) Battalion, Prince of Wales's Own Civil Service Rifles (TF), on 31 August 1914. Picked out for a commission, he was gazetted Second Lieutenant to 8 Battalion, Middlesex Regiment (TF) on 25 March 1915. Sent out to France on 29 April 1915, he was subsequently caught in a gas attack on Hill 60 and invalided home as a consequence. Once recovered, he successfully sought secondment to the RFC. Trained as a Pilot with 24 RS and at the CFS, before being confirmed and gazetted Flying Officer on 22 September 1916. He spent most of the following year instructing at Netheravon before, in August 1917, being sent to 50 TS to train on Bristol Fighters. Sent out to 22 Squadron on 9 September 1917, charged with bomber escort and offensive duties. Following a relatively brief tour with '22', during which he gained six victories between 25 January and 16 March 1918, he returned to Biggin Hill. A posting to 48 Squadron as a Flight Commander was crowned with immediate success as he gained his seventh victory on 21 March. Three further victories came on 23 March. Five days later on 28 March 1918, Wells and his Observer/Gunner, Corporal W Beales (Number 2565), in Bristol Fighter, 'C4701', were both wounded during an aerial combat. Corporal Beales, an Ace Gunner with nine victories, was subsequently awarded a Distinguished Conduct Medal in the *London Gazette* of 26 June 1918. Wells' wounds were so severe that they proved mortal and he died almost two months later on 16 May 1918. The first of his MCs was announced three days before his death in the *London Gazette* of 13 May 1918: 'For conspicuous gallantry and devotion to duty. On four occasions during three months he has been engaged with superior enemy formations, and has brought down completely out of control five hostile machines and sent down one other crashing to earth. He has displayed the greatest gallantry, courage and determination in dealing with enemy aircraft'.

The Bar came, posthumously, in the *London Gazette* of 22 June 1918: 'For conspicuous gallantry and devotion to duty. He frequently attacked enemy troops and transport with bombs and machine-gun fire during operations, often flying at a very low altitude under heavy fire. While attacking enemy troops from a height of 150 feet he was severely wounded but succeeded in bringing his Observer and machine back safely. He has destroyed five enemy machines and driven down five others out of control, and has always set an example of courage and determination to the flight which he commanded'.

William Wells is buried in St Sever Cemetery, Rouen, France.

NB: The RAF Museum Hendon has his medals in its collection: MC, 1914-15 Star, British War Medal 1914-20, and Victory Medal 1914-19.

WEST, Ferdinand Maurice Felix VC

The son of Lieutenant Francis West, East Lancashire Regiment, and his wife, the former Comtesse Clemence de la Garde de Saignes, of Princes Square, London W2, he was born on 29 January 1896. Francis West, who had resigned his commission in 1896, rejoined the colours when the Boer War broke out in 1899, only to be killed on active service in 1902, the third year of the war. The widowed Clemence returned to her native Italy with her son, taking up residence in Milan where Ferdinand, or 'Freddie', as he was known, received much of his early education. After graduating in International Law at Genoa University in June 1914, the trilingual Freddie obtained a position in a Swiss bank. When the war came, he felt obliged to return to his father's country to offer his services. Arriving in London in September 1914, friendless and alone, he was immediately persuaded to enlist as a Private soldier into the Royal Army Medical Corps. Picked out for a commission, he was gazetted Second Lieutenant to 4 (Extra Reserve) Battalion, Royal Munster Fusiliers on 13 May 1915. Sent out to 2 Battalion of his regiment, then in the trenches at Loos, on 8 November 1915. After serving for 17 months in the trenches and by then an A/Captain and Company Commander, West successfully sought secondment to the RFC in April 1917. Having trained as an Observer, he was sent out as such to 3 Squadron (Morane Parasols). His tour with '3' completed, in October 1917, he next trained as a Pilot, returning to Grantham in the UK for the appropriate tuition. His training duly completed, he was confirmed and gazetted Flying Officer on 20 December 1917. Posted out to 8 Squadron (AWFK8s) on 8 January 1918, he regained his rank of A/Captain when he was promoted to Flight Commander in June 1918. His MC, won with his Observer, Lieutenant J A G Haslam (qv), was announced in the *London Gazette* of 1 May 1918, details in the *Gazette* of 26 July 1918: 'For conspicuous gallantry and devotion to duty. While on patrol he, with another officer, observed fifteen enemy motor lorries. As these could not be engaged by our artillery by zone call, they flew 8,000 yards over the enemy lines at a height of 3,800 feet in the face of strong opposition from the ground, and dropped four bombs, obtaining direct hits on the lorries and doing considerable damage to their personnel. They then proceeded to attack them with machine-gun fire as they sought cover. A fortnight later they carried out, at a height of 150 feet, a reconnaissance of their corps front, on which an attack was expected. Despite the fact that the clouds were at 200 feet, and there was thick mist, they obtained most valuable information. During this flight they directed and located the fire of our artillery on a concentration of enemy infantry. Throughout the operations their work in co-operation with our artillery was always of the greatest value, and their enterprise in attacking enemy troops and transport with bombs and machine-gun fire was splendid'.

On 9 August 1918, West and his Observer, Lieutenant J A G Haslam, in AWFK8, 'D5138', on a tank patrol, had their engine shot up, which forced them to land near Caix. Despite this trauma, on the following day the same pair, in 'C8602', were again charged with conducting a liaison patrol with a convoy of tanks advancing on Roye. Visibility was poor and coming down low in a swirling mist, West and Haslam stumbled across a concentration of enemy tanks and transport which they immediately attacked. No sooner had they done so when they themselves were attacked by seven enemy scouts. West was hit in the left leg by five explosive bullets. The leg was virtually shredded and hanging off. Despite this terrible injury, West continued to help his Observer to fight off the attacking enemy machines. Haslam, too, was wounded in the ankle during this fight. Finding themselves in the clear at last, West crashlanded the 'Big Ack' in a field near to some Canadian infantry. Carried to a nearby Casualty Clearing Station, West, despite his frightful injuries, insisted on giving a full report before receiving medical attention. The citation for his Victoria Cross, *London Gazette* of 8 November 1918, tells the story: 'Captain West, while engaging troops at a low altitude far over the enemy lines, was attacked by seven aircraft. Early in the engagement one of his legs was partially severed by an explosive bullet, and fell powerless into the controls, rendering the machine for the time unmanageable. Lifting his disabled leg, he regained control of the machine, and although wounded in the other leg, he, with surpassing bravery and devotion to duty, manoeuvred his machine so skilfully that his observer was enabled to get several good bursts into the enemy machines, which drove them away. Captain West then, with rare courage and determination, desperately wounded as he was, brought his machine over our lines and landed safely. Exhausted by his exertions, he fainted, but on regaining consciousness insisted on writing his report'.

His injuries were such that it was necessary to amputate his left leg. Returning to London, he had an artificial limb fitted in time to attend an investiture at Buckingham Palace on 1 March 1919, for the bestowal of his Victoria Cross from the hands of the King. At first, intent on resuming his career as a Lawyer, he changed his mind soon after the war when he was offered a permanent commission in the RAF. West married Wynne Leslie in a ceremony held at Westminster Cathedral on 19 January 1921. His appointments, promotions and further honours during his RAF career included: Staff College; OC, 17 Squadron; instructing at the CFS; Service in Malta; School of Army Co-operation, Old Sarum; OC, 4 Squadron; and service in the Air Ministry's Diplomatic Corps which took him to Finland, Estonia and Latvia. A Group Captain in 1939, his war service included counter-intelligence work in Switzerland and Italy. Retiring from the RAF in March 1946, he worked in the Rank Organisation, becoming Managing Director of Eagle-Lion Distributors. Group Captain Freddie West, VC, died at the Princess Margaret Hospital, Windsor, on 7 July 1988.

WEST, Theodore James

From Queensland, Victoria, Australia, he was born on 12 June 1892. A qualified Surveyor, he was working in London when war came in August 1914. He enlisted immediately as a Private soldier into 23 (1 Sportsmans) Battalion, Royal Fusiliers. Picked out for a commission, he was gazetted Second Lieutenant to 9 (Reserve) Battalion, East Yorkshire Regiment, on 9 November 1914. Sent out to the Dardanelles as a replacement officer to 6 Battalion of his regiment on 13 September 1915, 6 East Yorks (Pioneers) having previously landed at Suvla Bay, Gallipoli, as part of 11 Division, on 7 August 1915. Following the evacuation from the Peninsula and his unit's return to Egypt, he successfully sought secondment to the RFC in the spring of 1916. Having trained as an Observer in Egypt, he was posted to 14 Squadron, subsequently being confirmed and gazetted Flying Officer (Observer) on 1 July 1916. On 24 July 1916, West and his Pilot, Second Lieutenant R P Wilcock, in a BE2c, were both slightly wounded during an aerial combat with an enemy machine. On 2 August following, West and his Pilot of the day, Lieutenant A S C MacLaren (qv), in DH1A, '4609', scored the first Allied victory on the Egyptian front when they sent a Fokker down near to Salmana. The enemy crew, Leutnant H Henkel and Oblt Stalter, were taken prisoner. West's MC was announced in the *London Gazette* of 25 November 1916: 'For conspicuous gallantry in action. He attacked an enemy machine and brought it down, displaying great courage and ability'.

West served subsequently at RFC HQ, Egypt, where he trained as a Pilot and, from 24 May 1917 to 17 March 1918, with 63 Squadron (RE8s) in Mesopotamia. He survived the Great War.

WHITAKER, John Tudor (also known as Powell-Whitaker)

Originally from Lee, Lewisham, London, he was born on 20 February 1894, his family later moving to live in Hastings, Sussex. Educated at University School, Hastings, where he was a member of the OTC, and at Felsted School, Essex (1908-10). He would later prefer to be known as 'Powell-Whitaker', his father's second name being 'Powell'. His mother, after becoming a widow, would also adopt the hyphenated name, signing herself in that fashion. He was living and working in Canada when the war came and subsequently enlisted into 103 Calgary Rifles before transferring for service with, firstly, 14 Company, CASC, and, secondly, with 3 Company, Canadian Army Service Corps. Picked out for a commission, he was gazetted Second Lieutenant to the Army Service Corps on 15 February 1916, with an almost immediate secondment to the RFC. His formal pilot training duly completed, he was confirmed and gazetted Flying Officer on 4 June following. On 1 July 1916, the first day of the Battle of the Somme, Powell-Whitaker and his Observer, Second Lieutenant T E G Scaife (qv), in BE2c, '2689', arrived over the devastation at 10am. Most of the casualties on that terrible day, 20,000 dead and 40,000 wounded on the British side, had already occurred by that time. Some of the infantry carried mirrors on their backs and, by this device, the airmen were able to spot some who had moved forward into the German positions. Powell-Whitaker and Scaife came down to 700 feet and strafed a machine-gun position in Bernafay Wood. Flying along the lines, the pair saw the men of 18 Division, mainly Liverpool and Manchester 'Pals', advancing near Montauban, the one successful point of attack. The airmen celebrated this singular success by wagging their wings as they skimmed the British troops, who, in turn, reciprocated with wildly waving arms. Their BE2c was then hit by anti-aircraft fire, but the pair escaped unscathed and managed to bring their damaged machine back safely. Just six days later, the same pair, in BE2d, '6236', were again hit by anti-aircraft fire over Montauban but, once again, got back safely without harm. Powell-Whitaker had transferred to 4 Squadron by 21 August 1916, when he and his Observer, Second Lieutenant E H Stevens, in BE2c, '2647', fought several successive combats with two Fokkers, one of which they may have sent down. Four days later on 25 August, Powell-Whitaker was wounded by a bullet in the abdomen during the course of another aerial combat. His MC was announced in the New Year *London Gazette* of 1 January 1917 (no citation). He was also Mentioned in Despatches on two occasions and the French awarded him the Croix de Guerre. Once recovered, he was posted as an Instructor to 54 TS, then at Grantham, where he also gained experience as a Squadron Commander. Powell-Whitaker would go on to serve as a Major on the Italian front in 1918 as OC, 66 Squadron, his service recognised by the awards of the Croce de Guerre, the Order of the Crown of Italy (Cavaliere) and the Silver Medaglia al Valore Militare. Staying on in the RAF after the war, he was given a permanent commission in 1920. He died in Bombay, India, on 10 December 1927.

WHITE, Lewis Scott

The son of Dr Edward White and Mrs White, of 2 Green Park, Bath, he was born on 7 December 1895. Educated at Bath College and at Kelley College. A trained Motor Mechanic, he enlisted (Number 1883) into the RFC on 20 October 1914. Served as a 1 AM with 10 Squadron in the UK and in France. Picked out for a commission, he was gazetted Second Lieutenant to the RFC, via the Special Lists, on 3 June 1916. His training had been on-going for some time and he was confirmed and gazetted Flying Officer on 5 June, just two days after his commissioning. Sent out to, and served with, 2 Squadron in France. On 10 January 1917, in accordance with a carefully prepared plan, White acted as Observer in a machine flown by Captain G C Bailey. The RFC Communiqué describes the subsequent events, thus: '[Bailey and White].flew over the enemy's trenches just north of the double Crassier at a low altitude and opened machine-gun fire. They fired Very Lights and generally attracted the enemy in the trenches, who thus had their backs turned to the front line and were firing at the aeroplane with rifle and machine-gun fire. The Germans were so occupied with this work that our troops were enabled to leave their trenches and cross no-man's land without being perceived, and without any previous artillery preparation. Two parties entered the German trenches, took eight prisoners, and bombed dugouts which were full of Germans. Captain Bailey's machine was hit in a few places by AA fire but was untouched by rifle or machine-gun fire. During the flight he and his Observer located 13 active hostile batteries'. For this brilliantly executed operation, Bailey was awarded the Distinguished Service Order, *London Gazette* of 3 March 1917, and White was awarded his MC, announced in the same *London Gazette*: 'For conspicuous gallantry in action. When acting as observer he co-operated in an infantry raid by flying over the enemy's trenches at a height of only 1,500 feet for more than an hour and a half in very adverse weather conditions. He attacked the enemy in the trenches with machine-gun fire, and located 16 active enemy batteries during this flight'.

A friend wrote to White's parents describing the action for which their son was given his award: 'His CO told us what a gallant performance it was for which he won the MC and how richly he and his pilot deserved the decoration. They were sent by night to draw the enemy's fire and make them believe there was an attack coming from that point. They sent rockets and signals as if to troops coming up behind, and entirely deceived the enemy, who brought up all his reserves there to meet the danger. They did their work so well that an attack planned in another part of the line came off without a hitch and without loss, while these brave boys were being fired at by every sort of gun, and when they returned, their machine was riddled with shot, but both were untouched'.

His tour with '2' completed, he was brought home as a Fighting Instructor with 28 Squadron, then stationed at Yatesbury. On 28 September 1917, White, by then an Acting Captain, was killed in a flying accident in Wiltshire whilst piloting Sopwith Camel, 'B6343', during a delivery flight from 7 AAP, Kenley, to Yatesbury. He is buried in Bath (Locksbrook) Cemetery, Bath.

WHITE, Victor Rodney Stokes

The son of Poulterer and Game Dealer, John White and Mary Jane White (née Seaton) of 95 Paris Street, Exeter, Devon, he was born on 22 May 1895. Educated at Heleb School, Exeter. A Bank Clerk when the war came, he enlisted as a Trooper into 1 Royal Devon Yeomanry (TF) on 3 September 1914. Picked out for a commission, he was gazetted Second Lieutenant to 3 (Reserve) Battalion, South Staffordshire Regiment on 20 March 1915, with an attachment to 1 Battalion of his regiment coming just ten days later. White was wounded on 14 July 1916, during the Battle of the Somme, hit by shrapnel in the forehead. The first of his MCs, earned for gallantry when acting as a Forward Observation Officer, was announced in the *London Gazette* of 26 May 1917. Seconded to the RFC in the spring of 1917, he trained as an Observer and was subsequently gazetted Flying Officer (Observer) on 28 April 1917. He served initially with the Sopwith Strutter-equipped 45 Squadron with which unit he gained his first victory on 13 July 1917. Next, he was posted to the FE2b-equipped 20 Squadron. Striking up a successful partnership with Captain H G E Luchford (qv), he gained a further five victories between 25 September and 21 October 1917. The Bar to his MC came in the *London Gazette* of 26 November 1917, details in the *Gazette* of 6 April 1918: 'For conspicuous gallantry and devotion to duty. While acting as an observer on an offensive patrol he and his pilot shot down an enemy scout in flames. Later, while on a reconnaissance with three other machines, he and his pilot engaged 8 enemy aeroplanes, and shot down and destroyed one of them. On another occasion they destroyed one of three hostile scouts, and also a hostile two-seater'.

White was given a permanent commission in the RAF on 1 August 1919, but, in the event, retired from the service with the rank of Flying Officer on 12 December 1922.

WHITESIDE, Arthur Barlow

The son of the Reverend Arthur Whiteside and Mrs Whiteside, of 2538 Quadra Street, Victoria, BC, Canada, he was born in Fort Quappelle, Saskatchewan, in 1990. Educated at McGill University. Enlisted into Princess Patricia's Canadian Light Infantry and subsequently fought with the CEF in France before being gazetted Second Lieutenant to the RFC on 10 May 1917. Gained his Royal Aero Club Certificate (Number 4763) on 5 June 1917. His formal pilot training duly completed, he was confirmed and gazetted Flying Officer on 1 July following. Accompanied the night-bombing and FE2b-equipped 102 Squadron to France on 24 September 1917. The first of his MCs was announced in the *London Gazette* of 26 March 1918, details in the *Gazette* of 24 August 1918: 'For conspicuous gallantry and devotion to duty. He carried out several night-bombing raids with great success, attacking enemy aerodromes, trains and billets, often from a low altitude. On one occasion he attacked a train with his machine-gun from a height of a 100 feet. He showed splendid skill and initiative'.

Research has unearthed the original recommendation for this award which provides much fuller detail than does the published citation: 'A B Whiteside. 102 Sqn 5/2/18: For gallantry and devotion to duty when carrying out night bomb raids during the period 20/10/17-2/2/18, notably on the following occasions. On 28/10/17 this Officer successfully bombed the railway east of Courtrai from a height of 2,000 feet. On 6/11/17 2/Lt Whiteside set out to attack troops, trains, etc, in the Cambrai area. He succeeded in dropping his bombs on troops at Moorslede in spite of machine-gun and rifle fire. On 7/11/17 his objective was Gontrude aerodrome. He bombed this from a height of 750 feet after which he followed an EA to the north-east of Theilt, making observations. He then proceeded to Lichtervelde and, descending to 100 feet, opened fire with his machine gun on a train. On the night of 30/11/17 he made three trips to Marquion. He successfully bombed the village, afterwards firing many rounds at lights and other suitable targets. On 3/2/17 this Officer again found his objective – Honnecourtville – in spite of a strong wind and considerable haze. He obtained direct hits on the village and emptied two drums at ground targets. On the night of 18-19/12/17, 2/Lt Whiteside carried out a fine piece of navigation. He flew over Gontrude and finding it deserted, returned to St Denis-Westem to drop his bombs. On 13/1/18 this Officer proceeded to bomb Menin. He experienced intense darkness, but eventually succeeded in obtaining direct hits. On 25/118 his objective was Marquion aerodrome which he bombed with great success, obtaining direct hits on the hangars. He also obtained direct hits on EA which he located by means of a parachute flare. This operation was carried out at a height of 500 feet. He afterwards dropped a bomb on a train. His machine was badly damaged and he was obliged to return on service tank. On 2/2/18 he located Scheldewindeke aerodrome with the aid of a parachute flare and dropped his bombs among the hangars. He also fired many rounds at trains and sent in a very valuable report. This Officer has done consistently good work since he has been with 102 Squadron. He has not been deterred by adverse weather conditions and his work has throughout been characterised by the greatest courage and determination to overcome difficulties'.

The Bar to his MC came in the *London Gazette* of 16 September 1918: 'For conspicuous gallantry and devotion to duty. This officer has taken part in over fifty night bombing raids, many of which, carried out at heights considerably under 1,000 feet, and in adverse weather conditions, were only successful through the skill and energy displayed by him in discovering and attacking his objective. On one night in particular, after having successfully bombed a large ammunition dump, which was set on fire and blown up, he proceeded to drop bombs on a town which held large numbers of the enemy, also firing from a low altitude with his machine-gun on the roads leading to it. Returning to his squadron he obtained more bombs and ammunition, and with the same Observer proceeded to drop bombs on a train behind the enemy's lines. On several occasions his machine was badly knocked about by enemy fire from the ground. The devotion to duty and disregard of danger displayed by this officer have been admirable examples to all members of his squadron'.

The Observer referred to in this citation is Lieutenant E F Howard (qv), who also received the MC in this *Gazette*. Whiteside's tour with '102' completed, he returned briefly to the UK before being allowed leave in his native Canada. Returning to duty in September 1918, he was sent as an Instructor to No 2 School of Navigation and Bomb Dropping, RAF. Having survived such an eventful operational career, Arthur Whiteside was killed in a flying accident on 22 April 1919. His funeral, with full military honours, took place at the Airmen's Cemetery, Penton Mewsey, on 25 April 1919, a Handley Page (HP 0/400, No F3758) flying overhead in salute. He is buried in Penton Mewsey (Holy Trinity) Churchyard, Hampshire.

WHITHAM, Robert Parker Musgrave

The son of Robert Musgrave Whitam and Margaret Whitham, of Craven Lodge, Burnley, Lancashire, he was born in 1895. Educated at Burnley Grammar School and at Manchester University, where he was a member of the OTC. Gazetted Second Lieutenant, 15 (Reserve) Battalion, Northumberland Fusiliers on 10 June 1915. After service in France with the regiment, he successfully sought secondment to the RFC which occured in the autumn of 1916. His formal pilot training duly completed, he was confirmed and gazetted Flying Officer on 17 January 1917. His MC was announced in the *London Gazette* of 26 July 1917: 'For conspicuous gallantry and devotion to duty. On four successive days he showed remarkable courage and ability in bombarding enemy positions, and working in conjunction with our artillery he rendered them most valuable information'.

He was also Mentioned in Despatches on one occasion during the Great War. Staying on in the RAF after the war', his appointments, promotions and honours included: Wing Flying Examining Officer; OBE, 1934; Deputy Director of War Organisation, 1938; Group Captain, 1939; Director General of War Organisation, Air Ministry, Air Commodore (T/Air Vice-Marshal), 1941; CB, 1942. He married, in 1939, Margaret Nutter, with whom he had one daughter. Lived at 'Barco', Broadlands Avenue, Shepperton-on-Thames. Air Commodore Whitham was killed on a flight while returning to England from the Middle East on 23 March 1943. He was in a

Liberator (AL587) of 511 Squadron in transit from Gibraltar, shot down by a Ju88 from 15/KG40, the German Pilot being Leutnant Ulrich Hanshen. Whitham's remains were never recovered and hence he is commemorated on the Runnymede Memorial, Panel 118.

WHITTET, Percy Henry Roy

Probably a Technical, not a flying, award

The son of Harness Contractor, Percy Lucknow Whittet and Mary Ann Whittet (née Martin), of 'Elmstead', London Road, Twickenham, Middlesex, he was born on 27 April 1888. Educated at Wellingborough School. A Coffee Planter in East Africa when war came in 1914, he served locally as a volunteer with the East African Mounted Rifles. The volunteers handed over their guarding duties of the area's villages and farms as soon as they were relieved by elements of the recently arrived Indian Army. Whittet sailed for the UK from Mombasa, via Naples, to offer his services (and subsequently made numerous, albeit unsuccessful, attempts to recover the cost of the voyage from the Air Ministry). Gazetted Second Lieutenant to the RFC, via the Special Reserve, on 22 July 1916. He was subsequently appointed Assistant Instructor (graded as Equipment Officer, 2nd Class) at the School of Aerial Gunnery with effect from 24 October following. He appears not to have qualified in any form of flying capacity and hence it has to be assumed that his MC was awarded for technical service. His MC was announced in the New Year *London Gazette* of 1 January 1918 (no citation) and was presented to him by the King at an investiture held at Buckingham Palace on 9 March 1918. Left the RAF in 1919 and was permitted to retain the rank of Captain.

WHITWORTH, William Hervey Allen

The son of the Reverend William Allen Whitworth, Vicar of All Saints, Margaret Street, London, and Mrs Sarah Louise Whitworth, née Elwes, he was born in East Grinstead, Sussex, on 24 February 1888. Educated at Westminster School (1900-05) and at Trinity College, Cambridge, where he was an Exhibitioner (1905-08), BA 1908. Appointed Assistant Master at Gresham's School, Holt, from 1909-11, before becoming Head Master at the Central High School, Coorg, India, from 1911 to 1913. Secured a position as an Assistant Schoolmaster at Lancing College from May 1913. Gazetted Second Lieutenant to 4 Battalion, Dorsetshire Regiment (TF), on 11 December 1914. Seconded to the RFC in January 1916. Gained his Royal Aero Club Certificate (Number 3028) on 1 April 1916. His formal training duly completed, he was confirmed and gazetted Flying Officer, 30 May following. Accompanied 52 Squadron to France on 21 November 1916. His MC was announced in the *London Gazette* of 10 January 1917: 'For conspicuous gallantry in action. He has carried out a great deal of artillery observation in the face of severe attacks from hostile machines. On one occasion he fought two hostile aircraft for 10 minutes until another machine came to his rescue'.

Whitworth was promoted to A/Captain and Flight Commander in January 1917. On 13 March 1917, Whitworth and his Observer, Second Lieutenant N J Brebner, in a BE2e, were both wounded by rifle fire from the ground, Whitworth seriously. It was February 1918, before Whitworth was sufficiently recovered from his wounds to take up instructing duties in the UK. He was presented with the insignia of his MC by the King at an investiture at Buckingham Palace on 9 March 1918. In August 1918, he was sent to 250 Squadron for anti-submarine patrols in DH6s. Whitworth was allowed to relinquish his commission to return to teaching at Lancing College on 30 November 1918. He was Head Master at Framlington from 1929 to 1935. Lived in retirement at Manor Farm, Rendham, near Saxmundham, Suffolk.

WILBERFORCE, William Robert Sargent

The youngest son of the Right Reverend Ernest Roland Wilberforce, Bishop of Chichester, and Emily Henrietta Maud Wilberforce, née Connor, he was born on 12 June 1893. His elder brother, Arthur, had been dangerously wounded in the South Africa War whilst serving with the Imperial Yeomanry. William was educated at Summer Fields and at Winchester (1907-11), House Prefect, Soccer XI, won Junior Steeplechase. On leaving school, he went out to Canada to learn practical farming before returning home in 1913 to study Land Agency, becoming Land Agent for Lord Caernarvon from 1913 to 1914. Gazetted Second Lieutenant to 7 Battalion, King's Royal Rifle Corps, on 9 September 1914. Accompanied his battalion to France on 19 May 1915. On 4 January 1916, and upon the recommendation of the C-in-C, he was commissioned to a Regular Army battalion of the King's Royal Rifle Corps with an almost immediate secondment to the RFC. Gained his Royal Aero Club Certificate (Number 2683) on 24 March 1916. His formal pilot training duly completed, he was confirmed and gazetted Flying Officer on 29 May following. Sent out to Egypt soon afterwards, he fought through the first Battle of Gaza in Palestine, with 14 Squadron, between July 1916 and May 1917. His MC being announced in the *London Gazette* of 16 August 1917: 'For conspicuous gallantry and devotion to duty. During a bomb attack on our lines by hostile aircraft he attacked them single-handed, although they were superior to him in speed, and after a running fight destroyed an enemy machine. His skill and courage throughout nine months' operations have been worthy of the highest praise'.

Fever and ill-health compelled him to return to the UK in the autumn of 1917. Once recovered, he was posted as an Instructor at the CFS, Upavon, where he was accidentally killed whilst testing a new machine on 2 June 1918. William Wilberforce is buried in Shedfield (St John the Baptist) Churchyard, Hampshire.

WILKINSON, Eric Russell

The son of Charles and Emily Wilkinson, of 55 St Mary's Mansions, Paddington, London, he was born in Cheshunt on 26 January 1894. Leaving his widowed mother, Wilkinson emigrated to Canada in 1913 and was 'fruit ranching' in British Columbia when the war came in 1914. Already a pre-war volunteer with the rank of Sergeant in 31 British Columbia Horse, he was amongst the first to offer himself for service with the CEF. Attesting into Lord Strathcona's Horse on 22 September 1914, he was, in view of his previous experience, given the rank of Lance Sergeant. Embarked for France on 4 May 1915. Picked out for a commission, he returned to England and was gazetted Second Lieutenant to 15 (Reserve) Battalion, Middlesex Regiment on 15 October 1915. Seconded to the RFC, he trained as a Pilot and was confirmed and gazetted Flying Officer on 26 July 1916. A 'founder member' of 47 Squadron, he accompanied a Flight of that unit to Salonika on 20 September 1916. Wilkinson was involved in a bizarre incident when horsing around in a sham fight with Ulsterman Second Lieutenant Joseph Lamont Bamford of 17 Squadron, the two colliding in mid-air over the aerodrome at Hadzi-Junas. The tail plane and rudder of Bamford's BE12 were swept away and he fell spinning to the ground. Fortunately, apart from concussion and extensive bruising, Bamford survived the crash. In the meantime, Wilkinson managed to land his DH2 which immediately 'collapsed like a pack of cards when it touched the ground'. Despite this unfortunate incident, Wilkinson was subsequently awarded the MC, announced in the Birthday Honours *London Gazette* of 4 June 1917 (no citation).

On 6 October 1917, eight British machines having bombed batteries at Nicolic from a low height, were returning when they spotted enemy infantry. Coming down to one hundred feet to attack the soldiers, the bombing machines found their fire returned from the ground. Wilkinson's machine received a direct hit on the engine and he was forced to land. It transpired that he had also been wounded in the abdomen and, despite receiving immediate medical attention, he died the following day at No 21 Stationary Hospital. Eric Wilkinson is buried in Sangol Military Cemetery, Kriston, Greece.

NB: His medals are in a private collection: MC (engraved: E.R.W*), 1914-15 Star* (Sjt. Lord Strahcona's Horse)*, British War Medal 1914-20, and Victory Medal 1914-19* (Lieut).

WILLCOX, George Talbot

From Newport, Monmouthshire, he was born in Cardiff in 1895. Educated at Wellington School, Somerset ,where he was a member of the OTC. Gazetted Second Lieutenant to 1/6 (City of Glasgow) Battalion, Highland Light Infantry (TF), on 18 October 1914. He accompanied his battalion to Gallipoli, landing there on 3 July 1915. Following the evacuation, he successfully sought secondment to the RFC, which came on 25 June 1916. His pilot training duly completed, he was confirmed and gazetted Flying Officer on 15 October following. Served on Home Defence duties with, successively, 33 and 36 Squadrons. Willcox accompanied the night-bombing FE2b-equipped 101 Squadron to France as a 'founder member' on 25 July 1917 and was promoted A/Captain and Flight Commander on 21 September following. The following extract from RFC Communiqué No 122, dated 21 January 1918, gives a fascinating insight into the difficulties of flying basically under-powered machines at night and in bad weather: 'On 9/10 [January 1918] Captain Willcox and 2/AM Rennie, 101 Squadron, left ground 5.20pm to test the weather. Having reached 1,000 feet the pilot decided to cross the lines, although the weather was getting worse and the wind stronger. He flew to Menin on which place he dropped eight 25lb bombs and then turned in order to re-cross the lines. He had a dead head-wind against which it was practically impossible to make any way, the wind having a velocity of about 50 miles per hour. The hostile anti-aircraft soon realised the difficulties with which the machine had to contend, and were not slow to take advantage of it. Owing to the very high wind, the machine drifted by Lille in spite of efforts to prevent it, and immediately a heavy barrage of machine guns and anti-aircraft guns firing tracer and burning shells (flaming Onions) was opened up at it. This lasted for some considerable time, as the machine was unable to get away. The machine having been fitted with wireless, the Aerodrome from time to time received messages from it and these proved to be of the greatest assistance. By this means intimation was received that bombs had been dropped and the whereabouts and condition of the machine. The aeroplane still continued to drift south and Captain Willcox was unable to do anything to prevent it. For a short time he was lost and a message was received asking for rockets. These were fired and the assistance of the searchlight section (anti-aircraft) was asked for. They put on their lights which proved to be very useful to the pilot, by this time, another message was received, stating that the machine was near Bethune, and being shelled heavily by our own anti-aircraft guns in spite of it having fired the colour of the night. Eventually No 23 was reached and the pilot shortly after saw the aerodrome. The Squadron Commander says, 'This flight is in my opinion the finest that any night flyer pilot has yet put up. It was impossible for Captain Willcox to go higher than 2,000 feet as the wind above that was 90mph: 30 miles an hour faster than the speed of the machine. Captain Willcox's machine was very badly hit while on this and the other side of the lines'.

Willcox's MC was announced in the *London Gazette* of 18 February 1918, details in the *Gazette* of 18 July 1918: 'For conspicuous gallantry and devotion to duty. On five occasions he carried out bombing raids at a low altitude on important enemy railway stations, aerodromes, and other targets, obtaining direct hits on each occasion. He has set a very fine example to his squadron by his gallantry and devotion to duty'.

His tour with '101' completed, he returned to the Home Establishment on 23 March 1918 and was posted as a Night Flying Instructor in the UK. Sent out again after the war, he joined 27 Squadron, then at Beauvois on 14 December 1918. His last, brief, posting was to 75 Squadron in February 1919, before he finally left the RAF, via the Unemployed List, on 8 March following. George Willcox died in Surrey in 1968.

WILLIAMS, Ernest Leslie

The son of Mercantile Clerk, Percy Howard Williams and Edith Susannah Williams (née Fyson), of 5 Gordon Road, Camberwell, London, he was born in Clapham on 15 November 1895. Educated at St Dunstan's College, where he was a member of the OTC. He was living and working in Southport, Lancashire, when the war came in 1914. Gazetted Second Lieutenant to 11 (2 Hull) Battalion, East Yorkshire Regiment, on 9 September 1914. Seconded to the RFC in the late autumn of 1915. His training duly completed, he was confirmed and gazetted Flying Officer on 4 March 1916. Sent out to BE2e-equipped 9 Squadron in France soon after qualifying for his 'Wings'. His MC was announced in the *London Gazette* of 17 September 1917: 'For conspicuous gallantry and devotion to duty in co-operating with our artillery, often under extremely unfavourable weather conditions. On one occasion in particular, although much hampered by mist and clouds, he ranged three of our batteries on to a hostile battery position and enabled them to demolish it. His splendid example has been of the greatest value to his squadron'.

Promoted to A/Major in June 1918, Leslie Williams, as he preferred to be known, survived the Great War.

WILLIAMS, Frank Emlyn

The son of Mr and Mrs T Williams of Troeddyrhiew House, Mountain Ash, Glamorgan, he was born in 1894. Educated at Colston's School, Bristol. A pre-war volunteer, he was commissioned into 1/5 Battalion, Welsh Regiment (TF). Mobilised with the rest of the TF on the first day of the war, 4 August 1914. Accompanied his battalion to Gallipoli, landing at Suvla Bay on 9 August 1915. Frank's wife Sybil, privately published her memoirs after the war and describes his early service thus: 'Frank was sent to Gallipoli and after fierce fighting and defeat, a sniper shot him through the cheek and the bullet lodged in his throat, but happily on the Hospital ship on the way home he coughed the bullet up and so saved his life'.

Once recovered, he successfully sought secondment to the RFC and, having trained as an Observer, was sent out to 14 Squadron in Egypt on 29 January 1917, the same day that he was formally confirmed and gazetted Flying Officer (Observer). His wife takes up the story again: 'After three months in Hospital at Southsea he changed to the RFC and when fully trained was shipped out to Egypt and was stationed at Ismailia. Before this happened he and I were married by the first Archbishop of Wales in Caerwys Church. It was a beautiful autumn day, 16 October. After a reception in the dear old Rectory [Sybil's family home], Frank and I left for Shrewsbury where we stayed at 'The Raven Hotel', leaving next day for 'The Hydro', Torquay, where we spent our honeymoon of three weeks. We returned to Mountain Ash, and after a few days at Troeddyrhiew House [Frank's family home] I went to see Frank off from Cardiff. He was posted to Egypt, Ismailia, to join the Corp [sic]'.

His tour with '14' completed on 16 December 1917, he was promoted to A/Captain and sent as an Instructor to 57 TS in Egypt. His MC, awarded under the heading of: '....military operations culminating in the capture of Jerusalem while serving as an Observer in the RFC', was announced in the *London Gazette* of 11 April 1918 (no citation). Tragically, after surviving Gallipoli and nearly 12 months of operational flying, he was very badly burned in a fire at his living quarters on 31 March 1918, dying from his injuries just seven days later on 7 April. His wife records these events and her great sadness at the news, in her memoirs: '....he distinguished himself by winning the MC for bravery in the shelling of Gaza. In a few weeks he was caught in a fire in the Desert Camp, and after seven days he died. In time I received his medal from Lord Haig in Liverpool. And so ended another phase of my life. If it had not been for my mother's care and nursing I doubt that I would have lived. For months I could not bear to see anyone, and I shed so many tears that I think I must have dried up the fountain, for I have never shed a tear since that time'.

Frank Williams is buried in Ismailia War Cemetery, Egypt.

NB: His medals were offered for sale by Buckland Dix & Wood (lot 276) on 2 December 1992: MC, 1914-15 Star (Lieut Welsh Regt), *British War Medal 1914-20, and Victory Medal 1914-19* (Capt).

WILLIAMS, Frederick

Born in the Maranoa district of Queensland, Australia. Served with 55 Squadron where he flew a large number of operations in DH4 machines. His work was rewarded with both the MC and later the Distinguished Flying Cross. Known as 'Billy, his MC appeared in the *London Gazette* on 16 September 1918: 'For conspicuous gallantry and devotion to duty during recent operations. He took part in a number of long distance raids and photographic reconnaissances showing great gallantry and skill under difficult conditions. He destroyed three enemy aircraft and drove down two out of control. Throughout he showed great keenness and determination'.

His Distinguished Flying Cross was announced in the *London Gazette* of 21 September 1918, which noted that he had flown a further 17 bombing raids and ten photographic operations. The French also rewarded his efforts with a Croix de Guerre. His final raid took place on 1 August 1918, a mission to bomb factories in Cologne, in DH4 'B3957'. On his sorties he flew a Union Jack pennant attached to a wing strut. When returning to Australia in 1923 he was lucky to survive a severe bout of Tuberculosis, but went on to live until 1963.

NB: The RAF Museum Hendon has his medals in its collection: MC, Distinguished Flying Cross, and Croix de Guerre (France) only.

WILLIAMS, Henry Daniel

A Kiwi, he was born in New Zealand on 8 September 1893. A Farmer and a married man by the time the war came, he immediately enlisted into 11 Battalion, Auckland Mounted Rifles. He sailed for Egypt on 14 February 1915, as part of the Third Reinforcing Draft. His regiment did not take part in the initial ANZAC landings on Gallipoli but was, instead, sent as reinforcements to that unhappy place on 4 May following. Williams was commissioned in the field, being gazetted Second Lieutenant to the New Zealand Military Forces on 15 July 1915. He survived the severe fighting, being evacuated from the Peninsula later in the year. Next he successfully sought secondment to the RFC, which followed in May 1916. Having trained as an Observer at RFC HQ, Egypt, he was sent as a Probationary to 17 Squadron. Appointed to 'B' Flight, he flew reconnaissance and bombing flights in the BE2c of the squadron against the Senussi tribes in the area around the Kharga and Dakhla Oases. In June 1917, the main body of '17' was sent to Salonika with Williams' 'B' Flight following a month later. His 'apprenticeship' satisfactorily completed, he was confirmed and gazetted Flying Officer (Observer) on 15 July 1916. Williams served on the Doiran front until ordered to England for pilot training on 6 September 1916. He had, by this time, accumulated one hundred hours of operational flying. He commenced flight training on 21 November 1916, gaining his Royal Aero Club Certificate (Number 4207) on 2 January 1917. However, all of this was interrupted by a spell of bad health and consequent hospitalisation on 27 February 1917. Following successful surgery, he recommenced pilot training and, having formally qualified, was posted to the BE2e-equipped 7 Squadron, then at Motigny in France, on 27 April 1917. As part of the preparations for the assault on the Messines Ridge, Harry Williams' Flight was ordered to work alongside 21 Squadron, then at Poperinghe. Both squadrons were heavily engaged in 'flash' patrolling and artillery observation throughout and beyond the Battle of Messines. In June 1917, 7 Squadron exchanged the BE2e for RE8. Williams, striking up a successful partnership with Welshman Sergeant J G Morris (Number 77982) from Llanelly, was next involved in the build up for, and execution of, the Third Battle of Ypre, later more often known as Passchendaele. With Morris in the observer's seat, Williams gained his only confirmed victory, sending down one of two attacking Albatros Scouts to crash in the vicinity of Langemarck. His MC was announced in the *London Gazette* of 26 September 1917, details in the *Gazette* of 9 January 1918: 'For conspicuous gallantry and devotion to duty whilst carrying out artillery observation. Although attacked by two machines, he carried on with his work, driving one off and destroying the other. He has consistently shown courage and perseverance in carrying out his work, and set a very fine example to his squadron'.

Sergeant Morris, too, was awarded the Military Medal in the *London Gazette* of 17 September 1917. Williams was promoted to A/Captain and given command of 'C' Flight soon after the award of his MC. His heavy workload continued until 29 November 1917, when he was sent back to England for a well-earned rest, having also been Mentioned in Despatches for distinguished work in company with Sergeant Morris and having accumulated 252 hours, 40 minutes operational flying. Promoted next to A/Major, he saw out the war as an Instructor and training expert at various training depots and training squadrons in the UK. Harry Williams finally left the RAF, via the Unemployed List, on 16 August 1919.

WILLIAMS, John Jordan Lloyd

The son of Headmaster, John Jordan Lloyd Williams and Ellen Augusta C L Williams, of the Grammar School, Oswestry, Salop, he was born in 1894. A pre-war volunteer, he was gazetted Second Lieutenant to the Denbighshire Yeomanry (TF) on 26 July 1913. Mobilised with the rest of the TF on 4 August 1914, he subsequently served with the Yeomanry in Gallipoli and, following the evacuation, in Egypt. Seconded to the

RFC, he trained as an Observer at RFC HQ, Egypt, and was sent as such to 111 Squadron in Palestine on 31 August 1917. Williams achieved five victories between 8 October and 8 November 1917, becoming an Observer Ace. On 8 October 1917, Williams and his Pilot of the day, Second Lieutenant R C Steele, in BF2b, 'A7194', drove Oberleutnant Ditmar and his Albatros DIII, '636/17', down into Allied lines, the first enemy machine to be captured in Egypt. Steele was awarded the Distinguished Service Order for this feat, *London Gazette* of 17 December 1917, details in the *Gazette* of 23 April 1918. On 9 January 1918, Williams and his Pilot of the day, Lieutenant C R Davidson, in a Bristol Fighter, were shot up during an aerial combat. Davidson was wounded in the action, but Williams emerged unscathed. John Williams' tour with '111' completed, he returned to RFC HQ, Egypt, for rest and recuperation on 29 January 1918. His MC was announced in the *London Gazette* of 23 April 1918: 'For conspicuous gallantry and devotion to duty in aerial fighting. He shot down three hostile aeroplanes in a very short period, showing great initiative and fearlessness on all occasions'.

Williams next trained as a Pilot and, after qualifying for his full 'Wings', served in that capacity from 15 June to 24 November 1918, when he returned to the UK. In later life he served with the Police Force, becoming an Inspector with the Met.

WILLIAMS, John Scott

From Vancouver, British Columbia, Canada, he was born on 22 February 1891. Educated locally. Enlisted as a Private soldier into the Canadian Army Service Corps and served with the CEF in France as part of 2 Divisional Supply Column. Successfully responding to a plea for volunteers for the flying service, he was gazetted Second Lieutenant to the RFC, via the Special Lists, on 31 May 1916. Having trained as an Observer, he was sent out as a Probationary to FE2b-equipped 22 Squadron in France in August 1916. Williams soon struck up an effective partnership with South African Pilot, Lieutenant G W Robarts (qv). The two did some particularly noteworthy work in attacking enemy ground troops on 9 September 1916. On 24 September following, the same pair encountered a number of enemy machines during an offensive patrol, and managed to account for two of them in quick succession. Both men received the MC for this feat, announced in the *London Gazette* of 14 November 1916: 'For conspicuous skill and gallantry when attacking enemy machines. On one occasion, with another officer as a pilot, he brought down two enemy machines'.

His 'apprenticeship' more than satisfactorily completed, Billy Williams was formally confirmed and gazetted Flying Officer (Observer) on 23 September 1916. After 201 operational hours, his tour with '22' was completed and he returned to the Home Establishment on 10 November 1916. Williams was allowed some leave back home in Canada in 1917, before, as soon as he returned, training as a Pilot in the UK. Once qualified for his full 'Wings', he was posted to a number of instructing posts, including, on 1 March 1918, that of Flight Commander at the School of Special Flying. Williams received a Mention in Despatches at this time, *London Gazette* of 13 March 1918. His outstanding work in the field of instruction was eventually marked by the award of an Air Force Cross in the *London Gazette* of 2 November 1918. He was finally repatriated to Canada on 15 August 1919, where he was appointed A/Squadron Leader in the newly forming RCAF. He rose to the rank of Wing Commander in the RCAF and, at one time, commanded the Training Wing at Camp Borden, before retiring and starting one of the first commercial airlines in Canada, offering an air mail service in the Northern Ontario goldfields. He later became a Test Pilot in the USA. During the Second World War, he held various Staff positions with the RCAF, before being appointed CO, 2 ITS, Regina, Saskatchewan, in April 1943. Bad health caught up with him, however, and he was obliged to relinquish this post in November 1943, due to a heart condition. Wing Commander John Scott Williams retired to Montreal, where he died on 1 January 1944.

WILLIAMS, Leslie Bernard

Born in Wrexham, in 1895, he was brought up by sister's husband, Furniture Manufacturer, John Baillie Lawson, of 'Baillieville', Mill Lane, West Derby, Liverpool. Gazetted Second Lieutenant to the Army Cyclist Corps, with an immediate secondment to 11 Battalion, King's (Liverpool Regiment), on 19 November 1914. The 11 KLR was the very first of the nationwide 'Service' Battalions to be raised and handed to the War Office and Lord Kitchener, ready for service. Converted to a 'Pioneer Battalion', they were sent to France on 30 May 1915. Seconded to the RFC in April 1916, he trained as an Observer and was sent out as a Probationary to 1 Squadron in June 1916. His 'apprenticeship' satisfactorily completed, he was confirmed and gazetted Flying Officer (Observer) on 1 November following. His tour with '1' completed, he returned to the Home Establishment to undertake pilot training on 30 December 1916. Having qualified for his full 'Wings' with 49 Squadron in the UK, he was next sent to train with the DH5s of 64 Squadron, before accompanying the unit to France as a 'founder member' on 15 October following. '64', a specialist low-level attack unit, were heavily involved on the first day of the Battle of Cambrai on 20 November 1917. Six of the squadron's DH5s were lost or damaged on the day. Williams, in DH5, 'A9486', was fortunate to escape only with wounds when his top wing was blown off in the air by ground fire. He was forced to crash in no-man's land near to Bullecourt, but was again fortunate to be rescued by nearby Tommies, who spirited him away to a Casualty Clearing Station. His MC was announced in the *London Gazette* of 25 April 1918: 'For conspicuous gallantry and devotion to duty. During an attack with machine-guns and bombs on enemy infantry he displayed great courage and endurance in spite of very adverse weather conditions, which caused the machine to become separated in the fog. Observing a hostile battery in action he released bombs on it, one of which was observed to be a direct hit. Afterwards, whilst continuing his attacks on the enemy front trenches, his main plane was blown away, and his machine crashed to earth in the open. Being wounded, he lay there unable to move, but was eventually rescued. This officer has always shown himself full of zeal, determination and courage'.

Once recovered, he was posted to instructing duties with 29 TS, but was again hospitalised in August 1918, with a reoccurrence of the health problems caused by the wounds he received during the Battle of Cambrai. Williams finally left the RAF, via the Unemployed List, on 16 May 1919. He was known to be living in Strete, Dartmouth, South Devon, during the 1920s. Leslie Williams died on 13 February 1969.

WILLIAMS, Sedley Gerald

Worked, pre-war, for the Bank of Montreal in London. Enlisted as a Private soldier into 1/5 (City of London) Battalion, London Regiment, London Rifle Brigade, as soon as war came in August 1914. After service in France with the LRB, he was picked out for a commission and gazetted Second Lieutenant to the New Armies on 28 November 1915. On 3 May 1916, he was attached to a Trench Mortar Battery of the Devonshire Regiment. He served in the trenches with the Devons and was awarded the first of his MCs in the New Year *London Gazette* of 1 January 1918 (no citation). Seconded to the RFC, he trained as an Observer and accompanied the night-bombing FE2b-equipped 102 Squadron to France as a 'founder member' on 24 September 1917. On 21 February 1918, Williams and his Pilot, Second Lieutenant B C W Windle, in FE2b, 'B451', were forced to land behind enemy lines and taken as prisoners-of-war. The irrepressible Williams failed in one escape attempt when jumping from the train during a transfer from one prison camp to another. He was soon re-captured but his second break was entirely successfully, and he returned to Allied lines on 1 May 1918. The Bar to his MC came in the 'Escapers Gazette', *London Gazette* of 16 December 1919: '....in recognition of gallantry in escaping from captivity whilst Prisoners of War'.

WILLIAMS, Thomas Frederic

Born in Ingersoll, Ontario, Canada, on 12 October 1885. He enlisted as a Trooper into 1 Canadian Dragoons as soon as war came in August 1914, subsequently serving with the CEF in France and Flanders in 1915 and 1916. Responding to a call for volunteers for the flying service in 1916, he was eventually gazetted Second Lieutenant to the RFC on 26 April 1917. His formal pilot training duly completed, he was confirmed and gazetted Flying Officer on 18 July following. Sent out to 45 Squadron (Sopwith Camels) in France soon after qualifying for his 'Wings', he experienced an inauspicious start to what would prove to be a highly successful combat career. Firstly, on 22 September 1917, he was shot down by elements of Manfred von Richthofen's JGI, but was, fortunately, only shaken by the experience. On 6 November 1917, he was shot down again, and this time by a Canadian machine gunner who mistook him, and his squadron colleague, Captain Firth, for German machines as they flew back from across the lines. During this period he himself claimed four victories, including one on 24 October 1917, when he took on, single-handedly, no less than seven Albatros Scouts. It was because of this one-sided contest that he was given the nom-de-guerre 'Voss' by his colleagues, an echo of that monumental last battle put up by the great German Ace Werner Voss. From France, '45' moved to the Italian front on 17 November 1917, where Williams went on to claim a further four victories between 10 January and 27 March 1918, before being posted to the Sopwith Camel-equipped 28 Squadron, also stationed on the Italian front, as an A/Captain and Flight Commander. Six further victories came to him between 19 June and 27 July 1918, the Italians awarding him their Silver Medaglia al Valore Militare. His MC was announced in the *London Gazette* of 16 September 1918: 'For conspicuous gallantry and devotion to duty. He destroyed four enemy aircraft and drove down one. Also, in conjunction with another officer, he was instrumental in forcing an enemy machine to surrender and land'.

Williams was said to have been recommended for the Distinguished Flying Cross at this time but, in the event, he never received it. Returning home to Canada after the war, he became a 'Barnstormer' in the 1920s, the holder of Flying Certificate (Commercial) Number 91, he also gained an Air Engineers licence. From 1927 to 1931, he owned and ran a commercial air service in south-western Ontario, before becoming a Flying Instructor at the London Flying Club in Ontario. He next flew for Skylines Express, but when that company ceased to exist, he switched to become a Charter Pilot and Instructor at Rouyen, Quebec. In 1939, he became Chief Test Pilot for the Fleet Aircraft Company of Ontario, a post he held until 1948. 'Tommy' or 'Voss' Williams continued to fly into old age. In 1971, age 87, he flew one last aerobatic flight, becoming recognised, as a consequence of this, as 'the world's oldest Pilot'. He also published a book of poetry age 97. Canadian aviation pioneer, Tommy Williams, died in Woodstock, Ontario, on 25 July 1985.

WILLIAMS, Thomas Melling

The son of Thomas Henry Williams and Sarah Elizabeth (née Melling), of South Africa, he was born on 27 September 1899. Educated at Germiston, South Africa. As soon as he was old enough, he enlisted as a Private soldier into 12 Battalion, SAI, and served with that unit in German East Africa in 1916 and 1917. Recruited in South Africa as a volunteer for the flying service, he travelled to the UK where he was gazetted Second Lieutenant to the RFC on 30 August 1917. His pilot training duly completed, he was confirmed and gazetted Flying Officer on 6 November following. Sent out to the low-level attack specialising 65 Squadron (Sopwith Camels) in France at the end of 1917, he achieved nine victories between 29 January and 1 August 1918. It is recorded that the first of these victories came when he got to within point-blank range of an Albatros DV, before firing into the fuselage and sending it down in flames. On 8 August 1918, the first day of the Battle of Amiens and the so-called 'Black Day for the German Army', Williams attacked the rear troop train of three, dropping two bombs from low altitude with such accuracy that the transport broke into two. He then descended to an extreme low-level and proceeded to attack the German infantrymen spilling out of the wrecked coaches with his machine guns, although coming under heavy retaliatory fire from the ground. When he returned to base, his Camel was found to be riddled with bullets. Also 8 August was 'a Black Day' for 65 Squadron, with no less than eight of their Camels shot up or sent down during the daylight hours. Williams ended the day unscathed and may well have added a tenth victory to his tally but, unfortunately, that remains unconfirmed. His MC was announced in the *London Gazette* of 16 September 1918: 'For conspicuous gallantry and devotion to duty. During recent operations he destroyed three enemy aircraft and drove down two out of control. He showed great skill and courage in his attacks, and set a fine example to all'.

He was also awarded the first of his Distinguished Flying Crosses in the *London Gazette* of 2 November 1918, this largely for his attack on the troop train on 8 August 1918. He was also awarded the Italian Medaglia al Valore Militare at this time. Staying on in the RAF after the war, he next served with the Allied Intervention Force in Russia, where he earned a Bar to his Distinguished Flying Cross, *London Gazette* of 22 December 1919 (Baltic). Williams was next attached to the Royal Navy, in a role akin to the Fleet Air Arm, from 1919 until 1926. His many appointments, honours and promotions thereafter included: Service in Malta, 1926 to 1931; Adjutant, Cambridge University Air Squadron, 1931 to 1934; RAF Staff College, 1935; Air Ministry, 1936-37; CO, RAF Andover, 1938; HQ, 1 Group, 1938-39; France, Air Striking Force, September 1939/June 1940; CO, RAF Station Watton, July 1940/June 1941; OBE, 1941; SASO, 2 Group, July/October 1941; D/SASO, Bomber Command 1941-42; SASO to Air Marshal Pierce in Java, January/February 1942; SASO, Air Forces in India, March/December 1942; AOC, Bengal Command, RAF India, 1943; Deputy Commander, HQ, Eastern Air Command (Air Command South East Asia), 1944; CB, 1944; Assistant Chief of Air Staff (Operations), 1944-47; Commandant, RAF Staff College, Bracknell, 1947-48; AOC-in-C, BAFO, Germany, 1948-51; knighted (KCB), 1950, and Inspector General of the RAF, 1951-52, before retiring in 1953. He married, in 1938, Patricia Joan Osmond, with whom he had one son and two daughters. He lived, in retirement, at Glovers, Kennington, Kent. Air Marshal Sir Thomas Williams died on 10 June 1956.

WILLIAMS, William George Bransby

The son of famous actor Bransby Williams and Emile Margaret Williams, of Broomsbank, Selsey, Sussex, and of 19 Eton Court, Elton Avenue, London, he was born on 6 January 1898. His brother, Eric Bransby Williams, also became an actor of some note. William was educated at St Winifred's School, Kenley, and at Dulwich College (1912-13). Volunteering his services as soon as he was old enough, he was gazetted Second Lieutenant to the RFC, via the Special Reserve, on 12 June 1915. His formal pilot training duly completed, he was confirmed and gazetted Flying Officer on 31 July following. Sent out to 2 Squadron in France in the late summer of 1915, still then only 17 years old. On 12 October, Williams and his Observer of the day, Lieutenant H B Davey (qv), whilst taking photographs over Pont-a-Vendin in a BE2c, were attacked repeatedly for over half-an-hour by an Albatros Scout. Only when the British pair got a burst into the enemy machine at close range, did the German decide that discretion was the better part of valour and dived away. The BE2c sustained hits in the engine, propeller and aileron, but still Williams got them safely home. His tour with '2' completed in mid-March 1916, he returned to the UK for a rest before taking up instructing duties at Dover. His MC was announced in the Birthday Honours *London Gazette* of 3 June 1916 (no citation). Although no formal citation was published in the *Gazette*, research has unearthed the original recommendation for the award: 'W G B Williams For conspicuous gallantry and skilful work in the air, between September 22nd 1915 and March 1916. Notably on January 22nd 1916, working far over the lines, when the clouds made it necessary to fly very low, he registered a 6 inch gun on Carvin under a very heavy fire. On March 9th he acted as leader to a successful bomb raid of 34 machines'.

Promoted to A/Captain and Flight Commander and thus becoming one of the youngest Captains in the British Army, he returned again to France on 12 October 1916, this time accompanying the Sopwith Strutter-equipped 45 Squadron as a 'founder member'. On 23 January 1917, Williams and his Observer of the day, Second Lieutenant J Senior, in Strutter, 'A1083', sent an Albatros DII down out of control over Menin, the pair also damaging another enemy machine in the same engagement. Williams next transferred, again as a Flight Commander, to the Spad VII-equipped 19 Squadron. On 12 May 1917, Williams in Spad VII, 'B1560', was shot down and killed over Izel by Leutnant Paul Billik of Jasta 12, the second of the German Ace's eventual 31 victories. William Bransby Williams' remains were never recovered and hence he is commemorated on the Flying Services Memorial, Arras, France.

WILLS, Oliver Byerley Walter

The son of Mr and Mrs George Tarlton Wills, of Sunningdale, Berkshire, he was born in Finchley on 27 June 1892. Educated at Elstree, Heddon Court, at Bedales School (1906-10), and at Trinity College, Cambridge (1911-14), where he studied Zoology. When the war came, he enlisted as a Private soldier into the Honourable Artillery Company (Infantry) (TF) on 6 October 1914. After service with the Reserve Battalion, HAC, in the UK, he was picked out for a commission and gazetted Second Lieutenant to the RFC on 22 April 1916. His formal pilot training duly completed, he was confirmed and gazetted Flying Officer on 28 July following. Sent out to France and 34 Squadron on 30 August 1916. Wills was soon heavily involved in the hard slogging artillery observation, reconnaissance and photographic work expected of a 'Corps' squadron. However, when in January 1917, '34' switched from the BE2e to the RE8 – the BE2e were sent on to 52 Squadron and it appears that Wills accompanied the older type machines to their new home. His tour with '52' completed on 6 October 1917, Wills returned to the Home Establishment for a rest and an onward posting to the Experimental Station at Orfordness. His MC was announced in the *London Gazette* of 18 October 1917, details in the *Gazette* of 7 March 1918: 'For conspicuous gallantry and devotion to duty. He carried out a reconnaissance on a hostile heavy howitzer emplacement nearly 8,000 feet over the line. He descended to a height of 2,000 feet, and carefully examined the position. Having decided the exact position of the gun, he successfully directed the infantry on to it, securing a direct hit on the emplacement'.

Wills married his fiancée, Ursula Carr, in 1918. On 10 November 1918, the day before the war finally ended, Wills was killed in a flying accident at Orfordness. It was reported afterwards that he had been up with a Pilot (presumably a pupil) and, 'just as they were landing, quite naturally and quickly, he was seen to fall from the machine, no one knew how, and was killed at once'. Oliver Wills is buried in Orford (St Bartholomew) Churchyard, Suffolk.

WILMOT, Edmund Percy

The son of Mr and Mrs Joseph Wilmot of Bungaree, Pootilla, Victoria, Australia, he was born on 12 August 1895. He was teaching at Salt Creek State School (Number 2334) when the war came in August 1914. Wilmot enlisted as a Private soldier (Number 670) into the AIF on 25 September 1914 at Ballarat and was sent for training at Camp Broadmeadows. On 25 February 1915, his basic training completed, he embarked aboard the Transport ship *Runic* at Melbourne, bound for the Middle East as a Sapper with 3 Reinforcement Group for the 2 Division, Signalling Company, Australian Engineers. He served subsequently in Egypt and, from 26 April 1915, in Gallipiloi with 14 Battalion, AIF. Wilmot was Mentioned in Despatches on 9 August 1915, for repairing telephone wires under heavy fire. Wounded in action on 12 August 1915, his 20th birthday, he was subsequently evacuated to England for medical care. Recovered and fit for duty again on 17 April 1916, Wilmot responded to an appeal for volunteers for the flying service. He was accepted and gazetted Second Lieutenant to RFC, via the Special Lists, on 15 July 1916. His formal pilot training duly completed, he was confirmed and gazetted Flying Officer on 14 December following. Sent out to 3 Squadron on 18 February 1917. On 15 March 1917, Wilmot and his Observer of the day, Lieutenant Morris, in Morane LA, 'A250', were shot down by anti-aircraft fire during an artillery observation patrol over Fremicourt. Fortunately, both men emerged unscathed from the wreck. His MC was announced in the *London Gazette* of 18 July 1917: 'For conspicuous gallantry and devotion to duty whilst co-operating with artillery. On one occasion he successfully ranged a siege battery on an enemy gun position in very bad weather, which necessitated flying at a very low altitude, during which he was subjected to an intense fire'.

3 Squadron's role changed in October 1917, when it was re-equipped with Sopwith Camel F1s, and was consequently designated a fighter unit. Edmund Wilmot was promoted to A/Captain and Flight Commander on 2 November 1917. Just four days later on 6 November, four Camels from 3 Squadron were victims of the atrocious weather conditions on that day. Battling their way through strong winds and poor light, they struggled to keep each other within sight. Realising that they were above enemy territory, but having no idea of their whereabouts, they decided, via hand-signalling, to land and find out. Having established that they were near to Namur, they took off again, or rather three of them did. Second Lieutenant T B Bruce (qv), in 'B6392', found that he was unable to take off and so burnt his Camel and went on the run. The remaining three continued their attempts to reach their own lines, but soon became disorientated again and were eventually forced to land as their petrol ran out, still in enemy territory near to Rheims. Wilmot and his colleagues, Second Lieutenants R

C Taylor and A G Cribb, were taken prisoner. Repatriated to the UK on 23 December 1918, Wilmot stayed on in the RAF for a period. Following a rest, he was sent first as an Instructor to 41 Training Depot on 14 February 1919. He later served with 29 TS and with the Army Co-operation Squadron. Wilmot left the RAF, via the Unemployed List, on 16 May 1920, before finally returning to Australia on 1 September 1921. Edmund Wilmot died on 10 May 1969.

WILSON, Arthur George

From Haxby, North Yorkshire, he was born in December 1894. A pre-war volunteer, he was a Corporal (Number 1416) in 1/5 Battalion, Yorkshire Regiment (TF), when war came in August 1914. Picked out for a commission, he was gazetted Second Lieutenant to his own battalion on 26 November 1914. Promoted to A/Lieutenant, he accompanied 1/5 West Yorks to France and Flanders on 15 April 1915. After extensive service in the trenches, Wilson was seconded to the RFC in September 1917. Having trained as an Observer, he was sent out again to the Western Front on 11 November 1917, eventually joining 7 Squadron (RE8s) on 30 December following. His MC was announced in the *London Gazette* of 26 July 1918: 'For conspicuous gallantry and devotion to duty, flying under most difficult weather conditions and obtaining, under heavy fire, valuable information, which he embodied in a series of excellent reports. On one occasion, when a smoke screen was put up by the enemy, he flew round and made a close reconnaissance from between 500 to 1,000 feet under heavy anti-aircraft and machine-gun fire'.

His tour with '7' completed on 26 August 1918, he returned to the Home Establishment and to instructing duties. Wilson finally left the RAF, via the Unemployed List, in December 1919. After leaving the RAF, Wilson went on to study medicine at Oxford University, eventually becoming a General Practitioner. Dr Arthur Wilson died in April 1990. In 1993, his son produced a biography of Arthur Wilson, entitled 'Peter'.

WILSON, Christopher William

The son of Mr and Mrs A H Wilson, of 11 Drummond Place, Edinburgh, he was born on 1 February 1878. Educated at Glenalmond (1892-95), Cricket XI, Rugby XV and Rowing VIII. After leaving school, he went on to attend Sandhurst in 1896, with the intention of making a career in the Army. He became Heavy and Middleweight Boxing Champions at Sandhurst but, for some reason, decided not to enter the Army at that time, but rather to go to the Argentine to live and work on the family ranch there, from 1896 to 1910, when he finally returned to the UK. Developing an interest in aviation, he gained his Royal Aero Club Certificate (Number 329) in a Graham White machine at the Graham White School at Hendon on 15 October 1912. Commissioned into the Seaforth Highlanders at last, his flying qualification facilitated Wilson's secondment to the RFC in 1913. On 12 May 1914, Wilson was involved in the first ever mid-air collision involving two aeroplanes of the RFC. Both were 5 Squadron machines - standard Sopwith three-seater tractor bi-planes, with 80hp Gnome engines. That afternoon, Lieutenant Wilson (in '325') had taken off from Farnborough at 16.00, en route for Brooklands. Almost an hour later, the other machine in the equation ('324'), crewed by Captain E V Anderson and Air Mechanic H W Carter (Number 133), took off from Brooklands on a routine practice flight. Whilst Anderson was still climbing, Wilson, returning from Farnborough, came gliding down. The two machines, each totally unaware of the other's presence, collided and fell out of control to crash quite close together. Anderson and Carter were killed outright, whereas Wilson had a miraculous escape, suffering only heavy bruising and a broken jaw. Technically, Wilson, as the Pilot of the higher of the two machines, was responsible for the crash. Wilson accompanied the original RFC contingent to France in August 1914, as a Flying Officer with 5 Squadron. He was promoted to A/Captain and Flight Commander on 16 September following. His work in the early months of the war was marked by the award of the newly instituted MC, in fact, he was only the second airman, ever, to be named as a recipient of the MC, announced in the *London Gazette* of 1 January 1915 (no citation). He was also Mentioned in Despatches on three occasions during 1914 and 1915. His tour with '5' completed, he returned to the Home Establishment in July 1915. Wilson was thereafter mainly employed in various training and Staff positions in the UK and in France, although he did command an operational squadron at the front from 25 February to 7 December 1917. With the rank of A/Lieutenant Colonel, he commanded 29 Wing, RAF, late in 1917 and early in 1918. His outstanding work in the instructing field was marked by the award of the Air Force Cross, *London Gazette* of 22 December 1919. Wilson relinquished his commission in the RAF on 7 February 1920, to accept a Captaincy in 1 Battalion, Seaforth Highlanders. He retired from the Seaforths with the rank of Major in 1923. Christopher Wilson died on Christmas Day 1963.

WILSON, David

The son of the Reverend David Wilson, MA, and May Wilson, of 14 Tavistock Square, London, WC 1, and a nephew of the first Lord Nunburnholme. Gazetted Second Lieutenant to 11 Battalion, East Yorkshire Regiment (2 Hull), on 29 October 1914. After service in the UK with 11 East Yorks, he was accepted as a volunteer to the flying service in December 1915. Gained his Royal Aero Club Certificate (Number 2275) on 14 January 1916. His formal pilot training duly completed, he was confirmed and gazetted Flying Officer on 9 March following. Sent out to 24 Squadron (DH2s), the first single-seater Scout unit, in France on 30 March 1916. His MC was announced in the *London Gazette* of 22 June 1916: 'For conspicuous gallantry and skill. After his machine had been damaged in a combat with an enemy machine and was difficult to control, he continued his patrol and assisted another officer to bring down an enemy machine. Later he found another enemy machine, dived at it, and brought it down in flames within our lines'.

Wilson died of wounds received in action on 30 July 1916. He has just been promoted to A/Captain and Flight Commander with another Squadron, being under orders for the transfer to take place on the following day. David Wilson is buried in St Pierre Cemetery, Amiens, France.

WILSON, Eric

From Clapham, London, he was born on 24 January 1897 and educated at Charterhouse. Gazetted Second Lieutenant to the RFC, he was confirmed and gazetted Flying Officer (Observer) on 28 March 1917. Sent out to 10 Squadron (AWFK8s) in July 1917, he transferred soon afterwards to 21 Squadron (RE8s). His MC was announced in the *London Gazette* of 26 September 1917, details in the *Gazette* of 9 January 1918: 'When he was in one of three machines engaged on photographic reconnaissances they were attacked by a formation of nine hostile scouts. A determined resistance was offered to this attack, which was beaten off, and the photographs were then taken. Whilst returning to the aerodrome, this officer turned back alone to take some further photographs, and, observing six hostile machines approaching, he promptly attacked them at close range, and after a sharp fight brought one down and drove off the remainder. He then completed his photography'.

He was also Mentioned in Despatches at this time. His tour with '21' completed, he returned to the Home Establishment on 7 December 1917. Sent out to RFC HQ, Egypt, on 18 December 1917, he served in that theatre of war until returning to the UK in July 1918. Wilson left the RAF, via the Unemployed List, in February 1919, but, for reasons unknown, was recalled briefly for temporary duty from 11 April to 4 June 1921.

WILSON, George Hamilton Bracher

The son of Charles John Wilson and Jane Wilson (née Snook), of Aylesbury Park, Dublin, Ireland, he was born on 14 May 1895. Educated at Marlborough (1908-12) and at Pembroke College, Cambridge, where he studied English and was a member of the OTC. Gazetted Second Lieutenant to 10 Divisional Train, Army Service Corps, on 10 November 1914. Posted to Gallipoli in July 1915, he next served in Salonika with 476 Company, 10 Divisional Column, Army Service Corps, from February 1916. He was hospitalised in Salonika on 12 July 1916, suffering from the dysentery and enteritis he had first contracted in Gallipoli. Following further medical treatment in Malta, he was next seconded to the RFC in the UK at the end of 1916. Having trained as a Pilot in the UK, he was confirmed and gazetted Flying Officer on 22 April 1917. Sent out briefly to 27 Squadron on the Western Front, he was next posted out to 113 Squadron on 13 August 1917 to fly operationally in Egypt and Palestine. His MC, announced in the *London Gazette* of 11 April 1918 (no citation) was awarded for: '.... military operations culminating in the capture of Jerusalem', His tour with '113' completed in January 1918, he returned to RFC HQ, Egypt, to take up instructing duties and eventual promotion to A/Lieutenant Colonel. His outstanding work in the instructing field was acknowledged with an Air Force Cross, *London Gazette* of 3 June 1919 (Egypt) and he was also created CBE. Wilson returned to the UK in March 1919, before leaving the RAF, via the Unemployed List, on 5 April following. A talented Engineer, Wilson then embarked upon what would prove an extremely successful business career. Joining the Dunlop Rubber Company in 1920, he subsequently became a director, later Chairman and, ultimately, Life President, of Raleigh Industries Ltd and subsidiary companies. He was also a director of Sturmey Archer Gears Ltd and of Tube Investments Ltd. He married in 1929, Elizabeth Violet Glenn, with whom he had one son and one daughter, living at 'The Curragh', Bramcote, Nottinghamshire. His civil appointments included: Chairman of Nottingham Savings Committee, 1939-48; President, British Cycle Manufacturers and Traders Union Ltd, 1945-48; President, Motor Trade Benevolent Fund, 1950-51; Member, Council of FBI, North-Midland Region, 1947-56; Member Council of Nottingham University, 1948; JP Nottingham, 1939; and High Sheriff of Nottinghamshire, 1949. He lived, in retirement, at The Old Rectory, Plumtree, Nottinghamshire. George Wilson died on 19 December 1963.

WILSON, Gordon Campbell

The son of Agnes Cecilia Wilson, of Hampton Avenue, Adamstown, New South Wales, Australia, he was born in Mimmi, New South Wales, on 6 October 1895. A Pattern Maker in Newcastle, NSW, he enlisted initially as a Sapper (Number 110) into 1 Field Company, Australian Engineers, on 22 August 1914. His basic training completed, he embarked, with the rank of Lance Corporal, at Sydney aboard the SS *Africa* (Transport A19), on 18 October 1914, bound for the Middle East. Promoted to Corporal on 24 February 1915, he landed in Gallipoli with his unit on 25 April 1915. After the evacuation from the Peninsula, he served again in Egypt and was promoted to Sergeant with 14 Field Company, AEs. He accompanied his unit to France in June 1916. He served subsequently with 'The Tunnellers' on the Western Front, winning an exceptional Distinguished Conduct Medal, *London Gazette* of 13 February 1917: 'For conspicuous gallantry in action. He exploded an enemy gallery single-handed. On one occasion he displayed great courage and determination when in charge of carrying parties to the front line, himself frequently passing through intense barrage'. He was next accepted as a volunteer to the flying service, arriving in Reading for tuition on 5 December 1916. Gazetted Pilot and Second Lieutenant to the AFC on 25 April 1917. Once qualified, Wilson and several other 2 Squadron, AFC, Pilots were sent out to France in July 1917, specifically to gain practical operational experience with RFC units at the front. After four weeks with 32 Squadron (DH5s), Wilson was subsequently promoted to A/Captain and Flight Commander with 2 Squadron, AFC (also DH5s) on 21 September 1917, the same day that he accompanied that unit to the front as a 'founder member'. 2 AFC arrived in France just in time to become heavily involved in the ensuing Battles of Cambrai and Gouzeaucourt. Wilson it was who witnessed and later reported upon his colleague Harry Taylor's (qv) extraordinary bravery after he (Taylor) had been shot down into the enemy's lines during a joint patrol on 20 November 1917. Taken ill, Wilson was evacuated to London for medical treatment on 13 January 1918. His MC was announced in the *London Gazette* of 4 February 1918, details in the *Gazette* of 5 July 1918: 'For conspicuous gallantry and devotion to duty. His work at low altitudes under very adverse conditions has been of the greatest value. On one occasion he scattered the enemy from a strong point with his machine gun. On another occasion he bombed and fired upon a field gun, killing two gunners. Despite the constant attacks of enemy scouts he held his formation together, which was out on a bombing raid, and enabled it to drop all its bombs on the objectives, an enemy aeroplane being also driven down. His dashing leadership has been a splendid example to his flight'.

Research has unearthed the original recommendation for this award, made by Brigadier General J F A Higgins, Commanding 3 Brigade, RFC, on 3 December 1917, which provides fuller detail: 'For continuous gallant work at very low altitudes in almost impossible weather. On 20-11-17 this officer scattered the enemy from a strong point near Flesquières with his machine gun. On 25-11-17 he bombed and shot on a field gun near Roumilly, killing two gunners. On 27-11-17 in spite of the constant attacks of enemy scouts he led a formation, carrying four bombs each, over Bourlon Wood. All the bombs were dropped on the objectives, and EA driven down. He then engaged a low-flying scout and fired 200 rounds at him at an average of 50 feet. His ammunition was then exhausted, and he had to return to his aerodrome. This officer has been out nearly every day attacking troops with bombs and machine-gun fire at very low altitude. His dashing leadership has been a fine example to his flight'.

Once recovered, Wilson was posted to HQ, 1 Wing, AFC, Cirencester, on 6 February 1918. He was next appointed to the command of 8 TS on 20 February 1919, his last job before leaving England for Australia and home on 6 May 1919. His outstanding work in this field was recognised by the award of an Air Force Cross, announced in the *London Gazette* of 3 June 1919. He was also Mentioned in Despatches on one occasion during the Great War. Gordon Campbell Wilson, MC, AFC, DCM, was killed in a road accident near Bogan Gate, New South Wales, on 11 March 1929.

WILSON, Percy

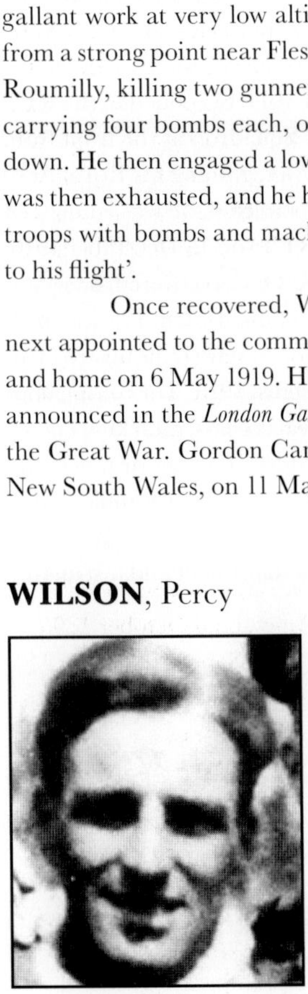

The son of publican, William Wilson and Margaret Ann Wilson, of The George and Dragon Hotel, 82 and 84 Grange Road, Birkenhead, Cheshire, he was born in Liverpool on 11 April 1895. He enlisted as a Sapper (Number 54064) into the Royal Engineers and, after training at Bulford, Salisbury Plain, he was promoted to Corporal and sent to France on 29 June 1915 as a motor-cycle despatch rider. Following service with the RE in France and Flanders, Wilson was accepted as a volunteer for the flying service. Gazetted Second Lieutenant to the RFC on 26 September 1916. His pilot training duly completed, he was confirmed and gazetted Flying Officer on 27 March 1917. He joined 28 Squadron (Sopwith Camels) in November 1917, just in time to accompany that unit to the Italian front. Wilson achieved seven victories between 25 January and 19 May 1918, including one balloon. On 3 May 1918, he attacked five enemy scouts that were escorting an Aviatik two-seater, shooting one of them down. Eight days later, when acting as escort to an RE8 of 34 Squadron, Wilson and his colleague, Lieutenant O W Frayne, each shot down Albatroses that were attempting to attack their charge. Wilson's MC was announced in the *London Gazette* of 16 September 1918: 'For conspicuous gallantry and devotion to duty in destroying six enemy aeroplanes and driving down three more out of control. He also destroyed an enemy balloon, which fell in flames'.

The Italians showed their appreciation of his services with the award of the Bronze Medaglia al Valore Militare as, indeed, did the French with a Croix de Guerre avec Palme. Wilson served with 79 Squadron in 1919, as part of the Army of Occupation in Germany.

NB: His medals were offered for sale by Dix Noonan Webb: MC, 1914-15 Star (54064 Cpl, RE), *British War Medal 1914-20, Victory Medal 1914-19* (Capt RAF), *Croix de Guerre avec Palme (France, bronze), and Bronze Medaglia al Valore Militare (Italy,* Percy Wilson, Trentino, Diverno 1917-18).

WINDSOR, Horatio Thomas Other

The son of Solicitor Thomas Other Windsor and Mrs Windsor, of 'Invermay', Hayward's Heath, he was born in Australia on 24 April 1892. Educated at Cheltenham (1904-08). He was living at 'Ellesmere', New Church Road, Sussex, when war came in August 1914. He had been a pre-war volunteer, holding a commission as a Midshipman in the Royal Naval Volunteer Reserve. Anxious to 'get into the fight', he resigned his commission in the RNVR and enlisted as a Trooper (Number 8269) into 9 (Queen's Royal) Lancers. Picked out for a commission, he was gazetted Second Lieutenant to 8 Battalion, Royal Munster Fusiliers, on 22 October 1914. Seconded to the RFC in the autumn of 1915, he first trained as an Observer and served as such with 12 Squadron at the front from 28 October 1915. Returning to the UK in the spring of 1916, he next trained as a Pilot, gaining his Royal Aero Club Certificate (Number 3033) on 22 May 1916. His formal pilot training duly completed, he was confirmed and gazetted Flying Officer on 23 November following. Sent out to 52 Squadron (RE8s) on 15 December 1916, the tour ended prematurely on 19 February 1917, when he was hospitalised in the UK. Once recovered, he served with 50 Squadron (BE 12s) at Throwley on Home Defence duties before joining 100 Squadron in France on 18 August 1917. His distinguished service with the night-bombing 100 Squadron was marked with the award of an MC, announced in the *London Gazette* of 26 March 1918, details in the *Gazette* of 24 August 1918: 'For conspicuous gallantry and devotion to duty. He carried out several night-bombing raids with great success, attacking enemy aerodromes and railway communications, often from a low altitude. He acted as leader of a long-distance raid in bad weather conditions, but reached his objective and obtained direct hits. He set a splendid example of skill and determination to the pilots of the squadron'.

His tour with '100' completed on 1 June 1918, he returned to the Home Establishment and instructing duties, never again to return to operational flying.

WINDSOR, John Stephen

The son of Foreman Hydraulic Fitter, John Charles Windsor and Elizabeth Gertrude Windsor (née Thomas), of 250 Dock View Road, Barry, Glamorgan, South Wales, he was born in 1894. Educated at Barry Elementary School and apprenticed as a Locomotive Engineer with the Barry Dock Railway. Despite his apparently basic and rudimentary education, he must have had exceptional ability, as he was allowed to enter the Royal Military College, Sandhurst, on a Scholarship in the summer of 1915. From Sandhurst, he was gazetted Second Lieutenant to a Regular Army battalion of the South Wales Borderers on 24 November 1915, with an almost immediate secondment to the RFC. Gained his Royal Aero Club Certificate (Number 2407) on 28 January 1916. His formal pilot training duly completed, he was confirmed and gazetted Flying Officer on 1 April following. Sent out to Mesopotamia and 30 Squadron on 6 July 1916, he flew operationally in that theatre of war (over 300 operational flying hours) until 23 May 1917, when he returned to the UK and instructing duties at the CFS. His MC was announced in the *London Gazette* of 25 August 1917 (no citation). It would appear from the South Wales Borderers regimental history for the Great War, that Windsor reverted to his regimental duties in the last months of 1917. He fought with 2 Battalion, South Wales Borderers, in the Battle of Cambrai and, indeed, was reported as 'missing' on 2 December 1917. He obviously turned up again, for he was soon back with the RFC, joining 1 Squadron (SE5As) at the front with the rank of A/Captain and Flight Commander on 13 April 1918. Just three days later on 16 April, Windsor, in an SE5A, was wounded in action by ground-fire during a low level patrol. Once recovered, he again returned to the CFS and instructing duties in November 1918. In April 1919, he was sent to serve with 92 Squadron, then stationed in Belgium, before going on to serve with 80 Squadron in Egypt from June 1919 until January 1920.

WINGFIELD, Lawrence Arthur

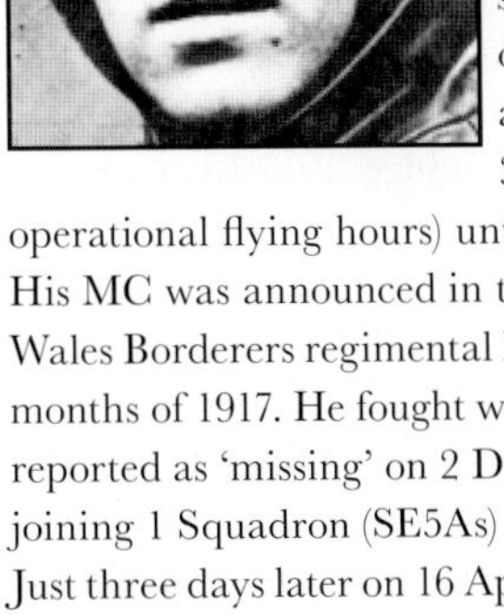

The son of Solicitor George Arthur Wingfield and Mrs Wingfield, of 4 Mount Row, Davies Street, London W1, he was born in Richmond, Surrey, on 17 April 1898. Educated at Aldenham (1909-14). After leaving school, he was articled to his father's practice at 74 Cheapside, London E1. Joined the Inns of Court OTC as a Private soldier (Number No4/2/4518), as soon as he was old enough on 28 June 1915. Gazetted Second Lieutenant to 6 (Special Reserve) Battalion, Royal Fusiliers, on 26 August 1915, with a secondment to the RFC coming in the following month after he had gained, at his own expense, his Royal Aero Club Certificate (Number 1781) on 22 September 1915. His formal pilot training duly completed, he was confirmed and gazetted Flying Officer on 20 December following. Sent out to 12 Squadron in France in January 1916. During a bombing raid on the opening day of the Battle of the Somme, 1 July 1916, Wingfield, in BE2c, '4196', was shot down to be taken prisoner near to St Quentin, possibly by Leutnant Wilhelm Frankl of Kek Vaux, one of the German Ace's eventual 20 victories. Remarkably, Wingfield would subsequently escape from Strohen Camp on 2 October 1917 and, despite many difficulties and considerable discomfort, successfully make his way to the Dutch border and safety, nine days later. That Wingfield flew operationally again is evidenced by the fact that he was awarded the Distinguished Flying Cross in the very first gazetting of the new award in the Birthday Honours *London Gazette* of 3 June 1918 (no citation). His MC, of course, came in the so-called 'Escapers Gazette', *London Gazette* of 16 December 1919: 'in recognition of gallantry in escaping from captivity whilst Prisoners of War'.

Leaving the RAF in 1919, Wingfield duly qualified as a Solicitor in the following year, becoming a partner in his father's practice. Retaining an interest in aviation, privately and professionally, Wingfield was, in time, appointed a Councillor to the Royal Aeronautical Society and Solicitors Clerk to the Guild of Air Pilots and Air Navigators of the British Empire, upon the formation of that body. After the Second World War, he had become a partner in the firm of Mackell and Company, Solicitors, 31 Bedford Street, London, with an appointment as Solicitor to the New Zealand Government in the UK. Lived at that time at 'Leverton', St George's Avenue, Weybridge, Surrey.

WINNICOTT, Russell

The son of Alderman Richard Weeks Winnicott, JP, and Annie Winnicott (née Proud), of 'Hyperion', Mannamead, Plymouth, Devon, he was born on 24 May 1898. Educated at Plymouth College and at The Leys, Cambridge (1913-15). Gazetted Second Lieutenant to 5 Battalion, Devonshire Regiment (TF), on 2 October 1915. Seconded to the RFC in August 1916, he trained as a Pilot and was duly confirmed and gazetted Flying Officer on 11 November following. Sent out to 41 Squadron (FE8s) in May 1917. The squadron converted to DH5s in July 1917, and Winnicott soon began accumulating victories, achieving seven between 6 September and 18 October. A further conversion to SE5As came in November 1917, with Winnicott gaining three more victories with this new marque in the same month. Coincidently, it was Winnicott who achieved 41 Squadron's first victories in both DH5s and SE5As. His MC was announced in the *London Gazette* of 27 October 1917, details in the *Gazette* of 18 March 1918: 'For conspicuous gallantry and devotion to duty in aerial combats. In a fight against the enemy scouts he drove down two out of control. On another occasion he destroyed an enemy scout, and on three previous occasions drove down enemy machines out of control. His dash and determination were of the highest order'.

Said to have been involved in more than 50 aerial combats, Winnicott was killed in action on 6 December 1917, almost certainly as a consequence of an aerial collision. Russell Winnicott is buried in Varennes Military Cemetery, Somme.

WINTER-IRVING, Stanhope Irving

The son of Stanhope and Frances Amelia Winter-Irving of 'Noorilum', Dandenong Road, Armadale, Victoria, he was born in Toorak, Victoria, on 13 November 1891. He was working as a Grazier in civilian life when he enlisted in the AIF as a 2 AM with 1 Squadron, AFC, on 17 February 1916. An unusually rapid promotion to Sergeant came on 1 March 1916, just 15 days before he embarked at Melbourne aboard the Transport A67, SS *Orsova*, as part of 'C' Flight, 1 Squadron, AFC, bound for the Middle East. After arriving in Egypt, he was posted to 17 Squadron, RFC, on 21 April 1916. Picked out for a commission, he was gazetted Second Lieutenant (Commonwealth Military Forces) on 12 June 1916. Sent to RFC HQ, Aboukir, for aviation instruction on 12 August 1916, he was duly confirmed and gazetted Flying Officer on 24 October following. Sent to 67 (Australian) Squadron in Heliopolis on 29 October 1916, he subsequently served on the Palestinian front. Promoted to A/ Captain and Flight Commander on 15 August 1917. His MC was announced in the *London Gazette* of 8 October 1917, details in the *Gazette* of 25 April 1918: 'For conspicuous gallantry and devotion to duty. When acting as escort during a reconnaissance, he repeatedly attacked and drove off single-handed a formation of three enemy aeroplanes, thereby enabling a most valuable reconnaissance to be made'.

Winter-Irving was also Mentioned in Despatches at this time. His tour with '67', later designated 1 Squadron, AFC, completed on 21 November 1917, he was allowed to return home to Australia, his appointment terminating there on 19 June 1918. Winter-Irving lived between the wars at 'Coolwoola', Nagambie, Victoria. He served again in the Second World War, this time with the RAAF at Maryborough, Victoria, before finally being discharged on 5 October 1945.

WISE, Cuthbert Walter

A Staff, not a flying, award

The son of Bank Officer W W Wise and Mrs Wise, of Streatham, Surrey, he was born in 1884. Educated at Epsom College. A pre-war volunteer, he was commissioned Second Lieutenant into 1 Volunteer Battalion, Queen's Royal Regiment, on 23 April 1902, with a promotions to Lieutenant coming in 1903 and Captain in 1907. Shortly after the outbreak of the Great War, Wise, by then a Major, was appointed Adjutant of 4 Battalion, Queen's Regiment (Royal West Surreys) on 24 October 1914. He held this appointment until the following January, but later reverted to the rank of Captain with 3 (Reserve) Battalion on 15 September 1915. Anxious still for active service, he subsequently accepted a commission and the rank of Lieutenant in the Army Service Corps, on 6 March 1916. Secondment to the RFC and appointment to Adjutant, Military Wing, followed on 10 November 1916. Wise was next appointed Staff Officer, 2nd Class, RFC, with grading, for purposes of pay, as Brigade Major on 6 September 1917. His MC was announced in the New Year *London Gazette* of 1 January 1918 (no citation). Wise was also Mentioned in Despatches on two occasions during the Great War. Further honours came from the Allies, the French awarding him the Croix de Guerre, *London Gazette* of 18 April 1918; and from the Serbs came the Order of the White Eagle with Swords, 4th Class, *London Gazette* of December 1919. Finally in this respect, he was also created an OBE in 1919. Wise was demobilised from the services and returned to civilian life on 6 May 1919. He was known to be living at 20 Eaton Garden Mansions, Hove, in the 1950s.

WISNEKOWITZ, Harry

Born in Covna, Russia, on 6 June 1895. Became a naturalised British subject in 1901, whilst living in Pearl, South Africa. Educated at the University of Cape of Good Hope, where he studied Engineering. He spent four years as a volunteer with the South African Defence Force from 1913 to 1917. He then enlisted, in 1917, into the Duke of Edinburgh's Own Rifles (South Africa). In May 1917, whilst stationed in Cape Town, he was recruited for the RFC by Captain A M Miller, who was in South Africa with the express purpose of seeking out suitable candidates for the flying service. After travelling to the UK, Wisnekowitz was gazetted Second Lieutenant to the RFC on 13 September 1917 (his name spelt in the *Army List* as 'Wisnekonitz'). Having trained as an Observer, he was sent out as a Probationary to 8 Squadron (AWFK8s) in France on 28 December 1917. His 'apprenticeship' satisfactorily completed, he was confirmed and gazetted Flying Officer (Observer) on 13 March 1918. On 23 March 1918, at the height of the German spring offensive which had started two days earlier, Wisnekowitz and his Pilot of the day, Second Lieutenant Lionel Conrad Hooton (qv), in 'C8430', were shot up by a ground-based machine gun over Chipilly during a contact patrol. Both men emerged unscathed from the incident. Four days later on 27 March, the same pair, in AWFK8, 'C3611', were again shot up near Morlancourt. Again, they escaped personal injury. Their MCs were announced in the *London Gazette* of 22 June 1918: 'For conspicuous gallantry and devotion to duty. On one occasion, during a very thick mist, he and his Pilot, by flying very low, despite very heavy machine-gun fire, succeeded in locating the enemy's positions. Though his machine was hit in all the vital parts, it was flown back to the aerodrome in safety. On a later occasion, when on a contact patrol, during failing light, they succeeded in locating accurately the position of the enemy. They have shown the utmost gallantry and skill during recent operations, and have carried out their duties with the greatest courage and determination'.

Harry Wisnekowitz survived the Great War to return to South Africa.

WOLTON, Richard Nigel

From West Garth, Ipswich, he was born on 21 June 1896. Educated at Ipswich School. A pre-war volunteer, he was gazetted Second Lieutenant to 'B' Battery, 2 Suffolk, 3 East Anglian (Howitzer) Brigade, Royal Artillery (TF). Wolton subsequently served in France from November 1915 with 272 Brigade, Royal Field Artillery. Seconded to the RFC in September 1916, he trained as a Pilot and was duly confirmed and gazetted Flying Officer on 10 February 1917. Sent out to the Cavalry Co-operation 35 Squadron (AWFK8s) on 4 April 1917. His exacting, if unspectacular, tour with '35' lasted more than a year. He was promoted to A/Captain and Flight Commander on 24 August 1917 and, despite being slightly wounded in action on 20 November 1917, continued on until 19 April 1918, when he returned to the Home Establishment for a well-earned rest. The first of his MCs was announced in the *London Gazette* of 26 March 1918, details in the *Gazette* of 24 August 1918: 'For conspicuous gallantry and devotion to duty. He performed most successful work in co-operation with artillery, often under the most adverse weather conditions and at very low altitudes. On one occasion during a flight of four and a half hours he successfully ranged a siege battery on one of the enemy's batteries and destroyed it, although he was attacked by enemy aircraft. He also attacked the enemy battery with bombs and machine-gun fire. By his courage and determination he has always set a splendid example to his squadron'.

Research has unearthed the original recommendation for this award which provides a little further detail: 'R N Wolton RFA 6/2/18 For conspicuously brilliant and successful work in co-operation with our artillery and our infantry, often flying under the most adverse weather conditions, and at very low altitudes. On January 29, 1918, during a flight of 6½ hours, he successfully ranged one of our siege batteries on a hostile battery position near Nauroy completely destroying it despite the fact that he was attacked by enemy aircraft. He also attacked this battery with bombs and with machine-gun fire. He has, by his courage and bravery, always set a magnificent example to the Squadron in which he serves'.

The Bar to his MC, the only one achieved by a member of 35 Squadron, came in the *London Gazette* of 22 June 1918: 'For conspicuous gallantry and devotion to duty. On discovering bodies of the enemy descending from motor lorries at a certain point behind the front, he sent down a wireless call, and having used his bombs and ammunition, he landed and reported to headquarters. He then went up again and dropped messages to several of our field batteries, with the result that heavy casualties were inflicted on the enemy. On the following day, noticing some hostile bodies crossing the bridges and failing to receive any answer from his wireless calls, he landed by the side of one of our siege batteries and personally directed the fire of the guns on to the enemy. His information has at all times been most reliable, and his work in co-operation with the artillery was of exceptional value'.

Posted next to instructing duties, he served at various training squadrons and training depot squadrons until finally leaving the RAF, via the Unemployed List, on 28 April 1919.

WOMERSLEY, John Herbert Greenwood

The eldest son of Mr and Mrs J Womersley of Swiss Cottage, Rufford Park, Yeaden, Yorkshire, he was born on 31 March 1896. He interrupted his studies at Leeds University to volunteer and was subsequently gazetted Second Lieutenant to 6 Company, East Riding of Yorkshire, RGA (TF), on 27 October 1915. After service with the Gunners in France, he was seconded to the RFC in October 1916. His pilot training duly completed, he was confirmed and gazetted Flying Officer on 1 April 1917. Sent out to 43 Squadron (Sopwith Strutters) in France on 18 April 1917, he achieved two victories before the unit converted to Camels in the following September. Three more victories followed before, on 12 November 1917, he took off on a practice flight and crashed, sustaining severe injuries which, effectively, brought his operational flying to a close. His MC was announced in the *London Gazette* of 18 January 1918, details in the *Gazette* of 25 April 1918: 'For conspicuous gallantry and devotion to duty in aerial fighting. He brought down four enemy machines and forced others to land. He also carried out reconnaissances at a low altitude'.

Womersley finally left hospital in March 1918, but was only allowed to perform 'light duties'. However, his injuries and poor health led to him being prematurely discharged from the service in September 1918. He was known to be living in Oversley Castle, near Alcester, Warwickshire, in the 1920s.

WOOD, Geoffrey Hunter

The son of Laundress, Mary G Wood of Mill Street, Buxton, Norfolk, he was born in 1893. Educated at Bury St Edmunds School, where he was a member of the OTC. After leaving school in 1910, he worked as a Rubber Planter in Malaya. Returning to England when the war came, he enlisted as a Private soldier (Number 1500) into 16 (Public Schools) Battalion, Middlesex Regiment, in September 1914. Wood accompanied his battalion to France with the rank of Corporal on 17 November 1915. Picked out for a commission, he was gazetted Second Lieutenant to the RFC on 9 May 1916. Having trained as an Observer, he was confirmed and gazetted Flying Officer (Observer) on 18 May following, and posted to 7 Squadron. On 9 August 1916, Wood and his Pilot of the day, Second Lieutenant Laurence Minot (qv), in BE2d, '5792', were shot up over Pozières during a contact patrol. Despite their machine being damaged, Minot nursed it back to their own aerodrome. On 2 November 1916, Wood and his Pilot, Sergeant Cecil Percy John Bromley (Number 1312), from Dover, in BE2e, '5760', were shot down whilst registering for the Artillery, crashing near to Le Sars. Bromley, who had been in the RFC since before the war and was entitled to a 1914 Star, was killed. Wood was very badly wounded, his left arm was subsequently amputated five inches below the shoulder, gangrene having set in. He also had a bullet in his left lung, which proved difficult to remove. No longer eligible for military service, Wood requested an early release as he had no father and his two brothers had already fallen in France. His MC was announced in the *London Gazette* of 14 November 1916.

WOOD, Harry Alison

From Toronto, Ontario, Canada, he was born on 16 March 1894. Educated at the University of Toronto, from where he graduated BASc in Civil Engineering in 1915. Volunteering for the flying service, he was gazetted Second Lieutenant to the RFC, via the Special Reserve, on 20 November 1915. Gained his Royal Aero Club Certificate (Number 2272) on 14 January 1916. His formal training duly completed, he was confirmed and gazetted Flying Officer on 18 April following. Posted to France and the DH2-equipped 24 Squadron in June 1916, he quickly established himself as an exceptional Pilot, achieving five victories between 6 July 1916 and 24 January 1917, although being shot down twice by ground fire himself in the process. He was promoted to A/Captain and Flight Commander on 5 December 1916. His MC was announced in the Birthday Honours *London Gazette* of 4 June 1917 (no citation). Although no citation was published in the *Gazette*, research has unearthed the original recommendation for the award: '10 March 1917, 4/Brigade HQ, RFC: For good work in leading his Flight on offensive patrols. He has been very active in attacking HA, and has brought down three machines on this side of the lines'.

His tour with '24 completed, he returned to the Home Establishment in March 1917. Following a short rest, he first instructed at the CFS, before being posted to 23 Wing at Lincoln, where he commanded 61 TDS with the rank of Major in August 1918. After leaving the service and returning home to Canada, he worked for the Canadian National Railways from 1920 until his retirement as Chief of Development in March 1959. He subsequently became a Director of a Montreal-based industrial company. For many years he was President of the Montreal Power Boat Squadron. Harry Wood died from a heart attack on 28 August 1959.

WOOD, Walter Bertram

The son of Consulting Engineer Walter James Wood, JP, and Annie Wood, of 'Ernecroft', Abbey Road, Grimsby, Lincolnshire, he was born on 25 October 1898. His brother, Ted, Second Lieutenant Edwin Leonard Wood, 'C' Company, 1 Battalion, Royal Scots Fusiliers, was killed in action in Flanders on 26 September 1917. The book, 'Two Soldier Brothers' by J Bygott(published in 1919 (Jarrold) tells both their stories. Walter enlisted as a Private soldier (Number 4567) into 28 Battalion, London Regiment (Artists Rifles), before being picked out for a commission and gazetted Second Lieutenant to 2/8 Battalion, Hampshire Regiment, on 4 June 1916, with an immediate secondment to the RFC. Having trained as a Pilot, he was confirmed and gazetted Flying Officer on 3 March 1917. Sent out to 29 Squadron (Nieuport XVIIs) in France on 23 April 1917, he achieved 13 victories between 11 May and 9 August 1917, including three 'doubles' on single days. His tour with '29' completed, he returned to the Home Establishment on 11 August 1917 and, following a short rest, reported for duty with 44 HD Squadron, based at Hainault Farm. The first of his MCs was announced in the *London Gazette* of 17 September 1917: 'For conspicuous gallantry and devotion to duty on many occasions when engaged with hostile aircraft, during which he has shown a fine offensive spirit and the utmost fearlessness. He has had no less than 23 combats, in the course of which he had destroyed and driven down numerous enemy machines, frequently attacking several single-handed, and on one occasion fighting with his revolver when he had run short of ammunition'.

The Bar to his MC came in the *London Gazette* of 26 September 1917, details in the *Gazette* of 9 January 1918: 'For conspicuous gallantry and devotion to duty in attacking enemy aircraft. On several occasions he has shown admirable dash and determination in attacking hostile machines single-handed, destroying some and driving others down out of control. He has also displayed great daring in attacking enemy infantry and transport with machine-gun fire at very low altitudes, in spite of attacks by hostile aircraft whilst so engaged'.

Wood had suffered with a debilitating bout of influenza and was probably still not fully fit when, on 11 November 1917, he took off in a Camel in company with another machine, to teach air fighting tactics. Unaccountably, his Camel suddenly dived into the ground near to Poulter's Farm, Hainault, Ilford, and he was killed outright. It was generally assumed that he had fainted at the controls. Walter Bertram Wood is buried in Grimsby (Scartho Road) Cemetery, Lincolnshire.

WOODCOCK, Frederick

The son of Solicitor F A Woodcock and Mrs Woodcock, of 'Ravenswood', Whalley Range, he was born in Derby in 1897. Educated at Riber Castle, Matlock, at Harrow (1911-14), and at Manchester University, where he studied Law. Articled to his father's practice, F A Woodcock and Company, Solicitors, of Manchester, in November 1914, going on to pass the Intermediate Examination for the LLB Degree at Victoria University, in June 1915. On reaching his 18th year in July 1915, he obtained a commission in the RGA, being gazetted Second Lieutenant on 2 August 1915, before going to France in the following November, where he joined 9 Brigade, Heavy Artillery. He remained at the front till March 1917, when he was seconded to the RFC and, after training, was confirmed and gazetted Flying Officer (Observer) on 11 April following. Sent out to 4 Squadron in France soon after qualifying, he was awarded his MC for his reconnaissance work in August and September 1917, announced in the *London Gazette* of 18 October 1917, details in the *Gazette* of 7 March 1918: 'For conspicuous gallantry and devotion to duty. He performed continuous and valuable work in contact patrols and reconnaissances, flying at a low altitude. On one occasion in a very strong gale, flying low, he obtained information of the greatest importance'.

Research has unearthed the original recommendation for this award, which provides a little more detail: 'F Woodcock. 7/9/17 Obs 4 Sqn. For conspicuous good and valuable work in carrying out contact patrols and reconnaissances at low level. On August 24th 1917, during a heavy enemy attack on our lines near Westhoek, he, by flying at a low altitude in a very strong westerly gale, obtained information of the greatest importance. This information was of special value as the enemy had placed a triple barrage behind our lines, so that it was most necessary that information as to the situation should be obtained'.

His tour with '4' completed, he returned to the Home Establishment in January 1918, where he undertook pilot training. Having qualified for his full 'Wings', he was sent out to the night-bombing FE2b-equipped 101 Squadron. Promoted to A/Captain and Flight Commander in August 1918. Woodcock was killed on 31 October 1918, near Roisel, in Northern France. He was manoeuvring for take-off when his FE2b came into contact with some explosives left on the ground, which, in turn, exploded a bomb in the machine. Woodcock was killed in the explosion, as was brother officer,33 year old Irishman, Second Lieutenant Thomas Pargeter Jones, MBE, who went to his assistance. Frederick Woodcock is buried at Roisel Communal Cemetery Extension, France.

WOODHOUSE, John Whitaker

The eldest of the three sons of the Reverend J T Woodhouse, the pastor of the Chapel Street Congregational Church, and Mrs Woodhouse, of Southport, Lancashire, he was born on 26 July 1888. One of his brothers was an Army officer, the other a Surgeon Lieutenant in the Royal Navy. Educated at Birmingham University. A Mechanical Engineer trained at Coventry, 'Jack' figured prominently before the war in motor track cycling at Aston, Birmingham, and in various motor reliability trials in the Midlands. In August 1914, he offered his services to the Belgian Army and served in that country for three months. Returning to the UK, he gained his Royal Aero Club Certificate (Number 1028) on 22 December 1914. Gazetted Second Lieutenant to the Military Wing, RFC, on 12 March 1915. His formal training duly completed, he was confirmed and gazetted Flying Officer on 24 June following. Sent out to BE2c-equipped 4 Squadron soon after qualifying. On 3 October 1915, Woodhouse made one of the first successful RFC 'spy drops' behind the German lines in France. The Official History, 'War in the Air', describes the event, thus: '....Woodhouse landed his BE2c at dusk, alongside a wood near Bantouzelle, about eight miles south of Cambrai. The passenger, with two baskets of pigeons, got clear into the wood, but returned when he saw that the pilot could not get his engine restarted. Woodhouse insisted that the agent return to the cover of the wood, eventually succeeded in restarting the engine alone, and scrambled into the aeroplane as it moved off. But he was not in the air long. The engine, which was over-oiled, was missing badly and he was compelled to land a second time. He ran the engine all out on the ground in short bursts to use up the surplus oil, got off again, and came down safely in the dark behind the British lines'. The first of his MCs was announced in the *London Gazette* of 14 January 1916 (no citation). Although no formal citation appeared in the *Gazette*, research has unearthed the original recommendation for the award: '4 Sqd. 'For repeated gallant acts, notably on August 30th, when he came down to 3,000 feet to attack an observation balloon under heavy AA fire, dropping 7 incendiary bombs and narrowly missing it; on Sept 25th when he attacked and broke the railway under heavy fire, and Oct 3rd when he carried out a difficult mission with great coolness and determination'.

His tour with '4' completed, he returned to the Home Establishment in November 1916. Following a brief period with 28 RS at Castle Bromwich, he served with 50 Squadron in Dover on Home Defence duties. On the night of 24/25 August 1916, Woodhouse in BE2c, '4142', pursued Zeppelin *L32* up the Channel, firing a drum and a half of the special Pomeroy ammunition at the airship before losing it in cloud and darkness. The Bar to his MC came in the *London Gazette* of 24 January 1917: 'For conspicuous gallantry on three occasions in attacking Zeppelin airships over land and sea'.

Next, promoted A/Captain and Flight Commander, he was posted to 66 Squadron (Sopwith Pups), then stationed at Filton, and subsequently accompanied that unit to France as a 'founder member' on 17 March 1917. He was appointed to command the Special Duties Flight on the Western Front and the wording of the citation for the Distinguished Service Order he received in the *London Gazette* of 17 September 1917 suggests that he continued to be employed in 'special duty' roles: 'For conspicuous gallantry and devotion to duty in carrying out special missions by night during which he had frequently been compelled to face very bad weather. In the course of numerous bombing expeditions by night he invariably descended to very low altitudes in order to use his machine-gun against hostile troops on the roads. He has consistently set a fine example'.

He was also Mentioned in Despatches and awarded a Croix de Guerre by the French. Promoted to Major, Woodhouse subsequently commanded the Flight Group at the School of Air Fighting, Ayr, in 1918. Staying on in the RAF, he commanded, successively, 55 and 207 Squadrons in Iraq during the 1920s. Promoted to Wing

Commander in the early 1930s, he commanded the Experimental Flying Department, RAE, in 1933. Promoted to Group Captain on 1 January 1938, he went on to serve in Africa during the Second World War.

NB: The RAF Museum Hendon has his medals in its collection: Distinguished Service Order, MC & two Bars (entitled to only one Bar), 1914-15 Star (Capt J W Woodhouse RFC)*, British War Medal 1914-20, Victory Medal 1914-19 with MID* (Capt J W Woodhouse RFC)*, 1939/45 Star, Africa Star 1940-43, Defence Medal 1939-45, War Medal 1939-45, Silver Jubilee Medal 1935, and Coronation Medal 1937.*

WOODHOUSE, Lionel Mostyn

The eldest son of Arthur L and Isabel Woodhouse, of 'Tofts', Little Baddow, Essex, he was born in 1896. His younger brother, Flight Sub-Lieutenant Mosley Gordon Woodhouse, RNAS, a Camel Pilot with 9 Naval Squadron, was killed in action over Nieuport, age 18, on 9 August 1917; another brother served as a Midshipman in the Royal Navy. Lionel was educated at Eton. Gazetted Second Lieutenant to the Essex Yeomanry on 1 July 1915. Seconded to the RFC, he trained as a Pilot and was subsequently confirmed and gazetted Flying Officer on 16 August 1916. He accompanied 52 Squadron (RE8s) to France as a 'founder member' on 21 November 1916. An exhausting and intensive tour through some of the most dangerous periods of the Great War came to an end in August 1917, when he returned to the Home Establishment. His MC was announced in the *London Gazette* of 25 August 1917: 'For conspicuous gallantry and devotion to duty. His work whilst observing for artillery has been of the greatest value. During one month of observation he has been responsible for the destruction of thirteen emplacements and for causing a large number of explosions and fires'.

In October of the same year, he was given command of the Artillery Department of the School of Aeronautics at Reading, but was again posted back to France in August 1918, this time as a Flight Commander with the RE8-equipped 59 Squadron. On 24 August 1918, Woodhouse and his Observer of the day, Lieutenant G M Thompson, DFC, in RE8, 'B6674', were shot up by ground fire. Despite damage to the 'Harry Tate', Woodhouse got the machine back safely. The records of 59 Squadron chronicle the frequency of missions and hardwork of the squadron during this period. Woodhouse and his Observers were out on patrol or on bombing or reconnaissance missions daily, and sometimes more than once in a day. On 1 September 1918, he received a direct hit from anti-aircraft fire to both his top and bottom right hand planes, compelling him to return. In an attempt to stabilise and balance their machine, the Observer leant out over the fuselage with, to add to his weight, the Lewis Gun in his hands. All their controls, with the exception of the elevator, were useless. Despite these difficulties, Woodhouse got the badly damaged RE8 back to his home aerodrome. On 27 September 1918, however, Woodhouse and his Observer of the day, Lieutenant Walter Sidney Peel, MC, Lincolnshire Regiment, attached RFC, in RE8, 'F6011', were sent down in flames to their deaths during an aerial combat over Grevillers. The award of a Distinguished Flying Cross for, amongst other things, bringing his machine down to 100 feet to attack enemy infantry, was announced posthumously in the *London Gazette* of 2 November 1918. Lionel Mostyn Woodhouse is buried in Grevillers British Cemetery, France.

NB: His medals were offered for sale by Glendining's (lot 349) on 28 March 1990: MC (engraved: Awarded 3/7/17, 1st battle of Somme, Lt RFC, 52 Sqd*), Distinguished Flying Cross (engraved:* Awarded 17/9/18, Capt., MC RAF 59 Sqd*), British War Medal 1914-20, Victory Medal 1914-19* (Capt RAF)*, and Next of Kin Memorial Plaque. Also sold at this sale (lot 349a) were the medals of his brother, Mosley Woodhouse: British War Medal 1914-20, Victory Medal 1914-19, and Next of Kin Memorial Plaque.*

WOOLLETT, Henry Winslow

The son of Major Sidney Winslow Woollett, OBE, Royal Army Medical Corps, and Mrs Woollett, of 47 High Street, Southwold, Suffolk, he was born in 1895. The son of a doctor, he was himself a medical student at the University of London when war came. Gazetted Second Lieutenant to 6 Battalion, Lincolnshire Regiment, on 26 August 1914. He landed with his battalion at 'V' Beach, Helles, on 20 July 1915, taking part in the subsequent landings at Suvla Bay on 6 August following. The 6 Lincolns were evacuated to Egypt in November 1915, before eventually being sent to the Western Front late in 1916. Seconded to the RFC, Woollett, a natural and gifted Pilot, gained his 'Wings' after only three and a half hours of dual instruction, being confirmed and gazetted Flying Officer on 27 October 1916. He suffered a crash in an Avro 504 that slightly delayed his eventual posting to the DH 2-equipped 24 Squadron in France in the following month. Woollett gained the first of his eventual 35 victories in a near-obsolete DH2 on 5 April 1917. '24' then took delivery of DH5s in May 1917 and Woollett proceeded to secure a further four victories by 17 August following. His tour with '24' completed, he returned to the UK shortly after gaining his fifth victory. The first of his MCs was announced in the *London Gazette* of 26 September 1917, details in the *Gazette* of 9 January 1918: 'For conspicuous gallantry and devotion to duty in engaging three enemy aircraft and following them down to a low altitude behind the enemy's lines, destroying one and driving down another out of control during the operations. He has done excellent work as a patrol leader, and has always displayed great gallantry in aerial combats, having brought down three other enemy machines in addition to those already mentioned'.

After a period instructing, Woollett returned to France in March 1918, as a Flight Commander with the Sopwith Camel-equipped 43 Squadron. Woollett then went on to achieve a further 30 victories (including 11 balloons) between 8 March and 9 August 1918. On 12 April 1918, he became the first RFC/RAF Pilot to gain six victories on a single day. His 'scoring' during this period also included one 'trio' and six 'doubles' on single days. Never self-effacing and something of an extrovert, he wore a leopard-skin flying helmet and gauntlets and had the spinner of his Camel painted to represent the face of a Red Indian. The Bar to his MC came in the *London Gazette* of 22 June 1918: 'For conspicuous gallantry and devotion to duty. On one occasion, when on offensive patrol, he dived on to an enemy plane which was attempting to cross our lines, and fired 100 rounds into it at 100 yards range, causing it to burst into flames and crash to the ground. He then dived onto another hostile machine, which went down in a spin and finally crashed to earth. On a later occasion he attacked and brought down in flames two enemy observation balloons. The gallantry and skill exhibited by this officer have been most inspiring to his flight'.

Woollett was also awarded a gallantry Distinguished Service Order in the *London Gazette* of 16 September 1918. The French, too, showed their admiration for his prowess with the Légion d'Honneur, *London Gazette* of 30 November 1918, and a Croix de Guerre avec Palme, *London Gazette* of 15 July 1919. He was also Mentioned in Despatches, *London Gazette* of 15 July 1919. Returning to the Home Establishment in August 1918, he took command of three training squadrons at Eastbourne. Staying on in the RAF, he toured the USA with other leading Aces between February and April 1919. He subsequently served in Iraq in 1924 and commanded 23 Squadron during 1930 and 1931, before finally retiring from the RAF, with the rank of Squadron Leader, in 1932. Henry Woollett died on 31 October 1969.

WOOLLVEN, Charles Henry Chapman

The son of HM Customs Collector, William Charles Woollven and Ellen Butler Woollven (née Chapman), of 35 Gaywood Road, King's Lynn, Norfolk, he was born in Folkestone, Kent, on 28 June 1897. From the Royal Military College, Sandhurst, he was gazetted Second Lieutenant to a Regular Army battalion of the Devonshire Regiment on 26 January 1916, with an immediate secondment to the RFC. Gained his Royal Aero Club Certificate (Number 2636) on 31 March 1916. His formal training duly completed, he was confirmed and gazetted Flying Officer on 27 May following. Sent out to the FE2b-equipped 25 Squadron on 19 June 1916, he gained five victories between 8 August 1916 and 1 May 1917, being promoted to A/Captain and Flight Commander on the intervening 31 December 1916. On 25 September 1916, Woollven and his Observer of the day, Lieutenant Charles Service Workman (qv), attacked a stationery troop train with six 20lb bombs and then swooped low to aim their machine-gun fire at the German troops spilling out of the wrecked train. Both men received the MC for this action. Woollven's award was announced in the *London Gazette* of 14 November 1916: 'For conspicuous gallantry in action. He dived down to a low altitude, attacked a train, causing many casualties, and displayed great courage and determination throughout'.

Charles Woollven appears not to have flown operationally again following the completion of his tour with '25'.

WORKMAN, Charles Service

The son of Dr Charles Workman MD, and Mrs Workman, of Glasgow, he was born on 30 November 1896. Educated at Merchiston Castle School (1909-14). Gazetted Second Lieutenant to 5 Battalion, Cameronians (Scottish Rifles) (TF) on 24 October 1914. Seconded to the RFC in the summer of 1916, he trained as an Observer and was sent out to FE2b-equipped 25 Squadron as a Probationary on 20 August 1916. On 1 September 1916, Workman and his Pilot of the day, Second Lieutenant N W W Webb (qv) in an FE2b, attacked two enemy balloons. Crossing the lines in cloud, they detected the first of these balloons upon which Webb dived, whilst Workman fired five drums of ammunition into it. As the balloon was lowered, they also dropped four bombs that exploded very close to the envelope. They then attacked the second balloon, which was about a mile away. Again, their machine-gun fire scored hits as the balloon was hauled down. The FE had suffered considerable damage from anti-aircraft fire and Webb was obliged to carefully nurse the machine back across the lines. His 'apprenticeship' satisfactorily completed, Workman was confirmed and gazetted Flying Officer (Observer) on 11 September following. On 25 September 1916, Workman and his Pilot of the day, Lieutenant C H C Woollven (qv), attacked a stationery troop train with six 20lb bombs and then swooped low to aim their machine-gun fire at the German troops spilling out of the wrecked train. Both men received the MC for this action. Workman's MC was announced in the *London Gazette* of 14 November 1916: 'For conspicuous gallantry in action. He and his pilot dived down to a low altitude, attacked a train, causing many casualties, and displayed great courage and determination'.

His tour with '25' completed, he returned to the Home Establishment on 10 November 1916, where, after a rest, he trained as a Pilot. Having qualified for his full 'Wings', he returned to France on 5 May 1917, this time reporting to the Sopwith Strutter-equipped 70 Squadron. On 15 June 1917, Workman and his Observer of the day, 2 AM S A Groves, in Strutter, 'A8230', narrowly escaped disaster when their machine was hit by anti-aircraft fire during a photo-reconnaissance. On 7 July following, the same pair suffered the same experience when their Strutter, 'A1206', was damaged, again by anti-aircraft fire. The squadron converted to Sopwith Camels days after this incident and, on 17 July, Workman, in Camel, 'B3779', became one of the squadron's first casualties in this new type, when he was shot down during an aerial combat with Leutnant Tuxen of Jasta 6. Mortally wounded and taken prisoner, he died three days later in Courtrai (German) Hospital. Charles Workman is buried in Kortrijk (St Jan) Communal Cemetery, Kortrijk, West-Vlaanderen, Belgium.

WRAY, Arthur Mostyn

The son of Chief Petty Officer Arthur Charles Wray and Annie Wray (Née Lipscomb), of 45 Balliol Road, Portsmouth, Hampshire, he was born in Cape Colony, South Africa, on 15 April 1896. He spent much of his early life with a surrogate family in Ireland, whilst his parents were living and working abroad. Educated at Monkton Coombe School (1907-10). Gazetted, initially, Second Lieutenant to 9 (Reserve) Battalion, East Kent Regiment (The Buffs), on 26 February 1915, he later had the opportunity of entering Sandhurst with the prospect of obtaining a permanent commission in the Regular Army. Resigning his temporary commission with 9 Buffs, he completed the course at the Royal Military College and was duly commissioned Second Lieutenant to a Regular Army battalion of the same regioment on 27 October 1916. Seconded soon afterwards to the RFC, he trained as a Pilot and was confirmed and gazetted Flying Officer on 21 March 1917. Sent out to 29 Squadron (Nieuport Scouts) in France soon after qualifying. Wray achieved conclusive victories on 13 and 20 May 1917, before, on 28 May, his Nieuport was shot up during an offensive patrol and he received a wound to his knee and his thigh bone was fractured. He would later be known as 'Hoppin' Wray as a consequence of this injury. His MC was announced in the *London Gazette* of 16 August 1917: 'For conspicuous gallantry and devotion to duty. While on offensive patrol he attacked a hostile two-seater at close range. He was at once severely wounded, and though his thigh was fractured and his machine fell several thousand feet, out of control, he managed to obtain control again and effected a safe landing. He has previously done splendid work'.

Once recovered, Wray was employed in instructing roles and his outstanding work in this field was eventually recognised with the award of an Air Force Cross, *London Gazette* of 1 January 1919. Staying on in the RAF after the war, Wray served in Waziristan between January 1922 and April 1923, flying Brisfits against local tribesmen and receiving the first of his Distinguished Flying Crosses for his services in that territory, *London Gazette* of 30 May 1924. Wray rose steadily through the levels of command in the years between the two World Wars: Flight Lieutenant, 1924; Squadron Leader, 1933; and Wing Commander in 1937. When the Second World War came in September 1939, Wray was posted to Bomber Command and promoted to Group Captain in 1940. An active Commanding Officer at RAF Hemswell with its three Polish Squadrons, he flew operations over Germany. After his Wellington bombers had attacked Essen, he was awarded the second of his Distinguished Flying Crosses in the *London Gazette* of 7 April 1942, for: '....deliberately descending to a low altitude in the face of fierce opposing fire, to bomb his objective'. The exiled Polish Government also awarded him their highest award, the Virtuti Militari, *London Gazette* of 24 July 1942. Promoted next to Air Commodore in May 1943, he was appointed AOC, 12 Base, RAF Binbrook. Still involving himself in operational flying, he was awarded a gallantry Distinguished Service Order in the *London Gazette* of 20 August 1943, for participating 'in numerous sorties, including an attack on Hamburg in July 1943'. He was also Mentioned in Despatches on three occasions during the Second World War, *London Gazettes* of 1 January 1943, 1 January 1945, and 1 January 1946. His last significant appointment, on 14 July 1945, was as AOC, 221 (Tactical) Group, RAF. He finally retired from the RAF on 10 May 1946, farming and living with his wife, Margaret and their three children, at East End Farm, Pitney, near Langport, Somerset. He next developed an interest in gliding and, at the remarkable age of 75, qualified for his Gold 'C' Certificate in May 1972. Air Commodore Arthur Wray died on 6 April 1982.

WRIGHT, Alfred John

From Barrie, Ontario, Canada, he was born on 28 September 1890. Educated at Toronto University, from where he graduated BASc in 1913. He worked as an Electrical Engineer, with Toronto Hydro Electrical Systems, Toronto, in 1914 and 1915. Enlisting into the Canadian Engineers as a Sapper in 1915, he served with various units before being promoted to the rank of Company Sergeant Major with 11 Field Company, CEs, which unit he accompanied to France and Flanders in August 1916. After service in Ypres and Kemmell, he successfully sought transfer to the RFC. Gazetted Second Lieutenant to the RFC on 10 May 1917. His pilot training duly completed, he was confirmed and gazetted Flying Officer on 28 July following. Sent out to 35 Squadron in France just three days after qualifying for his 'Wings'. After an exacting and exhausting tour with the 'Big-Acks' of '35', Wright returned to the Home Establishment on 28 March 1918. His MC, won with Lieutenant R W Hobbs (qv) as his Observer, was announced in the *London Gazette* of 26 March 1918, details in the *Gazette* of 24 August 1918: 'For conspicuous gallantry and devotion to duty. He carried out many reconnaissances at great distances over the enemy lines and often flew over new and difficult country. On many occasions, despite adverse weather conditions, he obtained successful photographs and brought back valuable information. He has always shown splendid courage, determination, and skill'.

Research has unearthed the original recommendation for the award, which provides much more detail: 'A J Wright. 25 Sqn Feb 1918. For courage and devotion to duty and continuous good work during the period 9/8/17-5/2/18, notably on the following occasions: On 19/11/17 he executed a very brilliant reconnaissance of enemy aerodromes on the line Meetkerke-Coolkerke-Oostcamp-Doomkerke and Maria Aalter-Thielt. On 28/1/18 this Officer took 44 photographs in the course of a very fine railway reconnaissance of the line Ghent-Melle-Audenarde-Renaix-Ath-Mons. On 3/1/18 2/Lt Wright undertook a reconnaissance of the railway line Audenarde-Brussels-Ath, bringing back with him 54 photographs which contained valuable information. On 2/2/18 he covered every pin-point and secured 31 exposures in a reconnaissance of the railway Valenciennes-Aulnoye-Hirson-Wassigny- Busigny. On 3/2/18, this Officer executed a successful reconnaissance of the line Laon-Marle-Virvins-Hirson-Aobentem-Rumigny-Liart-Mont Cornet in spite of most trying weather conditions. Layers of cloud interfered with his work and at one time he was obliged to fly through a heavy rainstorm. He would not be deterred and eventually succeeded in covering all his objectives. The work of this Officer has been marked by courage, skill and determination. He has always shown a high sense of duty and can be absolutely relied upon to carry out the duties entrusted to him. His reconnaissance work has been carried out at a great distance over enemy lines and often over new and difficult country. He has invariably found his objectives and often, when other machines have return on account of adverse weather conditions, he has persevered and brought back successful photographs. He is always anxious to go to places which may prove of interest, although this often necessitates a much longer course. His keenness and determination are always most marked'.

The French, too, showed their appreciation of his invaluable work with a Croix de Guerre. After a short rest in the UK, he was posted home to Canada, where he served as a Flight Commander with 43 Wing, RAF. Wright finally left the RAF, via the Unemployed List, on 19 April 1919.

WYNCOLL, Hugh Edmond Fowler

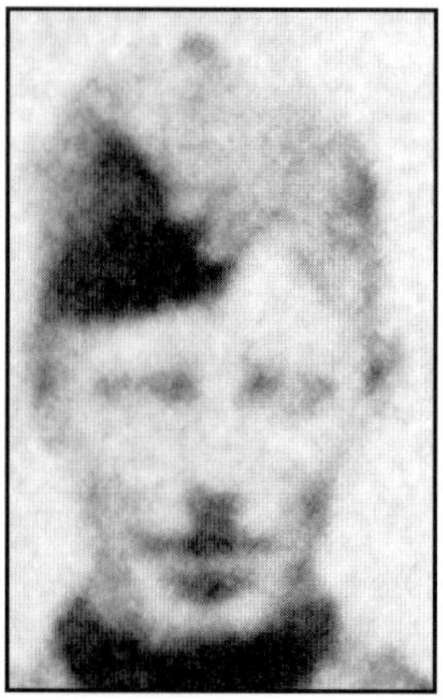

Born on 29 December 1889. A pre-war Regular Army officer, he was gazetted Second Lieutenant to 1 Battalion, Sherwood Foresters, on 24 October 1908. Wyncoll was in Deolali, India, with 1 Sherwood Foresters, when war came in August 1914. 'The Stubborns' were ordered home and left Bombay aboard the SS *Thongwa* on 2 September, arriving in Plymouth exactly one month later. Sent to France, they landed at Le Havre on 5 November 1914, with Wyncoll a platoon commander with 'A' Company, earning a 1914 Star. Wyncoll suffered a bad strain to his right foot on 13 November, when he was thrown from a cart and was obliged to return to England briefly for treatment. Once recovered, he returned to France and, by June 1915, was a Company Commander. Seconded to the RFC, late in 1915, he trained as an Observer. Already a qualified Instructor in Gunnery, Wyncoll was gazetted Flying Officer (Observer) on 21 March 1916 and accompanied the FE2b-equipped 22 Squadron to France on 1 April 1916. On 15 July 1916, during the Battle of the Somme, Wyncoll and his Pilot, Captain J G Swart (qv), together with squadron colleagues, Lieutenants Bowen and Mansell, attacked German infantry on the Flers-Longueval road with their machine guns. Swooping down three times, they caused the enemy to disperse and inflicted a number of casualties. They then attacked some wagons and a gun-limber, killing a horse and causing the drivers to run. His MC was announced in the *London Gazette* of 22 September 1916: 'For conspicuous gallantry and skill as an Observer, and in attacking troops on the ground from low altitudes. On one occasion, with Captain Swart as pilot, he successfully attacked three detachments of the enemy, his machine being subjected to heavy machine-gun and rifle fire from the ground'. His tour with '22' completed, he returned to the UK late in 1916, to take up instructing duties. On 19 January 1918, Wyncoll was appointed Gunnery Brigade Instructor (graded as Park Commander) with the rank of T/Major on the Home Establishment. For his work in this field, Wyncoll was created an OBE in the Birthday Honours *London Gazette* of 3 June 1919. Staying on in the RAF after the war, he eventually retired from the Aero Branch with the rank of Squadron Leader on 29 December 1932.

WYNNE-EYTON, Robert Mainwaring

The son of Mr and Mrs C E Wynne-Eyton, of North Wales, he was born in Whitchurch, Salop, in 1886. Educated at Wellington College (1900-01). A Farmer in North Wales, and a keen yachtsman, he was also a pre-war volunteer, being commissioned Sub-Lieutenant into the Royal Naval Volunteer Reserve. Transferring to the Army, he was gazetted Lieutenant to 3 (Light) Battalion, Motorised Machine Gun Section, Royal Artillery, on 1 September 1915. His unit accompanied 46 Division on its intended posting to Egypt, on 8 January 1916. However, soon after sailing, the Division was recalled to await deployment to the Western Front. This event seems to have decided Wynne-Eyton to seek secondment to the RFC, which came in the spring of 1916. His formal pilot training duly completed, he was confirmed and gazetted Flying Officer on 23 October following. Sent out to 47 Squadron for service in Macedonia and the Aegean. On 5 July 1917, he was credited with an Albatros two-seater sent down and destroyed whilst patrolling in a DH2 near to Cerniste. On 30 November 1917, Wynne-Eyton and his Observer of the day, Second Lieutenant W D Robertson, were both wounded in the air during a protracted and, in the end, indecisive combat with an enemy machine. Despite the damage to his machine and the wounds he had suffered, Wynne-Eyton, returned safely to his home aerodrome. His MC was announced in the New Year *London Gazette* of 1 January 1918 (no citation). Wynne-Eyton was sent back to the UK, via Malta, for medical treatment, arriving on 11 January 1918. Once recovered, he was promoted to A/Captain and sent to 6 TDS as a Flight Commander on 6 April 1918. Sent out to France and to 211 Squadron (DH9s) later in 1918. On 16

August 1918, Wynne-Eyton and his Observer, Second Lieutenant T B Dodwell, in DH9, 'C6348/C', were forced down into the North Sea after their engine was hit by flak whilst returning from a bombing raid over Bruges. Wynne-Eyton and the wounded Dodwell were rescued from the sea by Dutch sailors and interned in neutral Holland until four days after the Armistice, when they were repatriated to England. After leaving the service in 1919, Wynne-Eyton went to try his hand at farming in Central Africa.

Y

YATES, Henry Irving Frederick

The son of Journalist, Edmund S Yates and Lilian Yates of 20 Denmark Avenue, Wimbledon, Surrey, he was born on 20 July 1884. Served in the South African War, and was entitled to the Queen's South Africa Medal 1899-1902, with five clasps. A self-employed Mining Engineer, he developed an interest in aviation, gaining the French version of the Royal Aero Club Certificate (Number Fr 1551) on 1 December 1913. Yates was married and living in London, when he applied for a commission and was subsequently gazetted Second Lieutenant to the Military Wing, RFC, via the Special Reserve, 12 May 1915. His formal pilot training duly completed with 9 Squadron, then at Brooklands, he was confirmed and gazetted Flying Officer on 16 September following. Sent to 14 Squadron at Shoreham on 29 October 1915, he accompanied the unit to Arabia, via Egypt, as a 'founder member', during the following month. His MC was announced in the *London Gazette* of 30 March 1916: '14 Sqd., 5/Wing, RFC, SR. For conspicuous gallantry and skill. He was instructed to destroy an enemy waterworks, but on arrival, found the place defended by anti-aircraft guns and infantry lying on their backs, who opened a heavy fire. Notwithstanding this he pluckily descended to 600 feet and dropped a bomb into the centre of the waterworks. He thus succeeded in destroying them, and then attacked a machine-gun detachment and drove it from its position by fire from his own machine-gun. On a previous occasion his name was brought to notice for gallant and skilful work on a reconnaissance'.

Promoted to A/Captain and Flight Commander on 1 June 1916, his tour with '14' was completed just ten days later when he returned to RFC HQ, Egypt. Promoted to A/Major in May 1917, he served with a number of squadrons in the Middle East during 1917, and in the early months of 1918. Promoted to A/Lieutenant Colonel, he transferred to a Staff role in 1918. He was created an OBE (Military Division) in 1919 for his services with the Staff. After leaving the RAF, he returned to his mining and drilling work and was reputed to have attempted to win vast oil concessions for Britain in South America at the height of the petrol crisis in 1929. Yates apparently served again in some capacity during the Second World War. Henry Yates died of cerebral thrombosis and arteriosclerosis in Bournemouth, Hampshire, on 31 October 1976.

NB: Part of his group of medals was offered for sale by Christie's (lot 81) on 21 November 1989: OBE (first type, Military Division), MC, Victory Medal 1914-19 (Major RFC), *War Medal 1939-45.*

YOUDALE, Alfred Clarence

The son of John Beaumont Youdale and Rebecca Youdale, of 'Coniston', 43 Ormond Street, Ashfield, New South Wales, Australia, he was born in Burwood, NSW, on 18 January 1888. He was one of three brothers who all served in the AIF. A Commercial Traveller pre-war, he enlisted as a Private soldier (Number 971) into the Australian Imperial Force on 8 January 1915, being sent for training at camp Liverpool, NSW. His basic training completed, he embarked on 21 May 1915 at Sydney, boarding the SS *Karinga* (Transport A58), with 5 Reinforcement Group for 7 Battalion, Australian Light Horse, bound for Heliopolis, Egypt. Youdale subsequently served in Gallipoli with 7 Australian Light Horse from 6 August 1915, being promoted to Sergeant on 13 August and Sergeant Major on 14 November 1915. After an exhausting stint on Gallipoli and following the evacuation, Youdale was allowed to return to Australia on 20 January 1916. Volunteering for further service, he re-embarked on 12 March 1916, this time bound for the UK. After serving with the Australian Army Service Corps, Youdale volunteered for the flying service and, once accepted, was gazetted Second Lieutenant to the RFC on 21 February 1917. His formal pilot training duly completed, he was confirmed and gazetted Flying Officer on 9 May following. Sent out initially to 9 Squadron (RE8s) on 5 June 1917, he joined 27 Squadron (DH4s), 'on loan' just 22 days later on 27 June, before returning again to '9' on 2 July 1917. On 14 August 1917, during a violent storm, Youdale and his Observer of the day, Lieutenant R B Ashcroft (qv), aside from gaining valuable information during a reconnaissance, fired 350 rounds from very a low level into a concentration of enemy troops, causing many casualties. On 16 August 1917, the same crew attacked Au-bon-Cite with machine-gun fire from 400 feet in worsening light, as our infantry attacked; flying through a supporting 18-pounder artillery barrage several times in order to do so. The first of his MCs was announced in the *London Gazette* of 26 September 1917, details in the *Gazette* of 9 January 1918: 'For conspicuous gallantry and devotion to duty. Working in conjunction with our infantry, he rendered valuable assistance in the attack, flying several times through our heavy barrage and using his machine-gun at a very low altitude. His work has been consistently skilful and fearless during the whole of the operations, especially when engaged in contact patrols and in attacking enemy infantry from low altitudes'.

On his last day with '9', 20 September 1917, Youdale and the faithful Ashcroft, fired 300 rounds into an enemy-filled Eagle Trench in the morning, 800 rounds into trenches and shell holes in the afternoon and 950 rounds from 100 feet into Eagle Trench again in the same evening. Promoted to A/Captain and Flight Commander on the following day, he was sent next to 21 Squadron (RE8s). Four days later on 25 September, Youdale and his Observer, Second Lieutenant Eric Wilson (qv), were attacked by three enemy Scouts, one of which they shot down. Almost immediately after this, they were attacked by two enemy two-seaters, one of which they also destroyed. On 4 October 1917, Youdale received a slight wound to the face, but reported for duty on the following day. On 12 October 1917, Youdale and his Observer, Lieutenant Jacob Ernest Mott, Royal Irish Fusiliers attached RFC, came near to disaster, although both emerged unscathed when their RE8, 'B5072', was shot up by anti-aircraft fire and they were sent down to a forced landing. On the very next day the same pair suffered an almost identical experience, this time in RE8, 'B5026'. Yet again, on 28 October 1917, their RE8, '5885', was damaged by anti-aircraft fire, but this time they were able to return safely to their own aerodrome. The Bar to Youdale's MC came in the *London Gazette* of 27 October 1917, details in the *Gazette* of 18 March 1918. The luck the pairing of Youdale and Mott had enjoyed so far came to a sad end on 23 December 1917, when their RE8, 'B5088', was hit by flak and, on this occasion, sent down in flames to destruction. Youdale was subsequently awarded a second Bar to his MC which was posthumously announced in the *London Gazette* of 5 July 1918: 'For conspicuous gallantry and devotion to duty on contact patrol. When he was sent up to locate the positions gained by our troops, his first attempt was frustrated by a snowstorm. He made a second attempt, and, flying at a height of 200 feet, in spite of severe hostile fire, succeeded in locating all our positions'.

The gallant Alfred Youdale's remains were never recovered and hence he is commemorated on the Flying Services Memorial, Arras, France.